Psychology, Religion, and Spirituality

James M. Nelson

Psychology, Religion, and Spirituality

 Springer

Author
James M. Nelson
Department of Psychology
Valparaiso University
Valparaiso, IN 46383
USA
jim.nelson@valpo.edu

.b24234032
.01332764
7011 9826

ISBN 978-1-4419-2769-9   e-ISBN 978-0-387-87573-6
DOI 10.1007/978-0-387-87573-6

Printed on acid-free paper.

springer.com

Preface

Over a century ago, psychologists who were fascinated with religion began to study and write about it. Theologians and religious practitioners have responded to this literature, producing a fascinating dialogue that deals with our fundamental understandings about the human person and our place in the world. This book provides an introduction to the important conversations that have developed out of these interchanges.

The dialogue between psychology and religion is difficult to study for a number of reasons. First, it requires knowledge of both psychology and religion. People with a background in psychology often lack a solid understanding of the religious traditions they wish to study, and theologians may not be up to date on the latest developments in psychology. Second, it requires conceptual tools to organize the material and understand the basic problems involved in any attempt to connect the science of psychology with religion. These concepts can be found in many places, for instance in the writings of philosophers of science, but they are complex and often hard to follow for those without a proper theological and philosophical background. Finally, authors who write on the topic come to the study of psychology and religion from a variety of academic and personal backgrounds. This makes for wonderful diversity in conversations, but it makes understanding and mastery of the material quite difficult.

Given these problems, why should we try to understand this dialogue? Along with many other scholars, I believe that psychology and religion both have things to say to each other that are mutually beneficial. Psychology offers religion the resources of science to improve the accuracy of its self-understanding and the methods it uses to pursue desired goals. Religion offers psychology a vast store of accumulated wisdom on the nature of the human person and how a good life might be achieved. As each field hears what the other has to say, there is a response or critique, and these are of vital importance as well. For instance, theological responses to psychological theory and research provide valuable corrections that can help the field avoid mistakes and misunderstandings. Accordingly, this book is written from a *dialogical perspective*, looking at some of the important conversations and critiques that have been exchanged between psychologists, theologians and religious practitioners. The word "and" in the title of this book reflects this dialogical aim.

A dialogical approach to psychology and religion carries with it certain assumptions. First, psychology and religion are treated as equal conversation partners that are both worthy of respect. Thus, an attempt must be made to avoid privileging either field in our inquiry. Second, while dialogue produces many fascinating connections it does not produce a structure that fits both areas into a neat system. While psychology and religion have much to say to each other, they are different in their aims and methods, so that discontinuities between the fields will always be present.

While the book has a primary focus on Christianity—and I write from that perspective—Hinduism and especially Buddhism have also contributed greatly to the psychology and religion dialogue. Thus, major sections of the book also discuss information related to these two traditions. Unfortunately, some other major religions have not been well studied by psychologists, and so there is not a coherent body of dialogue available for discussion. Thus, there is very little discussion of Judaism in this book, and only a modest treatment of Islam. Hopefully, theory and research will progress in the future so that these important religious traditions will have a more central place in the conversation with psychology.

The Plan of This Book

The fields of psychology, religion, and spirituality have a vast, rich heritage that is beyond the scope of any single volume or set of volumes. Even the literature on the intersection between psychology and religion is enormous. Accordingly, in a book such as this, hard choices must be made about what to include and how it should be discussed. In general, I have tried to provide a bird's-eye view of the field, indicating important major issues and areas where dialogue is taking place. However, this is a textbook rather than an encyclopedia, so you will not find coverage of all the major writers or research related to psychology, religion and spirituality. Such an undertaking would be neither possible nor desirable in the confines of a single volume. Instead, it is important to be selective and focus on key figures or ideas as a way of introducing various points of view and issues of interest. In order to understand the current state of the dialogue, it is necessary to focus more on recent research findings and understandings of various issues, although older work is also considered when it is relevant to current debates. This includes discussion of research in the sociology and anthropology of religion that is of importance to psychology. Each chapter concludes with a discussion of a key issue or theme that emerges from the psychology and religion dialogue on that topic.

The material in the book falls into several sections. Part I deals with fundamentals in the psychology and religion dialogue. It is very helpful to consider this topic within the context of the larger conversation between science and religion. Thus, there is a chapter that introduces the philosophical concepts (e.g., naturalism, materialism) and historical information (e.g., positivist movements) needed to understand the science and religion relationship, particularly as it has worked itself out with reference to psychology. For those that are unfamiliar with the major religious traditions addressed in the psychology and religion dialogue, a chapter with a brief review of Hinduism, Buddhism and Christianity is also included.

Parts II and III cover basic areas in the psychology and religion dialogue as it has evolved over the past century. Part II also provides an overview of approaches to the topic that are likely to be central in the future, such as the perspectives provided by neuroscience and postmodernism. Part III summarizes material related to the important area of human development, and suggests how new advances in narrative psychology may help us to understand the process of spiritual growth.

Part IV deals with the practical applications of the psychology and religion dialogue. Religion and psychology share a concern with the quality of human existence. They hope to offer guidance to people seeking to find meaningful, fulfilled and even happy lives. Thus, a final goal of this book is to harness theory and empirical research in the service of practical applications. How can we in the 21st century build positive communities? In what ways can we help individuals deal with challenges and develop richly satisfying lives? The concluding chapters of this book will attempt to begin sketching out answers to these questions.

A difficult problem is how to handle terminology and references, which for this topic must come from a number of fields. For the most part, references utilize the system developed by the American Psychological Association, although this is not always ideal when referring to philosophical or theological works. Multiple author citations have been abbreviated somewhat in the text, although the full citation can still be found in the reference list. A glossary is included at the end of the book that provides quick definitions of terms as they are typically used by psychologists, theologians, and religious studies scholars.

The primary task of a book such as this is to present ideas that have been influential in the dialogue between psychology and religion. Once we have these ideas in front of us, the next critical task is to evaluate the value of these ideas and the evidence that supports them. This is important, as the ideas of many influential figures in the dialogue (e.g. Freud, Fromm) have little or no evidence to support them, while other less-known ideas appear on examination to be very attractive. However, evaluation is not easily done. A systematic critique of theories requires agreement on how they should be evaluated and a body of theoretical discussion or evidence relevant to the task. Unfortunately, one or both of these things is often missing in the science and religion dialogue. Scholars in different fields such as social psychology and religious studies often disagree on what constitutes evidence in support of a position. For instance, scientists often insist upon the presence of empirical data to support a theory, while a theologian might argue that other kinds of evidence are more relevant and persuasive. There is also much variability in the quantity and quality of critique directed at different positions. Some theories—even good once—have been the target of extensive critiques, while others have received little criticism even when there is little data to support them. So while evaluative sections have been included in situations where there has been a lot of scholarly discussion about the worth of a particular theory or position, it has not always been possible to offer an extensive critique of every theory. Absence of a critique does not mean a position is "proven" and presence of a critique does not mean a view has no value. Much remains to be done to evaluate the worth of the many strands in the psychology and religion dialogue.

The Community Behind the Book, with Thanks

Any writer is indebted to many people both past and present. One of the most painful parts of writing the book has been the need to cover rich systems of thought and lifetimes of study by many fine people in a few sentences. Thus, both thanks and apologies are due to colleagues. Hopefully this book will motivate the reader to pick up and read the original sources and authors involved in the psychology and religion dialogue.

Many of my students have contributed to this book in important ways. John Unrath did some of the background research for Chapter 12, and Mark Burek contributed some suggestions on Chapter 13. Kathryn Alfrey, Lisa Daube, Katie Patrick, Marla Tiebert, and Kathy Berg did much of the typing, editing and cross-checking of the reference list, a significant job in a book of this type. Julie Hamaide, Erin Westerman, and Jennifer Zimmer read large portions of the text and commented on them from a student point of view, suggesting improvement to make the book more user friendly. They also worked with Chrystal Frey and Anthony Nelson in helping to assemble the glossary. Catherine Renken and Megan Berning assisted in the production of the index. Several of my psychology and religion classes at Valparaiso University and in China have also endured earlier versions of the chapters in this book and made helpful suggestions.

A number of wonderful colleagues have read and critiqued portions of this book. Al Dueck, Ted Ludwig, Nancey Murphy, and Brent Slife have read selected chapters, while Kevin Mooney and Jeanne Brown read earlier drafts of the entire manuscript. Richard Gorsuch, Frank Richardson, and Fraser Watts were kind enough to read a final version of the book and offer comments. Throughout the whole process, the editors at Springer have been tremendously supportive and helpful, especially Jennifer Hadley and Sharon Panulla. All have made numerous helpful suggestions that have enriched the final product. Obviously, deficiencies that remain in the book are my responsibility.

Finally, I must acknowledge my faith community and my family, especially my wife Jeanne and children Anthony and Teresa, who warmly supported me during the incessant reading and periodic writing that went into this book.

Indiana, USA   James M. Nelson

Disclaimer

Although this book treats a number of important personal and mental health issues, it is not intended as a volume to provide spiritual or psychological guidance to people in distress. Individuals struggling with these problems should seek help from qualified religious and psychological professionals.

Contents

Chapter 1
Introduction to Psychology, Religion, and Spirituality

1.1 Introduction

The nature of the human person has been a subject of fascination since ancient times. We desire to understand ourselves and our place in the world, and at times we also look at broader human questions: Why am I here? What is the meaning or purpose of my life? Why do people suffer? This book is about two of the most important ways that people have attempted to answer these kinds of questions—religion and psychology. Especially over the past century, there has been a fascinating interchange of views between psychologists and religious practitioners about questions of daily life and broader meaning. In this book, we will seek to understand this complex and constantly changing dialogue and its implication for our understanding of the human person (cf. Henking, 2000). We will begin our quest in this chapter with a look at the basic concepts of religion, spirituality, and psychology, as well as some history of the dialogue between them.

1.2 Basic Concepts

1.2.1 What is Religion?

From prehistoric times to the present, religion has been a central part of human experience and culture. Religions are thought to have existed in all times and societies (Cela-Conde, 1998; Glock & Stark, 1965). Traditionally the term **religion** was used to refer to all aspects of the human *relationship to the Divine* or **transcendent**—that which is greater than us, "the source and goal of all human life and value" (Meissner, 1987, p. 119). More recently, scholars have started to understand religion as activities and a *way of life:* "the fashioning of distinctive emotions; of distinctive habits, practices, or virtues; of distinctive purposes, desires, passions, and commitments; and of distinctive beliefs and ways of thinking," along with "a distinctive way of living *together*" and a language for discussing "what they are doing and why" (Dykstra, 1986). Thus religion has to do not only with the transcendent as it is "out

J.M. Nelson, *Psychology, Religion, and Spirituality,*
DOI 10.1007/978-0-387-87573-6_0, @ Springer Science+Business Media, LLC 2009

there" but also as it is **immanent** in our bodily life, daily experiences, and practices. Some religious traditions like Islam are thought to emphasize transcendence, while Eastern religions tend to emphasize immanence. Christianity stresses both: the transcendent God is also the God who can be found within and around us, discernable in both a dramatic religious experience and in the simple, quiet love of a child for his or her parent (Maloney, 1992, p. 1; Spidlik, 1986, p. 134; Shannon, 2000; Macquarrie, 1982, p. 34). Religion is thus multidimensional, and its complexity must be understood if it is to be properly evaluated (Gorsuch, 1984; Snibbe & Markus, 2002).

1.2.1.1 Religion as Transcendence

All of us encounter the **transcendent** part of life, something that takes us beyond our current way of thinking, feeling, or acting. We master a foreign language, listen to a new kind of music or learn to pilot a canoe. All these things are examples of self-transcendence and they are also comprehensible; we can understand the system of processes, abilities, and decisions behind each of these new activities. We could refer to these situations as offering a kind of **weak transcendence**, something that is beyond us but also within our reach—transcendence "of an *internal* and human sort" (Nussbaum, 1990, p. 379). It is something that can be achieved or comprehended, often without a fundamental change in our way of life or outlook.

Sometimes, however, we encounter more radical forms of **strong transcendence** that defy comprehension, understanding, and control. This happens when we find that life cannot be put into a box or reduced to a set of propositions and rules despite our best efforts. In the words of philosopher Emmanuel Levinas (1969), we find that our world is not just a settled, controllable "totality" of a clearly understood system but is an "infinity" that sometimes goes beyond our human control and understanding. This infinity can appear in situations that challenge our settled view of things, as when the death of a loved one makes us realize the finitude of life. The psychiatrist-philosopher Karl Jaspers (1932) referred to these as **limit situations** or experiences. Strong transcendence also appears in the puzzles and **paradoxes** of life—things that seem to be simultaneously true but not reconcilable with each other. For instance, the world seems to have an underlying unity, but at the same time there is great diversity. Religious people can speak of God as love and at the same time acknowledge the presence of suffering in the world. Paradox appears when we ask big questions like why do things exist? Why is the world predictable and orderly? Finally, it is evident in our **human freedom** to make choices, pursue goals, react in different ways, and exercise creativity (Theophan, 1995, p. 72). No matter how carefully we study and plan, our own actions and those of others— even the effects of planful modern science and technology—continue to surprise us and defy prediction. Human action can be thought of as a struggle between this freedom and necessity (Arendt, 1998, pp. 230–235). In religious traditions, many thinkers speak of spiritual life as involving some kind of ascent and contact with this transcendence and that after returning from such an encounter we find ourselves changed in important ways (Shah-Kazemi, 2006, p. 1).

While most human philosophies and religions embrace at least some form of weak transcendence, views on strong transcendence vary markedly. Most forms of humanistic philosophy reject the idea of strong transcendence, arguing that sacredness is just another word for human power and ability (Ornstein, 1991, p. 274; Taylor, 2007; Vergote, 1969, p. 74). A view such as this emphasizes our ability to control the world instead of seeing it as a gift to be received. On the other hand, many religious systems would argue that while weak transcendence exists and is good, a view of the world or the human person that stops there is radically incomplete. We must also take strong transcendence into account.

For the majority of religious people in the world, this transcendence is not just an abstraction, but it has a personal quality. The something that is beyond relates to us in love, and we in turn offer it our love. This is known as **theism**, belief in a God who is free, transcending both us and the world, but who wishes to relate to us. As transcendent, God can become an object of devotion (Peters, 2007; Hay, Reich, & Utsch, 2006). Nontheistic religions may acknowledge strong transcendence but deny its personal quality. This is a traditional stance within Buddhism.

Strong transcendence poses problems for science in general and psychology in particular on a number of fronts. First, scientists generally prefer tidy models that attempt to explain things without reference to transcendence (Smith, 2000). Inclusion of transcendence in a model is an admission that the theory is limited in its explanatory power, while many model builders hope to continually expand their reach. Second, some scientists have a limited view of logic which conflicts with aspects of transcendence such as paradox. As Wolfhart Pannenberg has noted, some scientists have a tendency to confuse **rationality** (something that makes sense) with **rationalism** (something that conforms to a rigid understanding of logic; Tupper, 1973, p. 261), a stance that is quite restrictive and at odds with how most people—including scientists—actually arrive at knowledge (Watts & Williams, 1988, p. 56; Polanyi, 1962). This demonstrates that our ideas about logic and rationality are not neutral but have important implications (Watson, 1994). Third, freedom also poses problems for many scientific explanations. Like most aspects of strong transcendence, freedom is defined in a negative way as *not* chance or *not* necessity; as such it cannot be directly observed (Macquarrie, 1982, p. 13). In the words of Levinas it is a **trace phenomenon**; we can see its effects as in the free response we make to the demands of others (Treanor, 2005), but we can never see the thing itself. You can observe the fact that you are reading this book and understand how this is different than alternatives that you might have chosen, but you cannot measure or prove that freedom allowed you to make the choice. Some scientists assume that since something cannot be directly observed, it cannot exist. Scholars who accept the presence of strong transcendence argue that problems like rationalism or freedom show us a natural limitation of science in its quest to grasp the human being. They suggest that we cannot understand the human person solely by looking at ourselves from a non-transcendent point of view. We must also seek other ways of knowing, (Goldsmith, 1994, p. 95; Howard, Youngs, & Siatczynski, 1989; Powlison, 2003, p. 205; Macquarrie, 1982, pp. 26, 41–42; Zizioulas, 2006).

Since transcendence is an essential part of most religions, the study of religion using a system that excludes transcendence would appear to have limits in understanding its object of study. For instance, hope for an afterlife is an important part of religion for most theists, and an understanding of this phenomenon must accept that for believers this type of transcendence is entirely real. However, many scientists—including some psychologists—would find this difficult to accept because it is not directly observable. As a science, psychology suffers under limitations and needs to avoid "psychologism," the tendency to assume that all of religion can be explained by psychology when it obviously excludes critical aspects of the phenomena (Vergote, 1969, pp. 5–21).

1.2.1.2 Religion as Immanence or Human Activity

Many experts prefer to see religion as a particular type of human activity, and certainly all major religious traditions have developed philosophies on the nature of the human person and our place in the world (e.g., Hartsman, 2002). For instance, the sociologists Charles Glock and Rodney Stark see religion in relation to our **values**, things that we deem particularly important. They feel that individuals develop value orientations or "over-arching and sacred systems of symbols, beliefs, values, and practices concerning ultimate meaning which men shape to interpret their world" (Glock & Stark, 1965, p. 9), and they view religion as one manifestation of this phenomenon. By this definition, Marxism and other secular systems of thought are akin to religion as they provide value orientations. However, Glock and Stark also view religion as a social phenomenon with particular dimensions: (1) ritualistic, (2) experiential, (3) intellectual, and (4) consequential, i.e., having implications for behavior and ethics.

In a similar way, religious studies scholar Ninian Smart (1998) identifies religion as a human activity with some or all of the following dimensions: (1) practical and ritual, including prayer, worship, and meditation; (2) experiential and emotional; (3) narrative or mythic; (4) doctrinal and philosophical; (5) ethical and legal; (6) social and institutional; and (7) material, including buildings and other artifacts. He believes that the narrative or mythic element of religion is particularly important, as it includes the sacred stories and art that help define both the group and the sacred entities that are the focus of the religion. Smart argues that many secular movements such as atheism, humanism, or Marxism fit some or all of this definition but that it is not proper to call them religions, because "they conceive of themselves, on the whole, as antireligious" (1998, p. 26). However they can be thought of as offering a **worldview** (1999a,b)—a basic set of assumptions and way of thinking about self, the world and our place in it (cf. Kearney, 1984, p. 41). Secular worldviews often appear to fill some of the same functions as a religion by providing an **ideology**, or system of thought, that attempts to explain everything from a single premise. For instance, the ideology of **humanism** is based on a concept of the basic good and power of humanity. In the modern world, ideologies often claim to have a scientific basis to increase their persuasive power (Arendt, 1968, p. 468).

Other authors prefer to look at religion as an activity that is part of **culture**, the complex whole of "capabilities and habits acquired by man as a member of society" (Tylor, 1871), especially the "webs of significance" available in society that help us in the search for meaning (Geertz, 1973, p. 5). Belzen (1999) argues that seeing religion as merely another part of culture could provide a "religiously neutral" starting point for inquiry by psychologists. A cultural view of religion tends to see it as a human production, a multidimensional system or worldview that underpins a culture and allows members to construct meaning and make sense out of the world. This is a popular approach to religion in contemporary university settings (Marsden & Longfield, 1992; Vergote, 1997, p. 19).

There are two ways of approaching cultural phenomena. In the **etic** model, cultural forms are seen as universal phenomena with similar characteristics across all cultural settings. In the case of religion, an etic view assumes that all religions share certain attributes like having a view of transcendence, and that they can be broken down and analyzed according to a universal set of categories, as when we compare Christianity and Buddhism on their "devotional practices." In the **emic** model, each cultural form is thought to be unique and occurs within a given physical, social, and historical context. An emic view of religion would argue that two different religions are not just alternate varieties of the same thing; rather they are unique systems and each must be understood and evaluated on its own merit (e.g., Shuman & Meador, 2003, pp. 37–40). Both of these approaches can be found in the contemporary psychology and religion literature, with scientists tending to use etic models and theologians or religious studies scholars arguing more from an emic stance.

Definitions of religion that view it as a human activity often have two implications. First, if religion is defined as a worldview, it is possible to speak of everyone as being religious since everyone has a worldview. The Christian theologian Paul Tillich seems to have believed this, saying that it was impossible to be nonreligious because everyone has "confessed or concealed answers to the questions which underlie every form of religion" and if they don't profess a religion they at least belong to a "quasi-religion" (1963a, pp. 2–3). Second, when religion is viewed as a human activity it is natural to conduct a **functional analysis** and look at it in terms of its functions—what it does—instead of a **substantive analysis** that looks at its content and specific beliefs. For instance, a functional analysis might evaluate religion in terms of its ability to help us cope with life stresses, while a substantive analysis could look more at the truth value of religious doctrines. Functional analyses are commonly used in psychology (Zinnbauer, Pargament, & Scott, 1999; Ahmed, 2004) and offer a practical approach to study; the disadvantage is that functionalism can obscure underlying differences, sometimes labeling everyone as "religious" despite the fact that some people avoid or oppose it (Smart, 1999b, p. 57; McDargh, 1983, p. 9; Vergote, 1997, pp. 14–15). A functional analysis might conclude that there is no difference between a table lamp and a flashlight because both give light. However, a power outage or a battery failure after prolonged use would show that the functional analysis had overlooked some important substantive differences! Similarly, religion may function differently in those for whom it is a central part of life compared with individuals who seldom practice it. Finally, functional analyses can imply that religion is *only* about its functions and not about its substance such as its views on transcendent reality, a position that would certainly not be shared by adherents of religious traditions (Drees, 1998, p. 323; Berger, 1974).

Are religions more about transcendence or immanence? While some religions may emphasize one over the other, all the great religious traditions encompass both (cf. Shah-Kazemi, 2002, 2006, p. 69; al-'Arabi, 1980, pp. 72–75).

1.2.2 What Is Spirituality?

Over the last several decades the term **spirituality** has entered the common language as an alternate way to describe our search for the transcendent. In its original English meaning, "spiritual" was a term used to contrast church life with "worldly" or materialistic ways of being (Rizzuto, 2005). In the 19th century, "spirituality" was not a commonly used term and "Spiritualism" referred to contact with spirits and other psychic phenomena. In contemporary usage, the term has a number of common meanings (Zinnbauer et al., 1997), and definitions in the scholarly literature also vary. These differences reflect the fact that spirituality is a broad term encompassing multiple domains of meaning that may differ among various cultural, national, and religious groups (Roehlkepartain, Benson, King, & Wagener, 2006; Lewis, 2004; Takahashi & Ide, 2003). Today the term is often used to denote *the experiential and personal side of our relationship to the transcendent or sacred* (cf. Hill et al., 2000; Emmons & Crumpler, 1999). Those who use the term in this way typically contrast it with religion, which they define narrowly as the organizational structures, practices, and beliefs of a religious group (Zinnbauer et al., 1999). Theologians and religious practitioners, on the other hand, tend to prefer definitions that draw less of a strict division between religion and spirituality. In their eyes, spirituality is *the living reality of religion as experienced by an adherent of the tradition.*

Roof (1999, p. 35) argues that spirituality encompasses 4 themes: (1) a source of values and ultimate meaning or purpose beyond the self, including a sense of mystery and self-transcendence; (2) a way of understanding; (3) inner awareness; and (4) personal integration (cf. Tillich, 1958; Becker, 2001; MacInnes, 2003, p. 51; Ingersoll, 1994). The last characteristic is particularly important. Spirituality has an integrative and harmonizing function that involves (a) our inner unity and (b) our relationship and connectedness with others and to a broader reality that powers our ability to be transcendent (Schneiders, 1998; cf. McGrath, 2006; Kosek, 1996; Theophan, 1995, pp. 95–99). Thus, the fact that we are spiritual is not a separate nature or characteristic that we have but an inseparable part of all we are and do (Wagener & Malony, 2006; Wuthnow, 1998; Shafranske & Gorsuch, 1984, p. 231; May, 2004, p. 42; Wiseman, 2007). Most visions of spirituality also involve contact with the **sacred**, or "those forces whose dominance over man increases or seems to increase in proportion to man's effort to master them" (Girard, 1977, p. 31; cf. Roehlkepartain, 2004), so spirituality has a powerful, mysterious quality that cannot be reduced to a simple object of study (May, 2004, p. 183). Ideally, spirituality takes us beyond ordinary daily experience and has a transforming effect on our lives and relationships. It is not just about being and experience, it is also about doing. In contemporary practice, it involves a search for higher values, inner freedom, and things that give life meaning (Shannon, 2000, p. 47; Vergote, 2003). While in Western countries this search has typically involved a search for God, a nontheist can also be involved in the quest for meaning (Mansager et al., 2002).

Religious conceptions of spirituality generally involve **thick** definitions that are rich in allusions to specific beliefs and practices, as opposed to **thin** or generic "one size fits all" definitions that focus more on natural experiences, personal values, or connectedness (Zaehner, 1961; Walzer, 1994; Sheldrake, 1998, p. 56; e.g., Miller, 1999; Emmons, 1999, p. 92; Piedmont, 1999). For instance, Jernigan (2001) offers a thin definition of spirituality as "the organization (centering) of individual and collective life around dynamic patterns of meanings, values, and relationships that are trusted to make life worthwhile (or, at least, livable) and death meaningful." (p. 418). His thick definition of Christian spirituality is more specific: "the organization (centering) of individual and collective life around loving relationships with God, neighbor, self, and all of creation—responding to the love of God revealed in Jesus Christ and at work through the Holy Spirit." (p. 419). Thick definitions often are theistic, have a strong communal content and are multidimensional with experiential, relational, and behavioral components (Dykstra, 1986; Aumann, 1980, p. 18; Sheldrake, 1998, pp. 58, 82; Schneiders, 1994; Hall & Edwards, 1996, 2002). Thin definitions of spirituality are attractive to scientists because they are thought to tap universal human qualities related to invariant natural laws that the scientist can discover through research. However, some scholars believe that such definitions may distort the fundamental nature of spirituality (Slife, Hope, & Nebeker, 1999). Thicker concepts may contain important content and contextual information necessary for understanding a particular type of spirituality. Different groups and individuals have very diverse ideas about it, making thin or global interpretations difficult (Helminiak, 1987, p. 165; 1996; Richardson, 1996; Zinnbauer et al., 1997; Zinnbauer et al., 1999; Shahabi et al., 2002; cf. MacIntyre, 1988, 1990).

Given that religion and spirituality are complex concepts that have different meanings for different groups, it is difficult to articulate a single definition for either of them. However, their multidimensionality suggests that definitions that focus on only one aspect of religion or spirituality should be avoided.

1.2.2.1 Connections Between Religion and Spirituality

A number of scholars see spirituality and religion as conceptually different. Sinnott (2001), for instance, thinks spirituality involves one's relation to the sacred as distinct from religion which involves adherence to specific beliefs and practices, although he also admits that the two are sometimes hard to separate and are often not distinguished in theory and research (Sinnott, 2002a,b). Separating the two has the advantage of recognizing that a kind of broadly defined spirituality is quite possible for those outside of religious traditions and communities (Rayburn, 2004). Focusing on spirituality fits especially well within a Western framework that focuses on the individual and their experience rather than the needs and experiences of a larger community (Mattis, Ahluwalia, Cowie, & Kirkland-Harris, 2006; Bonnycastle, 2004). Continental European authors find the distinction particularly attractive, as some associate the decline in traditional values and religion with a turn toward spirituality and a focus on the "deeper" layers of the self (e.g., Houtman & Aupers, 2007).

There are numerous indications in the empirical literature that in Western samples it is possible to (1) develop definitions and measurement instruments that reliably measure religion and spirituality separately, (2) find that they have different qualities or effects, and (3) identify people who are either spiritual or religious, but not both, although in many people they are highly related (Halman & Riis, 2003; Shahabi et al., 2002). For instance, Dowling and her colleagues (Dowling et al., 2004) have found that religion and spirituality have independent effects on thriving, although spirituality also has an effect on religiosity. They found that spirituality involved orientation to help others and do good work, as well as participate in activities of self-interest. This was found to contrast with religiosity, which involved things related to beliefs and institutional influences. Some studies with adults also show that religion and spirituality can be separated and that they change differently during the aging process, with group averages on religiosity staying fairly steady across the life span, while spirituality increases, especially after age 60 (e.g., Dillon & Wink, 2003). Individuals who are spiritual but not religious may also differ in beliefs, for example, they have higher levels of **nihilism**, the belief that life has no purpose (Shahabi et al., 2002).

Others raise objections to the practice of making a strict separation between religion and spirituality. Certainly individuals in religious traditions generally reject the idea that these are separate (e.g., Merton, 2005b, p. 46). The psychologist Brian Zinnbauer and his colleagues have pointed out that researchers who draw a strict distinction between religion and spirituality often polarize the concepts in value-laden ways, with organized, communal religion defined in negative terms and individualistic spirituality in positive terms. In their view, these types of definitions can tell us more about the values or prejudices of the investigators than the phenomenon they are studying (Zinnbauer et al., 1999). They also note that the people we study generally do not draw a strict distinction between them. In their studies of US Midwestern adults, only 6.7% of their sample saw the two as strictly different, while the vast majority saw the two as interrelated in some way (Zinnbauer et al., 1997; cf. Musick, Traphagan, Koenig, & Larson, 2000). Similar results have also been found in Japan (Takahashi & Ide, 2003), and personality research suggests that those high in spirituality and religiousness share many things in common such as a compassionate attitude toward others (Piedmont, 2005). This suggests that in some cultural settings a distinction between religion and spirituality may not be meaningful and that even when the two can be distinguished they can support each other in positive ways (Verma & Maria, 2006).

Is it really possible to be spiritual without being religious? If by this we mean is it possible to engage in a spiritual quest without formal membership in a religious group, the answer is "yes." However, complete separation of spirituality from religion is difficult. The psychologist David Elkins has argued that it is possible and in his book *Beyond Religion* (1998) presents a program for spiritual life outside of religion. However, his program makes extensive use of practices and beliefs taken from major religious traditions, and he frequently quotes religious figures in support of his arguments! This illustrates the fact that in practice it is often impossible to divorce spirituality and religion from each other (Hill & Pargament, 2003; Eliassen, Taylor, & Lloyd, 2005) and that the practice of spirituality without the support of religious structures is difficult in many ways. In Christianity, religious practitioners and theologians have traditionally resisted the move to split religion and theology from spirituality as inaccurate and harmful, although it has occurred during periods of history. These writers would argue that ultimately the Christian religion and spirituality require each other, and the same is probably true in other religious traditions as well (Tillich, 1963a, pp. 88–89; Pannenberg, 1983, p. 13; Rahner, 1975, p. 40; Sheldrake, 1995, pp. 52–57; Rossler, 1999). Certainly the study of spirituality in those who are outside of religious groups is particularly difficult, so that most research on spirituality to date involves those who affiliate with churches or other religious groups (Emmons, 1999, p. 98).

If religion and spirituality are distinct yet related, there are two ways of understanding their connection. One way is to suppose that one of the constructs is actually a subset of the other so that religion is just an "add-on" or response to spirituality or vice versa. For instance, Kenneth Pargament defines religion broadly as "a search for significance in ways related to the sacred" (1999, p. 32) and sees religion as a broader concept than spirituality (Zinnbauer et al., 1999; Pargament, 1999). An opposite perspective is offered by the European researcher Stifoss-Hanssen (1999), who argues that spirituality is a broader construct because the quality of sacredness emphasized in religion is not experienced by atheists and agnostics. A third perspective is to see that religion is related to the sacred but that sacredness can be approached from other ways (e.g., Demerath, 2000). A sensible way to resolve the issue is to treat religion and spirituality as distinct but overlapping (e.g., Hill et al., 2000; Benson, Roehlkepartain, & Rude, 2003). Scholars who follow this line of thought have developed typologies that classify people into categories according to their levels of religiousness and spirituality (see Table 1.1).

Table 1.1 Typology of religion and spirituality

	Religiosity	
	High Engaged, Participatory (US Percentage)	Low Disengaged, Uninvolved (US Percentage)
Spirituality		
High	Traditional Integrated (59–74%)	Spiritual Seeker Individualistic (14–20%)
Low	Cultural Dogmatic (4–15%)	Uninterested or Antagonistic (3–12%)

Note: Figures for relative proportions are from multiple US studies as reported by Marler & Hadaway (2002). For use of the terms "Spiritual Seeker" and "Dogmatic" see Roof (2003).

1.3 Religion and Spirituality Today

What is the status of religion and spirituality in the world today? This is a difficult question to answer. Both are extraordinarily rich parts of our human experience and social life, and as such are resistant to easy description. The complexity of the topic and weaknesses in available statistics are complicated by the fact that different measures of religion may be appropriate for different cultures (Chaves & Stephens, 2003; Presser & Stinson, 1998; Sherkat & Ellison, 1999; Kisala, 2003). For instance, traditional research often measures religiosity by membership in a religious community such as a congregation. However, Asian Buddhists may be very religious but typically do not belong to a specific group—temples do not have membership lists.

Despite these problems, social commentators and sociologists have produced a number of descriptions of the current state of religion. These cluster around three points of view—secularization, religious transformation, and cultural divide.

1.3.1 The Secularization Hypothesis

Early 20th-century sociologists assumed that religion was a critical part of human life. The famous French sociologist Emile Durkheim, for instance, argued that religion would always be present because it performs necessary functions. This was challenged mid-century by the **secularization hypothesis** (Davie, 2003). This theory developed out of French Enlightenment and positivist views of history, which hold that religion is a primitive way of thinking that will eventually be displaced by modern science and technology (Gorski, 2003; Lash, 1996, p. 110; see Section 2.3). Steady declines in European religious participation beginning in the 19th century especially among younger adults seem to support the idea that religion is dying out. Other authors hold a milder version of the secularization hypothesis and argue that while religion may not die out, it will have declining influence in the public sphere. Belief may continue but will no longer be taken for granted or in some circles even considered a respectable option (Gill, 2001; Norris & Inglehart, 2004, p. 73; Taylor, 2007, pp. 1–14). In this view, the absence or negative portrayal of religious figures and practices in the media are surface manifestations of secularization (Clarke, 2005).

Taylor (2007) argues that secularization is about more than removing religious beliefs in God. He outlines the components of secularization as follows:

- It is a rejection of the possibility of strong transcendence, a move to a purely immanent and human-centered frame of reference that assumes life is about human flourishing and achieving purely human goals (cf. Arendt, 1998, p. 253). Goals beyond ordinary human flourishing or afterlife beliefs are seen as irrational, unscientific, enthusiastic, or fanatical.
- It removes the sense that the world is "enchanted" and affected by spiritual and moral forces or agencies.

- It sees the universe as at best impersonal, and at worst cold or threatening, rather than created by God with positive divine purposes in mind. Time is seen as infinite, homogeneous and empty as opposed to moving toward a particular conclusion.
- It rejects the idea that we are persons embedded in a social and natural world that has divine purposes; rather we are individuals with "buffered" identities disengaged from others. Expressive varieties of individualism that developed especially in the 1960s gave this aspect of secularization a big boost.
- It sees human rationality and power as key values, with an active, interventionist goal of controlling both nature and other people to achieve human goals.
- It works to exclude religion from important areas such as politics, economics, or ethics (cf. Vergote, 1969, p. 253).

Wilson (2001) provides a typical account of the secularization hypothesis. He argues that secularization is a global process affecting all religions. In the first phase of secularization, increasing material comforts cause salvation to be relocated from some future time and place—heaven or some state of rebirth—to the present. This removes the motive for spiritual and moral striving, which leads to a second phase in which morality is seen as simply following the rules so that one can participate in society. In the third and final phase, work and society become increasingly depersonalized, and the moral social order is abandoned in favor of mechanistic efficiency and productivity, which have minimal requirements in terms of personal relations or moral commitments. The sacred or transcendent is eliminated, and the focus shifts to pleasure through common participation in technological and financial structures. Religion has declining influence over the individual as well as social life and politics, although there may be continuing personal religiousness (Tschannen, 1991; Halman & Pettersson, 2003a; Greinacher, 1999; Procter & Hornsby-Smith, 2003). Scholars like Bruce (2001, 2002) see this as an irreversible process under current social, economic, and intellectual conditions. In this view, religion will cease to matter as a real force in society and the lives of individuals.

Many social commentators who agree that secularization is occurring argue that it is associated with a number of social problems including distrust, weakened social institutions, increasing rates of psychological problems, and a decreased sense of meaning and coherence. These problems lead to apathy, cynicism, and consumerism or materialism (Martin, 1978; Tillich, 1963a), although some see fewer negatives and more positives in these developments (e.g., Halman & Riis, 2003; Bréchon, 2003). Secularization can also lead to **atheism** which can take a number of forms: an active denial of God and the value of religion as in secular humanism and some forms of scientific atheism, or a more passive lack of affirmation where people may retain membership in religious organizations and participate in ceremonies like weddings or funerals but reject its daily role in their lives as in consideration of moral questions. While science is often associated with active forms of atheism, in fact science is not necessarily atheistic (Peters, 2007; Pannenberg, 1983; Tupper, 1973, pp. 27–32; MacIntyre & Ricoeur, 1969; see Chapter 2).

By the late 20th century, the secularization hypothesis had been severely challenged, and it has been rejected by a number of contemporary scholars

(Sherkat & Ellison, 1999; Berger, 1999, 2007; Davidman, 2007). Evidence against the secularization hypothesis includes the following:

1. *Statistics show continued strong interest in religion and low rates of atheism, even in technologically and scientifically sophisticated societies like the US.* The Gallup International survey in 1999 found that 84% of their sample identified themselves as part of a religious denomination. Rates of atheism were low, ranging from about 2% in North America to 15% in Western Europe. Even in Western Europe, some countries still have high rates of participation, and the evidence suggests that while disbelief has increased and religious practice has decreased, changes in belief or affiliation have been much less substantial so that the population might better be described as "unchurched" rather than "secularized" (e.g., Halman & Riis, 2003; Davie, 2000). People in countries with formal commitments to atheism such as China also appear to have a strong and increasing interest in religion (Tu, 1999).

2. *Trends in contemporary religion aren't really that different than the past.* While individualized spirituality may be more prominent today (Taylor, 1999), since at least the early 1800s there has always been a portion of American society that has identified with different spiritual movements and rejected mainstream religion. Also, while membership rates have fluctuated quite a bit, US attendance and participation rates have actually been quite stable at around 40% (Wuthnow, 1998, p. 40; Dillon & Wink, 2007, pp. 43–69; Ammerman, 1997; Presser & Chavez, 2007).

3. *Trends away from religion are really part of a more general trend away from social involvement.* Several authors (e.g., Chaves & Stephens, 2003; Putnam, 2000; Presser & Stinson, 1998) suggest that any trends away from organized religion are part of a general decline in participation in civic and voluntary organizations so that "secularization" is more about social disengagement than a move away from religion and spirituality.

4. *Secularization in apparently less religious areas such as Europe is an anomaly due to unusual sociocultural factors* (Davie, 1999, 2001). Some believe that higher rates of European nonparticipation are due to the traditional identification between government and religion in many of those countries, allowing religious non-adherence to become a form of social protest (e.g., Martin, 1978). The French sociologist Daniele Hervieu-Leger (2000, 2001) also argues that there is a unique amnesic quality in modern European society that makes it difficult to maintain access to traditional beliefs and practices that underlie communal religion.

While levels of strong religious commitment in the US remain stable, one change that does seem to be taking place is a decrease in those who are affiliated with a religion but minimally involved, and an increase in those who are completely disconnected. This trend is probably aided by increasing cultural support for alternative religious practices, as well as the idea that spirituality, morality, and religion can or should be separate. This suggests that increasing *polarization* rather than decreasing levels of genuine commitment is the trend in the US and perhaps elsewhere (Dillon & Wink, 2007, pp. 70–72, 119–128; Putnam, 2000, p. 75; Norris & Inglehart, 2004, p. 93). However, as a number of authors have pointed out (e.g., Abramowitz, 2001), declining participation or membership rates do not mean that people are necessarily becoming less religious or spiritual. The idea of a simple steady progression toward secularization does not fit the evidence and is leading scholars to look for alternatives (Ammerman, 2007b).

1.3.2 The Religious Transformation Hypothesis

Problems with the secularization hypothesis have led to the development of a revisionist or **religious transformation hypothesis** (e.g., Luckmann, 1967; Stark & Bainbridge, 1997; Roof, 1993, 1999). This theory rejects the secularization model of straightforward decline and argues that cultural changes like increasing individualism and social fragmentation will transform but not eliminate religion, making a more individualized spiritual and religious practice attractive (Hill et al., 2000; cf. Ammerman, 2007a, pp. 4–9; Taylor, 2007, p. 461). Hervieu-Leger (2001) notes that while participation in organized religion in Europe has dropped dramatically, there has been little decline in interest in spirituality or religion, just a shift from communal participation to a system where individuals choose their own constructed belief systems and participate in communal activities only as they advance their personal agendas. Taylor (2007) argues that the modernist and secularist view of life that rejects transcendence is unconvincing and unattractive to many people because it leads to a sense of absence or emptiness and lack of meaning, and so a turn away from traditional religion does not lead to unbelief for most people but to many alternate forms of religious seeking. Individuals may become "spiritual but not religious," or even engage in **vicarious religion,** where the persons themselves do not practice but support religious institutions and the practice of religion by others (Davie, 1999). Taylor predicts that when the secularization narrative does not pan out and the evils attributed to religion do not go away in secularized societies, the draw of unbelief will lessen, and the move to a transformed religion will gain further support.

This increasing individualism in religion is thought to fuel several trends:

1. *The increase in religious seeking both inside and outside of religious organizations.* Robert Wuthnow (1998) and Wade Clark Roof (1999) argue that disillusionment with religion has led some US residents to go from being **dwellers** or participants in a particular religious tradition to being **seekers** who have no firm commitment to a particular religious group. Seekers tend to see churches as providing religious goods and services to be sampled, with the primary purpose of personal satisfaction, enabling one to survive a busy contemporary life. The increase in seeking is thought to be a product of skepticism in the validity of any one religious or secularized spiritual path. It is also associated with certain kinds of family backgrounds marked by rigidity and less closeness. The shift toward seeking and away from dwelling changes the expectations and reasons people participate in religious organizations, which has provoked experimentation among religious groups for different ways of reaching out to seekers (D'Antonio, 1995; Wright, 1995). Seeking has advantages in terms of flexibility and adaptability, but it also has disadvantages. Roof and others argue that the personal individualistic spirituality of seekers often involves an incoherent and

unclear pattern of beliefs and practices. They also argue that it is hard to maintain commitment and identity without spiritual support from group interaction. Seekers that lack this community connection tend to lack strong commitments to particular beliefs and practices and so are more likely to remain spiritual "tourists" rather than pilgrims dedicated to growth (cf. MacIntyre, 1984, pp. 221–223).

2. *Religious and spiritual eclecticism.* The formation of individually constructed spiritualities often involves combining religious practices from different traditions and the many alternatives that are available, what Roof has called a *pastiche* style of religiosity (Roof & Gesch, 1995; Besecke, 2007). In North America and Western Europe only about 20% of the 1998 Gallup sample agreed with the statement "there exists one and only one true religion," while 55% of the Europeans and 71% of the North Americans endorsed the statement "there is truth in many religions." Similar results have been found in more recent polls (e.g., Pew Research Center & Pew Forum on Religious Life, 2002). This kind of syncretism can also been seen throughout the developing global culture, for instance, in Japan where people combine Buddhist and Shinto worship (Levitt, 2007; Pace, 2007; Musick et al., 2000). Interestingly, some scholars argue that globalization trends such as secularization and Westernization will eventually lead to homogeneity and *less* religious variety (Halman & Pettersson, 2003c).

3. *The rise of New Age spirituality and new religious movements, as well as the revival of ancient beliefs and practices like paganism.* Herrick (2003) argues that a "new religious synthesis" now exists for many people that combines the use of scientific rationality to enhance spiritual evolution with mystical ideas about nature and personal divinity. Hervieu-Leger (2001) sees New Age religious movements as individualistic expressions that emphasize the subjective nature of reality. In these groups, truth must be discovered through an individual quest for self-perfection that satisfies the needs of the seeker. Sociologists like Hervieu-Leger are somewhat critical of this development, as they question whether a truly individualistic spirituality can ever succeed in creating satisfying meaning, if individuals never have real affirmation of their views from others.

Taylor (2007, pp. 486–488, 505–529) argues that there are both positives and negatives to seeking religion. On the positive side, it focuses on authenticity and moving beyond a lifestyle purely focused on pleasure. It rejects a purely instrumental stance toward the world that leads to personal or environmental devaluation and fragmentation. It also is expressivist in nature and facilitates practices such as pilgrimages that fit in well with a seeking style of spirituality. On the negative side, it tends to be individualized and privatized, and since it lacks structure or support, it can lead people into practice patterns that are shallow and undemanding. Taylor argues that some seekers will find this unsatisfying and will be drawn back to traditional religious structures and practices. He believes the US will be particularly congenial to increased spiritual or religious seeking because of the independence of religion from government, its positive role in American society, and the long tradition in the US of nontraditional religious forms. However, not all the religious transformation that is taking place is of the individualistic seeking variety. For instance, some writers in the Christian tradition have commented that individuals coming to churches are highly interested in community, as well as experiential and participatory activities or rituals (Pleasants, 2004).

1.3.3 The Cultural Divide Hypothesis

Ronald Inglehart has proposed a new theory about global religious trends that attempts to update the secularization hypothesis (Norris & Inglehart, 2004; Inglehart & Welzel, 2005). Inglehart begins his analysis of sociological data with the observation that one of the strongest forces behind the importance of religion is a need for security (cf. Pannenberg, 1983, p. 74). He believes that in Europe, economic development has increased security and reduced physical constraints on lifestyle, while the welfare system has produced a sense of existential security, that one's survival can be assumed. This increased security, along with less constraint, leads to an emphasis on values of self-expression, personal autonomy, and well-being, as well as decreasing commitments to the family and childrearing. Together, these factors lead to lower birth rates in Europe, as well as secularization and less motivation for religious participation. In this environment, religion (as well as family) is seen as an extra that may or may not be desirable rather than a necessary way of life (Casey, 1996, p. 25). On the other hand, the developing world faces continued and increasing threats to security. This leads to increased religious observance, which in turn strengthens family values and leads to population growth. The combination of decreasing population in secularized areas and increasing numbers in more religious ones means that as a whole the world has actually become *more* traditionally religious over the past 40 years (Lippman & Keith, 2006, p. 113). Inglehart thinks this will produce an increasing **cultural divide** between secular and religious societies and provoke reactions from sections of the world that see themselves threatened by secular values. His theory is unclear about the reasons for continued religiosity in the US and differences in secularization in different parts of Europe; perhaps they are a result of complex differences in history and patterns of religious activity (Halman & Pettersson, 2003a).

   Although each of these sociological hypotheses has its weaknesses, all of them also have some supporting evidence. Secularization, transformation, and polarization are important parts of the contemporary religious landscape. An understanding of these trends is helpful as we consider psychological perspectives on religion.

1.4 Psychological Approaches to Religion and Spirituality

1.4.1 What Is Psychology?

Like the term spirituality, the meaning of the word **psychology** has changed over time. The term originally comes from the Greek words *psyche* or soul, and *logos* or study. This association of psychology with the human soul implies a focus on the interior life of the person, and historically most definitions of psychology have labeled it as the study of mental life or the mind. Prior to 1850, most works in psychology were written by philosophers, but in the latter half of the 19th century experimental laboratories for the study of psychology were established in Europe and North America, and researchers began applying methods from the natural sciences to the study of the mind. Psychology then became seen as *the scientific study of behavior*, and this definition is the one found in the contemporary textbooks and scholarly articles written by most psychologists. In North America, this emphasis on natural science led to a loss of contact between psychologists and scholars in fields like philosophy or theology that did not have an exclusively scientific outlook (Gorsuch, 2002a, p. 48; Fuchs, 2002). This type of split was much less pronounced in Europe, so interdisciplinary study and cooperation has a much stronger tradition there, especially on the Continent.

In the US, **behaviorism** was the dominant paradigm in psychology for the first half of the 20th century. Behaviorists believe that human behavior can be explained largely on the basis of learning and reinforcement from the environment. Secondary to this was the **psychodynamic** or psychoanalytic school of thought, which sees behavior as determined by internal and often unconscious forces and structures. The discovery of antidepressant and antipsychotic drugs in the 1950s led to increased interest in **neuroscience** theories that explained behavior on the basis of biological and genetic factors affecting the brain. Finally, progress in design of digital computers invited comparisons with the mind and helped fuel the development of **cognitive psychology**, which uses scientific methods to study mental processes like language, reasoning, and memory. The rise of these biological and cognitive models have displaced behaviorism as the dominant models in psychology (Miller, 2003), although behavioral and psychodynamic views continue to have some influence within the field.

While many early psychologists were interested in or sympathetic to religion, none of the four dominant approaches to psychology has been particularly friendly to religion, and in the US, psychologists tend to be less religious than the general population. This, along with the disciplinary isolation that began in the early 20th century, has kept psychologists and theologians or scholars in religious studies relatively unacquainted with current work in each other's fields. Christian theologians and scholars in other religious traditions often respond to older theories that are no longer of wide interest within psychology, and psychologists are often unaware of important aspects of the religious traditions that they study. However, recent writers have expressed more appreciation for alternative perspectives, as in the openness of some psychologists to more theoretical perspectives (e.g., Vande Kemp, 1999).

1.4.2 Early American Psychology of Religion

Many of the founders of American psychology had interests in religion, as well as personal religious backgrounds (Spilka, 1987), and were interested in applying scientific principles to its study. This included the two main founders of the field: William James (1842–1910) at Harvard and G. Stanley Hall (1844–1924) at Clark University. A second generation of scholars carried on the work of James and Hall, including Edwin Starbuck (1866–1947) and James Leuba (1868–1946). Starbuck and Leuba both did their Ph.D. work at Clark, and so together with Hall they are sometimes referred to as the "Clark school" in the psychology of religion (Vande Kemp, 1992), although Starbuck worked closely with James and shared many of his views. Two aspects of religion were of primary interest to these early authors: religious experience and religious development (Booth, 1981).

1.4.2.1   William James

William James (1842–1910) was the founding president of the American Psychological Association and one of the greatest American psychologists and philosophers. Originally trained in medicine, he moved into the field of psychology and become the first American professor of the subject. Later in his career, he became more interested in philosophical and religious topics, including the study of psychic phenomena. From 1899 to 1902 he spent a sabbatical in Europe, during which time he delivered one of the famous Gifford lectures in natural theology at the University of Edinburgh. His lectures were published in 1902 under the title, *The Varieties of Religious Experience*, which remains one of the great classics of psychological and religious literature (see Section 4.2).

1.4.2.2   The Clark School

Hall and the reinterpretation of Christianity. Hall is best known as a developmental psychologist and an early advocate of **genetic psychology**, which held that the development of the individual was a recapitulation or repeat of prior stages in the development of the human species. He thought that Darwinism and critical views of Biblical texts made it impossible for any intelligent, educated person to believe in traditional Christianity, but that the Christian religion contained vital truths worth preserving. He thought genetic psychology and secular ideas could help restructure Christianity, preserving essential psychological truths while rejecting intellectually unrespectable beliefs such as supernaturalism. His critique and proposal, contained in *Jesus the Christ in the Light of Psychology*, was published in 1917. In the book, he tried to apply psychoanalytic principles to explain Christianity as "a purely psychological projection" (Hall, 1924, p. 422). Hall believed in the existence of a vital force called the Mansoul that represented the highest nature present in humanity and contained our potential for development (Hall, 1924, pp. 280, 442–443). The goal of evolution was for us to surrender our individuality to this larger racial consciousness, which in his view is the real god. Hall thought that the racial soul was a residue from a past "probationary age" (p. 243) and that the function of religion was to bring us back to these older aspects of our psychic life, hopefully assisting us in our advancement. Jesus was thought of as an expression of this principle, who showed the inherent good in human nature and the possibilities our race might achieve through continued evolution. In this view, Jesus offered a kind of practical psychotherapy that would release us from guilt and fear.

Leuba and the triumph of science over religion. Leuba came to America from Switzerland and studied with Hall. Leuba had abandoned personal religious beliefs prior to beginning his professional work and became a sharp critic of traditional religion, although he viewed spirituality in a positive light (Wulff, 2000). In 1921, he conducted a famous study on the religious beliefs of scientists that indicated lower levels of religious belief in "greater men" of science as opposed to "lesser men," from which he concluded that "disbelief in a personal God and in personal immortality is directly proportional to abilities making for success in the sciences" (1925, pp. 324–325). A follow-up of Leuba's study suggests possible declining levels of personal belief and increasing levels of disinterest or disbelief among leading scientists across the 20th century (Larson & Witham, 1998).

Leuba (1912) agreed with Hall that traditional Christianity was no longer acceptable and that psychology could assist in the formation of something to take its place. He believed that all religious experiences or needs could be explained on a purely psychological basis, with the help of biological and evolutionary theory and an understanding of normal thought processes. He believed that all behavior is **instrumental**, designed to achieve gratification of needs and desires, and that religion was about how we relate to and use the powers of the psyche. Religion is thus a psychological phenomenon, and should be studied by psychological experts, not religious practitioners or theologians who he viewed as ignorant. Serious theology should only be conducted using scientific methods, and thus should become a branch of psychology. When this happened rapid spiritual improvement would follow (Leuba, 1925, p 332). He attacked research conducted by those with religious convictions as "hopelessly biased and blind," preferring work done by those who "have lived naively through religious experiences and then to have gained freedom from traditional convictions" (1912, p. 275). Leuba argued for the existence of a metaphysical, impersonal god, a "non-purposive Creative Force" (1912, p. 334), which he thought could form the basis of a reconstructed religion or morality.

Not surprisingly, Leuba's work was criticized by some including Joseph Marechal, a European Jesuit psychologist. Marechal (2004) questioned Leuba's objectivity and accused him of going beyond the limits of psychology to advocate personal views of atheism. He also criticized Leuba's simplistic and reductionist view of mystical experience as ecstasies that were psychopathological or sexual in origin. He argued that Leuba simply started with these conclusions and then arbitrarily interpreted his data so that it would support his views.

The work of the Clark school did not continue. By the 1920s, behaviorism and positivism had become the dominant paradigms in psychology; workers in these areas had little interest in religion, and it was marginalized in academic psychology (Delaney & DiClemente, 2004). Also, a reaction against the racist implications of early 20th century evolutionary thought limited the acceptance of Hall's genetic theory. However, a newer version of this line of thought has begun to appear recently in applications of evolutionary thought to psychology and religion (see Section 6.2).

1.4.3 European Developments

European investigations in psychology and religion during much of the 20th century have both parallels and divergences from US work. A main parallel would be a strong interest in phenomenology and religious experience, which can be seen in the early 20th century work of German authors like Friedrich von Hugel, Rudolf Otto, or Friedrich Heiler, the French author Joseph Mareshal, or the later work of the Belgian priest-psychologist Antoine Vergote (see e.g., Section 4.3). The divergences between Europe and the US reflect differences in intellectual and cultural situations. The split between psychology and fields like philosophy or theology did not affect Europe as much as the US, so psychological works by Europeans often show more familiarity with developments in other disciplines. Also, the religious climate in Europe is marked by much lower levels of religious participation and higher levels of unbelief, so psychologists of religion working in Europe have a significantly different object of study, sometimes leading to different questions and conclusions.

Within European academic circles there are also differences between national traditions. German writers have often held posts in departments of theology or religious studies and been exposed to work in Asian religious traditions like Hinduism and Buddhism. French work has been strongly influenced by the psychoanalytic thought of Freud and the French psychoanalyst Jacques Lacan (Vandermeersch, 2000). It also has been strongly influenced by French anthropological and sociological thought that owes much to Marxism in its formulation. British psychology shares many affinities with the US in both psychological and philosophical traditions, so its work resembles that of the US and has been particularly influential in North America. For instance, the British object relations school of psychoanalysis has been much more important in the US psychology of religion than the French varieties influenced by Lacan.

1.4.4 Psychodynamic Approaches

1.4.4.1 Sigmund Freud

One year before the publication of William James classic *Varieties of Religious Experience*, an unknown medical researcher named Sigmund Freud (1856–1939) published *The Psychopathology of Everyday Life* and began to make his views known to the world. Freud became the founder of psychoanalytic psychology and wrote on a variety of topics, including religion. In general, Freud saw religion as something that fostered illusion and prevented people from coming to grips with reality (see Section 5.1). Despite the fact that Freud was highly critical and even dismissive of religion, 20th century theologians like Paul Tillich and Reinhold Niebuhr were surprisingly sympathetic toward his work. Like Freud, they were aware of the potential for illusion in religion, and hoped to find in the psychodynamic approach some help for understanding the human person and dealing with issues in pastoral care. Psychoanalysis had a particular impact on Catholic writers, especially those in Europe such as Antoine Vergote (Vandermeersch, 2000).

1.4.4.2 Erik Fromm

Erik Fromm (1900–1980) was a psychoanalyst who had substantial impacts on humanistic psychology, transpersonal psychology, and the dialogue of psychology with Zen Buddhism. Although Fromm was ambivalent about religion, he was both personally and professionally interested in the topic, meditating on a daily basis and reading extensively in mystical literature, especially Zen and works by the medieval mystic Meister Eckhart (Funk, 2003).

Fromm defined religion broadly as "any system of thought and action shared by a group which give the individual a frame of orientation and an object of devotion" (1950, p. 21). He felt that psychoanalysis and religion have somewhat different interests but need not be opposed. In his view, the key to healthy spirituality is to reject all **authoritarian religion** and belief in a power greater than ourselves, such as that traditionally held within Christianity. He believed that submission to authority as in authoritarian religion leads to hate and intolerance, as well as interfering with the exercise of human reason. Rather, we should accept a **humanistic religion** "centered around man and his strength" in which God is understood only as a symbol of human power, "what man potentially is or ought to become" (1950, p. 37). He felt that philosophies such as Spinoza, some varieties of Buddhism, and the teachings of Jesus or mystical Christianity were all acceptable humanistic religions. Psychoanalysis could relate well to them because of their awareness of basic issues about existence, focus on "ultimate concerns" or the meaning of life, and their desire for oneness. On the other hand, religion that promoted belief in the existence of God and a lack of self-reliance should be rejected. The viewpoint of Fromm is similar to that of the rationalist psychologist and atheist Albert Ellis (1985), who saw most religion as a form of mental illness due to its supposed promotion of dependency and irrational ideas.

Fromm was pessimistic about the social role of religion. Following Freud, he argued that religion "…has the task of preventing any psychic independence on the part of the people, of intimidating them intellectually, of bringing them into the socially necessary infantile docility toward the authorities" (1963, p. 16). It also made life tolerable for people so that they would be less interested in change. Given these views, it is not surprising that he thought traditional religion was an "empty shell" that was no longer useful (Fromm, 1963, p. 100; Cooper, 2006, p. 116). However, he was also pessimistic about the contemporary alternatives. He believed that while modern society had freed itself from the totalitarian authority of the church, it had produced complacent, automated, alienated people absorbed in consumerism and the fulfillment of desires. He felt we must emerge from materialism to a level where spiritual values are important so that we could follow our humanitarian conscience.

Zen Buddhism attracted Fromm because he perceived it to be more anti-authoritarian. He became friends with the Japanese scholar D. T. Suzuki (1870–1966), the leading interpreter of Zen to the US and Europe. Fromm attended lectures by Suzuki, and in 1957, he arranged a conference in Mexico that involved Suzuki and a group of psychoanalysts. This meeting was an important early milestone in a dialogue between psychoanalysis and Buddhism that has remained very active (see e.g., Section 14.3.2).

1.4.5 Humanistic and Transpersonal Approaches

After the demise of the Clark school of psychology and religion, dialogue between the two fields languished outside of psychoanalysis. This began to change in the 1960s with two new developments: the rise of humanistic psychology, and the application of social-personality psychology to the study of religion (Gorsuch, 1988).

In the 1960s, **humanistic psychology** joined psychoanalysis and behaviorism as a "third force" within the larger field of psychology. It attempts to use scientific inquiry to study people in terms of their uniquely human positive qualities and potentials, including capabilities for self-transcendence and mystical experience. In general, humanistic psychology argues for a weak interpretation of transcendence, an individualistic and subjective view of the human person, and anti-traditionalist views of religion (Sutich, 1969). The three most prominent founders of the movement were Carl Rogers (1902–1987), the existential psychologist Rollo May (1909–1994), and Abraham Maslow (1908–1970). May (the most friendly of the three to religion) and especially Rogers have been influential in the psychology and religion dialogue primarily through their impact on the pastoral counseling movement (see Section 14.1.4). Maslow is important because he was vocal about religious issues and was a central figure in the creation of **transpersonal psychology**, a movement within humanistic psychology focusing on potentials for human development and experiences that extend beyond what is typical for the individual person. Transpersonal psychology has provided a forum for dialogue between psychology and some Asian religious traditions.

1.4.5.1 Abraham Maslow

Maslow is well known for producing a motivational theory of personality. He believed that people act to meet certain basic needs (e.g., food, safety) and that once these are consistently met we have the ability to develop further and begin seeking after higher needs. In his theory, the highest need and goal of life was the drive for **self-actualization**: "man's desire for self-fulfillment, namely, to the tendency for him to become…everything that one is capable of becoming" (1970, p. 46; 1964, p. 49). Satisfaction of higher needs would lead to better physical and psychological functioning and "greater, stronger, and truer individualism" (1970, p. 100).

Especially in his earlier work (e.g., 1964), Maslow had a largely negative view of religion. He was a member of the American Humanist Association, an organization that promoted atheism (Taylor, 1999, p. 269). He felt that while religion might have a role in helping people satisfy lower drives like safety needs, the "sophisticated" scientist will disagree with most religious answers to spiritual questions. He thought that a "humanistic faith" could be developed based on scientific study of the "natural" man using empirical procedures. This could allow scientists to discern basic values and answers to religious questions by identifying what contributes to the "actualization of the inner nature of man" (1970, p. 270). However in his last work (1999, p. 206), Maslow moved toward a less negative view and acknowledged that an authentically religious person might be able to use their faith to construct a set of genuine values.

One of Maslow's most famous contributions was his study of self-actualizers, reported in the classic book *Motivation and Personality* (1970). His subjects were a group of personal acquaintances, friends, and historical figures chosen by him as exemplary. His group largely excluded traditional religious figures, although the Buddhist scholar D.T. Suzuki and the Christian figure Thomas More made the list. Maslow found that these individuals had a variety of positive features, including deep interpersonal relations, creativity and more efficient perception of reality. They also had imperfections, could be ruthless, and struggled with guilt, sadness, or conflict like others. Not surprisingly, given the absence of traditional religious figures from his sample, he found self-actualizers were not religious. They were strongly ethical but unconventional and not always concerned with social politeness.

A key characteristic reported by his self-actualizing subjects was the presence of **peak experiences**—an ecstatic state of nonpossessive and self-transcending perception of the universe as an integrated whole. In his early work (1964), he argued that religious or mystical experiences were examples of peak states. He felt that religion should play no role in the understanding of these states because religious experiences are just part of human nature and can be explained naturalistically without any theological baggage or interference (1970, p. 164). Because the peak state is the core of all religious experiences, he believed that all religions are in essence the same and apparent differences can be safely ignored, a position that is questionable from a modern religious studies perspective.

1.4.5.2 The Transpersonal Psychology Movement

Maslow's work on self-actualization and peak experiences led him to speculate about the human potential to go beyond the personal and tap into universally available advanced states of cognition and development. He saw this transpersonal potential as very important, and so in the late 1960s, he worked with Stanislav Grof and Anthony Sutich to found a "fourth force" within psychology, the field of transpersonal psychology (Maslow, 1969; Valle, 1989). In this field, investigators begin with the assumptions that (1) higher levels of human functioning and potential are most evident in our ability to reach more advanced levels of human consciousness, and (2) while religions contain transpersonal elements, they also contain much specific content that is culture-specific and irrelevant to transpersonal concerns (Scotton, 1996). This latter view is sometimes known as the **perennial**

philosophy, the belief that all religions have a common, universal core (Wittine, 1989; Huxley, 2004; see Section 4.3). Along with these is a further assumption that (3) humans have untapped human potential which can be released and developed with sufficient effort and study (Valle, 1989; Frager, 1989).

While the basic concepts tying together the transpersonal movement are quite simple, in practice, the field of transpersonal psychology has encompassed the study of a wide variety of phenomena related to consciousness, including mystical, transcendent, and even psychic or parapsychological experiences (Sutich, 1969; Tart, 1975, 1992). Also of interest have been techniques used to alter consciousness such as meditation or drugs (e.g., Shapiro & Walsh, 1984; Grof, 1985). The transpersonal outlook is reflected in the work of the important religious philosopher Ken Wilber. In his early work such as *The Atman Project* (1996), Wilber focused on the evolution of consciousness and its relation to human development (see Section 7.5.1). In later work such as *Integral Psychology* (2000a), and *Sex, Ecology, and Spirituality* (2000b), he has critiqued modern rationality and scientific thought, arguing for a more holistic and unified view of the world.

Assessment. A number of critiques of the transpersonal movement have been offered, such as the one by Rubin (1996). He notes that while transpersonal psychology has made a contribution in its consideration of non-Christian religious systems, it has typically gone to the other extreme and become "Orientocentric" (Rubin, 1996), although some small steps have been taken recently to begin referencing Christian mystical thought (e.g., Judy, 1996). Transpersonal psychologists have also tended to focus on only those Asian traditions with minimal theistic content (such as Zen Buddhism) and ignore versions of even the same religious tradition with a more devotional orientation (such as Pure Land Buddhism), thus potentially biasing their work. He also argues that the transpersonal focus on consciousness as the key to development is individualistic and neglects vital relational aspects of spirituality, a complaint echoed by other critics of humanistic and transpersonal approaches (e.g., Liebert, 2000, p. 19).

1.4.6 Social and Personality Approaches

In the early to mid-20th century, some psychologists became interested in studying religion as a dimension in personality or as a form of social behavior. They attempted to develop a rigorous scientific methodology for the study of religion using questionnaires and other quantitative methods. Interesting findings from this work began a revival in the psychological study of religion that had languished in the US since the demise of the Clark school. Much of the modern field of psychology of religion has evolved out of this work by social psychologists interested in the scientific study of religion, especially their study of religious beliefs and behavior (Batson, 1997). This field has generated an impressive empirical literature looking at religion from a psychological perspective, and recently spirituality has also become a topic of interest.

1.4.6.1 Gordon Allport

The most important early figure in this school is Gordon Allport (1897–1967), a social psychologist and personality trait theorist. Like many early psychologists, Allport hoped to remove judgments about the human person from the sphere of morality and put the study of mature development on a scientific basis (Nicholson, 1998). Allport differed from some psychologists such as those of the Clark school as he had a more positive attitude toward Christianity, but he did believe that some kinds of religious involvement could be negative (Vande Kemp, 2000). Like Fromm, and many in the generation affected by Nazism and World War II, Allport had a strong interest in authoritarianism and prejudice. In his studies on the subject, he was surprised to find that many religious people displayed high levels of prejudice, even though the beliefs of their religion were opposed to that type of attitude. Allport was able to explain this by looking at why individuals had religious commitments. He found that some people were attracted to religion for instrumental or **extrinsic** reasons as a way of achieving specific goals, and that these people were more likely to be prejudiced than those who had an **intrinsic** attitude and pursued religion for its own sake (Allport, 1966).

Allport's theory has been modified and expanded over time and has been a dominant construct in the psychology of religion research for many years. For instance, Richard Gorsuch and his colleagues have conceptualized the intrinsic and extrinsic stances as reflecting types of basic **religious motivation**, and were able to replicate their existence in non-Western religious groups. They found that measures of genuine religious involvement such as attendance were correlated with intrinsic but not extrinsic religiosity (Schaefer & Gorsuch, 1992). Another proposed revision has been that of Batson, who identified a third orientation called the **quest** or seeking orientation. Thus it is now common for social psychologists to talk about three dimensions of religious motivation:

1. *Extrinsic or means dimensions*: The use of religion to meet self-serving ends such as dealing with feelings of weakness and impotence (Vergote, 1997, p. 53). Research indicates that this is a common religious orientation but is associated with no beneficial effects and perhaps some negative ones.
2. *Intrinsic or ends dimension*: Religious commitment is used as a "master motive" for life, part of a coherent worldview. This orientation may have positive and negative consequences, although research has generally connected it with positive outcomes.
3. *Quest or seeking dimension*: An "open-ended readiness to confront ultimate, existential questions, coupled with a skepticism of definitive answers to these questions" (Batson, Schoenrade, & Ventis, 1993, pp. 376–377). Batson argued that questers have the positive benefits of religion without having to tolerate the loss of freedom he believes is implicit in intrinsic religious commitment. Batson's views have led to many interesting studies but have not been consistently supported by research.

Schaefer and Gorsuch (1991) have argued that religious motivation is a central factor in religion. They have proposed a **Multivariate Belief-Motivation Theory** of **Religiousness** that divides religion into three interacting domains: (1) motivation (intrinsic-extrinsic), (2) beliefs such as our concept of God, and (3) problem-solving or coping style (see Sections 8.3, 9.3.1 & 10.2). On the other hand, researchers like Kirkpatrick and Hood (1990) have been critical of the concept of religious motivation because of perceived conceptual and methodological problems. Others have criticized its tendency to reduce the complex phenomenon of religion to simply a type of human motivation (e.g., Vergote, 1969, pp. 57, 94–96). As a result the concept of religious motivation has been less influential in recent research.

Social psychologists like Allport and Gorsuch wrote from a perspective sympathetic to religion and have frequently pointed out positive aspects of religious behavior on both personal and social levels (Wulff, 2003). Allport in particular was willing to consider the moral quality of various personality orientations, which he thought could be demonstrated scientifically. He argued that psychology and religion were both about truth and so that ultimately there could be no conflict between them, although he rejected what he called "psychologism" or the attempt to reduce religion to psychological categories (Vande Kemp, 2000). However, not all social psychologists believe that religion is beneficial or needed. For instance, Daniel Batson and his colleagues have argued that "the religious Stranger does not appear to be on our side" (Batson et al., 1993, p. 373). This more negative assessment has been challenged in important ways over the last 15 years, as we will see throughout this book.

1.4.7 Integration and Dialogue

In the post World War II period, many Christians entered psychology either as academic teachers and researchers or as clinical practitioners. They were dissatisfied with what they saw as an anti-Christian bias within the field that was problematic both for themselves and for the people they were trying to serve. A key work that expressed some of this dissatisfaction was a book by Paul Vitz entitled *Psychology as Religion: The Cult of Self-Worship* (1977). In that book, Vitz argued that psychology had become a secular religion that was anti-Christian, perhaps hostile to most religious traditions, and that this bias was causing negative effects on individuals as well as society. He argued that much of the academic prejudice against Christianity is an automatic, assumed position by people who are largely ignorant of Christianity or the issues involved. Vitz attacked the "selfism" inherent in the secular humanism of Fromm. He argued that the positive view of humanity articulated by humanists was plainly contradicted by psychological research that demonstrated the inherent tendency of humans toward destructive aggression. He concluded from this that humanist selfism is not scientific and is simply a religious position, a set of values that gain scientific prestige through their inclusion in psychology.

There is considerable support for this position. A highly critical stance toward Christianity is obvious in the views of many of the people mentioned in this chapter, such as Leuba, Freud, Fromm, and Maslow. Research studies have found that (1) psychologists have substantially lower levels of religious belief and participation than the general population, (2) few psychologists receive significant information or training in their graduate program related to religion or spirituality, and (3) very little psychological research concerns religion. For instance, an early 1990s review of 7 major APA journals found only 2.7% of studies assessed a religious variable (Weaver et al., 1998). A response to this bias and neglect can be found in the Christian integration and Biblical counseling movements.

1.4.7.1 The Christian Integration Movement

Since most university psychology departments were perceived as being inhospitable to religion or psychologists with religious affiliations, a movement began to start independent schools that would conduct research and train clinicians in a more religion-friendly atmosphere, as well as try to develop an approach to psychology that would integrate good scientific knowledge with basic Christian beliefs. The term **integration** began to be used in the 1950s as a way of describing theory and research that attempted to combine psychological and theological perspectives. The 1960s saw the organization of the first independent, faith-based clinical psychology training programs. The movement has spawned a considerable literature and grown to encompass a number of scholarly journals and training programs (Vande Kemp, 1996). Explicitly Christian organizations like the Christian Association for Psychological Studies (CAPS) were created to supplement more secular groups such as Division 36 (Psychology of Religion) in the American Psychological Association or the Association for Spiritual, Ethical and Religious Values in Counseling (ASERVIC) which is part of the American Counseling Association.

While there are a wide variety of approaches within the integration movement, there is broad agreement among its members that psychology and Christianity have the potential to illuminate each other (Ellens, 2004a). Through most of the 20th century the relationship was largely a unidirectional one, with psychologists studying religion and religious professionals and scholars (mostly Christian) studying psychological theories and techniques. However, more recently there have been attempts to critically evaluate psychological theories from a theological perspective, to make constructive use of religious ideas and practices in psychological theory and practice, and to engage in mutual dialogue (Jones, 1994). This critical evaluation has focused on the fact that psychological theories and practices are value laden and contain unacknowledged philosophical and metaphysical positions that may be at odds with a Christian view of the human person. Translation of Christian ideas into psychological categories thus has the potential to distort or alter theological beliefs and practices. Christian integration writers argue that they must prevent this by having a clear understanding of the theology and values underlying integration, as well as the implications of this theology for psychological theory and practice (cf. Jones, 2006; Murphy, 2005; Spilka & Bridges, 1989).

1.4.7.2 Biblical Counseling

While the integration approach gives a positive status to both psychology and Christianity, others have viewed the psychological contribution to integration with greater suspicion. Jay Adams (1970) and more recently David Powlison (2000, 2001, 2003) have argued that any Christian counseling strategy must be Biblically based and distinct from secular paradigms or theoretical commitments which can blind investigators and do not offer a coherent explanation of the human person. Powlison argues that non-Biblical models of counseling have a detached, impersonal quality avoided by the Bible and appeal mostly to human desire; they "systematically suppress awareness of our dependency on and accountability to God" (Powlison, 2003, p. 4) and our need for redemption. Biblical counselors generally believe that self-will, pride and personal sin are at the root of many problems. These factors are thought to lie behind our excessive focus on achievement and acquisition, problematic desires for superiority and control, and avoidance of the needs of others, all of which eventually lead to worry and anxiety. In this view, freedom comes when we give up attachments to power, set aside our pride and become more focused on others (see Section 14.3.1).

1.4.7.3 Asian Dialogues

The other two main psychology and religion dialogues that have taken place involve Buddhism and Hinduism. Conversations with Hinduism have largely been limited to appropriating specific techniques like yoga for use in clinical situations (see Section 10.3.2). The dialogue with Buddhism has been more extensive, probably due to its perceived commitment to a nontheistic view of the world and its complex understanding of human psychology (Wallace & Shapiro, 2006). Buddhist understandings have had a significant impact on psychological approaches to religion through their influence on Carl Jung and psychodynamic theorists like Erik Fromm. Particularly noteworthy was Fromm's work with the Zen scholar D. T. Suzuki, that made Zen Buddhism a religious tradition of primary interest for some psychoanalysts (Parsons, 2000). Specific techniques inspired by Buddhism are seeing increasing use in clinical settings (see e.g., Section 11.4.2) and the broader importation of a Buddhist worldview into psychotherapy has also had an impact, particularly in psychoanalysis (see Section 14.3.2). However, the Buddhist dialogue has been somewhat limited by the fact that it has been dominated by Westerners and attracted little interest from Asians in the various Buddhist traditions (Heisig, 1999; Bankart, 2003).

1.4.7.4 Approaches to Integration

Types of models. Many different schemes for relating psychology and religion have been proposed; but, as Richard Gorsuch has aptly noted, none of them has seen any wide adoption. Ideas about the relationship between psychology and religion can be described according to several characteristics including *congruence* (how well do psychology and religion fit together) and *priority* (should psychology or religion be counted as more important). There are three general positions that can be taken with regard to congruence—separation, conflict, and complement. In the **separation** model, it is assumed that psychology and religion each have their own areas of interest and approaches to truth and that both are necessary for a complete picture of reality. This was the traditional view in the science of the early modern period (see Section 2.2) and is still occasionally argued, as by the evolutionary theorist Stephen Jay Gould (1999, p. 65). Opposed to this is the **conflict** view, which holds that science and religion do have overlapping areas of interest (against the separation model) but that they provide different and conflicting truth claims (against the integration model). A third position is the **complement** view, which holds that science and religion deal with some of the same questions (against the separation model) but are congruent or complimentary (against the conflict model). In this view, both science and religion are vital because each provides important and irreplaceable viewpoints on human behavior (Ellens, 2004b). The latter position has been the traditional stance within the Roman Catholic Church. This view is congruent with the idea that psychology and theology have much to offer each other, and so interaction between them should be encouraged (Spilka & Bridges, 1989).

The complement model can be further divided into weak and strong versions. A weak position holds that some congruence is possible between psychology and religion but that in other areas there might be separation or conflict. In contrast, a strong complement model holds that it is possible to develop a single seamless system of truth that encompasses both psychology and religion. An example of weak complementarity is the position of Richard Gorsuch, who defines integration as "when two or more disciplines are jointly brought to bear on the same issue so that decisions about that issue reflect the contributions of both disciplines" (2002a, p. 6). Like Peter Homans (1968b) he argues that this integration can happen at both professional and personal levels. An example of the strong position might be that of John Carter and Bruce Narramore (1979). They argue that there is a unity of truth so that it should be possible to integrate truth from different sources, including psychology and theology (cf. Johnson, 1997).

The second issue in integration involves priority, whether psychology or religion will receive privileged status in the interaction of the two fields. This depends in part on one's views of science and religion, so that it seems likely that there will never be a single agree-upon way of doing integration, even within a specific religious tradition (Vande Kemp, 1998). Three positions can be taken here: **confessionalism**, which privileges the perspectives of a specific religious tradition over those of psychology; **scientism**, which argues that science is the superior or only way to gain true knowledge and thus should be privileged in the relationship with religion; and **dialogical integration**, which tries to give equal respect to each field, although the methods and conclusions of one might be preferred in certain areas.

An example of confessionalism is the work of Robert Roberts (1997a,b). Roberts argues that integration can never be based primarily on psychology, because the field does not offer a body of mutually congruent and coherent beliefs and that any privileging of psychology will undermine spirituality and provide unnecessarily reductionistic or simplistic explanations of human phenomena. He believes that Christianity will provide a better base for integration, because it includes a resistance to overly individualistic views of the person found in psychology, as well as strong concepts of agency and sin. He has a weaker view of the possibilities of integration because he believes that, while psychology and theology have many interests in common, there are fundamental differences in sources of data (e.g., the use of Biblical narratives). Gorsuch, on the other hand, argues for a position of dialogical integration, in which the positions of all parties in the dialogue are respected. He rejects scientism, saying that a true integration dialogue requires an acknowledgement that other sources of knowledge beyond science are useful (2002a). Current figures that argue for scientism would include some writers in the evolutionary psychology of religion movement, such as Pascal Boyer (see Section 6.2.3).

Current status. The integration and Biblical counseling movements continue to be very vital, attracting many adherents and generating lots of research and writing. It can also be argued that the integration movements have had a significant role in changing negative views toward religion and spirituality within the profession of psychology, although clearly other factors have been involved as well. However, there is tension and less dialogue than one would like. Clearly, integration is not easy for, along with areas of common ground, there are differences in goals and even strategies of inquiry, both in terms of theory and practical application (Jones, 1996). One issue that is often important but is left unaddressed has to do with the context of the discussion. As Browning and Cooper point out, an integration dialogue within an evangelical Christian faith community is in a different context than a dialogue in a more public forum (Browning & Cooper, 2004, p. 263).

1.5   Religious and Theological Responses to Psychology

During the early part of the 20th century the theological response to scientific psychology was muted. Protestant Christian theology was heavily influenced by the neo-orthodox position of Karl Barth (1886–1968), who believed that theology should be based totally upon "the Word of God" rather than human experience or psychological theory. Protestant dialogue during this period was mostly carried out in the context of the pastoral counseling and theology movements. In Roman Catholicism, the situation was somewhat different. Early Catholic psychologists like Edward Pace (1861–1938) and Thomas Verner Moore (1877–1969) were ordained priests with substantial training in theology and a commitment to working as psychologists within the Catholic context. While this situation was more favorable for dialogue, there was often opposition by suspicious members of the Catholic hierarchy (Gillespie, 2001). However, by mid-century more Protestant writers had begun to join the dialogue. Especially noteworthy are Paul Tillich (1886–1965) and Reinhold Niebuhr (1892–1971).

1.5.1 Paul Tillich

Theological responses to psychology are influenced not only by the individual views of the theologian toward psychology but also by their theological stance. Tillich adopted an *apologetic* approach to theology that began with human experience and tried to make the Christian message appealing to contemporary thinkers, rather than a *kerygmatic* stance (e.g., Karl Barth) that gives priority to the basic Christian message (Cooper, 2006, p. 196). Tillich called his apologetic approach the "method of correlation" (1951, pp. 60–63). He analyzed the human situation using materials from contemporary thought and then reinterpreted Christian theology to show how the Christian message provided answers to modern questions (1957, pp. 28, 239). His method was dialectical, and he tended to avoid the approach of later writers who wanted to critically evaluate the positions taken by secular and scientific writers (1963a, p. 51; Tracy, 1975, p. 46). He used two primary tools in building his system—the existential philosophy of writers like Soren Kierkegaard or Martin Heidegger, and the insights of psychoanalysis.

1.5.1.1 Tillich and the Human Existential Situation

Existentialism tries to understand the human person by looking at their connection to the ultimate characteristics of existence like freedom (we all have the power to make choices and change or transcend our situation) and finitude (we always work within limitations and eventually will die). Religion for him was intimately connected to these ultimate concerns and our attempts at self-transcendence, a focus shared with humanistic psychology (1963b, p. 107; Maslow, 1964, p. 45). In his theology, Tillich emphasized the transcendence of an infinitely free God who is not only the ground of all nature but beyond it as well. Tillich argued that this dialectic between nature and freedom is also repeated in our human situation. We are part of the natural world and thus finite, but we also transcend the natural world because we possess a finite version of God's infinite freedom. The tension between these forms the basis of what Tillich called an "existential gap" or existential situation. The dialectic between the constraints of existence and nature and our essential freedom is "the condition for man's religious existence" (1957, p. 10). The transcending possibility of spirit and freedom means that religion cannot be reduced to psychological dynamics or moral self-integration (1963b, pp. 118, 192).

1.5.1.2 Tillich and Depth Psychology

Tillich used psychoanalysis to help articulate the psychological dynamics involved in dealing with ultimate concerns. An individual who is able to stand at the balance point between the demands of existence and their essence as a free person he referred to as "centered" (1957, p. 60). He saw this state of balance or self-integration as the goal of a healthy life. However, Tillich argued that this ideal balance can never be realized because we are finite and unable to assimilate the many conflicting demands of existence. The result of this lack of balance is confusion, self-alienation, and meaninglessness, leaving us at the mercy of internal compulsions and external demands. It is our awareness of this situation of finitude, lack of meaning and helplessness that leads to **ontological anxiety**, a basic tension that is built into existence and must be accepted. This anxiety is different from **neurotic anxiety** that is caused by psychological problems and is open to psychological help (1957, p. 34; 2000; Cooper, 2006, pp. 37–52). Fleeing from ontological anxiety creates neurotic anxiety and irrational or unreasonable fears that tie up the person with inner conflicts. However, through the religious life and support of a spiritual community, people could embrace a capacity for transcendence and by making appropriate "moral" choices develop a genuine sense of identity (1963b). Science, on the other hand, is unable to understand or help with ontological anxiety because it detaches existence from transcendence and tries to explain and control everything on a purely natural basis.

Perhaps in part because of his correlational method and his own personal experience with traumatic anxiety as a chaplain during World War I, Tillich was quite open to the basic findings of psychoanalysis such as the existence and power of unconscious motives and their impact on some religious activities, as well as the problem of guilt and the need for acceptance (1957, p. 177; 1963b; Cooper, 2006, p. 41). He appreciated and accepted Freud's work, although he observed that it had limitations because it ignored our existential situation and our essential nature as free persons. Not surprisingly, Tillich also rejected Freud's apparent position of total psychological or biological determinism (1957, pp. 54, 66). He was more ambivalent toward behaviorism; for instance, he rejected the idea that life processes are oriented toward the pursuit of pleasure and avoidance of pain because hedonistic views ignored the presence of other forces like creativity (1963b, p. 56).

1.5.1.3 Tillich, Fromm and Rogers

Terry Cooper (2006) notes that there are a number of interesting points of agreement and disagreement between Tillich and humanists like Fromm and Rogers. Tillich and Fromm had a long acquaintance that went back to their days in Germany; both were influenced by Marx and Freud, but they had many disagreements as well. Tillich agreed with Fromm that selfishness and self-hate rather than self-love are the basic human problems. However, Tillich saw that these problems could not be solved apart from God, while Fromm wanted to eliminate God talk from the conversation altogether. Fromm thought that we have tendencies toward both good and evil and can choose good, overcoming our problems without help. Tillich believed our estrangement was too great for self-solution and that we had a need to wait for help, a passivity that was offensive to Fromm.

Tillich and the humanistic psychologist Carl Rogers also had some areas of agreement in addition to their differences. Rogers and Tillich both saw inner conflict or self-estrangement as a basic human problem, but they had different ideas about the nature of estrangement and how acceptance helps. Rogers saw self-estrangement as an incongruence between our true self and societal expectations or pressures that thwart our drive toward growth. His answer to this was an experience of unconditional positive regard by a therapist or other person who sets aside their values and is nonjudgmental. Tillich, on the other hand, argued that estrangement is ultimately built into existence, so we need more than human sources of acceptance (Cooper, 2006, p. 5). Tillich also rejected the claim made by Rogers that psychotherapy can and should be value free. In Tillich's view, any relationship—including the therapeutic relationship—involves a commitment to some kind of values. Cooper argues that Rogers viewed himself as making psychological claims but that actually his theory reveals many hidden theological or ontological assumptions that go beyond "scientific psychology."

While Tillich was extremely influential in the psychology and religion dialogue during the 1950s through the 1970s, he is less so today as his existential approach is not central to contemporary discussions (Polkinghorne, 2004, p. 51). Tillich tended to describe highly personal encounters with abstract concepts that are seemingly removed from qualities of personal care and love. Fromm even questioned whether Tillich's thought really represented an authentic statement of the Christian faith (Cooper, 2006). Nevertheless an understanding of his work is vital in the study of the psychology and religion dialogue.

1.5.2 Reinold Niebuhr

Another prominent 20th-century theologian and participant in the dialogue was Reinold Niebuhr (1955; 1996a,b), who produced some interesting theological perspectives on Freud. While Niebuhr approved of some of Freud's positions such as his vision of human complexity, he had a number of criticisms of Freud, including his denial of transcendence and freedom.

1.5.2.1 Niebuhr's View of the Human Person

Niebuhr believed that each of us is finite and thus bound by the laws of nature, but at the same time we are free and able to transcend our situation; we are "a unity of finiteness and freedom, of involvement in natural processes and transcendence over process" (1996b, p. 113). This self-transcendence is evident in the way that our natural impulses run beyond the bounds of nature, while nonhuman animals are restrained by natural instinct. This contradiction between finiteness and freedom or transcendence is the occasion—but not the cause—for many human problems. "This essential homelessness of the human spirit is the ground of religion; for the self which stands outside itself and the world cannot find the meaning of life in itself or the world" (1996a, p. 14).

In Niebuhr's view, the tension between our two natures has important consequences. It causes anxiety, which can be a source of creativity or a motivation to hide our finiteness and freedom. When we avoid our finiteness, we ignore our limitations, leading us to overestimate ourselves as individuals or as a race. This can lead to arrogance and fanaticism, either in rationality or religion. Avoidance of our freedom is also problematic, for it blinds us to human potentials such as the possibility for true altruism. It also hides from us the possibility that freedom has both creative and evil possibilities and so can be misused. Contemporary history is full of evidence of the potential for evil in modern systems of warfare, power, and economics, but we still deny this evil potential, supposing that somehow these problems are just due to ignorance, not enough science, or social forces which we are about to overcome, rather than seeing our poor choices. Remorse and repentance (as opposed to simple psychological guilt) are thus in some sense religious experiences, because they show an awareness of our situation of finiteness before God.

1.5.2.2 Avoidance in Freud

Niebuhr appreciated the fact that Freud recognized our finite nature, but criticized him for his naturalistic stance, which made it impossible for him to recognize the presence of freedom and transcendence. Freud rejected the possibility of transcendence or freedom, because he attributed all behavior to human drives, developmental events, or culture, leading to pessimistic views on individuals and society. Niebuhr saw this as an incoherent position, as the ego and even Freud's id, which was supposedly ruled by blind instinctual forces, showed themselves to be wily and smart, revealing "subtleties and strategies that are not part of nature" (1996a, p. 43). Also, while Freud saw reason and intellect as our best hope, he also claimed that we are totally controlled by instinct and culture and thus not truly responsible. The implication of Freud's denial of freedom is that all guilt must be neurotic guilt, denying the possibility that a person might have legitimate guilt from violating either personal or more universal norms and the claims that others have on us.

Niebuhr saw the problem of freedom as not confined to Freud but a general limitation of psychology. Freedom is something that allows us to transcend the boundaries of predictable time and space, but empirical psychology can only study things within those bounds. The mystery of freedom is apparent in the fact that "any previous event is an intelligible, but not a sufficient, cause for the succeeding event" (1955, p. 61). What we do can be understood in retrospect but cannot be predicted in advance. Human activity in history is more like a kind of practical wisdom than a predictable rationality (cf. Section 6.3.4). In his view, a psychology that wants a rich view of the individual will thus have to go beyond the boundaries of natural science.

Humanistic psychologists responded to Niebuhr in a predictably negative fashion. Carl Rogers (1962), while sympathetic to Niebuhr rejection of deterministic naturalism and his advocacy of freedom, disliked Niebuhr's claim to possess the truth and rejected his focus on human sinfulness. Rogers' view of human nature rejected both the notions of perfection and evil; he believed that people were inherently "positive, forward-moving, constructive, realistic, trustworthy" (Rogers, 1957). Niebuhr offers food for thought to those who want a view of human nature that tries to balance optimism and realism.

1.5.3 Hermeneutic Writers: Don Browning and Paul Ricoeur

Another influential response from the religion side of the dialogue with psychology came from practical theologian Don Browning, who offered a critique of psychological theories used in counseling. Browning based his approach in part on the interpretive or **hermeneutic** approach to understanding found in the philosophy of Paul Ricoeur. According to Ricoeur, any kind of understanding—including a psychological theory—comes into being through an interpretive process involving a series of dialectical relationships that move the interpreter from their original view of the world to a new understanding (Ricoeur, 1976; 1981, p. 93). This means that our understandings and theories are strongly influenced by our starting view of things, including our current beliefs, personal experiences, and the culture and history of any larger groups to which we belong. This starting point is known as our **pre-understanding**. In the hermeneutic view of things, knowledge is not some single verifiable fact but a set of new ideas "opened up" by our attempt to move beyond a pre-understanding. We gain new understanding as we appropriate these ideas and make them our own (Ricoeur, 1974, p. 87). Since knowledge is dependent upon the starting context, it is prudent to know and critique the relevant pre-understanding factors and understand their effect on a person who is advocating new knowledge claims (Ricoeur, 1981, p. 90; Packer, 1988; see Section 6.3). For instance, a hermeneutic investigator would be interested in the fact that Freud had a strong pre-existing personal belief in atheism, as this pre-understanding most likely had an influence on how he interpreted data about religion.

Browning has utilized a hermeneutic approach in a couple of ways. First, he has attempted to uncover the pre-understandings of the various schools of psychotherapy and subject these to a Christian critique (Browning & Cooper, 2004). In the hermeneutic perspective, all psychological theorists begin with implicit assumptions, worldviews, and ethical points of view that go beyond what is explicitly present in their research and often attempt to reduce all behavior to these implicit worldviews or metaphors without considering the validity of their pre-understanding and how it might distort the object of study (Browning & Cooper, 2004). This is an issue in all the sciences, but this is especially true in psychology and religion where personal beliefs for or against religion can be very strong. This does not mean that good science is not possible—just that we must be aware of our biases and those of others (Vergote, 1997, pp. 30–31; 1998, p. 40; but cf. Beit-Hallahmi, 1985). In Browning's view, the secular presuppositions of many psychological theories are questionable, and adjusting these presuppositions could result in a more adequate theory. Second, Browning has attempted to use the hermeneutic model to develop what he calls a practical theology that looks at how religious practices actually function in real life. This approach rejects a technological view of religious practice and argues that religious activities can only be understood when they are considered in the context of their relational, cultural, and theological surround. True religion is not something one does on the side; it is a way of life (Browning, 1991; see Section 6.3).

1.6 Current Research Approaches

The basic philosophical assumptions behind scientific approaches to religion will be explored in the next chapter. Here, we provide just a quick summary of commonly used research methods that will make it easier to evaluate and appreciate the large body of empirical research that exists on topics related to psychology and religion. These methods fall into two general groupings—quantitative and qualitative.

1.6.1 Quantitative Methods

Quantitative methods allow scientists to measure and look at relationships between important variables. In this process, important variables are operationalized through a process of **methodological reductionism** or simplification so they can be measured, and then measurement instruments are developed that measure the variable of interest and give a numeric value in relation to it. For instance, in religion research, we often want to study a person's religious commitment, but this is a very rich construct that cannot be grasped numerically, so we reduce it to a simpler variable like Sunday worship attendance that can be more easily measured. A key problem here is that the way constructs are defined and operationalized can affect how they are related to each other (Watson, 1994, p. 120). Also, quantitative surveys force individuals to respond according to categories or choices defined by the experimenter, when none of the categories may accurately represent its position (Berger, 2007).

How does one investigate relationships among variables using quantitative data? Assuming that one cannot take an **experimental** approach by manipulating variables in a controlled setting like a lab and seeing the effects, one is left doing what is called a **quasi-experimental** approach, which involves careful selection and observation of variables in a group of subjects and then generalization from sample subjects to the characteristics of the larger population they are drawn from. **Descriptive statistics** (such as averages) can be used to understand characteristics of the sample, and then **inferential statistics** (also known as significance tests) allow us to understand how confidently we may be able to generalize conclusions about a sample to a larger population. Typically the researcher comes to the project with a theory and specific hypotheses or predictions based on the theory that they want to test.

Quantitative research can proceed from one of two stances. In **exploratory analysis,** the researcher thinks that there are relationships among a group of variables but is unclear about the nature of the relationships. The exploratory analysis examines a wide variety of possible relationships using (1) an inferential statistical test to determine whether a significant relationship exists between variables and (2) descriptive statistics to determine the **effect size**, a measure of the strength and nature of the relationship. The classic measure of effect size is the **correlation coefficient**, which ranges from a positive relationship of 1.0 (perfectly related, where variables increase or decrease together) to 0 (not related) to a perfect negative relationship of −1.0 (perfectly related, where one variable increases while the other decreases).

It is extremely important to look at both inferential and descriptive measures in evaluating the results of a research study, as often a study may find results that are statistically significant in the inferential test but relatively unimportant when one examines the effect size. For instance, Krauss and Flaherty (2001) discovered a significant negative correlation between mood and quest scores, with higher quest scores related to lower levels of mood. This is an interesting finding, but how important is it? The size of the correlation coefficient is $-.15$, which means that only slightly more the 2% of the variance in mood is related to quest score, and 98% is related to error or other factors. Thus it is significant but relatively unimportant.

The second possible approach is the **confirmatory analysis**. In this procedure, the researcher identifies the hypothesized relationships between variables ahead of time and then asks the question, is my model consistent with the data? Confirmatory analytic procedures such as structural equations modeling can be powerful tools for testing elaborate models and are seeing increasing use in psychology of religion research.

Scientists look for law-like regularities that underlie the complexity of nature, so simplification is a natural part of the scientific enterprise. A number of statistical procedures like **factor analysis** have been developed to look for simple underlying dimensions in complex data. These analyses are helpful, although the presence of simple factors in data does not necessarily indicate that these dimensions have real existence— they are just statistically handy for simplifying things (D'Andrade, 1995, pp. 83–86).

Even though quantitative research seems straightforward, and it has added much to our knowledge about the human person, interpretive problems remain. For instance, most of the research in psychology of religion uses correlational or quasi-experimental methods that cannot establish whether religion is a cause or an effect of psychological factors (Batson et al., 1993, p. 373). Another problem is one of measurement, which is particularly difficult in psychology of religion research, since variables like "religiousness" or "spirituality" are difficult to define and measure. Generally a measurement instrument is thought to be satisfactory if it has good **reliability** (it gives consistent results) and **validity** (it measures what it is supposed to measure). A tremendous amount of effort has gone into devising instruments with good measurement characteristics, perhaps at the expense of research that could be devoted to more substantive questions (Gorsuch, 1984). Many of these are self-report measures, although some constructs with religious significance such as humility may not be measurable by self-report (Tangney, 2002). Finally, psychologists involved in the study of religion often have strong pro and anti views, so investigators must work hard to guard against bias and resist the temptation to offer judgments about the ultimate meaning and nature of religion (Gorsuch, 1988; Vergote, 1998, p. 39).

1.6.2 Qualitative Approaches

Qualitative methods provide a different and complementary approach to research. They are designed to be flexible, sensitive to social context, and focused on meaning and action as they emerge in real-life situations. A qualitative approach attempts to create holistic descriptions and understandings that may or may not be supplemented with quantification or statistical analysis (Mason, 2002). These methods are especially useful when you do not know much about an area and need to construct an initial understanding of a phenomenon. They are also helpful in situations where complex phenomena are being studied or where the individual meaning of certain experiences is of interest. There has been an increasing number of qualitative studies in the psychology and religion area (for a review, see Aten & Hernandez, 2005). Some authors argue that the holistic and experiential nature of spirituality is better captured by qualitative research (e.g., Hamilton & Jackson, 1998; cf. Hay, 1979). In fact, quantitative and qualitative approaches are both valuable, address different levels of complexity, and have different roles in the scientific process. Qualitative methods are particularly good at generating ideas and possible models, which may become the target of further research using quantitative procedures (Belzen & Hood, 2006).

1.6.2.1   General Characteristics

Basic philosophy. Qualitative research is often more a philosophy or attitude toward inquiry rather than a specific technical methodology. A key attitude is openness to having one's ideas changed and flexibility in the research process. Understanding is more important than prediction or control, and validity is more important that reliability in qualitative studies, so the investigator strives to use methods that will accurately describe the phenomenon in question. This can be seen in attitudes toward sampling: while quantitative researchers try to use standardized procedures and random samples of subjects, qualitative researchers focus on selecting informants who are experts and will provide the maximum amount of information. Clearly formulated research questions and the use of multiple methods are used to enhance the validity of qualitative studies.

Contextuality. Human behavior and experience always takes place in a particular environment, so good research provides relevant information about the context of the phenomenon being studied. Qualitative methods assume that these situations are complex and that a holistic understanding is valuable. This has several implications. First, a holistic understanding cannot afford to always ignore outliers or people whose pattern does not follow the norm. Second, the investigator himself or herself forms part of the context for the study, as the person doing the interpreting affects the interpretation.

Participant focus. A distinguishing feature of qualitative methods is their dependence on various types of interviews and the way they are conducted. First, in qualitative interviews, questions are not standardized; rather subjects are asked questions in a way that will best allow them to express their knowledge of a topic. Second, there is an assumption that the people you are interviewing have a valuable and unique knowledge about your research question. While the knowledge of the subjects may not be accurate, it is not automatically assumed that the investigator is the expert and the subjects possess only folk knowledge (Gabriel, 2004). Particularly in research asking about individual experiences and life stories, it is assumed that the participant has an expert's role. Third, qualitative researchers generally try to ensure that any research will be of benefit to the participants and that all parties will have a voice in the interpretation and dissemination of results from the investigation. The intensive, relational nature of the qualitative process makes it impossible to treat participants simply as objects of study. Devising an analytical scheme and categories that are not relevant to the participants is thought to be of questionable value (cf. Roff, 2001).

1.6.2.2 Specific Approaches

Grounded theory. **Grounded theory** (Strauss & Corbin, 1998) is a qualitative approach in which one begins with a research question rather than a theory and specific hypotheses and tries to construct a theory and categories on the basis of the data. The design, methods, and concepts of the study are allowed to emerge during the research process as a result of developing theory. Analysis in grounded theory is a continuous process of conversation between researchers and data. Description is used to identify the categories of phenomena, interrelationships among conditions (structure), unfolding action (process), and consequences. The theory and categories are then refined until theoretical saturation is reached, and new data produces no new understanding. The research is very participant-focused, and it is expected that the needs of the participants, as well as their ideas about interpretation should be taken into account, although the participants are not always assumed to be completely knowledgeable.

Ethnographic interviews and observation. Ethnographic research methods were originally developed to study various cultures, and thus their ultimate aim is the collection of information about groups. Ethnography generally involves (1) *fieldwork*, traveling to and living in or near the group under study; (2) *participant observation*, where you actually participate in the group, allowing you to blend in and get new insights in the context of real-life situations; and (3) *ethnographic interviewing* of informants selected for their knowledge of the group and ability to talk about it. The result is information that would not be attainable by other means (Bernard, 2002). While rarely used in psychology and religion research, studies of religious communities such as the work of Nancy Ammerman (1998) and James Hopewell (1987) have used these methods.

Phenomenological analysis. The phenomenological approach has its basis in philosophy rather than in psychology, but it lies behind most if not all methods of qualitative data collection. The philosophical roots of the work are typically traced to the writings of Husserl (e.g., 1970). The basic thrust of this type of investigation is to examine the subjective experience of the individual from a point of *epoche*, a detached objective stance taken by the investigator. Since the method focuses on subjective experience, it is typically used when we wish to understand a certain type of experience (e.g., a religious experience) or the reactions of people to a certain type of situation (Moustakas, 1994). The research begins with interviews that have both open-ended and guided questions. The goal of the interview is to perform a phenomenological reduction of the experience to gain a fresh perception of the source of the experience and its meaning. After setting aside or bracketing out things so that the phenomenon can be focused on, the researcher looks for the *horizon* or boundary of the experience, as well as its meaning and constituents such as temporal or spatial quality, causal inference, and intention. Individual descriptions are then integrated into a composite textural and structural description.

Hermeneutic analysis. Hermeneutic approaches have traditionally been used in the interpretation of discourse, textual materials, and narrative, with the goal of increased understanding. Methods inspired by hermeneutics have also been used generally in psychology and more specifically in the psychology of religion (Packer & Addison, 1989; Belzen, 1997). They will be discussed further in Chapter 6 (see also Chapter 9.3.3).

1.7 Conclusion and a Look Ahead

The fields of psychology, religion, and spirituality have a vast, rich heritage that is beyond the scope of any single volume or set of volumes. Even the literature on the intersection between psychology and religion is vast. The remainder of this book will provide a framework for understanding contemporary discussions in psychology and religion and some examples of the excellent work that is taking place at the intersection between these two fields of human endeavor.

In the next two chapters (Chapters 2 and 3), we will look at some basic concepts in psychology, science, and religion that underlie any discussions between the two fields. Then the next six chapters will consider specific approaches to the study of psychology and religion: experiential/phenomenological (Chapter 4), psychodynamic (Chapter 5), developmental (Chapters 7, 8, 9), and new approaches (Chapter 6). We will consider empirical research, as well as important theories and religious/theological critiques that have emerged within each of these approaches.

Religion and psychology share a concern with the quality of human life. They hope to offer guidance to people seeking to find meaningful, fulfilled, and even happy lives. Thus, a final goal of this book is to harness theory and empirical research in the service of practical applications. How can we in the 21st century build positive communities? In what ways can we help individuals deal with the challenges of life and develop richly satisfying lives? The concluding chapters of this book (Chapters 10, 11, 12, 13, 14) will attempt to begin sketching out answers to these questions.

Chapter 2
Science, Religion, and Psychology

Modern discussions about the relationship between psychology and religion are now over a century old. However, this dialogue is part of a more general conversation between science and religion that goes back hundreds of years. This general discussion provides a broad context for our study that is important in a couple of ways. First, it helps us better understand a number of problematic issues that have appeared in the psychology and religion dialogue. Second, it helps us to better understand the nature of science, including the strengths and limitations that any scientific discipline like psychology will bring to a conversation with another field of human endeavor.

In this chapter, we introduce some basic philosophical concepts that are involved in discussions about the nature of science. We will then look at how ideas about science have changed over time and the affect of these shifts on the relationships between religion, science, and psychology. We will see that the philosophy of science one adopts will have a large impact on whether science and religion are seen as partners or competitors. It will also become apparent that perceived conflicts between science and religion are mostly based upon philosophies of science that are problematic and have been rejected in contemporary thought.

2.1 Philosophical Concepts and Issues in Science and Religion

2.1.1 Empiricism

Any understanding of science must begin with the fact that it is an empirical endeavor. Empiricism is a philosophical position related to **epistemology**, a branch of philosophy that considers the ways we gain knowledge about the world and ourselves. **Empiricism** is the view that knowledge should be based on experience. It is often contrasted with **metaphysics**, an inquiry into the basic nature of the world that relies primarily on reasoning rather than experience. While metaphysics is thought to be desirable and necessary by many scholars (particularly in philosophy), empiricism is generally taken to be a fundamental beginning point for science, including scientific explorations of religion (Hawley, 2006; Helminiak, 1996). **Scientific**

J.M. Nelson, *Psychology, Religion, and Spirituality,*
DOI 10.1007/978-0-387-87573-6_2, @ Springer Science+Business Media, LLC 2009

empiricism limits the kinds of experiences that can be considered a basis for knowledge, excluding things that do not fit comfortably within a framework of scientific investigation (MacIntyre, 1984, pp. 80–81). Psychology generally adopts an epistemological position of scientific empiricism and tends to limit acceptable experience to things that can be directly observed by an investigator. Opponents of this strict scientific empiricism point out that many important aspects of the human person—including religious experiences—cannot be directly observed. Thus, scientific empiricism makes knowledge about some aspects of the human self difficult or impossible to acquire (Willard, 1998).

Scientific empiricism often makes the assumption that the experiencing observer is completely impartial and detached from the phenomenon being studied. This assumption is a touchy issue in the psychological study of religion, as many psychologists have personal commitments to a religious tradition or secular atheism. Proponents of the detached observer assumption argue that the religious convictions of investigators cause difficulties as they can lead to theory or research intended to defend religion rather than just explain it (Beit-Hallahmi, 1985). Opponents of this view argue that personal religious experience and involvement is essential for understanding religion and that in any event complete detachment of the observer from the subject is impossible (Vergote, 1998).

Empirical work in science is thought to take place at different levels of observation, with different scientific disciplines focusing on different levels. Many scientists consider physics to be the fundamental level of observation because it studies the basic components and characteristics of matter and energy. Successively higher levels of observation include chemistry, biology, psychology, and sociology. Some writers would consider spirituality as another level for empirical investigation above psychology and sociology.

2.1.2 Reductionism

Reductionism is a process of simplification used in science. It is an essential part of human life. Our minds are constantly sorting through the vast amount of internal and external information available to us. Through selective attention and simplification, this is reduced to a manageable quantity so that we can make sense out of the world. However, reductionism takes different forms, often with important implications for how we think about and study a phenomenon of interest. Nancey Murphy (1998c) identifies five kinds of reductionism (Fig. 2.1):

1. **Methodological** or **atomistic reductionism** is the simplification of a phenomenon for the purpose of study, typically by breaking it into parts. For instance, one might define religiousness in terms of worship service attendance and the performance of religious practices like prayer, and then study how each of these relates to some other variable such as mental health. The opposite of atomistic reduction is **holism**, the idea that "the underlying unity of the world is not only a matter of derivation from common underlying principles, laws and constants, but extends also to a common interrelatedness and interconnectedness" (Peacocke, 1993, p. 42).

Fig. 2.1 *Nancey Murphy.*
With earned doctoral
degrees in both philosophy
of science and philosophy
of religion, she is one of the
most important figures in the
science and religion dialogue.
Photo courtesy of Nancey
Murphy

According to this view, things are not merely the sum of their parts but also have an additional quality due to complex interrelationships (Slife & Hopkins, 2005; for an opposing view see e.g., Dawkins, 1987, p. 81). Atomistic and holistic perspectives are both helpful and do not necessarily exclude each other, but a rigid methodological reductionism can be quite limiting, especially when combined with other versions of reduction (Peacocke, 1993, pp. 39–40; Barbour, 1997, p. 230).

2. **Epistemological reductionism** is the idea that laws governing higher level, complex phenomena should follow from laws at lower levels (Stoeger, 2002). In this view, the laws of human behavior and human activities like religion should be similar to and deducible from the laws of biology and physics. This could also mean that the *methods and approaches* used in the study of biology or physics are also those that should be used in psychology. A scientist taking this position might argue that neuroimaging of brain functioning could deduce laws that could explain religious experience and behavior. An opposing position (e.g., MacIntyre, 1992) argues that it is not appropriate to equate psychological knowledge with knowledge in the physical sciences and that psychology needs to be free to pursue methods more in keeping with its subject matter.

Other critics who reject strict epistemological reduction often believe that different levels of organization have unique or **emergent properties** because of their complexity, and that these emergent phenomena cannot be derived or understood from the study of lower levels (Davies, 1998, p. 159; Murphy, 1998c; Marras, 2006; cf. Kim, 2006). In this view, there are connections between higher and lower levels of the system, and lower levels may be necessary to the operation of higher levels, but higher levels also have their own unique properties (Ellis, 2002; Baldwin, 1902,

p. 8; cf. Andler, 2006). For instance, many authors believe that human psychology and sociology have patterns that cannot be understood solely by looking at biology. Emergent properties can change the behavior of both the parts of the system and the systems as a whole in fundamental ways. For instance, carbon atoms are different when part of diamond or graphite, and it is impossible to understand the difference unless we consider not only the carbon atoms but the nature and quality of their interrelationships (Slife & Hopkins, 2005; Birch, 1998, p. 241). So while different levels of observation like psychology and biology certainly relate to each other, and we can work toward an understanding of their connectedness (Goldsmith, 1994, p. 141), we cannot ignore differences and unique emergent features in our study of the world. This view of things is congruent with holism. Some scholars view human consciousness and freedom—perhaps even the very experience of personhood—as emergent properties of complex neuronal networks in the brain (Hefner, 1998; Davies, 1996; Varela, Thompson, & Rosch, 1991; Peacocke, 2002).

3. **Logical or definitional reductionism** holds that the vocabulary and language used at one level of scientific inquiry should be able to be exactly translated into the language of another level. While many early theorists like William James and Carl Jung rejected this idea, much research in the psychology of religion accepts this principle and assumes that religion can be explained using the same psychological constructs used to explain other human behavior. This kind of reduction can also be found when scientists apply human language to nonhuman objects or bodily organs, as when evolutionary biologist Richard Dawkins (1989) labels genes as "selfish" or a psychologist incorrectly attributes things like action or language to the brain that are really activities of the whole person (Bennett & Hacker, 2003). An alternative view is that different levels of inquiry require a different kind of language and that descriptions at one level are somewhat unique. In this perspective, a psychological word like "willpower" cannot be translated entirely into neurological description.

4. Many philosophers of science see reality as operating at various levels: basic levels such as the subatomic or molecular level studied by physicists or chemists and higher levels that involve more complex biological and human systems studies by biologists or psychologists. **Causal reductionism** says that events at "lower" levels such as physics determine what happens at "higher" levels like psychology. This is also referred to as **bottom-up causation**. Less strict views of causal reduction suggest that levels are partly decoupled from each other and have some relative autonomy or that **top-down causation** can occur where higher levels influence activity at lower ones, a possibility implied in holism. For instance, a top-down causal view would suggest that subjective mental events such as religious experiences could influence chemical processes in neurons (Campbell, 1974; Peacocke, 1993, p. 53, 1995; Murphy, 1998c; Peters, 1996). In psychology, a strict causal reductionist might hold that our psychological life is completely determined by our biology. Those holding a decoupled view (e.g., Barrett, Dunbar, & Lycett, 2002, p. 2) would disagree, arguing that while biology is relevant to human nature, our personhood cannot be reduced to biology. Holistic or top-down theorists, who contend that mental activity can affect biological processes, also reject strict causal reductionism. In their view, full knowledge of the human person must involve an understanding of

both bottom-up and top-down causal processes. Knowledge at one level illuminates other levels without replacing them (Stoeger, 2002; Faucher, 2006).

Nancey Murphy has described the relationship between levels in the hierarchy as a **supervenience relationship** (Murphy, 1998c). In this type of relationship, (a) lower level events can constitute higher level events in given sets of circumstances but not in others, and (b) there is more than one pattern of lower level events that can lead to any given higher level event. The relation between depression and biology offers a good example of this. A person with cancer (a lower level biological condition) might feel depressed (a higher level psychological condition), if they knew that there is little chance for recovery but might feel no depression if they knew there was an easy cure for the disease. In addition, there are numerous biological conditions (e.g., drug use, hormonal irregularities), which can lead to the same psychological condition (depression). Thus there is no automatic link between lower level and higher level properties—they are related but somewhat independent of each other.

5. **Ontological reductionism** is the most extreme kind of reduction. It assumes that something has no real or unique existence—it is "nothing but" a combination of other types of things that are real. For instance, social psychologists who emphasize that religion is a cultural and psychological phenomenon might try to say that religion is only "our own creation, an illusion invented by society to curb self-gratification and to meet our desperate need for comfort and direction," (Batson, Schoenrade, & Ventis, 1993, p. 370). This type of ontological reduction turns "explaining" religion into "explaining away" religion (Pargament, 2002b). Another example is **ontological materialism**, the position that all things are ultimately and only material objects. Since ontological reductions cannot be proven empirically, they are metaphysical positions, assumptions that philosophers and scientists make about the nature of the world and our experience.

Many scientists and philosophers reject ontological reductionism as unhelpful, untrue or scientifically unjustified. While seldom found in the physical sciences it appears more frequently in psychology, including some work in the psychology of religion. Extreme ontological reductionism is rarely accurate, particularly in the biological sciences, although it can have considerable heuristic value (Polkinghorne, 1999a; Corveleyn, 1996; Watts, 2002c, p. 4; Kistler, 2006; Schaffner, 2006; Poirier, 2006). In fact it is a trade-off; reductionistic explanations gain in simplicity while losing in accuracy. Ontological reductionism seems particularly problematic with reference to a complex phenomenon like religion, where overly simplistic explanations will yield models that are misleading, mistaken, or useless (Vergote, 1998, p. 42; Watts, 2002c, p. 25; Taylor, 2007, p. 679). Allport viewed ontological reductions that attempted to make religion nothing but a psychological state as arrogance (Vande Kemp, 2000). Holism rejects ontological reductionism because the whole is greater than its parts and thus cannot be reduced to it (Barbour, 1998). Furthermore, ontological reductionism is unnecessary as other kinds of simplification can be carried out without making ontological assumptions (Ruse, 2000, p. 270). Advocates (e.g., Sagan, 1997, p. 275) argue that reductionism is one of the greatest achievements of science even when it turns out to be wrong.

2.1.3 Materialism

Materialism in psychology refers to "the *sufficiency* of the material of the body (biology) alone for explaining our minds and behaviors" (Slife & Hopkins, 2005, p. 122). It is a metaphysical position related to **ontology**, the nature of things, and is thus a philosophical position rather than a scientific fact. It is often closely related to materialism as an ethical philosophy (cf. Section 11.1.2). It has a long history in philosophy dating back to the ancient Greeks, but it was not a widely held position prior to the 19th century. Some philosophers argue that materialism is the dominant ontology in philosophy and science today (Moser & Trout, 1995, p. ix) and is so widely accepted that people are often unaware that it is a metaphysical position that they hold. However, materialism is still controversial in philosophy, as it has great difficulty accounting for things like mental life and our subjective experience, which are seemingly nonmaterial in nature (Madell, 2003; Nagel, 1986; Griffin, 2000, pp. 76–77).

A common version of materialism is **reductive** or **eliminative materialism,** a kind of ontological reductionism that says everything is really just a collection of material particles and the laws that govern them. Reductive materialists typically exclude consideration of any potentially nonmaterialistic (e.g., spiritualistic) phenomena or more "subjective" methods that might accumulate data contrary to materialistic assumptions. All mental events must ultimately be reducible to material ones (Griffin, 2000, pp. 70–71; Nagel, 1970). For instance, the neurophilosopher Paul Churchland argues that things like "mind" or "spirit" are simply "folk psychology" terms that describe **epiphenomena**—things with no reality or ability to affect other things. He predicts that someday we will engage in some necessary linguistic reduction and replace concepts like "thought" with ideas from neurobiology that better recognize their material character. This position is not widely accepted, as others have pointed out that such a linguistic reduction has never succeeded in the history of science (D'Andrade, 1995, p. 165). Reductive materialism involves a kind of **dualistic reductionism,** where mind and brain are split from each other, and then the term that is inconsistent with the philosophical assumptions of the materialist investigator—the mind—is eliminated (Olafson, 2001, p. 72). It is generally anti-holistic as it holds that only the stuff things are made out of has real existence, not their organization (Barbour, 1998). In psychology, theories as divergent as behaviorism, Freudian psychoanalysis, and some variants of cognitive neuroscience are constructed on reductive materialist views of the world. Philosophers of science generally reject the use of these eliminative strategies (Wimsatt, 2006), but they are commonly used in psychology.

In softer varieties of materialism, material objects are thought to occupy a prominent but not exclusive role in the foundation of reality. Sometimes, this takes the form of a **methodological physicalism** which holds that nonmaterial things exist but that we can only study the world through physical entities (Shoemaker, 1999; Butchvarov, 1999). In milder positions like **supervenience materialism**, nonmaterial aspects of reality not only exist but also can be described; however, they do not exist independently of physical processes, because any difference in nonmaterial states can only occur if there is a difference in physical states (cf. Murphy, 1998b). **Nonreductive materialism** is an even softer version of materialism, which argues that there are nonmaterial aspects to reality that at least initially owe their existence to material objects or processes but later function independently as emergent phenomena. These higher nonmaterial processes are able to exercise an influence on lower or physical levels of reality through top-down causation (Peacocke, 1993, p. 53). For instance, a nonreductive physicalist view of mind and brain holds that we are not just bodies, so that while mental events are embodied in brain activity they are not identical with it (Murphy, 1998a; Jeeves, 1998). Contemporary Christian theologians often hold softer versions of materialism, emphasizing the fact that we are embodied creatures and thus cannot be understood apart from our material nature but that reductive materialist positions cannot account for important aspects of the human person.

Materialism raises a number of philosophical and scientific problems. The definition of matter is problematic, as it is mass or energy—characteristics of matter, rather than matter itself—that appears in mathematical descriptions of the world produced by scientists. Quantum theory and other aspects of modern physics also deemphasize the importance of matter, as they suggest that the universe is more about structure and interaction than stuff (Stoeger, 2002; Heller, 1988). Reductive materialism also introduces problems into social scientific and psychological inquiries, since things of interest to psychologists such as cognition and emotion are often not material entitles or open to direct observation (Slife, 2005).

2.1.4 Naturalism and Scientism

The word "natural" has a couple of different meanings in reference to science. In the first place, it can refer to an area of study, the natural world, which in the early modern period was taken to mean the nonhuman world of stars, rocks, plants, and animals. It also forms the root of the term **naturalism**, which is the philosophical position that the world around us can be understood abstractly in terms of natural, lawlike processes. In this abstractionist way of thinking, things are looked at from a universal viewpoint; what is important to know is not the things we see in all their diversity, but the uniform laws that presumably stand behind what we see. Sometimes, these laws are taken metaphysically as having a real existence rather than just descriptions of regularities (Stoeger, 1996; Davies, 1996; cf. Arendt, 1998, p. 268), as when we say that something falls "because of the law of gravity" or that "Mother Nature" (the sum total collection of laws) makes certain things happen. The presumed regularity of laws invites one to see the world—including the human person—in a mechanistic way. We become machines made of pieces that operate according to certain fixed principles so that an understanding of the parts gives complete knowledge of the system as a whole. The scientist is able to relate to the world as an outside observer of these abstract laws, rather than as a participant (Slife, Mitchell, & Whollery, 2004; Vergote, 1969, p. 51). For instance, the cognitive psychologist Pascal Boyer argues that religion is a natural outcome of the lawlike workings of cognitive mental processes and thus is entirely predictable from psychological laws that can be derived by scientific observation (see Section 6.2.3).

Numbers (2003) distinguishes two varieties of naturalism: First is **methodological naturalism**, which is a commitment to produce lawlike explanations without recourse to supernatural forces. These explanations are abstractionist, and the methodology assumes that it is possible to understand a phenomenon from the position of an outside observer with objective neutrality (Drees, 1999, p. 26; Slife, 2005). This form of naturalism is widely accepted in psychology and in fact has been supported by Christians throughout the history of science. After 1750, a **metaphysical** or **reductive naturalism** also developed, which combines the tenants of methodological naturalism with epistemological reductionism (methods developed in the physical science are the best way to study everything) and reductive materialism (nothing exists except the material world; cf. Drees, 1999). The inclusion of these metaphysical beliefs makes naturalism into an ontology or view of the world rather than a methodological stance. It tends to blur the distinction between human and nonhuman (Olafson, 2001, pp. 5–6; Griffin, 2000, p. 37). The acceptance of metaphysical naturalism within psychology can be seen in a number of areas and can be found in the psychology of religion as early as the work of James Leuba (Murphy, 1928; see Section 1.4.2). The adoption of naturalism means that phenomena which fit most comfortably within a naturalistic frame will be privileged subjects of study, and methodologies best suited to the study of those objects will be held in highest esteem. Some scholars argue that it is possible to accept methodological naturalism while rejecting the limitations inherent in metaphysical naturalism. Others argue that both abstractionist and objectifying explanations are problematic, as even a milder methodological naturalism has metaphysical assumptions that bias investigations, particularly those related to religion (Slife & Whollery, 2006; Slife, 2005).

Many philosophers (e.g., Strawson, 1985, pp. 2, 67) have noted a connection between reductive forms of naturalism and **scientism** or "the attitude that the only kind of reliable knowledge is that provided by science, coupled with a conviction that all our personal and social problems are 'soluble' by enough science" (Peacocke, 1993, pp. 7–8; cf. Ruse, 2002) so that the domain of science has no boundary (e.g., Drees, 1999, p. 8). Along with scientism comes increasing cultural technification so that the superiority of science and technical solutions to problems is taken for granted or becomes commonsense and a never-discussed basis for thinking and practice. Extreme versions of scientism hold that science is the only truly valuable enterprise, thus limiting or eliminating the possibility of true dialogue with religion or for that matter with many other disciplines of human study such as the humanities (Polkinghorne, 2004, pp. 24, 179; Stenmark, 2001, p. 19). While some version of scientism is still a common belief among scientists, it has also been heavily challenged as a basic logical error or category mistake about what science is and can do (e.g., Peterson, 2003; Zahavi, 2004). Critics outside of science have pointed out that science has been unable to deliver on the grand promise of solving all our difficulties and has brought with it other problems. This has led to a lot of skepticism toward science in some quarters. As Kay and Francis remark, "scientism is not just bad for religion; scientism is bad for science itself, because it presents a false view of what science is and what science can properly be expected to achieve" (1996, p. 155). The fact that scientism is not scientifically demonstrable also suggests a problem with its rational coherence as well (Shanahan, 2004, pp. 243 n. 14, 318).

Richard Gorsuch points out that a naturalist metaphysic sits uncomfortably with the study of religion in a couple of ways. First, while a naturalist view of the world focuses on law, in fact we live in a world of rich diversity that is not completely captured by these laws (2002a, p. 51). This is particularly true of the human and mental realms which have few if any determinative laws, so some would argue that naturalism may be problematic for psychology (Polkinghorne, 1988, p. 136). Science tends to value the generality of law over specificity of particular situations. However, if the aim of science is to gain a better understanding of the world around us, specificity can be just as important as broad laws, for very general laws cannot reliably tell us what is the right thing to do in specific situations (Shanahan, 2004, p. 90). In this view, nonnaturalistic approaches could and should supplement naturalistic ones in our attempts to gain knowledge. Second, a lawlike view of the world is hard to reconcile with the idea of a God who acts in history: "By definition, God's individual acts do not replicate. So science can never identify them even if they happen a dozen times a day in every scientist's life" (Gorsuch, 2002a, p. 66). For this and other reasons, some authors have questioned whether metaphysical naturalism can be reconciled with Christianity or any of the major world religions (Richards & Bergin, 2004; Griffin, 2000, pp. 35, 65). Others have pointed out that reductive naturalism has a tendency to lead to a broader moral and ethical skepticism that is based on an ideological philosophical position, not on facts (Hurlbut, 2002).

2.1.5 Assessment

We now have a basic philosophical vocabulary that will help us understand some of the issues in the dialogue between science and religion. The positions that we have reviewed are important, but unfortunately are often adopted by participants in the dialogue without reflection, justification or understanding of their implications. We will see that the uncritical adoption of strong reductionist and naturalist positions has greatly affected the dialogue between science and religion, particularly within the field of psychology. As the 20th century saw a strong philosophical and scientific critique of these reductive positions, different ways of thinking about science and religion emerged that offer new possibilities for dialogue.

2.2   Early Modern Views of Science and Religion

2.2.1   Background to the Modern Period

Science and religion have coexisted in Western civilization since classical Greek times. Contrary to popular perception, for most of that period the relationship involved peaceful coexistence and even cooperation. For instance, in the Middle Ages, studies of the natural world, human behavior, and theology were part of a body of knowledge learned by all educated people. Relations between science and theology were generally harmonious, with science playing a subsidiary but increasingly independent role from theology as a separate but interrelated field. Theologians like Aquinas could write about the mutually beneficial interaction of science with theology as he worked to integrate Christian ideas with Aristotelian views of science and causation (Thomas, 1998, Pt. I, Q 79, Art 9; Aristotle, 1941, Bk. 2 Ch. 3, pp. 240–242). Applications of science to theology included reinterpretation of scriptural passages that were found to conflict with accepted scientific theory and observation (Grant, 1986). Problems in the relationship had to do more with professional rivalries rather than any perceived conflict between science and religion. In fact, many historians argue that medieval religion and later Puritanism actually played an important positive role in the development of modern science (e.g., Lindberg, 1992; Kocher, 1953; cf. Cohen, 1990). As late as the 16th and early 17th centuries, there was no firm dividing line between natural philosophy (science) and other branches of philosophical inquiry so that people worked in both areas and freely shared perspectives (Zagorin, 1998; Brooke, 1991, pp. 1–116). In the early modern period, however, a divorce began to develop between science and religion, particularly in the work of Francis Bacon.

2.2.2 Francis Bacon and the Beginnings of Modern Science

Francis Bacon (1561–1626) is often identified as producing the first systematic exposition of the modern scientific method, as well as the most important early modern statement about the relationship between science, metaphysics, and theology. As a result, his views set the tone for ideas about science and religion in the modern period. Bacon came to this topic not as a working scientist but as a man of learning who was interested in promoting the growth of knowledge and technology. He felt that science, like religion, should lead to "good works" (Zagorin, 1998).

While Bacon did not identify himself as a Puritan, he grew up in a Puritan home, and his work reflects Puritan and Calvinist Christian influence. His ideas were often seen as a natural part of Puritan eschatology and ethics (Perez-Ramos, 1988, p. 13). Puritans thought that the church would play a role in creating the Kingdom of God on earth through learning and progress. These ideas generated a positive and optimistic attitude toward the future and human works that is reflected in Bacon's writings.

2.2.2.1 The Purpose of Science and Learning

Bacon had a very practical or utilitarian view of knowledge. He was concerned with the broad social role that science could play in human life, as well as the advancement of knowledge for its own sake (Rossi, 1997). He viewed the relationship between utility and knowledge as important in a couple of ways. First, he saw knowledge and science as a means to power that would help us subdue nature so that we could gain resources and pursue human goals. For Bacon, knowledge and power were interchangeable concepts (Bacon, 2000). Second, the ability to make artifacts or achieve control over nature was a validation of knowledge, a way of verifying and demonstrating that our ideas about the world are accurate (Perez-Ramos, 1988, pp. 143–148). In this view, any kind of progress or increase in power is good, and in fact Bacon believed that advances in military technology were just as good as the invention of printing or ways to preserve food. He saw no need for science to have an ethic that would distinguish between various goals of progress, perhaps because he thought that morality was really the concern of religion rather than science (Bacon, 2001, pp. 32, 213; Perez-Ramos, 1997).

2.2.2.2   The Need for New Scientific Methods

In *The Advancement of Learning* (1605), and particularly in his later work, the *New Organon* (1620), Bacon articulated new ideas about scientific investigation. Prior to Bacon's work, scientific work was often guided by the method of Aristotle, who argued that explanations of the natural world should focus on the causes of phenomena. Aristotle believed that often things happened because of some end goal or purpose in nature, what he called **final causes** and that one could construct **teleological** explanations of the world based on an understanding of how things happen in order to reach certain ends or goals. Bacon thought that scientific explanations based on teleology were questionable. He believed that explanations based on final causes were really a human invention not derived from the nature of the universe, a position that seems defensible when examining inanimate phenomena but questionable in a full account of living things (Ayala, 1998a). Bacon believed that teleological explanations were uncertain because they were really part of metaphysics or philosophical speculation on the nature of the world. In his view, science should avoid teleology and primarily follow the interpretive method of induction, compiling large amounts of detailed information and then looking for generalities. He thought this **inductive method** was less prone to error, although he also acknowledged a role for the **deductive method**, where a scientist invents new experiments based on the generalities derived from inductive investigation. This "double ladder" of investigation involving inductive and deductive inquiry formed his complete view of science, which he envisioned as an undertaking of an organized community (2001, p. 95; Rossi, 1997, p. 32). He preferred inductive interpretation, because it involves gathering information from a broad range of sources, as opposed to deduction that is less open, looks at a limited range of familiar evidence and thus may produce little progress.

2.2.2.3   Science, Religion, and the Two Books

Early modern philosophers like Bacon and Thomas Hobbes (1962) struggled to define the relationship between science, religion and different fields of human inquiry. While Hobbes tended to subordinate religion to science, Bacon is well known for advocating separation between science and theology, a position widely held by his scientific contemporaries (Zagorin, 1998, p. 49). He used the **two books analogy** from Augustine (1994) to justify this, arguing that theological knowledge is based on revelation from God's "book," while science or natural philosophy is based on evidence from the senses and nature's "book" (cf. Bacon, 2001, p. 89). They should be separate, for "to seek heaven and earth in the word of God is to seek temporary things amongst eternal; and as to seek divinity in philosophy is to seek the living amongst the dead, so to seek philosophy in divinity is to seek the dead amongst the living" (2001, p. 220). In particular, the miraculous cannot be conceived as part of the natural world and as such has no place in science (2001, p. 75).

Bacon was skeptical of **natural theology**, the attempt to use what we see in the world as a support for our understanding of God. In the Middle Ages, natural theology was a favorite topic, and aspects of the world were used as the basis for proofs about the nature and existence of God. Bacon had a different and more limited view of the possibilities of natural theology (Barnouw, 1981). He certainly agreed with theologians like John Calvin (1960, p. 52) that God could be seen in the world because creation contains the imprint of the Divine mind. Contemplation on the book of nature could thus lead a person to meditate on things like God's omnipotence and might help bring religion to atheists who will not accept supernatural proofs. However, Bacon believed that an examination of nature cannot really provide safe religious knowledge, as the use of philosophy or science to support religion makes it dependent upon changeable current opinion and ultimately is an expression of a lack of faith (Bacon, 2001, pp. 92–93), a position also held by his contemporary Galileo. Even more foolish are attempts to derive natural philosophy from the scriptures, as the Bible is not intended to be a scientific book (Bacon, 2000). Thus, Bacon had a position that was closed to the possibility of a theologically informed science as well as skeptical of natural theology.

While Bacon separated science and theology, he thought the study of the human person involved both books. He considered psychology under the head of human rather than natural philosophy, although he thought that because of the relations between mind and body, the study of the mind could not be strictly assigned to either and that ultimately knowledge of the human person was also a type of religious knowledge and thus the province of theology (Bacon, 2001, pp. 109–110).

2.2.2.4 Problems and Prospects

While many of the specifics of Bacon's proposals were ignored, his ideas about the broad social role of science, technology, and advancement had a wide and continuing influence on Western modernity (Perez-Ramos, 1997). Many of these effects persist today and have been criticized by contemporary authors.

Change from contemplation to power. Koyre (1965, pp. 6–11) indicates that a prime effect of Bacon and others at the time of the scientific revolution was the destruction of a worldview that included value, purpose, and the qualitative aspect of human experience. His views moved society away from classical utopian ideals of contemplation, self-sufficiency and pursuit of the good rather than the conquest of Nature (Weinberger, 1985, p. 21). Dossey (1997) argues that Bacon's amoral approach has created problems for science. Many people associate science with an unbridled pursuit of power and that the technology developed as a result of this is responsible for many problems such as global environmental degradation. This leads people to oppose scientific study when it might be helpful.

Separation of fact and value. Bacon treated advancement as an end in itself that was separated from ethical or moral concerns, which were seen to be the province of theology. His thought introduces a distinction between *facts*, which he saw as related to science, and *values* that were the concern of theology. However, Bacon's scientific enterprise is in fact quite value laden. In his descriptions of science and the pursuit of knowledge, he privileges the values of progress, control, or manipulation of nature for human ends over contemplative religious values. In a sense, facts become more important than values.

Science and religion. While Bacon was an advocate of separating science and religion, he also provides some positive prospects for conversation or integration. Certainly his view of science was an open one that avoided reductionist positions and allowed for broad inquiry with little limitation of subject matter. While science and nature are separated from religion as a different "book," Bacon held that the book of revelation is also a valid and valuable way to knowledge. Both are viewed as necessary to an understanding of the human person.

2.2.3 Kant and the Problem of Empiricism and Skepticism

Other early modern philosophers also wrestled with the problem of scientific and religious knowledge. Bacon's positive view of experience and induction was challenged by the Scottish philosopher, David Hume (1711–1776), who argued that there was no way that definite knowledge could be based upon sense experience, because we can never prove that what we have experienced in the past will also be true in the future (Hume, 2001, pp. 61–65). This **problem of induction** threw into question the validity of Bacon's inductive empiricism as a methodology for scientific inquiry. Hume's skepticism led to a number of attempts to defend our ability to gain knowledge, including the important work of Immanuel Kant (1724–1804). Kant thought that there were three great questions of life: What can I know? What ought I to do? What may I hope? (1965, p. 635). The last question is primarily a religious one, but the other two are both psychological and theological in nature. His answers to those questions have had a great impact on the relationship between science and religion.

2.2.3.1 What can I know?

Kant believed there were three fundamental powers of the soul: (1) the *cognitive power* involved in our understanding of nature; (2) the *power of desire* which governs our **practical reason** about moral matters and is based on freedom and the moral law; and (3) the *feeling of pleasure and displeasure* which forms the basis of **judgment** (Kant, 1987, p. 16). Our cognitive powers operate through **analytic reasoning** that breaks things up into parts and explores what we already know and **synthetic reasoning** that adds to an original concept and give us two kinds of new knowledge: *a posteriori* knowledge dependent on experience and *a priori* knowledge that is necessary and universally true completely independent of experience. He referred to reasoning based on a priori knowledge as **pure reason** (1965, pp. 41–62).

Kant believed that our knowledge of the world was limited. He divided the world into two realms, the **phenomenal** world of objects as we experience them with our senses, and the **supersensible** world where the real things-in-themselves or **noumena** exist (1965, pp. 257–275). Kant thought we could never know real super-sensible reality directly or in full but that we could have intuitions of it through sense experience (1965, p. 105). Thus Kant had a **subjective** understanding of knowledge as created within the person, connected to reality without fully grasping it. He believed that this creative process was dependent upon basic *a priori* mental categories like time and space that help us interpret our experience. His position acknowledged that human reason has its limits but that things have a real existence and that we can know some things about them. For instance, Kant believed that God and human freedom are supersensible and as such cannot be known directly or be an object of scientific inquiry. However, through pure reason, we can infer their existence and some fundamental things about them (1965, pp. 297–300, 322–326; 2002, pp. 119–121). Importantly, Kant thought that *relationship* was a fundamental mental category for organizing experience; his idea marked the beginning of a trend toward seeing relationality as central to an understanding of the human person (Shults, 2003, pp. 20–21).

2.2.3.2   What Ought I to do?

Kant believed in the existence of a universal supersensible moral law that cannot be deduced from experience (1960, p. 15) but that all people are aware of *a priori.* Because of this awareness, it can be an object of pure reason and guide our practical reason (2002, pp. 43, 161). Pure reason allows us to derive the existence of freedom from the presence of the inner moral law we possess, since freedom is a necessary prerequisite to carrying out the law (1965, pp. 635–636; 2002, pp. 4, 29). However, since God and the moral law cannot be deduced directly from experience, they can-not be the object of scientific inquiry and must be kept separate (1960, p. 15). We can also reason that growth in virtue requires more than the time available in a finite human existence, suggesting the necessity for the immortality of the soul. Further-more, a Supreme Reason (God) must be postulated to ensure that the highest good of moral law and happiness can be achieved together (2002, pp. 122–129; 1987, p. 450). If reason were the complete determinant of our behavior, then we would unfailingly use our freedom to follow the moral law, but since that is not the case, we experience the law as a moral or "categorical imperative" of things we should do. Our relationship to the moral law should be one of dependence, duty, and obedience out of "moral feeling and respect for the law" (2002, pp. 20–21, 32–33, 75–82). Ultimately, he believed that following the moral law meant treating others as "ends in themselves" and not as "means to an end." This treatment of moral law as a matter of practical reason paralleled Bacon's separation of fact and value and cemented it in a comprehensive and influential philosophy (Barbour, 1997, p. 47).

In his later work, the *Critique of Judgment*, Kant argued that not only are God, freedom, and immortality necessary for fulfillment of the moral law, but a belief in the purposiveness of nature is also necessary and forms the basis of the faculty of judgment, although it cannot be a matter of scientific proof (1987, pp. 196–198, 435–436). Thus, Kant was uncomfortable with Bacon's removal of final purpose or **teleology** from any connection to our view of the natural world.

Kant thought that true religion is a moral religion founded on rationality, a "pure religion of reason" (1960, p. 140) with theology based entirely upon the moral law. It is morality, rather than the natural world, that leads us to religion and a view of God as Lawgiver. God is ultimately unknowable and engaging in acts of worship or devotion that attempt to bridge this gap is rationally indefensible and constitutes superstition or fanaticism (1960, pp. 5–6, 162). Kant viewed this compartmentalization of self, natural world, and God as a way of protecting religion and keeping science or rationality within appropriate bounds. However, his system also served to isolate religion from science and philosophy, increasing the divide between them. His orientation to religion was also very individualistic, a trend that will reappear in the work of William James (e.g., Kant, 1987, p. 273; Taylor, 2002, p. 14; see Section 4.2).

2.3 The Rise of Classical Positivism

Kant was a philosopher of the **Enlightenment**, the 18th century intellectual movement that hoped to make a society based on human reason. Some Enlightenment philosophers like Kant were concerned to maintain a role for religion in a rational society. In contrast, French Enlightenment thought put forward views that favored science and opposed theological or religious ideas. These currents converged in the philosophy of **positivism** developed by Auguste Comte (1798–1857), who created the first comprehensive philosophy of science since the time of Bacon. In this philosophy, Comte argued that human society and inquiry should be based only on positive, verified knowledge obtained through science. Positivism marked a shift to hard versions of naturalism, materialism, and scientism that went beyond separation and advocated the overthrow of theology. It included (1) a Baconian emphasis on science as a tool for power and control, (2) a reductionist view of inquiry, (3) a reductionist view of the unity of science, and (4) a view of history that emphasized scientific progress.

2.3.1 Basic Tenants of Classical Positivism

In addition to adopting Bacon's attitude of science as a means to power, Comte's positivist philosophy advocated a *strong empiricist and naturalist view of inquiry.* He believed that the only true knowledge is scientific or positive knowledge based on observed facts. He also argued against trying to understand the true cause of things, which he considered to be metaphysical speculation: "Instead of resorting to the old ways of pronouncing or imagining *why* it must be so, the positive philosophy instructs us to recognize the simple fact that it *is* so" (Comte, 1998a, p. 122). The most that we can do is observe "relations of succession and likeness" which he hoped would eventually lead to the discovery of invariant natural laws, which would make possible our prediction and control of the physical world and also perhaps the social world (1998a, pp. 160, 241–243; Ple, 2000). Thus, Comte adopted the Kantian skepticism about knowing the real nature of things, although for somewhat different reasons.

Comte also had a *strong reductionist view of the unity of science.* He constructed a hierarchical model of the interrelationship of scientific disciplines. Higher sciences on the list were "closely dependent" on those lower on the list, while more basic ones were wholly independent of higher ones (1998a, p. 144). The hierarchy was

- Social physics (Sociology)
- Biology and Physiology
- Chemistry
- Physics
- Astronomy
- Mathematics

Psychology was not included in the list, because he considered the mind to be a biological development and its study a branch of physiology. He viewed all psychological and social phenomena as ultimately governed by material, biological laws (1998a, pp. 255–257). He believed that as much as possible we should aim to explain things using the fewest possible concepts and that the use of scientific methodology should be extended to the study of individuals and groups. However, he also acknowledged that each field of study must modify this basic method to suit its object of study (1998a, p. 112).

In the narrative portion of his theory, Comte formulated what he called the *Law of Three Stages* of human history, arguing that it was inevitable that humanity would progress through three phases: "the primitive theological state, the transient metaphysical, and the final positive state" (1998a, p. 285). In the final stage, science would assist in the elimination of theological and metaphysical (philosophical) ideas and help found a new and more orderly society that would replace absolute ideas with the doctrine of relativism (1998a, pp. 212, 220). Comte argued in a seemingly paradoxical manner that the only force that could ensure this transition to a utopia was a religious or spiritual force. So despite his own personal atheism, Comte rejected atheism as a philosophical position (Pickering, 1993, p. 654). He proposed to construct a "Religion of Humanity" (1998b, p. 381) with humanity constituting the "Great Being" (1998b, p. 445). Included in the religion were a system of social worship, a positivist calendar and pantheon of saints, and a positivist library of 150 books (1998b, pp. 454–480) with others subject to destruction. The "ascendancy of Humanity" would substitute for "the utter exhaustion of the Kingdom of God" (1998b, p. 483).

2.3.2 Implications and Assessment

Comte's theory is very significant in several ways, although many of his ideas like the Religion of Humanity met with a lukewarm reception from his contemporaries. It articulated an influential philosophy of science that moved from milder versions of reductionism, materialism, and naturalism as found in Bacon to more reductive ones. It also moved the relationship between science and religion from a "two-books" doctrine to a stance of conflict. This attitude became increasingly common as the 19th century progressed and can be seen in books like Andrew White's *History of the Warfare of Science with Theology in Christendom* (1901), as well as the later work of authors like Bertrand Russell. Positivism became one of the major factors in ideological secularization (Marsden & Longfield, 1992, pp. 16–25; Senne, 2002).

One especially influential aspect of Comtean positivism is his view of history as inherently progressing toward a scientific ideal while primitive beliefs like religion are destined to disappear. Although this "subtraction narrative" view of history has been discredited by modern historiography (e.g., Leahey, 2002), it was and is quite influential within the field of psychology (Simon, 1963, p. 24; O'Connor, 2001; Leahey, 1987, 2002; Nelson, 2006). It is also central to humanist and secular self-understandings and views of religion (Taylor, 2007). In the general culture, it can be seen in the common assumptions that traditional practices are outmoded, and future progress will provide better solutions—a conclusion not always warranted by the data. It also remains an assumption among many in the scientific community. It can be seen in scientific statements and narratives that convey the impression that we have certain knowledge about something even though research findings do not support definite conclusions (Young, 2004a). Even more common is the habit of admitting flaws in a theory or data but then minimizing them by saying that they will be cleared up in the future (Arendt, 1968, p. 346). Writers like neurophilosopher Paul Churchland or the sociobiologist E. O. Wilson also put forward this kind of 19th-century viewpoint, when they argue that through science we are moving away from a "folk psychology" referring to the mind (Churchland, 1995, p. 155) and "primitive religious beliefs" to a new scientific vision of the world that is freer and more morally insightful (Churchland, 1996, pp. 17–18; Wilson, 1978, pp. 192–193, 200–201). This puts some neurobiologists who wish to move away from acknowledging the existence of the mind in the odd position of denying the reality of the phenomena they are studying, which seems at odds with scientific empiricism (Zahavi, 2004).

2.4 Logical and Neo-Positivism

At the beginning of the 20th century, attempts at reformulating the positivist system led to the development of **logical positivism**, a version of positivism incorporating analytic philosophy of language and logic. By the end of the 19th century, it become a goal of philosophers like Bertrand Russell (1872–1970) to analyze and reform language, purifying it of religious and philosophical content so that it could be a vehicle for logical analysis and statements of empirical, scientific knowledge. Russell's work combined logical analysis with both the empiricist and sociohistorical agendas advocated by Comte. Influenced especially by Russell's thought, and by their interpretations of the early work of Ludwig Wittgenstein in the *Tractatus Logico-Philosophicus* (1975), positivists picked up these trends in logic and language, combining them with positivist philosophy to form logical positivism.

Logical positivism flourished during the early part of the 20th century, thanks in part to the work of the Vienna Circle, a group of scientists and philosophers that met periodically to discuss various topics. Their initial goal was to propagate a scientific worldview, developing a unified science, and a definition of scientifically testable statements purged of metaphysical or theological ideas. Most of this group subscribed to a set of basic tenants relating to verification of truth and the nature of science, in addition to the basic concepts articulated by Comte.

2.4.1 Basic Tenants of Logical Positivism

2.4.1.1 Verification

Logical positivists believed that the truth of propositions could and should be verified by reference to simple empirical facts. In the original logical positivist formulation, verification was done empirically, by comparing "atomic" scientific statements with data (Wittgenstein, 1975; Russell, 1966). In this view, truth takes the form of representational propositions about the world, and the observer plays only a detached, mechanical role in the verification of truth claims. Initially, the group set up very strict criteria for verification. However, as time went on, the idea of atomic verification was discovered to be unworkable, and more relaxed criteria were proposed (Ayer, 1966; Feigl, 1956; Schlick, 1949b). Carnap (1949b) later retreated from the idea of truth value altogether, saying that scientific statements can never be definitely accepted or rejected, but they can only be confirmed to a greater or lesser degree by observation or comparison with previously accepted statements.

The logical positivist stance on verification carried with it three important corollaries. First, only certain kinds of statements were in fact verifiable, and statements not verifiable were considered nonsensical. Significantly, since metaphysical or theological propositions were not completely verifiable according to logical positivist standards, they were considered nonsensical and fit for elimination from discussion. For example, logical positivists would say that statements about life after death are neither true nor false, they are simply nonsensical. Scientific explanations were seen as superior to theological or metaphysical ones because of their testability and parsimony (Feigl, 1949a,b; Ayer, 1952, 1966; Ayer & Copleston, 1994) and their ability to make use of quantitative and experimental methods (Carnap, 1995). Most statements about ethics and values were considered to be metaphysical statements or simply expressions of feeling, so this area was of relatively little interest to them (Ayer, 1966). Logical positivists of course denied that they had any kind of metaphysical or religious presuppositions underlying their work (Feigl, 1956), a position that was challenged by their critics. They claimed that the scientific method of studying data and reaching conclusions generated "positive" knowledge, which seems contradictory to their tacit acceptance of Hume's skepticism.

Second, logical positivists thought that verifiable statements needed to be composed of precisely defined terms. They supported the development of **operational definitions** that put concepts in terms that would allow their inclusion in scientific studies that could evaluate their meaningfulness and fruitfulness (Frank, 1977; Feigl, 1949a). Statements were expected to be definite, logically consistent, and aimed at increasing predictiveness. Feigl (1949a) argued that one of the main reasons for the use of operational definitions was to purify science of any pre-scientific or nonscientific (e.g., metaphysical) elements, along with its practical purpose in clarifying meaning. Many authors (e.g., Schlick, 1949b) drew on the work of Percy Bridgman (1993), whose theory of operationalization stressed the importance of repeatability in scientific study. This latter point is quite important with regards to integration, because some (but not all) elements of religious truth (e.g., revelation) are inherently non-replicable and thus by this definition not scientific statements (Gorsuch, 2002b).

Finally, logical positivist standards of verification led to a reductive materialist position. Minds, feelings, and other internal phenomena could be said to exist as long as it was agreed that they were simply "abbreviations of physicalist statements" (Hempel, 1949). Schlick (1949c) claimed that this was empirically true and did not constitute a metaphysical presupposition, partly because he argued that quantification and agreement between observers was necessary to science and that only physical things could be measured quantitatively or allow for observer agreement.

2.4.1.2 Synthetic and Analytic Truth

Kant had argued that it was possible to learn new things through analytic logic or synthetic *a priori* reasoning from self-evident truths apart from experience. Logical positivists agreed with Kant's classification of reasoning but rejected his position that *a priori* principles could have a role in synthetic reasoning (Schlick, 1949a; Wittgenstein, 1975, p. 71). Thus, *new (synthetic) knowledge could only be gained through experience*, which they defined as verifiable sensory experience. Language could be analyzed to see if a particular statement or process of reasoning was analytic or synthetic *a posteriori* (from experience), and any statements that were neither were nonsensical. Furthermore, synthetic *a posteriori* reasoning was believed to be entirely objective and independent of any theory or factors related to the observer.

2.4.1.3 Reductionism and the Unity of Science

Logical positivists believed that science provided a unified approach to knowledge. Part of this had to do with the broad view of science held by writers like Carnap, who defined science as "all theoretical knowledge, no matter whether in the field of natural sciences or in the field of the social sciences and the so-called humanities, and no matter whether it is knowledge found by the application of special scientific procedures, or knowledge based on common sense in everyday life" (Carnap, 1949a). They also generally accepted the Comtean idea of a hierarchy of sciences with physics at its base, and chemistry, biology, psychology, and the social sciences on successively higher levels and used what they called *theoretical reductionism* to express one theory (e.g., a psychological theory of mind) using the concepts of another theory (e.g., a biological theory of brain). Hempel for instance argued that there was no inherent difference between psychology and the natural sciences. Psychology could be considered "an integral part of physics" (Hempel, 1949) and that eventually it could be derived from biology (Carnap, 1949a). They thus endorsed the ideas of logical and causal reductionism (see Section 2.1.2).

2.4.1.4 Logical Positivism and Religion

Like classical positivism, logical positivism typically had a negative attitude toward religion. For instance, Feigl (1980) argued that anything based on metaphysical or theological presuppositions was incompatible with modern science. Things like "magic, animism, mythology, theology and metaphysics" were all remnants of or regressions to prescientific thought characteristic of "less mature phases of intellectual growth." Nonscientific ways of knowing like "religious ecstasy" or artistic inspiration were not valid knowledge claims, although he did approve of religious devotion to values. As a consequence, positivists such as Russell and Ayer led a sustained, determined attack on religion (especially Christianity) and theological beliefs. In *Religion and Science* (1997), Russell wrote a paean of triumphal scientism, exposing how the steady progress of science had unmasked the flaws of religion and various nonsensical religious ideas such as free will. Interestingly, some of the triumphal character of his 1935 work disappears in his book *The Scientific Outlook* (2001), where he gives this description of a scientific society:

> In such a world, though there may be pleasure, there will be no joy. The result will be a type [of people] displaying the usual characteristics of vigorous ascetics. They will be harsh and unbending, tending towards cruelty in their ideals and their readiness to consider that the infliction of pain is necessary for the public good. ... The man drunk with power is destitute of wisdom, and so long as he rules the world, the world will be a place devoid of beauty and of joy (2001, pp. 212–213).

2.4.2 The Destruction of Positivism

By the mid-20th century, positivism was largely dead as a philosophy of science and prominent psychologists like Sigmund Koch were criticizing its presence in psychology (Passmore, 1967; Day, 1998). The destruction of logical positivism happened as a result of two devastating critiques. The first challenge came from philosophers of science like Karl Popper (2002), who disputed some of the key tenants of positivism. Much of this critique came from writers like Ludwig Wittgenstein and W.V.O. Quine, who at one time had connections with logical positivism. The second line of attack came from new studies showing that science actually works quite differently than the picture painted by positivism.

2.4.2.1 The Conceptual Critique

Collapse of positivist verification. A number of compelling arguments by scientists and philosophers caused the logical positivists themselves, as well as others, to abandon the idea of verification:

a. Several authors demonstrated that hypotheses could not be conclusively verified or proved *true* through simple observation and induction because there might be a counterexample. Under some circumstances, hypotheses can be tested and proven *false*, a principle that forms the basis of most research in the psychology of religion (Batson, 1997). However, even this kind of testing is difficult or impossible to do in complex situations (Popper, 2002), and some authors have pointed out that hypotheses are not verified or rejected on the basis of individual facts. Instead, theories are accepted or rejected as an interconnected whole after a weighing of all the evidence (cf. Quine & Ullian, 1978). Thus, contemporary philosophers of science have abandoned the view that science is about verifying propositions.
b. Verification statements are not just impartial representations of a bit of reality, because most language involves not *seeing* but *doing* things in a particular context. Language is a game with certain rules agreed upon by people in practical situations. Thus, any representation is not a universal law (a prime tenant of positivism) but simply true relative to the specific group and task at hand (cf. Wittgenstein, 1958).

Problems with reductionism. While many critics of logical positivism were sympathetic with a reductionist agenda, problems appeared with various aspects of their reductive strategies. For instance, the philosopher of science Carl Hempel demonstrated that no reductionist scheme and its associated theory are really verifiable, because there are numerous competing alternatives that may also be true (cf. Hempel, 2001a,b). An even more serious problem was the issue of **operational definitions**, the procedure by which various theoretical constructs of interest to psychologists (e.g., depression) are reduced to specific behavioral outcomes that can be measured (e.g., answers to questions on a survey). Positivists based their measurement ideas on the work of physicist Percy Bridgman, who developed the concept of operational definitions in physics (1993). However, Bridgman was critical of much of the positivist agenda and objected strenuously to the applications of his ideas in psychology. He felt that the situational context within which behavior occurs could not be reduced to pure operational definitions. He also felt that the standards for operationalization and verification of facts used in physics were different from those appropriate for psychology and sociology (1959, pp. 21, 51; cf. Lash, 1996, p. 103). For instance, repeatability is a necessity in scientific verification within physics, but introspection—a valuable technique in psychology—is often inherently unrepeatable (1959, p. 239). Overall, Bridgman thought that a distorted and rigid use of his principle of operationalism would render the results of psychological investigation irrelevant (Bridgman, 1950, p. 4; 1959, pp. 56–61; Taylor, 1998). Since that time, the idea that we can strictly and completely operationalize a concept has been rejected in most quarters outside of psychology (Bickhard, 2001).

2.4.2.2 The Historicist Critique of Neopositivism

Although original formulations of logical positivist thought ceased to be viable after the 1930s, **neopositivist** theorists such as Carl Hempel (2001a,b) attempted to continue aspects of the theory while dropping unrealistic claims about verification. However, neopositivism outside of psychology did not survive a second challenge from a group that questioned the fundamental approach of the positivists toward the philosophy of science. This group argued that the positivists were wrong, because their description of science as an exercise in logical verification did not accurately describe what scientists actually did in their work. This descriptive or **historicist** approach was carried on by several people, notably Thomas Kuhn (1922–1996), Michael Polanyi (1891–1976), and Paul Feyerabend (1924–1994). They moved progressively from Popper's view that science comprises competing individual theories to Kuhn's view of successive paradigms to the view of Imre Lakatos of competing research programs (Lakatos, 1978, p. 132).

Kuhn (1996) argued that science operates within **paradigms**, which are ideas about how the world works and how we can best study it. He thought that there are two modes of scientific practice: (1) *normal science* which makes slow steady progress within a given paradigm but resists attempts to modify the paradigm and tries to explain away conflicting data; and (2) *scientific revolutions* which involve paradigm shifts. Kuhn's analysis of the history of science showed that science progresses by stops and starts and is as much a social enterprise as a logical one. This was quite contrary to positivist claims that because of empiricism and logical method the scientific enterprise was totally objective and unbiased and that the personal beliefs of scientists played no part in their work.

Other scholars came to conclusions that paralleled that of Kuhn. For instance, in the book *Personal Knowledge* (1962), the British chemist Michael Polanyi argued that scientific statements cannot be completely objectively justified so that when scientists state beliefs it involves a personal commitment to a particular position—a commitment based on evidence but still a personal commitment with subjective elements. Paul Feyerabend (1993) argued that this was not bad because many of the illogical aspects of the process were necessary for scientific progress. The idea that scientists interpret their findings and results from within a paradigm suggests that science has an interpretive or hermeneutic aspect to it that is similar to other methods of gaining knowledge (Happel, 1996; see Sections 1.6.2, 6.3.2).

The actual science critique was formalized by philosopher Imre Lakatos (1922–1974), who proposed a new philosophy of science based in part on the historicist viewpoint. Lakatos critiqued the work of Popper, Kuhn, and others and came up with a theory that showed how scientific *research programs* were in fact structured and tested. In some ways, the research program theory attempted to combine the best elements of Popper and Kuhn. Lakatos liked Popper's refutation of verification, but denied that it was possible to falsify a theory, since in actuality theories are never rejected on the basis of a little contradictory evidence. He liked Kuhn's historical approach but denied the existence of a clean picture of normal science—revolution—new paradigm. Instead, Lakatos argued that research takes place in programs, which have a *hard core* of metaphysical ideas, as well as scientific beliefs and practices, that must be defended. However, over time, research inside and outside the program will accumulate evidence that does not fit with the hard core. When this becomes apparent, *auxiliary hypotheses* are then developed to explain these phenomena and protect the hard core beliefs. For instance, in evolutionary theory, the idea that we act to survive is a hard core belief, which is challenged by the fact that many people behave in altruistic ways that do not advance our survival or interests. Recognizing this, evolutionary theorists have developed an active research area to develop auxiliary hypotheses to protect the evolutionary hard core against this seemingly contradictory data. According to Lakatos, over time, the auxiliary hypotheses multiply and people increasingly spend their time defending the core beliefs rather than generating new knowledge, leading to a *degenerative* trend in the research program and its eventual abandonment in favor of another that offers more productive possibilities. In this view, science is often in a position where congruence with the reigning paradigm and protection of core hypotheses can take precedence over investigation and fit with actual empirical data.

2.4.3 Positivism's Persistence in Psychology and its Effects

Psychology as a discipline separated from philosophy or theology during the last half of the 19th century and early years of the 20th century. As the founders of modern psychology sought to create a science of the mind, and later a science of behavior, they looked to positivist and logical positivist ideas about science that were accepted at the time in the physical sciences and philosophy. Although positivism has since been discredited as a philosophy of science, most observers agree that it remains the core philosophy for most of psychology (Koch, 1992), an "unspoken grammar" (Stam, 1992, p. 18) that has a number of important behind-the-scenes effects and constitutes a kind of **neopositivism** within psychology. Characteristics of psychological neopositivism would include the following:

1. *Unreflective adoption of philosophical positions.* Positivists discouraged philosophical speculation and believed that their approach to science contained no assumptions (a view we have seen to be false). Given this kind of double blindness, it is not surprising that psychological theories and methods have unspoken positivist assumptions built into them such as (1) an observer can work completely independently of any presuppositions (a view shown impossible by many philosophers of science) and (2) psychological processes are ultimately explainable in terms of lower level processes in physics, chemistry, and biology. Positivism also introduces unspoken ontological assumptions like reductive materialism and naturalism (Yanchar & Hill, 2003; Griffin, 2000; Viney & King, 1998).

2. *Physics envy and the limitation of method.* Positivism argued a unity of science position that applied methods from physics to psychology independent of subject matter. This has discouraged qualitative research approaches that are often well suited to the study of religion or spirituality and discouraged conversations with investigators in disciplines using non-positivist methodologies.

3. *Narrowing of topics.* Psychological methodology was developed for use in a positivist framework, which assumes an eliminative materialism and strict rules of operationalism. This means that topics or questions of study that did not fit well in the positivist methods or worldview (e.g., things that implied the existence of non-objective phenomenon like consciousness) were largely excluded from study (Gadamer, 1981, p. 11). This has limited psychology to a 19th- or early 20th-century view of scientific practice in many areas (Taylor, 1998).

4. *Narrowing of theoretical approaches.* The paradigms in psychology with the widest acceptance have been those with positivistic and mechanistic orientations, such as behaviorism or computational models of the mind. This in not to say that there are not competing viewpoints (Yanchar & Hill, 2003) but simply that they are just that—competing voices that critique mainstream positivist views from the margins.

5. *Distorted perspective on current and new theories.* Positivism argues for a progressive view of history that discounts old ideas and automatically assumes that new scientific ideas are better (Leahey, 1987, 2002), potentially overvaluing new knowledge in relationship to old. Some theorists also take this view of progress to mean that problems with current theories will necessarily be eliminated by future progress, although there are no specific reasons to believe that this is true.

6. *Negative attitude toward religion.* Any of these five problems have the potential to affect the psychology and religion dialogue in a negative way by limiting topics, methods, and approaches. When we add to this the very hostile stance toward religion taken in positivist philosophy, psychology and religion dialogue would appear to be in serious trouble. However, the rejection of positivism opens new possibilities, and its demonstrated weakness is probably partly responsible for the revival in dialogue during the latter half of the 20th century.

2.5 Contemporary Issues in Science and Religion

The contemporary dialogue between science and religion outside of psychology is rich and vast. Much of this conversation has involved scientists—especially physicists—with broad training in theology or philosophy, as well as theologians and philosophers with scientific interests. Generally these thinkers reject the idea that science and religion are necessarily opposed to each other, a view similar to that held by medieval theologians (Taylor, 2007, p. 332; McGinn, 2001, p. 22). Most of the dialogue has taken place using a framework of Christian ideas about the world, although interesting parallels have been drawn between developments in modern physics and certain Hindu and Buddhist beliefs. Here, we will indicate some of the main themes of that dialogue so that we can better situate the interaction between psychology and religion.

2.5.1 Developments in 20th Century Physics and Cosmology

The new dialogue between science and religion is based on a number of scientific findings that challenge old positivist beliefs about the nature of the world. Four of these developments are of particular interest.

1. *Challenges to determinism.* Much of the problem in the relation between science and religion has resulted from models of the world developed in 18th and 19th century physics. These models were built upon a viewpoint of **strict determinism**, that is, they assumed that present and future events are completely controlled by events in the past. This of course makes it difficult to understand how free will can exist or how a God could be active in the world. However, *quantum theory* as developed by Niels Bohr and others suggests that at the subatomic level strict determinism does not hold, for instance, that the position of small particles cannot be completely predicted by past events, only the probability that the particle will be at a particular location (Peacocke, 1993, p. 47). This suggests that the universe is not mechanistic and has characteristics of both necessity and freedom, leaving the universe open to chance and creativity (Ward, 1996). Furthermore, quantum theory strongly suggests that particles do not attain a specific location until they are observed. This observational requirement has led to the controversial idea that consciousness—the ability to observe—must be a fundamental property of the universe (Davies, 1996).

Research on complex open dynamic systems such as living organisms shows that they operate in ways that violate traditional laws of determinism and entropy. This principle is developed in *chaos theory* (e.g., Crutchfield, Farmer, Packer, & Shaw, 1995). Complex systems fail to be predictable in several ways. First, small changes in initial conditions of the system can have unpredictably large effects, leading to what is called the *butterfly effect,* where a tiny action such as a butterfly landing on a leaf can change weather patterns in other parts of the world (Barbour, 1997, pp. 182–184). Second, while it is possible to specify how individual items of the system are related to each other, it is inherently impossible to predict the long-term behavior of the system as a whole even if all the relevant variables are known

(Wildman & Russell, 1995), as in the case of weather. Finally, complex dynamic systems exert effects of the whole on their components that are not strictly predictable from the sum of the parts (Peacocke, 1995). These properties make the system appear to be self-organizing and dependent on an interaction of chance or freedom and law or constraint that leads to properties of wholeness and emergence (Barbour, 1997, p. 193).

2. *Challenges to classical ideas of rationality.* Some phenomena behave in paradoxical ways. For instance, light appears to behave as both a particle and a wave. This is known as the principle of **complementarity**. It is a violation of classical Aristotelian logic, and at the quantum level various other violations also occur, suggesting that the nature of rationality in the universe can vary from that typically supposed in positivist science (Grib, 1996; Barbour, 1997, p. 167).

3. *Challenges to classical ideas of causation.* Standard materialist views of causation have held that causation happens when material particles interact and that causation ceases when there is no longer a material connection. However, quantum researchers have observed that once particles have interacted with each other, the behavior of the particles when observed remains linked even though the effects occur simultaneously and at a distance with no apparent material connection. This is sometimes known as the principle of **quantum entanglement** and is described by Bell's theorem (Tracy, 1995). Taken together, these three findings of quantum theory have made consciousness a more legitimate subject for research (Deikman, 2000, p. 75).

4. *Challenges to classical ideas about the universe.* Traditionally scientists have taken for granted the fact that the universe allows for the presence of life and that living creatures like humans can understand it. Contemporary writers find both of these facts to be remarkable; for instance, Einstein once remarked that the "most incomprehensible thing about the universe is that it is comprehensible" (quoted in Davies, 1996, p. 149). Modern cosmology suggests that the specific pattern of fundamental properties of our universe is extremely unlikely to occur by chance but is just right to allow for the presence of life, including intelligent beings. This is sometimes known as the **anthropic principle** (Barrow, Tippler, & Wheeler, 1988). This "fine tuning" of fundamental properties enhances the idea that the universe is an interconnected whole and relational (Ward, 1996; Barbour, 1997, p. 205). The fact that the universe not only exists but is also intelligible by us has been a point of dialogue for science and religion (e.g., Davies, 1993). Science presupposes and describes intelligibility, but cannot explain why it is so, an issue perhaps better treated by religious writers (Heller, 1995).

So far, there has been little or no attempt to revise psychological theory or methods in light of these developments, even though some of them pose challenges for current approaches within psychology. For instance, most psychological statistical procedures are designed to describe linear systems, where various elements are independent of each other, and the action of the whole is simply a combination of the individual actions of the parts. However, developments from modern physics, as well as anomalies found in behavioral research, suggest that many of the systems psychology attempts to describe are nonlinear in nature.

2.5.2 Understanding Divine Action

Authors in the science and religion dialogue have developed a number of ways to understand how God could exercise continuing activity in the world without violating modern understandings of the universe and its lawlike regularities. Robert John Russell (Russell, 1998; cf. Murphy, 1995) sees this happening at the level of quantum indeterminacy, which might in turn allow for God to act through the process of genetic mutations. John Polkinghorne (e.g., Polkinghorne, 1995) sees God acting by manipulation of chaotic system boundary conditions and the input of information. Arthur Peacocke looks at the effects of top-down or whole-part constraint, emphasizing that it is the interplay of chance and law that allows new forms to be created, to emerge, and to evolve (Peacocke, 1998, 1995, 2002). Some of these writers have used the **process philosophy** of Alfred North Whitehead (1861–1947) as a basis for their theoretical constructions. This philosophy emphasizes the changing nature of the universe and the interconnection of events, as well as the evolving nature of reality (Barbour, 1997, pp. 104, 285; Barbour, 2002; Griffin, 2000, pp. 82–106) (Fig. 2.2).

Other authors take a more **deistic** view, arguing that while God may have been involved at the time of creation, the Divine no longer acts directly in the world. An example of this would be the work of Paul Davies, who sees God's activity as the determination of natural possibilities at the time of the Big Bang, and that the complexity of current events is just a working out of these possibilities (Wildman, 1998; Davies, 1998; Barbour, 1998; Chela-Flores, 1998). In psychology, some authors

Fig. 2.2 *John Polkinghorne.* A physicist and an Anglican clergyman, he has written numerous books on science and religion issues from a critical realist perspective. Photo courtesy of Yale University Press

like Daniel Helminiak (1996) have also taken a deistic position, arguing that God as transcendent creator has little to do with human issues, and so thinking about God adds nothing to our understanding of psychology. The approach of Davies and Helminiak is less popular, because many authors want to find a way to understand the concept of agency and how God might be actively involved in the world on an ongoing basis (Polkinghorne, 1995).

The emphasis on constructing models of God's action that are in harmony with modern science has meant that many scholars have tried to avoid theories that use supernatural types of explanation. In **supernaturalism**, God acts by suspending natural law, while contemporary theorists try to picture a way that God acts in the world while respecting laws that are presumably of divine origin (Russell, 1998). This does not mean the rejection of transcendence or a supernatural agent, just a willingness to see God at work within the structures of creation, a position long held by Catholic theologians such as Thomas Aquinas (1998; Peacocke, 1998; Happel, 1995). These authors also try to avoid **God-of-the-gaps** explanations, where God is presumed to be active only in places that science cannot explain. Instead, they try to picture God as active within current scientific understandings of the world, as well as relevant to questions that science will never be able to answer like the mystery of origin (Coulson, 1955; Russell, 1998; Stoeger, 1995; Ayala, 1998a). There also has been a general rejection of solutions that posit some kind of absolute dualism or separation of mind from body, as has been found in much of Western thought since the time of Descartes (Brown, 1998a,b).

Is there teleology, a direction or purpose to the universe or God's working in the world? In contemporary science and religion dialogue, there is some variation in points of view, but a common position is that creation is moving toward some kind of an end point but that the process by which that end is reached is somewhat indeterminate and could be affected by human choice (e.g., Davies, 1996, 1998). The alternate position, which is to reject teleology, seems to necessitate the acceptance of a view that life and the universe are without inherent meaning, a position knows as **nihilism**.

2.5.3 Science and Values

Hillary Putnam (2002) notes that one of the consequences of the destruction of logical positivism has been the rediscovery of the relation between facts and values. In his view values are "entangled" with facts, neither identical nor strictly separate (cf. Smith, 2001; Midgley, 2002, p. 19). Like Kant, Putnam would argue that moral issues cannot be settled by science, although he would not agree with Kant that they were unrelated. Some relationships between science and values might include the following:

1. Science itself assumes a set of values such as coherence, simplicity, and a concern that we accurately describe and explain the world. These are sometimes called *epistemic values*. These values are presupposed by knowledge of facts.

It is of course a question whether these values are always appropriate outside scientific inquiry.

2. Since every scientist has a set of values that is part of his or her worldview, it may often be the case that these values influence the work of the scientist.

3. Since the results of science and technology have large implications for the human and physical world, the ethical implications of scientific research should be a prominent concern among scientists and others.

This issue of values is especially important for psychology. Most value systems contain a vision of the goods of human life, as well as virtues or vices, and qualities and behaviors that we may possess that will incline us toward success or failure in our pursuit of life goals (MacIntyre, 1984). In a similar way, psychological theories also contain a vision of the goals of human life and how they may best be achieved, so they inherently deal with questions of values and the ethical life (Browning & Cooper, 2004; see e.g., Section 11.1.2).

A contentious area with regard to the role of science is whether it can provide a basis for values and ethics. One position taken by writers is that while science may study ethics and depend on values like progress or rationality for its work, it cannot provide values and thus needs to get them from some external source. This is especially true of sciences like psychology because they are primarily descriptive enterprises. While psychology can evaluate the effectiveness of an activity in moving toward a particular goal, it ultimately cannot evaluate whether a particular goal is good or bad; that requires some kind of norm of the human person and an exploration of possibilities that stands outside of science (Macquarrie, 1982, pp. 3–5). Thus, science cannot provide values although it can determine whether a particular action might promote a certain value (Ellis, 1998). The importance of values for science, coupled with its inability to actually produce and justify those values, suggests a need for respect and dialogue with other fields, a stance taken even by scientists with no religious background or inclinations (Ayala, 1998a).

On the other hand, some scientists believe that values can be discovered by science. In a reductive naturalistic view, we can study the world and conclude from the nature of things what our values should be, a viewpoint taken by some humanistic psychologists (see Section 1.4.5) and evolutionary theorists (see Section 6.2). However, even many evolutionary scientists are skeptical of this possibility (e.g., Ayala, 1998b). Putnam's view is that scientific observation is relevant but is not the whole story. Those against the naturalistic view of ethics often accuse their opponents of what is called the **naturalistic fallacy**: that what is observed is what actually should be, e.g., observed standards of morality are "natural" and should be the goal of moral development.

The attempt to break down the barrier between fact and value is part of a general movement against dualistic understandings of the human person that separate mind and body, thinking and feeling, and events and their meaning. Dualistic approaches have been common among modern Western philosophers such as Descartes and Kant, but do not adequately account for the fact that we are *both* mind and body, thought and feeling, and that these are intimately interconnected (Macmurray, 1957, pp. 62–83). Alternatives to dualism can be developed in several ways. In **monism** all aspects of the person are seen as part of a single underlying reality. This type of understanding can be achieved through eliminating aspects of the human person that are deemed to be unimportant, as when eliminative materialists claim that all psychology can be understood in terms of brain processes. Monistic understandings can also be developed by imagining that all things are part of a universal oneness, as in varieties of Hinduism. Alternatives to monism are found in **dialogical** theories that argue that things like mind and body are separate but intimately related in some way. For instance, relational theories of human nature argue that both self and other are necessary constituents of our personhood—without both a strong sense of self and a strong orientation to others we cannot exist as unique and mature persons.

2.5.4 Critical Realism

Many of the authors above end up working from a stance of **critical realism**. In science, critical realism is the philosophical position that (1) science is able to give us knowledge of the real world, (2) this knowledge is steadily improving but imperfect because all models are partial, and (3) something like the entities described by science really exist. It also recognizes that knowledge is not directly obtained but involves an interaction between experiment and interpretation. Thus, in the critical realist view it is incorrect to claim that science is just about "fact" and other disciplines about "opinion" (Peacocke, 1993, p. 12; Barbour, 1997, pp. 117, 332; Polkinghorne, 1999b, p. 17). This position allows that there is a subjective aspect to scientific inquiry and that laws are constructions, but it argues that these regularities really do give us a partial understanding of nature that is valid regardless of cultural or social circumstances (Davies, 1996). This realism needs to be critical or willing to question our understandings because science can make mistakes, and some domains of realty like the quantum world have logic and properties that are very counterintuitive (Polkinghorne, 1995).

In a dialogue between science and religion, one can also think about theology from a critical realist perspective (e.g., Wright, 1992, pp. 32–37). In this view, theology and religion do provide us real information about God or ultimate reality and our relationship to it. This information is limited and inadequate and thus should be subject to critique, but both the knowledge and the language used to describe it are unique and necessary. Like science, religions also have processes of discernment by which they select data or evidence and test it against a variety of sources, which may include things like common sense, authority, and communal views or traditions. They assume that there is false religion that must be weeded out (Ellis, 1998). Thus, in a critical realist view of science and theology, both disciplines can be thought of as approaches to learning about reality (Peacocke, 1993, pp. 14, 20). Variants of critical realism such as **fallibilism** are less optimistic, arguing that while we can make positive statements about God, in practice it is difficult to construct and test such models because of the effects of pre–existing cultural and ideological structures (Hustwit, 2007).

2.5.5 Models for Science and Religion

Given the above, how should we approach the relationship between religion and science? Ian Barbour (1997, pp. 77, 90) has produced the most influential typology of views on this topic. He describes four models—conflict, independence, dialogue, and integration. *Conflict models* assume that there is an inherent incompatibility between scientific and religious thought, as in positivist metaphysics. *Independence models* argue, like Francis Bacon, that science and religion deal with separate areas and kinds of knowledge. *Dialogical theories* suggest that there is a relationship between science and religion, but it is a more distant one concerned with presuppositions, limit questions, and methodological parallels. *Integration* involves several possibilities: natural theology (we can find evidence of God in nature as revealed by science), a theology of nature (nature and science help us reformulate theology), and systematic synthesis as in process philosophy. Barbour's typology has been critiqued, for instance, by Stenmark (2004, pp. 257–259). He points out that Barbour's typology does not reflect the real historical process of model development and that terms like "integration" mean different things at different points in history. He also points out that the typology does not deal with the problems of expansionism, whereby science or theology try to take over the traditional domain of the other, a prominent feature of the science and religion relationship both in the past and today.

The overall effect of the general science and religion dialogue is hard to judge. Some observers would claim that there is a trend in science in the direction of a less eliminative stance toward religion, even within evolutionary biology, and an attitude that science and religion can work toward occasional shared goals (e.g., Bering, 2004; Cicirelli, 2006). Despite the presence of dialogue, hostile attacks on religion from scientists and scientific philosophers have continued, in particular from those associated with evolutionary biology such as E. O. Wilson, Richard Dawkins, and Daniel Dennett. They recount with somewhat more sophistication the standard positivist view of history, which is that religion is nonsensical, primitive, and harmful and will eventually be replaced by science. John Haugt (1998) has argued that these attacks are personal, ideological, or metaphysical in nature rather than scientific. George Ellis (1998) has argued that while these attempts may result in more power for science, the arguments are flawed because they are based on the following:

- Unjustified and often unstated assumptions or restrictions that are based in metaphysics, not science
- Misrepresentations of scientific findings
- Misrepresentation or dismissal without substantive argument of any positions or data contrary to their view
- Lack of understanding about the views of many religious people toward changing understandings of the human and natural world.

Much remains to be done to put the dialogue between science and religion on a firm and constructive basis.

2.6 Conclusion

Key issue: *Although positivist approaches to science have been largely discredited, they remain prominent within psychology, hindering our understanding of the human person and the dialogue with religion. A critical realist position is more philosophically defensible and helpful to the process of dialogue.*

Religion and science both relate to totality and infinity. When St. Paul encounters Christ on the road to Damascus or Einstein expresses wonderment at the natural world, they are encountering the transcendent part of life, although in science this quality of unpredictability might be known by other names such as "indeterminism" in quantum theory. The great efforts of Christian theologians to produce systematic theologies or statements of the Christian faith are efforts toward totality, just as when psychologists try to develop a comprehensive, naturalistic model of the human person. In the religious view, however, any model of totality will fail because it will be unable to reduce infinity to totality. Infinity cannot fit in a box! However, we need predictable ways of understanding the world around us, so both infinity and totality seem to be necessary parts of life that are in tension with one another. The dialogue between science and religion is a necessary and exciting part of that tension. Dialogue can facilitate understandings that support academic study and practical appropriation. It also has the potential to create new ideas that may be useful to both science and religion.

The Baconian and positivist vision of science as a tool for human power that will progressively wipe away ignorance and lead to an ideal human society has an ambivalent status at the present time. It contains a vision for the past and future that is widely accepted within psychology, and certainly science has given us advances in medical technology and other areas that have led to increased comfort, health, and longevity. Few people would want to give up these benefits. On the other hand, this view is under increasing pressure for a number of reasons (Taylor, 2007):

- A rejection of positivist views of science and history by philosophers and scholars
- The failure of rational secular experiments in social makeover, such as occurred in Stalinist and Maoist communism, or in Western societies such as in welfare systems and public housing projects
- Increasing environmental degradation such as global warming due to our instrumental, technological focus on nature
- Awareness that positivist views are metaphysical positions that shield us from confronting transcendence and the limitations of science, because it is assumed without proof that the advances of science have no boundaries

This puts science in the dangerous position of making claims it cannot fulfill and is ultimately bad for science.

The positivist stance of reductive naturalism also has an ambivalent status within psychology. It has been a powerful tool for simplifying the bewildering diversity of human behavior, looking for patterns that can increase our understanding. However, it does so by ignoring the particular and unique features of individuals in their life situations, seeing them as interchangeable and replaceable, depersonalizing them. Its emphasis on the lawlike quality of some behavior patterns also leaves little room to consider human freedom and transcendence, as well as more relational views of the person. This can be a particular problem when dealing with areas of human behavior such as ethics. While modernity with its emphasis on reduction of life to general rules sees morality as seeking an ideal rational code for behavior, others argue that morality is relational in nature and complex, relating to a variety of events, situations, and goals. Thus, it will always escape systematization and is best thought of as related to general principles or goals.

While reductionism in general has its advantages, it also has its dangers. The problem is that when we simplify, we risk eliminating things that need to be understood and are part of a complete picture of the world. This leaves us in a worse position than when we started (Zizioulas, 2006; Taylor, 2007, pp. 704–707). Reductionism may lead to these kinds of problems when it assumes that all aspects of religion can be explained psychologically, arguing that religion is nothing but social support or beliefs about morality (Watts & Williams, 1988, pp. 1–3). While scholars should be free to adopt a naturalistic perspective, they should be under no illusion that this is a neutral stance, or that when they use such models to explain religion that they have completely described what religion is or what it means to its followers (Smith, 2000). It is also well to keep in mind that explaining the immediate or proximate cause of something in no way answers questions about the ultimate cause of things. Such judgments put scientists who deny transcendence in the position of claiming they can transcend appearances and make religious pronouncements, a position that is self-contradictory (Cooper, 2007, pp. 30, 88).

The critical realist perspective offers an alternative to positivism. It avoids overly simplistic and reductionistic views of the world, while at the same time offering a positive assessment of how psychology and religion can both contribute to our understanding of the human person. It has provided a constructive platform for dialogue between science and religion and has the potential to enliven the more specific conversation between psychology and religion as well.

With this brief view of science in mind, we now move to an examination of some major religious perspectives.

Chapter 3
Religious Traditions

In the preceding chapters we began to sample the richness of the dialogue that has taken place between psychology and religion. However, it is impossible to really appreciate this conversation without an understanding of the religious traditions that have been involved. In this chapter, we will review the three main traditions that have been central in the psychology and religion dialogue: Hinduism and yogic practices, Buddhism and Zen practices, and Christianity.

The religious traditions we will discuss are the center of immense bodies of literature, produced both by adherents of the religions and the scholars who study them. Each tradition contains a tremendous amount of internal diversity in terms of beliefs and organizational structures. Thus, any summary given in the space of a few pages will leave out much of interest. In the following discussion, we will focus on those aspects of the traditions that will help us understand the psychology and religion dialogue, but a serious student will also wish to consult additional primary and secondary sources to gain a more comprehensive picture of these great religious traditions (see e.g., Ludwig, 2000; Smart, 1999a,b, 1998).

3.1 Hinduism

Hinduism is best understood as a grouping of diverse Indian religious traditions around a common core of sacred writings (Klostermaier, 2000a,b; Flood, 1996) (Figure 3.1). The beginnings of Hindu religious thought are found in the *Vedas*, an ancient collection of hymns, poetry, and text on a variety of religious subjects and rituals. It is believed that the earliest Vedic hymns originated in oral form before the 2nd millennium BCE and that they were present in written form sometime during the 1st millennium BCE. Four primary **samhitas** or collections of texts exist, the oldest and most important of which is the *Rig Veda*, which presents a number of ideas that became important in basic Hindu thought. Separate from the four samhitas, but also important for our purposes, is the *Ayur Veda*, a collection of texts that deals with healing practices and rituals (see Section 10.3.2).

Later writers began to reflect on the Vedas and develop other documents such as the *Upanishads* ("sitting down near" or "secret scriptures"), which include about

J.M. Nelson, *Psychology, Religion, and Spirituality,*
DOI 10.1007/978-0-387-87573-6_3, @ Springer Science+Business Media, LLC 2009

Fig. 3.1 *Hindu temple,*
Kathmandu. Devotion and
rituals of purification are
important in most branches
of Hinduism, and temples
in various parts of the world
provide pilgrimage sites,
where people can come
to engage in important
ceremonies. Photo by the
author

100 texts, a dozen of which are considered especially important and were composed early in the 1st millennium BCE. The Upanishads contain a number of concepts that have been a central part of Hinduism, including the essential relationship between our inner selves and ultimate reality around us, and the ongoing cycle of death and rebirth or **reincarnation** known as **samsara**. Hindus believe that our position in this cycle is determined by our actions or **karma**. These actions can condemn us to endless lives of suffering, but it is also possible to achieve liberation from samsara. In Hinduism, this liberation is pursued through several related methods, the most important of which are the paths of devotion, philosophical understanding, action, and inner development.

3.1.1 Hindu Devotion and Philosophy

Devotion. Many gods and goddesses inhabit the Hindu pantheon, although sometimes these are seen as manifestations of one god or underlying reality. The most important of these are Brahma the Creator, Vishnu the Preserver, and Shiva the Destroyer. **Vaisnavism** centers on devotion to Vishnu and his various **avatars** or incarnations such as Krishna, while **Saivism** focuses devotion to Shiva. Saivism also tends to be associated with ascetic and spiritual practices that promote inner development, such as yoga. Another stream of worship is **Saktism**, which centers on the female, the goddess Shakti who is the consort of Shiva. This form of devotion is often associated with secret practices of particular power, known as **tantra**.

Philosophy and Understanding. In Hinduism, individual spiritual practices or worship are more central to the religion than doctrinal beliefs (Flood, 1996, p. 12), but nevertheless systems of philosophy have developed that provide possible underlying metaphysics for Hindu belief. Philosophical writings in ancient India were put down in the form of **sutras** ("threads") or collections of pithy and often enigmatic sayings. These are often accompanied by **bhasyas** or commentaries that provide interpretations of the sutras.

A key issue that runs through Hinduism, as well as many other religious traditions, is the problem of **dualism**. A dualistic religion sees an essential separation between the *physical world* of the senses or the body, and a *spiritual reality* that also may include the human mind. The early Vedas often imply a dualistic point of view that was developed in some versions of **Samkhya**, the philosophic school that forms the basis for classic yoga. In contrast to this, a monistic or **nondual** view of the world argues that all parts of reality are essentially one, and that differences we perceive between things are inconsequential or illusionary.

In later writings like the Upanishads and the *Bhagavad Gita*, authors began to explore the possibility of a monistic view of reality, and more attention was given to the individual spiritual quest. Systems of thought based on the Upanishads and the later *Vedanta* or *Brahma Sutra* are known as **Vedanta** ("end of the Vedas"), since the Upanishads are the final sacred works in the Vedic tradition. The most important of the schools is probably the systematization known as **Advaita Vedanta**, a nondualist position developed by Sankara (6th century CE). Advaita thought equates **Brahman**—the total, universal, transcendental reality or mind that lies behind subjective reality—with **Atman**, or the totality of our individual mind which includes but goes beyond the ego and the action-oriented parts of our psychological life (Brett, 2003). In Hinduism, our realization of this identity is thought to be the key to liberation and freedom (Sankaracarya, 1975). Some varieties of Vedanta are **theistic** and hold that there is a god or gods who are different than the world but may be involved in it. In the Hindu tradition, theism is associated with Vaisnavism or Saivism. The alternative is the **nontheistic** view, which denies the existence of a separate god or gods. In Hinduism and Buddhism, monistic or nondualist views of reality are generally nontheistic. Sankara's nondualist position became and remains to some extent the dominant school of thought in Indian philosophy. Influence of this nondualist position can be seen in later schools of Yoga practice that depart from the dualism of classic yoga.

3.1.2 Inner Development: Asceticism and yoga

Action and asceticism. The path of action is ethical and personal in nature. In the *Bhagavad-Gita*, growth comes through testing and finding the proper ethical path in life that combines detachment and action. Also part of the active path is **asceticism**, a lifestyle and set of practices designed to discipline the body or mind and further one's spiritual development. Hindu ascetics are often known as *renouncers* because they frequently choose a lifestyle of homelessness, depending upon alms and eschewing possessions. Specific ascetical practices can involve fasting, lying on a bed of nails, or holding unnatural positions for long lengths of time. Many ascetic techniques date to Vedic times, and influenced both the development of yoga and Buddhist spiritual practices.

Table 3.1 Some primary schools of Hindu yoga

Name	Focus/Emphasis	Key classic text
Raja Yoga	The most classical form of yoga Dualist	*Yoga Sutra* (Patanjali, 2003)
Hatha Yoga	Transformation of and through the body	*Hatha Yoga Pradipika*
Bhakti Yoga	Devotion to a god or goddess Dualist	*Bhakti Sutra* (Narada) *Sri Bhasya* (Ramanuja)
Jnana Yoga	Development of transforming wisdom Nondualist	*Bhagavad-Gita*
Karma Yoga	Transformation of and through action	*Bhagavad-Gita*
Kundalini Yoga	Arousal of kundalini power	*Yoga Kundalini Upanishad*
Mantra Yoga	Transformation through chanting	*Mantra Yoga Samhita*

Inner development. While ascetic practices are thought to be helpful to spiritual development, the key lies in **yoga**, a general term that refers to a number of schools of inner spiritual practice (Feuerstein, 2001; see Table 3.1) These are an essential part of **sadhana** or the process of growth in the spiritual life that is facilitated through practices. It is somewhat artificial to label yoga as a "practice" rather than a "philosophy," since it is considered one of the six classic schools of Vedic philosophy along with Samkhya and Vedanta. The classic formulation of yoga ("joining"), also called **Raja Yoga**, can be found in the *Yoga Sutras* of Patanjali (2003), composed around 200 BCE. It is built on a dualistic metaphysic with theistic overtones. Patanjali saw an essential split between Nature or matter (**prakrti**) and Spirit (**purusha**). This separation results in **duhkha** or suffering and is made worse by **klesas** or problematic patterns of thinking (Feuerstein, 1989, pp. 59–65) such as misperceptions (*avidya*), misidentifications (*asmita*), excessive desire (*raga*), avoidance (*dvesa*) and insecurity (*abhinivesa*). The basic idea of yoga is that it is possible for us to achieve contact or unity with the underlying reality of the universe. This experience of unity is **samadhi**, a blissful state of consciousness in which the distinction between self and other dissolves. This is the goal of all the various yoga pathways. While study and other religious practices are helpful, there is no substitute for this personal experience in the process of spiritual growth (Sankaracarya, 1975, p. 41).

Patanjali's raja yoga includes eight "branches" that are a sequenced set of techniques for achieving samadhi and allowing the individual to assimilate with their true self (Feuerstein, 1989; cf. Shah-Kazemi, 2006, p. 24):

1. *Yana*: abstinence from ethically objectionable behaviors like greed; negative thoughts should be opposed by positive ones.
2. *Niyama*: observance of various practices like worship and study; together with yana, this results in purification and the ability to achieve **ekagrata** or "one-pointed" concentration. **Bhakti yoga** emphasizes the practice of worship and devotion.
3. *Asana*: steady, comfortable bodily postures that help to still the mind.
4. *Pranayama*: breath control, which involves a slow steady breathing, sometimes with retention, that also helps calm the mind; counting is sometimes used as an aid to control.

5. *Pratyahara*: sense withdrawal, which allows one to begin experiencing the pure mind that lies within.
6. *Dharana*: concentration, the "binding of the mind to one place, object or idea" (Feuerstein, 1989, p. 95); the practice of this along with the next two stages is referred to as *samyama*.
7. *Dhyana*: meditation, a progressive focusing of attention that results from the practice of dharana.
8. *Samadhi*: contemplation, "when there is the shining of the object alone, as if devoid of form" (Feuerstein, 1989, p. 99), the distinction between subject and object disappears, and knowledge is gained as well as special psychic powers or *siddhis*.

Yoga can affect the individual at several levels. In Hindu thought, people are believed to have several "bodies" including our physical body and a set of **subtle bodies** that support mental processes and consciousness. Some forms of Yoga such as **Hatha Yoga** devote more concern to the physical body, preparing and strengthening it for the experience of samadhi through the use of special asanas, and purifying the body through diet or other means. In a number of classical works such as the *Hatha Yoga Pradipika*, a goal is also to awaken energy that resides at the base of the spine using additional techniques of pranayama and samyama drawn from Raja Yoga. This **kundalini** energy, which is associated with the goddess Shakti, then travels along a channel through a series of subtle body centers or **chakras**, eventually reaching the top of the head where it is united with Shiva and triggers the experience of samadhi. Yoga practice designed to arouse this energy is sometimes referred to as *kundalini yoga*.

Some schools of Yoga, especially Hatha Yoga, have been strongly influenced by *tantric* writings and practices. The term **tantra** is used in a couple of different ways. In one meaning, tantra is a kind of scripture that was secretly revealed and then hidden, as opposed to **sutras** or scriptures that contain teaching given openly. However, the more important use of the term tantra is to describe a group of intense practices designed to tap powerful sources of psychic or spiritual energy and provide a rapid path to enlightenment, allowing one to achieve release from samsara in a single lifetime. Because of this power, tantric practices have traditionally been treated as **esoteric**, reserved to a select group of followers who pass through an initiation ceremony and take a pledge of secrecy (Powers, 1995, pp. 219–282). Of course in modern times this prohibition has broken down to some extent, and web pages, DVDs, and books purporting to reveal the secrets of tantra abound (Flood, 2004, p. 98). While tantric practices can be found in several Asian religions, its chief place in modern spiritual practice is in **Vajrayana** or Tibetan Buddhism.

Tantras typically emphasize the role of the physical body in spiritual experience. If nondualism is true, and there are no real divisions, then the visible world—including our physical self—must be part of ultimate reality. This means that it should be possible to experience samadhi in the phenomenal world through the transformation of the body, integrating it with higher spiritual realities. In Hinduism, tantra developed primarily within Saivism and Saktism but also within

Vaisnavism. Theistic versions of tantra see the techniques as a way to achieve union with a god or goddess, thereby attaining divine status (e.g., becoming another Shiva as in Saiva Siddhanta tantrism), or being inhabited by the Divine during tantric rituals. In certain circumstances, this unity experience involves engaging in normally taboo practices like alcohol consumption and meat eating. Followers of kundalini and hatha yoga often use tantric practices, such as purification rituals, **mantras** (repeated words or phrases), **mudras** (hand gestures; in Hatha yoga, also various body postures) and **mandala** (circle) **drawings** that represent important spiritual realities (see Fig. 5.3). Other techniques used in tantra include sexual activity, which is thought to generate energy that can be channeled into arousing the kundalini and furthering spiritual growth (Powers, 1995). The combination of tantra and yoga has been of significant interest to psychologists, as in some of Carl Jung's work (see Section 5.2.3).

The development of yoga continues with the creation of new schools of thought. One of the most important modern systems is *Integral Yoga*, developed by the 20th-century Indian mystic Sri Aurobindo (1872–1950). Integral yoga attempts to combine the philosophy and techniques of various yoga schools with evolutionary ideas. It is especially important because Aurobindo has influenced a number of writers in the transpersonal psychology movement, such as Ken Wilber (see Section 7.5.1).

All major religious traditions believe that spiritual development must involve the practice of certain techniques and that this practical component cannot easily be learned without guidance from some person or persons with experience—just as it is much easier to learn to drive a car if one has an experienced driver to teach you! Hinduism places considerable emphasis on this, holding that knowledge and practice can only be learned from an experienced teacher or **guru** who has achieved high levels of proficiency and spiritual growth. The guru becomes the focus of obedience and devotion for the postulant (see Section 14.1.2). Gurus who found religious movements are especially revered and might be thought of as avatars of a particular god or goddess. This kind of devotional orientation can be seen as a natural human characteristic or as something leading to psychopathology (Kalam, 1990).

3.2 Buddhism

Buddhism was founded in the mid 1st millennium BCE by Shakyamuni Gautama, the son of royalty in the North Indian kingdom of Maghda (Figure 3.2). Through a series of events, Gautama became acquainted with the suffering and transience of the world and became dissatisfied with his protected life. Leaving home he studied with some religious teachers and practiced extreme asceticism, none of which solved his problem. Finally, he relaxed some of his more extreme practices and focused more on meditation, seeking a middle path to freedom between an undisciplined life of pleasure and severe ascetic practice. While sitting under a bodhi true he had an experience of seeing the nature of reality and became an "enlightened one" or **Buddha**. He soon began teaching groups of disciples, and by the time of

Fig. 3.2 *Burning incense, Buddhist temple, China.* Psychological studies of Buddhism have focused on its intellectual views and individual meditation practices, but the practice of Buddhism in many parts of the world involve devotional and communal activities as well. Photo by the author

his death a large community had sprung up around him. This continuing community or **sangha** forms one of the three bases or "jewels" of Buddhism, along with the Buddha himself and the teachings of Buddhism or **dharma** (Harvey, 1990).

3.2.1 Early Buddhism and Basic Teachings

Early in Buddhist history there were many stories, writings and oral traditions about the Buddha and his teachings. Eventually several councils met and defined what is known as the **Pali Canon** of writings attributed to the Buddha and his immediate circle. These texts fall in three main groups of *Pitakas* ("baskets") and are thus known as the *Tripitaka.* They were written in the Pali language, a variant of Sanskrit that uses words like "sutta" instead of "sutra," "jhana" instead of "dhyana," and "dhamma" instead of "dharma." Writings in the original two baskets are somewhat unsystematic in their presentation of material, but later followers developed a more systematic philosophy that forms the third basket, the **Abidhamma**. Buddhism based strictly on the Pali canon and practices associated with it is known as **Theravada Buddhism**, which today is found in Sri Lanka and much of Southeast Asia. Theravada teachings and practice are the basis for much of the contemporary dialogue between psychology and Buddhism.

At the center of all schools of Buddhist philosophy are the **Four Noble Truths**, which by tradition are thought to have been given by the Buddha in his first sermon after enlightenment. These are given in the *Mahasatipatthana Sutta* from the *Digha Nikaya* (Walshe, 1995, pp. 344–350) as follows:

1. Suffering pervades life and is related to five "graspings" or kinds of mental activity: form, feeling, perception, mental formation, and consciousness. Buddhists generally hold that because these aspects of experience vary according to our psychological state, they are constructions that are "empty" and have no real ontological reality.

2. The origin of suffering is attachments or "cravings" which are based on mental activity and keep the person in the cycle of samsara. These attachments include problematic ways of thinking such as the graspings. An especially harmful habit is the making of illusory discriminations and creating dualities that can lead to the idea that we exist as a permanent, independent self. Buddhism thus rejects the concept of an immortal soul and finds even the idea of it problematic.

3. Enlightenment and the cessation of suffering can be found through detachment from the world, including our discriminatory or dualistic thinking and our belief in an independent, existing self. This leads to **nirvana**, a state in which suffering is left behind.

4. The practices necessary for the cessation of suffering are contained in the **Eightfold Path**, which includes knowledge to be learned (right view), a series of ethical prescriptions (right thought, right speech, right action and right livelihood), and practices for meditation and mental control (right effort, right mindfulness and right concentration). At the end of this process, one could become an **arhat**,or holy and enlightened being and eventually achieve final nirvana.

It is important to note several things here. First, a basic assumption of the Four Noble Truths is that enlightenment is in a sense the natural state of humanity and that all that needs to be done is the clear away the impediments of ignorance (Nanamoli & Bodhi, 2001, pp. 353, 358). Sometimes writers use the metaphor of a mirror with dust upon it—all that needs to be done is to clear away the dust for the mirror to reach its perfect condition. Second, as in Hinduism, the Buddhist path involves an entire makeover of the individual, including lifestyle, ethical practices, beliefs, and meditation. Early Buddhist scriptures like the *Dhammapada* (Kaviratna, 1980) strongly emphasize the ethical nature of spiritual seeking. In some branches of Buddhism, these activities are carried out in religious communities or temple settings, while in other places they are done mostly in the home (Musick, Traphagan, Koenig, & Larson, 2000). Third, the process of the Eightfold Path happens without reference to a god—Buddhism is in principle nontheistic, although many schools of Buddhism retain a strong element of devotion to spiritual beings. Fourth, Buddhism focuses on the empirical experience of reality and tries to avoid metaphysical speculation about its actual nature. For instance, Buddhist rejection of dualism simply says that ultimately reality seems nondualistic, and it produces less suffering to think of it that way, not that everything actually is one.

3.2.2 Early Meditative Practices

While there is a common core of Buddhist belief, there are different schools of thought and types of practice within Buddhism, each of which offers a somewhat unique perspective (Kawamura, 1995; Harvey, 1990). Early Buddhism had two types of meditative practices: **calm meditation** (*samathayana*) and opening or **pure insight meditation** (*suddhavipassanaayana*). These are outlined in *Tripitaka* texts and in the *Visuddhamagga*, the classic Theravada meditation manual, and are

often confused in psychological treatments of meditation. Calm meditation practices begin with focusing on one's breath, regulating or "counting" it and becoming
aware of its movement. As the individual becomes more proficient, **mindfulness**
(*sati*) emerges, a state of nonjudgmental awareness of reality involving changes in
both attention and comprehension (Wiseman, 2007). At this point one encounters
the five hindrances: sensual desire, ill-will (aversion to the task), sloth and torpor,
worry or doubt, and fear of commitment. As these are overcome one enters **jhanas**,
states of consciousness where one experiences peace and "one-pointed" concentration. Eventually one enters a realm of pure form and then formlessness where the
distinction between subject and object disappear. This distinction between concentrative and opening forms of meditation can also be found in Islam (e.g., al-'Arabi,
1980, pp. 156–158). Some authors argue that the emphasis on mindfulness in Buddhist meditation makes it different from yoga and other types of meditation that
emphasize concentration. However, concentration is a necessary prerequisite to the
practice of mindfulness meditation, so it is unwise to draw too strict a division
between the practices.

Mindfulness practices must, in later stages, be combined with insight or **vipassana**
to achieve progress toward nirvana. Insight involves gaining knowledge about certain psychological and metaphysical truths that will lead us away from suffering
and toward enlightenment. Traditionally this type of meditation begins with the four
foundations of mindfulness as found in the *Mahasatipatthana Sutta*: "contemplating body as body … feelings as feelings … mind as mind … and mind-objects as
mind-objects" (Walshe, 1995, p. 335), becoming aware of their impermanence and
emptiness. The experience of emptiness shows that certain things such as our mental
life are ultimately not where enlightenment is to be found (Gunn, 2000, p. 128). This
allows us to become detached from them. Eventually one moves into a condition of
detached abiding and achieves arhatship (see Section 13.5.1).

3.2.3 Mahayana Traditions and the Spread of Buddhism

The Buddhist tradition as developed in Theravada Buddhism implies a personal motivation for pursuing the Buddhist path—escape from suffering, becoming an arhat and
achieving final nirvana. Later schools of thought that were part of the **Mahayana** or
"Great Vehicle" Buddhist movement challenged the supremacy of this motive. In the
Mahayana tradition, one pursues the spiritual path in order to help others achieve Bud-
dhahood. While the Mahayana tradition has many points of agreement with Theravada
(Wiseman, 2007), a key difference lies in their vision of ideal spiritual development.
While in Theravada the goal is to become an enlightened arhat, in Mahayana the ideal
is to become an enlightened being called a **Bodhisattva**, who turns aside from the
quest for final nirvana and works to help others along the path. Mahayana Buddhism
began in India as early as 200 CE, developing a "perfect wisdom" literature and culminating in the work of Nagarjuna (2nd–3rd century CE), whose philosophy of **Madhyamika** tried to provide a synthesis of Buddhist thought that avoided the extremes of

nihilism and asceticism which were opposed by the Buddha. Nagarjuna's philosophy and Mahayana ideas are formative for a number of schools of Buddhism including Vajrayana or Tibetan Buddhism and Chan or Zen Buddhism (see Table 3.2).

Mahayana Buddhist metaphysics is based on the **doctrine of dependent origin**, which in brief states that all things are the product of causes and are in turn causes for other things. In the Buddhist context, this implies that nothing has any substantial or continuing existence, it is simply part of a chain of causes that reaches back into the past and forward into the future. Mahayana Buddhists thus believe that apparently stable things like the self are **empty**, that is, their apparent continuity is an illusion because they are constantly in flux. The distinctions that we make between things are also illusory, as everything is part of the great chain of interlocking causal processes. These ideas align Mahayana Buddhism firmly with the doctrine of nondualism, a position that is also sometimes taken by thinkers in other religious traditions

Table 3.2 Spirituality in the Mahayana Buddhist tradition

Period	Beg. Date	Schools	Founders	Key texts (Translation)
Indian	200	Early Wisdom thought		*Prajna-Paramita-Sutras, Heart* and *Diamond Sutras* (Conze, 1975, 2001)
		Madhyamika "Middle Way"	Nagarjuna	*Mulamadhyamak-Karika* (Nagarjuna, 1995)
	400	Yogacara "Mind-only"	Asanga	*Lankavatara Sutra* (Suzuki, 1999)
Chinese	6th cent.	T'ien-t'ai	Chih-i	*Lotus Sutra* (Watson, 1993)
		Hwa-yen	Tu-shun	*Avatamsaka Sutra* (Cleary, 1993)
		Pure Land	Various	Pure Land Sutras (Inagaki, 1995)
		Early Chan	Bodhidharma	*Zen Teachings, Platform Sutra of Hui-neng* (Bodhidharma, 1987, Price & Wong, 1990)
	12th–13th cent.	Classical Chan	Various	*Wumenguan* ("Gateless Gate") (Cleary, 1996)
Japanese	12th cent.	Jodo, Shin (Pure Land)	Honen, Shinran	*Senchakushu* (Honen, 1998)
		Zen: Soto	Dogen	*Shobogenzo* (e.g., Tanahashi, 1985)
		Zen: Rinzai	Eisai	*Blue Cliff Record, Transmission of the Lamp* (Cleary, 2005; Keizan, 2002)
Tibetan	8th cent.	Vajrayana (Tantric)	Various	Various

(e.g., Rumi, 2004, p. 190). However, some of these other nondualists such as the Hindu philosopher Sankara would reject the traditional Buddhist idea that things do not have a continuing existence (Leggett, 1981, pp. 389–392).

Much of the development of Mahayana Buddhism took place in China and Japan, where it become the dominant form of Buddhism. Buddhism entered China about 50 CE and was well established there by the 3rd century CE. It was often seen as a "foreign" religion and was forced to come to terms with indigenous Chinese religious beliefs. Particularly important was the influence of Taoism, which had developed a sophisticated cosmology and anthropology in the *I Ching*, and the later philosophical work of Laozi (e.g., the *Tao Te Ching*) and Zhuangzi. A basic belief in Taoism is the cyclic nature of the world, which is governed by the opposing forces of yin (earth) and yang (heaven). The sage is the person who is one with this essential principle of the Tao and allows all of their actions to be spontaneously guided by it (see Box 3.1).

Box 3.1 The Story of Wen Hui's Butcher

The *Book of Chuang Tzu* is one of the most famous works in Chinese philosophy and a primary text for philosophical Taoism. The text is traditionally thought to be written in the 4th century BCE by Zhuangzi and is a compilation of teaching stories and commentary. Perhaps the most famous story in the book is that of Wen Hui's butcher:

Cook Ting was butchering an ox for Lord Wen Hui. Every movement of his hand, every shrug of his shoulder, every step of his feet, every thrust of his knee, every sound of the sundering flesh and the swoosh of the descending knife, were all in perfect accord, like the Mulberry Grove Dance or the rhythm of the Ching-shou.

"Ah, how excellent!" said Lord Wen Hui. "How has your skill become so superb?"

Cook Ting put down his knife and said, "What your servant loves best is the Tao, which is better than any art. When I started to cut up oxen, what I saw was just a complete ox. After three years, I had learnt not to see the ox as a whole. Now I practice with my mind, not with my eyes. I ignore my sense and follow my spirit. I see the natural lines and my knife slides through the great hollows, follows the great cavities, using that which is already there to my advantage. Thus, I miss the great sinews and even more so, the great bones. A good cook changes his knife annually, because he slices. Now this knife of mine I have been using for nineteen years, and it has cut thousands of oxen. However, its blade is as sharp as if it had just been sharpened …."

"Splendid!" said Lord Wen Hui. "I have heard what cook Ting has to say and from his words I have learned how to live life fully" (Zhuangzi, 1996, pp. 22–23).

As in Hinduism, devotion plays a major part in the lives of many Buddhists. Despite the Buddhist views of emptiness and nonduality, various Buddhas and Bodhisattvas have become a focus for meditation and devotion, including *Avalokitesvara*, the Bodhisattva of compassion and *Amitabha Buddha*, who rules over the Pure Land. Buddhist practice built around devotion to the Amitabha Buddha is known as **Pure Land Buddhism**. It remains the most popular form of Buddhism in modern China and Japan, forming a kind of popular or **folk religion** when combined with different indigenous cultural traditions and beliefs (Vergote, 1998, p. 207). Devotees of Pure Land Buddhism will read and recite sections of the three Pure Land sutras (Inagaki, 1995), and stress is often put on reciting the name of the Amitabha Buddha, with the belief that this will gain the postulant merit and allow them to be reborn into the Pure Land (Unno, 2002). Western views and interpretations of Buddhism influenced by modernist thought have often tried to "purify" Buddhism of these devotional qualities, but they are an essential part of most traditional and contemporary Buddhist paths (Eckel, 2000).

Buddhism has been a significant force in Tibet since the 7th century. The Vajrayana version of Buddhism that dominates there is highly visible in the West due to Tenzin Gyatso, the Dalai Lama, who has spoken widely and written a number of popular books on Buddhism. Tibetan branches of Buddhism are heavily influenced by tantric practice, but retain a basic Mahayana orientation; well known in the West is the Tibetan belief in reincarnation and the *bardo* state, an interim period between death and rebirth. *The Tibetan Book of the Living and the Dead* describes the bardo and was one of the first Tibetan Buddhist works to be translated into English. It caught the attention of Carl Jung, who wrote a preface for the book.

3.2.4 Chan/Zen Buddhism

One of the most important schools of Buddhism within the Mahayana family is Chan or Zen Buddhism (Dumoulin, 1990, 2005). Tradition has it that Chan was founded by the Indian monk Bodhidharma, who went to China from India in late 5th century CE, staying briefly in the southern part of the country before moving to North China where he taught for over thirty years (Suzuki, 1970). A number of works are attributed to him, although authorship is controversial (McRae, 1986; Pine, 1987). However, Chan actually traces its origins back to an encounter between the Buddha and Kashyapa, one of his followers:

> In ancient times, at the assembly on Spiritual Mountain, Buddha picked up a flower and showed it to the crowd. Everyone was silent, except for the saint Kashyapa, who broke out in a smile. Buddha said, "I have the treasury of the eye of truth, the ineffable mind of nirvana, the most subtle of teachings on the formlessness of the form of reality. It is not defined in words, but is specially transmitted outside of doctrine. I entrust it to Kashyapa the Elder" (Cleary, 1996, p. 33).

This story illustrates several key features of Chan thought. First, teaching and learning happen on an individual basis, with wisdom passed down directly from master to student. Second, learning is experiential—it cannot be gained simply by study of texts and memorization of information. There must be an inner experience of enlightenment. Third, the truth to be gained through Chan is **ineffable**, not something that can be expressed in words. All of these ideas are certainly present in other forms of Buddhism, but they are especially emphasized in Chan.

A key issue that caused discussion and sometimes division in Chan Buddhism was over the nature of enlightenment. Was enlightenment a **sudden** experience that might come unexpectedly and perhaps involve a dramatic change, or was it a **gradual** process involving a slowly developing sense of awareness of one's true nature? Some writers tended toward one view or the other, while other thinkers like Nagarjuna of the Madhyamika school and Chih-i (539–597), founder of Tientai Buddhism, tried to strike a middle ground between the two approaches. This conflict was especially pronounced in Chinese Buddhism because it recapitulated the long-standing tension between Taoism, which emphasized more sudden religious experience, and Confucianism that emphasized more gradual training in morality (Gomez, 1987; Donner, 1987). This sudden vs. gradual issue is a fundamental one in philosophical/theological and psychological understandings of spiritual development (see e.g., Sections 4.5, 7.1).

Chan developed for many centuries in China, where it became the dominant form of Buddhism for a time and produced much of the classical literature still used today. It has continued to flourish in Japan, where it is known as **Zen Buddhism**, and it has also exercised considerable influence on Buddhism in Korea and Vietnam. The Buddhist monk Eisai brought Chan to Japan in the 12th century CE and founded the Rinzai school of Zen. This is perhaps the best-known form of Zen in the West due to the work of D. T. Suzuki (1870–1966), a member of the school who wrote extensively in English and corresponded with a number of famous psychologists and Christian religious figures like Carl Jung and Thomas Merton. The other main school of Zen in Japan is the Soto school, founded by Dogen (1200–1253). Deeply influenced by early experiences of emptiness such as the death of his mother (Gunn, 2000, p. 36), he taught extensively and produced the *Shobogenzo*, which is thought to be one of the greatest works of Japanese philosophy. The two schools of Japanese Buddhism tend to be divided on the sudden vs. gradual issue, with the Rinzai school emphasizing sudden and the Soto school gradual achievement of enlightenment (see Section 4.6.1).

Since Zen is experiential, an understanding of its practices is critical to an understanding of Zen. At the heart of Zen practice is the mindfulness practice of sitting meditation known as **zazen** or *shikantaza*. It involves "a sitting posture, control of breathing and a mental attitude of sitting in which extraneous thoughts are eliminated from the mind, allowing us to see our original nature" (Omori, 1996). Zazen stresses the need to eliminate effort to control mental processes and achieve a particular result, deepening the experience of emptiness (Gunn, 2000, pp. 63–64). This is typically combined with other meditative practices like *kinbin* (walking meditation), as well as the study of enigmatic teaching stories or sayings known as **koans**. Elimination of thought leads to a state of **samadhi** or deep meditation, which may be helpful in opening the individual to an experience of **satori**, a glimpse at reality and our true self as part of a unified world. Satori is thus an experience in which one gains **prajna**, or transcendental wisdom. This experience of a unitive state can also be found in Christian thought, such as in the writings of Meister Eckhart (McGinn, 2001).

Various forms of Buddhism differ in the emphasis they place on doctrinal beliefs versus practice. Especially in Western countries, Buddhism is strongly associated with practice and many beliefs are free to vary so that it is common for individuals to retain original Christian identification or beliefs while practicing Buddhist meditation (Scotton, 1998; Marek, 1988).

3.3 Christianity

Like Hinduism and Buddhism, Christianity is a richly diverse tradition that has a history of productive dialogue with psychology (for an overview of Christian history see Latourette, 1975a,b). A brief look at its history, beliefs, and practices will help us understand the dialogue (Figure 3.3).

3.3.1 History and Beliefs

Christianity arose as a movement within Judaism during the first century CE with the life and ministry of Jesus. After his death, the movement spread amongst both Jewish and Gentile (non-Jewish) groups. Towns and cities became headquarters for Christian communities presided over by a leader or *bishop* and a group of elders. Thus, from early times, Christianity has emphasized the importance of community in religious life.

Fig. 3.3 *Stained glass window of man praying, Los Angeles.* In Christianity, one goal of churches and religious communities is to provide support and inspiration for individual spiritual practices like prayer. Visual art like this can serve as a means of encouragement. Photo by the author

While Christianity is a richly diverse religious tradition like Hinduism and Buddhism, it tends to have stronger forms of internal organization and places more emphasis on agreements in belief as well as practice. As a result, Christianity has more of a central core of beliefs that are widely accepted in official Christian circles, although there are also many areas of disagreement. These common beliefs would include

- The existence of a transcendent, personal God who created the universe, loves, and cares for it
- Humanity was created in the image of God and thus has a special, unique status in the created order
- Although we are created in the image of God, we are sinful and stand in need of a redemption that we are unable to achieve on our own—a key difference between Christianity and Hinduism or Buddhism
- The presence of both God and man in Jesus, known as Christ, who sacrificed himself to redeem humanity and demonstrated this by rising from the dead. This presence of God in the flesh is referred to as the **incarnation** (Athanasius, 1994b). This gift or **grace** when accepted provides the core of a solution to the problems of sin, guilt, and separation from God (McMinn, Ruiz, Marx, Wright, & Gilbert, 2006)
- The continuing presence in the world of God in the person of the Holy Spirit, who works to further God's purpose for the redemption of all creation
- The possibility of eternal life so that our purpose is not limited to our immediate earthly existence
- The possession of sacred writings in the Bible, which are of special significance for the community.

Systematic works in Christian theology also agree on the types of subjects that are of interest, including the following:

- The nature of truth and revelation
- The nature of God and the Trinity
- The nature and purpose of creation
- *Christology*, the nature of the person and work of Christ
- *Pneumatology*, the person and work of the Holy Spirit
- *Ecclesiology*, the nature and work of the Church, including sacraments
- *Eschatology*, the final purpose of history and the end of a linear time process when God's kingdom will be established on the earth
- Practical applications of theology, such as in ethics

Some of these topics are of great importance to psychology. Writings about creation are of interest because they typically discuss basic human nature and the origins of suffering, while works on ecclesiology and ethics treat the fundamentals of communities and relationships. Theological writings produced in the last century are especially relevant for the psychology and religion dialogue, as theologians became increasingly sophisticated in their knowledge of psychology and made use of scientific theory and research in their work.

3.3.1.1 Trinitarian Thought and the Relational God

Modern Christian theology has tended to emphasize the relational character of God through a renewed emphasis on the ancient doctrine of the Trinity (Gunton, 1991, 1993; Grenz, 2001). Briefly, this doctrine is built on the idea that God contains both unity and diversity, relationality, and personhood. God is thought to consist of three Persons, the Father who creates, the Son who redeems and the Spirit who sustains. Each of these persons is unique, but they are also in some way One and their work is harmonious. The idea of God as distinct persons yet One is a strong statement that God has a relational character (Zizioulas, 1985, p. 84; Fiddes, 2002). Trinitarian language of Father and Son emphasizes this fact; a father cannot exist without a son (and son without father) because of the relationality inherent in the terms (Athanasius, 1994a; Gregory, 1994). Trinitarian theologies seek ways to express this combination of essential relationality or unity and unique personhood.

Different authors use different languages to describe the deep relationality present in the Trinity such as *constant presence* (Irenaeus, 2001), *mutual indwelling* (Gregory, 1994; Kelly, 1978, pp. 364–365; Torrance, 1994, pp. 10–14; Balswick, King, & Reimer, 2005), a constant *generativity* or mutual creativity (Origen, 1994; Pannenberg, 1988, p. 268), and an eternal *loving communion* (Augustine, 1956; Kelly, 1978, pp. 274–275) or characters in a narrative that has *dramatic coherence* (Jenson, 1997, pp. 64, 75). The relationship does not submerge the identities of the persons but acts to support and distinguish them, transforming each other without making them alike (Pannenberg, 1988, pp. 303–319; Jenson, 1997, pp. 149, 156).

Christian theology maintains a strong commitment to the idea that the Trinity is active in the world. While most theologians would say that we cannot ever directly know the essence of the persons and their relations, we can know them through their activity. This has led many writers to distinguish between the essence of God or **immanent Trinity** and God as acting in the world or **economic Trinity**. They point out that we can know the latter but not the former, although both are relational (Peters, 1996, p. 263). Some theologians deemphasize the difference between God's essence or immanent Trinity and work or economic Trinity (e.g., Rahner, 1974, pp. 22–23; Reid, 1997, pp. 55–66), while others tend to emphasize the differences (e.g., Irenaeus, 2001; Origen, 1994; Lossky, 1998, pp. 23–43, 67–90).

The active and relational nature of God has a couple of important implications for Christian theology. First, some theologians such as Robert Jensen (1997) have argued that since God is relational and active in the world through relating to other persons, both the essence and activity of God have an ethical character. Since the Divine reveals itself in action, we know something about this ethical nature, but because God is free and hidden, we will never know the entirety of God's moral intentions and purposes. We may understand them in retrospect but cannot fully predict them in advance. Second, since we learn about God through action and activity in the world, our knowledge of God is relational. The Trinity reveals itself freely through action, and through this gift of knowledge further establishes a relationship with us (Barth, 1932, pp. 362–381). So it is not just we who approach God, but God also approaches us. As action, this knowledge is not propositional but is *historical,* occurring as unique events at particular places and times. It has a narrative character (cf. Section 6.3.3). We discover the immanent Trinity through the economic Trinity, and while this knowledge does not eliminate the essential mystery of the Trinity, we can learn about and respond to the Divine.

There are fascinating parallels between Trinitarian relationality and the ideas of many modern scholars and theologians about human relationships and personhood (Ware, 1986a). For instance, the theologian Wolfhart Pannenberg (1985, p. 850) defines the human person as an individual capable of self-transcendence through his or her presence with others. The Christian philosopher Charles Taylor (1989, pp. 159–162) argues that we must reject a view of the human person as isolated but that people have a kind of interpenetration or mutual indwelling with each other in which personhood and relationality depend upon each other. Our uniqueness is not simply a personal characteristic but is due to the fact that we are at the center of a unique set of relationships with other persons and communities (Grenz, 2001, p. 303). There are also a number of other interesting implications:

1. While we do not know others directly in their essence (in part due to their freedom) we can gain partial knowledge of them through action. This is knowledge that ultimately is revealed in our relationship with them. Even individuals with Alzheimer's disease act upon others and call forth action so that they remain persons despite the loss of cognitive and emotional abilities.
2. People can neither be reduced to isolated individuals (as in individualism) nor can they be understood solely on the basis of their membership in a collective group or their relations with others. A strictly individual perspective is isolating, while viewing people only from a collective perspective risks intolerance and a lack of appreciation for distinctive personhood (see Section 12.3.1).
3. Our connectedness to others enhances our uniqueness. Relationships occur in specific historical situations and are unique and non-repeatable. They are also not reversible: a son and father cannot trade places, nor can two friends exchange places, for they have different points of origin and a different nexus of relationships. This perspective is quite different from that of psychologists like Piaget and to some extent Kohlberg, who pictured ideal relationships abstractly as completely reversible (Inhelder & Piaget, 1958, p. 272; Kohlberg, 1984, p. 256; see Section 7.4).
4. Ideal relationships involve a kind of interdependency with freedom that supports the other in their personhood, uniqueness and work. Thus freedom also carries with it obligation to fidelity which is unique to each person.
5. Since persons are ultimately unknowable in some respects and are constituted by relations, they cannot be completely described by rationalistic and propositional statements. Contrary to the positivist position, important knowledge about persons is of a practical or relational nature and relates to a certain nexus of persons and relations in a particular time and place in a practical situation, moral demand, and response. It is not entirely describable through thin, universal, and absolute descriptions but is known through concrete practical activity (cf. Sections 2.3, 6.3.4).

3.3.1.2 Diversity of Belief and Organization

Historically, Christianity consists of three main organized movements: Catholicism, Eastern Orthodoxy, and Protestantism. During the first four centuries of the Christian movement, no large-scale divisions took place. However, beginning at least by the 5th century CE, the Western part of Christianity, headquartered in Rome, began to drift away from the Eastern part of the Church that was based in Byzantium (Constantinople, modern Istanbul) and other cities in the Middle East. This division finally resulted in a formal rupture between the two groups in the 14th century over issues of Trinitarian theology and the authority of the Pope. Following the death of Mohammad in 632 CE many traditional Byzantine Christian areas were overrun by Moslem invaders, but Eastern Christianity continued to flourish in Greece, the Balkans and eventually Russia, forming the **Eastern Orthodox churches**. Western Christianity remained dominant throughout most of Western and Central Europe, where it divided into two groups—Catholic and Protestant. The **Catholic church** is headquartered in Rome and was the sole grouping of Western Christians until the European and English Reformations of the 16th century, when large groups of individuals broke away from the Catholic church over issues of church policy and doctrine, as well as papal leadership, marking the beginnings of various **Protestant churches**. The original Reformation churches (Lutheran, Calvinist/Reformed, and Anglican) became themselves the target of other dissenting and reform groups (Anabaptists, Methodists, Baptists, and Pietists), splintering the Protestant movement into a complicated diversity of groups.

Given the diversity of Christian groups, it is not surprising that there are differences and often conflicts over issues of belief (for an overview of issues in Western theology, see Bromiley, 1978; on Eastern theology see Lossky, 1998). Lindbeck (1984) divides these belief systems into three types. In traditional or **preliberal theology**, statements of belief are propositions that make truth claims, e.g., the existence of life after death. Beginning in the late 18th and early 19th century, an alternative **liberal theology** arose that saw most Christian beliefs as simply expressions of religious experience, feeling, and sentiment (e.g., Schleiermacher, 1999). More recently a third alternative known as **postliberal theology** has developed, which sees systems of doctrine as representing a kind of cultural and linguistic framework that undergirds the practices of a community, as well as how its members experience the world. Some Christian writers take these three approaches to theology as mutually exclusive and work within a single framework. Others work within two or more of the categories; for instance, when a writer argues that while religious beliefs reflect experience and cultural patterns, they also have truth value.

A number of specific issues are matters of debate within the spectrum of Christian belief. **Dualism** is an issue that has appeared in Christian thought, especially in two contexts. First is *good-evil dualism*. Since God is associated with the Good, is there an opposite but equal force for Evil that struggles with it? This type of dualism has largely been rejected in Christianity, which sees a good God as stronger than any evil. A typical view is that of Augustine, who saw evil as simply the absence of good. This position would later disturb the psychologist Carl Jung, who had a more dualistic view of good and evil. Second is *body-soul dualism*, which deals with the issue of separation or unity between our physical and spiritual natures. Historically, dualistic views that separate body and soul have been popular in both Christian theology and Western philosophy, although more recent theology and religious practice has tended to reject this type of dualism.

A second key area of disagreement in Christian thought is that of **human freedom**. Many Christians believe in the absolute sovereignty and control of God, which if carried to an extreme conclusion means that the lives of individuals are completely governed or preplanned by God. This doctrine of determinism or **predestination** is opposed by the **Arminian** position, which holds that individuals have free will, a view that is assumed by both Buddhism and Hinduism despite the doctrine of karma. In the Christian tradition, freedom means that we have the ability to "commit ourselves to being the person we believe God intended us to be, and to commit ourselves to the path of life we believe God invites us" (Lonsdale, 2000, pp. 135–136). The issue of free will posed by naturalistic determinism and causal reductionism has also been a significant topic of discussion within psychology.

A third doctrinal problem in Christianity centers on the nature and authority of the Bible. Beginning in the 18th and 19th centuries, Christian scholars and other writers began to look more critically at the Biblical text from the basis of Enlightenment rationalism and scientific naturalism, questioning its accuracy and trying to "de-mythologize" the faith. Liberal theologians beginning with Schleiermacher began to build a new Christian theology oriented more toward personal experience and Enlightenment social concerns. This provoked a strong conservative intellectual and political response that resulted in two counter-movements within Protestantism—evangelicalism and fundamentalism. Both of these groups emphasized the accuracy, value, and centrality of the Biblical witness for issues of faith. However, there were also differences, as evangelicals were critical of fundamentalists for their perceived lack of attention to philosophical and social problems and their lack of emphasis on the unity of the Bible as a witness to God's action in the world (Miller, 2000). Dialogue between Christianity and psychology tends to look quite different depending on whether one approaches it from a liberal or conservative standpoint.

A final area of disagreement is over the role of tradition. Some groups find the maintenance of traditional beliefs and practices very important, while others stress innovation. However, even groups that are closely tied to tradition recognize that the Christian witness must adapt to changing times (von Balthasar, 1995, p. 12), and communities that are anti-traditional maintain the importance of many basic rituals and beliefs.

3.3.2 Christian Spirituality

In the Christian tradition, spirituality has a much more specific meaning than the general usage discussed in Chapter 1 (see Section 1.2). Christian spirituality is the experience and development of one's relationship with God. The goal of this development is thought of in various ways by different authors. In medieval Catholicism, it was thought to be a state of final beatitude, when the individual has been perfected and has direct knowledge and experience of God (Thomas, 1998, I, q. 26, a. 1), "the intimate and joyful union of the souls of the blessed with God in glory" (Aumann, 1980, p. 42). In the Eastern Church, spirituality involves becoming "divinized" and experiencing participation in the inner life of the Trinity. For others, Christian spirituality is becoming like Christ, identifying with him in some way or conforming one's behavior to a Christian ideal with the help of a spiritually advanced elder. Since God is found both outside and inside us, this development was both an ascent to the God outside and a retreat to seek God within (von Balthasar, 1995, p. 167).

Histories of organized Christian spirituality in the post-Biblical period (e.g., McGinn, 1991, 1996, 1998, 2005; Mursell, 2001a,b) often trace its beginnings to St. Anthony and the Desert Fathers and Mothers, groups of individuals who went into the deserts of Egypt, Palestine, and Syria seeking solitude and God. Generally these seekers formed communities around a leader or teacher, which became the first Christian monastic communities of men and women. Along with traditional Christian worship, they participated in a set of intense spiritual practices revolving around prayer and ascetical techniques like fasting. These communities and their practices spread throughout the Eastern Church, where further development took place. John Cassian (c. 360–435) brought information on desert spirituality to Western Christianity, establishing monasteries in the south of France that would form the basis of spirituality in the medieval Catholic Church (see Table 3.3, Sections 12.2.3, 13.2).

There are two primary traditions or approaches in Christian mystical writings. In the **kataphatic** or positive theology approach, one tries to make positive statements about God, perhaps seeing the Divine as love or a sense of presence. This positive speech about God can take many forms (von Balthasar, 1995, pp. 22, 94; Turner, 2002). In the **apophatic** or **negative theology** school that first appeared in the 4th century work of Gregory of Nyssa, writers argue that because God is transcendent, we are ignorant about the Divine in fundamental ways, so the reality of God exceeds any positive statement we might make (Merton, 2008, pp. 75–76; Turner, 1995, pp. 19–20; Louth, 1996, p. 15). This can be due to (1) failures in language, (2) limitations of human thought, or (3) that unknowability is a basic ontological characteristic of God (Meredith, 1999, pp. 91–94). Earlier Christian writers such as Origen tended to attribute failures in understanding to limitations in the human mind, while later writers like Gregory Palamas saw them as an essential property of God (Thunberg, 1995, p. 407; Meyendorff, 1998b, p. 203). In this latter view, just as an attempt to describe what is special about a friend goes beyond any objective description of traits, any single definition of human person, of God, or of Trinitarian relationality, fails to encompass everything so that mystery is an essential characteristic and part of its perfection (Lossky, 1998, p. 121; Rahner, 1965, pp. 100–101; Williams, 2002). This kind of thinking is reflected in many Judaeo-Christian writings such as the Wisdom tradition in the Bible, as well as in aspects of Luther's theology (Fiddes, 2002; McGinn, 2002). It is also present in Islamic thought (e.g., Chittick, 1983, pp. 49, 234, 307). Some Christian authors (e.g., Eckhart, John of the Cross) represent this ignorance by using negative descriptive language, saying that God is *not* this or that, that the Divine is a kind of *darkness* beyond descriptive language or normal categories of thought (Shah-Kazemi, 2006, p. 9),

Table 3.3 Spirituality in the Orthodox and Catholic Traditions

Period	Date	Description	Key Authors and Works
Eastern Orthodox Tradition			
Desert Fathers	Late 3rd cent.	Writings about early seekers	Anthony, Evagrius and others *Sayings of the Desert Fathers* (Ward, 1975)
Early Byzantine Fathers	4th–7th cent.	Developed systems and monastic rules	Basil (c. 330–379) *Monastic Rules* (Basil, 1999). John Climacus (c. 525–606) *Ladder of Divine Ascent* (Luibheid, 1982)
Greek Monastic	7th cent. on	Mt. Athos monastery communities	Gregory Palamas (c. 1296–1359) *The Triads* (Palamas, 1983) Nicodemos (1748–1809), *Philokalia* (Nikodimos & Makarios, 1979–95)
Diaspora	8th cent. on	Russian	Various, including *A Pilgrim's Tale*
Western Catholic Tradition			
Formative	500–600	Desert Fathers	John Cassian (c. 360– c. 435), *Conferences*
		Confessional	Augustine (354–430), *Confessions*
		Monastic	Benedict (c. 480– c. 547), *Rule of St. Benedict*
		Apophatic	Pseudo-Dionysius (c. 500), *Mystical Theology*
Medieval	1000–1400	Monastic	Bernard of Clairvaux (1090–1153), *Sermons*
		Beguine and women writers	Hildegard of Bingen (1098–1179), *Scivias* Julian of Norwich (1343– c. 1413), *Showings*
		Apophatic	Meister Eckhart (c. 1260–1328), *Sermons* Unknown (c. 1370), *The Cloud of Unknowing*
Post-Reformation	1500 on	Carmelite	Teresa of Avila (1515–1582), *Interior Castle* John of the Cross (1542–1591), *Dark Night of the Soul*
		Ignatian	Ignatius of Loyola (1491–1556), *Spiritual Exercises*
Modern	1900 on	Post Vatican II writers	Thomas Merton (1915–1968), *New Seeds of Contemplation* Anthony de Mello (1931–1987), *Wellsprings*

while others go further and say that God in essence is utterly unknowable (e.g., Maximus Confessor) so that no language or categories are sufficient to describe the Divine (Turner, 1995, pp. 34–35, 195–204; Thunberg, 1995, p. 413). In either event, apophatic knowledge of God is something that cannot be gained through reason, only through experience (Louth, 1996, p. 147). Some writers (e.g., Carmelites like John of the Cross) consider the kataphatic and apophatic as separate stages with the apophatic usually coming as a later stage of growth that is marked by a move from complexity to increasing simplicity in views and experiences of God (Turner, 1995, p. 44). Other authors such as many medieval Catholic writers see individuals as inclined toward one or the other of these paths, so they are different styles within a tradition (Turner, 1995, p. 257). Other religious traditions like Buddhism also argue that crucial aspects of experience like emptiness are apophatic in nature (Gunn, 2000, p. 29).

Orthodox authors also describe a *mysticism of vision* that is spiritual and intuitive, without form or concept (Spidlik, 2005, pp. 242–244). Some writers describe this expansion of natural abilities as a vision of pure divine light, somewhat like a vision of the sun, where we see it but also see because of its light (Bartos, 1999, pp. 27–31). Palamas describes it as an intellectual and spiritual illumination that is visible only to those who have a purified heart, like the vision of light described in the transfiguration of Jesus. It enables a spiritual vision of the heart that can see divine things and know something of God (Palamas, 1983, pp. 33–34, 77–80; Louth, 1996, pp. 132–139). Two points are important here. First, such knowledge is limited. As Palamas points out, since God is transcendent and thus can never be fully experienced, it is not even possible to define "God." This takes us beyond the limits of Aristotelian logic (Meyendorff, 1998b, p. 131). Second, this knowledge comes through experience, which makes the distinction between theoretical and practical theology meaningless (Palamas, 1983, p. 79; Meyendorff, 1998b, pp. 200–228). Christian spirituality thus has both an intellectual and an affective character, with different writers sometimes emphasizing one or the other of these features of the mystical life, although ultimately agreeing that we need both (McGinn, 2001, pp. 37, 152).

The Protestant Reformation argued for a somewhat different view of Christian spirituality, rejecting the monastic ideal and its focus on human effort as a way to God. Groups of Protestants developed their own diverse but vibrant forms of spirituality (see Table 3.4). They retained the basic Christian spiritual practice of **prayer**, which is usually thought of as an active conversation between the believer and God, rather than simply an open or focused awareness of the Divine that is characteristic of **meditation**, although the division between these is sometimes hard to make in practice. Other practices and beliefs differ from group to group but often include ascetical techniques like fasting, periods of solitude, study of holy writings, and a simple lifestyle.

The difference between Protestant and non-Protestant understandings of spirituality can be thought of in terms of the sudden vs. gradual issue that we encountered in our examination of Zen Buddhism. Protestants see that the key event for the Christians comes in the acceptance of God's gift of love by faith, which results in **justification** and marks the sudden beginning of the individual's Christian life. When this event is

Table 3.4 Key figures in spirituality from the Western Protestant tradition

Period	Date	Description	Key authors and works
Reformers & Anabaptists	1500– 1600	Lutheran	M. Luther (1483–1546), *Freedom of a Christian*
		Calvinist	John Calvin (1509–1564), *On the Christian Life*
		Anabaptist	Menno Simons (1496–1561), *Writings*
Early English	1500– 1700	Literary	George Herbert (1593–1633), *The Temple*
		Theological	J. Taylor (1613–1667), *Holy Living and Dying*
English and Continental Dissenters	1600 on	Quakers	George Fox (1624–1691), *Journal*
		Puritans	John Owen (1616–1683), *The Mortification of Sin*
		Pietists	Philipp Spener (1635–1705), *Pia desideria*
		Baptists	John Bunyan (1628–1688), *Pilgrim's Progress*
Great Awakening	18th century	English and	John Wesley (1703–1791), *Journal*
		American revival	J. Edwards (1703–1758), *Religious Affections*
Later Anglicanç	20th century		C. S. Lewis (1898–1963), *Mere Christianity*
			Evelyn Underhill (1875–1941), *Mysticism*
Later American	20th century		ML King (1929–1968), *The Measure of a Man*
			Billy Graham (1918), *Just As I Am*
			Dallas Willard (1935), *The Divine Conspiracy*

accompanied by struggle and emotion, it is often referred to as a **conversion** event, a topic of vital interest to psychology of religion researchers (see Section 4.5). After conversion a person then begins to realize their new faith in everyday life through a process of **sanctification**. The emphasis here is on God's work rather than on human effort. Catholics and Orthodox Christians tend to think more in terms of gradual progression toward an ultimate goal. Either approach presupposes the desirability of religious or spiritual development (see e.g., Section 7.1, 7.2). Also in either approach, religious experience can be important. When this involves the direct experience of God, it is often referred to as **mysticism** (see Section 4.1.1).

Almost all religious practices in Christianity are either public rituals or things that can be done either in public or private. Worship services that combine discourse, music, and prayer are at the center of any Christian community. One especially important public ritual is performance of the **sacraments**. Various Christian groups define them differently, but all would agree that they are special acts related to the presence and work of God amongst the community and individual believers. In the Eastern and Western Christian traditions, sacramental acts play a central role in the worship experience, while in Protestantism they tend to have a more peripheral, symbolic role. The two primary Christian sacraments are the Eucharist, which is a reenactment of Jesus' final supper with his disciples, and Baptism, which is given when a person joins the Christian faith.

Public practices tend to take place in spaces designated as holy or sacred, so in artificially constructed spaces it has been important to use art, architecture, and music to create a suitable environment for ritual and prayer. The visual and spatial aspects of religious practice have been little studied in psychology but are important for most religious traditions and have been generating much scholarly interest in other disciplines (e.g., Morgan, 1998).

3.4 Conclusion

Key issue: *Any detailed and accurate understanding of world religions will find similarities and differences between traditions and within them as well.*

Our brief review of Hinduism, Buddhism, and Christianity demonstrates a number of important facts about religious traditions. First, there is considerable diversity within individual religions. Statements like "Buddhists believe X" or "Christians believe Y" are risky and may misrepresent significant subgroups and ways of thinking within a tradition. Second, religion does not stand completely independent of culture. Great world religions that have spread into different parts of the world adapt to the indigenous intellectual and cultural landscape, as Buddhism did in its long dialogue with Taoist and Confucian thought. Third, religions are a comprehensive way of life that integrate a worldview and beliefs with religious practices. It is potentially problematic to assume that individual religious practices can be removed from their context. Finally, while religious traditions often overlap each other in terms of common concerns or beliefs, there are also substantial differences and areas of uniqueness (e.g., Barth, 1932, p. 359).

A true rather than a superficial pluralism acknowledges both similarities and differences between traditions, as well as the benefit of dialogue. It respects the fact that any system of comparison or coordination of thought between different religious systems has its problems and limitations (Smith, 1982). It does not absorb traditions into each other but is not exclusivist, saying other traditions have nothing to offer (Senne, 2002). So, for instance, while Buddhism at least in its Theravada variety cannot really be reconciled with Christianity, there are a number of points of useful dialogue (Smart, 1993). However as Paul Tillich argued, we must be open to the possibility that not all beliefs are equally adequate so that dialogue must also involve critique as well as appreciation (Mead, 1962).

Now that we have a basic working knowledge of several religious traditions, in the next several chapters, we will turn to psychology and see in more detail how various thinkers have approached the task of dialogue.

Part II
Dialogue—Past, Present, and Future

Chapter 4
Phenomenological Approaches to Religion and Spirituality

4.1 Introduction

At the heart of the spirituality of every person and group, one can find experiences that are both personal and compelling, sometimes life changing in their impact. Because of this, a proper understanding of religion and spirituality must involve the study of experience. Over the past century, scientists and philosophers have been refining the study of **phenomenology**, or the lived experience of human beings, and applying these new techniques and knowledge to the analysis and understanding of our spiritual life. Phenomenology takes us beyond simple functional analyses of religion to look at its substance and the experience of transcendence (Berger, 1974). In this chapter, we will look at what scientists, philosophers, religious studies experts, and mystics have learned about spiritual and religious experience.

4.1.1 Definitions and Concepts

4.1.1.1 Consciousness and Subjectivity

Experience can be thought of as a way we gain knowledge, "an intuitive and affective grasping of meanings and values" perceived in the world (Vergote, 1969, p. 27). The primary way that we have this mental experience is through **consciousness**, "*the system, context, or field* within which the different aspects of the mind... including thoughts, feelings, sensations, perceptions, images, memories, and so forth, function in patterned interrelationships" (Metzner, 1989, p. 331). This experience of perception and consciousness is **subjective**, that is, personal to each of us individually. In a famous article entitled "What is it like to be a bat?" the philosopher Thomas Nagel (1974) notes that each of us operates from a single point of view that is always different from that of others, sometimes so completely different that we cannot possibly imagine their experience. While our bodies can be understood from several points of view, e.g., a doctor or a friend who knows us well, subjectivity can only be understood from our own point of view. Consciousness and subjectivity are thus unique phenomena that are not easily studied but cannot be avoided if we wish to understand religious experience.

J.M. Nelson, *Psychology, Religion, and Spirituality,*
DOI 10.1007/978-0-387-87573-6_4, @ Springer Science+Business Media, LLC 2009

For our purposes, it is useful to talk about states of conscious experience as lying along two dimensions—differentiation and relationality. At one end of the first dimension is our normal everyday consciousness or **differentiated** experience. In this type of experience, consciousness is directed toward *objects* different or separate from ourselves, the *subject.* In phenomenology, this directedness of thought is known as **intentionality**; it is believed to be a fundamental component of consciousness and an indicator that people are agents who actively construct their world (Vergote, 1998, p. 226). As we direct our attention toward these conscious contents, we take an instrumental or purposive attitude toward them, analyzing and separating them from each other and ourselves using traditional logical thought (Deikman, 2000). These things exist within a field of consciousness that has a **horizon** of awareness involving the presence of *space* and the passage of *time.* In the temporal aspect of consciousness, a "window of simultaneity" is present that allows for the integration of different cognitive components into a "lived present" (Varela, 2001, p. 215). This makes consciousness an ongoing process—a "stream of thought" rather than a static fixed state (James, 1890, pp. 224–290). Just outside of this horizon is a fringe consciousness or **subconsciousness** that we can become aware of, sometimes unexpectedly, lending an air of mysteriousness to the experience (Pratt, 1971, pp. 50–64).

At the opposite end of our first dimension lies **nondifferentiated** experience. In this state, there is a loss of distinction between things or between us as a subject and any other object. Mild versions of this happen often, as when we become wrapped up in a beautiful sunset or piece of music and briefly cease thinking about ourselves. In religious and mystical experience, people frequently report a much more profoundly nondifferentiated state. Some people describe this state as a **pure consciousness experience** (PCE), a raw state of awareness that contains no objects or intentional content at all—just awareness. A state of stillness while engaged in thought or a sense of unity with objects around us may lead to such an experience (Forman, 1998b). Others describe this state as a **monistic experience,** where all things are seen as one and we may become dissolved or absorbed into this great absolute unity (Austin, 2006, p. 343). Since it has no content, it has sometimes been described as an experience of nothingness (Matt, 1990). Mild versions of PCEs probably happen in everyday life, for instance, in unconscious fantasies and dreams, where conventional roles and distinctions become fuzzy (Eigen, 2001) or when we are in a more receptive or intuitive mode of thinking.

A second dimension of consciousness is relationality, the experience we have with another person. At one end of the continuum we perceive events or objects as things without human qualities, while at the other we experience a **relational consciousness** in which we recognize the presence of another person who is connected with us in some way. People are different from objects because we share with them the experience of subjectivity. We can reach joint understandings about things and learn to empathize, approximating their point of view. We also experience a sense of presence that is absent when we relate to an object so that we see them as "who" rather than "what" (Hurlbut & Kalanithi, 2001; cf. Ricoeur, 2007; Arendt, 1998, p. 179). The quality of this experience is known in phenomenology as **intersubjectivity**. Our experience in relationships is a combination of this feeling of relationship and intersubjectivity with our own sense of subjectivity, difference, and personhood. Thus in relational consciousness there is a tension between subjectivity and intersubjectivity, between myself as a unique person but also as one who relates to others.

Relational consciousness is a normal state of affairs, but it can also become unordinary when a spiritual or religious experience involves this kind of consciousness, such as when a person senses the presence of God or some powerful Other. Some extremely powerful and rare experiences seem to combine aspects of nondifferentiated and relational consciousness in an experience of deep communion with a personal God. Any of these religious experiences involve a loss of isolation from others and the world. Instead, we acquire a different, non-instrumental attitude toward them (Hogan, 2004, p. 140; Deikman, 2000).

Shifts in our state of consciousness or subjective awareness that are perceived to be unusual are referred to as **altered states of consciousness** (ASCs). ASCs can be produced in a variety of ways through alterations in sensation, emotion, or cognition. They can also include changes in time sense, body image, or the meanings we attach to events. The experience may involve a sense of **ineffability** or inability to communicate the full import of the experience to others because of its secret, hidden, or incommunicable quality (Merton, 2008, p. 67; Vergote, 2003). It can also have a **noetic** or illuminative quality, a sense that something fundamental about the nature of reality was learned (Streng, 1978, p. 142). These states can be adaptive (e.g., used for healing) or maladaptive (Ludwig, 1990). When they involve a congruence of our body with both the mind and surrounding environment, these experiences also have an embodied quality to them (Thandeka, 1997).

4.1.1.2 Religious and Spiritual Experiences

The generic concept of a religious or spiritual experience is relatively new, as the term is not found in traditional religions. As Bernard McGinn says with reference to mystical experiences, "No Mystics (at least before the present century) believed in or practiced 'mysticism.' They believed in and practiced Christianity (or Judaism, or Islam, or Hinduism)" (McGinn, 1991, p. xvi; cf. p. 252). Nevertheless, psychologists have found the concept of religious experience to be a useful way of talking about features of spirituality that are found in various religious traditions.

General characteristics. Religious experiences are extremely diverse and complex (Hardy, 1983, pp. 26–29; Hay, 2001). Sometimes, they involve unusual sensory experiences and other phenomenon (Spilka, Ladd, McIntosh, Milmoe, & Bickel, 1996, pp. 99–100), but on other occasions they simply involve viewing ordinary experiences from a religious perspective. In either case, the experience can be personal and powerful (Saver & Rabin, 1997; Vergote, 1997, pp. 175–180; Moltmann, 1980, p. 9; Atchley, 1997a). Religious experiences can be classified into a number of types. For instance, the sociologist Rodney Stark (1997b) lists the following four types:

- *Confirming*: a feeling of sacredness or a sense of presence
- *Responsive*: an experience of having been seen or helped

- *Ecstatic*: a confirming and responsive feeling of connectedness
- *Revelational*: having received special knowledge from the Divine

Emotional qualities. Many religious experiences are accompanied by profound emotional states that can include a sense of desire or yearning (Vergote, 1969, pp. 80–82; 1997, p. 192), emotionally powerful physical experiences such as *glossolalia* or speaking in tongues (Spilka, Hood, Hunsberger, & Gorsuch, 2003, pp. 267–268), or a sense of presence that is regenerative and renewing (Davis, 1989, p. 45). These aspects of the experience suggest that religious knowledge—probably like most kinds of knowledge—can have a strong emotional component (Watts & Williams, 1988, p. 75). Hill and Hood (1999) argue that this affective quality is central to the experience and can interact with the person's belief system in powerful ways. For instance, an experience in which we sense that the world is meaningful can transform negative emotions or events into positive ones, and a feeling of trustworthiness of people and the world can provide an affective base for relationships. This idea is congruent with the positive emotions theory of Fredrickson (2001), who argues that positive emotions act to open us up and broaden repertoires of thought and action, building additional personal resources, undoing narrowing negative emotions, and fostering resiliency. Modern accounts of religious experience tend to focus on these emotional aspects rather than other kinds of content (Vergote, 1998, pp. 134–135). While ethical and mystical experiences are different (Robbins, 2005; cf. Levinas, 1969, pp. 201–204), the latter can have profound moral consequences. For instance, the religious experience of Thomas Merton when he was in his 40s provided a sense of solidarity with others that motivated his deep concern for social issues (Mott, 1984, p. 311; Brewi & Brennan, 1988, p. 8; see Box 4.1, Fig 4.1).

Fig 4.1 *Thomas Merton.* An adult convert to Christianity, Merton became a Catholic monk and wrote on a wide variety of topics including spirituality, social justice and interreligious dialogue. Photograph of Thomas Merton by Sibylle Akers. Used with permission of the Merton Legacy Trust and the Thomas Merton Center at Bellarmine University

Box 4.1 Thomas Merton's Louisville Experience

Reported in *Conjectures of a Guilty Bystander* (1966, pp. 156–158).

In Louisville, at the corner of Fourth and Walnut, in the center of the shopping district, I was suddenly overwhelmed with the realization that I loved all those people, that they were mine and I theirs, that we could not be alien to one another even though we were total strangers. It was like waking from a dream of separateness, of spurious self-isolation in a special world, the world of renunciation and supposed holiness. The whole illusion of a separate holy existence is a dream. Not that I question the reality of my vocation, or of my monastic life: but the conception of "separation from the world" that we have in the monastery too easily presents itself as a complete illusion: the illusion that by making vows we become a different species of being, pseudoangels, "spiritual men," men of interior life, what have you.

Certainly these traditional values are very real, but their reality is not of an order outside everyday existence in a contingent world, nor does it entitle one to despise the secular: though "out of the world" we are in the same world as everybody else, the world of the bomb, the world of race hatred, the world of technology, the world of mass media, big business, revolution, and all the rest. We take a different attitude to all these things, for we belong to God. Yet so does everybody else belong to God. We just happen to be conscious of it and to make a profession out of this consciousness. But does that entitle us to consider ourselves different, or even *better*, than others? The whole idea is preposterous.

This sense of liberation from an illusory difference was such a relief and such a joy to me that I almost laughed out loud. And I suppose my happiness could have taken form in the words: "Thank God, thank God that I *am* like other men, that I am only a man among others." To think that for sixteen or seventeen years I have been taking seriously this pure illusion that is implicit in so much of our monastic thinking.

It is a glorious destiny to be a member of the human race, though it is a race dedicated to many absurdities and one which makes many terrible mistakes: yet, with all that, God Himself gloried in becoming a member of the human race. A member of the human race! To think that such a commonplace realization should suddenly seem like news that one holds the winning ticket in a cosmic sweepstake.

I have the immense joy of being *man*, a member of a race in which God Himself became incarnate. As if the sorrows and stupidities of the human condition could overwhelm me, now I realize what we all are. And if only everybody could realize this! But it cannot be explained. There is no way of telling people that they are all walking around shining like the sun.

(continued)

This changes nothing in the sense and value of my solitude, for it is in fact the function of solitude to make one realize such things with a clarity that would be impossible to anyone completely immersed in the other cares, the other illusions, and all the automatisms of a tightly collective existence. My solitude, however, is not my own, for I see now how much it belongs to themand that I have a responsibility for it on their regard, not just in my own. It is because I am one with them that I owe it to them to be alone, and when I am alone they are not "they" but my own self. There are no strangers!

Then it was as if I suddenly saw the secret beauty of their hearts, the depths of their hearts where neither sin nor desire nor self-knowledge can reach, the core of their reality, the person that each one is in God's eyes. If only they could all see themselves as they really *are*. If only we could see each other that way all the time, There would be no more war, no more hatred, no more cruelty, no more greed... I suppose the big problem would be that we would fall down and worship each other. But this cannot be *seen*, only believed and "understood" by a peculiar gift.

Again, that expression, *le point vierge*, (I cannot translate it) comes in here. At the center of our being is a point of nothingness which is untouched by sin and by illusion, a point of pure truth, a point or spark which belongs entirely to God, which is never at our disposal, from which God disposes of our lives, which is inaccessible to the fantasies of our own mind or the brutalities of our own will. This little point of nothingness and of *absolute poverty* is the pure glory of God in us. It is so to speak His name written in us, as our poverty, as our indigence, as our dependence, as our sonship. It is like a pure diamond, blazing with the invisible light of heaven. It is in everybody, and if we could see it we would see billions of points of light coming together in the face and blaze of a sun that would make all the darkness and cruelty of life vanish completely.... I have no program for this seeing. It is only given. But the gate of heaven is everywhere.

Interpretive framework. Religious experience involves the attribution of religious meaning to an event (Rizzuto, 1991, p. 47), and thus contemporary Christian theologians and psychologists tend to agree that an experience cannot be religious unless the person has a framework of religious beliefs, symbols, and language by which to interpret it. An individual without such a framework might interpret an experience differently, and use other language to describe it with potentially different meanings. Of course, the presence of such a frame neither guarantees that a situation will be taken religiously nor does it exclude that other interpretations might occur along with religious ones (Sheldrake, 1998, p. 21; Spilka et al., 2003, p. 262; Vergote, 1997, pp. 172–182; 1998, pp. 135–144; van der Lans, 1987). An interesting example of this is the case of the positivist philosopher and atheist A. J. Ayer, who reported an unpleasant near-death experience during a cardiac arrest. While many people attribute religious or spiritual meanings to such an event, he did not interpret the experience in a religious way, although on some occasions, he did say it weakened his belief that life ends with death (Sabom, 1998, pp. 209–210; Belling, 2004). The presence of an interpretive framework does not necessarily suggest that the experience arises from the beliefs; clearly in many religious traditions, beliefs come from historical experience rather than the reverse (Murphy, 1995). It also does not rule out the possibility that some experiences are more intrinsically religious, as they involve the feeling of an outside force or perception of an ultimate reality, while others (e.g., visions) are more tied to culture and personal interpretation (e.g., Davis, 1989, pp. 30–31). These interpretive frameworks most commonly come from a religious tradition and will govern the importance attached to religious experiences, how they are described, which ones are valued, and how their truth value can be interpreted (Geels, 1996; Wildman & Brothers, 2002). They can have powerful effects; for instance, research has found that religious experience scores are higher in traditions that emphasize them (Hood, 1994).

Frequency. Spiritual and religious experiences of the types mentioned above are common. Studies from the 1970s done in the US by Thomas and Cooper (1978) and in Britain by Hay and Morisy (1978) found that about 1/3 of their adult samples reported having religious or spiritual experiences. For some individuals, these experiences are infrequent, while for others they are common (Laski, 1962, p. 43). Both studies found that greater age, higher social class, and more positive levels of psychological well-being were associated with higher frequencies of religious experience. Hay and Morisy found that church attendees were more likely to have experiences but that many religiously active people did not, and that 24% of atheists reported such experiences. Thomas and Cooper found that the types of experiences were quite diverse, including experiences of consolation (12%), psychic or supernatural experiences (12%), and mystical experiences (2%). Religious experience may be even more common in some groups. Christian Smith (2005) found in one study that over half of US adolescents reported one or more religious experiences, and rates among US adult church attendees appear to be even higher, in the 65–75% range (Spilka et al., 1996).

Associated factors. Research has identified a number of sensitizing factors that will trigger or increase the chance a person will have a religious experience. These factors include an intrinsic religious orientation (Hood, 1975), availability of a religious language and framework, living in a receptive or stimulating sociocultural context, and older age (Atchley, 1997a,b). Triggers associated with the beginning of an experience include participating in individual spiritual practices or public rituals like prayer and worship (Bartocci, 2004; DeConick, 2001), nature experience (Marechal, 2004, pp. 147–215), creative activity (Averill, 1998) or personal factors like the occurrence of distress or crisis, especially when connected with life marker events like death or birth (Hood, Morris, & Watson, 1989; Spilka et al., 1996; Vergote, 1997, pp. 152–154; Geels, 1996). Expectations of the nature of the experience and perceived desirability are also related to the type of experience and chances of occurrence.

4.1.1.3 Mysticism

Mysticism has long been prized in all the world's spiritual and religious traditions (Geels & Belzen, 2003). The term originated in Christianity, where it refers to a reaching out and "non-conceptual knowing of God" accomplished through experiences of union (Vergote, 2003, p. 81) or "some form of immediate contact with the divine presence" (McGinn, 2005, p. 371; cf. Vergote, 1969, pp. 145–146; Merton, 2008, p. 29). Paul Tillich once said that "without a mystical element—namely an experience of the immediate presence of the divine—there is no religion at all" (Tillich, 1963a, pp. 88–89). While there is no commonly agreed upon definition of mysticism among scholars (or among mystics!), a number of characteristics are common to most definitions. William James (1961, pp. 299–300) identified the following as central features of **mystical experience**:

* *Ineffability*: a felt inability to describe the experience
* *Noetic quality*: a sense that something fundamental was learned
* *Transiency*: the experience lasts for a brief period of time
* *Passivity*: a sense that the experience was not under the person's control.

Mystical experiences can be negative (apophatic) or positive (kataphatic) in character, or an interplay of the two (Turner, 1995, p. 271; see Section 3.3.2). They can occur in milder or stronger form but commonly involve an experience of transcendence beyond normal categories. Different kinds of mysticism also vary according to whether they emphasize the noetic or relational aspects of the experience (Leavy, 1995, pp. 359–360; Stoeber, 2001; Stoddart, 2007). The encounter with transcendence that is a central part of mystical experience can lead to the perception of the presence of a powerful Other with whom we can have relationship and communion. Such experiences are often carried back into everyday life, changing and enhancing it (Zizioulas, 2006, pp. 286–291; Freeman, 2003; Taylor, 2003). In the Christian tradition, this has sometimes resulted in a kind of love mysticism centered on the person of individuals like Jesus or Mary (Johnston, 1995).

Mystical experiences are diverse and complex; because of this it is difficult or perhaps impossible to reduce their description to a short list of characteristics. In addition to the classical criteria of William James, other authors see that a **unitive experience**—a sense of union with God or the universe—is a central and distinctive part of mysticism (Vergote, 1998, p. 137). These experiences involve both a perception of an underlying unity and a sense of participation in the unity to such an extent that the self is lost or transformed (Hayes, 1997; Leavy, 1995; Hood, 2001, pp. 3–5, 84–85). Along with this can come a cessation of normal intellectual operations and their replacement with different and intuitive modes of thinking (Gimello, 1978). Medieval Christian mystics like Richard of St. Victor noted that at the highest stages of their mystical journey, things that were encountered were beyond or even against normal reason (Richard of St. Victor, 1979, p. 161). This leads to the recognition and acceptance of the idea that **paradox**—the simultaneous truth of two seemingly incompatible things—is an essential feature of reality (cf. Section 1.2.1). However, mystical experience can occur without this paradoxical quality (Hood, 1975).

A strong affective tone (pleasurable, fearful or serene) and intense realness are also common characteristics. Other perceptual aspects of the experience such as visions are frequent but generally considered to be secondary features and are typically viewed with caution by religious practitioners (Gimello, 1978; Deikman, 1990; Douglas-Klotz, 2001; Meissner, 2003; Veilleux, 1980, p. 356).

A way of life in which mystical states are valued and sought after is known as **mysticism** (Hood, 2001, p. 155; Vergote, 2003). In the Christian context, mysticism involves a deep desire and need to bridge the gap between ourselves and the Divine that transcends us. This desire becomes the driving force for participation in a variety of activities in both individual and communal contexts. In this view, mysticism is not so much a kind of experience but an orientation or way of life (Merton, 2008, p. 3). Writers argue about the extent to which mystical experience can flourish and affect us apart from a way of life and practices that support it.

The problem of ineffability. The criterion of ineffability has caused considerable discussion among scholars, especially theologians who tend to see language as vital to religious life (e.g., Tillich, 1957, p. 31). Ninian Smart (1978, p. 19) has rightly pointed out that mystical experiences cannot be *completely* ineffable, because mystics do use language to refer to and even describe their experiences. It is better to talk about degrees and types of ineffability. Some kinds are common and involve the trouble we have sharing any kind of personal experience (Moore, 1978). In mystical experiences, ineffability might include (1) an inability to conceptualize what has happened or (2) an ability to conceptualize it but not communicate it (Tart, 1992, p. 51). Communication problems might be due to a lack of vocabulary and conceptual structures in the person's language and culture; it would be easier for those living in a community with adequate vocabulary and others who had similar experiences (cf. McGinn, 2005, p. 20). However, it is also likely that there are conceptual problems (Bambrough, 1978; cf. Section 3.3.2). These could be due to cognitive or sensory overload from a stimulus too novel, rich, and complex, a likely possibility in a unitive experience, but they could also be related to the nondualistic nature of the experience. A unitive consciousness would involve no differentiation between objects or between subject and object, and since all conceptual structures depend on such differentiation, they would be unable to encompass such an experience (Braud, 2002; Prigge & Kessler, 1990; Masters & Houston, 2000, pp. 270, 297). Music, poetry, or even silence might be better choices than speech in such a situation (Leavy, 1995, pp. 355–357).

Do different religious traditions describe different kinds of religious experiences? This is an important and controversial point. Theistic religions such as Christianity are built around belief in a God who is active in the world but not identical with it. In these groups, the longing to have unity with God and the experience of divine love are the essential traits and driving forces of the mystical life. For these religions, mystical experience is relational in nature (Vergote, 1998, p. 244; 2003; Butler, 2003, p. 143). On the other hand, monistic religions like Buddhism argue that everything is ultimately one, so that there is no God separate from the created order. Many authors (e.g., Underhill, Stace and Smart) argue that monists and theists are having the same experience, just interpreting or representing it differently.

Stoeber (1994) disputes this and argues that they are really significantly different experiences, as monistic states are nondual, strictly impersonal and described in negative terms. Stoeber suggests that monistic experiences provide the foundation for theistic experiences of unity, a view similar to that found in some Hindu writers (e.g., Ramanuja, Sri Aurobindo) and the Christian mystic John Ruysbroeck. In this view, we are first united with the Divine and then are able to become a channel for an active personal encounter (Stoeber, 1994, pp. 18–24, 45–58). On the other hand, some authors in the Christian tradition (e.g., Maximus Confessor) argue that it is in God that things find their unity so that an experience of God is foundational for any kind of unitive experience.

Hood believes that mystical experiences are not inherently important, and certainly some deeply religious figures like C.S. Lewis claim little in the way of mystical experience (Hood, 1997, p. 229; Dorsett, 2004, p. 51). If they occur to someone who eschews spiritual or religious beliefs, they may be set aside as incompatible with the rest of the person's experience. However, those who belong to spiritual or religious traditions that value and describe these experiences are better able to cultivate and incorporate them into their view of the world (Hood, 2001, p. 159). On the other hand, Zinnbauer and his colleagues (1997) found that both religious and spiritual and spiritual but not religious individuals were higher than non-spiritual groups on ratings of mysticism, although the spiritual but not religious group was higher on types of mystical experience less commonly found in the Christian tradition. Little is known about mysticism in this latter group, and therefore more research is needed.

Related factors. Personal and situational characteristics related to mystical experience seem to be similar to those reported for other types of religious experience. For instance, religious motivation (see Sections 1.4.6, 9.3.1) appears to be a factor in mysticism. Individuals with high levels of intrinsic motivation—those who seek religion for its own sake—have higher mysticism scores, and when those high in extrinsic motivation do have mystical experiences they tend to not report the experience as religious in nature. Those people who are indiscriminately high in both intrinsic and extrinsic religiosity also have higher mysticism scores (Hood, 1973, 2001). Gender role also appears to be a factor in mysticism, as individuals endorsing a feminine or androgynous sex role orientation report higher levels of mystical experience. Women overall have more frequent and intense mystical experiences, and their religious experiences are more likely to be mystical in nature (Mercer & Durham, 1999; Hood, 2001; Sjoerup, 1997). There is a small but significant trend toward more mystical experiences in older age groups (Lange & Thalbourne, 2007). Situational factors are also sometimes involved (Hood, 1978). Scores on measures of mysticism are generally unrelated to psychopathology (Mehrabian, Stefl, & Mullen, 1997).

Changes in attention seem to be an important part of the mystical experience. Deikman (2000) argues that in normal consciousness our attention is mostly directed to our thoughts, and our perception of the world around us is relatively automatic. He believes that in mystical states this process is reversed, with attention to the perceptual world going through a process of deautomatization. This makes perception more intense and allows us to become aware of aspects of reality not previously perceived. Studies have found that mysticism is related to the ability to become absorbed or devote total attention to a stimulus, and it has also been connected with higher levels of hypnotizability, which reflect an ability to set aside conventional assumptions about perception or behavior and enter various kinds of trance states (Spanos & Moretti, 1988).

4.1.1.4 Anomalous and Drug Experiences

Psychic and paranormal experiences. Religious experiences have also been compared with various types of anomalous or unusual states, including parapsychological phenomena such as extrasensory perception (ESP). Studies have shown that reports of these phenomena are about as common as religious experiences and that there is a low positive correlation between frequency of anomalous experience and religiousness or reports of mystical experience. However, among Christians there is no relationship between anomalous experiences, religious affiliation, and belief (Spilka et al., 2003, pp. 312–314; Thalbourne & Hensley, 2001; Thalbourne, 1995, 2004; Thalbourne & French, 1995; Mehrabian et al., 1997). Some religious traditions such as Hinduism and Buddhism suggest that at certain stages of spiritual development a person may gain psychic powers such as the ability to see the future (Rao, 1994; cf. Hollenback, 1996, pp. 135–300), although generally these traditions see the occurrence of psychic phenomenon as peripheral to the central task of spiritual growth. This is a very controversial area of study, in part because it sits uneasily in a naturalistic framework (Griffin, 1997), with many investigators vehemently labeling the study of anomalous states as "pseudoscience" and not worthy of scientific study, while others maintain that there is good scientific evidence for the existence of these states (Utts, 1996; Cardena, Lynn, & Krippner, 2000; Radin, 1997; Beloff, 1993; see Box 4.2). Some studies suggest that dissociative phenomenon like déjà vu or out of body experiences are relatively unrelated to mystical experience (Fox, 1992; Spanos & Moretti, 1988).

Drug-induced experiences. Since the time of William James (1997, p. 305) a connection has been noted between religious experiences and ASCs obtained through the use of psychedelic drugs like psilocybin or LSD. Most major religious traditions do not recognize drug-induced states as religious experiences, but there are some points of similarity. The majority of psychedelic drug users report religious imagery during drug-induced ASCs, perhaps from the same biochemical processes that are involved in religious experience during meditation. From the standpoint of self-definition, such experiences might be considered religious (Spilka et al., 2003, p. 286; Masters & Houston, 2000, p. 247–254; Davis, 1989). However, there are also phenomenological differences. In a famous experiment, Pahnke (1966; Pahnke & Richards, 1966) gave psilocybin to some seminary students during a Good Friday service, provoking experiences that he labeled mystical. However, the drug experiences were marked by considerable fear, distress, and self-doubt which are untypical of mystical states, as are the frequent perceptual changes

Box 4.2   Near Death Experiences and Mysticism

A near death experiences (NDE) is a type of powerful experience that often has religious or spiritual effects on an individual.

Sobom (1998) gives a striking example of an NDE by a neurosurgery patient. In order to repair a brain aneurism, she underwent an unusual surgery that involved cooling her body and stopping both her heart and brain activity so the blood could be drained from her head during a portion of the operation. Instruments attached to her verified that during portions of the surgery she had no measurable electrical activity in the cortex or brainstem. Nevertheless, she was able to report aspects of the surgery from a vantage point out of her body and had an experience of going down a tunnel to a place of light, where she met and conversed with a number of family members who were deceased. Then she was sent back and returned to her body, which was revived by the surgical team following successful repair of the aneurism.

Experiences such as this are difficult to explain from a reductive materialist point of view. Nevertheless, their interpretation is somewhat dependent upon the worldview of the individual who has the experience. The atheist and positivist philosopher A. J. Ayer had a NDE experience and at one point said that it "slightly weakened" his disbelief in life after death, although he still hoped it would be true (*National Review*, October 14, 1988). He claimed that the experience did not alter his atheist beliefs at all, despite the fact that a witness says Ayer reported meeting a divine Being during his experience.

and occasional psychotic states that go with drug use (Doblin, 1991; Pahnke & Richards, 1966). Linguistic analysis of drug, mystical, and schizophrenic states also reveals significant differences in description. Schizophrenics tend to describe their experience in terms of deviancy and illness, drug users describe perceptual changes like altered space and sensation, while mystics focus on the connection of their experience to daily events and their religious life (Oxman, Rosenberg, Schnurr, Tucker, & Gala, 1988). A largely unexplored area is how drug use (e.g., antidepressants) might interact with meditation in the production of ASCs (Bitner, Hillman, Victor, & Walsh, 2003).

Creative and other states. Another experience with parallels to religious experience is the *flow state* described by Csikszentmihalyi (1990). This is a condition that occurs during enjoyable and absorbing artistic creative states. The flow experience has characteristics of an altered state like feelings of exhilaration, altered time sense, and a loss of awareness of self. Certainly there are a number of parallels between creative and mystical states, but there are also differences. Flow states typically occur in goal-oriented task situations, and the person may leave the experience with an enhanced sense of personal control, while mystical experiences generally have a more passive quality and end with a feeling that they have been given a gift, rather than gotten something through effort (Raab, 2003; cf. Nixon, 1996). A state with more similarities to mysticism is the **peak experience** described by Maslow in his study of self-actualizing individuals. In this state of being or *B-cognition*, objects are fully attended to and seen as a whole, independent from their possible usefulness. The experience has a number of features similar to religious and mystical experience, including a quality of timelessness, uniqueness, passivity and receptiveness, and a sense of unity with the world that overcomes polarities. Emotional reactions include "a special flavor of wonder, of awe, of reverence, of humility and surrender before the experience as something great" (Maslow, 1999, p. 98). In its most intense form, this experience appears to be similar to a unitive experience, although the qualities of ineffability and noesis do not seem to be present in the same ways as in a mystical experience. Imagery, visions, and hallucinations can also be an important part of religious experience, although most religious traditions would give these phenomena a subsidiary role (Spilka et al., 2003, pp. 270–277; Merton, 2006, p. 307; Meissner, 2003).

Many authors have speculated about the parallels between religious and psychotic experiences. Those who see parallels point out that religious delusions are found in at least a quarter of psychotic states (Siddle, Haddock, Tarrier, & Faragher, 2002), and that there is no specific form or content difference between spiritual and psychotic experiences, so it is wrong to label one as "illness" and the other as normal (Jackson & Fulford, 1997). Isabel Clarke (2001c) argues that both spiritual and psychotic experiences involve a common process of transition from ordinary to transliminal consciousness but that in psychotic experiences there is a problem returning to normal consciousness, and that this problem is what leads to distress and dysfunction. Other authors argue that while there are points of similarity there are also differences between psychotic and religious experiences (e.g., Marzanski & Bratton, 2002a,b). Psychotic experiences tend to have a more negative or frightening emotional tone and a focus on trivial details, in contrast to the positive and unitive quality of mystical experience (Chadwick, 2001; Davis, 1989; Davies, Griffin, & Vice, 2001). Psychotic experiences—especially when they are frequent—are also often distinguished by the negative effects they have on the person's life, while religious or mystical experiences are more life enhancing as well as acceptable to religious peers (Pierre, 2001; Jackson, 2001; Siddle et al., 2002; Peters, Day, McKenna, & Orbach, 1999; Davis, 1989; Bartocci, 2004; Freeman et al., 2005).

4.1.2 Challenges in Studying Religious and Spiritual Experience

4.1.2.1 Methodological Issues

There are a number of methodological problems that bedevil the study of consciousness and of religious experience (Pekala & Cardena, 2000). As we have seen, religious experience is a broad phenomenon so coming up with a definition precise enough for scientific work is difficult. There are also other problems.

Sources. The sources of our data on mystical experience have important limitations. Religious studies scholars primarily work with texts written by mystics, while psychologists typically depend upon interviews or questionnaires in their studies. Unfortunately, neither approach allows the investigator direct access to the subjective experience or its cultural and religious context (DeConick, 2001; Moore, 1978, p. 101; Keller, 1978, pp. 77–79, 95; Bender, 2007). Texts are a special problem because they often discuss the author's views on the mystical journey rather than report specific experiences. This is especially true of Hindu mystical documents (Gupta & Lucas, 1995; Moltmann, 1980, p. 55). Working with individuals through interviews or questionnaires has advantages over the textual approach, but it is still generally not possible to study people while they are having a religious experience, because it is impossible to predict when they will occur so that they can be observed or questioned during the experience. Also, much of the psychological research on mysticism has focused on a normal college age or adult population rather than accomplished mystics who perhaps are more appropriate subjects for study (e.g., James, 1997, pp. 22–24).

Methods. Mysticism can be thought about from a number of perspectives that involve different conceptual and linguistic frameworks. However, research questionnaires are generally created from a single theoretical framework, which may leave out things of importance (Perovich, 1990, p. 248; DeConick, 2001). For instance, Hood's M scale (Hood, 1975; Hood et al., 1989)—the most widely used psychological measure of mystical experience—conceptualizes mysticism in unitive but nontheistic terms. Does such a test really measure religious experience for a theist? Or does it confuse two phenomena that may be quite different from each other (Zaehner, 1961)? Furthermore, how does one meaningfully quantify a mystical experience, especially when the subject says parts of their experience are beyond description? Qualitative methods like phenomenological investigation may be better suited in this situation, since the person having the experience is in the best position to report what actually happened (Hood, 2002; Davis, 1989, p. 21; Valle, King, & Halling, 1989). However, psychologists only infrequently use these methods in their studies.

4.1.2.2 The Problem of Veridicality

The problem of veridicality. Scholars outside of theology generally avoid the question of religious truth. However, as Ninian Smart (1978) argues, a real theory of mystical experience must address issues of validity. There are a number of reasons for this, one of which is that people who have religious experiences—especially mystical ones—say that the experience conveys something important about the nature of reality, making its truth value or **veridical** quality an essential part of the experience (Proudfoot, 1985, pp. 174–177). Another reason is that the position researchers take on this issue may affect their theoretical framework and how they interpret the empirical data. Those who reject the veridicality of the experiences, such as Leuba (1925), point to their confused and puzzling character and develop naturalistic explanations often related to dysfunctional biological or psychological processes. Others (e.g., Pratt, 1971, pp. 456–458) accept at least some aspects of religious experiences as veridical, pointing to the fact that people in many different religious traditions appear to report similar types of experiences. This provides cumulative evidence of veridicality that is difficult to explain reductionistically (Davis, 1989, pp. 174–177, 233–235; Macquarrie, 1982, pp. 216–220). Most transpersonal and some humanistic psychologists take this point of view.

Religious views. Major religious traditions generally take a critical realist view toward religious experience, with Buddhism as a possible exception (Marek, 1988). Even those following mystical paths generally insist that not all religious or spiritual experiences are veridical; they admit to mistakes, criticize others, and have tests or checking procedures just like scientists (Moore, 1978, p. 126; Meissner, 2003). An experience is tested against a variety of sources, which include communal views and tradition or foundational theological beliefs, consistency, and especially the moral and spiritual fruits produced by the experience (Ellis, 1998, p. 273; Sheldrake, 1995, p. 60; Davis, 1989, p. 71). Thus, just as religious experience is critical to the religious life and the development of theology, theological beliefs are critical to a sound mystical life. Thomas Merton puts it this way: "There is no theology without mysticism (for it would have no relation to the real life of God in us) and there is no mysticism without theology (because it would be at the mercy of individual and subjective fantasy)" (Merton, 2008, p. 65). Pike (1978, p. 219) finds two tests are primary in the Christian mystical literature: the spiritual effects of the experience and its lack of conflict with scripture, although in practice great mystics like Teresa of Avila (1515–1582) used the compelling truth quality of the experience as their primary guide (Mavrodes, 1978, p. 256). Avoiding extremes in practice can also minimize errors. Attachment to spectacular aspects of religious experience such as visions or revelations, and relying on too much or too little effort and intellectual activity, are also considered to be problematic (Merton, 2008, p. 211).

While most psychologists adopt a skeptical stance toward religious experience, some have not done so. One of these was William James.

4.2 William James and Varieties of Religious Experience

Many historians of psychology (e.g., Boring, 1950, p. 743) have identified William James (see Fig 4.2)as the greatest American psychologist, and he remains the most prominent figure in the American psychological study of religion. A gifted psychologist and philosopher, James was fascinated with religion although his background and beliefs were untraditional (Hollinger, 1997). While he had some personal experiences that might be termed mystical, he did not feel connected to a religious tradition and tended to interpret his experiences as a type of psychic phenomena. His strongest attraction to religion occurred in his struggles with depression, which plagued him throughout his life along with recurrent physical problems. He hoped that the religious temperament, which he saw as opposed to his own melancholic or "sick-souled" temperament, would help him find ways to reject philosophical pessimism. He also hoped that his religious and psychical researches would help support the development of religion (Capps, 1997b, pp. 26–28, 67; Taves, 1999; Hay, 1999).

Fig 4.2 *William James.*
One of the most important
American psychologists and
philosophers, his work on
religious experience is over a
century old but it remains one
of the best phenomenological studies of religion. Photo
courtesy of the National
Library of Medicine

4.2.1 Basic Beliefs: Radical Empiricism, Pragmatism and Pure Experience

James thought that all knowledge rested on conscious experiences, and he held a position of **radical empiricism** (1996a), that nothing besides experience should form a datum for psychological investigation. He also believed that **introspection** or personal examination of our own mental states could provide valuable information about the world and ourselves. He rejected a positivist approach to experience that tries to study it by breaking it up and examining its parts (see Sections 2.1.2, 2.4.1). Rather, he took a holistic view that conscious experiences form an indivisible whole between subject and external object, with the connections themselves becoming part of the experiences. This indivisible given experience was self-contained and valid in itself and could not be analyzed in an entirely atomistic manner. He termed this phenomenological state **pure experience** (1996a, pp. 1–91). While experiences have similarities and are interconnected, no one connection runs through every-thing—the universe is essentially diverse and discontinuity is an essential feature of experience. This ultimate lack of final connection forms the basis of novelty, indeterminism, and freedom, leading to what James called a **pluralistic universe** with many unities rather than a single unity (1996a, p. 90; 1996b, pp. 310–311; 2003, pp. 57–65). He saw reality as a group of many partial stories where different things work together toward a conclusion, interfacing with each other but having no absolute unity that we can construct in our minds, although all things are aiming toward a final convergence point (2003, pp. 62–70).

Of course, experience at times offers conflicting possibilities of truth. James argued that in these situations one should determine truth by the **pragmatic maxim**, which is to look at "what practical consequences would be different if one side rather than the other were true" (1996a, p. 72). Sometimes, this meant that one must make a commitment to something that cannot be completely established as true by rational and scientific means because its practical consequences are desirable. He thought that religious truths often fell in this category (1897, pp. 11, 56). Pragmatism allowed for the preservation of both religion and "the richest intimacy with the facts" (2003, p. 15), what he called a rich "thick" rather than an abstract and "thin" method (1996b, pp. 308–309). It rejected a priori materialism and the positivist antitheological bias, simply evaluating religion on the basis of its "value for concrete life" such as establishing a basic attitude of trust (1996b, pp. 33, 120; 2003, p. 36).

4.2.2   The Varieties of Religious Experience

James most influential treatment of religion has been his Gifford lectures, which were based in part on material from his 1896 Lowell Institute lectures (Taylor, 1984). These later became the *Varieties of Religious Experience* (James, 1961).

4.2.2.1 Approach

The methodology of the *Varieties* reflects the radical empirical stance taken by James and his acceptance of pure experience—including religious experience—as a fundamental datum for investigation. James saw the essence of religion as lying in these experiences rather than in some particular set of beliefs (Brown, 2000, p. 13). His method also reflects his pluralistic philosophy in that he assumed that there would be no single universal model of religious experience that would exactly fit each individual. Accordingly, he used what today would be called a qualitative approach, reviewing individual accounts of religious experiences collected by others and building a narrative that picked out patterns without leaving out the richness of the individual account (Mounce, 1997, pp. 103–104).

4.2.2.2 Key Points

Religion as individual feeling. Like the liberal Protestant theologian Friedrich Schleiermacher (1999), and many others of the 19th century, James valued passion, energy, and vitality and thought that these feelings lay at the basis of religion. For James, religious feeling was foremost a personal and individual matter. Each individual had his or her own character structure with a different susceptibility to emotional excitement and associated impulses and inhibitions. In addition, each person had different abilities and needs so that the function of religion was different for everyone, and its pattern did not conform to a particular set of stages. He saw the institutional aspect of religion as problematic and less fundamental than the personal, although he acknowledged that individual religion does not have the richness and complexity of institutional religion. Given his emphasis on feeling and the individual, religion for James became "the feelings, acts, and experiences of individual men in their solitude, so far as they apprehend themselves to stand in relation to whatever they may consider the divine" (1961, p. 42).

Types of religious experiences. The *Varieties* is rich with personal accounts of many kinds of religious experiences. However, two were of particular interest to him. The first is what he called "the reality of the unseen," a sense of a very real but immaterial presence in the world (1961, p. 62). This experience could be brief or habitual, but it had the potential to be profoundly motivating beyond the power of rationality, leading to "belief that there is an unseen order, and that our supreme good lies in harmoniously adjusting ourselves thereto" (1961, p. 59). The second kind of experience was the mystical experience. Mystical experiences involve a unity consciousness in which one experiences an insight and reconciliation of opposites (see Box 4.1). They are real experiences, a kind of subliminal perception as valid as scientific truth, although we should not necessarily accept them uncritically (Taves, 1999, p. 263).

Religious types and psychopathology. James gave the relationship between psychopathology and religion a central place in his theory of religious experience. He noted that many great religious figures were very sensitive and had "abnormal psychic visitations," as well as a conflicted and melancholy inner life (1961, p. 25). He thought that emotionally and attitudinally, people lay on a continuum between two types. The **healthy-minded** were people who had a natural sense of happiness and optimism, believing that things are good and that evil can be overcome. On the other hand, the **sick-souled** person sees life as insecure with real evil as an essential part of things. James believed that the sick-souled individual had a more complete but also more conflicted view of the world, so that they often struggled with melancholia and philosophical pessimism. Religious experience and mystical states could help the sick-souled person, because they have an optimistic quality and help us accept our ultimate dependence on the universe. So in general, James saw religion not as *causing* emotional problems but as a way of *responding* to them. He saw the religious point of view as a sympathetic one wanting intimacy with the universe and struggling against pessimism, while antireligious materialism was aligned with cynicism. He thought that most people at heart were in need of this kind of intimate relationship (1996b, p. 33).

Conversion and religious transformation. James felt that individuals, especially the sick-souled, experienced life as a divided self and looked for a way to achieve unification. He saw religion as one way to achieve this inner unity. Those who were able to invest their excitement and "the habitual center of [their] personal energy" into a religious system (1961, p. 165) would experience a religious **conversion**, a gradual or sudden change which led to a new personal equilibrium and level of spiritual vitality. He thought that some people could never have this type of experience, either due to intellectual reasons such as a commitment to materialism, or because they were incapable of religious sensibility or emotion. James rejected the idea that there is some distinctive feature of the new person after conversion. Those who are healthy-minded or sick-souled will remain that way, but the latter would now have more resources to combat their essential pessimism.

The value of religion. James evaluated the value of religion using his pragmatic maxim. Along with the "luminousness" and philosophical reasonableness of ideas (1961, p. 33), he thought we should judge religion on the basis of its practical effect. James believed that the key impact of religion on the individual lay in the development of **saintliness**, a condition that occurs when our personal energy becomes centered on the spiritual. For James, saintliness has practical consequences that could be found in all religions, such as sacrifice and self-surrender, patience and fortitude, and purity of spirit and increasing charity (Higgins-D'Alessandro & Cecero, 2003). However, his view of the value of saintliness was deeply influenced by his pluralistic philosophy and individualism. While he approved of the characteristics of saintliness like purity, charity, and feelings of harmony, he thought one should not be too saintly. He thought that spiritual excitement needed to be balanced by other things, or it will become excessive, interfering with our mission and vocation in life.

4.2.3 Influence and Critique

The views of James on religion and his phenomenological method were very influential and helped open the area to later investigation. His description of sick-souled mysticism found in figures like Paul, Augustine, Luther, and Kierkegaard influenced 20th-century theologians like Niebuhr and Tillich and has influenced virtually all psychological treatments of the topic of religious experience (Edie, 1987, p. vii; Browning, 1980, pp. 249, 262). James' method mirrored the dialectical quality of his philosophy; it developed a central vision but retained flexibility, allowing conflicting ideas to remain unresolved and in tension with each other. This approach anticipates modern hermeneutic thought (e.g., James, 2003, pp. 3–5; Leary, 2003; Seigfried, 1990, pp. 198–199; see Sections 1.6.2, 6.3.2). However, many aspects of James' approach to psychology and religious experience were displaced as positivism and behaviorism became dominant in psychology. His work has been criticized on a number of fronts (Wulff, 1997, pp. 499–502). Some significant points that recur in the literature include the following:

1. James drew selectively from religious traditions, mostly focusing on Protestant Christianity and leaving out altogether some major religious groups like classical Buddhism (Stace, 1960a, p. 43).
2. While James attempted to portray individuals in a rich descriptive manner, his descriptions decontextualized them from religious institutions, which is not how religious experience functions for most people (Gale, 1999, p. 265; Taylor, 2002,

p. 23). Capps (1997b, pp. 25–26) argues that virtually every account cited by James supports the view that there is no purely individual, decontextualized religious experience.

3. Some believe James overemphasized the role of feeling in religion. For instance, Vergote (1997, pp. 135–139; cf. Belzen, 1999) complains that identifying religious experiences as a type of emotional intensity is simplistic and expands the definition of religion too much, making it difficult to justify what is meant by "religious."

4. James' philosophical presuppositions and agenda have also been criticized. It is interesting to note that he viewed himself as collecting data without any *a priori* system (1961, p. 261) and just letting experience speak for itself, when it is quite obvious that his definitions, views of empiricism, and pluralism all had a large impact on his work. Contemporaries like Leuba also criticized his religious agenda and attacked James for attempting to use reports of religious experience to support the idea of a spiritual reality beyond that of the psychological or rational (James, 1996a, p. 274).

4.3 Perennial and Universal Views

While James believed in a pluralistic universe, he also talked about a core in religious experience that cuts across personal and religious backgrounds. The idea that there is a shared body of universally true and valid knowledge in all religious traditions and experiences throughout history is called the **perennial philosophy** (Schuon, 1984, 2007). While philosophers such as Leibniz had used the term since the 18th century, it was popularized in the 20th century by Aldous Huxley (2004), who characterized the philosophy as holding the following positions:

1. The ultimate goal of life is "liberation and enlightenment." This is achieved by developing one's spiritual life through coming to a unitive personal knowledge and harmonious relation with the "spiritual Ground of things" (2004, pp. 65, 76–79). This condition is a higher state of development beyond the ordinary (Shapiro & Walsh, 2003).

2. Salvation is not found in material possessions or social progress, but through an inner journey that leads us to the Ground. This journey demands an attitude of selflessness, purity of heart, and trust toward others and the world. It also requires participation in spiritual disciplines and practices that help us to die to ourselves and eliminate the "self-regarding ego" that separates us from the Ground. Progress in the journey reflects back upon our lives in a reciprocal manner, leading to the development of charity, humility, and peacefulness. Religions are ideally a means to these ends, although each religion overlays the perennial philosophy with unnecessary beliefs and practices.

3. The Absolute or God we seek in salvation is timeless and more real than the world as we observe it in our daily life. It is ineffable in terms of normal rational

thought but contrary to Kant can be "directly experienced and realized" (2004, p. 21) especially in experiences of union.

4. This Absolute Ground has a personal, loving quality, and gives spiritual grace to help us achieve our final end and return to the Ground. The Ground can sometimes be found among us in incarnations or **avatars** and can be seen in divinized human beings who have followed a contemplative path.

Perennialists vary according to whether they believe there are one or several cores to religious experience. They also disagree about the extent to which religious tradition plays a role in these experiences (Parsons, 1999, pp. 110–115). Often, they express their belief saying that all traditions share a similar aim in terms of mystical experience but provide unique paths to the same summit (e.g., Hayes, 1997; Coomaraswamy, 2007; Stoddart, 2007). This view is particularly evident among scholars influenced by Hinduism and to a lesser extent by Islamic thought. Some perennialists such as the *traditionalist school* headed by Frithjof Schuon argue that religious traditions are of inherent value because they contain within them a core of universal truths and practices that assist believers in connecting themselves to what is Real. Writers in this version of perennialism value the **exoteric** outer forms of religion as possessing symbolic power, as well as the more universal **esoteric** inner truth gained through immediate experience of the transcendent. The former provides a means for the average person to relate to transcendence, while the latter is a path for an elite few (Schuon, 1984; Minnaar, 2007; Cutsinger, 2002; cf. al-'Arabi, 1980, pp. 131–132, 279–282; Shah-Kazemi, 2006, p. 250). Psychoanalytic approaches to mysticism have been strongly influenced by the perceived legitimacy and value of mystical ways of knowing and have tended to respond to and follow perennialist views of religious experience (Parsons, 1999, pp. 109–115). Most transpersonal psychologists hold to some degree the main tenants of the perennial philosophy. However, Funk (1994) identifies a number of differences of opinion among transpersonal thinkers, including the following:

- The validity of postmodern constructionism (see Section 6.3.1) that has challenged the idea of the universality of experience
- How various states of consciousness are to be ordered in relation to each other
- The relationship of personal material to transpersonal material
- How the highest level of development or consciousness should be conceptualized

4.3.1 Plotinus

The work of Plotinus (ca. 204–270) is cited by many scholars as one of the early expositions of the perennial philosophy. He is important in the Christian tradition because his mystical and philosophical work the *Enneads* influenced Augustine and the apophatic writings of other early Christian writers (Majercik, 1995; Hadot, Davidson, & Wissing, 1990; Hadot, 1993; Davidson, 1990). His writings present a vision of the spiritual seeker as one who escapes from the world to seek union with the Divine (Hadot, 1986a).

Connectedness of all things. Plotinus (1991) believed that higher reality beyond the realm of matter consisted of three *Primals* or fundamental principles upon which everything is based. The highest is a primal simple unity or One. From this One comes two other primals, the Logos or Intellectual Principle and the World Soul that gives form to matter and reason to life. Our reason is a reflection of this Logos. Matter is distant from higher reality but is also related to it and because of this is not evil. Evil instead is an absence or a falling short of the Good that lies at the heart of existence.

Approaching the One. Some people are able to approach the One from which we have descended. They have the inborn "nature of a lover" and a philosophical temperament (1991, p. 258), as well as courage for the task and the ability to undertake the moral discipline necessary to purify and free the soul from the passions. Our love and yearning for the One are based on a recognition of kinship and the Universal Love of the One for us. The seeker begins the path through a contemplation of external beauty, but must go beyond this, withdrawing within to contemplate the beauty of the soul and eventually to the source of its loveliness. The journey involves a retreat within oneself that also results in self-knowledge and self-awareness, and because of our essential nature with the One, "to find ourselves is to know our source" (1991, p. 544). As we progress, our souls become like a mirror, reflecting this ultimate good and beauty.

The experience of Union. The experience of Union with the One is a vision that cannot be produced by our own effort; we can only prepare ourselves and then wait for it. In absorbed contemplation there is an ineffable vision of light beyond all statements, knowing and objective thought, so that we join with the One in nondifferentiated unity. This is a state of utter simplicity, rest, and stillness without passion, desire, or movement; the self disappears and there is no diversity. We are able to experience this vision because we have something of the supreme principle within us. The experience cannot be described in a positive manner: "if we are led to think positively of The One, name and thing, there would be more truth in silence" (1991, p. 398).

4.3.2 von Hugel, Pathology, and Religious Experience

The idea of a universal core to religious experience dominated psychological and religious treatments of the topic during the first half of the 20th century. These early works were also concerned about the relationship between religious experience or mysticism and psychopathology. One of the most interesting early treatments of this was the study of the Christian mystic Catherine of Genoa (1447–1510) by the German lay Catholic scholar Friedrich von Hugel (1852–1925).

4.3.2.1 von Hugel on Mysticism in Catherine of Genoa

Von Hugel (1999) thought there were 3 elements of religion: (1) the *institutional and historical* involving tradition, sense and memory, a child's way of getting religion;

(2) the *synthetic-philosophical* using reasoned argument as in formal theological discussions, appropriate for youth; and (3) the *mystical and experimental,* involving feelings states and appropriate for the mature adult. Von Hugel thought that all three are necessary and present in religious traditions like Christianity and that religious crises occur as people pass from one stage to the next (cf. Pratt, 1971). These stages also interact in complex and important ways. He did not believe that there was a "specifically distinct, self-sufficing, purely Mystical mode of apprehending Reality" (1999, p. 283) because the non-mystical always contains a mystical component and vice versa. While true mystics are rare, they offer much because regardless of their religious tradition they point to the presence of the Infinite. However, each individual mystic is different and will possess God differently, focusing more on the relationship with God or God's oneness, experiencing different stages, as well as sudden or gradual modes of progression.

Von Hugel thought that the mystical life went beyond mere mystical experiences to involve the deepest activity of the soul. He believed the key to the spiritual life of the true mystic is their ability to maintain a complex balance between different opposing tendencies, such as initiative and passivity or love and contemplation. In a lack of balance, passivity could become **quietism**, a fanatical concentration on the inner life to the exclusion of the important normal means and duties of human and religious life, such as prayer, religious practice, and moral action.

4.3.2.2 Psychopathology and Mysticism

Catherine of Genoa struggled with depression and experienced unusual ecstatic and physical states during her life. Like James, Von Hugel saw her depression as a nervous disorder that was present before her conversion and unrelated to her spiritual life, except as she used it as a catalyst for growth. Von Hugel thought that ecstatic states, including visions or other physical symptoms, were not a pathological condition but were related to a sensitiveness that was part of her temperament and a necessary preexisting affinity for mysticism. Whether they became a positive or destructive influence depended on the ability of the person to filter these experiences and make use of them in constructive ways. Part of Catherine's uniqueness was her ability to judge between healthy and morbid states and use them in ways that promoted positive spiritual growth and ethical fruits. Von Hugel thought that without her strong intelligence, and the institutional support she received from the Church, her temperament would have ruined her or at least made her ineffective.

While some contemporary authors have argued for a more pathological view of some or all aspects of mystical experience (e.g., Frenken, 2000; Kennedy & Drebing, 2002), most empirical work has found that higher scores on mystical and religious experience are related to better subjective well-being (Byrd, Lear, & Schwenka, 2000), higher scores on ego development tests (Hood, 2001, p. 9), as well as higher levels of life satisfaction, life purpose, and religious satisfaction, although it accounts for a relatively modest 10–15% of the variance (Poloma & Pendleton, 1989, 1990). Mystical experiences can also serve as a primary catalyst for spiritual growth (Atchley, 1997a).

While religious experience may not be an expression of pathology, pathology might make religious experience problematic. Hagglund (2001) notes that the sense of timelessness in a unity experience could provoke fear of death or disintegration and loss of self, especially in a person with emotional problems. Mystical experiences could also feed narcissism, or seekers could mistake their pathology for higher states of consciousness (Hunt, 2003; Engler, 1984). Pathology might also be a factor in certain specific types of experience, such as diabolical experiences (Spanos & Moretti, 1988). Motivational changes coming from the experience might lead to loss of interest in old activities and giving up things to pursue new priorities so that the post-mystical life may include important losses as well as gains (Baumeister & Exline, 2002).

4.3.3 Rudolf Otto

During the early to mid-20th century, German scholars studying religion developed a descriptive tradition that made a number of contributions to the study of mysticism (Wulff, 1997). The most well-known works in this tradition are those of Rudolf Otto (1869–1937; see Fig 4.3) and Friedrich Heiler (1892–1967; see Section 13.4.2).

Fig 4.3 *Rudolf Otto.* One of the first scholars to study both Christian and non-Christian religious experience, Otto elaborated a number of key concepts that have been influential in psychology, anthropology and religious studies. Photo courtesy of Universitatsbibliothek Marburg

Otto grew up in a strict evangelical Lutheran home. He traveled widely and was deeply influenced by other religions and points of view—he had his first reported spiritual experience when visiting the Sphinx in Egypt (Almond, 1984, pp. 10–25). Although he had periods of depression, he was a prolific scholar and published a number of works, the most important of which were the *Idea of the Holy* and *Mysticism East and West*, a detailed study of the Christian mystic Meister Eckhart (c. 1260–1327/8) and the nondualist Hindu writer Sankara.

4.3.3.1 The Idea of the Holy

Otto (1950) believed that the religious life has both rational and nonrational aspects. On a rational level we can think about a God who has purposes, morality, and rational qualities, and develop reasoned systems of description about the Divine. However, we also experience a God who is transcendent and beyond normal rationality. Both of these are necessary and support the religious life in different ways. Because of transcendence, we think about God in a different way than other things. Otto believed that each of us had the capacity to develop the **holy** as a "category of interpretation and valuation peculiar to the sphere of religion" (1950, p. 5). Because this category was a unique interpenetration of rational and nonrational he considered it to be *sui generis*, a category that exists on its own and is irreducible to any other. The holy thus has an *a priori* and universal nature, functioning like a Kantian category that allows us to make sense out of the world (Belzen, 1999; see Section 2.2.3). Religion happens when the mind recognizes and attributes holiness to something using this category (Almond, 1984, p. 57).

The **numinous** is the nonrational component of the Holy that is experienced when a religious "object" activates it. Otto identified 3 elements of the numinous (1950, pp 10–36; Hunt, 2003, pp. 16–17):

1. A feeling of creatureliness or nothingness in contrast to "that which is supreme above all creatures" (1950, p. 10).
2. A feeling of *mysterium tremendum*, which includes a sense of mystery, "that which is hidden and esoteric, that which is beyond conception or understanding, extraordinary and familiar" (1950, p. 13), combined with a sense of religious awe or dread, a feeling of an overpowering and consuming presence with great power (cf. Keltner & Haidt, 2003).
3. A feeling of fascination and yearning that can lead to a search for something beyond; thus the experience has a special value that is intrinsic to it. Everyone has the capacity to develop this although not all do.

4.3.3.2 Otto Mysticism East and West

Otto believed that there were universal mystical impulses that were reflected in similarities in descriptions of spiritual experience between different religious traditions.

For instance, he saw many similarities between the Hindu writer Sankara and the Christian preacher Meister Eckhart in their view of religious life as a way of salvation that develops an experience of the ultimate Being. However, he rejected the idea of a mysticism "independent of circumstances and conditions" (1932, p. 139) and saw essential diversity in various expressions of mystical experience. For instance, he distinguished between a "cool" quietistic and monistic mysticism of writers like Sankara that emphasized transcendence and union and a dynamic "hot" mysticism of Eckhart and Ramanuja that focused on a personal and loving relationship with God as a necessary part of unitive experience.

4.3.3.3 Evaluation

Otto's work has had a lasting impact on the psychology and religion dialogue, particularly through the conceptual structures and vocabulary of the numinous that he created. He has also influenced many important figures such as Paul Tillich. However, a number of criticisms have also been voiced.

1. The data he cites in his work is much more supportive of religious diversity than unity, suggesting he really started with the idea rather than finding it in his research (Almond, 1984, pp. 63, 85; cf. Vergote, 1998, pp. 169–171).
2. He neglects some important religious or cultural traditions and settings like Theravada Buddhism that do not fit easily within his framework (Smart, 1996, p. 29; Vergote, 1997, pp. 142–144).
3. Otto focuses on the content rather than the process of religious understanding, making it difficult to understand the symbolic quality of religious concepts and thinking (Vergote, 1998, p. 67).
4. While he claimed to combine rational and nonrational elements, in fact the nonrational dominates the theory and his combination of the two is problematic (Almond, 1984, pp. 26–27).

Like Kant, Otto was concerned about the protection of religion from scientific skepticism. His construction of an *a priori, sui generis* category of the holy was a way of separating religion from scientific naturalism, demonstrating that there is something special about religion that cannot be explained by reducing it to natural categories (Almond, 1984, pp. 54, 91–95). This is an important position that is currently being challenged by some evolutionary theorists (see Section 6.2.3).

4.3.4 W. T. Stace

One of the most important taxonomies of religious experience in the perennial tradition is that of W. T. Stace (1886–1967). He considered mysticism to be a new kind of consciousness whose central characteristic is "an ultimate nonsensuous unity in all things" (1960a, p. 14; cf. 1960b). Like James and the perennialists, Stace saw mystical experiences in various religious traditions as essentially similar (Hood, 2003). He did not see mysticism as a necessarily religious phenomenon, although a description of it in theistic terms as "union with God" is appropriate given the qualities of the experience (1960a, pp. 23–25). He argued that unity mysticism could be broken into two main types of experience. In the **extrovertive** type, the mystic senses unity in the world and a sacredness that is living and present in all things, as in some kinds of nature mystical experiences. **Introvertive** mysticism involves a unitary state of consciousness that is contentless and independent of time sense, a state of pure consciousness and loss of self as in the Void of Buddhism. Both types are universal and lead to a perception of a One or ultimate Unity, which then may be interpreted in theistic or other terms based on the culture and beliefs of the mystic. Either type of experience could include feelings of bliss or joy, holiness, or sacredness, although extrovertive experiences are generally spontaneous, and introvertive ones are acquired through effort. Stace argued that while mystics tend to assume that both kinds of experiences are the same, in reality the extrovertive is an incomplete version of the introvertive and thus should be placed on a lower level. Studies have suggested that the extrovertive type of mysticism is the most common, although within a given religious tradition, the pattern of types of experiences may be affected by cultural background (Lazar, 2004). Intensive introvertive experiences appear to be rather rare, although they are more important in the history of mysticism (Masters & Houston, 2000, p. 307; Gimello, 1978).

Stace's theory has been the target of critique. Some object to the fact that he (along with Zaehner) gives priority to certain kinds of experiences, while scholars like Smart prefer to avoid rankings (Davis, 1989, pp. 188–189). Others (e.g., Watts & Williams, 1988, p. 19) argue that in practice there is no clear distinction between introvertive and extrovertive experience and that it is better to talk in terms of pure experience and interpretive factors. However, the most sustained critique has been from constructionist thought, to which we now turn.

4.4 Constructivism and Responses

Versions of the perennial philosophy lay behind much of the psychological research on religious experience through the end of the 1960s. However, this viewpoint was open to criticism from a couple of theoretical perspectives. First, from a Kantian perspective, all experience of reality is essential subjective, mediated by categories of reason, and thus a universal experience that is independent of a person's beliefs or cognitive structures is impossible. Kant himself thought that mysticism was a kind of fanaticism and false (Perovich, 1990, pp. 241–243). Second, anthropologists and culture specialists note wide differences between religions in different cultures: Christianity is not the same as Buddhism, and a vision of the Virgin Mary is not the same as one of Amida Buddha. It seemed obvious from the data that a person's beliefs and culture formed an essential part of their religious experience, a position known as **constructionism** or constructivism.

4.4.1 Sunden and Role Theory

One of the first theories to look at religious experience from a social perspective was developed by the Swedish psychologist Hjalmar Sunden (1908–1987). He was interested in answering the question, how is it psychologically possible for religion to happen? Rejecting Otto's framework and the idea of an *a priori* category of religious experience, Sunden developed **role theory**, a model that attempted to understand the perception of religious experience from the viewpoint of the social conditions of its production (Kallstad, 1987; Holm, 1995, 1997; Belzen, 1995).

Sunden defines *role* as a sum or group of cultural patterns that act to pattern perception (Stifoss-Hanssen, 1995). In his view, roles are learned from the social environment and create expectations about how others will act. The reference frame of a role provides patterns for giving meaning to perception. In the Christian religious situation, these roles are learned in part from reading stories in the Bible. As we hear these narratives, we take the role of Biblical figures that have particular defined relationships with God. We assume that God will act in a similar manner toward us, for example as a helping partner, and we structure our experiences according to these role assumptions. Learning of these latent roles and adopting them helps us feel connected to people of the past and prepares us for the possibility of religious experience (Wikstrom, 1987; Kallstad, 1987). Sunden opposed trends in modern philosophy, theology, and society that worked to demythologize and take away stories, as these provide the primary cultural resource from which we learn our roles (Belzen, 1995).

Sunden believed that religious experiences occur when a stimulus triggers the activation of latent learned roles, for instance, when old mechanical patterns are not sufficient to cope with a situation. When this occurs, a religious frame of reference is adopted, and we take a dual role of both the figure from the Biblical tradition and also that of God. Suddenly, we see things from God's perspective and perceive the world differently, creating a "phase-shift" and a new experience. Sunden's model is thus very focused on perception. While it is relational it also has a passive quality, although he did comment on active role-taking techniques like the Spiritual Exercises of Ignatius (Wulff, 1997, p. 144; Kallstad, 1987; see Section 13.3.4). His theory differs from other constructivist theories that discuss role from a narrative point of view, as these tend to focus on action and emplotment rather than role (van der Lans, 1987; Belzen, 1995),

4.4.2 The Basic Constructivist Position

One of the first people to articulate an argument against the perennialist position from a Kantian and constructionist perspective was Steven Katz, who argued that there are no pure and unmediated experiences. In his view, "all experience is processed through, organized by, and makes itself available to us in extremely complex, epistemological ways" (Katz, 1978, p. 26). Katz attacked the idea of Stace that it is possible to separate an experience from its interpretation. Rather, he argued that interpretation is an inseparable part of the experience, shaping it and the form of its report in every way, although he did not indicate how that process might work or how religious experience might have a reciprocal effect on interpretive structures (Almond, 1990; Franklin, 1990). According to this position, religious experience in different traditions such as Hinduism and Christianity will be inherently different. He used the example of Buddhism to point out that the tradition has a preexisting understanding that describes what is being sought and the experiential character- istics of what will be found, and that it was bizarre to suppose that these were somehow separate from the actual Buddhist mystical experience. He also attacked the idea of a set of common characteristics for religious experience (e.g., ineffabil- ity, noesis), arguing that these are just an outgrowth from the presuppositions of the investigator and were generally so broad as to be meaningless. He rejected the perennial philosophy and argued for pluralism of mystical experience, accusing the perennialists like Stace, Smart, or James of being overly reductionistic and over- looking evidence for differences (cf. Proudfoot, 1985).

While the difference between an experience that is interpreted and an experi- ence that includes interpretation seems trivial, it has significant implications for scholars like Katz. For instance, he argued that since all parts of experience are dependent on context, "no veridical propositions can be generated on the basis of mystical experience" (Katz, 1978, p. 22). This does not mean that these experi- ences are not true—just that they cannot provide evidence about the ultimate nature of reality, a point of view shared with Buddhism (Lax, 1996). He also argued that since all experience is interpreted and conditioned by the person, a state of pure consciousness is impossible. Exercises like yoga that attempted to decondition con- sciousness were actually just substituting one form of contextual conditioning for another (Woodhouse, 1990).

4.4.3 Objections to Constructivism

Although the constructivist position was the dominant one within religious studies during the latter part of the 20th century, it has been strongly challenged, and a num- ber of scholars are attempting to move beyond it while retaining its insights (Herman, 2000; White, 2000). One response to Katz was led by Robert Forman (1998a). He argued that an important variety of mystical awareness was the Pure Conscious- ness Event (PCE) "a wakeful though contentless (nonintentional) consciousness" (1990a, p. 8). In his view, a PCE is a form of Stace's unitive introvertive mysticism, and that like other ways of knowing it uncovers something that is already present rather than construct it. Forman pointed out that mystics from many traditions such as Buddhism and even Christianity report PCEs (cf. Bernhardt, 1990; Griffiths, 1990). Forman used the example of Eckhart as a Christian mystic who like Paul in the New Testament had PCEs something like Stace's introvertive experience. These PCEs occurred n defiance of their own religious traditions and thus could not have been constructions (1990b, pp. 108–111). The existence of PCEs with no content that could be influenced by cultural or religious interpretation refuted constructivist claims that experience depended solely upon culture or belief.

Other authors have brought up additional objections to the position of Katz. Almond (1990), for instance, pointed out that while the arguments of Katz suggest a *correlation* between context and experience, this does not mean that experience is *entirely produced* by context. In fact, we know that religious creativity and novelty exist because mystics have gone beyond their tradition, sometimes even transforming it. Just because context is involved it does not mean that there are no cross-cultural experiences. Rothberg (1990) attacked the supposed neutrality of the constructivist position, arguing that Katz simply introduces his own set of biases. The constructivist position is based on an implicit rejection of the tradition it is trying to study by invalidating any truth claims and denying the possibility of pure consciousness—a prime tenant of those traditions (Rothberg, 1990; Prigge & Kessler, 1990).

Empirical findings have also challenged extreme constructivist positions like that of Katz. For instance, Ralph Hood has confirmed and replicated in some cross-cultural research the extrovertive-introvertive structure of mystical experience described by Stace. He has also found a religious interpretation factor separate from these that seems partly related to the numinous quality of some mystical experiences (Hood, 1975; Hood et al., 1989; Hood, 2001, p. 34; Hood & Williamson, 2000; Hood, 2003; Hood et al., 2001; Lazar & Kravetz, 2005a, b). These findings challenge the idea that mystical experiences are entirely dependent upon culture or tradition as claimed by Katz. Hood also argues that the existence of a separate interpretive factor supports the idea that spiritual and religious mysticism can be thought of independently from religion, although individuals who separate the two are the exception rather than the rule (Hood, 2003).

4.4.4 Moderate Positions

The debate between perennialists and constructivists shows up the weaknesses and unnecessary reductionism in both positions. It suggests that extreme positions are more about ideology and interpretation than facts (Watts, 2002a, p. 93; Shah-Kazemi, 2006, pp. 229–252). Perennialists have good evidence for the presence of a type of universal mystical experience, but any such account is obviously incomplete without taking constructionist concerns about interpretive structures into account. Likewise, constructivist thought has problems in that it is unable to account for common experiences or explain exactly how cultural interpretive structures function in relation to experience. Christian and Buddhist mysticism may include common experiences but each gets it's meaning from within its own cultural and religious frame of reference (Vergote, 1997, p. 300; e.g., Eugene, 1997). What is needed is a theory that can bridge the two positions. The phenomenology of William James includes both universal and individual features of religious experience, but his theory has some weaknesses as well (Stoeber, 1994, p. 8; Godby, 2002).

An alternative is the intersubjective theory of Mary Frohlich (1993), which is built upon the work of the Catholic theologian Bernard Lonergan. Frohlich begins with the phenomenon of **intersubjectivity** as an experience that unites subjectivity and social context. It is a kind of implicit consciousness and awareness that functions as the background or ground of our intentional, discriminating consciousness, a horizon within which things are experienced. We cannot examine it directly because to do so brings up our normal discriminating consciousness, drowning it out. It has no content and cannot be described, only talked about using apophatic language. This sense of implicit awareness of self and other persons as subjects is what we share with each other. It is a sense of presence. As the experience becomes more intense it helps us transcend ourselves, understand and reach out to others, thus leading to communion. Frohlich believes that a mystical experience represents the far limit of this consciousness. In mysticism, our typical mental life is stilled, and we experience directly the full measure of the implicit, intersubjective consciousness that is at the base of our own awareness and our bonds with others. It is an awareness of communion, a unity experience and state of intersubjectivity that has the potential to produce transformation, shifting the horizon within which we view the world, and increasing both autonomy and communality. In theistic traditions, this unity is experienced as both personal and active; it is the place where we meet God.

Another theoretical approach that offers a bridge between perennialism and constructivism is found in cognitive psychology. From a cognitive processing perspective, constructivism is simply an observation that the organization and interpretation of experience is dependent upon mental processes, beliefs, and attitudes. For instance, Hill (1997) has noted that attitudes affect both the accessibility of experience, the degree of control an individual may have over the experience, and how it is evaluated. Cognitive systems of belief or **schemata**, and **attributions** or explanations we make about events, may have parallel effects (cf. McIntosh, 1997; Ozorak, 1997; Proudfoot & Shaver, 1997; Spilka, Shaver, & Kirkpatrick, 1997). Sunden's role theory has a similar view—that our perception of things influences the meaning they have for us and their effect on our lives (Wikstrom, 1987). However, little has been done to develop cognitive processing models for understanding mystical or religious experience.

4.5 Conversion

The study of conversion experiences has a long history in psychology, probably because of its importance historically in the US among Protestant Christians. **Conversion** is still a phenomenon of great importance today: One third of US adolescents and adults report being born-again Christians or having a conversion experience (Benson, Donahue, & Erickson, 1989; Roof, 1993). It is an emotional experience of awakening, perhaps triggered by an awareness of the reality and nature (love) of God, or our place and purpose in the universe, leading to an act of will and commitment. As a result, there is an "emergence of the self from 'the prison of I-hood'" and senses of liberation/victory and nearness as well as love toward God. This may occur abruptly or develop over time. As a result of the experience, a rereading of one's past can occur (Vergote, 1969, pp. 218–223).

4.5.1 Classical Research: Edwin Starbuck

The first textbook in the psychology of religion was written by Edwin Starbuck (1915), a graduate student of James and Hall who compiled results of hundreds of autobiographical interviews about conversion experiences written in response to a list of questions. Although his findings are over a century old, and were drawn from what today would be an atypical sample of cases from Protestant Christian revivals (Woody, 2003), some ideas emerged from the work that are still widely held by scholars.

1. For most people, conversion is a positive life event, which typically results in substantial moral and psychological changes in the individual, although conversion is just the beginning of a process that carries on into later life. The positive nature of the change in contemporary samples has been documented by Zinnbauer and Pargament (1998), who found that those who had conversion experiences or became more religious without conversion had greater improvement in overall sense of self-confidence, identity, spirituality, and identification with the sacred than those who did not change. Factors related to personality also seem to change, especially behavior, attitudes, goals, identity and one's sense of meaning and purpose rather than basic temperament (Paloutzian, Richardson, & Rambo, 1999). At least some elements of this process are probably not unique to religious change, as models of change developed in psychotherapy research have also been found relevant to religious conversion (e.g., Bockian, Glenwick, & Bernstein, 2005).

2. Conversion usually happens in adolescence, the "great formative period" in religious life (Starbuck, 1915, p. 195) when we transition from childhood to adulthood both physically and psychologically and engage in a larger picture of life, a fact that is still true today (Spilka et al., 2003, p, 347). Conversions do not come out of nowhere but are the end result of a process. In Starbuck's samples, the peak period for conversion was mid-teens. Women reported more emotional storm and stress prior to conversion, men more intellectual doubt.

3. Parental and family environment had a significant impact on conversion. For instance, about 1/3 of the conversion experiences in Starbuck's sample reported gradual acceptance rather than sudden conversion, and this was associated with warm parental religiosity and training. The importance of family environment in the development of religious belief has been replicated in numerous contemporary studies (see Section 8.1).

4. Conversion occurred for a variety of reasons that varied by temperament, but emotion was of fundamental importance. The most common case was an individual who was struggling with a sense of estrangement from God, helplessness, and

depression. Feelings of sadness, anxiety, or helplessness were reported by well over half of the subjects. These negative emotions greatly decreased after the experience. Conversion related to an active struggle for a better life was less common. In contemporary samples, the frequency of people who convert because they are looking for peace and stability remains much higher than those looking for answers to truth questions (Ullman, 1989), and conversion has been found to be consistently related to objective or subjective measures of stress or crisis.

4.5.2 Types and Motifs of Conversion

Late 20th century researches on conversion attempted to expand on the temperamental differences found by Starbuck and identify different types of conversion. Lofland and Skonovd (1981) identified six types of conversion motifs, which they believed varied in a number of ways including involvement of social pressure, temporal duration, type and level of affective arousal, and whether participation or belief came first. The types have been identified in both Christian and Islamic convert groups (Kose & Loewenthal, 2000):

1. *Intellectual*: involving extensive research prior to participation; it is relatively uncommon but increasing in frequency because of increased privatization of religion
2. *Mystical*: less prevalent, a sudden experience with high affective arousal, e.g., Paul on Damascus road; this type was the focus of James and Starbuck
3. *Experimental*: more prevalent recently, active exploration to see whether the religion might be personally beneficial; a lower level of affective arousal than others
4. *Affectional*: motivated by the person's experience of love from a group or individual in the group
5. *Revivalist*: meetings with emotional arousal and crowd conformity effects; less common now in industrialized societies and rare in Islam
6. *Coercive*: involving high social pressure, arousal and negative emotions as in pressure to join a cult; it occurs rarely.

The other prominent theory of conversion types is that of Rambo (1995), who has developed a holistic model of conversion as a change process that includes multiple determinants such as cultural, social, group, personal, psychological, and experiential factors. Like many contemporary theories of conversion, Rambo emphasizes the relational, contextual, and active nature of the person and group in the conversion process. He identified 5 types of conversion: (1) *Tradition transition*, e.g., Christian to Islam; (2) *institution transition* e.g., changing denominations; (3) *gaining an affiliation*; (4) *abandoning previously held beliefs or religious affiliation*; and (5) *intensification or revitalization* of a previous commitment.

Like Lofland and Sconovd, Rambo believes that conversion types and processes change during different periods of history. He also argues that conversion was neither just sudden or gradual, but occurred in a series of interactive and cumulative stages including (1) surrounding *context*, (2) crisis or *catalyst* such as stress or a religious experience, (3) *quest* or active search, (4) *encounter* with a group or individual, (5) *interaction*, including personal relationships and communal rituals, (6) *commitment*, and finally (7) *consequences*. Rambo's model has been tested, for instance, by Kahn and Greene (2004) who factor analyzed a conversion experience questionnaire and found that the dimensions corresponded to the different phases of conversion in the model.

Paloutzian (2005) has recently attempted to develop a meaning system analysis of conversion that would apply to both spiritual and religious change and describe some of the underlying psychological processes in Rambo's model. A **meaning system** is a structure that makes sense out of the world by integrating ideals, feeling, behavior, and motives or ultimate concerns. In this theory, conversion or spiritual change begins when life discrepancies and doubts—limit experiences—force people to construct a new meaning system, which then leads to changes in things connected to the meaning system. Since the components of the system are interconnected, a change in the system will lead to potential changes in all the parts, thus causing the startling shifts that can be seen as a result of conversion experiences. The model has some potential problems, as it assumes that religious and spiritual transformations work by a common psychological process, despite the fact that different religious meaning systems have unique features. It also tends to focus on crisis factors, making it more difficult to understand gradual conversion that may take place over a longer period of time (cf. Gooren, 2007).

4.6 Religious Perspectives

All major religious traditions give religious experience an important role. The traditions that have had the greatest impact in the dialogue with psychology on these issues have been Zen Buddhism and Christianity.

4.6.1 Zen Enlightenment and Nontheistic Religious Experience

All schools of Buddhism give religious experience a central focus, beginning with the enlightenment experience of the Buddha. In Zen Buddhism (see Section 3.2.4), this enlightenment experience is called **satori**. It involves leaving behind our normal state of consciousness to experience a condition of nonduality (Dumoulin, 1979, pp. 15–21). Different schools within Zen interpret the experience and the process of coming to it differently. They also differ from other schools of Buddhism like Pure Land, which is much more widely practiced than traditional monastic Zen in contemporary East Asia (Unno, 2002).

4.6.1.1 The Soto Perspective

In the Soto school of Zen founded by Dogen (1200–1253), the emphasis in experience is on a slow gradual finding of the Buddha nature that is already within the person and can provide the basis for our awakening and realization of freedom. In this view, an enlightenment experience is not a dramatic event that changes our being; it is simply a point when we become aware of our true nature, what is already there. The practice of techniques such as meditation does not produce Buddha nature; however, it can provide the occasion for our mental awakening and realization of its presence. Since it is already present, the experience of awakening can have an effortless quality. Rather than an experience of dramatic insight or exultation, it is an experience of cosmic consciousness and non-differentiation ("nothingness") as opposed to the more personalistic experience common in Christianity. However, for Dogen, the experience is religious in nature because it is connected with religious practice, and religious structures provide important help in providing necessary stability for practice and the experience. Since the enlightenment experience is impermanent like everything else, practice is necessary after satori to help us continue to realize our spirituality and our Buddha nature. In keeping with a nondualistic way of looking at the world, practice and attainment are not really separate. This differs from forms of Buddhism like Pure Land, which believe that some power beyond us is necessary for our realization (Dumoulin, 1979; Abe, 1992a).

4.6.1.2 The Rinzai Perspective

The Rinzai school of Hakuin Ekaku (1685–1768) and D. T. Suzuki (1870–1960) uses more active techniques to break down distinctions and move the person toward an enlightenment experience (Dumoulin, 1979; Suzuki, 2002, pp. 4–124; 1955, pp. 81–82). Like the Soto school, Rinzai practitioners believe that religious problems cannot be solved by deep thinking or reasoning but require a personal experience and a practical approach. However, a definite enlightenment experience is more central in Rinzai Zen than in the Soto school. In Rinzai practice, the first step in the process is to awaken one's consciousness of spiritual issues through active techniques like riddles or **koans** that make us aware of the paradoxes and contradictions in life. The koans shake our confidence in ordinary views of the world, producing a state of Great Doubt that becomes acute as time passes (Gunn, 2000, p. 41). Eventually this drives the person into an active and creative state of satori or pure experience: "the mind seeing itself as reflected in itself" an "act of self-identification, a state of suchness" only possible "when the mind is devoid of all its possible contents except itself" (Suzuki, 2002, p. 23). The experience is more than just a feeling as it also has a noetic quality that one has learned something fundamental. The experience influences our attitude on many levels including moral, spiritual, and metaphysical outlook. It moves us beyond dualistic thinking and can trigger reorganization of the personality.

4.6.1.3 Points of Contact

The Zen experience has similarities to other types of mystical experience. For instance, Suzuki saw parallels between Zen experience and the writings of the Christian mystic Meister Eckhart, who described the mystic experience as a transformative awareness of our identity with God, the Ground of existence (McGinn, 2005, p. 183). According to Eckhart, the experience involves an absorption or sinking into God. It is a stillness and state of self-annihilation, where we find a monistic point from which we see both finite and infinite, creature and God (e.g., Eckhart, 1981, pp. 183–184; 1986, pp. 265–267). Like Dogen, Eckhart speaks of the experience as an awareness of an already existing state of affairs rather than the creation of something new. Suzuki also saw that the intent of Zen practice had parallels with the Spiritual Exercises of Ignatius (see Section 13.3.4). Certainly the Zen experience has parallels with the PCE, and its transiency, ineffability, and noetic qualities place it as a type of mystical experience. However, Suzuki rejected a number of key Christian teachings and was unclear about whether Christian mysticism described the same kind of process and experience as Zen. He felt that terms like "union" when used by Christian mystics imply a difference between us and God and thus are ultimately dualistic and contrary to Zen thought. He also acknowledges that Eckhart—and certainly other Christian mystics—have experiences that are much more personalistic, while the Zen experience is more metaphysical. Eckhart and other Christian mystics generally argue that changes in conscious state are peripheral and not central to the spiritual journey. Eckhart also maintains a sense of transcendence and an emphasis on rationality that is not apparent in many Zen writings (McGinn, 2001, pp. 57–64; e.g., Eckhart, 1981, p. 164; 1986, p. 333). Suzuki attributed this to cultural constraints (Suzuki, 1949, pp. 263–286; 1996, p. 199; 1999, pp. 106–295; 2002, pp. 80, 95; cf. Smart, 1996, p. 49). These discussions highlight the fact that Christian mysticism is based on communion, while maintaining our uniqueness and particularity, rather than a monistic absorption into God or creation. It is primarily a relational phenomenon rather than an experience of consciousness (Zizioulas, 2006, pp. 292–306).

Erich Fromm (see Section 1.4.4) was deeply influenced by Suzuki, and the two men worked to find parallels between Zen thought and psychoanalysis (Fader, 1986; Fromm, 1986). Fromm saw monotheistic religion as dead, but Zen Buddhism was of interest because it could provide the rationality and personal independence of the monotheistic outlook, while giving meaningful answers to the questions of life (Suzuki, Fromm, & DeMartino, 1960). In terms of specific parallels between Zen and psychoanalysis, Fromm pointed out that both emphasize knowledge and grasping the truth of things as they are as a way to transformation or transcendence. They both see the need to go beyond intellectual knowledge and conscious thought to a more experiential awareness. In Fromm's psychological language, satori was a state of complete attunement to reality that enlarges our consciousness and leads to a character transformation in which self-centeredness is left behind. Both he and Suzuki saw a parallel between the Zen experience of new perceptions about reality, and the psychoanalytic process of things emerging into awareness from the unconscious. However, they also acknowledged substantial differences. Suzuki admitted that in Zen the unconscious or "no mind" is not a psychological category but a metaphysical one—it is ultimate reality perceived apart from discrimination (Suzuki, 1996, pp. 185–191). Fromm acknowledged that the two fields used different methods—meditation and koan practice versus psychoanalysis—and also admitted that the goals of Zen were more radical. So, while Fromm and Suzuki saw Zen and psychoanalysis as congenial, their work highlights important differences between the two ways of thought.

The comparisons that Suzuki and Fromm made between Zen, psychoanalysis, and Christianity are potentially problematic due to their limited understanding of both Zen and Christianity. Fromm acknowledged that his understanding of Zen was incomplete (Fader, 1986), and many contemporary scholars have criticized Suzuki's understanding of Zen as deficient. He is often thought to have painted Zen in an oversimplified and anti-intellectual way tailored to suit Western interests at the time he wrote (Keenan, 2007; cf. Suzuki, 1986a,b; 1999, p. 285). It is also true that Suzuki primarily presented Rinzai Zen to his readers so that the important works of others like Dogen and the Soto school were neglected (Abe, 1986). In particular, he argued strongly for the suddenness of enlightenment, neglecting the rich developmental tradition found in Soto thought (1949, pp. 363–364; 1999, p. 104).

4.6.2 Jonathan Edwards and the Religious Affections

The famous early American theologian Jonathan Edwards (see Fig 4.4) articulates a Christian point of view on religious experience. For Edwards, the question of religious experience was "What is the nature of true religion? And wherein do lie the distinguishing notes of that virtue and holiness that is acceptable in the sight of

Fig 4.4 *Jonathan Edwards.* Thought by many to be the most important American theologian, Edwards wrote extensively about religious experience and its role in the Christian life. Printed by permission of the Jonathan Edwards Center, Yale University

God?" (2004, p. 15). The conclusion of his work was that "True Religion, in great part, consists in Holy Affections" (2004, p. 23). While this sounds like Edwards is building an emotional view of religion similar to Von Hugel or Otto, Edwards had a much broader view of religious experience. For Edwards, affections were vigorous exercises of our heart (2004, pp. 24–25) that involve all aspects of the person including body and spirit, feeling, and action. In this anti-dualistic view, action must be motivated by emotion, and true affections will be more than feelings but also have an active component.

4.6.2.1 Detecting True and False Affections

While Edwards believed that true religion requires affections, he did not believe that all affections are true religion, and that learning to distinguish "the wheat and the chaff" (2004, p. 50) was vital to the Christian life. Edwards approached the topic by comparing the experience of the spiritual and natural person. The *spiritual person* is the one who believes in Christ and is a recipient of the Spirit of God with whom they have an inner relation that is special and personal. Along with this comes a special knowledge or understanding and the ability to judge, as well as special virtues like meekness. This is in opposition to the carnal or *natural person*, who is prideful, self-righteous, and trusts in his or her own wisdom. The spiritual person is not the creation of a new psychological nature but "a new foundation laid in the nature of the soul" that allows us to use our abilities in different ways and inclines us toward different kinds of actions (2004, p. 134).

Edwards did not think that all religious experiences were necessarily genuine; it was the source of the affections that ultimately determined their value. Natural people can have religious affections just like the spiritual person. However, the experience of the natural person lacks a spiritual sense and is really just a reflection of mental or physical weakness, as in the experience of melancholy. Nor is a sense of assurance a good guide, because the prideful natural person can be blinded by hypocrisy and lack of self judgment, while the true saint may be plagued with doubts which can only be overcome through action and pressing on in one's spiritual life and development. Edwards was thus acutely aware of the human ability to create illusion and self-justification.

What are the positive characteristics of truly religious affections? Edwards thought that first of all they have to do with the motives we bring to the experience. He said: "The primary ground of gracious affections is the transcendently excellent and amiable nature of divine things as they are in themselves and not any conceived relation they bear to self or self interest" (2004, p. 165). One should seek the Divine for its own sake and qualities, and the experience of a transcendent God will help us develop a sense of humility and a softening of the heart that would assist us in our moral progress. People with holy affections feel that grace and power are given to them from the outside. They have an attitude of humility toward their experience.

Second, Edwards found the mark of genuine religious affections in their effects. Occasionally affections might bring about dramatic events, but most of its effects were practical changes in the life of the person. These might include a decrease in confusion and the development of spiritual understanding or moral changes in the person's conduct and the production of different desires. He thus rejected any kind of a division between Christian religious experience and practice. It was the effect rather than the manner of its coming that determined whether an affection was a genuine experience. These outer effects could and should be judged by the community, but the inner experience could only be judged by the persons themselves, and was often best done in retrospect when they could see the long-term impact of the experience. Others should not attempt this, as we do not have the wisdom to judge others.

4.6.2.2 Conversion

Edwards saw conversion as an affective and moral experience, a great and universal change turning the individual from sin to God and holiness. The affective quality of the experience was important but variable. Conversion could be preceded by intensely negative feelings of wretchedness and awareness of personal evil but not always. Post-experience changes and feelings of comfort and joy were common but not necessarily evidence of conversion, and the absence of these stages is not a sign that a genuine conversion has not taken place. What is important is not the order of doing but "the spiritual and divine nature of the work *done*, and effect *wrought*" (2004, p. 91). In particular, one needed to look not at transient effects but the spirit and temper of the person over the long term.

4.7 Conclusion

Key issue: *Any detailed and accurate understanding of religious experience will find both universal and tradition-specific characteristics.*

The perennialist-constructivist debate continues to divide scholars seeking to expand our understanding of religious experience. Psychologists have often taken a modernist or perennialist view of the topic, seeing these experiences as the working out of universal natural law. In this view, Christian and Buddhist religious experiences are the same in all their important characteristics. Religious studies scholars, on the other hand, have been profoundly influenced by the postmodern critique, and in recent years have followed the constructionist position and attempted to understand religious experience within its surround of culture and belief. The idea of universal natural laws of religious experience or even comparisons between different cultural groups can become nonsensical in this point of view. Fortunately, there is movement toward a middle position that would allow psychologists, religious studies scholars, and theologians to have a more constructive dialogue. As we saw in Chapter 3, all religious traditions are not alike and there are many indications that the modernist position leaves out important aspects of the story. However, extreme constructivism assumes that different religious traditions and cultures are completely isolated from each other. Many scholars have pointed out that this is simply not the case. While it is true that culture and belief affect our interpretation of events, it is possible to enter into a sensitive investigation of the experiences of others and to have a dialogue with them about common concerns.

Another issue related to the perennialist view of religion is the extent to which religion or spirituality is universal in nature. If religious experience is an essential part of authentic religion, then religion is not universal, as some people will never have a "religious" experience. Different individuals seem to have different levels of ability to perceive and think in religious ways (Watts & Williams, 1988, p. 5), suggesting that for some religion is not a "natural" way of being. However, if spirituality is thought of as a relationship to transcendence or immanence, then presumably these relationships are ontological—built into the world—and while they may be ignored they cannot be escaped.

A final issue has to do with the limits of phenomenology. Psychologists have always been keenly aware of the limits and disadvantages of the phenomenological method. It is difficult for people to accurately report their experience and for others to understand it. This issue is also important from a theological perspective, because if God or the object of religion is truly beyond description, the knowledge we gain from analysis of accounts of our experience of the divine will always be incomplete. Yet to the extent that God can be thought of as real and active in the world, description is possible and tells us valuable things about the nature of the Divine (Mensch, 2005).

Chapter 5
Psychodynamic and Relational Approaches

Two years before William James published his classic *Varieties of Religious Experience*, a relatively unknown doctor named Sigmund Freud authored his first great work, *The Interpretation of Dreams*, ushering in the new field of psychodynamic psychology. Ten years later, Freud published *Totem and Taboo*, his first major work that attempted an analysis of religion. In the following years, the work of Freud and other psychodynamic theorists would provide a rich—and sometime contentious—platform for a religion-psychology dialogue.

Psychodynamic theories focus on cognitive, emotional, and relational dynamics within the individual, especially mental processes that are unconscious and outside of awareness. In particular, psychodynamic approaches focus on one or more of three different types of processes: (1) **drives** or instinctual processes that motivate behavior, (2) **structures** or internal patterns that provide organization for the personality, and (3) relations between the self and external or internal objects. Each of these types of processes has provided a basis for a psychological perspective on religion. In this chapter, we will consider Freud's drive-oriented approach to religion, the theory of Erik Erikson that has important structural features, and the object-relational theories of Harry Guntrip and David Winnicott. We will also consider the unique contributions of the psychodynamic theorist Carl Jung.

5.1 Sigmund Freud: Master of Suspicion

Sigmund Freud (1856–1939) was no friend to religion from the beginning of his career. Along with personal experiences that alienated him from Christianity, he was an admirer of some of the most important opponents to traditional religion such as Ludwig Feuerbach and Friedrich Nietzsche. His mentor Ernst Brücke was Vienna's most ardent positivist and a reductive materialist (Gay, 1998, pp. 12–34; Ramzy, 1977). Freud was thus influenced by Comtean positivism, which acted to constrain his choices in the development of psychoanalysis so that spiritual issues were neglected or reduced to material processes (Domenjo, 2000; Grotstein, 1992). Positivism carried with it a view of history that placed religion as a primitive phenomenon destined to be replaced by science, an idea that Freud elaborated in his work (see Section 2.3) (Fig. 5.1).

J.M. Nelson, *Psychology, Religion, and Spirituality,*
DOI 10.1007/978-0-387-87573-6_0, @ Springer Science+Business Media, LLC 2009

Fig. 5.1 *Sigmund Freud.*
One of the most influential
figures of the 20th century,
Freud had generally negative
views on religion, although
many theologians appreciated
aspects of his work. Photo
courtesy of Mary Evans
Picture Library

Freud's initial outline for his vision is contained in the manuscript *Project for a Scientific Psychology* (1953). In this work, Freud developed the idea that the psyche could be entirely described using material processes that operated in the mechanistic fashion of 19th-century physics. The activity of the human psyche was simply "neuronal motion" (1953, p. 310). This material basis of his theory continued to be a principle in his later work, even if it was not explicitly articulated (Mackay, 1989, p. 222). Along with positivist and materialist ideas Freud also adopted the doctrine of **recapitulation**, the idea that the stages of development in human evolution, including psychological and cultural evolution, are repeated in the stages of development of each human being.

5.1.1 Basic Concepts

Freud thought that all behavior was motivated by instinctual drives, particularly forces related to sexuality and aggression. He thought these drives were primarily active at the **unconscious** level of the personality, completely outside our awareness but able to govern our behavior. These drives govern the **id** or instinctual part of the psyche, which along with the **superego** or conscience and the **ego** or executive function make up the three main structures of the personality. The drives express themselves in different ways depending on the person's stage of development. For instance, Freud thought that around age 4 or 5 the sexual drive sets up an unconscious attraction between boys and their mother, leading to competition with the father and unconscious fantasies of murder. He termed this the **Oedipus complex**. Many of these urges are culturally inappropriate and threatening, so the ego utilizes **defense mechanisms** to try to express them in more socially approved ways. For instance, during **projection** the ego attributes unacceptable unconscious feelings like anger to other people or things.

5.1.2   Views on Religion

Freud developed positions on the cultural origins of religion, as well as its genesis in the individual (Watts & Williams, 1988, p. 24). He had a long-standing interest in culture and in *Totem and Taboo* (1950) offered a psychoanalytic explanation for the **totem**, a special sacred object of devotion found in many societies that serves as a guardian spirit or helper. Totems are the focus of a number of prohibitions or restrictions for a group, and Freud argued that these prohibitions were the original source of many human moral ideas, such as the Kantian categorical imperative and incest taboos (see Section 2.2.3). While totems are usually animals or other natural objects, Freud believed that sometime in the distant human past there existed a "primal father" who served as a totem for a group but was murdered by them. He thought that the root form of every religion was a longing for this father and that religious ceremonies of atonement or celebration are recapitulations of the ancient murder. God is simply a replacement for the totem animal and father, although Freud did not know the source of this new idea. The assumption behind his idea is that there must exist a collective mind that retains a sense of guilt over the original murder, as well as progress made in human evolution. He thought that this collective mind developed by an unconscious reading of other people through their reactions. In essence, Freud argued that "God" is a projection of these human figures, a view that has some parallels in Epicurean philosophy (Long, 1986).

In the 1920s, Freud wrote about his concerns for the future of civilization and its ability to make continued material progress. In *The Future of an Illusion* (1961b) he built a case for the elimination of religion that has many similarities with Comte's Law of Three Stages. Freud argued that a key role of civilization is to combat and tame nature, which he viewed as a cold cruel destroyer that we must defend against. Our feelings of helplessness in the world are similar to our childhood feelings that our parents—especially the father—help us to combat. The value of religious ideas is that they offer a similar kind of protection and are thus really a form of a longing for a protective father. However, these traditional beliefs are not to be accepted because of their contradictions and lack of confirmation. Instead, human reasoning—Logos—can be our god, and we must turn to science as the only way can know about reality outside of ourselves. Religion retards the intellectual development of the individual, and it is ineffective as it has not made us happy. Instead, science should replace it. Freud believed that such antireligious ideas should be kept away from the masses but that eventually a turning away from religion is bound to occur. It will be difficult for those brought up with religion, but for others "sensibly brought up" the prospects may be better. While we must admit our "insignificance in the machinery of the universe" we can leave behind infantile attachment to a good God and move to confront the hostile world using our own resources, hopefully with the increased power that science will provide and a state of resigned endurance for things that cannot be changed (1961b, p. 63). Freud's thought here echoed that of Feuerbach (1957), who had argued the God is just a representation of a purified human nature and that reason needs to be applied to religion to destroy illusions that deprive us of power. Erik Fromm also held similar views, as he believed that God is really a human creation and a representation of our potential (Cooper 2006, p. 117).

Freud's theory of religion did not address the issue of religious experience. Soon after the publication of *The Future of an Illusion*, the French writer Romain Rolland sent Freud a letter asking about an unbounded, "oceanic feeling" that occurs in many people and is used as a source of energy in many religions. Freud responded to this by saying that he could not discover such a feeling in himself but that he presumed it was a regression to an early undifferentiated state of ego-feeling and narcissism that later became connected with religion. Thus, he minimized or denied the possibility of a state of pure consciousness or nonsensory and nonintellectual experience of reality (Leavy, 1995, p. 349). He rejected the idea that this could be a source for religion, thinking that nothing could be stronger than the sense of help-lessness sustained by the fear of superior powers (1961a, pp. 11–21).

5.1.3 Impact and Evaluation

As might be expected, Freud's ideas on religion met with some critical response from theologians. Albert Outler sardonically remarked, "If religious faith reflects an infantile regression, so [Freud's] naturalistic faith looks a good deal like the ado-lescent rejection of the father…" (Outler, 1954, p. 252). Freud's view of ethics as simply a regret for primal murder or other unacceptable desires challenged deeply held beliefs of many Christian groups, who believed that moral laws were univer-sal imperatives of divine origin (MacIntyre & Ricoeur, 1969; Pannenberg, 1983, pp. 19–20). However, other religious writers, particularly liberal Protestants, had more sympathy for Freud's work. These writers recognized that religion could have illusion connected with it and found that Freud's work provided some useful ways of understanding this. They also appreciated the fact that psychodynamic theory con-tains a relational component that can be useful in the analysis of religious experience and development (Lietaer & Corveleyn, 1995; Jonte-Pace, 1999; Homans, 1970, pp. 14–15, 1968b). Niebuhr (1957, pp. 260–270) liked Freud's realistic view of the limits of reason, and pessimism is certainly the dominant tone in much of Freud's work (Burns-Smith, 1999). However, Niebuhr rejected Freud's naturalism as being unable to deal with the issues of transcendent freedom and historical context in their creative and destructive possibilities. Maritain (1957) argued that the problem with Freud was not his psychology but his metaphysical assumptions and rationalism that turned useful insights into reductionistic, hardened positions of limited validity.

Most of Freud's theory—including the details of his views on religion—is no longer widely accepted within psychology (Watts & Williams, 1988, pp. 26–28). Some of his basic premises about the material nature of brain processes and the doctrine of recapitulation have been rejected by modern biology and neuroscience. In addition, his cultural explanations such as developed in *Totem and Taboo* have been rejected by anthropologists because they lack any supporting data and simply assume at the beginning what he set out to prove (Girard, 1977, p. 193). Although many academics followed Freud in associating religion with pathology, some prominent scholars like Karl Jaspers rejected his conclusions and argued that psychopathology in religion was mostly to be found among fringe supporters (Jaspers, 1963, pp. 723–724). Nor does Freud's own psychoanalytic data provide support for his views on religion; he himself admitted that his religious views were not based upon his psychoanalytic investigations but were simply a restatement of older ideas using a psychological language and framework (Ricoeur, 1970, p. 234). Many today would agree with Belzen that Freud "transgressed flagrantly the frontiers of his professional competence" (Belzen, 1996, p. 28). At best his observations only apply to aspects of religion that appear at an immature stage in development (Vergote, 1969, p. 136).

A number of scholars have attempted to expand Freudian theory and apply it in a more constructive way to religion. One of the most active of these has been the Jesuit psychoanalyst William Meissner (1984). In his view, psychoanalysis, if properly expanded, can go beyond some of Freud's errors or religious prejudices and develop a respectful view that can coexist with and reinforce a religious perspective. Meissner accepts Freud's insight that religion can have an illusionary quality but points out that (1) this is only one type of religion or religious experience and that a consideration of development beyond infantile levels reveals many other more sophisticated types of experience; (2) illusion is not the same as delusion—it retains ties to reality but transforms it in ways that give it significance and is thus a vital and constructive part of human experience; and (3) Freud's analysis focuses exclusively on the father, while clearly the mother and other models are also important in religious development and experience.

Meissner argues that the philosophical neutrality of science is a myth, and he takes issue with two of Freud's assumptions. First, he challenges Freud's passive and mechanistic view of the human person, which does not fit the active, open, dynamic quality of how people really live. Second, he disputed the reductionistic tendencies in Freud's system. His objection to reductionism is its abstractionist quality, which removes psychoanalysis from lived experience. This empties the theory of meaning, giving it less value and validity. It also ignores the fact that the study of the psyche is interpretive in nature and not able to completely separate the observer and observed. By contrast, religion is sometimes excessively anti-reductionist, so psychoanalysis and religion have the potential to complement each other. However, Meissner admitted that the tension between religious and psychoanalytic views might not be resolvable due to the supernaturalistic quality of some aspects of religion such as mystical experience. Meissner went on to develop a theory of religious development that combined some traditional psychoanalytic ideas with concepts from object relations theory.

5.2 Carl Jung and Archetypal Religion

Carl Jung (1875–1961) had a diverse personal and professional background that was reflected in his work. His father was a Swiss Protestant minister and his mother's side of the family had strong interests in spiritualism and the occult. Ultimately, he rejected his father's Christianity but continued to be deeply influenced by Christian thought, Eastern religions, and spiritualism, all of which figure prominently in his theories (Koss-Chioino, 2003; Jung, 1989, p. 210; Bishop, 1999; Davis, 1996). In adulthood, he was exposed to Hinduism, Buddhism, and especially Taoism with its emphasis on the pairing of opposites (McGuire, 2003; Karcher, 1999). Jung was also influenced by a number of psychologists, including William James. He worked closely with Freud for a time but eventually came to a parting of the ways over a number of differences, including Freud's resistance to Jung's spiritual preoccupations (Shamdasani, 1999, 2000; Charet, 2000). The breakup with Freud affected Jung greatly, leading to a psychotic breakdown that lasted several years. Jung's work on alchemy and Taoist texts led also to his study of **synchronicity** or the simultaneous occurrence of apparently unconnected psychic states and external events (Jung, 1973, 1969a, p. 441; Haule, 2000) (Fig. 5.2).

5.2.1 Basic Ideas

5.2.1.1 Knowledge

Jung took a Kantian stance toward human knowledge (see Section 2.2.3). He believed that we have no way of knowing things-in-themselves because our mental structures

Fig. 5.2 *Carl Jung.*
A creative figure with diverse
interests, Jung's ideas still
play an important role in
the psychology and religion
dialogue. Photo courtesy
of Snark/Art Resource,
New York

are ultimately responsible for our observations about reality. He took this to mean that our psychological existence is an autonomous realm *sui generis* (1969b, p. 58, 1970, p. 79; cf. Section 4.3.3) so that while events like religious experience are very real they do not tell us about the world, only about ourselves (1967a, p. 86, 1969c, p. 194, 1969d, 1989, pp. 347–348). He drew from a vast array of sources in art, literature, religion, and psychology as he developed his ideas (Dourley, 1995a, 1995b; Helal, 1999). He was also a perennialist and believed that different kinds of literary, philosophical, and religious material displayed many common themes (Becker, 2001; see Section 4.3). Overall, this resulted in his taking a position that avoided the extremes of positivist objectivism or extreme relativism, although he did tend to emphasize the emotional and irrational aspects of human nature (Kotsch, 2000; Hauke, 2000, pp. 231–233).

5.2.1.2   Libido and Balance

Jung followed Freud in utilizing the concept of **libido** or energy to understand the workings of the human psyche, although Jung thought that libido was a kind of general instinctual energy rather than specifically sexual or aggressive. Jung thought that psychic energy worked according to several principles similar to those of physics. According to **the principle of opposites**, structures in the psyche often work in opposed and antithetical dualistic pairs, each of which can be invested with energy, creating tensions between opposites that provide essential sources of psychic power. However, these pairs are also governed by the **principle of entropy**, which states that in situations of imbalance the psyche will act to neutralize energy differences and restore balance. This energy is not lost but conserved and redistributed according to the **principle of equivalence**, the view that the total amount of energy in the psychic system remains equal across time, although the location and function of energy may change (1967a, 1967c, p. 63, 1969a, pp. 18–28, 1969c, p. 197, 1969d, p. 584).

5.2.1.3   The Self

A central concept in Jung's system is the **Self**. In psychology this term is often used to refer to the "conscious, perceiving center of awareness and agency" which we observe (D'Andrade, 1995, p. 163; Browning, 1968). However, Jung used the term to refer to the *totality of the human person* (1969b, pp. 186–187, 1969d, p. 82). Jung believed that there were three levels to the Self. The first level is the conscious mind, which Jung generally equates with the ego. The ego thus is subordinate to the Self, although it plays an important role in consciousness and the maintenance of the **persona**, our system of adaptations and the face that we present to the world. Underneath the conscious is the **unconscious**, an autonomous realm of emotional and instinctive forces out of our awareness. It is divided into the **personal unconscious**, which includes material specific to the individual that was at one time conscious but now forgotten or repressed, and the **collective unconscious**, which contains materials of a universal and impersonal character that are inherited. The unconscious is unlimited in scope and is thus ultimately unknowable and ineffable. Much of the content of the Self consists of pairs of opposites with one pole of the pair in our conscious mind, while the other pole resides in the unconscious and may be dormant (1969b, 1969c, p. 5).

5.2.1.4 Archetypes

Jung thought that important aspects of our psychological life are determined by the collective unconscious. Especially important are the influence of **archetypes**, which are not specific contents but *"patterns of instinctual behavior"* (1969b, p. 44) or "a possibility of representation that is given *a priori"* (1969b, p. 79). These can assume different content depending on personal or cultural contexts. They are like the Kantian categories except that they are categories of imagination rather than reason (1969d, p. 518; see Section 2.2.3). They are ultimately unknowable; their meaning cannot be completely described but only indicated from what we see in consciousness. Throughout our lives, situations corresponding to the archetype activate them and produce primordial images in consciousness. The energy attached to archetypes gives them a numinous quality that is particularly evident in religious experiences and encounters with religious symbols (1969c, pp. 149, 184, 1967a, p. 232). Jung believed that many things in religion—like God—are either archetypes or have an archetypal quality connected with them. It is the relationship we develop with these archetypes and symbols—positive or negative—that lies at the basis of religion. In fact, religious symbols and practices have been the primary way that humans have learned about and related to our archetypes (1969b, pp. 5–7, 153–156, 1969d, p. 81).

The Self and God as archetypes. Because the Self encompasses the collective unconscious, as well as other parts of the personality, it also has an archetypal aspect and is ultimately unknowable in full (cf. Baumeister, 1998). Jung believed that the Self-archetype represents our potential for unity and self-transformation and that this archetype was indistinguishable from an image or archetype of God. He supported this idea by quoting Christian writers who said that God could be found within (1969c, p. 22). Jung believed that the God image is an archetype charged with powerful libido or energy so that it has a particularly numinous quality. As an archetype it acts as a living figure in a dialectical relationship with us, moving us toward a goal of wholeness (1967a, pp. 56–60, 85–90). Theistic views of God come about when we associate the Divine with characteristics of our parental **imagoes**, representations or images of our parents that are formed during the first four years of life (1969b, pp. 62–66).

Other archetypes. The collective unconscious also includes a number of other archetypes such as the shadow, anima, and animus (1969b, 1969c, p. 8). The **shadow** is the dark side of the personality, a trickster part of us that is childish and at times uncertain or self-defeating and in need of help. Although it has negative features, we must eventually accept it as part of our growth toward wholeness. The **anima** is a feminine principle with a spontaneous and youthful quality that is fascinating (1967a, pp. 324, 437, 1969c, pp. 28, 268; 1969d, pp. 75–78). This archetype takes many positive or negative forms, and is connected with the feelings of awe or devotion one might experience in church or nature. It is paired with the **animus** or masculine principle, which is more associated with aggressiveness, dominance, and utilitarian attitudes. Everyone possesses both anima and animus, although the feminine is hidden in men and the masculine in women until we discover them later in life.

5.2.1.5 Symbols

While archetypes are not directly knowable, their contents can be experienced indirectly in visual and other forms as **symbols** (1967a, 1969b, 1969c, 1969d; see Section 12.4.1). In Jung's view, symbols serve a couple of necessary functions. First, they enable us to learn about contents of the collective unconscious while protecting us from the power of a direct contact. They offer new knowledge and a compensation for what is missing or has been forced out of consciousness. Second, symbols act to facilitate and empower the transformation process in the human psyche by reconciling tensions, bridging the conscious and unconscious and leading us toward wholeness. Since symbols are dynamic representations they have a numinous quality and must be experienced rather than passively viewed or rationally analyzed (Clift, 1982, p. 13). Since the Self is the key archetype of the personality (Heisig, 1999), symbols that represent the self or the God archetype are particularly important. They often take the form of pairs or circles as in a **mandala** drawing (Gollnick, 2001; see Fig. 5.3). In Christianity, Christ functions as such a symbol (Kings, 1997). Jung believed that one of the great potential contributions of religion was to provide symbols that could help with the process of personal transformation.

Fig. 5.3 *Mandala of Jnanadakini* (from Sakya Monastery, Tibet). Like other mandalas, the image gives a symmetric, visual representation of an aspect of the world using concentric circles, squares, and religious symbols. Mandalas are used in Hinduism as well as Tibetan Buddhism. Photo courtesy of Metropolitan Museum of Art/Art Resource, New York

In his view, psychological forces appear in religious symbols, and thus it is impossible to completely separate religious and psychological issues. He believed that this interrelationship becomes particularly acute at midlife so that the problems of people after age 40 have an essentially religious aspect (Gunn, 2000, p. 189; Hillman, 1967, p. 54; Haule, 2000).

5.2.1.6 The Problem of Modern Man

Jung (1964) believed that trends in contemporary Western culture cause great problems for the modern person. In the past, the unconscious and irrational side of the Self was recognized in society, and symbols helped to harmonize conscious and unconscious forces. However, the rise of rationalism and scientific materialism has led to the devaluing or repression of our psychic life, particularly material that is archetypal in nature and unconscious (1970, p. 81). With the severing of links between the conscious and unconscious the individual develops a "rootless consciousness" and unconscious forces assert themselves in unpredictable ways to compensate (1969b, p. 157). This problem was made especially acute by the devaluing and rejection of religious perspectives, as religious dogma and symbols are the best means we have to access material in the collective unconscious. Jung blamed this partly on the inability of science to comprehend the irrational and imagistic aspects of human nature. He thought that the move to devalue or reject religion was foolish, even dangerous (1967a, 1969a, p. 367, 1969c). However, like Paul Tillich, he also criticized Christian theologians for their inability to articulate a religious message of relevance to modern man. He questioned the liberal Protestant abandonment of traditional symbols, sometimes in favor of a Freudian theory hostile to spiritual values (Dourley, 1995b, pp. 135–139; Jung 1969b, p. 104, 1969c, p. 333; Chapman, 1997). He argued that the real message of Christianity needed to be restated (1967a, p. 435, 1989, p. 210). While Jung denied that his psychology was a religion or even a worldview, he did see his depth psychology as a rediscovery and restatement of Western spirituality. He hoped that through belief and faith in symbols, people could once again participate in a religious message (1967a, pp. 230–231; Homans, 1968a).

5.2.1.7 Individuation

Jung's key concept for describing spiritual and personal growth was **individuation**, a maturational process that involves the reuniting of unconscious materials with the conscious so that the person can achieve wholeness. The holistic Self and God archetypes provide a form for the process and drive it (1967a, 1969b, 1969c, 1969d, p. 207). The groundwork for this is laid in the first half of life, as we move from a kind of vague unified consciousness which Jung called **participation mystique** to a clearly defined and functioning ego based in consciousness (Dourley, 1995a, p. 284). This growth of the ego is necessary for development, but its increasing dominance creates a split between the conscious and unconscious aspects of our psyche. This leaves us in a state of disunity, with parts of our personality available in consciousness while opposite aspects necessary for balance remain submerged in the unconscious and inaccessible. At midlife, however, we start to become aware of these opposite, unconscious aspects of the Self such as the shadow and work to reintegrate them (Jung, 1969a, 1969b, 1969c; Schaer, 1950, pp. 120–126). Jung called the use of these opposites by the psyche to facilitate growth the **transcendent function** of the personality, a process he saw as similar to the union of opposites or *coniunctio oppositorum* discussed by medieval alchemists (1963, 1967b, 1968, 1969d, p. 489). The acceptance of the shadow and other unconscious material is experienced as a healing process and can be associated with religious experiences (Jung, 1967a, p. 433; Coward, 1985, p. 72).

While Jung's theory suggests that the highest levels of development are open to all, growth is a painful process, and in practice he seems to have believed that only a few will approach the goal of development (Rich & DeVitis, 1985; Jung, 1969b, p. 382). This goal is a numinous state of unity of consciousness and unconsciousness similar to samadhi or satori that he called **unus mundus** (1963, p. 540). This final growth requires an experiential process that is dependent both on our conscious activity and our choice to step aside and let the action of the Self or God archetype guide us toward wholeness. It is an emotional process that reflects the numinous quality of archetypal activity (Jung, 1969d, Dourley, 1995a, pp. 273–276; Haule, 2000; Becker, 2001). In this view, religious development is a coming to know our archetypes, particularly the God image, and our acceptance and integration of them into our personality.

Jung thought that the process of integration of conscious and unconscious could be speeded along by the technique of **active imagination**, where the individual is consciously presented with images from the unconscious and interacts with them. This allows the person to work through paradoxes and conflicts using symbols from the unconscious. The technique is similar to that utilized by Ignatius of Loyola in the *Spiritual Exercises*, a point which Jung expanded upon in later work (Jung, 1977, 1978; Becker, 2001; see Section 13.3.4). Jung himself was ambivalent about the role religion might play in the individuation process. Although he acknowledged that religious people might be able to use their faith as a path to growth (Jung, 1969d, p. 308; Haule, 2000), he also stated that it was impossible to utilize a religious system for individuation, because its inherently narrow understanding of God and the self might limit the active imagination (Becker, 2001). So while he saw religions as having a healing role, he seemed to view psychotherapy and the process of active imagination as superior, particularly for modern Europeans (Jung, 1967a, p. 356; Gomez, 1995; Coward, 1985, p. 73). However, his position on this important issue is often not clear or consistent.

5.2.2 Jung on Christianity

Jung wrote two longer works on aspects of Christianity. In the first work, *A Psychological Approach to the Trinity* (1969c, pp. 107–200), Jung analyzed the Christian doctrine of the Trinity as an archetypal and powerfully numinous but impersonal symbol of the Self that can help in the process of individuation. He viewed sets of three like the Trinity as powerful symbols because they contain a third which is able to unite opposites. Nevertheless, Jung saw threesomes as defective in that they did not include a set of perfect oppositions. He argued that one way to correct the problem with regard to the Trinity would be to expand it to a *quaternity* with two pairs of opposites by adding a female figure or an evil figure to balance the good of Christ (Chapman, 1997). In *Answer to Job* (1969c, pp. 355–470), Jung developed this position further and argued that the almighty God of Job is also a dark God who is unfair, internally divided and not to be trusted, a God of opposites that includes evil as well as good (Gollnick, 2001; Boorer, 1997, p. 279). In a similar way, Jung also saw Christ as a numinous, impersonal symbol for the Self archetype (Edinger, 1992), but he thought that the symbol was incomplete because it did not include an evil or dark side.

In his second work on *Transformation Symbolism in the Mass* (1969c, pp. 201–296), Jung argued for the psychological efficacy of the Christian ritual that portrays the transformation process through rich symbolism. The mass portrays the eternal character of a divine sacrifice and represents the destruction of the self. He believed that the spontaneous manifestation of the Self archetype in the mass combined with the ego's choice to participate in sacrifice have an integrative function. In this view, the transformation accomplished in the mass can be seen as a rite of individuation.

Jung attempted to take an agnostic position on the existence of God, arguing that his Kantian position forbade him to make statements about the true nature of reality. Accordingly, he attempted to focus his theory on religion as a psychological reality in the individual and avoid dealing with its claim to truth (Jung, 1967a, p. 61; Bockus, 1968). His views on the subject beyond this are unclear. In an interview, he once said about his belief in God, "I don't need to believe, I know" (cited in Clift, 1982, p. 3). On the other hand, he also stated in his late work that the existence of a being like God was "highly improbable" (1963, p. 548).

5.2.3 Jung on Yoga

Jung visited India briefly and wrote about parallels between his theories and some versions of yoga. Jung saw yoga as a way of disciplining psychic instincts that had parallels with his own ideas about psychic transformation (1969c, p. 560). However, his treatments of yoga were largely carried out to illustrate various aspects of his own ideas rather than to understand the nuances of yoga philosophy and practice, and he actually rejected important aspects of yoga philosophy (Coward, 1985). He was also selective in his choice of sources, emphasizing the more dualistic Samkhya philosophy and avoiding devotional or monistic versions of Hinduism, or discussions of the Hindu concept of purusha or Self (Jones, 1993, p. 177). Some parallels that he drew include the following:

- Transformation as in yoga and his ideas of individuation
- The concept of Brahman–Atman and his idea of the Self
- The concept of prajna and his idea of libido
- The concept of enlightened mind and the collective unconscious
- Development through transcendence of opposites

Jung developed some of these ideas in his lectures on Kundalini Tantric Yoga (1975, 1976). In his view, the chakras discussed in yoga writings were symbols of transformation, and the awakening of the kundalini in yoga was a description of the transcendent process. Jung seemed to pass over a number of differences and discrepancies between his system and the chakra system of yoga. A major difference is that yoga practitioners believe that their philosophies actually describe the nature of the world and the human person, while Jung believed that they only described our inner psychological makeup. Other aspects of yoga philosophy that were rejected by Jung include the following:

1. The belief that we can realize the identity between Brahman and Atman and a blissful state in this life. In contrast, Jung believed the individuation process was never complete (Moacanin, 1992).
2. The belief that unconscious contents of the mind are obstructions to be removed. Jung argued that they were essential parts of the human person to be used in the process of growth (cf. Feuerstein, 1989, pp. 99–100).
3. The belief that a state of ego loss and pure consciousness is both possible and desirable. Jung believed that pure consciousness was impossible because consciousness requires an ego, and any egoless state was thus necessarily unconscious (Jung, 1969b, p. 288, 1969c, pp. 484–505, 1975, pp. 21–22; 1976, p. 17).

5.2.4   Jung on Zen

One of Jung's most interesting dialogues with religion occurred in 1958 when he met with the Zen scholar Shin'ichi Hisamatsu (Shore, 2002). They noted many similarities in language and concern between them, particularly with regard to the Self. Jung shocked Hisamatsu by agreeing that one can and must free oneself from compulsions and the collective unconscious (Muramoto, 2002b; Meckel & Moore, 1992, p. 111), which seems quite at odds with his other views. However, there were also many obvious differences between Jung and Hisamatsu:

1. Jung sees the unconscious as ultimately unknowable, while the closest Zen equivalent to the unconscious, the state of no-mind, is actually a state of awareness that can be clearly experienced in awakening (Jones, 1993, p. 176),
2. While Jung and Zen both talk about the Self, they have different meanings for the term (Muramoto, 2002b; Okano, 2002). While the Jungian self is a phenomenon of the psyche, the Zen self lies beyond the parts of the psyche such as the collective unconscious, it is simply pure nondualistic awareness (Sato, Kataoka, DeMartino, Abe, & Kawai, 1992; Abe, 1992b).

3. Jung viewed individuation as a never-ending process and suffering as something that can be reduced but not eliminated, while Zen thinks that enlightenment and the removal of suffering are attainable in this life. This is because Zen practitioners believe they are able to remove the root cause of the problem—bondage to things like the collective unconscious (Meckel & Moore, 1992, pp. 109–117; Muramoto, 2002a).

Kasulis (1992) notes that there are a number of parallels between Jung's idea of individuation and Zen concepts like the need for active involvement on the part of the person, a desire to develop an inner freedom from compulsions or conflict, and a present orientation. However, there are also differences such as the Zen focus on total experience rather than just inner analysis, an orientation away from the self or ego, and the importance of a spiritual mentor (Kawai, 2002). So, while Jung often seemed to believe that he and Zen were talking about the same thing (Serrano, 1966, p. 100), there were really significant differences, which Jung seemed to attribute to mistakes on the part of Zen.

5.2.5 *Jung's Ambivalence About the East*

While Jung admired and studied Eastern thought (e.g., 1969d, p. 537), he frequently interrupted his discussions of Eastern texts with arguments against their widespread use in the West. We cannot copy or steal from other's ways, he would say; each must pursue their own path, you cannot graft one onto the other or onto each other's collective experience (Coward, 1985). In his view, Westerners were unable to assimilate the spiritual, pre-Kantian ideas behind Buddhism or Hinduism, and they were unable to place their trust in a spiritual guide like a guru. Instead, Westerners should exploit the resources in their own traditions, and make use of psychotherapy that offered a more dialectical kind of helping relationship (1964, 1966, pp. 58–59; 1969c, 1976, p. 31). He also believed that yoga and many Eastern practices were too structured and intuitive; they would strengthen the conscious mind that is already too strong in Westerners, thus inhibiting rather than stimulating growth (1975, p. 9).

5.2.6 *Continuing Conversations*

Jung's work has been marginalized within the field of psychology (Morey, 2005), but it still attracts interest from a variety of scholars. Contemporary writers in the New Age and pagan movements draw on Jungian concepts, although there has been little involvement of professional Jungians in these applications, and Jung would likely have rejected them (Tacey, 2001). More recently, some scholarly authors have taken a more critical look at Jung, including some of the unflattering aspects of his background and alleged problems such as anti-Semitism, Nazi sympathies, and sexual affairs with patients (Bishop, 1999; Charet, 2000; Budziszewski, 1998). However, there remains a small but devoted group of followers that use Jung as a basis for constructive dialogue between psychology and mainstream religious traditions.

5.2.6.1 Christian Uses

Christian authors like Ann Ulanov (1997) or Wallace Clift (1982) have found much to like in Carl Jung. They agree with his views on the importance of experience, the close relationship between self and God, and the centrality of religion and the effects on modern society from growing disconnection from traditional symbols (Ulanov, 1999, pp. 9–11). However, most Christian authors that make use of Jung have developed systems that depart from some of his positions or reinterpret him in significant ways. Christian adaptations of Jung all agree that religious rituals and practices can be helpful in the process of individuation and spiritual growth and cite numerous examples in support of this (e.g., Welch, 1982). They see Jung as overly individualistic, ignoring the importance of community and relationships as instruments of love and forgiveness that can promote growth.

Other critiques of Jung have focused on his metaphysical or theological views about the nature of evil and the role of God in human life. Christian authors would argue that evil is not found within God but in the fracturing of the psyche and our relationship with God (Becker, 2001; cf. Tillich, 1951, pp. 249–252; Jung, 1976, pp. 283–297). In a Christian Jungian view, the crucifixion provides the point where good and evil meet and reconciliation takes place (Clift, 1982, p. 74). These authors would also reject the idea that God is simply a symbol for the human psyche. For instance, Welsh draws a distinction between the psyche or human personality and the soul, which is the aspect of personality, and the interior life that links the person to God. The two are separate although intimately related (Welch, 1982, p. 65).

5.2.6.2 Relationship to Hinduism and Buddhism

Hindu and Buddhist religious writers and practitioners have not responded much to Jung (Heisig, 1999), but scholars studying these religious traditions have been highly critical of his writings. In their view, Jung provided his own meanings for Hindu and Buddhist texts that ignored their original meaning. He also rejected reports of religious experiences that conflicted with his theory, such as the pure consciousness experience (Gomez, 1995; Coward, 1992, pp. 248–250). This disregard for sources extended to Christian writings and practices as well (Boorer, 1997, pp. 287–294; see e.g., Jung, 1967a, p. 367). He has been accused of **orientalism**, a problem in 20th-century Western scholarship of Asian religions and thought systems marked by the following assumptions (Said, 1978):

1. Many distinct ideas and practices can be combined under one category of "Oriental" or "Eastern" without regard to important differences so that we can draw broad, universal conclusions about them.

2. These ideas are inferior to those of Europe and in need of corrective study or at the least need help from Europeans to properly express and interpret them
3. Asian ideas are not important in themselves, but only in terms of how they help Europeans better understand the world and themselves.

Jung's work is certainly marked by most or all of these problems, although it is also fair to say that he had great respect for the achievements of Eastern religions before it was popular to utilize them in psychological theory or research. However, his selective use of religious texts means that his assessments of religious traditions were likely inaccurate and thus of limited usefulness (Becker, 2001; Jones, 1993).

5.2.7 Critique

It is difficult to give a fair evaluation of Jung's work because of the great range of sources and theoretical concepts, as well as the relative lack of relevant empirical data (Drake, 1996). As Chapman (1988, pp. 152–157) notes, Jung really develops three different theories in his work. First, Jung had a psychological theory based on energy, as in his principles of entropy and equivalence. Second, one can see in Jung's writings a phenomenological and mythological quest model focused on meaning and value, which is reflected in much of his work on symbols and archetypes (Hudson, 1996). Finally, Jung had a metaphysical or theological model that took positions on basic characteristics of human existence. It can be argued that it is not possible or desirable to evaluate these three theories together, as they have different levels of scope and focus on different activities and tasks. Nevertheless, his theory invites critique, both for its positive, innovative ideas and the numerous problems identified by psychologists and theologians (e.g., Loder, 1998, pp. 307–309).

Jung deserves commendation for his efforts to open a dialogue between psychology and both Christianity and Eastern religions. On the negative side, in addition to some of the difficulties already noted, his theory had a number of concealed and unproven metaphysical presuppositions that profoundly affected his conclusions. Jung made many statements claiming that his theory avoided metaphysics and did not represent a worldview (e.g., 1969a, pp. 376–379). However, it is abundantly clear that he actually took a number of important epistemological and metaphysical positions. Foremost of these was his Kantian stance that we are unable to have any knowledge or experience outside of the psyche (Dourley, 2001). More importantly, while Jung claimed neutrality with regard to the things he studied, he interpreted religion as a psychological reality and denied the possibility that religions might have any valid truth claims or that there is a possibility for transcendental encounter outside of the psyche—a position that is not particularly neutral (Jung, 1953, 1969c, pp. 360, 476; Dourley, 1995b; Vergote, 2003). So, while he championed the absolute, indisputable quality of religious experience (1969c, p. 104), he emptied it of substantive meaning. Other key concepts in Jung's theory such as the Self or collective unconscious are also metaphysical in nature (Coward, 1985, pp. 178–183) in that they are not directly observable and require significant reinterpretation of experience to make them fit with the data. Jung in fact admitted that metaphysical and religious ideas must be called into use at times, for instance, in understanding the experience of unity in the emergence of the Self (1963, p. 547). This makes his stated position of neutrality on religious issues even harder to understand. God could find a place in his theory, although Jung himself made efforts to distance himself from thinking of God as any more than a psychological reality (Bidwell, 2000; Bower, 1999).

Jung has been accused of claiming to offer an objective science but really offering his own private religion (e.g., Gomez, 1995). Richard Noll, one of Jung's most trenchant critics, claims that as early as 1910 when he was working with Freud, Jung expressed hope to transform psychoanalysis into something like a religious movement (Noll, 1997, p. 64; cf. Homans, 1995) and that his theory has ended up as a variety of European occult philosophy (Davis, 1996, p. 10). However, his theory seems to fall short of being a real religion. It lacks an ethical vision and seems to embrace a version of moral relativism strikingly at odds with his insistence that evil be recognized as a real power (Jung, 1969c, p. 197; Coward, 1995). Nor does it have a community of worshippers, a God to worship, or a theory of belief apart from experience (Segal, 1999; Storr, 1999). Nevertheless, the debate shows the strong positive and negative feelings that Jung's ideas continue to inspire in others.

5.3   Erik Erikson

Erikson (1902–1994) was an innovative thinker who used Freud as a starting point to produce the first fully articulated psychological theory of life span development (Erikson, 1964, 1982; Homans, 1978a, p. 15; Fuller, 1996). He was especially intrigued by exceptional development and did interesting work painting book-length verbal portraits of the great religious leaders Martin Luther and Mahatma Gandhi, who became his norms for development (Capps, 1996b; Zock, 1990, p. 118). Erikson rejected the idea that health simply involved a lack of sickness; rather the healthy personality was one that (a) actively works to master the environment, (b) shows a sense of unity within the self and relationally with those around them, and (c) accurately perceives self and world (Erikson, 1968, pp. 91–92, 1987, p. 598; Zock, 1997; Capps, 1984). He is often thought of as offering a functionalist approach that does not look at the nature of the objects or qualities but how they adapt to the environment. When applied to religion, functionalism avoids truth questions but asks how it assists persons in their development (Fuller, 1996). Functionalism is often a way of getting rid of transcendence, although this was probably not the case for Erikson (Zock, 1990, pp. 180–181) (Fig. 5.4).

5.3.1   Basic Concepts

Erikson's general theory of development is founded on an **epigenetic principle** which states that (1) we have an inbuilt plan for growth into wholeness that unfolds throughout life, (2) this plan unfolds in a particular sequential order which includes

Fig. 5.4 *Erik Erikson*. One of the most creative and complex psychodynamic thinkers, Erikson rose from humble beginnings to become a pioneer of life span development theory and research. His later writings in particular contained numerous references to religious or spiritual issues that remain important in contemporary discussions on psychology and religion. Photo courtesy of Harvard University

specific tasks that must be accomplished at various points, and (3) proper development at earlier stages is essential to success at later ones. This plan proceeded in eight stages, with each stage marked by a **developmental crisis** or turning point that provided the opportunity to add a particular strength, or the possibility of a failure that would lead to maladjustment, either of which could persist throughout life (1964, pp. 138–140; see Table 5.1). Especially important was the stage of *infancy*, which provided the opportunity for the formation of basic trust in others and the environment. *Adolescence* is also critical because it is during this period that we develop our **identity** a "sense of personal sameness and historical continuity" (1968, p. 17). An optimal sense of identity is important, because it gives us a sense

Table 5.1 Erikson's stages of development

Stage (age)	Crisis	Developmental task	Virtue
Infancy (0–2)	Trust vs. mistrust	Develop trust in self and others sense of continuity	Hope
Toddlerhood (2–4)	Autonomy vs. shame and doubt	Develop self-control without loss of self-esteem	Will
Early school (5–7)	Initiative vs. guilt	Independence in goals	Purpose
Mid-school (8–12)	Industry vs. inferiority	Independence/success in tasks	Competence
Adolescence (13–22)	Identity vs. role confusion	Develop identity	Fidelity
Early adult (23–30)	Intimacy vs. isolation	Form and nurture adult friendships Marriage and family	Love
Mid-adult (31–50)	Generativity vs. stagnation	Productivity and creativity Training the next generation	Care
Late adult (51-on)	Integrity vs. despair	Develop mature ideas of meaning Life review	Wisdom

Source: Erikson, *Insight and Responsibility* (1964)

of inner assurance and positive life direction, as well as supporting our physical and psychological well-being (Erikson, 1968, p. 165). It also provides resources for the development of intimacy, fidelity, and love in later stages of development (Markstrom & Kalmanir, 2001).

Erikson believed that identity is initially formed in adolescence through a combination of positive and negative movements (Erikson, 1968, p. 303). In **positive identity** we affiliate or identify with people and an ideology that we want to emulate. This kind of identity is traditionally formed with the help of community; it thus has links to the past, as well as an orientation to the future (Erikson, 1968, p. 310). However, it is also possible for us to form a **negative identity** that is developed as a reaction against or rejection of a particular community, set of ideals, or beliefs. In negative identities, we decide that whatever we are, we do not want to be like a particular individual or group we abhor. In extreme cases, groups of people with negative identities can become a **pseudospecies**, thinking themselves different and special, perhaps the only worthwhile group of people on the planet (1987, p. 580). This is a more common outcome among individuals or groups who have not achieved an identity, have lost it, or find it threatened in some way (Hoare, 2000; Erikson, 1968, p. 172, 1969, p. 431). Urban gangs can be seen as a secular example of pseudospecies behavior.

5.3.2 Application to Religion

Erikson never articulated a systematic psychology of religion (Homans, 1978b, p. 233), so it is not often appreciated that religion had an important role in Erikson's work (Capps, 1996a). At about his mid-career mark he published *Young Man Luther*, a psychological study on the great Christian reformer, and *Gandhi's Truth*, a work on the Hindu religious and political leader. In these books, and his later work, he moved away from functionalism and developed existential aspects of his thought (Hoare, 2000, p. 29; Zock, 1990). While he was not involved in institutional religion, he claimed he was a Christian follower, and especially in his later works, he talked about the importance of our relationship to the Ultimate. These views likely were a reason for his declining popularity in psychology and the increasing interest in his work from theology (Hoare, 2000; Fuller, 1996). As a result, his work has not been especially influential in the psychological study of religion, but a number of religious writers with theological agendas have appropriated his work (e.g., Whitehead & Whitehead, 1979).

5.3.2.1 Religion and Development

Several stages in the Eriksonian framework have implications for religious development. The stages of infancy, with its development of trust, and the stage of adolescence and the formation of identity, are of particular importance.

Infancy and Trust. In Erikson's early work such as *Childhood and Society* (1950), religion was primarily linked with developmental issues such as trust (Zock, 1990, pp. 83–84). Erikson believed that we have a drive for essential wholeness that requires the development of basic trust in the environment. This gives a generalized sense of ourselves and the world around us as interrelated and good. He believed that organized religion is the major social institution that provides this sense of reassurance through teachings and practices like prayer and rituals. This trust is an early manifestation of religious experience and a basis for hope (Weigert, 1962, p. 7). Unfortunately, religious institutions can at times also be unhelpfully cold and cruel, which leads to a struggle to find other ways to find safety and wholeness (Erikson, 1968, pp. 83–84).

Adolescence, Identity, and Ideology. Especially beginning with *Young Man Luther*, Erikson began to explore the connection between identity and religion. His idea about identity as a center of the individual's life was similar to the concept of faith in Paul Tillich (Elhard, 1968). He believed that at various stages in our life we confront what can be called basic or existential anxiety over our dependence on others. This requires development of an existential identity that is separate from other aspects of identity (Erikson, 1958, pp. 177–182, 1969, pp. 396–400). For most people, the ideological resources of a religious tradition are used to do this; although as a functionalist Erikson believed that other ideologies might also satisfy this requirement (Zock, 1990, pp. 89–97; Homans 1978b, pp. 239–240). Furthermore, Erikson believed that a select group of people face the struggles of their age, reach beyond the answers provided by others and resolve this issue directly. They are the **homines religiosi** or religious geniuses like Luther or Gandhi who blaze new paths for humanity (Browning, 1973, p. 149).

Later stages of development. For Erikson, religion and spirituality are aspects of human experience that become a permanent feature at midlife (Hoare, 2002, p. 75). Erikson thought that religion also had a particularly vital role to play in old age by promoting integration and helping the individual deal with ultimate concerns. Other scholars have noted the religious nature of midlife in Eriksonian thought. For instance, religious themes appear in his concept of **generativity**, the midlife task of giving oneself to care for a younger generation, which provides an altruistic normative image of the human person (Browning, 1978, p. 264, 1973, pp. 163–164; cf. Clark, 1995). Recent research has found that the characteristics of highly generative persons such as strong hope, trust, and faith very often have a religious base and that generativity can be linked to a search for personal immortality (McAdams, Hart, & Maruna, 1998; McAdams & de St. Aubin, 1998; McAdams, 2006).

5.3.2.2 Virtue

Erikson also developed an ethical and social aspect of his developmental theory that has relevance to religious life (Zock, 1990, p. 115). While he rejected automatic adherence to the moral dogma of a religion, he did think that each person needs to develop a principled ethic based on mutuality and the Kantian principle of treating others as ends and not means (see Section 2.2.3). He thought this adult ethical sense should be based on the integration of ideology with the superego in the adult personality. He equated the ideal ethical sense with the Christian concept of unconditional love, rather than a formal sense of justice as found in Piagetian developmental theorists like Lawrence Kohlberg (Hoare, 2000; see Sections 7.4.1 and 7.4.2).

In his later work, Erikson began to look at the positive virtues that emerged from each stage of development. He saw these as basic strengths that provide vitality for other positive characteristics. The virtues as portrayed by Erikson develop through living in a multigenerational community and are closely tied to religion (Erikson, 1964, pp. 113–114, 1968, p. 232; Zock, 1990, p. 205). For instance, Erikson saw that the virtue of hope or *"the enduring belief in the attainability of fervent wishes"* (1964, p. 118) is both the basis of and nourished by adult faith. The virtue of fidelity, *"the ability to sustain loyalties freely pledged in spite of the inevitable contradictions of value systems"* (1964, p. 125) is central to identity and is supported by ideology and affirming others, both of which can be provided by religion. His culminating virtue was wisdom, which involved a continued concern with life but a freedom from attachments (Erikson, 1964, p. 133; Capps, 1984). Work in the area of virtue has become very popular within psychology (see Section 11.1.2).

5.3.2.3 Ritualization

Erikson thought that adult religious rituals were related in part to a common daily childhood activity he called **ritualization**: "an agreed-upon interplay between at least two persons who repeat it at meaningful intervals and in recurring contexts" (1966, pp. 602–603). The earliest ritualization was the greeting or affirmation and recognition of face and name between a mother and her baby. Such encounters have a paradoxical quality; they are both formal and familiar because of repetition but also playful and surprising. The earliest affirmation between mother and child carries with it a special emotional quality; since it is an exchange between unequals, it has a sense of "hallowed presence" (1987, p. 578). This gives a numinous quality to the encounter that will later form the foundation for the sense of numinous presence in adult religious rituals, especially personal devotions. Ritualization also provides a foundation for hope and for individual identity (Erikson, 1966, p. 605, 1968, p. 105, 1977, pp. 82–92; Capps, 1984).

Erikson believed that ritualization is intensely relational and becomes more complex, as new elements are added during development and an expanding circle of persons becomes involved. Adolescent and adult rituals are particularly important as they demonstrate our attachments to persons and ideologies. Some rituals like marriage sanction us to become parents and ritualizers to others—our children. Overall, Erikson had a positive view of ritual as making many important contributions to our life. However, he recognized that sometimes ritual can become separated from its natural social context. He termed this **ritualism**, the compulsive compliance or repetition of rituals on an individual basis that can become legalistic

(Erikson, 1966, pp. 609–618, 1977, pp. 90–105, 1987, 1996; Zock, 1990, p. 98; cf. Section 12.4.1).

5.3.2.4 Transcendence, Subjective Identity, and the I

Along with our basic identity, Erikson thought we also developed a subjective identity, an awareness that we exist and have an enduring individual style that provides continuity in our relationships. Erikson developed a transcendent, almost mystical aspect of this thought through his writings on the "I" or numinous sense of awareness, existence, and life that goes with consciousness (1968, pp. 216–221, 1996). He believed that the "I" emerges from mutual recognition and interactions with an Other, who in early life is our maternal caretaker. Erikson thought that ultimately the "I" in each of us has a religious quality and that it is this inner "I" that Jesus addresses in the Gospels. If our experiences of recognition and interaction have been positive, God works during adulthood to play the role of a numinous Other that helps develop both our sense of "I" and our connectedness toward others, as well as helping us confront the issue of a possible eternal identity (Erikson, 1968, 1982, 1996; Capps, 1997a; Zock, 1990, pp. 100–101; Browning, 1973, pp. 153–154). However, if the person experiences rejection or lack of recognition, the Other is perceived as malevolent, encouraging the labeling of other groups as dangerous. This aspect of Erikson's thought has many parallels to the work of Niebuhr and even more closely resembles that of Tillich (Homans, 1978b).

5.3.3 Assessment

Wulff (1997, pp. 405–408) has summarized some of the chief complaints about Erikson's work from the standpoint of psychology, including lack of clarity and consistency in his writing, shifting and vague theoretical constructs, and lack of overall systematic focus. The universality and nature of the individual stages in Erikson's theory of development have also been questioned. These problems make it difficult to construct an empirical test of Eriksons's ideas. His treatment of gender has also been labeled as inadequate or even offensive by some, as he associated the homo religiosi with a "feminine" mode of inclusiveness, holding, and passivity (Capps, 1996b; Zock, 1997). Critiques from theology have focused on the functional and outer-directed nature of his theory that tends to neglect religious experience. Specific complaints have also been directed toward his psychobiographical methods. For instance, Erikson's biography of Luther has been attacked as depending on unreliable primary sources and excessively focusing on Luther's psychological problems such as anxiety to the exclusion of other aspects of his story and character (Hendrix, 1995).

Erikson also differs from some religious writers in his view of the central aspect of the human person. For Erikson the center of the person was the ego and the identity that it constructs through interactions with the environment. In the traditional Christian view, the center of the personality is the **heart**—not our physical heart but the central part of the personality around which a true unified self can be built. This heart is known directly only by God—we must infer its existence and characteristics. It is *discovered*, not made; finding it is one of the goals of Christian life (Rahner, 1963, p. 277; Ulanov, 2001, p. 130; cf. Pannenberg, 1985, pp. 197–224; see Section 13.2.4).

Nevertheless, Erikson's theory offers some valuable insights. It can be used to understand issues that go on in the background of spiritual and religious development, or it may be taken as a model for understanding the stages and tasks of spiritual development (e.g., Tate & Parker, 2007). His focus on development throughout the life span offers a reminder of the importance of middle age and older adulthood, and his work on early trust has provided an enduring contribution to the psychology and religion dialogue. Scholars point out that trust is the foundation of hope, which allows us to develop purposeful intention and to move from willfulness to willingness, breaking our attachment to the present and opening up new possibilities (Meissner, 1987, pp. 186–187, 204–205).

5.4 Object Relations Approaches to Psychology and Religion

Object relations theory (ORT) developed as a movement within British psychoanalysis during the mid-to-late 20th century. It moved away from the Freudian emphasis on drive and structure and assumed instead a fundamental interrelatedness that does not idealize individualism (Chodorow, 1999, p. 117). Many of the British object relations theories had religious backgrounds and were sympathetic toward religion, partly because historical and cultural factors had caused the British Enlightenment to take place within instead of against Christianity (Watts, 2002c, p. 2).

5.4.1 Basic Concepts

In ORT, motivation revolves not around sexual, or aggressive instincts (Freud), or inner conflict and balancing (Jung) but around a need to develop a significant existence that allows for self-realization through our relationships with other persons. Anxiety is produced not by conflict but threats to our ability to establish satisfactory relationships with others. This has led ORT theorists to develop the concept of object. For Freud, objects were anything that could satisfy a need, which in his system were instinctual in nature. In ORT, an **object** is "some person or persons to whom we can relate ourselves significantly so that life can be positively enjoyed, and come to have a meaning and value, and to be worth preserving" (Guntrip, 1957, p. 43). Objects that should fulfill that function but do not or have the opposite effect are referred to as *bad objects*. Many objects are external, but others exist as representations within the psyche that affect us even when the physical object is absent. For example, our parents continue to exercise an important influence on us through our internalized representations of them even when they are absent. These **internalized objects** may be incomplete; thus we can refer to *part* or *whole objects*. Furthermore, people may be unable to construct cohesive representations due to inconsistencies and conflicts; the different irreconcilable parts are separated into different objects; this process is known as **splitting**. Since objects are generally constructed from people and relationships we have early in life, they are laden with attached emotions and pre-linguistic experiences (Hill & Hall, 2002; Beit-Hallahmi, 1995).

In ORT, all psychic processes are viewed as reactions to our internal or external object environment (Guntrip, 1957, pp. 58–59). Object relations theories of religion contend that God appears in us as an object that at first is modeled after our parents. Later as we get older, the God object dissociates from them, becoming more universal and complex (St. Clair, 1994, p. 12). Since spirituality in a theistic context is thought about in terms of one's relationship to God, spirituality will be healthy or unhealthy depending on the quality of our God object and the relationship we have with it (Hall & Brokaw, 1995). ORT can be used in this context to (1) uncover the developmental roots of God images, religious practices or problems, (2) expose unconscious factors underlying religious practices and ideas, and (3) suggest additional ways of thinking about religion from a relational perspective (Miller, 2000; Jonte-Pace, 1999). This has generated a large and fruitful theoretical and empirical literature in the psychology of religion (see e.g., Section 8.3).

5.4.2 Harry Guntrip

The object relations theorist who wrote most prolifically about religion was Harry Guntrip (1901–1975). He developed the work of his mentor W. R. D. Fairbairn (1889–1964) and tried to apply it to problems encountered by pastors (Hoffman, 2004; Guntrip, 1996).

5.4.2.1 Psychopathology

Guntrip (1957) believed that our unconscious is populated with the mostly unhappy, negative, and frustrating figures that we would like to forget but cannot because of our strong emotional attachments to them. He thought that negative emotional states were due to interactions with internalized bad objects. The tantalizing figure that promises but then disappears or withholds becomes a "Desirable Deserter," while the aggressive and persecutory figure forms a "Hated Denier." These objects cause deep divisions and conflict in the rest of the personality including the ego so that we actually interact with the world in different modes depending on which object is dominant. Dominance of the Deserter can lead to a *schizoid position* toward life, where we are afraid to love, while the Denier can lead us to a *depressive position* marked by fear and anger. Divisions in the personality can also occur when important figures behave inconsistently, leading to splitting of objects into good and bad parts. This splitting can then lead to further internal conflict and inconsistency in our behavior and mental life. Different psychopathologies develop as ways of dealing with these internalized bad objects. These bad objects can also become centers of meaning and value: in the Christian view they are false gods that we give ourselves to in devotion (Crosswell, 2000). Solving the problem of anxiety requires correcting problems with bad objects, but instead we often just use substitute gratifications that we hope will reduce anger or pain. Guntrip believed that lasting satisfaction could only be achieved by modifying object relations.

5.4.2.2 Development and Transformation

Guntrip thought that mutuality rather than adaptation was the key to development. In early development, it is the relational environment provided by the mother that makes growth possible. Ideally our parents are not overly frustrating or dominating but provide an atmosphere of love and respect that encourages development of our personality without guilt or fear and with increasing competence in personal relations. This also increases our sensitivity to the environment, opening us to religious experience (1957, p. 72). Development progresses from an initial state of immature dependency to a mutual or mature dependency where we are capable of being alone but prefer to be together. This happens by (a) realization of our potential in good personal relationships marked by freedom, reciprocity, and mutual valuation and (b) development of a sense of personal reality and stable selfhood that provides defense against anxiety. Together, these represent what Guntrip called the *spiritual plane of life* (Guntrip, 1957, p. 130, 1969, 1973; Paul, 1999).

5.4.2.3 Psychotherapy

According to Guntrip, **anxiety** is a kind of mental pain (1957, p. 24), and that when dealing with the pain and its source on our own becomes too difficult, we develop defenses such as depression or physical illness to cover up. Psychotherapy was designed to correct these problems by providing a positive relationship in which the therapist assumes the role of a good parent object, helps the person experience things within that have been concealed or ignored, and protects the person against the emotional dangers of the healing process. Thus, while psychotherapy might benefit from scientific study, it is most of all a personal healing relationship designed to restore confidence, faith, and hope and is not a scientific activity (1957, p. 185).

5.4.2.4 Religion

For Guntrip, religion is *"an overall way of experiencing life, of experiencing ourselves and our relationships together; an experience of growing personal integration or self-realization through communion with all that is around us, and finally our way of relating to the universe*" (1969, p. 326). This definition implies that religion is relational in nature, ideally an experience of personal communion with an ultimate, all-embracing reality. Other experiences like work and family may thus have a broadly religious aspect, (1957, pp. 186–199) and rich relational experiences can provide a way of understanding religious experience. The definition also suggests that a prime function of religion is to lead us toward a sense of unity and integration that will impact the way we relate to others, our environment, and ourselves.

5.4.2.5 Religion and Psychotherapy

Guntrip thought that psychotherapy and religion were both therapeutic in their goal. He believed that they had a bidirectional relationship. Religion could impact therapy: a sound religious faith and capacity for religious experience were desirable prerequisites for psychotherapy, and religion might have a therapeutic effect. On the other hand, therapy or help with psychological problems might help the religious life of the individual (1957, pp. 186–189). There were limits to this, however, as he believed that many personality structures from childhood were permanent and that all religion or therapy could do is help "maintain faith, courage and determination in facing and resisting difficulties that cannot be removed from the deeper levels of the psychic life" (1957, p. 192). Religious leaders needed to understand these therapeutic needs so that religion could promote and not harm mental health. Guntrip, as with other writers of his period, offered a therapeutic vision of religion that has been very influential but more recently has been challenged by some theologians and other scholars (see Section 10.3.1).

5.4.2.6 Religion, Science, and Ethics

While Guntrip had great respect for science, he thought the idea that science could solve all our human problems was "simple minded" (1957, p. 197). While science can teach us a great deal, he believed that mechanistic science could not penetrate the subjective nature of relationality and that it could not discover the meaning, value, and purpose that lay at the heart of human existence. He saw reductionistic science as undermining basic human values and mental health. Ultimately, if we are to grow it must *matter* that we are mature and mentally healthy; thus a moral stance is necessary for personality change to take place and skepticism—scientific or otherwise—makes for poor prognosis in therapy. Moral values are important because they involve commitment to the kinds of personal qualities necessary to sustain the good human relationships that lie at the base of our life. It is values rather than mechanistic causes that form the basis of our motives, and it is these values that allow us to control the destructive potential of science (Guntrip, 1957, pp. 165–196, 1969).

5.4.3 David Winnicott

Although Guntrip wrote extensively about religion, it is his other mentor David Winnicott (1896–1971) who is currently most influential in the psychology and religion dialogue. Winnicott was raised in a religious home and introduced to psychoanalysis by Oskar Pfister, a Christian friend of Sigmund Freud. Although he did not speak much about his faith, Winnicott had a lingering religiosity and theism that revived later in his life (Hoffman, 2004). Certainly many Christian ideas and attitudes are present in his work.

5.4.3.1 Distinctive Contributions

Winnicott (1990) is best known for his theory of development. He conceptualized childhood as moving in three stages from *absolute dependence* to *relative dependence* and finally toward *independence* (Abram, 1997). Like Erikson, he believed that good development was facilitated by a stable but responsive environment that promoted the formation of trust, confidence and a sense that the environment around us is a benevolent one (LaMothe, 1999). He referred to this as a **holding environment**. Most important in providing this environment is the relationship between child and mother, where the mother who in a "good-enough" way responds to the needs of the child. Winnicott looked at a quiet resting condition with the mother as a kind of original state of goodness. Good-enough parenting allows us to develop the freedom to express our true self, while failures in parenting lead to the development of a false self that simply complies with the demands of the environment (St. Clair, 2000, p. 67).

While this early dependence on the mother is essential, the child must eventually move away and establish independence. Winnicott believed that this crucial step occurred when the child was able to substitute other objects for the mother during her absence. He called these substitutes **transitional objects** or transitional phenomena (Winnicott, 1953). These transitional objects are formed in the individual prior to the onset of language abilities; thus they are emotional and experiential in character. Like all objects, they have an external and internal reality or meaning. They also have the ability to both connect and separate internal and external reality (Eigen, 1999; Abram, 1997, p. 311). For children, a blanket or teddy bear can serve as a transitional object.

After the transition to adulthood, the ability to form substitute representations that have emotional value remains in the individual. Winnicott and others often refer to this as the **transitional space** in the person, "an intermediate area of *experiencing*, to which inner reality and external life both contribute" (Winnicott, 1975, p. 230). It is a realm of symbolism that is the nexus for cultural activity, play, creativity, and religion (Winnicott, 1975, p. 224; St. Clair, 1994, pp. 14–15). In a Winnicottian framework, psychotherapy, spiritual direction—or even prayer—provides a holding

environment and transitional space where creative work and growth can take place
(Hardy, 2000; Meissner, 1984, p. 182). As with Erikson and some other writers, he
recognized the sometimes playful quality of psychological processes (cf. Smith,
2004). Extending this idea, Ulanov (2001, p. 11) has argued that for reality to be
real, we must encounter it in this transitional space and contribute an illusory, playful, and creative component, or it will have no meaning for us.

5.4.3.2 Applications to Religion

According to Winnicott, religion does not happen inside or outside of us but in
our transitional space, where it is centrally placed to affect all aspects of the self
(Winnicott, 1975, p. 96; Meissner, 1987, p. 43). The space begins to assume religious functions early in life with the formation of a God-object or **God image** in
the space that can act as a transitional object (Winnicott, 1990, pp. 100–101). Our
initial God image is based on interactions with our parents, but it goes beyond this
as well (Underwood, 1997). Perhaps it can be thought of as a kind of generalized
sense of presence of what the world and others are like. Like other transitional
objects, the God image has both objective and subjective components. However,
unlike other objects, the God object is not abandoned by the psyche during development but remains a powerful part of our inner reality, especially in relation to
the creative and symbolic capabilities of the transitional space (Banschick, 1992;
McDargh, 1986). In this view, development of the symbolic is relational rather
than instinctual (Jones, 1997). For Winnicott, mystical or religious experiences
in part involve an encounter with this God object that is part of our subjective
reality. Religious rituals like communion can create a kind of transitional space
that might facilitate this encounter (Winnicott, 1990). Our religious life reflects
the changes that take place in our God image over time. Religion can also assist
the process of growth through training and practices that facilitate imaginative
thinking (Pruyser, 1985).

Ulanov (2001) has developed an elaborate treatment of the God image based
on Winnicott's theory. She notes that material for the image probably comes
from a variety of sources, including personal experiences, ideas of family and
friends, and official images from religious tradition and culture. It also sometimes includes projected materials, things about us that we have difficulty
accepting and would rather push off onto God. Our God image thus has the
potential to reveal things about ourselves to us. Depending on the materials that
go into the image, we may see God as a positive and supporting, challenging, or
very punitive.

For Winnicott, the self is a subjective sense of feeling real that develops as the
child moves toward independence. If our needs mesh with the environment, this
sense of self reflects our genuine feelings and needs. When there is a disconnect
between the environment and our needs as in the failure of the holding environment, the person constructs a different self—a **false self** or mask—that helps the
person comply with social obligations and feel better about deficits we may have in

identity. This means that everyone develops a false self, that is, who we would be, if we were able to meet the demands of the environment and cope with its failings while meeting our own needs (Abram, 1997, pp. 268–269; cf. Winnicott, 1990). This kind of distinction between true and false self can also be found in religious thought, as in the writings of the Christian Spanish mystics and the work of Thomas Merton (Welch, 1996, p. 40; see Section 13.3.2). The false self is an illusion, and the problems that it causes play a prominent role in both Christian and Buddhist analyses of the human condition.

5.4.4 Assessment

An implication of object relations views of religion is that to some extent our experience of God is affected or mediated by our personal history of relationships with others. Traditional theologians like Karl Barth would argue that this is the reason why theology cannot be built solely on personal experience, as the temptation is to construct a God according to human need or assumption rather than reality (Martyn, 1992, p. 147).

The application of ORT to God representations alters the Freudian understanding of religion in several important ways. First, it provides a nonreductive account of the origins of the religious and symbolic world and the relational organization of the religious imagination (McDargh, 1993). God representations are no longer thought to relate only to instincts and the father figure, and their use by the psyche has a healthy rather than purely defensive function. Second, the special nature of the God object suggests that it has the potential to change and influence behavior into adulthood (McDargh, 1992). As an early object, it can also influence the formation of other internalized objects that have transformational powers (Shafranske, 1992; J. Jones, 1997). Third, it moves toward a relational model of the human person that captures important aspects of experience. It is a model that works well in theological dialogue.

5.4.4.1 Limitations of the Object Relations Model

The strengths of the object relations model can also be its weaknesses. Jones (1997) notes that its focus on bonding as a key early developmental process can obscure other important issues like social context or the effects of instincts and drives. Also, by identifying people as objects, an object relations view of relationality sometimes leads to the faulty assumption that relations with people are the same as the relationships with nonhuman things that fulfill needs for us. However, when we relate to other people we typically see them not as an object (like, say a sandwich) but as a subject who is also a center of consciousness. There is an experience of mutuality that recognizes similarity of the inner experience of being human and the confirmation we receive from others. There is also an unpredictableness and tension that occurs between recognizing the other and asserting the self (Benjamin, 1999; cf. Sections 4.1.1 and 4.4.4).

The view of Winnicott that the goal of development is independence has been criticized as ignoring the fact that we are always dependent. Critics argue that dependency is a natural state that can have a healthy function in the context of a positive relationship and is not something we outgrow. Religions like Christianity call on us to recognize dependence and see gaps in development including parenting failures as inevitable (Ulanov, 2001). When it works well, religion can contribute positively to age-appropriate dependence. McDargh (1983, pp. 84–96) argues that our capacity to be alone but also tolerate dependency develops faith and trust in our relationship to a real, meaningful world and that this in turn supports development of the self and our ability to love. Refusal to accept dependence can be connected to a lack of faith.

The use of Winnicott's conception of the God object by religious writers has been criticized. Jones (1997) argues that analysts like Meissner who make use of Winnicott's work focus too much on the representational aspect of God images and neglect the fact that for Winnicott a transitional object is also a capacity for experience. In this second meaning, transitional phenomena are not objects but also types of experiences. They have an in-between or **liminal** character that offers a kind of psychological space between fantasy and the demands of reality that allows for renewal and creativity (see Section 12.4.1).

Another problem is that uncritical commentators often assume that adult transitional objects are exactly equivalent to Winnicott's childhood examples. For instance, religious rituals or narratives are often transitional in the sense that they involve both our inner and outer reality, but they have broader shared meanings and deal with many issues in addition to dependency such as identity (LaMothe, 1999). These adult transitional phenomena serve not only a protective function but also have transformative effects (Bollas, 1978). In fact, the transformative quality of the experience can itself become an object of representation so that our experience of change during adulthood can draw upon earlier experiences of change, raising old excitements and worries. God representations can include this transformational quality (Shafranske, 1992; Paul, 1999). Furthermore, it is not only the object itself but the relationship to the object which becomes key for adults.

From a theological perspective, ORT carries with it certain assumptions and limitations that can be problematic. Psychoanalysts rightly point out that they are limited to descriptions of experiences or objects and cannot speak about the God that the experience points at (St. Clair, 1994, p. 17). Some theological writers have also argued that ORT has a limited view of human nature. For instance, Burns-Smith (1999) points out that Winnicott assumes a highly optimistic view of human nature. He assumes that many human problems are not inherent in our experience but simply due to preventable failures in the environment. This would appear to leave little or no role for factors like faulty personal choices, biology, or instinct (Hoffman, 2004; Guntrip, 1973, pp. 133–136).

5.5 Conclusion

Key issue: *Any detailed and accurate understanding of the human person that hopes to comprehend our religious and spiritual life needs to account for our essential relational nature as well as individual uniqueness.*

Psychodynamic theories have contributed more than any other field of psychology to the dialogue with religion. One of the most important benefits of this interchange has been to highlight the important role of development in the spiritual and religious life. We will look at other views of religion, spirituality, and development in subsequent chapters (see Chapters 7, 8 and 9).

One of the strengths of psychodynamic approaches is that they contain explicitly worked out views of the human person. While these theories agree that human life is dynamic, worked out in tension between different competing forces, they disagree about the basis or ontology of personhood and what brings a person into being and makes them what they are. Zizioulas (2006) distinguishes between two different ontologies of personhood—substantialist and relational. In **substantialist ontologies**, it is assumed that there is some substance, quality, or essence of the human person that makes them what they are. Freudian theory is substantialist, because it argues that the power or energy from drives within the person is the primary factor behind human development. Substantialist ontologies are also found in other branches of psychology. For instance, cognitive views of the human person assume that rationality is the most important human quality, while neurobiological views argue that certain material processes and structures within the body are key. Substantialist ontologies are attractive to scientists because they are especially compatible with **monism**, the idea that everything can ultimately be reduced to a unified system or whole with no essential differences, an idea rejected by psychologists like William James (see Section 4.2.1). They also fit well in a culture that values individualism and places the independent, conscious self at the center of things. The alternative is a **relational ontology**, which argues that people gain their identity in their relations with others who are different from us in important ways but offer us the possibility of relationship. Relational ontologies emphasize the uniqueness and irreplaceability of each individual and their freedom, while substantialist ontologies focus on uniformity and conformity to law. According to relational ontologies:

- Gratitude should be a central response to life, since who we are is in large measure received from those around us
- Love is more than a feeling, it is a free relationship that helps provide identity and uniqueness
- Since our personhood is dependent upon relationship, it is not a quality we possess—it is *what we are*, and while it can be distorted in separation or our refusal to accept freedom and uniqueness, it cannot be lost
- If persons are essentially relational, they are best known in relationship.

Relational ontologies are of particular interest in the psychology and religion dialogue as most contemporary Christian theology (as well as key elements of classical Christian thought) is relational rather than substantialist in nature. Both relational and substantialist ontologies are influential in contemporary approaches to the dialogue. We examine some of these developments in the next chapter.

Chapter 6
Contemporary Approaches and Debates

So far we have been concerned with great historic movements in the dialogue between psychology and religion. Where is the field headed next? While predictions about the future are dangerous to make, in this chapter we review three prominent movements within psychology that are likely to affect the dialogue with religion. These are: (1) neurobiological approaches that utilize our expanding knowledge of the structure and workings of the brain; (2) evolutionary and cognitive psychology, which have developed a combined approach to the study of religion; and (3) postmodern perspectives, which challenge many of our conventional understandings of the human person and suggest new ways to think about religious life and the spiritual quest.

6.1 Neurobiological Approaches to Religion

Since the mid-20th century there has been increasing interest in the biological bases of behavior. The growing sophistication of research methodology and knowledge in this area has allowed researchers to begin investigating the biological underpinnings of religious experience. These attempts assume that there is a relationship between the brain and our mental life. In the early modern period, mind and brain were treated as largely separate from each other. This **dualistic** position was embedded in the philosophy of Rene Descartes (1596–1650) and has been very influential in modern thought. However, 20th century developments in neurobiology have questioned this position and today it has largely been rejected in theology as well (e.g., Rahner, 1963, p. 216). This has led to discussions about the **mind-brain problem**, how our mental functioning (which appears to be nonmaterial) is related to the physiological processes in our brain (which appear to be material).

A number of solutions to the mind-brain problem have been proposed as replacements for dualism, generating an enormous literature that is beyond the scope of this book. In the neuroscience community, a popular philosophical position is that the mind and brain are the same thing, a version of **monism**. There are various versions of this with important differences. In **reductive materialist monism,** mental events are thought to be merely brain processes. Generally, scholars who take this

J.M. Nelson, *Psychology, Religion, and Spirituality,*
DOI 10.1007/978-0-387-87573-6_6, @ Springer Science+Business Media, LLC 2009

view assume that consciousness and subjective awareness are **epiphenomena** with no real effect or importance. However, many believe that this kind of eliminative dualism is inadequate, and that consciousness and subjectivity are vital parts of our humanity (e.g., Varela, 2001; cf. Nagel, 1986). In this view, finding a way of looking at mind and brain that preserves the integrity of both is the most sensible way of approaching their relationship.

While it is entirely possible that the mind-brain problem is philosophically and scientifically insoluble, there are several non-reductive possibilities available that avoid dualism and allow mind and brain to relate to each other without being the same thing. One sophisticated version is *dual-aspect theory*, which argues that mind and brain represent two aspects of a single substance, just as light is both a wave and a particle (Barbour, 2002; Velmans, 2000, pp. 247–250). Another possibility is to consider consciousness as an *emergent phenomenon* of the brain (Murphy, 2002; Stoeger, 2002; see Section 2.1.2). In this view, mental processes supervene on physical ones—they are dependent upon them without being reducible to them. This means that it is impossible in principle to describe mental events completely as brain events, as emergent levels must be described on their own terms in addition to their relation with other levels (Clayton, 2002). Another more speculative view is that of some quantum theorists (e.g., Grib, 1996) who believe that pure consciousness is a *property of the universe* (see Section 2.5.1)—a position taken in traditional Hindu thought.

6.1.1 A Brief Introduction to the Brain

A basic knowledge of the brain is a helpful prerequisite to understanding neuroscience research related to religion and spirituality. On a cellular level, the brain is a collection of neurons that transmit signals using chemicals called **neurotransmitters**, which are released by a nerve cell and link up with receptor structures that stimulate or inhibit activity in other nerve cells. At the level of gross anatomy, the brain can be thought of as a collection of structures. In the **localization hypothesis**, it is assumed that particular locations in the brain carry out specific functions. There is considerable support for this, particularly with regard to basic sensory and motor functions. However, many functions (e.g., memory) do not seem to have a single specific location connected with them. This gives support to the **mass action hypothesis**, the idea that the whole brain or widely distributed networks of brain cells are involved in many brain functions. This **connectionist** view of the brain has generally replaced older **computational** models, which pictured the brain as a computer that processes instructions in a linear fashion. Connectionist theories help us understand how emergent processes can develop in the brain, helping it solve problems and increase its **plasticity** or ability to change (Varela, 2001; D'Andrade, 1995, pp. 10, 149; LeDoux, 2002, p. 43).

At a structural level, the brain can be generally divided into two main areas: cortical and subcortical (e.g., Cummings, 1985, p. 78; for maps of the brain see the digital atlas at www9.biostr.washington.edu/da.html). The **cortex** is the outermost, wrinkled and folded part of the brain and consists of four lobes—the **occipital lobe** located at the back of the head, the **parietal lobe** on top and to the rear, the **temporal lobe** on the lower sides and to the back, and the **frontal lobe**. Many higher cognitive functions are thought to be related to processing in these parts of the brain. The **subcortical** area of the brain contains a maze of small structures, pathways, and systems that carry out a variety of functions. One of these is the **limbic system**, which comprises a number of structures including the amygdala, hippocampus, and cingulate gyrus. The limbic system is thought to be related to emotional functioning, socioemotional perception, memory, and attention (see e.g., Paton, Belova, Morrison &, Salzman, 2006). It is connected to a number of other important subcortical structures, including the thalamus, which functions as a sensory relay station for the brain, and the hypothalamus, which exercises control over the body's hormone system. It is thought that the limbic system is able to regulate sensory input and focus through its connections with the thalamus (for a database of interconnections see brainmaps.org). Some of the functions of cortical and subcortical structures appear to be **lateralized** and more concentrated in either the left or right side of the brain, although contemporary research has tended to downplay the idea that some functions are strictly "left brain" or "right brain" (cf. Springer & Deutsch, 1998).

Another key part of the nervous system is the **autonomic nervous system (ANS)**, which helps regulate basic bodily functions. It includes the **sympathetic** or *ergotropic* **nervous system**, which is involved in arousal and stimulation, and the **parasympathetic** or *trophotropic* **nervous system** that has rest and rebuilding functions. Studies of brain waves using an **electroencephalogram** (**EEG**) have led some authors to suggest that ergotropic activity is connected with desynchronization or disconnection of brain wave activity in different regions, while trophotropic activity is related to synchronized EEG, relaxation, and suspended judgment. The ANS is regulated by the hypothalamus and indirectly by the limbic system through limbic-hypothalamic interconnections.

Traditional theories of brain function (e.g., Luria, 1973) view the brain as organized in hierarchical levels of primary, secondary, and tertiary or integrative functioning. In the sensory systems, primary functioning involves reception of basic sensory information. At this level, sensory information is processed independently for the different modalities: auditory information is handled in the temporal lobe, visual in the occipital lobe, and somatosensory (e.g., touch, body sensation, body image, and location) in the parietal lobe. At the secondary level, this basic information is associated with prior learning, allowing for identification and interpretation of sensory information. At the highest or tertiary level, information is processed in **sensory association areas** that integrate information from different sensory modalities (cf. Hunt, 1989). This probably takes place in the lower parts of the parietal lobe where it abuts the temporal and occipital lobes. Some authors refer to the tertiary area on the left side of the brain as the *verbal association area,* and the corresponding area on the right as the *visual association area* because of the tendency for language functions to be carried out on the left side of the brain and visual functions on the right. In the motor system, which has important controls in the frontal lobes, primary function involves the interface of the brain with motor neurons that trigger movement in various parts of the body. At the secondary level, the complex motor programming and sequencing necessary for activities is carried out. Finally at the tertiary motor area, the brain integrates information from the sensory areas and limbic system, as well as supports planning and decision-making functions related to goal-directed behavior. This tertiary area is sometimes referred to as the **attention association area**. In the motor unit, information moves from the tertiary level though the secondary to the primary level, where it triggers nerves that run to muscles and other parts of the body.

6.1.2 Evidence for Biological Factors in Religion

Most of the research on biological factors in religion has focused on physiological and neurological changes connected with meditation and religious experience (see Section 13.6). Older research has explored the connection between religion and epilepsy, while newer research has begun exploring possible structural, neurochemical, and genetic factors in religious experience or practice.

6.1.2.1 Epilepsy Studies

Epilepsy is a condition marked by **seizures** or uncontrolled electrical activity in the brain, as well as physical or mental changes. There are two main types of seizures—*generalized seizures* that affect the entire brain and *partial seizures* that affect only parts of the brain and have more varied effects. The most common site for partial seizures is the inner portion of the temporal lobe near the limbic system, with seizure activity often spreading to the hypothalamus. These seizures are typically complex, involving transliminal alterations in normal consciousness or awareness. In addition, individuals frequently report spiritual or religious feelings during seizures or abnormal temporal lobe activity (Thalbourne, Crawley, & Houran, 2003). There have even been reports of religious conversions following epileptic seizures (Saver & Rabin, 1997). This led Persinger (1987; Persinger & Makarec, 1987) to speculate that transient temporal lobe electrical activity forms an important base for God experiences. Persinger has found correlations (in the 0.4–0.66 range) between reports of complex partial epilepsy symptoms and various paranormal experiences, including a sense of presence, as well as a number of negative personality traits like aloofness and judgmentalness. He argues that these experiences reflect transient temporal lobe activity, perhaps triggered by changes in magnetic fields, which might be more likely to trigger paranormal experiences in those with seizure predispositions (Persinger, 2001; Persinger & Healey, 2002; McKay & Persinger, 2006). However, his experimental findings have not been confirmed by other investigators (Austin, 2006, p. 157).

Although quite interesting, Persinger's research has a number of limitations. First, it relates seizures to paranormal experiences and sense of presence, rather than strictly religious experiences. MacDonald and Holland (2002) partially confirmed this when they found that spirituality, but not religiousness, was related to a self-report measure of complex partial epileptic-like signs. Other investigators have found that temporal lobe epilepsy patients do not have a higher rate of mystical or religious experiences and religiousness than others and that the phenomenology of the seizure experience is typically different and more unpleasant (Sensky, 1983; Wildman & Brothers, 2002, p. 368; Watts, 2002a; Jeeves, 1997, p. 69). Persinger's work also contains a number of questionable philosophical and neurological assumptions; for instance he assumes a strict localization hypothesis (Persinger, 2001) that is not compatible with more recent neuropsychological understanding.

6.1.2.2 Neurotransmitter Findings

Recently, research has been appearing looking at the relationship between religiosity and neurotransmitters. In one study, Borg, Andree, Soderstrom, and Farde (2003) found that higher levels of serotonin inhibition in subcortical structures connected with sensory functioning were strongly related to higher levels of materialistic and rationalistic attitudes and lower levels of spiritual acceptance and self-transcendence. Kurup and Kurup (2003) compared neurochemical activity in the hypothalamus in spiritually inclined and atheistic individuals and found that differences in serotonin and dopamine functioning seemed to sensitize the perceptual system in spiritually inclined persons while increasing the chance of epileptic activity. They also suggest that this sensitization might produce subliminal types of perception—sensory activity outside of our normal conscious awareness. This would be consistent with phenomenological studies that found sensitivity to be a frequent characteristic among mystics and those who have religious experiences (see Sections 4.2.2 and 4.3.2), while atheists and those not spiritually inclined may not have easy access to such experiences. However, other studies have found different kinds of changes (e.g., Kawai et al., 2001), and this research suffers from small sample sizes and a lack of control over confounding variables. Additional brain chemical such as endorphins and melatonin are also being identified as potentially related to ASCs or mystical experiences, further confusing the picture (Hill & Persinger, 2003).

6.1.2.3 The Heritability of Religion

Could religion be inherited as part of the genetics of human nature (Anderson, 1998)? Answering this question is difficult in a couple of ways. First, the relationship between one's genetic information or **genotype** and its expression in the **phenotype** of a particular organism is complicated. Most genes have multiple effects on the phenotype, and multiple phenotypes can come from the same genotype in response to different environmental conditions and needs. Furthermore, the phenotype manifests itself in different ways depending on the environment and our personal choices, so the effect of genotype on behavior is quite indirect, making simple reductionistic models impossible (Geary & Bjorklund, 2000; Soto & Sonnenschein, 2006; cf. Pannenberg, 1985, p. 34). The second problem relates to the estimation and interpretation of the **heritability coefficient**, which indicates the amount of correspondence between genetic variability and the occurrence of a characteristic (Lerner & von Eye, 1992). Like a correlation coefficient, heritability coefficients do not necessarily imply causation. For instance, membership on a men's soccer team has a 1.0 (perfect) heritability index because sex-linked genetic variability (male vs. female) completely predicts team membership, but no one would say that the makeup of the team was completely due to sex-linked genetics.

An important procedure used in heredity research is the **twin study**, which compares identical twins having very similar genotypes with fraternal twins who have a normal level of genetic similarity. Twin studies have consistently found that religious affiliation—where you go to church—is not heritable but that religiosity and religious attitudes have a significant genetic component. One of the earliest studies was that of Waller, Kojetin, Bouchard, Lykken, and Tellegen (1990) who looked at a group of Minnesota twin pairs and found that roughly 50% of variance in religious values and interests was accounted for by genetic factors. Later studies have confirmed that pattern but found substantially lower heritability estimates. One of the best studies is the Virginia 30,000 study (D'Onofrio, Eaves, Murrelle, Maes, & Spilka, 1999), which has studied 14,781 twin pairs and their families, looking for **concordance** or agreement between the members of each twin pair on religious variables. While religious affiliation was related to culture or family rather than genetics, modest genetic effects for religiousness were present. Genetic-only effects for church attendance were 14.5% for men and 14% for women, and conservative religious attitudes had additive genetic effects of 35.8% for men and 17.3% for women. Personality variables did not appear to account for the relationship. These heritability figures are in line with Australian twin studies from the late 1980s that found figures in the 0.22–0.35 range (Eaves, Martin, & Heath, 1990), which corresponds to heritability figures on personal devotion behavior found in one study (Kendler, Gardner, & Prescott, 1997). Higher heritability figures have been reported among African Americans (Heath et al., 1999). However, heritability estimates typically make assumptions (e.g., about the independence of heredity and environment) that may not be valid in research on religious variables, so that research findings in this area may be highly misleading (D'Onofrio et al., 1999).

The findings on heritability are interesting and have led some writers to speculate that perception of a spiritual reality is an inherited ability that people possess in varying degrees, much as different people are more or less able to ride a bicycle. In this view, religiosity or atheism are related to high or low levels of this trait (Alper, 2001; Thalbourne & Delin, 1999). Specific gene locations have not been proposed, but given the fact that much of the effect of genes is through complex patterns of interaction, rather than specific effects of single genes, such a location is unlikely to exist.

6.1.3   The Mystical Mind

The only detailed attempt to construct a comprehensive biological model of religion has been that of Newburg and d'Aquili (d'Aquili & Newberg, 1999; Newberg & d'Aquili, 2000; Newberg & Newberg, 2005). They follow the perennialist model of Stace and focus on two possible universal dimensions of religious experience: (1) intermittent emotional episodes involving awe, peace, tranquility, or ecstasy and (2) varying degrees of unitary experience. They also follow Stace in separating the experience of the mystical event from its interpretation so that while the experiences are cross-culturally invariant there may be interpretive differences (Laughlin, McManus, & d'Aquili, 1993, pp. 160–164). They are particularly interested in a model that will explain the occurrence of states of *absolute unitary being* (AUB) and other mystical experiences. They believe such a theory could provide a basis for a new overarching universal metatheology that is not tied to a particular technique or religious tradition.

Newberg and d'Aquili believe that religious and spiritual experiences are supported by activity in many parts of the brain. Sustained attention, which is necessary in most religious practices such as prayer and meditation, is assisted by activity in the cortex, particularly the right frontal area, and in subcortical areas such as the cingulate gyrus. This in turn causes changes in structures such as the thalamus that are involved in the processing of sensory information about our body and the outside world. However, they believe that much of religious experience is due to patterns of ongoing "tuning" or activity in the autonomic nervous system. Under normal conditions, the ergotropic and trophotropic branches of the ANS act to inhibit each other, but under special conditions the system can be altered so that intense stimulation in one branch can spill over and activate the other branch as well, producing unusual mental experiences as well as physiological changes that are often associated with meditative practice. This retuning can be driven from the "bottom up" by physical activities like dancing and fasting, or it can be driven from the "top down" through imagery or meditative concentration, which activates different neurotransmitter systems (Laughlin et al., 1993; Newburg & Iversen, 2003). They identify five categories of excitatory events relevant to religious experience (d'Aquili & Newberg, 1999, pp. 255–256):

- Trophotropic, producing a relaxed yet vigilant mental state as in meditation
- Ergotropic, which produces aroused alertness as in flow states
- Trophotropic with ergotropic spillover, leading to feelings of energy or "oceanic bliss"
- Ergotropic with trophotropic spillover as in ecstatic experiences
- Maximal stimulation of both systems, leading to the most intense mystical experiences

Another important part of their view of the brain is their concept of *cognitive operators*, "general methods or functions by which the brain interprets the world" (Newburg & d'Aquili, 2000, p. 253). They identify a number of operators including a **holistic operator**, which enables us to see gestalts and put things in larger

contextual frameworks. They connect the holistic operator with activity in association areas of the right parietal lobe. In their view, all religious experiences involve
the operations of the holistic operator, which generates a sense of unity and thus of
self-transcendence and transformation (d'Aquili & Newberg, 1999, pp. 159–161).

D'Aquili and Newburg (1999) have also applied their theory to understanding
myth and ritual. Their basic thesis—like that of Kant and evolutionary psychologists
(see Sections 2.2.3 and 6.2.3)—is that ideas found in myth and ritual are shaped by
mental structures such as cognitive operators. They believe that myths, rituals, and
religious practices trigger holistic operators that allow all areas of the brain to work
together so that paradoxes and ultimate problems like death can be both perceived
and overcome. Thus while religion has its problems, overall its adaptive benefits
outweigh the negatives. Although they decline to take a position on whether the
brain is the cause or the occasion for mystical phenomena, they point out that there
is no reason to assume that mystical and other experience do not point to what is
real (cf. Laughlin et al., 1993).

While the first stage of all mystical experiences probably involves activation of
the frontal cortex as the will operates to clear the mind (Newburg & Iversen, 2003),
they argue that different types of experiences will be related to activity in other
areas of the brain. For instance, kataphatic experience will involve the visual association area while numinous and apophatic experiences will have its activity reduced
or blocked (d'Aquili & Newberg, 1999, pp. 102–117, Newberg & d'Aquili, 2000,
p. 258; Jourdan, 1994; cf. Section 3.3.2). They believe that less intense activation,
meditation, and ritual or spontaneous events cause discharges in the hypothalamus
and the limbic system leading to feelings of fear, awe, or ecstasy but at higher levels
of activation the holistic operator blocks the association areas in the parietal lobe
and produces a sense of absolute unitary being and breakdown of the dichotomy
between self and other.

6.1.4 Evaluation and Critique

The work of Newberg and d'Aquili has been critiqued by a variety of scholars.
Watts (2002a) notes that the theory has a number of strengths, including its attempt
to creative a comprehensive model that is based on the normal brain. However, he
and Andresen (2001) criticize the tendency of the theory to collapse all religious
paths under the single label of meditation and focus on a limited range of religious experiences such as those found in yoga and Tibetan Buddhism (Newberg,
Newberg, & d'Aquili, 1997; d'Aquili & Newberg, 1999, p. 256). They tend to
invent vocabulary (e.g., cognitive operators) that is not commonly used in the
neuroscience field and sometimes fail to adequately specify constructs. They also
seem to be inconsistent at times, for while they argue that it is possible to make
universal generalizations about religious experiences (Laughlin et al.,1993), they
also argue that it is impossible to generalize between individuals of different levels
of experience and different traditions (e.g., 1999, p. 159). Their theory is considered

speculative, because while it is mostly consistent with available data, there are few directly relevant studies, and it has not been tested against a competing model. Of course, religious experience is so diverse that it may not be possible to develop a single theory that encompasses all of it (Watts, 2002a). However, the theory does identify possible mechanisms for the perception of unitary states, weakening arguments by psychologists like Jung that such states cannot exist.

Some scholars offer a more general critique of the neuroscience perspective. On a technical level there are a number of problems. For instance, current imaging techniques are often noisy, disrupting the atmosphere needed for spiritual practices. They also lack the resolution and speed to pinpoint activity in small brain structures on a timely basis. So, while neuroimages are often taken to represent the same level of evidence as a photograph, in fact they provide a much more indirect type of data. Thus, the current data do not allow us to draw firm conclusions about the relation between brain states and mental states (Newberg & Iversen, 2003; Roskies, 2008; Farah, 2008). On a practical level, neuroscience findings may help us understand the biological mechanisms behind religious experiences, but they have limited ability to tell us their meaning or how they are integrated into the life of the individual (e.g., Wildman & Brothers, 2002). Finally, there are questionable metaphysical assumptions made by many neuroscientists, for instance that because an experience depends upon neurological mechanisms that it must be due to those mechanisms. That is like saying that our perception of a flower or of a kind action on the part of a friend is "nothing but" neurological activity and that the flower or actions are not real—a position of extreme skepticism that few would endorse. Clearly we need to avoid extreme reductionism that says only biological factors are relevant to understanding religion and embrace a multilevel approach, although extreme reductionism is becoming very fashionable among some neuroscientists (Watts, 2002a; Cacioppo, 2002; Bickle, 2006). There is no such thing as a wholly biological person; for instance, biology constrains culture but does not exist without it. Also, just because a phenomenon is brain based does not mean it does not have spiritual significance (MacIntyre, 1984, p. 161; Saver & Rabin, 1997). This of course does not mean that neuroscience research cannot be valuable and interesting—just that one should be aware of philosophical prejudices that might lead one to overinterpret findings. However, neuroscience explanations are fascinating, even if the neuroscience component of the explanation is of limited relevance or practical importance (Weisberg, Keil, Goodstein, Rawson, & Gray, 2008). Thus, it seems likely that neurobiological investigations of religious or spiritual phenomena will continue.

6.2 Evolutionary Psychology and Religion

The last 20 years have seen the increasing use of evolutionary theory to study religion. On the surface, this seems strange, as scientists or philosophers with an atheistic orientation (e.g., Dawkins, 1987, 1989; Dennett, 2006; Tooby & Cosmides, 2005) and conservative religious writers both see evolutionary theory and religion as in direct conflict. Although science cannot prove that God does not exist or is uninvolved in the world, some reductionist evolutionary theories seem to offer a kind of natural theology that substitutes evolution for God (Badcock, 2000, p. 17; Buller, 2005, pp. 422–426, 472–479; Cooper, 2007, p. 37). On the other hand, a number of scholars argue that while the reductive materialism and naturalism of some evolutionary thinkers may be incompatible with religion, some readings of theology and evolutionary thought may work well together (Peacocke, 1998; Russell, 1998; Ayala, 1998a; Ruse, 2000; Teo, 2002). In this view, incompatibility between evolutionary theory and religion is due to the personal metaphysical beliefs of the writer that people have "smuggled in and then given an evolutionary gloss" (Ruse, 2001, p. 128). These metaphysical beliefs require additional nonscientific arguments to support them, such as an outmoded positivist view of science which forces people unnecessarily into a conflict model of science and religion (McGrath, 2005, pp. 92, 140).

A full review of evolutionary theory with its problems, successes and challenges is beyond the scope of this book. Here, we will review some fundamentals of evolutionary thought, discuss the primary model in use for its application within psychology, and then discuss its current use in the study of religion.

6.2.1 Basics of Evolutionary Theory

6.2.1.1 Evolution and Selection

Evolution is the change in organisms that takes place over time due to genetic alterations. Like all science, evolutionary thought is built on both empirical observation or "fact" and theory (Goldsmith, 1994, p. 13). Facts would include the fossil record and observations of the evolutionary process that can be made in the laboratory, such as changes in bacteria that make them resistant to antibiotics. For most scientists, there is no doubt that evolution occurs; the debate is over how the process works (Plotkin, 2004, p. 128). The goal of evolutionary theory is to develop explanations of **ultimate cause**, or how the genotypes of organisms came to be the way they are, rather than the explanation of the **proximate cause** behind the development of the phenotype for a particular organism. Ideally, both explanations are necessary and complement each other.

Evolutionary explanations of change require three things. First, there must be a structure of law and constraint that is imposed by the basic laws of physics and biology, as well as requirements of the environment. Second, there must be freedom in the system in the form of novelty and variation. Novelty enters the creative process in several ways (Goldsmith, 1994, pp. 29–30), for instance though genetic changes, which can be produced by (1) mutation or recombination, (2) the movement of genes within populations or between groups known as **gene flow**, and (3) self-organizing processes that occur in complex systems (Barbour, 1998). Other events can also introduce **random drift** into a population, such as the meteor impact that ended the Cretaceous Period and the reign of the dinosaurs. A third and final requirement for changes is that there must be a way of sorting novelty and retaining helpful features (Ayala, 1998b). In evolutionary theory, this is done by natural selection, the process discovered by Charles Darwin (1809–1882).

In Darwin's original theory, selection referred to the retention of characteristics that helped organisms in the struggle for existence (Darwin, 1872, p. 60). In the modern synthesis of evolutionary theory, however, **natural selection** refers to the retention of characteristics that increase **reproductive fitness** or successful reproduction, for survival is meaningless in evolution unless your genes are passed on. This fitness is of two types, **Darwinian fitness** or the person's own reproductive success and **inclusive fitness**, which includes not only your own reproductive success but also that of your kin (Hamilton, 1964; Burnstein, 2005). The latter kind of fitness brings up the dilemma of **parental investment** (Trivers, 1972), which is that parents want to invest in their offspring to maximize inclusive fitness, but these investments are costly and must be balanced against other needs. An unanswered but controversial question is whether natural selection works solely with regard to individual organisms or might also work at a group level (Sober, 2002).

Darwin believed in a gradual evolutionary process of slow and steady change. This model does not fit easily with observed gaps in the fossil record, so some theorists like Gould (1988) have argued for a punctuated equilibrium model, where periods of stability alternate with rapid progress. Another issue has to do with the direction of the change process. While evolutionary theorists generally avoid the position that evolution is directed or moving toward a particular conclusion (e.g., Dawkins, 1989, p. 13), it seems difficult to deny some kind of directionality, a least a movement toward more complex forms within a range of possibilities established by evolution, a key issue for theological interpretation of the evolutionary process (Stoeger, 1998; Watts, 2002b; cf. Dawkins, 1997).

Earlier writers in **sociobiology** and behavioral ecology (e.g., Wilson, 1975) believed that the selection process could apply to specific behaviors, but today most scholars believe that it is the structures or mental mechanisms that produce behaviors rather than the behaviors themselves that are selected and passed on (Goldsmith, 1994, p. 92; Symons, 1995; Shanahan, 2004, pp. 260–261; Buller, 2005, pp. 50–53; Tooby & Cosmides, 1992, 2005; Batson, 1998). The idea that behaviors could be directly inherited is termed the **sociobiological fallacy** by its opponents. Sociobiology introduces a kind of functional reductionism, where for instance insects' sacrificing each other for the sake of the hive is equivalent to human altruism and is thought by some to be mostly pure speculation. This has led even evolutionary theorists to reject all or part of sociobiological explanations (Lerner & von Eye, 1992; Watts, 2002c, p. 17; Schloss, 2002b). Nevertheless, this type of reasoning can still be found in the professional literature (e.g., Roes & Raymond, 2003).

6.2.1.2 Adaptation

Adaptation is a key concept in evolutionary theory, but it is a confusing word because it has several meanings. In psychology we use the term **adaptive** to describe helpful changes that people make in response to environmental demands. If the temperature drops, we adapt by putting on a sweater. In evolutionary language, however, an **adaptation** is a characteristic that was selected in the past because it increased the reproductive fitness of an organism—its ability to survive and reproduce. It is of course difficult to determine what is an adaptation because we cannot look at the history that led to the present (Goldsmith, 1994, pp. 32–35) or at the **environment of evolutionary adaptiveness** (**EEA**) in which the adaptation arose. While it is easy to assume that current adaptive qualities originally developed as adaptations, there are many possible exceptions to this. First, a characteristic could be fitness enhancing now but not originally designed for its current role, either because it had a different original purpose or no original purpose at all. Gould and Vrba (1982) call these **exaptations**. They use bird feathers as an example, which are now adaptive because they assist flight but originally appear to have had a thermal regulation function. Another possibility is that something could be a **spandrel**, a necessary by-product of an adaptation that originally had no adaptive value but later found an adaptive function (Gould & Lewontin, 1979). For instance, it is likely that the ability to be a scientist has no adaptive value—it does not increase reproductive fitness—but it is a byproduct of intellectual development that does improve our ability to survive and reproduce. The presence of exaptations and spandrels makes it difficult to determine the original purposes of things by examining their current use, making it hard to develop evolutionary explanations. Also complicating matters is that various adaptations can interact, and organisms can act to modify their environments, changing the context for selection or even producing genetic or anatomic changes, an effect known as the *Baldwin effect* (Buller, 2005, pp. 41–42; Birch, 1998; Barbour, 1998).

Adaptationism and Darwinian pluralism. How does the importance of the natural selection process compare to that of novelty or freedom and constraint in the evolutionary process? While all are necessary and work together (Stoeger, 1998, p. 176), there are debates on which should be considered the primary process. Gould and Lewontin (1979) have argued that constraints such as environmental conditions are often more important or interesting explanations for evolutionary change than selection. This is called **Darwinian pluralism**. Opposed to this is the position that is called **adaptationism** or **Darwinian fundamentalism** (Gould, 1997), the idea that non-selection factors have at most a minor role in evolution. Darwin himself was uncomfortable with adaptationism (Shanahan, 2004, p. 137), and in general the field of evolutionary biology has moved toward a more pluralistic position over the past 20 years (Richardson, 2000).

6.2.1.3 Implications

Metaphysical assumptions. The metaphysical assumptions behind evolutionary theory have been the subject of comment. A number of authors have pointed out that evolutionary theories typically assume a lack of purpose or meaning to the universe (cf. Russell, 1998). The universe is seen as fundamentally a place of struggle for survival in a zero-sum environment of limited resources so that some must win and others lose (Barrett, Dunbar, & Lycett, 2002, p. 3). Critics argue that the assumption of lack of purpose makes it difficult or impossible to develop categories of value or virtue and, that while it is obvious that struggle exists and that life must be preserved, it is just as easy—perhaps easier—to argue that the universe has a moral order with elements of surplus, generosity, gift, and sacrifice (Hurlbut & Kalanithi, 2001; Ellis, 1998, 2002; Murphy & Ellis, 1996; Happel, 1996). Recognizing this noncompetitive side of life can enhance understanding of our biological condition and embeddedness in the natural world. A view of the universe as more than a struggle also appears to be a primary component in the development of generative individuals (McAdams, 2006, p. 8).

The metaphysical assumption that life is primarily about struggle is particularly problematic when applied to the study of religion. In the traditional adaptationist view, life consists of competing for a share—perhaps as big a share as possible—of limited resources and that when some win others must lose. However, this does not appear to be the situation with religious and spiritual goods. While there is no doubt a competitive factor in some aspects of religion (e.g., only one person can be Pope at a time, although many may wish to do so), religions commonly advertise that the benefits of allegiance and practice are available to all. A competition and limited resources model does not seem to make sense, and an application of such a model to the study of religion seems likely to distort its subject.

6.2.2 Evolutionary Theory in Psychology

Evolutionary theory and psychology have had an uneasy relationship. Early psychologists like Hall were influenced by the theory to take a developmental outlook on human behavior, leading to a tremendous research program with many positive benefits (see Section 7.3.1). On a more negative note, 19th-century figures like Herbert Spencer (1820–1903) and the psychologist Francis Galton (1822–1911) used evolutionary thought to develop **social Darwinism** and ideas about **eugenics**, the improvement of the human species through competition and manipulation of genetics (Plotkin, 2004, p. 43). Spencer in particular used the concept of "survival of the fittest" to justify various social policies that have since been strongly criticized (Badcock, 2000, p. 7). Darwin himself believed that men were intellectually superior to women and proposed an evolutionary explanation for this "fact" (Arnhart, 1998, p. 125). Modern evolutionary theorists are sensitive to this history and have tried to avoid these reductionistic traps.

The latest attempt to apply evolutionary theory in psychology is known as **evolutionary psychology (EP)**. While much of the effort of evolutionary psychologists is devoted to the explanation of sexual behavior (e.g., on rape see Hartung, 1992; Kanin, 1985; Palmer, 1991) or human traits like altruism and morality (Krebs, 2005), some evolutionary psychologists have also attempted to apply a version of evolutionary theory to religious phenomena. This effort has met with a mixed reception, just as critiques or alternative explanations have been proposed for evolutionary explanations of sexual behavior and morality (e.g., on rape see Lisak & Ivan, 1995; Malamuth & Brown, 1994).

The theoretical manifesto for EP has been given by Tooby and Cosmides (1992, 2005). They have a broad vision for EP, which is that it will provide a unifying theory that will transform the social sciences, which are "descriptive, soft and particularistic into theoretically principled scientific disciplines with genuine predictive and explanatory power" (2005, p. 6). They identify three ideas that they believe are widely held in psychology but are problematic and need to be removed:

1. *The universe is designed with a moral and spiritual order.* They believe that this is untrue because the universe is constructed by nature using the mechanism of natural selection and has no moral or spiritual order or purpose.
2. *Human nature is a blank slate that is quite variable and is aided by a mind that uses general-purpose problem solving mechanisms.* They argue that the mind that is at the center of human nature is made of a collection of domain-specific information-processing mechanisms that are not learned but represent a universal preset human nature.
3. Worst of all, *the value system of the social sciences privileges the different, particular and variable over the uniform, which gives a minimalist view of human nature.* This makes it impossible to discover the invariant natural laws that govern humanity. The social sciences are also infected with holistic thinking, which is thought to be problematic as it makes it difficult or impossible to analyze things in terms of their parts (Badcock, 2000, p. 228).

Several authors have noted that this description is an inaccurate caricature of most work in the social sciences, and Tooby and Cosmides admit this (Tooby & Cosmides, 1992, p. 31). Despite this, EP proposes the following assumptions in their place:

1. *Human nature is a mind that is an information-processing machine.* EP bases its view of human nature on aspects of modern cognitive science. EP sees the mind as central to human nature, as it is the cause of all behavior and bodily regulation. The mind in their view is very much like a computer—it is a set of information-processing devices that regulate behavior in response to information. Like a computer it is composed of thousands of problem-solving machines or **modules** that are evolved adaptations to specific problems, just as a Swiss army knife has many blades for specific functions. This **massive modularity hypothesis** (MMH) is preferred to the idea of the mind as a general-purpose problem solver, as a modular brain may be faster and is perhaps easier to explain within an evolutionary framework. However, more recently, Tooby and Cosmides (2005) have retreated from the position somewhat and speculated that emotions might also be an important part of human nature and aid in information processing.
2. *All aspects of human nature are adaptations produced through natural selection.* EP takes a Darwinian fundamentalist position, arguing that everything in the body has evolved to perform a function through natural selection, although they acknowledge that all behavior is not necessarily functional. In particular, they

dismiss the idea that culture is a source for functional behavior (Buss, 2001). These adaptations form a common human nature that took shape during the EEA of the Pleistocene period (about 1.8 million years ago to about 10,000 BC) when we lived in small groups and followed a hunter-gatherer lifestyle (Cosmides, Tooby, & Barkow, 1992). The adaptations form a developmental program or possibility for development of mental structures that is inherited and which might or might not be realized in everyone (Buller, 2005).

3. *EP can produce a general framework for both explanation and prediction of behavior.* Grantham and Nichols (1999) have noted that there are two general approaches within EP: explanatory and predictive projects. In explanatory projects, one works from an observed function and speculates about its adaptive source. For instance, Boyer argues that the degree of grief we feel about a loss is related to their reproductive potential, so that we feel less loss over the death of an infant or an aged parent than a young child or particularly a teenager, and that a loss of a group member engenders grief because of the loss of information and cooperation (Boyer, 2001, p. 25). In the predictive project, the researcher thinks about problems that our ancestors must have confronted and what solutions must have been necessary to solve them, and then reasons forward about what our minds should be like today.

6.2.2.1 Critical Views

Evolutionary theory certainly offers possible benefits to psychology, and evolutionary theorists have trumpeted its superiority over other models and its ability to put forward a progressive research program (e.g., Buss & Reeve, 2003; Ketelaar & Ellis, 2000; Ellis & Ketelaar, 2000, 2002). It is attractive when it advances our understanding of human nature and aids clinical practice (Hinde, 1991). However, the particular ideas about the mind and evolution embraced by EP have been heavily criticized (cf. Caporael & Brewer, 2000). Some of the key concerns are as follows:

1. *The EP view of the mind based on the massive modularity hypothesis is flawed.* EP calls for hundreds or thousands of modules, but evidence has only been found for the existence of a few. Some of these appear to be the product of both genetic and environmental factors, questioning the EP view that the modules are universal and invariant (Hughes & Plomin, 2000). The MMH also seems inconsistent with what we know about the brain, for instance, its developmental flexibility (Samuels, 2000; Badcock 2000, p. 23; Buller, 2005, pp. 130–137) and the fact that important parts of the brain appear to be multipurpose. Certainly the EP assumption that flexible, general-purpose mechanisms could not have been favored by selection is questionable (Buller, 1999, 2005, pp. 140–160). The computer model of the brain that lies behind the MMH also seems problematic; many things act like computers or have a computational character but are not computers—just because something can be used as a chair or acts like one does not mean it is one (Searle, 1993)!

2. *The fundamentalist view of adaptation taken by EP is flawed.* Extreme or "naive" views of adaptationism are no longer held in evolutionary biology (Freyd & Johnson, 1992; Lloyd & Feldman, 2002), and critics argue that they are certainly not an appropriate basis for an evolutionary psychology. Reducing everything to selection and adaptation is questionable as a scientific theory, because many behaviors cannot be interpreted in this way; instead, it is likely that there are several mechanisms shaping things besides natural selection, and evolution may involve multiple responses to problems. For instance, scholars like Mithen (2000) argue the archaeological evidence suggests that the creation of cultural artifacts, rather than the adaptation process, has stimulated much of recent mental evolution and development. This means that many human abilities are best conceptualized as exaptations or spandrels and that the idea of a single monolithic human nature is questionable (Teo, 2002; cf. Goldsmith, 1994, p. 34; Archer, 2001; Buller, 2005, pp. 14–15; cf. Gould & Lewontin, 1979).

3. *The explanatory and predictive projects as outlined by EP are flawed or overly ambitious.* While the concept of an explanatory project has not been criticized, in practice it has proved difficult, because it is hard to tell whether or not something is an adaptation and thus can become the proper object of an evolutionary explanation (Simpson & Campbell, 2005). The predictive project has met with much broader criticism. Grantham and Nichols (1999) argue that EP underestimates our ability to study psychology outside of the evolutionary framework and overstates the accuracy with which we can make predictions from the past. Many authors including paleontologists (e.g., Mithen, 2000; Cela-Conde, 1998; Cela-Conde & Marty, 1998) argue that our limited knowledge of the EEA reduces the specificity with which evolutionary problems, tasks, and possible adaptations can be ascribed to statements like "get a good mate" or "find food" which are so general as to be of little value. The lack of specificity means that EP explanations can be vague, speculative, and difficult to test. They are theoretical possibilities, not empirical realities (Buller, 2005, pp. 95–110; Thornhill & Thornhill, 1992; Shapiro, 1999; Bering, 2004; Teo, 2002; Batson, 1998). The dilemma for EP is that to the extent the EEA and current environment are different, it is difficult to establish meaningful comparisons, but if they are the same an evolutionary explanation adds nothing to hypotheses we can gather by traditional social science research (cf. Davies, 1999).

4. *EP theories do not meet traditional scientific standards for verification or falsifiability.* Since the evolutionary situation cannot be directly observed, many have accused EP theories of being unfalsifiable and have dismissed them as fairy tales (e.g., Girard, 1987, p. 89). Some EP scholars deny this (e.g., Buss, 1995; Kirkpatrick, 2005, pp. 180–182) and argue that it is possible to generate specific falsifiable hypotheses within the evolutionary paradigm, although it is impossible to test the paradigm as a whole. This is a questionable strategy, as it admits that it is impossible to test evolutionary explanations against competing views such as cultural ones. Other EP scholars (e.g., Ketelaar & Ellis, 2000) admit that evolutionary explanations are not falsifiable but say that this is not a problem, because EP operates within a Lakatosian model of science

(see Section 2.4.2), where the criteria of success for a given hypothesis are compatibility with the core beliefs and the progressive, heuristic nature of the program. In this view, demonstrating that an explanation is "speculative but plausible" (e.g., Murphy & Stich, 2000, pp. 70–71) or offering examples of where it might be true (e.g., Buss, 2001) are considered adequate verification. This is a misreading of Lakatos (Caporael & Brewer, 2000) and has raised many concerns, even within the EP community, that there are lots of theories but little testing against the data (e.g., Wynn, 2000; Hurlbut & Kalanithi, 2001). Richardson (2000) has commented that without such testing, there is no way of knowing whether EP theories are any better than Ptolemy's theory of epicycles. The strategy of claiming that EP methods do not need falsification is also risky, as EP dismisses other theories such as creation science because they are not falsifiable (Buss, 1995).

5. *EP theories contain many unrecognized and unsupported metaphysical positions.* Given the strong presence of positivist metaphysics within psychology (see Section 2.4.3), it is not surprising that the EP takes a view of evolutionary theory that best fits within the positivist framework. EP explanations are marked by atomism, simplistic reduction of phenomena to a basic cause (such as adaptation) and rejection of holism. While these stances are defensible in certain situations, we have seen that their broad use has many disadvantages. A second metaphysical position implicit in EP is that the purpose of life is reproductive fitness. However, many would argue that quality of life and human flourishing are important goals that are not reducible to reproductive fitness. This is a particularly important issue if evolutionary psychology is to be applied to religion, where spiritual advancement is considered a central goal. Finally, some express concerns about the metaphysical and ethical implications of EP. For instance, the evolutionary theorist Hagen, after providing a spirited defense of EP against moral objections, closes an article on the following note:

"More worrisome, EP challenges the foundations of crucial enlightenment values, values we undermine at our peril. Perhaps the mix of secular and religious values on which the priceless institutions of democracy rest are like a tablecloth that can be quickly yanked out, leaving everything standing on some solid, though as yet unknown, base. But I wouldn't bet on it. We are at a crossroads. A vibrant science of human thought and behavior must always be able to question its own premises and is thus utterly unsuited to be that solid base. Yet, if we discard the secular, quasiscientific notion of the blank slate, or even subject it to genuine scientific scrutiny, we may threaten institutions far more valuable than a science of human nature. The vital question is not, as most critics seem to think, whether EP is correct, but whether any real science of the brain is prudent" (Hagen, 2005, p. 171).

6.2.3 Evolutionary Psychology of Religion

Evolutionary psychologists conceptualize religion as a solution to adaptive problems (Buss, 2002). This can be done in a couple of ways. First, religion can be considered as an adaptation, an ability or strategy that conveyed some advantage and so enhanced reproductive fitness. This is a sociobiological conception of religion (e.g., Wilson, 1975; Broom, 2003), which has been rejected by most writers, since there is little or no evidence that specific behavior like religious ones can function as adaptations and be inherited (e.g., Hinde, 2002). Second, religion can be seen as related to human cognitive capacities and other abilities that are produced by evolution, so it is the abilities and not religion itself that is the evolutionary product (e.g., Clement, 2003). This is the stance taken by most contemporary investigators in the psychology of religion, as well as by anthropologists and cognitive scientists working to develop a cognitive science of religion.

6.2.3.1 Psychology of Religion and Evolutionary Thought

In psychology, the leading advocate for an evolutionary approach to the psychology of religion is Lee Kirkpatrick (1999, 2005). Kirkpatrick begins from the standard EP model and argues that religion is not an adaptation but built on other evolved mechanisms and that it acts along with the rest of our evolved nature (cf. Bering, 2004). Kirkpatrick believes that evolutionary theory will provide an overall paradigm for psychology of religion research that will help us understand the universality that lies under "superficial" variability (2005, p. 184). While Kirkpatrick does not offer a comprehensive evolutionary theory of religion, he points out a number of places where an evolutionary perspective may help us understand factors that are related to religion such as interpersonal attachment (see Section 8.2), the role of status, dominance or power figures, and our understanding of altruism, cooperation, and outgroup behavior. Many of Kirkpatrick's suggestions are interesting, although his broad adoption of the EP model brings with it the many problems we have discussed above. It is also unclear how much will be gained by the use of EP. Kirkpatrick notes that bringing an evolutionary perspective into his attachment research "does not fundamentally change my theory of attachment and religion in any way" (2005, p. 189) and that it is difficult to empirically test evolutionary explanations against standard attachment ones.

6.2.3.2 Cognitive Science of Religion and Evolutionary Thought

In the **cognitive science of religion** (CSR), scholars take insights from anthropology, evolutionary theory, or cognitive science and apply them to the understanding of religious thinking. The general thesis of CSR is that human thought processes have a certain character that leads us to make meaning or think religiously and to do so in certain ways (Klinger, 1998). While there are many parallels between CSR and EP, in practice CSR scholars vary in terms of their allegiance to specifics of the EP model and the amount they utilize evolutionary thinking in their theories. The hope of many CSR scholars is to "free religion from the realm of metaphysical speculation and to anchor it instead in the empirical" while respecting it and avoiding unnecessary reductionism (Andresen, 2001, p. 1), although some writers embrace reductionist explanations more than others.

In CSR theory, religion is considered to be a spandrel or exaptation based on the standard set of evolved cognitive capacities shared by all humans. It rejects the position of Otto (see Section 4.3.3) that religion is a phenomenon that is *sui generis* with unique characteristics (Pyysiainen, 2002; cf. Murphy, 1998b). Rather, CSR scholars generally believe that religious thinking is built on the tendency of our minds to detect the presence of persons and agents. When inexplicable events occur, it is cognitively easy and natural to attribute them to agents because it allows us to use our normal thinking about the category "person" to understand what happened (Boyer, 2001). However, these agents must have abilities that violate our expectations of the laws of nature so that the agent has additional supernatural qualities. Ideas that have both natural and supernatural aspects are referred to as **minimally counterintuitive ideas**, and CSR scholars argue that our minds find them attractive because they provide the opportunity for imaginative stories with many different kinds of inferences. Since they are attractive they tend to be transmitted from person to person. Explanations based on supernatural agents and minimally counterintuitive ideas constitute a **cognitive optimum position** that is a natural way of thought and is described in theories like those of Pascal Boyer and Harvey Whitehouse (Day, 2005; see e.g., Whitehouse, 2004a, 2004b). The cognitive optimum position is personalistic and utilizes the representational and attributional functions of the mind. This is in contrast to science, which offers mechanistic views of the world that are also counter-intuitive but non-personalistic (Pyysiainen, 2001a, pp. 197–228).

Stewart Guthrie and anthropomorphism. Guthrie (1993, 2001) has argued that the cognitive optimum position for humans is one of *anthropomorphism*, the attribution of personhood and agency to non-agentic phenomena. Barrett (1998, 1999; Barrett & Keil, 1996) argues that this is because it provides a quick and easy way for us to think about certain topics. He draws on cognitive research to note that the brain processes information in two ways: a fast mode that is intuitive and narrative in form, and a slower mode that is less intuitive, more complex and theological. In research with Hindu subjects, Barrett found that anthropomorphism was much more common in narrative than in theological descriptions, suggesting that one reason for anthropomorphism is that categories like "agent" are a quick and efficient way to understand God and conceptualize religious ideas. However, he notes that Guthrie's thesis that anthropomorphism is a general cognitive bias still needs empirical support.

Pascal Boyer and naturalized religion. While some CSR theorists have tried to pursue non-reductionistic strategies, others like Boyer (1994, 2001, 2005) have used the cognitive optimum position as a tool to produce reductive naturalist accounts of religion. For Boyer, an explanation of religion need not be of any humanistic or practical interest, but the focus should be on reducing diversity to develop a parsimonious account of general mechanisms; his final account of "The Full History of All Religion (Ever)" occupies only 2–1/2 pages (2001, pp. 326–328)! His focus is on the question of why anyone would hold religious ideas, which he sees as illogical, of no straightforward adaptive value, and often costly to the people who hold them and to others. Given his reductive naturalist position his answer is not surprising: he finds them to be a natural function of the general operations of the human mind rather than some special ideas and practices developed by religious people, and they are transmitted because they follow the cognitive optimum position (cf. Boyer & Ramble, 2001). This naturalness explains "the dogged pursuit of the paranormal and the miraculous" (Boyer, 2001, p. 76), rather than supposing that the explanations and rituals of religion have any actual value as in providing meaning, purpose, or deliverance from mortality.

Boyer's work has met with increasing criticism from other CSR scholars. Many object to his reductionistic labeling of many things as counterintuitive or supernatural and his implicit scientism that discounts other approaches to the study of religion (Pyysiainen, 2002). Hinde (2005) has challenged a number of specific features of the theory, including its focus on a narrowly defined set of cognitive characteristics and standards of rationality and its exclusion of emotion and religious experience. Bering (2004) also notes that while Boyer may not see a connection between religion and issues of immortality and meaning, many others find the connection extremely important and thus a vital part of any understanding of religion. Some scholars find aspects of his theory highly speculative (Pyysiainen, 2001a, p. 233) and question the testability of the theory or the extent to which it is congruent with available evidence (Whitehouse, 2004a, p. 79).

Harvey Whitehouse and modes of religiosity. Whitehouse has worked to extend the work of Boyer by trying to create a testable theory of religious transmission that goes beyond the narrow range of phenomena considered in Boyer's theory (Day, 2005; Whitehouse, 2004a, 2005). Like Boyer, Whitehouse defines religion in terms of beliefs and actions that relate to a supernatural agency, and his primary interest is in how religious beliefs are transmitted. However, he also rejects Boyer's view of religion as an unconscious process, which he sees as limiting the explanatory power of a theory. Instead, Whitehouse argues for a broader layered approach that takes seriously the explicit statements people make about their beliefs, because they have real motivational salience and thus cannot be ignored. He also widens the focus of his model and is interested in the context that constrains religious concepts and practices and acts as a filter or motivator for religious transmission.

Whitehouse is best known for his **modes theory** of religious transmission. He believes that methods of religious transmission tend to cluster in combinations called *attractor positions*, rather than follow a rigid set of lawlike rules. The cognitive optimal position is one attractor position. However, many religious things that are valued are not cognitively optimum. They are more conceptually dense and may be transmitted by methods that cluster around different attractor positions or *modes*. Like the cognitive optimal position, these modes provide ways for people to remember and motivations for passing on teaching.

Whitehouse has identified two modes of religious transmission. The *doctrinal mode* is found in complex thought as is typically present in large religious communities. Transmission in the doctrinal mode involves calm, ritualized, routine, and automatic repetition. This need for repetition makes the doctrinal mode very labor intensive, and it must balance problems of tedium in repetition against the needs of the priestly hierarchy to transmit doctrine. In the more ancient *imagistic mode*, which involves simple thoughts and small groups, transmission is oriented around emotionally intense, seldom-performed practices. In the Christian tradition, weekly worship services might be examples of the doctrinal religious mode, while ceremonies structured around baptism or conversion could be more imagistic. Transmission can trigger an extended search for the meaning of the experience that requires conscious thought and sometimes the help of experienced elders. The two modes of Whitehouse invite comparison with the fast/implicit and slow/complex processing modes of Barrett, suggesting a dual process mode of religious cognition (Mailey, 2004; Tremlin, 2005).

Almost all aspects of the modes theory have been challenged, including its focus on only certain aspects of religion, and problems with testability and measurement. A key criticism revolves around whether one can categorize religions as doctrinal or imagistic, as all religions seem to have elements of both (Laidlaw, 2004a, 2004b; Bloch, 2004; Whitehouse, 2004b; Pyysiainen, 2005). Some religious groups do not seem to fit well within the model. For instance, in American evangelicalism, repetition is designed to increase relevance more than to remind, and the movement as a whole gets energy from individual emotional experiences rather than small groups (Malley, 2004). Boyer (2005) has criticized the theory for its descriptive quality and lack of causal explanation.

6.2.4 Positives, Problems, and Prospects

There is no question that evolutionary theory is a powerful tool that has advanced our knowledge of the living world. It also seems likely that despite the history of failed attempts such as eugenics and sociobiology, further efforts will be made to apply evolutionary thought in psychology. We will probably learn valuable things from this, particularly as it is applied to areas of psychology closely related to reproductive fitness.

However, there are problems. We have already seen that general evolutionary theory contains metaphysical assumptions about the nature of human life that are quite limiting and that there are significant methodological and metaphysical limitations inherent in the current EP model. Some of the same problems may apply to CSR. While the goal of CSR is to bring religion out of the realm of metaphysical speculation, CSR like any other approach in science, has metaphysical presuppositions that need to be examined, understood, and critiqued. In particular, it is important to see how reductionism and naturalism influence this work.

6.2.4.1 Reductionism

As we noted earlier (see Section 2.1.2), reductionism is a natural part of science and of our daily way of looking at the world. However, EP and CSR often pursue it in ways that are unwarranted or unhelpful, particularly with regard to the study of religion.

1. EP engages in *methodological reductionism* by attempting to explain everything in terms of behaviors or thoughts that enhance reproductive fitness (cf. Kirkpatrick, 2005, pp. 161–163). This means that things like emotion, religious experience, or consciousness are ignored as are the broad effects of these things beyond fitness enhancement. It gives the theories something of a passive and atomistic quality that ignores holistic processes and the effects of human agency (Hinde, 2005; Pyysiainen, 2001b).

2. EP follows a strict *causal reductionism* by assuming that cognitive and evolutionary processes affect religion but not the reverse. This neglects a basic principle of evolutionary biology that context and environment—including cultural and religious environment—can affect the development of human characteristics and abilities (Jensen, 2002; Day, 2005).

3. Some EP and CSR authors seem to engage in *ontological reductionism* by assuming that if religious capacities have evolved and make use of common cognitive abilities, then religion is not unique and is nothing but a product of evolution. These are assumptions, as it is perfectly possible for religion to make use of common cognitive abilities but still be unique and have truth value (Watts, 2002b; Elkind, 1970).

6.2.4.2 Naturalism and Scientism

Reductive forms of naturalism and scientism also show up in EP and some versions of CSR. *Reductive naturalism* appears as **abstractionism**, an assumption that the general and abstract is of greater worth or more real than the particular and that science or nonscience approaches that embrace the particular are worthless. This is problematic for the study of religion because (a) examination of particular, exceptional religious persons offers valuable information about religion that cannot be gained by studying group averages, and (b) religion cannot be understood apart from transcendence, which typically manifests itself in the different rather than the uniform. *Positivistic scientism* follows in part from reductive naturalism when science or non-science approaches that give attention to the particular are deemed worthless or harmful. It appears in the assumption that anyone who criticizes details of evolutionary and EP approaches must be unscientific and resistant to change (Day, 2005). It also is apparent in the tendency of EP and some CSR authors to overstate findings and understate possibilities for other models, a problem which is compounded by a worrying lack of empirical data (Watts, 2003). These positivistic attitudes serve to shield EP and CSR from dialogue, criticism, and verification, thus hindering their ability to achieve true knowledge of their subject.

All of these forms of reductionism and naturalism involve metaphysical assumptions that are almost always left unstated and unsupported. The extent to which they affect various theories in CSR (or EP) varies. Whitehouse, for instance, seems to make an effort to avoid unnecessary reductionism, while writers like Boyer embrace it with its attendant problems. The extent to which EP and CSR can make genuine contributions to the study of religion and spirituality will depend on their ability to make appropriate use of reductionistic strategies and to understand the limitations an evolutionary metaphysical position places on their ability to understand religion. It seems likely that complex behaviors like altruism or religion cannot be understood simply within an evolutionary framework but require insights from other models and disciplines as well (Schloss, 2002a).

Above all, the presence of biological and evolutionary explanations of religion should not be taken as a criticism of either the truth or social value of religious traditions. As the evolutionary theorist Broom (2003, p. 29) notes:

> The existence of a biological explanation does not devalue spirituality. It may well encourage people to be a part of a religion because they understand it and its benefits better. Writers who criticize and denigrate religion generally pick on what are actually rather peripheral structures and rituals, apparently without appreciating the central tenants. Some general statements by evolutionary biologists, see for example Dawkins (1993), such as 'religion is just like a computer virus' are bad science and indicate a failure to understand either evolutionary mechanisms or the complexities of organisation of societies.

6.3 Postmodern Perspectives, Psychology, and Religion

One of the most significant intellectual and cultural changes of the later 20th century was a move away from what is known as **modernism**. This is a worldview that formed as a result of the developments from the Renaissance (late 15th and 16th century), and the Protestant Reformation (16th century), as well as the rise of science and the Enlightenment (late 17th to 18th century). The modernist worldview emphasizes the universality of truth and the centrality of the individual who stands apart from the world and others; it forms that basis of much scientific philosophy, including positivism, and helps to drive the increasing technification of our culture. In recent years, this worldview has come under criticism, and some scholars have abandoned all or part of it in favor of what is called a late modern or **postmodern** worldview. In this section, we will consider details of these paradigms and possible applications of postmodernism to the psychology and religion dialogue.

6.3.1 Modernism and Postmodern Critique

6.3.1.1 Basic Issues

Ideas of Truth. The classical modernist position on truth is that it is universal and can be discovered not through tradition but by procedures of inquiry, leading to a general theory or **metanarrative** of the world and existence. This idea of truth and knowledge is very congruent with positivism but is rejected by postmodernists in a couple of ways. First, postmodernists reject the possibility of metanarratives (Lyotard, 1984), because they believe all truth exists within a particular cultural or historical context and for a particular purpose. In this view, what is true for people in one culture may not be true for those from a different tradition or cultural background (MacIntyre, 1988; Ratner, 1989). Since truth is dependent on social and communal context, knowledge can be viewed as a product of **social construction** (cf. Berger & Luckmann, 1966; Gergen, 1999). In extreme statements of this position, postmodernists seem to argue that there is no fixed truth at all (e.g., Gergen, 1994, p. 79), a position at odds with that traditionally taken by religious traditions (Rizzuto, 2005). Second, postmodernists reject the idea that more knowledge will necessarily result in human progress. Rather, since knowledge is socially constructed, it is subject to political and economic processes and may be used as a tool for power and oppression. Picking apart this darker underside of human inquiry is a primary goal of **deconstructionist** critiques of knowledge. For instance, writers like Foucault (1965) and Cushman (1995) argue that economics and the need for social control have been primary factors in the medicalization of mental illness and deviant behavior (cf. Section 10.3.1). This analysis of hidden structures of power or oppression is a key agenda item for much postmodernist work, although sometimes this has been taken to excess. Deconstructionism in the hands of a writer like Foucault is primarily destructive, pointing out flaws in the current system, while other writers like Alasdair Macintyre also offer constructive alternatives (Carrette, 2000; Doniger, 2000).

Centrality of the individual. A second critical component of the modernist paradigm is its view of the human person as an isolated, autonomous individual—what Taylor (1989) has called a "punctual self." This can be seen in positivist views of the human person, and also surprisingly in some humanistic and transpersonal accounts like that of Maslow (1970, pp. 194–199). Since postmodernists believe that the individual cannot be understood apart from the social and historical context within which they live, they often take a relational approach to understanding the person (e.g., Balswick, King, & Reimer, 2005; Evans, 2004). This relational view is part of a broader "relational turn" found in contemporary Christian theology, as well as social science and humanities disciplines. In a **relational ontology** or approach, since each person has a unique history and stands in the center of multiple and perhaps contradictory relationships and contexts (de Certeau, 1984, p. xi), each person is *unique* and any understanding of the human person must encompass that uniqueness. In the traditional modernist view, the *typical* is what is important and the focus of attention (Taylor, 1989, p. 209), while uniqueness presents a problem for the model to be overcome by a better model with more variables, improved measurement techniques, or at last resort by simply calling it "error" and dismissing it.

Spectator vs. Actor. Modernist views of persons tend to treat them as detached observers controlled by the forces of natural law, lacking free will and agency. Postmodernists, on the other hand, see people and societies as agents who are active in constructing themselves and their world. This view of the person as active agent fits well with traditional Christian views of the soul as the center of action; it also implies that a view of human behavior will contain within itself an ethical perspective on how action may be evaluated (Happel, 2002; Thomas, 1998, I q 76 a3, q77 a1; Talbot, 1997).

Critical stance toward science. Many postmodernists are ambivalent about aspects of scientific approaches to knowledge and problem solving. They point out:

1. While science portrays itself as the means to find unshakable and objective truth, in fact current scientific theories frequently make contradictory claims, and truth is established only to find out later that it is either partial or false. Total objectivity in science is also impossible, for experiments and interpretation of data are determined by theory, which is partly imaginative opinion that can overwhelm facts. Also, interest groups and the profit motive can affect the conduct and application of scientific studies (Hauke, 2000, pp. 237–239).

2. Science promotes technological solutions that can have positive effects, but they also carry with them threats like weapons of mass destruction or global warming. It also promotes a view in which nature is attacked, and things are stripped of meaning and value, becoming just resources and products for consumption (Polkinghorne, 2004, pp. 25–26, 40–41).

3. Science promotes the values of efficiency and control and with them the idea that decisions should be made by expert managers, who are morally neutral authorities on their subject and able to effectively solve problems. However, the values of efficiency and control are not morally neutral, and the knowledge needed for effective control of problems often does not exist, so that the decisions made by experts frequently are just an exercise of personal will or preference (MacIntyre, 1984, pp. 74–77).

Critical stance toward universalism in religious studies. Postmodernists have challenged early 20th-century perennialist thought that tended to see all religions as similar to each other. They argue that such as position pays insufficient attention to differences and the context of belief and practice, and that such views are strongly influenced not by the facts but by the modernist presumptions of the scholars doing the work (Holdrege, 2000; cf. e.g., Tyler, 1986; Rabinow, 1986; Ray, 2000). In this view, religions need to be understood on their own terms, rather than as imperfect examples of some kind of universal phenomenon. Postmodernists have also pointed out the effects of culture on the psychology of the individual (e.g., Stigler, Shweder, & Hendt, 1990), suggesting that relationships between psychology and religion are not universal but are specific to a particular cultural setting. This critique has been quite influential, so many researchers are now including cultural considerations in their theory and research (Vande Kemp, 1999; cf. Section 4.4).

Importance of culture and relationality. Since postmodernists believe that reality is constructed by the individual, their explanations of human behavior focus on systems that make construction possible. While Kant believed that universal thought structures lay behind the formation of knowledge (see Section 2.2.3), postmodernists argue that culture is a primary tool in this process. The beliefs and practices that are part of a given culture are thought to influence us in many ways, for instance, in how mental illness is defined and conceptualized (e.g., Foucault, 1976, pp. 60–88).

6.3.1.2 Effects of Postmodernism

Levels of adoption. Although the dominance of positivism in psychology has made it resistant to ideas that question the modernist paradigm, postmodern influence in the discipline has been increasing. It is particularly noticeable in the fields of psychotherapy and family therapy (e.g., Michael White), psychoanalysis (e.g., Steven Mitchell), cognitive psychology (e.g., Jerome Bruner), developmental psychology (e.g., Richard Shweder), personality (e.g., Dan McAdams), and social psychology. It also has influenced later versions of feminist theory and theology (Chopp, 1997; Keller, 1997). Psychologists influenced by postmodernism do not necessarily reject every aspect of modernism and adopt all the postmodern alternatives. In fact, mixtures of ideas are common, which make it inappropriate to issue blanket assessments of postmodern influence; some scholars even refuse to use the term postmodern, preferring late modern or some variation as an alternative. An example of this in psychology would be the work of Gergen, who has adopted constructionist views of truth but retained much of modernist individualism. The result is a radical position of individualistic relativism, where each person develops fragmented or "saturated" selves and is free to have multiple identities and constructions of reality to suit the needs of different situations (Gergen, 1991). This view has been rejected by other postmodernists with a more relational stance (e.g., Balswick et al., 2005) as espousing **relativism**, the idea that there is no truth that can be discovered. Such a view makes it difficult to develop a coherent concept of moral action (Baumeister, 1998). A more moderate position is that of **postfoundationalism** (e.g., Godfrey, 2006), which argues that one can move toward increasingly better views of the world but that dialogue between traditions provides a crucial critical perspective on one's beliefs which assists in the process. This view fits well with **critical realist** views of science (see Section 2.5.4).

Development of postmodern alternatives. Postmodern thought not only offers a critique of modernist presuppositions but also an alternative strategy for inquiry and a different understanding of the human person. This is developed in three ways: (1) a hermeneutic approach to knowledge, (2) a narrative understanding of how we look at the world and construct ourselves, and (3) a consideration of everyday practices and practical reasoning.

6.3.2 Hermeneutics and the Postmodern Approach to Knowledge

Hermeneutics is a theory about how we interpret meaning in discourse and actions (Ricoeur, 1981, p. 43). In a hermeneutic psychology, what is important about life is not a series of factual events but the meaning that is attached to those events. In this view, it is believed that statements and events can be seen in multiple ways and so must be interpreted (Crowe, 2005; Bruner, 1991). Unlike the traditional positivist approach, hermeneutics acknowledges that interpretation cannot occur in a vacuum. Any statement or action, even in the physical sciences, is made with reference to an observational frame that forms a **pre-understanding** or context from which interpretation proceeds (Ellis & Stoeger, 1996; Gadamer, 1989). In the human realm, the context for understanding statements or actions includes (1) the personal worlds and history of the actor/speaker and the interpreter, and (2) any larger context within which the action took place or the thought was expressed, including the beliefs, current situation, and history of larger groups to which the actor/speaker and interpreter belong. The interpretive process occurs when the discourse or action we seek to interpret interacts with our personal and global contexts to from a new insight or understanding, which in turn alters the beliefs that form the context for interpretation. This dialectical or back-and-forth process where the speaker/actor and interpreter affect each other and their interpretive frameworks is sometimes called the **hermeneutic circle** (Ricoeur, 1974, p. 87, 1976, 1981, p. 93, 1984, pp. 46–77, 1995, p. 240). This dialogical process can be used as a model for understanding human behavior and action. It can also be used as a framework for conversation between disciplines, such as between religion and science (Browning, 2002) (Fig. 6.1).

Hermeneutics questions traditional psychological explanations of action that emphasize rationality and logical rules (e.g., Piaget and Kohlberg, see Section 7.4) or empirical explanations that aim at prediction and control through formulation of universal causal laws. These are thought to oversimplify and assume that human systems can be described in the same way as physical ones. Instead, hermeneutics offers a framework that escapes this kind of reductive naturalism (Richardson, 2006). In the hermeneutic view, action always has a holistic character and can only be understood by understanding the meaning it has in the specific context and situation

Fig. 6.1 *Paul Ricoeur.* One of the most important French philosophers of the 20th century, he brought a sophisticated and sympathetic understanding of psychology and theology to his work on hermeneutics and narrative. Photo courtesy of University of Chicago

where it occurs. Since this is constantly changing and always somewhat unique, timeless ahistorical laws cannot adequately describe human action, and other formats such as narrative may be required (Packer, 1985, 1988; Polkinghorne, 2004, pp. 77–79). Thus the hermeneutic or interpretive approaches to religion within psychology are often seen as at odds with traditional empirical methods (Luyten & Corveleyn, 2007), although they also can be seen as complementary to each other. Hermeneutic approaches have become increasingly popular in recent years, particularly in the field of pastoral care (Schweitzer & Mette, 1999).

6.3.3 Narrative Aspects of Knowledge and Self

As we remarked before, postmodernists are interested in the lived experience of the human person and feel that accounts—scientific or otherwise—that leave this out are incomplete. This means that explanations must deal with *time*, because the temporal character of life is one of its most important attributes. Postmodern theorists view narrative as the best way for us to understand this aspect of existence (Ricoeur, 1984, p. 3; Bruner, 1991, p. 4). They accept the thesis (e.g., Arendt, 1998) that a characteristic of the human person is that their life comprises events and actions that have enduring effects and are put into story form. By dealing with action and the intensions of actors in the story, narrative provides explanations for why things happen.

    The nature of narrative. Narrative is both a kind of discourse and a way of thinking (Bruner, 1991). Narrative begins with action—isolated episodes of practical action or more deliberative acts—and through the creative work of **emplotment** that weaves actions and characters together into a coherent story or **narrative**. Narratives thus include **mimesis** or representations and schemas of action that establish concordance among a collection of conflicting themes and events. This struggle to establish coherence is at the core of authentic experience. Emplotment in narrative accomplishes this task by (1) showing the relation between individual events and story as a whole; (2) bringing together heterogeneous elements like circumstances, agents, or goals; and (3) providing a temporal unity that overcomes discordance. This unity gives meaning to the story, helping us to understand past events and allowing us to picture ways we might pursue future goals; narrative thus can lead to action (Polkinghorne, 1988; de Certeau, 1984, pp. 70–79). Narrative also includes an ethical component, revealing character by connecting individuals to actions and their consequences. The specific emplotment we develop depends on several things: the events that happen, their temporal quality or relationship, and our interpretation of actions by others and ourselves. It also depends on the kinds of plots or patterns that we expect to see in events. These expected patterns form a set of beliefs that is a pre-understanding to our construction of narrative, giving the process of emplotment a hermeneutic character (Ricoeur, 1984, pp. 56–66; Bruner, 1991). Narrative manages to find patterns, but leaves room for the uniqueness of the individual human story.

Narrative and the self. Ricoeur (1992) believes that we construct our personal identity by building narratives about ourselves through a dialectical interchange between self and others. This **narrative identity** has three aspects. First is the experience of physical sameness based on our body. Second is character or lasting dispositions found in habits or identifications such as values or ideals that we gain from others. Third is self-constancy, the keeping of one's word to act in particular ways and is an ethical component of identity. The loss of any of these threatens identity; fragmentation may result, as when we form multiple self-narratives for presentation to different audiences (Downing, 1998; Day, 1993).

Narratives help us understand or form our identity in several ways. Because they present material in a temporal framework, they help convey that aspect of our experience (cf. Ricoeur, 1995, p. 114). The emplotment of action helps link discordant events into a common framework. Stories draw connections between intentions, roles, actions, and outcome that help us reflect upon and understand ourselves and our values or goals. The story helps us to see and pull together different fragmented and conflicting parts of our lives, bringing them to a conclusion that combines diversity, discontinuity, and instability with permanence. It thus provides a unifying force to our identity (Ricoeur, 1995, pp. 140–166; MacIntyre, 1984, pp. 217–219). It can also highlight specific aspects of identity, showing for instance how self-constancy can be maintained in the face of challenges to one's character and values. Finally, narrative allows us to not only consolidate our sense of self but also to try out innovative and imaginative possibilities through "what-if" kinds of stories. However, narrative does not always succeed in bringing harmony, as in the case of suffering, when a story may be tellable only as a "tragic" narrative that articulates an insoluble conflict (Ricoeur, 1992, p. 243).

Narrative and religion. Ricoeur has also written about narrative and hermeneutics from a theological perspective. Since narrative allows us to think about lived experience, it can also help to articulate religious experience and meaning (Ricoeur, 1995; Polkinghorne, 2004, p. 135). A key aspect of religious experience in narrative is when our story is disrupted by **limit situations**, either positive or negative (see Section 1.2.1). Narratives have *expressive power*, allowing us to voice our deep struggles and feelings in such situations. They also have *transformational power* in that they move a person from a beginning to an end. In the Christian view, religious narratives also tell stories about a God who is an actor in history, an ethical god who keeps faith, and whose divine narrative intertwines with human ones. These narratives provide ways of expressing or understanding religious meaning as it unfolds in the experience of the individual (Crowe, 2005). In some cases, these narratives may have a powerful role for the Other (e.g., God) who has a "face" or presence that makes special demands upon us (Levinas, 1998).

Religious narratives can provide a foundational identity for a people or a community attempting to maintain a religious life (Ricoeur, 1995; Hopewell, 1987), and an analysis of these narratives can advance our understanding of religious individuals and groups (e.g., Bartkowski, 2007). Smart (1996, pp. 133–134) argues that narratives provide a history that helps define both the group and the sacred entities of the religion. These narratives also provide scripts for ritual or explanations of key doctrines, and links the individual to their past. In Christianity and other religious traditions, the narrative serves to bring assurance from the past; it also connects the person to the future, to hope, and thus to freedom (Moltmann, 1980, pp. 3–12). Ammerman (2003) has analyzed and identified several types of these narratives: autobiographical tales, public stories of groups or institutions, and metanarratives or "paradigms for how stories go." These religious narratives have a special character because they include religious actors, beliefs or concepts, as well as experiences of the sacred. She believes that the decline in US liberal Protestant churches has been due to the abandonment of unique features of the Christian narrative, which erases the boundary between religious communities and the broad secular culture.

6.3.4 The Human Person as Actor

A final common feature of the modern paradigm is the view that human persons are spectators. As spectators, we construct representations of the world, and the part of the human person responsible for this—the mind—becomes our most important feature. We are pictured as passive observers who lack freedom and are at the mercy of nature or social forces that we must fight against and try to control, often unsuccessfully. The brain is viewed as an information-processing machine that constructs these representations (Slife, 1995). Postmodernists, on the other hand, typically have a more active view of the human person as embodied agent who engages in social practices. In their view, relationality—which lies at the heart of religion and spirituality—cannot be understood apart from action, and an analysis of action requires an examination of practices (Loder, 1999). Here the human person is viewed as a person of action rather than an information-processing device.

6.3.4.1 The Actor at Work in Practice

There are a number of definitions of **practices**, a good one for our purposes is that of Frohlich: "the free committed engagement of the human subject in morally significant action" (1993, p. 35). Practices thus involve action that affects others and that is done in service of goals in a particular situation. They are socially established (MacIntyre, 1984, p. 187) and may vary from culture to culture. Some authors see practices as overlearned, "common sense" activities and approaches to problems; they typically operate in the background out of awareness but occasionally need to be supplemented with reflective reasoning (Polkinghorne, 2004, p. 152). Practices also involve what Greek philosophers called **phronesis** or practical reasoning and wisdom, which are deliberations about how to act in the pursuit of good life in a particular situation. This type of reasoning forms an essential part of our religious and spiritual journey (Polkinghorne, 2004, pp. 111–115). Practical reasoning helps us actively respond to specific and constantly changing real-life circumstances where there are multiple conflicting values.

Practice and practical reasoning are somewhat different from scientific reasoning, which makes them hard to study and appreciate from a scientific point of view. Because practice is focused on action in specific situations, practical reasoning goes beyond the simple, decontextualized application of general rules that science tries to apply (Polkinghorne, 2004; Bruner, 1991; MacIntyre, 1984, pp. 161–162). Furthermore, science tends to look at action as the product of past causes. In contrast, practical action is directed toward specific ends in particular situations, and so to understand it we must be able to capture its goal-directed quality (Howard, Youngs, & Siatczynski, 1989).

In postmodern thought, practical reasoning is seen as superior to scientific thinking when it comes to forming a basis for everyday action. It has a logic that is flexible according to situation and is attentive to individual variability and our relational interdependence with others and our surroundings (de Certeau, 1984, pp. 20–21; Varela, 2001). In this view, scientific descriptions that focus on process miss a full understanding of the thing they try to study. If we take a car apart and understand its pieces, and even if we put it together again and understand how the parts work together, we still do not know how to drive a car in London or understand the meaning of it for the people who do (Bourdieu, 1990, p. 18). Practical knowledge involves "ways of operating" or doing everyday things (de Certeau, 1984, p. xi), a non-propositional knowledge that to be evaluated must be translated into life practice and judged according to its outcome—a position taken many years ago by William James. Spiritual and religious activities can be thought of as these sorts of practices (Wuthnow, 2001; Hefner, 1998).

6.3.4.2 Theories of Practice

A number of writers conceptualize human activity primarily from a practice perspective. Hermeneutic theorists like Ricoeur often have a strong practice element to their theories (Whitehouse, 2000). Another important example of this approach can be found in the work of Pierre Bourdieu (1977, 1990).

The nature of practice. Bourdieu argues that there are three kinds of knowledge of the social world: (1) *phenomenological,* which too uncritically accepts lived experience; (2) *objectivist,* that looks for universal law but ignores issues of meaning, as well as the tremendous diversity and unpredictability in how practices really happen, eluding description by rules; and (3) *practical* knowledge which is found between subjectivism and objectivism. Practical knowledge does not obey a universal law and thus is not accurately studied by classical objective technique. In everyday life, rigid rules do not work because of constantly changing, ambiguous, and uncertain situations. Instead, real practices are based upon *strategies,* as these allow for constant vigilance and adjustment. The practice theorist de Certeau (1984, pp. 35–38) offers a helpful additional distinction between *strategies,* which work within an established system or space and everyday *tactics,* which are heterogeneous popular practices of those without power that work on the margins and through the loopholes of the established system. In this view, practices can be a product of strategies or function as a tactic.

Practices have a particular temporal character. Good practice cannot be determined ahead of time; it is a matter of the moment, and we only can make a positive judgment after the fact that we acted in the best way possible. One of the keys to practice is its mastery of time, its knowledge of the proper time and tempo for action. Science has trouble grasping practices because it tends to assume that actions are atemporal: an action can be done at any time or context and one done at one time is the same as that done at another. This ignores the fact that the meaning of events is dependent upon the response they elicit. Two acts at different times will typically have different responses and meanings; from this perspective, they are not identical actions even if the same behavior was involved (de Certeau, 1984, p. 54).

The habitus. One of Bourdieu's important contributions is the concept of the *habitus* or "systems of durable, transposable *dispositions*" that generate practices (1977, p 72). These systems are learned early in life and function mostly unconsciously. In Bourdieu's thought, specific practices are generated by a *habitus* in a way that is not rule bound but allows for the development of coherent strategies to help the agent deal with unforeseen circumstances. The *habitus* sets boundaries for what is impossible, possible or probable but allows flexibility so that the individual can accomplish diverse tasks in response to specific situations. Because they circumscribe action without limiting it to specific rules, practices produce statistical regularities but not strictly predictable behavior. They create both a commonsense world that is intelligible and practices of coordination and adjustment that are not necessarily logical but are coherent and economical (1977, pp. 72–88).

6.3.4.3 Critique

Bourdieu's theory has been criticized for containing metaphysical views that seem unnecessary to a theory of practice. For instance, he believes that the dispositions of the *habitus* are all-powerful so that any apparent free will or future orientation in our behavior is an illusion (1977, pp. 73–76). Also, since the *habitus* are really dispositions generated by social class, an individual history is just a specific example of the collective history of a group, or a deviant personal style (1990). Other practice theorists have criticized Bourdieu's concept of *habitus* as something that has not been observed but is needed in order for his theory to work. In addition, although Bourdieu argues against structure and objectivity, one wonders whether his tightly worked out system is able to break free of what he criticizes (de Certeau, 1984, pp. 58–69). A final problem is that Bourdieu seems to think that practices work independently of belief, while others (e.g., Taylor, 2007, pp. 212–214) argue that practices are inseparable from the mode of understanding and the worldview that underlies them.

6.3.5 Evaluation and Critique

In psychology, postmodernism has been more ignored or dismissed as a fad than critiqued due to the dominance of positivism (e.g., Teo & Febbraro, 2002). This is unfortunate, as it has much to offer in terms of identifying limitations in the positivist worldview and suggesting new approaches. Nevertheless, postmodernism has its problems. Many of the objections to postmodernism in the scientific community are due to its perceived antiscientific relativism (Lau, 2002). Extreme versions of postmodernism seem to reject all ideas of truth in favor of skepticism or **nihilism**, which has led scientific critics to call postmodernism a "skepticism that refutes itself," since a position that there is no truth also means that the postmodern position itself is not true (Locke, 2002, p. 458)! These criticisms of extreme postmodernism are well taken; as Terry Cooper notes, "Recognizing the sociohistorical limitations of one's thought does not mean that all thought is of equal value" (Cooper, 2006, p. 214; cf. MacIntyre, 1984, pp. 12–31). Relativism is particularly troubling for the application of psychology in counseling and mental health settings, which implicitly require some kind of authority for defining concepts like "health" and "adaptation" and are expected to talk in terms of goals and means with individuals in counseling (Lee, 2004).

In religious studies, postmodernism has been used to attack any attempt to compare or see common themes among various religious traditions. While this has been positive in that it has sensitized people to the importance of cultural context and differences between traditions, it has also been reductionistic, attempting to explain everything on the basis of culture or power, and has privileged difference over similarity, sometimes unnecessarily. This misses the point that comparisons can be done which increase our understanding of the topic. It also treats cultures and religious traditions as self-contained entities, which particularly in the contemporary world is simply untrue (Patton & Ray, 2000; Doniger, 2000; Eck, 2000; Patton, 2000; Paden, 2000).

Nonetheless, some criticisms seem to miss the point. Postmodernism offers a rich and diverse set of possibilities, some of which are aimed not at a rejection of truth claims but a questioning of crass materialism and a call for a positive attitude toward spirituality and human values (Allen, 2006). Charges that postmodern methods are subject to bias and unreliability (e.g., Haig, 2002) ignore the availability of high-quality qualitative approaches, as well as the bias and validity problems present in traditional methods. The complaint that postmodern emphases like relationality offer nothing new misses the point that while there is nothing new about relationality, current methods do not address it well. Postmodern emphases on plurality have been criticized for introducing too much complication (Kruger, 2002, p. 456), but this simply recognizes the fact that human behavior *is* complicated and psychology must attempt to describe it—a basic task of science (cf. e.g., McAdams, 1996). Nor does postmodern questioning of truth necessarily leave one in a moral vacuum with no possibility of rational discussion, as it opens the possibility for argument and comparison between different approaches to problems (Slife, 2000; Edwards, Ashmore, & Potter, 1995).

Each form of discourse has its own strengths and weaknesses. There is no need to choose, but there is a need to be explicit about our presuppositions and choices and to provide adequate justifications for the ones we make (Dueck & Parsons, 2004). The case of practices suggests that there is an important area of the psychology and religion dialogue that cannot be easily addressed from the modernist frame, positivist or otherwise. Likewise, the modernist frame offers certain advantages that should not be lightly cast aside. An approach that takes advantage of both perspectives will have the best chance to capture human experience.

6.4 Conclusion

Key issue: *The ability of current approaches to facilitate dialogue is dependent upon the theoretical and methodological assumptions of the investigators who employ them.*

Neurobiology, evolutionary psychology, and postmodernism all offer new perspectives that are influencing the psychology and religion dialogue. This influence plays out in different ways. Neurobiology has a long history in psychological studies of religion that is being revitalized by advances in technology and its increasing importance within the larger discipline of psychology. Evolutionary and postmodern influences are less important within psychology but have tremendous potential in the dialogue with religion, particularly because of the impact of postmodernism on other conversation partners in theology and religious studies. Time will tell whether these approaches broaden our perspective. Each of the new strategies can be used selectively, and history suggests that when this is done it has the potential to enrich the conversation between psychology and religion. On the other hand, reductionistic strategies that use a single model to explain everything tend to curtail discussion, a problem that has plagued the field for the past century. The work of Pascal Boyer and Harvey Whitehouse illustrates how two people working within a common framework can either stimulate or close off dialogue through different presuppositions and attitudes toward reductionism. This issue is also prominent in the psychology and religion conversation on development, our next topic.

Part III
Human Development

Chapter 7
Fundamentals of Human Development, Religion, and Spirituality

A central feature of both religious and psychological understandings of the human condition is that people are not static entities. Life from birth to death involves many changes in our physical, psychological, and spiritual makeup. In psychology, this issue has been explored through two major schools of thought—the psychodynamic tradition (see Chapter 5) and the cognitive-structuralist school. In this chapter, we will look at variations on the structural approach. In the following two chapters, we will expand our understanding of religious and spiritual development during childhood, adolescence, and adulthood by considering the empirical literature and some other approaches in the context of these theories.

7.1 Basic Issues in Developmental Theory

The most fundamental issue confronted by developmental theory is that of stability and change, an issue that has caused sharp disagreements in Western thought ever since the debates of Plato and the Presocratic philosophers. It is obvious that as we grow older we change, but at the same time we remain the same *person* in some essential way. Is this true, and if so how does it happen? How do change and stability apply to our religious and spiritual lives?

7.1.1 The Nature of the Change Process and Time

In general, three different kinds of developmental metaphors appear in human thought. In the first set of models, development is thought of like climbing a ladder. As we age, we climb higher and higher on the ladder through a universal, fixed set of stages and reach increasingly sophisticated levels of development, while still dealing with basic issues raised at lower stages (cf. Spidlik, 1986, p. 71, 2005, pp. 207–209; Casey, 1995). These **hierarchical** theories of development can be found in both Eastern and Western religious thought, as well as in psychologies as diverse as those of Jean Piaget and Abraham Maslow. In a second metaphor, life is seen as a circle, which proceeds through a series of predictable periods. During

J.M. Nelson, *Psychology, Religion, and Spirituality,*
DOI 10.1007/978-0-387-87573-6_0, @ Springer Science+Business Media, LLC 2009

the early part of the cycle, we grow and add abilities as we encounter predictable, age-related life tasks, while in the later part of life we decline or reflect over what had gone before. This metaphor is developed in **life span** theories of development, which can be found in South Asian religious literature and in the work of psychodynamic psychologists like Erik Erickson. Both hierarchical and life span theories often think of development as taking place in stages. In hierarchical theories, only a few individuals reach the final stages of development, while lifespan theorists think of all individuals as passing through the various stages of life if they live into old age. In a third metaphor, development is thought of like a journey or—to use religious language—a **pilgrimage**. In this view, while certain kinds of experiences or processes may be shared between different individuals, each person follows a unique path in their life, and no particular stage has a special value above the others (von Balthasar, 1995, p. 82). Aspects of this can be found in certain Buddhist and Christian writings and form the basis of narrative theories of psychological development. This approach moves beyond stage theories and attempts to describe the complex phenomenological experience of development (cf. Hay, Reich, & Utsch, 2006).

Development involves change, but does any type of change qualify as development? Liebert (2000, p. 56) argues that in order to qualify as development, changes must involve (1) increased complexity, (2) a new way of psychological ordering that encompasses and surpasses prior stages, and (3) permanence. All three types of developmental models have ways of understanding complexity and how it both surpasses prior stages and acquires permanence.

Development takes place *in time*, and thus how a theory understands time and its relationship to human life will affect the nature of the theory. In philosophies such as Kant's, time is thought to be a mental category that underlies our ability to understand the world (see Section 2.2.3). In traditional religious theories, time is thought of on a cosmic or divine scale, with segments of earthly time set apart as sacred. In this view, our development is a small movement in a larger order, and the real nature of time is concealed from our ordinary vision. In East and South Asian religions, this development can be a process that extends across many lifetimes (Marek, 1988).

Brent Slife has noted that since the work of Sir Isaac Newton, Western science has held a different idea of time. Slife argues that in the Newtonian model, time is as follows:

- *Objective* and exists independently of the mind or consciousness
- *Continuous* and smoothly flowing
- *Linear*, an irreversible arrow moving from past to future so that the past is the sole determinant of the present.
- *Universal*, following the same mechanical laws everywhere
- *Reductionistic*, in that time can only be examined at particular moments or intervals, e.g., a particular age or phase of life, never as a whole.

Slife argues that this version of time is foundational for much of psychology but that when considering human experience from a developmental point of view it does not work. He points out a number of anomalies that challenge a Newtonian view of time:

1. Human time appears to have a *subjective* aspect, because our perception of it is influenced by the culture and personal situation of the observer. Time as it is lived by us has a different quality for each person (Carr, 2004). For instance, time passes much more slowly for a young child than for an 80-year-old adult.
2. Developmental time appears *discontinuous*, with sudden breaks and lack of connection. This implies the possibility that "aspects of early development are temporary adaptations which have little to do with later development" (1993, p. 49) and that development emerges through a dialectical process rather than a smooth learning curve. Conversion experiences are a religious example of discontinuity (see Section 4.5).
3. Subjectively, people perceive time to be *nonlinear.* Linear views of time assume that causation moves in one direction from past to present, while nonlinear views hold open the possibility that what we anticipate about the future can also determine psychological phenomenon in the present. Christian understandings of hope are built around this nonlinear view of time.
4. Psychological laws appear to be different at different points in time, making them nonuniversal and *context-specific.* For example, older and younger adults may differ in how they relate to situations at work or in relationships.
5. Time has a *holistic* quality, because the meaning of events in time is not in the events themselves but how they stand in relation to other events, as in a narrative.

The perception of time as interconnected facilitates our ability to act and make meaning in various situations, rather than just passively process information (Slife, 1995). This critique suggests that development is more than just change over time (Scarlett, 2006). These issues will become apparent as we consider psychological theories of development, which are largely built on the Newtonian view of time.

7.1.2   The Nature and Goal of Development

Most theories of development, whether they are psychological, philosophical, or religious, presuppose a goal or endpoint to the development process, an ideal to be achieved, as well as a way of life to achieve it (cf. Hadot, Davidson, & Wissing, 1990; Hadot, 1995, p. 59; Druker, 1994). This is particularly true of hierarchical theories of development that need an understanding of what lies at the top of the hierarchy. While these goals may be based in part on empirical observations, they also carry with them cultural, philosophical, or theological assumptions about the nature of life, the human person, and the ideal society. These presuppositions are based on value judgments and are not "provable" in the scientific sense (Browning & Cooper, 2004, p. 214). They affect the entire theory of development and the kind of life that is described by it, since all aspects of growth are conceptualized as leading up toward

that goal. Global goals of development could include happiness, a sense of complete-
ness or well-being, reproductive success, achievement of one's unique potential, a
sense of meaning and purpose, and positive relationships or autonomous self-mas-
tery (Ryff, 1989). Some goals may be more modest: becoming competent, functioning successfully within society, or simply shielding others from a toxic past (Kotre &
Kotre, 1998). Our thinking about developmental goals may also depend on whether
one focuses on generic spirituality (e.g., Benson, Roehlkepartain, & Rude 2003;
Helminiak, 1987, p. 121) or a more specific religious conception of development.
Hierarchical theories in Christianity or other religious traditions contain a tension
between spirituality as a goal only achievable for a few and a vision of a religious life
that is for everyone in everyday walks of life (Sheldrake, 1995, p. 136).

Pilgrimage theories can have multiple views of the goals and process of development. Religious models often envision a particular end goal of development that
has a transcendent or mystical dimension beyond psychology and argue that there
may be many paths to that endpoint (Butler, 2003, p. xxiv; Sparkman, 1986). On
the other hand, some secular pilgrimage theories—including some versions of postmodern or evolutionary theories—begin with the view that there is no particular
goal or meaning to life. Religious pilgrimage theories often view development as a
process of discovering our true self, in which every stage in the journey is necessary
and has its own value (von Balthasar, 1967, p. 244; Schweitzer, 1991). Relational
views of this process might use images such as journey by which a bride and bridegroom develop love for each other (e.g., Bernard, of Clairvaux, *Sermons on Song of
Songs*) or an increasing clarity of vision of the beloved (e.g., Mechtild of Madeburg,
Flowing Light of the Godhead). Since most of our life journey is spent as adults,
these theories often focus on adulthood as a key time for spiritual development
(Helminiak, 1987).

7.2 Religious Models of Spiritual Development

7.2.1 Christian Perspectives

Early Christianity possessed no specific, developed models of spiritual growth. As
in the classical philosophical traditions, writers produced works intended to give
practical help with spiritual development rather than provide systematic statements
of principles (Davidson, 1990; Hadot et al., 1990). These didactic writings began to
be formulated in the third and fourth centuries when Christians founded religious
communities in the Egyptian and Syrian deserts to pursue intense lives of spiritual seeking. Writers from this early period such as Evagrius Ponticus (345–399)
believed that the Incarnation opened up new possibilities for development (see
Section 3.1.1). If a person was willing to open themselves to God through physical
and mental discipline, they could gradually become like God in a process of transformation known as **theosis** or *divination*, and at the highest level of development
participate in the inner life of God (Athanasius, 1994b; Maximus, 2003; Sherwood,

1955, pp. 71–72; Palamas, 1983, pp. 76–85; Meyendorff, 1998b, pp. 143–145; Spidlik, 1986; Bartos, 1999, pp. 9–20). Similar ideas can be found in the writings of Reformation theologians like Martin Luther and modern Protestant writers, although they often use terms like **sanctification** or holiness rather than divination (Kärkkäinen, 2004, p. 5; Habets, 2006).

The concept of theosis was especially developed in the thought of Maximus Confessor (c. 580–662). Maximus argued that theosis is a lifelong process involving all aspects of the person. In this view, deification is not just a private mystical experience of union but a relational, cooperative activity involving God, the human person, and a supportive community. It leads to an interpenetration or mutual reciprocity based on the action of love so that we are caught up by God and reproduce the pattern and likeness of the Divine in virtuous conduct, inner simplicity, and unity. This likeness does not imply that we *are* God, just that we are able to resemble the Divine and have communion with it (Russell, 2004; Makrakis, 1977, p. 21; Louth, 1996, p. 101; Finlan & Kharlamov, 2006; Vishnevskaya, 2006; Pseudo-Dionysius, 1987, pp. 197–198; Cauchi, 2005). Maximus talks about four aspects or characteristics of the theosis process (Louth, 1996, pp. 88–91; Maximus, 2003, pp. 51–66, 117–118; Thunberg, 1995, pp. 118–131):

1. *Effort and Non-Effort*: While we need to engage in the kind of lifestyle and practices that make the process possible, deification ultimately takes us beyond our natural abilities and is a gift of God. The kind of challenges we must overcome will change with the developmental process, with some problems fading into the background and others becoming more acute.
2. *Transformation*: Deification makes us into a likeness of God through an ongoing personal encounter and imitation, which leads to new knowledge and the imitation of divine virtues like love. As a result, God is manifested through us in our virtues so that eventually our body and soul become "the clearest of mirrors" reflecting God (Louth, 1996, p. 115).
3. *Unification*: For Maximus, divinization is the uniting with God of those who have become like him. This union is a kind of mutual interpenetration (*perichoresis*) that respects the nature of each. It happens in part through love that draws us together with God, is embodied in our actions, and provides the ultimate meaning of life (Bartos, 1999, p. 331). It also overcomes divisions that are present within us and with the world, and increasing unity is associated with greater complexity in our spiritual life (Williams, 2003; Magaletta, 1996).
4. *Love and Freedom*: The evidence and result of theosis is the growth of love and freedom in our lives. As we become like God, we become united in love with the Divine and develop love and compassion for all other things that are also loved by God. Love thus promotes unity. This compassion helps us fight the problem of arrogance, which is always a temptation as we reach higher levels of development. In addition, theosis leads to spiritual freedom, a state of rest and satisfaction of desire as opposed to enslavement to passions. Life without this freedom is incomplete; with it, we can use our gifts to their full potential (Welch, 1996; Theophan, 1995, pp. 36–44).

In the Eastern Church, the Biblical story of the Transfiguration provides a model for deification, whereas in the Western church the sacrifice of the Cross and the Resurrection experience has greater emphasis (Spidlik, 2005, pp. 304–305).

In Western Christianity, during the Middle Ages, ideas about the goal of spiritual development changed in a couple of ways. First, more general ideas about human development began to emerge. As early as the 7th century, elaborate models dividing the lifespan into childhood, adolescence, and adulthood were developed, and by the 13th century, these models had entered theology and could be found in the works of monks like William of St. Thierry. These medieval works often made use of pilgrimage allegories to describe human life (Goodich, 1989). Second, models took on more of a relational and affective emphasis. The development of a deep relationship and identification with Christ was emphasized, resulting eventually in the experience of a **beatific vision**, "the intimate and joyful union of the souls of the blessed with God in glory" (Aumann, 1980, p. 42), a direct experience and knowledge of God (Thomas, 1998, I, q. 26, a. 1).

Western Christian descriptions of development typically contained three or four stages of the journey toward God. Central to these theories were three modes or "ways" of the spiritual life: the *Via Purgativa* (purgation), *Via Illuminativa* (illumination) and *Via Unitiva* (union). Some authors, especially those in Protestant Christianity, also added an initial stage, that of **awakening**. This is an emotional event that typically occurs in the context of a conversion-type experience of the reality and love of God. As a result of the experience and our response to it, there is a sense of liberation, an "emergence of the self from 'the prison of I-hood'," as well as feelings of nearness and love toward God (Underhill, 1990; Aumann, 1980; Merton, 2006, pp. 283–284).

Awakening is followed by the stage of **purgation**, when one is purified and develops the underlying character, personal habits, and mental attitudes necessary for progress in spiritual life. This is a painful process that involves significant suffering, but this pain is necessary and thus is a positive good that promotes growth. In this stage, there is a moving away from sin, formation of basic trust at conscious and unconscious levels (Groeschel, 1995), and development of **humility,** "a basic honesty about who one is and is not" (Frohlich, 1993, p. 193) that is essential in later stages of development. Specific goals and practices at this stage include the following:

- Moral reform and confession to promote self-knowledge and humility
- Physical discipline for control of things like food and sexuality
- Mental discipline, "guarding the heart" from unwelcome thoughts and images
- Detachment from created things through self-denial
- Detachment from the will through poverty and obedience

As purgation proceeds, we experience **illumination** or an increasing sense of God's presence, as well as feelings of love and unity toward all things (Inge, 1910, pp. 236–237). In this stage, one is "proficient" as opposed to a beginner but not yet perfected (Thomas, 1998, II–II, q. 24, a. 9). As the process continues, there is a sense that effort is needed to prepare the self for growth but that more and more of development is due to the work of people or forces outside the person (Frohlich, 1993, pp. 206–207).

In the final stage of development, there is an increasing sense of **union** with God. The highest stage of development is described by many Christian writers in metaphorical terms using a variety of images such as a beatific vision, the intimacy of mutual love between bride and bridegroom (e.g., Bernard of Clairvaux, 1987, pp. 270–278), a vision of dazzling light (Mechthild, 1998, pp. 40–42), becoming like God (William, 1971, p. 96), a boiling over of God within (McGinn, 2001, p. 71), a state of *ecstasis* or going out of oneself, and a state of *epectasis* or increasing desire for God and penetration into the divine light (Merton, 2008, pp. 79–82). The use of metaphor in these descriptions is due to the intensely ineffable nature of the experience of "things that he who from that height descends, forgets or cannot speak; for nearing its desired end, our intellect sinks into an abyss so deep that memory fails to follow it" (Dante Alighieri, 1995, p. 379). In the Christian context, the emphasis is on a union of wills—a joining together in love for others rather than an experience of metaphysical union (Merton, 2008, p. 249; cf. Teresa of Avila, 1979, pp. 97–102).

Contemporary Christian authors have critiqued this traditional model of purgation, illumination, and union. For instance, Sheldrake (1995) points out that standard models obscure the individual nature of spiritual growth and the religious quest. They promote the idea that one leaves behind earlier stages as one develops, when in fact the states are constantly intermixed. In his view, spiritual development is more like an increasing refinement of vision, or increasing awareness of a voice or music; one learns to filter out competing images or sounds and come closer to the source of vision or music. Furthermore, progressive models obscure the fact that growth often involves gaining new abilities or ways of doing things only to give them up so that we can move on to something even better. This pattern of gains and losses is implicit in many Christian descriptions of development such as that of Teresa of Avila (Frohlich, 1993).

7.2.2   Concepts of Development in Hinduism and Buddhism

Traditional Hindu thought sees spiritual development in the context of the human life span. For instance, the *Laws of Manu* (Olivelle, 2004b) divide the life of the upper-caste Hindu worshipper into four stages or **ashrama**. The process begins during *bramacharya* when the child or adolescent works as a student and family member. They try to master the basic skills and cultural abilities necessary for life and study the Vedas under a teacher. In the second quarter of life or *grihastha*, one marries after mastering the Vedas and becomes a productive householder. The individual continues their spiritual study and observes traditional religious rituals and requirements for offerings. After the birth of grandchildren and around midlife one moves into *vanaprastha* or simple retirement and becomes a forest dweller. This stage marks the beginning of more intensive spiritual seeking, reciting the

Vedas and practicing compassion. Finally at the end of life, one enters *saanyasa* and becomes a renunciate, taking up an ascetic lifestyle and engaging in deep meditation. In practice, these last two stages are not sequential but represent different end paths of development. The stages refer to both a place of residence for religious exertion and also a mode of life. The model specifies the things that are possible and needful at various stages of life, providing a framework by which these may be normalized and valued, although the renunciate appears as the paradigm for the ideal holy person (Tilak, 1989; Olivelle, 2004a).

Since spiritual development in Buddhism happens in relation to meditation practice, many Buddhist views of development cannot really be understood without a knowledge of those practices (see Section 13.5.1). A somewhat more accessible example of development in the Zen Buddhist tradition is provided in the *Ten Oxherding Pictures* (Loori, 1999; Sekida, 1975, pp. 223–236). This series of pictures depicts the journey toward the Buddhist goal of discovering the emptiness of the false self and leaving it behind for our true self and a state of nondualism. It is a journey that begins with a state of emptiness and ends with a different experience of it (Gunn, 2000, p. 1). The pictures use the metaphor of the mind as an ox that must first be disciplined and then later forgotten. One version of the series of pictures goes like this:

- The herder realizes there is an ox (one's true nature) and searches for it
- The herder finds traces of it, confirming the search
- The herder sees the ox: an experience provides a first glimpse of enlightenment
- The herder catches the ox, which is wild and undisciplined
- The ox is tamed and tethered, discipline has begun
- The herder rides home on the ox, we remain at peace among difficulties
- The herder forgets the ox and is in repose: meditation is effortless
- The herder also disappears: a unity experience
- There is a return to the source where all is simple and effortless
- There is a return to the marketplace where the benefits are brought to others

At the end, the person has discovered his or her true self, which in Zen is paradoxically no self at all!

7.3 Early Genetic Theories of Religious Development

For over a century, psychologists have been actively creating innovative theories of psychological development. Many of these theories are relevant to an understanding of religious and spiritual growth. Some of these are important general theories of human growth, while others are more specific theories of moral development with concerns that overlap those of spiritual or religious formation (Worthington, 1989). Early theories in psychology moved away from a philosophical analysis of adult thought, such as that produced by Kant, and began to look at the genesis or source of mental life, how our abilities emerge or evolve from their earliest beginnings in childhood. This emphasis on genesis led to the development of **genetic psychology**, which focused not on heredity (which was not well understood at the time) but on the developmental sources and processes behind the psyche. G. Stanley Hall and James Mark Baldwin developed early theories of genetic psychology and logic, which later formed a background for the genetic theories of Jean Piaget.

7.3.1 G. Stanley Hall

G. Stanley Hall (1844–1924) is an important figure in the early history of the psychology of religion (see Section 1.4.2). One of his contributions was the formulation of a theory of development that gave an important place to religion. The genetic psychology of Hall was built on the concept of **recapitulation** (cf. Freud, 1950), which is the view that the various states of development in the individual (*ontogeny*) recapitulate or repeat the stages in evolution or development of the species (*phylogeny*). For instance, Hall believed that the attempt to establish psychic unity that occurs in adolescences was a recapitulation of an earlier, paradisiacal time when humanity and nature were in harmony. Not unlike Plotinus (see Section 4.3.1), Hall believed that each person was "a fragment broken off and detached from the great world of soul" (1916, p. 66) and was born with a racial knowledge formed from past human experiences. While largely unconscious, this buried knowledge can surface, reinvigorating the person and forming the basis of new aesthetic, ethical, and religious sentiments. An implication of the theory of recapitulation is that the religious thought of children is like that of primitive peoples, and that teaching modern religious beliefs to children would be impossible or counterproductive (Wells, 1918), an idea later taken up by followers of Piaget.

Hall thought that adolescence was the key time for religious development, while older adulthood was a time of "senescence" and declining capacity (Hall, 1923). He saw the teenage years as a time of turmoil when unconscious materials from our racial past become available to us, and the psyche attempts to establish a new balance and mental unity. This turmoil meant that adolescence was a peak time for conversion experiences, which he saw as a natural or even necessary process. Adolescence was also a time for development of sexuality and increased capacity for love, which allows us to make connections with others and with our past. Hall believed that the adolescent transition should include a change in one's attitude toward religion, which can help us achieve our true place in the world. Like the liberal Protestant theologian Friedrich Schleiermacher, he believed that religion should be interpreted subjectively and independent of any particular doctrinal belief.

7.3.2 James Mark Baldwin

James Mark Baldwin (1861–1934) was an important figure in the beginnings of North American psychology who also had professional and personal interests in religion. Among other things, Baldwin was interested in *interpretation*, how we go about thinking about reality and giving meaning to experience. He believed that our logic of interpretation passed through a series of stages, and he developed a theory of "genetic" logic to describe these changes (Wozniak, 2001; Baldwin, 1930). His theory is of interest in its own right but also because it provided the starting point for the work of Jean Piaget (Kohlberg, 1982).

Several key ideas underlie Baldwin's genetic theory. First, he accepted the concept of recapitulation as found in Hall. This means that early in development the individual tends to interpret things in the way they were interpreted in early human societies. Second, Baldwin had a social view of development, where growth in the real self occurs in dialectical social relationships between the individual and others. In this view, social relationships are vital for growth (1902, pp. 15–36). He argued that the individual is not only a passive recipient of information from the environment but also actively reacts, thus introducing novelty into the world (Valsiner, 2000, p. 29). He believed that these patterns of interaction and activity were relationally transmitted, learned through interactions with individuals and the group. In particular, he believed that children actively construct a view of an ideal self from things they appreciate and imitate, especially the moral and ethical behavior they see in others. The sense of self and other are thus closely related. The child is able to experiment with different ideal images through play and imitation, which in early development becomes the driving force of growth. This ideal—which is typically reflected in our understanding of God—then becomes the basis for religious development. Emotional connections are made with the idealized object, such as (1) a sense of dependence, where dependence refers to feelings of trust and faith, and (2) a sense of mystery toward the object (cf. awe, fear, holiness, sacredness) that makes the object worthy of respect (Baldwin, 1902, pp. 339–340). The object is looked up to because of these emotional connections. It becomes religious as the individual—through social learning from the group—comes to understand that this object has some real existence, and they experience a personal presence of the object. Like significant others, it can become an object we identify with and try to follow. Baldwin believed that our moral development was based on these affective activities of willing and role taking, along with our increasing ability to distinguish between inner and outer reality (Kohlberg, 1982).

Baldwin (1975) thought that some areas of cognitive experience lie outside the laws of formal logic, and thus a description of mental life in solely objective terms would be inadequate. In particular, he thought that traditional logical analysis could not account for biological and social aspects of reasoning, and that there are assumptions about reality buried in traditional logic that if used exclusively would distort our thinking. He favored an understanding of mental life using genetic logic, which is a logic of the knower. According to genetic logic, thoughts are not fixed entities but a continuous flowing process. Each thought is a unique entity that cannot be subdivided or equated with any other thought, although they can be subdivided into types or modes according to the type of object at the center of the thought. Critically, he believed that different kinds of logic applied to different sorts of objects so that, for instance, logic as applied to moral objects would be different from that applied to sensory information. Paralleling Kant's distinction between pure and practical reason, he saw religious logic and reasoning as more connected with practical (utility) and affective interests. This type of logic allows for paradoxical thinking and also stresses the idea that the truth or meaning of a statement might depend upon context. Religious logic provides motivational interest directed toward a number of goals, including forming and becoming an ideal self (Wallwork, 1982).

Baldwin (1902, pp. 304–366) thought that religious development proceeded through a number of stages. In the early or *prelogical* stage, thinking is marked by spontaneity and a unity or nondifferentiation between the basic modes of emotional, practical, and intellectual thought. Religious dependence begins in this stage with a sense of trust in the environment and one's caretakers; it also involves growth of a sense of mystery. In early development, this sense of mystery and our image of the ideal become identified with God, who like our parents is a person who defies prediction and draws forth a reaction from us of reverence and awe. This is the beginning of religion, which Baldwin defined as "*emotion kindled by faith,* emotion being reverence for a Person and faith being dependence upon Him" (1902, p. 366). Our conception of this Person grows and matures as we develop because religious sentiments are dependent upon our ethical and social ones and thus change as these develop. However, religious thought often struggles in the second or *logical* stage when emotional, practical, and intellectual thinking becomes separated from each other, with discursive and critical intellectual thought gaining predominance. While logical thought is freeing, it also results in ignoring or disparaging certain kinds of experiences that do not fit within the logical categories of this level. This leads to a dualism between subject and object, mind and body.

In higher stages of development, one becomes freed from these problems through a reunion of the emotional and intellectual, as well as the redevelopment of imagination in religious thought. First comes a *hyper-logical* or aesthetic stage marked by contemplative intuition and immediate perception of knowledge and value. At this level, the person is able to directly perceive and interpret objects, bypassing practical and intellectual reason. Finally at the highest level was the *extra-logical* or moral and ethical stage of development. The ethical self that develops at this point is a social self which is conscious of its ability to do right or wrong. It is driven by sentiment and a sense of obligation to go beyond habit and strive toward an ethical ideal (1902, pp. 42–46, 304–306). It forms when the individual is able to overcome the antithesis between self-serving attitudes and compassion for others. At this stage, the person moves beyond emotion and intellectual thought to reasoning that is practical, active, and socially oriented. This ethical self is strongest if it is attached to a public self and anchored in a community with shared ideals.

A key characteristic of early psychological theories of religious development is that they primarily focused on childhood and adolescence. Although this perspective is contrary to the experience of many religious traditions, it formed the basis of cognitive-structuralist theories of development, which we will consider next.

7.4 Cognitive-Structuralist Theories of Development

Psychological theories of religious and spiritual development have an odd history. While there has been much written about religion and related topics from a developmental perspective, virtually none of the theories used by psychologists were specifically developed to help us understand religion or spirituality. Rather, most efforts have involved taking theories of emotional, cognitive, or moral development and applying them to the topic, viewing religion as using the same cognitive capacities, and following a similar developmental trajectory to other normal mental processes (Johnson & Boyatzis, 2006). Along with psychodynamic approaches (see Chapter 5), the main group of developmental theories used to understand religion has been **cognitive-structuralist theories** developed by researchers like Jean Piaget and Lawrence Kohlberg. These theories attempt to understand the human person by trying to identify underlying organized structures or schemas of mental activity. Cognitive-structural theories of moral development have been particularly popular, because morality is central to most religious traditions, even though it has features that are developmentally unique (Worthington, 1989). In this cognitive view, religious or spiritual development can be thought of as a kind of learning or change with transformational properties (Mulqueen & Elias, 2000).

7.4.1 Jean Piaget

Jean Piaget (1896–1980) stands as a giant among 20th-century developmental psychologists. While his theory has come under criticism from a variety of sources, almost all developmental theorists share the assumptions of his theory. These assumptions include the characterization of human life as a dynamic and changing natural process and the view that forces within move us toward progressively more complex and adaptive internal organization and structure (Vandenberg & O'Connor, 2005; Fetz, 1988) (Fig. 7.1).

Piaget was primarily interested in **epistemology** or how we acquire knowledge. Like Baldwin, he took a developmental or genetic view toward mental function (Piaget, 1971, p. 45, 1982). Unlike Baldwin, however, he took a more mechanical and structural approach to understanding the human person, seeing mental functions as governed by underlying organized structures or **schema** that act as lawlike systems and govern our ability to acquire knowledge, act, and solve problems (Piaget & Inhelder, 1969, p. 4). He believed that human mental processes often paralleled mathematical forms and should be studied using the procedures of natural science. His research was based upon observing and questioning children (including his own), while engaged in particular tasks.

Unlike Kant, Piaget thought there was no *a priori* beginning point to development (1997, p. 399) but that it proceeded through various structural equilibrium points marked by increasing scope, complexity, and stability. These equilibrium points are often referred to as stages, although he did not himself emphasize the

Fig. 7.1 *Jean Piaget.* One
of the most important
psychologists of the
20th century; his views
of development had an
enormous impact on the
psychological study of moral
and religious development.
Photo courtesy of Jean Piaget
Society

concept of stage in his work (Broughton, 1981b). Each of the equilibrium points
marked a level of adaptation to the environment that balanced *assimilation* or incor-
poration of things into existing structures with *accommodation* and adjustment of
structures to the demands of the environment. He believed that this development
proceeded in a sequence governed by biological maturation rather than culture so
that environmental factors could only speed or slow the process, although social
interaction was necessary for it to proceed (Broughton, 1981a; Inhelder & Piaget,
1958, p. 338; Piaget, 1954, p. 361, 1971, p. 47). He did agree with Kant, however,
that the process of knowing does not allow us to speculate about the nature of the
reality behind that experience (Seltzer, 1977).

In the view of Piaget, children seek coherence and organization, and early in
development acquire basic structures for processing sensory and motor information. This *sensorimotor* stage is later surpassed by *preoperational* or intuitive ways
of thinking. This type of cognition is egocentric and marked by creative play with
elements of fantasy and symbolism, which he saw as undesirable because of its
tendency to reinforce the self-centered state of the individual (1954, p. 362, 1968,
p. 90). As development progresses, egocentric stages are displaced, and thinking
becomes more mathematical in quality. Intuitions become *concrete operations*,
structures that allow for the grouping of similar elements and perceptions of equivalence or reversibility among patterns. During adolescence the development process
culminated in *formal operations*, when verbal statements are substituted for objects.
This abstract reasoning allowed for prediction of experience, as well as the development of propositional logic and scientific forms of thought that are valid for any
content. Piaget believed that emotional factors did not need to be considered in this

process, for while they are present in values and life commitments, they come from the same structural base as cognition and thus add nothing to our understanding of the process of gaining knowledge (Inhelder & Piaget, 1958).

7.4.1.1 Moral Development

In his early work, Piaget (1997) became interested in the study of moral development. He thought that while the affective aspect of morality cannot be studied, we could enquire about its rational base. Like Kant, he saw the essence of morality in the respect an individual acquires for moral law (see Section 2.2.3). These rational rules correspond to "the deepest functional constants of human nature" and form the basis of moral emotions (1997, p. 186), although he believed that emotions should have no part in decision making as they led to false interpretations of reality. Piaget conducted his research on morality by observing children playing marbles and seeing how they actually made decisions about right and wrong in various situations. Other moral researchers like Lawrence Kohlberg have used similar methodologies, giving people situations like the Heinz dilemma, and seeing the reasoning they use in deciding what to do (see Box 7.1). The focus is not on what the person does—the content of the moral decision—but the *process*, how they come to conclusions about what to do.

Piaget saw "two moralities" emerge during development (1997, p. 194). The first is dominant during preschool years and is an external or *heteronomous* form of morality that involves a focus either on egocentric needs or conformity and unilateral respect for others. While this form of morality is problematic it is not a stable system, and given freedom and the ability to interact with peers independent of adult influence, one's moral reasoning would eventually change. This would lead to a superior system of *autonomous* morality and justice reasoning based on mutual respect and reciprocity

---

Box 7.1　The initial Heinz Dilemma (Kohlberg, 1984)

Dilemma III: In Europe, a woman was near death from a special kind of cancer. There was one drug that the doctors thought might save her. It was a form of radium that a druggist in the same town had recently discovered. The drug was expensive to make, but the druggist was charging ten times what the drug cost him. He paid $400 for the radium and charged $4,000 for a small dose of the drug. The sick woman's husband, Heinz, went to everyone he knew to borrow the money and tried every legal means, but he could only get together about $2,000, which is half of what it cost. He told the druggist that his wife was dying, and asked him to sell it cheaper or let him pay later. But the druggist said, "No, I discovered the drug and I'm going to make money from it." So, having tried every legal means, Heinz gets desperate and considers breaking into the man's store to steal the drug for his wife.

Should Heinz steal the drug? Why or why not?

of relations as in Kant. Piaget thought that the transition to autonomous morality began around age 7 or 8 and concluded by age 11 or 12, with the development of a sense of distributive or egalitarian justice. He thought that this cooperative moral style formed the foundation of the mature personality. At this point, the individual begins to adopt adult roles and a life program that includes plans for changing society and becoming more successful than his predecessors (Inhelder & Piaget, 1958, pp. 335–343).

7.4.1.2 Religious Development

Piaget came from a liberal Protestant Christian tradition and sought to find a rational basis for religion and morality (Burman, 1994, p. 159). While he did not write extensively about religion or collect much meaningful data on the subject, he did have a conception of religious development and ideals that drew on positivist concepts, although he criticized certain aspects of positivism. He believed that values and religious ideas were evolving toward a superior understanding that should replace older views of morality and religion, so that traditional metaphysics and theology should be eliminated. His ideal religion was an individualistic one that adjusted religion to modern thought (Vidal, 1987). He also tended to accept the positivist model of conflict between science and religion. In his early treatise *The Mission of the Idea* (1916), he painted religious orthodoxy as an enemy of science and social salvation. He generally approved of Comte's ideas about history and saw societies evolving in similar ways, "from gerontocratic theocracy in all its forms to equalitarian democracy" (1997, p. 325, cf. pp. 336–337).

Piaget (1997) associated mystical experience and religious orthodoxy with immature and egocentric thought. He thought that mysticism comes from feelings of unilateral respect for parents and adults and is associated with imposed rules of ritual, taboo, and moral realism. He also believed that mysticism is connected with egocentrism in which individuals confuse their own wishes with those of God. This means that feelings of transcendence and the myths associated with them are irrational and have no value as beliefs. In more advanced stages of development, we should abandon these myths and substitute rational experiment and naturalistic explanations for supernatural mysticism. This development should climax in adolescence with the integration of a new rational religion into our life system and plans in which God and individual cooperate with each other.

Piaget's thinking had a strong influence on religious education. In the mid-1960s the British writer Ronald Goldman published *Readiness for Religion* (1968), a system for applying Piagetian insights to the religious training of children. Goldman thought that the Bible contained many highly abstract concepts that exceeded the concrete cognitive abilities of the child, leading to problems in religious education (cf. Lawrence, 1965). He thought that early education should focus on the life experience of the child and the Bible should be introduced later. This position has been widely rejected, as a number of studies have shown that children are perfectly capable of understanding scriptural narratives at early ages (e.g., Slee, 1990; Elkind, 1962; Hoge & Petrillo, 1978; Ashton, 1997; Csanyi, 1982). In fact, these narratives provide both inspiration and direction for action (Coles, 1990, p. 121). Religious identity appears to be acquired initially through *practices*—things that we do—rather than *beliefs*, and even young children can absorb teachings about practices from Biblical stories.

7.4.1.3 Critique

Piaget's theory has been criticized on a number of fronts. First, a variety of aspects of Piaget's cognitive structural framework have been questioned:

1. *Inappropriate use of reductionism.* Piaget has been criticized for making a number of unwarranted reductionistic assumptions, including that (a) all of development can be explained on the basis of a single mechanism of assimilation and accommodation, (b) this mechanism is universal to all times, places, and individuals, and (c) moral or religious reasoning is just a subset of other kinds of reasoning and develops in the same way (Alexander, Druker, & Langer, 1990; Elkind, 1964, 1996; Rich & DeVitis, 1985). Many scholars reject this, arguing that different areas of cognition may utilize different developmental mechanisms.

2. *Neglect of agency.* The passive nature of the assimilation and adaptation process as described by Piaget appears to ignore the possibility of active learning and offers no explanation for important aspects of human experience such as goal-directed action, expressive activity, or the development of meaning and consciousness (Broughton, 1981c, 1981d; cf. Seltzer, 1977).

3. *Neglect of important process factors* such as (a) the relational, social, and cultural components of the developmental process, (b) the role of emotion in thought and behavior, and (c) the value of active imagination in the lives of both children and adults (Vygotsky, 1986; Cole & Wertsch, 1996).

4. *Neglect of the content and meaning of cognition,* even though Piaget realized that process and content were not entirely separate (Exline, 2002a; cf. Piaget, 1997, p. 85; Baldwin, 1902, p. 20).

5. *Unnecessary inflexibility in the Piagetian model.* The model has a limited number of categories, and this restricts the kinds of trajectories and growth outcomes that can be considered (Langer et al., 1990). Piaget's idea that the goal of development is a kind of distant objectivity that can be achieved in adolescence neglects the possibility of relational goals or cognitive development during adulthood (McGuinness, Pribram, & Pirnazar, 1990; Cartwright, 2001).

Second, his methodology has come under criticism because slight changes in the Piagetian tasks can produce large changes in performance (Burman, 1994, p. 156). In fact, Piaget himself noted that the children he interviewed provided answers closer to his theory than those interviewed by others (1997, p. 210). His use of a sample limited to middle class, male children and a small number of tasks and questions with a limited number of possible responses meant that his observations were generated using his own explanatory framework, making it impossible to truly test his assumptions (Broughton, 1981c; Vygotsky, 1986, p. 15; Rich & DeVitis, 1985). This means that his emphasis on the autonomous moral conscience may be a reflection of cultural practices or his own liberal Protestant beliefs and values (Broughton, 1981e). Third, there is also a question as to whether subsequent data support his ideas of moral development. Some studies have found his notions of the differences between children and adults to be exaggerated (Vianello & Marin, 1989). Even preschool children offer justifications for moral decisions based on concern for others rather than authority (Eisenberg-Berg & Neal, 1979), and Piaget himself complained that adults did not fit his model because of their poor psychological insight, tendency to adhere to custom or external influence, and their belief in the reality of moral laws (1997, pp. 190–191, 262–268; cf. 1968, p. 64). Research has not supported his contention that give and take with peers necessarily leads to higher moral development (Rich & DeVitis, 1985, p. 50) or that the age ranges for the thinking he describes are culturally invariant (Tanuwidjaja, 1974). This raises questions about the appropriateness of applying his model to moral or religious development.

7.4.2 *Lawrence Kohlberg*

Lawrence Kohlberg (1927–1987) initially set out to construct a theory of **justice reasoning**, or how people decide what is just or right behavior in situations where there are competing claims among persons. His approach to moral judgment thus focuses on the *process* rather than the *content* of decision making, which in his view allows for constructing a universal theory that need not account for individual and cultural differences in moral content. His approach was based on Piaget's cognitive theory and methodology, as well as the psychological ideas of Baldwin and John Dewey (e.g., Dewey & Tufts, 1932; Carpendale, 2000) and the philosophical ethics of Kant and John Rawls. There are two important ideas that are presuppositions to his work:

1. Like Kant, he believes there is a universal human capacity for moral judgment, as well as a set of values, rules, and principles for moral reasoning, including the concepts of reciprocity and equality, that can be agreed upon by all thinking individuals (1984, pp. 222–224).
2. These universal principles and values cannot be derived from simple observation. Just because something *does* happen (e.g., murder) does not mean that it *should* happen (i.e., that it is morally right). Deriving matters of value from fact commits a **naturalistic fallacy** (1984, p. 285; see Section 2.5.3). Rather, these rules must be presupposed and judgments made on a conscious rational basis.

On the basis of research evidence available at the time, Kohlberg believed that cognitive structuralism was the most powerful explanation for moral behavior, since social development and emotion are affected or mediated by cognitive structures. He felt that things like parental factors and the handling of "basic drives" were unrelated to the development of moral attitudes or behavior, although parental warmth encouraged learning of social norms (1984, pp. 27–28). Psychodynamic developmental factors like attachment were explainable using imitation and cognitive-structural concepts (Kohlberg, 1984, p. 158), although specific attachments might speed up or slow down development and give it particular content and affective significance.

7.4.2.1 Stages

Like Piaget, Kohlberg believed that the development of justice reasoning proceeded in universal, fixed stages in an invariant sequence. His stage model was constructed after analyzing responses to situations like the Heinz dilemma (see Box 7.1). Unlike other moral thinkers like Baldwin and Levinas, he also privileged the idea of reciprocity or equality as the ultimate goal in human relations. Each stage in his theory of moral development is a whole worldview that represents an increasingly complex, universalized form of reciprocity (Burman, 1994; Kohlberg, 1984, p. 73). He referred to his model as a **hard stage model** with a fixed set of stages applicable to everyone, as opposed to hierarchical or **soft stage models** where development to higher stages is optional, and the final stages have a mystical or post-rational quality (Kohlberg, 1984, p. 248). However, Kohlberg rejected the idea of simple progress from heteronomy to mutual respect contained in Piaget's moral theory; rather, each level had two stages that showed a progression toward reversible thinking within that stage (see Table 7.1). At the lower and middle levels of development, moral reasoning revolved around obedience or social conformity. The reasoning given by Adolf Eichmann for his support of Hitler and the Holocaust is often used as an example of this kind of reasoning (see Box 7.2).

Kohlberg struggled with his ideas about the endpoint of moral development. He found that he could not reliably identify individuals who functioned at his hard Stage 6. He also believed that there were optional soft stages of development that occurred after age 30. He thought these additional stages would help to explain the existence of Christian moral virtues like agape love or altruism which did not fit well within the framework of reciprocity, but he was reluctant to include them in his model because it would introduce an ethical or religious philosophy into his theory that went beyond rational judgment (Kohlberg, 1981, pp. 345–356; 1984, pp. 212–249; cf. Dawson, 2002). However, he acknowledged that soft models might be more adequate for describing adult development. He considered the possibility of including a soft Stage 7 in his model. This stage would be reached when an individual begins to ask ontological or religious questions about the meaning or purpose of life and morality, and finds an answer in experiences of a transcendental, nondualistic, and post-rational nature that provides a cosmic perspective on reality and a loving relationship with it (1981, pp. 369–371; Kohlberg & Ryncarz, 1990).

7.4.2.2 Religious Development

Although Kohlberg wrote primarily about the development of moral reasoning, he also expressed thoughts about religious development and attempted to relate his theory to it. In his view, religious development may parallel but also differs from moral development as it deals with different kinds of questions. He argued that

Table 7.1 Kohlberg's Stages of Moral Development

Stage		Description
Level A;	Preconventional	Moral value resides in external acts or needs rather than persons or standards
Stage 1:	Punishment and Obedience	Literal obedience of rules to avoid punishment; egocentric focus *God pictured as powerful figure*
Stage 2:	Instrumental purpose	Right is meeting your own interests and having agreements that allow others to do the same *God will help you if you do what God wants*
Level B:	Conventional	Moral value in roles, conventional order and experiences of others
Stage 3:	Mutual relationships and conformity	Acts in ways that will gain or maintain approval and trust of others, as well as self-approval *God is a loyal trustworthy friend; you should behave correctly so you don't offend*
Stage 4:	Social system and conscience maintenance	Need to uphold laws and duties and make contributions so that society is upheld *God as supreme lawgiver over natural and Moral orders*
Level:B/C	Transitional; Postconventional, but not principled	Personal and subjective basis for choice based on what the individual thinks or feels is right
Level C	Postconventional	Moral value in shared standards, rights, duties
Stage 5:	Prior rights and social contract; utilitarian ethics	Rules are relative to the group but must be upheld because of mutual obligation; Rational decisions of morality based on "the greatest good for the greatest number" *God and individual mutually involved*
Stage 6:	Universal ethical principles	One should act in accord with universal ethical principles, which may conflict with laws; Principles include equal rights, individual dignity

Source: Kohlberg (1981) and Kohlberg & Ryncarz (1990)

Box 7.2 Eichmann's stage 1 reasoning

But to sum it all up, I must say that I regret nothing. Adolf Hitler may have been wrong all down the line, but one thing is beyond dispute: the man was able to work his way up from lance corporal in the German army to Fuhrer of a people of almost eight million.

I never met him personally, but his success alone proves to me that I should subordinate myself to this man. He was somehow so supremely capable that the people recognized him. And so with that justification I recognized him joyfully, and I still defend him (cited in Kohlberg, 1984, pp. 54–44).

---

morality deals with the nature of the good life and the good person, while religion concerns fundamental questions about human nature and the human condition. Kohlberg believed that morality was a "logically independent realm" from religion because (1) moral development occurs in people with no religious beliefs, and (2) individuals at a high stage of moral development can have very different religious views (1981, pp. 336–337). Some research data support this, suggesting that religious people often distinguish between universally applicable moral laws and those specific to their group (Nucci & Turiel, 1993; cf. Lourenco, 2003). As in the case of morality, Kohlberg assumed that there are universal issues like our relationship to the eternal, which people try to answer through their religious reasoning in an attempt "to affirm life and morality as related to a transcendent or infinite ground or sense of the whole" (1981, p. 321). He also speculated that a sixth stage of religious development such as the agape ideal might be a competitor for his own vision of a highest moral Stage 6. However, he later argued that agape assumes a Stage 6 morality; thus religious development depends on moral development (1981, p. 351).

7.4.2.3 Critique

Two types of critiques have been mounted against Kohlberg's theory. Narrower critiques have focused upon problems in his description of justice reasoning, while broader ones have questioned his presuppositions and methodology. Critics point out the following:

1. People cannot be placed at a single stage of moral reasoning or development, because different kinds of ethical dilemmas elicit different levels of moral reasoning from people. For instance, people deciding whether to drink and drive typically use lower levels of reasoning then when talking about the Heinz dilemma (Carpendale, 2000; Grover, 1980).
2. The theory ignores the possibility that moral development in general or justice reasoning in particular might vary according to gender or culture (Gilligan, 1982; Gibson, 2004; Gorsuch & Barnes, 1973). In Indian samples, researchers have tended to find similar stages, but the subjects responding to the Heinz dilemma also make use of moral and philosophical values that do not fit within Kohlberg's framework (Parikh, 1980; Vasudev & Hummel, 1987).
3. Rational views of justice reasoning neglect the relational character of morality (Gilligan, Murphy, & Tappan, 1990). A relational view focuses less on reasoning about principle or reciprocity and more about personal or group commitments, empathy, or the ability to take the perspective of others (Carpendale, 2000; Nucci & Turiel, 1993). Religious types of ethical reasoning, especially in theistic religions, often have a strong relational and communal component (Johnson, 1996a, 1996b; Gibson, 2004). Because of this, narrative might provide a better framework for understanding moral reasoning (Hermans, Kempen, & van Loon, 1992).
4. While Kohlberg attempted to define moral reasoning as a separate domain, studies with Western samples show that people think that (1) moral maturity cannot be defined solely on the basis of justice reasoning but involves characteristics of moral character and virtue such as integrity, dependability, self-control, and degree of care (Colby, 2002; Baumeister & Exline, 1999; cf. Baumeister & Leary, 1995);

and (2) morality and religion cannot be clearly separated because while it is possible to think of moral people who are not religious, morality is an essential part of religion (Walker & Pitts, 1998a, 1988b). Thus, Kohlberg's claim that religion and morality are independent is at the minimum overstated and clearly wrong for some individuals (Walker & Reimer, 2006).

5. Like many hard stage models, Kohlberg's theory has good reliability but a narrow range of application (Reich, 1993). For instance, a theory of moral development that focuses solely on justice reasoning has trouble offering an effective explanation of moral action (Batson, 1998). This is because moral judgment and action in real situations may be more related to other factors like character, courage, moral emotions like guilt, and the specific situation and self-structure of the individual (Blasi, 1983; Colby, 2002; Arnold, 2000; Grover, 1980; cf. Kohlberg, 1984, p. 337). Kohlberg himself admitted that judgment is not the only predictor of moral action (1984, pp. 70–71).

A final issue with regard to theories like Kohlberg's is the extent to which an understanding of moral development is relevant to religious or spiritual development. Some writers (e.g., Kant, see Section 2.2.3) have closely associated the two, while others have seen them as potentially separate. Recent work by Kevin Reimer (e.g., Walker & Reimer, 2006) has indicated an asymmetrical relationship between these concepts in the minds of many religious people. In this view, morality and moral thinking is a necessary prerequisite to religious practices and spiritual development, but moral thinking does not require spiritual underpinnings, although religious individuals will be influenced in their moral thinking by their religious beliefs and practices.

7.4.3 James Fowler and Faith Development

Probably the most influential modern theory related to religious and spiritual development has been that of James Fowler. Fowler is a theologian who worked at Harvard with Kohlberg and absorbed the outlook of the structural tradition in developmental psychology (Lownsdale, 1997).

7.4.3.1 Fowler's Conception of Faith

Fowler (1981, 1996) has articulated a theory of faith development. Drawing on ideas from Tillich and H. Richard Niebuhr, he defined **faith** as an evolving sense of sprit and relatedness to others that provides meaning and coherence and allows participation in "an *ultimate environment*" (1996, p. 21). It is a universal feature of human beings that gives coherence and direction to life, links people to each other and to a larger frame of reference, and enables them to deal with the limit conditions inherent in human life. In his view, faith is a more fundamental category than religion, which involves beliefs, practices and images that express and inform faith (Fowler & Dell, 2004). Faith involves patterns of (1) knowing or belief, (2) valuing or commitment, and (3) meaning construction, typically expressed through narrative (1987, p. 56) (Fig. 7.2).

According to Fowler, faith is based in our sense of self that develops on several levels: an *emergent self* in infancy that forms the basis of imagination, a core or *embodied self* that appears in physical rituals, and an *intersubjective self* that allows us to develop shared frameworks and fantasies (Fowler, 1989). This faith creates triadic relationships between ourselves, others and "shared centers of value and power" (1996, p. 21). In this view, different kinds of personal identities in people can be thought of as coming from various sorts of relations with potential centers of value. Some people have multiple centers of value with no center; they have many compartmentalized identities and move between different interests and situations. Fowler called these people *polytheists*. This pattern is often found in contemporary culture, particularly in people who suffer from personality disorders (Haynes, 1998). Others are *henotheists*, who have an identity unified around a single center of power that is not of ultimate concern, such as money or status. A last group is made up of *radical monotheists*, who have "loyalty to the principle of being and to the source and center of all value and power" (1981, p. 23).

Fig. 7.2 *James Fowler.*
A central figure in psychology and religion dialogue; his view of faith development has been enormously influential in both psychology and Christian theological circles. Photo courtesy of James Fowler

7.4.3.2 Stages of Faith

Fowler has developed a structural model of faith development that draws on the work of Piaget and Kohlberg. In Fowler's view, faith development parallels cognitive development and involves shifts between stages, each of which are "patterned operations of knowing and valuing" (1996, p. 56) that help us find and make meaning. Faith stages become increasingly complex as we move to higher levels, and each stage includes a worldview as well as a whole set of values, myths, stories and symbols that articulate them (See Table 7.2). Fowler believed his stages were invariant, sequential, hierarchical and universal, although in his later writing he has backed away from claims of stage universality (1996, pp. 57, 297; cf. 1999b). His stages parallel the stages of cognitive and ego development as outlined by Piaget, Erikson and the early childhood psychologist Daniel Stern (2000). Each stage typically involves being a member of a community that shares this faith. Transition to a new stage is triggered by a sense that old structures are no longer adequate, leading to disenchantment with old patterns and then a new beginning following a period of confusion and searching. Fowler explicitly argues that these new stages

Table 7.2 Fowler's states of faith development

Stage of faith (age)	Emergent strength/virtue	Other characteristics
0. Undifferentiated/primal (infancy)	Mutuality, trust pre-images of the ground of being	Parents most important source
1. Intuitive-projective (early childhood/preschool)	Imagination Images of numinous and Ultimate environment	Pre-operational magical thinking, fantasy Aware of God, religious issues (e.g., death)
2. Mythic-literal (school age)	Narrative ability Hearing and telling stories of faith	Concrete operations Faith based on shared traditions Synthesis by narrative form
3. Synthetic-conventional (adolescence)	Forming of identity, personal faith, typically without reflection	Formal operations Integration of what has been taught into a system; development of personality, attached to value system
4. Individuative-reflective (young adulthood)	Reflective construction of ideology Vocational dream	Evaluation of received values, critical choice of beliefs and values; self-persona differentiation
5. Conjunctive (mid-adulthood and later)	Awareness of paradox, depth of issues intergenerational responsibility for the world	Openness to other perspectives; move beyond questioning stance to acceptance
6. Universalizing	Detachment from ideology	Results in a "keonosis" or emptying of self, very rare

Source: Fowler (1981, p. 290, 1996)

are qualitatively different, although not necessarily better or more desirable than the old ones (Fowler & Dell, 2004). Conversion experiences do not necessarily bring about stage transitions, they tend to be involved when the individual shifts to an entirely different center of power or value.

7.4.3.3 Evaluation

Fowler's theory has been widely influential. It has all the advantages of a structural approach. It helps us understand universal features of faith and ways of knowing, allowing for comparisons between diverse groups and among individuals within a group, including those following non-religious paths of development. It also allows for comparisons between faith stages and with other types of development (Fowler, 1981; Rizzuto, 2001a). Fowler has even used it to conceptualize the process of cultural evolution in interesting ways (de Kock, 2000). He has also argued that congregations and religious groups have modal levels of development (1987, p. 97), a concept that might provide a useful framework for understanding religious communities.

Fowler's theory has also been subject to a number of criticisms:

1. His definition of faith is thought by some to be too broad, putting believers and unbelievers alike under the same heading, blurring distinctions between ethics, spirituality, and religious faith (Vergote, 1994, p. 234). This makes it difficult to understand how these things are different and might function in diverse ways in different contexts such as theistic and nontheistic religions (Kohlberg & Ryncarz, 1990; Wallwork, 1982) or how various aspects of a person's life might function at different levels of faith development (Rizzuto, 2001b).
2. The theory does not place faith development in the context of broader developmental issues including psychodynamic, emotional, experiential, relational, gender, and cultural factors (McFadden, 1999; McDargh, 1983; Parks, 1991; Streib, 2001a, 2001b).
3. It focuses on process over content and thus tends to assume all centers of value are the same, a questionable position (Hyde, 1990; cf. Fowler, 1981, pp. 273, 301).
4. It provides no account of the transformational mechanisms that help a person grow from one stage of faith to another (Wallwork, 1982), perhaps because these processes are not universal but vary according to object structure and socioreligious context (Rizzuto, 2001b).
5. It has weak empirical support, with little or no quantitative data and conceptual links that would tie the theory to other research (Hyde, 1990). Additionally, available research has been unable to identify many individuals at his highest stages of faith, which suggests that his conception of the goal of development may be problematic. Certainly his theory does not have a clear role for many of the higher stages of religious development such as illumination and union (Haynes, 1998).

6. It privileges individual autonomy over the important role of community, although he has tried to address this in later writings (Johnson, 1996a; Fowler & Dell, 2006).

7. It assumes that faith development proceeds in stages that are invariant, sequential, and hierarchical, a position rejected by many postmodernists (Streib, 2001a, 2001b). Fowler has responded to this, claiming that he is open to postmodern hermeneutic and interpretive insights, as well as the role of emotions and the unconscious (1996, p. 157). He has suggested some additions to his theory (e.g., Fowler, 2001); however, these are not well integrated with the rest of his thought and have not attracted much interest.

Fowler has been sensitive to the criticisms raised by postmodernists, although he has serious problems with parts of the postmodern movement because of its tendency toward relativism and minimizing the need for a core self, as in Kenneth Gergen's work (Fowler, 2001).

7.4.4 Fritz Oser and Religious Judgment

A different perspective on cognitive development and religion is provided by Fritz Oser and his colleagues (Oser & Gmunder, 1991; Oser, 1991a, 1991b), who have developed a theory of religious judgment. According to their definition, **religious judgment** is how the individual deals subjectively with the process of meaning making, coping with contingencies, and creating subjective security in a world of objective insecurity. It also involves how people think about their relation with the Ultimate. It provides a deep reflective or "mother-structure" that operates in the background most of the time but can be seen when crises challenge the way we understand the meaning of events (Oser, 1991a). As in other structural theories, the emphasis is on process, although Oser admits that "structures in the religious domain can never be entirely purified of content-aspects" (Oser & Gmunder, 1991, p. 61). Religious judgment is a part of a *religious consciousness*, which also involves construction of a relationship with an Ultimate being that can help us solve life problems.

Although Oser studied with Kohlberg and was certainly influenced by him, there are also important differences between the two scholars. Kohlberg was interested in religion only as it related to morality (Oser, 1997), while Oser is interested in describing a theory of religious rather than ethical judgment. Oser describes the differences between Piaget, Kohlberg, and himself in terms of how subject and object relations are handled. In Piaget, the focus is on intellectual development and the relation of subject to object. Kohlberg, on the other hand deals with social development and the subject-subject relation. Oser's theory differs from both as he deals with religious development and the relation of subjects to the Ultimate and thus to each other. As a result, Oser's theory is often thought to be less of a hard stage model than that of Kohlberg, although not as soft as Fowler's theory (Power, 1991, p. 128).

Oser sees that development is a process where the individual seeks equilibrium on seven bipolar dimensions that are important for religious judgment: transcendence vs. immanence, freedom vs. dependency, trust vs. fear or anxiety, sacred vs. profane, hope vs. absurdity, eternity vs. ephemerality, and functional transparency (seeing how things work) vs. opaqueness (having a hidden or magical quality). During different stages of growth, these dimensions are balanced in various ways, but development seeks a complex equilibrium that is finally achieved in the last stage (see Table 7.3). Stage transitions are often triggered by important life experiences or changes that cannot be dealt with adequately within existing cognitive structures and call for the integration of new elements of thought. Each stage is a holistic unity that involves the rejection of previous ways of looking at things while incorporating parts of the past. It contains a new worldview and way of interpreting experience,

Table 7.3 Oser's stages of religious judgment

Level	Orientation	Description
Stage 0	Undifferentiated	No distinction drawn between interior and exterior
Stage 1	Absolute heteronomy	Ultimate is exterior and may or may not help
		Direct activity of the Ultimate in the world
		We are dependent upon the Ultimate
		People react to the Ultimate, should follow its plan
Stage 2	"Do Ut Des"	Ultimate is exterior and will help if we pass tests and care about the Ultimate
		Direct activity of the Ultimate in the world
		People can influence the Ultimate
Stage 3	Absolute autonomy (Deism)	Ultimate has a separate sphere of influence
		The Ultimate is not active in the world but provides underlying order
		People are autonomous, responsible for themselves
		Religious and other authority may be rejected
		Atheists do not usually progress beyond here (Oser, 1991a)
Stage 4	Mediated autonomy	There is an unexplained part of life that only makes sense in relation to the Ultimate
		Ultimate is both transcendent and immanent
		Ultimate provides the basis for possibility of action, e.g., freedom, hope
		Ultimate acts in the world according to a plan through us; the world is the image of the Ultimate
		People recognize some dependence on an Ultimate without negating autonomy
		People engage in various forms of religiosity
Stage 5	Intersubjective religious	Ultimate seen as love for self and others
		Ultimate being part of all commitments but also transcends them in infinite freedom
		Ultimate is seen in others, mystical experience
		Loyalty to Ultimate shown in relations with others
		People are independent of religious community or salvation plan

Oser and Gmunder (1991) and Oser (1991b)

and with it a new subjective perception of our relationship with God. The outcome of each stage produces a set of competencies, which may or may not translate into action for various personal or situational reasons.

Like Kohlberg, Oser has tested his theory using participant responses to dilemmas. Early research utilized a sample of 112 individuals aged 8–75 from a town in Switzerland, but other research has been conducted in a variety of places with different samples, including some non-Western groups. Oser found that people could be assigned to different stages of religious judgment and that individuals in older age groups showed an increasing sense of autonomy and partnership with God (Oser, 1997). Oser also speculates about a possible 6th stage of development based on the themes evident in earlier stages. This stage would be a version of Stage 5 with an orientation toward "universal communication and solidarity" (Oser & Gmunder, 1991, p. 81). However, researchers have not identified people fitting this description, so its place within the theory is tentative.

7.4.4.1 Critique

Like other psychological theories of development, parts of Oser's theory are based in data, but other parts are dependent upon philosophical or theological assumptions. These are not empirically validated and color the way in which the data are interpreted (Oser & Gmunder, 1991, p. 7). In particular, theories like those of Oser and Fowler contain a final stage of development that has not been verified empirically (virtually no one fits the stage), but the theory is built around the value-laden assumption that this is the best and ultimate goal of development (Fowler, 1991, p. 36). This can mean that the theory does a good job of explaining things that fit within its assumptions, but a poorer job otherwise. It may also explain why theories like those of Oser and Kohlberg are similar in lower stages but diverge in higher ones (Oser & Gmunder, 1991, p. 3)—different conceptions of end goal lead to increasingly different pictures of development when one reaches higher stages.

Oser's theory is based on a typical 20th-century liberal Protestant view of Christianity that emphasizes individuality and downplays the role of community, although like Kohlberg he would agree that major religious traditions help sustain higher levels of development. As a result, his theory has been criticized as being unable to explain growth toward maturity in groups outside of liberal Protestantism, such as conservative or evangelical Christians. Research on Oser's stages also suggests that they do not capture important aspects of religious development during adulthood (Oser, 1997; Tamminen, 1994a). By ignoring the specific context provided by different religious groups, the model ignores the content of religious reasoning and risks neglecting the effects of environment on the developmental process (Bronfenbrenner, 1977).

The focus on reasoning in Oser's theory—as well as that of Fowler—carries with it other limitations as well. For instance, it does not provide a clear understanding of how reasoning translates into action, how affect and unconscious processes contribute to religious judgment, or how religious experience interacts with judgment when interpreting the meaning of events (Power, 1991; Rizzuto, 1991; Tamminen, 1994a). Oser has acknowledged the validity of some of these criticisms (Oser, 1991b).

7.5 Integrative Approaches to Religious Development

7.5.1 Ken Wilber

One of the most sophisticated integrations of Eastern perspectives with modern psychology can be found in the work of Ken Wilber. In an early work entitled *The Atman Project* (1996), Wilber outlines a transpersonal theory of development that draws upon sources in religion, psychology, and philosophy. While he recognizes the effects of culture on the individual, Wilber aligns himself with the perennial philosophy (see Section 4.3) and argues that there is a universal aspect to development. He rejects a mechanistic, materialist worldview in favor of a holistic and hierarchical one (see Wilber, 2000b) but nevertheless argues that many aspects of spiritual development show a stage-like progression (Wilber, 2000a, p. 134).

Like the perennialists, Wilber believes that we all have a drive toward Spirit. The process of ascent follows a hierarchical stage model of development, with lower stages in the model resembling those of Piaget (Rothberg, 1998). Wilber rejects the idea that we might have spiral paths of development where temporary regressions to lower levels may help us achieve higher ones; rather the spirit draws us on in a progressive, ascending path (Washburn, 1998). Unfortunately, we tend to pathologize, misunderstand, or feel threatened by stages higher than our own (Walsh, 1998).

Like many Eastern writers such as Sri Aurobindo (e.g., 1996), Wilber draws close parallels between development and evolution. However, the transpersonal framework views evolution as more than successive adaptations to the material world that convey reproductive advantage (see Section 6.2.1). Rather, **evolution** and development are progression toward transcendence—they are ultimately religious or spiritual in nature. Drawing on Hindu thought, Wilber believes that the goal of evolution is "Atman, or ultimate Unity Consciousness in only God" and is part of the "drive of God towards God" (1996, p. xvii). Development proceeds toward increasing differentiation and hierarchical integration, which is a reflection of universal processes of growth.

Wilber has outlined a stage model describing the path of personal evolution. Each stage involves the creation of *basic structures* such as sensorimotor abilities or formal operational reasoning. These structures remain available to the person in all stages subsequent to their emergence. At each stage, the individual also develops *transition structures* that are present at that stage but will disappear when the person moves on to a new level of development. Our experience of the self is an example of a transition structure, as it changes to new unique forms as we move from stage to stage (Wilber, 1986a).

During the first half of life, development proceeds in an "outward arc" of developing subconscious and conscious awareness of self and environment (see Table 7.4).

Table 7.4 Ken Wilber's stages of personal-transpersonal development

Stage (Substage)	Cognitive style Affective atmosphere	Conative or Motivational factors	Temporal/self Mode
Prepersonal (pleromatic)	Adualistic "Oceanic"	Instinctual	Pretemporal Oceanic
Prepersonal (uroboric)	Recognition of other Euphoria and fear	Survival and Physiological Needs	Pretemporal Reflexive
Typhonic (physical/ emotional bodies)	Differentiation of objects from self and each other Distinguishing various kinds of emotions	Survival Pleasure Principle	Momentary Narcissistic
Typhonic (image body)	Primary process Sensorimotor completion Sustained emotions	Wish fulfillment Anxiety reduction Survival and safety	Extended present Nonreflexive body-image
Mental-egoic	Secondary process Concrete/formal thought Dialogical language, emotions (e.g., love)	Goal direction Willpower Self-esteem needs	Linear, historical Extended past, future Egoic-syntaxical Personae
Centauric	Transverbal Vision-image, fantasy Spontaneous	Creative wishing Meaning seeking Self-actualization	Grounded in present Integrated
Low-subtle	Extraegoic Transpersonal	Paranormal siddhi	Sees past, future Out-of-body
High-subtle	Intuitional Sensory revelations Rapture, bliss	Compassion Love and Gratitude	Transtemporal Archetypal-divine
Low-causal	Final illumination Radiant bliss	Love-in-oneness karuna	Transtemporal Vanishing into God
High-causal	Cessation Samadhi; Ecstasy	Love-in-oneness Spontaneity	Transtemporal Formless realization
Ultimate	Ultimate Unity		

Wilber (1996)

These are the *prepersonal* and *personal* phases of development. This is followed in some individuals by a *transpersonal* phase, an "inward arc" that involves development of higher states of consciousness. The outward arc involves a series of stages at the gross level of development and perception that include many of the cognitive, emotional, motivational, and experiential changes discussed by Piaget and other developmental psychologists. The peak of the arc is the centauric stage, which is a creative, spontaneous way of being that has characteristics similar to the state of self-actualization described by Maslow. Following this in the inward arc are a series of subtle and causal stages that are marked by increasing experiences of connectedness with the world and others, including paranormal experiences. The final goal is an experience of unity with the world in which the self dissolves.

A key point made by Wilber is that there are both similarities and differences between less and more advanced stages of development, so that sometimes very advanced states of consciousness may be mistaken for immature ones. In this way of thinking, earlier modes of development like fantasy that are preverbal may have equivalents at transverbal or transpersonal stages of development that look like fantasy but are actually fundamentally different, because they are experiences of transverbal and transpersonal realities rather than internal states. He calls this tendency to confuse higher and lower experiences that are superficially similar the **pre-trans fallacy.** Wilber points out frequent examples of it in the writings of psychologists like Freud, who in his view mistakenly equated higher states of consciousness like the "oceanic feeling" with the undifferentiated consciousness of infancy and early childhood.

Wilber's ideas about psychopathology are built around his developmental theory. He believes that certain kinds of psychopathology tend to be characteristic of each level of development. Adults who are still in the prepersonal phases typically suffer from personality disorders, while in the personal phase one might suffer from existential problems such as concerns about personal authenticity or the meaning of life. In the transpersonal stages, one can also experience a variety of unusual experiences and problems such as surges of uncontrolled energy or "dark night" depression-like experiences that come, as the individual begins to detach from things that formerly provided pleasure (1986b).

7.5.1.1 Critique

Wilber's work is creative and offers a number of advantages. His theory attempts to go beyond strictly materialistic and naturalistic theories and embraces a holistic view of reality. It provides a framework for understanding **nondualistic** experience in a developmental perspective. His concept of the pre-trans fallacy provides a structure for understanding confusions that may plague a number of theories of psychological and spiritual development (Reynolds, 2004).

Wilber's work has been criticized by a number of writers, including some within the transpersonal movement. For instance, Frager (1989) notes that Wilber's view (1) is one-dimensional, linear, and hierarchical, unlike the inner growth process experienced by most; (2) tends to take concepts from traditions and use them outside of the supporting conceptual structure, drawing comparisons that ignore important differences; and (3) uses his own idiosyncratic terminology that is distinct from others in psychology. Others have suggested that his theory does not account for some critical data of experience, such as the presence of higher transpersonal experiences at lower levels of development, or the apparent effects of cultural or gender differences, and it tends to romanticize Eastern religious traditions like Buddhism (Rothberg, 1998; Rubin, 2003). Evolutionary theorists have attacked him for his view that neo-Darwinism is unable to explain some important aspects of our world such as the origin of life, the beginnings of sentience, and human self-awareness. Finally, some have criticized the overly synthetic and non-relational quality of his theory (Reynolds, 2004). As a result, it may not be testable using traditional scientific methodologies.

7.5.2 James Loder

The work of James Loder (1931–2001) is important because he offers one of the few models of development that has both theological and psychological sophistication. He believed that theological as well as psychological perspectives were necessary to understand human development. This is not because he disagreed with theories like that of Piaget, Kohlberg or Fowler. Rather, he believed that human uniqueness, issues of purpose or value, as well as some more specific interpretive tasks either demanded or benefited from a theological perspective (1998, xiii, 4). As a result, Loder's theory is based on the idea that human development is shaped by spiritual transformation, while more psychological theories like Fowler's argue that spiritual transformation is embedded in human development, a view which tends to privilege psychological concerns over theological or spiritual ones (Balswick, King, & Reimer, 2005, p. 274)

A model that truly integrates theological and psychological categories is necessarily complex, and Loder's work *The Logic of the Spirit* (1998) is no exception. In his view, development takes place in two orders, divine and contingent, with the former surrounding the latter. The divine order is the source of grace that can remake human life and the environment within which development occurs, while changes in the body, soul (psychological ego), and sociocultural contexts lie within the contingent order. Spiritual development takes place on the boundary between the two and thus is affected by both divine and contingent orders. The divine order has the potential to affect the contingent order when surprise intrudes upon the fixed patterns of contingent time, providing the potential for transformation.

Loder argues that relationality has priority over rationality both developmentally and in terms of our "quality of being" (1998, p. 8). He defines relationality as the unity that is possible within a polarity of two things that are apparently opposed and possibly asymmetrical. This relationality is foremost an interaction between the person and the environment, sometimes between people, and most importantly between the person and God or the "ultimate ground of being" (1998, p. 10). Systems of meaning are constructed utilizing these relationships, and transformation occurs when something questions the current system of coherence and calls for a reordering. Inattention to incoherence leads to potentially destructive use of our abilities and must be avoided. Development is thus a series of coherences and is a fundamental human drive; incoherence such as between soul and spirit requires transformation or re-creation.

Loder provides a description of how the axes of psychological development, spirituality, and transcendence interact at various stages of life. Like Erikson, he believes that there are fundamental developments that take place at each stage which are important for later stages of development. His theory focuses primarily on the early foundational stages, although he also addresses some developmental concerns of adulthood.

Infancy. The task of the first stage of life is to construct a trustworthy world out of chaos, "a future that is indebted to but not controlled by the past" (1998, p. 88). Symbolic of the kinds of processes that take place at this stage is the response of the infant to a face. The prototype of religious experience that develops at this level is the sense of recognition, affirmation, and presence that one receives from an Other that provides satisfaction and harmony. This sense of the Face of the Other fights the "underlying negation of human existence" that manifests itself in loneliness, dread, and mistrust (1998, p. 105). It has analogies to later Christian religious experiences of the Creator Sprit, the face of Jesus as the face of God, and the experience of negation and original sin.

Toddler and Oedipal. Interactions with the environment produce autonomy, but also separation from the source of that autonomy, which leads to shame and inner doubt. These early childhood issues are of great significance, for here is formed the foundations of human freedom. This is the stage at which symbols and transitional objects are especially important, as the child's inner world is elaborated through imagination and play. It is a crucial period for religious development, for it is at about age 2–1/2 or 3 that the God representation begins to take shape. Successful negotiation of this stage will give the child a sense of imagination and an ability to construct and believe in a vision, as well as identify with parental models of good and bad.

School age. The beginnings of a coherent structure of life and work are laid down during the early school years. The child comes to this stage with two worlds, one that is literal, linear, rational, and socially controlled, and the other that is mystical, imaginative, and playful. During this stage, the child begins to form life narratives and structures that hold these two worlds together in a coherent picture. Role-taking that is active at this stage provides a prelude to work and participation in community, although this is only an approximation of true community or *koinonia* as envisioned in Christian religious thought. The problem comes when work and the linear world are emphasized at the expense of other areas, and personal worth becomes confused with work, as is possible in achievement-oriented societies. When this happens we develop attachments or even addictions to work, putting tremendous amounts of energy into them, trying to make them solve problems and meet needs for which they were not designed. Loder indicates that one of the values of a theological critique of development is to point out problems like this and remove the obsessive quality to work, reestablishing our worth on its original ground—the love of God.

Adolescence and young adulthood. Loder believes that in adolescence the individual begins a more explicit search for order. Developing a sense of this at the psychological level requires that we build up the ego and our identity in terms of things like ideology, values, and work commitments, as well as views of authority and love. We also begin to see that it is relationality that underlies all forms of order. We discover that friends can serve as transitional objects, as we develop our sense of identity. Because of this need for relationality, we have a need to behold its Face and develop a relationship with it. This is a religious task, and each culture and religion has its own version of what a *homo religiosus* should look like. Relationality with God is thus also developed in the context of our relationship with individuals, important groups, and the culture within which we live.

Young adulthood. In the ideal situation, this is a stage where creating and maintaining a dream with integrity have primary authority. This dream relates to individual concerns like work, but it also involves intimacy, the ability to create a shared dream and ultimately a love that is accepting, appreciative, and not possessive. All of this involves a restructuring of development at the level of the ego. We need to reverse our growth patterns and become more childlike. Through taking an active risk and expressing our identity to another person, we can overcome isolation, as well as confront negative aspects of our prior development. Ego identity and faith will end up stronger for this process. The paradox of going back to previous stages to move forward, and stripping ourselves of things to gain more, is a characteristic feature of religious concepts of development, especially those elaborated by theologian-psychologists with psychodynamic leanings (McDargh, 1983, pp. 56–57).

Middle and older adulthood. Loder's treatment of midlife and beyond is disappointingly short but thoughtful. Loder pictures the time of middle adulthood as one of ambivalence. Whether we have attained success or feel that we have not achieved our goals, there is typically a sense of depression or even stagnation that people experience. This forces us to reevaluate our lives, look again at where we have invested our energy, and seek a transformation of the ego to achieve balance. Loder views old age as a time of losses such as physical decline, decreasing work involvement, and declining independence. However, he sees that these losses have a benefit, in that they bring simplicity to our life and strip away things that distract us from the pure love of God.

7.5.2.1 Critique

Loder's theory is an innovative example of how modern psychology might be combined with theological insights to produce an interesting theory of development. Unfortunately, theories like those of Loder and Wilber have generated relatively little discussion among psychologists. This may be due in part to their generality, which makes it difficult to apply the theories in research or practice. Also, more strictly psychological theories like those of Kohlberg and Fowler come with built-in research methodologies that make it easy for investigators to test or develop them further, while Loder's ideas may be difficult to test.

7.6 Conclusion

Key issue: *Developmental approaches to the psychology and religion dialogue are heavily dependent upon the theoretical presuppositions of a theorist, including general views about the nature of time and specific ideas about the goal, trajectory, and diversity of development.*

Even a brief review of theories from psychology and several religious traditions reveals the complexity of the issues involved when talking about religious or spiritual development. Some of the fundamental questions that must be considered include the following:

1. How does development *function in time*? Psychological theories tend to be built upon Newtonian versions of time that emphasize its objective and linear qualities; they assume that time functions similarly in all situations. Religious views of development often look at time from a non-Newtonian point of view and consider its subjective, forward-looking and holistic character.
2. What is the *goal* of development? In general, religious theories of development tend to emphasize transcendence, the ability of the individual to surpass the ordinary and find profound transformation. Psychological theories, on the other hand, tend to map out what is expected and predictable, with development involving a progression toward increasingly sophisticated ways of adapting to the demands of life within a linear time framework. Some theories such as that of James Loder attempt to do both.
3. What is the *trajectory* of development? When does religious development occur? Traditional religious views see childhood and adolescence as simply precursors to the primary period of growth that occurs during adulthood. Psychological theories have emphasized the importance that childhood patterns have for adulthood.
4. What is the *diversity* of development? How much similarity exists in the developmental trajectories of people across the life span? Religious and psychological theories have both pointed out common patterns, although it could be argued that many religious theories allow for more diversity in developmental process and outcome, while reductive naturalist theories emphasize their common pattern.

We will encounter these issues frequently as we turn to the specifics of child, adolescent, and adult religious or spiritual development in the next two chapters.

Chapter 8
Religion and Development in Childhood and Adolescence

The study of childhood religion and spirituality has had little place in either Christian theology or child psychology (Boyatzis, 2003; Benson, Roehlkepartain, & Rude, 2003). This is surprising, as psychologists since the time of G. Stanley Hall have recognized that childhood and adolescence are important periods in religious development, and the nurturance of children has been an important concern of Christian work, particularly during the Reformation and in the 20th century (Bunge, 2001, pp. 3–11). This lack of attention to children and adolescents is unwarranted, for if one defines spirituality as a craving for transcendence and meaning, then certainly children have a strong spiritual nature. They seek these things and experience awe and wonder as much or more than adults (Ratcliff & May, 2004). Nevertheless, some good empirical research exists on the topic, which we will examine in this chapter.

Another problem is that existing research on religion and spirituality among children and adolescents has been narrowly conceived as is also the case of much psychological research about children (Nye, 2004). Childhood and adolescence are seen mostly as precursors to adulthood, and as a result research often focuses on the implications of childhood and adolescence for adult spirituality, rather than seeing childhood as a period of life with its own importance. This is a key issue, for children are not just little adults; their spiritual and religious life has unique characteristics and considerations, such as the role of family (Pendleton, Benore, Jonas, Norwood, & Herrmann, 2004). Even early work in psychology recognized that the child does have religious needs and that these are not the same as the adult's (Wells, 1918). Childhood and adolescence are rich, complex periods of life, and researchers need to consider multiple domains in understanding religious development during this period. The cognitive, social, emotional, and moral aspects of childhood are all of importance and are directly or indirectly related to religious life (King & Boyatzis, 2004).

If spirituality and religion are thought of as concerned with a relation to ultimate meaning and transcendence that involves the whole person, childhood spirituality can be thought of as spontaneous experiences of a relational consciousness. This relational awareness can manifest itself in a number of ways, including feelings of presence and sometimes dependency, a reaction of wonder and awe at the world around us, and a sense of ultimate goodness and meaning. For the

J.M. Nelson, *Psychology, Religion, and Spirituality,*
DOI 10.1007/978-0-387-87573-6_8, @ Springer Science+Business Media, LLC 2009

most part, children do not separate such experiences from religion (Hart, 2006; Ratcliff & May, 2004; Hay & Nye, 2006; Scott, 2003; Tamminen, 1991, p. 34; Scarlett & Perriello, 1991; Shelton & Mabe, 2006; Loomba, 1942). These types of experiences can be found throughout childhood and adolescence. For instance, in a large study of Lutherans, Tamminen (1994b) found that religious experiences involving a sense of presence were common in childhood, often triggered by emergencies or personal troubles, loneliness, and fear. Adolescents also commonly reported them, although they were often given a secular interpretation. Adolescents who reported experiences of presence were more likely to report them in devotional and church situations, especially prayer, and in relation to death or loss rather than more common personal troubles. Those reporting nearness experiences had more positive attitudes toward school and were more altruistic. They were also more emotional, conscientious, and concerned about the opinions of others and were closer to their parents.

Three topics related to childhood religious development have been of particular importance to researchers: (1) the importance of socialization in the development of religious consciousness, (2) the role of early attachment relationships to later religiosity, and (3) the formation of concepts of God and their influence on adult life. We will consider each of these in some detail.

8.1 Religion and Religious Socialization in Childhood

Most psychologists and religious practitioners would agree that the family is central to the development of religiousness and spirituality (Boyatzis, Dollahite, & Marks, 2006). Although religious attitudes and practices have a moderate relationship with genetic makeup (see Section 6.1.2), religious affiliation as well as many aspects of attitudes and practices are primarily transmitted through socialization in family and community (D'Onofrio, Eaves, Murrelle, Maes, & Spilka, 1999; Mehta, 1997). This early socialization by parents, church, and school appears to be more important than other life course factors in determining adult religion (Sherkat, 1998). While church and peer factors are important in religious transmission, the strongest effect is that of parental religiosity on the child (Regnerus, 2003). The specific effect depends upon a number of relational and environmental factors in the home, including the following:

1. Warm, caring behavior from both mothers and fathers is predictive of strong adolescent religiousness, and mothers' caring is predictive of attendance (Dudley & Wisbey, 2000). The relational quality of family closeness, a good marital relationship, and traditional family structure also seem helpful (Ozorak, 1989). Doubt or non-belief in adolescents is related to lower parental affection and religious practice (Potvin, 1977). Some studies have found relationships between parental beliefs and the development of intrinsic religious motivation in their children (e.g., Kaldestad, 1996).

2. Parental religiosity can affect parenting style, which in turn can affect child and adolescent religiosity. Research has focused on two parenting styles: **authoritative parenting** that involves a combination of warm parental support with firm, demanding expectations, and **authoritarian parenting**, which combines high levels of demand with a cold, rigid emotional tone. In a study involving a national sample of over 400 families, Gunnoe, Hetherington, and Reiss (1999) found that maternal and paternal religiousness was predictive of the presence of authoritative parenting, which in turn predicted transmission of parental values like religiousness (Wilcox, 1998). Increased maternal religiousness predicted less use of authoritarian parenting. They also found a strong relationship between adolescent social responsibility, authoritative parenting, and parental religiousness. Thus parental religiousness appears to have multiple direct and indirect effects on religion in their children and teenagers.

3. Other parental characteristics such as agreement on beliefs between mother and father also appear to promote transmission, while large dissimilarities in religious belief or participation can have negative effects on well-being (Dudley & Wisbey, 2000; Beit-Hallahmi & Argyle, 1997; Petts & Knoester, 2007). Mental health issues also have an effect; for example, maternal depression decreases intergenerational transmission and its beneficial qualities. Religious transmission in nondepressed mothers seems to be related to lower risk of depression in their children, while transmission in depressed mothers is associated with higher risk (Gur, Miller, Warner, Wickramaratne, & Weissman, 2005).

4. Family involvement in religious activities and conversations at home promote religious transmission by teaching religious beliefs and helping to make them plausible. Unfortunately, relatively little is known about family religious activities and how they relate to other aspects of family life. Erikson's work on ritualization suggests some possible lines of investigation (Beit-Hallahmi & Argyle, 1997, p. 97; Mahoney, Pargament, Murray-Swank, & Murray-Swank, 2003; see Section 5.3.2).

There is also a beneficial effect of religious involvement on family relationships. Using longitudinal data collected in the 1980s, Pearce and Axinn (1998) found that mothers with greater religious service attendance and higher or increasing religious salience had more positive relations with their children. Positive mother-child relations were further enhanced in families that had multiple members with high religious salience. Greater mother-child congruence in religiousness also predicted positive mother-child relationships 5 years later. They argue from their data and other research that religion appears to have an integrating effect in families, increasing cohesion between family members. Religion does this by (1) promoting the desirability of positive relationships among family members, (2) offering activities like worship that promote interactions and (3) creating a shared set of social ties with people that have similar values. In some cases, these relationships may become sanctified and take on a spiritual character and significance that leads to better functioning (Mahoney et al., 2003). This effect has also been found in adolescents. Using the National Longitudinal Survey of Youth from the late 1990s, Smith and Kim (2003) found that teens involved in multiple religious activities, when compared with uninvolved youth, had stronger parental relationships and participated in more family activities. Teens with parents who frequently attended church services or engaged in prayer also had better relationships with their parents. In particular, teens of frequent attendees had parents who knew more about their lives and fathers who were supportive and served as role models.

The beneficial effects of religion on family relationships also extend to the marital relationship. Religiousness is a protective factor against divorce and problems like domestic violence. A number of studies (e.g., Smith & Kim, 2003) have also found that frequent religious involvement is associated with higher levels of marital satisfaction and more positive relationships on a wide variety of measures. This appears to be especially true in certain circumstances (Mahoney & Tarakeshwar, 2005):

- When the two individuals, particularly the husband, are in good mental health
- When both individuals have strong and similar religious commitments
- When religiousness includes frequent religious participation

However, problems like marital infidelity may be more distressing in religious couples because of conflict with religious beliefs.

It is often assumed that children receive religious transmission from their parents, but research suggests that it is co-created by parent and child in reciprocal dialogue. In a study of communication in Christian families, Boyatzis (2004; Boyatzis & Janicki, 2003) found that children initiate conversations about religious topics (e.g., God, prayer) as frequently as adults. Mothers were more involved than fathers. There was a wide variation among families as to the directedness of the conversation, with some parents trying to convey their beliefs while others simply provided guiding questions and a structure to support the search for understanding. While conversations on religious topics were frequent, correction by parents was relatively rare. It is also the case that transmission is dependent upon the child's *perception* of parental beliefs, rather than their actual views (Okagaki & Bevis, 1999).

Some of the effect of parents appears to be due to **channeling**, where the parents direct youth into groups and activities that reinforce home teaching. However, studies have shown that much of the effect of parents on their children is direct and unmediated by channeling. The influence of parents also appears to continue through adolescence, although effects of ethnicity, congregational climate, and peer church attendance are also significant during this time of life (Gunnoe & Moore, 2002). Research is varied on gender effects, but in general while both parents contribute, the mother seems to be more important (Martin, While, & Perlman, 2003; cf. Sherkat, 1998). Interestingly, adolescents from economically stressed families reported valuing religion more but attending less. More research is needed, and qualitative approaches such as narrative should be used more often in order to better understand the meaning that religion has for individuals in the context of family life (Boyatzis et al., 2006).

8.2 Attachment and Religion in Children and Adults

Attachment theory comes out of the work of John Bowlby (e.g., Bowlby, 1988). Bowlby observed that over time infants develop attachments to caretakers that respond to calls for help. This kind of relational **attachment** is an internal, emotional bond to a trusted person, who can serve as a secure base for exploration and a safe haven when threatened (Labouvie-Vief, 1996, p. 105). An attachment bond can form the basis of **attachment behavior** as when the trusted person is sought out for protection in times of anxiety or other need (Oksanen, 1994, pp. 34, 57; Kirkpatrick, 1992, 2005, pp. 169–187).

Baumeister (Baumeister & Leary, 1995) has argued that attachment is an example of a basic human need to form strong, stable interpersonal relationships marked by concern for the welfare of the other person and that a few stable consistent relationship of this type are more important and helpful than many superficial ones. These relationships may be difficult to replace when lost because they have special unique benefits. Presumably, people should be reluctant to break these bonds and will do a lot to maintain them and will be negatively affected by loss or threat of loss of these relationships. This need to belong may be related to religious behavior, such as in the desire to seek supportive relationships in a religious community.

Attachment appears to work through a couple of fundamental processes. First, attachment assists in the formation of positive, stable internal representations of others and our relationships. In object relations theory (ORT), these representations are referred to as **objects**, while in attachment theory they are called cognitive-affective schemas or **internal working models** (Balswick, King, & Reimer, 2005, p. 126). They develop out of early caregiver interactions and act as guides for subsequent relationships with others. Unlike psychodynamic ORT, attachment theory tends to assume that these models are fairly accurate representations of reality and not highly affected by fantasy (Levy & Blatt, 1999). However, attachment theory and ORT agree that internalized objects and working models are not strictly intellectual representations but have emotional and experiential components. Attachment can thus be an alternative framework for looking at object relations phenomena that has parallels but also points of divergence (Ainsworth, 1969; Kirkpatrick, 1997).

8.2.1 Attachment Styles

Bowlby's work on attachment was expanded on by Mary Ainsworth (1969, 1978). She thought that the Freudian drive theory and its conceptualization of development as moving from dependence to independence were inaccurate in a couple of ways. First, some dependency relationships coexist well with increasing independence. Second, mature adulthood is marked by the continuation of attachment relationships that are enduring, loving connections to others. Ainsworth extended Bowlby's work by identifying several fairly stable styles or patterns of attachment. The most common pattern is **secure attachment**, when children feel that they can depend upon their caretaker and thus are able to tolerate their departure as well as seek them out when they return. In the **insecure,** anxious or ambivalent pattern, the child is more isolated and hostile, shows distress on departure of the caretaker, and does not soothe on their return. In this situation, the caretaker does not appear to the child as offering either a secure base or safe haven. Insecurely attached children may be either excessively preoccupied or prefer distance (Schottenbauer, Fallot, & Tyrrell, 2004; Kirkpatrick, 1992).

More complex taxonomies of attachment have also been developed and have advantages over simpler schemes (Leak, Gardner, & Parsons, 1998). Bartholomew and Horowitz (1991) have divided attachment according to characteristics of internal working models of self and other, whether we see ourselves as the sort of person that others are likely to help and whether we view others as likely to respond to our needs. These working models result in four attachment patterns:

- **Secure**: positive views of self and other; nondefensive
- **Preoccupied**: positive view of other, but negative view of self; anxious and/or ambivalent
- **Dismissing**: positive view of self, but negative view of other and intimacy
- **Fearful**: negative views of self and other; socially avoidant

Some scholars believe that secure attachment requires success at two developmental tasks: (1) learning to form stable mutually satisfying relationships; and (2) establishing a healthy, realistic and positive identity. Healthy identities have two characteristics. First, they are **differentiated**, rich with many different interests, values, and coping mechanisms. Second, they are **integrated** so that the many aspects of the individual are able to work together in harmony. From an attachment perspective, patterns like the fearful and dismissive ones represent developmental levels related to different degrees of integration and differentiation (Levy & Blatt, 1999).

Although people do not uniquely fit one style all the time (Bartholomew & Horowitz, 1991), a large body of research shows that people have persistent attachment patterns and that these have significant effects on a wide variety of behaviors. Attachment patterns affect many different things, such as our goals for interaction, our models of the self, and our emotional connections to others. Secure attachment helps promote compassion and altruism by reducing personal distress and fostering a strong sense of self that can remain balanced while facing the demands of needs from other people. Secure attachment also affects parenting, as individuals with this pattern are more likely to have secure attachment bonds with their children (van IJzendoorn, 1995). In contrast, insecurely attached people are not comfortable with closeness and have negative models of others, and anxiously attached individuals may become emotionally overwhelmed by the distress of others, lacking a clear line between them and the self (Gillath, Shaver, & Mikulincer, 2005). Attachment may also facilitate social support because it builds positive perceptions and comfort with intimacy, and it may help to protect against stress by fostering a sense of security and social competency (Kenney, 2000).

8.2.2 Attachment and Religion

There are obvious reasons to believe that attachment and religious behavior might be related. As Kirkpatrick (1992) notes, theistic religions often refer to God as a kind of available and responsive attachment figure, who can serve as a haven to turn to in prayer, or a secure base that can be experienced as friendly and trustworthy. Religious people turn to God through prayer or other means in situations where this type of figure would be helpful, such as in times of crisis. This attachment relationship with God becomes more central as children become more independent of their parents (Granqvist & Dickie, 2006). Image of God studies also fit well in the attachment framework. Nearness to God and a loving, protective parental factor have been consistently found to be aspects of our God image, and these seem to be descriptions of secure attachment (Kirkpatrick & Shaver, 1990), while avoidant attachment is related to an image of God as not loving but controlling (Rowatt & Kirkpatrick, 2002).

Some aspects of adult religiousness can be predicted from childhood attachment patterns. Sudden conversion experiences seem to be more common among those with insecure attachments, while securely attached individuals have more gradual conversions (Granqvist, 2003). Positive beliefs about God and one's relationship to the Divine, as well as whether we have a sense of having a personal relationship with God, are enhanced in individuals with strong childhood attachment patterns. Those with secure attachments also tend to feel more secure in their relationship to God and less threatened by the possibility of religious change. Not surprisingly, adult intrinsic religious motivation is positively related to secure attachment and negatively related to avoidant attachment in childhood. However, the relationships between childhood attachment and adult religiousness are complex and go beyond any simple mental models hypothesis. Furthermore, attachment is not good at predicting other aspects of religiousness such as participation. More work on the topic is needed in order to gain a clearer picture of these relationships (Granqvist & Hagekull, 2000; Kirkpatrick & Shaver, 1990; Rowatt & Kirkpatrick, 2002).

How does attachment have these effects on our religious and spiritual life? Lee Kirkpatrick has identified two main hypotheses that have been pursued by investigators. In the **correspondence hypothesis**, it is believed that our relationship with God matches the pattern of attachment we developed as children; thus people with secure attachment might be expected to have better relationships with God. In this view, an *experience* of love is a necessary foundation of our *ability* to love (von Balthasar, 1986, p. 105). The alternative view is the **compensation hypothesis**, which predicts that people without early secure attachment are more likely to turn to religion, because they are looking for a substitute (Kirkpatrick, 1992, 2005).

Evidence from research is supportive of both hypotheses. The *correspondence hypothesis* is supported by research suggesting that those with secure attachments and more comfort with closeness will participate in more communal and individual religious activities. They also have greater religious commitment, higher levels of theological exploration, more positive images of God, and lower rates of loss of faith. Individuals who come from emotionally cold or authoritarian homes have attachment patterns similar to the dismissing or fearful styles and report more avoidance or anxiety in their relationship to God (Schottenbauer et al., 2004; Kirkpatrick & Shaver, 1992; Beck, 2006; McDonald, Beck, Allison, & Norsworthy,, 2005; cf. Oliver & Paull, 1995). Evidence for the *compensation hypothesis* is found in longitudinal studies which show that insecure, avoidant, and anxious individuals are twice as likely to report new relationships with God compared with secure attached people, and that religious experience or conversion is more than twice as common among the anxiously attached than those with avoidant or secure patterns. Some research has also found high rates of sudden religious conversion precipitated by transitional times, emotional turmoil, or personal crises like marital problems among those with avoidant or insecure attachments. In these situations, God seems to act as a substitute attachment figure, while gradual religious change is more related to socialization factors (Kirkpatrick, 1997; Kirkpatrick & Shaver, 1990; Oksanen, 1994, pp. 153–157; Granqvist & Kirkpatrick, 2004). Kirkpatrick has suggested that correspondence and compensation behavior are both present but found in different kinds of situations. He believes correspondence behavior is related to the formation and continuity of internal working models and has more of a long-term longitudinal effect, while compensation is related to substitute attachment figures and seeking a fit between attachment models and current relationships. These latter effects are more evident in cross-sectional studies (Kirkpatrick, 1992, 1997, 1998).

8.2.3 Critique

Religion has many possible connections with attachment-related issues, so this literature has rich potential utility in the psychology of religion, particularly as a way of operationalizing some important psychoanalytic insights. However, effect sizes in attachment studies tend to be small, and even advocates of the model recognize that life cannot be reduced to attachment (Kirkpatrick, 1992). The way the theory has been conceptualized to date also has certain limitations. It compares child attachment with adult behavior but does not say much about how attachment affects religious life during childhood. Attachment styles are described as static, while in fact representations change and become more complex over time (Levy & Blatt, 1999), and positive adult attachment experiences can potentially alter one's attachment style. The theory also ignores the possibility that attachment and separation have a dialectical relationship, that these develop in interaction with each other and are both needed for the development of a stable, differentiated identity and strong relatedness to others. Concepts from other psychodynamic theories like that of Erikson might help broaden the attachment model to take into account some of the very complex features of the process (Blatt & Blass, 1990).

Attachment has been an attractive concept for Christian writers engaged in integration work, but it has also met with criticism. Miner (2007) argues that attachment models can become overly reductionistic, ignoring important relational factors like beliefs and experience, as well as neglecting the importance of religious community for relationships and our spiritual life. Especially important from an integration standpoint is that attachment models often lack any kind of developed theological understanding of the concept.

8.3 God Image and Representation

A prominent idea in both psychological and theological literature is that each person contains within them an image of God. In Christian thought, the idea of a God image stretches back to the Judaic scriptures that proclaim humans were created in the image of God. Eastern Christian thinkers commonly distinguish between this *image of God*, or what we are created to be, and the *likeness of God,* the extent to which we display or reflect that potential (e.g., Lossky, 1974, 1998). The image of God thus relates to some essential aspect of our nature as persons.

In psychological studies of religion, the concept of **God image** has a more limited meaning, referring to a representation or internal working model that we have of God, which is powerful but not easily explainable in functionalist terms (McDargh, 1983, p. 5). The idea of a psychological God image was first developed in psychodynamic thought and is related to ideas about object relations. Freud thought that our internal representations of God and supernatural beings like devils were related to male or father figures, as well as our own self-representations, ignoring the mother or the effects of interactions between the parents (Goodwin, 1998; Rizzuto, 1976). Erikson extended this idea and distinguished three kinds of God images—a loving and accepting image related to our material experience, a guiding conscience related to the father, and a preparental image "where God is pure nothing" (1958, pp. 263–264). Jung thought that God images were archetypal, and thus the specific personal characteristics of the image were less important than its universal quality. Current discussions about the God image are mostly based in object relations theory and Winnicott's idea of transitional objects (see Section 5.4.3). Schaefer and Gorsuch (1991) argue that religious beliefs, as manifested in the God concept of the individual, are one of the three foundations of religiousness along with motivation and coping or problem-solving style (see Sections 1.4.6, 9.3.1 and 10.2).

8.3.1 Early Psychoanalytic Work

The first major work on psychological aspects of the God image was done by Rizzuto (1974, 1979). Her work was largely rejected by the psychoanalytic establishment and has been criticized for its reliance on a case study approach using a clinical sample of people who were not well integrated (St. Clair, 1994, p. 28). However, it has been very influential among many clinicians and researchers (McDargh, 1997). She reached a number of conclusions, which have largely been supported by later work:

1. All people raised in Western culture have some sort of God image or internal working model of God, in addition to a *God concept* or intellectual definition, although they do not necessarily recognize its presence (Meier & Meier, 2004). This image is separate from other internalized images in the psyche such as the self-image, although it can impact other images and be affected by them. Like other images, it can be complex and can be a transformational object with integrating or fragmenting effects throughout the lifespan (McDargh, 1992).

2. Elements used to form God images are found in early object representations and interactions. Unlike Freud, she believed that these images include both maternal and paternal material. In her sample, those who were aware of a benevolent God tended to have God images primarily drawn from the relationship with the mother, while those who were questioning and had more fearful feelings about God as controlling or angry had their image drawn from their paternal relationship. She found that God images are also affected by God representations found in official religions, as well as by our own personal experiences (Rizzuto, 1991).

3. It is possible to develop a typology of God images and different attitudes toward the image. In her patients she found four groups of people: those (a) aware of God, (b) questioning God, (c) not interested and surprised that others are, and (d) aware of a demanding God that they would like to eliminate (Rizzuto, 1974). Similar groups of people were found in a study of adolescents by Banschick (1992), although he also identified a fifth type of image where God is seen as an impersonal force.

8.3.2 Gender of God Images

In monotheistic religions, God representations have tended to be built around a male, parental figure. This raises the question of whether psychological God images also have gendered characteristics. The answer to the question appears complex, for gender qualities in these images are based on individual experience with our parents, social and cultural views of what mothers and fathers are like, and religious teachings about possible gender-specific characteristics of God (Vergote, 1981a). Cross-cultural studies have found that maternal and paternal images are typically described in terms of (1) availability and (2) authoritarian or legalistic qualities, with the former more primary in maternal descriptions and the latter in paternal ones. These same factors appear as important aspects of God image descriptions found in both Christian and non-Christian religious groups (Tamayo, 1981; Meier & Meier, 2004; Kunkel, Cook, Meshel, Daughtry, & Hauenstein, 1999; Desjardins & Tamayo, 1981). Using European samples, Vercruysse and de Neuter (1981) found that the maternal image was more dominant but that other qualities including paternal ones were also included. In the US, studies suggest that this changes with age, with image descriptions more like the father in early childhood and more like both parents or the mother in middle childhood. The trend toward maternal or bi-gendered image characteristics has also been found in other studies of older children and adolescents (e.g., Meier & Meier, 2004; Dickie et al., 1997; Ladd, McIntosh, & Spilka, 1998) suggesting that this period of life is an active time for redefining our God image. These differences can have important effects; for example one study found that boys tend to see God as closer in problem situations if the Divine is seen as male, while girls see a non-male or female God as closer (Eshleman, Dickie, Merasco, Shepard, & Johnson, 1999). Vergote (1997, p. 68) argues that in secular Western societies, adults can only remain believers, if they transform their child-hood God representation using alternatives from available religious language and symbols.

Other factors also appear to affect the gender characteristics of the God image. Vergote (1981b) found that religious believers tend to have God images that emphasize availability, while doubters see law as a primary characteristic and thus are more likely to view God as a threat to their autonomy. Studies with European adolescents seem to confirm this picture, as teenagers with the lowest spiritual and religious attitudes have the highest scores for fear of God (Vergote, 1969, p. 193). Lambert and Kurpius (2004) found in a study with Catholic university students that feminine gender identity was related to having an image of God as female, regardless of whether the subject was male or female. They also found that femi-nine rather than masculine images of God were more related to nontraditional and less negative attitudes toward women. A number of writers, drawing on feminist psychoanalysts like Nancy Chodorow and theologians like Rebecca Chopp, have expanded on this. They argue that exclusively male patriarchal images can limit the image of God, while feminine, nurturing, and natural world images are a positive addition (Stone, 2004). Names connected to the God image can also have special significance because of their connection with gender (Fisher, 1988, pp. 53–73).

8.3.3   Development of the God Image

The trend in scholarly research has been to move away from the Piagetian view that children have limited and primitive understandings of God toward a view that chil-dren are imaginative and capable of surprising sophistication in their understanding. Barrett and Richert (2003) advance an alternative "preparedness" hypothesis that states (1) children are able to form concepts of intentional agents that are not limited to humans, (2) supernatural assumptions are the default position for children rather than an aberration applied to God, and (3) children as young as age 3 or 4 are perfectly capable of distinguishing between divine and human activity (cf. Harms, 1944).

In general, psychodynamic psychologists such as Meissner (1984, pp. 138–140, 150–157) see the God image or images as rooted in experiences and creative activ-ity from as early as the first year of life. These images are thus pre-linguistic and highly affective in nature. Early events such as experiences of trust and immer-sion develop emotional tones and interpersonal resources that can impact later mystical or religious experiences and images of God, giving them a numinous quality (McDargh, 1983; Balswick et al., 2005, pp. 128). In this view, the self begins and forms images in a dialectic between biologically undergirded motives and caregivers who are emotionally available. As early as age 3, these interactions build a prerepresentational affective core that supports self-regulation, empathy, and a moral self that has rules and emotional signals able to guide behavior. Children at this point can articulate stories with a moral component (Emde, Biringen, Clyman, & Oppenheim, 1991). After this early stage comes a differentiation of the self that involves a tension between autonomy and adoption of familial religious structures and values. The individual forms an image of God that has a numinous quality due to a fusing of cognitive and affective processes. Religion at these early stages often serves a defensive function of protecting against anxiety. As the child ages they become more aware of the shared and communal quality of beliefs as well as the distinction between fact and fancy, the problem of religious paradoxes, and the moral issues that come with the development of the superego and conscience. Gradually the child shifts from judgments based on authority to personal responsibility for sorting through these issues, hopefully with the help of institutional support. This can be seen in drawings that children make of God (see Figs. 8.1 and 8.2). When the individual reaches maturity, religion no longer needs to serve a defensive role, as the individual has hopefully found other ways to deal with anxiety. Instead, tensions are embraced, affirmed, and resolved, resulting in an inner harmony that combines meaningful object relations with a mystical, numinous quality of experience. Freud's accounts deal with early types of this religious experience, while adult religious experience is more typical of the later levels.

Shafranske (1992) has argued that the God image contains material not only about our parents, but it is a personal statement of our relationship with the source of otherness and all of existence, as well as the transformational power this has or could have in our lives. The God object is thus a *transformational* object as well as a *transitional* one. Its presence suggests to us that change is possible, and the views of God and change contained within the object help determine what kinds of changes we think are possible and desirable. Unlike other transitional objects, God is not abandoned after childhood and can play a continuing functional role in the

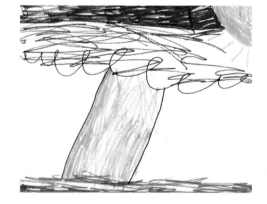

Fig. 8.1 *God in the Light.*
Drawing by T.X., girl, age 7.
Young children often have a
God image that combines a
sense of numinous awe with
childhood playfulness
Q: Where is God?
A: In the light.
Q: Where are you?
A: I'm off to the side having
   a snack

Fig. 8.2 *Meeting God.* Drawing by C.A., boy, age 11. As children move into adolescence, God images become more sophisticated and relational. Boys in particular tend to focus on the moral and guiding qualities of the relationship

developing adult (Banschick, 1992). The God image has the potential to grow and change throughout adulthood. From a theological perspective, this is not surprising, for any image falls short of the reality of the Divine and thus has the potential for change (Lonsdale, 2000, p. 60).

Empirical research suggests that religious socialization from both parents and church are influential in offering resources for constructing a God image (Meier & Meier, 2004; Nazar & Kouzekanani, 2003; Spilka, Armatas, & Nussbuam, 1964). As with attachment, data support both a correspondence and a compensation relationship between these influences and the God image. Correspondence is supported by evidence that when parents are perceived as nurturing (especially the father) and powerful (especially the mother), God is seen that way as well (Dickie et al., 1997). Also, God images that form in negative environments are often negative, or if they are positive they will be set aside and God will not be perceived as close (Roberts, 1989; Bellous, de Roos, & Summey, 2004; McDargh, 1983, pp. 128–132). On the other hand, a compensation view is suggested by the finding that both boys and girls see God as closer in problem situations, if the parents are less involved or the children are older (Eshleman et al., 1999).

Not surprisingly, traumatic events that affect one's views of relationships can affect one's relationship with God and our religious behavior. For instance, sexual assault victims often report **spiritual injury**, including a broad sense of alienation and malevolence in the world, personal feelings of impurity, difficulty trusting or believing in God, feelings of anger at God, perceptions of God as wrathful and distant or disapproving, and problems with lack of meaning and hopelessness. Studies suggest that sexual assault victims have lower levels of religious attendance but increased frequency of prayer, along with higher levels of depression and lower levels of mental health. The use of religion as a source of strength weakens the relationship between trauma and depression, although it does not protect against all kinds of mental health problems (Chang, Skinner, Zhou, & Kazis, 2003; Hall, 1995; Lawson, Drebing, Berg, Vincellette, & Penk, 1998; Pritt, 1998; Kane, Cheston, & Greer, 1993).

8.3.4 Dimensions of the God Image

Empirical research suggests that theistic God images are multidimensional and include several relatively independent characteristics. Following early work (e.g., Spilka et al., 1964), Gorsuch has identified a number of possible types of God image qualities that fall into three factor groupings, providing a typology of God images. First are characteristics describing an active, benevolent, guiding, and stable God with omniscient and omnipresent characteristics similar to the traditional Christian conception. Second are descriptors of a severe God who is wrathful and condemning; these are uncorrelated with the higher-order Christian God factor. Third is a set of characteristics describing a distant or uncaring God who is deistic-like, impersonal, inaccessible, irrelevant, and passive. This categorization is similar to that developed by Vergote (1969, pp. 291–292) who divides descriptors into objective, moral, and affective attributes such as greatness (objective), kindness (moral), and strength (affective). Most of the participants in college student samples had God images similar to the Christian one, and the presence of this kind of image was related to higher levels of religious participation and spiritual importance, as well as complex relationships with well-being and coping style (Gorsuch, 1968; Schaefer & Gorsuch, 1991, 1992; Wong-McDonald & Gorsuch, 2004). Scores on the benevolent and active God factor most strongly related to an intrinsic religious orientation, which in turn was related to higher levels of attendance and a sense that God is in control. Religious attendance appears to help maintain feelings of God-control (Krause, 2007). Other research looking at more relational rather than conceptual aspects of the God image have connected intrinsic motivation with better scores on measures of awareness and relational quality (Hall & Edwards, 1996, 2002). God concept descriptors were largely unrelated to quest motivation, suggesting that seeking can take place in the context of any of these God concepts.

While various types of God descriptors can be separated from each other conceptually and statistically, in practice they overlap each other. Potvin (1977) found that among US adolescents the most common was a loving and punishing God (45%) followed by loving and non-punishing (19%). A combination of punishing and non-loving was rare (2%). The specific pattern of God image descriptors was related to type of parental control and education, supporting the idea that socialization and projection of parental images are related to development of the God image. The interaction in types of descriptors appears to vary in different religious groups, with evangelical

Protestants higher on vindictive, stern, and powerful descriptors than mainline Protestants or Catholics, and mainline church members seeing God as more distant and less kind than the perceptions of evangelicals (Noffke & McFadden, 2001).

8.3.5 Impact of the God Image

A number of relationships have been found between the God image of the individual and important psychological variables. For instance, our image of God is related to religious salience and participation, as well as the kinds of attributions we are willing to make with regard to God—whether things are due to God's will, God's response to us, or just plain luck (Maynard, Gorsuch, & Bjorck, 2001; Mallery, Mallery, & Gorsuch, 2000). Images of God that are benevolent may assist in helping deal with life traumas like sexual abuse (Gall, Basque, Damasceno-Scott, & Vardy, 2007). Another major impact of the God image is on our object relations status. Todd Hall (Hall & Brokaw, 1995; Hall, Brokaw, Edwards, & Pike, 1998; Hill & Hall, 2002; Hall & Edwards, 1996; cf. Brokaw & Edwards, 1994) has argued that the search for the sacred, particularly in the Christian theistic context, is really a relational one, and the God image is not just a belief but has relational qualities and implications. In his view, spiritual maturity is relational in nature, a matter of mature dependence or interdependence, and these qualities can be related to relational aspects of the God image. This has been confirmed in studies with Christian church members, which have found strong correlations between spiritual well-being, religious involvement or spiritual maturity, positive object relations, perceived quality of relationship with God, and positive God image qualities like benevolence and eternality. Not surprisingly, these positive relational qualities are associated with greater effectiveness and stress tolerance in ministry situations (e.g., Barnett, Duvall, Edwards, & Hall, 2005; Lewis-Hall, Duvall, Edwards, & Pike, 1999). Other studies have found relationships between positive God images (e.g., benevolent) and good interpersonal relationships (Schottenbauer et al., 2004), higher self esteem (Benson & Spilka, 1973) and lower levels of anxiety (Schaefer & Gorsuch, 1991), while harsh and punitive views of God are more common in families with psychological dysfunction (Wilson, Larson, & Meier, 1983). Psychological treatment that addresses spiritual and religious issues has been found to positively alter the God image toward more good, loving, and supportive qualities (Tisdale et al., 1997).

8.3.6 Limitations

A criticism of God image theory and research is that it is insufficiently relational because it concentrates on our *representation* of the Divine and not the *relationship* we have with God (LaMothe, 1999). These scholars see the religious imagination as having a relational organization (McDargh, 1997) and thus a typology of God objects should take into account types of relational bonds that are possible, such as attachment (providing security and comfort), affiliation or community, alliance and commitment to well-being of others, collaboration, nurturance, and receiving help or guidance. In this view, our perception of God is related to the type and nature of these bonds (Hill & Hall, 2002), and it is these connections with a real God who relates and acts that puts God's love into terms that are believable, meaningful, and relevant to our experience (Meissner, 1987).

The concept of God image has also been criticized as being unnecessarily static. Shafranske (1992) has argued that it is the powerful process of transformation or the experience of that process which is represented in early objects, and that the trace of this initial transformational object can be found in other later object representations that have transformational power. God image theory has not yet been developed to help understand how it relates to transformation, other aspects of religious experience and belief, or other developmental and object relationship issues (cf. Schottenbauer et al., 2004; Kunkel et al., 1999). Research on the God image is also almost entirely dependent upon self-report measures, a limitation that this area shares with other research projects based on an object relations model (Piedmont, 2005).

8.4 Adolescent Description

Adolescence has been a topic of keen interest to psychologists and scholars in religious studies since the early 20th century (see e.g., Adams, 2000; Whittaker, 1932). Psychologists like G. Stanley Hall were convinced that adolescence was a key time for religious and spiritual development. Hall viewed adolescence as a new birth, a recapitulation of an ancient period of "storm and stress" (1905, p. xiii) associated with increased incidence of both psychological problems and religious change. He thought this was due in part to the onset of sexuality and other biological factors. Research over the years has continued to confirm that this period of life is an active one in terms of religious experience, and that this is true in both Western and non-Western cultural settings (Ahmed, 2004). For instance, in a study of high school students from the early 1960s, Elkind and Elkind (1962) found that religious experiences were frequent among adolescents, especially among honor students. These included experiences that strengthened and maintained faith, as well as testing experiences such as the death of loved ones or times of religious initiation ceremonies. While experiences occurred when alone or in prayer, they also frequently occurred within group settings, although they found ritual experiences to be less common among Protestants. Acute experiences seemed more related to chance factors, while recurring ones were related to subjective choices to seek out and engage in practices supportive of these experiences.

Contemporary scholars continue to find that the teenage years are very important for spiritual and religious development and the quest for meaning (e.g., King & Boyatzis, 2004; Bruce & Cockreham, 2004), although the perspective has changed somewhat from that of Hall. Many researchers now view adolescence as a social construction related more to social, economic and political factors than to biology

(Elkind, 1999). A number of recent studies conducted by sociologists of religion have expanded our understanding of the religious life of adolescents. These studies have used large national databases from the late 1990s (e.g., Smith & Faris, 2002a) and more recent data from the US National Study of Youth and Religion (NSYR), a longitudinal study which involved in-depth telephone interviews with a national representative sample of over 3000 teens and their parents, as well as follow-up face-to-face interviews with a subsample (Smith, 2005; Schwadel & Smith, 2005; Smith & Denton, 2003; Denton & Smith, 2001).

The NSYR found religion to be an active force in a large number of teens, although there is a wide range of adolescent religiosity and religious practices. About half say religion is "extremely important" or "very important," and although 2/3 do not believe it is necessary to be involved in a congregation in order to be "truly religious and spiritual," about 40% say they attend religious services or other activities once a week or more. Substantial numbers of these also engage in other religious practices like prayer, fasting, Bible study, etc. The most religious teens tend to build lifestyles with other religious friends and religious activities, although in general most religious teens have a mix of friends. About 16% identify themselves as "nonreligious," although they may have religious beliefs or occasionally participate in religious activities. Only about 3% identify themselves as atheists. Overall attitudes toward religion—even among those not involved—tend to be quite positive.

Religious participation tended to decline across the teenage years in the NYSR study, a pattern also observed in Europe where it is associated with declining positive attitudes toward Christianity and increasing negative attitudes toward religious practices (Kay & Francis, 1996; Goosen & Dunner, 2001). However, the effects of development on attendance and religious importance are different so that while *attendance* may decrease through adolescence, *salience* tends to remain constant (Kerestes, Youniss, & Metz, 2004). Other researchers have argued that adolescence is a time of religious polarization, when less religious adolescents drift toward increasingly less participation, and religiously active teens become more committed and involved (Ozorak, 1989). Some US research has supported this hypothesis (King, Elder, & Whitbeck, 1997), suggesting that religious development in adolescence may be for many a continuation of trends established in childhood.

In the NSYR study about 25–30% of teens said religion was unimportant; half of these could be described as alienated from religion, the other half as disengaged (Smith, Faris, & Denton, 2004). These rates are about the same as for the adult population and are about the same as the mid-1970s. Among those who were raised in a religious home, the most common reasons for lack of participation were lack of interest (about 50%) and intellectual skepticism (about 30%). Life disruptions (10%) and dislike of religion (7%) were smaller factors. Teens that were not religiously involved tended to live in what Smith called a "morally insignificant universe" characterized by a lack of inherent meaning or moral significance to human action, whereas highly religious teens saw themselves in a universe with ultimate moral significance, meaning, and purpose.

Parental religiousness, religious affiliation, and practice were the most important influence on teen religiousness and religious participation, particularly in families with religious parents (Smith, 2005, p. 57). Other sociological variables connected with religiousness and/or religious participation included quality of family life (intact family, positive caring relationship with parents) and peer relationships. Interestingly, low attendance was more common in families with less education. Regnerus (Regnerus, Smith, & Smith, 2004) found a strong relation between parental religious attendance and adolescent attendance and ratings of importance but also some influence by the attendance patterns of friends. They interpreted this as providing support for modeling and channeling hypotheses.

Although teens typically report religion as important, Smith argues that its visible salience appears low for the average teenager. In the NYSR study, teens often had a hard time articulating ways that religion made a concrete difference in their lives. It operates in the background; it is not something that they think about all the time or operate from on a conscious intentional basis. Smith argues that this is a consequence of intense competition for time and attention from other aspects of life such as school, sports, and the media, none of which provides opportunities for working out or integrating religion and spirituality. He characterizes the dominant religious view among US teens as that of "Moralistic Therapeutic Deism," which includes the following beliefs:

- A God exists who created and orders the world and watches over human life.
- God wants people to be good, nice, and fair to each other, as taught in the Bible and by most world religions.
- The central goal of life is to be happy and to feel good about oneself.
- God does not need to be particularly involved in one's life except when God is needed to resolve a problem.
- Good people go to heaven when they die (Smith, 2005, pp. 162–163).

Smith sees this as directly related to the American cultural worldview of "therapeutic individualism" that views the self as the source of authentic knowledge and institutions as barriers that constrain individual self-fulfillment, the ultimate purpose of life (Smith, 2005, p. 173). In this environment, religion becomes part of a consumer mentality. It is seen not as an end in itself but as a means to achieve personal goals such as happiness and personal development, or to overcome problems and gain perspective on life (see Section 10.3.1).

Although there is a lot of publicity in the US and Europe about teen (and adult) participation in alternate spiritualities like paganism, the actual number of US teens who identify themselves in this way is very low—less than 1%. The percentage of teens that identify themselves with a non-Christian religious tradition (Islam, Hinduism, Buddhism, Judaism) is around 2–3%, the majority of which identify with one of the main branches of American Judaism. The numbers of teenagers affiliating with a non-Christian religious tradition seems to be increasing, as is the number of nonaffiliated, suggesting a trend toward religious pluralism and perhaps polarization in US society (Smith, Denton, Faris, & Regnerus, 2002). Overall about 52% identify with a Protestant Christian tradition and 23% with Roman Catholicism.

However, this does not mean that they subscribe to all the beliefs of their particular group. For instance, 10% or more of teens in various Christian groups indicate that they do not believe in life after death, and 60% of teens (including 50% of conservative Protestants) agree with the statement "many religions may be true." There also appears to be a general lack of knowledge about the actual beliefs of their church group. Most tend to hold a highly individualistic stance toward truth and moral judgment—you should believe whatever you think is true.

8.5 Identity Development, Gender, and Religion

How do religious and spiritual changes in adolescence relate to other aspects of psychological development during this period? A key way appears to be through the process of identity development.

8.5.1 Old and New Conceptions of Identity Development

Traditional views of identity formation are based on the work of Erik Erikson. In his view, **identity** was a necessary human quality that involved continuity over time and a sense of historical sameness (see Section 5.3.1). He believed that each person needed to make a strong commitment to a particular identity, ideology, and group at the end of adolescence, but that this should be preceded by a period of exploration or struggle, and that the well-developed identity should be flexible and open to change. This view of identity development parallels many Biblical stories where identity development was often connected with personal struggle (Marcia, 1980; Parker, 1985). Marcia (1966; cf. Griffith & Griggs, 2001) developed a typology of identity status that placed people according to their level of identity exploration and commitment. His four categories were *achievement* (strong commitment with exploration), *foreclosure* (strong commitment without exploration), *moratorium* (no commitment but exploration), and *diffusion* (no exploration or commitment). In this view, identity is about choices made by an individual rather than social or cultural factors (Taylor, 2007, p. 482).

Recent work on identity has expanded and sometimes altered this traditional picture of identity formation. For instance, psychological views of identity have typically conceptualized it as an individual creation and accomplishment. As a consequence, people who do not go through a personal identity "crisis" during adolescence (e.g., foreclosed) are seen as inferior in accomplishment compared to those who search and struggle individually. Bosma and Kunner (2001) have questioned whether this picture is accurate. They found diffused or foreclosed identities in 50% of their adolescent sample, a high percentage for what is considered by some to be a pathological outcome. It would appear that the Marcia model is not very sensitive to or descriptive of developmental changes, and that there are many pathways to identity rather than just a fixed progression of stages. A kind of fluctuating status is the most common, with periods of equilibrium and disequilibrium triggered by conflict or change and a clear progression toward "higher" levels in only 25% of cases. Identity formation is thus a long process affected by contextual and individual factors, and optimal development appears to involve a balance of differentiation and integration rather than achieving some ideal end state. In other words, identity is something that is continually achieved, not gained and then never altered (Cady, 1997).

Contemporary work also develops the idea that identity does not exist in a vacuum but is relational in nature and can be defined in terms of one's connection to family, religion, community, and culture. In this model, identity development involves deepening relationships with others, as well as changes in commitments and in the process of forming them. Commitments that were once externally motivated became internally driven, and the individual seeks to carry through on these in their everyday life (Newman & Newman, 1988). Family is central to this, but peer and other relationships become increasingly important during adolescence. Overall, identity may be more a product of intimacy than foundational for it, which is the reverse of the picture drawn in Erikson's theory (cf. Balswick et al., 2005, p. 180; Kneezel & Emmons, 2006; Schwartz, Bukowski, & Aoki, 2006). This relational effect can be seen in our **personal identity** or sense of unique personhood and in our **collective identity** that involves our self-concept as a member of various social or cultural groups (Templeton & Eccles, 2006). The traditional view—that identity formation must involve struggle and individualistic rejection of the expectations of family and community—is viewed by relational theorists as a feature of Western culture rather than as a human imperative. In this way of looking at things, destruction of community through geographical mobility, separation of religion from other aspects of life, and family disintegration are all barriers to identity formation (Koteskey, Walker, & Johnson, 1990). A way of dealing with this problem is to construct multiple identities based on the practices and worldview of all the communities a person may be a part of at different times (Jensen, 2003). However, this kind of pastiche identity (Gergen, 1991; cf. Lifton, 1999) sits uncomfortably with traditional psychological views that emphasize the importance of forming a core, consistent self.

If identity development is thought of as occurring in the context of relationships and community, then it becomes apparent that race and **ethnicity**—belonging to a group with common descent or national origin—can have a large impact on identity. Ethnic and religious identities can be intertwined, especially in cases where people of a common ethnicity or racial background all tend to practice a certain religion. In the US, this has traditionally been the case with African Americans, who have high rates of church membership, attendance, and participation in devotional practices. In this situation, a particular conception of spirituality may be part of one's ethnic identity development. However, the effect of race and ethnicity is complex, and racial labels ignore the diversity that exists within groups due to cultural and personality factors (Chae, Kelly, Brown, & Bolden, 2004; Mattis, Ahluwalia, Cowie, & Kirkland-Harris, 2006; Taylor, Ellison, Chatters, Levin, & Lincoln, 2000).

8.5.2 Religion and Identity Development

Religion and identity development appear to have a bidirectional relationship, each affecting the other in complex ways. Traditionally, research has focused on how factors related to identity development affect our religious life. When the traditional model of identity formation is applied to religious development, the assumptions are that (1) religious crises are a normal part of adolescence, (2) rebellion against the church is inevitable because questioning is a normal part of adolescence, and (3) transition to higher levels of faith development is facilitated by dissonance in a supportive milieu (Hill, 1986; Meilman, 1979). So for instance Mischey (1981) in a study of college-age Canadian teens, found that low scorers on Fowler's faith development scale had identities marked by confusion or conformity and uncritical trust, while those at higher levels were more critical, challenging, and actively searching and had an identity status of achievement or moratorium. In the traditional view, this is a way in which the adolescent constructs a faith that is not a blind acceptance of institutional religion but more intensely personal (Elkind, 1999).

The other side of the religion-identity relationship is the effect that our religious life may have on our identity formation. Involvement in a religious community teaches a vocabulary and scheme for interpreting behavior, and this system can have an integrative function that assists in identity development, particularly among those for whom a search for security is important (Dykstra, 1986; Meissner, 2001; Vianello, 1991). Tightly knit communities with strong religious beliefs such as in fundamentalism might have an especially prominent role in identity formation (Elkind, 1999). Research with adolescent and college student samples does indicate that religion has a number of connections with positive identity development. Church attendance, religious commitment, and participation in practices like prayer are all related to lower levels of ideological, interpersonal, and identity moratorium or interpersonal diffusion (Donelson, 1999; Youniss, McLellan, & Yates, 1999; McKinney & McKinney, 1999). Development of a strong religious identity is also associated with lower levels of depression and higher levels of personal meaning, as well as prosocial activities and community service (Koteskey, Little, & Matthews, 1991; Furrow, King, & White, 2004). Religious ceremonies such as baptism or confirmation may play an important role as markers of the identity development process (Mattis et al., 2006).

Some research has considered how religious motivation may affect identity status. In a study using Christian undergraduate students, Fulton (1997) found that Marcia's achieved identity status—strong commitment with exploration—was associated with high intrinsic and low extrinsic-social motivation, while identity foreclosure or commitment without exploration was related to low intrinsic and high extrinsic motivation. The nonachieved identity statuses varied on their quest scores: moratorium had the highest quest values, foreclosed the lowest, and diffused fell in between. All three of the nonachieved statuses were associated with low values of intrinsic motivation. Results were consistent with the idea that achievement is a temporary condition that alternates with periods of seeking and reevaluating. Other studies have confirmed this pattern with achieved and foreclosed identity status and have found attendance related to commitment identity, either foreclosed or achieved (Markstrom-Adams & Smith, 1996; Markstrom-Adams, Hofstra, & Dougher, 1994).

Meissner (1987) has argued that there is an inherent connection between spiritual development or the deepening of spiritual identity and the internalization of religious values systems in personality and life experience. For him, the ultimate expression and development of spiritual identity is disinterested love. The idea that identity and identity development are intimately related to practices and actions toward others has been confirmed by a study of community service by James Youniss and his colleagues (Youniss et al., 1999). They found that religious adolescents were more likely to engage in service activities, and that those who engaged in church-sponsored service were more likely to adopt religious rationales for the meaning of what they were doing, strengthening their religious identity. Their analysis of data from the Monitoring the Future project of data from the 1970s through the 1990s showed that almost 3/4 of those who rated religion highly were doing regular service vs. about 1/4 of nonreligious peers (cf. Section 12.4.3).

8.5.3 Prosocial Effects of Religion in Adolescence

The link between religious identity and service is part of a broader literature that has found adolescent religiosity related to a number of positive effects on health and prosocial behavior. Parents often give religious training to children and adolescents hoping that it will affect their ethical upbringing, providing a religious orientation and habits or regulatory skills that will lead away from deviant behavior (Vergote, 1997, p. 91; Litchfeild, Thomas, & Dao Li, 1997). A number of studies with adolescents have found that high or increasing religiousness does indeed have a variety of positive effects. It appears to act by (1) promoting positive behaviors and (2) acting as a protective factor against risk behaviors and delinquency. Those with low or declining religiosity have higher levels of problems such as alcohol and drug use. This is true even when controlling for a number of possible confounding variables (Benson et al., 2003; Kerestes et al., 2004; Smith & Faris, 2002a, 2002b; Duncan, Duncan, Strycker, & Chaumeton, 2002; Donahue & Benson, 1995).

Positive behaviors identified in the literature as related to adolescent religious participation include (1) better diet and exercise, which in turn are related to enhanced physical heath; (2) more seat belt wearing and responsible alcohol use leading to lower mortality rates in accidents (Jessor, Turbin, & Costa, 1998; Wallace & Forman, 1998); and (3) greater altruism and service orientation, which appears to persist into adulthood (Hodgkinson, Weitzman, & Kirsch, 1990; Smith & Faris, 2002a; Youniss et al., 1999; Wilson & Musick, 1997). Better school performance is also reported, especially for the students with the strongest and weakest academic records (Regnerus, 2000; Regnerus, Smith, & Fritsch, 2003).

In the mental health literature, studies about protective effects have focused on suicide, substance abuse, and sexuality, with significantly fewer problems reported by religiously active teens, especially in groups with traditionally high levels of religious involvement like African Americans (Donahue & Benson, 1995; Weaver et al., 2000; Heath et al., 1999; Wills, Gibbons, Gerrard, Murry, & Brody, 2003; Ball, Amistead, & Austin, 2003). In Britain, positive attitudes toward Christianity are associated with stricter attitudes toward alcohol use (Francis, Fearn, & Lewis, 2005). Lower rates of depression and higher levels of well-being and life satisfaction are also associated with higher levels of religiousness, perhaps because of the enhanced sense of purpose and hope for the future that can be provided by religion (Wright, Frost, & Wisecarver, 1993; Hunsberger, Pratt, & Pancer, 2001; Leffert et al., 1998; Markstrom, 1999; Smith & Faris, 2002b). Lower levels of danger-seeking and risk-taking behavior, including less premature sexual involvement and lower frequency of sexual activity with fewer partners have also been found (Smith & Faris, 2002a; Wallace & Forman, 1998). Some protective effects are substantial but appear to be less in families where there are considerable differences in religious affiliation or involvement between the parents (Petts & Knoester, 2007). Chandy, Blum, and Resnick (1996) found that self-reported religiosity or spirituality was the strongest protective factor out of 55 variables against the negative effects of sexual abuse or parental alcohol misuse.

Studies with adolescents or college-age adults find that religiousness has a moderate deterrent effect on crime, especially minor or nonviolent crime like underage alcohol use. The effect is stronger in more religious samples—those from conservative Protestant families, and for women and individuals of color. On the other hand, higher delinquency rates are associated with religious disagreements with parents (Gorsuch, 1995; Bayer & Wright, 2001; Johnson, Jang, Larson, & Li, 2001; Smith & Faris, 2002a; Regnerus, 2003). In at least some cases, this deterrent effect may be due to reduced alcohol and drug use, especially by those who engage in personal religious practices like prayer and Bible study (Benda & Corwyn, 1997; Corwyn & Benda, 2000; Gorsuch, 1995).

The positive and protective effects of religious involvement persist even after ruling out possible confounding variables and self-selection factors. Some of the positive effects of religion might be indirect, as when religion causes people not to associate with drug users, thereby lowering the risk of drug use. This kind of indirect effect seems especially important in protecting against early or risky sexual behavior. Other effects are more direct such as through dense community networks of social support, moral direction that promotes self-control and virtue, and spiritual experiences that help solidify moral commitments and constructive life practices, as well as positive role models (Regnerus, Smith et al., 2003; Smith, 2003a, 2003b; Wallace & Forman, 1998).

Much of the research on positive and protective effects has been done without any kind of guiding theoretical model, other than vague ideas that religious identity development may be a contributing factor. A stronger theoretical view is the *developmental asset model*, which has been influential in recent work on adolescence and religion. This model is based on an ecological view of development as an increasingly complex reciprocal interaction between the person and the environment (e.g., Bronfenbrenner & Evans, 2000; Bronfenbrenner, 1995). In this interaction, an individual actively works to acquire external and internal developmental assets from contact with cohesive communities and adults that provide a repeated, consistent message promoting values and standards. These assets are thought to be more effective than prevention programs in preventing problematic behaviors, as they are more likely to produce sustained change (Leffert et al., 1998). External assets include social support from extended family, mentors, and the community. These assets lead to positive behaviors and values, as well as empowerment through meaningful roles, opportunities for constructive use of time, and clear boundaries or expectations. Internal assets include social competencies and self-perceptions, commitment to learning, positive values, and positive identity or view of self. Research has found a strong negative relationship between these assets and at-risk or antisocial behavior, especially among males. The assets also appear to have an additive or cumulative effect, boosting resiliency and coping ability (Benson, Leffert, Scales, & Blyth, 1998; Wagener, Furrow, King, Leffert, & Benson, 2003; King & Furrow, 2004; Benson, Masters, & Larson, 1997). In this model, religion has the possibility for producing positive effects in multiple ways by providing access to a number of external assets and supporting the development of internal ones.

Development of religion and spirituality in childhood and adolescence can be part of a general orientation in the family toward generativity, the passing on of gifts to others. Dollahite (e.g., Boyatzis et al., 2006) argues that a generative spirituality develops when the family shares (1) a common spiritual paradigm or set of beliefs about the transcendent, (2) a set of common spiritual practices, and (3) a spiritual community of care. This generativity becomes an important part of what gives life meaning. However, in contemporary society many traditional religious beliefs and practices are seen by some as outdated or irrelevant, leading to a sense of meaninglessness, which may in turn be connected to at-risk behaviors, violence, and suicide in adolescents (Verma & Maria, 2006; see Section 5.3.2).

8.5.4 Gender, Identity, and Religion

One of the most consistent findings in social scientific studies of religion is that women appear to be more religious than men on a variety of measures. In general, researchers have rejected the idea that there are inherent sex differences between men and women with regard to religiousness. Rather, explanations have focused on the issue of **gender**, "the socially constructed roles of men and women implicating different social norms and cultural expectations for both sexes" (Möller-Leimkühler, 2003, p. 2; cf. Fulkerson, 1997). In Western cultures, female gender identity tends to have a relational emphasis, while for men it is more defined in terms of achievement and competition.

Despite the observed differences between men and women, there has been surprisingly little specific research on the subject of gender and religion, although the topic is of increasing interest (Miller & Stark, 2002; Anderson & Lewis-Hall, 2005). Early figures in the field like Freud, James, or Jung neglected gender, and issues dealing with gender and sexuality are hard to investigate due to concerns that research might promote bias or discrimination (Jonte-Pace, 1997; Sherkat, 2002). The effect of gender is often thought to interact with culture and ethnicity, either when culture with its gender roles affects religious practices, or when religious identities support the formation of more traditional gender roles, as in American Muslim female adolescents. These interactions further complicate attempts to study gender as a variable (Elkind, 1999; Markstrom, 1999; Abu-Ali & Reisen, 1999). The lack of attention to gender in psychology is in contrast to contemporary theology, which has seen more intensive conversations about the relationship between our gendered and embodied nature and the religious life (e.g., Anderson, 2007).

Perhaps because of the neglect of the topic in research, few studies have been done that have identified specific gender effects beyond general differences in religiousness. Specific effects that have been found include a stronger relational orientation for women than for men, with stronger correlations between religiousness and social activities, while there are indications that religion for men may be more practical and rule oriented (Dillon & Wink, 2007, pp. 31–32, 196; Tamminen, 1994b). In adolescents, occasions for religious experience appear somewhat different for boys and girls. Girls report strengthening religious experiences more often when alone, anxious, or fearful, while boys have them more often in prayer or when involved in ethical situations (Elkind & Elkind, 1962). In men, gender role conflict—not living up to gender role expectations—has been linked to lower levels of spiritual well-being (Mahalik & Lagan, 2001).

Interestingly, while research in Western societies has consistently found higher levels of religiousness in women and older adults, no gender or age differences appear in agrarian societies, suggesting that the effects are related to socioeconomic or cultural differences (Norris & Inglehart, 2004, pp. 70–78). Two specific theories have been proposed to explain this effect. First, *social structure theory* argues that social forces like patriarchal domination force women to assume roles such as religious ones, perhaps as a way of coping with a repressive situation. Second, *socialization and personality theory* argues that women are socialized to participate in religion and develop personality structures that find it attractive (Thompson, 1991). Taylor (2007, p. 494) believes that the emphasis on family and childrearing in Western churches are a primary factor in this differential attractiveness. Presumably these factors are present in Western societies but not in agrarian ones, explaining the difference in gender effects. However, it is of interest that monastic movements have often included more women than men; this appears to have been true of ancient Christian communities at the time of the Desert Fathers, as well as more recent examples such as 20th-century Russian monasticism (Bolshakoff, 1976, pp. 222–223).

Social structure and socialization theories are influenced by feminism, which has had a minimal impact in psychology but a significant role in molding the study of religion in the social sciences, humanities, and theology. Woodhead (2001) has identified three phases of this influence. First wave feminism includes the late 19th and early 20th centuries that emphasized equality between men and women and discouraged theories or research that would find substantive differences. Second wave feminism from the 1960s through the 1980s critiqued the system of male patriarchy as tied to traditional religion and sought liberation for women. This critique has had a strong impact in the humanities, theology, and religious studies. Third wave feminism, which began in the 1990s, has focused on understanding gender as a complex construct that is only loosely connected to our bodily makeup. These researchers see the feminine and masculine as gender roles or identities and argue that it is feminine attitudes and values which incline people toward religion, not their biological sex. This viewpoint is sometimes known as **gender identity theory**.

Gender identity theory has been supported by empirical work, indicating that gender differences in religiosity disappear when sex role or gender orientation is introduced as an explanatory variable (Thompson, 1991). In UK research, personality characteristics that are negatively related to religiousness like psychoticism appear to be associated with masculinity and negatively related to femininity (Francis, Lewis, Brown, Philipchalk, & Lester, 1995; Francis & Wilcox, 1998; Maltby, 1999). Using data from the US General Social Survey and the World Values Survey, Miller and Stark (2002) found that religiousness was not related to socialization or empowerment but to feminine personality and gender role characteristics. They did find a relation between religion and aversion to risk which was more common in women, suggesting that in some situations women are more religious than men because to be less religious is risk taking (e.g., Miller & Hoffman, 1995). Thompson and Remmes (2002) have expanded the model by drawing the helpful distinction between masculine gender orientation and gender ideology or endorsement of traditional masculine ideas of toughness and seeking status. In a study of older adults, they found that intrinsic motivation as well as higher levels of attendance and private religious activity were related to feminine gender orientation, while extrinsic motivation was related to the acceptance of masculine toughness ideology. Quest motivation was more related to masculine gender orientation.

Third wave feminism has affected the dialogue between psychology and religion in several other ways. It has been associated with the turn toward relationality in theology and the psychology of religion field, and an understanding of how social changes for women related to work and family have affected women differently than men. These changes may have impacted their ability to participate in religious communities and activities and thus affected the institutions as a whole (Ammerman & Roof, 1995; Marler, 1995; Hertel, 1995). Jonte-Pace (1997, 2006) argues that feminist influence in the psychology of religion has led to three projects: a critical project, looking at how and why women have been excluded; an inclusive project, bringing in women's experiences and issues; and an analytic project, studying how gender affects experience and vice versa. Consideration of personal and social factors that have excluded women and broadening a view of experience to be more inclusive of their perspective has affected therapy and how it might be applied to religious issues (McKay, Hill, Freedman, & Enright, 2007). Feminism has also profoundly affected the companion fields of theology and religious studies, producing such important movements as feminist theology (Briggs, 1997).

Finally, feminism has affected religious practices. Some new religious movements have grown from feminist attempts to define a spirituality of women outside of traditional religion as an alternative to systems that are perceived to be patriarchal and repressive. These alternatives often draw on New Age beliefs or practices (see Section 12.4.3) and have encouraged revivals in neopaganism, Goddess worship, and even witchcraft. This retreat into past spiritualities is sometimes related to the belief that earlier societies were matriarchal and worshipped female rather than male gods (Eller, 1991).

Consideration of gender and its influence on religion is critical, but much remains to be done. One danger is to assume that "female" or "feminine" are somehow unitary categories, when modern feminist thought would argue that there is no single experience of women (Davaney, 1997a, 1997b; Jones, 1997).

8.6 Conclusion

Key Issue: *One of the three great contributions by psychologists in the dialogue with religion has been an understanding of the importance of childhood and adolescence for adult faith.*

While religious traditions have tended to treat childhood as a precursor to adulthood and genuine spiritual accomplishment, it is obvious that for most people the foundations for adult faith are laid in childhood. However it is true that, contrary to Piaget's view, childhood is not the end of the story, as we will see in our next chapter. It is also the case that both psychologists and religious writers have yet to really explore and appreciate childhood faith on its own terms. The vital connections between childhood religion and other important aspects of development suggest that a better understanding of childhood spirituality may teach us much about a number of important aspects of development.

Chapter 9
Religion, Spirituality, and Development in Adulthood

Most religious traditions contain a rich body of wisdom about how to move beyond childhood faith to a mature religious and spiritual life (Casey, 1996, p. 59; see Section 7.2). In contrast, psychological research has tended to focus more on childhood or adolescence, and the psychological studies of adult development that do exist mostly neglect spiritual and religious issues. However, an interesting body of work does exist that casts light on a number of features of spiritual development during adulthood.

9.1 Issues in Adult Development Research

Psychological studies on adult development are difficult to conduct as most possible research methodologies have drawbacks. The most common approach is the **cross-sectional study**, which compares groups of different ages on selected variables and then concludes that differences between groups are due to development. However, these studies have the problem that the comparison groups of different ages or **cohorts** are born at different times and thus grew up under diverse circumstances. This means that the different age groups may not be comparable with each other, a difficulty known as the **cohort effect**. This problem is especially important in religion research as different cohort groups such as US baby boomers appear to have aspects to their spirituality that are unique (Schaie & Hofer, 2001; Rudinger & Rietz, 2001; Roof, 1993). An alternative approach is the **longitudinal study**, which follows one group of people over a period of years to look for changes. However these studies are difficult to conduct and take years to produce meaningful data, so studies that combine cross-sectional and longitudinal features are often best. Developmental research on religion and spirituality in adulthood has been criticized as suffering from other problems as well, such as the following:

- Lack of a theoretical framework
- A focus on the functional aspects of religion while ignoring other important aspects such as religious experience and consciousness
- Neglect of important variables such as gender or spirituality
- Superficial assessment of constructs, e.g., equating religious participation with frequency of attendance

J.M. Nelson, *Psychology, Religion, and Spirituality,*
DOI 10.1007/978-0-387-87573-6_9, © Springer Science+Business Media, LLC 2009

• Neglect of qualitative approaches to research that if done well may be better suited to the study of spiritual and religious development (Blieszner & Ramsey, 2002).

Research on religious and spiritual development in adulthood has also confronted three major theoretical questions in addition to these methodological problems. First, are adult spirituality and religiousness similar to those of childhood? Research suggests that there are substantial differences, which means that we must be cautious in applying childhood developmental models to the adult situation. For instance, while our understanding of child religiousness is probably enhanced by considering it in relation to the level of cognitive development, assuming that the same is true of adult religiousness introduces the potential for unexamined bias based on the values and preconceptions of the experimenter (Seifert, 2002). Furthermore, people's conceptions of these things and their religious motivations may change during adulthood. For example, some studies suggest that quest motivation is more typical of earlier stages of adulthood while intrinsic religious motivation increases later in age (Watson, Howard, Hood, & Morris, 1988).

The second major theoretical issue confronting researchers is the question, what is the goal of development? Contemporary psychologists often describe it as "successful aging" which includes (1) a low probability of disease and related disability, with a life style that minimizes risk factors for problems, (2) a high physical and cognitive functional capacity, and (3) an active engagement with life, including good interpersonal relationships, productive activity that is socially valued, and resilience or rapid recovery from stress and other life changes (Rowe & Kahn, 1997). This defines the goal of human life in terms of health, productivity, and social adaptation. Other psychological definitions go beyond health and adaptation to consider human potential. For instance, Paul Baltes (e.g., Baltes & Staudinger, 2000) defines development as increasing *wisdom*, which involves our ability to coordinate personal resources such as tolerance or creativity so that we can pursue well-being and the meaningful good life for self and others.

Traditional definitions of psychological maturity are largely silent on the issue of religion or spirituality, but recent work in psychology has tried to rectify this problem. For instance, Koenig and his colleagues (e.g., Crowther et al., 2002) talk about the concept of **spiritual maturity**, which involves the development of a relationship with the transcendent or sacred that reflects positively on the welfare of others and ourselves. These conceptions of spiritual maturity generally have two characteristics: (1) They include at least weak forms of transcendence as a necessary part of life (e.g., Young-Eisendrath & Miller, 2000), and (2) they are holistic, arguing that spiritual maturity encompasses a wise variety of factors including relational, emotional, ethical, and cognitive strengths (e.g., Ray & McFadden, 2001). This raises the issue of whether spiritual development may be thought of as a separate life task or whether it is simply integral to many aspects of development (Gold & Mansager, 2000). Empirical evidence certainly supports the inclusion of practice, relational, and religious experiences (e.g., a sense of God's presence) as independent important factors, in addition to cognitive ones in the developmental process (Bassett et al., 1991; Kass & Lennox, 2004).

Relationality is especially prominent in new conceptions of spiritual maturity, such as the one developed in the collaborative work of theologian Ron Shults and psychologist Steven Sandage (Shults & Sandage, 2006; Sandage & Shults, 2007). In their view, spirituality is ultimately relational in nature and involves developing connections to God, others, and ourselves. These relationships develop within a social context and are dependent upon relational schemas developed in life. They are essential for personal knowing and the formation of the self and can promote (or inhibit) transformation. In this view, the goal of development or maturity is not just about happiness or well-being, it must involve a search for wholeness as well as the development of a fruitful, secure love and intimacy with God and others. This mature spirituality requires a balance between **seeking**, which involves openness to change and reflective wisdom, and **dwelling**, which is more about attachment (see Section 1.3.2). Transformation toward maturity is fostered by (1) relationships and communities that support both seeking and dwelling, and (2) stress or difficulties that can form a crucible within which transformation can take place.

A third major theoretical issue revolves around the question, are stage theories an effective approach to describing adult development? While stage theories of development have dominated both the child and the adult literature, a number of scholars (e.g., Worthington, 1989; Studzinski, 1985; Vergote, 1994; Overton, 1998) argue that as one enters adulthood the developmental process becomes increasingly variable due to both biology and experience (McFadden, 1999). Rigid stage models function poorly in this kind of situation; more flexible approaches that attend to the interplay between cognitive, affective, and relational factors may provide a better understanding of the developmental process. In this situation, **pilgrimage** models may be especially attractive ways to think about development (see Section 7.1.1).

For instance, Streib (2001a, 2001b) has proposed modifying Fowler's theory using postmodern insights. He suggests replacing the current hierarchical stages with a list of religious styles or modes that are alternative ways of being religious. The modes include ritual, symbolic, cognitive, and narrative components that are rooted in life history and are more relational in nature than cognitive. The styles include the following:

- *Subjective and intuitive*: prominent in early childhood
- *Instrumental-reciprocal*: based on give and take; God seen as a parental authority
- *Mutual*: based on needs for respect, love, and identification; God seen as partner
- *Individuative-Systemic*: based on view of world as a system with us as a part
- *Dialogical*: based on the ability to let go and learn from others

Many authors argue that adult spiritual development may not involve a movement to new and distinct stages but rather a spiral process where issues from early life reappear and are dealt with at increasingly deeper levels (cf. von Balthasar, 1995, p. 174). For instance, issues of intimacy will be important in early adulthood in the context of marriage and childrearing, but in later adulthood will be confronted again as relationships mature or are lost. In this view, spiritual development involves the steady deepening of religious meaning and practice in ways that are not reducible to brain states. Stages of development are more like challenges to be confronted, the nature and timing of which may be dictated by culture in addition to biology and will be profoundly affected by context (Roehlkepartain, 2004; Studzinski, 1985, p. 97; cf. Wink & Dillon, 2002; Damasio, 2003, pp. 284–286; Singer, 1996). Shults and Sandage talk about the process of spiritual development or transformation in terms of *intensification* and increasing complexity of relationships, rather than a series of new tasks or preoccupations (2006, pp. 18, 29).

9.2 Young Adult and Midlife Development

9.2.1 Life Span Patterns

Recent research by social psychologists and sociologists of religion has significantly expanded our understanding of changes in religion and spirituality across the life span. These studies have begun to use sophisticated methodologies, including qualitative interviews with older adults, and looked at multiple dimensions such as religious affiliation, organizational participation, religious practices, and commitment. They have also tried to understand religious change in the context of other aspects of life and the surrounding culture. Currently, the most extensive analyses of longitudinal data on adult religious and spiritual development come from the work of Michelle Dillon and Paul Wink, who have been studying subjects from the Berkeley Institute of Human Development (IHD) longitudinal study, a long-term follow-up of a group of individuals born in Northern California during the 1920s (Dillon & Wink, 2007; Wink & Dillon, 2002, 2003; Dillon, Wink, & Fay, 2003; Wink, 2003). Although the sample is not representative in some ways (e.g., lower levels of parental religiousness) and includes some single-item measures of religiousness, spirituality, and well-being, it provides a rich picture of change in this group of adults (Ingersoll-Dayton, Krause, & Morgan, 2002).

Is religiousness stable across the life span? Dillon and Wink have found that the answer to this question depends on how you look at the data. When you compare group averages for different ages, studies indicate that religiousness shows small decreases during adolescence and young adulthood to a midlife low point and then increases later in life, with perhaps a few up and down fluctuations over the course of the life span. However, an examination of individual patterns tells a somewhat different story. In the IHD study, Dillon and Wink found that individually people displayed very stable high or low patterns of religiosity. Significant upward or downward movement occurred in only in about 6% of cases, and these changes typically happened in adolescence or early adulthood. At the group level, the early and midlife dip occurred later in women and did not occur among conservative Protestants. External events connected to decreases usually involved work demands, recreational opportunities, and children leaving home, although life transitions or historical events were sometimes involved in larger changes. Less frequently, negative experiences were involved in decreased religious involvement, generally a disillusionment with church members in reaction to excessive strictness, but occasionally other factors like disagreements with church policies about moral issues. Dillon and Wink argue that involvement with religion in adolescence provides a social engagement foundation that leads to higher religiousness, as well as a number of positive mental health benefits.

While most people in the IHD group displayed little change in religiosity over the life span, more marked changes occurred in spirituality. Beginning around midlife and especially after age 60 or so, Dillon and Wink found steady and substantial increases in spirituality, particularly for women, although other studies have found that roughly 80–90% of older adults report similar levels of importance in religiousness and spirituality (Musick, Traphagan, Koenig, & Larson, 2000). These changes have also been found in non-Western settings (Takahashi & Ide, 2003). The small changes in religion compared to the much larger changes in spirituality suggest that religion is fairly consistent throughout the life span while spirituality is more of a later life phenomenon. However, they also found that while religiousness levels typically do not change, there are changes in the *meaning* of religion, with shifts toward a more universal morality, a decrease in religion as a social focus, and an increase in the importance of faith and theological issues (Ingersoll-Dayton, Krause, & Morgan, 2002; Wink & Dillon, 2002).

The studies by Wink and Dillon also indicate that spirituality functions differently in religious and nonreligious individuals. Increases in spirituality in nonreligious individuals appear to be related to (1) personality characteristics like introspection, openness to experience (cf. McCrae, 1999), intellectual independence, unconventionality or creativity, and (2) the occurrence of personal turmoil and negative life events such as conflict with spouse or parents and financial strain. In these cases, spirituality is marked by a strong self-focus and search for personal growth. In contrast, the combination of strong spirituality and religiosity appears to be a stable, lifelong pattern unrelated to personal problems. These individuals are more social and report more close warm relationships and community involvement. They score higher on personality characteristics like conscientiousness and agreeableness. In a similar manner, religiousness and nonreligious spirituality are both related to generativity and purposive involvement, but in different ways. Nonreligious spirituality is more connected with a self-expanding generativity that is focused on desires for immortality, power, and leaving a creative legacy. Generativity connected with religious spirituality is more about communal concerns, developing strong relationships, caring and giving to others, and displaying personal altruism. Wink and Dillon interpreted their data as supporting Robert Wuthnow's division of people into (1) religious **dwellers** who are generally religious and spiritual, and (2) spiritual **seekers** who score high on spirituality but low on religiousness. They argue that psychology is biased against dwellers in favor of seekers but that these are equally valid and in some cases overlapping styles (Wink, 2003).

9.2.2 Emerging Adulthood and Religious Switching

Traditionally, adulthood was thought to begin somewhat abruptly in the late teenage years at the end of adolescence. However, cultural changes in postindustrial societies have caused some scholars to identify **emerging adulthood** as a new and sometimes difficult transitional time running from the end of adolescence through the mid-to-late 20s. Characteristics of this period include prolonged independence from family responsibilities, role, and relationship exploration or instability, and reevaluation of important aspects of one's worldview and religious practices. Identity formation is now thought to extend beyond adolescence into emerging adulthood, and this prolonged instability in the context of a complex postindustrial and global culture may lead some to construct multiple or bicultural identities (Arnett, 2000a, 2002).

The current US cohort in this age range is a diverse, post-Baby Boomer group with some characteristics that stand out as important for religious and spiritual development. Contemporary US emerging adults have grown up in a time of great social change, and while optimistic about their personal prospects for success, they tend to be pessimistic about the outlook for their generation and have struggled with increasing levels of psychological and emotional problems. Surveys suggest that over 80% of this group continue to find issues of spirituality, religion, and life philosophy or meaning very important. However, many cultural influences such as the media now tend to separate spirituality from religion, and members of this cohort tend to be skeptical of religious institutions because of dull or negative previous experiences and a fear that religion will inhibit individual freedom. University environments are also typically unsupportive of religious or spiritual development and reflection (Eckstrom, 2004). So while parental influence is still the predominant influence on the formation of religiosity among emerging adults, it is becoming more likely that individuals in this group will choose to decouple spiritual seeking from parental religious practices, leading to the formation of individualized combinations of religious and nonreligious spiritual beliefs. Personal relationships such as marriage and family also have ongoing importance for this group, both as a general foundation for future happiness and as an important factor in religious life (Bishop, Lacour, Nutt, Vivian, & Lee, 2004; Day, 1994; Arnett & Jensen, 2002; Arnett, 2000b; Burke, 1999).

The separation of spiritual beliefs from religious practice among some people in this group may have important implications. In a study involving in-depth interviews with British and Indian spiritually mature individuals, Thomas (1997) found that early mystical and religious experiences can have important effects on development throughout life, but that in order for this to happen there must be participation in subsequent spiritual disciplines, and that this is much easier if one is in a community that understands the experiences and has disciplines available to help the person incorporate them into their life. Maintenance of these practices outside of a framework of tradition and community is possible but much more difficult.

One specific kind of religious change that can happen during emerging adulthood or later in life is **religious switching**, the change from participation in one religious group or tradition to another. It is common, found perhaps in a third of

US adults (Roof, 1989). The odds of switching appears to be increased by a number of things, including desire for increased social status (Stark & Glock, 1968), changes in family, friendship or marital relationships, geographic moves, theological dissatisfactions, or lapses in religious practice. Strong parental religious commitment and similarity between mother and father, as well as their intention to transmit religious faith appear to be the primary factors connected with resistance to switching. Other factors that support remaining in one's religious tradition of origin are having children, and residence in parts of the US more supportive of religion such as rural areas. Childhood membership in a church decreases the odds of switching, and the factors involved in switching appear to be different for different groups. For instance, higher levels of education are positively related to switching among fundamentalists but negatively related to change in evangelicals. This may be because, while education does not affect participation, it does have a negative effect on Bible beliefs—a staple of fundamentalist religious communities (Loveland, 2003; Sherkat, 1998; Smith & Sikkink, 2003).

A number of sociological models have been devised to explain religious switching. Some explanations focus on switching as a way of enhancing social status. Other models fall into three groups (Sherkat, 2001; Finke, 1997):

1. **Supply side theories** argue that it is the structure of religious supply—churches in Christian contexts—that determines switching. For instance, some supply side theories explain the switching of people to conservative churches and away from mainline ones as a function of the higher commitment demanded by conservative groups, which enhances retention and makes them more distinctive in comparison to secular organizations. This type of reasoning lies at the basis of some cognitive-economic models of religious stability and change, such as rational choice theory (see below, Section 9.3.2).

2. **Demand side theories** attempt to explain switching by looking at factors that affect demand such as personal preferences and social sanctions that might limit or encourage choices. Secularization theory (see Section 1.3.1) is a type of demand side theory, because it argues that cultural and socioeconomic changes in Western society are reducing demand for religious activities.

3. **Human capital theories** point out that involvement in a particular religious group allows one to gain religious value through learning the teachings and practices of the group. This value would be lost if the person changed to a very different group, so there is a motivation for people to stay or change to a similar group. This theory is probably better at explaining retention than switching.

A number of family factors are connected to religious stability. Parental closeness is predictive of retention or return to childhood religion, while parental divorce is related to switching or abandonment. Family cohesion is related to retention, while family conflict or differences in belief with one's parents are associated with doubt. Return is connected to major relational events like marriage or having children, although religious differences in the marriage can lead to decreased participation. Interestingly, one study has found that women who change patterns of attendance have higher levels of anxiety disorders, while changing in men is associated with lower rates of depression. A possible explanation for the findings is that women are more likely to reduce religious activities in response to emotional problems, while men tend to continue participation (Maselko & Buka, 2008).

The level and type of religious participation in individuals is also related to stability and change. Retention is most common among those raised in evangelical Protestant and Catholic churches, special groups like Latter-Day Saints, and those with traditional beliefs. It is least common among those raised in liberal Protestant churches. Those leaving evangelical churches tend to switch rather than abandon religion altogether. Not surprisingly, those who were at one point committed and participating members are more likely to retain membership or return after an absence (Wilson & Sherkat, 1994; Roof & Gesch, 1995; Hertel, 1995).

9.2.3 Midlife and Turning Points

Since the time of Carl Jung, psychologists have seen midlife as a time of transition and change with important implications for religious and spiritual development. This happens in several ways. Midlife is a time in which polarities, inconsistencies, and even paradoxes in our life are confronted. We have needs for attachment but also for separateness, so how are we to resolve these apparently opposite forces in our life (Levinson, 1978, pp. 209.)? How shall we deal with the personal and career limitations that become more obvious as we grow older? These are issues confronted with particular intensity at midlife. Also, midlife is thought to be a time of increasing **generativity**, the movement described by Erikson (1950) involving a deepening responsibility for others and a desire to contribute something of worth to the world (see Section 5.3.2).

An important type of change that is extremely common during young adulthood and midlife is a **turning point**, something that redirects our life on a long lasting basis. This could include changes or recommitments in roles or important goals as family members die, or we experience failures in relationships and career. It can also involve changes in our identity as relationships and commitments change, and our aging brings about physical limitations and an awareness of mortality (Kristeva, 1987; Kunnen & Wassink, 2003). Midlife turning points can be sudden affairs provoked by a crisis or struggle, but more commonly they involve a slow steady acceptance of changes that lead toward increasing responsibility and maturity. In either case they involve experiences of emptiness—limit experiences—that challenge our previous frameworks and are not solvable on our own. These experiences can be denied, buried under distractions, or confronted (Wethington, Cooper, & Holmes, 1997; Fuller, 1988; Gunn, 2000, pp. 1–16). Turning points are often only recognized in retrospect and can be experienced initially as a feeling of estrangement or as a sense of **accedie**—discontent, apathy or boredom—rather than severe emotional turmoil, depression, or anxiety (see Section 11.2.1). Signs that a turning point has passed include a change in direction, identity or role commitment, and resistance to a return to old patterns (Brewi & Brennan, 1988; Wheaton & Gotlib, 1997).

The issues faced by people at midlife can be seen as having spiritual components that are addressed in the teachings and practice of most religious traditions
(Studzinski, 1985; Wethington, Cooper, & Holmes, 1997). For instance, religion
can help us achieve better integration in the face of life's conflicting demands and
paradoxes. Spirituality involves the movement toward a holistic inner balance and
a strong sense of connectedness, so changes toward recognizing and learning to
live with paradoxes and limitations represent movements toward spiritual maturity. Jung thought that most of the second half of life dealt with these kinds of
inner spiritual issues, for instance in the acceptance of our shadow side (Jung, 2001;
Brewi & Brennan, 1988, pp. 55–1; see Section 5.2.1). Religion can help in this
process by providing a system of beliefs and practices that move a person toward
self-knowledge and self-acceptance—an honest recognition of their limitations and
a willingness to accept them.

Religion and generativity are intimately connected. Highly generative individuals often report that it is religious beliefs, practices, and examples that motivate their
generative efforts. This generativity can lead to profound social and religious innovation as in the case of **homines religiosi** like Gandhi, who became driven to actualize for other people the religious faith and values they have accepted for themselves
and found helpful (Erikson, 1969, pp. 397–402; cf. McAdams, 2006).

Finally, religion and spirituality can be deeply involved in midlife turning points.
Many turning points have a spiritual and holistic quality that involves trying to find
a sense of balance and connectedness to the larger world. They can be triggered by a
limit experience that leads to a crisis involving a loss of control and meaning. These
can have a broadening effect, which if managed and resolved from a religious or
spiritual framework can make the situation a *spiritual* turning point, leading to religious or spiritual change (James & Samuels, 1999; Fiori, Hays, & Meador, 2004;
Elder, 1995; Wethington, Cooper, & Holmes, 1997; Musgrave, 1997). Religion
can help us negotiate these turning points and seek necessary changes in our life.
Instead of losing hope and giving up, or trying to avoid dealing with the problems
and losses that occur at midlife, the support of a religious faith and community may
help us to mourn our losses, seek transformation and move on, as we prepare for
the second half of our life journey. This transformation could include a shift in time
perspective, taking the "long view" on our life, or becoming more involved in the
present moment. Changes could involve a new balancing of priorities, a reevaluation of relationships or other life structures like job and place of residence. It could
also lead to a reinterpretation of some life events and a change in our images of self
and God. These kinds of transformations can change the scripts or structures we use
to organize experience and make meaning from events, and thus have the potential to fundamentally alter our identity and experience of life (Kunnen & Wassink,
2003; Tomkins & Demos, 1995).

What must happen for turning points to produce spiritual change? Balk (1999)
argues that there are three factors: (1) a crisis or change creating psychological
imbalances that are hard to correct, (2) time for reflection, and (3) a continuing
and permanent "coloring" of our life by the experience. The kind of reflection we
make on events is affected by a number of factors; for instance, if God is seen as

reliable, able to help, and open to communication, reflection tends to be positive and optimistic (Hays, Meador, Branch, & George, 2001). Because turning points involve problems that we are unable to solve on our own, another factor in spiritual and religious change is our willingness to admit our need for help and to accept it, surrendering our will to a higher power that will help us find wholeness. In this view, happiness in later life depends on moving away from egoism and toward personal integration with these sources of support (Fuller, 1988, pp. 103–112; see also Section 11.3.1).

9.2.4 Belief and Unbelief

Up to now we have mostly spoken about the increase or change in religious and spiritual life during adulthood. Another possibility is that the individual may reject religion and perhaps spirituality altogether, adopting a stance of unbelief. In the US, these individuals typically identify themselves on surveys as having no religious preference. Primarily drawn from people who have been loosely or never attached to religion, their numbers have leveled off recently at about 14% of the US population, with a smaller percentage of these identifying themselves as active atheists (Hunsberger & Altemeyer, 2006, pp. 15–18; Sherkat, 2001). With the exception of some areas in Europe, most parts of the world have similar or lower rates of religious unbelief.

Taylor (2007) argues that unbelief is generally not based on rational arguments against religion. Unbelief is not required by science or philosophy, and the religious views attacked by unbelievers are typically those of childhood Sunday school rather than real mature adult faith (see Sections 2.5 and 6.2). Instead, it is the moral "spin" of unbelief narratives that makes them attractive to its adherents. Unbelievers see themselves as courageous, mature adults by opposing religion, which they view as antirational, authoritarian (and thus restrictive of freedom), and distracting from the pursuit of happiness and human benefit. For unbelievers, the throwing off of religion provides a feeling of power and invulnerability. Religion is thus not something to be ignored but something bad to be opposed and stamped out. Power and the impersonal disengaged reason of the individual are seen as the best way to increase human dignity, an ethical stance typically rejected by religious individuals and groups as overly reductionistic, utopian, and mistaken. The viewpoint of unbelief forms a restricted "closed world structure" (2007, p. 551) that makes it seem unarguable to its followers, even though the positivist views of history and religion on which it is based are highly questionable. The need to maintain this structure in the face of belief means that unbelief, like belief, is not a completely stable position and must be continually supported. Taylor's argument parallels neurobiological findings that suggest that both belief and unbelief are strongly hedonic in nature (Harris, Sheth, & Cohen, 2007).

Unbelief can be looked at in a couple of ways. In the more traditional view, unbelief is an end-state condition in which people reject the truth value of religious teachings and may even deny the value of any type of spiritual quest or awareness. This condition might be reached through **cultural unbelief**, where a person grows up without any religious background. It also can occur because of **apostasy**, when a person is raised with belief but later actively rejects it. Apostasy may result in the adoption of **nihilistic** views with its attendant **existential sickness** and need to disconfirm the beliefs of others (see Section 11.1.2). Strongly held positions of unbelief tend to be associated with the latter and are defined in opposition to belief and negative conceptions of religion (Taylor, 2007, pp. 269–274). An alternate viewpoint sees unbelief or religious doubt as a fundamental component of the spiritual and religious life of all people, not just those who reject religion. For instance, those influenced by the apophatic traditions in Christianity may reject beliefs about God because they fall short of the divine reality (Turner, 2002; see Section 3.3.2). The idea that unbelief is an important feature of religion is elaborated by the European researcher Antoine Vergote, who has articulated a well-developed theory of unbelief.

9.2.4.1 Vergote on Belief and Unbelief

For Vergote, religion is "a system of belief" and "an ensemble of conceptions, forms of behavior and experiences related to (a) 'supernatural' being(s) which is (are) not the object of a knowing comparable to other forms of knowledge" (1997 pp. 208–209). This belief is not just an ideology but involves relationships and everything that makes up the life of an individual (1997, pp. 26–40). Vergote (1998, p. 44) argues that since religion deals with the most fundamental desires in human life, it automatically stirs up conflict so that along with the desire to seek God there is also a pressure to doubt and distance ourselves from the Divine. Belief and unbelief thus exist in reference to each other in a tension that changes over time. In a sense, parts of us accept belief, while other parts ignore it or struggle against it (Kristeva, 1987, p. 39). Belief is thus somewhat unstable—it at least in part involves faith (Bishop, 2007)—and must be constantly maintained through active involvement, just like a relationship. Believers must repeatedly decline human inclinations to follow a different way of life. Likewise unbelief is a system of belief that requires maintenance. For those in an environment that has eliminated religious symbols or who have distanced themselves from religion for a long period of time, this is easy, and unbelief can become a matter of indifference (Vergote, 1997, pp. 207–214). However, substantive exposure to religion and the evidence supporting it challenges unbelief and can produce a crisis similar to a crisis in belief, although more personal. The irritation, scorn, and even hatred of nonbelievers for religion is quite different from the feelings the believer encounters in a crisis:

> "These feelings cannot be compared to any other experience. People with a deep-rooted hate of Marxism or capitalism feel that they are attacked or threatened by a hostile force; but given the fact that the enemy is seen to be external, this does not touch upon their sense of human value. When it comes to a hatred of religion, however, there is a certain

contempt, even a disgust, as though the enemy were within. We cannot understand this phenomenon unless we realize that the very fact of religion raises a question with regard to the individual's very person, and that this question is, by nature, felt as an intrusive and threatening summons. The psyche defends itself by throwing out the call as an illness" (Vergote, 1997, p. 213).

This negative reaction is often justified by reference to events from the past, either personal experiences or historical events like the Inquisition or the condemnation of Galileo. From a rational perspective, the reasoning can seem odd: One would not refuse to take advantage of modern medicine because physicians used to practice bloodletting or give medicines later found to be harmful! However, Vergote argues that this loathing of unbelievers for religion occurs because religious belief represents a danger, contradicting basic certainties in the life of the unbeliever, including the primacy of one's own reason to set goals and the ways we will attain them. A fundamental aspect of atheism is thus a defense against a threatening God (Vergote, 1969, pp. 259–266).

Vergote thought that both cognitive and emotional factors separated believers and unbelievers from each other. In terms of cognition, Vergote argued that believers and unbelievers stress different conceptions of God. In his empirical research, Vergote found that believers and unbelievers used similar categories to talk about God, but that Christian subjects emphasized maternal characteristics of God, while unbelievers emphasized the paternal ones. These different conceptions of God were related to motives for belief or unbelief. Unbelievers focus on rejection of authority, because acceptance of a superior force implies a loss of control and highlights human deficiencies. Christian subjects, on the other hand, focused on trust and an acceptance of their existential dependence on a dependable reality. Vergote thus sees the essential issue in the decision about belief or unbelief to be the conflict between autonomy and dependence. While believers see God as a help and an ally, unbelievers see God as a competitor and a threat to their absolute autonomy. Unbelief then is often accompanied by a sense of triumph over a rival, a sense of freedom, and relief that religion does not offer truth so that we may seek it by human striving and move away from the past. Vergote saw this cognitive tendency as rooted in the psychological disposition and history of the individual, leading them to favor certain types of God images (1997, pp. 226–245, 272–273; 1998, p. 96).

Vergote argues that emotional issues like resentment and disappointment are also primary factors in the development of unbelief. These are problems that are particularly acute in the case of unbelievers, who see evil in the world as incompatible with the existence of a good God and who have unrealistic, utopian ideas about what organized religion should be like. These resentments destroy the emotional base necessary for belief by reducing the capacity for trust and attachment and fueling questions about the goodness of persons and of God. This promotes a focus on external blaming that makes it difficult to see how we sometimes suffer from the same impure motives and actions we criticize in others. Vergote argues that forgiveness is the best antidote to these feelings of resentment so that forgiveness is not just a consequence of faith but a precondition for it and a liberation from the emotional memories that resentment and vengeance are unable to erase. Vergote thus has a relational view of feeling as embedded in our relationship with God and others. He argues that good religious development involves an enhancement of the emotional qualities and a leaving behind of childlike, magical views of religion for a realistic and mature faith (1969, p. 285; 1997, pp. 251–266).

9.2.4.2 Other Empirical Perspectives

Sociologists of religion have recently begun to comment more extensively on unbelief. Wuthnow (1999) has found that while some individuals who leave their faith of origin because of bad experiences or boredom will reject religion and even spirituality entirely, it is more common for unbelievers to still talk about spirituality. They do not reject the sacred; they just disagree with or question the beliefs of others and want a set of views that are more acceptable. Thus, those leaving religion seldom escape their past entirely; they continue to see religious meaning in events. These people may become questers or spiritual seekers, have some continuing sense of the sacred, and may continue to engage in religious practices, reflect on religious issues or even maintain a peripheral level of participation in a religious organization. However, Wuthnow notes that people seldom continue to perform religious practices on their own, so maintenance of a vibrant spirituality apart from religion is difficult.

Psychological research specifically targeting unbelievers is rather limited, with the notable exception of some work by Canadian researchers Altemeyer and Hunsberger. In one study (1997, pp. 209–214), they looked at university students who chose belief or unbelief at odds with their familial background. In particular, they looked at *Amazing Apostates* (AAs), who came from religious families and *Amazing Believers* (ABs), who came from nonreligious backgrounds. They found significant differences between the two groups. AAs gave intellectual reasons for becoming apostates and talked about it as an individual decision relatively detached from peer influence. ABs reported that they made the change to help deal with emotional problems and issues; familial divorce was much more common in AB families, suggesting that conversion could be part of a compensation process (see Section 8.2.2). The change process was also different for the two groups, as AAs reported that their transition began earlier, lasted longer and caused more familial disruption than was the case for ABs. ABs were higher on measures of right-wing authoritarianism than AAs. These findings would seem to be in accordance with Vergote's theory, which predicts that unbelievers would attribute more salience to authority issues and be more anti-authoritarian, while believers would view the issue as less salient or perhaps be positively attracted to the structure provided by religious communities and beliefs.

A more recent study by Hunsberger and Altemeyer (2006) looks at North American atheists in general, rather than just those who come from religious backgrounds. The pattern from the data suggests that these individuals typically have little religious socialization in childhood and have serious doubts about religious beliefs beginning in adolescence, although many had at least a period in which they considered religion or had some attachment to it. The primary reason for unbelief was a dismissal of religion for lack of acceptable rational proof, a contrast to the European situation where perceived lack of flexibility and irrelevance of belief are more common reasons (Ganzevoort, 1994). The majority of US atheists reported that their stance produced difficulty with family and/or friends. Despite this, they were strongly committed to their unbelief. The majority of them were likely to proselytize their beliefs (just over 60%), although they had lower levels of interest in passing beliefs on to their children. They reported high levels of dogmatism about atheistic beliefs—they said that nothing could change their mind on the topic—and also had high levels of prejudice toward those with strong religious views like fundamentalists.

Atheism in Europe comes about in a different social and religious context, so it is difficult to make comparisons or apply information about one group to the study of the other. Researchers have identified 4 kinds of atheism in the European setting: (1) *transitional*, a temporary condition when moving from one kind of religious belief or affiliation to another; (2) *philosophical*, a worked through position including humanism or scientific materialism; (3) *unchurched*, maintaining some aspects of religious belief but eschewing connection to a religious organization; or (4) *indifferent*. Common issues reported as reasons for unbelief include need for autonomy and control, fatalism, relationship with others, specific intellectual problems like evil or suffering, and negative experiences with religious education (Oser, Reich, & Bucher, 1994). This data offers broad support to Vergote's conceptualization of unbelief.

What does one believe about the world and life issues, if a person embraces a stance of religious or spiritual unbelief? If one rejects religion on rational grounds, one is likely to also reject magical models like New Age spirituality, leaving one with secular beliefs such as scientism and Marxism. However, the collapse of communism and increasingly severe problems caused by scientific technology have rendered these alternative worldviews less attractive, and most secular alternatives also lack the affective, relational, and organizational resources offered by religions (Helve, 1994; Vergote, 1994). This leaves many individuals outside religious traditions in a vacuum that may or may not seem problematic to them.

Given the problems with nonreligious alternatives, it is not surprising that many apostates return to church in later life (Wilson & Sherkat, 1994). However, many do not, and the stability of cultural unbelief or nonaffiliation is increasing in younger age groups (43% vs. 30% in older adults; Sherkat, 2001). An interesting study of older US nonattendees by Black (1995) found that continued noninvolvement was associated with three beliefs: (1) spiritual achievements are not real successes and are unimportant for living life, (2) religious involvement would distract from pursuing unrealized goals related to financial success and work, or (3) the persons saw themselves as possessing superior qualities and personal achievements, so they did not need to consider spiritual issues, which they perceived as involving naive beliefs. Those who did have a concept of the Divine thought God to be uninvolved, so while unbelievers may continue to think in religious categories they exclude God from life. The older adults in Black's study articulated a vision of the ideal person, who is a youthful hero, solitary, physically strong, and possessing great sexual prowess. Once solidly established, unbelief can become a set perspective for life, and even profound religious experiences will not alter it, for these will be interpreted or explained away from a nonreligious framework (Ganzevoort, 1994; Bachs, 1994).

Since the Enlightenment, there has been a strong tendency for intellectuals and academics to resist religion, so unbelief has been a common position among people with advanced university educations such as psychologists (see Section 14.2.2). The well-known developmental researcher Susan McFadden, for instance, tells the story of how her department chair advised her to never use the words "religion" or "spirituality" in a paper title for fear of being denied tenure or promotion (Ray & McFadden, 2001). However, some observers think that there may be at least some small changes taking place. For instance, in a study of Brazilian academic physicists, de Paiva (1994) found a decrease in hostility toward religion compared to 20 years ago, when adherence to Marxism and atheism was a prerequisite for professional recognition. While almost all the academics in her sample were detached from institutional religion, there was now a strong tendency to treat religion as a private issue that does not necessarily interfere with science.

9.3 Mechanisms of Stability and Change

Current research on development highlights one central fact: powerful forces for both stability and change in religion or spirituality are active in the lives of adults. The persistence of patterns across adulthood suggests stability, and traditional psychological theories of adulthood have tended to focus on these static elements of behavior and experience, or on problems of physical decline (Valsiner, 2000, p. 8). On the other hand, examples of profound transformations that involve self-transcendence, growth, and a death of the former self also abound (Liebert, 2000, pp. 126–127). What are the mechanisms promoting stability or change? Some researchers have considered personality as a factor, but while there are some modest relationships between personality and spirituality or religiosity in certain situations, many important things like an orientation to spiritual transcendence are unrelated to personality variables (Piedmont, 1999). This has led researchers to consider alternate ways to explain spiritual or religious stability and change. In this section, we consider three possible frameworks—religious motivation, cognition or rational choice, and life narratives.

9.3.1 Stability and Religious Motivation: Internal, External, and Quest

Psychologists studying religion tend to argue that adults engage in religion because of internal motives, and that each individual has a particular pattern of motivation that is fairly consistent throughout the lifespan, providing a kind of stability to their religious

Fig. 9.1 *Richard Gorsuch.*
One of the world's leading
psychologists of religion,
Gorsuch has made important
conceptual, methodologi-
cal, and empirical research
contributions in a number of
areas, including research on
religious motivation and our
internalized images of God.
Photo courtesy of Richard
Gorsuch

behavior. Schaefer and Gorsuch (1991) see religious motivation as one of the three important factors that determine religious behavior, along with beliefs, coping styles, and their important interactions (Hathaway & Pargament, 1990) (Fig. 9.1).

Religious motivation theory goes back to the work of Gordon Allport on intrinsic and extrinsic religiosity (see Section 1.4.6). In the original theory, Allport identified two types of religious motivation. The first is an **extrinsic motivation** (E) that sees religion as a means so that religious involvement is motivated by instrumental or utilitarian goals and self-interest. The second is an **intrinsic motivation** (I) that sees religion as an end in itself worth doing for its own sake regardless of other benefits, a "master motive" that has ultimate significance above other things and provides a creed which an individual will try to internalize and follow. Allport originally thought that perhaps 10% of church members would qualify as purely I, and that this inner experience of religion was related to the development of tolerance, while E was connected with prejudice (Allport, 1966; Allport & Ross, 1967, pp. 434–435; Reiss & Havercamp, 1998).

The **Multivariate Belief-Motivation Theory of Religiousness** (Schaefer & Gorsuch, 1992; see Section 1.4.6) predicts that religious motivation will have impor-
tant interactions with beliefs, coping styles, and other important variables such as psychological well-being. This has been verified in a number of studies that have revealed intricate relationships. For instance, religious attendance has moderate positive correlations with I but not with E motivation. There is also a positive correlation between attendance and certain features of the God image (e.g.,

benevolent, guiding) and a negative relationship with other aspects (e.g., deistic). Other characteristics of the God image are unrelated to attendance. The complexity of the relationships between motivation and well-being can be seen in factor analyses, which have found I (but not E) related to positively worded well-being items but unrelated with existential well-being or religious/existential confusion (Eggers, 2003).

Attempts have been made to expand the concepts of I-E motivation, and revised scales of measurement have been developed that appear to be reliable in groups as young as fifth grade (Gorsuch & McPherson, 1989; Gorsuch & Venable, 1983). An early attempt at expansion was made by Allport and Ross, who argued in their later work that I and E motivation were not separate characteristics and that it was possible to be high or low in both, positions they labeled as **indiscriminately proreligious** and nonreligious, respectively. However, other researchers observed that high I individuals are similar in many ways to the indiscriminately proreligious, while high E persons resemble the nonreligious group, so this expansion of the I-E construct is not very helpful (Donahue, 1985). Researchers continue to be somewhat divided over whether it is better to think of E and I as motivation types at ends of a bipolar continuum, or independent and orthogonal characteristics. Kirkpatrick (1989) has argued for the latter view, but research has found that E and I are negatively correlated in groups like conservative Protestants, which supports the traditional bipolar or typological view (Saroglou, 2002).

A second expanded approach to religious motivation used factor analysis to refine the analysis of extrinsic motivation by breaking it into two subfactors—seeking rewards of personal security or comfort (Ep) or developing social relationships, gains, and rewards (Es). This distinction has been found meaningful in both US and UK studies, and appears in much of the work on religious motivation (Gorsuch & McPherson, 1989; Kirkpatrick, 1989; cf. Gorsuch, 1988; Maltby & Day, 2003). Some have argued that intrinsic motivation also has a social component and may help meet personal needs for companionship, so that it is inaccurate to characterize intrinsics as uninterested in rewards (Burris, Batson, Altstaedten, & Stephens, 1994)

A number of explanations have been proposed for the existence of intrinsic religiosity. Some investigators have argued that seeking religion "for its own sake" is really a search for the rewards that religion has to offer. However, this ignores the data that shows intrinsic motivation to be separate from extrinsic motivation. Gorsuch (1997) argues that intrinsic motivation may have multiple sources and that individuals raised in a religious faith may develop intrinsic motivation for different reasons than those who are later converts. Cognitive consistency with one's values and experiences, as well as emotional factors, are likely to be important.

A final major expansion to the theory has been made by Daniel Batson, who has proposed a third type of religious motivation known as **quest**. He describes this as a pattern that includes (1) a readiness to criticize self and to face complexity or existential questions, (2) perception of doubt as positive and resistance to clearcut answers or commitments, and (3) openness to change (Batson & Schoenrade, 1991a; Batson, Schoenrade, & Ventis, 1993; Saroglou, 2002; see Section 1.4.6).

Batson thought that quest comes from cognitive restructuring in response to existential questions, such as those provoked by a contemplation of death, tragedy, or contradiction in life, a connection that has been found in some studies (e.g., Krauss & Flaherty, 2001). He also argues that quest is a type of motivation completely separate from intrinsic or extrinsic religiosity, although some researchers have found evidence that it is modestly related to extrinsic motivation (Kojetin, McIntosh, Bridges, & Spilka, 1987; Wong-McDonald & Gorsuch, 2004). A helpful distinction has been made by Beck and Jessup (2004), who have identified two questing patterns—a soft quest marked by tentativeness and exploration within tradition, and a hard quest associated with doubt, negative emotions, less orthodoxy, and decreased well-being. It is this latter pattern that appears to be connected with lower values of intrinsic and higher values of extrinsic motivation.

There has been an extensive debate about the nature of quest. A fundamental issue is whether quest is a type of religious motivation or a personality characteristic. While quest does appear to be related to religious conflict and anxiety, quest scores are not much related to other measures of religion and spirituality. Quest motivation does have a relationship to a number of psychological factors including higher scores on cognitive complexity and the personality factor of openness to experience and lower scores on measures of prejudice or authoritarianism. This suggests that quest is really better thought of as a personality characteristic or a general reactive, negativistic stance that represents a resistance to identity foreclosure (Donahue, 1985; Simpson, Newman, & Fuqua, 2005; Burris, Jackson, Tarpley, & Smith, 1996; Saroglou, 2002; Futterman, Dillon, Garand, & Haugh, 1999; Klaassen & McDonald, 2002). Some UK research has suggested that quest is more about conflict and distress than searching for a religious or spiritual change (Joseph, Smith, & Diduca, 2002; cf. Kahn & Greene, 2004).

One area of debate has been whether the intrinsic or the quest styles of motivation are superior to each other. Research results on this question have been somewhat inconsistent, and interpretation of the findings depends in part on the values of each researcher and their conception of maturity. Early writers such as Alexander (1962) defined emotional maturity in terms of ability to become interested in things outside the self, so that things like intrinsic religiosity and altruism are highly desirable and superior to a self-centered quest. Other researchers argue that quest develops later in life than intrinsic or extrinsic religiosity and so is a more advanced type of motivation (Socha, 1996). Finding that individuals high in I also score higher on some measures of self-deception and impression management, and that Stage 5 development in Fowler's scheme is not associated with high I values could also be used to support the superiority of quest (Burris, 1994; James & Samuels, 1999). However, in a US study, Kristensen, Pedersen, and Williams (2001) looked at religious motivation and three components of attitude: affect, cognition, and conation (behaviors and intentions). They found that people high on quest had high scores on cognitive motivation but low scores on affect and conation, a pattern similar to those with a more extrinsic motivation. The authors argued that the dissociation of quest from behavior and intention suggests that it is not a good description of spiritual maturity. These findings parallel other work that suggests quest is tied to cognitive motivations, I to seeking spiritual perfection and E to personal superiority (Grzymala-Moszczynska, 1996). Pargament (1997, p. 63) argues that all three orientations involve means and ends, just different ones. He argues that means are embedded for intrinsic, compartmentalized for extrinsic and complex, and conflictual for quest motivation, while ends are more relational for intrinsics, focused on status or safety for extrinsics, and about meaning or self-development for questers.

The concept of religious motivation has been a key one in the scientific study of religion and appears in many studies. While the I-E theory has generated interesting findings, some researchers like Kirkpatrick and Hood (1990) have been critical of it. These criticisms include following:

- The I-E model is conceptually flawed as the constructs are not clearly defined, have multiple meanings, are value-laden, and may relate more to personality.
- The scales used for research on religious orientation have measurement problems (cf. Griffin, Gorsuch, & Davis, 1987; Batson & Schoenrade, 1991b).
- The model is too simplistic in its attempt to reduce religious motivation to 2 or 3 categories and is not based on a strong theory (Reiss, 2000).
- Researchers often treat intrinsic or extrinsic religiosity as a type rather than a characteristic that varies from person to person or between groups (Lazar, Kravetz, & Frederich-Kedem, 2002).
- It does not describe a characteristic relevant to nonreligious people (Donahue, 1985; but see Rowatt & Schmitt, 2003).

As a result of these criticisms, religious motivation has become a less popular construct in scientific research on religion, and researchers have been actively looking at other explanatory frameworks. However, a large body of high quality research attests to the importance of motivation in explaining a number of important aspects and consequences of religion.

9.3.2 Cognitive Perspectives on Change and Development

Psychological theories of religious development, especially those that concentrate on childhood and adolescence, have frequently focused on factors related to cognition. These types of theories can also be found in the adult development literature. Two are especially important—postformal and rational choice theories.

9.3.2.1 Postformal Development Theory

Sinnott (1994, 1998, 2000) has argued that the growth in spirituality and mysticism during adulthood happens in tandem with cognitive changes that take place. According to Piaget, cognitive development ends in adolescence with the move to formal operations thinking and Aristotelian or scientific logic. Sinnott rejects this view, as he believes that in adulthood people may move to a higher or postformal stage. This **postformal thought** or logic allows us to organize contradictory information that is encountered when one begins to deal with spiritual issues and is thus necessary for mature spiritual development. Instead of being rigidly limited to one system with certain interests and goals, postformal logic allows us recognize the limits of our perspective, accept the existence of paradox and inherent unknowability of certain things, and begin to see multiple possibilities. Some authors (e.g., Cook-Greuter, 2000; Cook-Greuter & Soulen, 2007) associate this kind of postformal thought with flexible systems of meaning-making that are found at transpersonal levels of development.

Postformal systems of thought are ideal for achieving balance and integration, both of which are central to spirituality. This is because postformal thought is more than just a form of logic. It is multimodal, involving emotions, as well as the logical mind, and it is multiperson and relational, developing in the context of our interpersonal experiences, our connections to others, and to God. It is a kind of cooperative cognition that involves the union of mind and emotion and allows judgment to be made on the basis of *either* or *both* depending on what is best for the particular time and context. As spiritual issues become more prominent during adult development, postformal thought supports the perception of multiple realities and unitive states of consciousness.

Postformal thought involves the ability to see that more than one type of reasoning system can be valid, and to see that dealing with a particular problem in different contexts may require different solutions. It sees problems as practical rather than abstract and that they should be understood more concretely with attention to both general features and those specific to the case. This type of reasoning is thus pragmatic and complex, able to see multiple causes and even paradoxical aspects operating in a problem. It allows for the creation of multiple goals and solutions, recognizes multiple methods that are possible approaches, picks one that is best, and takes ownership for it. This flexibility allows us to rise above conflicting truths and make choices appropriate to our situation.

Sinnott's theory is interesting and has some scattered support in the adult development literature on wisdom, which has some characteristics similar to postformal thought. His theory also has many parallels with postmodern and practice approaches to religion and spirituality (see Section 6.3.4). However, few people have begun to explore the theory, so empirical evidence for it remains limited.

9.3.2.2 Rational Choice Theory

A more popular theory has been **rational choice theory**, which involves the application of rational decision-making models from economics to the study of religion. The theory was pioneered by Lawrence Iannaccone (1990, 1995b), who argued that religion is something that produces products like personal satisfaction, as well as **compensators** or substitutes for desired rewards such as immortality. Since religion produces products, it is subject to laws of supply and demand and can be subjected to economic analysis (Iannaccone & Everton, 2004; Stark, 1997a). In his view, religious products such as satisfaction can be measured by looking at concrete variables like denominational adherence. These can then be thought of as produced by money, scarce resources, and acquired skills or **human capital**, allowing for the development of complex quantitative explanatory models. The assumptions of this theory are that (1) people act rationally; (2) these rational decisions utilize cost-benefit analyses that are based on a fixed set of personal needs and preferences so that changes in behavior are because of changes in external constraints; (3) people choose actions that maximize benefits, sometimes with reference to the needs and wishes of others, as well as their own; and (4) because religious capital is acquired in a specific group, people avoid changing affiliation to prevent loss of value (Ellison, 1995; Iannaccone, 1990, 1997a).

Rational choice theory has been used to develop models about a couple of religious phenomena. First, it has been used to explain why religion in the US has remained strong, while European religion has followed the predictions of secularization theory and seen declining rates of participation. The rational choice model says that the free market style of US religion is responsible for its resilience against the corrosive effects of modern culture by promoting competition between different groups and keeping them strong. In this model, groups like Catholics are more successful in resisting secularization, because they maintain internal competition by allowing diversity (Finke, 1997). This is in contrast to secularization models like the sociopolitical conflict model (e.g., Martin, 1978), which says that European nonparticipation is not due to lack of competition but because of identification between government and religion, allowing religious nonadherence to become a form of social protest. There is significant evidence against both of these theories as an explanation for differences between Europe and the US, although the rational choice theory continues to attract interest (Gorski, 2003). It also goes against older theories such as those of Peter Berger (1967; Ammerman, 1997), which said that religious pluralism weakened rather than strengthened religion by questioning its truth, value, and plausibility.

Rational choice explanations have also been used to understand why conservative churches are growing in membership, while mainline churches are declining. In the view of Iannaccone (1996), conservative churches are growing and attract higher levels of financial commitment, because they are stricter and thus stronger. Strict churches are more distinctive or exclusive, distancing themselves from worldly and secular alternatives. Raising the level of commitment weeds out "free riders" that are less dedicated and take more from the organization than they give to it, and increased expectations attract enthusiastic members who participate and build up others. The removal of free riders and retention of committed ones increases resources and enhances the net benefits of membership, which leads to higher retention rates and more switching in from other less strict groups, a pattern that has been found in sociological studies and within denominations (Sherkat, 2001; Olson & Perl, 2001, 2005). The distinctiveness hypothesis is also supported by research that finds a negative relationship between market share and religious commitment (Perl & Olson, 2000). Of course, at some point strictness reaches a level where the cost is too great, and churches must moderate their demands; this level appears to vary for different groups (Iannaccone, 1994, 1997b; Neitz & Mueser, 1997). However, in a social climate not favorable to religion, liberal churches are more likely to lose members than conservative ones because of their lower level of strictness (Wilson & Sherkat, 1994).

Given the focus on money in society, it is not surprising that economic metaphors and theories would eventually be used to study religion (Ammerman, 1997). However, rational choice theory has been subjected to a broad critique (e.g., Neitz & Mueser, 1997; Ammerman, 1997). Some of the objections raised about the theory are as follows:

1. The key idea of rational choice theory—that people make decisions on the basis of costs and benefits—does not allow us to make specific predictions or to rule out alternative explanations such as demand side theories or demographic changes (Bruce, 1993; Finke, 1997; Iannaccone, 1995a; Beyer, 1997; Perl & Olson, 2000). Instead, the theory is dependent upon other assumptions that are unsupported (Chaves, 1995)
2. It offers a limited definition of rationality and decision-making—economic and short term. This overlooks the possibility that loyalty to religion may be different from loyalty to a brand of coffee. A broader view of rationality will also consider meaning-making, values and emotional factors in decision-making and commitment (Demerath, 1995; Hechter, 1997; Bruce, 1993)
3. It ignores important relational, cultural, and social factors. Since it is culture that provides standards of value, it is impossible to understand decision-making about value without reference to culture (Ellison, 1995). Research also suggests that choices are not just due to cost and benefit but are also affected by social relations factors such as example setting, social sanctions, and what we think will please others. Rational choice needs to be combined with demand side theories if it is to adequately account for these factors (Sherkat & Wilson, 1995; Sherkat, 1997, 1998).
4. It ignores differences in the content of religious belief that appear to affect participation rates. For example, mainline denominations that are losing members are also those groups who have leaders that have become skeptical about basic Christian beliefs (Sherkat, 2001).
5. It ignores or minimizes the "nonrational" aspects to religion that may influence choices such as emotion, religious experience or mysticism, and the appeal of novelty (Young, 1997; Sherkat, 1997; Collins, 1997).
6. It does not explain important aspects of choices and changes in Europe, for instance why Nordic countries have low rates of attendance but strong support for finances and rituals, or why people are abandoning religion completely (Bruce, 2000; Marwell, 1996).

9.3.3 Narrative Perspectives on Stability and Change

Dissatisfaction with motivational and cognitive models of change and stability has opened the door to the consideration of new approaches to understanding development. One of the most important of these is narrative theory. Modern narrative theory in psychology goes beyond the early work of writers like Erikson or Freud and includes material from cognitive psychology (e.g., Bruner, 1986, 1991), analyses of literary and historical theory (e.g., Polkinghorne, 1988), and personality theory (e.g., McAdams, 1997; Singer & Bluck, 2001). Its application in developmental theory fits well with what has been called the contextual turn in research (e.g., Bronfenbrenner, 1977), and it has links to postmodern and practice understandings of the human person (see Section 6.3). It also has attracted the interest of theologians (e.g., Stroup, 1981), making it an interesting framework for considering development from both psychological and religious perspectives.

Narrative theorists argue that humans have two modes of representation, *propositional* or scientific and *narrative* (Bruner, 1986, p. 11). Scientific thought is rational and is good at manipulating abstract ideas but tends to be inefficient for responding to particular situations in everyday practical life. On the other hand, **narrative** is more about human action as embodied and lived experience. It is experiential, intuitive, creative, and emotionally engaging, focusing more on procedures than ideas. It is thus more the kind of reasoning that actually motivates most human action; we are story-telling animals that judge what we are to do by the stories we inhabit. As a result, a narrative theory should have inherent advantages in helping us to understand many aspects of the human person (Epstein, 1994; Polkinghorne, 1988, pp. 125, 142; Hermans, Kempen, & van Loon, 1992; MacIntyre, 1984, p. 216).

Psychologists and other narrative theorists note that narrative thinking in individuals has a number of important specific functions. Along with adding meaning to events (Neimeyer & Levitt, 2001), narrative brings integration and harmony to our inner world and thoughts through organization of memory and emotions. Along with other dispositions and characteristic patterns of behavior, these form the basis of our character, personality, and identity (McAdams, 1996, 2001; see Section 6.3.3). Narrative also has a practical role in understanding and planning practical action in space and time (see Section 7.1.1). It thus helps to internalize moral principles and provide guidance about moral choices in concrete situations (de Certeau, 1984, pp. 117–125; Crossley, 2000, pp. 47–51; Vitz, 1990; cf. Ricoeur, 1992). It is especially helpful in planning action, because stories contain an imagined future or goal for our action, preserving the temporal component of action so that it is easy to see the importance of the process of working toward a goal and not just attaining it (McAdams, 2001; Sommer & Baumeister, 1998).

9.3.3.1 Narrative Elements and Framework

Organization of information in life narratives has four primary characteristics. First, experiences and memories are arranged *temporally* in chronological sequences using **emplotment**. It thus involves more than a focus on the moment (Farb et al., 2007). The plot organizes events and shows connections; the ordering provides interpretations and explanations for why things happened and the meaning, worth, and purpose of events. The narrative is also **teleological**, pointing toward the goal of the story, showing the possible consequences to action, as well as the reactions they trigger. Narrative thus considers the relational connections to action (Neimeyer & Levitt, 2001; Polkinghorne, 1988, pp. 18–19, 60; McAdams, 1996, pp. 25–26).

Second, narrative focuses upon *uniqueness* or **particularity**; each event and its context are thought to be special in some way and never able to be exactly repeated. This is true in part, because the temporal positioning of two events and their context can never be the same. The particularity of the event and the context influences the interpretation (Bruner, 1991; Ganzevoort, 1994). This way of thinking is somewhat different from the stage theory view of development, which emphasizes similarities of events between people rather than their particularity.

Third, narrative constructions of life are generally *complex*. Even within the narrative structure, people have different styles (e.g., in terms of richness or thinness of description) and tell the story at different levels of involvement (e.g., protagonist, narrator, or reader; Randall, 1995). A key feature of personal narratives is that they are **multivocal**, and there is typically not a single story or voice. Rather, there are multiple story lines and voices that may be incompatible or are in tension and dialogue with each other (de Certeau, 1984, p. 125; Hermans, 2001; Hermans & Josephs, 2003; Hermans et al., 1992; Toomela, 2003; cf. Bakhtin, 1981, p. 45). So while narrative helps to bring unity to events, it does not necessarily provide a neat and tidy framework, a single deep plot by which a narrative proceeds (Polkinghorne, 1988, pp. 78, 112).

Finally, narrative organization *presumes a space-time setting* or **chronotype** and a cultural background that provide organizing centers for the narrative. Some chronotypes are biographical in nature and depict people moving through a whole life course, while others have a structure that views life sequences in terms of concepts like beginning or guilt and redemption, providing a different feel to events (Bakhtin, 1981). This background also includes (1) assumptions about the culture, practices, and community within which the narrative takes place and (2) a personal ideology or **worldview** that has ideas about how the world works and how life should be lived (Bruner, 1991; MacIntyre, 1984, p. 220; de St. Aubin, 1999; Tomkins & Demos, 1995).

Life narratives involve memory for events and a winnowing process by which some things are selected and others left out. Thus they are based on facts but they are also constructions (McAdams, 1996; Crossley, 2000, p. 52). Research suggests that memory for autobiographical events is fairly good so that the process of constructing a narrative is more about selection and interpretation of events rather than distortion (McAdams, 2001). When combined into a narrative these events then help to direct and sustain action (Pillemer, 2001; Ganzevoort, 1994). These events include the following:

- *Originating events* that set a person on a particular life course
- *Anchoring events* that provide a cornerstone for ideology and belief
- *Transitional events* that direct the person and provide life lessons
- *Crisis or limit events* that cannot be understood within the context of the story and force a reappraisal and new understanding through inner and social dialogue

Populating the narrative are characters, representations of the person, and others in action. These characters are typically built around **imagoes** or idealized concepts of the self or other person (McAdams, 1996). Emotions are also interwoven into the narrative. They are important as they help engage us and add meanings and evaluative qualities to stories. They constitute a language within narrative, either connected to memories or directed to the future or values. These can be emotions related to a specific episode or extended in time, for example, life as bitter or sweet (Goldie, 2004; Ruth & Vilkko, 1996).

9.3.3.2 Development of Narrative

McAdams (1996, 2001) and other scholars believe that narrative abilities develop in a consistent fashion during various periods of life. While some authors trace the beginning of narrative to late preschool years (e.g., Polkinghorne, 1988, pp. 112, 160; Bluck & Habermas, 2001), McAdams argues it begins in early childhood around or before age 2 when autobiographical memory begins to emerge. This early period is a prenarrative one where others stimulate our memory, and we begin to develop our **narrative tone**—the general form of optimism or pessimism our stories will take. We begin to learn about the expected features of stories from imagery and examples in our culture or faith tradition, for instance, through hearing or reading children's stories. As childhood progresses, this cultural learning becomes more detailed, and we learn specific features of stories—patterns of goals and how they are pursued, as well as possible *master narratives* that can be used as examples of how life stories are constructed. These master narratives are critical in traditional societies as the basis for expected life narratives, while in postmodern societies people must construct their own patterns. In adolescence, these master narratives might become the basis of the first true **narrative identity**, as people acquire the beliefs and values necessary to construct an identity, and reflect upon important episodes in their life that can form materials for their own story (Fig. 9.2).

Research suggests that our narrative changes across the life span. Especially important is a time known as the memory or *reminiscence bump*—a period from about age 15 to 25, when most people have more memory for autobiographical events. At different times during the life span we tend to work on different aspects of story. After an emphasis on identity and thematic coherence in adolescence, early and middle adulthood narrative work tends to focus on our self-imagoes. In middle age, work begins anew on created coherence in life narratives, producing a generativity script that leads to new beginnings in our life story and the lives of others. Reflection on this narrative is thought to be particularly acute in later adulthood when we engage in **life review**, an integrative remembering that includes critical analysis of our life story and what we have done. With increasing age, these life reviews tend to become more positive, and while they are focused on the past, the life narratives of most individuals continue to have a forward-looking component (Pillemer, 2001; Staudinger, 2001; Bluck & Habermas, 2001).

Fig. 9.2. *Dan McAdams.*
One of the world's leading
personality psychologists,
McAdams has pioneered
the use of narrative as a
conceptual and research tool
for studying personality and
adult development. Photo
courtesy of Dan McAdams

9.3.3.3 Narrative, Religion, and Spiritual Autobiography

Narrative theory provides a way of approaching spiritual or religious thinking and development. Narrative techniques can help us understand our spiritual life, and narrative also offers a way of understanding and facilitating narrative change. Narrative is effective for a number of reasons:

1. Narrative deals with issues of unity, meaning and coherence, and prominent themes in religious and spiritual development. Its framework for conceptualizing the problems of authenticity and the failure of any single human narrative to encompass life are powerful ways of understanding religious and spiritual struggles (Irwin, 2002, pp. 87–133).
2. It allows us to conceptualize and understand the meaning of a spiritual or religious journey. MacIntyre (1984, p. 219) argues that it is the narrative quest for a *telos* or goal that brings unity to life. This goal need not be fully clear at the beginning of the journey, part of the quest may include the discovery of a worthy goal to pursue. However, this goal and the journey itself both have meaning and are revealed in narrative. Religions are rich with possible master narratives and visions for character and life goals that can help shape our own narratives

(Frank, 2004). Narrative also helps us understand the meaning of our life narratives, how we discover them and how they motivate action. In this framework, virtues and practices described by religious traditions are things that will sustain us in the quest described by our narrative.

3. Since narrative taps the experiential system rather than the rational system (Epstein, 1994), it is able to encompass the meaning aspect of the religious life, the subjective quality of spiritual or mystical experiences, and the postformal sense of paradox they bring with them.

4. Narrative does an excellent job of portraying relationality by showing how characters and their actions influence and affect each other. In older adults, the communal aspect of narrative promotes interdependence and self-worth in the face of suffering, a good alternative to late life dependency or isolated individualism (Ramsey & Blieszner, 1999, pp. 129–133). The dialogical interchange between figures in narrative is especially appropriate for religion, as in dialogues with God or other exchanges with religious significance (Bakhtin, 1981, p. 351).

Spiritual Autobiographies. One way that narrative can be helpful in the process of religious development is through the writing of a **spiritual autobiography**. This is an autobiographical document that traces the movement of spiritual and religious changes in a person's life so that they can understand more about their past and present situation, and gain ideas about future directions that might be followed. It may be particularly helpful for people in transitional times, helping them gain a sense of control or direction and thus increasing their spiritual well-being (Hateley, 1984).

A small but important literature exists on how to construct spiritual narratives and autobiographical accounts for use in personal reflection and growth (Peace 1998a, 1998b; Crossley, 2000; Progoff, 1980, 1992). These authors suggest that development of an autobiography proceeds in stages, and much of the work takes place prior to doing any writing. During an initial preparation period, the writer determines the purpose of the autobiography and who will be its intended readers. Examining examples of spiritual autobiographies or memoirs written by others (e.g., Augustine, 1992; Lewis, 1955) can provide helpful ideas. It is important to frame the project in such a way that it deals with important issues like self-honesty and past hurts but not to attempt a narrative that would be too large or emotionally overwhelming. Next comes a collection phase when the author gathers materials through prayer, reflection, and guided imagery. These materials should include (a) important experiences such as *originating events*, a point of call where God entered our life for the first time or in a new way, (b) special *experiences of presence* or empowerment—religious or mystical experiences, (c) *connecting experiences* that link us to others or tie together different aspects of our life, (d) *anchoring events* important for development of our ideology or beliefs, and (e) *crisis events*, disappointments, and disillusionments. The latter can include visions that we have about ourselves and our lives that seem partly true but do not fit comfortably. When collecting these materials it is important not to edit or exclude things that seem to be important, and it is also essential to focus on not just what happened but the meaning and emotion connected to the events and experiences.

Once the preparatory work is mostly complete, the author can begin to write the autobiography. While the document can be structured with separate sections for themes or important influences, it is usually organized temporally around a structuring timeline of at most a dozen or so life periods or phases. Each of these periods should have a unity and unique character. They are defined in part by **boundary events**—important experiences or changes in ways of looking at things that occurred at a particular time. The autobiography should describe each period in some detail. Things to be considered could include (a) experiences, crises, and growth outcomes; (b) key people, activities, creative involvements or ideas; (c) internal and external events, including physical health; and (d) tests or challenges for each period or transition. Also described should be turning points, steppingstones that move a person in a new direction and transitional or **hinge events**. While narrative typically focuses on choices made and their consequences, it can also be important to describe paths *not* taken, especially if strong emotions are connected to them. The journal can also include imaginative pieces such as dialogues with others or God, a summary testament and possible future scripts, as well as a final reflection on the process of writing the journal.

Spiritual Change Through Narrative. The advantage to the constructed nature of narrative is that as adults we can choose to rethink our personal narrative though self-reflection or collaboration with others (Irwin, 2002; Crossley, 2000, pp. 59–62). We can rewrite the self through an Augustinian process of recognizing that all is not well, distancing ourselves from the narrative to locate problems, articulating new possibilities, and then appropriating the changes through our actions. These new narratives may be less negative and self-defeating, helping us confront responsibilities and plan effectively. They can help us appreciate the good aspects of life and accept forgiveness (Freeman, 1993, pp. 44–45; Magee, 2001). Religious narratives can make use of new or altered religious symbols. It might also be possible to develop standards that would help us evaluate religious narratives and pinpoint areas for needed change. McAdams (1996) has proposed a number of categories for judgment—coherence, openness, credibility, differentiation, reconciliation, and generative integration.

Narrative theory highlights two problems that may be barriers to constructive change. First, it is possible for stories to be deceptive, where the story lacks congruence with the events and characters it contains. This often appears as inconsistencies in stories (Sarbin, 1986). Such narratives are problematic because in order to motivate action and produce transformation, stories must have credibility (de Certeau, 1984, pp. 148–149). Second, it is possible that a person may not make choices among stories (Polkinghorne, 1988, p. 154). In postmodern society, people may use multiple narratives in different situations and so have no true identity (Gergen, 1991), leading to the development of identity disorders. These problems are especially acute in narratives that contain much suffering or tragedy and are inherently difficult (Gabriel, 2004).

9.3.3.4 Critique

As we have seen, a narrative approach to religious and spiritual development has much potential. Its use is only beginning in research, primarily in qualitative studies. The use of narrative may help address gaps in the literature, including subtle but important differences in the meaning of religious terms and issues that are largely untreated or not easily conceptualized using reductionistic models. Some possible topics might include gender effects on spirituality, development of wisdom, issues of meaning, or understanding the communal and relational context of development (Blieszner & Ramsey, 2002; Levenson & Crumpler, 1996). On a practical level, narrative work can help people identify features of their spiritual life and directions for possible change. The study of positive narratives can help people find models for successful aging, providing inspiration and instilling hope (Ramsey & Blieszner, 1999, pp. 125–127).

A narrative approach also has limitations and potential problems. Human thought *can* be representational, working with images or descriptions, as well as stories, and this other kind of thinking also offers strengths when it comes to systematic tasks (Russell & Lucariello, 1992). Also, narrative like any single approach tends to concentrate more on certain aspects of human experience like the unity and coherence of the human life, at the expense of other things like the nature of the self who does the narrating (Loewenstein, 1991). The effects of culture on narrative are also relatively unknown. For example, does narrative mean the same thing in cultures that have cyclic views of time in contrast to our own linear perspective (Crossley, 2000, p. 54)? These are important questions that will need to be addressed, as narrative work becomes a more prominent model in the study of religious and spiritual development.

9.4 Religion and Spirituality in Older Adulthood

Psychologists refer to the period of life beginning in the mid-50s and following midlife as **older adulthood**. Two visions of this time of life can be found in Western culture. The traditional view found in Christianity, and shared by many other religious traditions, is that the later years can be a time of great accomplishment in religious life. In this view, aging is seen in a positive light (Lyon, 2004). In contrast to this, the modernist view that has been influential in psychology is that older adulthood is a time of "senescing" or downward development, a return to a kind of second infancy (e.g., Levinson, 1996, p. 21; Hall, 1905, p. vi). In contemporary Western societies, one of the goals of older adults is to not be older (!), to try to escape the physical and other changes that happen naturally during the aging process (Katz, 1995; Hummel, Rey, & d'Epinay, 1995).

Actually, there are positive and negative elements of older adulthood, and both have vital connections to spiritual and religious development. If spirituality represents a search for the sacred in connectedness and meaning, then older adulthood is clearly a prime time for spiritual development. Older adults must cope with a number of physical, emotional, relational, or existential losses and changes (Leder, 1996). These challenge the individual to maintain a sense of meaning and hope in the face of loss and potential or actual disability. They also call the person to maintain relationships rather than surrender to isolation (MacKinlay, 2001). In this view, successful aging might be thought of as maintaining meaningful life in the face of declines and challenges (Wong, 1998a). Spirituality involves a struggle to persevere, reframe worldviews to explain and cope with suffering, and maintain a sense of balance and self-reliance. Thus, there is a close connection between spirituality and the search for meaning in old age and the ability to be resilient in the face of life's challenges (Sorajjakool, 1998; Wagnild & Young, 1990; Langer, 2004). Exactly how these changes are viewed is strongly influenced by cultural attitudes toward aging and the body, which tend to be quite negative in Western cultures (Lyon, 2004).

Despite the obvious connections between spirituality, religion, and issues of older adulthood, research in the area is somewhat sparse, and a theoretical framework has been lacking (Payne, 1990). However, recent research has begun to identify the importance of religion and spirituality during this period of life. For instance, prayer and communal religious activities have been found to be a central practice and way of coping for older adults, particularly for US minority groups like African Americans (Armstrong & Crowther, 2002). High rates of religious participation and practice have also been found in older US Hispanics, particularly women, with over 3/4 engaging in prayer at least once a day and reporting that their religious faith was very helpful in dealing with life problems (Magee, 2001). In these groups, as well as in the current cohort of older adults in the US and other countries, religious practices and spirituality are strongly related (cf. Musick et al., 2000). In a recent qualitative study, older Lutheran women in the US and Germany reported that the emotional and relational support found in a religious community was an important part of their resiliency that helped them maintain a rich and meaningful life, while coping with issues of aging (Blieszner & Ramsey, 2002; Ramsey & Blieszner, 2000).

However, aging is more than coping; there are also potential gains to be claimed in older adulthood. These could include a freedom to relax defenses, reveal inner thoughts and redefine one's status, enabling us to establish positive dependencies and a new, generative creativity. The focus of life can shift from preoccupation with the future to living well in the present, finding a new assurance of order, meaning, and purpose (Pruyser, 1975; Erikson, Erikson, & Kivnick, 1986; McFadden, 1999). Older adulthood can also be a time to find new standards and perspectives by which to evaluate one's life. Some researchers have found that older adults often move away from narcissism to a more transcendent perspective in later life, with corresponding changes in attitudes and relationships. This includes a move away from a materialistic and pragmatic view of the world toward one that involves connectedness, appreciation of mystery, authenticity, and an emphasis on relationships. This change is accompanied by increases in life satisfaction, and some authors suggest that it is related to the development of postformal ways of thought (Bertman, 1999; Tornstam, 1997, 1999; Grams, 2001). Certainly older adulthood is not a time for declining religious interest; even when attendance declines due to health or other problems, religiousness and engagement in private devotional practices will generally continue (Sorajjakool, 1998).

One possible gain that can be claimed in older adulthood is accepting and making peace with the past. Religious ideas of forgiveness and practices of confession or Ignatian examen (see Sections 11.4.1 and 13.3.4) can assist in this process, as can techniques of spiritual life review that help us recall incidents from the past, confront our responsibility, and give or accept forgiveness (Lewis, 2001; Magee, 2001; Moberg, 2002b). Accepting the past does not mean resolving every troubling situation or trying to have no regrets by claiming we would do everything the same way—including our mistakes! Also, some situations are not resolvable, because others are involved and reconciliation cannot be achieved. However, we can relish happy memories and present painful ones to God. We "die" to our past in a potentially positive way, if we are able to say with our whole heart that we renounce our mistakes and would do things differently if we had the opportunity (Hughes, 1999; Anthony, 1999).

There are striking similarities and a few differences in how older adults of different religious traditions engage in spiritual pursuits. In a study with Moslem, Hindu, and Christian older adults in Singapore, Mehta (1997) found all groups made extensive use of spiritual practices such as prayer or meditation to deal with problems of aging. Moslem and Christian older adults engaged in a number of regular communal practices such as worship or prayer times. Hindus were less focused on issues of morality and conduct, while Moslems were more concerned about holding themselves as role models for a younger generation.

9.4.1 End of Life Issues

Older adults confront death and dying in a couple of ways. First, if one is privileged to live into old age, one will witness the disability and death of many family members and friends. Married women will most likely experience the death of their spouse. Second, one must eventually confront and experience one's own mortality. Religion and spirituality enter into both these situations.

Many studies have associated religiosity with a positive role in coping with the disability and death of others. For instance, qualitative studies with caregivers of family members suffering from Alzheimer's disease have found that Christian beliefs, religious practices like prayer, and social support were all helpful in dealing with the demands of caring for an increasingly disabled loved one. Caregivers reported three helpful aspects of their faith: (1) *beliefs* (e.g., the idea that God has a plan and things happen for reason) that helped construct a framework bringing meaning and purpose to the situation; (2) *ethical injunctions*, such as the call to do good and values like a positive outlook; and (3) *optimism*, making the most of situations. These caregivers did not find the distinction between religion and spirituality to be meaningful (Stuckey 2003, 2001).

Bereavement or the loss of a loved one through death is a major event related to negative physical and psychological changes. However, most people find that religious beliefs and support, as well as rituals like funerals offer considerable help. These do not always provide help with immediate coping or buffer the person from the pain of the loss, but they are strongly associated with better long-term outcomes. Research in both the US and UK suggests that religious beliefs are associated with better resolution after bereavement and a lower incidence of delayed or complicated grief, including depression or other psychological problems. These latter difficulties are connected with a view of death as a meaningless event and high levels of attempted self-reliance. There is also a greater possibility of positive spiritual changes as the person works to resolve feelings of loss and find new roles in life. Religious beliefs and practices are thought to be associated with positive outcomes and process in bereavement because (1) these beliefs help support feelings of comfort and guidance as well as a sense of both personal and divine control; (2) afterlife beliefs make death a meaningful event, reducing questioning or blaming of God which is associated with less well-being; and (3) religion increases social support which reinforces positive beliefs. There is an especially strong correlation between hope produced by religious faith and grief resolution. Some research has also indicated that roughly half of bereaved individuals report some kind of positive and reassuring continuing contact with the deceased person (Frantz, Trolley, & Johil, 1996; Walsh, King, Jones, Tookman, & Blizard, 2002; Balk, 1999; Wuthnow, Christiano, & Kuzlowski, 1980; Spilka & Bridges, 1989; Herth, 1990; Golsworthy & Coyle, 1999).

The evidence is more mixed regarding the positive effects of religious belief on fears about one's own mortality. The approach of death intensifies the process of separation and loss which is a prominent feature of older adulthood, but religious traditions have beliefs about life after death that look beyond these losses (Barbre, 2004). In general, belief in eternal life is correlated with higher levels of well-being. Spiritually mature individuals have more confidence and positive attitudes toward death, and individuals higher in intrinsic religious motivation have lower levels of death anxiety (Ellison, Boardman, Williams, & Jackson, 2001; Thomas, 1994; Thorson & Powell, 2000). However, Dillon and Wink (2007, p. 199) found in their developmental studies that the lowest levels of death anxiety were found in both the very religious and nonreligious members of their sample, with the highest levels of anxiety in the middle religiousness group.

9.4.2 Religious Perspectives on Older Adulthood and Aging

Although there is a diversity of opinion within and between religious traditions on issues of aging (Firth, 1999), in general they have tended to view later life as offering the possibility of great spiritual accomplishments and wisdom. The Hindu view of older adulthood has been briefly discussed previously (see Section 7.2.2); here we look at a Christian perspective on the topic.

Contemporary Christian views of spirituality and aging are formulated in opposition to modernist attitudes toward older adulthood. In the view of religious writers and critics, societal attitudes in the West toward aging are based on three presuppositions:

1. *Aging is a problem.* Since late 19th century, and the increasing dominance of positivist and modernist attitudes, aging has been seen as a process of decline with decreasing potential for growth. In this view, aging represents a failure in biological material processes leading to decay, dependency, and death (Stoneking, 2003; Shuman, 2003; Hauerwas & Yordy, 2003; Leder, 1996).
2. This problem is especially acute because *the worth of persons is dependent upon qualities or capabilities of the individual that are affected by the aging process,* such as our cognitive skills and our ability to produce or consume. For instance, in his early work, Engelhardt (1986) argued that personhood is defined by our ability to be rational, free, and self-conscious moral agents so that humans with impaired cognitive ability or limited ability to act freely are not really persons, as in the case of those with dementia (McNamara, 2002; Jones & Jones, 2003).
3. Since aging is a set of physical and medical problems, *the "problem" of aging can be solved through technology.* In this view, modern experts familiar with scientific knowledge and technology know more about all aspects of aging than ordinary people or our predecessors, who often follow traditional practices and beliefs that are mistaken (Stoneking, 2003). We should follow the lead of technical experts who can develop solutions for the medical problem of aging using scientific techniques of explanation, control and management (McNamara, 2002; Heckhausen, Dixon, & Baltes, 1989). In this view, images and attitudes about aging and its meaning are separated from the "facts" of the aging process and the technology used to solve its problems, so the answers to the problems of aging may be developed independently of questions of meaning or value.

Contemporary Christian writers have attempted to offer a corrective response to this position. While valuing many of the contributions of modern science and medicine, they also argue the following:

1. *Aging is good, although the suffering connected with aging should be opposed.* Christian thinkers generally see aging as a separate issue from things connected with older adulthood like suffering and death. Life is thought to be a gift of God and of fundamental value, and continued life allows for continued opportunities for growth and service. However, longevity for its own sake is not necessarily the highest good, a short life can be well lived, while a long one can be senseless or even toxic (McNamara, 2002; Hays & Hays, 2003).

Suffering can sometimes be connected with aging and is to be opposed (Aers, 2003; Buddhaghosa, 1999, p. 508). However, contrary to the hedonistic perspective (cf. Section 11.1.2), aging in the presence of suffering can continue to be meaningful. Spiritually mature people with poor health often report high levels of life satisfaction and transcendence over suffering, and common problems can lead to hope, intimacy, and growth. It is loss of meaning and hope in the face of suffering that leads to depression, isolation, and loss of freedom. One of the key functions of religious traditions is to nurture that hope (MacKinlay, 2001, 2002; McNamara, 2002; Thomas, 1991; Stoneking, 2003; Meador & Henson, 2003).

2. *Our worth is not reduced by the aging process or problems related to old age.* In the Christian view, human persons are essentially relational creatures and find their meaning in relation to others and to God. These connections are the essence of Christian spirituality, and they do not vanish with aging or disability (Jernigan, 2001). The limitation in community participation due to old age and poor health is a significant issue (Maldonado, 1994), but even those with reduced participation or serious cognitive impairments such as found in Alzheimer's disease remain and can feel part of the community; they can respond to visits or participate in rituals and other community events. If community is thought of from a narrative perspective as a group of people who make a common story together, even very impaired individual can participate in storytelling or just be part of the story (MacKinlay, 2001, 2002; Firth, 1999; Jeeves, 1997, p. 67; Idler, Kasl, & Hays, 2001).

3. *Technological answers cannot solve all of the "problems" related to aging and in fact they can create new difficulties.* While medical technology can certainly prolong life, and in many cases improve its quality, some problems cannot be solved in this way. In fact, because technology has trouble dealing with issues of meaning, it can miss the distinction between caring for the body and just trying to perpetuate it with machines and technology, leading to various well-known ethical conundrums and sometimes making the situation worse rather than better. These kinds of situations illustrate the impossibility of completely separating facts from values and issues of meaning (Hendricks, 1986, p. 127).

In aging, one must identify what cannot be lost (our status as a human person), mourn but not be overly concerned about what must be accepted (our mortality or limitations and the suffering that goes with them), and find realistic possibilities. This is a difficult transition; we cannot bring back the past and try to do things we are no longer able to do. Instead, facing our limitations and accepting help improves our quality of life and can actually help us maintain our functioning and independence. This is a contemplative stance to the problem of dependency that allows us to surrender control to others as needed and receive graciously what we get from them (Cloutier, 2003; Jernigan, 2001; Anthony, 1999; Hendricks, 1986, pp. 129–135; McNamara, 2002; cf. Section 11.3.1). Modern society with its value of autonomous individualism resists this approach out of concern about being a burden to others. However, all of us are dependent on others throughout our lives and will be burdens on many occasions (Shuman & Meador, 2003, p. 132). Finitude before God means that we can yield to this reality and be guided by it without loss of dignity (Lash, 1996, p. 243).

Christian thinkers typically see community as providing a necessary aspect of care that cannot be done by technology. In the Christian conception, community is important because it provides (1) a context for care of spiritual and physical needs

(Aers, 2003); (2) ideals and practices that treat aging in a positive manner, allowing people to care and be cared for (Shuman, 2003); (3) a context for cross-generational friendships that enrich life (Hauerwas & Yordy, 2003); and (4) a role for the elderly in maintaining memory, which is essential for community life and identity, both communal and personal (Lysaught, 2003).

9.5 Conclusion

Key issue: *Traditional psychological views of development based on positivist and reductive naturalist assumptions may be inadequate to understand some aspects of adult spiritual development. Religious and narrative perspectives may offer correctives to this problem.*

The psychology and religion dialogue on adult spiritual and religious development is still in its infancy. Conversations to date highlight differences in opinion about the goals, trajectory, and diversity of spiritual or religious development. However, several broad conclusions can be drawn from the literature:

1. While it may be possible to speak of an ideal goal of development, it is certainly not the case that everyone ends up in the same place. Some people end their lives with profound spirituality, while others ignore or are openly hostile to such development.
2. Given the vast differences in end points of religious and spiritual development, it seems likely that different individuals may have quite different developmental trajectories. This is particularly true of development during adulthood. While these pathways may often be influenced by common factors like attachment or religious motivation, it is quite likely that these factors operate in different ways or configurations, and that individuals may also have unique influences that are important. A corollary to this is that naturalistic models emphasizing hard-and-fast laws of development will fail to capture essential features of spiritual and religious journeys (cf. Vergote, 1969, pp. 22, 285).
3. Given the observed diversity in developmental outcomes and paths, models that allow for flexibility and diversity are worthy of special consideration as ways of understanding development. Thus, while traditional approaches that try to identify common mechanisms and processes will continue to be important, newer approaches like narrative offer an important corrective that helps us appreciate the rich variety of religious and spiritual life.

Spiritual and religious processes of development are an important part of the human experience. They also can have important effects on the physical and mental health of the individual, topics to which we now turn.

Part IV
Applications

Chapter 10
Religion, Spirituality, and Physical Health

All major religious traditions have a long-standing interest in working to promote health and to cure physical, mental, or spiritual illnesses. More recently, psychology has also become a major provider of health care services, and psychologists have taken on healing roles previously reserved for doctors or religious professionals. This joint interest offers many possibilities for dialogue between psychology and religion about issues related to health and healing. In this chapter, we look primarily at issues related to physical health; in the next chapter, we will consider mental health.

10.1 Scientific Approaches to Religion and Health

Although religious individuals have generally seen their traditions as promoting health, psychologists beginning with Freud have frequently challenged this association, claiming instead that religion is associated with pathology. Much of the dialogue between psychology and religion during the 20th century revolved around this issue. One of the largest shifts in that dialogue has been mounting scientific evidence that religion does indeed promote health, challenging long held antireligious views in the psychological community.

10.1.1 Definitions of Health

Health can be defined in one of two ways. In the modernist view that is current in Western societies (see Section 6.3), health is generally defined as an absence of illness or disease and is thought of as an ultimate human good. Illness is thought of as something that invades the body of an individual from the outside and disrupts its complex mechanical functioning. Modern medical care is defined according to the **allopathic principle** of countering this outside force through chemical and mechanical intervention. Specialist experts are considered essential to the task of countering disease and maintaining normal functioning. This is sometimes referred to as the **medical model** of health. This view of health and the human person can

J.M. Nelson, *Psychology, Religion, and Spirituality,*
DOI 10.1007/978-0-387-87573-6_10, @ Springer Science+Business Media, LLC 2009

be extended to many areas of life by seeing various legal, social, and religious problems as illnesses to be counteracted by specialists. This is sometimes referred to as the **medicalization of culture** (Kinsley, 1995, pp. 9–11, 170–178).

In the medical model, disease can be said to progress in two phases—(1) a prepathogenic phase in which characteristics of the person, environment, and specific problem interact to determine risk; and (2) pathogenesis, when actual problems and symptoms develop. Health care measures in the prepathogenic phase involve **primary prevention** to reduce the risk of developing a disease. After pathogenesis, the choices are **secondary treatment** on an outpatient basis or **tertiary treatment** in a hospital. During the prepathogenic phase, there may be **protective factors** that either slow disease or move the person toward health. These are also sometimes known as *salutatory* or *salutogenic factors.* Researchers often see spirituality and religion as general protective factors rather than as treatments for specific illnesses (Levin, 1996, 2003).

The traditional medical model also tends to distinguish between physical health and mental health, depending on whether the symptoms of disease are primarily "physical" or "mental" in nature. This distinction reflects a dualistic understanding of mind and body as somehow separate, a belief which many historians trace to the early modern philosophy of Rene Descartes (1596–1650). This dualism is rejected in most contemporary thought, and there is substantial research indicating that physical and mental health have strong connections with each other (e.g., Merrill & Salazar, 2002).

A broader definition of health that goes beyond the medical model sees wellness as more than an absence of illness. Along with avoidance of disease, health can be thought of as including positive qualities like meaningfulness of life, active engagement, and productivity. In this view, illness is more than a disruption of mechanical processes; it also can interfere with our relationships and raise questions of meaning; as such, health and illness have an essential spiritual component (Rowe & Kahn, 1997; Kinsley, 1995, p. 152). This is a more **holistic model** of health that (1) focuses on the interrelationship and interconnectedness of many factors rather than a piecemeal approach to health and (2) focuses on health as more than the absence of illness but the global status of many aspects of our life.

Most research exploring the connections between religion and health has been conducted from the perspective of the medical model. This research has suffered from a number of methodological problems, including (1) simplistic or inconsistent definitions of health and religion that leave out important aspects of spiritual experience and religious life; (2) problems in research design, sampling, and measurement such as a lack of longitudinal studies following the course of health and illness over time; and (3) a lack of good theoretical models that include important variables such as coping and personality (Rew & Wong, 2006; Chatters, 2000; Kier & Davenport, 2004; Dein & Stygall, 1997; George, Ellison, & Larson, 2002). Some critics also argue that research has been hindered by the stereotypes, prejudices, misconceptions, and personal antagonism toward religion of some investigators, leading to continuing skepticism among researchers and practitioners (Thoresen, 1999; Chatters, 2000). Nevertheless, over the past 10–15 years, increasingly sophisticated research has been published in first rank journals (Koenig, Hays et al., 1999), and while it is possible to find flaws in individual studies, the volume and consistency of the findings is very impressive. These results have challenged negative stereotypes toward religion and suggest that it does indeed have positive effects on health and illness (Miller & Thoresen, 2003).

10.1.2   Effects of Religion on Health and Illness

Over a century of research on the connections between religion, spirituality, and health has found a moderate association between religious involvement and better health status. This positive effect is found at both the individual and group levels, even when many possible confounding variables are controlled. Quite a bit of research suggests that this association is causal, that is, religious involvement appears to protect individuals against disease and promote health (Ellison & Levin 1998; Thoresen, Harris, & Oman, 2001; Chatters, 2000; Levin, 1994; Levin & Chatters, 1998). Only a few investigators now claim there is no relation between religion and health (e.g., Sloan & Bagiella, 2002), but their work has been criticized for selectively ignoring important studies and minimizing strong overall patterns (Koenig, Hays et al., 1999).

Mortality rates. Persuasive and consistent evidence from methodologically sophisticated cross-sectional and longitudinal studies indicates that frequent church attendance and, perhaps, some other factors like subjective religiosity are associated with a longer life span. Frequent attendance is associated with reductions in mortality rates of 25% and increases in life span of up to 7 years. This means that the gains from frequent religious participation are roughly equivalent to the health benefits of not smoking. The effects appear to be even stronger for some groups like African Americans and perhaps women (Levin, Chatters, & Taylor, 2005; Ellison & Levin, 1998; Hummer, Rogers, Nan, & Ellison, 1999; Koenig, Hays et al., 1999; McCullough, 2001b; McCullough, Hoyt, Larson, Koenig, & Thoresen, 2000; Koenig, 2001b). The biggest differences in mortality rates have been found for those who are (1) generally physically healthy, (2) highly religious, (3) frequently attend religious functions, and (4) indicate they are both religious and spiritual compared to only spiritual or religious (e.g., Mueller, Plevak, & Rummans, 2001; Shahabi et al., 2002). Differences persist even when possible salutary factors due to religion are taken into account. Effects are generally smaller in studies that focus on death from particular causes like cancer (Strawbridge, Cohen, Shema, & Kaplan, 1997). In more secular European environments among older religious individuals, even modest levels of religious affiliation and attendance are related to better survival rates, although effect sizes are smaller than in the more religious environment of the US. Interestingly, variables related to health seem to differ between religious and secular samples. For instance, the giving or receiving of help and the presence of bigger, more active social networks have a stronger connection to health among the more religious (la Cour, Avlund, & Schultz-Larsen, 2006).

Specific illnesses. Religious involvement is also associated with lower rates of some specific illnesses like depression, as well as some other severe chronic problems. This is particularly true among African Americans (Koenig, 1995; Krause, 2002; Levin et al., 2005; Steffen, Hinderliter, Blumenthal, & Sherwood, 2001). There is considerable evidence that religion or spirituality protects against cardiovascular disease, perhaps by reducing blood pressure and hypertension (Seeman, Dubin, & Seeman, 2003; Levin & Vanderpool, 1989). When cardiac surgery is necessary, some studies suggest that people with higher religiosity have fewer complications and shorter hospital stays, and that those who felt a great deal of comfort and strength from religion also had lower death rates (6 vs. 16%; Contrada et al., 2004; Oxman, Freeman, & Manheimer, 1995). In hospitalized men, Koenig, Cohen, Blazer, Pieper et al. (1992) found religious coping related to less depression. However, the relationship between religion and specific problems is complex, so results are not always consistent. For instance, more private religious practice is associated with slightly greater hypertension, and more attendance is associated with longer postoperative stays in people with weaker beliefs, perhaps due to religious struggle (Krause et al., 2002; Levin & Markides, 1985).

There are also some indications that religious involvement has positive effects on a wide range of other health problems. In more religious older adults, research has found higher levels of general self-rated health status, as well as better outcomes with regard to stroke, pulmonary or GI problems, and cognitive decline (Maselko, Kubzansky, Kawachi, Staudenmayer, & Berkman, 2006; Van Ness & Kasl, 2003). Intrinsic religiosity is associated with shorter recovery times in medically ill older patients, and spiritual well-being is associated with better self-reported health status among geriatric outpatients (Koenig, George, & Peterson, 1998; Daaleman, Perera, & Studenski, 2004). Religious attendance appears to be connected with long-term improvements in disability and coping with chronic pain among medically ill elderly in terms of self-rated reports of health, finding sources of strength or comfort and discovering meaning in suffering (Idler, 1995; Idler & Kasl, 1997a, 1997b; Cohen & Pressman, 2006; Kirby, Coleman, & Daley, 2004). Attendance is not associated with better mortality or disease progression in cancer patients, although there is some evidence that being prayed for improves recovery from acute illness (Powell, Shahabi, & Thoresen, 2003; Ellison & Levin, 1998; Koenig, 2001b).

Prayer and health. Trying to prove or disprove that prayer "works" or is "ineffective" has been an irresistible topic to some researchers. One of the earliest studies of this type was conducted in the 1870s by Galton (2001). He concluded that prayer does not work, because British royalty who are the target of prayers for long life in fact do not live longer than others. Like many other studies on prayer, Galton's work had many methodological problems and was dismissed by no less an authority than the great statistician Karl Pearson (Finney & Malony, 1985; Wulff, 1997, p. 207). Since then, research has tended to support the overall helpfulness of prayer, but findings are very inconsistent and relationships are weak (Francis & Evans, 2001a; Dossey, 1997). Often cited as demonstrating the efficacy of prayer is a study by Byrd who found a small but significant improvement in ratings of hospital treatment course and adverse outcomes in coronary CCU patients, who were given intercessory prayer (e.g., Byrd, 2001; Harris et al., 2001), but this has not been consistently supported by other research. Other studies have found that prayer helps decrease depression and distress after coronary bypass surgery (Ai, Dunkle, Peterson, & Bowlling, 1998). However, the methodologies of these studies suffer from many problems. While the theoretical model of prayer used by these studies is seldom made explicit, most seem to view prayer as a mechanical process that is expected to produce effects upon demand, regardless of the religious status of the recipient or the degree of skepticism of the investigator and participants. This is a magical view of prayer that is generally not held within Christianity; the attitude of both parties and gifts of the person doing the praying are thought to be vital components in the process. Most studies also have a limited theoretical rationale and focus on curing disease, not promoting optimum health or protection from illness (Levin, 1996, 2001, p. 102; Dossey, 1997; cf. Miller, 2001; Francis & Evans, 2001a; see Section 13.4.3).

10.1.2.1   Models and Mechanisms of Action

In general, religion appears to convey health benefits by providing a buffering or protective effect against adversity. Longitudinal studies have found that while the religious well and ill differ little in life satisfaction or depression, the nonreligious ill have much lower levels of life satisfaction and higher levels of depression. Religion thus appears to act as a preexisting resource drawn upon in time of need to help provide meaning, patience, a sense of God's closeness and protection, and/ or a belief that all events are part of a plan. Spiritual seeking does not appear to have these effects, although it does help to maintain a sense of control (Dillon & Wink, 2007, pp. 138, 186–193; Wink, 2003; Dillon & Wink, 2003). The **buffering model** predicts that religion will become more helpful as stress increases and that stressors have less impact on active participants. It also implies that while religion may help in coping with significant trauma, it does not necessarily help with daily hassles. Prayer especially fits this stress buffer model, as studies indicate that it increases in frequency with distress or pain and assists with coping so that increased prayer is sometimes associated with poorer physical health but better mental health and well-being (Ellison, 1991; Plante, Saucedo, & Rice, 2001; Ellison, Boardman, Williams, & Jackson, 2001; Argyle, 1999; McCullough, 1995; Meisenhelder & Chandler, 2000).

   Three more specific models have been proposed to explain the relationship between religion and health: the moderator, suppressor, and counterbalancing or distress-deterrent models (Krause & Tran, 1989; Chatters, 2000; see Table 10.1). The **distress-deterrent model** is a kind of **mediating model**, arguing that the effects of religion on health happen indirectly through an in-between variable. For instance, religious activity may enhance coping skills that act to deter distress or improve health. The moderator and suppressor models both hold that religious involvement has a direct positive effect on health, but they differ from each other in

Table 10.1 Models of how religion buffers effects of stress on health

Model	Religious practice	Protective effect	Mechanism
Moderator	Constant across all levels of stress	Greatest in high stress situations or with more involvement	Direct effect reduces stress or negative effects
Suppressor	Greater with increased stress	Greater with more involvement	Direct effect reduces stress or negative effects
Mediating/dis tress-deterrent	Constant across all levels of stress	Greater with more involvement	Indirect effect enhances coping which reduces stress or negative effects

their view of how this process may work. In the **moderator model**, religion has a greater impact when stress levels are high, although stress does not affect the actual level of religious practice. In the **suppressor model**, increases in problems lead to greater levels of practice that suppress the effects of stress. There is considerable evidence supporting the moderator model, as religion does appear to provide a cushion against negative events, reducing depression and physical problems. Some research with older adults is also consistent with the suppressor model, while the distress-deterrent model probably has the least support (Pargament, 1997, p. 306; Levin & Chatters, 1998).

Current research about religion and health is focused on trying to identify specific mechanisms by which religion exercises its buffering effects. The exact nature of these mechanisms is unclear, perhaps because spirituality and religion are very complex, although it is clear that religion is somewhat unique both in the combination of things that it offers and the way they interact (Thoresen et al., 2001).

One of the most important mechanisms that enable the buffering effects of religion is the provision of positive relationality and social support. This relational support is of three types. First, it includes direct effects like social resources, social integration or harmony, and support from a sense of caring in community. This is gained from interpersonal exchanges but also through participation in practices such as group worship and prayer. Second, there are also indirect social effects such as greater marital stability and changing the way we respond to social influences. Both of these are examples of horizontal support on the level of human relationships. A third type of support is vertical or **spiritual support**, the sense that God is friendly and available to help (Pargament, 1997, p. 210; Maton, 1989). All three types are especially important in the process of coping with and finding meaning in loss, and are more likely to be experienced in cohesive religious communities (McIntosh, Silver, & Wortman, 1993; Mackenzie, Rajagopal, Meilbohm, & Lavizzo-Mourey, 2000).

There is consistent evidence that many people see religion as a source of support, and that they resist giving up this strong social network even in the face of serious medical problems that might limit participation. These social influences are related to health and life expectancy; in fact, some studies have found that when social support is separated from attendance, there is no longer a connection between attendance and health indicators like mortality or depression. Recent research indicates that church-based social support has independent effects different from secular social support, although the nature of these differences is still unclear (Nooney & Woodrum, 2002). Social support appears to reduce the sense of threat in difficult situations, and it promotes positive psychological states that have desirable physiological effects, perhaps affecting immune performance. Giving support to others also appears to have positive health benefits for the giver as well as the recipient. Of course, negative interactions or social isolation related to religion can have the opposite effect. However, it is not clear whether the health benefits connected with religious practice will have the same benefits if divorced from their supportive, communal context (Krause, 2002, 2006; Masten & Reed, 2002; Strawbridge et al., 1997; Cohen & Lemay, 2007; Dein & Stygall, 1997; Benjamins, Musick, Gold, & George, 2003; Cohen, 2004).

Researchers have proposed several other types of mechanisms to explain how religion has a salutary effect on health (Pargament, 2002a; Ellison & Levin, 1998; Levin et al., 2005; McFadden & Levin, 1996; Idler et al., 2003). They include the following:

1. *Promoting a healthy lifestyle* and discouraging destructive habits like smoking or excessive alcohol consumption, as well as encouraging compliance and participation in health care services and preventive practices (Peltzer, 2004; Koenig, Hays et al., 1999; Aaron, Levine, & Burstin, 2003).

2. *Supporting positive beliefs* such as (a) positive perceptions of self or others; (b) a healthy worldview leading to optimism, hope, and reduction of uncertainty; (c) positive ideas about God; or (d) specific beliefs and explanations such as ideas about a good afterlife. Some research suggests that the *content* of specific beliefs that provide comfort or existential security and help the person cope with suffering is more important than the *coherence and structure* of beliefs (Krause et al., 2002; Chatters, 2000; Musick, Traphagan, Koenig, & Larson, 2000; Schwab & Petersen, 1990).

3. *Providing religious resources and skills for coping*, such as prayer or devotional reading. The use of these coping skills is a powerful predictor of recovery and survival once one is ill.

4. *Regulating emotions* to generate emotional stability or produce positive feelings, such as positive affect during ritual or prayer. This may be facilitated by relational attachments (Watts, 2007; McFadden & Levin, 1996).

5. *Encouraging transcendent religious experiences or religious practices* such as prayer, meditation, and service that have positive effects (Kennedy & Drebing, 2002; Krause & Tran, 1989; Levin & Chatters, 1998; Koenig, 2001b; McCullough, Pargament, & Thoresen, 2000; Kim et al., 2005). While public participation appears to be the most important factor in the religion and health or mental health connection, private religious practices like prayer also predict health status even after controlling for public religiosity (George et al., 2002;

Levin, 2001, p. 76). Christian older adults who report stories of physical healing often indicate that faith, prayer practices, and Bible reading were important in addition to participation in worship (Arcury, Quandt, McDonald, & Bell, 2000). The possibility of healing activity outside of normal lawlike natural regularities might also be considered (Levin, 2003; 2001, pp. 139–140).

Many researchers assume that religion ultimately has its effects on health through biological pathways. For instance, Levin (2003, 2001, pp. 71–72) uses a 3-stage model where (1) religious commitment and identification promotes (2) healthy behaviors, social support practices, and beliefs, which then lead to (3) positive emotion and associated physiological effects. Explicit models linking social and biological factors are lacking (McCullough, 1995; Levin, 1996), although it is clear that these links exist. Physical changes from higher levels of attendance and religious commitment appear to include better lipid profiles and immune functioning. Although there are few studies with Christian devotional practices, research involving religious practices from other traditions such as Zen or yoga has found connections with less oxidative stress and hormone reactivity, as well as lower cholesterol and blood pressure. More of this work on biological factors remains to be done in Christian settings (Kiecolt-Glaser & Glaser, 1995; Seeman et al., 2003; Kim et al., 2005).

10.1.3 Critique

Scholars who evaluate the research on religion and health caution against over-interpreting or under interpreting its findings. Just because religion is beneficial, it cannot be concluded that everyone will benefit from it. Its effects also appear to be limited. Research shows that its greater effect is to help prevent disease rather than heal, although it is possible that things like prayer might also have healing functions in certain specific situations. It is also the case that factors outside of religious participation such as genetics have an even bigger role in health. However, we do not want to under interpret findings either. Just because it is possible to isolate specific factors like social support does not mean that this disproves a connection between religion and health—just that the relation is sometimes indirect. It is religious practice that sets social support in motion and is thus the ultimate cause of the beneficial effects (Levin, 1996; Thoresen et al., 2001; Watts, 2001).

Critics of the importance of religious involvement on health can point out a number of negatives. Religious practices are demanding and might sometimes promote problems like negative religious coping or low self-esteem. Since religion requires involvement in a community, it subjects a person to anything in that environment that could be problematic. This might include things like extreme criticism, negative views of human nature and self, withdrawal of community support, and interpersonal or group conflicts, annoyances, and threats. One prominent area of concern among health professionals is that religion might discourage people from seeking appropriate medical treatment, either because of advice from a religious professional, personal beliefs, or reliance on religious means of healing. This is especially true of religious groups like Christian Scientists or Jehovah's Witnesses that object to dependence on some or all modern medical procedures. Surveys suggest that the prevalence of this type of problem is very low (Trier & Shupe, 1991), but cases like this are troubling to health professionals and may be a significant factor in harming the already poor relations between religious organizations or professionals and their medical counterparts (Ellison & Levin, 1998; Chatters, 2000; George et al., 2002; Koenig, McCullough, & Larson, 2001).

10.2 Religion, Health, and Coping

Much of the research we have reviewed implies that religion provides resources for coping with difficult situations, and that these resources have either direct or indirect effects on health. How does religion affect coping? Considerable research has been devoted to the question, and the results are one of the most interesting areas of empirical work on the psychology and religion connection. In general, scholars believe that there are several coping styles that are related to religion and that these have different kinds of effects on health. Schaefer and Gorsuch (1991) argue that problem-solving or coping style is one of the three fundamental domains of religion, along with motivation and belief, and that coping style is the mediating link between belief and its positive (or negative) effects on health and adjustment. Recent research has proposed that religious coping is one of the mechanisms most influential in mental health outcomes (Nooney & Woodrum, 2002), and there is evidence it can affect physical health status as well.

10.2.1 Psychological Views of Coping

When confronted with threats to health, people respond with **coping behavior** "ongoing cognitive and behavioral efforts to manage specific external and/or internal demands that are appraised as taxing or exceeding the resources of the person" (Lazarus, 1993, p. 237). Coping is triggered as a result of **cognitive appraisals** or judgments that what we are confronting is stressful, representing (1) a threat of harm or loss, (2) a challenge with possibility of growth, or (3) something beneficial (Folkman & Lazarus, 1985; Bjorck, 2007). This appraisal is dependent on a number of cognitive factors, including beliefs about ourselves and the world, as well as the meaning and value we attach to events and people. Thus, coping involves our understanding of an event, something that can be facilitated or hindered by religious beliefs and practices. Our coping response impacts the effects of a situation on both our physical and mental health (Kreitler & Kreitler, 1991; Heilman & Witztum, 2000).

Coping with change or crisis is an ongoing process, not a single event, and there are many factors that contribute to positive outcomes. These factors include

(1) things related to the nature of the crisis event such as severity, controllability, or expectedness; (2) personal factors such as social class, prior crisis experience, or temperamental factors like optimism; (3) environmental factors such as social support or the post-crisis environment; and (4) cognitive appraisal of the situation and our personal ability to deal with it. As these factors change, the type of coping needed and the possibilities for growth will also change. Outcomes of successful coping might include increased social resources such as deeper relationships, or greater personal resources and coping skills. Changes in the way we look at the world, the stories we tell about our lives, and an enhanced appreciation of paradox are also common positive outcomes (Schaefer & Moos, 1992; Lazarus, 1993; Tedeschi & Calhoon, 1995; Emmons, 1999, p. 142).

There are several types of coping. In **emotion-focused coping** the individual focuses on managing distressing emotions by changing attention to the problem or the meaning of what is happening. Examples of this include wishful thinking, distancing, self-blame, and tension reduction. This is different than **problem-focused coping**, which involves trying to change what is causing the distress by acting on the environment or self, such as by analyzing the problem and making a plan of action. People generally use both problem and emotion-focused coping and sometimes mix them together. Western culture tends to value problem-focused coping, although in uncontrollable situations it may be less helpful than emotion-focused coping (Folkman & Lazarus, 1985; Lazarus, 1993). A third type of coping is **religious coping**, the use of religious beliefs or practices to respond to a perceived stress, threat, or loss. In US studies, religious coping is found in 80% of the population, particularly those who (1) practice and identify with a religion, especially those for whom religion is very important and intrinsically motivated, (2) have higher levels of education, and (3) those with chronic conditions such as depression (Ferraro & Kelley-Moore 2000, 2001; Schaefer & Gorsuch, 1991, 1992; Pargament, 1997, p. 143; Bjorck & Cohen, 1993). Among children, spiritual or religious coping is found more in those who are affiliated with a specific religious tradition (Shelton & Mabe, 2006).

10.2.2 Pargament's Theory of Religion and Coping

The most influential theory of religion and coping is that of Pargament (1997). For Pargament, coping is the "continually changing process through which individuals try to understand and deal with significant personal or situational demands in their lives" (1990, p. 198). This definition assumes that people are active agents who seek to cognitively construct the significance of events and things of value through appraisal of their meaning, as well as hold on to a sense of value and meaning in life during times of transitions when demands may exceed capabilities. It also assumes that individuals have some kind of coherent orienting system that provides a way of looking at the world and dealing with concrete situations (Fig. 10.1).

Fig. 10.1 *Kenneth Pargament.* A central figure in psychology of religion research, he is probably best known for his fundamental theoretical and empirical work in the area of religious coping. Photo courtesy of Ken Pargament

When and how does coping involve religion? Pargament views religion as a particular way that people search for meaning: It is the process of "*a search for significance in ways related to the sacred*" (1997, p. 32). Among other things, it is a process that can allow people to deal with life's difficulties (Pargament, Poloma, & Tarakeshwar, 2001). Religious individuals who are theists typically believe that life has a purpose or ultimate goal that is transcendental in nature, lying beyond the realm of science, and that there is a God who is benevolent and active in the world. These beliefs form the basis of a religious orienting system that is very resistant to the effects of trauma and serves as a resource in dealing with difficult situations. **Religious coping** happens when events, our goals, and the means we use to reach them are actively interpreted in relation to the sacred, and this enhances our sense of meaning, control, comfort, intimacy, or support. Religion thus has a functional aspect, helping the person to either conserve or transform their goals, the pathways by which they seek their goals, or both. The outcome of the religious coping process can be judged as good or bad depending on how well it meets situational demands, has a good balance of goals, and fits well with the person's social system (Pargament, 1997, p. 237; Harrison, Koenig, Hays, Eme-Akwari, & Pargament, 2001; Pargament, Koenig, & Perez, 2000; Overcash, Calhoun, Cann, & Tedeschi, 1996; Pargament & Park, 1995; Butter & Pargament, 2003).

An implication of Pargament's theory is that religious and non-religious coping are different but intimately related. In his view, coping need not use religion and religion need not involve coping. However, some people construct meaning in relation to the sacred; for them religion can be an essential part of the coping process and contribute in a variety of ways, for example, by decreasing high-risk behaviors. However, religion can also be affected by the coping process, for instance when religious faith is strengthened as we find consolation in the face of chronic problems or limitations. Thus, the relationship between religion and coping is a bidirectional one. Sometimes coping can become religious even when the person does not truly believe in the sacred, as when unbelievers request a Christian funeral. Religious and nonreligious coping both predict good outcomes, although in some studies religious coping predicted better adjustment above and beyond nonreligious coping, especially with regard to religious outcomes such as perceived spiritual growth (Pargament, Ensing, et al., 1990; Pargament, 1990; Fitchett, Rybarczyk, DeMarco, & Nicholas, 1999; Pargament, Cole et al., 1999).

Positive religious coping is common among adults and is frequently used to cope with difficult situations. For instance, studies of US and British psychiatric inpatients have found that 70–80% use religious coping, including prayer and worship service attendance, and roughly 2/3 of these perceive it as effective, especially those with more severe psychotic or bipolar disorders. It is a little less common in college students but still very frequent (Rogers, Poey, Reger, Tepper, & Coleman, 2002; Reger & Rogers, 2002; Harrison et al., 2001; Pargament, Smith, Koenig, & Perez, 1998; Pargament, Koenig et al., 2000). Not surprisingly, religious coping is more likely to be found among people with higher levels of religiosity, and among those that have less access to secular power and resources, such as members of minority groups or those who are elderly, poor or less educated. For religious people, religious coping may be more likely in limit situations with harmful events that seem unmanageable and involve a loss or threat to the well-being of the self or to important others (Pargament, 1997; Maynard, Gorsuch, & Bjorck, 2001).

10.2.2.1 Religious Coping Styles

Pargament argues that there are three main styles of religious coping (Pargament, 1997, pp. 180–182; Pargament, Kennell et al., 1988). In a **self-directing coping** style the individual acknowledges the presence of the sacred but relies on one's self rather than on God to solve a problem. The emphasis here is on personal autonomy and control, similar to Fromm's ideal humanistic religion (see Section 1.4.4). The opposite of this is a **deferring coping** style in which responsibility for a problem is deferred to God. It is thus more passive and dependent upon authority and is associated with lower personal control and self-esteem. Finally there is the **collaborative coping** style which involves an active partnership between the individual and God. This is related to high personal control and self-esteem and is probably related to intrinsic religiosity. Religious coping styles are at least partly due to learning from significant others and one's religious community, as there is a strong correlation between one's coping style and the perceived beliefs and coping style of others (Schaefer & Gorsuch, 1991, 1992). Some studies on religious coping have also identified additional styles such as pleading to God.

Two aspects of one's God concept are particularly relevant to coping and the development of coping style. First, those who see God as benevolent and caring are more likely to adopt collaborative or deferring coping styles, while those that have less positive views tend toward self-directing coping. Second is the issue of whether we see God as in charge and involved in the world, sometimes referred to in the literature as one's **God locus of control**. Those who have a strong God locus of control tend to use collaborative or deferring coping styles, while those who see God as distant or unpredictable will be more likely to adopt a self-directing style.

Religious motivation also impacts coping. Individuals with intrinsic motivation tend to see difficult situations not just as threats but also as opportunities for growth. This motivational pattern is related to the use of collaborative or sometimes deferring styles and avoidance of the self-directed style. Intrinsic motivation is also connected with less problem avoidance and higher problem-solving scores. In contrast, extrinsic motivation is more about religion as a help to deal with threats to personal development and less about positive growth. It is associated with less personal control and more problem avoidance, focusing on positive aspects of situations, while attempting to ignore possible threats. It is sometimes related to pleading with God. Extrinsics who are comfort-seekers with high extrinsic-personal (Ep) scores tend to use deferred coping, while those with high extrinsic-social (Es) scores and a motivation centered on social gains will gravitate to the self-directing style. Quest motivation can be related to a collaborative style of working together with God for self-discovery, but it is more often related to self-directing coping. These patterns of religious motivation and religious coping style also interact with God concept beliefs to affect anxiety and psychological adjustment in complex ways (Pargament, 1997, p. 195; Pargament, Kennell et al., 1988; Wong-McDonald & Gorsuch, 2004; Schaefer & Gorsuch, 1991).

In his original theory, Pargament argued that the collaborative and self-directing coping styles were the most desirable. Research since that time has found that the collaborative style is most consistently associated with positive adjustment (e.g., Bickel, Ciarrocchi, Sheers, & Estadt, 1998), while other styles have more mixed results. Pleading is probably the least effective, and while self-directing is generally better than the deferring style, the latter can be occasionally helpful (Kinney, Ishler, Pargament, & Cavanaugh, 2003; Pargament, Ensing, et al., 1990). Interestingly, the deferring and collaborative styles are often used together (Pargament, Kennell et al., 1988; Kinney et al., 2003; Pendleton, Benore, Jonas, Norwood, & Herrmann, 2004; Bickel et al., 1998). Commonly found relationships with the three styles are as follows (Pargament, Kennell et al., 1988; Hathaway & Pargament, 1990; Yangarber-Hicks, 2004; Schaefer & Gorsuch, 1991):

1. The *self-directing style* is negatively related to prayer, intrinsic motivation, religious orthodoxy, and God locus of control. It is positively related to feelings of personal control, self-esteem, but also higher levels of anxiety. Individuals with this style who suffer from serious mental illness tend to have poorer outcomes.

2. The *deferring style* is positively related to orthodoxy, religious involvement, intolerance, and higher God locus of control. It is negatively related to personal control, self-esteem, psychosocial competence, and anxiety.

3. The *collaborative style* is positively related to prayer, religious salience and involvement, greater personal control, higher self-esteem, and psychosocial competence. It is related to lower anxiety, less belief in control by chance, and higher God locus of control. In coping with serious mental illness, the collaborative style is related to more empowerment and participation in recovery-enhancing activities.

While some of these religious coping styles appear to be more helpful overall, research indicates that no strategy is best all the time. This suggests that coping styles need to be matched to the situation and that personal adjustment will be facilitated by the use of multiple coping methods (Pargament, Koenig et al., 2000). For instance, church members dealing with uncontrollable single events had less depression when using collaborative coping, but a study of dementia caregivers found greater depression when using collaborative coping with this chronically uncontrollable situation (Pargament, 1997, p. 330; Kinney et al., 2003). Children in particular seem to benefit from the use of a variety of styles (Pendleton et al., 2004).

The relation of God locus of control to some of these styles may also affect their helpfulness. Higher levels of God locus of control are associated with many of the benefits of internal locus of control. It is correlated with positive health habits and coping skills, as well as lower levels of depression in some groups (Welton, Adkins, Ingle, & Dixon, 1996; Wong-McDonald & Gorsuch, 2004; Bjorck, Lee, & Cohen, 1997). Not surprisingly, belief in a benevolent God who is in control and a supportive partner is connected with better outcomes from religious coping (Pargament, Ensing, et al., 1990). God locus of control appears to be weaker in individuals who have suffered early parental losses or felt alone as children; it is possible that it might be enhanced by later experiences of caring (Rizzuto, 2001a).

Other religious coping styles have been proposed in the literature. One of these is the **surrender to God coping** style, which involves an active surrender to God in a situation, rather than the passive waiting of the deferring style. Not surprisingly, it is correlated with higher God locus of control. This style has been found in some studies to be related to higher levels of spiritual well-being and religious importance, as well as better coping with traumatic situations. It is positively correlated with the use of deferred and collaborative coping and negatively related to self-directing coping. In terms of religious motivation, it is negatively related with extrinsic comfort seeking and quest but positively related with intrinsic motivation (Wong-McDonald & Gorsuch, 2000, 2004; Schaefer & Gorsuch, 1991, 1992; Ting and Watson, 2007). Surrender is facilitated by belief in a just God who is in control, which then contributes to coping through finding meaning and purpose in events (cf. Mackenzie et al., 2000).

Much of the research on religious coping has also used a broader classification of coping styles into positive and negative groups. **Positive religious coping** involves a positive focus on problem solving with a religious dimension. God is seen as benevolent, forgiving, loving and in control, a partner in dealing with difficult situations, and the person feels a sense of spiritual and congregational support. Efforts to do good deeds and live a better life are part of this style, along with occasional avoidance. **Negative religious coping,** on the other hand, involves a sense of spiritual discontent and a lack of congregational support. God is seen as punishing or helpless, so the person may see themselves as afflicted by God, leading to passive forms of coping like deferring or pleading. Individuals with quest motivation who are alienated from both God and organized religious communities may fit this pattern (Pargament, Ensing, et al., 1990; Harrison et al., 2001; Pargament, Koenig et al., 2000). In older adult samples, there is a positive correlation between both private and public practices and positive religious coping. There are indications that people tend to use either a positive or negative style somewhat consistently, and that negative coping is less commonly found in children than in adults (Bosworth, Park, McQuoid, Hays, & Steffens, 2003; Pendleton, Cavalli, Pargament, & Nasr, 2002).

There is a substantial literature connecting positive religious coping with beneficial outcomes, and negative religious or nonreligious coping with poorer outcomes (Chatters, 2000; Harrison et al., 2001; Pargament, Kennell et al., 1998; Pargament, Koenig et al., 2000; Pargament, 1997, pp. 282–285; Pearce et al., 2002). This is particularly true for those who identify themselves as both religious and spiritual (Bussing, Ostermann, & Matthiessen, 2005). Positive religious coping is related to better physical health, self-esteem, and life satisfaction, as well as better adjustment to negative life events. In college student and hospital samples, it is correlated with stress-related growth and positive religious outcomes. Cross-sectional and longitudinal studies have shown that positive religious coping is related to lower levels of depression and is superior to religiousness as a predictor of depression (Bosworth et al., 2003). It appears to buffer the effects of negative events (Bjorck & Thurman, 2007). On the other hand, negative coping is associated with higher illness risk, more emotional distress and poorer adjustment to negative life events. Higher levels of negative religious coping are found among those with multiple conditions or functional limitations, and this is predictive of lower functional ability or less improvement with treatment. Better psychological and spiritual outcomes (e.g., less depression and more spiritual growth) from positive religious coping and poorer outcomes from negative religious coping (e.g., more feeling of spiritual struggle or discontent) have been found in trauma victims (Smith, Pargament, Brant, & Oliver, 2000) and in a variety of specific medical patient populations, including those in rehabilitation (Fitchett et al., 1999), older medical patients (Pargament, Koenig, Tarakeshwar, & Hahn, 2001), cancer patients (Cole, 2005), chronic pain patients (Rippentrop, Altmaier, Chen, Found, & Keffala, 2005), and children with cystic fibrosis (Pendleton et al., 2004). Poorer outcomes have mostly been associated with extrinsically motivated religious coping, where religion is a peripheral part of life just called on in certain occasions for help (Pargament, 1997, p. 281).

While research generally supports a positive association between religious participation and physical or mental health, the relationship is sometimes weak, and results have not been entirely consistent. Some researchers have suggested that this is because religion mostly works indirectly through the mediating variable of religious coping rather than acting directly to moderate the effects of stress on health. In this view, religious participation or belief stimulates religious coping in a particular style, which in turn alters or blocks the potentially negative effects of stress on health (e.g., Hathaway & Pargament, 1990). Research has partly supported this position, although the relationships involved appear to be complex. For instance, Fabricatore, Handal, Rubio, & Gilner (2004; cf. Chatters, 2000) found that collaborative coping in undergraduate college students was a mediating (intermediate) and not a moderating variable between stress and mental health variables, while deferring coping had a partial moderating but no mediating effect. Pargament (1997, p. 307) has argued that there is evidence for both distress-deterrent and moderator effects of religious coping, while Nooney & Woodrum (2002) using sociological data have shown that the effects of prayer on depression were mediated by religious coping. Smith et al. (2000) found both direct and mediating effects of religious variables on psychological and spiritual outcomes after trauma.

10.2.3 Critique

The coping framework has generated a large body of useful information about the religion-health connection. It has the potential to alter the way we think about the helping process. In the traditional view, helping (e.g., counseling) is a practice directed to individuals after problems occur and is best done by professionals. In the religion and coping view, primary prevention, as well as helping after the fact is appropriate, and efforts can move beyond the individual and utilize many kinds of service providers (Pargament, 1997, p. 389).

However, coping theory has limitations. The coping construct is important but has limited explanatory power, as its effect size is modest (Pargament, 1997, p. 312). While coping styles can be identified, they are too broad to explain variations in the ways an individual copes with specific situations, so this sort of general all-inclusive functional approach has limited value. Also, current process approaches to coping are not well integrated with other aspects of a person such as goals and beliefs (Koenig, 1995).

A key limitation in the theory as it stands is that it can be simplistic and ignore many other factors of importance to the coping process. Potential complicating factors that are not well understood include (1) the individual's level of cognitive and spiritual development, (2) the type of problem or stressor, (3) the specific situational and cultural context within which coping takes place, (4) changes in the coping process over time, (5) the specific group or population being studied, and (6) the multidimensional nature of religion and spirituality (Pargament, Koenig et al., 2000; Koenig, 1995; Pargament, 1997; Chatters, 2000; Ark, Hull, Husaini, & Craun, 2006; Bjorck et al., 1997; Nooney & Woodrum, 2002; Butter & Pargament, 2003). Models probably need to be expanded to include more important variables like religious experience, motivation, affect, values, and actual coping behavior (Koenig, 1995; Lazarus, 1993; Maynard et al., 2001). Inconsistencies in findings suggest research design and methodology problems (Harrison et al., 2001; Pargament, 1997, p. 285).

A more nuanced view of possible outcomes from coping is also needed. We need to distinguish between psychological and religious outcomes, as religious coping may help one but not the other (Smith et al., 2000). It is important to identify situations when religious coping might be problematic, as when religion is used as a defense to support social policies or personal behavior that is damaging (Pargament, 1997, p. 323). We must also recognize that while religion often provides comfort, it might also be connected with disquiet, for instance when it increases concern about the meaning of events for others who are undergoing persecution or social injustice (Seybold & Hill, 2001; Pargament, 1997; Harrison et al., 2001; Plante & Chanchola, 2004). Research has the potential to help religious communities understand how best to equip people to use the resources of their faith in a helpful way and utilize religious coping as a positive force.

10.3 Religious Perspectives on Health

All major religious traditions have a perspective on health that stems from several aspects of religious life and practice. First, all spiritual traditions have a way of relating to the body, although this is more prominent and well developed in some groups than in others. This includes religious practices that focus on the body such as hesychasm or charismatic prayer in Christianity, tantric practices in Hinduism and Buddhism, or body- oriented practices in esoteric spiritualities like the mysticism of Gurdjieff (Louchakova & Warner, 2003; see e.g., Sections 13.2.2 and 13.2.4). Second, religious traditions generally have a concern for others and their care. Thus, they have been at the forefront of efforts to understand and treat physical and mental conditions that cause suffering. Third, religious groups articulate an idea of the goal of human life, which affects their attitudes toward how they would define health. Generally, they view health as not the absence of illness but in a broader way as a movement toward goals of the spiritual life, such as wholeness and freedom. Finally, religious traditions often have a holistic approach to mind, body, and spirit that emphasizes their interconnections (Tong, 2003).

On the other hand, religion is also about more than health, and this fact affects the attitudes of religious groups toward physical and mental illness. For religious people, religion is not a health practice but a way of life that may have health benefits. It is practiced because it is good in its own right (Arcury et al., 2000). This runs counter to some modernist and popular attitudes that appear in surveys, showing that people rank health as more important than aspects of life such as love or religious faith (Vergote, 1969, p. 257). Therapeutic ideas of religion thus can sit uneasily with members of religious groups, as can be seen in current Christian writings on the topic of health and illness.

10.3.1 Christian Views

From its very beginning in the ministry of Jesus, Christianity has been concerned with healing and health. In the early church, healing was popular from the 2nd century on, although the emphasis was on healing of the soul. Healing the body was a lesser preoccupation pursued so that individuals could continue their work and Christian service. While physical suffering was a concern, and the church reached out to individuals in need, early Christians also viewed suffering as an opportunity for growth and to identify with the person of Christ. This perspective on suffering was very different from the view in the classical world at the time, which abhorred suffering as something to be avoided or endured (Spidlik, 1986, pp. 135–136; Veilleux, 1980, pp. 214–216). In these early Christian views, health was a very broad concept that referred to the whole person including body, soul, and spirit. As a holistic and all-inclusive phenomenon, it manifested itself not only in the absence of physical illness but also in positive emotional states like joy and in loving conduct toward others. Healing thus involved not only the body but also the restoration of the soul (Merton, 2006, pp. 198–202).

Despite this history, there is not a unified viewpoint on health, healing, and illness within the Christian tradition. However, the general shape of Christian attitudes on the topic can be discerned from looking at contemporary theological critiques of the modern view of health, as well as the writings of Christians in the health and healing movement.

10.3.1.1 Critique of Modernist Views of Health

Many Christian theologians see contemporary views of health as coming out of modernist and positivist views of the human person that are quite problematic. They see the modern world as an essentially **therapeutic culture**, where problems are defined as illnesses, and elimination of these illnesses is the ultimate goal of life and society. Philip Rieff first articulated this insight into modern culture in a book entitled *The Triumph of the Therapeutic* (1966). In this work, Rieff argued that modern culture represents a rejection of religious views of health and an acceptance of what he calls the **therapeutic**: things that will maintain the adjustment and social functioning of the individual. He believes that therapeutic culture contains a number of ethical and philosophical presuppositions:

1. Health is morally neutral and can exist in many different frameworks of values and personality organization, so compelling central values need not be a part of health.

2. Human perfection is achieved when our inborn instincts are satisfied. Thus (a) impulse release must be a primary therapeutic tool rather than self control or depravation, and (b) hope of transformation is not a meaningful ideal.
3. A healthy life should focus on the present and everyday, turning attention away from things "ultimate" or "divine" (1966, p. 54). Freud for instance thought that even asking questions about the meaning of life was a sign of illness, since there is no meaning apart from satisfying private wants of the individual.
4. Cure or perfection are impossible; instead, we should aim for increasing personal capacity to satisfy instincts. This is the ideal of Baconian science that hopes to increase our power and freedom to choose without reference to ideals (cf. Section 2.2.2). Psychoanalysis is an example of this, as it provides a technology for increasing freedom but no way of ordering choices and determining what is worthwhile.
5. The idea of community as a positive force is rejected. Rather, community is something to be managed so people can live together and find release of impulses. For instance, Freud argued that community or culture cannot be therapeutic, rather the individualistic self must be in the center, and rejection of commitment is therapeutic.

Rieff argues that every culture has a therapeutic aspect that generally supports religion and moral demands as helpful. However, in our current society the therapeutic has become completely dominant, and old religious and ethical contents are now preserved only to the extent they have therapeutic potential. Morality has become medicalized. Faced with this change, one obvious route for religion is to become therapeutic, turning into a religious psychology. Rieff thought that liberal Protestantism had followed this path. In his view, this surrenders essential aspects of religion and accepts presuppositions at odds with both a religious and ethical life. Thus, he views these propositions as flawed and problematic in many ways. A number of contemporary secular authors have joined in this critique, arguing that the medicalization of normal states and problems such as sadness is not helpful (Horwtiz, 2002; Horwitz & Wakefield, 2007; Conrad, 2007).

A number of Christian authors have followed Rieff and criticized contemporary research on religion and health as holding these same flawed therapeutic presuppositions. A good statement of their argument is given by Shuman and Meador (2003). They begin by rejecting the view that religion is therapy. In their view, religious truth claims are not all or even partly about health but about proper conduct, as well as the nature and destiny of life. Religious traditions are about helping people to live in the world together regardless of whether they are sick or well. This involves spiritual healing that takes place at a deep level and may or may not lead to bodily healing (Tillich, 1958; Chamberlain & Hall, 2000, p. 338). In Christianity, the hope and the promise of the future lies elsewhere, and healing is a sign of new things to come rather than an end in itself. Health care is not about advancing individual needs but is based in the ideal of hospitality of community members to each other and to the stranger. Devotion to health as an ultimate goal in place of God is not only limited and idolatrous, but it represents an abandonment of the Christian perspective and the ideal of hospitality; it changes attitudes toward the sick in unhelpful ways (cf. Vergote, 1998, p. 266).

Next, Shuman and Meador reject the narcissistic focus of the therapeutic. They argue that in therapeutic culture everything is aimed toward the development of physical and mental capacity or power. The focus on power manifests itself in a number of ways, including the youth orientation of the culture. The term "spirituality" fits comfortably in this framework, as it is individualized, self-interested, and therapeutic. Missing is an examination of whether the desires we pursue and the political system that supports them constitute a good way of life. In a capitalist framework, religion becomes just a means to satisfy the ends of the individual rather than an end in itself; it becomes a commodity to be sampled or used to obtain particular objectives. This kind of religious consumerism is destructive of community traditions, making God simply a producer of commodities, not an object of worship (cf. McCullough, 1995). The narcissistic focus of therapeutic religion implies that people can and should adopt religion as a product that will give them better health; however, there is no evidence that if people adopt religion for utilitarian, extrinsic purposes it will have these kinds of beneficial effects.

Finally, Shuman and Meador reject the technological orientation behind therapeutic culture. In their view, the idea that religion is a therapeutic technology represents a magical view of the world where all things are finite, and everything has a sympathetic interdependence, so manipulation of some things will affect others. The Christian religion rejects this as it deals with our relation to infinite power and transcendent values. Instead, it involves a consciousness of dependence. The difference between a technological and Christian orientation can be observed in attitudes toward prayer that have changed during the 20th century (Dillon & Wink, 2007, pp. 46–47). Technological prayer is about wish fulfillment, using divine power for personal purposes. While this is a common phenomenon in history (religious and secular), it is a magical distortion of prayer. Real prayer is focused on God, and prayer heals us as whole people when we are reconnected with our spiritual center. It is about relationship, not technology. Studies of Christian meditation and prayer indicate this relational focus, as individuals who are involved in the practices develop more positive attitudes toward others, as well as toward sickness and suffering, and are less oriented to seeking personal fulfillment (Kulik & Szewczyk, 2002).

10.3.1.2 The Healing Movement: A Contemporary Christian View of Healing

Christian writers have also produced positive statements about healing and health, in addition to the critical views of writers like Rieff, Shuman and Meador. An example of this kind of work can be found in the *healing prayer movement* that exists in many churches but especially those influenced by the charismatic movement. This broad grouping of as many as 500 million people worldwide holds a theology of healing that has been articulated by a number of authors, including Agnes Sanford, Francis McNutt, Ruth Carter Stapleton, and Gary Seamands. Their approach to healing is centered on individual and group prayer, and their theology includes many premodern, modern, and postmodern ideas. In charismatic healing prayer, the prime focus is on facilitating one's relationship with God and a sense of presence (MacNutt, 1999, pp. 27–36); healing is a secondary outcome to these relational and experiential goals.

Charismatic healing prayer does not involve a fixed method or system, but does operate according to a couple of general principles. First, it is carried out in the context of a holistic view of health and healing. Prayer is intended to have broad effects, addressing both our outer circumstances and our inner spiritual condition. Its transformative power is about healing the soul and the whole person, not just our body or superficial emotional concerns (Sanford, 1966). It is also true that any illness has many facets: a man with prostate cancer may become depressed, and all aspects of this situation can be addressed through healing prayer (Khouzam, 1996). A health problem might include several kinds of sickness: (1) **spiritual sickness** or problems arising from personal sin, (2) emotional illness such as anxiety or depression that is related to past hurts, emotional wounds or traumas, and (3) physical illness. MacNutt (1999) argues that while suffering due to external trials can have constructive effects and produce growth, the inner suffering connected with spiritual and emotional sickness is not the will of God and can be commonly healed through prayer.

Although charismatic thought emphasizes the holistic nature of healing, prayers are generally targeted to a specific problem. The tone of health prayer is positive, focusing on the help and increased health the person will receive, and then giving thanks for the help. The general method of prayer is selected based on the type of problem (Sanford, 1966, pp. 53–57; MacNutt, 1999, pp. 146–162). Spiritual sickness is generally addressed using prayers of repentance and forgiveness. Prayers of self-examination are sometimes helpful in this case but should be avoided with some problems like depression, as they simply make the problem worse. Emotional sickness is approached through prayers for inner healing, bringing painful memories from the past to light and praying for release from their binding effects. An offering of positive and loving imagery in the place of former memories can be helpful. Since physical illness directly involves the body, prayer for these types of problems should also have a physical component such as a laying on of hands. Prayers for deliverance from external oppression, persecution, or opposition may also be appropriate with any of these kinds of illnesses.

A second general principle of healing prayer is that it is not a technology and does not work according to a mechanical process, although most charismatics would argue that God works through medicine and doctors, as well as prayer (MacNutt, 1999, p. 131). This view of prayer as different from technology results in a number of specific attitudes and beliefs. In the technology view, healing is carried out by a therapist expert who is trained in particular techniques; when applied in the correct situation, the procedures have a beneficial effect regardless of the inner attitudes of the therapist and the person seeking help or the nature of their relationship (cf. MacIntyre, 1984, pp. 28–31). For instance, a surgeon can successfully remove a ruptured appendix even if he or she dislikes the patient and the individual on the operating table is unenthusiastic about the surgery. Healing prayer is different. While some specific technical knowledge about psychology might enhance the work of a person doing prayer for inner healing, the power of healing is a gift from God that is specially given to an individual or group and involves an intensification of natural gifts. The healing is highly relational, requiring sharing and trust between the individuals, and especially an attitude of love on the part of the healer. It also requires that the patient be aware of the reality of God's power, open to this gift, and ready to receive healing. Prayer can lead to profound emotional experiences that can be healing but may simply increase internal strain, if the person is not prepared to receive them (Sanford, 1966; Richardson, 1958). This is why valid spiritual healing is best done in a community with careful controls about how authority and power are used in a beneficial way (Oates, 1958).

The holistic and gifted nature of healing prayer means that it resists systematic description and study. Those with a charismatic healing ministry like MacNutt argue that healing through prayer cannot be reduced to a single experience, system, or method that produces effects upon demand (1999, p. 109). Participants in healing prayer frequently report experiences of partial or total healing, but that what was healed was not always the original problem, and healing involved more than the restoration of a past state—it was the beginning of something new (Hurwitz, 2004; Frank, 2004). In addition, the healing was often not superficially obvious and thus was resistant to study by outside observation (Garzon, 2005; Chamberlain & Hall, 2000, pp. 67–70). These characteristics mean that healing through prayer is difficult to study statistically and that skeptics looking at occurrences of healing can normally explain them as coincidence (Booth, 1958; Polkinghorne, 2001, p. 34).

10.3.2 Hinduism and Health: Ayurveda and Yoga

In contrast to Christianity, Hinduism has a more systematic metaphysics and theory of health and illness. This approach to physical and mental health includes the ayurvedic system of medicine and various techniques of yoga.

While adherents of modern ayurveda commonly trace its roots back to early Hindu Vedic literature such as the *Atharvaveda*, the current system probably came into being much later, perhaps around the time of the Buddha. **Ayurveda** developed over a long period of time and has assimilated a number of concepts. For instance, early ayurveda did not include the system of chakras and energy paths found in yoga philosophy (Wujastyk, 2003, p. 260), but modern treatments often include them and incorporate aspects of yoga. Its philosophical base draws on the dualistic Samkhya philosophy of Isvarakrsna, which also forms the basis of Patanjali's classic system of yoga, although elements of Vedanta are also present (Chapple, 1990; see Section 3.1.1). The system is thus ancient and complex but has recently been the focus of renewed interest (e.g., Lad, 2002; Sharma & Clark, 1998; Frawley, 1999).

10.3.2.1 Basic Metaphysics and Psychology

In Samkhya philosophy, above all is **Brahman**, a state of pure awareness and consciousness. Brahman has two fundamental manifestations, the first of which is **purusha** or an energy free of the world of action. It is pure consciousness, providing the basis for thought processes. Second is **prakrti**, a primordial will and creative potential, sometimes referred to as a divine Mother that manifests itself in the material world (see Section 3.1.2). In human experience, this pure unified consciousness is initially split into three parts: the knower (*rishi*), the process of knowing (*devata*) and the object of knowledge (*chhandas*), which alternate back and forth in our awareness. The three aspects of consciousness acting with prakrti generate three humors or energies called **doshas**: *vata* from rishi, *pitta* from devata, and *kapha* from chhandas. These form a basis and governing principle for matter, including the operations of the human body (Chapple, 1990, p. 58). Thus unlike Western materialism, Samkhya thought holds that matter ultimately comes from consciousness rather than the reverse, a view that has some parallels in modern quantum theory (cf. Polkinghorne, 1999a; see Section 2.5.1). This view also implies a kind of dualism in which consciousness and the self exist independently of matter, although all is unified in Brahman. One can thus speak of the self or soul as being of two kinds, an individual soul or **atman** and the universal soul or Brahman. The soul cannot be directly measured, but its causative effects can be observed and experienced (Lad, 2002, pp. 15–16). In writings like the *Katha Upanisad* (Easwaran, 1996, pp. 88–90), an analogy of a chariot is used to describe the relation between our various parts, with the body as chariot, the soul as charioteer, the mind as the reins and self as the owner (Wujastyk, 2003, p. 203).

10.3.2.2 Doshas

In ayurvedic thought, physical and mental functioning is assumed to be governed by dharma or laws, some of which are universal, while others are particular to our individual nature. At the level of the physical body, the three doshas of vata, pitta, and kapha form the governing principles of bodily function. Health and well-being or blissful states occur when the doshas are balanced; one feels alert, sleeps well, and body processes are normal. When imbalances occur a number of physical and mental problems develop. Each person has their own ideal balance that relates to their normal physical, cognitive, and personality characteristics, and so ayurveda (as well as yoga) emphasizes that each individual will have a somewhat unique path to wholeness (Sharma & Clark, 1998, pp. 35–44; Frawley, 1999, pp. 9–12). The doshas move through physical pathways in the body but also through energy channels known as **srotas**. Problems occur when there are blockages or excess flow in these channels due to emotional problems, physical imbalances, or poor diet. Chemicals in body tissues can alter the qualities of the doshas and are related to positive or negative emotional and cognitive qualities.

Much of ayurvedic theory is built around the idea that there are characteristic physical and mental effects when one of the doshas is out of balance (Lad, 2002). The effects of each dosha tend to be concentrated in particular areas of the body, so that problems with that dosha will lead to a corresponding set of symptoms. Problems with *vata* (wind) affect motion and energy, as well as the colon and lead to problems such as constipation or lower back pain, as well as grief, sadness, anxiety, and fear. Pitta (bile) is connected with the metabolic and digestive system, as well as some brain neurotransmitters and the heart chakra, so problems with it will lead to inflammatory disorders, anger, jealousy, and criticism. Kapha (phlegm) is connected to bodily structures, tissues, and immunity and when in balance can promote feelings of love and forgiveness. Kapha imbalance is associated with attachment, greed and congestive disorders; it can also affect *agni*, the digestive fire and metabolism of the body that promotes positive mental qualities like mental clarity or reasoning, and emotions like joy or patience.

Subtle doshas. At the level of the subtle body—the electrical aspect of the body that gives rise to consciousness—the doshas have three subtle counterparts that work to sustain vitality and promote health, as well as support the deeper levels of yoga and meditation practice. *Ojas* is related to vitality and immunity and is influenced by nutrition and psychological factors like stress, imbalances in diet or activity, and the quality of our relationships. It maintains consciousness, connecting it to matter, and is the source of our freedom and ability to love. *Tejas* is related to energy and digestion, while *prana* is connected to cerebral activities and forms a bridge between purushi and prakrti. Modern practitioners who follow ayurvedic theory believe these doshas to be superfine substances or essences that have biochemical equivalents, and, in combination, they form the basis of the kundalini that flows in the pathways of the chakra system (Lad, 2002, pp. 212–229; Sharma & Clark, 1998, pp. 31–32; Frawley, 1999, pp. 87–94).

The gunas. There are three universal qualities or **gunas** which are aspects of prakrti based on prana: (1) *sattva* which is the energy of cognition, right action, and spiritual purpose or potential that moves us toward purification of mind; (2) *rajas*, a quality of movement, excitability, and active vital force; and (3) *tamas*, the quality of inertia, confusion, and reflexive or unconscious activity that contrasts with the inaction and pure consciousness of purusha (cf. Sankaracarya, 1975, pp. 54–55, 78–80). While these alternate and interact, each person has a particular guna that tends to predominate, and various combinations of gunas are possible, some of which are more positive than others. For instance, a combination of raja and tamas is found in people who enjoy harm and destruction, while raja and sattva produce a healing transformative power that brings integration and wholeness. Yoga and ayurveda tend to emphasize sattva development, although yoga does it as a platform for spiritual development, while ayurveda wants to restore a state of balance that will allow for physical healing (Frawley, 1999, pp. 26–33).

10.3.2.3 Theory of Disease

Western medicine is allopathic, that is, it treats disease by introducing contrary forces. Classical ayurveda views this as just suppressing symptoms and instead seeks a more permanent solution by removing imbalances or blockages and working to restore normal harmony and flow. Western medicine also assumes that there is a typical normal state that is universal for all individuals, while ayurveda believes that what is normal differs for each person depending on the doshas that dominate in the individual. Some people are born with balanced humors and are not illness-prone, while others must continually strive to correct imbalances. Pathogenesis begins with over accumulation of a dosha, which then spreads to areas of the body where it does not belong. This can manifest as physical signs such as a rash and may become chronic without corrective action (Wujastyk, 2003, pp. 18–19; Sharma & Clark, 1998, pp. 52–54).

Early key ayurvedic works, such as the *Heart of Medicine* by Vagbhata, saw disease as due to an unbalanced lifestyle. In the ayurvedic system, health problems are generally attributed to one of three kinds of mistakes: improper diet, a lack of appropriate daily or seasonal routines, and problematic mental activity or behavior. These lead to doshic imbalances or clogging of the srota channels and thus to illness. Health is associated with moderation, following a middle way that is in harmony with the seasons and involves regular diet, exercise, and periodic cleansing of the system. Virtuous conduct is part of this middle way, refraining from evil and practicing positive acts toward others, while madness or mental illness is associated with loss of self control, becoming a slave to desires and the senses (Muktananda, 1980, p. 62). Treatment consisted either of purging the body to correct excesses or pacifying the psyche through mental activity that seeks wisdom, steadfastness, and knowledge of the self (Wujastyk, 2003, pp. 207).

In ayurveda, true health is not limited to an absence of physical disease. Rather, optimum human health is the state of enlightenment, where we are free from suffering and live in constant awareness of pure consciousness. The early ayurvedic physician Vagbhata produced one of the world's first formulations of mental illness based on this principle. He saw mental problems as due to destruction of heart pathways caused by improper diet, unbalanced behavior, failure to perform religious rituals, and mental anguish. He distinguished between 6 kinds of problems (Wujastyk, 2003, pp. 245–246):

- Vata imbalances producing hyperactive, uncontrolled or psychotic behavior
- Pitta imbalances leading to threatening, aggressive behavior
- Kapha imbalance leading to loss of appetite, motivation, and social isolation
- Problems related to imbalances in all three doshas
- Problems caused by loss, leading to depression, lack of sleep, and agitation
- Poisonings and delirium

10.3.2.4 Ayurvedic Treatment

Since doshic balance is affected by food, ayurvedic practitioners believe that alteration of diet can be a good beginning place for efforts to correct imbalances and
health problems. Different foods relate to various combinations of elements and
thus can promote different emotional states, affecting the gunas and the quality of
one's spiritual life. Because of individual differences, a diet should be based on one's
personal constitution; there is no standard ayurvedic diet. Diet therapy can then
be supplemented with other techniques. These might include yoga and behavioral
rasayanas such as practice of religious observances or simplicity of life. Rasayanas are positive factors that strengthen immunity, the opposite effect produced by
negative emotions such as anger and depression (Lad, 2002; Sharma & Clark, 1998,
pp. 30–34).

Even very early ayurvedic works covered treatment of psychological and
emotional problems, because these were seen as highly connected to physical illness. The *Compendium* of Caraka lays out three kinds of therapy. Sacred
therapy included meditation, offerings, and pilgrimages to foster religious and
spiritual development. Rational therapy involved adjustment of diet and use of
medicine. Therapy for character focused on turning the mind from what is not
good, replacing bad habits with good ones, and working to gain knowledge of
self, others, and the world. Character therapy was assisted by avoiding association with those who are greedy and without compassion, and seeking out those
with integrity who are mature and at peace. Successful treatment was thought
to restore balance amongst the three goals of life: virtue, prosperity, and pleasure. This happens by directing pleasure away from problematic attachments and
toward inner well-being and spiritual fulfillment. Some of Vagbhata's proposed
treatments like comforting, changes in diet or lifestyle revision. and religious
ritual seem quite reasonable by modern standards, but other suggestions such as
frightening, bloodletting, beating or scolding seem out of place (Glaser, 1994;
Wujastyk, 2003, pp. 18–33, 240–251).

10.3.2.5 Yoga and Health

The Hindu Samkhya philosophy that lies at the base of ayurvedic medicine is also
fundamental to the practices of yoga. While ayurvedic approaches to health are not
widely used or studied outside of India, yoga has become extremely popular in the
West as a way of promoting physical and psychological health. In a 1998 US survey, roughly 15 million had used yoga at least once, 7.4 million in the past year. By
2004, these numbers had increased substantially (Riley, 2004). Its use is more common among individuals with certain demographic characteristics: female, college
educated, urban baby boomers that typically have also used other non-Western
approaches to health.

Hatha yoga (see Section 3.1.2) is the most common type of yoga used for health
promotion. There are a number of different styles of Hatha yoga, but all attend to

posture and breathing. A meditation component is also typically part of Hatha yoga practice. Common uses of yoga include promoting general wellness or treating specific health problems like back or neck pain (21% of users) and depression (6.6%). Users rate their health higher than nonusers but are also more likely to report specific health problems like pain, anxiety, and depression (Saper, Eisenberg, David, Culpepper, & Phillips, 2004; Riley, 2004). Studies have also been done about its use with other conditions; for instance Nagendra and Nagarathna (1986) have developed and tested a successful program for asthma patients that uses yoga techniques.

Relatively little research has been done to investigate how physical states like posture and breathing affect emotions or the mind, and studies that do exist suffer from various methodological problems. However, in a number of groups and with different kinds of yoga, practice is found to increase subjective well-being and decrease depression or anxiety symptoms compared with control groups, even among those with no prior yoga experience (e.g., Pilkington, Kirkwood, Rampes, & Richardson, 2005; Shannahoff-Khalsa, 2003; Kumar & Ali, 2002; Waelde, Thompson, & Gallagher-Thompson, 2004; Watts, 2000). The aerobic aspect of exercise does not appear to be necessary for these benefits to occur. Psychological benefits are greater for regular attendees, but the source of the improvements is not known and could be due to a number of factors (Berger & Owen, 1992; Woolery, Myers, Sternlieb, & Zeltner, 2004).

Weintraub (2004) has developed a program based on a type of Hatha yoga to help individuals who suffer from depression. In her view, depression occurs when we are bound by kleshas or afflictions like ignorance that lead to attachments and fear of change or loss, as well as imbalances in gunas which can cause lethargy and anxiety or too much energy and aggressiveness. Western treatments for depression like antidepressant medications can be helpful, but they treat the symptoms and not the cause of the problem and so are not enough. She begins with the normal yoga progression followed by Patanjali (see Section 3.1.2) and addresses lifestyle through abstentions (*yamas*), ethical conduct, and inner observances (*niyamas*). These lifestyle changes promote contentment and surrender. Next, physical techniques are introduced including postures (*asanas*) and breath control (*pranayama*). The last four stages of yoga involve a series of mental exercises: sense withdrawal (*pratyahara*), concentration (*dharana*), and meditation (*dhyana*), culminating in **samadhi** or contemplation and promoting acceptance of our self and condition (Pankhania, 2005). Additional techniques can also be used that focus more on posture or alignment. These in turn can be combined with different kinds of yoga like **bhakti yoga**, tantric techniques, and even Christian or Buddhist meditation. Unfortunately, yoga programs have fairly high dropout rates, so it is unclear how practically useful the technique may be with many individuals (Shannahoff-Khalsa, 2003).

Yoga techniques can also be combined with other practices from the Hindu healing tradition such as ayurveda. Ayurveda and yoga have a common philosophical and religious foundation and can have complementary roles in treatment, with ayurveda working through techniques of lifestyle management, diet, and behavior, while yoga works more through meditative practices. Depending on the specific problem and the makeup of the individual, different combinations of diet, herbs, meditation, and types of yoga might be prescribed. Practitioners claim that these could eliminate psychological problems like anxiety, anger, and depression (Frawley, 1999). Ayurveda and Transcendental Meditation can also be combined, with meditation helping to increase awareness of the body and build mental discipline (Schneider et al., 2002; Sharma & Clark, 1998, p. 7).

Watts (2000) has recently offered a critique of yoga research that is available from Western sources. Along with critiquing aspects of research design and subject selection, he notes that most research approaches yoga as a consumer technique for enhancing physical or mental health, but that it is intended to be a philosophical and practical way of life that has a goal of spiritual purification (Weintraub, 2004, p. 121; Laungani, 2005). This Western research philosophy takes yoga out of context and looks at short-term benefits, when in fact it is long-term practice that is most likely to be helpful, especially if it is kept in its original ethical and philosophical framework.

10.3.3 Buddhism and Health

Buddhism also has a perspective on health and a set of practices designed to enhance it. This is probably most well developed in Tibetan Buddhist medicine, which combines Buddhist ideas with concepts from Hinduism and traditional Chinese medicine.

In Buddhist thought, all except the enlightened are sick and suffering. We are subject to mental disease, cravings, and delusions that lead to discontent, anxiety, and depression, even though disease might not be apparent now (Donden, 1986 p. 15; de Silva, 2000, pp. 123–124). Ultimately the cause of illness lies in these cravings and delusions, although they manifest themselves in immediate causes such as alterations in the balances of the three doshas or humors of the body: wind, bile, and phlegm.

In Tibetan Buddhist medicine, disorders can be classified in a couple of ways. First, they may be categorized by the humor that is out of balance. Bile disorders are considered "hot" problems that are believed to come from hatred, while phlegm disorder are "cool" and thought to be related to ignorance. Wind disorders are also "cool" and are related to desire or attachment as in addictions and can be fed by behavior, mental excesses, or an unbalanced lifestyle. Second, disorders may be labeled according to their root cause. In this system, problems are labeled as (1) minor or superficial, due to correctible problems with diet or behavior; (2) spiritual, due to spirit possession, requiring a spiritual approach using rituals conducted by a *lama* or holy person; (3) problems beginning in early life but manifesting later, which may require medicine or surgery; and (4) karmic disorders, resulting from the negative effects of behavior in past lives (Donden, 1986, pp. 16–17; Thrangu, 2004; Yun, 2005).

Like Christianity, Buddhism views all people as in need of healing, but is skeptical of a technological approach to health. Tibetan Buddhism does make use of physical techniques such as diagnosis by pulse taking or urinalysis, and treatments may include alteration of diet, cleansing emetics, or traditional Chinese medical remedies such as acupuncture or herbal medicine (Donden, 1986). However, Buddhism argues that what is needed is not a treatment but a new way of life and thinking that would include an orientation toward reality, a non-dualistic outlook, a change in behavior toward more self-aware actions, and deepened relationships marked by charitable conduct toward others (de Silva, 2000, pp. 125–137). This outlook does not separate the spiritual and physical so that spiritual techniques are intertwined with physical ones. **Mantras** and prayer rituals are used to produce and strengthen the action of herbal medicines, as well as remove mental or physical imbalances. Medicines not only have physical benefits but also can work to remove obstacles to meditative practice. Techniques of repentance and confession are intermixed with meditations of devotion to the Buddha and contemplations. In particular, greed is curable by contemplating impurity, anger by contemplating and practicing kindness, and ignorance by acquiring wisdom through contemplating the nature of things (Yun, 2005).

A specific practice used in Tibetan and Buddhist medicine is meditation and veneration involving the Medicine Buddha, who is believed to be a bodhisattva who made vows to help others with physical healing and liberation (Yun, 2005, pp. 16–19, 107–110). Medicine Buddha meditation involves some standard Buddhist techniques like visualizations, mantra practice and vipassana meditation, but it also involves *yidam* practices of generation and completion. Since mind, body, and spirit are interconnected, these practices are thought to lead to the supreme attainment of liberation, as well as more common attainments like physical health. In the generation stage of yidam, the person first works to develop devotion and faith that the process will work (Thrangu, 2004). Then the meditator repeats the name of the Medicine Buddha or other mantra and visualizes themselves in the presence of the Buddha, who is surrounded by a mandala. The goal of the meditation is clarity of visualization, and a mandala may be placed in front of the person to assist in the visualization process. **Mudras** or ritual gestures and acts of veneration may also be used, as well as the reciting of material from sutras. As the person becomes proficient, they are asked to imagine rays of light linking them to the Medicine Buddha and other buddhas or bodhisattvas. The person can also visualize a small Medicine Buddha in a part of the body that is afflicted, in combination with a laying on of hands by a lama or holy person. The practice is thought to empower and purify the individual and lead them toward a completion stage when they dissolve the visualization and allow their mind to rest in emptiness.

10.4 Collaborative Approaches to Health

Since both psychologists and individuals in religious traditions have interests in health, it seems natural that they would find ways to collaborate in efforts to heal others. Practitioners and scholars both see many possible benefits to cooperation, but instances of collaboration are few and many barriers stand in the way of effective joint efforts.

Expressions of interest about collaboration in religion or theology journals peaked during the 1980s, but attention to the topic has been gaining in secular journals. Several themes appear in this literature, including (1) the frontline role of clergy in treatment and prevention of health problems, especially those related to mental health; (2) mutual benefits to collaboration, especially for mental health workers; (3) the importance of shared values and respect, eliminating negative views about religion; (4) needs for more education and training; (5) obstacles to collaboration; and (6) possible roles of clergy and mental health professionals in collaboration (Oppenheimer, Flannelly, & Weaver, 2004).

10.4.1 Frontline Roles and Benefits of Collaboration

A motivation for collaboration from a religious perspective is that many people seek help for heath problems from religious communities and especially from clergy. This is particularly true with regard to mental health issues. In the early to mid-1990s, 40% of people with mental health problems were seen by clergy, and ministers reported spending about 15% of their time in direct pastoral counseling. Currently, over 100 million hours of counseling services are provided each year by US clergy, as well as many hours of informal contacts over long periods of time. This means that clergy actually deliver more mental health services than psychologists (Oppenheimer et al., 2004; Weaver, Flannelly, Flannelly, & Oppenheimer, 2003).

Health care professionals should also be motivated to collaborate, because many of their patients come to them with spiritual and religious issues. This is true of physicians in general medicine, as well as in psychiatric practice, although the latter encounter these issues more frequently in both positive and negative ways (Koenig, 2002, p. 5; Koenig, Lawson, & McConnell, 2004, pp. 79–80; Curlin, Lawrence & Odell et al., 2007). In a US study of hospital patients (King & Bushwick, 1994), 77% said that physicians should consider spiritual needs, and 48% said they would like their physicians to pray with them. Obviously, the desire of patients to have their religious issues addressed and the positive effects of religious involvement on health are major reasons why collaboration should occur. However, these needs are not being met, for 80% of hospital patients said their physician had never or only rarely discussed religious beliefs with them. A recent study using videotaped interviews of patient-physician interactions found that physicians made no efforts to support or facilitate religious participation, even when the issue was raised by the patient (Robinson & Nussbaum, 2004). A recent large study of advanced cancer patients found that 72% felt their spiritual needs had minimal or no support from the medical system (Balboni et al., 2007).

Collaboration could also be of benefit to health care professionals for a couple of other reasons. First, religious communities and clergy have access to large numbers of individuals from groups in need of health care like the elderly, or groups that are underserved by the health care industry such as minorities and those living in rural areas. For these individuals, religious communities provide a trusted place that people turn to as a first source of help, especially for problems like marriage and family disruption or depression. These communities are also a first source of help for those strongly connected to religion, such as frequent church attendees, conservative Christians, and groups with strong traditional religious affiliations. For these groups, the church could be used as a way of building bridges and disseminating information about programs (Musgrave, Allen, & Allen, 2002; Hatchett, 1999; Chalfant et al., 1990; Kloos, Horneffer, & Moore, 1995; Taylor, Ellison, Chatters, Levin, & Lincoln, 2000). The fact that older adults have high rates of religious participation but receive less treatment for depression suggests that religious organizations may be helpful in outreach to them as well (Puffer & Miller, 2001).

Churches are also attractive collaboration partners, because they can provide services in unique ways. In many cases a congregation may be better able than a professional setting to provide personal assistance because of the different type of relationship it offers. Churches tend to be effective at helping patients to feel more like people being cared for and served, rather than clients visiting a business (Maton & Wells, 1995; Anderson, Maton, & Ensor, 1991; Chatters, 2000). Perhaps because of this, clergy have the highest satisfaction rates from people who only visit one source for mental health assistance (Taylor et al., 2000). Collaboration is also good because religious communities are not tied to government, allowing for more flexibility and the ability to use a strong network of volunteer support (Voss, 1996). Partnerships with churches, faith-based organizations and volunteers may be especially attractive at a time when government services are no longer expanding or are even contracting, while health care needs are growing due to the aging of the population (Sherr & Straughan, 2005; Koenig, Lawson et al., 2004). Certainly programs offered by churches can impact the health practices of members in positive ways (Koenig, 2003). However, shrinking numbers of clergy and often declining levels of cultural and emotional support for them may make it increasingly difficult for churches to meet demands without innovative programming and better training. Collaborations could utilize the strengths of churches, while professional support helps them improve the quality of what they do (Worthington, Kurusu, McCullough, & Sandage, 1996; Zondag, 2004; Weaver, 1995; Kloos et al., 1995).

10.4.2 Importance of Shared Values

There are few reports of collaboration between health care and religious professionals in the literature, and a number of authors have argued that this is because of problems of respect and differences in values between the professions. In a survey of Midwest religious communities, clergy indicated that they were more interested in collaborative models of joint work that respect the expertise of both parties, in contrast to a consultation model that viewed the psychologist as the expert. The most common concern voiced by pastors was that psychologists would not respect their beliefs (Kloos et al., 1995). In fact, clergy and psychologists both report negative experiences involving arrogance or dismissive attitudes of people in the other group toward their goals, values, and potential contributions. This is even true of those who worked together regularly and had positive attitudes toward collaboration. Clergy have become especially pessimistic, because while most religious professionals make at least occasional referrals to health care providers, clergy receive few referrals even when spiritual issues are involved. In hospital settings, most referrals to chaplains come from nurses and social workers, only rarely from physicians and psychologists (Weaver, 1995; Lukoff & Lu, 1999; Larson et al., 1988; Worthington et al., 1996; Thiel & Robinson, 1997; McMinn, Aikins, & Lish, 2003; McMinn, Chaddock et al., 1998).

Clergy are also concerned about respect for religious values among health care professionals. Differences in values are reflected in a number of problems, including (1) use of similar language by both groups but with different meanings; (2) different ways of thinking about problems, goals, or strategies; and (3) stereotyping of individuals in the other group (Anderson et al., 1991). For instance, both clergy and mental health professionals frequently help people with marital problems, but mental health workers may see their task as helping individuals escape a situation that is not conducive to their personal well-being, while clergy may be more committed to the sanctity of marriage and the benefits that can come from lasting commitment in the face of problems. Secular professionals may be concerned that these religious values may cause clergy to defend behavior that is abusive (Foss & Warnke, 2003). As a result of these issues, collaboration probably needs to involve dialogue about values and ways to build mutual respect and trust (Oppenheimer et al., 2004).

10.4.3 Education and Other Barriers to Collaboration

Health professionals and clergy both complain that they are poorly prepared for collaborative work. Few educational programs for physicians or mental health professions include training about how to deal with the interface between health, mental health, and religion, or how to work together in collaborative efforts (Shafranske, 2001; cf. Chatters, 2000). Specialists in practical theology note that when training does occur, it tends to be from a psychiatric perspective, limiting the broader outlook that clergy could bring to health care work (Browning, 1999; Forrester, 1999; Oppenheimer et al., 2004). Low rates of religious involvement, particularly among mental health professionals, probably exacerbate the problem of unfamiliarity with spiritual or religious issues, as well as possibly contributie to the problem of value differences (see Section 14.2.2).

Health care professionals often resist making referrals out of concern that clergy might interfere with necessary medical treatment. For instance, the clergyperson might encourage them to seek spiritual or religious healing in place of regular medical treatment or encourage them to discontinue medications. This does happen on occasion: for instance Mitchell and Romans (2003) found in a study of bipolar patients in New Zealand that 32% reported a spiritual healer had told them that they no longer needed medications. This was especially true for those of non-European ancestry. However, a number of writers point out that in some cases a referral to clergy from health care professional may actually increase support for treatment and compliance, thus leading to a better outcome, while refusal to collaborate or include a spiritual component in treatment may drive away religious individuals for whom this is important (Post, Puchalski, & Larson, 2000; Kirov, Kemp, Kirov, & David, 1998; Keks & D'Souza, 2003; Koenig, 2000).

Many writers (e.g., Sloan, Bagiella & Powell, 2001; Tan & Dong, 2001; Levin et al., 2005; Koenig, 2002) have pointed out that there are a number of potential ethical barriers to collaboration. Some of these involve concerns about the role of the therapist, their competency to discuss issues, and potential boundary problems when the therapist assumes an ecclesiastical role. Another set of difficulties relates to how proactive a health care professional should be in bringing up spiritual or religious issues and pressing for a referral. Support of patient autonomy requires that all available options and issues be made known and discussed so that the patient can make an informed choice. However, this might violate the moral agency of the physician who opposes a referral and also introduces potential coercion where the professional might inadvertently or deliberately impose their beliefs and values on the patient. The alternative is to never discuss the issue or to do so only if the patient insists upon it. This raises the issue of what to do with people who do not participate but might gain great benefits from religious involvement. Many ethicists and professionals suggest that a middle road must be followed that balances conflicting claims. Physician agency and full disclosure are both important, and solutions should avoid the extremes of religious skepticism or an exclusively religious approach (Curlin, Lawrence, Chin et al., 2007; Chatters, 2000). However, no easy universal principles exist to determine how this should work. A case-by-case approach to the problem that is sensitive to the particular nuances of the situation, illness, and individuals involved is probably necessary, as is good communication and dialogue. Failure to make an appropriate referral for collaboration when it is indicated could be construed as an act of negligence from a legal and ethical point of view (Post et al., 2000).

10.4.4 Collaborative Roles

Collaborative work can be motivated by feelings of necessity or by a belief that collaborative work will actually improve the quality of health care for individuals. In either case, there are many different possibilities for collaborative work (Arcury et al., 2000). While collaboration between religious communities and health care professionals has been rare, and there is little research about how it might best be conducted, it is also true that it has been successfully done in the past and a number of innovative collaborative programs exist (Weaver et al., 1997; Court, 1997; McMinn, Meek, Canning, & Pozzi, 2001). Collaborative relationships with clergy have been helpful in a number of areas including parish nurse, caregiving, hospice and bereavement programs, as well as collaborative community programs and research focused on specific religious subgroups (Flannelly, Weaver, Smith, & Handzo, 2003; Post et al., 2000). In the mental health area, programs of lay counseling and visitation of individuals at risk for problems have also been done (Koenig, Lawson et al., 2004; Tan & Dong, 2001). These successful efforts can provide models for other joint work. They suggest that ideal collaborative relationships are those where health care workers and religious professionals or communities each provide unique and complimentary services that work well together in the interest of the people being served (McMinn, Aikins et al., 2003).

In general health care settings, most authors believe that at a minimum every patient should be assessed to determine their spiritual or religious needs and the possibility of collaboration. In fact, the Joint Commission for the Accreditation of Healthcare Organizations (JCAHO) now requires that hospitals and nursing homes perform a spiritual assessment on all patients. Assessment should involve at least a screening with simple questions about (1) whether persons consider themselves spiritual or religious and also should ask about (2) its importance and influence in persons' health and ideas about health care, (3) their connections to religious community, and (4) whether they have any specific spiritual concerns and if so whether there are preferences about how such issues might be addressed. These questions can reveal a lot of emotionally rich information that may be related to problems and coping strategies, as well as information on positive and negative aspects of the individual's religious life (Post et al., 2000; Puchalski & Romer, 2000; Koenig, 2002, p. 22). More in-depth interviews could include family history, religious affiliation, personal religious practices and spiritual experience. The interview allows the health professional to express openness and respect for patient religious beliefs and spiritual concerns, as well as explore their impact and potential use. It is most easily done when the clinicians have clarified their own positions and prejudices (Chirban, 2001).

10.5 Conclusion

Key issue: *The second great contribution that psychology has made to the dialogue with religion is an understanding of the positive impact of religion on health and some of the reasons for its effects.*

It is hard to overstate the importance of health as a topic in the psychology and religion dialogue. One of the main prejudices against religion among psychologists has been the perception that it has a negative impact on health. Even when most of Freud's ideas were discarded within psychology, his association of religion with pathology continued to have credibility with many scholars and practitioners. The research by Harold Koenig, Ken Pargament, and others has greatly changed this picture and with it the terms of the whole psychology and religion dialogue.

What are the practical implications of the findings on religion and health? At first glance, they suggest that religious participation should be encouraged, as it will lead to better health. However, religion is not just a set of discrete behaviors and attitudes, or a variety of alternative medicine—a kind of "God pill" that one takes to get healthy. Rather, it is a culture, a way of life and worldview with many implications for people who adopt it (Chatters, 2000). Some may find themselves unable or unwilling to make this kind of commitment.

One of the most fascinating aspects of the interchange between psychologists, theologians, and religious practitioners has been the argument over our vision for human life. Should it be "normality" or absence of disease? Or should human wellness be thought about in broader or more challenging terms? This issue recurs when we consider mental health issues, our next topic.

Chapter 11
Religion, Spirituality, and Mental Health

The relationship between religion or spirituality and mental health has been a subject of intense interest. Most of the thousands of studies on the topic in both the psychological and religious literature take the position that there is an important connection between religious activities, mental health, and spiritual wellness. However, the nature and importance of the relationship remains a topic of contention (Hathaway & Pargament, 1990). Some authors like Freud have argued that the relationship is essentially negative, with religion representing a kind of psychological pathology. More recent work has often suggested that religion has a positive effect on mental health and that good mental health is an important prerequisite for spiritual development (e.g., Stoeber, 1994, p. 98). A third group of authors (e.g., Welch, 1996, p. 98) argues that while there are important connections between the two, they are also somewhat independent of each other so that a person might have a rich spiritual life while suffering from mental illness, or be psychologically healthy but have deep spiritual problems.

Conceptual and definitional issues are of great importance to this topic. The views an investigator takes about the nature of religion, spirituality, and mental health will influence the kinds of questions they ask and the answers they receive. As we have seen, spirituality is not just a specific human characteristic but involves the way that we function as a whole in relation to the world, others, and the Divine (see Section 1.2.2). Thus, we might expect that there would be complex connections between spiritual wellness and mental health. Spiritual problems might involve issues of balance more than a specific and predictable set of psychological problems. We begin with a review of three important psychological approaches to the topic.

11.1 Psychological Models of Mental Health

11.1.1 The Medical Model

The most influential view of mental health in the US is the **medical model**, which forms the basis of the *Diagnostic and Statistical Manual of Mental Disorders* (DSM; American Psychiatric Association, 2000). It is a framework consisting of several beliefs:

J.M. Nelson, *Psychology, Religion, and Spirituality,*
DOI 10.1007/978-0-387-87573-6_11, @ Springer Science+Business Media, LLC 2009

1. Mental or psychological health is the normal state of human functioning and can be defined as a condition in which the person is functioning well in their environment with a minimum of personal distress. A person is healthy in the absence of problems.
2. Mental problems are factual entities that can be grouped into discrete illness categories just like physical problems. Each illness has a particular group of symptoms associated with it that are related to a common cause, and knowledge of the illness category will help devise and apply appropriate treatments.
3. Mental illness is an abnormal condition caused by problems either within the individual or in their external environment. Internal causes of mental illness might include biological dysfunctions or problems during development such as those caused by child abuse or neglect. External causes would include things like loss of a job or a situation perceived by the person as difficult or threatening.
4. Spiritual or religious issues are generally not relevant to mental health, but on occasion may be causes or manifestations of pathology (Lukoff, Lu, & Turner, 1992).

While the medical model is perhaps the dominant way that mental health is approached in many Western countries, it has been the target of criticism from both secular (e.g., Maddux, 2002) and religious authors (e.g., Yarhouse, Butman, & McRay, 2005, pp. 77–78). These criticisms challenge all aspects of the model:

1. A definition of health as absence of illness is negative and ignores the presence or absence of human strengths. Furthermore, terms like "normal" or "functioning well" are vague. For example, it is very difficult to find a point of reference that allows us to draw a firm line between delusional, spiritual, and "normal" experiences or beliefs (Clarke, 2001a; Brett, 2003; Peters, Day, McKenna, & Orbach, 1999). People without psychiatric diagnoses endorse many unusual beliefs, and those with mental illness have largely typical ideas about the world (e.g., Peters, Joseph, & Garety, 1999), leaving the line between mental health and illness unclear. Furthermore, "normal" is not necessarily best; as Pargament (1997, p. 337) has noted, those who helped Jews escape the Holocaust in Europe were not "normal" but certainly constitute a model of human development and spiritual health.
2. Mental problems are not self-evident facts. Rather, labeling something as "abnormal" or "illness" is a judgment which depends upon an ideology and a set of cultural values by which those in power interpret the meaning of a condition, identify it as a problem, and propose a solution (Woolfolk, 1998, pp. 35–45; Vergote, 1988, p. 14). Ignoring the value component of this process commits the **naturalistic fallacy** (Moore, 1903), pretending that value judgments derive from matters of fact. Even strictly utilitarian views of the world deal with meaning, although many argue that pragmatic worldviews—which are often found in psychology—are too limited (Arendt, 1998, pp. 154–156). "Factual" descriptions and illness categories are thus social constructs that may be misleading or provide relatively little help in finding a solution to a particular problem. In fact, diagnosis may make the situation worse by pathologizing essentially normal parts of life (Lopez et al., 2006).

3. The medical model tends to focus attention on certain kinds of causal conditions and to unnecessarily label them as different from normal problems. Individualistic and biological views of mental disorder and treatment are unnecessarily favored over explanations that include personal choices or social and relational factors (Nesse, 2005).

4. Spiritual and religious concerns are in fact very important to mental health. As many as 1/3 of client sessions include references to religious issues, depending on how that is defined and measured (Lukoff, Lu, & Turner, 1996). Neglecting religion or holding a negative view of it is biased and may amount to a kind of cultural insensitivity or prejudice (O'Connor & Vandenberg, 2005).

5. While a view of mental disorder as illness was designed to remove guilt and restore the dignity of people with problems, in fact it dehumanizes them, picturing individuals as pathological or underdeveloped and in need of outside manipulation from an expert. It also ignores the moral component and consequences involved in many forms of mental disorder and discourages us from taking responsibility for others and ourselves. The results can be even crueler than the original problem (Taylor, 2007, pp. 620–634, 697–743).

A number of recent attempts have been made to adapt the medical model and address these concerns. Psychoanalysts have published a *Psychodynamic Diagnostic Manual* (Psychodynamic Diagnostic Manual Task Force, 2006) designed to complement the DSM and look at the person more holistically. In addition to covering traditional topics like the patient's subjective experience of problems (S axis) and personality difficulties (P axis), the new system also includes an axis of mental function (M axis) that examines personal assets such as relational and emotional capacity, the ability to observe oneself or others and form internal representations, and the capacity to form personal standards or ideals. However, the definition of mental health in the new system is still based on adaptiveness, flexibility, and lack of distress rather than a broader model of health that more directly addresses spiritual and religious concerns.

11.1.1.1 The Medical Model and Religion

Recent revisions of the medical model now allow for the possibility that spiritual problems might be considered as treatment issues. These changes were spearheaded by a group of transpersonal psychiatrists, and the modifications are part of an overall trend toward greater cultural sensitivity in diagnosis and treatment. In addition to revising codes of ethics for the helping professions to require respect for client religious beliefs, the DSM has been modified to include the diagnostic category of Religious or Spiritual Problem:

> This category can be used when the focus of clinical attention is a religious or spiritual problem. Examples include distressing experiences that involve loss of faith, problems associated with conversion to a new faith, or questioning of spiritual values that may not necessarily be related to an organized church or religious institution (American Psychiatric Association, 2000, p. 741).

In the new category, religious problems are conceptualized as difficulties related to institutional practices, while spiritual problems are related to our relationship with a higher power or transcendence. Types of religious problems might include a change in level of faith or altered connection to a faith community. Spiritual problems could include spiritual experiences or dealing with problems that have a spiritual component such as a terminal illness or an addiction (Turner, Lukoff, Barnhouse, & Lu, 1995). Some transpersonal authors also distinguish between a **spiritual crisis**—a life event with a spiritual component—and a **spiritual emergency** which is distress related to a spiritual experience or the outcome of spiritual practices (Grof, 2003, pp. 50–75; Sperry, 2001; Lukoff, Lu, & Turner, 1998). An important limitation of the new category is that it is listed as a "V" code in the DSM, which means that services for treatment of the problem will not be reimbursed by US insurance companies or government agencies.

What differentiates healthy and pathological states in the medical model? It can be difficult to draw a firm distinction between them as health and pathology occur in different degrees and mixtures (cf. Peters, 2001). Wagener and Malony (2006) note that several approaches can be used to identify pathological conditions. In psychology a functional approach is often taken, considering the effects of the experience on the person's life and its developmental progression. In this view, pathological states tend to be marked by a slow onset and deterioration in functioning. Non-pathological religious states come on more quickly, and are seen by individuals as enhancing their lives. Within religious traditions, community norms and the experienced judgment of religious figures can also be used to tell whether a condition is healthy or pathological. In fact, a purely individualistic and mechanical approach to distinguishing pathological and non-pathological religious phenomena is probably doomed to failure, as experiences that might be considered problematic in one person may be normal or healthy in another (Lukoff et al., 1996, 1998; Beit-Hallahmi, 1996; Claridge, 2001).

It is now believed that there is a small positive correlation—but not an automatic relation—between religiosity and good mental health. This relationship is found in a broad spectrum of religious groups but is especially true among individuals who are both spiritual and religious compared with those who identify themselves as neither (Larson et al., 1992; Koenig, Hays, et al., 1999; Hall & Brokaw, 1995; Corveleyn, 1996; Koenig, 2001a; Rippentrop, Altmaier, Chen, Found, & Keffala, 2005; Moberg, 2002a; Merrill & Salazar, 2002). Historical treatments of religion that emphasized its negative role in mental health (e.g., witch trials) have been balanced by information about the positive role of churches and religious communities in the development of hospitals and compassionate care for the physically and mentally ill (Koenig & Larson, 2001; Koenig, 2000). Although the research is somewhat inconsistent due to methodological and definitional problems (Crawford, Handal, & Wiener, 1989; Hackney & Sanders, 2003; Bergin, 1983; van Uden & Pieper, 1996), its quality is steadily improving, and good longitudinal studies are finding positive relationships between variables such as religious attendance and mental health (e.g., King, Cummings, & Whetstone, 2005). The size of this correlation varies according to how mental health is defined and is probably stronger in some groups such as women or the elderly but holds for both adolescents and adults (Strawbridge, Sherma, Cohen, & Kaplan, 2001; Crawford et al., 1989; Koenig, George, & Titus, 2004). Studies that define mental health as an absence of illness generally find a small positive relationship between health and religious involvement, while research that uses a more challenging benchmark such as self-actualization, personal integration or existential well-being finds stronger positive relationships (Worthington, Kurusu, McCullough, & Sandage, 1996). Attempts to find systematic psychopathological characteristics in religious communities have largely failed, even when studying unusual groups like charismatics (Newberg, Wintering, Morgan, & Waldman, 2006). So while Freud associated religion with negative mental health, in fact the opposite appears to be the trend (Koenig, 2006).

Studies have found religiosity to be associated with lower levels of many kinds of psychological problems including psychosis, borderline personality, and schizotypal symptoms. UK studies have also found negative relationships between religiousness and **psychoticism**, a personality trait marked by asociality, as well as lower level of empathy and social conformity (Koenig, 2001a; Joseph & Diduca, 2001; Tateyama, Asai, Kamisada et al., 1993, Tateyama, Asai, Hashimoto et al., 1998; Siddle, Haddock, Tarrier, & Faragher, 2002; White, Joseph, & Neil, 1995; Maltby, Garner, Lewis, & Day, 2000; Maltby & Day, 2002; Joseph, Smith, & Diduca, 2002; Hills, Francis, Argyle, & Jackson, 2004; Francis, Lewis, Brown, Philipchalk, & Lester, 1995; Diduca & Joseph, 1997). Some religious experiences such as possession states have often been attributed to psychosis. However, research indicates that there are significant differences between psychotic states and religious experiences, and that when psychotic delusions do have religious content they do not have a negative effect on treatment outcome. Thus, normal or even unusual religious experiences are not necessarily connected to mental health problems, although psychological problems might occasionally interfere with one's ability to participate in religious practices. Overall, while there are no doubt specific instances where religious involvement has negative effects on mental health, these are not commonplace (Wilson, 1998; Noblitt & Perskin, 2000, pp. 45–46; House, 2001; Siddle, Haddock, Tarrier, & Faragher, 2004; English, 1954; Pargament & Park, 1995).

Now that researchers have largely accepted the presence of a positive relationship between religion and mental health, the focus of work has shifted toward identifying the mechanisms for this effect. A number of possibilities have been proposed (e.g., Koenig, 2001a, 2001b; van Uden & Pieper, 1996), including (1) beliefs supporting a positive worldview that provides meaning, purpose, and an optimistic attitude in the face of difficulties; (2) beliefs favoring a healthy lifestyle and positive relationships with others; (3) generation of positive emotions through participation in personal and communal religious practices and rituals; (4) involvement in a community that provides social and spiritual support; and (5) perceived support by God. Overall these factors appear to act by strengthening resilience to deal with difficult situations (Watlington & Murphy, 2006; Fiala, Bjork, & Gorsuch, 2002). In their longitudinal studies, Dillon and Wink have found that this buffer effect appears to relate to religiousness but not to spirituality (Dillon & Wink, 2007, e.g., pp. 187–193, 2003; Wink, 2003). Intrinsic religiosity appears to have an especially strong buffering effect, while extrinsic religiosity is related to difficulty processing emotions such as guilt (Ventis, 1995; Linley & Joseph, 2004; Maltby, 2005). Paralleling this is the finding that spiritual integration by itself appears to be unrelated to affective well-being, but the relational effects of religious beliefs such as a concern for social justice are correlated with lower levels of depression and higher levels of positive affect (Powers, Cramer, & Grubka, 2007). Interactions between various factors or some kind of overall holistic effect of religion may also be involved in its positive relationship to mental health, although these possibilities are still largely unstudied.

Research that finds positive effects of religion on mental health deals with large group averages, not the results for every individual or small religious community. This raises the possibility that while the overall effect of religion is beneficial, it may be negative with certain individuals, subgroups, or types of religious practices (Bergin, 1983; Fetzer Institute, 1999; cf. Maselko & Buka, 2008; Oates, 1955) or that there may be a limited group of psychological symptoms such as obsessive thoughts that are more frequent among religious individuals (Abramowitz, Deacon, Woods, & Tolin, 2004; Sorotzkin, 1998). Under what circumstances could religion be related to negative mental health outcomes? Some possibilities would include (1) interpersonal problems or religious struggles related to beliefs, community participation or the effects of religious practices (Exline, 2002b); (2) unbalanced beliefs, such as stress on sinfulness leading to excess guilt (Spilka, 1986); and (3) **spiritual abuse**, "the misuse of social or political power in a spiritual context" (Wagener & Malony, 2006, p. 146; cf. Wehr, 2000). Presumably, religious or spiritual activities performed out of a sense of obsessive need rather than free choice will also have less desirable outcomes (cf. Vallerand, 2008). On the positive side, consistent spiritual practices within the support and guidance of a strong spiritual community may be associated with greater resilience in the face of adversity.

11.1.2 Positive Models of Mental Health

Dissatisfaction with the negative medical model approach to mental health has led many psychologists to consider positive alternatives. In these new approaches, human health is conceptualized as more than an absence of illness. Instead, an attempt is made to propose a broader vision of what the "good life" or goal of human existence is like and how it should be achieved (Hardy, 2000; Ryff & Singer, 1998). Ryan and Deci (2001) have noted that positive models of mental health tend to follow two different approaches that have different visions for the goal of human life. In the **hedonic** approach, positive mental health is equated with **happiness**, the short-term experiences of pleasure and avoidance of negative emotions (Ellison, 1991; Diener, Suh, Lucas, & Smith, 1999; Keyes & Lopez, 2002; Lawton, 1996; Myers & Diener, 1995; Urry et al., 2004; cf. Pressman & Cohen, 2005), or **subjective well-being** (SWB), which is the individuals' evaluation of the quality of their lives (Diener & Lucas, 1999; Diener, 2000; Diener, Lucas, & Oishi, 2002). This approach is based upon the moral claim that the self-interest of the individual in seeking pleasure and avoiding pain is the fundamental human motive (Higgins, Grant, & Shah, 1999, p. 244; Slife, Mitchell, & Whollery, 2004). Hedonic factors are thought to broaden and build positive patterns of thought and behavior and probably have a positive impact on physical health and longevity (Fredrickson, 2005, 2006; Danner, Snowdon, & Friesen, 2001; Pressman & Cohen, 2005).

In the **eudaimonic** approach (e.g., Ryff, 1989), mental health is thought of as a dynamic process rather than an end state of pleasure, and is described in somewhat broader terms as **psychological well-being** (PWB), the position of a fully functioning individual who (a) engages life, seeking to actualize their potential and find meaning; (b) develops quality relationships; and (c) develops competence and seeks to master the environment (van Dierendonck & Mohan, 2006; Ryff & Singer, 1998). This is similar to the ethical position taken by the Greek philosopher Aristotle.

The most prominent school of thought within psychology following the eudaimonic approach is the **positive psychology** movement, which hopes to develop a science that will maximize human happiness and potential, helping people to live well (Seligman & Csikszentmihalyi, 2000; Snyder & McCullough, 2000; Seligman, 2002; Emmons, 2004). Positive psychologists argue that the key to achieving these goals lies in individual strengths, character traits, and moral virtues (McCullough, Kilpatrick, Emmons, & Larson, 2001; Davidson, 2005). After reviewing a list of virtues from religions and philosophies, Seligman and his colleagues (e.g., Seligman, Steen, Park, & Peterson, 2005; Peterson & Seligman, 2004; Dahlsgaard, Peterson, & Seligman, 2005; Peterson, 2006) have compiled a list of 24 strengths and virtues that fall into 6 core groups: wisdom, courage, relations and care for others, justice, temperance, and transcendence. Factor analytic studies suggest that the virtues fall in two broad categories, warmth-based virtues like empathy and conscientiousness-based ones like justice (Worthington, Sharp, Lerner, & Sharp, 2006). Some positive psychologists see these strengths as a kind of antithesis of the DSM categories of mental illness, and that increasing virtuous activity could enhance mental health and happiness. The eudaimonic and positive psychology traditions fit well in European psychology, which tends to oppose the idea of humans as hedonistic or passive and helpless (Pleh, 2006). However, they have been criticized for offering a shotgun approach to virtue with lists of strengths that are overly simplistic and have no common core or coherent idea about the nature of the good life (Hackney, 2007).

Factor analytic studies have suggested that hedonic or subjective well-being and eudaimonic or psychological well-being are distinct but related, perhaps with SWB or happiness as a by-product of PWB (Keyes, Shmotkin, & Ryff, 2002; Ryff & Keyes, 1995; Ryff & Singer, 1998; cf. Scheier et al., 2006). Some scholars define **flourishing** as a condition where people are high in both SWB and PWB, while free of mental health problems (Keyes & Lopez, 2002; Keyes, 2002; Fredrickson & Losada, 2005). SWB is affected by a number of things, including micro worries about personal health or success, and macro worries about broader issues like the environment. Gender is related to emotions connected with SWB, for example, women tend to report higher levels of sadness than men (Schwartz & Melech,

2000; Nolen-Hoeksema & Rusting, 1999). Emotions connected with SWB can have important effects in terms of directing and motivating behavior in specific situations, as well as affecting more global values and priorities (Frijda, 1999).

11.1.2.1 The Hedonic Model and Religion

In general, studies have found positive connections between religion and SWB, although the results depend on measures used, the sample studied, and other variables examined (Paloutzian & Kirkpatrick, 1995; Lewis, 2002; Atchley, 1997b; Robbins & Francis, 1996; Fiori, Brown, Cortina, & Antonucci, 2006). Some empirical studies in the US and Europe find that religion accounts for 5–7% of the variance in life satisfaction, which would mean that its impact is similar in magnitude to the effect of physical health on well-being (e.g., Mookherjee, 1998; Diener, Suh et al., 1999; van der Lans, 1996; Ellison, 1991; Levin & Taylor, 1998). In some US data, this relationship is stronger in groups with higher levels of religiousness such as African Americans, immigrants, and older adults (Fry, 2000). In UK research, the connection tends to be found when looking at long-term measures of happiness (Lewis & Cruise, 2006). In the continental European setting, vanishingly small or negative correlations between SWB and religiosity in former communist countries have often been found, perhaps because religion was less culturally sanctioned (Krause, 2003; Harker, 2001; Diener & Clifton, 2002; Ferriss, 2002).

Dimensions of religion related to SWB include intrinsic religious motivation; individual beliefs, religious experiences, and devotional practices that generate positive feelings; participation in organized activities, and identification with a supportive community. Various aspects of religiosity have different relations to life satisfaction for different groups (Byrd, Hageman, & Isle, 2007; Ellison, Gay, & Glass, 1989; Musick, 2000; Cohen, 2002; Maltby & Day, 2003; Levin, 2001; McCullough, 1995). In an important study, Wink and Dillon (2003) found that religiousness but not spirituality was related to relational aspects of well-being through service, generative, and creative activities, while spirituality was related more to self-perceived personal growth. A number of other ways that religion might affect SWB have been suggested, including having a personal relationship with a divine Other, reducing self-focus, and providing a system of meaning, purpose, and coherence (Ellison, 1991, 1998; Koenig, 1994; Plante & Sharma, 2001; French & Joseph, 1999; Michael & Snyder, 2005; Smith, 2000; van Dierendonck & Mohan, 2006; Levin & Taylor, 1998). Religion might also have indirect effects through supporting other things that have strong effects on SWB such as marital status, healthier lifestyles, or academic achievement (Myers & Diener, 1995; Zautra & Bachrach, 2000; Martin, Kirkcaldy, & Siefen, 2003). Subjective well-being is more strongly affected by our perceptions of the world than our actual circumstances (Diener, Lucas et al., 2002), so religious beliefs might well have an impact on SWB.

A by-product of well-being research has been a support for religious views questioning the value of ethical materialism. Often closely linked to metaphysical materialism (see Section 2.1.3), **ethical materialism** argues that pleasure is the main goal of life and that this is achieved primarily through acquiring and possessing material goods. Research on materialism indicates that it has two aspects: a striving for money and possessions, and a focus on image, appearance, and social status and recognition. In samples of US individuals, students who rate themselves as more materialistic have higher levels of distress, depression, and anxiety, more substance use or personality problems, less frequent experiences of positive emotion, and lower scores of well-being (Ryan & Deci, 2001). Dramatic increases in income in the US, Europe, and Japan since World War II have generally led to no changes in SWB, suggesting that once a basic level of material comfort is achieved, further increases do not enhance well-being (Diener & Oishi, 2000; Inglehart & Klingemann, 2000; see Fig. 11.1). Materialistic people tend to be more extrinsically motivated, place a lower value on relationships, and are more manipulative and less empathetic. Especially when combined with high levels of individualism (see Section 12.3.1), these patterns interfere with the social connectedness and sensitivity to emotional factors necessary for the development of well-being, fueling a focus on wealth and status which conflicts with other values like benevolence, justice, and environmental protection (Kasser, 2006; Csikszentmihalyi, 1999). Some scholars (e.g., Lane, 2001; O'Connor, 2005; Moltmann, 1980, p. 37) see materialism as a primary factor behind a loss of meaning, declining levels of happiness, and increasing rates of depression in many countries. Materialism as an ethic thus appears to have limited validity at best and toxic effects when followed exclusively as a way of life—a position taken by most religious traditions.

Critique. A number of criticisms of the hedonic model have been articulated.

1. Some research suggests that the goal of the hedonic model—happiness—is not something that people can strive for; rather, each individual has a personal emotional level or **hedonic set point** which is determined by genetics, temperament, personality variables, biology, and other factors (Weiss, Bates, & Luciano, 2008). This level is generally positive, and efforts to increase it have only temporary

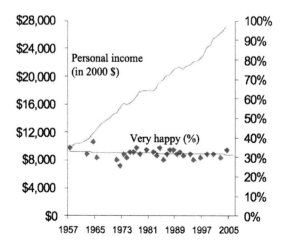

Fig. 11.1 *US Personal Income and Happiness, 1957–2005.* The disconnection between material wealth and happiness is evident in US data that shows no change in the percentage of people calling themselves "very happy" despite a tripling in personal income over a 50-year period. Chart courtesy of David Myers

effects so that people striving for additional happiness must get on a **hedonic treadmill** of increasing efforts in order to get and maintain a level of happiness above their set point (Hamer, 1996; Lykken & Tellegen, 1996; Ryan & Deci, 2001; Frederick & Loewenstein, 1999; Suh, Diener, & Fujita, 1996; Diener & Lucas, 1999; O'Connor, 2005; Diener & Diener, 1996; Lawton, 1996; Emmons, 1999, p. 156; but cf. Davidson, 2005; Diener, Lucas, & Scollon, 2006).

2. Studies use simplistic measurement procedures, such as reducing all emotions to pleasure and pain. Most are cross-sectional with no theoretical rationale and ignore the sociocultural context in which behavior occurs. Since the measures focus on momentary mood states, it is not clear they would even detect changes related to issues of meaning that manifest themselves over longer periods of time (e.g., Shorey, Snyder, Rand, Hockemeyer, & Feldman, 2002, p. 327; Berenbaum, Raghavan, Huynh-Nhu, Vernon, & Gomez, 1999; Lewis & Cruise, 2006; Levin & Taylor, 1998; Bufford, Paloutzian, & Ellison, 1991; Diener & Clifton, 2002; Diener & Oishi, 2000; Davidson, 2005; Sommers & Kosmitzki, 1988; Ellison et al., 1989; Antonovsky, 1994).

3. The concept of SWB as pleasure is limited. It ignores many other important domains in life such as purpose and growth (Ryff, 1989; Lane, 2001, p. 6). The hedonic model assumes that well-being will follow from the satisfaction of any desire or completion of any task as long as it is valued and chosen by the individual (Cantor & Sanderson, 1999); however, not all desires will lead to well-being if achieved (Ryan & Deci, 2001). In addition, the limitation of the model to the pursuit of pleasure ignores the fact that negative emotions and adversity are given parts of life that may bring benefits and provide important incentives for growth (Vash, 1994; Exline, 2002a, 2002b; Hacker, 1974). For instance, Buddhist thought argues that pursuit of positive emotions and avoidance of negative ones eventually affects our ability to see life in a realistic manner, leading to a variety of problems (Gunn, 2000, p. 57).

11.1.2.2 The Eudaimonic Model and Religion

Positive psychology relates to religion in a couple of ways. First, religion can be seen as a source of moral inspiration and a dialogue partner that helps to provide more sophisticated and useful definitions of concepts (Watts, Dutton, & Gulliford, 2006; Schulman, 2002). Second, religion or spirituality can be seen as a kind of goal-directed activity or striving for the sacred that can have positive benefits (Emmons, 2006; Pargament & Mahoney, 2002). These views have led psychologists to examine virtues traditionally advocated by religious traditions as potential contributors to positive mental health.

Gratitude. From a positive psychology perspective, gratitude is a virtue with roots in early attachment experiences. It is relatively uncommon, first appearing during childhood but mostly found in highly generative adults. Like humility, gratitude is a virtue not emphasized in contemporary culture, so theorists have turned to traditional religious and philosophical sources in an attempt to understand it (Emmons, 2004; Emmons & Shelton, 2002; McAdams & Bauer, 2004). From a philosophical perspective, gratitude is a social phenomenon. It implies that there is a benefactor and a beneficent act that is intended for a recipient, who may experience feelings of indebtedness toward the benefactor. These emotions act as a moral indicator that we have received something good, and counter feelings of resentment, superiority, and dissatisfaction. Expressions of gratitude motivate others to behave in helpful ways. Narcissism inhibits the experience and expression of gratitude because of feelings of entitlement and lack of empathy (Roberts, 2004; McCullough, Kilpatrick et al., 2001). Spiritual experiences and Christian affiliation appear to be connected with higher levels and expressions of gratitude (Emmons & Kneezel, 2005). A grateful outlook is linked to a number of indicators of well-being, including optimism, more positive and less negative affect, and tolerance for unpleasant emotions during difficulties (Emmons & McCullough, 2003).

Hope. Hope is a prominent theme in Christian theology (Dutney, 2005; Moltmann, 1967), and research on hope by Snyder (2002) and others has generated considerable literature. For Snyder, all human action is goal directed, and hope is an essential prerequisite for successful striving. He defines **hope** as the perceived capability to (1) engage in *pathway thinking* about how to reach desired ends and (2) keep ourselves motivated with *agency thinking*—positive self-talk about how to accomplish our goals. In this view, hope is about thinking rather than emotions, although a positive emotional state can be a by-product that helps sustain our activity (Snyder, Harris et al., 1991; Roesch & Vaughn, 2006). Pathway thinking develops in infancy and is related to secure attachment relationships, interaction with caretakers, and learning to think about goals in more sophisticated ways, although later interventions should also be able to increase pathway and agency thinking (Snyder, 2000a; Snyder, Rand, & Sigmon, 2002; Snyder, Lehman, Kluck, & Monsson, 2006; Snyder, 1995). Hope appears to have both dispositional and situational components (Snyder, Sympson et al., 1996). It appears to correlate with a wide variety of positive things, including measures of adaptation, PWB and perceived meaning in life (Gilman, Dooley, & Florell, 2006; Shorey, Snyder, Yang, & Lewin, 2003; Wrobleski & Snyder, 2005; Rodriguez-Hanley & Snyder, 2000; Irving et al., 2004; Snyder & Taylor, 2000). Like other qualities that develop positive emotions, hope is associated with decreased likelihood of developing diseases like hypertension or diabetes (Richman et al., 2005). The model appears to explain at least some of the effectiveness of cognitive-behavioral approaches to counseling (Snyder, Ilardi et al., 2000). Although Snyder has avoided any references to religion in his formulation of hope, he sees agency and pathway thinking as important in religion (Snyder, Sigmon, & Feldman, 2002).

Critics have challenged the adequacy of Snyder's concept of hope as too ego-centered, tied to personal control and competency, while leaving out ideas of basic hope or trust in the world or God that are powerful, as well as more fundamental and phenomenologically unique (Smith, 2007; Trzebinski & Zieba, 2004; Aspinwall & Leaf, 2002; Feldman & Snyder, 2005; Peterson, 2006). Snyder seems to argue that hope is always positive regardless of situation and goals (Snyder, 2000b; cf. also

McCullough & Tsang, 2004), confusing hope and blind optimism. This is problematic because hope is only helpful in situations where a sought-after outcome is both possible and desirable, while hope for an unattainable goal is illusive and leads to failure. Too much or too little hope is not good (Watts et al., 2006; Baumeister, 1998; Polivy & Herman, 2002; Peterson, 1999; Menninger, 1962; but cf. Snyder, Rand, King, Feldman, & Woodward, 2002; Snyder & Rand, 2003). Religious versions of hope that combine optimism with humility may be more desirable formulations (Meissner, 1987, pp. 186–187, 204–205; Harter, 2002).

Positive psychology research on hope and other virtues also suffers from the positivist tendency to atomize and focus on single virtues or characteristics, typically those that support the idea of the good life held by the investigator. This positivist approach assumes that virtues operate independently of each other. It contrasts with religious thought, which tends to emphasize that virtues like hope or love depend upon and strengthen other virtues, and that spiritual crises involve the whole person, although they may start in relation to a specific issue (e.g., Maloney, 1992, pp. 214, 266; Thunberg, 1995, pp. 309–322; Guntrip, 1949, p. 31; Merton, 2005b, p. 80). Some researchers suggest that a dialogue between positive psychology and theology would help it avoid becoming too simplistic and allow it to see things in a broader framework (Watts et al., 2006).

Meaning. In positive psychology, an outcome of engagement with the world is **meaning**, a feeling or idea that life has value, we have a place in the world, and we can seek ends through activities, caring relationships, and involvement in life (Wong, 1998a, 1998b; Hefner, 1998; Hermans, 1998; Heidegger, 1962, pp. 370–380; Korotkov, 1998; Wong & Fry, 1998; Halama, 2003; Baumeister, 1991, p. 312; cf. Sommer & Baumeister, 1998). Meaning thus involves a global *state* or feeling we have about things. It also involves a *process* of meaning-making, by which we attempt to gain meaning or restore it, if it has been lost or threatened, for instance, in the aftermath of a trauma. Religion appears to be generally related to a higher sense of meaning and to a stronger meaning-making process that helps individuals cope with trauma and grow from it (Park, 2005). Emmons (1999) refers to the pursuit of meaning as **spiritual striving** and sees it as an inherent part of the personality that brings inner unity, minimizing conflicts between goals and making painful experiences comprehensible (Petersen & Roy, 1985; van der Lans, 1996; cf. Baumeister, 1991, pp. 29–31). Our age and developmental status provide a context for this search (Seifert, 2002). Loss of meaning is a significant issue in contemporary culture, as there are many reports of feelings of emptiness, especially from younger individuals (Ramsey & Blieszner, 2000). A lack of meaning leads to what Maddi (1998) has described as **existential sickness**. It has three components: (1) *vegetativeness*—loss of interest, apathy, and boredom; (2) *nihilism*—a need to disconfirm the possible positive meanings of others, and along with it anger, distrust, and cynicism; competitiveness and combativeness; and (3) *adventurousness*—attempting to counter lack of meaning and boredom through high-risk activities. Critics of modernity argue that many aspects of contemporary culture such as its technological and instrumental focus make the finding of meaning difficult and increase the risk of existential problems (Hefner, 1998).

11.1.3 Mental Health as Spiritual Well-Being

Some scholars argue that religion also produces a kind of well-being that is different from the hedonic or eudaimonic varieties described by psychologists. Craig Ellison (Ellison, 1983; Paloutzian & Ellison, 1982; Ellison & Smith, 1991) has developed the concept of **spiritual well-being** to describe this unique effect. In his view, in addition to desires for pleasure or self-fulfillment, humans have needs for transcendence, "The sense of well-being that we experience when we find purposes to commit ourselves to which involve ultimate meaning for life" (Ellison, 1983, p. 330). This type of well-being provides integration, harmony, and freedom within the personality and is of two types. First, it involves a *vertical relation* or well-being in connection to God, which he calls **religious well-being**. Second, it includes a *horizontal relation* to the world around us, including a sense of life purpose and satisfaction, or **existential well-being**. Spiritual well-being can be an expression of spiritual health or maturity but is not identical with them (cf. Mansager, 2000). It is different than psychosocial well-being because it goes beyond material aims to fundamental questions. Spiritual well-being has a relational focus rather than a goal-directed striving focus and has less of a set pattern of development (Ai, 2000; Mohan, Mohan, Roy, Basu, & Viranjini, 2004). Because psychology lacks a spiritual or theological theoretical base, traditional psychology has had a hard time incorporating concepts related to spiritual well-being (Charry, 2001).

Spiritual well-being is associated with higher religious salience, participation, and satisfaction, as well as better physical and psychological well-being, lower anxiety, and less depression, especially in evangelical Christians (Poloma & Pendleton, 1990; Ellison & Smith, 1991; Ellison, 1983; Ellison, Boardman, Williams, & Jackson, 2001; Davis, Kerr, & Kurpus, 2003). It is also related to self-realization, as individuals who have higher levels of self-realization have greater spiritual well-being, stronger intrinsic religious commitments and a greater frequency of spiritual experiences (Park, Meyers, & Czar, 1988). Development of spiritual well-being is related to positive relations with parents, personality characteristics like conscientiousness or agreeableness, and the presence of religious experiences. It is also related to beliefs that emphasize acceptance or less self-focus, the establishment of healthy dependencies, as well as the development of a relationship with a religious community (MacDonald, 2000; Hodges, 2002; Cecero, Bedrosian, Fuentes, & Bornstein, 2006). Unity and coherence of goals and acting in accordance with them also seem related to spiritual well-being, as well as other positive characteristics such as freedom from compulsions, self-esteem, higher empathy, and likelihood of helping behaviors (Sheldon & Kasser, 1995; Harter, 2002). Spiritual well-being is challenged by the loss or violation of things seen as spiritually significant or sacred, such as can happen in an illness, injury, or relationship problem such as divorce. These losses can be devastating because the sacred occupies a highly valued part of our world. Violation or desecration can be particularly problematic, especially in those with more negative styles of religious coping such as blaming, leading to reactions of anger (Pargament & Mahoney, 2005; Pargament, Magyar, Benore, & Mahoney, 2005; Emmons & Crumpler, 1999).

11.2 Spiritual and Religious Models of Mental Health

11.2.1 Christian Views

There is no single Christian theory of mental illness and health. Mental illness is not a dominant concern in Christian thought, and treatments that do exist generally place it in a holistic context that emphasizes the interdependence of body, mind, and spirit (e.g., Larchet, 2005, pp. 1–33). Despite the diversity of opinions, certain traditional formulations about the nature of spiritual struggles have been very influential in Christian communities. One of the most important of these is the theory of the Eight Deadly Thoughts developed in Orthodox thought by Evagrius Ponticus and expanded upon by later writers like Maximus Confessor.

11.2.1.1 The Eight Deadly Thoughts

Evagrius and other Orthodox thinkers believed that mental disturbances—unwelcome and unwholesome or "deadly" thoughts—were a universal occurrence, and that different kinds of problematic thoughts were characteristic of particular stages of development. In their view, we have no choice in whether or not we have these thoughts. However, we can make choices about how to deal with the thoughts and the situations that provoke them. For instance, in the first stages of spiritual development, we deal with basic desires for things that satisfy our bodily needs and bring pleasure. Evagrius thought that these desires were perfectly normal but could be misused (cf. Merton, 2005b, p. 168). Instead of simply eating enough to satisfy our hunger or obtaining enough material possessions to meet our basic needs, we think that more is better, and we become inordinately focused upon the objects that satisfy or bring pleasure, building our lives around them. These objects become **disordered attachments**. They are disordered because they unbalance our life, causing us to focus our efforts excessively on them at the expense of other things we need and alienating us from normal desires (cf. Thomas, 1998). They are thus very different than the **relational attachments** described by developmental theorists and psychoanalysts (see Section 8.2). Healthy relationships ultimately serve to increase our freedom, while disordered attachments and passions limit our freedom—they become addictions (see below, Section 11.3.1). Thus in the Christian view, human freedom is not doing whatever we like, but a freedom from disordered attachments that ultimately limit our choices and negatively impact our life in many ways (Merton, 2006, pp. 311–315).

In the Evagrian system, there are two ways that we can respond to this potential for disordered attachment—vices or virtues. **Vices** are the repeated seeking of objects in excess of need that interfere with other aspects of our life. They are opposed by **virtues,** which are acts or patterns of behavior that rightly use our desires and resist the formation of disordered attachments. Love is the chief of these virtues because it helps all of them work together in harmony (von Balthasar, 1995, p. 113). If we repeatedly seek the objects of our attachments we develop **passions**, irrational desires for these objects that reinforce habits of inordinate seeking and vice. These passions can increasingly dominate us, overshadowing our rational power of decision-making and ultimately leading to inner conflict, confusion, and a loss of freedom. Normal emotional states like joy, peace, courage, and love give way to anxiety, anger, dejection, depression, and relational problems (Maximus, 2003; Louth, 1996, p. 99; Thunberg, 1995; Spidlik, 1986, pp. 245–246; Hausherr, 1990, p. 157; Schimmel, 1997; Theophan, 1995, pp. 227–256). Through self-examination and struggle against disordered attachments and passions, we learn about their source and how they can be combated. This is where we gain true knowledge of spiritual life (Merton, 2006, pp. 46–52).

Evagrius had a developmental view of psychopathology. He believed that eight thoughts—and the virtues needed to overcome them—tended to happen in a certain order, affecting different parts of us at different stages of development (see Table 11.1). His view of the human person was based on Plato's division of the human person into immaterial **soul** and material body, and the soul into a passionate part and a rational aspect (*nous*) that brings us knowledge of God. Plato (1997, p. 1071) further divided the passionate part of the soul into two faculties: the *concupiscible* or **desirous faculty** and the forceful, irascible, angry or **incisive faculty**, a model followed by many other Orthodox writers (Sherwood, 1955, p. 84; cf. Helminiak, 1996). Evagrius believed that early in development most problems related to disorders in the desirous faculty—gluttony, lust, and avarice. If these problems were

Table 11.1 The Eight Deadly Thoughts of Evagrius

Deadly Thought	Opposed Virtue	Ascetic Techniques
A. Problems of desire	abstinence	
Gluttony, inordinate desire	self-mastery	fasting, vigils
Lust, craving for pleasure (*porneia*)	temperance	self-denial, prayer; anger
Avarice, envy	perseverance	almsgiving, hope
B. Problems of irascibility	love	
Grief , sadness (*lupe*)	hatred of pleasure	charity, hospitality, good deeds; thanks for misfortunes
Wrath, anger (*orge*)	long-suffering	compassion, gentleness; gifts or almsgiving; psalmody
Sloth, weariness (*acedie*)	patience	perseverance, tears; manual labor; prayer
C. Problems of Rationality	rational knowledge	
Vainglory, conceit	humility	self-examination obedience
Pride, arrogance	humility	self-examination obedience love in community

Source: Evagrius, (1972); Sinkewicz, (2003, pp. 36–37, 63–65, 154–163); Thunberg, (1995, pp. 268–276); cf. Thomas (1998, 2.148 ad 1; 2.36 ad 3; 2.118 ad 1; 2.158 ad 2; 2.25 ad 1)

overcome and the person progressed spiritually, they would then encounter difficulties connected to the incisive faculty such as sadness and anger (Sinkewicz, 2003, pp. 214–215; Dysinger, 2005, p. 21; cf. Cassian, 1999, pp. 69–193). At the highest level were the problems of the rational faculty, especially irrational ideas about our accomplishments and ourselves. These are connected to the problems of **vainglory** or craving of praise from others and lack of humility or **pride**. In this view of things, psychopathology and arrested development are related to attachments and passions that trap us, while progress and freedom come from the development of **apatheia** or detachment from inordinate desires. This progress manifests itself in a number of ways, including emotional harmony, behavioral control and freedom from distractions in prayer (Driscoll, 2005, pp. 22–24). A key point here is that detachment does not mean disinterest, just freedom from excessive or misaimed desire.

For Maximus, **phronesis** or the practical life involved finding the right use of our desires. This involved (1) **wisdom,** or the ability to discern what is right use, and (2) virtue, or how to do it (Thunberg, 1995, p. 80). Ideally, phronesis involves finding a way for the desirous, incisive, and rational faculties of the soul to work dialectically in a unified, balanced way and for the right purposes. Specific ascetic techniques could be used to help combat problems with each of the deadly thoughts. However, love for God was ultimately the key to the solution. It is a unifying factor that helps overcome divisions, transforms desire to its proper use, and enables us to perform virtue. It binds all the virtues together into an interdependent system that helps us live in freedom. Love combined with an active process of apatheia also resists extremes of passion that lead to imbalances and harmful emotional states. Development involves a constant struggle between these opposing forces. He referred to the process of purification of desire and growth of love as **theosis** (Louth, 1996, pp. 147–158; Maximus, 2003, pp. 117–118, 163–169; Chrysostomos, 1988; Maloney, 1992, pp. 150, 214; Spidlik, 1986; see Section 7.2.1).

Although the early Fathers recognized that some mental illnesses might be physical in their origin (Larchet, 2005, pp. 34–43), they saw many problems as psychological or spiritual in nature. Over 1500 years before Freud, Evagrius developed a sophisticated understanding of the relationship between desire, depression, and anger. He saw that unhealthy attachments and frustration of desire could lead to depression or anxiety. He viewed anger as an outgrowth of depression, although on occasion anger could also lead to depression as when thoughts of revenge go unfulfilled. He divided depression into two types—mourning because of loss of attachment and "demonic" sadness that strikes for no apparent cause. This latter condition of melancholy was dangerous and different from usual sorrow because of the lack of hope that typically accompanied it (Evagrius, 1972, pp. 98–101; Cassian, 1999, pp. 139–142). In its milder varieties, he thought it could be used as a tool to help the person see the downsides of attachment. On the other hand, severe depression that could come in dwelling over losses was a great evil that could "wither the flesh" (Sinkewicz, 2003, p. 34) and make it impossible for the person to pray or feel spiritual pleasure. This kind of condition needed to be challenged through perseverance in love. The feelings in and of themselves were not thought to be sinful but surrendering to them or preferring them was thought to be an act of will which separated the person from God and thus was a kind of sin (Merton, 2005b, pp. 179–185).

One condition described by Evagrius that is often confused with depression is **accedie**, more akin to what we might call "burnout" in today's idiom. It is a spiritual disorder that cannot really be directly equated with any type of psychological problem (Chrysostomos, 2007, pp. 103–104). Called the "noonday demon" because of the tendency for it to strike between 10 am and 2 pm, Evagrius described it as the most oppressive of all the deadly thoughts (Evagrius, 1972, p. 99). Signs of accedie include a sense that time is moving slowly, laziness in prayer, a dissatisfaction with one's current state, and a desire to move from one activity to the next while finding satisfaction in none of them. While sadness involves troubles with others, accedie is about dissatisfaction with ourselves and our current state of life (Merton, 2005b, p. 183). The most important cure for it is perseverance and work, along with gentle treatment by others (Sinkewicz, 2003, pp. 34–35, 84–85; Cassian, 1999, pp. 151–155).

The Christian model developed by Evagrius, John Cassian, and the other early Church fathers differs from the medical model in several important ways. Mental or psychological health is the normal potential for every individual but is not a normal state of functioning. Rather, most people lack freedom from passions and attachments, leading to a variety of problems. Emotional problems are not generally due to some breakdown in a person's internal functioning or external environment but occur when normal abilities and desires are applied toward problematic ends and become subject to inordinate attachment and loss of freedom. If this is true, many emotional problems labeled as "psychological" may be more properly thought of as "spiritual" in nature.

11.2.1.2 Modern Formulations

In the Western world, models of soul care like that of Evagrius or Western authors like Gregory the Great dominated spiritual and emotional healing until the rise of medical psychiatry in the 19th century. The decline of a distinctively Christian perspective was due to several reasons, including (1) fascination with secular approaches which led to neglect of wisdom in the religious tradition, and (2) the separation between psychological and spiritual aspects of care. However recently there has been a resurgence of interest in formulating a distinctively Christian view of psychopathology that takes into account modern scientific knowledge. The recent work of Yarhouse et al., (2005) is an excellent example that has parallels to other work in Christian psychology and theology. They argue that a Christian view of mental illness will contain (1) a particular view of the human person, (2) a set of values that defines what it means to be healthy, (3) a theory of the causes of human suffering, and (4) a view of the helping process. Secular views of psychopathology also have these elements, but a Christian theory will base its view on theological and Biblical teachings that attempt to understand our connection to larger things (Cooper, 2003).

The Human Person. Yarhouse and his colleagues argue that in a Christian view, creation and humanity are seen as good but are also broken and incomplete, in need of grace. A holistic view of the person is emphasized in which the individual is not isolated but exists in relationship to God and as part of a community with mutual responsibility to others. Sin refers to behaviors or attitudes that rupture these relationships, and health is a condition of strong relationships that is promoted by virtuous conduct. Since humanity has a fundamentally broken aspect, sin is thought to be typical, and health is found in rare individuals rather than in the state of the average person. In their view, psychology has moved to relabel sinful behavior as illness, even when this may not be the most appropriate viewpoint, and has tended to attack or disdain traditional morality and religious structures that help to regulate behavior and promote strong relationships and community (Schimmel, 1997).

Mental Health. Modern authors like Yarhouse et al. argue that religious and spiritual development are related to psychological wholeness but not necessarily connected with mental health. In this view, Christians are not immune from mental illness and people who are maladjusted can respond well to God, although increasing union with God is usually connected with a more integrated personality (Welch, 1982, pp. 75–76). Another example of this way of thinking can be found in the work of Merton (1991), who argues that while the Christian ascetic life presupposes a normal level of psychological maturity and freedom from serious anxiety or depression, the goal of religious life is to bring the person into union with God in Christ, not promote normal or smooth functioning as is the case in psychiatry. The ascetic life does not offer an answer to serious mental problems, and in fact might make them worse because of the rigorous demands of religious practices and community life (cf. Rahner, 1965, p. 52).

Human Suffering. In contrast to a hedonic view of the human person that sees depression (unhappiness) as the ultimate human suffering, modern Christian authors have tended to see anxiety as the central psychological problem. These writers frequently distinguish **neurotic anxiety** due to psychological problems from **existential anxiety** resulting from our fundamental limitations and separation from God and others. While neurotic anxiety is problematic and a mental health issue, existential anxiety can be positive or negative. It is positive if it helps us to progress, identify with others in need, or is a sign that we do not fit in with a modern society that pursues dysfunctional aims—adaptation is not always good. It is negative if it leads to loss of hope or isolation. This latter kind of anxiety is conquered through an awareness of God's love, not through psychology (Merton, 1991; O'Connor 2005, p. 53; von Balthasar, 2000).

Cooper (2003) has advanced a Niebuhrian-Augustinian formulation of the problem of anxiety. In his view, humans are a mixture of nature and spirit—partly bound by history and thus limited, but as spiritual beings filled with the desire and ability to transcend nature and a life limited to meeting basic needs. This leads to striving, but because of our limitations it ultimately leads to failure, engendering feelings of self-contempt, hostility, and anxiety. Christian faith and hope counter this by increasing trust and love and decreasing our self-focus and need for control. Cooper argues that the main secular solution to this problem is hedonism, which tries to deny transcendence or give us feelings of power over our anxiety and limitations. Unfortunately, these feelings of power lead to pride and feelings of superiority that are both unrealistic and damaging to relationships. They also lead us to develop attachments to things like wealth, alcohol, or food that give us power or help us avoid unpleasant feelings. When these attachments become strong enough they become addictions. Pride and attachments mask our real self and lead to disordered desires, which further compounds our problem.

Helping Processes. In the Christian view, helping is not just about removing suffering, because while fighting it is often a good, it may not be possible to eliminate it (Vergote, 1998, pp. 272–275). Rather, helping is about assisting people to reevaluate their suffering and find meaning in it. This involves moving beyond just trying to eliminate negative aspects of our life and instead to find positive benefit in suffering and the practice of virtue (May, 2004 pp. 39–40; von Balthasar, 2000; Schimmel, 1997). This kind of helping is an essential part of the Christian mission to bear one another's burdens and minister to all. Finding meaning in suffering gives it the power to be transformative so that it can actually contribute to coping and creativity (Rahner, 1963, p. 280; Yarhouse & Turcic, 2003).

11.2.2 Islamic Perspectives

Although Islam is one of the world's major religions, it has attracted little attention in Western psychology. However, since the 1980s a few articles referencing Islam have begun to appear in English-language publications, a significant proportion of them critical of Islam (Sheridan & North, 2004). As of yet, this literature is spotty and does not address many topics in the psychology and religion dialogue that are extensively treated with reference to other traditions such as Christianity and Buddhism. Nevertheless, a critical mass of articles has emerged on the topic of mental health so that it is possible to discern the possible outlines of some Islamic views of psychopathology.

11.2.2.1 Islamic Views of Psychology

As early as the mid-20th century, Western psychology was well developed in a number of Islamic countries, including Egypt, Iran, Pakistan, Indonesia, and Turkey. Arab and Moslem countries typically imported Western ideas with little filtering, and original research done in these countries was carried out within Western frameworks. Recently psychologists in these countries have become much more critical of this approach. Critics believe that traditional Western psychology is not culturally neutral but in fact is based upon individualistic values incompatible with a community-focused culture (Dwairy, 2006, p. 48; Pridmore & Pasha, 2004). As a result, what was imported was of questionable value to the daily lives of Moslem and Arab peoples. These critics also believe that psychological studies of religion are of limited value, as they explain only small proportions of the variance and are not necessarily valid when translated into another cultural setting. A strictly Western psychology has also ignored the long history of civilization in Arab and Moslem worlds. Even in the medieval period, Islamic scholars developed sophisticated views of medicine and psychology, including systems that distinguished between psychosis, anxiety, depression, and other conditions (Abou-Hatab, 1997; Khalili, Murken, Reich, Shah, & Vahabzadeh, 2002; Murken & Shah, 2002).

Western psychology has not disappeared in Islamic countries as a result of this critique, but there have been a number of responses. In deeply religious and Islamic countries like Malaysia, religion is viewed as superior to science, and so psychology has traditionally been done within a religious framework. In more secular countries like Turkey, some operate within a traditional religious framework, while others, especially younger adults, come from a more secular orientation (Aygun & Imamoglu, 2002). Recently in some Islamic countries a movement has formed that is similar to the Christian psychology movement in Western countries (see Section 1.4.7). The Islamic psychology movement seeks to construct a psychology that is based on Islamic fundamentals. Differences of opinion exist as to the details, such as whether to follow the religious psychology of early Muslim scholars or more modern ones, and the degree to which it might be possible to use Western approaches, while rejecting underlying metaphysical ideas that are deemed incompatible with Islam (Haque & Masuan, 2002).

Scholars working to construct an Islamic psychology argue that it must be based on ideas about truth found in the religion. In Islamic thought, true knowledge can be gained only through the use of all our faculties. Since we have a spiritual, as well as an intellectual component to our nature, the search for truth cannot be based upon just intellectual or scientific knowledge but must include a spiritual dimension. There are four levels of the search for truth: (1) knowledge and principles from the Qur'an, (2) the *sunnah* or sayings of Mohammed, (3) *inma* or consensus opinion of Muslims, and (4) *quays*, deduction within the framework of Islamic law. This means that knowledge must also be subject to guidance from other areas of Islamic belief. It should be carried out by someone who is based in this framework and is sensitive to the impact of teaching on others. Investigation that does not proceed from that framework risks disrupting Islamic law and leading toward moral degradation (Kadri, Manoudi, Berrada, & Moussaoui, 2004; Haque & Masuan, 2002).

11.2.2.2 Islamic View of the Person

While there is not a single Islamic view of the human person, in general Islamic theory rejects reductionistic and dualistic models that focus just on our cognitive or biological aspects (Dwairy, 2006, pp. 49–52). Rather, it holds that each person comprises four parts. The (1) heart (*qalb*) and (2) intellect (*'aql*) allow us to understand knowledge as given to us in the Qur'an and other sources. The heart in particular is critical, as it is the essence of our spirit and the place where we meet God, a mirror which can be polished to reflect the Divine and the Names that disclose

God's attributes and actions (Nasr, 2002; Samsel, 2002; al-Ghazali, 1980, p. 87). These help us follow (3) the spirit (*ruh*) given by God to each person that contains a template of potential for that person, and (4) the self (*nafs*) which encompasses the biological and psychic aspects of the individual, our animal nature. This latter part also includes the passions and anger that underlie our negative potential for rebellion against God. However, rebellion is not our core purpose, for we were created with *fitah*, "a God-given innate state or inclination to believe in God and to worship Him" (Mohamed, 1995, p. 2), in which the four parts of the person are in harmony, and we experience contentment. Through belief, worship, and submission to God we can actualize this potential. Resisting it will lead to imbalance, discontent, and the possibility our powers can become evil and will be abused for selfish ends. In this view, satisfaction of materialistic and sexual needs does not lead to harmony but simply a condition of overstimulation. Rather, we need to practice self control and live in a society that supports this way of life. However, the exact nature of the path is different for every person. In the mystical Islamic thought of **Sufism**, each individual is believed to have a fixed personality structure that offers a particular kind of path toward God. This personality structure is represented in the **Enneagram** system, which is also popular among some contemporary Christian spiritual directors (Mohamed, 1995; Khalili et al., 2002; El Azayem & Hedayat-Diba, 1994; Inayat, 2001; see Section 14.2.2).

11.2.2.3 Islamic Practices and Perspectives from Sufism

Islam includes an extensive set of religious practices, and since there is no real division between spirit and self, these are believed to have beneficial effects on both our psychological and spiritual state. Islamic theory divides all *sharia* or actions into five groups: obligatory, meritorious, permissible, reprehensible, or forbidden (Pridmore & Pasha, 2004). In the obligatory group are the Five Pillars of Islam, a group of practices that provide a basic life structure (Johansen, 2005). These include (1) confession of faith in the transcendent God and Mohammed his prophet, (2) daily prayer, (3) almsgiving, (4) fasting during the season of Ramadan, and (5) a pilgrimage to Mecca at least once during a person's life. Each of these pillars is thought to have beneficial effects. Prayers are traditionally said five times a day either alone or in a group. They are often preceded by purification rituals, and are thought to link faith to life and help guard against anxiety and depression. Almsgiving is believed to produce feelings of compassion, generosity, or gratitude, and fasting works to regulate excess and build willpower, helping to prevent over stimulation and imbalance.

In Sufism (e.g., Rumi, 2007), practice is focused on gaining knowledge through actual personal experience of God. This is thought to be superior to intellectual systems that are unable to encompass the reality of a transcendent God (al-Ghazali, 1980, p. 81). Man stands as an "isthmus" between the Divine and the natural world and through experience and practice can become like a polished mirror reflecting the Divine (Rumi, 2004, p. 6). A small elite takes this mystical path, while most will relate to God through the outer exoteric forms of religion (e.g., al-'Arabi, 1980). Those who take the inner path of ascent to God eventually may experience ecstatic states, loss of self and absorption with the Divine (Shah-Kazemi, 2006, p. 92; Chittick, 1983, pp. 175–181, 220–223). Schimmel (1975, pp. 98–148) has described the Sufi path of ascent in terms of a series of stages or stations (*maquamat*) on a path leading to purification of the self (*tasawwuf*). These stations include

- Repentance
- Renunciation and ascetic practice to tame the *nafs*
- Trust in God and surrender to the Divine
- Physical and spiritual poverty
- Patience
- Gratitude
- Fear, which is gradually overcome by hope
- Love
- Annihilation of the self

Sufi practices are diverse, using prayer, dance, story, poetry, fasting or other means to help the individual awaken and recognize their relationship with God and place in the world. The practices promote attitudes of seeking, desire, and passionate love of God, with whom our innermost being or heart truly lies (cf. e.g., Chittick, 1983, pp. 206–210, 325–326). A key to successful practice is the mentoring relationship that takes place between the teacher and the student, which is reminiscent of guru devotion in Hinduism or the Christian practice of spiritual direction (Douglas-Klotz, 2003; Rumi, 2004, pp. 180–183; Schimmel, 1975, p. 103; Kabbani, 2004, pp. 44–47; see Section 14.1.2). The mentoring relationship is also supported by community life, in which practitioners are inducted into a particular branch or order of Sufi practice and often live with others of their group. Both the object and practice of Sufism are thus relational in nature. Perhaps the most important practice is *dhikr* or the continual remembrance and recollection of God. This is done through silent or vocal prayer and repeating the Divine Names, often while engaging in breath control (Schimmel, 1975, pp 167–78; cf. e.g., Theophan, 1995, pp. 186–193; Kabbani, 2004, pp. 95–121; cf. Section 13.2.4).

11.2.2.4 Mental Health, Counseling, and Therapy

Although hospitals for psychiatric care appeared in Islamic countries as early as the 8th century, in traditional settings most people first seek help from an *imam* or spiritual leader, as Muslims generally see mental health difficulties as due to spiritual problems or weaknesses in faith. In general, there is a negative view of psychology and the mental health system, partly because of the social stigma attached to people with serious mental illnesses but also because of fears that religious views will not be respected (Pridmore & Pasha, 2004; El Azayem & Hedayat-Diba, 1994; Khalili et al., 2002; Johansen, 2005; Kadri et al., 2004). Views of treatment are influenced not only by the Qur'an but also by the views of traditional healing in the societies where Islam has flourished, and the extent to which religious beliefs are central for personal and social identity (Okasha, 1999; Haque & Masuan, 2002; Hortacsu & Cem-Ersoy, 2005).

Islamic countries have some diversity in terms of the types of psychopathology that are prevalent, which in turn affects the kinds of treatment strategies that need to be used (Wahass & Kent, 1997). For instance, dissociative or trauma-related disorders may be more prevalent in some countries. Symptom patterns and triggers for problems may also differ from what is typically seen in Western settings. Depression and other emotional problems may tend to present as agitation or be intermixed with physical complaints; psychotic symptoms tend to be more florid and stress related (Alansari, 2005). Obsessive-compulsive disorder may appear in the context of purification rituals specific to Islamic practice. Information on some types of problems such as suicide and alcohol abuse is limited, because religious prohibitions make it difficult to study them. However, it is known that these problems are common enough in Islamic countries to be of concern (Dwairy, 2006, pp. 84–92; Okasha, 1999; Pridmore & Pasha, 2004). The situation among US Muslims is somewhat different, in part because many are refugees, and about 40% are African American. Specific issues in this group include trauma history, dealing with discrimination and women's issues, as well as differences in family and marriage practices (Lumumba, 2003; Ali, Liu, & Humedian, 2004).

Islamic counselors working with Islamic clients generally see their religion—particularly in its intrinsic versions—as a resource that helps guard against problems like depression and suicide, as well as providing coping resources for other types of problems (Ali et al., 2004; Watson, Tuorila, Detra, Gearhart, & Wielkiewicz, 2002). Explicit religious interventions used with clients include listening to tapes of religious readings, prayer, and **reciprocal inhibition** or setting up patterns of thoughts and behavior that oppose problematic ones. The explicitly religious approach appears to be especially helpful with highly religious clients, who can take advantage of their religious beliefs to help them live with problems. Problem and emotion-focused coping are both evident in these situations (Wahass & Kent, 1997; Hussain & Cochrane, 2003; Azhar & Varrma, 1995; Inayat, 2001; see Sections 10.2.1 and 14.2.2). In true Islamic therapy, therapists must be practicing Muslims, and they may view thoughts and behaviors not in line with Islamic tenets as potentially problematic. The emphasis in treatment is social, including care for the family and parents, as well as the individual (Khalili et al., 2002; Okasha, 1999; El Azayem & Hedayat-Diba, 1994).

11.3 Psychological and Spiritual Views on Specific Problems

A vast literature exists on the relationship between religion or spirituality and many specific mental health problems. In this section, we take an in-depth look at two of these—addictions and depression.

11.3.1 Addictions

It has long been thought that religion and spirituality are very helpful in the understanding and treatment of addictive disorders. While the empirical literature is somewhat problematic because of vague definitions or simplistic measurement of spirituality and religion (Cook, 2004), virtually all studies of alcohol use or abuse and other drug problems have found that religiousness—especially intrinsic religiosity—is associated with fewer problems. Across a wide variety of types of studies and groups, the odds of alcohol or drug dependence in actively involved religious people are 30–40% less that the rest of the population (Koenig, 2001a; Plante & Sharma, 2001; Hatchett, 1999; Strawser, Storch, Geffken, Killiany, & Baumeister, 2004; Musick, Blazer, & Hays, 2000). The strength of the relationship between religion and alcohol use is dependent upon a number of factors, including childhood religion and current religious affiliation of self and spouse, level of commitment or participation, and how the person interprets his or her religious tradition. Beliefs such as whether or not God is involved in the world, the centrality of hope and forgiveness, and whether a religious tradition is more supportive or condemning affect the individual's experience of religious life and the psychological benefit it might provide. Level of personal devotion and feelings of closeness to God have an inconsistent relationship with addictions (Gorsuch, 1995; Kendler, Liu et al., 2003; Booth & Martin, 1998; Forthun, Bell, Peek, & Sun, 1999; Cochran, Beeghley, & Bock, 1992; Kendler, Gardner, & Prescott, 1997; Perkins, 1985). Similar patterns may be present for online addictions such as cyberporn, although there may also be differences (Stack, Wasserman, & Kern, 2004; Abell, Steenbergh, & Boivin, 2006).

Religion seems to have its biggest effect in preventing initial problems rather than helping after a problem with addiction has developed (Gorsuch, 1995). It does this by providing a community environment, social norms and beliefs that reduce opportunities for use, and providing non-drug-related ways of coping. Social norms and beliefs about alcohol use differ significantly among religious groups, so patterns of use and abuse also differ (Chen, Dormitzer, Bejarano, & Anthony, 2004; Cochran et al., 1992; Booth & Martin, 1998). Although this is its primary effect, religiousness also predicts better recovery from substance abuse. People who are successful in treatment have higher levels of religious faith and spirituality, which is related to a number of helpful factors such as optimistic life orientation, greater perceived social support, better resilience in response to stress, and lower anxiety (Booth & Martin, 1998; Plante & Sharma, 2001; Pardini, Plante, Sherman, & Stump, 2000).

11.3.1.1 Spirituality and Addictions: Alcoholics Anonymous

While research on the etiology of alcoholism has focused on the importance of religion, the concept of spirituality has been more influential in treatment. The prototypical means of help for addictions are 12-step programs like Alcoholics Anonymous (AA; Alcoholics Anonymous World Service, 2004, pp. 59–74), which involve a series of steps aimed to produce spiritual transformation with the help of others who have similar problems (Levy, 2000). The steps take place in the context of group meetings, where individuals share their weaknesses, successes, and struggles with alcohol. The model is particularly popular in parts of the world with traditional ties to Protestant Christianity, perhaps because the type of problem drinking described by AA is more typically found in those countries (Peele, 1997).

The first set of steps (1–3) address issues of power and control: The alcoholics are asked to be honest, admitting their powerlessness and limitations, particularly with regard to alcohol. They also need to express belief in a higher power that can provide help, and turn themselves over to this higher power. Typically this is thought of as involving a spiritual experience, which may be gradual or sudden. Included in the experience may be a leveling of pride, an awareness of help that is available from God and others, and a willingness to accept assistance, thus replacing hopelessness with hope. It requires accepting experience, letting go and giving up attachments, especially needs for perfection and continual control. This surrender leads to (1) emotions of gratitude for receiving something we did not get through our own efforts, (2) honesty and awareness of our imperfections, and (3) acceptance of imperfections through forgiveness of self and others. While this may not involve traditional theistic religious beliefs, atheism or skepticism can be a kind of intellectual pride that may prevent the person from acknowledging powerlessness and accepting needed help (Kurtz & Ketcham, 1992). Qualitative studies suggest that AA members—even those without religious inclinations—do change in their perception of self and world. Through the spiritual aspect of the program they move toward some relinquishment of control, accepting help from something outside the self. They also frequently report spiritual awakenings and those that do have the best chance of maintaining sobriety (Sommer, 1997; Kaskutas, Turk, Bond, & Weisner, 2003).

The remainder of the program involves applying this spiritual reorientation to various aspects of life. In the second set of steps (4–9), the alcoholics are asked to confront their own imperfection and abandon self-delusion through making a moral inventory, including wrongs they have done to others and resentments or lack of trust they harbor. They ask for help in removing their imperfections and attempt to make amends for wrongs done to others. Family and interpersonal issues are usually especially painful and important, and a supportive relationship with a spiritual advisor or sponsor is thought to be helpful in this process (Sommer, 1997). The third set of steps (10–12) involves establishing a set of regular practices and a way of life based on AA philosophy, including continuing moral examination, seeking contact with God through prayer or meditation, and working to help others with alcohol problems. Studies suggest that these regular practices have a moderate-to-strong correlation with purpose in life and a low but significant correlation with length of sobriety (Carroll, 1993).

Although it is difficult to assess the effectiveness of AA due to high initial dropout rates and other problems, it certainly helps many individuals. About half of the people that join become long-term members and probably 2/3 of those are abstinent or decrease drinking. Ratings of perceived helpfulness are quite high, and roughly 20% report additional belief in a higher power as a result of participation. This spiritual component is commonly thought to be the most important part of the program, and increases in religiosity and spirituality that can accompany AA participation are related to more success in controlling drinking (Robinson, Cranford, Webb, & Brower, 2007; Gorsuch, 1995). However, many clinicians dislike the spiritual focus of AA, and certainly other factors connected with 12-step programs are also important such as work with the sponsor and lifestyle or employment changes (Alexander, Robinson, & Rainforth, 1994; Levy, 2000, p. 596; Booth & Martin, 1998; Nealon-Woods, Ferrari, & Jason, 1995). Overall, there is a weak-to-moderate relationship between religiosity and substance abuse treatment outcome, although the reason for this relationship remains somewhat unclear (Shields, Broome, Delany, Fletcher, & Flynn, 2007).

11.3.1.2 Gerald May and a Contemplative Approach to Addictions

The most thoroughly worked out theory of the relationship between spirituality and addiction is that of contemplative psychiatrist Gerald May (1982). In his view, Western psychology tends to view life's difficulties as due to problems coping with stress, not doing the right things to produce happiness, or a failure to seek and actualize one's potential. All of these are versions of *willfulness*, which focuses on control, striving, and manipulation. In this view, **mystery** or things outside of our control or knowledge are simply confusions or incomplete understandings that will eventually be eliminated. May says that this view is inadequate, because it fails to recognize that mystery is inherent in the universe and that this apophatic quality of existence must be confronted experientially and with acceptance. This kind of open attentiveness to the world and acceptance of its mysterious and transcendent quality, without attempts to manipulate it, forms the basis of **contemplative spirituality**, "an experienced and interpreted relationship among human beings and the mystery of creation" (1982, p. 22). It is characterized by a loving, receptive attitude toward the world, a *willingness* to take it on its own terms and appreciate it for what it is, and an understanding and acceptance of our dependency on things beyond our control, realizing that the expectation and desire for control can be illusionary (cf. Bjorck, 2007). This willingness stands at the center of the spiritual life (cf. Theophan, 1995, p. 180). Willingness does not mean passivity or putting aside efforts to meet basic needs for food, shelter, protection, and companionship. It involves a conscious, intentional act to set aside the desire to control, acknowledge the reality and beauty of mystery, and accept both good and bad aspects of life and ourselves. Contemplative spirituality is thus paradoxical; it is not passive, but it is also not about striving to acquire or control (see Section 13.3.1).

In the contemplative view, a willful rather than a willing and accepting response to mystery creates problems. When we respond willfully we identify objects or behaviors that we think will control or combat our troubles. Two problems can come from this. First, since some important parts of life like our own mortality are beyond our knowledge and control, willfulness is often bound to result in failure. Second, things that help us escape mystery by producing temporary relief and maintaining illusions of control offer powerful attractions. Initially, we seek them because they help us deal with particular situations, but as time goes on we begin to seek them for their own sake regardless of whether or not they continue to offer help. They become disordered attachments that serve to limit our freedom and distort our perception of the world (May, 1982, pp. 227–228). These attachments can be to anything: drugs, self-image, stress, unhealthy religious practices, even aversions to food (as in anorexia), or people (as in prejudice). They can involve feelings of power so strong they becomes compulsions or **addictions**—things that we must do or obtain even when they lead to problems. As they become central to our life, our attention becomes fixated on them, and we lose perspective, deceiving ourselves about their hold on us (cf. Maloney, 1992, p. 154). Eventually the attachment becomes so powerful that we lose the freedom to follow our true desires and rid ourselves of it; we must have outside help. The potential for addiction in Western culture is especially strong because of the importance that the culture places on control. In fact, some have commented that rejection of a contemplative view of the world is one of the primary features of the modern secular worldview (cf. Arendt, 1998, pp. 289–304). This means that in Western countries addiction is a common state rather than an unusual medical problem.

According to May (1982), there are several ways to deal with addiction. One is to avoid dealing with the underlying problem of attachment and to simply substitute another less damaging addiction. This helps us avoid the empty feeling of freedom and mystery but does not really solve the underlying problem. A second possibility is to use psychological techniques or even spiritual techniques like meditation to decrease the negative affects of addictions. This can also be positive, but meditation when used in this way is no longer a spiritual technique because it does not deal with the underlying spiritual issue. The third approach is a spiritual one: to give up false security and detach from addictive behaviors or objects. This does not necessarily mean giving them up (although often we must), but we must discover that we can exist without them (May, 1988, p. 96). Medical neuroscience cannot cure addiction or replace this spiritual aspect of recovery, so eventually this realization is necessary (May, 2004 pp. 160–161). However, it is difficult to do; we become accustomed to the loss of freedom that goes with attachments and addictions, so the new freedom can be frightening. The process works best when we are powerless and thus most open to change. Spiritual practices such as meditation and contemplative prayer (see Section 13.3) can help the process, and overcoming addiction in return furthers our relationship with God (Milhailoff, 2005, p. 86). May also believes that we eventually need to become located within a valid spiritual and religious tradition for spiritual progress to continue.

11.3.1.3 Other Religious Approaches to Addictions

Some individuals object to the spirituality implicit in AA and similar approaches to addictions and argue that "consumer choice" demands more alternatives (e.g., Marlatt et al., 2004). As a result, efforts have been made to develop other strategies, especially ones that avoid any kind of theistic content (e.g., Vick, Smith, & Herrera, 1998). One possibility is to use Hindu-inspired techniques like **Transcendental Meditation** (TM; e.g., O'Murchu, 1994; see Section 13.5.3). TM work for addictions involves individual and group instruction as well as daily practice. The theory is that substance abuse is caused by attempts to optimize psychophysiological function, and so if we maintain a positive psychological state through meditation, it removes the incentive to use drugs. It also reduces risk factors for substance abuse like stress, anxiety, or depression, thus addressing deeper causes of addiction (Goodman, Walton, Orme-Johnson, & Boyer, 2003; Hawkins, 2003). Studies suggest that TM significantly reduces drug and alcohol use. Effect sizes appear to be larger in at-risk populations than in general ones. It also appears to be more effective for cigarette and illicit drug use than alcohol (Alexander et al., 1994; Walton & Levitsky, 1994).

Approaches based on Buddhist philosophy or techniques are also possible. In Buddhism, addiction is conceptualized as a disease of the mind. It involves attachment to behaviors that promise relief from suffering but actually increase craving, because they do not address our basic problem of ignorance. In this view, meditation is key to the recovery process by enhancing mindfulness and breaking the power of attachments (Marlatt, 2002; Dudley-Grant, 2003; cf. Section 13.5.1). However, initial studies with mindfulness meditation have shown less promise (Alterman, Koppenhaver, Mulholland, Ladden, & Baime, 2004).

11.3.2 Depression

Depression is a condition that can involve sadness, loss of interest in activities, changes in cognition such as negative thoughts, and a number of physical problems such as disturbed sleep. It is also associated with problems in mood regulation such as a tendency toward automatic, stronger, and persistent responses to negative stimuli (Davidson, 2003; Davidson, Pizzagalli, Nitschke, & Putnam, 2002; Larson, Nitschke, & Davidson, 2007; Jackson et al., 2003). It is common all over the world, and in Western countries it has increased dramatically in the last 50 years; in the US, depression rates have doubled in the last generation so that about 1 in 6 adults can be expected to have at least one serious episode of depression in their lifetime. Women appear to be particularly affected by the growing problem (Compton, Conway, Stinson, & Grant, 2006; Norman, 2004; Murphy, Horton et al., 2004). These increasing rates seem to be connected with modernization, which appears to increase narcissism and promote a loss of meaning and hope (Seligman, 1990; Stone, 1998). For many, depression is a chronic and highly disabling condition requiring continuing treatment. It is associated with increased mortality, as well as decreased quality of life and productivity (Murphy, Nierenberg et al., 2002; Ebmeier, Donaghey, & Steele, 2006; Hollon, Thase, & Markowitz, 2002; Westen, Novotny, & Thompson-Brenner, 2004).

11.3.2.1 Religion and Rates of Depression

Overall, religious involvement and affiliation appears to be related to fewer problems with depression, higher levels of well-being, and quicker recovery from depressive episodes when problems occur, especially in those with an intrinsic religious motivation (McCullough & Smith, 2003; Koenig, 2001a; Loewenthal, Cinnirella, Evdoka, & Murphy, 2001; Koenig, George, & Peterson, 1998). This has been found in both the US and Europe using well-controlled cross-sectional and prospective longitudinal studies (Miller, Warner, Wickramaratne, Weissman, 1999; Larson & Larson, 2003; Coleman, Ivani-Chalian, & Robinson, 2004). Although the relationship between religious involvement and depression is complex, and the correlation between them is somewhat inconsistent, individuals with no religious involvement have a 20–60% greater chance of a major depressive episode than those who are involved (Smith, McCullough, & Poll, 2003; Koenig & Larson, 2001; McCullough & Larson, 1999; Eliassen, Taylor, & Lloyd, 2005; cf. Kennedy, Kelman, Thomas, & Chen, 1996). There is even stronger evidence for a relationship between religiousness and suicide. Higher rates of suicide are observed in countries with lower rates of religious participation, and lower rates of suicide may be associated with specific religious beliefs and prohibitions (Koenig, 2001a; Clarke, Bannon, & Denihan, 2003; Dervic et al., 2004; Stack, 1991; cf. Zhang & Jin, 1996). A stronger connection between religion and lower rates of depression can also be found among groups that tend to be more religious, such as older adults, those that live in rural areas, and US minority groups such as African Americans and Mexican Americans (Mitchell & Weatherly, 2000; Cummings, Neff, & Husaini, 2003; Koenig, Cohen, Blazer, Kudler et al., 1995; Levin, Markides, & Ray, 1996; Braam, Beekman et al., 1997; Braam, Sonnenberg et al., 2000; Braam, van den Eeden et al., 2001; Braam, Hein et al., 2004; cf. Hill, Burdette, Angel, & Angel, 2006). The connection may be weaker for those who live in cultural settings not supportive of religion. As in the case of other health problems, religion seems to act by providing a buffering effect, so it is more likely to be effective in groups of people under greater stress or at risk for depression (Flannelly, Koenig, Ellison, Galek, & Krause, 2006).

While religion appears to have a generally positive effect on depression, religious problems can be associated with higher rates of depression, and some religious groups such as Pentecostal Christians appear to have more problems (Meador, Koenig, Hughes, & Blazer, 1992). College students reporting religious strain, such as religious doubts or disagreements with family over religious issues, reported higher levels of depression and suicidality independent of religiousness and the degree of comfort provided by religion. In these students, depression is associated with alienation from God. Those with higher levels of strain were also more interested in discussing religious issues in counseling (Exline, Yali, & Sanderson, 2000). Thus, the presence of positive religiousness does not mean that a person may not have religious problems that are negatively impacting their mental health.

Inconsistencies in the research appear to reflect a number of factors. Results can be affected by the aspect and type of depression that is measured, for instance religion effects seem to be bigger with cognitive than with physical symptoms of depression (Koenig, 1995). It can also be affected by the specific aspects of religion or spirituality that are assessed, with sophisticated multiple measures more likely to find results (e.g., Mitchell & Weatherly, 2000). The most consistent results appear to be an association between participation or group involvement and lower rates of depression, while studies about the effects of individual spirituality or personal devotion are more inconsistent (McCullough & Smith, 2003; Davidson, Pizzagalli, Nitschke, & Putnam, 2002; Baetz, Griffin, Bowen, Koenig, & Marcoux, 2004; McCullough & Larson, 1999; Kendler, Gardner et al., 1997; Bosworth, Park, McQuoid, Hays, & Steffens, 2003). Results also seem to be related to high levels of religiousness, as some studies have found that moderately religious individuals have higher rates of depression than those with low or high religiosity, perhaps because of problems related to religious ambivalence or conflict (Miller, Weissman, Gur, & Greenwald, 2002; McCullough & Smith, 2003; Schnittker, 2001; Nordin, Wasteson, Hoffman, Glimelius, & Sjoden, 2001).

11.3.2.2 Mechanisms

A number of models and mechanisms for the relation between religiosity and depression have been proposed (Kennedy, 1998; Smith, McCullough et al., 2003; Plante & Sharma, 2001). Three commonly discussed possibilities are:

1. Religiousness influences depression by buffering stress, acting as a suppressor or moderator, and providing positive coping or appraisal mechanisms. In the **suppressor model**, religious practices increase in response to stress and act to buffer its potential to trigger depression. In the **moderator model**, religious practices do not increase, but they become more effective at higher levels of stress, buffering against the possibility of depression. The presence of a perceived loving relationship with God appears to have an especially strong buffering effect (Levin, 2002; cf. Section 10.1.2).
2. Religiousness helps the person cope with the emotional effects of depression, perhaps providing a way of seeking comfort or deterring distress.
3. Religiousness helps prevent depression by discouraging behaviors that increase the risk of stress or depression, such as substance use.

There is evidence supporting all of these models, as well as evidence that there might be common developmental or biological influences that affect both religiousness and depression. Most research has suggested that the main helpful effect comes from long-term involvement in beliefs, practices, and community life that then exercise a protective factor, buffering the negative effects of stress on mental health and psychological well-being (Williams, Larson, Buckler, Heckmann, & Pyle, 1991; Wink, Dillon, & Larsen, 2005). Spirituality when separated from religion does not have the same effect. There is support for both suppressor and moderator models, as the negative correlation between religion and depression is stronger in high stress situations (Smith, McCullough et al., 2003; cf. Table 10.1). The public involvement aspects of religiousness appear to have a stronger buffering effect, but some studies (e.g., Schnittker, 2001) have found that devotional activities and spiritual help-seeking can have a buffering effect in the presence of multiple negative life events. Some specific factors that buffer, provide comfort or prevent depression include the following:

1. Specific beliefs, including (a) afterlife beliefs, which may reduce depression and anxiety particularly among the bereaved (Flannelly et al., 2006; Patrick & Kinney, 2003); (b) God image beliefs, with a stern God image related to higher levels of depression in men (Greenway, Milne, & Clarke, 2003); or (c) beliefs that reduce hopelessness (Murphy et al., 2000a, 2000b; P. Murphy, Ciarrocchi et al., 2000).
2. The use of positive religious coping such as seeing God as a partner. Negative strategies such as pleading are associated with higher levels of sadness (Koenig, Cohen, Blazer, Pieper et al., 1992; Smith, McCullough et al., 2003; see Section 10.2.2).
3. Social support from others in a religious community, or **spiritual support**, a sense that a person is loved by God and can love in return. Both kinds of support are related to protective effects against stress, lower levels of depression, and higher levels of life satisfaction. Familial agreement on religion has a similar effect (Fiala et al., 2002; Levin, 2001; Wright, Frost, & Wisecarver, 1993; Nelson, Rosenfeld, Breitbart, & Galieta, 2002; Harris et al., 2008; Miller, Warner, Wickramaratne, & Weissman, 1997).
4. Religious motivation. US and UK studies have found that adults with high levels of intrinsic motivation are associated with lower levels of anxiety and depression, fewer signs of character disorder, and higher ego strength, while those with extrinsic motivation have higher levels of depression. However, there is considerable individual variation in the relationship, and there are likely complex relationships between religious coping, motivation, type of stress, and depression that are not adequately understood (Laurencelle, Abell, & Schwartz, 2002; McCullough & Smith, 2003; Maltby & Day, 2000; Nelson et al., 2002; Miller, Weissman et al., 2002; Parker et al., 2003; Strawbridge, Shema, Cohen, Roberts, & Kaplan, 1998). There is probably an additional holistic effect among beliefs, coping, support, and motivation that goes beyond the individual components (Westgate, 1996).

11.3.2.3 Theological Perspectives on Depression and Spirituality: The Dark Night

Much of the psychological literature on depression assumes that it is an abnormal state to be avoided. An alternate view is that there might be cases in which depression-like conditions are normal, natural, or even an essential part of spiritual development. This is the position taken by the Carmelite Christian mystic John of the Cross (1542–1591), who described what he called a **dark night experience**, a kind of purification and stripping away in preparation for advancement to a higher level of spiritual development. The experience increases our sensitivity so that we become aware of God's presence and work within us in ways that were previously beyond our awareness. Ultimately it frees us to love (May, 2004).

John described two kinds of dark night experiences (John of the Cross, 1973, pp. 311–352). In the *dark night of the senses*, it is our sensory abilities that are purified and accommodated to the Spirit. He believed that this is a fairly common experience. It involves moving away from a dependence on sensory pleasure that characterizes prayer in the beginner, to a focus on spiritual delight. This initially manifests itself as a dryness in prayer and meditation, where spiritual practices that previously were pleasurable are no longer satisfying. Paradoxically, this is combined with an increased longing for God and a desire to be alone with the Divine in a quiet state without thought. In this new state of open awareness, we become aware of changes taking place within us that seem beyond our natural powers. These changes manifest themselves in our psychological life through increasing inner harmony, peacefulness, self knowledge, and humility. External manifestations include a strengthened practice of virtue and increased love for those around us. All of this involves a new state of spiritual satisfaction.

A second and much rarer kind of experience is the *dark night of the spirit*. In this experience, we become deprived of spiritual satisfaction. This is sometimes experienced as a loss of meaning and direction, or as alienation from God, and a crisis of faith (Turner, 1995, p. 232; O'Connor, 2002). It is a painful experience involving feelings of desolation that may last for an extended period of time. In John's view, this darkness is actually God at work in a very intimate way, with a kind of pain resulting from the nearness and purity of God working to perfect us beyond our normal capacities. It is an experience of **infused contemplation** (see Section 13.3.1). As the experience progresses, we have increasing periods with a sense of freedom, abundance, peace, and an intimate relationship with God. We come to know and love God not because of what God does for us, but because of who God is. We desire God without a need to possess. This work prepares us for experiences of union with God, which become increasingly more common and persistent (Turner, 1995, pp. 236–244).

John of the Cross describes a process that bears some similarities to depression. It involves experiences of loss and removal of pleasure, as well as inner pain. Like depression, it affects our psychological self: our appetites, experiences, and how we think or talk about ourselves, possibly leading to feelings of emptiness, hopelessness, and lack of motivation. However, John and his contemporaries like Teresa of Avila (1515–1582) also distinguished between dark night experiences and depression (Turner, 1995, pp. 227–251; Welch, 1982, pp. 144–145; May, 2004, pp. 155–157):

- The dark night is really a normal process, whereas most people consider depression to be an abnormal condition.
- The causes of the condition are different. Depression is related to losses of objects such as a job or relationship, while the dark night is related to losses in our experience of God. John also thought that severe depression had physiological causes that were not a factor in dark night experiences.

- In dark night experiences, work and relationships may continue normally or even be enhanced, while in depression they typically suffer.
- In depression, there is destruction that feels forced with nothing to take the place of what is lost. In dark night experiences, a person can acquiesce to the experience and gains inner transformation.

While there are clear differences between a dark night experience and depression, this does not mean that in practice the conditions are always separate. They could coexist or be triggers for each other (O'Connor, 2002). The relationship between depression and dark night experiences is a reminder of the complexity of trying to understand the convergences and divergences between mental health and spiritual growth. A key insight is that "feeling good" is neither necessarily a sign of spiritual progress nor is "feeling bad" a sign that things are not going in productive directions (Dieker, 2005). In fact, feeling bad can be an opportunity for further spiritual exploration and growth (Anthony, 1966, p. 49). Using psychological language, negative moods can have a regulatory function that motivates the person to make positive corrections in their life (Damasio, 2002). All of this raises a fundamental issue: mood states which are labeled "abnormal" in the medical or hedonic models may in some situations be a natural, expected reaction to life and developmental events (Tillich, 1962), and that attempts to remove the symptoms may at the least miss their true significance and at most actually hinder our development.

11.4 Religion and Spirituality in Mental Health Treatment

Recently the psychology and religion dialogue has shifted in important ways. Through much of the 20th century, the conversation was primarily psychology talking about and studying religion. With some notable exceptions (see e.g., Sections 1.5.1 and 1.5.2), religious voices were silent, and their contribution to psychology was behind the scenes. This one-sided conversation has changed in the last couple of decades, as the field has seen more and more instances of psychology trying to learn from religion and borrow techniques that might be of help in mental health treatment. In this section, we examine two of these practices: forgiveness, which is borrowed from Christianity, and mindfulness, which is an importation from Buddhism.

11.4.1 Forgiveness

Forgiveness is a central virtue and practice within Christianity and other religious traditions. It allows us to move forward without being controlled by the past (Schreiter, 1998, pp. 56–63). It has obvious relevance to many situations involving relational difficulties, abuse, or trauma that can lead to mental health problems (Lin, Mack, Enright, Krahn, & Baskin,, 2004; Reed & Enright, 2006). Because of its intensively interpersonal nature, forgiveness was generally ignored by traditional research that operates out of a **substantialist ontology** of the human person. More recently, **relational ontologies** of the human person have become more popular (see Sections 5.5 and 6.3), which are more sensitive to issues like forgiveness. In the 1990s, the work of Robert Enright, Robert McCullough, and Elliott Worthington began to highlight this area. As expected, most studies have found connections between forgiveness and a variety of mental health or therapy outcome variables, including enhanced well-being and decreased substance use. Forgiveness is also connected with some positive measures of physical health. There are also many indications that religious participation enhances this virtue (Worthington, Mazzeo, & Canter, 2005; Witvliet, 2001; Ryan & Deci, 2001; Maltby, Day, & Barber, 2005; Wuthnow, 2000; Knight et al., 2007; Worthington & Scherer, 2004).

11.4.1.1 Definitions and Concepts

The psychological literature typically defines forgiveness as a gift that is extended to another person who has wronged us. It begins when persons perceives themselves as wrongly treated by another resulting in (1) negative emotions like anger, (2) changes in cognition such as loss of respect, and/or (3) altered behavior such as avoidance or aggression. These negative changes lead to disruptions in relationships and social harmony. Many people in these situations respond by insisting on reparation or taking revenge on the perpetrator of the wrong. In **forgiveness**, the person recognizes that they have the right to reparation or revenge but they renounce it and instead choose to respond with compassion and love toward the perpetrator, leaving open the possibility of better relations. It is thus not the same as forgetting or excusing (Enright, Eastin, Golden, Sarinopoulis, & Freedman, 1992; Enright & Fitzgibbons, 2000; Pingleton, 1997; Gould, 1993, p. 118). In the Christian tradition, the idea of forgiveness is intimately related with the virtue of humility (Harmless, 2004, p. 237). This forgiveness can take two forms—*decisional forgiveness*, which involves acting toward a person as one did prior to the wrongful treatment, and *emotional forgiveness* or the reduction in negative emotions such as anger or fear that can come from perceived wrongful treatment. This complex of negative emotions is sometimes referred to as **unforgiveness** (Worthington & Scherer, 2004).

Given this definition, it is obvious that forgiveness is a complex phenomenon that raises a number of conceptual issues:

1. *Who is the forgiver and who is forgiven?* In most articles on forgiveness, the focus is on a person who might forgive someone else that has wronged him or her. However, there are other possibilities to forgiveness: we might choose to forgive ourselves, or realize that we have wronged someone else and need to receive forgiveness. These other types of forgiveness are especially connected with Christian visions of the practice (Gulliford, 2004a, 2004b; Walker & Gorsuch, 2004).

2. *How are forgiveness and unforgiveness related to each other?* They would seem to be opposites, so it could be argued that forgiveness can be used as a

kind of emotion-focused coping strategy to reduce unforgiveness that occurs in response to stressful interactions (Worthington & Scherer, 2004). However, research suggests that they are not simply opposites but somewhat independent processes. For instance, unforgiveness is more related to situational variables and forgiveness to traits like **empathy**, "the ability to identify with and understand the situations, motives, and feelings of another" (Hurlbut, 2002, p. 314). This means that forgiveness may not be the only or best way to reduce unforgiveness (Worthington & Wade, 1999; cf. Wade & Worthington, 2003, 2005).

3. *How are forgiveness and reconciliation related to each other?* Some authors argue that forgiveness is an emotional state within a person that can be generated without external changes in the relationship. Others believe that reconciliation should be the real goal of forgiveness.

Berry, Worthington, O'Connor, Parrott, and Wade, (2005) note that there are three primary approaches to forgiveness in the literature: (1) the emotion-based model of Worthington and Wade; (2) the model of McCullough that looks at reconciliation and reduction of avoidance; and (3) the approach of Enright, which looks at the interplay of cognition, behavior, and emotions like anger.

For Worthington, the key barrier to forgiveness is avoidance and withdrawal. Forgiveness, like bereavement, involves grief and mourning, as it requires that we accept loss and let go feelings of self-righteousness and anger (Gulliford, 2004a; Worthington, Mazzeo et al., 2005). For this we need empathy, which involves both perspective taking and an emotional response to the person congruent with their welfare. Empathy is important because forgiveness is easier when we feel compassion, and the positive feelings of empathy help us overcome fear or other negative emotions that drive avoidance or withdrawal. Empathy is also helpful because it increases altruistic behavior and the possibility of reconciliation. Empathy can be facilitated by a number of things, such as looking at our own guilt in past situations (humility) or by an apology from the offender that can reduce unforgiveness. Although empathy is a disposition with its roots in infancy, religion may assist here by promoting the values of mercy and commitment to virtue and values supportive of relationships. (Worthington, O'Connor et al., 2005; Worthington, Sharp et al., 2006; Gulliford, 2004b; Batson, Ahmad, Lishner, & Tsang, 2002; McCullough, Worthington, & Rachal, 1997; Wade & Worthington, 2005; Konstam, Holmes, & Levine, 2003).

McCullough emphasizes reconciliation and avoidance reduction in the forgiveness process. For him, forgiveness is a prosocial activity related to well-being, and so it is intimately involved with relational wholeness. In the short term, forgiveness is about altering motivations, especially decreasing motivations to avoid or seek revenge, thereby enhancing the possibility of harmonious relationships. It is affected by dispositional factors like neuroticism that increase the chance of avoidance or by agreeableness that enhances forgiveness. It is also impacted by situational factors such as the history of the relationship between the two individuals and nature of the offense. Empathy also plays a key part in the process by activating our capacity for altruism toward the offender and inclining us toward forgiveness (McCullough, 2001a; McCullough, Worthington et al., 1997). Although he acknowledges that reconciliation is different from forgiveness and more difficult, he argues that it is a more desirable goal than simple emotional change and should be the ultimate objective of the forgiveness process (cf. Gulliford, 2004a).

Robert Enright (e.g., Enright & Fitzgibbons, 2000; Enright, 2001) takes a more cognitive-behavioral approach to forgiveness. He views it as an individual rational decision, which unlike reconciliation is not dependent on action by the other person. It can also be seen as a virtue, a skill, or a coping strategy. In this approach, it is assumed that a person feels anger about some real hurt or injustice and that removal of this anger by forgiveness can help the person with problems like depression. The focus is thus more on removal of anger than empathy or reconciliation. The forgiveness process proceeds in four phases: (1) uncovering and looking at the hurt, (2) making a decision to forgive, (3) humanizing the offender, and (4) deepening the forgiveness experience. We make the offender more human by developing compassion for them using techniques like role-taking, gift giving, and empathy. We deepen the forgiveness experience through finding meaning and purpose in the events and becoming aware of the effects of forgiveness. The process is seen as transformative, whereby the person's motives change from concern about the self to disinterested love with a focus on the other and their worth and humanity, changing the quality of the relationship (cf. Pope, 2002).

11.4.1.2 Barriers to Forgiveness

Research has been helpful in clarifying the kinds of things that can act as barriers toward forgiveness. Not surprisingly, specific characteristics of the situation like the reception of an apology are related to forgiveness. Aspects of the relationship with the other person like closeness, commitment, and satisfaction are also important (McCullough, 2001a). Some more global barriers include the following:

1. *Low levels of dispositional forgiveness.* Walker and Gorsuch (2002, 2004) have found four dimensions of dispositional forgiveness: forgiving others, receiving forgiveness from others, self-forgiveness and receiving God's forgiveness. These categories are related to personality variables such as neuroticism and agreeableness. Failures to feel forgiveness from God, give it to others, or forgive oneself probably have different sources, although each kind of forgiveness can probably support or inhibit others (Pingleton, 1997; Watts, 2004). Negative moods like anxiety due to dispositional or situational characteristics can also decrease forgiveness (Ryan & Kumar, 2005).

2. *Specific personality patterns.* Narcissistic entitlement blocks forgiveness because the person is self-focused and attuned to the possible benefits of collecting on debts, as well as the costs of forgiving such as loss of self-respect (Exline, Baumeister, Bushman, Campbell, & Finkel, 2004). From the object relations perspective, inability to forgive is due to splitting or other primitive defenses that make it impossible for us to see good and bad simultaneously in a person (Gartner, 1992; see Section 5.4.1).

3. *Cognitive patterns.* Rumination or tendencies toward self-justification enhance negative emotions and decrease positive ones like empathy (Bassett, Bassett, Lloyd, & Johnson, 2006; Berry et al., 2005).

11.4.1.3 Interventions

True forgiveness seems both rare and difficult, but it can be cultivated. Increasing it may be a desirable goal in therapy, particularly when working with couples or families (Pingleton, 1997; Worthington, Mazzeo et al., 2005). Research indicates that forgiveness attitudes can be increased at least temporarily in therapy with positive benefits (e.g., Hebl & Enright, 1993; Coyle & Enright, 1997). These studies suggest that strictly cognitive approaches based on decisional forgiveness are not effective, but process-based ones that address emotion and empathy are effective, producing reductions in anxiety and depression, as well as higher levels of forgiveness and hope (Baskin & Enright, 2004). Most current outcome research uses group interventions although individual interventions appear to have larger effect sizes (Freedman & Enright, 1996; McCullough, Worthington et al., 1997; Wade & Worthington, 2005). In Christian contexts these approaches could be supplemented with reflection through spiritual journaling, ritual, or education about Christian ideas of forgiveness (Enright & Fitzgibbons, 2000, p. 17; Gulliford, 2004a; Wade, Bailey, & Shaffer, 2005; Lampton, Oliver, Worthington, & Berry, 2005). Similar interventions could be designed to assist people in identifying needs for forgiveness and seeking it from others (e.g., Enright, 2001, pp. 245–261).

Worthington and his colleagues (e.g., Wade & Worthington, 2005; Lampton et al., 2005) use a 5-step pyramid model for change that includes the following: (1) recall of the hurt in helpful ways in a supportive environment; (2) empathy building with the transgressor, including self-reflection and seeing one's own offenses; (3) altruistic giving of forgiveness; (4) commitment to forgiveness; and (5) holding on in the midst of doubts, while controlling rumination. In the altruistic gift phase, the person is asked to imagine how they might have benefited from being forgiven in various situations, thus emphasizing the development of humility along with forgiveness. The effectiveness of an intervention such as this to increase forgiveness is related to the length of time the person spends empathizing with the transgressor. The procedure works by increasing forgiveness rather than decreasing unforgiveness, although adding post-decision empathy and humility-building exercises can decrease unforgiveness and revenge motivations (Worthington, Kurusu, Collins et al., 2000).

11.4.1.4 Critique

Current models of forgiveness have been criticized in a number of ways. Commentators point out that these models assume that the process of forgiveness is the same regardless of the individual level of development and psychopathology or the religious context of the individual (Pingleton, 1997; Burns, 2004;

McCullough & Worthington, 1999). The effect size of therapies built on these models is also quite modest. In the case of the Worthington model, this may be because of the fact that altruism is a very complex behavior that typically is multiply motivated (Oliner, 2002). A specific objection to the Enright model is that it is built on unilateral forgiveness as an unconditional gift (cf. Lamb, 2005). This is in contrast to a negotiated model that focuses more on reciprocity and addresses issues of reconciliation. Andrews (2000) argues that negotiated models, such as in the truth and reconciliation commissions established in Chile and South Africa, have an advantage because they require transactions between the wronged and wrongdoer; this allows confession, ownership, repentance, and remorse to take place, thus changing both people. Reconciliation is a complex concept, so while powerful it can have many different meanings (Schreiter, 1998). A final criticism is that the models do not address the possibility that forgiveness might not be desirable in some situations, such as in the case of women who are dealing with issues of victimization, anger, and abuse of power. Lack of forgiveness and maintenance of anger in these situations might help to protect individuals and motivate efforts to address social problems (McCullough, 2001a; Worthington, Mazzeo et al., 2005; McKay, Hill, Freedman, & Enright, 2007). It also may not be appropriate in situations where we need to forgo the impulse to blame and simply acknowledge the potential for failure that is inherent in the human condition (Coate, 2004).

An interesting critique of the psychological forgiveness literature has come from theologian Stanley Jones (1995a). He believes that contemporary views of forgiveness are deficient. In the modernist view, forgiveness has become part of the therapeutic model, which assumes (1) forgiveness is a personal matter, a psychological act within the individual; (2) everyone is a victim in some way who needs compassion; and (3) as victims our need is to forgive others rather than to be forgiven for our own transgressions. Jones rejects these views. He argues that forgiveness is not an act but an embodied way of life aimed at deepening our relationships with God and others. It is about more than self-interest, it involves habits and patterns of relationship that aim toward justice (Watts, 2004). The idea that everyone is a victim and that only others are in need of forgiveness produces a kind of moral anesthesia, which ignores our failings and needs for repentance, and makes it impossible to address the real goal of forgiveness, which is restoring communion. Therapeutic versions of forgiveness are simply cheapened versions of the real thing that help us feel better but lack the transforming power of real forgiveness. Some psychologists have welcomed the involvement of theologians in forgiveness research, arguing that scholars like Jones help to provide a broader picture to the questions being studied (Watts et al., 2006; Enright & Fitzgibbons, 2000).

Exline, Worthington, Hill, and McCullough (2003) recently summarized the debate on forgiveness that is taking place in a number of fields and have pointed out key unanswered questions. What is forgiveness? Does it invite repeated offenses? Should some things be considered unforgivable? While some questions seem answerable by empirical investigation, others challenge basic philosophical and theological beliefs that are not so easily settled. It is likely that this will continue to be a rich area of investigation for the foreseeable future.

11.4.2 *Mindfulness and Vipassana Meditation*

A prominent appropriation of religious practices in the mental health field has been the integration of mindfulness meditation techniques into versions of psychotherapy (Williams & Swales, 2004). Drawn from traditional Buddhist Vipassana meditation practice (see Sections 3.2.2 and 13.5.1), the goal of mindfulness meditation is to become detached observers of our mental activities. This allows us to see distortions and eliminate attachments to fleeting pleasures and problematic habitual patterns of thought that lead to suffering (Kutz, Borysenko, & Benson, 1985; Goldstein & Kornfield, 2001; Shapiro, 1992b). Psychological descriptions of mindfulness tend to emphasize two components. First, mindfulness involves self-regulation of attention and sustained focus on events, while inhibiting mental self-talk and analysis of experience. Second, it involves a particular orientation away from an instrumental or control view of experience toward a stance that is participant and present-centered, nonjudgmental, and thus open to novelty (Deikman, 2000; Bishop, Lacour, Nutt, Vivian, & Lee, 2004; Germer, 2005a, 2005b; Kabat-Zinn, 2003a). Acceptance is a particularly crucial aspect of mindfulness, for Buddhist thought takes the paradoxical position that what is to be changed must first be accepted (Rand, 2004). More than a computational process, it is a cognitive style or preferred way of thinking that heightens awareness to the present and the environment, as well as to oneself. It has some parallels with dissociative conditions, although there are also important differences (Sternberg, 2000; Langer & Moldoveanu, 2000a; Waelde, 2003).

Psychologists have taken two general approaches when appropriating Buddhist or Hindu techniques such as mindfulness meditation. In the first approach, meditation is considered a technology that can be appropriated for scientific or therapeutic purposes. For instance, Benson and his colleagues (e.g., Kutz et al., 1985) believed that concentrative meditation could be "conceptually denuded of its cultural and religious biases" and used as a technology to manipulate attention, promote relaxation and self-exploration, or to intensify the psychotherapy process (Langer & Moldoveanu, 2000a; cf. Kabat-Zinn, 2003a). This technology idea is still popular in the field, although aspects of it are no longer widely accepted (e.g., Lazar, 2005). In the second approach, psychologists have not attempted to separate the technique from its worldview but have incorporated part or all of the underlying religious thought. In the case of mindfulness meditation, this has meant exploiting parallels between Buddhist Abidhamma philosophy and Western psychology in terms of cognitive analysis and modification (Kutz et al., 1985; Epstein, 1999). Zen Buddhist principles are sometimes also used (e.g., Chen, 2005). Buddhist views of reality and the person might also be used to question traditional Western psychological ones and advocate an alternate metaphysical basis, for instance, using the Buddhist idea that the self is contextual and without enduring identity (e.g., Germer, 2005a; cf. Salmon et al., 2004). Experienced meditators generally take this approach, as they find it increasingly important to embrace a connection to a community and the support of a set of religious beliefs and practices, typically Buddhist or some combination of Buddhist and Christian ideas (Shapiro, 1992b;

Goldstein & Kornfield, 2001, p. 227). Historically, those who see meditation as a technology have joined with transpersonal thinkers to encourage its use in therapy, perhaps in combination with other techniques, while psychoanalysts using meditation have also adopted aspects of Buddhist philosophy. Advocates of integration argue that meditation and psychotherapy have similarities or are at least complementary to each other, although therapy may be more appropriate than meditation in people with more severe disorders (Bogart, 1991; Brown & Robinson, 1993; Delmonte, 1990).

Mindfulness and other Buddhist practices can be integrated into therapy in one or more of three ways. First, it can be a practice for the therapist. Second, it can provide a framework of reference that informs the therapy process, as when Buddhist ideas about suffering provide guidance for the counselor. Third, it can be taught as a skill or used as the basis of an educational program (Kabat-Zinn, 2003a; Germer, 2005b; Langer & Moldoveanu, 2000b). Clinical mindfulness programs typically include a conscious change of attention to nonjudgmental awareness. This begins with observing our breath, although other foci of attention can also be used such as parts of the body, sounds (e.g., a bell), thoughts, feelings, or activities like walking. A quiet state of hypoarousal and nonjudgmentalness is produced that is designed to enhance present-moment awareness and diminish habitual patterns and automatic reactions (Salmon et al., 2004). In the traditional Buddhist framework, insight meditation is also dependent upon an initial set of moral precepts. These can be positive acts such as a commitment to generosity or negative such as avoidance of mind-altering substances and refraining from harmful acts. This restraint helps normalize our lives so that we are able to better concentrate and develop states of mindfulness and insight (Goldstein & Kornfield, 2001, p. 117). However, most psychological adaptations of mindfulness neglect or reject this framework.

11.4.2.1 Specific Approaches

Mindfulness-Based Stress Reduction (MBSR). While there were reports about the use of mindfulness in therapy at least as far back as the mid-1970s (Sternberg, 2000; e.g., Deatherage, 1975), one of the first people to adapt mindfulness techniques for systematic use in psychological settings was Jon Kabat-Zinn, who developed a program called Mindfulness-Based Stress Reduction. His goal was to remove mindfulness from its "religious, cultural and ideological forms" and use it as a technique for self-regulation of chronic pain by helping people detach from it (Kabat-Zinn, Lipworth, & Burney, 1985, p. 164). The application he developed involves 8 weekly sessions of instructions, as well as a silent retreat and regular practice. Along with successful reductions in chronic pain and pain-related psychological problems, MBSR has been found to reduce ruminative thinking, anxiety or depression and increase quality of life in some groups. It is also associated with increased scores on measures of spiritual experience (Salmon et al., 2004; Kabat-Zinn et al., 1992; Tacon, McComb, Caldera, & Randolph, 2003; Ramel, Goldin, Carmona, & McQuaid, 2004; Bedard et al., 2003; Astin, 1997). Although the technique is called "mindfulness-based," in fact it includes a number of techniques, including concentrative and walking meditations, yoga stretching, and visualizations (Smith, 2004a; Baer, 2003). Mindfulness is developed through developing focus and awareness on the breath, or through the *body scan meditation*, which develops awareness by progressively focusing on various parts of the body (Kabat-Zinn, 2005a, 2005b). While there are relatively few good-quality studies on MBSR and little data on long-term effects, a meta-analysis of available research shows that it is moderately helpful with a wide variety of physical and psychological problems (Grossman, Niemann, Schmidt, & Walach, 2004). Short-term mindfulness courses have been shown to increase left anterior brain activation that is associated with positive affect and approach behavior, as well as increase antibody response (Davidson, Kabat-Zinn et al., 2003; Davidson, 2003; Kabat-Zinn, 2003b). MBSR has had mixed results in reducing relapse in substance abuse treatment, although it may help with emotional aspects of the problem (Breslin, Zack, & McMain, 2002; Marlatt & Kristeller, 1999).

Mindfulness-Based Cognitive Therapy (MBCT). Another major application of mindfulness procedures has been its integration with cognitive-behavioral therapy (CBT), as in Mindfulness-Based Cognitive Therapy (Segal, Teasdale, & Williams, 2004; Segal, Williams, & Teasdale, 2001). MBCT differs from traditional cognitive therapy in that it focuses on cognitive or attentional *process* rather than *belief*s. In traditional cognitive therapy, cognitions are thought to be the cause of problems and therapy aims at disputing problematic beliefs. MBCT aims at the person's thinking about their thoughts and sees these *metacognitions* as a factor in the continuation and recurrence of depression (Carney & Segal, 2005; Orsillo, Roemer, Lerner, & Tull, 2004; Melbourne group, 2006; Salmon et al., 2004; Scherer-Dickson, 2004). The therapy has been especially designed to help prevent relapse in people with a history of multiple, chronic episodes of depression, and while using some techniques that are similar to MBSR it has a broader focus (Baer, 2003).

MBCT is an eight-session structured small group therapy often combined with individual therapy (Williams & Swales, 2004). It is based on the idea that relapse in depression is caused by a kindling phenomenon, where negative thoughts and feelings like those experienced during previous depressions trigger ruminative thinking, which increases the chance of relapse. This results from a person living in a "doing" mode that pursues wishes and "oughts" that leave the person unsatisfied. MBCT aims to develop a state of mindful awareness and a nonstriving "being" mode marked by a nonjudgmental acceptance of experience. This helps us to detach from problems and automatic intrusive memories of the past (Baer, 2003; Williams, Teasdale, Segal, & Soulsby, 2000; Teasdale et al., 2000). During the first three sessions, participants are introduced to mindfulness techniques, including the breath and body scan exercises from MBSR, as well as the "raisin" exercise, where a person explores without evaluation the sensations of a raisin using all sensory modalities. A fourth session continues mindfulness training and introduces educative material on depression and basic Buddhist philosophy (Carney & Segal, 2005). During the last four sessions, mindfulness and CBT techniques are used to teach the participant how to handle mood shifts and formulate relapse prevention strategies. Four follow-up sessions help maintain gains made during the class. Studies in the

US and UK have found that MBCT is effective, increasing metacognitive awareness and detachment of self from thoughts and feelings. This leads to a 40% reduction in relapse rates for individuals with 3 or more previous depressive episodes and a 50% drop in scores on the Beck Depression Inventory, although it is apparently not beneficial in those with less chronic depressions. Completion rates for the program are quite good, around 75% in larger studies, although regular practice levels after the program are below 50% (Teasdale et al., 2000; Baer, 2003; Breslin et al., 2002; Ma & Teasdale, 2004; Teasdale et al., 2002). It is similar to Action and Commitment Therapy (Hayes, Strosahl, & Wilson, 2003; Wilson & Murrell, 2004), although it lacks the emphasis on values clarification of the latter procedure (Bach, Gaudiano, Pankey, Herbert, & Hayes, 2006).

Dialectical Behavior Therapy (DBT). The paradoxical techniques of Zen Buddhism make their appearance in Dialectical Behavior Therapy (Linehan, 1993a, 1993b). DBT is a strategy for treatment of borderline personality disorder (Koerner & Linehan, 2000), a chronic and disabling condition which is associated with frequent suicidal behavior, self-mutilation, and other problems that severely affect the person's quality of life. DBT is based on a dialectical worldview that reality is a constantly changing pattern of interrelated oppositional pairs that form new syntheses, which in turn form the basis of new opposing pairs. It assumes that nothing has a truly stable independent existence (Linehan, Tutek, Heard, & Armstrong, 1994, pp. 28–33; Robins, 2002). This idea helps combat the black and white thinking about people and relationships that is characteristic of borderline personality and leads to interpersonal problems. While DBT has similarities to Zen thought, there are also differences, as Zen deals with normal kinds of suffering and tries to provoke crisis to change ways of thinking, while DBT deals with situations of unusual suffering and crisis (Anbeek & de Groot, 2002).

DBT is a lengthy, comprehensive approach that involves individual psychotherapy and group skills training (Linehan, Comtois et al., 2006). Focus on breathing helps to increase ability to attend nonjudgmentally. DBT uses dialectical strategies, including a teeter-totter procedure of alternately supporting or opposing the client's views to lead them toward an integration of reason and emotion, and an appreciation of the paradoxically good effects that bad situations can have. This is supplemented with skills building to increase capabilities for emotional regulation, distress tolerance, and motivation. Thus DBT is explicitly oriented to change, in contrast to Zen that is more oriented toward acceptance (Williams & Swales, 2004). DBT also teaches core techniques including "what" skills like observing or attending and also "how" to do them nonjudgmentally to help resolve problem situations (Baer & Krietemeyer, 2006). A number of studies have supported the effectiveness of DBT in reducing anger, suicidal behavior, hospitalizations, and treatment dropout, as well as increasing treatment compliance (Linehan, Comtois et al., 2006; cf. Linehan, Armstrong, Suarez, Allmon, & Heard, 1991; Linehan, Tutek et al., 1994; Koerner & Linehan, 2000). It does not appear to reduce depression, a sign that its effect comes through increasing distress tolerance (Robins, 2002). While the dialectical aspect of the therapy is presumed to be responsible for its effectiveness, research has not yet established this.

11.4.2.2 Critique

A number of cautions and criticisms have been offered to the contemporary use of mindfulness within psychology and counseling.

1. The concept of mindfulness is vague, and it is unclear who it will work for and what kinds of problems it will solve (Bishop, 2002). It is also unclear what groups of people will do well with meditation, although there are indications it is less well-suited for severely depressed individuals (Beauchamp-Turner & Levinson, 1992). Mindfulness is not an easy skill to learn; it requires extensive work and persistence, must be practiced consistently to maintain its benefits, and may need to be practiced by therapists who want to use it (Williams & Swales, 2004; Baer & Krietemeyer, 2006; DeBerry, Davis, & Reinhard, 1989).
2. The concept of mindfulness as operationalized in psychology differs from its original Buddhist use (Marlatt et al., 2004), so while new applications of mindfulness may be helpful they may be quite different from their original effect. For instance, MBSR is a combination of Buddhist nonstriving and a pragmatic Western symptom-focused emphasis on change. The point of vipassana is detachment and acceptance, which is the opposite of the kind of goal-oriented striving envisioned by the various therapies (Salmon et al., 2004). MBSR and other therapies also avoid critique of client goals or feelings, but in Buddhist thought some goals and emotions are problematic and others are good and to be pursued (Robins, 2002; Ekman, Davidson, Ricard, & Wallace, 2005).
3. Studies have been criticized for weak design and the use of small or atypical samples and the choice (or absence) of control groups. This makes it difficult to compare procedures like MBSR with other techniques. While significant changes in some target variables are found, the studies do not address the clinical significance of these changes, whether mindful states are actually produced, or the extent to which mindfulness is the factor involved in any positive effects (Smith, 2004a; Baer, 2003; Breslin et al., 2002; Salmon et al., 2004; Bishop, 2002; Williams & Swales, 2004). Parallel techniques are also found in the Christian tradition, for instance in the "guarding of the heart" used in Orthodox spiritual practice or in techniques of contemplative prayer (Williams & Swales, 2004; see Sections 13.2 and 13.3), but these have been little studied.
4. Vipassana meditation is a powerful technique, so it is not surprising that it can lead to disturbing experiences and have adverse effects especially when used more intensively with people who are unprepared (Melbourne group, 2006; Emavardhana & Tori, 1997; Walsh, 1977, 1978). In one study of long term meditators after a vipassana retreat, Shapiro (1992a) found that almost two-thirds of participants experienced at least one negative effect, and about 7% reported severe negative effects including interpersonal problems, increased feelings of social isolation, and intrapersonal difficulties such as negative emotions and disorientation.

11.5 Conclusion

Key issue: *Religious and spiritual perspectives on mental health offer great resources for individuals and societies that seek psychological and spiritual growth.*

The large body of mental health literature reviewed in this chapter reinforces the views developed in the last chapter on physical health. Traditional ideas within psychology that religion is a negative force are generally false. Particularly noteworthy is the destruction of the supposedly scientific view held during much of the 20th century that organizational religion is particularly problematic and to be avoided. In fact, research suggests that involvement in institutional religion may be more important to the maintenance of positive physical and mental health than individual spiritual practices, although it is also obvious that it is difficult to strictly separate the individual and communal. These positive benefits of religion are still largely ignored within the professional mental health community, which is unfortunate (McNamara, 2002). Details of these communal and individual practices are the topic of our next three chapters.

A comprehensive look at the mental health literature reveals a deep inconsistency in some contemporary ideas about spirituality and religion. In some models of human health, spirituality is about power, and religious practices are tools for increasing human power and control in the search for happiness and well-being. However, as the literature on addictions demonstrates, power is neither an unreserved good nor is control possible or desirable in all situations. Spirituality that leads to freedom may involve relinquishing constant needs for power and control, accepting mystery that is inherent in life, and welcoming with gratitude what others have to offer. Acceptance of that is a key to a genuine spiritual life, as well as to freedom from illusions and attachments that lead to pain and suffering. Furthermore, the pursuit of happiness as the most important or sole good in life can lead to attachments that are destructive of freedom and happiness. These realities need to be taken into account in any effort that hopes to address the serious mental health problems and needs of our time.

Chapter 12
Practices and Religious Communities

For most people with a religious orientation, religion is not a *thing* but it is something that they *do*, a set of individual and communal **practices** that they perform to develop and express their spiritual nature (cf. Section 6.3.4). Thus, no consideration of the topic of religion and psychology is complete without a thorough examination of the individual and communal actions performed in pursuit of religious or spiritual goals.

12.1 Religious and Spiritual Practices in Community

There are two ways of approaching the study of religious and spiritual practices. In the modernist and positivist view, practices are a technique or technology engaged in for a particular purpose. These techniques can be learned and performed regardless of the beliefs and lifestyle of the person performing them. In this view, a person can practice Buddhist meditation without holding any Buddhist beliefs or engaging in any other Buddhist practices or community life. This is quite different from a postmodern perspective (see Sections 6.3.1 and 6.3.4), which holds that all activity is contextual and thus assumes a particular set of beliefs or worldview. In this view, any single practice cannot be understood apart from other practices and the community life that supports them. Studying or using a practice in an isolated way, even if possible, is somewhat like taking an electronic part out of a cardiac pacemaker and expecting it to work on its own, or inserting it into an entirely different device like a computer and supposing that it will perform the same function. The part may (or may not) function in its new context; it may even have a helpful effect, but its function is likely to be different. In the postmodern view, any attempt to understand religious practices outside of their context may lead to fundamental errors.

There is value in both modern and postmodern approaches to practice. In support of the modernist perspective, it is true that people can and do engage in spiritual practices while divorced from the communities and traditions that produced them, such as in the use of Buddhist approaches to the treatment of psychological problems (see Section 11.4.2). It is also true that research in a positivist framework has helped us understand some biological and psychological factors connected with practices like meditation (see Section 13.6).

J.M. Nelson, *Psychology, Religion, and Spirituality,*
DOI 10.1007/978-0-387-87573-6_12, @ Springer Science+Business Media, LLC 2009

However, the postmodern approach has particular advantages when considering practices because of the inherently contextual nature of spirituality (cf. Section 1.2.2). In the religious perspective (and many nonreligious ones), spirituality is where all the aspects of life meet and run together; it is the common theme that brings unity and coherence within ourselves and with the world. This means that everything affects our spirituality and so "working on our spirituality" is not picking a single practice that we do every once in awhile but choosing a *way of life* that supports spirituality and leads us toward wholeness. It involves the whole person, including the body as well as our beliefs, attitudes, values, and actions. Addressing this whole person requires a system of intertwined practices. This way of life will inevitably affect our relationships and actions toward others and our connections to the communities that surround us; it thus has a moral quality (Polkinghorne, 2004, pp. 1–9; Wuthnow, 2001). Religious and spiritual practices exist within this contextual and communal framework, and religious communities and traditions have been the primary places where these practices have been developed and refined over many generations.

Postmodern approaches are popular in the contemporary study of religious practices done by Christian theologians and religious studies scholars. An example can be found in the practical theology of Browning (1991) and others, which draws on hermeneutic philosophy, practical early Christian thought, and theologies like that of Reinhold Niebuhr or David Tracy (see Sections 1.5.2 and 1.5.3). It emphasizes that (1) religion involves practices; (2) these practices take place within a communal ideological context and cannot be understood apart from the context, so they are theory laden; and (3) practices are responses to the specific needs of individuals in particular situations and thus cannot be comprehended by reductionist statements of general laws (Forrester, 1999; Fowler, 1999a, 1999c; Tracy, 1975, p. 46; 1983, p. 76). Practical theology argues that practices and their descriptions in religion— and also in psychology—are theory laden. This means that their effect is dependent upon the ethical and theoretical assumptions of the individual and community that stand behind the practices, as well as the concrete situation within which they are performed. Transformation is thought to be multidimensional and include all these aspects (Browning, 1999; Viau, 1999).

Postmodern approaches to spiritual practice have largely been absent from psychology. One of the main reasons for this is that psychology has generally ignored the communal and social aspects of religion or been unsophisticated in its approach to the topic (Pargament & Maton, 2000; Pargament, 2002b). This is understandable, as a thorough understanding of community dynamics includes a wide variety of areas including (1) sacred space, symbols or rituals; (2) community relationships, including patterns of leadership; (3) community climate, what it feels like for members; (4) beliefs and values; and (5) practices (Roehlkepartain & Patel, 2006). However, it is also unfortunate, as there are many indications that community life forms a vital part of religious or spiritual development, although the kind of community best suited to the individual may vary according to their stage of development (Love, 2002).

In this chapter, we will consider religious communities, as well as practices that are typically done in group settings, while in the next chapter we will focus on individual practices such as prayer and meditation. While these are treated separately, in fact it is not truly possible to put practices into strict categories like "individual" or "communal." Individual practices like prayer can intensify social support and are dependent upon a rich communal tradition of goals and methods (Ladd & McIntosh, 2008). Likewise, communal practices like worship have a deeply individual aspect to them. Our discussion will highlight these connections.

12.2 Religious Self-Understandings of Community

From the very earliest times, spiritual seeking has brought people together into religious communities. Central to the life of a religious community is an **ideology**, a set of beliefs that has three components—(1) descriptive statements about the world, (2) normative statements about how we ought to act, and (3) sociological imperatives that define social existence for believers (MacIntyre, 1984, pp. 118–119; 1988, pp. 349–369). Also important for the community are shared practices that are sometimes performed individually but are often done in small or large group settings. In psychological language, the community and the supportive mentoring relationships within it are designed to provide a container within which transformation can be supported and worked out in positive ways (Gunn, 2000, pp. 126–127, 276–280; see Sections 14.1.1 and 14.1.2). In this section, we consider the understandings of community developed within two religious traditions—Buddhism and Christianity. In contrast to social scientific views of religion that attempt to study communities *as they actually are in society*, religious understandings focus on communities *as they should be* and discuss typical barriers and problems that occur in attempting to attain this goal. Of course, social scientists studying religious communities bring their own values and ideas about ideal communities to their work, so in practice these two approaches are not strictly separated.

12.2.1 Buddhism and the Sangha

The **sangha** or community is considered to be so important in Buddhism that it is included as one of its Three Jewels along with the Buddha and dharma (see Section 3.2). Although probably not the original intent of the Buddha, the earliest sangha were **monastic communities** of men, and later women, who lived in unisex groupings apart from society and were distinguished from lay Buddhists who remained in the world. A man who lived in one of these communities was known as a *bhikkhu* or **monk**. In early Buddhism, the term *sangha* referred to a particular monastic community, but in later times the term was also applied to a more universal collection of all monks, or even all practicing Buddhists, and as a model for the ideal society. Over time, these communities settled in particular locations and built buildings or **monasteries**, initially just as dwelling places but later to provide facilities for teaching and learning. Initially monks lived on alms, but more sophisticated forms of support also developed over time (Putuwar, 1991).

In order to join the community, one had to have a certain level of moral purity and traditionally be at least 15 years of age. The prospective member often had a sponsor who presented the person to an assembly where the community decided on admittance. On presentation the person recited the formula "I take my refuge in the Buddha, I take my refuge in the Dhamma, and I take my refuge in the Sangha" (Hazra, 1988, p. 181). Once admitted, there were two levels of ordination for monks. At the first level, one became a novice (*samanera*) and chose two teachers—a general teacher (*upajjhaya*) and a person to train them in meditation techniques (*acariya*). Many leave after a couple of years, but those who stayed went through a second ceremony to become a bhikkhu (Hazra, 1988, pp. 81–97).

The sangha had two social structures: First, there was an administrative structure for managing community affairs. The early sangha did not have a monastic community leader or **abbot**; instead, most important decisions were made by democratic vote and generally required unanimous approval. Thus, there was no requirement of obedience to a superior and equal rights among members were emphasized. However, moral conduct (*sila*) including obedience to outward rules (*vinaya*), and following inner beliefs or attitudes (*dhamma*) was expected as essential support for teaching and practice. These rules included prohibitions of sexual behavior and owning personal property (Putuwar, 1991, pp. 36–60). Second was a more hierarchical teaching structure. Offices or ranks included the (1) *thera* or chief monk, (2) theras of lesser degrees who acted as teachers, and (3) junior bhikkus still undergoing training. Criteria for advancement to the status of a thera included observance of rules, accomplishments in learning and study, satisfaction with life, and proficiency in meditation (Hazra, 1988, pp. 195–196).

In more modern thought, while Buddhist monasteries still exist in large numbers particularly in Asia, a sangha need not be a collection of monks but simply a group of friends who practice mindfulness together, inspired by each other, the historic Buddha and his teachings. In other words, Buddhism is about practice (Lawlor, 2002a). Taking refuge in the sangha is taking refuge in practices supported by friends with similar ideas. These practices are thought to help provide stability, joy, and collective energy, as well as lead to increased awareness and compassion (Hanh, 2002, pp. 9–27). Historically in the West, members of a sangha knew little about each other, but more recently the formation of spiritual friendships has been increasing in importance (Lawlor, 2002a, 2002b), along with a number of other practices including the following:

- Mindfulness retreats and weekly gatherings where members can share teachings, discuss problems of practice, and support each other (King, 2002)
- Acts of compassion and service, although some see Buddhism's primary social role as offering values (Dockett & North-Schulte, 2003)
- Participation in regional, national and international events (Hanh, 2002)
- Outreach to others, for instance by starting mindfulness practice centers that are open to members of other religions.

Buddhists have always recognized the problems of community and their potential to interfere with practice (cf. Casey, 1995, p. 98). For instance, the early Buddhist meditation manual the *Visuddhimagga* contained lists of the faults of a monastery (Buddhaghosa, 1999, p. 118). Some modern treatments of Buddhist communities also discuss problems, including autocratic leadership, intolerance, internal divisiveness or conflict, members with serious mental illness, and sexual or financial misconduct by community leadership (Lawlor, 2002b, 2002c; Schmied, 2002). Some commentators see these problems as more serious in Buddhist groups outside of the Asian context, although specific data on this are not available. Many of these problems are found in all kinds of organizational or workplace settings, although the degree of similarity or difference between religious and secular organizational settings is not clearly known. At any rate, like all groups, Buddhist sangha developed ways of dealing with rule-breaking and other problems of community life. Early sangha distinguished between disciplinary or disputable matters and nondisciplinary or nondisputable problems. Disciplinary matters included rule breaking and immoral conduct, while nondisciplinary matters involved things like appointments of officers for managing community affairs. Disciplinary matters were handled according to a set of formal procedures for accusation and trial (Hazra, 1988, p. 107). Buddhist communities in the West tend to have less systematic ways of dealing with disciplinary problems.

12.2.2 Religious Communities in Zen Buddhism

Dogen (1996) and other Zen writers also developed visions for an ideal religious community. While Zen communities tend to have a less egalitarian structure than the classical sangha, all, regardless of rank or wisdom, are viewed as equal members, and writers recognized that wisdom is often unrelated to rank. A number of temple administrators from the chief cook or *tenzo* to the abbot or head of the monastery are described by Dogen. He taught that the most important attitude of an abbot is to serve the community for the benefit of others, maintaining high standards and respectfully following in the footsteps of predecessors. Temple administrators should strike a middle ground in terms of strictness: They should be gentle but not overly compassionate, welcoming to strangers but also screening out potential monks who do not possess the proper faith and habits. Leaders were to have an attitude of service and use skillful means when helping monks in training or **novices**. Newcomers were to be provided with basic necessities and education about the local region and rules of the community. In return, monks were expected to live according to Zen and not be critical of faults or hardships; rather they were to maintain a joyful attitude and avoid contentiousness.

The daily schedule at a monastery included early rising (4 am!), gatherings for meditation and sutra-chanting or study in a dignified atmosphere, meals and work time, with the monks retiring at about 9 pm. Annual observances throughout the year would include Buddha's birthday, enlightenment and death, remembrance services especially for the founder of the order, and repentance services (Foulk, 1988). Simple events like meals were structured to become times for contemplation and abandonment of flaws like greed.

12.2.3 Christian Communities

In the Christian tradition, monastic communities for men and women began to form in the early 4th century near towns and in more isolated areas of Egypt, Syria, and Palestine. These communities were in part a response to social conditions that were thought to present obstacles to following a truly Christian way of life (Gould, 1993, pp. 139–140). Especially in Western Christianity, a supportive community of like-minded individuals following a common rule of practice was thought to offer the best atmosphere for pursuit of Christian ideals and spiritual development. It was thought that most people would flourish better in a community setting than following a hermit life of individual seeking (Goehring, 1999; Spidlik, 1986, p. 151; Welch, 1996, p. 81; Merton, 2005b, p. 39; Driver, 2002, p. 23; Veilleux, 1980, pp. 151, 238). This idea of mutual accountability and encouragement also lies at the foundation of a number of Protestant communal traditions such as Methodism (Watson, 1986).

However, Christian texts like the Bible clearly recognize the existence of both good and bad religion, and as Luther once noted, even good communities have problems (Hendricks, 1986, p. 17; Kärkkäinen, 2004, p. 61). There is a need to steer a course between the extremes of rampant individualism and excessive organization that can become mechanical or even totalitarian (Merton, 2005b, pp. 44–45). As a result, Christian communities have worked to define rules for common life that would minimize problems and maximize benefits, turning problems of community life into opportunities for spiritual growth. The earliest monastic rules, the *Rule of Pachomius* (Veilleux, 1981, pp. 141–223; Merton, 2006, pp. 72–114; Harmless, 2004, p. 124) and the *Rule of St. Basil* (Holmes, 2000) were based on Biblical principles and early church practices. They not only emphasized community life as a way of withdrawal from distraction and worldly concerns, but also made it clear that love of others and love of God are interrelated and are best learned together in community. Basil referred to a harmonious religious community as "a stadium for athletics, a method for traveling forward, a continual exercise (gymnasia) and a practice of the Lord's commandments" (Holmes, 2000, p. 142). He saw intense community life as a practice for all Christians, not just for monks (Merton, 1973, pp. 68–69). Others offer us an insightful perspective on our gifts and flaws, and the community provides a framework for the pursuit of relational goals like service, mentoring and hospitality. The community also supports individual devotional practices that help us develop inner stillness and awareness. These inner states help us to advance spiritually and deal constructively with the anger and judgmentalness that can occur in a community (Gould, 1993). In the ancient world, the communities also provided education such as basic literacy so that members could read the Bible and sacred texts. At various times in history these rules were more or less successful in achieving their ideals, although periods of decadence also provided an opportunity for the flourishing of the mystical life and creativity as communities struggled to reform (de Certeau, 1992, p. 25). Some rules like that of Basil were designed for general use by Christians, while others like that of Pachomius were for separated monastic communities. The intention was to provide a framework for growth while maintaining flexibility for individual needs, aptitudes and capacities (Merton, 2006, p. 125; Veilleux, 1980, p. 83).

In the early 5th century, Christians like John Cassian from Western Europe brought back news of Eastern monasticism and began forming their own religious communities. The basic ideal of these groups is stated in the *Rule of St. Augustine* as: "Mutual love expressed in the community of goods and in humility" (Canning, 1986, p. 11). In the early 6th century, the monk St. Benedict developed the *Rule of St. Benedict* (Benedict, 2001), which provided a detailed vision of community for Western Christians. Areas covered by the various monastic rules included the following:

1. *Leadership.* The abbot should be one who shows no partiality, governing by deeds as well as words. While they have the final authority and responsibility, power should not be used in an arbitrary fashion, and the abbot should consult with all about any important matter. Humility was considered to be a key virtue (Veilleux, 1980, p. 316). The Western rule tends to be more hierarchal than Basil's rule.

2. *Relational practices.* Monks were directed to practice mutual obedience and develop humility in order to foster spiritual growth of both the individual and the community.

3. *Communal religious practices.* Most of the day was structured around set times for prayer and worship known as the **Daily Office**. During the day this included the prayer times of *Prime, Terce, Sext, None, Vespers,* and *Compline,* and at night a period of silence or *Vigils.* Prayers were to be reverent, short, and pure. Some of the prayer times were individual, while others took place in an assembly (Harmless, 2004, pp. 128–129).

4. *Discipline.* Discipline for rule breaking should not be arbitrary but for good reason and only after private and public admonishment. Patience was encouraged. In more serious cases, a person might be excluded from some or all community activities and given the guidance of a mature brother, while others prayed for him. If problems remained, then expulsion from the community was allowed.

5. *Communal life.* Private property was not allowed; goods were to be distributed based on need rather than rank or social status, and while equality was stressed there was also attention to the individual, for instance that all should work according to their ability. Duties included kitchen work and a regular daily schedule of manual labor with time set aside for reading and the Daily Office. Life was to be regulated with the goal of spiritual advancement and the needs of others in mind.

6. *Membership.* While hospitality and reception of guests, pilgrims, and prospective members was important, full membership in the community was more difficult to attain. Individuals joining the community needed to make difficult vows of stability (remaining with the community), reformation of life, and obedience. Age and other limits were established to make sure people had the personal stability necessary to take these vows, and a preparatory period of novitiate helped determine whether the individual was suited to the way of life offered by the community.

12.2.3.1 Modern Views

Modern Christian thought continues to emphasize the importance of community in human development and spiritual formation. A Christian psychological view is provided by Balswick, King, and Reimer (2005) who argue that (1) people are essentially relational, and so (2) community and the intimacy it can provide are necessary to human growth. Strong communities produce a "reciprocating self" that is integrated with good resources and stands in the middle of a continuum between the extremes of a "fortress self" that is highly defended and a "fragmented self" with few resources. This kind of relational self allows for moral development and full faith and intimacy in God without sacrificing the particularity of the individual. Thus, most Christians reject the idea that community and personhood are somehow opposed to each other, and argue that any spirituality must have access to a tradition that provides community and a set of concrete spiritual practices designed to foster growth. This connection to community allows one to separate authentic and inauthentic spiritual experience. In Christianity, the Trinitarian focus of belief and practice means that spiritual growth is relational in nature and should be reflected in interactions; it is not just a solitary quest or pattern of ethics (Rahner, 1963, pp. 122–126, 235–239; Herrera, 2000; Sheldrake, 1998). Community also provides support for Christian belief that is increasingly important in a culture dominated by secular ideas and ways of thinking (Pannenberg, 1996).

While some modern Christian religious communities aim for isolation or avoidance, most try to connect the individual with society. Along with evangelism, types of mission include (1) social activism—social justice which involves changing existing structures, (2) civic activism—supporting existing structures that meet social needs, or (3) social service—improving existing structures. Other mission priorities involve providing sanctuary and protection to individuals in need (Pargament & Maton, 2000).

Within the Christian tradition, there is a large diversity of community practices and ideals. Many of the issues discussed in the ancient rules of Basil and Benedict continue to be wrestled with by Christians in popular literature and in **ecclesiology**, the branch of theology devoted to the study of religious community. Differences of opinion exist about a number of issues (Kärkkäinen, 2002, p. 84; Dulles, 2002). For instance, some see the visible Church as the presence of God in the world (e.g., Calvin, 1960, pp. 1011–1053), while others see the true Church as invisible, operating in the midst of a community that externally may seem quite broken. Others like Luther hold that it is both, offering a "hospital for the sick." Other debates within ecclesiology revolve around the relative importance of various aspects of community, such as (1) institutional and hierarchical or episcopal structures, (2) sacramental practices, (3) personal holiness, (4) traditional customs and beliefs, (5) proclamation through preaching or evangelism, (6) personal mysticism, and (7) outreach to other groups and religious traditions or **ecumenism** (cf. Gilkey, 1994). Some Christian groups emphasize institutional, traditional, and sacramental aspects of communities, while others stress more personal and mystical aspects. This debate contains both a discussion of the goals for an ideal community and a debate over the best way to deal with problems that regularly occur in community life. This discussion takes place amidst constant social, cultural, and economic shifts that put pressures on groups to change and adapt. This constant pressure for change often leads to conflict and is a significant problem in contemporary US Christian communities (Dudley & Roozen, 2001).

12.3 Psychological Perspectives on Religious Communities

Research by social scientists and psychologists adds a valuable complement to self-understandings of religious communities. We begin by considering aspects of modern culture that affect the nature and status of community and then move to research that focuses specifically on Christian communities.

12.3.1 The Modern Backdrop to Community Life

General patterns of social organization in our culture have a large impact on the functioning of communities, including religious ones. Research suggests that these overall patterns can be classified into three types—individualist, collectivist, and communitarian (Hofstede, 1980; Triandis, 1995). In the pattern of **individualism**, society is thought to be a collection of loosely linked individuals who are motivated by personal preferences, needs, and rights. It is assumed that the autonomy, goals, values, and successes of the individual should govern our association with others and have priority over group objectives. The individual should be protected against group forces that are assumed to inhibit the individuals in their quest for success or happiness. In this view, the individual becomes the authority on what is true or right. Freedom and power are stressed as primary virtues (Bloom, 1992, pp. 21–26). Modernist societies such as the US are thought to be primarily organized around individualist values. Interestingly, a strong dominance of religion at a societal level can promote a more individualistic approach to religion, as has been the case in Iran (Kazemipur & Rezaei, 2003).

Collectivism is a social pattern that emphasizes giving priority to the goals of the collective over personal needs of the individual. Harmonious functioning and obligation to others are primary, and interdependence is assumed. This does not necessarily translate into close or affectionate relationships; it is possible to be superficially polite without trust or love. In this system, morality is based on duty and reciprocity rather than personal caring of individuals (Fiske, Kitayama, Markus, & Nisbett, 1998). Societies like China are traditionally thought to be collectivist in orientation.

In early research, individualism and collectivism were thought of as contrasting worldviews on opposite sides of a continuum. However, recent research has found that they are independent dimensions. For instance, many regions of the modern world such as the US, other English-speaking nations, and countries in

South America tend to be relatively high on measures of individualism, but the US and many English-speaking countries are also low on collectivism, while countries in Latin America are high on both (Oyserman, Coon, & Kemmelmeier, 2002). The issue of social organization is also complex because differences are sometimes subtle, and everyone from a particular national, racial, or ethnic group does not follow the same pattern (Williams, 2003). Other factors that can alter the effects of social organization are as follows: (1) the presence of a *vertical structure* that accepts inequality and difference or a *horizontal structure* that emphasizes equality and sameness, (2) the amount of flexibility and complexity allowed, and (3) the way control is exercised, either through a *grid* of social classification or through *group* influence and social pressure on the individual (Douglas, 1996, pp. 59–62).

   A third type of social organization that offers an alternative to individualism and collectivism may be called **communitarian**, which holds that the ideal form of social organization promotes both (1) a strong sense of individual autonomy and uniqueness, and (2) a deep commitment to relationships, community values, and goals. In this view, the individual person and community support each other, and the goals of each are balanced in the context of specific practical situations. It recognizes both our experience of finiteness and our sense of shared belonging, values, and perspectives (cf. Steinbock, 2004). Some religious communities are built around this communitarian ideal. For instance, monastic communities promote an intensely relational way of life, but they also support autonomy through requiring members to voluntarily choose to affiliate with them. They also support uniqueness by individually modifying the responsibilities and benefits of membership depending on need and ability, as well as individualizing the pattern of suggested spiritual practices for each individual.

12.3.1.1 Effects of Social Organization on Religious and Other Communities

It is clear that the dominant form of social organization in a society has important effects on individual and community life, although the exact nature of these effects is still a matter of debate. Traditionally, scholars and Western political theorists have argued that more individualism is better and that it is impossible to get too much of it (e.g., Veenhoven, 1999). However, an increasing number of researchers argue that extreme individualism has a corrosive effect on social institutions and groups, as it is hard to combine individualism with social bonding (Almond, Appleby, & Sivan, 2003, p. 231; Taylor, 2007, p. 477). Critics of individualism point to its apparent effects in the US, where surveys have found that 25% of the population says they have no close confidante they could talk to about a serious personal problem, and 50% says they have none outside their immediate family. These percentages have doubled since the 1980s, suggesting that individualism in American society is increasing and having negative effects on social support, one of the most important factors connected with positive mental health (McPherson, Smith-Lovin, & Brashears, 2006). (Robert Putnam 2002; Putnam & Goss, 2002) note that advanced democracies all over the world have declining rates of participation in beneficial social organizations and increasing levels of distrust and cynicism, particularly in young adults. He attributes this to the increasing anonymity and technological orientation of modern society that fosters withdrawal and individualism, while working against the formation of social networks. Extreme individualism is related to increased levels of loneliness and loss of meaning, less social support, higher divorce and crime rates, more stress-related illness, and higher rates of depression. In Western societies this appears to be especially the case for men, who tend to be socialized into roles of more extreme individualism. It is especially problematic in poor societies, those that are undergoing rapid social change, or those that do not value things connected with individualism (Ahuvia, 2002; Scott, Ciarrochi, & Deane, 2004; Reid, 2004; Diener, 2000; Möller-Leimkühler, 2003). Extreme individualism, which promotes disconnection from the group, is also thought by some to be one of the prime prerequisites for totalitarianism, as the disconnected individual is more likely to offer total loyalty to a leader (Arendt, 1968). In terms of religion, some researchers argue that individualistic trends in society hinder cohesiveness in congregations (Pargament & Maton, 2000).

The evidence collected by Putnam and others would seem to argue that individualism is a problematic system and that an alternative like collectivism might be preferable. However, collectivist societies generally have lower levels of self-esteem and subjective well-being among their members and may have lower scores on some indicators of mental health (Triandis, 1995, p. 108). Also, some aspects of individualism are connected with positive conditions like freedom, spontaneity, privacy, and respect for human rights that often suffer in collectivist societies (Veenhoven, 2000; Myers, 1999). This leads some to conclude that a kind of a communitarian balance between individual and collective needs is desirable (Diener & Suh, 1999; cf. Kirsh & Kuiper, 2002). For instance, research with college students has found that those with a communal orientation are more likely to help a person and respond to sadness than those who are not. Low communion males are more likely to endorse flattery, withholding affection or physical aggression as acceptable means of getting what they want. They also are more likely to complain about doing a favor for someone and are less likely to listen to other points of view. They rate power and wealth as important, while those high on the communal dimension rate duty and service as more important (Clark, Ouellette, Powell, & Millberg, 1987; Bankart & Vincent, 2001).

How can a communitarian system manage to support individuals and the community at the same time? In approaching this question, it is helpful to distinguish between individualism and autonomy (Ryan & Deci, 2001, 2006; cf. Ricoeur, 1966). Extreme individualism is based on the assumption that all our choices should be based on our own personal needs and desires. **Autonomy** does not make this assumption; it is perfectly all right to concur with the preferences of others, as long as we freely chose to do this and the choice is congruent with our values. We can choose to be dependent on others or sacrifice our personal goals in the interests of the community, as long as the individual freely elects these decisions (Inglehart & Welzel, 2005, pp. 136–139; cf. Dwairy, 2006, pp. 49–52). It is forced choice and loss of control that are associated with lower levels of well-being and higher levels of suffering or psychopathology, while autonomy is associated positively with intimacy and creativity (cf. Shults & Sandage, 2006, p. 113). In practice, autonomy might or might not also be associated with religious participation. Dillon and Wink (2007, pp. 66, 207) argue that in the US, autonomy has meant freedom from cultural elites with an antireligious agenda so that autonomy results in increased religious participation. Those interested can become involved, and those who are dissatisfied can explore.

In their ideal form, religious communities in the Christian and Buddhist traditions are communitarian in nature. For instance, monastic communities support autonomy and freedom of choice; no one is forced to join, for each person freely elects membership and has opportunities during a trial period to withdraw. They also recognize and support the uniqueness of each individual in the spiritual guidance process and the fitting of spiritual disciplines to the specific gifts and problems of each person (see e.g., Section 14.1.1). On the other hand, religious communities also support the idea of individual sacrifice in support of the community and its goals. Examples of this in the Christian tradition include the sharing of material resources and labor according to ability and need, as well as the emphasis on development of obedience and humility. This of course does not mean that every religious group is communitarian in nature. It is easy to find examples where religious groups—either deliberately or by accident—have adopted structures that were either excessively individualist or collectivist in nature.

The communitarian ideal is congruent with contemporary Christian views of the human person. For instance, Zizioulas (2006) argues that personhood involves three primary characteristics: (1) communion and relationship, (2) uniqueness, and (3) the freedom to open ourselves to communion while maintaining our uniqueness. He believes that modern individualism confuses difference with division and that real communion respects difference without creating divisions. Individualism tries to maintain uniqueness but ends up creating division and destroying communion, while collectivism destroys uniqueness that forms the basis for authentic relationships. The union of human and divine in Christ and models of relationality in the Trinity provide models of how this should work, although in practice human fallenness and fear limit our ability to attain this dynamic interaction of uniqueness and communion.

12.3.2 Christian Churches and Congregations

While psychologists have devoted relatively little attention to religious communities, quite a bit is known about them from the work of scholars in sociology and religious studies. In the US, church members tend to be older than the US population average, although some communities are mostly young adults and children. Communities known as **congregations** are mostly small—under 200 members—but more than half of church attendees go to the 10% of congregations that are larger—over 350 participants. Regular participants in worship number about half of membership;

80% or more of regulars report worshipping every week and always or usually experience God's presence during worship (Ammerman, 2005; Woodberry & Smith, 1998). In the Christian tradition, most congregations are voluntary religious communities, although in Europe and some American Christian groups, a congregation is also defined geographically. Since membership is voluntary, churches must actively recruit members, and so the community is under continuous creation (Warner, 1994). Churches have resemblances to other voluntary associations but are also different. In industrial and post-industrial societies they embody the sacred in a secular world, both at the broad level of life narratives and the mundane level of everyday concerns or problems (Woolever & Bruce, 2002; Browning, 1994).

Congregational life includes a variety of activities, which are frequently aimed at specific gender and age groupings (Ammerman, 2005). Surveys of congregational leaders in the US suggest that members give the highest ratings to (1) a style and quality of worship and preaching that builds close connection to God; (2) educational and small group activities that foster spiritual growth, and in conservative churches opportunities for evangelism; and (3) fellowship activities that are structured around normal life events but also give support in more difficult times. These activities are relationally intensive and affective in character, leading to high rates of friendship and social connection among attendees (Wuthnow, 2004, pp. 97–98). More frequent attendees report bigger and more diverse social networks, as well as a higher quality of social relationships that are more supportive (Bradley, 1995; Ellison & George, 1994). In general, surveys show that over 80% of members report that their congregation is meeting their needs, and the majority of those reporting strong growth in their faith attribute this to their congregation (Woolever & Bruce, 2002, p. 27).

Differences in activities and relational patterns, as well as community history and context, lead to different styles of community environment. Pargament, Silverman, Johnson, Echemendia, and Snyder (1983) found a number of dimensions of congregational climate including sense of community, activity level, degree of social concern, openness to change, stability, expressiveness of feelings, order and structure, and levels of intrinsic or extrinsic orientation. Some types of churches have a wider range of climate styles, with small African American Protestant congregations showing the most variability and uniqueness. Small white Protestant churches were higher on expressiveness of feelings, had a stronger sense of community, and were more open to change than some larger white Protestant churches. Large Catholic churches reported lower expressiveness and sense of community but higher levels of activity, stability, and social concern. Members of fundamentalist congregations reported more expressiveness and involvement in religious beliefs, and greater autonomy among their members was linked with higher self-esteem and life satisfaction. It is likely that this culture evolves developmentally over time (cf. Liebert, 2000, pp. 146–161), but little is known about the existence and nature of these patterns.

Congregations are grouped into **denominations** and other larger affiliations. In the US, Protestants dominate with about 80% of congregations, 2/3 of which are conservative with more traditional beliefs and include **Pentecostal** or **charismatic** churches that focus on spiritual gifts. Conservative and charismatic groups are growing rapidly worldwide, and traditional or mainline ones are shrinking; in the US, between the mid-1960s and 1980s, some 13,000 mainline congregations disappeared, while more than 13,000 conservative churches were set up (Gilkey, 1994). So, while some authors argue that US religion is suffering from decreased participation and connectedness, this evidence is mixed especially in conservative churches (e.g., Wuthnow, 2004). Roughly a third of US Christian communities strongly identify with a denomination and another third more modestly, although there is some evidence that these denominational bonds are weakening (Warner, 1994; Becker & Dhingra, 2001; Dougherty, Johnson, & Polson, 2007). Denominational bonds mean that congregations and the people in them are not isolated but embedded and interrelated, although the implications of this vary according to the culture of the denominational group (Ammerman, 2005, pp. 206–210). Congregations thus exist at several points of tension between (1) a local culture vs. transnational organization, (2) local or historic past tradition vs. evolving future, and (3) a public organization related to the greater community vs. a private grouping that exists to serve its members. Each of these tensions contributes to the construction of identity of the group and the individuals in it (Marty, 1994; Bass, 1994). While congregations take some character from their denomination, each is unique and members certainly feel this uniqueness and a strong sense of belonging. Community narratives hold the group together and convey a shared sense of unity and purpose (Wind & Lewis, 1994; Woolever & Bruce, 2002; Webb-Mitchell, 2001; Hopewell, 1987; cf. Macintyre, 1984, p. 205).

12.3.3 Specific Religious Communities and Movements

Perhaps because of the negative view of organized religion held by many social scientists, existing research on religious communities has tended to focus on movements or groups perceived to be unusual or pathological in some way. Nevertheless, this research has yielded interesting findings in a variety of groups.

12.3.3.1 Fundamentalism

Definition and characteristics. Although the origins of Christian fundamentalism go back into to the 19th century, the term was first used by a Baptist periodical in 1920 to describe a group willing to do battle to preserve fundamentals of Christian religion against attacks from liberalizing seminaries and universities (Johnson, 2004). The most thorough exploration of this type of religious movement is the Fundamentalism Project of the American Academy of Arts and Sciences (Marty & Appleby, 1991, 1993, 1994, 1995; Almond et al., 2003). According to them, **fundamentalism** is a broad type of pattern found in all major religious traditions and can be defined as "a discernible pattern of religious militance by which self-styled 'true believers' attempt to arrest the erosion of religious identity, fortify the borders of the religious community, and create viable alternatives to secular institutions and behaviors" (Almond et al., 2003, p. 17). This pattern has both ideological and organizational components. Ideological characteristics include the following:

1. *A negative reaction to social trends* such as individualism, the marginalization of religion by modernist secular societies, and corruption within mainstream religious groups who are failing to resist these trends. This is the key behind all other characteristics. Groups vary according to elements in the mainstream religious tradition they embrace and what parts of secular culture they oppose or use to gain their goals.
2. *A view of religious texts as presenting absolute truth* in a literal and inerrant fashion. These texts become authoritative and define the nature of virtue or vice and the boundary of who stands within the group and on the side of good.
3. *A dualistic view of the world* as composed of light and dark, pure and impure, and good and evil. History is viewed as pointing toward an upcoming culmination of this conflict, which will happen in the near future.

The beliefs underlie a characteristic organizational structure:

1. *Membership is selective and voluntary*, and those within the group tend to see themselves as an elect group who are specially chosen. There is a sharp division between members and nonmembers, with those on the outside seen as potentially harmful or dangerous. Membership might involve ethnic, political, or geographical criteria as well as religious status. Members follow strict rules for behavior that affect all aspects of life, and the social life of the person revolves around the fundamentalist community.
2. *There is a charismatic leader and an authoritarian leadership structure* that carries out the dictates of the leader or perhaps a small leadership group. In contrast to cults, however, allegiance of the members is to the movement, not to the leader.

Overall, the group is marked by selectivity, rigid boundaries, a sense of uniqueness and confidence in the group and its leadership.

Causes. Three primary approaches have been taken attempting to explain why fundamentalist movements develop. Within psychology, the traditional approach has been that fundamentalism is a psychological phenomenon, a form of personal rigidity that can affect any organization but is found particularly in religious ones. It occurs when people are threatened either with the beliefs of others or the ambiguity inherent in human existence (Ellens, 2004a). It can be thought of as a phenomenon of arrested development (Fowler, 1996, p. 63) or an expression of a certain type of character structure such as the authoritarian personality that tends toward submission to authority, aggression, and conventionalism (Altemeyer, 1996, p. 161). Certainly it is the case that fundamentalists often place their religion at the center of their identity (Kreidie, 2004). Psychological theorists like Altemeyer (2003) argue that this personality pattern and us-them mentality can be produced by strict religious training and identification in fundamentalist communities, although he acknowledges that the data on this question could be interpreted differently.

Scholars in the Fundamentalist Project and Islamic writers generally reject a strictly psychological interpretation of fundamentalism and take a more sociological approach. They hold that fundamentalisms are not just religious movements but instead are reactions to sociopolitical circumstances such as secularizing trends, socioeconomic development, and increasing moral and cultural fragmentation. Short-term and chance factors such as policies of local governments and especially leadership choices act as triggers, promoting the movement and determining whether it will pursue a *renouncer* strategy of withdrawal or a *conqueror* strategy of attack. In this view, Islamic fundamentalism is seen as a reaction to the formation of secular and repressive governments in the Middle East, as well as the perception that globalization is a cultural aggression against Islamic society that will lead to social misery and narrow control by outside interests (Almond et al., 2003; Mol, 1989; Moaddel & Talattof, 2002; Ali, 2002; Moaddel, 2005; Arkoun, 2000).

Recently other psychologists have argued that fundamentalism is ideological in nature, rather than psychological or sociopolitical in its origins. In this view, fundamentalism is seen as a type of religious meaning system that emphasizes transcendence and helps determine the goals and activities of a group. It is a set of beliefs about the world and the self that is built around a particular *text* and the principle of *intratextuality*, which is the belief that the text is (1) sacred, (2) speaks for itself, and (3) contains absolute truths. It is a response to the principle of *intertextuality* of modern and postmodern society, which holds that no text speaks for itself and all possess some authority. Fundamentalism as a meaning and value system provides a unifying philosophy, way of life. and sense of coherence organized around this single text. Other meaning systems are valuable only if legitimated by the text (Hood, Hill, & Williamson, 2005, pp. 2–39).

Effects. It has been presumed for a long time that fundamentalism was synonymous with a wide range of pathology, but recent research paints a more nuanced picture of fundamentalists that departs from these stereotypes. Fundamentalists do not generally have higher levels of pathology than other groups and score well on many measures of mental health (Wulff, 1997, p. 247; e.g., Burton, 1993).

One stereotype is that fundamentalism and perhaps conservative Protestant Christianity in general is associated with toxic family environments. However, research has shown that these concerns are at least overstated and in many cases untrue (Sherkat & Ellison, 1999; Bartkowski, 2007). One problem in the older literature was an assumption that a way of life that includes high standards for conduct and morality would lack warmth. Recent research has found that conservative Protestantism is associated with an **authoritative parenting** style that combines high demand with high levels of expressed support and warmth. This is in contrast to an **authoritarian parenting** style that is cold and demanding. The authoritative style is advocated in prominent conservative Protestant parenting literature, and surveys indicate that this style is associated with more positive emotional interactions in the family and healthy outcomes as well as enhanced transmission of parental values like religiosity (Wilcox, 1998). Some researchers suggest the pattern leads to enhanced autonomy, moral development, and emotional maturity (McAdams, 2006, p. 56). There are mixed findings about whether child abusers are more likely to come from fundamentalist backgrounds. Child abusers and fundamentalists have some similar attitudes toward child rearing, but abuse rates do not appear to be higher in fundamentalist groups (Neufeld, 1979). Fundamentalists are also thought to have negative attitudes toward education, but fundamentalism has been found to affect attitudes toward education in both negative and positive ways (Sherkat & Darnell, 1999).

Another issue that has been debated is whether fundamentalism promotes racism and prejudice. It seems logical that belonging to an elect group would encourage rejection and intolerance, and many studies support the idea that religion—especially of an orthodox or conservative variety—is associated with ethnocentrism, racism, and hostility toward groups like homosexuals (Hunsberger, 1996). In studies from the early 1990s with parents of Canadian college students, correlations of fundamentalism with prejudice were in the 0.3–0.4 range, suggesting a low-to-moderate association (Altemeyer, 1996, p. 159). However, this research is correlational and some suggest that the relationship between fundamentalism and prejudice is really a product of other factors like extrinsic religious motivation or authoritarian personality patterns, rather than fundamentalist teachings or social influences (Batson, Schoenrade, & Pych, 1985; Altemeyer & Hunsberger, 1992). Other research has suggested that fundamentalists are not higher in racism although as a group they are less tolerant, in part because of a different moral vision which translates into strong positions on issues like abortion, pornography, or homosexuality (Woodberry & Smith, 1998; Sherkat & Ellison, 1997). Saroglou (2002) argues that fundamentalism is not about intolerance per se but a need for closure and meaning along with an aversion to inner disorder. Members of both traditional and conservative groups score high on need for closure, and a preference for predictability is associated with discomfort with ambiguity. This is not to say that fundamentalism is never connected with problems—just that research does not support the idea that these groups are inherently or typically problematic.

Critique. All of the academic approaches to the study of fundamentalism have been criticized. The Fundamentalist Project perspective has been attacked for conflating various religious, political, and militant groups together under one head, while brushing over differences among various religious and cultural contexts and within each tradition (Woodberry & Smith, 1998; Moaddel, 2005, p. 7; Schimmel, 2000). For instance, fundamentalism in the Christian West seems more related to intellectual issues with modernity, while in Islam the focus is on political and social concerns. The concept of fundamentalism also does not work well in the nontheistic Asian context and brushes over the fact that secular ideologies can have fundamentalist qualities. All this suggests a need to avoid stereotypes (Almond et al., 2003, pp. 14–15). There have been arguments in the literature about the methodology of Altemeyer, which has provided much of the empirical basis for connecting fundamentalism with prejudice (Gorsuch, 1993; Altemeyer & Hunsberger, 1993). Some scholars have argued that Altemeyer's questionnaires are ideologically biased against conventional religious beliefs and assume a conflict stance between science and religion. Critics contend that when his questions are reworded to reduce bias, correlations between fundamentalism and authoritarianism disappear. A different reading of the data then suggests that fundamentalism is not connected to a distinctive personality type such as authoritarianism and is only weakly linked with dogmatism or inflexibility of beliefs. This has raised the possibility that some of the research critical of fundamentalism reflects cultural stereotypes or prejudices of social scientists rather than any real religious phenomenon (Hood et al., 2005; Watson et al., 2003).

12.3.3.2 New Religious Movements and Cults

New religious movements and groups known as cults have also attracted the attention of researchers. A **new religious movement** (NRM) is a group of individuals that affirm a common identity and unique set of religious beliefs distinct from those in the world's main religious traditions. These beliefs may be entirely new, or they may include elements of other current or ancient religious traditions and practices. While some groups are rejecting and separatist in nature, many are affirming of some individual or deity, or the revival of ancient religions in a kind of "repaganization" of Western culture (Braaten & Jenson, 1995, p. 1). Probably the most commonly discussed NRM is the **new age movement**, which holds that "inner spirituality—embedded within the self and the natural order as a whole—serves as *the* key to moving from all that is wrong with life to all that is right" (Heelas, 1996, p. 16). New agers typically believe that we have been indoctrinated by our culture into materialism and inauthenticness and that each individual needs to find their own spiritual path to seek their inner being. When this happens, the world will move toward a new age in the evolution of humanity (Jones, 1995b; Bloom, 1992, pp. 225–226).

Cults can be seen as a type of NRM. The exact definition of cult is a matter of debate, but scholars often distinguish them by comparison with other groups such as churches and sects. According to a distinction developed by Troeltch and others, **sects** are offshoots of churches that follow somewhat different doctrines, emphasize voluntary commitment, and have a membership that is less diverse and more underprivileged than a mainline church. **Cults** are like sects in most of these ways except that they do not have or maintain any connection with a church or other religious group of origin. They tend to have a set of common characteristics including (1) a primary focus on a charismatic, powerful, authoritarian leader, (2) a claim to possess and teach esoteric knowledge that offers a sure and clear path to salvation, and (3) a loose organizational structure that changes frequently over time. Cults also often have strong interest in sexuality or gender issues, and are often known for aggressive recruiting tactics, allegedly trying to separate new members from family and friends (Dawson, 2006, pp. 26–29; Hunter, 1998). The clear beliefs and practices of a cult can be especially attractive to adolescents anxious to establish their identity in an uncertain world (Richmond, 2004b).

NRMs are often portrayed negatively in the psychological and popular literature, and former members of cults are often thought to have high levels of serious psychopathology as a result of their experience. Recent research has revised this view, deemphasizing the level of psychopathology in these groups, as well as questioning the methodology of previous work (Saliba, 2004). For instance, high levels of psychopathology in former members are now thought to reflect psychological problems that predate their entrance into the NRM, although certainly people with no history of psychopathology join cults. Also, charges of "mind control" or brainwashing that have appeared in popular literature have not been substantiated by scholarly research. Nevertheless, criticism of the effects of NRMs continues, particularly with respect to cults, and certainly it is possible to find examples of cults with conditions that can produce high levels of psychopathology (e.g., Kliger, 1994). While mind control is no longer thought to be a central problem, opponents of cults point to examples of deceptive information and approaches by cults when recruiting new members. They also note that the tight organization of these groups around a single leader often leads to conflict and problems. In extreme cases, it can also lead to violence and ritual or other types of abuse (Kraus, 1999; Noblitt & Perskin, 2000, p. 43; Dawson, 2006, pp. 96–101, 144–166). Exiting a cult can also be difficult, as persons must reconstruct their lives and deal with psychological issues such as depression, loneliness or low self-esteem when they cut their dependency upon the group. Those with bad experiences in a cult may also experience guilt, paranoia, or even posttraumatic types of symptoms (Singer & Lalich, 1995, pp. 295–297). However, NRMs and cults are difficult to study, and there is a tremendous diversity among the groups, so lumping all NRMs and cults together to produce neat descriptions and explanations is problematic (Dawson, 2006, p. 11).

How do NRMs form, and why do people join them? The answer to this probably varies, depending somewhat on the group in question. NRMs in general are often thought to result from cultural and social changes, such as dissatisfaction with traditional religion that leads to exploration of religious alternatives (Partridge, 2004). In the case of cults, many scholars point to individual psychological factors. Despite the fact that people who join cults come from egalitarian and upper socioeconomic status (SES) families, cult joiners tend to be alienated from their families, as well as mainstream social groups, culture, and religion. They also tend to be younger and struggling with issues of personal identity. The NRM offers approval, strong affective ties, a supportive social group, and a focus for structuring an identity (Hunter, 1998; Dawson, 2006, pp. 77–80).

Meissner (2000) has articulated a psychodynamic theory of cultic or religious group process that might help explain some of the characteristics of cults and NRMs. In his view, **cultic process** is a normal defensive tendency of religious groups to form exclusive subgroupings that are at odds with dominant social hierarchies and environment. This exclusive group has a number of positive effects: it bolsters identity and self-esteem, increases feelings of power, and acts as a mechanism to cope with anxiety. This process operates in all religious groups, but under conditions of great social or personal uncertainty, it directs inner anxiety and anger toward objects that are perceived as a threat. This external enemy, along with any remembered traumas, becomes an organizing point for individuals, who fight the enemy as a way of dealing with internal anxiety and anger. Especially if traditional authority structures are failing, the cultic process encourages the idealization of a leader who offers protection. Once the cult forms, the group becomes a powerful motivating force because it supplies many needs: a sense of belonging and affiliation, shared tasks, a sense of meaning and identity, as well as control of internal aggression and anxiety which can be displaced externally.

12.3.3.3 Religious Communities and the Internet

The Internet affects many aspects of modern life, and some researchers have become interested in its impact upon religion. However, the Internet is rapidly evolving so that any snapshot of online religious activity will probably be out of date before it can be published. In 2003 data, the US had about 128 million Internet users, and 64% of these used the Internet for religious or spiritual purposes. The most common uses were personal correspondence such as email with spiritual content, and visiting Web sites for information about religious organizations and practices such as where to attend services for a particular group. About 84% of religious Internet users belong to religious communities or organizations, although they may tend to view themselves as outsiders. Evangelicals are strongly represented. However, internet religious users have a higher percentage of people who identify themselves as spiritual but not religious than is true of the general population, and individuals identifying themselves as neither religious nor spiritual tend to have the highest Internet usage (Dawson & Hennebry, 2004; Hoover, Clark, & Rainie, 2004; Larsen, 2004).

Religious activities on the Internet can be thought of as taking one of two forms (Prebish, 2004; Dawson & Cowan, 2004; O'Leary, 2004). First, Internet sites can provide **religion online**, activities and materials designed to supplement existing activities that are not online. These additions might include (1) increased communication and convenience, e.g., learning about community events, support through email or IM prayer requests, and staff contact; (2) information and educational materials or discussion forums with links to denominational information; or (3) a virtual temple or church with worship activities. Evangelism and outreach is also a possible function, although most sites currently do that by links to other sites specifically oriented to that purpose (Sturgill, 2004). Other possible functions include encouraging attendance by visitors, providing information about the community like a mission statement, providing devotional materials such as sermons, and publicity about activities (Larsen, 2000). Web-based services might parallel existing offerings or provide completely new types of activities; even those web functions that are similar to current community activities may have a different effect when translated to the web (Lovheim, 2004). Currently, Internet usage about religion is mostly of this supplemental and conventional type and involves both frequent attendees and new seekers (Larsen & Rainie, 2001). Perhaps because of this, Internet usage does not appear to be connected with lower religious participation or social involvement (Campbell, 2004). However, a small negative correlation between religiosity and Internet use that has appeared in a few studies has raised concern that the bias in the media against religion is also becoming dominant on the Internet (Armfield & Holbert, 2003).

A second option is that Internet sites can provide **online religion**—an entirely online community. This is much less common than religion online, but virtual churches and temples have begun to appear and seem to be increasing in popularity (Young, 2004b). Virtual communities allow people from diverse locations to interact and reach out to others not currently involved. This ability may be especially important for NRMs and other groups not already established. However, online religious groups have at least indirect connections with existing religion. For instance, teenagers using the Internet for spiritual seeking often depend on word of mouth from people they know when selecting sites, and they tend to trust the information they get on the Internet much less than from other sources like parents, teachers, friends, and religious leaders (Lutz & Borgman, 2002).

Internet NRMs include a number of groups, including witchcraft, pagan, Goddess, and Egyptian religious sites. It is hard to say how much old research on communities and conversion will apply to these new ones. Early studies have noted that NRMs tend to operate multiple linked pages in an attempt to maximize their visibility but do their recruitment mostly through existing social contacts with friends and family. Studies focusing on Wiccan sites have noted a high degree of transience, and that individuals who participate offer a great variety of points of view and a mixture of reverence and irreverence. Different sites have competing voices, making it difficult for any one of them to attract many followers without becoming increasingly radical. As a result, some scholars are unsure how much an Internet presence will help NRMs in the long term (Dawson & Hennebry, 2004; Lovheim, 2004; O'Leary, 2004).

The rise of religious groupings and networks on the Internet challenges traditional definitions of what constitutes a religious community. Churches and other religious groups are typically **geographical networks** formed in proximity to where people live and work. Internet groupings, on the other hand, are **associative networks** based on common interest and in theory are independent of geography. Such networks can be found in the history of religious traditions, as in letter writing that formed social bonds in early Christianity. They certainly resemble traditional communities in that they involve (1) interactive relationships, (2) personal concern for others, and (3) the ability to gather periodically in a kind of public space. However, many think that such networks are too shallow to count as the kind of real communities that form a necessary basis for religious life (Dawson, 2004; Dawson & Cowan, 2004; Campbell, 2004; Foltz & Foltz, 2003). Scholars have pointed out a number of limitations of Internet communities:

1. Group memberships on the Internet can be constantly changing, leading to more short-term and fragmentary relationships with weaker bonds. The authenticity of these relationships is also a question, as people can select any identity they choose and the accuracy of their self-disclosure cannot be verified. In this situation, relationships are going to become more anonymous, and the focus of interactions will be more exchange-oriented, specialized, and aimed at accomplishing some specific purpose. These relationships may not be adequate for the establishment of true community.

2. Internet groups have limitations in terms of their ability to control boundaries and appropriate behavior. In unmoderated interactive forums, skeptics can visit sites of different traditions and turn them into debating sites, so struggles for control can become public. However, these sites have insiders who exercise some control, with insider status defined by frequency of contribution, technical skills, and taking on the convictions dominant in the group (Lövheim, 2007). Established groups with authority structures do sponsor popular sites, and these have more control over content, but users more often visit informal, popular, and unofficial sites such as those devoted to Isidore of Seville, the informal patron saint of the Internet (Helland, 2004).

3. Technical factors structure and limit the kinds of interactions that can take place on the Internet. Since all Web sites appear on a computer screen and utilize common features like hyperlink navigation or blog interaction, a visit to a religious site has a similar feel to visiting an online retailer. Individuals visiting a site can visit links in any order, making it difficult for site managers to develop important kinds of structure such as narrative that are dependent upon sequence. Some argue that this encourages people to view religion as another part of consumer culture, a resource to be selected at the need or whim of the participant (Dawson & Hennebry, 2004).

A positive evaluation of online religion is that it is different, not inauthentic. It orients users toward a more self-directed spirituality outside of a hierarchy and emphasizes personal religious experience. It allows people to belong to many communities with weaker connections rather than a single more tightly connected group (Campbell, 2004; Cowan, 2005). It offers an alternative method of religious identity construction for adolescents and young adults when traditional channels for this have become less attractive. However, such identities are likely to be eclectic, and building a coherent identity outside of the support of a traditional organization is more difficult. For the foreseeable future, it appears that online identity construction will continue to be strongly influenced by offline structures (Lutz & Borgman, 2002; Lovheim, 2004).

12.4 Religious Practices in Community

Many religious practices take place in a community context or are dependent upon community support. Here we consider three important examples of religious practices— ritual, pilgrimage, and service.

12.4.1 Ritual

Ritual is an important form of religious practice and a central aspect of religious commitment (Stark & Glock, 1968, pp. 14–16; Fig. 12.1). Ritual is difficult to

Fig. 12.1 *Pilgrimage ritual on Buddha's Birthday, Lhasa.* All religious traditions include important rituals such as pilgrimage that have powerful psychological effects. Photo by the author

define because it is extremely varied; any definition except a very broad one misses some examples (Bowie, 2000, p. 154). It can be broadly defined as "the performance of more or less invariant sequences of formal acts and utterances not entirely encoded by the performers" that are dependent upon tradition and community influences (Rappaport, 1999, p. 24). Rituals generally include some kind of standard or traditional elements, although rituals also change over time, particularly in cultures that are antitraditional like current Western society. They are intentional activities, generally sanctioned or carried out by some authority, that create an ordered world separating sacred from profane and helping us interpret experience (Bell, 1997; Vergote, 1997, p. 309).

There are a number of different kinds of rituals such as (1) rite of passage or life crisis, (2) commemorative, (3) sacrificial, (4) healing or purification, (5) festive, and (6) organizational or political. These exist in hierarchies with some rituals thought to be more important than others (Bell, 1997, p. 94; Fuller, 1988, pp. 117–121; Forest, 1997, p. 67). Sequences of rituals such as **liturgical orders** that take place at set times also have a special meaning by making a period of time (e.g., Advent and the Christmas season) or the entire year sacred. These often use music and other devices to link individual spiritual activities like prayer to other aspects of ritual (Rappaport, 1999, p. 169; Begbie, 2001).

Religious rituals are also important within families, as they help maintain religious identity, reaffirm relationships, and teach correct behavior. These can include big festivals like Christmas or everyday practices at meals. Marriage brings together two people from different families of origin, offering an opportunity to construct new patterns of ritual that have special meaning. Most families construct rituals by drawing on traditions in both families, although some couples form their practices mostly around those of only one family, and about 20% of couples create entirely new patterns (Visscher & Stern, 1990). Participation in joint ritual activities increases marital satisfaction, and couples report that both the shared meaning of ritual and the act of practice are important (Fiese & Tomcho, 2001).

12.4.1.1 Theories and General Perspectives on Ritual

Many different theories about ritual exist that offer perspectives on their nature and function. Anthropologists who have reflected on the psychological and cultural importance of ritual have produced much of this literature. Early theories tended to focus on analysis of the rituals themselves. In the **mythic** school (e.g., Otto, 1950; Eliade, 1963; cf. Arlow, 1996), ritual is seen as related to master narratives we have about reality, the place of humanity in the world, and explanations for the universe or social order. In this view, religious myths tell stories in relation to some kind of divine reality; this content can be reenacted and experienced in a ritual so that people can understand and identify with it. Ritual thus has a communicative aspect (Vergote, 1998, pp. 59–65; Bowie, 2000, pp. 157–158; Bloch, 2004). The emphasis in the mythical school is on the *content* of ritual, in contrast to the **structuralist** school of Levi-Strauss (1963), which finds the meaning of ritual in its *form* or *structure*. Both schools touch on important aspects of ritual, although they have been criticized as promoting an unnecessary separation of thought and action, neglecting the physical aspect of ritual, and using categories of analysis that are irrelevant to the participants (Bell, 1997, pp. 10–12, 80–82).

An alternative is to think of rituals as **practices** (see Section 6.3.4). In this view, rituals offer a framework or strategy for action to be used in a particular situation that sets things apart from the ordinary (cf. Erikson, 1966, 1977; see Section 5.3.2). It involves the body, physical action, and structuring of the environment in a way that has a practical coherence. Like other practices, people can participate in ritual and understand some of its practical aspects or implications without understanding all the details of the meaning system behind them (Bourdieu, 1977, p. 118; 1990). This theory fits well with explaining ritual in the European situation, where people often participate in rituals without believing in their underlying meaning or have others do them on their behalf (Davie, 2007).

Recent psychologically oriented perspectives on ritual have tended to reject a practice view that deemphasizes meaning, as well as structuralist or cognitive views that separate the structure of ritual from its content. In **interpretive theories** developed by writers like Victor Turner or Clifford Geertz, the meaning that ritual has for participants is its central feature (Ouwehand, 1990; D'Andrade, 1995, p. 19; Heimbrock, 1990). Geertz (1973) emphasizes that (1) religion and ritual are cultural systems of meaning, (2) ritual does not just express culture but changes people's perceptions and interpretations through kinesthetic or other kinds of learning, and (3) people are active agents in the process (Bell, 1997, pp. 62–74; Geerts, 1990). In other words, religion and ritual help people actively interpret events and make sense of their world. Some psychological interpreters use Winnicott's concept of transitional object or space as a framework for explaining the interpretive process (cf. Section 5.4.3).

However, others have pointed out that ritual is more than a transitional object so that this framework cannot capture the full complexity of ritual (LaMothe, 1999; Moore, 2001, pp. 138–139). Another approach has been to focus on the **symbolic** nature of ritual as a structure for the representation of meaning. Rituals are supposed to have power through their use of symbols; they connect our existence with that of a different world, thereby altering our own in some way (Vergote, 1997, pp. 306–307). Community rituals are especially powerful because they involve an entire group in a sacred place with multiple symbols including objects, actions, and **liturgy** or special ritual language (van der Lans & Geerts, 1990).

While it is sometimes possible to place a theory or theorist within a particular school of thought such as structuralist or interpretive, many theorists treat some or all of these themes and are thus not easily placed in a typology of ritual theory. Rituals involve an interaction between a socially transmitted worldview or practice and the emotional needs and representation of God in the individual. Ritual is thus a different experience for everyone that cannot be entirely explained by a single theory (Wikstrom, 1990).

12.4.1.2 Victor Turner and communitas

One of the most influential and psychologically sophisticated theories of ritual is that of Victor Turner (1920–1983). In his view, religion is not just a reflection of economic or political relationships, rather it is important for understanding how people think and feel. Central to religion and to human thought are symbols, which form the basic building blocks of ritual and a primary means by which people interpret the meaning of their world (Schechner, 1988; Turner, 1988, p. 160). These symbols can take a number of forms including images, objects, physical movements, and language. Turner believed that symbols naturally occur in dyads or triads and that ritual is a *performance* that both highlights polarities in symbols and reveals their unity. Rituals and the symbols that are part of them thus have a paradoxical, mysterious, and affective quality that is beyond classic Aristotelian logic (Turner, 1969, pp. 37–65). For instance, in baptism water is a symbol both for death of our old life and birth of our new one.

Turner also related religion and ritual to feelings and social relationships. Drawing on the work of van Gennep (1960), Turner believed that we generally relate to others in structured hierarchical systems but that it is possible to change these structures or our position in them. This involves separating and detaching the individual from normal space and time and entering an in-between, ambiguous or **liminal** state of anti-structure and potential in which old characteristics are erased, so new ones can be substituted. Turner believed that ritual controls this powerful process by providing practices that symbolize crisis, detachment, separation, and return (Turner, 1969, pp. 94–109, 166–169). Religious rituals in particular are associated with the mysterious, powerful and sacred quality of liminality; when this is shared among members of a group a strong emotional experience of unity or *communitas* results. This experience has a powerful simplifying and leveling effect, breaking through structure so that people experience a spontaneous and transforming bond of commonality (Turner & Turner, 1978, p. 13; Turner, 1988, p. 157; Bradley, 1978, pp. 8–46; Moore, 2001, p. 46). This anti-structure experience works in dialectic with the normal social structure, leading to a balance of stability and change that supports the individual and society (Turner, 1969, pp. 127–142).

Although Turner's theory is based on extensive fieldwork, critics have questioned its empirical base, pointing out that *communitas* does not occur in many situations and that rituals can produce conflictual experiences. They also argue that it is too reductionistic, reducing ritual to the satisfaction of emotional needs and ignoring its intellectual, social and spiritual elements that may vary with different religious traditions and practices. Thus, while *communitas* may occur as a kind of temporary state, they argue that it is not transformational or fundamental to ritual (Morinis, 1992, p. 8; 1984, pp. 236–238, 257–261; Moore, 2001, p. 49; Bilu, 1988; Bradley, 1978, pp. 14–36). However, it does offer a phenomenology of ritual experience and symbolic process that is valuable. This aid to the understanding of symbolism is especially important, as it has been neglected by psychologists studying religion (Boudewijnse, 1990).

12.4.1.3 Effects of Ritual

Rappaport (1999) and others argue that ritual has a number of important effects. For Rappaport, ritual is a form of action that helps generate and bring together the conceptual, experiential, and other parts of religion. In particular, ritual joins ideas about the sacred with numinous experience. Some other specific effects includethe following:

1. Providing a focus for community life and identity that helps sustain the group, develop social solidarity and coordinate religious practices among members. More active involvement in liturgical ritual is associated with stronger community bonds (Hinde, 2005; Bell, 1992, p. 171; van der Lans & Geerts, 1990).
2. Making religious truths a socially important and meaningful fact through rehearsal. Rituals embody historical or spiritual realities, making them tangible and concrete in space and time. These truths include what Rappaport calls Ultimate Sacred Postulates, fundamental beliefs that form the basis for society. Rehearsal helps reinforce their truth value and establish a religious identity in the believer (Rahner, 1963, p. 117; Vergote, 1997, pp. 312–314; Geertz, 1973, pp. 112–114; Ammerman, 2003).
3. Helping to integrate action and belief, as well as highlighting important aspects of conduct such as ethics. In this way, ritual provides direction, increases conviction, and strengthens commitment to moral action (Reich, 1990; Hinde, 2005).

Scholars of ritual, like Rappaport, argue that although ritual is an essential way by which we construct the beliefs and worldview of the human world, its power has been damaged in modern culture without providing an effective replacement, although some modern practices like psychotherapy can have ritualistic aspects

(Anderson, 2005; Cole, 2003). Turner believed that modern society has moved away from supporting rituals that produce powerful liminal states to optional, individualized, and commercialized activities like sports that produce **liminoid** states lacking in transformational power (Moore, 2001, p. 49; Turner, 1969, pp. 49–50; Turner & Turner, 1978, p. 253). Although rituals meet basic needs for structure, safety and reliability, many scholars see ritual as declining in contemporary world due to the erosion of community life and emphasis on autonomy (Faber, 1990; Vergote, 1997, pp. 102–103).

12.4.2 Pilgrimage

Pilgrimage is an ancient and complex practice found in all major religious traditions. It involves a journey from a familiar place and routine to someplace unfamiliar, typically a location that is special or sacred and difficult to reach. The journey may be done as an act of devotion. It can also be part of a search for something or pursuit of an ideal, perhaps a cleansing or renewal that will allow us to connect with another worldly power and solve some current and seemingly intractable problem.

Pilgrimage takes place in personal, cultural, social, and physical planes that interact in unique ways. It is personal because going on a pilgrimage is an individual and voluntary decision. Whether or not a journey is a pilgrimage involves the individuals' perception of their activity as religious rather than recreational as in tourism (Cohen, 1992). It is cultural and social in that it involves symbols, history, legends, and ritual locations that are part of a religious tradition and culture. In most cases, a social group exists that maintains the site, passes on its meaning, and provides specialists who mediate contact between pilgrim and deity. Pilgrimage is often done as a solitary activity, but at times huge groups journey together, as in the *hajj* to Mecca or a Christmas journey to Bethlehem (Morinis, 1984, pp. 212–221; 1992, pp. 1–26; McKay, 1998; Turner & Turner, 1978, pp. 30–31; Forest, 2003; Blasi, 2002).

There is tremendous diversity in the motives and socioeconomic backgrounds of pilgrims. General goals of a pilgrimage may be (1) *devotional*, seeking an encounter with the sacred, perhaps to express love, give thanks, or ask for forgiveness; (2) *instrumental*, worldly goals like health, perhaps seeking a miracle or hoping to earn merit; (3) *religious*, part of a ritual cycle, obligation or initiation; or (4) *undefined*, with no predetermined goal (Morinis, 1984, pp. 278–282). Specific motivations are numerous and might involve profound religious or spiritual reasons like answering an inner call, achieving pardon or reclaiming parts of the self, or simply curiosity and for escaping routine. In modern pilgrimage, there is also a blurred line between pilgrimage and vacation, so visits to a site can be more about adding adventure, interest, and beauty to a trip than advancing toward a spiritual goal (Clift & Clift, 1996; van Spengen, 1998). Motives of pilgrims may also be specific to a particular site and religious tradition. For instance, common reasons among pilgrims visiting Lourdes in Europe include (1) deepening of faith, (2) asking for a cure and a blessing for self and others, especially the young, and (3) looking for peace and quiet reflection. Especially important for most pilgrims is construction of meaning, a personal quest for identity or a revitalized sense of faith (Voyé, 2002).

Pilgrimage sites have important and complex psychological meanings for the visiting pilgrims. The site is thought to be a place of spiritual power and immanent divine presence, typically because of its association with miraculous events, a famous religious personage, or because of geographical features such as difficulty of access and the presence of water or mountains (Jenson, 1995; Brenneman, 1993; Clift & Clift, 1996, p. 20). Some sites have regional appeal and might be visited often, while others like Jerusalem or Mecca might be the target of a once in a lifetime journey. They may have a formal connection to an organized religion or be more popular in nature. Some are open all the time and are important social and religious centers, while others operate only at annual festivals. The importance of the site may vary across time, gaining in popularity, or becoming a mere tourist spot, and eventually being abandoned (van Spengen, 1998; Markus, 1999; Buffetrille, 1998; Turner & Turner, 1978). The physical layout of the site may also have special meaning. If it is difficult of access, the journey to the site and the surrounding geography can have a sacred quality and symbolize the struggles of the spiritual life or increasing proximity of God, facilitating the production of transitional states (Vergote, 1998, pp. 198–220; Voyé, 2002; McKay, 1998; Morinis, 1992, pp. 2–6, 50–51). The site itself often consists of mundane zones separated from sacred ones, centered on a main shrine that may be staffed by people who offer rituals related to worship, sacrifice, or purification. Historical artifacts and stories about the site allow the collective memory of tradition to speak and be experienced. The layout of the site in circles or other shapes can also symbolize religious meanings (Friedland & Hecht, 2006; Morinis, 1984).

There are interesting connections between pilgrimage and ritual. In a Jungian view, pilgrimage is a ritual and also contains rituals that the pilgrim may perform at the pilgrimage site to facilitate connection to the sacred. Along with special activities as the person approaches the site such as traveling around it, or **circumambulation**, common motifs of pilgrimage rituals might include (1) water rituals and cleansing, associated with purification; (2) symbolically leaving part of oneself at this site, such as through an offering; or (3) taking a sacred object home from the site, typically some physical or religious artifact (Clift & Clift, 1996, pp. 9–20, 70–82; Loseries-Leick, 1998; cf. Morinis, 1984, pp. 222–224). From a Turnerian perspective, pilgrimage has some aspects of the liminality of passage rites: (1) a release from structure and production of *communitas*, (2) a ritual enactment of correspondences that reflects the meaning of religious and cultural values and movement from mundane to sacred, and (3) simplification of dress and behavior. Many pilgrimages are voluntary and not part of religious routine and so are technically a liminoid or quasi-liminal experience, although there are liminal features in liturgical rituals performed at the site. Often, smaller shrines are more likely to be liminal than larger ones that become tourist sites (Turner & Turner, 1978, pp. 232–239).

Individual and group pilgrimages can be special, powerful events. The effects of such pilgrimages depend upon the extent to which the event has been personally experienced and may have positive or negative long-term benefits. Successful pilgrimages are marked by considerable preparatory work and an emotional connection to the activity, either positive or negative (Watson, Tuorila, Detra, Gearhart, & Wielkiewicz, 1995; Poland, 1977). For instance, follow-up studies with older and younger pilgrims to Lourdes do not reveal physical improvements at the group level (cf. Section 10.3.1) but do find that both groups show decreases in anxiety and depression after the pilgrimage. Differences were larger for older pilgrims, especially those with more existential than recreational motives for the visit (van Uden & Pieper, 1990). Change of environment, spiritual atmosphere of shrine, hope for future in this life and next all apparently contributed to the beneficial effects (Morris, 1982).

12.4.3 Service

Most religious traditions encourage service to others as a central practice, and scholars have typically seen these kinds of actions as one important aspect of religious commitment. In the US, Europe, and other parts of the world, religious traditions and organizations provided much of the impetus for the creation of modern social services (Wuthnow, 2004, p. 9). This service orientation is true of both Christian and non-Christian religious groups, although at least in the US there is a tendency for non-Christian groups to focus more on care for their own communities rather than service as a general obligation (Stark & Glock, 1968, pp. 14–16; Ammerman, 2005, p. 115). Survey data suggest that religion and religiosity is indeed associated with more giving to the poor and involvement in volunteering: for instance about 75–80% of church members give to the poor, while the figure for nonmembers is about 55–60%. Social ties and religious beliefs are both factors in this impulse toward service, linking volunteering with community identity (Regnerus, Smith, & Sikkink, 1998; Ammerman, 2005; Putnam, 2000, p. 67; Park & Smith, 2000). This has led a number of sociologists to argue that religion in the US plays a positive role in helping lower income families and strengthening civil society, although there are exceptions (Wuthnow, 2004, p. 2; Curlin, Dugdale, Lantos, & Chin, 2007). In Christianity, this service takes place at a number of levels: individuals, churches or religious communities, and larger groupings such as denominations.

At the congregational level, it is only during the 20th century that the size of some US congregations grew to where they could offer specialized services and staff for them. Today about 2/3 of churches—including most larger ones—offer formal service programs. Fewer small churches have specific community programs as most assistance is provided on an informal basis; however they devote a larger percentage of their budget to charitable work. Small and large churches also support service work by providing volunteers, offering frequent sermons on topics like poverty, caring or forgiveness, and organizing small groups that engage in service work (Wuthnow, 2004, pp. 3, 66). These congregational programs tend to be oriented toward family and youth issues such as day care or education, but food pantry or soup kitchen ministries are also common—about 80% of congregations support one or the other of these services. Churches also frequently support homeless shelters. Other than the effect of congregational size, it is difficult to find a clear pattern as to what kind of churches are likely to offer service programs. Social change has traditionally been prominent in the agendas of African American, Catholic, and some mainline Protestant churches, and these groups are in fact more likely to sponsor service programs. However, researchers have found more generosity among theological and political conservatives, and there are many exceptions to any of these trends (Regnerus et al., 1998; Ammerman, 2005).

The amount of funds devoted toward service by any single church is generally modest, an average of perhaps $25,000–30,000 per year for churches with a membership of over 200. However, the totals for groupings of churches can be significant. For instance, in 2000, the Presbyterian Church–USA altogether spent close to $150 million on service activities. The total spent on formal service programs by all churches in the US is probably around $15–20 billion per year. When one includes the cost of clergy and staff time spent on programs, as well as building and utility costs, probably 10% of church operating budgets goes toward service work (Ammerman, 2005, pp. 47–50; Putnam, 2000, p. 67).

Churches also offer indirect service, either through denominational ministries or nondenominational networks. These networks can be formal ties to a service agency or informal coalitions among churches. Almost every US church has at least one outside service partner, and on average contributes about $2000 per year, sends volunteers to 2.8 organizations, and provides space for 1.8 service groups. Types of partner organizations include human service (e.g., food banks), self-help groups (e.g., Alcoholics Anonymous), and missions groups (e.g., Habitat for Humanity) at both the national and international level (Wuthnow, 2004, pp. 159–185).

12.4.3.1 Faith-Based Organizations

Another service activity that is indirectly connected with religious communities is the **faith-based organization** (FBO). These are groups generally founded by religious people that get contributions from them and would include something related to faith or religion in their mission statement and regular activities (Wuthnow, 2004, p. 138). In their daily activities, FBOs may not be particularly religious, but they do retain some sense of religious identity and mission. In 2001, four of the ten largest nonprofits in the US were FBOs, including Catholic Charities, Lutheran Social Services, United Jewish Communities, and the Salvation Army. Probably about 18% of private human service provision in the US comes from FBOs (Ammerman, 2005, pp. 179–181).

While FBOs have a religious base, they actually resemble secular agencies in many ways, and their services and clientele differ in some ways from those helped by individual congregations. Part of this is due to the fact that FBOs must follow the same legal and professional standards as secular groups. The main difference between FBOs and secular agencies appears to be the type of service provided. FBOs are more likely to be involved in day care, family counseling, and mental health issues, while secular nonprofits focus on job training and health. Congregations tend to be different from both FBOs and secular nonprofits. People seek them more for spiritual or emotional assistance, and churches tend to be particularly good at building whole-person relationships and communicating care to individuals seeking services. In addition, many poor people looking for help are themselves religious and may appreciate the caring community environment that churches try to provide. In surveys, clients generally report high levels of trust and satisfaction with congregational services, and the lowest levels with public welfare agencies (Wuthnow, 2004; Wuthnow, Hackett, & Hsu, 2004; Bonnycastle, 2004).

12.4.3.2 Volunteering and Social Capital

Church attendance and religiousness are also connected with increased volunteering, although not with informal helping. Weekly church attendees are twice as likely as nonattendees to volunteer, although individuals with very high levels of attendance tend to limit their volunteering outside of the church setting. While this trend is equally true for conservative and more liberal Christian groups, the meaning of the experience is somewhat different. Conservatives tend to see volunteering as a spiritual obligation that offers opportunities for growth, while individuals in more liberal groups view it more as an obligation of citizens to society. Volunteering is correlated with the amount of religious practice—especially devotional reading and prayer—as well as the self-rated importance of spiritual growth, while the effect of theological beliefs is less prominent. Also a key factor is the social network of the individual. The majority of volunteering happens because the person has a connection to someone else who is working in or is served by the program where they volunteer (Becker & Dhingra, 2001; Wuthnow, 2004; Lam, 2002). This helping no doubt has personal benefits to those who are involved: helping others improves mood and self-evaluation, particularly among those who value communal (e.g., friendship) rather than exchange (e.g., business-type) relationships (Williamson & Clark, 1989). However, the evidence for the existence of altruism and empathy as motives for helping is also very strong (Batson, 1998).

The relationships developed by congregations in service and volunteering have led some sociologists to note an indirect benefit of religious organizations and service: the development of social capital. Developed by Bourdieu (1985), the concept of **social capital** refers to the value produced by "social networks and the norms of reciprocity and trustworthiness that arise from them" (Putnam, 2000, p. 19). This is an issue of concern in contemporary society; US surveys find that large percentages of the population are dissatisfied or even alarmed by declines in community life that are related to decreased civility and lower moral standards and attitudes of trust. In addition, institutions like schools that depend upon social bonds for their functioning are having increasing problems.

Social capital comes in two varieties: **bonding capital** that holds groups together, facilitating emotional support, and **bridging capital** that builds ties between different cultural or socioeconomic groups, thus strengthening society. Robert Putnam

(2002, pp. 22–27, 66–74) argues that congregations through their regular and service activities may be the most important source of social capital in US society. There is no question that congregations are rich sources of relationships and social capital. Surveys suggest that almost half of church members have more than 10 close friends in their congregation, while only 7% indicate they have no close friends—figures that are very different than general values for the US population. Frequent participants more often have strong social networks, especially if there is a good fit between the identity of the congregation and the personal values or beliefs of the individual. Talking with friends in these social networks is seen as helpful in times of crisis. Church members are also more likely to have relationships with people in a different socioeconomic group than nonmembers, although membership does not by itself increase the odds of cross-ethnic or interracial friendships (Wuthnow, 2004, pp. 82–94; Wuthnow, 2002; Becker & Dhingra, 2001). However some European researchers have questioned the link between religiousness and social capital at the individual level (Halman & Pettersson, 2003b).

12.5 Problems of Religious Communities

While religious communities offer many benefits to their members and society as a whole, they also have problems ranging from hypocrisy of church members to cruelty and strife (Schulman, 2002; Altemeyer, 2004a). We have seen previously that religious traditions are well aware of the potential for trouble and have tried for many years to devise structures to deal with the common problems found in their communities. In this section, we look at psychological and social scientific research related to these problems. When reviewing the psychological literature on religious communities, one is immediately struck by the fact that the issues of interest to psychologists have mostly diverged from the issues pinpointed by religious traditions as areas of concern. The advantage of this is that the literature tells us about potential problems that may have gone unrecognized by religious groups. The disadvantage is that the literature is often of little help in understanding many of the problems of concern to religious communities and how they might best be improved.

12.5.1 Prejudice

The self-understanding of most religious traditions is that they promote love, not prejudice. Traditional research has shown that religious individuals are indeed more helpful to strangers, more kind and honest, and contribute more to charities but are also more prejudiced and judgmental (Argyle, 1985). A large amount of research in the social scientific study of religion has been devoted to understanding this odd combination.

Quite a bit is known about prejudice from the general social psychological literature. Groups exert a powerful force on identity formation, judgment, and behavior.

As we have seen previously (e.g., Sections 5.3.1 and 8.5.2), identification with a group and ideology is one of the primary ways that people form identity. However, identification with a group carries with it other consequences. It leads to perceptions of people as members of groups, either our own **ingroup** to which we relate, or an **outgroup** that is perceived as different from us. These categorizations are subject to common social psychological processes. We tend to see members of outgroups as homogenous and possessing similar characteristics, and in situations where we belong to an ingroup that is central to our identity, but in a minority position in society, we also think of its members as homogeneous. This perceived similarity could lead to **stereotyping**—cognitive judgments about individuals based on their group membership. As these opinions become emotionally laden and touch on our basic sensibilities of good and bad, they can become **prejudice** directed against others, which when acted upon lead to differential treatment or **discrimination**. Research has shown that problems with stereotyping and prejudice become more common under conditions of negative emotion, if the other group is seen as a threat or as interfering with important goals. Under these circumstances, we rate fellow group members as more trustworthy and peaceful and members of the other group as untrustworthy and dishonest. This kind of thinking is pervasive even in the face of good intentions and becomes more likely with increasing emotional prejudice, leading to avoidance or attack directed at people in the other group.

Prejudice can be entirely secular, related to sociocultural factors like nationalism, class or ethnicity; however it can also be related to religion (Allport, 1966). Religious groups have unique characteristics that might make them either less or more susceptible to ingroup-outgroup thinking, stereotyping, and prejudice. Religious belief systems often hold all people to be of equal worth and thus oppose prejudice and discrimination. On the other hand, religious traditions can promote strong identification of their members with the group, and the strong philosophical and moral convictions associated with religious belief systems might increase the tendency for outgroup judgments to become emotional and prejudicial. This may be even more likely if belief systems promote in-group superiority by holding that the group has exclusive possession of the truth, or that the group is chosen especially by God, and if membership is also limited along lines of class and ethnicity (Eisinga, Billiet, & Felling, 1999; Allport, 1966; Allport & Ross, 1967; Allport, 1979, pp. 444–449).

Given this conflicting situation, it is not surprising that the relationship between religion and prejudice is a complex one. In general, research has found higher levels of prejudice among religious people, although much of the fight against prejudice has been religiously motivated (Allport, 1966). A number of things seem to affect the relationship. It is less likely in those with high commitment or those who have had positive, equal status contacts with other groups. It is more likely if religious beliefs encourage discrimination, there is a history of negative interactions, or high levels of authoritarianism are present (Brewer & Brown, 1998; Fiske, 1998; Eisinga et al., 1999). Allport and others have also argued that religious motivation is related to prejudice, with intrinsic religiosity associated with lower levels of prejudice and authoritarianism. However, this conclusion has been challenged because of methodological and measurement problems in the research, as well as data that suggests it is not true with respect to certain kinds of prejudice (Allport, 1966; Allport & Ross, 1967; Donahue, 1985; Spilka, Hood, Hunsberger, & Gorsuch, 2003; Wulff, 1997, pp. 223–229; Tsang & Rowatt, 2007). Because societal attitudes toward prejudice have changed, older research may not reflect current relationships.

12.5.2 Authoritarianism (The Sin of the Pharisees)

Another problem apparently connected to religion is the increased incidence of **authoritarianism** and the authoritarian personality (Adorno, 1950), a style marked by conservatism, intolerance, rigidity, and prejudice. Altemeyer has identified a variety of authoritarianism correlated with some forms of religion called **right-wing authoritarianism** (RWA): a tendency toward submission to authority, conventionalism, and aggression toward others if sanctioned by authorities. RWAs tend to uncritically accept what others tell them, so they are susceptible to manipulation; they also tend to externalize and compartmentalize things and so have double standards, criticizing others for the things that they are guilty of as well (Altemeyer, 1996, pp. 28–31, 93–95). Some researchers believe that prejudice in religious people is really an expression of authoritarianism. This is supported by European and North American research, which has found no relation between church involvement or Christian belief and ethnic prejudice when adjusted for other variables. In this sophisticated research, predictors of ethnic prejudice are authoritarianism and nationality, suggesting that authoritarian personality patterns are the problem behind prejudice in religious individuals. This may be particularly the case in fundamentalist groups, as some research has found correlations between fundamentalism (not religious orthodoxy) and RWA (Eisinga et al., 1999; Altemeyer & Hunsberger, 1992). Spiritual seeking appears to be negatively related to authoritarianism, while religiousness is positively related (Wink, Dillon, & Prettyman, 2007). However, instruments used to measure RWA have questionable validity in other cultures, suggesting that findings may not generalize to all groups. Certainly not all religious people can be described as authoritarian or prejudiced (Rubinstein, 1997; Altemeyer, 1996, pp. 147–163).

The problem of prejudice in RWAs is even more striking in a subgroup who are high in both RWA and social dominance. While most high social dominators lack religious backgrounds, those that are involved have different attitudes from other religious individuals. In a Canadian study, Altemeyer (2004b) found them to be highly prejudiced, dogmatic, and amoral with little genuine religious belief. They were more likely than the rest of the congregation to believe in lying, cheating, or manipulation and to prefer a system that benefits them, regardless of its effects on others. His description of high social dominating RWAs is similar to that of the authoritarian personality as described by Hannah Arendt (e.g., 1968). Leadership by social dominating authoritarians is a major factor in the development of totalitarian governments and organizations.

What makes authoritarians, and what is its association with religion? Social psychologists like Allport argued that a common underlying dynamic was the prejudiced personality, a pattern marked by fear and insecurity coupled with poor insight and low tolerance for ambiguity. Individuals confronted with these problems seek definiteness, order and stability, which can be provided by structure and authority. This leads to authoritarianism, a willingness to follow a strong individual, externalize problems, and accept accusations against other groups. Allport believed that authoritarianism was a multi-determined personality trait related to both inborn temperament and education (1979, pp. 396–436). In this way of thinking, authoritarianism is connected to religion because authoritarians seek out religious authority structures they find attractive, not because religion necessarily leads to authoritarianism. Instead, intolerance and authoritarianism come from temperamental factors, as well as the basic human desire for structures and views of the truth that can provide security. Since religion tries to seek truth and build groups, it can become ensnared when these processes become dysfunctional, although any human organization or belief system is also susceptible (Vergote, 1997, pp. 93–97).

Other explanations for the relationship between religion and authoritarianism have also been proposed. Altemeyer has argued that RWA is more related to experiences such as religious training associated with fear of God's wrath or obedience to rules (Altemeyer, 1996, pp. 148–149; Altemeyer, 2004b). However, recent developmental research has questioned this link, suggesting that authoritarianism is much more related to personality and temperament than early religious socialization (Dillon & Wink, 2007, pp. 151–152). Meissner (2000, pp. 3–9) attributes authoritarianism and prejudice to a dysfunctional working out of the **paranoid process**, a normal function of the ego that helps sustain and integrate our self and identity by contrasting us with those around us. The paranoid process helps to build strong groups but can shift toward pathology under life stress or social change and perhaps particular styles of leadership.

12.5.3 Leadership and Its Abuses

As we have seen, religious communities are concerned about the need for good leadership. Early community rules provided guidance on the choosing of leaders and how they should fulfill their responsibilities. There are many fine leaders of religious organizations; however, problems with individual leaders and leadership structures continue to plague religious communities. While Christian leadership scandals are the ones noticed in the West, financial and sexual improprieties within Hindu and Buddhist communities have also been reported on a number of occasions (e.g., Taylor, 1999, p. 276), suggesting that leadership is a potential problem in all religious traditions.

Little systematic research exists in psychology on the problems of religious leadership. We do know that leaders are a focus point for their communities, attracting both more social support and negative interactions than rank-and-file members (Krause, Ellison, & Wulff, 1998). A significant literature exists on psychological evaluation of candidates for the ministry, and many religious groups have systematic procedures for screening candidates, looking for potential problems, as well as indications that the individual will be successful in a pastoral role (e.g., Malony, 2000). The sociological and religious studies literature also contains research on the problem of burnout among religious professionals, a particular problem among US Roman Catholic clergy who face increasing demands with decreasing numbers of priests (Knox, Virginia, & Lombardo, 2002).

The sexual abuse scandal in the Roman Catholic Church has attracted the attention of a number of psychologists, so there is a small body of work on this leadership failure. It provides some clues to the nature of leadership problems and their solution.

The sexual abuse scandal became public in the US in January 2002 with a number of accusations by individuals that priests had sexually abused them. A number of studies examining the extent of the problem suggest that probably about 2% of priests are implicated, most of the time involving a single incident but sometimes a priest who abused multiple individuals. Most abuse incidents occurred during the 1970s and 1980s; about half the victims were children at the time, while the other half were adolescents. The rate is similar to the rate of child abuse in US adults during that period, so the problem is unfortunately not a unique one. However, the religious office of the abuser makes the problem especially damaging, leading to feelings similar to incest and causing a dissociative pattern of stress response and spiritual injury (Gartner, 2004).

Most observers agree that the response of church leadership to the crisis was defective (Plante, 2004; Coleman, 2004; Jenkins, 1996; Markham & Mikail, 2004). Prior to 2002, the power of clergy abusers and attitudes toward them within the church discouraged people from reporting problems and impeded investigations. When problems were identified, effective action was often not taken, and priests were transferred rather than removed from roles where they had contact with potential abuse targets (Doyle, 2006; Gartner, 2004). As has been the case in other helping professions (including psychology), outside pressure from the media and lawsuits was necessary to mobilize effective action. In June 2002, a conference of Catholic bishops adopted a charter for protection of children, and set up a series of oversight review boards comprising mostly lay people to handle accusations of sexual abuse (de Fuentes, 2004).

Psychologists and others studying the problem have identified a number of structural and leadership problems within the church that impeded an effective response (Gonsiorek, 2004; Doyle, 2004; Spohn, 2004):

1. *Systemic problems*, including lack of separation of powers, and an absence of checks and balances in the hierarchical leadership system of the church. This was compounded by the aristocratic leadership style of some church leaders and the development of a siege mentality that sometimes led to cover-up attempts. Errors in judgment and decision-making by figures in power positions with no outside checks is consistent with social psychological research that associates power with automatic information processing and disinhibited behavior (e.g., Keltner, Gruenfeld, & Anderson, 2003).

2. *Poor knowledge base*, including a lack of information and unrealistic ideas about abuse, for instance, believing that priests are somehow magically immune to temptation. This was compounded by difficulties discussing sexuality within the church, a difficult topic in part because of debates over celibacy issues.
3. *Individual factors*, including a variation in the quality of investigative mechanisms, outside evaluators and mental health professionals. Also, adversarial relationships between churches and mental health workers developed on occasion.

12.5.4 Violence

Major religious traditions all value peace and oppose the taking of human life (Arinze, 2002, pp. viii, xiii). However, the religious record does not match this ideal, with many instance of violence between and within religious groups, involving both physical and psychological injury (Bellinger, 2001, p. 100; Selengut, 2003, p. 9). This anomaly has been remarked upon for many years by critics of religion and has recently become a target of psychological investigation.

The topic of violence and religion also includes the problem of secular violence directed against religious individuals. Religious people who die as a result of antireligious violence may be victims who have no choice or **martyrs**—those who choose to die rather than give up their religious commitment under coercion (Bergman, 1996). Sometimes these individuals are missionaries sent to another country to provide service or spread a religious message (Mariani, 2002, p. 47), but most often they are people living in their homeland. Persecution ranges from harassment by others when attempting to carry out religious practices (e.g., Forest, 1997, p. 32) to death as a victim or martyr. It is an enormous problem, as the 20th century saw the worst persecution of Christians since Roman times. For instance, millions of Orthodox believers perished in purges by atheists in the former Soviet Union. In the anti-Christian campaign by Stalin and Soviet communism, many churches were closed, and monks were arrested and deported to labor camps. As many as 40,000 Orthodox priests were killed or died from abuse during the first half of 1936 alone, and it is believed that the total number of priests, monks, and nuns killed during the purges of the 1930s are in excess of 200,000 (Forest, 1997, pp. 134–149; Wynot, 2004). Estimates of the total number all Christian martyrs in the former Soviet Union are about 12 million. Estimates from the 20th century of Christians who died from secular antireligious violence worldwide are over 25 million, more than all previous centuries combined (Bergman, 1996).

12.5.4.1 Causes

In the social sciences there are a number of competing theories to explain religious violence, but no one viewpoint is widely accepted (Bellinger, 2001, p. 4). Types of causes considered include the following: (1) *theological*, looking at the role of religious writings, beliefs, or practices; (2) *psychological*, asking whether religious violence meets inner needs and goals; or (3) *sociological*, tying religious violence to social trends such as cultural threat (Selengut, 2003, p. 11). Within psychology, no consensus exists about whether violence is individual or social in origin (Cooper, 2007, p. 212).

Theological explanations. Some people argue that religious beliefs or structures inherently lead to violence. Evidence supporting this view is (1) the power of appeals to religion in support of national power and authority or military campaigns, and (2) the presence of patriarchal structure and warrior motifs in religious writings that can be used to legitimize violence. An assumption of some theological critiques is that religion is an obstacle to world unity, and that peace would prevail if religion was marginalized or eliminated (Anderson, 2004). Recent versions of this thesis sometimes associate violence with a particular religion like Islam, a type of religious thought or system like theism, or the passionate conviction that can be generated by any religious beliefs, a condition thought to promote both violence and irrationality (Jacobs, 2003, pp. 224–228).

These explanations have been criticized by religious studies scholars and theologians (e.g., Noll, 2003; Arinze, 2002). While not wanting to minimize the problem of violence, they have raised a number of objections to the idea that religion is a source of violence and so should be eliminated:

1. Christianity and other religions are not the unique or even main source of social evil or violence found in the world. Societies as well as religions can have a myth of redemptive violence. Comic book heroes are a case in point (Wink, 2004).
2. Religion has also been a force for good and positive social change in the world; any fair assessment of religion must look at Gandhi and Mother Teresa, as well as Osama bin Laden (Kimball, 2002, pp. 32, 187; Pargament & Park, 1995). When not entangled with the status quo political order, religions have a history of challenging elitist cultural forms that can lead to violence, and the religious teaching or leadership of monotheistic and other religious traditions have provided the foundation that allows for moral critique (Mabee, 2004). Currently there are many religious and interreligious dialogues under way about peacemaking issues (Arinze, 2002, pp. 99 ff.). Religion can and does engage in constructive dialogue on common problems, promote reconciliation and goodwill gestures that build peace, and promote values like humility and forgiveness.
3. Sometimes religion becomes involved in conflict when it is justified or inevitable, and this can have a positive result. Writers who take this view often argue that peace is not just an absence of violence or war but includes freedom and justice, conditions necessary for the development of the human person. Promoting peace means encouraging these things. This may lead to struggle, for instance, when preaching for social justice arouses opposition from the status quo, or when violence is necessary to gain reforms to restore social balance or right wrongs (Arinze, 2002, p. 34; Millbank, 2003, p. 197; Davis, 2004; Anderson, 2004). This highlights the problem of the **ambivalence of the sacred**: religious individuals want peace and tolerance but have strongly held beliefs for which

they may be willing to fight, so a sacred obligation may take different paths. The possible need to use force in the service of transforming society and eliminating injustice can make it difficult to automatically judge violence as either good or bad (Appleby, 2000; Taylor, 2007, p. 674; Ellens, 2004d).

4. Often the involvement of religion in violence is a betrayal of religious teachings—it happens in spite of religion not because of it. Terror is not generally condoned by religious traditions, even in Islamic jihad or Christian just war doctrines; sacrificial motifs are more dominant (Davis, 2004). For instance, in Islam the main form of jihad is not political but the *jihad al-akhbar* or struggle with the self (Thurston, 2005; Rumi, 2004, pp. 86–87). Violence more often happens when a religious group becomes involved in political affairs or is in an actual alliance with the state, so that religious membership is automatically granted to everyone in a particular national group, and then national interests are given religious justifications. Religion then becomes a façade for justifying violence (Wink, 2004; Bellinger, 2001, pp. 105–108; Greinacher, 1999, p. 248; cf. Aden, 2004). In a secular society, religion can then become an easy target to blame when in fact the problem lies elsewhere (Anderson, 2004).

5. Sometimes the involvement of religion in violence is due to human error rather than religion per se. Christianity does not argue that the church is a perfect community; rather it is a group of sinners seeking perfection. This recognition of fallibility means that Christians must constantly engage in the examination of conscience and need to have the willingness to ask for forgiveness and seek reconciliation (Arinze, 2002, pp. 34–35, 84–93). Also while religions can help by uniting people in communities, they must be alert for separatist forces that promote division, if communities are based on ethnicity or social class. A consideration of the relational aspects of spirituality is necessary for understanding these kinds of problems (Sandage & Shults, 2007).

It is also possible that while religion in general does not foster violence, certain kinds of religious beliefs and structures might. For instance, a theology or community structure that emphasizes legalism and control can lead to shame, which in turn can set the stage for violence (Sloat, 2004a, 2004b).

Explanations based on social conflict and resistance to secularization. Many scholars see violence as an act, process, or relationship that is a response to social and cultural factors, which can produce spirals of violence (Ellens, 2004c). Changes associated with modernity and secularization pose powerful challenges to traditional identities, often directly attacking those based on religion. This can lead to what is called the **good copy problem,** where a person cannot construct a fully satisfactory identity that is both acceptable to modernity and loyal to one's culture (Moghaddam, 2005, p. 1039). Scholars like Juergensmeyer (2003) argue that these threats trigger a process of seeking empowerment through acting in a great cause—often a religious cause—in a chaotic and problematic world. Religious conviction provides a platform for response to a perceived attack by secular society and failure of social structures. Individuals fighting these trends may see themselves as engaged in cosmic conflict that provides a framework for understanding their suffering. These ways of thinking are dependent on a black-and-white view of the world that discourages compromise, and may encourage religious violence as a way of reasserting religion as a force, or simply as a demonstration of power that counters feelings of powerlessness and social marginalization. Many of these factors also apply to other types of political, ideological, or ethnic violence, although religious violence may be more symbolic and tied to religious claims of absolutism or moral justifications.

There is considerable evidence for the idea that religious violence is intimately connected to political and economic issues. For instance, many scholars believe that Islamic religious violence directed at the US and other Western countries is related to political policy issues and social conditions. Studies have found that dislike for the US rather than religiosity is related to support for violence among people in the Middle East (Haddad, 2003). Some religious conflicts such as the violence in Northern Ireland are obviously more political than religious in their origin (Juergensmeyer, 2003, pp. 37–41), but religion can become entangled or hijacked by political and secular groups (Selengut, 2003, pp. 224–227). However, it is important to avoid simplistic explanations that draw an arbitrary line between political and religious violence. This is particularly true in Islam, where the interweaving of legal, political, and religious institutions is very important, and so the idea of a secular political state divorced from religion is not a natural one (Moghaddam, 2005; Davis, 2004).

Psychological explanations. Many psychological explanations for religious violence have been proposed; one of the most significant is that of Rene Girard (Bellinger, 2001, p. 72). Girard (1977, 1986, 1987), argues that violence is not an aberration but a fundamental human problem caused by our tendency toward imitation or mimesis, and religious practices actually work to prevent violence. In this view, violence begins with what Girard calls *acquisitive mimesis* or **mimetic desire**. This occurs when we identify with others and seek to emulate them by copying their desires, polarizing individuals and putting them in competition for desired objects (Stirling, 2004). This creates a **double bind** in which we are both imitators and rivals, leading to **conflictual mimesis,** where we focus on defeating our adversary at any cost. This process leads to escalating vengeance and violence. As we copy our adversary, we become more like them—a **mimetic double**—although because of polarization we see ourselves as different and blame the other for the escalating competition and violence.

Girard argues that religion is one way humans deal with the problem of keeping peace and preventing vicious circles of mimetic vengeance and reprisal. Religions offer moral prohibitions to prevent mimetic conflict. They also prevent escalation through the practice of **scapegoating** and sacrifice, where a member either actually or ritually takes violence on themselves. This sacrifice and its healing effect raise powerful emotions, transforming potential conflict and disintegration into cooperation and unity, and preventing the mimetic process and spread of violence. Girard criticizes modern secular society for removing helpful religious rituals and prohibitions, or even making religion the scapegoat, thus eliminating one of the primary mechanisms we have for resisting mimesis. This increases the chance of violence and other kinds of psychopathology (Stirling, 2004). In his view, Christian answers to the problem of mimetic desire such as the message of Jesus to avoid vengeance, revenge, or recrimination offer a new message of love that is needed to control the problem of mimetic violence.

Girard claims that at least aspects of his theory such as his analyses of individual situations are testable, although some question whether the empirical data supports his positions (Selengut, 2003, p. 54). Certainly behind his theory is an implicit view of the human person influenced by the work of Freud and Jung, which some might doubt (Ellens, 2004e). Others have also questioned whether his theory goes far enough. Simply saying violence is an outcome of sin or mimetic process (or other explanations like childhood trauma) is an inadequate stopping point. It does not explain important aspects of the problem such as the lack of proportion of the initial problem to its effect. It also evades questions of moral responsibility. Finally the question is, why do we feel a lack that we try to fill through imitation? This is an existential and spiritual issue left unanswered by Girard (Bellinger, 2001, pp. 6–25, 73–77).

Social psychologists have also been active in attempts to explain religious violence. For instance, Struch and Schwartz (1989) have looked at the relationships between inter-religious group aggression and in-group vs. out-group attitudes. They found that strong identification with a religious in-group was generally unrelated to aggression, but under certain conditions aggression was much more likely. Contributing or mediating factors related to aggression included (1) beliefs that dehumanized the out-group, (2) a lack of empathy for individuals in the out-group, and (3) a perception that there was a conflict between the interests of the two groups. Dehumanization has been identified in an important factor in other research on violence (e.g., Zimbardo, 2007). This suggests that interventions to humanize out-group members, increase empathy, and build shared interests can be effective in reducing aggression. Of course, it leaves unanswered the question of why some people who are subjected to an aggression-promoting environment go along with it and others do not.

12.5.4.2 Conclusion

Ideas that religion is the source of violence in the world or that eliminating religion would somehow reduce or eliminate violence are obviously too simplistic (Jacobs, 2003, pp. 230–233). Instead, it is clear that any viable explanation for the relationship between religion and violence must take into account many factors, including sociopolitical, economic, and historical forces and differences between various religious traditions (Kimball, 2002, pp. 25–35). The best way to understand the problem is a holistic approach, looking at the unique theological, historical, economic and psychological features of each case rather than imposing a particular theoretical framework at the outset. We also need to understand subgroups with different attitudes toward violence and peace making (Selengut, 2003, pp. 228–234).

However, research to date does suggest some factors occasionally connected to religion that can make violence worse. These would include the following: (1) autocratic, hierarchal leadership that needs external enemies to maintain power (Lotufo & Martins, 2004), (2) teachings by leaders that violence is sanctioned by God (Bushman, Ridge, Das, Key, & Busath, 2007), (3) group anonymity, (4) feelings of superiority of one group toward others (Mabee, 2004), (5) claims of special access to truth and moral standing (Pearlin, 2002), (6) apocalyptic beliefs (Bromley & Melton, 2002), and (7) other beliefs such as moral nihilism or indifference that dehumanize people, stripping them of their inherent worth (Levinas, 1998; Pontoriero, 2006). This means that religion does not necessarily cause violence but can provide justifications and potentially escalate it—as well as helping to solve it. Secular causes in pursuit of a higher good may be liable to similar problems, as was seen in the terrible persecution of Christians by the atheistic Soviet government (Juergensmeyer, 2003, p. xi; Kimball, 2002, pp. 4–11; Taylor, 2007, p. 687).

12.6 Conclusion

Key issue: *An understanding of potential problems in religious communities is a potential major contribution of psychology to the dialogue with religion. However, this addition has been seriously limited by flawed and partial psychological understandings of these communities.*

The disdain for religious communities obvious in much of the older psychological literature has proved to be one of the biggest errors in the 20th-century scientific study of religion. The research on religion and physical or mental health (see Chapters 10 and 11), as well as some of the material reviewed in this chapter, is enough to suggest that communities offer tremendous power for positive change in the lives of individuals and society at large. However, many areas of the communal life, practices, and problems of religious communities remain unexplored. Fortunately, some researchers recognize this failure and are working to further our understanding of the benefits and problems of religious communities.

Religious self-understandings of community and its problems offer a good beginning point of a dialogical approach to understanding the power of community. The communitarian ideal put forward by both Christianity and Buddhism is interesting for a number of reasons, one of which is that it fits well with what we know about social organizations that are most effective at promoting the well-being of their members. The communitarian vision provides a balance of communal dwelling and individual seeking that is an essential foundation for religious life (Wuthnow, 1998).

Like every type of social group, religious communities have their problems and difficult people. It is a fact recognized for thousands of years by religious traditions, which have wrestled with the best format for community life that promotes spiritual development (Forest, 1997, p. 33). The *Rule of Benedict* as well as some of the other authors we have reviewed in this chapter suggest that strong and healthy communities

- Offer strong caring leadership but avoid the trap of blind obedience to an authority figure in a hierarchical system that lacks checks or balances (Kimball, 2002; Pargament, 2002a)
- Promote relational practices that foster close, supportive relationships among members, as well as respectful attitudes toward others
- Encourage communal religious practices such as rituals that have an important role in supporting spiritual development.
- Deal with problematic behavior in a sensitive, constructive but firm manner.
- Promote community life while meeting individual needs—communitarianiam
- Welcome others but have a strong sense of identity, only accepting members who will be able to live within the beliefs and practices of the community.

One thing that may be obvious from this review is that there is a large disconnect between the problems of religious groups discussed by psychologists (e.g., prejudice) and those of concern to religious communities and their members (e.g., leadership problems). However, both groups recognize that religious organizations designed to help people confront the realities of life and grow spiritually may sometimes have the opposite effect (Merton, 1973, p. 36). Social and organizational psychologists could contribute much to the understanding and solution of these problems. A dialogical approach here would be helpful so that psychologists could understand the nature of the problems from the perspective of the community. In return, religious communities may offer to psychology a model for how to construct a stronger community life, a pressing need in our contemporary global culture (Arnett, 2002, 2003).

No religious tradition or community is all good or all bad (Pargament, 2002a). It seems likely that some communities are more helpful than others, but even traditions sometimes thought to be more problematic may have advantages. Overall, connection to community is probably more helpful when the involvement is well integrated into the person's whole life. It is also a valuable support to those in need and facing stressful situations. Communities appear to be more problematic when they are (1) hierarchical and without checks or balances, (2) directive or cold, and (3) providing no balance of individual freedom and community. These are effects that can be studied by psychology, and the results can help religious traditions achieve the aim of providing a community life that facilitates spiritual growth.

Chapter 13
Individual Religious and Spiritual Practices

In the last chapter, we examined communal aspects of religious and spiritual practice. In this chapter, we will look at practices that are more individual in their orientation, although as we shall see they have communal aspects as well. In particular, we will look at the practices of prayer and meditation, as well as ascetic or lifestyle practices that support these spiritual disciplines.

13.1 Religious and Spiritual Practices: Prayer and Meditation

Prayer and meditation are perhaps the most important individual spiritual practices. They have also been the focus of an important dialogue with psychology. An understanding of both prayer and meditation is thus very important.

Prayer is a central feature of many religious traditions, an activity that gives voice to religious experience (Hartford Institute for Religion Research, 2003, p. 6; Putt, 2005). It is typically associated with Christianity, although many people in the devotional traditions of Hinduism and Buddhism also practice it. In the early Christian Orthodox tradition, **prayer** was variously defined as a petitioning of God for what is fitting (Basil), and ascent of the mind or spirit to God (Evagrius), or a conversation with God (Origen, 1994; Spidlik, 1986, pp. 308–311; 2005, pp. 34–36). This activity can be of two types: an effortful, **expressive prayer** involving speech and the imagination or an effortless letting go that allows God to speak as found in **contemplative prayer**. Christian and Buddhist approaches to prayer contain examples of both types (Pennington, 2001, pp. 60–61; Barry, 2001, pp. 98–99).

In the Christian tradition, prayer is ideally a transformative experience. In advanced prayer experiences as described by masters like Teresa of Avila, our previous ways of looking at the world and ourselves are called into question in a kind of **liminal** state that opens up possibilities for conversion and transformation (Welch, 1982, pp. 24–38; see Section 12.4.1). Ideally, prayer moves us away from illusion, although some have pointed out that like any spiritual practice, prayer can become magical or illusionary if practiced in the wrong way or for the wrong reasons (Nouwen, 1975; Fuller, 1988, p. 124; Johnson & Boyatzis, 2006). It also orients us toward a deep relationality, trust and recognition of dependence and away from

J.M. Nelson, *Psychology, Religion, and Spirituality,*
DOI 10.1007/978-0-387-87573-6_13, @ Springer Science+Business Media, LLC 2009

a more anonymous, instrumental way of looking at the world. We become more attuned to others and our connections with them (Vergote, 1997, p. 286; Elliott, 2001). Ultimately prayer can become a kind of continual process—"prayer without ceasing" in the Christian vocabulary—so that even daily activities become transformed and are seen in a different way (Benson & Wirzba, 2005; Wirzba, 2005). It is however a practice, not a commodity, requiring hard work and proper preparation (cf. Engler, 2003).

Meditation has a different emphasis than prayer, although in practice the two overlap to some extent. While prayer usually has a conversational or discursive aspect in which thoughts and feelings are directed out of us toward someone or something (God, in theistic traditions), **meditation** involves non-discursive procedures aimed at altering attention, clearing the mind of normal thought patterns and establishing a more receptive mode of consciousness. It is often thought of as a practice of Eastern religions like Hinduism or Buddhism rather than Christianity, but activities like meditation can be found in all three traditions (Andresen, 2000). While meditation and prayer are unique in some ways, they also share many features. Meditation is known as a technique for control of attention, but many versions of prayer also emphasize this (e.g., Kadloubovsky & Palmer, 1992, pp. 152–161); prayer is known as a way of seeking transformation, but meditation is also potentially a transformative experience, opening our consciousness to new perceptions of the world.

13.2 Early Christian and Orthdox Prayer and Ascetic Practice

Christian prayer developed in the early church as part of a rich set of spiritual practices. Members of the earliest communities were a minority in a largely pagan culture and drew upon Jewish, New Testament and other sources to fashion a distinctive way of life. After Christianity became the state religion of the Roman empire, people began moving to isolated desert areas in Egypt and Palestine to maintain the distinctive character of their practice and engage in intensive religious seeking (Robinson, 1995). This Desert spirituality has been decisive in the development of Christian spiritual practices, forming models of both individual and communal spirituality (Meyendorff, 1998a, pp. 8–12; Spidlik, 1986).

The earliest influential systematizer of Desert spirituality was Evagrius of Pontus (c. 345–399). He lived in the Egyptian desert during the 4th century AD. He and his Western European popularizer John Cassian helped establish a common vocabulary and approach to Christian spiritual practice (cf. Merton, 2005b, pp. 99–102; Stewart, 1999). They saw Christianity as a way of life that involves all aspects of the human person, rather than just a set of beliefs or membership in an organization—although these are also important (Driscoll, 2005, pp. 1–6). Evagrius combined knowledge of the practical wisdom of the Desert Fathers with a Greek philosophical view of the human person.

13.2.1 Models of Development

The works of Evagrius (Sinkewicz, 2003; Harmless, 2004, pp. 345–354) and other later writers like Maximus Confessor (Maximus, 2003; Louth, 1996) offer sophisticated models of spiritual growth and experience in prayer (Chirban, 1986). Evagrius and Maximus believed that development proceeds in three stages. During the first stage of **praktike,** one engages in lifestyle changes and ascetic practices to purify the passionate part of the soul. This eliminates vices and attachments while gaining virtues, ultimately leading toward a state of purity of heart. As purification is achieved and our emotions and desires function normally, we are able to quiet our mind and move on to the second stage of **natural contemplation,** where we see the inner *logoi* or laws and meaning of things in relation to the activity of God, appreciating the world as it is rather than as something to exploit (Thunberg, 1995, pp. 75–81; Allchin, 2003; Montaldo, 2003; Merton, 2003b, 2008, pp. 121–136). The assumptions here are as follows: (1) It is impossible to truly appreciate nature unless we have achieved some purity of heart and detachment through praktike (Pennington, 2003) and (2) part of the perfection of creation is the uniqueness and diversity of things that at the same time are in an overarching harmony; the universal and the particular require each other (von Balthasar, 1995, pp. 41–50). Finally comes **theoria** or *spiritual contemplation*, the vision or seeing of God, which includes ineffable experiences of formless light, union, and participation in a divine reality that exceeds traditional rational concepts (Spidlik, 2005, pp. 152–158; Dysinger, 2005; Driscoll, 2005, pp. 77–83; Cutsinger, 2003; Meyendorff, 1998b, p. 168; cf. Theophan, 1995, p. 131; Bolshakoff, 1976, p. 122). At this stage of theoria, divine activity dominates, and the soul becomes so pure that one can see God in it as if in a clear mirror (Sherwood, 1955, pp. 87–88; Spidlik, 1986, pp. 78–79, 334–338). Later writers tended to emphasize this kind of contemplation, speaking of it as pure prayer (Palamas, 1983, pp. 35–38, 61–65) or mutual sharing (*perichoresis*) that leads to **theosis**. While Evagrius seems to have treated these stages of development as sequential, later writers like Maximus tended to argue that they were parallel processes (Thunberg, 1995, pp. 332–359, 417–422), so ascetic practices of praktike are important at any level, and one's higher prayer life could lead to greater purity at the level of praktike (Spidlik, 2005, pp. 176–179; Driver, 2002, p. 101). The path of development is thus like a helix that ascends toward God as the person moves back and forth between ethical or practical struggles and the experience of contemplation.

13.2.2 The Ascetic Life

Eastern Orthodox spirituality created a range of **ascetic** practices, which are training activities or exercises designed to help create the kind of physical and mental state necessary for attaining virtue and achieving spiritual development toward perfection (Harmless, 2004, p. 61; Merton, 2008, p. 19). These practices have been particularly important among Orthodox and Roman Catholic groups but have also influenced Protestants like Martin Luther (Senn, 1986). Asceticism is built on the assumption that there is an essential interconnection between the physical, mental, and spiritual aspects of life (e.g., Theophan, 1995, p. 38; Allen, 1997). This is an area of considerable contemporary discussion due to an increase of interest in understanding the role of the body and emotion in spirituality and religious practices (McGuire, 2007; Kearns, 2005; cf. Peters, 2002; Ryff & Singer, 1998). Ascetical practices and disciplines include simplicity of diet, fasting, vigils (long periods of prayer, typically at night), almsgiving, manual labor, participation in the sacraments, and moral or sexual restraint. They were designed to foster a particular kind of intensified subjective experience and a way of life supportive of spiritual advancement and deep experiences in prayer or meditation (Chrysostomos, 2007, pp. 90–91; Flood, 2004; Sinkewicz, 2003, pp. 5–9; Okholm, 2001). Obedience to a superior was also thought to be important in giving a person the strength to overcome destructive passions (Merton, 2005b, p. 148). These practices were based on certain assumptions about the nature of spiritual perfection, how it should be pursued, and how the ascetic should view and relate to the surrounding culture (Kaelber, 1995):

1. While psychology has often assumed that bodily desires or pleasures are natural and thus should be satisfied, ascetic writers claim that in many situations the satisfaction of material desires simply increases the desire, leading to a loss of freedom. Spiritual desires on the other hand when satisfied have a transformative effect and lead to greater freedom (e.g., Sinkewicz, 2003, pp. 73–76; Sherwood, 1955, p. 116; Palamas, 1983, p. 51). Interestingly, experimental research has shown that ascetic techniques like fasting lead to changes in drive and reward mechanisms that reduce desire and provide less stimulation of brain chemicals involved in addictions. Fasting also appears to enhance inner tranquility, positive mood, and health, as well as retard aging (Bushell, 1995).

2. Freedom is not found through eliminating desires, but through purifying them, so that we are free to use our natural abilities and respond to God's presence. Ascetic discipline allows us to control, moderate and harmoniously direct our desires. This moves us toward virtue and spiritual advancement and away from compulsive following of our passions or the pressures of the surrounding culture. We develop a state of **apatheia**, an inner peace or detachment from compulsions that bind us, leaving us free to better love others and to pursue spiritual development (Louth, 1996; Nikodimos & Makarios, 1981, p. 67; Sinkewicz, 2003, pp. 110–112; Wilken, 1995; Ware, 1995; Makrakis, 1977, p. 137; Malina, 1995; Maloney, 1992, p. 190; Merton, 2008, p. 103).

3. Early Christian writers reject the idea that mind and body can be separated. For Evagrius and especially for later writers like Maximus or Gregory Palamas, it is dualistic to suppose that mind or spirit can be purified without attending to the body or developing a lifestyle that can support sanctification and spiritual development (Dysinger, 2005, pp. 28–34; Meyendorff, 1998b, pp. 143–150). In their

holistic view, we are a composite of body and soul that are separate in nature but interpenetrate (*perichoresis*) so that they are intimately related and actively reciprocal, unable to exist apart from each other (Maximus, 2003, pp. 71, 87; Thunberg, 1995). Thus, purification of the body sanctifies the soul and vice versa (Sherwood, 1955, pp. 105–125).

4. Ascetic practices were thought to be helpful for every Christian, and while withdrawal from the anxieties of daily life was thought to be helpful, exclusively solitary and individualistic forms of spirituality were discouraged, as they were found to be harmful to most people (Rubenson, 1995; Sinkewicz, 2003, p. 5; Spidlik, 1986, p. 214; Louth, 1996, p. 35; Gould, 1993, p. 168; Spidlik, 2005, pp. 95, 115; Meyendorff, 1998a, p. 13).

5. The goal of asceticism is not just a cleansing of vices and attachments but the development of positive virtues like humility and love. For writers like Maximus, it is virtue rather than the elimination of vice that leads to happiness and supports contemplation, which in turn leads to freedom and our increasing likeness to God. Thus, ascetic practices both required love and were a prerequisite for it (Kadloubovsky & Palmer, 1992, p. 55; Louth, 1996; Sherwood, 1955, pp. 81–93). Likewise, techniques of asceticism were not ends in themselves but simply tools for developing virtues (Nicodemos, 1989, p. 185).

6. No one system of practice will work for everyone. Each individual has his or her own needs, problems and abilities, so any system of ascetic discipline and prayer must be designed for the individual and balanced, avoiding extremes (Merton, 2005b, pp. 157–158, 220–225; 2006, p. 117).

13.2.3 The Life of Prayer

In the Orthodox view, prayer depends on the support of ascetic practices and disciplines that help to cleanse the passions and allow the mind to engage in deep prayer (e.g., Palamas, 1983, pp. 41–49). Mental discipline and cultivation of qualities like gentleness are needed because of the problem of *logismoi* or evil thoughts such as anger or resentment that arise during prayer. Some of these interfering thoughts are so powerful and out of place—seemingly contrary to nature—that Evagrius spoke of them as *demonic*, a term that did not necessarily refer to a spiritual entity (Hausherr, 1990, pp. 249–255). Self-observation in these cases is particularly important so that one can know the deceptive nature of the thoughts and their source. Reading, working with the hands and **psalmody** or vocal, prayerful recitations from the psalms have a calming effect and help control the problem of distractions (Sinkewicz, 2003; Dysinger, 2005; Kadloubovsky & Palmer, 1992, p. 57). They also help develop virtues like detachment and love, which are antidotes for the anger and spiritual pride that are particularly troublesome for more advanced practitioners. Ideally these practices lead to a state of pure prayer without ceasing, an inner state of detachment and attentiveness to God (Spidlik, 1986, p. 316; 2005, p. 285; Sherwood, 1955, p. 117).

There was considerable flexibility in early prayer practices. Various postures were used included standing with hands raised, kneeling, or seated and listening. There was an emphasis on short prayers said at frequent times during the day. Free prayers were often simply short phrases like the *Kyrie Eleison* ("Lord, have mercy") or even single words expressing our need for God's help (Spidlik, 2005, pp. 76–83; Gould, 1993, pp. 167–169; Merton, 2003c, p. 456; Meyendorff, 1998a, p. 18). These were a way of filling the mind and directing it rather than trying to empty it by force. Short prayers could be repeated, which over time led to a kind of continuous unconscious repetition of the prayer. Especially in larger communities, a formal system of prayer at various hours of the day began to evolve around the 4th century to become what is known today as the *prayer of hours* or the **Daily Office** (Cassian, 1999 pp. 15–39). This schedule also includes times for meeting with a spiritual advisor, communal assembly and prayer, meals, and worship (Sinkewicz, 2003, pp. 42, 51–56).

From the time of the 5th century (John, 1979) people began using the **Jesus Prayer** ("Lord Jesus Christ, Son of God, have mercy on me, a sinner") as an invocation to guard the soul (McGinn, 2001, pp. 38–44; Ware, 1986b, 2002; Maloney, 1992, p. 116; Anthony, 1966, pp. 84–88; Theophan, 1995, p. 59). The prayer is short and imageless; it can be said during passing moments or repeated continuously in a regular, rhythmical manner. It produces a silent but active, vigilant state, and by forcing out unproductive trains of thought and attachments it produces spiritual freedom. Its focus on Jesus helps make him present in an effective way and the prayer for mercy emphasizes our need for God (Sherwood, 1955, pp. 26–31; Spidlik, 2005, p. 335; Ware, 2003a, 2003b).

13.2.4 *Mysticism and the Guarding of the Heart*

Orthodox spirituality focuses on the inner unity of the person as the natural state in which we should live. They used the Biblical term **heart** (*kardia*) as representing the ground of the soul, the inner directing center of the person, a unifying principle and symbol of wholeness that affects all aspects of us and is affected by every aspect of ourselves. It is the place where we meet God, so it has a mysterious, unconscious, and transcendent aspect (Spidlik, 1986, pp. 105–106; Maloney, 1992, p. 116; Palamas, 1983, p. 43; Spidlik, 2005, pp. 250–256; Nicodemos, 1989, pp. 153–156; Louchakova, 2007; Ware, 2003a, 2003b). The Desert Fathers, particularly those in the Syrian tradition, understood that the practice of prayer depended upon the attainment of an interior state of the heart that supported it, moving away from attachments and passions that disrupt the proper functioning of our spiritual center (Merton, 2005b, p. 87; Theophan, 1995, p. 59). They described this as a state of **hesychia** or inner calmness, attentiveness, and attention to God that is free from distraction (Gould, 1993, p. 172; Rossi, 2002; Nikodimos & Makarios, 1995, p. 125). This allows the development of a contemplative state of *pure prayer* or **prayer of the heart** that involves the whole person in a feeling of boundlessness and a sense that Divinity is within us (Bartos, 1999, pp. 29–30; Ware, 2003a, 2003c). While involving concentration, it is also a kind of rejection of thought. In this state, the subject-object dichotomy between God and us is eliminated, and we lose awareness of self and the act of praying. It is a noetic state in that it involves contact with reality, allowing to see our mortality and the illusory nature of some of our ideas (Anthony, 1966, p. 57; Rossi, 2002). In the West, the heart became associated with emotion and this became a focus of prayer (Brock, 1999). It also is central in Islamic Sufism, which developed prayer techniques that resemble those of hesychasm (Thurston, 2005; Dieker, 2005).

Several aspects of practice were designed to foster hesychia including physical solitude, participation in ritual and psalmody, and maintenance of good relationships with others (Gould, 1993, p. 167). Especially important was the practice of *nepsis*, watchfulness or **guarding the heart** from things that could interfere with prayer. This involved vigilant attention to both outside influences or inordinate desires for pleasure, and from our inner imagination, which can dwell on things and magnify our attachments to them (Nicodemos, 1989, pp. 67–85, 107–112). These intruding thoughts could be cut off using an *antirrhesis* or **counter statement**, or using short scripture passages and prayers to help focus the mind against distractions (Spidlik, 2005, pp. 321–326; Kadloubovsky & Palmer, 1992, pp. 31–32). In some writers like Climacus (1979), hesychia was a returning within to seek a state of unity and simplicity or **spiritual poverty** that severed attachments and promoted a listening attitude, opening us to the presence of God, allowing a state of contemplation to develop (Ware, 2003b, 2003c).

In the 14th century, a **psychophysical method** of hesychastic prayer developed that involves the body as well as the mind. In this practice, the individual sits on a stool and recites the Jesus prayer, often in coordination with breathing or heartbeat. A prayer rope or *komboschini* can also be used to develop a regular prayer rhythm. The gaze and thoughts are fixed on the place of the heart to seek God. Physical sensations and feelings of light, warmth, or energy often occur. A clearing of the mind and awareness of the body help us to see more of our true internal state. This type of hesychastic prayer has been compared to yoga and some Islamic Sufi techniques; however, there are differences in content. Also, the aim is different: yoga is a physical technique which tries to bring about a certain result, while hesychasm brings quiet so we can be receptive to God's action and help. Since the psychophysical method involves altering basic bodily processes like breathing, it is recommended that it only be done under the supervision of an experienced master (Spidlik, 2005, pp. 341–346; Kadloubovsky & Palmer, 1992, pp. 74–89; Palamas, 1983, pp. 43–52; Ware, 2003a, 2003b; Bebis, 1989, p. 54; Nicodemos, 1989, pp. 159–168; Meyendorff, 1998a, 1998b; Chryssavgis, 2002).

13.2.5 Icons

An important part of Orthodox spiritual life is the **icon**, an artistic symbol of religious realities. Created in an atmosphere of reverence according to traditional rules and methods, icons serve several purposes. Famous icons like those by Andrei

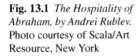

Fig. 13.1 *The Hospitality of Abraham, by Andrei Rublev.* Photo courtesy of Scala/Art Resource, New York

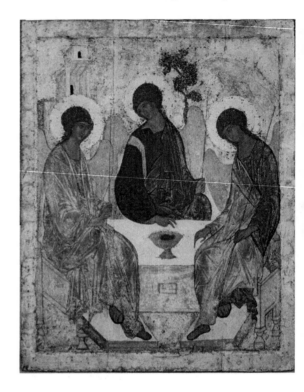

Rublev (See Fig. 13.1 and Box 13.1) convey tradition, providing a visual representation of belief and practice. They are also living, in the sense that they are designed to convey a sense of communion with a sacred presence. In this way they are spiritual objects, pointing not to themselves or the iconographer who created them but to spiritual realities. Since they generally involve pictures of people and places from Biblical and historical narratives, they are seen as witnesses to the incarnated reality of spirituality and its power to transfigure and transform. They also help the viewer to identify with the figures in the narratives. The fact that they fall short of the reality they refer to is a suggestion of the ultimate mystery that lies behind spirituality.

Icons are used to facilitate prayer in homes, as well as in churches. In the home, people often create an icon corner that is dimly lit and illuminate the icon with a vigil candle. This provides something to look at while standing before the icon, praying with eyes open in an attitude of silence. The atmosphere may be difficult to appreciate or even disturbing for the newcomer, as in contemporary society we are accustomed to noise and may find silence difficult. At the least it makes us aware of our busyness and lack of integration. Silence allows for the growth of prayer, a listening attitude and awareness of presence (Ouspensky & Lossky, 1999, pp. 21–36; Martin, 2002; Forest, 1997, 2003).

Box 13.1 A Rublev Icon

The Hospitality of Abraham by Andrei Rublev is probably the best known icon to most modern Western Christians (Williams, 2003, 2004, p. 45). A representation of the story of three angels visiting Abraham—it is seen as an image of the Trinity, three persons and one substance in loving relationship. The presence of angels or physical objects like the table shows an embodied, historical, and narrative aspect of spiritual truth. The minimal aspect of the background provides a setting without detracting from the meaning of the image and the relationship between the viewer and the figures, giving the picture a timeless quality.

The central figure in the icon is generally taken to represent the Son, with the Father to the left, and the Holy Spirit on the right. The circular positioning of the figures shows them to be distinct but of equal rank, and the inclined heads, posture, and gestures indicate peace but also a circular motion and action (Ouspensky & Lossky, 1999, pp. 200–202). The chalice in the middle contains a sacrificial animal, and its position in the center indicates the sacrificial nature of the Trinity's work.

What is important in the icon is not only what is represented but also how it is done. The symbolic values of the colors add to the meaning and impact of the icon: The blue and red clothing worn by the central figure represent heaven, the mystical life, and sacrifice. The gold background conveys sanctity, imperishability, and a sense of divine energy, the uncreated light of God (Forest, 1997, pp. 15–27). In most Western art, depth is shown by making objects in the back smaller to create the illusion of depth. In this icon, perspective is reversed; things in the back are larger which throws the figures forward. This and the open space at the table invite us to join the figures and participate with them in communion (Martin, 2002, pp. 88, 133). However, the figures do not directly face us, introducing mystery.

13.3 Prayer and the Western Contemplative Tradition

Roman Catholicism has developed its own unique forms of the prayer techniques pioneered by the Desert Fathers. In the Catholic tradition, it is common to divide the process of spiritual growth in prayer into four modes: *lectio* or prayerful reading, *meditatio* or meditation, *oratio* or prayerful response, and finally *contemplatio* or contemplation. These categories describe modes of spirituality centered on God that might operate in chronological succession but might also be simultaneous or separated. Growth involves intensification and simplification of our love for God and others, which in turn can result in transformations and a qualitative change in the nature of the prayer experience to a simpler state of absorption and presence, a willing expression of dependence and acceptance of love (Merton, 2003b, pp. 60–65; Broderick, 1991; von Balthasar, 1986). Thus prayer and the spiritual life can be described as climbing a spiral staircase in which one repeatedly returns to the same place but at a different level (Keating, 1992, p. 106). The flow will differ between individuals and at different times in seemingly unpredictable ways (Martin, 1997, pp. 218–220; Pennington, 2001; Casey, 1995, p. 59).

Lectio divina or divine reading is an ancient practice that is currently expanding in popularity. The intent of *lectio* is to engage the whole person in an experiential listening to God. Ideally, *lectio* is part of a broad pattern of practices and daily habits that develop our attentiveness (Pennington, 1998). In this practice, scriptures such as the psalms, gospels, or other spiritual writings are read slowly and prayerfully, looking for guidance in one's spiritual life and moral applications. The period of *lectio* may begin with prayer, and ends with the person taking a word or thought with them for later meditation (Pennington, 2001, p. 198; Casey, 1995; Spidlik, 2005, pp. 130–145). In **meditatio**, the person praying uses a word, phrase, or idea they have taken from *lectio* and reflects on the meaning it has for them—a meaning that will tell the person something about themselves, about the Divine and what God has to say. When properly done, meditation is a regular practice that requires good physical and emotional health, a supportive environment and attention to posture and breathing. This can lead to **oratio**, a spontaneous, prayerful response of gratitude, love, or need that comes from the heart and establishes a dialogue based on our innermost desires. The basis of true prayer lies in these kinds of desires and our relationship with God (Casey, 1996). Many different procedures such as imaginative visualizations can facilitate *meditatio* and *oratio*, but the process also involves an attitude of openness to receiving guidance and help and a willingness to respond (Flood, 2004, p. 193; Merton, 1971, p. 34; Hall, 1988, pp. 28–43).

13.3.1 Contemplation

Contemplation in the Western tradition has many similarities to its use in Orthodox descriptions and practices, although there are differences in emphases and descriptive language. The Catholic monk Thomas Merton describes contemplation as "an obscure, experiential contact with God beyond the senses and in some way even beyond concepts" (2003b, p. 71; cf. Deikman, 1990). Because it involves a kind of intuitive knowledge and vision that is beyond the intellect or the senses, Western Christians often refer to it as a kind of darkness, a language not typically found in Orthodox writings. Catholic descriptions of contemplation also may have a more emotional quality so that experiences of communion or participation with God are often described in the language of passionate love, involving intense feelings of spiritual longing and an intimate sense of an indwelling God. As a way of life, contemplation is viewed as an abiding state of this union where we live in purity of heart (Pennington, 2001, pp. 82–92; Teresa, 1979, pp. 126–194; cf. Keating, 1992, pp. 14–17; Merton, 2006, pp. 64–67). From a phenomenological view, early stages of prayer like *lectio, meditatio,* or even *oratio* are modes of intentionality that direct our attention toward God (Wright, 2005, p. 135). Contemplation, on the other hand, is a unique state of consciousness that is not intentional and dependent on the self but is a free response to the demand of God. It comes from outside our "horizon of expectation," so it can only be grasped poorly and tentatively. It is asymmetrical as the outside voice has priority, challenging our self-centeredness (Levinas, 1969; Andrews, 2005; Westphal, 2005).

While contemplation can happen at any stage in the spiritual life, it often follows a pattern of development. In the early stages of prayer, the will is active, and there is a reaching out for God. As contemplation progresses, this activity is succeeded by states of intense absorption referred to as **recollection** or the Prayer of Quiet (Welch, 1982, p. 2; Hollenback, 1996, pp. 539–540; Teresa, 1979, pp. 77–84) and then by a more passive or **infused contemplation,** where thoughts and feelings of spiritual consolation come unbidden. These types of higher prayer leave behind the laborious work of meditation and are considered a gift. They can be profoundly transformative, and there is a sense that God is intensely at work within the individual, leading to increasing love and humility (May, 2004, pp. 114–134; Turner, 1995, p. 198; Keating, 1995, pp. 91–92; von Balthasar, 1986, pp. 201–210; Welch, 1996). Painful **dark night experiences** can happen as previously satisfying modes of prayer seem unfulfilling or impossible, and new ways of experiencing God's love take their place (Hall, 1988, p. 47; Mansfield, 1991a; John of the Cross, 1973, pp. 140–142; see Section 11.3.2). Thus, while contemplation ultimately has a healing quality, intensive spiritual development involves some painful experiences. For those with serious emotional problems, or people unwilling to accept the necessary difficulties, attempts at contemplation could be damaging or degenerate into mere self-indulgence (Keating, 1992, pp. 75–77; von Balthasar, 1986, pp. 155–162; Merton, 2003b).

13.3.2 *Prayer and the Discovery of Our True Self*

Prayer is an interior activity that can bring us into contact with the deepest aspects of ourselves. Contemplative masters like Thomas Merton emphasize that an essential part of genuine prayer is a confrontation with our false self and a discovery of our true one. The **false self** consists of superficial or illusionary ideas about ourselves and the patterns of behavior we mistakenly believe to be essential to us. It is based upon emotional programs and unconscious motivations from early childhood that are reinforced when we identify with cultural shoulds and oughts that are contrary to our true nature. This false self is not free; it fragments us and puts us at odds with reality, others, and our self; because of this, it produces a general feeling of dread, guilt, or anxiety (Pennington, 2001, p. 124; Williams, 2003; Merton, 1973, pp. 97–102; Hall, 1988, p. 43; Keating, 1995, p. 3). We become aware of its falsity in experiences of emptiness, such as loss, impermanence, apparent meaninglessness, or helplessness (Gunn, 2000, pp. 140–154). The **true self** is the real person

Table 13.1 The false and true selves

False self	True self
Unaware of true motives and illusions about self and others	Self-aware, seeks the truth about self and others
Can be objectively described, an empirical object related to others who are also objects	Cannot be completely known, a spiritual subject related to others who are also subjects
Dualistic; sees the world and others as objects to be manipulated for pleasure	Nondualistic; we are a part of the world and should seek unity in love
Built completely around achieving egocentric desires	Built around a sense of receptivity, has no projects
A social construction; the ego	A real person who is discovered
Built around an ideal self, who we would like to be	Built around a real self, who we really are
Blames self and others when illusions are not fulfilled	Accepts self and others as they are
Is not known to God	Is known to God
Not free; tied to compulsive seeking of pleasure or approval	Free to enjoy things but is not bound by them
Fragmented	Unified
Constantly changing emotions	Stable feelings of love
Cannot tolerate mystery	Accepts and appreciates mystery

Source: Merton (2003b, pp. 15–25), Shannon (2000, pp. 120–126), and Merton (1961, p. 166)

hidden under this false exterior (see Table 13.1). Merton (1966, p. 142) describes it as a "virgin point," a deep heart in the soul that is pure and belongs to God (see Box 4.1). It cannot be completely known or objectified, nor is it possible to develop a psychology of it because it does not involve the superficial consciousness that we can reach through any psychological or even spiritual technique. Only God knows the true self in full, and so in the contemplative view the only real way to find the true self is to seek God (Ware, 2002; Shannon, 2000; Merton, 1961, pp. 1–5; Merton, 2003b; Keating, 1992, p. 2). Self-knowledge and spiritual progress thus go hand-in-hand, a view also held in Sufism (Chittick, 2005).

In the contemplative view, we must dismantle the false self although this is not an easy task. The first stage of the process is active confrontation with illusions about ourselves and expansion of awareness through prayer. This will lead us to confront problematic thinking, actions or behavior in relationships, and help us see our need for others (Casey, 1996, p. 15). However, the patterns of the false self are deeply ingrained on both conscious and unconscious levels, so a kind of resistance or **spiritual warfare** can occur as we begin to dismantle it, including feelings of anger, anxiety, or loss. Experiences of trust and support can assist in this process (Hall, 1988, pp. 2–19; Pennington, 2001, p. 104). Modern contemplatives use psychological models like object relations theory to help understand this false self and its resistance to change (Gunn, 2000, pp. 190–191; see Section 5.4.3). Contemplative prayer can provide healing by allowing access to unconscious levels (Keating, 1995; Shannon, 2000, p. 170). Contemplative thought parallels Buddhist ideas as both strive to eliminate the false self; it differs from Buddhism because it holds that there is a true self that can be discovered.

Merton and many contemplative authors argue that one of the chief obstacles to finding the true self is modern culture with its busyness and intrusions (Pennington, 2001, pp. 458–462). For Merton, the distractions of modern technological society increase rather than decrease illusions and lead to complacency and apathy or a search for more intense diversions with destructive potential. Contemporary life encourages materialism, a focus on immediate gratification, a lack of balance, and excessive competition that promotes division (Merton, 1985, p. 178; Shannon, 2000, pp. 265–268). Contemplation, on the other hand, rejects dependence on materialism and is not interested in escape; it tries to engage life and confront our fears and limitations. It manifests itself in an attitude of simplicity, humility, faithfulness, and love in small, everyday matters, and an awareness of presence and union with God in our life activities (von Balthasar, 1986, p. 137). This sense of identification and compassion can motivate activities of peacemaking and justice (Kilcourse, 2004; Merton, 1960, p. 73). Attachments such as needs for power and control—including spiritual and religious power—must be reduced as these inhibit our freedom and spiritual seeking (Hall, 1988; Merton, 2003b).

13.3.3 Centering Prayer

A number of techniques have been developed to facilitate the progression from *lectio* to contemplation. An imageless and less active method that has become popular is **centering prayer** (Pennington, 2001, 2004; Keating, 1992). It is designed to reduce obstacles to contemplation and intimacy with God by establishing interior silence, which enables us to become aware of our spiritual level of being separate from the superficial false self. The method was developed by the Cistercian monk Thomas Keating, but it draws on materials from both the Orthodox and medieval Catholic traditions.

In centering prayer the practitioner chooses a prayer word of 1–2 syllables that expresses love and desire for God and their intention to consent to God's presence. Then twice daily with eyes closed the person has a 20-minute prayer time that includes (1) an initial buffer time of several minutes for quieting down from daily events, (2) repeating the prayer word without particularly attending to it, or when possible simply remaining silent before God, and (3) a winding-down time including an active prayer like the Lord's prayer as a way of connecting the quiet time to our life. Details like place, time, or posture are important but should not be rigidly applied. Breath control can also be used, but simplicity is usually preferred. The prayer is generally combined with other kinds of individual spiritual practices like *lectio* and communal religious activities.

The beginner quickly discovers that mental silence is not easy to find, as they are plagued by various thoughts about daily affairs, self-reflections, or fantasies. Sometimes, emotionally charged thoughts and images from the unconscious appear. If not disturbing, they should be ignored and allowed to pass by without notice. After all, wandering thoughts are part of reality, and forcing thoughts from the mind, even if successful, just reinforces the false self that cannot listen but must always be in control. Distressing thoughts should not be ignored but embraced and experienced, allowing the pain or uncomfortable feeling to become a prayer word that is lifted up to God.

13.3.4 The Spiritual Exercises

A more active, effortful, and systematic approach to prayer is the **Spiritual Exercises** of Ignatius Loyola (Fig. 13.2). The Exercises were based on his own personal experiences and practices during a critical time in his spiritual growth and formation (Meissner, 1992, p. 87), and are intended to provide a "concrete way in which Christianity can become a living religion in us" (Rahner, 1965, p. 11). They are designed for people with a solid religious faith and relative freedom from psychological problems, who desire to deepen their relationship with God and gain additional inner freedom or a sense of direction in their lives (Veale, 1991a; Mansfield, 1991a; Grogan, 1991c).

General approach. In contemporary practice, a spiritual director (see Section 14.1.1) gives the Exercises individually, either as a concentrated experience in a retreat setting, or as a more extended process while the person remains involved in their regular daily life. Most retreat directors adapt the Exercises to the needs and circumstances of the individual, so sometimes there is only vague connection between the text of the Exercises and what happens (Lonsdale, 2000, p. 18; Sheldrake, 1991; Mariani, 2002, p. 81; Ivens, 1991). The focus of the Exercises is primarily relational, about intimacy and love of God or others rather than self-actualization or achieving better problem-solving strategies (Barry, 2001, pp. 4–5). The Exercises provide a system for meditating on scriptures and Christian themes (Ignatius, 1978, p. 19) with the following goals:

- *Self-examination that leads to a greater awareness of our real desires* and inner feelings, as well as weaknesses, attachments, and conflicts that limit our freedom (Barry, 2001, pp. 27–55; Hughes, 1991)

Fig. 13.2 *Ignatius of Loyola.* Roman Catholic saint and founder of the Jesuit order, Ignatius produced a system of spiritual exercises that are still widely used within Christianity. Image courtesy of the Society of Jesus

- *Discernment and making decisions* that build the relationship with God, as well as revise our views of the Divine based on personal experience (Houdek, 1996, pp. 128–131; Broderick, 1991; Meissner, 1992, pp. 97–99; Skinnider, 1991)
- *Promoting union with God* through identification with Christ and redefining our own identity to be like that of Christ (Barry, 2001, p. 124)
- *Conversion of heart* leading to a new quality of life and way of service (Ivens, 1998, p. 1; Buckley, 1995; Broderick, 1991). The social implications of the Exercises are stressed by many contemporary writers and were important to Ignatius as well (Shea, 1991; McVerry, 1991; Hellwig, 1991; Lonsdale, 2000, p. 51). Thus, the Exercises have a strong orientation toward action, which is less emphasized in some other currents of Christian spirituality (Veale, 1991b).

Role of director. The role of the director is important in the Exercises. They pray for the individual, provide appropriate directions and help the directee reflect on their experience, trying to help the person discover their authentic desires. In order to prepare, directors need to have done the Exercises themselves. They also need appropriate experience, listening skills and knowledge, and to be in personal spiritual direction. The director must help the retreatant find an appropriate setting for prayer and meditation, set an appropriate pace, and be alert to signs that the retreatant is ready to move on to the next stage of the Exercises (Mariani, 2002; Grogan, 1991a, 1991b, 1991c; Barry, 2001, p. 70). Some will progress though the entire Exercises, while others may not progress beyond the first week; either can be good (Sheldrake, 1991).

Process and Experience. The Exercises involve general activities that are repeated throughout the process. These include the *particular examen* that monitors and works to change a specific personal defect, and the *general examen* of conscience aiming for overall personal renewal (Ignatius, 1978, pp. 31–32, 38). There are also specific meditations, where the person is asked to picture a scene and engage in a colloquy or conversation with its characters while attending to emotional reactions. Multisensory imagination is encouraged to engage both mind and body (Savage, 2001; Herrera, 2000). The intensive use of imagination is powerful and promotes a sense of immediacy and intimacy, opening the person to new possibilities (Byrne, 1991; Wickham, 1991; Barry, 2001, pp. 95–103; Mariani, 2002).

Discernment. A distinctive feature of the Exercises is a complex system for **discernment**, or identifying spiritual movements and the will of God. Discernment involves looking for what is spiritually authentic. It promotes freedom to follow God and involves attention to external circumstances and the opinions of others, as well as internal senses and an awareness of the potential for self-deception (Ivens, 1998, pp. 205–208; Lonsdale, 2000, pp. 91–92). A primary tool of the rules for discernment is learning to identify *consolations* or things that move us toward God and inner unity, as well as *desolations* or things that move us away and produce inner confusion, restlessness, or division (Ignatius, 1978, pp. 152–159; Buckley, 1991; Barry, 2001, p. 130). Ignatius thought that the emotional signs of authentic consolation depended on the person's level of development. For those beginning the spiritual life in the purgative phase, things that promote development will be painful and perhaps trouble the conscience, while those that move away from God will be pleasurable. In the later illuminative phase, the opposite will be true. In the more advanced stages, additional rules need to be followed that deal with more subtle deceptions (Herrera, 2000; Newman, 1996; Ignatius, 1978, pp. 152–153, 160–164; Lonsdale, 1991).

Structure. The Exercises are divided into four "weekly" periods. The first week marks the purgative stage of the Exercises. The focus is on developing a realistic knowledge of ourselves and others so that we can improve our relationships and better respond to God's movement in our life (Barry, 2001, pp. 137–142; Veale, 1991a). The first week tries to promote habits of self-reflection, as well as encourage giving up attachments that limit our freedom and ability to respond to God. This is facilitated by a number of meditations, as well as confessions of how personal sins and failings have negatively affected others (Ignatius, 1978, p. 30; Meissner, 1992, p. 91; Rahner, 1965, pp. 69–74; St. Louis, 1991). The second week contains meditations on the life of Christ designed to promote experiential understanding and increase our identification with Christ. Its intent is to call the retreatant toward a decision or recommitment known as an *election* that will enable the person to further develop their relationship to God and service toward others. The third week involves meditation on the crucifixion, identifying our suffering and struggles with that of Christ (Mansfield, 1991b; Broderick, 1991). The fourth week culminates in the Contemplation to Attain Love (Ignatius, 1978, pp. 119–122), where the retreatant asks for an intimate knowledge of God's gifts. At the end, the director helps develop a plan for continuing the habits, insights, and commitments from the Exercises (Mariani, 2002, pp. 260–270).

Jung on the Exercises. While Jung never observed the Exercises, he was interested in them as a means to transformation that he thought had parallels to some Yoga and Buddhist texts (Jung, 1977, 1978). He produced a series of lectures on the Exercises that illuminate but suffer from many of the same problems as his selective use of Eastern texts; for instance, he neglected the entire last half of the Exercises. Jung criticized the Exercises as reflecting the Western attitude about prayer that focuses on outer reality. He also rejected the idea that a person like Christ would suffer for someone else, although he approved of the Ignatian idea that suffering can be formative and results from situations of conflict. He was more approving of the Ignatian emphases on identification with Christ, as Jung saw Christ as a symbol for human totality that promotes individuation. He also thoroughly approved of the awareness of the sinful potential of every individual that can be found in the Exercises. He noted that modern society has widely rejected the idea of a sinful nature and that most people think of themselves as basically good. He argued that this idea is a kind of arrogance at odds with the personal unhappiness and social catastrophes of the 20th century, which demonstrate that people are also capable of the worst vices and often deceive themselves about this fact.

13.4 Christian Protestant and Modern Views of Prayer

13.4.1 Martin Luther

Prayer in the Christian Protestant tradition is quite diverse, but many of its principles can be found in the writings of the great Reformation writer Martin Luther (1483–1546). Teachings on prayer are scattered throughout Luther's writings (2002, see especially Volumes 10–14 and 21). He himself had a strong personal prayer life and is said to have prayed the Lord's Prayer eight times a day. He also had some experiences healing others of illnesses through prayer (Berg, 2002). While he thought that basic moral discipline and other spiritual practices like fasting and doing acts of kindness could be appropriate if done for the right reasons, prayer occupied a special place in his vision of the daily life of the Christian (Wengert, 2004).

For Luther, real or earnest prayer is "the lifting up of heart or mind to God" (Luther, 1969a) and is one of the main aspects of the religious life. In particular, prayer is an activity of the heart involving the whole mind and body, including our thoughts, feelings and desires. Real spiritual prayer should be passionate, confident, and reflect our innermost yearnings and desires. He believed that this kind of prayer is essential but difficult, and ultimately it is a gift of God. Luther resisted the idea that prayer or religious practice would have any meaning or effect if used mechanically. In his view, this kind of prayer simply produces discord, pride, and misery.

Luther believed that spiritual practices like prayer played an essential role in personal discernment, learning about God and understanding the Scriptures (Peters, 2000, p. 17). Luther rejected the idea that knowledge of God could be gained by reason alone or without a clear view of our personal situation. Our experiences in prayer help us by teaching us about God and ourselves (Lohse, 1999, p. 41). Prayer also helps us understand Scripture, which Luther believed was the foundational source of our knowledge about God, and so he encouraged the practice of *meditatio* based on the prayerful reading and rereading of scriptures. This leads to *oratio*—our prayer response to reading or personal need—where we encounter the Holy Spirit who enlightens us and opens up the real meaning of the scriptures (Luther, 2002, pp. 34, 285–286; 1969a). In return, the Bible also opens and supports our prayer life. The promises and works of God discussed in the Bible strengthen our faith for prayer, and make us aware of our need and the depth of God's helping response to it (1969b). This crushes our pride and banishes confidence in the attachments of our old way of life, but we should not dwell too much on it as that leads to despair. Rather, we must seek the help and forgiveness offered by Christ, freeing our conscience so that we can confidently follow God.

Luther thought that prayer was also connected to our learning about God through what he called Anfechtung or *tentatio*. **Anfechtung** is a complex concept, rendered by different translators as distress, anxiety, testing, assault, or temptation. Anfechtung is a kind of experiential learning based on two basic attitudes: a feeling of need and dependence or poverty of spirit, and faith or hope that God is a refuge who will accept us, respond to our need, and keep us from despair. It was an essential part of Luther's own spiritual experience (1969a; Senn, 1986). Anfechtung is both an exercise of faith and a gift of God that allows us to interpret suffering in a positive manner so that it will build us up and help us know ourselves and God. Eventually it produces consolation and hope, fighting despair, and moving us forward in sanctification (Nestingen, 2002; Scaer, 1983). Prayer was not about badgering God for things but a gift of confidence and finding hope as we receive forgiveness and comfort during trials (Berg, 2002). Severe trials can thus be an asset for prayer as they give us power and longing in prayer, driving us in our suffering to seek Christ and the help that is available.

Luther believed that genuine prayer should be matched by attitudes and actions compatible with a Christian way of life. He had little use for people who prayed to make an impression on others or who did not follow in deeds what they prayed about in words. People who believed themselves pious but whose behavior did not match were profaners of prayer and "the worst and most harmful people in Christendom" (1969a, p. 30). He also saw pride and anger as special problems. Prayer is supposed to be based upon and promote a penitent condition, but we cannot gain mercy if we do not need it. Pride leads to arrogance, while what we need is to focus on our own sins and forgive those of others (Sander, 1998; Luther, 1969a).

Luther was a popular teacher of prayer (1968b, 1969a; Russell, 2002). Along with encouraging regular prayer practices, Luther taught a relational attitude toward prayer. The center of our prayer should not be ourselves but God or the people we pray for. He also tried to present a flexible method that could be used by many different people at various stages in their prayer life. For instance, while he seems to have preferred simple mental prayer, he also encouraged people to use verbal exterior prayer as a teaching tool and to prevent stray thoughts. He thought the Lord's Prayer provided an excellent model, because it expressed a feeling of dependence and a need for deliverance, although he supplemented it with psalms and expansions of each of its specific petitions. He also encouraged *lectio* and placed a great stress on intercessory prayer, encouraging people to pray not for a single individual or situation but for everyone.

Luther's treatment of prayer hits many themes developed by Orthodox or Catholic writers: the need of prayer from the heart, participation of the whole person, and the idea that prayer is often a response to some inner condition that we express to God. On the other hand, there are also differences. For Luther, prayer is more about expression, letting ourselves and our needs be known to God. It is a kind of speech. This was especially true of some of his later writings on prayer that were more focused on saying petitionary prayers for help with physical needs (Robinson, 1999). This is not to say that Luther neglected the listening and learning aspect of prayer—just that he did not emphasize it and preferred to stress its affective quality. More recent treatments of prayer by Protestant authors have returned to a broader picture of prayer, and contemplative practices are becoming popular once again among Protestant Christians.

13.4.2 Modern Views of Prayer

Psychological treatments of prayer have generally followed Protestant views that stress the expressive aspect of prayer. This can be seen for instance in the work of the early psychologist of religion Friedrich Heiler (1932), a convert to Lutheranism from Catholicism who produced the first major psychological treatment of prayer. For Heiler, prayer is speech with another as well as oneself that involves an awareness of dependence and trust. Because of this it is social in its essence and will become difficult or impossible if God becomes depersonalized. Prayer begins as an emotional discharge or outpouring from the heart but can lose its force if it becomes fixed, formulaic, and impersonal or is performed simply as a custom. Although he acknowledged that there is a great variety and mixture of prayer types, Heiler argued that prayer falls into two general categories—*mystical* and *prophetic* (see Table 13.2). While he recognized the presence of mystical prayer in the Christian and other religious traditions, he tended to view expressive and prophetic prayer as a higher form.

Heiler's classical typology is partly confirmed in factor analytic work by Ladd and Spilka (2002), who found that prayer had three dimensions. The first was an awareness factor, which included concern for others and self-awareness. Prayers of confession were described by this factor. The second dimension was an upward reaching, which included sacramental and ritual prayer, as well as quiet restful prayer times and seeking solace. The final factor was an outward reaching, including petitionary prayer. While the third factor clearly describes expressive or prophetic prayer, the second factor, as well as aspects of the first, appears to represent more receptive or mystical types.

Later psychological treatments of prayer have also focused on its expressive aspect. For instance, the Jungian psychologist Ann Ulanov (Ulanov & Ulanov, 1982) calls prayer "primary speech," an expression of who we are that begins early in infancy with our response to emotions and desires. In this view, the enemies of prayer are anything that breaks the link between our desires and prayer: dishonesty about our true desires, fear or doubt that leads us to avoid expressing our desires, or set and frivolous prayer. Strong feelings like aggression can in the right circumstances become an enabling force for prayer. As we progress through prayer, we may discover that our true desires are greater than any specific thing; limited

Table 13.2 Characteristics of mystical and prophetic prayer (Heiler, 1932)

Mystical prayer	Prophetic prayer
Denial or dissolution of self	Desiring a self that does God's will
Denial of the world	Challenging the world, with an ethical focus on others
Passive, resigned	Active
Subjective	Objective, historical, universally binding
Individual	Social
Monistic	Dualistic
Experience of union	Experience of emotion, struggle
Morality prepares for union	Morality is valuable in itself

attachments do not satisfy. Prayer thus allows us to help sort out our desires and find what truly satisfies us.

While Ulanov emphasized the expressive aspect of prayer, she also implicitly recognizes that prayer is more than this. Since prayer is relational and directed to God, she argues that our prayer life is affected by our image of the Divine. This image is not the reality, as sometimes it reflects past experience or expectations that give us an unrealistic view of God. What we need is a willingness to see a God who may be the same or different from these images or what we have been taught. Ulanov also argues that fantasy plays a constructive role in prayer. It helps avoid daydreaming or mechanical repetition, and it opens us to new possibilities, assisting us to better understand and express ourselves. It thus can have a transfiguring quality.

13.4.3 Empirical Studies of Prayer

Empirical studies of Christian prayer date to the late 1800s, but the quality and range of the studies has generally been poor. Scholars reviewing research in the area (e.g., Masters, 2005; Brown, 1994; Krause, Chatters, Meltzer, & Morgan, 2000; Finney & Malony, 1985) have a number of complaints, including the following:

- Overly simplistic views of prayer that ignore the complexity of techniques and treat prayer as a coping mechanism asking for things rather than a multidimensional practice
- Use of models that ignore differences between individual and group prayer
- Use of measures that focus just on frequency of prayer without reference to what is happening during the prayer time
- Lack of attention to mystical or contemplative prayer practices which offer parallels with Eastern meditative techniques (Hood, Morris, & Watson, 1989)
- Methodological problems with sampling, control groups, and study design
- Lack of a coherent theoretical or theological framework.

Despite the poor quality of studies on prayer, the empirical literature does provide some useful information. We know that prayer is a frequent practice, with about 3/4 of the US population praying at least once a week (Bader et al., 2006). We also know that while prayer can be found among all groups of people, it is clearly a religious practice that does not thrive outside of that environment. For instance, among nonchurchgoing UK teenagers, only 3.3% reported daily prayer and 66.8% indicated that they never prayed, while 35.7% of churchgoers reported daily prayer and only 12.6% reported not praying outside of church (Francis & Evans, 2001a, 2001b). European research suggests that prayer is most often motivated by problems and need for help or support, and it becomes more likely in emotionally intense situations such as a life-threatening emergency (Janssen, de Hart, & den Draak, 1990; Vergote, 1997, pp. 56–57).

Empirical studies have demonstrated that while prayer of the expressive or prophetic type is common, contemplative or meditative prayer practices are also frequent, at least in the US population. Using a large community sample, Poloma and Pendleton (1989, 1991) found four main types of prayer:

- *Meditative prayer*, including simple listening, adoration, quietly thinking about God, or experiencing a sense of presence; this type of prayer appears to be related to higher levels of subjective well-being (Maltby, Lewis, & Day, 2008)
- *Ritualist prayer*, including reciting written or memorized prayers
- *Petitionary prayer*, asking for things for self, friends, and relatives
- *Colloquial prayer*, a conversation with God seeking guidance or forgiveness, expressing thanksgiving, or talking about the relationship.

Petitionary and colloquial prayer are mostly expressive types of prayer, but meditative prayer is clearly a more mystical type and was common in their sample. Frequent occurrence of more contemplative types of prayer has also been found in other populations (cf. Ladd & Spilka, 2002). From a theological standpoint, the kind of meditative prayer of praise described here is especially significant, as it offers a way of saying something about a God who is beyond description (Gschwandtner, 2005). There is some evidence that personality characteristics influence one's preferred type of prayer (Francis & Robbins, 2008).

Expressive prayer can probably be divided into subtypes. Laird and colleagues (Laird, Snyder, Rapoff, & Green, 2004) used a multidimensional prayer inventory to distinguish between *problem-focused* prayer involving supplication or confession and *emotion-focused* prayer like adoration and thanksgiving (cf. Section 10.2.1). These types of prayer can be spontaneous or involve reading from expressive texts such as the Psalms (Driver, 2002, p. 85). Laird believes that emotion-focused prayer is more likely to be used by those with chronic problems or in situations where they have little control. It is a seeking for security, perhaps at the expense of freedom (Anthony, 1966, p. 27). Both types of prayer have moderate to strong correlations with intrinsic but not extrinsic religiosity. Authors like Hood (e.g., Hood et al., 1989) have argued, based on their studies, that intrinsics are more likely to attribute religious significance to prayer experiences and thus to have a different phenomenological—perhaps more mystical—experience of prayer.

While the effect of prayer on God is a topic outside the competence of science, empirical studies can illuminate the effects of prayer on those who engage in the practice (Menninger, 1954). Poloma and Pendleton (1989, 1991) examined the relationship between prayer practices and a variety of measures of mood, satisfaction, and well-being. They found prayer frequency negatively correlated with happiness and positively correlated with religious satisfaction. However, positive prayer experiences like sensing an answer had small positive correlations with life satisfaction, existential well-being, happiness and religious satisfaction. Interestingly, these correlations differed according to the kind of prayer. They found that meditative prayer was correlated with existential well-being and religious satisfaction, as well as feelings of closeness to God and a sense of purpose to life. Colloquial prayer was correlated with happiness. On the other hand, petitionary prayer had no correlations with well-being or mood, and ritual prayer had a small positive correlation with negative affect. They believe that unhappy people use petitionary prayer to feel better but that they typically have few prayer experiences and thus experience little help, while those who pray frequently and use meditative forms of prayer are more likely to have positive experiences. These results parallel those of Finney and Malony (1985) who found that mental health had a mixed or negative relation with verbal prayer but a positive relation with contemplative prayer. This relationship needs to be viewed in the context of the person's overall coping styles, as European studies (e.g., Banziger, van Uden, & Janssen, 2008) have found a connection between religious types of prayer and collaborative or deferring coping styles. Overall, cross-sectional surveys report low but positive correlations (about 0.3) between prayer and life satisfaction and feelings of purpose for both churchgoers and non-churchgoers. This is also found in longitudinal studies where previous prayer practices are found to predict subsequent positive effects on a variety of measures. However, Robbins, Francis, and Edwards (2008) found that personality characteristics of the people praying may account for much of this effect. A number of studies have been devoted to looking at health benefits and have found some positive results (e.g., Francis, Robbins, Lewis, & Barnes, 2008), although this is not consistent, and the methodology of these studies is very problematic (see Section 10.1.2). A number of pathways by which prayer may affect health have been hypothesized, including (1) placebo effect, (2) altering focus and attitudes toward the illness, and (3) activating natural or supernatural processes of healing (cf. Breslin & Lewis, 2008).

Some literature suggests that the helpful effects of prayer are stronger in more difficult situations. For instance, Mary Robinson and her colleagues (Robinson, Thiel, Backus, & Meyer, 2006) have studied spirituality in the parents of terminally ill children on an intensive care unit and found that prayer was reported as one of the most helpful ways of coping with the illness and impending loss.

13.4.3.1 Concepts of Prayer

Conceptions of prayer appear to change and become more sophisticated with development. In an older study that draws upon Piagetian concepts, Long, Elkind, and Spilka (1967) found that child conceptions of prayer went through three stages. In the first stage, children aged 5–7 were found to have a vague conception of prayer without a clear conception of how their needs might differ from those of God. In the second stage, children aged 7–9 had a clearer conception of what is involved in prayer, a view that it involves verbal activity and that the needs of the child are clearly differentiated from those of God. In the third stage beginning around age 10, the child develops a more abstract conception of prayer as an internal activity, a two-way communication between the child and the Divine. Through the process there was a movement toward more altruistic desires and a more meaningful involvement of feelings in prayer.

Research on prayer in adolescence, while limited, suggests that in the teenage years people begin to develop individual styles of prayer that vary in terms of intimacy and intensity. Prayer becomes a talking *with* rather than *at* God, and a sense of presence develops. In adolescence, the most common forms of prayer appear to be petition for self and family, thanksgiving, and prayer about relationships (McKinney & McKinney, 1999; Scarlett & Perriello, 1991, pp. 65–66). Some studies have found a negative correlation between prayer frequency and identity moratorium, indicating that frequent prayer is associated with resolution of identity issues.

Data about conceptions of prayer in adulthood is rather sparse. One fairly recent study (Krause et al., 2000) explored conceptions of prayer in late-life White and African Americans using focus groups. They found

1. Ideas about how prayer operates and is answered related to the overall belief system of the individual and their view of God. Some believed prayers are never answered, but it is helpful to pray anyway. Most believed that answers to prayer depend on the attitude and actions of person doing the praying, as well as the nature of the request. They believed that you need to wait for an answer to prayer and that when it comes you will get what is most needed, not necessarily what you asked for originally.
2. Interviewees thought there were significant differences between group and individual prayers. They saw group prayers as dealing with collective rather than individual concerns and that they were beneficial in a number of unique ways, including increasing awareness about the needs of others and producing special experiences of love and unity. They thought that group prayers were likely to be answered and that they helped the people praying, as well as the object of prayer.
3. Most felt that the use of prayer during difficult times such as turning things over to God was not at all a passive response; it is an active surrender of the outcome and a move to differentiate what cannot be changed. This allows you to focus energy on what can be changed and disengage from the rest.

13.5 Meditation: Eastern Perspectives

While psychologists have largely avoided the serious study of Christian prayer, meditation has been an important focus of investigation. It is difficult to define meditation, as different religious traditions use the term in different ways. As we have seen, the Christian tradition often uses the term to refer to quiet reflection and thinking (Driskill, 1989). Eastern traditions do not always use the word **meditation**, but when they do, it typically refers to a practice designed to develop voluntary control over concentration and awareness (Hollenback, 1996, p. 94; Walsh & Shapiro, 2006). The Christian concept of contemplation is probably closer to the Eastern idea of meditation as both offer access to a kind of transitional space, although there are important differences as well (Pennington, 2001, p. 20; Finn, 1992; Driskill, 1989). Research by psychologists has largely ignored Christian equivalents of meditation, and so psychological definitions are usually based on Eastern practices.

Meditation has become increasingly common in Western settings, with an estimated 10 million practitioners currently in the US (Walsh & Shapiro, 2006). It is common to divide meditations into two types, **concentrative** where there is a focus on an object such as a mantra or image, and passive, receptive, or **mindfulness** types of meditation where one simply tries to be aware of the present moment. They can be distinguished according to whether the meditator is trying to observe or modify their cognitive processes. In general, meditations related to yoga are more concentrative in focus, while most kinds of Buddhist meditation emphasize mindfulness (Murata et al., 2004; Shapiro, 1982; Engler, 2003; Waelde, 2003; Newberg & Iversen, 2003; Laughlin, McManus, d'Aquili, 1993, p. 147).

13.5.1 Classical Buddhist Meditation

Psychologists have been particularly interested in approaches to meditation based on classical **Theravada** Buddhist practices. These are found in the *Tripitaka* compilation of early Buddhist teachings, as well as the *Visuddhimagga* (Buddhaghosa, 1999) and other commentaries (e.g., Anuruddha, 2000). Classical Buddhist practice is built upon a sophisticated psychology that sees the origin of suffering in two interconnected problems: (1) cravings for material objects or conditions that lead to clinging and attachment, and (2) ignorance. In their view, undeveloped consciousness is sensual, rootless and unstable, or controlled by defilements or **klesas**, things like greed, hate, and delusion that tie people to suffering. Freedom from suffering requires purification from these cravings and removal of ignorance.

The first type of purification undertaken involves lifestyle, virtue, and character development. As in Christianity, Buddhists believe that some actions and wrong behavior (such as materialism) increase suffering, while an ethical transformation and the development of virtue are prerequisites for spiritual development and higher levels of meditation (Brown, 1986; Hayes, 2003; Putuwar, 1991; Marek, 1988). Development of virtue does not happen automatically through meditative or mystical experience (Butler, 2003, p. xlv). Rather it involves establishing a number of habits and patterns of conduct through (1) restraint from immoral acts like killing; (2) proper verbal and bodily conduct, including loving-kindness toward all living things; (3) "purification of livelihood" by avoiding certain kinds of occupations; and (4) avoiding exposure to sights and sounds that distract the mind and foster cravings. The *Visuddhimagga* counsels a middle path that avoids severe asceticism and encourages moderate practices such as simplicity in food or clothing and willingness to live a more solitary life.

The eventual goal of early Buddhist practice is to produce the purification necessary for the development of insight or **vipassana**. There are two approaches to vipassana. In **calm meditation** (*samathayana*), concentration is developed though a meditation and purification process that provides a basis for insight. In **pure insight meditation** (*suddhavipassanaayana*), the meditator contemplates the ever-changing flow of their own mental experience. The Buddha himself used the first approach, but contemporary Buddhism tends to favor the second as more uniquely Buddhist in contrast to concentrative techniques similar to yoga. However, both are part of the Buddhist tradition (King, 1980, pp. 15–48).

13.5.1.1 Calm Meditation

Calm meditation involves a set of concentrative techniques that lead to states of absorption or **samadhi**, which involves unified or one-pointed concentration (**ekagata**) on an object. This helps to eliminate distractions, calm the mind, and help the meditator reach a state of equanimity or detachment from feelings that provides a basis for insight. Classical Buddhist calm or concentrative meditation begins with sitting in the lotus position in a quiet place while focusing on breathing and contemplating things like our mental life, and the impermanence of all things. Working under an experienced teacher, persons are also given a meditation subject that matches their temperament and problems. Those of more speculative mind should avoid thoughts and focus on the body and breathing (King, 1980, p. 72), while those fighting anger could be helped by contemplation of peaceful topics or meditations on **kasinas**, things like a clay disk or colors that can serve as objects for visualization.

As the meditator becomes more advanced in absorption concentration they experience a series of **jhanas** or modes of consciousness that help overcome hindrances to practice such as sensual desire, ill will, sloth, and restlessness. The *Visuddhimagga* uses a four-stage model. The first two stages involve the acquisition and eventual surpassing of applied thought (which directs the mind to objects) and sustained thought (which keeps thought in place). The latter stages involve the development of mindfulness, detachment, positive emotional states, and supernatural powers such as acute sensory abilities or recollection of past lives. In each jhana, the achievements of previous stages are rejected as inadequate, and a new level of development is reached allowing us to experience reality beyond our normal perception (King, 1980, p. 41).

13.5.1.2 Mindfulness Meditation

An important concept in Buddhist psychology is **mindfulness** (*sati*). Mindfulness actually refers to a number of related concepts (Flood, 2004, p. 138). First, like concentration, mindfulness is an important mental ability. It involves full awareness and attentiveness to the present and assists the spiritual seeker in many ways (Newman, 1996). Second, mindfulness refers to a steady guarding of the mind that provides a foundation for moral development. At the level of virtue, mindful awareness helps persons exercise mental restraint so that they do not attend to things that may become objects of craving, freeing them to develop the concentration and other kinds of skills necessary for advanced meditation. Third, mindfulness is a technique of meditation in which the individuals "enters directly into the mindful contemplation of the changing mental and material processes in his own experience" (Anuruddha, 2000, p. 348). It produces a mental state that stands between total concentration, on the one hand, and daydreaming, on the other. Mindfulness is accompanied by increasing control over attention and balance of mental and emotional factors, and can lead to important insights about the nature of reality. Some research suggests that these classical descriptions of meditation fit well with the experiences of modern meditators who undertake mindfulness meditation (Brown & Engler, 1986b).

Newman (1996) has suggested that there are similarities between mindfulness and the practice of the Ignatian Exercises. In both practices, there is a direction of attention to emotion and thought. They also agree in the belief that emotions have a cognitive component and thus can become disordered or mistaken and become the basis of cravings or attachments. Both attempt to transform these disordered emotions through insight or discernment, working to break habit patterns. However, there are also differences. The Exercises are more concentration and content oriented. Rather than *reducing* affect and desire, they are about *directing* it toward God.

While psychologists and many Buddhists (especially Western ones) make a firm distinction between concentrative and mindfulness meditation techniques, and associate Buddhism with the latter, in fact the distinction is not so clear. Early Buddhist meditation systems are in fact a combination of parts of concentrative yoga practice and metaphysics with Buddhist innovations (King, 1980). Mindfulness requires the ability to exercise some control over attention and the will, and concentration requires the application of mindfulness. Characterizing Buddhist meditation as "mindful" and not "concentrative" is especially questionable with regard to Tibetan Buddhism, which employs many tantric techniques with a concentrative focus (Newman, 1996, p. 35; Dasgupta, 1974).

13.5.1.3 Development of Insight (Vipassana)

At the end of calming meditation, one enters the level of **supramundane consciousness** and the paths of liberation. Consciousness at this level is developed through applications of mindfulness and other techniques that promote insight or **vipassana,** which helps eliminate attachments and develops the faculty of wisdom "knowing things as they really are" (Anuruddha, 2000, p. 90). In this type of meditation, one attends to the changeability of mind, matter, and body, leading to an intuitive perception of reality as impermanent and the self as nonexistent. Its effect is to develop balance and break up aggregates of clinging and eliminate defilements or attachments, while hopefully avoiding attachment to the experiences of tranquility or unity that can result. While these insights are often reached after passing through the various jhanas, some are able to bypass these stages and reach them through *sukkavipassaka* or **bare insight**, although their mental and emotional experience of insight will be different.

In Buddhist psychology and metaphysics, a key idea is that what we perceive to be the self or enduring center of our being is "empty" and does not exist, for there is no "knower" or "experiencer" behind our consciousness. This idea is based in part on the Buddhist **doctrine of dependent origin**. In this view, reality consists not of some Kantian **noumena** but is a matrix of multiple dependent origins and causal chains; it is a **conditioned reality** (see Sections 2.2.3 and 3.2.3). All conscious states (*cittas*) and mental factors are part of this conditioned reality. As we examine our thoughts and actions, we can see their contextual nature, how they come and go, lacking permanence, and how cravings or compulsions for things lead to unhappiness (Newman, 1996). If a person were able to achieve complete detachment and leave behind the entanglements of craving they would be in an immaterial and uncondi-tioned realm arrived at through knowledge. In Buddhist thought, this unconditioned realm is **nirvana** and is the ultimate goal of human striving (see Section 3.2.1).

Insight, mindfulness, and concentration are distinct concepts in Buddhism, but they are also related. Insight depends upon basic concentration skills (Newman, 1996, p. 27), but it is different from concentrative meditation in that it aims more at detachment from the world rather than power over it. Insight also depends upon mindfulness, but it is distinct because mindfulness is a process that operates at many levels and is important in several types of Buddhist spiritual practices (King, 1980, p. 33). This has resulted in some confusion in the psychological literature that tends to either equate or separate the three concepts and stress some over others when all are vital skills (Conze, 1956, p. 19).

Insight and mindfulness approaches are of current interest to counselors and psychologists involved in mental health work (see Section 11.4.2) but there are often significant differences between these applications and real meditation as it is practiced in Buddhism. Vipassana in particular is different as it points beyond our normal reality, rather than attempting to help the person adjust to life within it. The intensity of training makes it unsuitable for everyone, especially those with serious health or psychiatric problems. It is designed to be used in conjunction with a spiri-tual guide or friend, not a professional fee-for-service healer (Fleischman, 2000). It is part of a set of spiritual practices that encompasses lifestyle changes and ethical commitments, not a stand alone technology that will automatically solve problems. It is also designed to function in a different cultural context, so its use in Western contexts may lead to unexpected difficulties and problems (Engler, 2003).

13.5.2 Zen Buddhist Meditation

Zen stands within the **Mahayana** tradition of Buddhism, which emphasizes the ability of all persons to reach enlightenment. The practice of true Zen does not involve intellectual understanding or even any particular kind of activity; it is not doing anything, just the process of experiencing fully (MacInnes, 2003, p. 67). In the Zen view, our normal state of consciousness does not involve full authentic experience; rather it is automatic, and we often view the world as something to be controlled or manipulated, setting up a separation between ourselves and the world. In Zen, we try to break this egocentric control so that we can begin to think beyond ourselves and see reality as it truly is rather than as we want it or think we need it to be (Sekida, 1975).

Zen offers a set of techniques designed to help achieve full experience, with dif-ferent schools in Zen placing particular importance on certain practices. Common techniques would include the three pillars of Zen: the **dokusan** or private meeting with a master teacher or **roshi**, the practice of sitting meditation or **zazen**, and the **teisho**, a master's commentary or lecture often from a **koan** or teaching story

(Kapleau, 1988). Those living outside of monasteries can participate in a **sesshin** or a week-long retreat of zazen and other activities that supplements and reinforces daily meditation practice (Dumoulin, 1979, pp. 128–129). All schools of Zen do similar early training in posture and how to focus on breath to concentrate (Foulk, 1988), but they also diverge. In the majority Soto school founded by Dogen, the individual is considered to be already enlightened, and Zen practice simply helps one realize what is already present in a slow gradual process following the pattern of the *Ten Oxherding Pictures* (see Section 7.2.2). The primary method emphasized in Soto is **shikantaza** or just-sitting meditation (Foulk, 1988; Dubs, 1987), while the Rinzai school founded by Hakuin Ekaku emphasizes koan practice as part of sitting meditation (see Section 4.6.1).

13.5.2.1 Roshi: The Zen Teacher

Like many religious and spiritual traditions, Zen believes that instruction from an experienced teacher is vital to the process of spiritual advancement. Although the roshi is not considered an especially holy or powerful figure as is the case with teachers in some Hindu guru traditions (see Section 14.1.2), the relationship between Zen master and student is a close one. The roshi questions a beginning student to determine their level of understanding and realization and then gives assignments such as meditation subjects, as well as instructions related to details of practice. Advanced students are tested through questions or confrontations that try to make them demonstrate or experience a more advanced level of understanding (Kapleau, 1988). Hakuin thought that the student needed to bring three essentials to these meetings and their practice: trust in their teacher and tradition, awareness of their lack of insight (the "great ball of doubt"), and courage to continue practice despite obstacles (Soko, 1988).

13.5.2.2 Zazen and Sitting Meditation

In all forms of Zen, a key element of practice is **zazen** or sitting meditation that allows attainment of a state of absorption or **samadhi** (Sekida, 1975, p. 29). The practice has some similarities to yoga in its physical aspects of sitting, breathing and posture, and the central role of the guru-roshi or teacher. However, the idea behind zazen practice is different, as it is not a technique to bring about a particular state of consciousness but a way of preparing the mind to experience what is already present, our "Buddha nature" (Dumoulin, 1979, pp. 20, 94–95).

Some types of samadhi occur naturally, as in flow experiences (see Section 4.1.1) when our attention becomes sharply focused on an activity to the exclusion of other things. However, Zen aims at a samadhi that involves an inward absorption or one-pointed consciousness, when the activity of the mind is stopped and automatic or reflecting thoughts disappear in an experience of oneness and altered time sense (Flood, 2004, p. 75; Chihara, 1989). This latter type of samadhi clears the mind of its normal patterns of attachment and is especially important in Soto meditation. When coming out of samadhi the mind is clear, and the meditator may have a sudden intense, uncluttered experience of pure existence, recognition of one's purified mind and true nature. This is called a **kensho** experience, which has similarities to other types of unitive experiences (see Section 4.1.1). Over time, the kensho experience can become a more permanent state leading to **satori** or enlightenment (Sekida, 1975).

In basic zazen or *shikantaza*, clothing and environment should be comfortable and the meditation place should be quiet. The meditator then sits cross-legged on a cushion in a lotus position with erect posture, eyes open, and mouth closed; respiration is regulated through counting breaths. Early Zen figures like Bodhidharma practiced zazen while facing a wall; in modern practice people often gather in a **zendo** or meditation hall. Implicit in this practice is the idea that mental states—even basic ones like concentration—must involve the body through posture and breathing, which help generate meditative power (Sekida, 1975). Once breathing is regulated, the meditator does not attempt to concentrate but simply tries to be aware of thoughts and allow them to vanish, to "think not-thinking" (Dogen, 1985, p. 30; 1996, pp. 70–72). A key goal is to eliminate ideas of grasping, including grasping after experiences or enlightenment, or even benefits for others. Dogen considered the development of Zen practice to be a long process, "the great matter of a lifetime" (Dogen, 1985, pp. 34–36; Bielefeldt, 1988).

13.5.2.3 Koan Practice: The Teaching Story

Zen practitioners also utilize the **koan**—a teaching story or puzzle—to generate doubt and break up our typical, automatic ways of thought. Hakuin used three kinds of koans: *hosshim* which focus on universal oneness (e.g., the "mu" koan), *kikan* which look at paradoxes such as the fact that things are both one and many, and *gonshen* which look for limits and weaknesses in language (Shimano, 1988). Koans are not used for speculation or debate, as they pose problems that are not resolvable by Aristotelian rationality. Instead they are used as catalysts; the goal is to experience the koan and its solution (MacInnes, 2003). As one repeats the koan over and over slowly and carefully, it "infiltrates" the brain and interrupts habitual patterns of thought. Suddenly there may be a moment when the passage acquires a tremendous meaning, and we can have a kensho experience of original nature or self, pure existence, or consciousness (Sheng-Yen, 1988; Sekida, 1975, pp. 99–100). Although Dogen accepted koan practice, he preferred other methods (Dumoulin, 1979, pp. 94–95; Bielefeldt, 1988, p. 185), while in the Rinzai school they are emphasized as a tool leading to sudden enlightenment and conversion.

13.5.2.4 Comparison with Contemplation

Christian and Zen authors (e.g., Johnson, 1997) have remarked on a number of points of contact between Christian and Zen meditation and their divergence from what Abe (1985) calls the *anti-religions* like **scientism, nihilism,** and some forms of **humanistic philosophy**. Merton certainly believed that contemplative-like experiences occurred outside of Christianity, especially in Zen, but was undecided about whether states like satori were really identical with Christian ones. Some points of contact are:

- Descriptions of seemingly similar experiences that include disruption of subject-object dualities
- The idea that one must look beyond appearance to a reality that is beyond concepts and that interfering illusions and attachments must be left behind
- That essential knowledge about reality can only be gained through experience and the development of relationships (MacInnes, 2003, pp. 32, 50–51).

However, Christianity and Zen Buddhism also have differences (Abe, 1985; Dumoulin, 1979, p. 11; MacInnes, 2003, p. 118; Flood, 2004, p. 125). Christianity in general has a stronger emphasis on transcendence, ethics, and relationality. Altered states of consciousness are a by-product rather than a goal of meditation (Moltmann, 1980, p. 62; Savage, 2001). In addition:

- Buddhism stresses the eradication of desire and volition, while Christianity is more about the transformation of desire and fulfillment of meaning, although the two are closer in practice than in theory (Shannon, 2000, pp. 216–226)
- Christians believe that there is an enduring true self under the false one and that pursuit of the true self leads toward God; Merton (2003a, pp. 8–11) believed that satori was a natural experience of the true self (von Balthasar, 1986, pp. 54–55)
- In Eastern thought, it is the method that produces the effect, and so adherence to a particular method is important, while in Christianity it is God at work within us and details of technique are less essential (Pennington, 1998, p. xii; 2001, p. 67).

13.5.2.5 Critique

Zen practice provides some powerful techniques for attacking what Christian contemplatives call the false self. However, like any human tradition there are potential problems that have been raised by critics. These include the following:

1. *Maintenance of practice.* In Western contexts, meditation practice is often plagued by high dropout rates, especially in early stages and among younger subjects. Feeling emotionally overwhelmed by the experience, a lifestyle that did not allow sufficient time or energy, or just a sense of no need are common reasons for dropout (Dubs, 1987).
2. *Problems with community support.* Zen communities boomed during the late 1960s and early 1970s, but in the years following had many of the problems that sometimes plague Christian communities, like internal divisions, leadership struggles, and unethical sexual or financial conduct on the part of leadership (Kraft, 1988; Collcutt, 1988).

3. *Appropriateness of integration with psychological techniques.* Some writers have argued that Zen techniques are similar or complementary to those used in psychotherapy. For instance, Magid (2003) argues that shikantaza is like psychoanalysis in its ability to work though emotional issues. However, some Zen experts argue that while Zen techniques may offer positive benefits as part of psychotherapy, it is no longer true Zen as the uprooting from Buddhist foundations makes fundamental changes in emphasis that are alien to it (Dumoulin, 1979, pp. 8–11).
4. *Unrepresentative focus.* The focus on Zen and mindfulness meditation is not representative of Buddhism as generally practiced in China and other parts of Asia. Other Buddhist groups like the Pure Land Buddhism of Shinran think that practice is not enough; we must rely on the power of a vow to the Buddha and eventual rebirth in a Pure land (Abe, 1992a). In Shin Buddhism, the Nembutu prayer to the Amida Buddha is thought to have a special power when repeated constantly like the Jesus prayer in Orthodox practice (Suzuki, 2002).
5. *Potential negative effects.* Meditation experiences can have powerful physical and emotional aspects that may be threatening, if they have no explanatory framework and can be mistaken for a psychotic episode (Clarke, 2001b).

13.5.3 Transcendental Meditation

Transcendental Meditation (TM) was developed by Maharishi Mahesh Yogi and brought to the West in the 1950s. Based on the Hindu tradition, TM is supposedly neither a contemplative nor concentrative exercise but a developmental technology, and advocates claim that it requires no change in lifestyle or belief system. It simply involves an effortless 15–20 minute practice of meditation during the day with eyes closed while reciting a sound or mantra. This procedure acts to accelerate the development of consciousness (Orme-Johnson, Zimmerman, & Hawkins, 1997; Alexander, Druker, & Langer, 1990). The training occurs in groups, but each individual also meets with a teacher and receives a mantra that is especially suited to him or her. It is believed that the sound of the mantra has vibratory effects in the nervous system that are beneficial. The regular TM training can be followed by the TM-Sidhi program, which focuses on application of the pure consciousness state in daily life and may include more overt religious activities such as recitation of sutras and development of paranormal abilities. TM can also be combined with the purification and herbal medicine techniques of ayurveda to help prevent disease and promote health (Sharma & Clark, 1998, pp. 7–20, 142–146; Schneider et al., 2002; Sands, 1994; see Section 10.3.2).

TM is based upon a seven-stage model of consciousness and organization drawn from the Hindu Vedic tradition (Dillbeck & Alexander, 1989). The first three stages are everyday temporary ones: waking, dreaming, and dreamless sleep. Above these ordinary stages are higher levels of transcendental or purse consciousness, which allow contact with the true Self and are the immediate goal of TM practice. These stages are marked by an enduring state of pure consciousness during daily activities, refinement of personality or emotional qualities, and increasing unity between subject and object. In their view, the ultimate purpose of life is to participate in this evolution of consciousness (Nidich, Nidich, & Alexander, 2000; Orme-Johnson, 1988). The Maharishi's descriptions of transcendental consciousness are similar to the pure unity consciousness of Stace: an unbounded consciousness or awareness with no content, absence of time or body sense and peaceful feelings (see Section 4.3.4). He claims this can be developed within a couple of months with TM practice and is related to a variety of positive effects (Gelderloos & Beto, 1989; Travis & Pearson, 2000). This relaxed, blissful, and wakeful state also is congruent with the goals of some types of Buddhist and Hindu meditation (Jevning, Wallace, & Beidebach, 1992).

Early research on TM (e.g., Wallace & Benson, 1972) found that TM produced many physiological changes, including decreased EEG frequency, oxygen consumption, heart rate, blood pressure, and increased skin resistance. Subsequent articles (e.g., Jevning et al., 1992; Walton et al., 2002) have reported a variety of physiological benefits including the following:

1. Changes in brain wave activity including increased intensity/amplitude of slow alpha, bursts of high voltage theta, and higher EEG coherence/synchrony in frontal areas, most frequently in regular practitioners; along with this, increased blood flow in frontal areas suggesting alertness (Orme-Johnson et al., 1997; Travis & Wallace 1999; Hebert & Tan, 2004; Alexander, Cranson, Boyer, & Orme-Johnson, 1986; Jevning, Anand, Biedebach, & Fernando, 1996; Travis, Olson, Egenes, & Gupta, 2001; Travis, Tecce, Arenander, & Wallace, 2002).
2. Physiological changes similar to a relaxed state of decreased autonomic activity and metabolism such as decreased blood pressure and oxygen consumption. In addition, possible changes in body chemistry include reduction in cholesterol and lipid levels or lowered adrenocortical activity, suggesting decreased levels of stress.

Other benefits proposed by TM advocates include the following:

1. Increased coherence in surrounding consciousness, affecting crime rates and other social phenomenon; this is referred to as the *Maharishi effect* (Orme-Johnson et al., 1997; Orme-Johnson 1994).
2. Increased self-actualization, positive emotions, cognitive performance, and psychological health, in part through reduction of anxiety, depression, anger, impulsivity, aggressiveness, and substance abuse (Alexander, Rainforth, & Gelderloos, 1991; Cranson et al., 1991; Alexander, Robinson, & Rainforth, 1994; Gelderloos, Hermans, Ahlscrom, & Jacoby, 2001; Israel & Beiman, 1977; Eppley, Abrams, & Shear, 1989).

The TM literature has provoked an intense debate. A number of criticisms of TM research have been advanced (Parks, 2004) including:

• Problems with research design, including extensive use of correlational studies
• Unrepresentative samples or control groups

- Questionable measurement reliability and validity
- Use of unusual or obsolete statistical techniques
- Most research is published in non-refereed journals and is done by researchers who are ardent TM practitioners with financial connections to TM organizations.

In the early 1990s, TM research was a target of investigations by the National Research Council, a US group that studies research accused of being "pseudoscientific." They issued reports arguing that TM is a religion not a technology and that research on it is flawed. Other researchers suggested that TM is really no different than any other kind of relaxation procedure in its effects or even inferior (Travis, Kondo, & Knott, 1976; Cauthen & Prymak, 1977; Israel & Beiman, 1977; Puente & Beiman, 1980: Zuroff & Schwarz, 1980; Carlson, Bacaseta, & Simanton, 1988; Jevning et al., 1992), or that it could even lead to problems such as depersonalization or anxiety (Castillo, 1990). TM researchers responded to these findings with a flurry of studies and meta-analyses demonstrating that TM was better than resting on some physiological variables like plasma lactate (Dillbeck & Orme-Johnson, 1987), and that it was better than relaxation procedures on other biological measures like respiration or blood pressure. It also appeared to be superior on some psychological variables like anxiety and self-actualization, as well as some health outcome measures of risk factors, morbidity, and mortality (Alexander et al., 1994). However, the ideological and financial ties of most TM researchers with the TM community have made it difficult for other investigators to accept these findings (Parks, 2004).

13.6   Meditation: Psychophysiological Perspectives

While some research on meditation has focused on psychological variables, most studies have focused on its medical uses and its physiological effects (Shapiro & Walsh, 2003). Interest in the topic was first prompted by the studies like those of Bagchi and Wenger (1957, 1958) on yoga. These initial field studies were often done in remote areas of India with portable recording equipment and yielded significant but conflicting results, suggesting that meditation produced important changes in brain wave and autonomic activity. Some results were startling, as in the experiment conducted at the Menninger clinic with the Hindu yogi Swami Rama who was able to voluntarily stop and start his heartbeat (Green & Green, 1977; Taylor, 1999, p. 276). Later studies (e.g., Anand, Chhina, & Singh, 1961a, 1961b; Elson, Hauri, & Cunis, 1977) differed as to the significance and direction of changes in measures such as heart rate and skin resistance. Decreases in oxygen consumption caused speculation that some of the effects of meditation were produced by an anoxic state (Woolfolk, 1975; Watanabe, Shapiro, & Schwartz, 1972). Some research looked at shifts in the frequency spectrum of brain waves measured by an **electroencephalogram** (**EEG**), with meditators displaying fewer **beta waves** (13–29 cps) and more **theta waves** (4–7 cps) or **alpha waves** (8–12 cps). However, these patterns were also not always consistent.

Zen meditation techniques are more uniform than those of Hinduism, and research studies into the effects of zazen have produced more consistent results (Woolfolk, 1975). Early studies showed a slowing in brain wave frequency and in other physiological functions such as respiration and heart rate (Kasamatsu & Hirai, 1969; Goyeche, Chihara, & Shimizu, 1972). Studies of Zen masters (e.g., Hirai, Izawa, & Koga, 1959) found large amplitude theta waves, as well as alpha patterns typical of relaxation. In general, the research on Zen meditation indicates that zazen brings about a physiological slowing in the meditator similar to some of the effects observed in yoga. Theta wave activity in this context is thought to reflect internalized attention and mindfulness (Jevning et al., 1992; Takahashi et al., 2005; Fromm, 1992).

13.6.1 Relaxation or More?

Early researchers such as Herbert Benson (e.g., Kutz, Borysenko, & Benson, 1985) argued that meditation is simply an effective technology that can and should be separated from its religious content and placed in the ideological surround of psychotherapy and the medical model. In this way, religious practices could be used to construct and maintain a secular self and intensify the therapy process (Charry, 2001). They were particularly interested in Buddhist methods, which they viewed as more ideologically neutral. Benson argued that various meditation techniques all produced a relaxation response, and a number of studies have supported this, although other types of relaxation techniques and prayer also produce this effect (Shapiro, 1982; cf. Worthington, Kurusu, McCullough, & Sandage, 1996; Collings, 1989; Francis & Evans, 2001a, 2001b). More recent studies have suggested that meditation has both an initial relaxation effect and a later excitation effect, with greater alertness found in more advanced meditators (Laughlin et al., 1993, p. 147). The idea that meditation could be a technology for altering physiology has led to studies that have connected it with a wide range of physical and mental health benefits (Monk-Turner, 2003; see Section 11.4.2). However, critics contend that evidence for the therapeutic effectiveness of meditation is weak and confined to problems that are clearly stress related (Canter, 2003). It is also true that some of the health benefits claimed for meditation can come from relaxation practice as well (e.g., Leserman, Stuart, Mamish, & Benson, 1989).

Experts from religious traditions, as well as some psychological researchers have objected to the reductionist view that meditation is a technology that just produces relaxation, or that all types of meditation produce the same effects. They argue that such a view obscures the richness of underlying religious psychologies and does not account for the data. It also lifts the techniques out of their ethical and cultural context, with potentially negative effects (Walsh & Shapiro, 2006; Andresen, 2000; Engler, 1986). At the least, studies suggest that different kinds of meditation produce specific changes in addition to some type of general relaxation effect (Davidson, Goleman, & Schwartz, 1976). For instance, researchers have found that concentrative and mindfulness meditations produce different physiological changes that go beyond simple relaxation (Dubs, 1987). Cahn and Polich (2006) found that open mediation (e.g., vipassana) vs. concentrative meditation (e.g., kundalini yoga) both altered functioning in the dorsal cingulate gyrus but activated different cortical areas such as posterior structures during imagery, prefrontal areas during effortful focus, and the dorsolateral cortex when focusing on the self or internal process and during psalmody. Religious practices that require less attentional control such as *glossolalia*, or speaking in tongues, have been associated with decreased frontal activity, while experienced Zen meditators have increases (Newberg, Wintering, Morgan, & Waldman, 2006; Ritskes, Ritskes-Hoitinga, Stodkilde-Jorgensen, Baerentsen, & Hartman, 2003). These and other studies suggest that relaxation is a relatively minor factor in terms of distinguishing between techniques, and that modes of engagement or disengagement and awareness were more important (e.g., Smith, Amutio, Anderson, & Aria, 1996). The relative importance of relaxation vs. other kinds of effects might also be related to individual differences. For instance, in a study with inexperienced Zen meditators, Murata et al. (2004) found that those with lower trait anxiety more readily induced meditation with a predominance of internalized attention, while individuals with higher trait anxiety more readily had states with a relaxation focus. This is not surprising, for relaxation procedures that employ both psychological and physical means of relaxation have different effects, including greater relaxation and positive psychological effects like mental quiet (Ghoncheh & Smith, 2004). It also suggests that control over anxiety facilitates more advanced states of attention.

In religious traditions with a devotional element such as Christianity, parts of Hinduism, or Pure Land Buddhism, meditation has a relational component and is usually viewed as more than a way of seeking personal enlightenment or fulfillment. Kulik and Szewczyk (2002) found that a relational orientation does not result in a more positive evaluation of the practice or a better ability to provide a sense of meaning, but they did find that relational practitioners had more positive views toward sickness or suffering and less need to escape from a difficult situation. A large Australian study using the Eysenck Personality Questionnaire, (Kaldor, Francis, & Fisher, 2002) found that prayer was associated with lower **psychoticism** scores, and Eastern meditation with higher scores. This suggests that nonrelational meditation is more often associated with a cold, impersonal, unsympathetic, and distrusting outlook, while prayer is associated with warmth, empathy, and altruism.

As research has challenged overly simplistic views of meditation, researchers have begun studying a larger variety of types of meditation, including mindfulness, vipassana and Vajrayana Buddhist techniques (Andresen, 2000). Mindfulness meditation is clearly more than simple relaxation. For instance, in a study of short-term and long-term retreat participants, Kornfield (1979) found that 80% of meditators reported unusual experiences including somatic sensations like energy flow or pain, visual or auditory intensification or hallucination, strong mental emotions like anger fear or depression, and changes in time awareness or out of body experiences. Sometimes these effects can become detrimental. Several authors (e.g., Sethi & Bhargava, 2003; Yorston, 2001) have documented cases of psychosis or manic episodes triggered by yoga, Zen, and other standard meditation techniques. These appear to be related to two kinds of situations. First are cases of vulnerable individuals who do not have sufficient ego strength to engage in meditation. The odds of problems in these individuals seem to increase, if the meditation is accompanied by ascetic techniques like sleep deprivation or fasting. Second are situations where advanced levels of development and practice lead to psychiatric complications such as changes in mood or reality testing abilities. These are a reaction to the intense experiences that can come with deeper meditation practice (Epstein & Lieff, 1986). These kinds of problems are one reason that religious traditions emphasize the need for a guide or teacher who can evaluate whether or not a practice is having unwanted effects. It has led some to argue that meditation should not be undertaken by individuals with serious psychological problems who are looking for a curative technique. In this view, meditation is more appropriate for those with a solid psychological foundation, who want to move on to higher stages of development (Helminiak, 1981; Wilber, 1986c).

13.6.2 Modern Neuroimaging and Neurophysiology Studies

Advancing technology has enhanced our ability to study brain activity during meditative states. Research suggests that meditators typically pass through different stages of meditation that are associated with various physiological effects and relative amounts of various brain wave frequency patterns. Gellhorn and Kiely (1972) note that in early stages, meditators show trophotropic relaxation, with alpha waves of increasing amplitude (Andresen, 2000; Cahn & Polich, 2006). Later stages are quite different and include the appearance of large amplitude theta waves in midline frontal areas as meditation deepens. This is particularly characteristic of yoga meditation but is also found in Zen and TM. Thus, meditation may produce two different effects—relaxation and shift of consciousness—with two entirely different sets of physiological changes (Walsh, Goleman, Kornfield, Pensa, & Shapiro, 1978).

The role of theta activity is poorly understood, but may be related to the move from relaxation to states of focused attention and absorption with accompanying changes in consciousness (Laughlin et al., 1993; Don, 1977–1978). During meditation, theta activity begins in bursts and then develops into rhythmic patterns that become synchronized between anterior and posterior parts of the brain. They are particularly dominant in anterior regions of the brain, while alpha is more concentrated in posterior areas (Andresen, 2000). This theta coherence is especially found in more experienced meditators and those doing mindfulness rather than concentrative meditation, although the presence of coherence in mindfulness states has been challenged (Cahn & Polich, 2006; Travis & Arenander, 2004). This theta activity may be generated in limbic structures linked to memory functions and emotional processing, as well as increased anterior cingulate and dorsolateral prefrontal cortical activity, as many meditation procedures like yoga produce changes in the functioning of subcortical structures (Lou et al., 1999; Kakigi et al., 2005; Kjaer et al., 2002). In yoga, this is accompanied by a major initial increase in prefrontal blood flow early in meditation with later decreases (Austin, 2006, pp. 216–218).

In experienced yoga meditators, theta power has a moderate positive correlation with positive emotional experience and a negative correlation with mental activity. Austin (2006, pp. 166–167) argues that changes in frontal lobe activity account for a number of aspects of the kensho experience in Zen, such as the pleasurable feelings and losses of sense of self and distinctions, reduction in directive activity, and loss of time sense. Coherence between prefrontal and posterior cortex may be connected with intensification of information processing, increases in positive, blissful experience, and decreases in negative emotion (Aftanas & Golosheykin, 2003, 2005).

Recent research has started to explore changes in the high frequency **gamma wave** spectrum (30–70 cps). In a study with long term Tibetan Buddhist meditators, Lutz, Greischar, Rawlings, Ricard, and Davidson (2004) found that experienced meditators had higher initial gamma amplitude in the medial frontal area and stronger increases in gamma patterns and power while meditating. The experienced meditators also showed increases in long-distance gamma synchrony between the frontal and parietal lobes (cf. Davidson, 2005). While not well understood, it is thought that this gamma synchronization may be related to the binding of diverse brain locations into neural networks (Austin, 2006, p. 46). Increased gamma power in the superior frontal gyrus may be related to the sense of dissolution of self, while posterior gamma changes are found in meditations of a more visual nature (Cahn & Polich, 2006). Increased anterior-posterior coherence in other frequencies has also been found in TM and yoga meditators, perhaps related to the activity of multifunctional networks, more efficient cortical functioning, greater attentional control, and deeper mental silence in the meditative state (Aftanas & Golosheykin, 2003, 2005; Travis, Arenander, & DuBois, 2004; Harrison, Manocha, & Rubia, 2004).

Although there is relatively little research involving visualization meditations in either the Eastern (e.g., Tibetan) or Western (e.g., Ignatian) traditions, it is apparent that during visualizing or verbalizing meditations, the corresponding visual premotor and language areas of the brain are active (Laughlin et al., 1993; Austin, 2006, p. 208; Lou et al., 1999). Interestingly, psalmody not only produces changes in dorsolateral prefrontal and dorsomedial frontal activity but also in parietal zones connected to visual memory (Azari et al., 2001).

13.6.3 Critique

Even after many years of research, most studies on the neural mechanisms of meditation provide more speculations than established findings. Literature reviews constantly report that more studies are needed to make sense of the often conflicting data. Specific problems in the research include the following:

1. *Failure to adequately specify important variables* such as the exact type of meditation, length of time needed for mastery, qualification and level of practice of teachers or trainers, as well as details about the meditative environment, level of effort and the specific meditative state of the individual (Austin, 1998; Caspi & Burleson, 2005).

2. *Failure to study individual differences* in response to a technique, which are often greater than differences between various approaches to meditation (Herzog et al., 1990; Beauchamp-Turner & Levinson, 1992).
3. *Failure to study long-term effects of meditation*, which are very important (Austin, 2006, p. 224; Smith et al., 1996). Studies find that long-term meditators have stronger physiological responses during their practice and more positive psychological indicators, suggesting there is a cumulative effect to long-term practice (Dubs, 1987; Corby, Roth, Zarcone, & Kopell, 1978; Aftanas & Golosheykin, 2003; Lutz, Brefczynski-Lewis, Johnstone, & Davidson, 2008). Inexperienced meditators may not be performing the meditation adequately, making it unclear what is really being tested when they are used as subjects (Brown & Engler, 1986a). However, studies of long-term meditators suffer from dropout rates of 50% or more, limiting the quality and applicability of findings (Walsh & Shapiro, 2006).
4. *Poor research designs*, vague research questions, and small sample sizes. Experimental and control groups tend to differ on multiple variables, making it difficult to compare studies or isolate effects (Andresen, 2000; Walsh & Shapiro, 2006; Cahn & Polich, 2006; West, 1979; Caspi & Burleson, 2005). Some research takes place under distracting laboratory conditions that are different from where the meditation is normally done. Statistical analyses assume linear relationships when there is evidence that nonlinear relationships hold for both physiological and psychological variables (Aftanas & Golosheykin, 2003; Compton, 1991). It is also not clear to what extent findings can be generalized, as individuals willing to volunteer for meditation studies may not be typical of the general population (cf. Watts & Williams, 1988, p. 87).
5. *Failure to study subjective experience* during meditation, making it impossible to relate this to physiological data (Austin, 2006, pp. 214–215). It also means that different states are equated with each other, even though their subjective experience and worldview are quite different (van der Lans, 1987). More use of qualitative methods would be helpful (Andresen, 2000; Caspi & Burleson, 2005).
6. *Problems with measurement instruments and procedures.* Available techniques such as EEG and even modern imaging instruments provide only a gross measure of brain function (Andresen, 2000), and experienced mediators have questioned the use of forced-choice questions in research instruments that do not allow for adequate descriptions of experience (Compton, 1991). Some have suggested that this is because investigators lack personal experience with the mental states they are studying (Walsh, 1980).

13.7 Conclusion

Key issue: *Individual religious practices are best understood as part of a way of life that unfolds within the context of particular religious communities and traditions.*

Individual practices represent a rich area for the psychology and religion dialogue. Much good work has been done in this area but much remains, particularly with regard to Christian approaches to practice that are relatively unstudied compared to those from Eastern traditions. Another area for conversation will be the relationship between these practices and community life. While prayer and meditation are often thought of as "individual" practices, they have been developed in religious traditions, and religious communities remain the primary means of supporting practices, which can be hard to maintain without this support and motivation (Taylor, 2007, p. 486). The increasing appreciation for the public role of religion that can be seen in both the psychological and theological literature will help open up this important topic.

Another issue that remains to be addressed is how practices work together in a way of life. Practices are a means to an end, not an end in themselves. and they are directed to the whole person, not just a part (Merton, 2005b, pp. 17–19). Sensible writers like Merton argue that balance in religious practices is a key thing and that the particular balance that is appropriate for each person will probably differ because of their individual history and problems. This means that the study of religious practices as mechanical procedures detached from context may miss some important aspects of how they can have a positive or negative role in the life of the individual. Finding this balance in practice may best be done with assistance from an experienced helper—our next topic.

Chapter 14
Helping Relationships: Counseling and Spiritual Growth

The path of religious and spiritual growth is in many ways a positive one filled with exciting possibilities. However, it is neither a smooth path, nor is it something that can easily be done outside of a relational or communal context. Because of this, it is not surprising that most or perhaps all people at some point in their lives seek others for help and support with their spiritual journey. In response to these needs, various religious traditions have developed relational strategies for guidance and help. These helping relationships play a key role, as modern research suggests that there is a strong relationship between involvement of others and success in achieving personal transformation (Baumeister, 1998). In the Christian tradition, this kind of assistance is sometimes referred to as *spiritual direction*, while in some forms of Hinduism and Buddhism the focus is on a relationship with a special teacher or *guru*. Catholic and Protestant Christians have referred to aspects of these helping practices as the *cura animarum* or care of souls and viewed them as providing healing for spiritual problems. This soul care model of helping lies at the basis of two modern practices of helping—*pastoral counseling* and *psychotherapy*. As interest in spirituality and religion has been rising, spiritual directors have seen a substantial increase in requests for their services, and counselors have become more aware of the need to address religious and spiritual issues in the course of their work (Ruffing, 2000; Mursell, 2001b, p. 470; Miller, 1999).

14.1 Religious Approaches to Guidance and Helping

14.1.1 Spiritual Direction

In the Christian tradition, **spiritual direction** is an ancient practice where an experienced spiritual master forms a relationship with a disciple who wants to profit from their knowledge (Hausherr, 1990, pp. 1–2). The Jewish and Christian scriptures contain many stories of people giving and receiving spiritual guidance. The custom became even more important in the early church with the beginnings of the monastic movement. Starting in the 3rd century, individuals began moving into the deserts of Egypt and Syria, seeking solitude and a place to devote themselves to spiritual growth. Some of these men and women—known as the Desert Fathers and Mothers—developed reputations for achieving two special qualities: (1) an exceptional level of holiness, piety, care, and love (e.g., Veilleux, 1980, pp. 28, 331) and (2) a gift of **discernment**, the ability to sense the needs and capabilities of their students and provide the appropriate kind of guidance and encouragement. They become spiritual elders and were sometimes referred to as doctors or healers of spiritual sickness. Some had official church positions while others remained simple spiritual seekers (Ware, 1990; Gould, 1993, pp. 37–41, 77–79). Other Christians began flocking to them, seeking a word of wisdom or the opportunity to live with them and emulate their lives and teachings. Communities quickly formed that clustered around the master for mutual learning and support. Together they sought the goal of **theosis**, becoming like God as much as possible in this life. Members of these communities also reached out to serve as confessors and spiritual guides to others (McNeill, 1951, p. 307).

Two principles from these early practices have persisted through the years and form the basis for most modern varieties of spiritual direction. First, people do not *decide* to be directors, they are *called* to that role by others who recognize some kind of special quality in the person. In this system, relational abilities like spiritual maturity or holiness matter more than educational attainment (Spidlik, 1986, p. 284; cf. Bolshakoff, 1976, p. 179). Second, direction generally assumes a communal context, a set of practices and beliefs that are shared at least in part by the director, directee, and others (Rogers, 2002).

Direction typically involves periodic meetings where the directees discusses their spiritual life and practice with a director. This helps them to learn, avoid deceptions, and maintain progress in their spiritual growth. In situations where the directee lives in close proximity to their director, much learning takes place from simply observing and emulating the life and practices of the master. The relationship thus combines aspects of authority and friendship (Gould, 1993, p. 69; Hadot, 1986b). Topics discussed are wide ranging so that all aspects of life and the self-system may be integrated around the person's spiritual life (Sacks, 1979). Some procedures and practices that are commonly used in the direction process include the following (Gould, 1993, pp. 28–32, 48):

- Listening and careful attention to thoughts, feelings, and events, trying to discern spiritual movements in one's life, especially as these occur in prayer
- Self-examination and confession, with the view of developing humility and promoting moral reform, revision of life, and self-knowledge
- Training in spiritual disciplines, such as prayer and meditation, or ascetic practices such as fasting and obedience, and discussion of how to deal with spiritual problems and temptations that arise; readings in scripture or other spiritual texts are often suggested.

Carrying out these tasks involves work on the part of both the director and the disciple. The director is expected to be personally involved in the life of the disciple, visiting frequently with them, praying for them, and being willing to make sacrifices on their behalf to promote their spiritual advancement (Hausherr, 1990). They should be flexible, adapting the process to the needs and developmental level of the directee. The directee needs to be active in selecting a trustworthy model as director and then submitting to his leadership. They need to be diligent in self-examination and willing to share all aspects of their life with the director so that healing can take place. The sharing of thoughts is considered to be especially important (Gould, 1993, pp. 31–32, 72–75; Spidlik, 1986, pp. 246–247; Harmless, 2004, p. 229). The effectiveness of direction is thought to depend on the gifts of the director, the ability of the disciple to imitate the master, and the quality of the relationship between the two. Especially important was the issue of trust: the ability of the directee to trust, and the ability of the spiritual father to provide a secure, stable, and supportive relationship (Studzinski, 1985, p. 123; Oman & Thoresen, 2003). It is thus a relational, as well as an educational and experiential process. Accounts of this process provided the basis for early works on spiritual development, such as the writings of John Cassian (Driver, 2002, p. 66).

Subsequent to the Desert Fathers, a number of traditions of spiritual direction developed within Christianity (see Table 14.1). Some traditions emphasize the equality of the director and directee as fellow travelers or spiritual friends (Aelred, 1974), while other models focus more on the experience (and perhaps authority) of the director. Different traditions also think about the goal of the religious life—and thus the purpose of spiritual direction—in different ways. Medieval Catholic Christianity saw the goal of the spiritual life as a *beatific vision*—an intimate knowledge and joyful union of the soul with God that also entails the perfection of the individual (Thomas, 1998, I. q. 26, a. 1). Protestantism has used terms more like discipleship, **sanctification,** and holiness to describe the goal and progress of the spiritual life, emphasizing the conforming of one's life to the model of Christ rather than a particular ongoing inner experience. In these groups, the term "spiritual director" is seldom used although the process still occurs (e.g., McMahan, 2002). Orthodoxy emphasizes the moral perfection and deification (*theosis*) of the individual in their relation with God, as in the writings of the *Philokalia* (Nikodimos & Makarios, 1979, 1981, 1984, 1995). Theoretically, different ideas about goals should lead to different types of direction experiences, but in reality it is often difficult to distinguish the actual practice of direction in these different traditions.

After some years of relative neglect, direction has become a vital contemporary practice. In modern language, the aim of the direction relationship is to create a kind of transitional space that promotes spiritual growth (Hardy, 2000). In theistic contexts, this translates into the task of helping the directees grow closer in their relationship with God and become more aware of divine presence through community involvement, grounding in a tradition, and attentiveness to the mysterious and emotional qualities of human experience. Individuals in direction look at the current movement of God in all aspects of their life and look for ways they can open themselves to further growth. In direction, this is done through attentiveness and mutual listening to each other, contemplating God at work in the life of the person (Rice, 2000; Bowen, 2005; Langer, 2005; Guenther, 2000, p. 106; Liebert, 2005).

Table 14.1 Some major traditions of Christian spiritual direction (Byrne, 1990)

Tradition	Founder/Date	Key/Sample texts	Characteristics of Director; typical philosophy, focus, and methods
Desert	Anthony c. 275 AD	*Sayings of the Desert Fathers* (Ward, 1975; Chryssavgis, 2000)	Director as spiritual master Direction as obedience, emulation Focus on spiritual warfare, transcendence, *theosis* Methods: spiritual disciplines, especially prayer
Monastic Benedictine Cistercian Carmelite	Benedict (c. 480–547)	*Rule of St. Benedict* (Benedict, 2001) *Way of Perfection* (Teresa of Avila, 1991)	Director as community leader Direction as seeking Focus on vocation and development; seeking God and the beatific vision Methods: group and individual spiritual practices; communal life
Celtic/ Spiritual Friendship	Various c. 400 AD Aelred (1109–1166)	*Spiritual Friendship* (Aelred, 1974)	Director as fellow seeker, friend Direction as mutual support Focus on relation with others, God Methods: self-disclosure, penance
Ignatian/ Jesuit	Ignatius of Loyola (1491–1556)	*Spiritual Exercises*; (Ignatius, 1978; Houdek, 1996)	Director as guide Direction as glorifying God Focus on discernment, inner freedom Methods: Flexible, uses *Exercises* to promote listening, confession Done often in a retreat setting
Modern	Various c. 1920 on	Various (Guenther, 1992; Leech, 2001; Edwards, 1980; Edwards, 2001)	Director model similar to Celtic Direction as exploration Focus on wholeness Methods: traditional but adapted for the modern situation Use of psychological insights

The opening lines from Aelred's classic work entitled *Spiritual Friendship* convey the hoped-for quality of this interaction:

> Here we are, you and I, and I hope a third, Christ, is in our midst. There is no one now to disturb us; there is no one to break in upon our friendly chat, no man's prattle or noise of any kind will creep into this pleasant solitude. Come now, beloved, open your heart, and pour into these friendly ears whatsoever you will, and let us accept gracefully the boon of this place, time, and leisure (Aelred, 1974, 1.1).

Current spiritual direction practices maintain continuity with the basic tenants of classical direction but draw on selective developments in theology and psychology, especially psychodynamic techniques that help identify hidden aspects of the person that hinder growth. Along with deep experience in the spiritual life and personal qualities like humility, directors are expected to be in ongoing spiritual direction themselves and continue their own growth process (Langer, 2005). Modern direction often follows a model of private meetings between a director and directee on a regular basis, typically once a month. However, group spiritual direction is becoming increasingly popular, especially in retreat or workshop contexts. Other formats are also possible: C.S. Lewis did enormous amounts of spiritual direction through letters, and the Internet opens up other possibilities (Dorsett, 2004, p. 24). Modern direction also tends to be less hierarchical in nature, a development that is especially important when dealing with individuals who have been negatively impacted by power structures. Feminist perspectives on direction are particularly attuned to these issues (Fisher, 1988).

14.1.1.1 Spiritual Direction and Psychotherapy: Parallels and Divergences

Despite the selective appropriation of psychology, the practice of spiritual direction or friendship remains quite distinct from counseling or psychotherapy. While both involve helping relationships marked by mutual trust and intimate disclosure, direction differs in its conceptualization of the nature of the helping relationship, as well as its goals and methods. Counseling is a professionalized, non-egalitarian undertaking, a dyadic relationship between counselor and client. It is seen as a service, and the therapist is a service provider who must meet specific education and training requirements. Their work is problem-focused and centered on the psychological issues of the individual. Therapists are monitored by professional organizations, governmental agencies, and funding entities. Spiritual direction, on the other hand, uses a nonprofessional model, usually more egalitarian and often described by terms like hospitality or friendship. Personal qualities of the director are the key, and there is more variability in educational background. It is a triadic relationship involving the director, the person in direction, and God. The focus is on spirituality, transformation and development of the person's relationship with God, celebration, and movement toward wholeness rather than symptom reduction, adjustment, or solving problems. Direction also generally assumes some kind of connection to a spiritual or religious community or tradition that supports the work. Thus, psychotherapy is often more appropriate than spiritual direction for dealing with severe life disruption and mental illness, although in many situations they might work well together. Both methods involve dealing with psychological issues and make use of psychotherapy techniques, but directors hear more spiritual issues and focus more on spiritual practices such as prayer and meditation. So, if an individual has many psychological and life adjustment problems, referral to a counselor or psychotherapist may be in order. This is particularly the case if there is any threat of danger to self or others (Sperry, 2005; Guenther, 2000; Langer, 2005; Moon, 2002a, 2002b; Rogers, 2002; Ganje-Fling & McCarthy, 1991;

Blanton, 2005; Vergote, 1998, pp. 272–275; May, 1992, pp. 179–198; Merton, 2008, pp. 284–285).

14.1.2   Guru Relationships

There are some parallels between helping relationships like spiritual direction and the guru relationship that has developed in Hinduism and some forms of Buddhism (Levinson, 1978, pp. 97–101; Bogart, 1997). An examination of these similarities, as well as divergences provides another perspective on the helping relationship.

14.1.2.1   Nature of a Guru

The **guru** is a special individual, a person "who has found the truth of brahman and is always concerned for the welfare of his disciples" (Sankaracarya, 1975, p. 130). Generally they are considered to be the transmitters of a salvific tradition that they have received by transmission from another guru, although in Hinduism it is possible for a new guru to appear and begin their own tradition. The specialness of the guru varies according to the specific Hindu or Buddhist group being considered. For instance, in versions of Mahayana and Zen Buddhism, guru devotion and respect are important, but the guru is simply a teacher pointing the way for the student. In Tibetan Buddhism and much of Hinduism, what is important is not so much what the guru does but who they are—a holy person who is a manifestation of Brahman or a reborn bodhisattva or Buddha. Transmission of spiritual teaching and progress is dependent upon *persons* rather than *techniques*, it is conveyed from the person of the guru to the student. In the Buddhist and Hindu traditions, gurus are traditionally men, but the presence of women gurus has become widespread, particularly within Hinduism (Pechilis, 2004; Erndl, 2004; Cleary, 1993, pp. 1174–1180; Capper, 2002; Bogart, 1997, pp. 23–41; Kamilar, 2002).

An individual looking for a guru must therefore seek a person who not only has knowledge, practical experience, and technical skills but also certain personal qualities. Most important is a sense of inner bliss or calmness that is a sign of spiritual perfection. This manifests itself in personal qualities like joy, freedom from desire or negative emotions, and compassionate relationships that are forthright and without falsehood. The guru must also possess the skills needed to guide disciples. Gurus who lack these qualities or who are conceited or arrogant should be avoided (Tsongkhapa, 1999; Sankaracarya, 1975, p. 37).

14.1.2.2   The Guru Relationship

Religious traditions like Hinduism and Buddhism believe that relationship with a guru is essential for spiritual advancement. We need someone outside of ourselves who has an independent perspective on our passions and attachments, and can go beyond the limits of our current mental life. Reading texts is not enough; growth also requires love, compassion, and kindness (Muktananda, 1980, pp. 64–69). In Tibetan Buddhism, a guru or teacher is especially necessary because the intense esoteric techniques of **tantra** can lead to puzzling, problematic mental states and can be harmful without supervision. The Tibetan guru offers guidance from their tradition and personal experience, monitoring the person's readiness before allowing an initiation ritual to be held (Capper, 2002).

The basis of the guru relationship is identification. The disciple strives to emulate the guru. Since the guru is a special individual, mantras or teachings given by the guru are thought to have a special significance. Even the presence of the guru is beneficial, acting as a mirror for the self and a catalyst for change (Muktananda, 1980).

The relationship between guru and student progresses through what Bogart (1997, pp. 4–5) calls the nine stages of spiritual apprenticeship. The early stages of the guru relationship revolve around commitment and instruction. These stages include (1) choosing a teacher, (2) initiation, (3) discipleship and (4) testing. The initiation stage varies greatly in length from days to years and can include a preparatory period, purification rituals and finally a ceremony that formalizes the commitment of student and guru to each other. The initiation and discipleship periods generally involve instruction in various practices aimed at weeding out distractions and developing inner freedom. This requires a degree of surrender and trust in the guru. Individuals raised in the Hindu tradition are accustomed to this directive approach to development and often expect it of counselors when they enter therapy, leading to potential conflicts with professionals who may use a more non-directive approach (Juthani, 1998).

The fifth stage of spiritual apprenticeship is guru devotion. In this stage, the focus is on the blessing the person receives from the presence of the teacher. The student listens, meditates on qualities of the guru, bows or makes offerings to them, and does acts of kindness toward them (Muktananda, 1980, pp. 128–165). This devotion is typically very intense, although the extent of guru devotion varies among Buddhist and Hindu groups. It is particularly important in Tibetan Buddhism, but even in less devotional traditions like Zen, the teacher still has great authority and is an object of admiration (Dumoulin, 1979, p. 41; Capper, 2002).

The later stages of the guru relationship are marked by a process of **individuation**. They include (6) glimpses of the goal, (7) separation from the teacher, (8) finding the teacher within, and (9) teaching others. Early in the relationship with the guru, the student needs to focus on the good qualities of the guru as this leads to increasing accomplishment. In the separation process, the disciple begins to see and accept the dark side of their teacher, learning to avoid the extremes of over or under valuation. They move toward a more independent relationship in which the students begin to assume guru functions for themselves and others (Capper, 2002). This movement toward independence is critical, for one of the dangers of the guru system is that the student can become addicted to the power of the teacher and dependent upon them. Gurus who promote this type of problem through coercion should be avoided, and unreasonable requests by gurus should be refused (Bogart, 1997, pp. 42–45; Tsongkhapa, 1999, pp. 61–64).

14.1.3 The Cure of Souls

Spiritual direction offers many potential benefits, but it does not directly address a number of problems. First, it is not designed to assess and treat serious emotional difficulties. Second, direction does not offer a direct answer to important questions confronting the religious community as a whole. For instance, how should people be helped who are having difficulty functioning in a community, and how can the community protect itself when a person becomes a problem for others? How should people be helped who fall into serious moral and spiritual lapses? These questions of the larger social context are important for religious groups and their leaders. They were pressing questions in early Christianity as it dealt with persecutions and a rapid influx of new members. The response was the development of theory and technique in what was known as the **cure of souls** (*cura animarum*). It involved an application of religious teachings and practices to the overcoming of problems of the soul, restoration of wholeness, and spiritual growth (Fuller, 1988, p. 132; Dysinger, 2005, pp. 113–115).

In the early church, problems in an individual's moral and spiritual life were often seen as a community concern. Christians who were guilty of moral or spiritual lapses were expected to engage in **confession** of their failings and show signs of repentance or a change of heart. Repentance was demonstrated by a change in life and also by acts of **penance**, designed to repair the damage caused by moral lapses and restore the spiritual life. In the early church, confession and penance were often public affairs but over time became private (McNeill, 1951, p. 112). Penitential manuals that drew on the Celtic traditions of confession and penance were in wide circulation during medieval times and gave advice about the kinds of penance that should be required in various situations.

Since soul cure in the early church was seen as a community matter, it was the responsibility of community leaders—priests and pastors—to undertake the cure of people under their care. The classic manual of soul care for pastors was that of Gregory the Great (c. 540–604). He articulated several important principles of soul care:

1. Soul cure and leadership is ultimately dependent upon the ability of the pastor to maintain high standards of conduct and make themselves heard with deeds, not with words. This requires humility—a personal honesty and awareness of our own problems—along with a strong interior life to counter the temptations to pride and misconduct that come with a position of power.
2. Soul cure requires great skill. It requires care for all parts of the person. It also requires discernment, for sometimes vices can be disguised as virtues, and wounds of the mind are more deeply hidden than those of the body. It is also a constant process because spiritual growth is never stagnant; if one is not progressing they are regressing.
3. Spiritual guidance should follow the principle of the golden mean. Discipline should avoid the extremes of laxity and harshness, although the pastor should work with fervor to oppose the problems of each person under their care. Guidance

should be sympathetic without condoning problematic actions or attitudes. Even good emotions like peacefulness should be balanced, as suffering can have a positive cleansing role.

4. Spiritual guidance should be individualized, adapted to the character or temperament of the person under care, as well as their gender, age, social status, and type of problem. Guidance should be done in such a way as to maximize the possibility of getting a good effect, which in some cases may mean ignoring lesser problems in order to focus upon more serious ones (Gregory the Great, 1978).

While the use of penance and especially confession could be a good tool to help those troubled by issues of guilt, the use of different penitential systems led to unevenness, and the system was further troubled by unscrupulous priest-confessors and others who took advantage of the system for financial and personal gain. Abuses in this system were thus both structural and individual, and formed one of the motivations for the Protestant Reformation (see Section 3.3.1).

Luther and the other reformers were certainly not opposed to practices like confession but saw them more from the perspective of the individual rather than the institution. His doctrine of the priesthood of all believers shifted the focus of confession to the laity. His teachings, particularly his view that confession was the privilege and duty of all, spurred development within Lutheranism of the mutual care of souls by groups of lay persons. Other early reformers like Zwingli, Martin Bucer, and the German pietists also produced works on the subject. Luther and other writers also became more concerned about the problem of spiritual care for those in distress; he himself made frequent visits to the sick and dying, even plague victims (McNeill, 1951, pp. 177–200). In Anglicanism and the English Reformation, involvement and outreach to the laity was furthered through the publication of the *Book of Common Prayer*, first issued in 1549, and the translation of the Bible into popular languages (e.g., German, English). This empowered individuals to take responsibility for their own spiritual growth, as well as that of others. Protestant practices of soul cure and spiritual direction thus took a less authoritarian path, although many similarities with Catholic direction remained.

14.1.4 Pastoral Counseling

Social and intellectual changes in the late 19th and early 20th centuries led to a number of changes in how the church viewed its helping ministry. Social developments included the use of a scientific and technological vocabulary to talk about the human person in terms of mastery and vitality rather than nurturance, the increasingly complex role of churches, and the professionalization of the pastoral ministry. Especially significant was the birth of modern psychology in the late 19th and early 20th centuries, which excited some with the promise of scientific resources that could be devoted to the care of souls (e.g., Hiltner, 1954a). In general, pastoral care workers in Protestant groups tended to embrace the new psychology, while attitudes in Catholicism and especially Orthodoxy were much more cautious. The influx of psychological theory and technique led to a new specialty in ministry—the pastoral counselor—and new attitudes toward religious and spiritual formation that emphasized individual fulfillment (Kemp, 1947; Holifield, 1983, pp. 169–176, 211–218).

14.1.4.1 Early Developments

The Emmanuel Movement. The first large-scale use of psychological healing techniques in a pastoral setting was launched at the Emmanuel Episcopal Church in Boston in 1906 (Taylor, 1999, p. 177). The founder of the group, Elwood Worcester, was a clergyman who had a Ph.D. from the University of Leipzig where he had studied under the experimental psychologists Wundt and Fechner. He wanted to hold groups that would combine religious and psychological healing techniques in the treatment of individuals with "functional" (nonorganic) neurological and psychiatric problems. The work included (1) classes that combined worship, lecture and social activity; (2) individual meetings with a minister that utilized self-disclosure, prayer and psychological suggestion techniques; and (3) follow-up visits from supportive visitors (Clinebell, 1990). The Emmanuel model spread and was employed in churches all over the country. It encountered resistance and peaked around 1910 but persisted until the death of Worcester in 1940. It marked an important trend toward scientific approaches to health and away from traditional ones.

Anton Boisen and the foundation of Clinical Pastoral Education (CPE). The next step in the pastoral counseling movement was the formation of clinical training procedures. This came from the work of Anton Boisen, a pastor who suffered from mental illness and became fascinated with the relationship between psychological problems and religion. He thought there were few psychiatrists capable of dealing with religious issues in mental illness and few clergy able to deal with abnormal mental states (Vande Kemp, 1985). He hoped to change this. In 1925 he began meeting with small groups of individuals to discuss these issues and provide training experiences. The more psychologically inclined members set the agenda for the group and formed the Association for Clinical Pastoral Education (ACPE) in 1967 (Leas & Thomas, 2005). Arguments continue over whether CPE should embrace secularization as a way of becoming involved with more patients (e.g., Lee, 2002) or follow an integrative strategy that combines psychological sophistication with religious wisdom (e.g., Foskett, 2001).

14.1.4.2 Modern Pastoral Counseling: Psychological Approaches

Pastoral counseling exploded in the years following World War II, stimulated by increases in church membership and a sense that psychology was becoming the new religion of America so that churches needed to incorporate psychology to remain relevant. It shifted away from the old view of soul cure with its emphasis on community, confession and penitence that seemed too legalistic and oriented toward self-control and denial. Instead, goals of self-realization and subjective well-being took their place, and the role of the community or tradition was viewed with suspicion (Browning, 1991,

p. 245; Holifield, 1983, pp. 269–305). Sin, when treated by these authors, was explored in terms of its psychological causes, and categories like pride or sloth were given psychological interpretations (e.g., Berthold, 1968; Hiltner, 1954b). Important writers like Steward Hiltner and Howard Clinebell privileged psychological theory over traditional religious writings. References to traditional pastoral authors like Gregory disappeared and were replaced by psychologists such as Freud and especially the humanistic psychologist Carl Rogers, often to the exclusion of other possible theological and psychological models. Some contemporary theologians like Paul Tillich retained some influence, and a minority argued that psychological models of the human person were limiting (Bunting, 2000; Stinnette, 1968; cf. Tillich, 1963b; Homans, 1968b).

This new approach to pastoral care and counseling was pragmatic or skill centered, although attempts were made to retain some type of Christian orientation (Aden, 1968). Its focus on skills meant that the movement as a whole had no common theoretical or conceptual base in either theology or psychology, although ideas from humanistic psychology and psychoanalysis were quite important. Training for pastoral counselors in this model focused on (1) the use of therapy techniques in the kinds of settings where pastors typically work, such as churches or hospital chaplaincy offices; and (2) dealing with typical issues encountered by pastors such as grief and bereavement, marriage and family, crisis situations and illness, or ethical concerns and religious issues. As this movement developed, its members became increasingly specialized and often moved out of church settings to offer fee-for-service counseling like more secular psychotherapists (Chalfant et al., 1990). Professional organizations like the American Association of Pastoral Counselors (AAPC) were established which drew up specific standards for practice, education, and training.

A good example of pastoral counseling in the liberal Protestant tradition following the pragmatic school can be found in the work of Clinebell (1984, 1993). A key figure in the establishment of the modern pastoral counseling movement, Clinebell was a United Methodist clergyperson and founding president of the AAPC. Clinebell felt the goal of counseling was to support growth toward wholeness in a variety of ways, including (1) enlivening the mind and revitalizing the body, (2) renewing or enriching intimate relationships, (3) deepening one's relationship with the biosphere, (4) growing in relation to institutions in one's life, and (5) deepening and vitalizing one's relationship with God. Clinebell emphasized the use of psychological techniques in counseling, especially those developed by Carl Rogers and other humanistic psychologists. He tended to de-emphasize the use of traditional methods of soul cure, although he acknowledged that spiritual direction techniques could be useful in dealing with spiritual issues. However, these techniques were not included as a typical or required part of CPE or AAPC-recognized training programs, effectively eliminating their use in most pastoral counseling work in Protestant churches.

14.1.4.3 Response to Psychological Pastoral Counseling Models

As the 20th century drew to a close, theologians became increasingly uneasy with psychological models of pastoral care based on self-realization and professionalism, and pastoral counselors began to look beyond the humanistic model for inspiration (Forrester, 1999; Holifield, 1983, pp. 311–314; Schmidt, 1999). One of the first to offer a sharper critique was Albert Outler (1954). Outler saw psychology as both an ally and a rival. It was an ally because of common concerns about health and well being, and it provided a great deal of practical wisdom about human development, helping relationships, and the potential for religion to be delusive. However, he also pointed out that psychology brought with it a different worldview. In particular, he noted that

1. Psychoanalysis is shaped by the Enlightenment, which supposes that the "good life" is here and now and that we can gain it through our own efforts with the use of rationality and the elimination of ignorant and superstitious practices like Christianity. Obviously, this is a rejection of the Christian tradition and the substitution of a humanist alternative.
2. Psychology adopts a reductionistic and naturalistic philosophy, an alternative "basic faith" associated with scientism and the idea that nature is self-contained and self-intelligible. This reductionism distorts and weakens Christianity by trying to reduce it to psychological material, removing God from the picture (cf. Section 2.1).

While Outler argued that Christianity is not tied to a particular understanding of the psychological structure of the human person, he believed that the humanist worldview in particular undermined basic Christian beliefs. As a result, Outler did not see any possibility for an alliance between Christian and humanist world views, and scientism in particular must be rejected. Nor did he see any possible advantage to humanism, as in his view "…the effect thus far, in three centuries of militant secularism, is modern man's disenchantment, despair and mass demoralization. Man's secularized devotion to 'humanity' has not turned out to be more actually humane than his old-fashioned sinful inhumanity to man" (1954, p. 254). If psychology was to be of help to the pastoral counselor, its practical wisdom must be separated from a naturalistic worldview.

Other theologians have also criticized the pragmatic pastoral counseling approach of Clinebell. Don Browning (e.g., Browning, 1991; Browning & Cooper, 2004) argued that psychological approaches such as those embraced by the pastoral counseling movement go beyond their empirical base and contain hidden theological and philosophical assumptions. These at times function as quasi-religious systems that need to be subjected to theological and philosophical critique. Oden (1984) also offered a critique of the assumptions of modernity which he felt are connected to positivist psychology. He argued that extreme stances of individualism, narcissistic hedonism, and reductionism have been toxic to social structures. He criticized ideas of acceptance based only on human forgiveness, and argued that pastoral care needs to recover its identity by looking to classical authors like Luther or Gregory the Great to provide an alternate vision of pastoral care. These critiques have been at least indirectly responsible for movements toward Christian psychology and spiritual direction within mental health and religious circles (cf. Bunting, 2000).

14.2 Spiritual and Religious Issues in Psychotherapy

14.2.1 Psychotherapy

Psychotherapy can be broadly defined as "the application of psychological insights to the growth, healing, or the process of maturing of a person" (Kalam, 1980). This application occurs in the context of a helping relationship with another individual who serves as attendant to the process. Psychotherapy is similar to healing in many traditional societies as it involves (1) a dynamic healing relationship; (2) an ideological component including a worldview, theory of illness, and healing wisdom; (3) ritual and symbols; (4) a placebo, suggestion or encouragement factor; and (5) a moral component (Kinsley, 1995, pp. 151–157; McClenon, 1997). A more exact definition is difficult to construct, as hundreds of kinds of psychotherapy exist. Another complicating factor is that many people distinguish between psychotherapy as a therapeutic procedure for treatment of mental illness and **counseling**, which is a helping relationship that focuses on assisting people to overcome problems and achieve their personal potential (Merton, 2008, pp. 280–284). The difference between psychotherapy and counseling is important at a theoretical level, but in research and practice the two are not consistently distinguished, so here the terms will be used interchangeably.

In general, psychotherapies assume that the individual is suffering from some inner problem or **psychopathology** that can be helped through counseling. Thus even growth-oriented humanistic psychologists like Elkins (1995) view psychotherapy as "the art of nurturing and healing the soul" from psychopathology or relieving "the suffering of the soul." Three general approaches have been taken that seek to understand how a helping relationship or technique might be applied to psychopathology. These are the *traditional theoretical*, *common factor*, and *empirical* approaches.

14.2.1.1 Traditional Theoretical Approaches

The 20th century saw the development of many different schools of psychotherapy that had contrasting views of the causes of psychopathology and the ideal manner of treatment or change (see Table 14.2). These schools departed markedly from the older traditions of spiritual direction and the cure of souls. Discussions of spirituality and religious issues that form the center of spiritual direction were not included in formulations of psychotherapy, as they were deemed peripheral to the mechanisms underlying psychopathology and treatment. The emphasis on confession in the cure of souls tradition is also alien to most traditional schools of psychotherapy, although stories of a confessional nature occur frequently during counseling sessions. Adler, for instance, thought the idea of contrition was inappropriate for psychotherapy (Vande Kemp, 1985). However, both soul cure and psychotherapy have traditionally focused on insight—a kind of healing contact with truth—as a central aspect of the helping process (LeFevre, 1968). More recently, the centrality of narrative for the process of

Table 14.2 Important theoretical schools of psychotherapy

Approach	Representative figures	Causes of behavior or psychopathology	Mode of change
Psychodynamic	Freud Adler Fromm	Unconscious drives Personality structures Social factors	Transference Catharsis
Humanistic	Rogers Maslow	Environmental barriers to growth	Nondirective listening, reflection
Behavioral	Watson Skinner	Learning or environment	Modification of environment or reinforcement
Cognitive	Ellis Beck	Dysfunctional beliefs or thought patterns	Thought restructuring
Interpersonal	Weissman	Grief Role disputes/transitions Interpersonal skill deficits	Analyze current relationships and losses; form new relationships

meaning-making has been recognized, and so narrative approaches are being increasingly incorporated into assessment and treatment (Russell & Wandrei, 1996).

Although there has been considerable debate on the effectiveness of psychotherapy, a large body of research indicates that many of these therapies are effective, and guidelines have been set up for evaluating treatment approaches (e.g., American Psychological Association, 2002a). There have been two interpretations of these findings. Some believe that the broad effectiveness of therapy indicates that there are common mechanisms at work within the various schools of therapy that explain their effectiveness and that helping relationships are effective when these **common factors** are maximized. The other approach holds that therapies do have differential effects, and it is possible to match particular therapies with specific diagnoses. This has led to what is sometimes called the **empirically supported treatment** (EST) approach.

14.2.1.2 The Common Factor Model

Michael Lambert and his colleagues (e.g., Asay & Lambert, 1999) believe that the common factor model best describes what happens in the psychotherapy helping relationship. After a massive meta-analytic review of the treatment outcome literature in psychotherapy, Lambert has identified four factors that accounted for most of the outcome variance and estimated the general importance of each factor. These factors are as follows:

- *Quality of the therapeutic relationship*, including empathy, warmth, acceptance and encouragement of risk taking: 30%
- *Extratherapeutic factors*, including client factors (e.g., coping skills) and environmental factors (e.g., social support): 40%
- *Expectancy ("placebo") factors* and things that develop hope in the client: 15%

- *Specific techniques*: 15%, although probably more important for some disorders (e.g., behavioral treatments for phobias)

The results of this research are quite compelling, as it suggests that traditional theoretical approaches to counseling that focus on specific techniques are somewhat misguided. Common factor model research also suggests that relational factors between the client and therapist, as well as general social support have a strong influence on helping effectiveness. However, the fact that the importance of specific technique varies according to the disorder suggests that the model does not account for all the important factors related to effectiveness.

14.2.1.3 The Empirically Supported Treatment Approach

In the EST approach, empirical research is used to determine what treatment strategies are effective for specific mental illnesses. In the EST paradigm the key to effective helping is using a treatment method that meets a certain standard in terms of research support and utility (American Psychological Association, 2005). Acceptable research support must be produced, and standards for research studies are patterned after the methodology used by pharmaceutical companies to establish drug efficacy. In order to qualify as an empirically well-established treatment, a procedure must have research support that meets stringent criteria, and it must be **manualized**, that is, conducted using a standardized set of instructions in a treatment manual that can be reliably followed in a similar manner by all therapists using the procedure.

There are advantages to the EST approach. A major benefit is that it encourages the use of effective helping practices, a benefit to the client as well as the practitioner. Well-established treatments—mostly of the cognitive-behavioral or interpersonal variety—have been identified for a number of disorders, including marital/couple problems, eating disorders, enuresis, chronic pain, depression, and various anxiety disorders (e.g., Weissman & Markowitz, 2000). The EST criteria are also influential because they have been widely adopted by managed care companies who are anxious to reduce costs. Some advocates of the paradigm also applaud the fact that the use of EST recommendations and manualized procedures will reduce the use of clinician judgment. Attempts to separate efficacy and cost as treatment decision factors remain a key issue (American Psychological Association, 2002a).

While the EST approach has a number of potential advantages, it is not popular with practitioners and has been severely criticized.

1. The EST paradigm has been attacked as unrealistic because it studies treatment effectiveness for single problems, when people typically have multiple chronic conditions. It confuses unvalidated and invalidated treatments, assuming that a procedure is not effective if it has not been validated (Westen, Novotny, & Thompson-Brenner, 2004).
2. The EST approach ignores important data that supports the common factor model. It also lacks data demonstrating the effectiveness of ESTs with ethnic

minority groups (Scharron-del Rio & Bernal, 2001). The quantitative research methods preferred by the paradigm may not be sensitive to issues related to spiritual growth, which may be better studied using qualitative methods (Tan, 2001b, 2002, 2003a; Westen & Bradley, 2005).

3. The EST requirement that treatments be manualized is flawed. Opponents point out that many forms of therapy—especially those dealing with spiritual and religious issues—cannot be reduced to a fixed set of instructions, and thus by definition they can never succeed in becoming ESTs even if they are highly effective.

A more fundamental critique of EST is that any type of routinized treatment represents a fundamental misunderstanding of the helping process. For instance, Polkinghorne (2004) argues that ESTs represent a "technified" approach to care that is appropriate in the physical realm but inappropriate for use in situations with humans. According to his argument, the rote treatment guidelines of modernist technical approaches assume that the particular problems and situation of the person are unimportant, while in fact they are essential. This leads one to make the false assumption that a treatment will always have a certain effect regardless of situational and contextual specifics. In his view, care needs to be based more on a **practice** approach, where therapist judgments about applying technique take into account the particular circumstances of the case and its context. This approach recognizes that treatment decisions are based on a system of values that cannot be derived empirically. Technical information can inform such judgments but never replace them (see Section 6.3.4).

Recently EST has been subsumed under the new label of **evidence-based practice in psychology** (EBPP), "the integration of the best available research with clinical expertise in the context of patient characteristics, culture and preferences" (APA Task Force, 2006, p. 273; cf. Institute of Medicine, 2001, p. 147). A more comprehensive concept, this approach avoids a sole focus on brief, manualized treatments and tries to accommodate a broader research base, a wider variety of treatments, and more flexibility for consideration of specific circumstances of each case. However, it still retains a medical view of the clinician as an expert making use of techniques to achieve focused goals. Nevertheless, researchers are working hard to suggest ways that findings from EST research can be combined with insights from clinical practice to improve the quality of care given in therapy (Kazdin, 2008).

14.2.2 Spiritual Issues in Therapy

The past decade has seen an explosion of interest in ways to address spiritual and religious issues within the context of a psychotherapy session. In the past, counseling has often seemed like a secular ritual designed to replace religious ones (Vandermeersch, 1990), so that spiritual or religious issues had no place in psychotherapy. However, many practitioners and scholars now argue that these issues must be allowed into counseling. There are a number of reasons why this seems like a good idea:

1. It is impossible to avoid, as clients generally do not separate moral or spiritual issues from psychological ones, and therapists cannot avoid having their values and spirituality influence their interactions with the client (Jones, 1994). Religious issues may thus be a source of conflict or alliance between therapist and client (Worthington & Sandage, 2001)
2. It is part of multicultural sensitivity that is mandated by professional codes of ethics (e.g., APA, 2002b) and necessary to avoid cultural conflicts that might interfere with therapy (Worthington, Kurusu, McCullough, & Sandage, 1996; Mansager, 2002).
3. It is a key aspect of life, and exploring it gives valuable information about the person (Sperry & Shafranske, 2005b; Spilka, 1986; Rizzuto, 1993).
4. It is a potentially helpful resource. Counselors frequently see religion as influencing the course and outcome of treatment in positive ways. It can help with coping through encouraging prayer and a positive lifestyle, providing social and religious support, nurturing a sense of coherence and hope, and helping to maintain positive goals like authenticity. Clients also see this and may request the discussion of religious topics or inclusion of spiritual practices in treatment (Fallot, 2001; Shafranske & Malony, 1990).
5. It may be central to the problems the person brings to therapy, as when the person is engaged in intensive spiritual seeking or experiencing a religious conflict (Juthani, 2001; Sperry & Mansager, 2004; Shafranske & Sperry, 2005). In these cases, spiritual interventions may be appropriate along with psychological ones, either by the therapist or a competent religious professional (Wilson, 1998).

14.2.2.1 Models of Inclusion

Once the decision is made to address spiritual or religious issues in therapy, the question is how to do it. The answer to this question will be greatly influenced by one's view of the relationship between psychological issues and spiritual or religious ones. A number of different models have been proposed for understanding this relationship (cf. Shafranske & Sperry, 2005; Sperry & Shafranske, 2005a; Sperry & Mansager, 2004):

1. In *reductionist models*, spiritual and psychological issues are seen as the same thing, and presenting problems of religious and spiritual issues really are a different way of talking about psychological problems. Generally people holding this model argue that the content of issues discussed in therapy is irrelevant, it is only the process that matters (Hinterkopf, 2005; cf. Gaines, 1998). This kind of reductionism can fit well with a hard scientism that sees science as able to understand and explain all aspects of human experience (Noam & Wolf, 1993).
2. In *hierarchical models* the two areas are thought of differently, but one is seen as a subset of the other, and the more inclusive concept is given primacy (cf. Sperry & Mansager, 2007). For instance, spirituality may be seen as one aspect of a person, perhaps dependent upon good psychological functioning so that

including material about it in therapy just adds on an additional specific focus. This often assumes that spirituality is a separate human quality rather than a holistic phenomenon (Noda, 2000).

3. In *dialogical models* they are thought of as different but overlapping and have equal importance. This view is congruent with a more holistic understanding of the human person (cf. Sperry & Mansager, 2007). The implication of this model is that since psychological and spiritual issues overlap, it will often be necessary to address both. Sometimes addressing problems in one area will help the other, but sometimes they might be largely independent (e.g., Vergote, 1988, p. 32; Benner, 2005; Willard, 1998; Blass, 2001). For instance, changes in God image can only be accomplished through explicitly spiritual techniques, but these changes can impact psychological variables like agreeableness and neuroticism (Cheston, Piedmont, Eanes, & Lavin, 2003). Approaches that combine techniques from counseling and spiritual direction like spiritually attuned counseling (Moon, 2002b) fit well in this framework. Harry Guntrip seems to have held this view; he distinguished between psychological work for adjustment and religious cure for skepticism and cynicism but argued that both are about the cure of souls (1949, pp. 23–25, 37–44; see Section 5.4.2). In a different way, Thomas Merton also seems to have a dialogical view, arguing that while psychological and spiritual health often go together, psychological help is often more about helping a person live with their problems and the expectations of society, rather than move to genuine spiritual growth (Merton, 2005a). Some models of therapy such as object relations or cognitive-behavioral approaches seem to work especially well in dialogical frameworks (Strawn & Leffel, 2001).

4. In *uniqueness models*, the two areas are seen as mostly separate and should not be confused, so that each set of issues needs to be addressed separately by psychological and spiritual counseling (Tan & Johnson, 2005; Bogart, 1997, p. 174). This view is often held by people who see large differences between psychological approaches that are focused on prediction or control, and spiritual or contemplative approaches that emphasize mystery and acceptance (May, 1982, p. 10; Howard, McMinn, Bissell, Faries, & VanMeter, 2000). An implication of this view is that it is possible to have a good spiritual life in the midst of poor psychological functioning or vice versa.

Another factor that can influence how spiritual issues will be included in counseling is how one sees the relationship between spirituality and religion. Helminiak (2001), arguing from a humanistic perspective, believes that the two should be kept strictly separate. In his view, spirituality deals with big questions of life—meaning, purpose, and universal values like self-transcendence, authenticity or openmindedness—while religion is simply a social vehicle to support spirituality. He believes that for ethical reasons counselors need to remain neutral and should deal with spirituality but not religion, although one might validate, try to change or reject some aspects of religious belief depending on what is helpful for healing and integration.

This position has been challenged by writers like Slife and Richards (2001). They argue that while Helminiak supports the need for neutrality, his own position is by no means neutral. It advocates certain values like open-mindedness that are part of his humanistic worldview but not universal. Furthermore, although he claims to be neutral, he is willing to reject religious positions that he does not like or to argue that different religious beliefs like theism or nontheism make no difference, when people from religious traditions holding those beliefs would strongly disagree. Slife and Richards argue that (1) counseling must address both spirituality and religion because people connect them, and (2) a neutral position on these issues is impossible because ethics and values are a part of therapy; therapists see some goals as desirable, certain kinds of behaviors as positive, and other actions to be avoided. This inherent ethical component to therapy should be recognized but cannot be removed (cf. Tjeltveit, 1999).

14.2.2.2 Barriers

While commentators often remark that there is increased tolerance for religion and spirituality within psychology and so fewer barriers to integration (Richards & Bergin, 2004; McMinn, Ruiz, Marx, Wright, & Gilbert, 2006; Myers, 1996), obstacles to the full treatment of spiritual and religious issues in counseling still exist, such as financial structures and hesitancies of both clients and counselors (Sperry & Mansager, 2004; Chrysostomos, 2007, p. 27). Traditionally, mental health professionals have lower levels of religious belief and commitment than their patients (Pierre, 2001), higher levels of atheism and skepticism, and are relatively uninformed about religion even though most report being raised in a religious tradition. Psychologists and mental health professionals are much more likely than their clients to identify themselves as spiritual but not religious, have a quest motivation, or hold somewhat vague nontraditional spiritual beliefs (Elkins, Lipari, & Kozora, 1999; Baker & Wang, 2004; Crossley & Salter, 2005). They may see religion as a system competing with their psychological framework, and studies suggest that this makes them less interested in religious issues and more likely to see spiritual experiences as pathological, although the number of counselors who are actively hostile to religion appears to be relatively small (Koenig, 1995; Allman, de la Rocha, Elkins, & Weathers, 1992; Walker, Gorsuch, & Tan, 2004; Breakey, 2001). Thus, it is not surprising that many psychologists and counselors can experience problems working with religiously committed clients (Ragan, Malony, & Beit-Hallahmi, 1980; Shafranske & Malony, 1990; Crossley & Salter, 2005; Worthington et al., 1996; Worthington, 1989). It is also unfortunate because some clinicians with a religious background indicate that this part of their heritage was an important and helpful part of their professional development (e.g., Rizzuto, 2004).

The effect of this is that the majority of clients—including those not affiliated with a religious tradition—want to discuss spiritual or religious issues but say that counselors seldom bring them up (Worthington & Sandage, 2001). Studies also suggest that people avoid therapy or will not discuss religious or spiritual issues, either due to the general reputation of mental health professionals or because of specific cues the therapist gives off (Sommer, 1997). Studies with AA members found them reluctant to discuss religious concerns because of fears that their beliefs would not be taken seriously, or they would be asked to do things against them, although there is not a lot of real data on how frequently active disrespect for religious beliefs occurs (McDargh, 1993; Crossley & Salter, 2005; Richards & Bergin, 1997, p. 123; Post, 1993). Obviously, these perceptions and attitudes represent a barrier to the treatment of spiritual and religious issues in counseling.

14.2.2.3 Therapy with Religious Clients

Spiritual and religious issues become particularly important in counseling when dealing with clients who have strong religious commitments. While religiosity is generally associated with lower rates of mental illness, even a person with a healthy spirituality can encounter psychological difficulties. Some specific groups may have higher rates of certain kinds of problems but may be reluctant to seek help due to religious beliefs about healing and suffering or suspicions about psychology (Trice & Bjorck, 2006). Religious differences do appear to affect clinical judgment and behavior with religious clients; for instance, the moral stance of some clients can provoke strong emotional reactions in counselors (Worthington et al., 1996; Eriksen, Marston, & Korte, 2002). Very religious clients—especially women—tend to prefer a counselor with the same values and may prefer a religious intervention in counseling. They may avoid services, if this is lacking or their religious convictions and values are discounted, for example beliefs about the importance of staying in marriage (Foss & Warnke, 2003). However, it is not clear whether having a therapist of similar religious views is crucial to the outcome. Some studies indicate that this makes no difference in therapy effectiveness; however, this may not be true for those with high intrinsic religiosity, or when outcomes like client values are measured (Schaffner & Dixon, 2003; Worthington & Sandage, 2001; McCullough, 1999; Ventis, 1995; Mueller, Plevak, & Rummans, 2001; Worthington, 1988). This suggests the possibility that a two-tiered approach to spiritual and religious issues in counseling may be necessary, with an accommodative approach available for highly religious individuals. An unwillingness to discuss religious and ethical concerns with this group could be a kind of negligence (Yarhouse, Butman, & McRay, 2005, p. 439).

14.2.2.4 Training Issues

In the 1980s, very little training with regard to religion or spirituality existed in psychology programs. Shafranske and Malony (1990) found that only 5% of clinical psychologist members of APA had these issues covered in their training. This is less surprising given the high rates of atheism or indifference to religion in APA at that time (Ragan et al., 1980). Nor was there a large database on religious or spiritual issues. In the early 1990s, less that 5% of studies in the most relevant APA journals included any types of measures on religion or spirituality, and most of these studies only included a single question about religion. Few studies have addressed any issues relevant to training (Weaver et al., 1998; Bartoli, 2007). Since that time, curriculum standards for counseling and other programs have begun to mention spirituality and religion, often as part of a list of sociocultural factors that should be attended to in treatment. Although this has resulted in some inclusion of spirituality-related course-work in medical schools and residency programs, training is still very minimal, and little is known about what knowledge and skills need to be passed on to practitioners. Within psychology, there is some inclusion of material in training programs, but it is unsystematic and uneven between schools (Brawer, Handal, Fabricatore, & Wajda-Johnston, 2002). This lack has spurred the development of outside resources such as continuing education workshops that are now fairly plentiful (Eichelman, 2007; Puchalski, Larson, & Lu, 2001; Burke et al., 1999; Tisdale, 2003). Program directors and faculty report little competence in addressing these issues and a skeptical culture continues to exist among them. This is despite the fact that people in training iden-tify religion as a critical issue in psychotherapy (Walker et al., 2004; Bartoli, 2007; Roskes, Dixon, & Lehman, 1998).

The counseling profession has had a long-standing interest in addressing spiri-tual issues in counseling (Richmond, 2004a). Recently the American Counseling Association incorporated religion and spirituality in training standards as part of its diversity competencies. These standards require that counselors be able to

(1) explain the relationship between religion and spirituality, including similarities and dif-ferences, (2) describe religious and spiritual beliefs and practices in a cultural context, (3) engage in self-exploration of his/her religious and spiritual beliefs in order to increase sensitivity, understanding and acceptance of his/her belief system, (4) describe one's reli-gious and/or spiritual belief system and explain various models of religious/spiritual devel-opment across the lifespan, (5) demonstrate sensitivity to and acceptance of a variety of religious and/or spiritual expression in the client's communication, (6) identify the limits of one's understanding of a client's spiritual expression, and demonstrate appropriate referral skills and general possible referral sources, (7) assess the relevance of the spiritual domains in the client's therapeutic issues, (8) be sensitive to and respectful of spiritual themes in the counseling process as befits each client's expressed preference, and (9) use a client's spiritual beliefs in the pursuit of the client's therapeutic goals as befits the client's expressed preference (Burke, quoted in Miller, 1999, p. 500).

The outlook for improving this situation is cloudy. Clearly, the first step in train-ing is to promote self-awareness on the part of the prospective counselor with respect to religious and spiritual issues and how their personal background might affect their ability to work with someone from a different background. This approach is strongly supported by the multicultural literature (Bartoli, 2007; Hagedorn, 2005). However one question is whether adequate competencies can really be taught in a formal training program (Kopp, 1971; Albee, 2000), and the extent to which a thera-pist must be an experienced religious or spiritual practitioner themselves, in order to be a competent guide for others. Also, self-knowledge is clearly not enough; for instance one cannot do a religious assessment without background knowledge of what is normal for different traditions (Hage, 2006). The proliferation of programs for training in psychology that have a specifically religious orientation has perhaps been aided by the difficulty of addressing these issues in other programs.

14.2.2.5 Assessment of Spiritual and Religious Issues in Counseling

Assessment is a good place to begin in dealing with spiritual or religious issues with a client. This allows the counselor to gain information so that they do not make assumptions about the person's belief system based on affiliation or ethnic factors. It also allows the counselor an opportunity to establish a respectful atmosphere for discussing spiritual issues and gives the client an opportunity to say whether they would like these issues discussed and if so how (Harper & Gill, 2005; Aten & Hernandez, 2004). Assessment should examine both the individual and their family and include (Rizzuto, 1993; Fallot, 2001; Darden, 2005; Fitchett, 1993) the following:

- A religious and spiritual history, especially including any spiritual experiences
- A review of current religious or spiritual practices, rituals, and community involvements, including their attitudes toward authority and guidance
- Discussion of beliefs, especially as they affect current problems
- How the person would like religion or spirituality addressed as part of their counseling.

Interview techniques can be supplemented with a variety of other procedures. **Spiritual genograms** and other visual display techniques allow the individual to diagram their family and personal history, and indicate the effects of religious and spiritual involvement on that history (Hodge, 2003). Questionnaires and psychological tests can also be used. Along with inventories that measure things like spiritual well-being or religious commitment (e.g., Fetzer Institute, 1999; Worthington et al., 2003), the Myers-Brings Type Inventory (MBTI) is sometimes used to assess personal style to help individualize the process of direction. Although the test generally has poor psychometric properties, some research suggests that it does measure some relevant variables. For instance, intuitive types on the MBTI tend to be more open to religious change, while sensing types see a clear separation between sacred and secular, place more importance in rules and are troubled more by religious doubt (Ross, Weiss, & Jackson, 1996; Rice, 2000).

One assessment procedure used sometimes by spiritual counselors is the **Enneagram**. Developed in part by the early 20th-century mystic Gurdjieff, it draws on a number of sources that probably include Orthodox Christianity, Islamic teaching from Sufi mystics, and Tibetan Buddhism (Shirley, 2004, p. 107; Speeth, 1989). The Enneagram works on the principle that everything is the result of three spiritual laws of Holy Affirming, Holy Denying, and Holy Neutralizing. The creative impulse from these three laws generates what is called the Law of Seven, positions in the Enneagram drawing that represent different individual types. In contemporary use, the person takes a questionnaire (e.g., Riso & Hudson, 2000, pp. 174–187) that places them in one of nine basic structures of personality, value, and being. These include feeling types (Helper, Achiever, Individualist), thinking types (Investigator, Loyalist,

Enthusiast), and instinctive types (Reformer, Challenger, Peacemaker). There are holy ideas, virtues, and passions and fixations connected with each position, and each type contains specific imbalances that can be corrected through certain types of practice. Gurdjieff himself warned against using the Enneagram as a kind of mechanical system (Shirley, 2004, pp. 162–164). He favored more indirect Sufi-inspired practices of self-remembrance and observation and techniques using the body such as movement and dance to heighten self-observation and remembrance (Gurdjieff, 1999, pp. 134–136; Hunt, 2003, pp. 226–227; cf. Hinterkopf, 2005). Although spiritual directors and counselors frequently use the Enneagram, critics say that it lacks empirical support, and that in its current use it is more a psychological technique than something with religious significance (MacInnes, 2003, p. 57).

14.2.2.6   Explicit and Implicit Strategies

All counseling takes place within a context of accepted professional ethics. This means that methods for discussing spiritual or religious issues must take into account relevant ethical guidelines. For example, the American Psychiatric Association has practice guidelines regulating discussion of religious issues (1990). They state that the clinician should (1) obtain information about patient religion and beliefs so that they can be attentive to them, (2) handle conflicts or differences with respect for patient beliefs, (3) avoid imposing religious, antireligious, or ideological beliefs on patients, and (4) avoid substituting one's own beliefs or practices in place of accepted procedures.

How does one deal with spiritual issues in a secular counseling session? Many authors (Frame, 2003; Walker et al., 2004; Shafranske, 2001; Tan, 1996, 2007) draw the useful distinction between explicit and implicit intervention strategies. **Implicit strategies** generally involve (1) basing a counseling approach on some system of spiritual and religious principles such as theistic ones, (2) identifying spiritual issues such as meaning, purpose and connectedness and discussing them, and (3) avoiding the use of spiritual or religious practices and discussion of the supporting spiritual or religious framework. Sometimes these strategies are disconnected from the beliefs of the counselor, but typically they depend upon **personal integration**, a process by which the counselor connects their own religious experience, beliefs, and practices with their counseling approach (e.g., Heynekamp, 2002). Personal integration can be reflected in implicit strategies, as when a therapist prepares for a session with private prayer, or it can impact other aspects of their professional life, as when religious individuals working in secular agencies deal with value conflicts (Gubi, 2001; Baker & Wang, 2004).

In **explicit strategies**, the counselor openly discusses religious or spiritual issues with the client, and may teach or engage in religious practices with them. Usually this is done in the context of individual counseling, but it can also be carried out in group settings (e.g., Segalla, 2003). Consultation with a religious professional is not often done but can be very valuable in this approach. The use of explicit strategies assumes that the counselor is familiar with a repertoire of relevant issues or practices and can help the client discuss or learn about them in a meaningful way. It also assumes that the client desires and consents to the use of such a strategy (Elkins, 2005; Tan, 2007). The most commonly used explicit interventions include (1) discussions and readings of religious ideas or scriptural teachings, (2) practice of virtues such as forgiveness, service or confession, (3) prayer for clients in or out of session, (4) teaching prayer or meditation practices, (5) use of religious imagery, (6) ritual, and (7) encouraging communal practices like worship (Sperry, 2005; Walker et al., 2004; Worthington, Mazzeo, & Canter, 2005; Cole, 2003). The use of spiritual direction techniques in counseling might be considered an explicit strategy in some cases, but it is relatively uncommon; the use of psychological techniques in direction is much more frequent (Benner, 2005; Worthington et al., 1996). Less than 10% of psychologists use explicit strategies, although it is more common among practitioners with religious faith. The majority of mental health profession-als question the appropriateness of explicit strategies because of ethical concerns and feel that they should only be used occasionally or when other alternatives are not available (Shafranske & Malony, 1990; Post, Puchalski, & Larson, 2000; Koenig & Larson, 2001; Gubi, 2001; Tan, 2003b). This is particularly true when dealing with individuals coming out of a repressive religious environment who might react negatively (Tan & Johnson, 2005). However, explicit strategies might be very appropriate in some circumstances, particularly when dealing with clients from a cultural background with strong religious elements (Abernethy, Houston, Mimms, & Boyd-Franklin, 2006), and there is evidence that the use of explicit strategies such as contemplative prayer can assist the therapy process (Finney & Malony, 2001).

A key issue with regard to spiritual and religious approaches to helping is whether the helper needs to be personally involved in the practice in order to teach or use it. Many argue that to do this requires an active spirituality on the part of the thera-pist (Elkins, 2005). While it is possible that a person might be mechanically able to teach various practices, dealing with the experiences and changes that occur as a result of those practices seems to require some personal experience of them. Tan (2001a) argues that for Christians some type of personal integration of Christian belief and practice is essential before professional or theoretical integration can be successfully undertaken.

A number of schools of psychotherapy theory and practice can provide a hospita-ble framework for the use of implicit or explicit strategies. Jungian therapy provides good possibilities for work with individuals who are spiritual but not religious, as it deals with spiritual issues but uses a nonreligious vocabulary (Corbett & Stein, 2005; see Section 5.2). Cognitive-behavioral therapy (CBT) can be congruent with a religious approach because it stresses importance of belief and is very practically focused. Spiritually oriented CBT with religious clients is as effective as secular CBT for treatment of depression but better than the secular approach at increas-ing spiritual well-being (Tan & Johnson, 2005). Interpersonal therapy deals with a number of issues of relationship, connectedness and meaning that have spiritual and religious significance (Miller, 2005). Finally, transpersonal therapy (Lukoff & Lu, 2005) uses a perennial philosophy approach to religious and spiritual experience that may resonate with some clients, as well as sometimes utilizing Buddhist mindfulness techniques.

14.3 New Religious Approaches to Psychotherapy

Implicit and explicit strategies allow for the discussion of spiritual and religious issues in counseling, and explicit strategies add the possibility of importing religious practices into therapy. However, all of these techniques are set within traditional psychological frameworks. Another possibility for integration is to design an approach to counseling which is entirely based upon theological or religious concepts. Especially during the last 20 years, writers have explored this option and constructed **religious psychotherapies** based on either Christian or Buddhist perspectives.

14.3.1 Explicitly Theistic or Christian Models

Christian versions of religious psychotherapy have come from individuals working in the integration and Biblical counseling movements (see Section 1.4.7). In their view, real integration and treatment of spiritual or religious issues is not just adding a couple of new techniques or topics for discussion to the therapy session. Rather, it involves trying to conceptualize the human person, mental health issues, and the practices of the therapeutic endeavor in a way that is at least compatible with Christian beliefs, values and practices. It assumes a strong personal spirituality on the part of the therapist, respect for the values and needs of the client, and recognizes that the counselor has a broad responsibility to the Christian community. Integrationists generally say that Christian thought and scripture provide an important and distinctive view of the human person but do not offer a detailed, comprehensive theory of personality. They need to be supplemented and integrated with theoretical models and data from psychology in order to construct a fully articulated Christian psychology and psychotherapy.

Counselors operating from an integrative Christian context generally see Christian counseling as distinctive and that it offers substantial benefits over secular approaches. Sometimes it involves simply adapting secular techniques with religious content, but more importantly it gives a central role to religious practices like prayer, scripture reading and teaching about religious concepts (Ball & Goodyear, 1991). The Christian acceptance of God's love and forgiveness by the therapist allows the counselor to have personal confidence and to identify with the client as a fellow child of God. Secular therapy has lost the sense of sin but retains a focus on failure and problems, making it difficult to have a genuinely positive focus in counseling (Bretherton, 2006). In Christian counseling, Jesus provides a model of a trusting and encouraging relationship that can look honestly at failings, while maintaining a positive outlook and hope (Propst, 1988).

All approaches to a Christian religious psychotherapy have both critical and constructive elements. In the *critical* part of integration, secular therapies are examined and critiqued (e.g., Jones & Butman, 1991; Browning & Cooper, 2004). A key area of concern is the belief that secular approaches trivialize the problem of human sin and brokenness, and their exclusive and often narcissistic focus on the person does not adequately take into account the person's connections to others and to God. The *constructive* aspect of integration then takes acceptable ideas and techniques from psychology and combines them with Christian beliefs and practices that are applicable to the counseling situation. Many integration authors believe that Christian scriptures should be the touchstone in terms of deciding what psychological knowledge can be validly used (McMinn, 1996; Jones & Butman, 1991; Collins, 1988). This process of criticism and construction tends to result in two general perspectives. In the *integrative approach*, the Christian counselor attempts to put together academic knowledge of psychology and Christian beliefs and apply them to the solution of practical problems in the counseling setting, with attention to training and ethical issues. Practitioners taking this approach tend to be more muted in their criticism of psychology, more optimistic about the use of psychological theory or technique, and less focused on the use of specific beliefs taken from the Bible or traditional practices. This is the approach taken, for instance, by Siang-Yang Tan in his proposed program for lay counselors in churches (Tan, 1991). In the *traditional approach*, teachings from the Bible and beliefs or practices from the Christian tradition are strongly privileged over psychological concepts, which are viewed with suspicion and used sparingly if at all.

14.3.1.1 Integrative Approaches and Theistic Psychotherapy

One sophisticated system built on the integrative model is the theistic psychotherapy of Richards and Bergin (1997, 2004), Richards (2005) and Bergin and Payne (1997). They wish to combine spiritual and psychotherapeutic techniques using a theistic framework. They hope their system will be helpful in working with people from a theistic background, as well as others who are struggling with problems such as depression or addictions.

In the critical part of their project, Richards and Bergin argue that current psychology is dominated by a naturalistic worldview that believes (1) there is no transcendent meaning, purpose, or force in life, (2) the good life involves the pursuit of happiness or power, and (3) spirituality and the human person are reducible to natural psychological, physiological, and cognitive processes. This worldview largely excludes spirituality or religious perspectives such as theism. Richards and Bergin reject this worldview and instead accept a worldview that includes a strong view of transcendence (see Section 1.2.1). They argue that reductive naturalist and atheistic worldviews are unable to account for the holistic interconnectedness, complexity, and mystery of life, as well as phenomena like altruism. They also believe that naturalism should be rejected because the worldview has toxic effects on mental health and relationships, including therapeutic ones.

Richards and Bergin base the constructive part of their integration on two principles: theistic realism and epistemological pluralism. **Theistic realism** states that God exists, we are creations of God, and that the Divine continues to maintain a link with us. Thus, we are not autonomous beings but exist in relation to God and others. It also holds that morality is not arbitrary but there are objective moral laws and guidelines that we can discover. It is good to live by these laws as they promote spiritual growth and harmony, and it is desirable to transmit these values to others. **Epistemological pluralism** is the view that any of our understandings of the world are only limited and partial, and because of this we need multiple ways of knowing. In particular, Richards and Bergin reject scientism and argue that we need spiritual ways of knowing in addition to scientific empiricism.

Theistic realism has implications for the counselor and how they conduct therapy. Since God is real, a therapist should have a relationship with the Divine, pursing spiritual well-being as well as psychological health. In addition, since reality has a moral framework, therapy needs to be conducted within this framework, at a minimum based on general moral values found in world religions. Richards and Bergin reject the idea that therapy can avoid questions of value, for a counselor's values influence the therapy relationship even if the therapist does not explicitly state them. However, deliberately imposing the values of the therapist on the client is also problematic. They prefer an **explicit minimizing strategy** in which the counselor is explicit about their values but also respectful of the autonomy of the client and their beliefs (Richards & Bergin, 1997, p. 131–132). While the therapist needs to be up front about their values, they should minimize the amount of undue pressure they place on the client to conform to a particular set of beliefs. Detailed self-disclosure and displays of explicitly religious symbols, pictures or dress should be avoided. Spiritual interventions are especially contraindicated when (1) spiritual issues are not relevant to presenting problems, (2) the client does not want to participate, (3) they have impaired thinking as in the case of psychosis, or (4) spiritual interventions are not allowable because of legal or professional restrictions.

Theistic psychotherapy begins by establishing basic rapport, trust, and a working alliance with the client, conducting a religious assessment and setting appropriate goals. The core goal of the approach is to "help clients experience and affirm their eternal spiritual identity and live in harmony with the Spirit of Truth" (Richards & Bergin, 1997, p. 116). Other goals might include helping the client to (1) attend to religious or spiritual needs and problems; (2) examine the impact of religious or spiritual beliefs and practices on their life; (3) use these resources to assist with coping, healing or change;and (4) make decisions about the role religion and spirituality will continue to play in their life. Sessions are based on positive values, and God is seen as an available healing resource. Explicit spiritual techniques can be employed such as prayer, theological discussions, and forgiveness. Consultation with religious leaders is frequently appropriate (Richards & Bergin, 1997, pp. 117–124; 2004).

14.3.1.2 Traditional Approaches

Biblical Counseling. The Biblical counseling movement is based on a much stronger critical project and weaker acceptance of psychology than theistic psychotherapy. The movement is based in the work of theologians, pastors, counselors, and psychologists coming from more conservative theological traditions, who not only question key tenants of psychology but feel that it has little of value to add to a Christian perspective or is even counterproductive (Jones & Butman, 1991, p. 18). The work of Adams (1970) and the more recent writing of Powlison (2000, 2003) exemplify this line of thought. Adams and Powlison both believe that psychology is mostly a liability rather than an asset in the helping relationship, and that many problems experienced by people are due to the acceptance of a psychological viewpoint within mainstream secular culture. They advocate a return to traditional Biblical models of care, although there are some differences between them in how such a model should be formulated and executed. Adams developed a *nouthetic* model of counseling that emphasizes the identification and removal of sin, which is seen as the primary cause of the client's problems. Powlison's version of the Biblical model is much more nuanced and dwells on many dimensions in the Biblical view of healing. He argues that dealing with sin occasionally requires loving confrontation on the part of the counselor, which must be done in a sensitive manner and with an awareness that the counselor deals with the same human realities and frailties. It should take place in the context of a warm and personal relationship that avoids moralizing and pridefulness. The ideas of Powlison, and particularly those of Adams, are quite different from those of modern psychotherapy and more liberal views of pastoral counseling. However, when looked at from a historical perspective, they are perhaps not quite so radical and bear some similarity to the cure of souls tradition in Christianity.

Orthodox Psychotherapy. From an Orthodox perspective, relations between science and religion remain problematic, in part because of potent religious intolerance that exists within the scientific community and contemporary culture. An Orthodox psychotherapy must be built on traditional ideas of the Greek Fathers who emphasize (1) unity of body and soul, (2) spirit is a higher power of their composite and an essential feature of the human person, and (3) all can be divinized and Christ is a divine archetype of divination. The key to Orthodox psychotherapy is pursuing the goal of divination or **theosis** using Orthodox methods such as a supportive lifestyle, ascetic disciplines, and spiritual techniques like watchfulness or hesychastic prayer (see Section 13.2). A helping relationship with a spiritual advisor is essential to the success of this process as is support of a religious community. In the Orthodox view, there are some points of convergence between mental health and religious psychotherapy, but the fundamental goal of Orthodox psychotherapy is not the treatment of disorders; rather it deals with existential dilemmas and fundamental problems behind those illnesses. Thus, it will often use different techniques, and when it employs similar techniques it will use them with different assumptions and purposes. Orthodox psychotherapy is about more than the restoration of health; it focuses on the potential for growth, perfection, and spiritual renewal. It is not however a substitute for psychotherapy which might be used to treat serious mental illnesses (Chrysostomos, 2007).

14.3.2 Buddhist Approaches

While Hindu philosophy and theology could be used to produce a theory of psychotherapy (Mukherjee, 2002), in practice it has been Buddhism that has dominated the literature seeking to develop a non-Christian religious approach to counseling. Buddhism is attractive to some because it provides an apparently non-theistic alternative and has a sophisticated system of beliefs about human psychology that can form a basis for dialogue and understanding. It shares with psychology the goal of alleviation of suffering. Classical Theravada Buddhism and, to a lesser extent, Zen and Vajrayana Buddhism have been the schools most used. This integration project has been of much more interest to Western psychologists than Buddhists living in Asia, although Japanese scholars like Enryo Inoue (1858–1919) and practitioners associated with the Kyoto school of Japanese philosophy (e.g., D. T. Suzuki, Masao Abe) have been active conversation partners and interested in a synthesis between psychology and Zen (Rubin, 2003, 1996; Young-Eisendrath & Muramoto, 2002; Onda, 2002; Payne, 2002). Western writers have tended to focus on Buddhism as an individual practice, which varies somewhat from its Asian context, where it is more intimately related to community and family (Masis, 2002).

14.3.2.1 General Approaches

The Buddhist integration literature has followed two paths. In the assimilationist school of thought such as that of Kabat-Zinn, Buddhism offers a technology that can be removed from its belief system and used to further therapeutic goals. Many applications of mindfulness practice follow this path (see Section 11.4.2). **Buddhist psychotherapy** differs from this in that it accepts most fundamental Buddhist beliefs and tries to construct a theory and practice of counseling within this framework. Much recent work has followed this path (Muramoto, 2002a).

Buddhist psychotherapy writers tend to stress the differences between Western psychology and Buddhism, while seeing that the two practices can complement each other in a number of ways. Writers vary in the extent to which they see Western psychology and Buddhism as compatible and how they might interact (Payne, 2002). In general, they agree that Buddhism and psychotherapy share a desire to alleviate suffering and both work through attempting to alter awareness and attention. These similarities mean they have the potential to be mutually supportive (Rubin, 1996, p. 155; Kamilar, 2002; Miller, 2002). Authors tend to diverge after this point, following either hierarchical or dialogical models. In the *hierarchical* model, Buddhist practices, including meditation are seen as a more encompassing approach than counseling, as Buddhism is designed to produce a better way of living and address fundamental issues such as narcissistic attachment to the self. This is in contrast to Western psychotherapy, which is limited to reducing distress or psychopathology and helping people adapt their individual lives to contemporary life. So while Western therapy and Buddhist practice may be complementary, the latter is more comprehensive and stands at the center of this vision of psychotherapy (Conze, 1956, pp. 37–38; Anbeek & de Groot, 2002; Kamilar, 2002; Epstein, 1995, pp.130–131; Young-Eisendrath, 2002).

In the *dialogical* model, authors argue that meditation by itself without the support of Western therapy techniques may not be sufficient to unearth unconscious conflicts and solve psychological problems. Also, deconstructing the self as in Buddhism is not appropriate early in our spiritual growth, when we need a strong sense of self that can be developed using Western methods. These authors suggest that neither Buddhism nor Western systems like psychoanalysis have a complete psychology, and some kind of combination of the two is desirable (Aronson, 2004, pp. 9, 53; Epstein, 1995; Rubin, 1996, 2003; Falkenstrom, 2003; Rosenbaum, 2003; Tatsuo, 2002).

14.3.2.2 Specific Principles

Most statements of Buddhist psychotherapy begin by articulating a view of the self that is different from the Western conception. Self can be thought of in two ways: an experiential or *process self* observed in the flow of consciousness, and a *representational self* including unconscious organizing structures and ideas we have about ourselves (cf. Pickering, 1997). Buddhism thinks the latter sense of self is a construction without real existence and needs to be surrendered. For Westerners, giving up the representational self can be frightening but liberating (van Waning, 2002; Young-Eisendrath & Muramoto, 2002, pp. 95–96). Mindfulness meditation is the key to solving this problem, as it not only breaks identification with the self but also provides a transitional space that helps to detach from and manage feelings of pride, hatred, and greed (Epstein, 1995, pp. 122–125). This does not mean giving up healthy secure attachments to others or destroying our functioning ego but giving up unhealthy attachments, false pride and striving that just lead to greater suffering (Aronson, 2004, pp. 71–79, 153–164).

Most branches of Buddhism see practice as the center of the religion, so it is not surprising that articulations of Buddhist psychotherapy tend to focus on details of practice while acknowledging some broad operating principles (Daya, 2005; Kamilar, 2002). Buddhist psychotherapy begins with the practice of the therapist, who must have a genuine spiritual life in order to work with a client (Wegela, 2003). Goals with the client revolve around two related areas—First, changing client beliefs, such as developing acceptance of our problems and not blaming the environment or others, as well as rejecting dualistic ideas and accepting the presence of paradox in life (Puhakka, 2003) and second, developing mindfulness practice as is found in vipassana or zazen meditation. It is this latter part of Buddhist psychotherapy that is most compatible with traditional Western views of counseling (Khong, 2003; Epstein, 1995, p. 147).

14.3.2.3 Problems and Critique

Writers both in and out of the Buddhist psychotherapy movement have pointed out a number of conceptual and practical problems. At a very basic level, it is not clear what a specifically Buddhist psychotherapy has to offer beyond other approaches. For instance, Christian contemplative practice may result in the same or greater mental health benefits (Payne, 2002). Some more specific problems have also been discussed:

1. Rubin (1996, 2003) has pointed out that there are many documented instances of self centered or exploitative behavior and misuse of power among both American and Asian teachers in US Buddhist groups, raising questions about constructive involvement and Buddhist claims about transformation. Buddhism seems to lack a theoretical or practical structure for examining these types of problems in depth.
2. In general, Buddhism tends to lack appreciation for narrative, historical, and individual contextual factors related to the specific problem and situation of an individual. It has less of a focus on relational issues such as intimacy (Kamilar, 2002; Rubin, 1996, 2003; Falkenstrom, 2003; Segall, 2003).
3. Buddhist psychotherapy as practiced in the West is inherently individualistic in nature. This is quite different than Buddhism as practiced as a living religion in Asia, where it assumes a spiritual tradition and community support that psychology cannot provide. When Buddhist practices are put into this individualistic context, they may strengthen tendencies in Westerners that are not optimal such as isolation and relational problems. This difficulty was also pointed out by Carl Jung (Conze, 1956, pp. 39–41; Epstein, 1995, pp. 177–179, 216–217; Aronson, 2004; see Section 5.2). It is especially a concern for individuals with severe psychological problems who are not emotionally ready for the rigors of intense meditation practice (Criswell & Patel, 2003; Masis, 2002).
4. Techniques such as meditation that are central to Buddhist therapy might be used simply as a technique for hedonistic ends, making the person feel better. In this situation, meditation would not lead to its desired goal of increasing insight and might actually be used to help the person avoid facing their problems (Masis, 2002).
5. Meditation and other techniques that might be used in a Buddhist psychology presume at least a minimal level of ego strength and organization. Thus, they are probably not appropriate for use in therapy with individuals who have severe personality disorders (Engler, 1986).

There are many important differences between Christian and Buddhist religious psychotherapies. However, they do share some things in common (Olson & McBeath, 2002).

1. They reject **modernist** emphases on hedonism and instead stress the importance of spiritual development and ethical aspects of experience.
2. They reject **scientism** and embrace a position of **critical realism**, which acknowledges the importance of experience and rational inquiry but also argues

that human reason has limitations. They reject views of logic that are limited to black and white thinking and affirm the importance of dialectical thought, as well as the presence of paradox and mystery. They reject the model of therapist as scientific expert, and focus more on the personal qualities of the therapist and the therapeutic relationship as healing.

3. They reject reductionistic views of the human person and experience that can have nihilistic and pessimistic implications. Rather, they tend to have an optimistic view and support the idea that human freedom exists and is a central aspect of personhood. They believe that religious beliefs and practices can support the development of personhood, with positive psychological implications.

14.4 Conclusion

Key issue: *The conversation between psychology and religion is shifting from monologue to dialogue, to the potential benefit of both parties. This new dialogue has the potential to improve helping relationships and better prepare people for helping roles.*

The literature on helping relationships illustrates the changes that have taken place in the psychology and religion dialogue over the past century. Beginning in the early part of the twentieth century the conversation between the two largely became a monologue, with religion submitting to scientific study and trying to adopt new approaches to helping that were supported by prominent psychologists. Since the high point of this movement in the 1960s, the direction of dialogue has changed markedly in a couple of ways. First, religious practitioners are rejecting a dependence on psychology and working to mine the resources of their tradition to conceptualize and build strong helping relationships. Second, psychologists are beginning to look to religious ideas and practices as a way of enhancing their own efforts to help others. This mutuality of conversation offers richer possibilities for a psychology and religion dialogue and bodes well for the future.

Chapter 15
Looking Back

What kind of conclusions can we draw from the dialogue between psychology and religion? As we have seen, the field is rich and complex so that any simple answer to this question will be inadequate. However, it is worthwhile to reflect on general trends as they have much to teach us.

15.1 Lessons from Dialogue

A first conclusion that must be drawn is that many views of religion held by psychologists in the 20th century were very wrong. Freud and many others viewed religious participation as psychologically unhealthy and viewed organized religious communities with disdain. These positions were advanced by well-meaning psychologists who viewed them as scientific facts. However, the evidence is that (1) religious participation is generally associated with positive physical and mental health, and (2) this positive effect is more related to participation in communal activities than individual devotional activity or spiritual seeking (see Chapters 10 and 11).

Science is a human enterprise and accordingly makes mistakes. Nevertheless, the fact that psychologists missed the mark by such a wide margin for many decades is an embarrassment for science in general and psychology in particular. We have much to learn from this failure. It teaches us about the limits of science, the value of nonscientific ways of knowing and the dangers of scientism that can lead us to wrong and hasty conclusions. Such conclusions are obviously bad for religion, if people wrongly perceive that there is something inherently problematic in religious participation. However, it is also the case that this kind of mistake is bad for science, as it undermines its credibility as well as places psychologists on the wrong side of the evidence.

Despite these problems, another conclusion that quickly presents itself is that psychological science has much it can offer to religious traditions. While religion is more than psychology, it is also true that every member of a religious tradition is an embodied, psychological being who is subject to the biological, relational, and social forces that are studied by psychologists. Failure to recognize this fact and take advantage of the knowledge and critical perspective provided by psychology would

J.M. Nelson, *Psychology, Religion, and Spirituality,*
DOI 10.1007/978-0-387-87573-6_15, @ Springer Science+Business Media, LLC 2009

be unfortunate. For instance, it is largely because of psychology—not religious thought—that we now understand the crucial role of childhood in the development of spirituality and religion in the individual (see Chapters 5, 7 and 8). Problems with prejudice and authoritarianism among religious individuals that have been revealed in psychological studies provide a healthy challenge to religious organizations to make sure they are moving toward the goals that they want to reach (see Section 12.5).

A final conclusion that is evident in recent dialogue is that religious traditions are a rich store of wisdom that could generate hypotheses to be investigated by psychologists, as well as offer critique and correctives (Ross & Konrath, 2002). Some of the most important contemporary movements in psychology, such as the expansion of therapy techniques and the development of positive psychology, are heavily dependent upon religious insight and practice (see Chapter 11). There is every reason to believe that more good material awaits.

The bottom line of all of this is that both psychology and religion have a vested interest in dialogue. No real scientist wants to pursue a mode of investigation that will conceal the truth or lead to falsehood. In like manner, no genuine, authentic follower of a religious tradition wants to ignore things that are problematic. If neither science nor religion is thought of as possessing a perfect understanding of all aspects of human experience, the ideal relationship between them becomes one of dialogue. In this model, science may study the human person in general and our spiritual life in particular, and this study will help expand and correct religious beliefs and practices. On the other hand, religion may react to this study and show ways in which it is deficient. It may also offer a more general critique of scientific approaches to human experience and suggest new ways of understanding the human person. We learn the most by fully participating in such a dialogue.

The terms of this dialogue have changed markedly over the past hundred years. During much of the 20th century, the conversation was largely one-sided, with psychologists talking and religious people listening. Even Freud received a good reception among some religious writers. However, in the past few years, psychologists have become much more interested in what religion has to offer, and religious professionals have become more circumspect about how they make use of psychological theory and research. This makes a more level playing field for dialogue.

15.2 Approaches to Dialogue

Under what conditions is a psychology and religion dialogue most likely to be successful? The best work over the past century has been based on six fundamental principles. It has been:

- *Knowledgeable* about relevant material in both psychology and religion.
- *Appreciative of complexity* that is involved in the issues under discussion. A corollary to this is that no single system or reductionist framework is likely to contain or explain all facets of the relationship between psychology and religion.

- *Transparent to self and others* about the philosophical and religious presuppositions behind the positions taken in the dialogue.
- *Fair* in evaluation of the evidence on a given issue.
- *Open to learning*, correction, and new perspectives. It involves a willingness to take seriously what the other side has to say, to recognize that one does not have all the answers, and to admit mistakes.
- *Useful* to the individuals or community who are the object of study.

Is any one approach to the psychology and religion dialogue more likely to be productive according to these criteria? While this is an important issue for discussion and debate, an examination of the field suggests that many approaches can lend themselves to either dialogue or monologue depending on the specific stance of the investigator. A good example of this can be found in applications of the evolutionary paradigm to the psychology of religion. Reductionist approaches such as that of Pascal Boyer are conversation stoppers of doubtful validity or utility, while the more open approach of someone like Harvey Whitehouse has much potential for promoting dialogue (see Section 6.2.3).

15.3 Barriers to Dialogue

We have the knowledge needed to undertake constructive dialogue between psychology and religion. What might prevent that from happening? At this time there seem to be two main types of barriers: ideological positions and cultural values.

15.3.1 Ideological Barriers

1. *Scientism.* Science is a wonderful tool, but it is not the only way we learn about the world. Given its limitations and the nature of human action, it seems likely that it is not always the best way to learn about people. Contemporary science is strongly influenced by naturalism and the search for universal, invariant laws. However, action takes place in specific contexts that are non-repeatable in their complexity, so while science can provide useful information, it can never give a complete guide to action. Other ways of knowing and deciding also need to be part of the picture. This is in keeping with the vision of the founders of modern science, who never argued that science is the best way to answer all questions.
2. *Positivism.* The dead hand of positivism continues to impair psychology in general and its dialogue with religious traditions in particular. While it has been many years since it was taken seriously as a viable philosophy of science, many psychologists—including some psychologists of religion—still subscribe to its beliefs and practices. Of particular importance for the psychology and religion dialogue is the positivist view of history, which sees the world as leaving behind religious superstition in favor of scientific progress. This view of history is not

a scientific fact—it is an ideological or philosophical position. Obviously, true believers in this particular ideology will ultimately be uninterested in what religion has to say. The increasing social and environmental problems linked to our modern, individualistic and technological culture reveals another picture of history that challenges the positivist model of progress. Ultimately, in a positivist strategy of reductionism and conflict, everyone is a loser.

3. *Hedonism.* Although specific religious traditions differ in both beliefs and practices, most have sought ways for individuals to transcend what is typical and achieve what is possible. Some psychologists would ask, why bother? Isn't life more about adjustment, fitting in, and being happy? Taylor (2007) argues that lying behind this is the idea that the pursuit of transcendence interferes with pleasure and so should be avoided. An ordinary life is best and the cost of growth is too much. An ideological position of this type leads to little interest in many aspects of religion, with the possible exception of things perceived to enhance well-being. From a religious perspective this is unfortunate, as (1) there is more to life than pleasure, (2) the pursuit of pleasure through methods such as materialism is ultimately self-defeating, and (3) a comprehensive sense of well-being requires the pursuit of transcendence and spiritual connectedness. Research to date in the social sciences is generally supportive of the religious position on this issue.

15.3.2 Cultural Barriers

Several aspects of belief and values that are enshrined in contemporary Western culture also can be seen as potential barriers to integration. One of the most important of these is extreme individualism.

The individual stands at the center of Western society, and an attempt to provide individual freedoms certainly has many benefits. However, individualism as it is practiced in Western countries often assumes that groups and relationships impede the individual in their search for happiness and growth. This attitude toward the group has led psychologists to ignore or look negatively upon religious organizations and communities. The anti-religious ideas endemic in positivism reinforce this tendency and constitute a barrier to a complete and fair examination of the role of religious communities in the life of the individual. This has proved to be a big mistake in several ways. First, a large body of research now shows that participation in organized religion is associated with significant physical and mental health benefits. Second, there is increasing evidence that it is difficult to understand the religious behavior of individuals without an appreciation for the religious culture and community within which they live. Third, it ignores the self-understanding and experience of religious traditions, which generally see communal life and relationships as vital to spiritual growth.

Individualism has also influenced the separation of religion from spirituality. Contemporary academic definitions of these terms tend to define religion in terms of community and spirituality with reference to the individual. Some authors appear to prefer an individualistic spirituality and to privilege it over more communal ways of seeking. However, studying spirituality from only an individualistic perspective runs the risk of ignoring the considerable effect of religious communities and the cultural context within which spirituality is lived for most people.

As we have seen, many scholars and individuals are observing a number of negative social and cultural trends. The newspapers carry stories of environmental degradation and global warming. The past century has seen unprecedented levels of warfare and cultural or physical genocide, which continue in the world today. Yet many people seem resigned to a conclusion that "progress" is inevitable, and these losses are things we must accept. One message of this book is that we need not accept this fate. Religious traditions offer great resources for the solution of many modern problems, and psychology can offer assistance in this endeavor.

It is clear from the theory and research reviewed here that the human person is both an *individual person* and a *relational being*. Thus, we need to avoid the extremes of an individualism that ignores the necessity of social relationships and a collectivism that ignores the uniqueness of the individual. This position has considerable support in the scientific literature, as well as important positions taken by religious and philosophical writers. Psychology in particular has often been guilty of stressing individuality at the expense of the vital relational connection a person needs to exist and flourish in their daily life.

15.4 Prospects and Directions for Dialogue

Assuming that barriers to dialogue can be overcome, what are the potential areas for dialogue in the future? Some encouraging current trends point to possibilities.

First, it seems likely that the psychology and religion dialogue will benefit significantly from postmodern and practice insights. Many scholars on the psychology side of the conversation, as well as those on the religion side, have begun to make use of postmodern concepts and methods, while avoiding the extreme relativism that has plagued postmodern thought in some areas of social psychology and philosophy. The willingness to consider qualitative approaches to investigation, sensitivity to differences among various religious traditions, and an understanding of the importance of context in religious behavior or experience are all valuable outcomes of a conversation influenced by postmodernism. It seems likely that these trends will continue.

Second, there are many exciting possibilities for expanding the depth and breadth of topics related to religion or spirituality that are part of the dialogue. While religious traditions are being exploited as a potential source of therapeutic techniques, other aspects of their thinking have been relatively neglected and may provide valuable insights. For instance, religious theories of psychopathology offer fascinating perspectives on important problems like depression, anxiety, or addictions. A broader consideration of religious traditions and practices is also at hand, with Islamic and Orthodox traditions taking their rightful place as partners in dialogue.

Finally, the psychology and religion dialogue is poised to explore the importance of community and the relational context for spirituality. Many contemporary authors on both sides of the dialogue have become deeply conscious of this important aspect of human experience. It may be that this conversation will also have an impact on the broader field of psychology, sensitizing it to these issues.

Predicting the future is hazardous. Fifty years ago, the British psychoanalytic writer Harry Guntrip argued that our culture needed a move away from a focus on human power and "a rebirth of the major interest in the needs of the heart and the end of existence toward which all our, at present, fevered and anxious activity tends" (Guntrip, 1957, p. 197). A strong dialogue between psychology and religion can help us move toward that goal while retaining the benefits that science has to offer us.

Glossary

Note: Numbers following the definitions refer to sections in the text where the term is discussed.

A

A posteriori knowledge Kant's term for knowledge built on experience (2.2.3).

A priori knowledge Kant's term for knowledge that is necessary and universally true completely independent of experience (2.2.3).

Abbot The leader of a monastic community (12.2.1).

Abidhamma A collection of Pali language writings that forms the most systematic early presentation of Buddhism (3.2.1).

Abstractionism An assumption found in many versions of naturalism, it is the belief that the general and abstract is of greater worth or more real than the particular, and that science or nonscience approaches that embrace the particular are of limited value (6.2.4).

Accedie A sense of discontent with one's current state, which can be accompanied by feelings of apathy, boredom, "burnout," or estrangement. It commonly occurs at midlife, and was described by Evagrius as one of the eight deadly thoughts that interfere with spiritual development. It is a spiritual disorder commonly confused with depression (9.2.3 and 11.2.1).

Active imagination A Jungian growth process where the individual is consciously presented with images from the unconscious and interacts with them in an attempt to overcome conflicts (5.1.2).

Adaptation In evolutionary theory, it is a characteristic that was selected in the past because it increased the Darwinian or inclusive fitness of an organism (6.2.1).

Adaptationism or **Darwinian fundamentalism** The belief that natural selection is the main or only factor responsible for evolutionary change (6.2.1).

Adaptive A general psychological term for a helpful change that people make in response to environmental demands (6.2.1).

Addictions A condition where we feel we must do or obtain certain things even when this leads to problems (11.3.1).

Advaita Vendanta A nondualist philosophy developed by Sankara (6th century) that equates Brahman with Atman (3.1.1).

Allopathic principle The basic principle of most modern medical care, it involves using chemical and mechanical intervention to counter forces that invade the body and cause illness (10.1.1).

Alpha waves Brain waves in the frequency range 8–12 cycles per second that frequently occur during relaxed states (13.6).

Altered state of consciousness (ASC) A shift in our state of conscious or subjective awareness that is perceived to be unusual (4.1.1).

Ambivalence of the sacred The fact that religious individuals want peace and tolerance but have strongly held beliefs for which they may be willing to fight (12.5.4).

Analytic reasoning Kant's term for reasoning that breaks things into parts and explores what we already know (2.2.3).

Anfechtung A complex concept in the thought of Martin Luther rendered by different translators as distress, anxiety, testing, assault, or temptation. It is a kind of experiential learning based on two basic attitudes (1) a feeling of need and (2) faith that God is a refuge who will accept us, respond to our need, and keep us from despair (13.4.1).

Anima The Jungian archetype representing the feminine principle. He believed that it has a spontaneous and youthful quality that is fascinating and is connected with experiences of awe or devotion (5.2.1).

Animus The masculine archetype in Jungian thought, it is associated with aggressiveness, dominance, and utilitarian attitudes (5.2.1).

Anthropic principle The observation that the fundamental properties of the universe are set just right to allow for life, but that the odds this might happen by chance are extremely remote (2.5.1).

Anxiety An important concept in psychology and existential philosophy, it is a kind of mood or mental pain that occurs when a person confronts conflicting demands or threatening situations (5.4.2).

Apatheia A state of detachment from inordinate desires and compulsions that provides a necessary foundation for spiritual development and freedom (11.2.1 and 13.1.2).

Apophatic or **negative theology** The theological position that it is difficult or impossible to make meaningful positive statements about God; rather, we know the Divine strictly through experience and excluding inaccurate conceptions of God (3.3.2).

Apostasy A type of unbelief that occurs when a person is raised with belief but later actively rejects it (9.2.4).

Archetypes A preexisting pattern of representation or instinctual behavior found in the collective unconscious. Jung believed that many important contents of the personality such as the Self or God were archetypal in nature (5.2.1).

Arhat (Sanskrit) or **Arhant** (Pali) An enlightened being (3.2.1).

Arminian theology The view taken by some Christian writers that we have free will and so every action is not necessarily predetermined by God (3.3.1).

Ascetic practices Activities designed to help create the physical and mental state necessary for spiritual development (13.2.2).

Asceticism A lifestyle and set of specific practices designed to discipline the body or mind and further one's spiritual development (3.1.2).

Ashrama A stage of life and spiritual development in the Hindu tradition (7.2.2).

Associative networks A social grouping of people based on a common interest. Membership may be independent of geography. Many Internet groupings fit in this category (12.3.3).

Atheism An active disbelief in God or a failure to allow belief in God to have a meaningful role in one's daily life (1.3.1).

Atman A Hindu term for the totality of our individual mind (3.1.1 and 10.3.2).

Attachment In psychology, the term refers to an internal, emotional bond to a trusted person who can be a secure base for exploration and a safe haven when threatened. These attachment relationships are an essential developmental asset. In Christian spirituality, attachment refers to a disordered or inordinate focus on some object or person that is perceived to satisfy a need but does so at the expense of other important things. In this framework, addictions are a type of attachment (8.2 and cf. 11.2.1).

Attachment behavior The behavior resulting from attachment to a trusted person, as when the individual or object of attachment is sought out for protection in times of anxiety or other need (8.2).

Attention association area Located in the frontal lobe of the brain, it includes the tertiary motor area where the brain integrates information from sensory and limbic structures, forming a basis for planning and decision making related to goal-directed behavior (6.1.1).

Attributions A term used in cognitive psychology that refers to explanations that people make of behavior and events (4.4.4).

Authoritarian parenting A cold and rigid style of parenting that is connected with lower rates of religion transmission and poorer mental health (8.1 and 12.3.3).

Authoritarian religion A concept discussed by Eric Fromm, it refers to any religion that has a belief in a power greater than humanity (1.4.4).

Authoritarianism A style of personality marked by conservatism, intolerance, rigidity, and prejudice (12.5.2).

Authoritative parenting A parenting style where the parents are warm and supportive but also firm and demanding. This parenting style is connected with good mental health and higher rates of religious transmission (8.1 and 12.3.3).

Autonomic nervous system (ANS) A key part of the nervous system that helps regulate basic bodily functions (6.1.1).

Autonomy The ability to make decisions without external coercion. These decisions may involve not following personal preferences if the choice is congruent with our values and beliefs (12.3.1).

Avatars In Hinduism, an incarnation of a god. In the perennial philosophy, they are individuals who embody the Absolute Ground of existence (3.1.1 and 4.3).

Awakening In Christian thought, an emotional event that occurs at the beginning of the spiritual life (7.2.1).

Ayurveda The system of health and illness that comes from the Hindu tradition (10.3.2).

B

Bare insight (*sukkavipassaka*) A means of attaining insight in Buddhism without passing through preparatory stages produced by calming meditation (13.5.1).

Beatific vision The medieval Catholic term for the ultimate goal of life, "the intimate and joyful union of the souls of the blessed with God in glory" (Aumann, 1980, p. 42), which results in a direct experience and knowledge of God (7.2.1).

Behaviorism A school of psychology that sees human behavior as determined by learning and reinforcement from the environment (1.4.1).

Beta waves Brain waves in the frequency range 13–29 cycles per second that are often found during normal waking activity (13.6).

Bhakti yoga A form of yoga that emphasizes the practice of worship or devotion (3.1.2).

Bhasya In Hinduism, an authoritative commentary on a sutra (3.1.1).

Bodhisattva A being that is spiritually mature and could leave the cycle of samsara but chooses to stay in order to help others achieve enlightenment. Achieving Bodhisattva status is the ideal of Mahayana Buddhism (3.2.3).

Bottom-up causation Also known as causal reductionism, it is the idea that events at higher and more complex levels such as psychological or social phenomena are determined by what happens at the lower levels of biological or chemical processes (2.1.2).

Boundary events Important experiences or changes in ways of looking at things that occur at a particular time (9.3.3).

Brahman In Hinduism, the total, universal, transcendental reality or mind that lies behind subjective reality (3.1.1 and 10.3.2).

Bonding capital A variety of social capital that holds groups together, facilitating emotional support (12.4.3).

Bridging capital A variety of social capital that builds ties between different cultural or socioeconomic groups, leading to a stronger society (12.4.3).

Buddha A term referring to (1) an enlightened person, or (2) Gautama Buddha, the founder of Buddhism (3.2).

Buddhist psychotherapy An approach to psychotherapy that accepts most fundamental Buddhist beliefs and tries to construct a theory and practice of counseling within this framework (14.3.2).

Buffering model A theory that religion contributes to health by buffering the effects of adverse circumstances (10.1.2).

C

Calm meditation (*samathayana*) Also sometimes referred to as concentrative meditation, it is a set of meditation practices designed to increase awareness by calming the mind and eliminating problematic patterns of mental activity. In Buddhist practice it prepares the way for *vipassana* or insight (3.2.2 and 13.5.1).

Catholic churches One of the three main branches of Christianity, it is headquartered in Rome and was the main form of religious practice in Western Europe prior to the Protestant Reformation (3.3.1).

Causal reductionism Also known as bottom-up causation, it is the idea that events at "lower" levels such as physics determine what happens at "higher" levels like psychology (2.1.2).

Centering prayer A simple mode of prayer developed by the Cistercian monk Thomas Keating, it attempts to establish a kind of genuine inner silence that is designed to reduce obstacles to contemplation and intimacy with God (13.3.3).

Chakras In Hindu thought, energy centers found in the subtle body that are related to various kinds of mental or spiritual activity (3.1.2).

Channeling A socialization technique where parents direct youth into groups and activities that reinforce home teaching (8.1).

Charismatic A Christian individual or group that focuses their religious life on the experience and practice of spiritual gifts (12.3.2).

Chronotype A space-time setting presumed by a narrative (9.3.3).

Circumambulation A circular path of travel around a religious site (12.4.2).

Cognitive appraisals Judgments about whether a situation represents a threat of harm or loss, a challenge with possibility of growth, or something beneficial (10.2.1).

Cognitive optimum position A term used in the cognitive science of religion to describe a natural way of thought (6.2.3).

Cognitive psychology A branch of psychology that sees behavior as a product of mental processes like language, reasoning, and memory (1.4.1).

Cognitive science of religion (CSR) An approach to the study of religion that looks at how the specific characteristics of human thought processes might lead us to think religiously and to do so in certain ways. CSR theories often make extensive use of concepts from evolutionary theory (6.2.3).

Cognitive-structural theory Approaches to understanding the human person that focus on the role of underlying organized structures or schemas of mental activity (7.4).

Cohort A group of people born during a particular period of history (9.1).

Cohort effect A problem in cross-sectional research on adult development that occurs when comparison groups of different ages are born at different times and grow up under diverse circumstances so that the groups may not be comparable with each other (9.1).

Collaborative coping A coping style involving an active partnership between the individual and God (10.2.2).

Collective identity The part of our identity that involves our self-concept as a member of various social or cultural groups (8.5.1).

Collective unconscious A concept developed by Carl Jung, it refers to the part of the unconscious containing materials of a universal and impersonal character that are genetically inherited (5.2.1).

Collectivism A social pattern that emphasizes giving priority to the goals of a group over the personal needs of the individual (12.3.1).

Common factor model The idea that there are common mechanisms behind the effectiveness of various approaches to psychotherapy (14.2.1).

Communitarian A type of social organization that promotes a strong sense of individual autonomy and uniqueness, as well as a deep commitment to relationships, community values, and goals (12.3.1).

Communitas A strong emotional experience of unity experienced when rituals produce a liminal state that is shared among members of a group (12.4.1).

Compensation hypothesis The hypothesis that people without early secure attachment will turn to religion as a substitute (8.2.2).

Compensators A term from rational choice theory, they are substitutes for desired rewards such as immortality that are provided by a religious organization (9.3.2).

Complement model Takes the position that science and religion deal with some of the same questions in a congruent or complementary manner so that each provides an important and irreplaceable viewpoint on human behavior. Since they overlap, each has the potential to assist and illuminate the other (1.4.7).

Complementarity The phenomenon in which something can behave in two seemingly incompatible ways. For instance, light appears to act as both a wave and a particle (2.5.1).

Computationalism In cognitive psychology, the older view that the brain works like a computer and processes instructions in a linear fashion (6.1.1).

Concentrative meditation Techniques to alter attention that involve a focus on an object such as a mantra or image. Yoga and Buddhist calming meditation are examples of concentrative techniques (13.5).

Concordance Agreement between the members of a twin pair on a variable of interest (6.1.2).

Conditioned reality The Buddhist view that reality is a matrix of multiple dependent origins and causal chains and thus has no permanent, enduring existence (13.5.1).

Confession A Christian practice of personal or public honesty about failings, especially when guilty of moral or spiritual lapses (14.1.3).

Confessionalism An approach to integration that privileges the perspectives of a specific religious tradition over those of psychology (1.4.7).

Confirmatory analysis An analysis that tests whether or not a hypothesized model is consistent with data (1.6.1).

Conflict model Holds that psychology and religion have overlapping areas of interest but that they provide different and conflicting truth claims (1.4.7).

Conflictual mimesis In the theory of Rene Girard, a situation where people focus on defeating an adversary at any cost, leading to escalating vengeance and violence (12.5.4).

Congregation An individual religious community in the Christian tradition (12.3.2).

Connectionist The view that distributed networks of brain cells and structures are involved in many brain functions (6.1.1).

Consciousness The field of awareness that forms the background for our mental life (4.1.1).

Constructionism The view that a person's beliefs and culture form an essential and inseparable part of their experiences, including religious experiences. It is sometimes distinguished from constructivism but as there is not a consistent usage the terms are used synonymously here (4.4).

Contemplative prayer Prayer involving an effortless letting go that allows God to speak. It is receptive in orientation (13.1).

Contemplative spirituality An approach to spirituality based on a loving, receptive attitude toward the world, a willingness to take it on its own terms and appreciate it for what it is, and an understanding and acceptance of our dependency on things beyond our control (11.3.1).

Conversion A change to a new status in one's religious life that often involves struggle and strong emotions. William James thought that individuals converting to religion would change and center their personal energy on the new religious system (3.3.2, 4.2.2, and 4.5).

Coping behavior Involves "ongoing cognitive and behavioral efforts to manage specific external and/or internal demands that are appraised as taxing or exceeding the resources of the person" (Lazarus, 1993, p. 237). It is triggered in situations that are perceived to be threatening or challenging (10.2.1).

Correlation coefficient A statistic commonly used as a measure of effect size or relationship between two variables (1.6.1).

Correspondence hypothesis The hypothesis that our relationship with God will match the pattern of attachment we developed as children; thus people with secure attachment might be expected to have better relationships with God (8.2.2).

Cortex The outermost, wrinkled and folded part of the brain that consists of four lobes: occipital, parietal, temporal, and frontal (6.1.1).

Counseling A helping relationship that focuses on helping people overcome problems and achieve their personal potential (14.2.1).

Counter statement (*antirrhesis*) Brief phrases, scripture passages or prayers to help focus the mind and repel distractions (13.2.4).

Critical realism The philosophical position that (1) science is able to give us knowledge of the real world, (2) this knowledge is imperfect but steadily improving, and (3) something like the entities described by science really exists. It is *critical* to the extent it is willing to subject our current understandings of the world to critique (2.5.4).

Cross-sectional study The most common approach to the study of adult development, which compares groups of different ages on selected variables and then concludes that differences between groups are due to development (9.1).

Cult A type of religious sect that does not have or maintain any connection to a church or other religious group of origin (12.3.3).

Cultic process A normal defensive tendency of religious and other groups to form exclusive subgroupings as a protection against anxiety or threat (12.3.3).

Culture A system of beliefs, values, and practices that provides a way of living a meaningful life (1.2.1).

Cultural divide hypothesis A sociological theory that cultural and demographic trends will lead to increasing global religiosity and a divide between advanced secular societies and developing religious ones (1.3.3).

Cultural unbelief A condition of unbelief in someone who grows up without any religious or spiritual background (9.2.4).

Cure of souls (*cura aminarum*) A Christian term for the application of religious teachings and practices to the overcoming of problems of the soul, the restoration of wholeness, and spiritual growth (14.1.3).

D

Daily Office Also known as the Divine Office or Prayer of Hours, it is a daily structure of times for prayer and worship in Christian monastic communities (12.2.2 and 13.1.3).

Dark night experience Described by the Christian mystic John of the Cross, it is an experience of purification and stripping away in preparation for advancement to a higher level of spiritual development. It is sometimes confused with depression (11.3.2).

Darwinian fitness A person's own reproductive success, it is a type of reproductive fitness (6.2.1).

Darwinian pluralism The belief that many factors are responsible for evolutionary change (6.2.1).

Deconstructionism A postmodern analysis that attempts to see how truth can be subject to political or economic pressures and may be used as a tool for power and oppression (6.3.1).

Deductive method A scientific method that involves the testing of hypotheses based on generalities derived from empirical investigation or other deductive studies (2.2.2).

Defense mechanisms Strategies used by the ego to express culturally inappropriate and threatening urges in more socially approved ways (5.1.1).

Deferring coping A more passive coping style in which responsibility for a problem is deferred to God (10.2.2).

Deism The view that God exists but no longer directly acts in the world (2.5.2).

Demand side theories Theories that attempt to explain religious behavior by looking at personal preferences and constraints on choice by social forces (9.2.2).

Denomination A large grouping of Christian congregations (12.3.2).

Descriptive statistics Summary measures of sample characteristics (1.6.1).

Desirous faculty The concupsicible part of the passionate aspect of the soul, it includes desires for things like food or sex (11.2.1).

Developmental crisis A turning point in development that provides the opportunity to succeed and add a particular strength or suffer a failure leading to maladjustment (5.3.1).

Dharma The Sanskrit term for duty or path, it is sometimes used in Buddhism to refer to the body of Buddhist teachings. It is one of the Three Jewels of Buddhism (3.2.1).

Dialogical integration A view that tries to give equal respect to psychology and religion in any dialogue, although the methods and conclusions of one might be preferred in certain areas (1.4.7).

Dialogical theories Theories that see things as related and in conversation with each other but not identical (2.5.3).

Differentiated experience Experience in which we perceive other things as *objects* separated from each other and from ourselves, the *subject* (4.1.1).

Differentiated identity A complex identity that is rich with many different interests, values and coping mechanisms (8.2.1).

Discernment In the Christian tradition, it refers to the process of gaining accurate perceptions of spiritual reality. In the context of spiritual direction, this involves the capacity of the director to accurately sense the needs and capabilities of their students (13.3.4 and 14.1.1).

Discrimination Differential treatment of a person based on group membership, stereotype or prejudice (12.5.1).

Dismissing attachment An attachment style that includes a positive view of self but negative views of others and intimacy (8.2.1).

Disordered attachments Excessive focus upon an object that satisfies a need or brings pleasure. This unbalances our life, causing us to focus on the object at the expense of other things that are important, leading to a loss of inner freedom (11.2.1).

Distress-deterrent model A model that sees religion as having indirect effects by enhancing coping mechanisms that then deter distress and promote health (10.1.2).

Doctrine of dependent origin The Buddhist belief that all things are the product of causes and are in turn causes for other things. In the Buddhist context, this implies that nothing has any substantial or continuing existence (3.2.3).

Dokusan A private meeting with a master teacher or roshi. It is one of the three pillars of Zen Buddhism (13.5.2).

Doshas A term from Hindu ayurvedic medicine, they are energies or humors that are believed to form a basis for our physical and mental functioning (10.3.2).

Double bind A situation where people are called upon to do two incompatible things. For instance, Rene Girard argues that people are called to be both imitators and rivals, leading to conflict (12.5.4).

Drives Instinctual processes that motivate behavior (5.0).

Dualism A philosophical and religious term that refers to a separation between two things that is thought to be fundamental and essential. For instance, some dualistic religious and philosophical thought draws a sharp contrast between the spiritual and physical worlds, or between the mind and body (3.1.1 and 6.1).

Dualistic reductionism A philosophical technique where two related things are separated from each other and then the unwanted item is discarded or viewed as merely a by-product of the other. For instance, materialists often separate mind and brain from each other and them argue that the mind has no reality (2.1.3).

Duhkha The Sanskrit term for suffering used in Buddhism and Hinduism (3.1.2).

Dwellers A term used by some sociologists to describe active participants in a particular religious tradition (1.3.2).

E

Eastern Orthodox churches One of the three main branches of Christianity, it is the main form of religious practice in parts of Eastern Europe (3.3.1).

Ecclesiology The branch of Christian theology devoted to the study of religious community (12.2.2).

Economic Trinity In Orthodox Christian theology, the term that is used to describe the Trinity as it appears and works in the world (3.3.1).

Ecumenism Outreach and dialogue between members of different religious groups and traditions (12.2.2).

Effect size A descriptive statistic that measures the strength and nature of the relationship between variables (1.6.1).

Ego A term used in psychodynamic theory for the part of the personality that carries on executive and decision-making functions (5.1.1).

Eightfold Path Part of the Four Noble Truths in Buddhism, the Path provides the basic way that people can eliminate suffering and attain enlightenment (3.2.1).

Ekagrata In yoga and Buddhist practice, the Sanskrit term for "one-pointed" or focused concentration (3.1.2 and 13.5.1).

Electroencephalogram (EEG) A technique for recording electrical activity in the brain (13.6).

Emergent properties Unique characteristics apparent at a particular level of organization that cannon be derived or understood from the study of lower levels (2.1.2).

Emerging adulthood A transitional period in development running from the end of adolescence through the mid-to-late twenties (9.2.2).

Emic models Models that view human behaviors as having unique characteristics that occur within a given physical, social, and historical context (1.2.1).

Emotion-focused coping A type of coping in which the individual focuses on managing distressing emotions, for instance by trying to alter the meaning of what is happening (10.2.1).

Empathy "The ability to identify with and understand the situations, motives, and feelings of another" (Hurlbut, 2002, p. 314), it probably underlies our ability to forgive (11.4.1).

Empirically supported treatment (EST) A therapy that has been shown by a specific research protocol to be an effective treatment for a particular mental illness (14.2.1).

Empiricism The view that investigations into the basic nature of reality should be based on experience and experiment rather than reasoning (2.1.1).

Emplotment The process of weaving actions and characters together into a coherent story or narrative (6.3.3).

Emptiness In Buddhism, the belief that apparently stable things like the self are in fact constantly changing and are thus have no real, continuing existence (3.2.3).

Enlightenment The 18th-century intellectual movement that hoped to build a society based on human reason (2.3).

Enneagram A system of personality types based on Islamic Sufi thought that is also popular among some contemporary Christian spiritual directors (11.2.2 and 14.2.2).

Environment of evolutionary adaptiveness (EEA) The environment in which an evolutionary adaptation originally arose and was selected (6.2.1).

Epigenetic principle The idea the people have an inbuilt plan for growth into wholeness that unfolds throughout life in a series of stages and that proper development at earlier stages is essential to success at later ones (5.3.1).

Epiphenomenon Something that has no reality or ability to affect other things. Reductive materialists often argue that our mental life is an epiphenomenon and that only our body is truly real (2.1.3 and 6.1).

Epistemological pluralism The view that any of our understandings of the world are only limited and partial, and because of this we need multiple ways of knowing (14.3.1).

Epistemological reductionism The idea that laws governing higher-level, complex phenomena should follow from laws at lower levels (2.1.2).

Epistemology A branch of philosophy that studies the ways we gain knowledge about the world and ourselves (2.1.1).

Esoteric practice A spiritual practice that is reserved for initiates of a religious tradition. The details of the practice are frequently kept secret and not revealed to outsiders (3.1.2). In the perennial philosophy, the universal truth behind all religions is referred to as esoteric truth (4.3).

Ethical materialism The view that pleasure is the main goal of life, and that this is achieved primarily through acquiring and possessing material goods (11.1.2).

Ethnicity A group of people who identify with each other, typically on the basis of perceived common decent or national origin (8.5.1).

Etic models A view that sees human behaviors as universal phenomena with similar characteristics in all times, settings, and places (1.2.1).

Eudaimonic models An approach in which mental health is thought of as a state of psychological well-being and engagement with life (11.1.2).

Eugenics The improvement of the human species through the manipulation of genetics and reproductive practices (6.2.1).

Evidence-based practice in psychology (**EBPP**) Psychotherapy practice that tries to take into account situational and contextual factors when applying research findings in practical situations such as mental health treatment (14.2.1).

Evolution In evolutionary biology, the change in organisms that takes place over time due to genetic alterations. In transpersonal theory, evolution is spiritual in nature, and is a progression toward transcendence (6.2.1 and 7.5.1).

Evolutionary psychology (**EP**) The most recent attempt to apply evolutionary theory to psychology, typically employing a Darwinian fundamentalist model of evolutionary change (6.2.2).

Exaptation An evolutionary term for a characteristic that is fitness-enhancing now but was not originally designed for its current role, either because it had a different original purpose or no original purpose at all (6.2.1).

Existential anxiety Anxiety resulting from our fundamental limitations and separation from God and others. This is a religious or spiritual problem that cannot be eliminated with psychological treatment (11.2.1).

Existential sickness An outcome of nihilistic beliefs characterized by boredom, adventure seeking, and a need to disconfirm the possible positive meanings of others (11.1.2).

Existential well-being A sense of life purpose and satisfaction that is part of spiritual well-being (11.1.3).

Existentialism A school of philosophy that tries to understand the human person by looking at their connection to the ultimate characteristics of existence like freedom and finitude (1.51.).

Exoteric religion In the perennial philosophy, the external forms of religion that may have great symbolic power (4.3).

Experimental method A scientific method that involves having an experimenter produce changes in a variable and then observing the effects of the changes on other variables (1.6.1).

Explicit minimizing strategy A philosophy of counseling integration proposed by Richards and Bergin, it argues that the counselor should be explicit about their values but also respect the autonomy of the client and their beliefs (14.3.1).

Explicit strategies A counseling approach where the therapist openly discusses religious or spiritual issues with the client, and may teach or engage in religious practices with them (14.2.2).

Exploratory analysis An analysis that is conducted to search for possible relationships among variables in a set of data (1.6.1).

Expressive prayer An effortful prayer that is directed toward God and involves language or imaginative activity (13.1).

Extrinsic motivation A desire to engage in religious activities as a way of achieving specific personal goals (1.4.6 and 9.3.1).

Extrovertive mysticism A category of mystical experience described by W. T. Stace, where a mystic senses unity in the world and a sacredness that is living and present in all things, as in some kinds of nature mystical experiences (4.3.4).

F

Factor analysis A statistical procedure used to find dimensions in complex data (1.6.1).

Faith A central term in Christian thought and the developmental theory of James Fowler, who defines faith as an evolving sense of sprit and relatedness to others that provides meaning and coherence (7.4.3).

Faith-based organization (FBO) An organization generally founded by religious people that gets contributions from religious groups and would include something related to faith or religion in its mission statement and activities (12.4.3).

Fallibilism A version of critical realism in theology that argues we can make positive statements about God but that in practice it is difficult to construct and test such models because of the effects of preexisting cultural and ideological structures (2.5.4).

False self A superficial and illusionary picture of the self that we present to others and ourselves (5.4.3 and 13.3.2).

Fearful attachment An attachment style built upon negative views of self and other, leading to social avoidance (8.2.1).

Final causes One of Aristotle's four types of causes, final causes assert that things sometimes happen because of some end purpose or goal (2.2.2).

Flourishing A condition where people are high in both subjective and psychological well-being (11.1.2).

Folk religion A popular version of belief and practice in a religion, which may differ from the beliefs and practices taught by religious leaders (3.2.3).

Forgiveness A Christian practice where a person who has been wronged recognizes that they have the right to reparation or revenge but they renounce it, and instead choose to respond with compassion and love toward the perpetrator, leaving open the possibility of better relations (11.4.1).

Four Noble Truths Four basic Buddhist principles about the causes and nature of suffering, as well as ways we can reach enlightenment (3.2.1).

Frontal lobe The portion of the cortex located in the front of the brain that has important roles in motor activity, planning and decision-making (6.1.1).

Functional analysis Explanations that focus on what a behavior does; for instance, functional analyses of religion focus on effects it creates or the goals it achieves (1.2.1).

Fundamentalism "A discernible pattern of religious militance by which self-styled 'true believers' attempt to arrest the erosion of religious identity, fortify the borders of the religious community, and create viable alternatives to secular institutions and behaviors" (Almond, Appleby, & Sivan, 2003, p. 17). This pattern has both ideological and organizational components (12.3.3).

G

Gamma waves High frequency brain waves in the range 30–70 cycles per second that may assist in binding different brain areas together in networks (13.6.1).

Gender "The socially constructed roles of men and women implicating different social norms and cultural expectations for both sexes" (Möller-Leimkühler, 2003, p. 2), which are thought to affect religious behavior (8.5.4).

Gender identity theory Theory that sees the feminine and masculine as gender roles or identities and argues that it is feminine attitudes and values which incline people toward religion, not their biological sex (8.5.4).

Gene flow Genetic changes caused by the movement of genes within populations or between groups (6.2.1).

Generativity The Eriksonian task of midlife, it involves giving oneself in care for a younger generation (5.3.2).

Genetic psychology A term used in early 20th-century psychology that referred to the study of the developmental sources and processes behind the psyche. Many genetic psychologists held that development in the individual is a recapitulation of prior evolutionary stages (1.4.2 and 7.3).

Genotype The specific genetic code of an individual (6.1.2).

Geographical networks A social grouping formed by people who live and work in geographical proximity to each other (12.3.3).

God image In psychology, an internal object representation or working model of God that forms early in life but changes during the course of development. Judeo-Christian scriptures state that humans were created in the image of God, and so the term in Christian theology refers to essential aspects of human nature or potential (5.4.3 and 8.3).

God locus of control The extent to which we see God as in charge and involved in the world (10.2.2).

God-of-the-gaps The view that God acts only with regard to phenomena that cannot be explained by science (2.5.2).

Good copy problem A problem found in many societies where a person cannot construct a fully satisfactory identity that is both acceptable to modernity and loyal to one's culture (12.5.4).

Grace The term used in Christian theology for an unearned gift, e.g., of God's love for us (3.3.1).

Gradual enlightenment The idea that enlightenment happens over a long period of time (3.2.4).

Grounded theory A qualitative approach in which one begins with a research question rather than a theory and specific hypotheses and tries to construct a theory and categories on the basis of data (1.6.2).

Guarding the heart (*nepsis*) A state of inner and outer watchfulness for things that might interfere with our prayer and spiritual life (13.2.4).

Gunas Universal qualities that are described in Hindu ayurvedic medicine (10.3.2).

Guru The term used in Hinduism to refer to a spiritual teacher of advanced attainment (3.1.2 and 14.1.2).

H

Happiness The short-term experiences of pleasure and avoidance of negative emotions (11.1.2).

Hard stage model A model for development comprised of fixed stages that are applicable to everyone (7.4.2).

Hatha Yoga A form of yoga that emphasizes the preparation or strengthening of the physical body to encourage spiritual development (3.1.2 and 10.3.2).

Health In the Western medical model, health is seen as an absence of illness. In more holistic models of heath it also includes wellness and positive characteristics of functioning like living a meaningful, active, and productive life (10.1.1).

Healthy-minded A term used by William James to refer to people who had a natural sense of happiness and optimism, believing that things are good and that evil can be overcome (4.2.2).

Heart A Christian term for the ground of the soul, the inner directing center of the person, and a unifying principle and symbol of wholeness that affects all aspects of the person and is affected by them. It is the place where we meet God, so it has a mysterious, unconscious, and transcendent aspect (5.3.3 and 13.1.4).

Hedonic models Approaches that tend to equate mental health with the experience of happiness or subjective well-being (11.1.2).

Hedonic set point A personal emotional level of happiness that is determined by temperament, personality variables, biology, and other factors (11.1.2).

Hedonic treadmill The phenomenon that increasing efforts must be made in order to get and maintain a level of happiness above one's hedonic set point (11.1.2).

Heritability coefficient A coefficient that ranges from 0 to 1, it indicates the amount of correspondence between genetic variability and the occurrence of a characteristic (6.1.2).

Hermeneutic circle A circular process of interpretation that includes the speaker/actor and hearer, their preunderstandings, what is said or done and the context in which it takes place. In the interpretive process, each of these things is affected by and impacts other parts of the circle (6.3.2).

Hermeneutics A school of philosophy that studies how we interpret meaning in discourse and action. Hermeneutics sees all knowledge as acquired through an interpretive process that is dependent upon both our personal history and the context provided by our culture and groups to which we belong (1.5.3 and 6.3.2).

Hesychia A state of calmness and attention to God that is free from distraction (13.2.4).

Hierarchical theories Theories of development that see life like climbing a ladder. As we age we climb higher and higher on the ladder through a universal, fixed set of stages and reach increasingly sophisticated levels of development (7.1.1).

Hinge events Turning points or other events that mark the transition between life periods (9.3.3).

Historicist critique A critique of philosophies of science carried on by studying how scientists have actually conducted their work in the past (2.4.2).

Holding environment Winnicott's description of a stable but responsive environment that promotes the development of trust, confidence and a sense that the environment around us is a benevolent one (5.4.3).

Holism The idea that the interconnectedness of things adds an essential component to them (2.1.2).

Holistic theory A model that focuses on the interrelationship and interconnectedness of many factors. It is opposed to a reductionistic approach that focuses on few factors and neglects interrelationships. Holistic models of health focus on it as more than the absence of illness but the global status of many aspects of our life (1.2.2 and 10.1.1).

Holy Something of transcendent value (4.3.3).

Homines religiosi Erikson's term for religious geniuses like Luther or Gandhi, who face the struggles of their age and find new paths for humanity (5.3.2).

Hope In positive psychology, it is a type of thinking that helps us to maintain goal-directed behavior. In other psychological and religious views, hope is a sense that the world and God are trustworthy (11.1.2).

Horizon A term in phenomenology that refers to the boundary of conscious awareness (4.1.1).

Human capital In sociological thought, it refers to skills and capacities people acquire that allow them to produce desired products (9.3.2).

Human capital theories Theories that explain religious retention by pointing out that involvement in a particular religious group allows one to gain religious value through learning the teachings and practices of the group, and that leaving the group would cause one to loose this value (9.2.2).

Human freedom Our ability to make choices, pursue goals and be creative that exceeds what might be expected (1.2.1 and 3.3.1).

Humanism An ideology that assumes humans are basically good as well as powerful, and that advancing human power and achievement is a fundamental goal of life (1.2.1).

Humanistic psychology A branch of psychology that attempts to study people in terms of their uniquely human positive qualities and potentials (1.4.5).

Humanistic religion A concept of Eric Fromm, referring to a religion centered on human power and strength. In humanistic religion, God is considered to be a symbol for humanity (1.4.4).

Humility "A basic honesty about who one is and is not" (Frohlich, 1993, p. 193), it is a virtue that is a key component of most Christian models of development (7.2.1).

I

Icon A visual representation of religious reality that forms an important part of Orthodox Christian practice (13.2.5).

Ideology A set of beliefs at the heart of a group that includes (1) descriptive statements about the world, (2) normative statements about how we ought to act, and (3) sociological imperatives that define social existence for its members (12.2).

Id In Freud's theory, a structure that contains the instinctual part of the psyche (5.1.1).

Identity Our "sense of personal sameness and historical continuity" (Erikson, 1968, p. 17) that can change over time (5.3.1 and 8.5).

Ideology A system of thought that attempts to explain everything from a single premise (1.2.1).

Illumination (the *Via Illuminativa*) In the Christian tradition, a more advanced stage of spiritual development marked by an increasing sense of God's presence (7.2.1).

Imago An internal idealized representation of the self or another person, such as a parent (5.2.1 and 9.3.3).

Immanent Something that is present in a tangible way, as in our bodily life, daily experiences and practices (1.2.1).

Immanent Trinity In Christian Orthodox theology, the term that is used to describe the essence of God, the Trinity as they fully are to each other, which we can never fully know (3.3.1).

Implicit strategies An approach to counseling that is based upon some system of spiritual and religious principles but deals with these issues without direct reference to this framework or any religious practices (14.2.2).

Incarnation In Christian theology, the belief that Jesus was not only human but was God in the flesh as well (3.3.1).

Incisive faculty In Greek and early Christian thought, the forceful, irascible, or angry part of the passionate aspect of the soul (11.2.1).

Inclusive fitness Reproductive success that is not merely concerned with the individual, but also the kin of that individual; it is a type of reproductive fitness (6.2.1).

Indiscriminately pro-religious A person who has high levels of both intrinsic and extrinsic religious motivation (9.3.1).

Individualism The view that society is a collection of loosely linked individuals motivated by personal preferences, needs, or rights, and that society exists to help people pursue these individual agendas (12.3.1).

Individuation A Jungian term for spiritual and personal growth, it is a maturational process that involves the reuniting of unconscious materials with the conscious so that the person can achieve wholeness (5.1.2).

Inductive method A scientific method advocated by Bacon that involves compiling large amounts of detailed information and then looking for generalities (2.2.2).

Ineffable A truth that cannot properly be conveyed in words because of its secret, hidden or incommunicable quality but must be experienced directly to be understood. This is thought by many scholars such as William James to be a typical characteristic of mystical experience (3.2.4 and 4.1.1).

Inferential statistics Tests that tell whether or not the characteristics of a sample can be generalized to a larger population (1.6.1).

Infused contemplation An experience of God's presence where we sense the Divine directly at work within us (11.3.2 and 13.3.1).

Ingroup A group of people with which we identify and relate (12.5.1).

Insecure attachment An attachment pattern that develops when a child perceives their caretaker as undependable. Children in this situation are generally more isolated and hostile, shows distress on departure of the caretaker and don't soothe on their return. Insecurely attached children may be either excessively preoccupied with intimacy or prefer distance (8.2.1).

Instrumental Actions designed to gratify a need or gain a goal, or relationships that occur when we see something or someone primarily as an object that will help us satisfy a need (1.4.2).

Integrated identity An identity that allows different aspects of an individual to work together in harmony (8.2.1).

Integration Theory and research that attempt to combine psychological perspectives with theological or religious views (1.4.7).

Intentionality A term in phenomenology that refers to the fact that consciousness is generally directed toward specific objects (4.1.1).

Internal working models In attachment theory, cognitive-affective schemas that form and provide mental representations of others. The concept of object in psychodynamic theory has a similar meaning (8.2).

Internalized objects Representations of objects within the psyche that affect us even when the original physical object or relationship is absent (5.4.1).

Interpretive theory The view that the primary function of religion is helping people to construct meaning that allows them to interpret and make sense of their world (12.4.1).

Intersubjectivity A term from phenomenology, it describes the experience of understanding that another individual is also a person who has a state of subjective awareness and a point of view (4.1.1).

Intrinsic motivation A desire to engage in religious activities because they have inherent value, regardless of any personal benefits that may be gained from them (1.4.6 and 9.3.1).

Introspection A method of phenomenological investigation where an individual examines his or her own mental states (4.2.1).

Introvertive mysticism Mysticism that involves a unitary state of consciousness that is contentless and independent of time sense, a state of pure consciousness and loss of self. It is one of W. T. Stace's categories of mystical experience (4.3.4).

J

Jesus Prayer A short prayer to Jesus such as "Lord Jesus Christ, Son of God, have mercy on me, a sinner" used in Christian Orthodox religious practice (13.2.3).

Jhanas Modes of consciousness produced in Buddhist concentrative or calming meditation that help overcome hindrances to practice and advance the individual toward insight and liberation (13.5.1).

Judgment Kant's term for reason and decision-making based on feelings of pleasure and displeasure, including aesthetic judgment (2.2.3).

Justice reasoning How people decide what is just or right behavior in situations where there are competing claims among persons. Lawrence Kohlberg has developed the most well-known theory and description of justice reasoning (7.4.2).

Justification In Christianity, the changed status before God that marks the beginning of the individual's Christian life (3.3.2).

K

Karma The Hindu and Buddhist term for human action, which is thought to affect our status when we are reborn into our next life (3.1).

Kasinas Objects like a clay disk or colors that can serve as objects for visualization in Buddhist concentrative or calming meditation (13.5.1).

Kataphatic theology Theology that attempts to make positive statements about God (3.3.2).

Kensho A state of consciousness discussed in Zen Buddhism in which the mind is clear and the meditator may have a sudden intense, uncluttered experience of pure existence, a recognition of one's purified mind and true nature (13.5.2).

Klesas In Hinduism, a group of problematic patterns of thinking that lead to our separation from reality, such as greed, hate or delusion (3.1.2 and 13.4.1).

Koans Enigmatic stories or sayings used in Zen Buddhism that move an individual toward appreciation of the contradictions in life (3.2.4, 4.6.1, and 13.5.2).
Kundalini In Hinduism, a term for psychic energy that flows upward from the base of the spine through channels in the subtle body. It is sometimes associated with the goddess Shakti (3.1.2).

L

Lateralized In neuroscience, a term indicating that a particular structure or function is more concentrated on either the left or right side of the brain (6.1.1).
Lectio divina The Roman Catholic spiritual practice of "divine reading," where scriptures such as the psalms or other spiritual writings are read slowly and prayerfully, looking for guidance in one's spiritual life and moral applications (13.3).
Liberal theology A position in theology initially developed by Friedrich Schleiermacher, which says that theological statements are simply expressions of religious experience, feeling and sentiment (3.3.1).
Libido The energy that powers the human psyche (5.2.1).
Life review An integrative remembering that includes critical analysis of our life story and what we have done. Erikson believed that this was a task of older adulthood (9.3.3).
Lifespan theories Theories of development that have a circular view of life. During the early part of the cycle we grow and add abilities as we encounter predictable, age related life tasks, while in the later part of life, we decline or reflect over our past (7.1.1).
Limbic system A subcortical brain system comprising a number of structures, including the amygdala and the hippocampus. Neural activity in the limbic system is thought to be related to emotional functioning, socioemotional perception and memory (6.1.1).
Liminal experience An experience where a person is in between two states but is in neither of them. This transitional state allows separation from old patterns so that new ones can be adopted (5.4.4 and 12.4.1).
Liminoid experience A weak kind of pseudo-liminal state that is individualized and commercialized, causing it to lose its transformational power (12.4.1).
Limit situations or experiences Situations either positive or negative that challenge our accepted view of life (1.2.1).
Liturgical orders Sequences of rituals involving worship and commemoration of past events that take place throughout the year (12.4.1).
Liturgy Special language that is used in a religious ritual (12.4.1).
Localization hypothesis The view in neuroscience that particular locations in the brain carry out specific functions (6.1.1).
Logical or **definitional reductionism** The idea that the vocabulary and language used at one level of scientific inquiry should be able to be exactly translated into the language of another level, e.g., that psychological phenomena can be completely described and understood using neurological language (2.1.2).

Logical positivism A version of positivism that used analytic philosophy of language and logic to analyze and reform language, purifying it of religious and philosophical content so that it could be a vehicle for logical analysis and statements of empirical, scientific knowledge (2.4).

Longitudinal study An approach to studying adult development where researchers follow one group of people over a period of years to look for changes (9.1).

M

Madhyamika A Mahayana philosophy developed by Nagarjuna that attempted to provide a synthesis of Buddhist thought. His work is foundational for most schools of Tibetan Buddhism (3.2.3).

Mahayana Buddhism The largest group of Buddhist schools of thought, including most Chinese, Tibetan and Japanese varieties of Buddhism. Mahayana emphasizes the Bodhisattva ideal of helping others to achieve enlightenment (3.2.3).

Mandala In Hinduism and Buddhism, a name for drawings and artistic constructions that are thought to represent spiritual or religious realities. They are often symmetrical in form and include concentric circles or squares, as well as religious images. Carl Jung saw them as symbols of archetypal material (3.1.2 and 5.1.2).

Mantras A repeated word or phrase used in various kinds of meditation, prayer and spiritual practice (3.1.2).

Manualized therapy Conducting a psychotherapeutic procedure using a standardized set of instructions in a treatment manual that can be reliably followed in a similar manner by all therapists (14.2.1).

Martyr An individual who chooses to die rather than give up their religious commitment (12.5.4).

Mass action hypothesis In neuroscience, the idea that the whole brain or widely distributed networks of brain cells are involved in brain functions (6.1.1).

Massive Modularity Hypothesis (MMH) The view that the mind is very much like a computer, and is made up of thousands of problem-solving machines or modules (6.2.2).

Materialism The philosophical position that the ultimate reality of things is found in their physical or material nature. In psychology, it is the assumption that sufficient explanations for our mind and behavior can be constructed based only on characteristics of our material body (2.1.3).

Meaning The feeling or idea that life has value; we have a place in the world, and can seek valued ends through activities, caring relationships, and involvement in life (11.1.2).

Meaning system A structure that makes sense out of the world by integrating ideals, feeling, behavior, and motives or ultimate concerns (4.5.2).

Mediating model A theory that religion does not have direct effects on variables like health, but it affects them indirectly by causing changes in other variables (e.g., social support) that do have direct effects on health (10.1.2).

Medical model The view that physical or mental illness is caused by disruptions to the proper functioning of our bodily or psychic mechanisms, which must be countered by chemical or mechanical actions performed by experts (10.1.1 and 11.1.1).

Medicalization of culture When many legal, social, and religious problems are viewed as medical ones in need of expert treatment (10.1.1).

Meditatio The traditional Latin term for meditation in Roman Catholic thought. It involves taking a word, phrase, or idea and reflecting on its personal meaning, leading to increased self-knowledge and understanding of the Divine. The Catholic term *contemplation* is probably closer to the Buddhist meaning of the term (13.3).

Meditation A non-discursive procedure aimed at altering attention, clearing the mind of normal thought patterns and establishing a more receptive mode of consciousness. In the Christian tradition, it becomes a technique for increasing one's awareness of the presence and love of God (3.3.2 and 13.1).

Metanarrative A general or universal theory of the world and existence that is true in all times and places. Modernism searches for metanarratives, while most postmodernists reject the possibility of truth that is not affected by social or cultural context (6.3.1).

Metaphysical or **reductive naturalism** A commitment to produce abstract, lawlike explanations without recourse to supernatural forces using methods from the natural sciences in which the investigator is seen as an impartial, outside observer of a world that is strictly material in nature. Typically it is also assumed that a system of laws exists that can explain all events (2.1.4).

Metaphysics Investigations into the basic nature of reality that are based primarily on reasoning rather than experience or experiment (2.1.1).

Methodological or **atomistic reductionism** Simplification of a phenomenon for the purpose of study, typically by breaking it into parts (2.1.2).

Methodological naturalism A commitment to produce abstract, lawlike explanations without recourse to supernatural forces using methods in which the investigator is seen as an impartial, outside observer (2.1.4).

Methodological physicalism The philosophical view that nonmaterial things exist but that we can only study the world through physical, material entities (2.1.3).

Methodological reductionism Simplification of a complex concept so that it can be measured in scientific research (1.6.1).

Mimesis The Greek word for the process of making representations or schema (6.3.3).

Mimetic desire Also called acquisitive mimesis, it is a concept developed by Rene Girard to explain religious violence. Mimetic desire occurs when we identify with others and seek to emulate them by copying their desires, polarizing individuals and putting them in competition for desired objects (12.5.4).

Mimetic double The way in which people become similar to someone they copy. Girard argues that adversaries become increasingly like each other, a factor in escalating violence (12.5.4).

Mind-brain problem The problem of how our mental functioning (which appears to be non-material) is related to the physiological processes in our brain (which appear to be material). This issue is currently unresolved but is of great interest in philosophy (6.1).

Mindfulness (*sati*) A state of unattached, nonjudgmental awareness of reality (3.2.2 and 13.5.1).

Mindfulness meditation A passive or receptive type of meditation in which one simply tries to be aware of the present moment. Development of insight (*vipassana*) in Buddhism usually involves the practice of mindfulness meditation (13.5).

Minimally counterintuitive ideas A term used by cognitive theorists to describe ideas that have both natural and supernatural aspects (6.2.3).

Moderator model The view that religion has positive effects by moderating the effects of stress. This model predicts that religion will have a greater positive impact when stress levels are high (10.1.2 and 11.3.2).

Modernism The dominant worldview in Western culture that began to take shape in the Renaissance and Protestant Reformation and become more central with the advent of the Enlightenment. Modernism emphasizes the universality of truth and the centrality of the individual who stands apart from the world and others; it forms the basis of much scientific philosophy, including positivism (6.3).

Modes theory A cognitive theory of religion developed by Harvey Whitehouse, which argues that there are different modes or types of religious thinking that involve different levels of effort and complexity (6.2.3).

Modules In evolutionary psychology, problem-solving mechanisms or processes within the brain that are evolved adaptations to specific problems (6.2.2).

Monastery A complex of buildings in which a monastic community resides and pursues religious devotion, study, and service. In the Christian traditions, monasteries housing communities of women are sometimes known as *convents* (12.2.1).

Monastic communities Groups of men or women, generally unisex in composition, who live apart from society in order to pursue a life devoted to religion and spiritual growth (12.2.1).

Monism The view that all aspects of a person are parts of a single underlying reality or system with no real differences. The assumption often made in neuroscience that the mind and brain are really the same thing is a monistic philosophical position (2.5.3, 5.5 and 6.1).

Monistic experience An experience where all things are seen as one and we may become dissolved or absorbed into this great absolute unity (4.1.1).

Monk A man who is a member of a monastic community. In Theravada Buddhism they are known as *bhikkhu*. In Christianity, women monastics are sometimes called *nuns* (12.2.1).

Mudras Hand gestures or body postures used during meditation or prayer that are thought to have special spiritual or religious significance (3.1.2).

Multivariate Belief-Motivation Theory of Religiousness A theory developed by Schaefer and Gorsuch that divides factors related to religion into three interrelated domains: motivation, belief or God concept, and coping style (1.4.6 and 9.3.1).

Multivocal A feature of the personal narrative in which there is more than one story line or voice (9.3.3).

Mystery A quality of life in which things are seen to be outside of our understanding and control (11.3.1).

Mystical experience An experience of the immediate presence of the Divine or of ultimate reality, or of union with that reality (4.1.1).

Mysticism A way of life in which mystical states are valued and sought after, although sometimes authors also use the term to refer to mystical experiences (3.3.2 and 4.1.1).

Mythic A school of thought that sees ritual as an expression of master narratives we have about reality. It sees the content of ritual as of primary importance (12.4.1).

N

Narrative A coherent story that weaves together action, characters, events circumstances and goals. It allows for the portrayal of embodied human action in lived experience (6.3.3 and 9.3.3).

Narrative identity A concept developed by Paul Ricoeur and others, a narrative identity is a story that we construct about ourselves, which forms the basis for our personal identity (6.3.3 and 9.3.3).

Narrative tone The general mood of optimism or pessimism in a narrative (9.3.3).

Natural contemplation The second stage of Christian growth discussed by Evagrius, it is when we see the inner laws and meaning of things in relation to the activity of God (13.2.1).

Natural selection In Darwin's theory, it is the evolutionary principle that genetic characteristics which *enhance the possibility of survival* are more likely to be retained or selected and passed on to succeeding generations. In the modern synthesis of evolutionary theory, it is characteristics that *enhance successful reproduction* that are selected (6.2.1).

Natural theology Theological inquiry that attempts to use what we see in the natural world as a support for our understanding of God (2.2.2).

Naturalism The philosophical position that the world around us can be understood abstractly in terms of natural, lawlike processes (2.1.4).

Naturalistic Fallacy The fallacy that what is *observed to be* people's values or actions is what *should be* people's values or actions (2.5.3).

Negative identity Identity that is developed as a reaction against or rejection of a particular individual, community or set of ideals and beliefs (5.3.1).

Negative religious coping A coping style that involves a sense of spiritual discontent, and a lack of congregational support. God is seen as punishing or helpless, and so the people may seem themselves as afflicted by God, leading to more passive forms of coping (10.2.2).

Neopositivism Technically, a form of logical positivism developed during the mid 20th century that involved abandoning previous claims to verification while maintaining other aspects of logical positivist theory. This was discredited through the historicist critique. However, versions of positivism continue to exist within psychology and may be termed neopositivist (2.4.2 and 2.4.3).

Neuroscience In psychology, the view that behavior is related to biological and genetic factors affecting the brain (1.4.1).

Neurotic anxiety Anxiety that is caused by unnecessary internal conflicts or psychological problems and can be helped through psychological interventions (1.5.1 and 11.2.1).

Neurotransmitter Chemicals released by a nerve cell that facilitate the transmission of a signal to other nerve cells (6.1).

New age movement A type of new religious movement that focuses on the inner spirituality of the individual (12.3.3).

New religious movement (NRM) A group of individuals that affirm a common identity and unique set of religious beliefs distinct from those in the world's main religious traditions (12.3.3).

Nihilism The belief that life and the universe have no real meaning or purpose. In some individuals, nihilism leads to a need to disconfirm or destroy the possible positive meanings held by others, and is associated with combativeness, distrust and cynicism (1.2.2, 2.5.2, and 11.1.2).

Nirvana In Buddhism, a state of enlightenment in which suffering is left behind (3.2.1).

Noetic experience An experience where an individual feels that they have learned something of great importance about the fundamental nature of reality. It is frequently a characteristic of mystical experience (4.1.1).

Nondifferentiated experience A state of consciousness with a loss of distinction between things, or between us as a subject and other things as objects separate from us (4.1.1).

Nondualism The religious or philosophical view that all parts of reality are essentially one, and that differences we perceive between things are inconsequential or illusionary (3.1.1).

Nonreductive materialism The philosophical view that there are nonmaterial aspects to reality that at least initially owe their existence to material objects or processes but later function independently as emergent processes. These higher nonmaterial processes are able to exercise an influence on lower or physical levels of reality through top-down causation (2.1.3).

Nontheism or **atheism** The belief that there is no god separate from the world (3.1.1).

Noumena Kant's term for things as they actually are, not as we perceive them (2.2.3).

Novices An individual living in a monastery or convent who is in training to become a full member of the community (12.2.2).

Numinous The term used by Rudolf Otto to refer to the nonrational aspect of our response to the Holy, including a sense of nothingness, mystery, and fascination (4.3.3).

O

Object An important term in psychodynamic thought. For Freud, objects were anything that could satisfy an instinctual need. In object relations theory, an object is "some person or persons to whom we can relate ourselves significantly so that life can be positively enjoyed, and come to have a meaning and value, and to be worth preserving" (Guntrip, 1957, p. 43). This concept is similar to the idea of internal working model in attachment theory (5.4.1 and cf. 8.2).

Object relations theory (ORT) A movement within psychoanalysis that focuses on relational aspects of our internal dynamics (5.4).

Occipital lobe The portion of the cortex located at the back of the head, it has a primary role in visual processing (6.1.1).

Oedipal crisis In Freud's theory, a period during preschool development when the sexual drive sets up an unconscious attraction between boys and their mothers, leading to competition with the father and unconscious fantasies of murder (5.1.1).

Older adulthood The stage in life following midlife. Most psychologists place the beginning of older adulthood around age 55 or 60 (9.4).

Online religion A religious community that exists entirely online (12.3.3).

Ontological materialism A type of ontological reductionism, it is the assumption that things are only real if they are material objects. This is sometimes known as reductive or eliminative materialism (2.1.2 and 2.1.3).

Ontological reductionism The assumption that something has no real existence, and is "nothing but" a combination of other types of things that are real (2.1.2).

Ontology The branch of philosophy that asks about the ultimate nature of things (2.1.3).

Ontological anxiety Anxiety that is an inherent part of existence, because of our limitations and the conflicting demands of life (1.5.1).

Operational definition A definition that puts a concept in terms that would allow its inclusion in scientific studies. In psychology, operational definitions reduce various theoretical constructs of interest like depression to specific behavioral outcomes that can be measured, such as answers to questions on a survey (2.4.1 and 2.4.2).

Oratio A spontaneous, prayerful response of gratitude, love, or need that comes from the heart and establishes a dialogue based on our innermost desires (13.3).

Orientalism A problem in 20th century Western scholarship of Asian religions, which tended to undervalue their importance and ignore important distinctions (5.2.6).

Outgroup A group of people that we perceive as different from us (12.5.1).

P

Pali Canon A group of Buddhist writings or sutras attributed to the Buddha and his immediate circle of followers. The writings were originally recorded in Pali, a version of Sanskrit (3.2.1).

Paradigm A system of thought containing ideas about how the world works and how we can best study it (2.4.2).

Paradox Two or more things that appear to be simultaneously true but not reconcilable with each other. An appreciation of paradox is often an outcome of a mystical experience (1.2.1 and 4.1.1).

Paranoid process A normal function of the ego that helps sustain and integrate our self and identity by contrasting us with those around us. Some psychologists like Meissner attribute authoritarianism and prejudice to a dysfunctional paranoid process (12.5.2).

Parasympathetic or *trophotropic* **nervous system** The part of the autonomic nervous system that has rest and rebuilding functions (6.1.1).

Parental investment The evolutionary dilemma that parents want to invest in their offspring to maximize inclusive fitness, but these investments are costly and must be balanced against other needs (6.2.1).

Parietal lobe The portion of the cortex located on the top and rear part of the brain that has an important role in body perception (6.1.1).

Participation mystique Jung's term for a kind of vague unified consciousness experienced in early childhood (5.1.2).

Particularity A characteristic of narrative, it is the assumption that each event and the context within which it occurs is unique and unrepeatable in some ways (9.3.3).

Passions Irrational behaviors or desires for objects that reinforce habits of inordinate seeking and vice (11.2.1).

Peak experience An experience described by Abraham Maslow that involves an ecstatic, non-possessive and self-transcending perception of the universe as an integrated whole (1.4.5).

Penance A Christian spiritual practice of performing actions designed to repair the damage caused by moral or spiritual lapses. It aims to restore the spiritual life of the individual and community (14.1.3).

Pentecostal church A Christian church that focuses on the experience and practice of spiritual gifts (12.3.2).

Persona A concept in Jungian theory that refers to the system of adaptations and the face that we present to the world (5.2.1).

Personal identity The aspect of our identity that is built upon our sense of unique personhood (8.5.1).

Personal integration A process by which the counselor connects their own religious experience, beliefs, and practices with their counseling approach (14.2.2).

Personal unconscious In Jungian theory, the section of the unconscious that includes material specific to the individual (5.2.1).

Perennial philosophy The view that all major religions and philosophies at different periods in history have held a common set of core beliefs (1.4.5 and 4.3).

Phenomenal world Kant's term for the world of objects as we experience them with our mind and senses (2.2.3).

Phenomenology A branch of philosophy that studies the lived experience of human beings (4.1).

Phenotype The expression of one's genetic information or genotype in our physical makeup as influenced by the environment (6.1.2).

Phronesis Practical reasoning or wisdom; deliberations about how to act in pursuit of the good life in a particular situation (6.3.4 and 11.2.1).

Pilgrimage A journey from a familiar place and routine to someplace unfamiliar motivated by a religious or spiritual purpose (12.4.2).

Pilgrimage theories A theory of development that sees life like a journey that has unique aspects for each person. This is a common model for religious theories of development (7.1.1).

Plasticity The brain's ability to change in response to a problem (6.1.1).

Pluralistic universe The idea that the universe contains many unities but no one single overarching system. William James saw this as a basis for understanding novelty, indeterminism and freedom (4.2.1).

Positive psychology A movement that hopes to develop a scientific psychology that will help us to maximize human happiness and potential (11.1.2).

Positive religious coping A coping style that involves a positive focus on problem solving with a specifically religious dimension (10.2.2).

Positivism A philosophy developed by Auguste Comte that human society and inquiry should be based only on positive, verified knowledge obtained through science, and that other ways of thinking such as religious ones should be rejected (2.3).

Postformal thought An advanced type of logic with emotional and relational aspects that develops in some people during adulthood. It allows adults to organize paradoxical information and serves as a basis for flexible systems of meaning-making that recognize the limits of our knowledge and help us to see multiple points of view (9.3.2).

Postfoundationalism The view that one can move toward increasingly better views of the world, but that dialogue between traditions provides a crucial critical perspective on one's beliefs that assists in the process (6.3.1).

Postliberal theology A theological position developed by George Lindbeck and influenced by postmodern philosophy. It argues that theological statements are part of the cultural and linguistic framework that governs a religious community and how its members see the world (3.3.1).

Postmodernism An alternative to modernism that developed in the 20th century and has affected many aspects of contemporary intellectual life and popular culture. Postmodernists generally reject the modernist view of the universality of truth (6.3).

Practical reason Kant's term for reason and decision-making related to practical and moral matters (2.2.3).

Practices Things that we do to accomplish ends or goals, or "the free committed engagement of the human subject in morally significant action" (Frohlich, 1993, p. 35). Religious practices are actions performed that attempt to accomplish the religious goals of an individual or community. For instance, religious rituals can be seen as a practice that allows for construction of meaning (6.3.4, 12.1 and 12.4.1).

Pragmatic maxim A criterion for judging truth used by William James and other pragmatic philosophers. According to this criterion, one judges truth by looking at the practical outcomes of various views of reality. This meant that sometimes ideas such as religious truths should be accepted because of their desirable consequences (4.2.1).

Prajna The Sanskrit term for transcendent wisdom used in Hinduism and Buddhism (3.2.4).

Prakrti In Hinduism, the term used to refer to Nature or the creative potential which manifests itself in matter and other ways. It is one of the two fundamental aspects of Brahma (3.1.2 and 10.3.2).

Praktike In the Evagrian Christian tradition, it is the first of three stages of spiritual growth, where one engages in lifestyle changes and ascetic practices to purify the passionate part of the soul, eliminating vices and attachments while gaining virtues, ultimately leading toward a state of purity of heart (13.2.1).

Prayer In theistic religions, prayer is traditionally considered to be a way of talking with God or having communion with the Divine (3.3.2 and 13.1).

Prayer of the heart A contemplative state of pure prayer involving the whole person when the mind feels boundless and senses Divinity within (13.2.4).

Predestination A theological position in Christianity, which holds that events are predetermined or preplanned by God (3.3.1).

Prejudice An emotionally laden reaction to another person based on a stereotype or their group membership (12.5.1).

Preliberal theology The traditional type of Christian theology, which holds that theological statements are propositions that make truth claims (3.3.1).

Preoccupied attachment An attachment style marked by positive view of others, but negative view of self, and feelings of anxiety or ambivalence (8.2.1).

Pre-trans fallacy A concept in the transpersonal theory of Ken Wilber, it is the tendency to confuse higher and lower level experiences that are superficially similar (7.5.1).

Pre-understanding The starting point on which we base any attempt to interpret the world and gain new knowledge. This pre-understanding includes our current beliefs, historical influences, and the beliefs and history of any larger groups to which we belong (1.5.3).

Pride A vice that stems from lack of humility. It involves an irrational, unrealistic view of ourselves, our capabilities, and failings (11.2.1).

Primary prevention Measures taken before a person becomes ill which reduce the risk of developing a disease (10.1.1).

Principle of entropy The Jungian idea that in situations of imbalance the psyche will act to neutralize differences and restore balance (5.2.1).

Principle of equivalence According to Jung, psychic energy is never lost but may be redistributed as in a closed mechanical system (5.2.1).

Principle of opposites In Carl Jung's theory, the idea that structures in the psyche often work in opposed and antithetical, dualistic pairs, creating tensions between opposites that provide essential sources of psychic energy (5.2.1).

Problem-focused coping A type of coping which involves trying to change what is causing the distress by acting on environment or self, such as by analyzing a problem and making a plan of action (10.2.1).

Problem of induction An issue raised by the philosopher David Hume, who argued that there was no way that definite knowledge could be based upon sense experience, because we can never prove that what we have experienced in the past will also be true in the future (2.2.3).

Process philosophy A 20th century philosophical system developed by Alfred North Whitehead that emphasizes the changing nature of the universe and the interconnection of events, as well as the evolving nature of reality (2.5.2).

Projection A defense mechanism where the ego attributes unacceptable unconscious feelings like anger to other people or things (5.1.1).

Protective factors Individual or environmental factors that either slow disease or move a person toward health. These are sometimes referred to as salutatory or salutogenic factors (10.1.1).

Protestant churches One of the three main branches of Christianity, Protestantism consists of a complex grouping of Western Christian churches that have broken away from the Catholic church (3.3.1).

Proximate cause In evolutionary theory, the cause behind the development of the phenotype for a particular organism, which typically includes both genetics and environment (6.2.1).

Psalmody A type of prayer in the Christian tradition that involves vocal recitations from the Psalms in the Bible (13.2.3).

Pseudospecies A kind of thinking that can develop in groups with strong negative identities when members believe themselves to be different and special, perhaps the only worthwhile group of people (5.3.1).

Psychodynamic psychology The view that internal and often unconscious forces or structures determine behavior. These unconscious factors have cognitive, emotional and relational components (1.4.1 and 5.0).

Psychological well-being (PWB) The position of a fully functioning individual who engages and masters life, seeking to actualize their potential, find meaning, cultivate quality relationships, and develop competence (11.1.2).

Psychology Traditionally the study of human mental life, in contemporary usage it refers to the scientific study of human behavior (1.4.1).

Psychopathology Inner psychological problems that lead to suffering (14.2.1).

Psychophysical method A method of Orthodox Christian prayer that combines recitation of the Jesus prayer with special patterns of breathing and posture (13.2.4).

Psychotherapy "The application of psychological insights to the growth, healing, or the process of maturing of a person" (Kalam, 1980), typically in the context of a helping relationship with another individual (14.2.1).

Psychoticism A personality trait marked by asociality as well as lower levels of empathy and social conformity (11.1.1).

Pure consciousness experience (PCE) A state of nondifferentiated consciousness or awareness that contains no objects or intentional content (4.1.1).

Pure experience The idea of William James that each experience forms an indivisible whole that is valid in itself, and thus not understandable by breaking it into parts (4.2.1).

Pure insight meditation (*suddhavipassanaayana*) Meditation designed to produce insight into the essential nature of reality as a way of achieving enlightenment. This can involve contemplation of the ever-changing flow of mental experience (3.2.2 and 13.5.1).

Pure Land Buddhism A version of Buddhism that focuses on devotion to the Amitabha Buddha (3.2.3).

Pure reason Kant's term for reasoning based on a priori knowledge, concepts and structures (2.2.3).

Purgation (the *Via Purgativa*) An early stage in spiritual development where one is purified and develops the underlying character, personal habits, and mental attitudes necessary for progress in the spiritual life (7.2.1).

Purusha In Hinduism, the term used to refer to Spirit, one of the two fundamental aspects of Brahma. It is an energy that is pure consciousness free of the world of action that provides the basis for thought processes (3.1.2 and 10.3.2).

Q

Quantum entanglement The phenomenon that particles can have simultaneous effects on each other at a distance even when there is no continuing material connection (2.5.1).

Quasi-experimental method A scientific method that involves careful observation of relationships between variables in a group of subjects (1.6.1).

Quest motivation A desire to engage in religious or spiritual activities out of a seeking impulse (1.4.6 and 9.3.1).

Quietism A fanatical concentration on the inner life that neglects important normal means and duties of human and religious life (4.3.2).

R

Radical empiricism A doctrine espoused by William James, it states that psychological investigations should be based only on experience (4.2.1).

Raja Yoga The classic dualistic form of yoga developed by Patanjali in the *Yoga Sutras* (3.1.2).

Random drift Evolutionary changes due to unexpected events, such as the meteor impact that ended the Cretaceous Period and the reign of the dinosaurs (6.2.1).

Rational choice theory A theory that applies rational decision-making models from economics to the study of how we make choices about religious involvement (9.3.2).

Rationality An explanation or way of thinking that makes sense and can have truth value (1.2.1).

Rationalism An explanation or way of thinking that complies with traditional Western standards of logic (1.2.1).

Recapitulation A term used in early 20th-century developmental psychology, it is the idea that the various states of development in the individual (ontogeny) recapitulate or repeat the stages in human cultural evolution or the development of the species (phylogeny) in important ways (5.1 and 7.3.1).

Reductionism A process of simplification used in science in which complex phenomena are explained using a few simple variables (2.1.2).

Reductive or **eliminative materialism** A kind of ontological materialism that claims everything is really just a collection of material particles and the laws that govern them (2.1.3).

Reductive materialist monism In psychology, the philosophical position that mental events are completely reducible to brain processes (6.1).

Reincarnation In Hinduism and Buddhism, the belief that we are reborn into a new life after our death (3.1).

Relational consciousness An experience that involves recognition of another person who is connected with us in some way (4.1.1).

Relational ontology The philosophical view that people gain their identity from relations with others who are different from us, rather than from some internal substance or quality. Since a pattern of relationships exists for everyone but is different in each case, every person is both interconnected and unique (5.5 and 6.3.1).

Relativism The idea found in extreme versions of postmodernism that argue there is no such thing as truth that can be discovered (6.3.1).

Reliability A measure of the quality of a measurement instrument, focusing primarily on the consistency of the results it produces (1.6.1).

Religion a set of beliefs and practices centered around human relationship to the Divine or transcendent (1.2.1).

Religious coping The use of religious beliefs or practices to respond to a perceived threat or loss. In Pargament's theory, religious coping happens when events, our goals and the means we use to reach them are actively interpreted in relation to the sacred, and this enhances our sense of meaning, control, comfort, intimacy, or support (10.2.1 and 10.2.2).

Religious judgment A term used by Fritz Oser that refers to the process by which individuals deal subjectively with the process of meaning making, cope with contingencies and think about their relation with the Ultimate (7.4.4).

Religious motivation A term used by psychologists like Gordon Allport to refer to the reason that people make religious commitments or engage in religious activities (1.4.6).

Religious psychotherapy An approach to counseling that is entirely based upon theological or religious concepts, such as Christian or Buddhist perspectives (14.3).

Religious switching A change from participation in one religious group or tradition to another (9.2.2).

Religious transformation hypothesis A sociological theory that cultural and social changes will lead to more individualized forms of religious and spiritual practice (1.3.2).

Religious well-being A component of spiritual well-being that includes a personal evaluation of our vertical relation to God (11.1.3).

Reproductive fitness A term in evolutionary theory that refers to successful reproductive potential. It includes Darwinian and inclusive fitness (6.2.1).

Ritualism The term used by Erik Erikson for compulsive repetition of rituals that can become legalistic (5.3.2).

Ritualization An Eriksonian concept for "an agreed-upon interplay between at least two persons who repeat it at meaningful intervals and in recurring contexts" (Erikson, 1966, pp. 602–603).

Role theory A theory of religious experience developed by Hjalmar Sunden that attempts to understand the genesis of religion and religious experience from a social perspective (4.4.1).

Roshi In Zen Buddhism, the title given a master teacher who has had an authentic enlightenment experience (13.5.2).

Recollection A state of intense inner absorption found in more advanced stages of prayer (13.3.1).

Right-wing authoritarianism (RWA) A variety of authoritarianism that includes a tendency toward submission to authority, conventionalism, and aggression toward others if sanctioned by authorities (12.5.2).

Religion online Religious activities and materials found on the Internet that are designed to supplement existing activities that are not online (12.3.3).

Reciprocal inhibition A technique used in Islamic counseling of setting up patterns of thoughts and behavior that oppose problematic ones. It is similar in theory to the Christian techniques of asceticism and counter-statement (11.2.2).

Relational attachments Attachments that act to build inner security and freedom. Typically these involve relationships with trusted, supportive individuals (11.2.1).

Ritual A practice that involves "the performance of more or less invariant sequences of formal acts and utterances" (Rappaport, 1999, p. 24) that are at least partly dictated by tradition (12.4.1).

S

Sacraments In Christian religious practice, sacraments are rituals that mark the presence and activity of God in the community, and the group's response to that presence (3.3.2).

Sacred Transcendent forces that have power over us and have a special mysterious quality that sets them apart (1.2.2).

Sadhana In Hinduism, a general term for the process of growth in the spiritual life that is facilitated through spiritual practices (3.1.2).

Saintliness According to William James, a state in which our personal energy becomes oriented around the spiritual (4.2.2).

Saivism A branch of Hinduism centered on devotion to the god Shiva the Destroyer. It is commonly associated with ascetic and spiritual practices such as yoga (3.1.1).

Saktism A group within Hinduism that focuses on devotion to the goddess Shakti. Members of this group often engage in tantric spiritual practices (3.1.1).

Samadhi A state of deep meditation in which the individual loses the distinction between self and other. In Hinduism and Buddhism, this is thought to involve contact with the underlying reality of the universe (3.1.2 and 3.2.4).

Samhita A collection of ancient Hindu religious texts from the Vedic period (3.1).

Samkhya The dualistic philosophical school that forms the intellectual basis for classical Yoga (3.1.1).

Samsara In Hinduism, the cycle of death and rebirth that constitutes normal existence. Buddhism emphasizes the belief that samsara involves a state of suffering (3.1).

Sanctification In Christian thought, the process by which a person grows in holiness and becomes transformed so that they can live out their religious faith in everyday life (3.3.2, 7.2.1, and 13.1.1).

Sangha The Buddhist community, one of the Three Jewels of Buddhism (3.2).

Satori In Zen Buddhism, an enlightenment experience leading to awareness of the fundamental nature of reality and our true self (3.2.4, 4.6.1, and 13.5.2).

Scapegoating A practice in which a member of a group either actually or ritually takes violence on themselves in order to prevent escalation of conflict (12.5.4).

Schema A term from cognitive theory that refers to underlying organized structures of belief or thought that govern our ability to acquire knowledge, act and solve problems (4.4.4 and 7.4.1).

Scientific empiricism The view that knowledge should be based on experiences that meet standards for inclusion in scientific inquiry (2.1.1).

Scientism The belief that (1) science is the best or only way to obtain knowledge, and/or (2) any problem is solvable through the application of the scientific method (1.4.7 and 2.1.4).

Secondary treatment Care for an illness on an outpatient basis (10.1.1).

Sect An offshoot of a church or mainstream religious group that follows somewhat different doctrines. It has a membership that is less diverse and more underprivileged than a mainline group but retains connections with older groups or traditions (12.3.3).

Seekers Individuals interested in religion and/or spirituality who avoid a firm commitment to a particular religious group or tradition (1.3.2).

Secularization hypothesis A sociological theory that religion will either die out or lose public influence and respectability because of advances in science or other cultural changes (1.3.1).

Secure attachment A positive pattern of attachment that can be seen when a child is able to tolerate the mother's departure and seek her out when she returns (8.2.1).

Seizures Physical or mental changes produced by uncontrolled electrical discharge in the brain (6.1.2).

Self An important term in psychology, religion and philosophy whose meaning varies and is often left undefined. In psychology this term is commonly used to refer to the "conscious, perceiving center of awareness and agency" that we observe (D'Andrade, 1995, p. 163). Carl Jung used the term to refer to the totality of the human person (5.2.1).

Self-actualization Our desire and need to achieve our potential, it is a concept in Abraham Maslow's theory of personality (1.4.5).

Self-directing coping A coping style in which the individual acknowledges the presence of the sacred but relies on themselves rather than God to solve a problem (10.2.2).

Sensory association area Located in the lower part of the parietal lobe, it is involved in integrating information from different sensory modalities at the highest or tertiary level (6.1.1).

Separation model A model of integration holding that psychology and religion each have their own areas of interest and approaches to truth, and that both are necessary for a complete picture of reality, although each needs to keep to its own domain (1.4.7).

Sesshin An extended Zen Buddhist retreat involving zazen and other activities that supplements and reinforces daily meditation practice (13.5.2).

Shadow In Jungian theory, an archetype that represents the dark side of the personality, a trickster part of us that is childish, at times self-defeating and in need of help (5.2.1).

Shikantaza Just-sitting meditation; the primary method of zazen emphasized in the Soto school of Zen Buddhism (13.5.2).

Sick-souled An individual who sees life as insecure with real evil as an essential part of things. William James believed that the sick-souled individual had a more complete but also more conflicted view of the world, so that they often struggled with melancholia and philosophical pessimism (4.2.2).

Social capital Individual and societal benefits that come from participation in social networks, such as increases in trust and reciprocal care (12.4.3).

Social construction A term in postmodernism for the view that truth is dependent on social and communal context and can thus be considered a social construction (6.3.1).

Social Darwinism The idea that some societies are fitter than others and will survive, while less fit societies will be eliminated. This idea has lost favor as it was used to justify destructive colonial practices in Africa and other places during the 20th century (6.2.1).

Sociobiological fallacy The idea that behaviors could be inherited adaptations, rather than the mechanisms that produce behavior (6.2.1).

Sociobiology The idea that social and other kinds of behaviors could be adaptations and part of the natural selection process. This is now largely rejected in favor of the view that it is the mechanisms that produce behaviors that are selected (6.2.1).

Soft stage model A hierarchical model for development in which movement to higher stages is optional and the final stages have a mystical or post-rational quality (7.4.2).

Soul In Greek philosophy and some strands of Christian thought, the term used to refer to the immaterial part of the human person. In Plato's philosophical system, it was divided into passionate and rational aspects (11.2.1).

Spandrel An evolutionary term for a necessary by-product of an adaptation that originally has no adaptive value but later finds an adaptive function (6.2.1).

Spiritual autobiography An autobiographical document that traces the movement of spiritual and religious changes in a person's life (9.3.3).

Spiritual injury A broad sense of alienation and malevolence in the world, which can include (1) personal feelings of impurity, (2) difficulty trusting or believing in God, (3) feelings of anger at God, (4) perceptions of God as wrathful and distant or disapproving, or (5) problems with lack of meaning and hopelessness (8.3.3).

Spirituality An important term with many meanings. It is often defined as the experiential and personal side of our relationship to the transcendent or sacred; for those in religious traditions, it is the living reality of religion as experienced by an adherent of the tradition (1.2.2).

Spiritual abuse "The misuse of social or political power in a spiritual context" (Wagener & Malony, 2006, p. 146) that often leads to negative health or mental health outcomes (11.1.1).

Spiritual crisis A life crisis or event that has a spiritual component (11.1.1).

Spiritual direction An ancient Christian practice where an experienced spiritual master forms a relationship with a disciple who wants to profit from their guidance (14.1.1).

Spiritual emergency Distress related to a spiritual experience or practice (11.1.1).

Spiritual Exercises A system for development of our relationship with God formulated by Ignatius of Loyola. It forms the basis for Jesuit spirituality (13.3.4).

Spiritual genogram A visual representation of the spiritual and religious history of a family (14.2.2).

Spiritual maturity In psychological treatments of spiritual growth, the term refers to development of a relationship with the transcendent or sacred that reflects positively on others or our own welfare (9.1).

Spiritual poverty A state of unity and simplicity that severs attachments and promotes a listening attitude, opening us to the presence of God (13.2.4).

Spiritual sickness A term used in the Christian healing prayer movement for any kind of illness or problem that has its roots in personal sin (10.3.1).

Spiritual striving A term used by Robert Emmons to describe the pursuit of meaning. He views it as an inherent part of the personality that brings inner unity, minimizing conflicts between goals and making painful experiences comprehensible (11.1.2).

Spiritual support The sense that God is friendly and available to help (10.1.2).

Spiritual warfare A Christian term for the process of overcoming inner and outer resistance to spiritual growth (13.3.2).

Spiritual well-being "The sense of well-being that we experience when we find purposes to commit ourselves which involve ultimate meaning for life" (Ellison, 1983, p. 330). It includes religious well-being in our relationship to God, and existential well-being or a sense of life purpose and satisfaction (11.1.3).

Splitting A process that occurs when people are unable to construct cohesive representations of objects due to inconsistencies and conflicts, so that different irreconcilable parts are formed into separate objects (5.4.1).

Srotas In Hindu thought and ayurvedic medicine, a term used to describe energy channels in the body that can become clogged, leading to disease (10.3.2).

Stereotyping A cognitive judgment about an individual based on their group membership (12.5.1).

Strict determinism A type of causal reductionism widely held by positivist philosophers, it is the assumption that present and future events are completely controlled by events in the past (2.5.1).

Strong transcendence An aspect of human life or experience that involves encounters with things that defy human comprehension, understanding and control (1.2.1).

Structuralism An approach to understanding ritual and other aspects of religious practice that analyzes its form and internal structure rather than content (12.4.1).

Structures In psychodynamic theory, the term refers to internal patterns that provide organizing mechanisms within the personality (5.0).

Subconscious Mental contents outside of consciousness that we can become aware of under certain conditions (4.1.1).

Subcortical area of the brain A large number of small structures in the brain that lie under the cortex and carry out a variety of important functions (6.1.1).

Subjective Something as it occurs or is perceived within the personal mental life of the individual. Kant believed that human knowledge is subjective because it is created within the person and is not a direct representation of reality (2.2.3 and 4.1.1).

Subjective well-being (SWB) A state resulting from the individual's evaluation of the quality of their life (11.1.2).

Substantialist ontology A philosophical position that assumes there is some substance, quality or essence of the human person that makes them what they are (5.5).

Substantive analysis Explanations of human activity that focus on actual behaviors; substantive analyses of religion concentrate on its specific beliefs and practices rather than the functional role that it plays in the lives of religious people (1.2.1).

Subtle bodies In Hinduism, bodies made of subtle physical or mental forms and energies that support cognition and consciousness (3.1.2).

Sudden enlightenment The idea that enlightenment happens in a sudden, powerful experience (3.2.4).

Sufism The mystical branch of Islam, comprised of a number of different schools (11.2.2).

Sui generis Something that is unique, a category that does not depend upon anything else for its existence (4.3.3).

Superego A personality structure that provides our conscience of shoulds and oughts (5.1.1).

Supernaturalism The view that God can act in the world even if it involves suspending existing natural laws (2.5.2).

Supersensible world Kant's term for the world as it actually is, not as we experience it (2.2.3).

Supervenience materialism The philosophical view that nonmaterial aspects of reality not only exist but can be described; however, they do not exist independently of physical processes because any difference in nonmaterial states can only occur if there is a difference in physical states (2.1.3).

Supervienience relationship A relationship in which (a) lower level events (e.g., chemical changes) can constitute higher level events (e.g., psychological events like mood) in given sets of circumstances but not in others, and (b) there is more than one pattern of lower level events that can lead to any given higher level event (2.1.2).

Supply side theories Theories arguing that it is the structure of religious supply (e.g., churches) that determines the likelihood of affiliation or group switching (9.2.2).

Suppressor model The theory that increases in stress lead to greater levels of religious practice, which then suppress the negative effects of stress (10.1.2 and 11.3.2).

Supramundane consciousness Advanced levels of consciousness achieved in Buddhist meditation that allow for the development of insight and liberation (13.5.1).

Surrender to God coping A coping style that involves an active surrender to God in a situation, rather than the passive waiting of the deferring style (10.2.2).

Sutra In Hinduism and Buddhism, a religious text typically composed of a number of pithy, often enigmatic sayings (3.1.1).

Symbol A broad term of importance in religion and psychology, a symbol is something that stands for something else without completely representing it. In Carl Jung's thought, it is a partial but tangible representation of an archetype that allows us at least partial knowledge of an archetype. Religious practices like rituals have an important symbolic component, as do material aspects of religion like buildings or artwork (5.2.1 and 12.4.1).

Sympathetic or *ergotropic* **nervous system** The part of the autonomic nervous system that is involved in arousal and stimulation (6.1.1).

Synchronicity A phenomenon studied by Carl Jung and also in modern physics, where apparently unconnected psychic states and external events occur simultaneously and are found to have a causal relationship with each other (5.2).

Synthetic reasoning Kant's term for reasoning that adds to a current concept or idea and thus produces new knowledge (2.2.3).

T

Tantra A term used to describe (1) a set of esoteric practices within Hinduism and Buddhism that are thought to possess particular power, and are thus reserved for initiates thought ready to handle them; or (2) a type of secret scripture that is revealed only to a select few (3.1.1 and 3.1.2).

Teisho A master's commentary or lecture, often related to a koan or teaching story. It is one of the three pillars of Zen Buddhism (13.5.2).

Teleology The study of how things are related to some final goal or end, what Aristotle called a *final cause*. Narratives often provide these types of explanations (2.2.2 and 9.3.3).

Temporal lobe The portion of the cortex located on the lower sides and to the back of the brain, it has important roles in memory and the perception of spoken language, as well as some aspects of visual processing (6.1.1).

Tertiary treatment Treatment for an illness in an inpatient or hospital setting (10.1.1).

Theism The belief that there is a God or gods who are free and separate from the world, transcending us but also perhaps active and wishing to relate to it. This is different than *pantheism*, a philosophical position that equates the world and the Divine, or *monism*, which considers all things to be one (1.2.1 and 3.1.1).

Theistic realism The view that God and objective moral laws exist and that we can learn about these laws as well as the Divine (14.3.1).

Theoria The final stage of Christian growth that involves spiritual contemplation, the vision or seeing of God. It can involve ineffable experiences of formless light or union and participation in a divine reality (13.2.1).

Theosis The Orthodox Christian term used for the process of transformation in which a person gradually becomes more like God (7.2.1 and 14.1.1).

Therapeutic A broad term, it often refers to anything that will maintain the adjustment and social functioning of the individual (10.3.1).

Therapeutic culture A culture in which problems are defined as illnesses and elimination of these illnesses through therapeutic means is the ultimate goal of life and society (10.3.1).

Theravada Buddhism A version of Buddhism that is centered on the teachings and practices found in early Buddhist writings. It is the primary form of Buddhism found in modern Sri Lanka and much of Southeast Asia. It is also one of the schools of Buddhism that has been most influential in psychology (3.2.1).

Theta waves Brain electrical activity in the range 4–7 cycles per second. High amplitude theta waves are sometimes found in meditation practice (13.6).

Thick definitions In religion, a definition that has many allusions to the beliefs and practices of a specific religious tradition (1.2.2).

Thin definitions In religion, a definition that is generic and may apply to all religious groups (1.2.2).

Top-down causation The idea that events at higher levels like psychology can affect what happens at lower levels such as biological or chemical processes (2.1.2).

Totem A special object of devotion that is sacred and serves as a guardian spirit or helper for a group (5.1.2).

Trace phenomenon Something that cannot be directly observed, although we can see its effects (1.2.1).

Transcendent Things that are greater than us, which may be comprehensible (*weak transcendence*) or totally beyond our understanding and abilities (*strong transcendence*) (1.2.1).

Transcendent function The Jungian term for the process where opposites in the psyche unite to facilitate growth (5.1.2).

Transcendental Meditation (TM) A system of meditation developed by Maharishi Mahesh Yogi that is based on Hindu thought (13.5.3).

Transitional objects Objects that can substitute for the mother and other critical figures in our life when they are not available (5.4.3).

Transitional space In object relations theory, "an intermediate area of *experiencing*, to which inner reality and external life both contribute" (Winnicott, 1975, p. 230). Winnicott believed that this allowed for the creation of transitional objects (5.4.3).

Transpersonal psychology A movement within humanistic psychology focusing on potentials for human development and experiences that extend beyond what is typical for the individual person (1.4.5).

True self The term used by Thomas Merton to describe the real person hidden under the false self. In his view, our true self is only known fully by God and thus cannot be approached except by a search for the Divine (13.3.2).

Turning point An event or internal realization that redirects our life on a long lasting basis (9.2.3).

Twin study An important procedure used in heredity research. Identical twins having very similar genotypes are compared with fraternal twins who have a normal level of genetic similarity to determine the influence of genetics on a particular characteristic (6.1.2).

Two books analogy Used to justify the separation of science and theology, it argues that science should be based on our reading of the "book" of nature, while theology should come from our reading of the Bible, the "book" of divine revelation (2.2.2).

U

Ultimate cause In evolutionary theory, the reason the genotypes of organisms came to be the way they are (6.2.1).

Unconscious The term used in psychodynamic theories to refer to an autonomous realm of the personality containing emotional and instinctive forces that are out of our awareness but able to govern our behavior (5.1.1 and 5.2.1).

Unforgiveness The complex of negative emotions such as anger or fear that can come from perceived wrongful treatment (11.4.1).

Union (the *Via Unitiva*) The final stage of spiritual development in Western Christian models, it involves a kind of interpenetration between the individual and the Divine where they are united yet remain separate (7.2.1).

Unitive experience An experience of union with God or the universe that is often part of mystical or religious experiences (4.1.1).

Unus mundus Jung's term for the highest state of development, a numinous state of unity of consciousness and unconsciousness that is similar to the Yoga and Zen experiences of samadhi or satori (5.1.2).

V

Vainglory A vice that involves inordinate craving of praise from others (11.2.1).

Vaisnavism A branch of Hinduism that centers its spiritual practices around devotion to the god Vishnu the Preserver (3.1.1).

Vajrayana Buddhism One of the main schools of Mahayana Buddhism, it is practiced primarily in Tibet (3.1.2).

Validity A measure of the quality of a measurement instrument, focusing primarily on whether or not the instrument measures what it is supposed to measure (1.6.1).

Values Things we deem particularly important (1.2.1).

Vendanta Hindu systems of thought that are based on the Upanishads and some later writings (3.1.1).

Veridical Something that has truth value (4.1.2).

Vicarious religion Indirect religious involvement, where a person does not practice a religion but supports religious institutions and the practice of religion by others on their behalf (1.3.2).

Vice A pattern of repeated seeking of an object in excess of need that interferes with other aspects of our life and reduces our inner freedom (11.2.1).

Vipassana The Pali Buddhist term for insight into the fundamental nature of things through personal experience, which leads to enlightenment (3.2.2 and 13.5.1).

Virtues Acts or patterns of behavior that rightly use our desires and resist the formation of disordered attachments (11.2.1).

W

Weak transcendence Something that is beyond us but also within our reach. It is something that can be achieved or comprehended, often without a fundamental change in our way of life or outlook (1.2.1).

Wisdom A broad term, it often refers to an ability to discern what is appropriate and helpful in specific practical situations (11.2.1 and cf. 9.1).

Worldview A basic set of assumptions and way of thinking about self, the world and our place in it (1.2.1).

XYZ

Yoga A general term that refers to a number of schools of inner practice that originated in Hinduism but can also be found in Buddhism (3.1.2).

Zazen Sitting meditation that is practiced in Zen Buddhism as a way of deepening our experience of emptiness and seeing our true nature (3.2.4 and 13.5.2).

Zen Buddhism The name for Chan Buddhism in Japan, it is a school of Mahayana Buddhism that emphasizes the need for personal meditation practice and experience on the path to enlightenment (3.2.4).

Zendo A Zen Buddhist meditation hall used in the practice of zazen (13.5.2).

Bibliography

Aaron, K. F., Levine, D., & Burstin, H. R. (2003). African American church participation and health care practices. *Journal of General International Medicine, 18*, 908–913.

Abe, M. (1985). *Zen and Western thought* (W. LaFleur, Ed.), Honolulu: University of Hawaii Press.

Abe, M. (Ed.). (1986). *A Zen life: D.T. Suzuki remembered.* New York: Weatherhill Press.

Abe, M. (1992a). *A study of Dogen: His philosophy and religion* (S. Heine, Ed.), Albany, NY: State University of New York Press.

Abe, M. (1992b). The self in Jung and Zen. In D. Meckel, & R. Moore (Eds.), *Self and liberation: The Jung-Buddhism dialogue* (pp. 128–140). New York: Paulist Press.

Abell, J. W., Steenbergh, T. A., & Boivin, M. J. (2006). Cyberporn use in the context of religiosity. *Journal of Psychology and Theology, 34*, 165–171.

Abernethy, A. D., Houston, T. R., Mimms, T., & Boyd-Franklin, N. (2006). Using prayer in psychotherapy: Applying Sue's differential to enhance culturally competent care. *Cultural Diversity and Ethnic Minority Psychology, 12*, 101–114.

Abou-Hatab, F. (1997). Psychology from Egyptian, Arab, and Islamic perspectives: Unfulfilled hopes and hopeful fulfillment. *European Psychologist, 2*, 356–365.

Abram, J. (1997). *The language of Winnicott: A dictionary and guide to understanding his work.* Northvale, NJ: Jason Arson.

Abramowitz, L. (2001). Prayer as therapy among the frail Jewish elderly. In L. Francis, & J. Astley (Eds.), *Psychological perspectives on prayer* (pp. 368–374). Leominster: Gracewing.

Abramowitz, J. S., Deacon, B. J., Woods, C. M., & Tolin, D. F. (2004). Association between Protestant religiosity and obsessive-compulsive symptoms and cognitions. *Depression and Anxiety, 20*, 70–76.

Abu-Ali, A., & Reisen, C. A. (1999). Gender role identity among adolescent Muslim girls living in the U.S. *Current Psychology, 18*, 185–192.

Adams, G. (Ed.). (2000). *Adolescent development: The essential readings.* Malden, MA: Blackwell.

Adams, J. (1970). *Competent to counsel.* Phillipsburg, NJ: Presbyterian and Reformed.

Aden, L. (1968). Pastoral counseling as Christian perspective. In P. Homans (Ed.), *The dialogue between theology and psychology* (pp. 163–181). Chicago: University of Chicago Press.

Aden, L. (2004). The role of self-justification in violence. In J. Ellens (Ed.), *The destructive power of religion: Violence in Judaism, Christianity and Islam, Volume 2: Religion, psychology, and violence* (pp. 251–264). Westport, CT: Praeger.

Adorno, T. (1950). *The authoritarian personality.* New York: Harper.

Aelred of Rievaulx, St. (1974). *Spiritual friendship* (M. Laker, Trans.). Kalamazoo, MI: Cistercian Press. (Original work written c.1165 AD).

Aers, D. (2003). The Christian practice of growing old in the Middle Ages. In S. Hauerwas, C. Stoneking, K. Meador, & D. Cloutier (Eds.), *Growing old in Christ* (pp. 38–62). Grand Rapids: Eerdmans.

Aftanas, L. I., & Golosheykin, S. A. (2003). Changes in cortical activity in altered states of consciousness: The study of meditation by high-resolution EEG. *Human Physiology, 29*, 143–151.

Aftanas, L. I., & Golosheykin, S. A. (2005). Impact of regular meditation practice on EEG activity at rest and during evoked negative emotions. *International Journal of Neuroscience, 115*, 893–909.

Ahmed, S. S. (2004). Religion and youth. *Journal of Indian Psychology, 22*, 20–35.

Ahuvia, A. C. (2002). Individualism/collectivism and cultures of happiness: A theoretical conjecture on the relationship between consumption, culture and subjective well-being at the national level. *Journal of Happiness Studies, 3*, 23–36.

Ai, A. (2000). Spiritual well-being, spiritual growth, and spiritual care for the aged: A cross-faith and interdisciplinary effort. *Journal of Religious Gerontology, 11*(2), 3–28.

Ai, A., Dunkle, R., Peterson, C., & Bowlling, S. (1998). The role of private prayer in psychological recovery among midlife and aged patients following cardiac surgery. *The Gerontological Society of America, 38*, 591–601.

Ainsworth, M. (1969). Object relations, dependency, and attachment: A theoretical review of the infant-mother relationship. *Child Development, 40*, 969–1025.

Ainsworth, M. (1978). *Patterns of attachment: A psychological study of the strange situation.* Hillsdale, NJ: Lawrence Erlbaum.

Alansari, B. M. (2005). Beck depression inventory (BDI-II) items characteristics among undergraduate students of nineteen Islamic countries. *Social Behavior and Personality, 33*, 675–684.

Albee, G. W. (2000). The Boulder model's fatal flaw. *American Psychologist, 55*, 247–248.

Alcoholics Anonymous World Service. (2004). *Alcoholics Anonymous: The story of how thousands of men and women have recovered from alcoholism* (4th ed.), New York: Alcoholics Anonymous World Service.

Alexander, C. N., Cranson, R. W., Boyer, R. W., & Orme-Johnson, D. W. (1986). Transcendental consciousness: A fourth state of consciousness beyond sleep, dreaming, and waking. In J. Gackenbach (Ed.), *Sleep and dreams: A sourcebook* (pp. 282–315). New York: Garland.

Alexander, C. N., Druker, S., & Langer, E. (1990). Introduction: Major issues in the exploration of adult growth. In C. Alexander, & E. Langer (Eds.), *Higher stages of human development* (pp. 3–32). New York: Oxford University Press.

Alexander, C. N., Rainforth, M. V., & Gelderloos, P. (1991). Transcendental meditation, self-actualization, and psychological health: A conceptual overview and statistical meta-analysis. *Journal of Social Behavior and Personality, 6*, 189–248.

Alexander, C. N., Robinson, P., Orme-Johnson, D. W., Schneider, R. H., & Walton, K. G. (1994). The effects of transcendental meditation compared to other methods of relaxation and meditation in reducing risk factors, morbidity, and mortality. *Homeostasis, 35*(4–5), 243–263.

Alexander, C. N., Robinson, P., & Rainforth, M. V. (1994). Treating and preventing alcohol, nicotine, and drug abuse through transcendental meditation: A review and statistical meta-analysis. *Alcoholism Treatment Quarterly, 11*(1–2), 13–87.

Alexander, F. (1962). Emotional maturity. In S. Doniger (Ed.), *The nature of man in theological and psychological perspective* (pp. 123–130). New York: Harper & Brothers.

Ali, S. R., Liu, W. M., & Humedian, M. (2004). Islam 101: Understanding the religion and therapy implications. *Professional Psychology: Research and Practice, 35*, 635–642.

Ali, T. (2002). *The clash of fundamentalisms: Crusades, jihads and modernity.* London: Verso.

Allchin, A. M. (2003). The prayer of the heart and natural contemplation: A foreword to Thomas Merton's lecture notes on St. Maximus. In B. Dieker, & J. Montaldo (Eds.), *Merton & Hesychasm: The prayer of the heart: The Eastern Church* (pp. 419–429). Louisville, KY: Fons Vitae.

Allen, D. (1997). Ascetic theology and psychology. In R. C. Roberts, & M. R. Talbot (Eds.), *Limning the psyche: Explorations in Christian psychology* (pp. 297–316). Grand Rapids, MI: Eerdmans.

Allen, W. L. (2006). Editorial introduction: Christian spirituality in the age of growing secularity. *Perspectives in Religious Studies, 31*, 5–45.

Allman, L. S., de la Rocha, O., Elkins, D. N., & Weathers, R. S. (1992). Psychotherapists' attitudes towards clients reporting mystical experiences. *Psychotherapy, 29*, 564–569.

Allport, G. W. (1966). The religious context of prejudice. *Journal for the Scientific Study of Religion, 5*, 447–457.

Allport, G. W. (1979). *The nature of prejudice* (Unabridged, 25th anniversary ed.), Reading, MA: Addison-Wesley. (Original work published 1954).

Allport, G. W., & Ross, J. M. (1967). Personal religious orientation and prejudice. *Journal of Personality and Social Psychology, 5*, 432–443.

Almond, G., Appleby, R., & Sivan, E. (2003). Strong religion: *The rise of fundamentalism around the world.* Chicago, IL: The University of Chicago Press.

Almond, P. (1984). *Rudolf Otto: An introduction to his philosophical theology.* Chapel Hill, NC: The University of North Carolina Press.

Almond, P. (1990). Mysticism and its context. In R. K. C. Forman (Ed.), *The problem of pure consciousness: Mysticism and philosophy* (pp. 211–219). New York: Oxford University Press.

Alper, M. (2001). *The "God" part of the brain: A scientific interpretation of human spirituality and God.* Brooklyn, NY: Rogue Press.

Altemeyer, B. (1996). *The authoritarian specter.* Cambridge, MA: Harvard University Press.

Altemeyer, B. (2003). Why do religious fundamentalists tend to be prejudiced? *The International Journal for the Psychology of Religion, 13*, 17–28.

Altemeyer, B. (2004a). The decline of organized religion in Western civilization. *International Journal for the Psychology of Religion, 14*, 77–89.

Altemeyer, B. (2004b). Highly dominating, highly authoritarian personalities. *The Journal of Social Psychology, 144*, 421–447.

Altemeyer, B., & Hunsberger, B. (1992). Authoritarianism, religious fundamentalism, quest, and prejudice. *The International Journal for the Psychology of Religion, 2*, 113–133.

Altemeyer, B., & Hunsberger, B. (1993). Reply to Gorsuch. *The International Journal for the Psychology of Religion, 3*, 33–37.

Altemeyer, B., & Hunsberger, B. (1997). *Amazing conversions, Why some turn to faith & others abandon religion.* Amherst, NY: Prometheus Books.

Alterman, A. I., Koppenhaver, J. M., Mulholland, E., Ladden, L. J., & Baime, M. J. (2004). Pilot trial of effectiveness of mindfulness meditation for substance abuse patients. *Journal of Substance Abuse, 9*, 259–268.

American Psychiatric Association (1990). Guidelines regarding possible conflict between religious commitments and psychiatric practice. *American Journal of Psychiatry, 147*, 542.

American Psychiatric Association (2000). *Diagnostic and statistical manual of mental disorders* (4th ed., text rev.). Washington, DC: American Psychiatric Association.

American Psychological Association. (2002a). Criteria for evaluating treatment guidelines. *American Psychologist, 57*, 1052–1059.

American Psychological Association. (2002b). Ethical principles of psychologists and code of conduct. *American Psychologist, 57*, 1060–1073.

American Psychological Association. (2005). *Report of the 2005 presidential task force on evidence-based practice.* Retrieved August 18, 2007 from http://www.apa.org/practice/ebpreport.pdf.

American Psychological Association Presidential Task Force on Evidence-Based Practice. (2006). Evidence-based practice in psychology. *American Psychologist, 61*, 271–285.

Ammerman, N. T. (1997). The market and beyond. In L. A. Young (Ed.), *Rational choice theory and religion: Summary and assessment* (pp. 119–132). New York: Routledge.

Ammerman, N. T. (1998). Culture and identity in the congregation. In N. Ammerman, J. Carroll, C. Dudley, & W. McKinney (Eds.), *Studying congregations: A new handbook* (pp. 78–104). Nashville, TN: Abingdon.

Ammerman, N. T. (2003). Religious identities and religious institutions. In M. Dillon (Ed.), *Handbook of the sociology of religion* (pp. 207–224). Cambridge: Cambridge University Press.

Ammerman, N. T. (2005). *Pillars of faith: American congregations and their partners.* Berkeley, CA: University of California Press.

Ammerman, N. T. (2007a). Introduction: Observing modern religious lives. In N. T. Ammerman (Ed.), *Everyday religion: Observing modern religious lives* (pp. 3–18). New York: Oxford University Press.

Ammerman, N. T. (2007b). Studying everyday religion: Challenges for the future. In N. T. Ammerman (Ed.), *Everyday religion: Observing modern religious lives* (pp. 219–238). New York: Oxford University Press.

Ammerman, N. T., & Roof, W. C. (1995). Introduction: Old patterns, new trends, fragile experiments. In N. T. Ammerman, & W. C. Roof (Eds.), *Work, family, and religion in contemporary society* (pp. 1–20). New York: Routledge.

Anand, B. K., Chhina, G. S., & Singh, B. (1961a). Studies on Shri Ramanand Yogi during his stay in an air-tight box. *Indian Journal of Medical Research, 49*, 82–89.

Anand, B. K., Chhina, G. S., & Singh, B. (1961b). Some aspects of electroencephalographic studies in Yogis. *Electroencephalography and Clinical Neurophysiology, 13*, 452–456.

Anbeek, C. W., & de Groot, P. A. (2002). Buddhism and psychotherapy in the west: Nishitani and dialectical behavior therapy. In P. Young-Eisendrath, & S. Muramoto (Eds.), *Awakening and insight: Zen Buddhism and psychotherapy* (pp. 187–204). New York: Taylor & Francis.

Anderson, M. (2005). Psychotherapy as ritual: Connecting the concrete with the symbolic. In R. Moodley, & W. West (Ed.), *Integrating traditional healing practices into counseling and psychotherapy* (pp. 282–292). Thousand Oaks, CA: Sage.

Anderson, P. (2004). Religion and violence: From pawn to scapegoat. In J. Ellens (Eds.), *The destructive power of religion: Violence in Judaism, Christianity and Islam, Volume 2: Religion, psychology, and violence* (pp. 265–284). Westport, CT: Praeger.

Anderson, P. (2007). Feminist challenges to conceptions of God: Exploring divine ideals. *Philosophia, 35*, 361–376.

Anderson, R. W., Jr., Maton, K. I., & Ensor, B. E. (1991). Prevention theory and action from the religious perspective. *Prevention in Human Services, 10*, 9–27.

Anderson, T., & Lewis-Hall, M. E. (2005). Introduction to the special issue: Gender and Christianity. *Journal of Psychology and Theology, 33*, 163–165.

Anderson, V. E. (1998). A genetic view of human nature. In W. S. Brown, N. Murphy, & H. N. Malony (Eds.), *Whatever happened to the soul? Scientific and theological portraits of human nature* (pp. 49–72). Minneapolis, MN: Fortress Press.

Andler, D. (2006). Federalism in science–complementarity vs. perspectivism: Reply to Harré. *Synthese, 151*, 519–522.

Andresen, J. (2000). Meditation meets behavioural medicine: The story of experimental research on meditation. In J. Andresen, & R. K. C. Forman (Eds.), *Cognitive models and spiritual maps: Interdisciplinary explorations of religious experience* (pp. 17–73). Thorverton, UK: Imprint Academic.

Andresen, J. (2001). Introduction: Towards a cognitive science of religion. In J. Andresen (Ed.), *Religion in mind: Cognitive perspectives on religious belief, ritual, and experience* (pp. 1–44). Cambridge, UK: Cambridge University Press.

Andrews, M. (2000). Forgiveness in context. *Journal of Moral Education, 29*, 75–86.

Andrews, M. (2005). How not to find God in all things: Derrida, Levinas, and St. Ignatius of Loyola on learning how to pray for the impossible. In B. Benson, & N. Wirzba (Eds.), *The phenomenology of prayer* (pp. 195–208). Bronx, NY: Fordham University Press.

Anthony, M. (1966). *Living prayer.* Springfield, IL: Templegate.

Anthony, M. (1999). The spirituality of old age. In A. Jewell (Ed.), *Spirituality and ageing* (pp. 30–38). London: Jessica Kingsley.

Antonovsky, A. (1994). A sociological critique of the 'well being' movement. *Advances, 10*, 6–12.

Anuruddha, A. (2000). *A comprehensive manual of Abhidhamma* (B. Bodhi (Ed.), M. Narada & B. Bodhi, Trans.). Seattle: BPS Pariyatti.

Appleby, R. S. (2000). *The ambivalence of the sacred: Religion, violence and reconciliation.* Lanham, MD: Rowman & Littlefield.

al-'Arabi, I. (1980). *The bezels of wisdom* (R. W. J. Austin, Trans.). Mahwah, NJ: Paulist.

Arbel, D., Afzal, C., Davila, J., Deutsch, C., Gieschen, C., & Golitzin, A., et al. (2001). Early Jewish and Christian mysticism: A collage of working definitions. *Society of Biblical Literature Seminar Papers, 40*, 278–304.

Archer, J. (2001). Evolving theories of behavior. *The Psychologist, 14*, 414–419.

Arcury, T. A., Quandt, S. A., McDonald, J., & Bell, R. A. (2000). Faith and health self-management of rural older adults. *Journal of Cross-Cultural Gerontology, 15*, 55–74.

Arendt, H. (1968). *The origins of totalitarianism* (New ed.). San Diego, CA: Harvest.

Arendt, H. (1998). *The human condition* (2nd ed.). Chicago: University of Chicago.

Argyle, M. (1985). New directions in the psychology of religion. In L. B. Brown (Ed.), *Advances in the psychology of religion* (pp. 8–17). Oxford: Pergamon.

Argyle, M. (1999). Causes and correlates of happiness. In D. Kahneman, E. Diener, & N. Schwarz (Eds.), *Well-being: The foundations of hedonic psychology* (pp. 353–373). New York: Russell Sage Foundation.

Arinze, F. (2002). *Religions for peace: A call for solidarity to the religions of the world.* New York: Doubleday.

Aristotle. (1941). *The basic works of Aristotle* (R. McKeon, Ed.), New York: Random House.

Ark, P. D., Hull, P. C., Husaini, B. A., & Craun, C. (2006). Religiosity, religious coping styles, and health service use. *Journal of Gerontological Nursing, 32*(8), 20–29.

Arkoun, M. (2000). Present-day Islam between its tradition and globalization. In F. Daftary (Ed.), *Intellectual traditions in Islam* (pp. 179–221). London: I. B. Tauris.

Arlow, J. (1996). Ego psychology and the study of mythology. In R. Segal (Eds.), *Psychology and myth* (pp. 1–23). New York: Garland.

Armfield, G. G., & Holbert, R. L. (2003). The relationship between religiosity and Internet use. *Journal of Media and Religion, 2*, 129–144.

Armstrong, T. D., & Crowther, M. R. (2002). Spirituality among older African Americans. *Journal of Adult Development, 9*, 3–12.

Arnett, J. J. (2000a). Emerging adulthood: A theory on development from late teens through twenties. *American Psychologist, 55*, 469–480.

Arnett, J. J. (2000b). High hopes in a grim world emerging adults' views of their futures and "generation x". *Youth and Society, 31*, 267–286.

Arnett, J. J. (2002). The psychology of globalization. *American Psychologist, 57*, 774–783.

Arnett, J. J. (2003). The moral dimensions of globalization. *American Psychologist, 58*, 815–816.

Arnett, J. J., & Jensen, L. A. (2002). A congregation of one: Individualized religious beliefs among emerging adults. *Journal of Adolescent Research, 17*, 451–467.

Arnhart, L. (1998). *Darwinian natural right: The biological ethics of human nature.* Albany, NY: State University of New York Press.

Arnold, M. L. (2000). Stage, sequence, and sequels: Changing conceptions of morality, post-Kohlberg. *Educational Psychology Review, 12*, 365–383.

Aronson, H. (2004). *Buddhist practice on Western ground: Reconciling eastern ideals and western psychology.* Boston, MS: Shambhala.

Asay, T., & Lambert, M. (1999). The empirical case for the common factors in therapy. In M. Hubble, B. Duncan, & S. Miller (Eds.), *The heart and soul of change: What works in therapy* (pp. 33–55). Washington, DC: American Psychological Association.

Ashton, E. (1997). Readiness for discarding? An examination of the researches of Ronald Goldman concerning children's religious thinking. *Journal of Education and Christian Belief, 1*, 127–144.

Aspinwall, L. G., & Leaf, S. L. (2002). In search of the unique aspects of hope: Pinning our hopes on positive emotions, future-oriented thinking, hard times, and other people. *Psychological Inquiry, 13*, 276–288.

Astin, J. A. (1997). Stress reduction through mindfulness meditation. *Psychotherapy and Psychosomatics, 66*, 97–106.

Atchley, R. C. (1997a). Everyday mysticism: Spiritual development in later adulthood. *Journal of Adult Development, 4*, 123–134.

Atchley, R. C. (1997b). The subjective importance of being religious and its effect on health and morale 14 years later. *Journal of Aging Studies, 11,* 131–141.

Aten, J. D., & Hernandez, B. C. (2004). Addressing religion in clinical supervision: A model. *Psychotherapy: Theory, Research, Practice, Training, 41,* 152–160.

Aten, J. D., & Hernandez, B. C. (2005). A 25-year review of qualitative research published in spiritually and psychologically oriented journals. *Journal of Psychology and Christianity, 24,* 266–277.

Athanasius, St. (1994a). Four discourses against the Arians. In P. Schaff (Ed.), *The Nicene and Post-Nicene Fathers, Second Series, Volume 4: Athanasius: Select Works and Letters* (pp. 303–447). Peabody, MA: Hendrickson. (Original work written c. 360 A.D.).

Athanasius, St. (1994b). On the incarnation of the Word. In P. Schaff (Ed.), *The Nicene and Post-Nicene Fathers, Second Series, Volume 4: Athanasius: Select Works and Letters* (pp. 36–67). Peabody, MA: Hendrickson. (Original work written c. 320 A.D.).

Augustine, St. (1956). On the holy Trinity. In P. Schaff (Ed.), *The Nicene and Post-Nicene Fathers, First Series* (Vol. 3 pp. 18–312). Grand Rapids: Eerdmans. (Original work written c. 428).

Augustine, St. (1992). *Confessions* (H. Chadwick, Trans.). Oxford: Oxford University.

Augustine, St. (1994). Reply to Faustus the Manichaean. In P. Schaff (Ed.), *Nicene and post-Nicene fathers, First Series* (Vol. 4 pp. 191–481). Peabody, MA: Hendrickson. (Original work published 400).

Aumann, J. (1980). *Spiritual theology.* London: Sheed and Ward.

Aurobindo, S. (1996). *The synthesis of yoga.* Twin Lakes, WI: Lotus Light.

Austin, J. (1998). *Zen and the brain: Toward an understanding of meditation and consciousness.* Cambridge, MA: MIT Press.

Austin, J. (2006). *Zen-brain reflections.* Cambridge, MA: MIT Press.

Averill, J. R. (1998). Spirituality: From the mundane to the meaningful-and back. *Journal of Theoretical and Philosophical Psychology, 18,* 101–126.

Ayala, F. J. (1998a). Darwin's devotion: Design without Designer. In R. Russell, W. Stoeger S. J., & F. Ayala (Eds.), *Evolutionary and molecular biology scientific perspectives on divine action* (pp. 101–116). Vatican City State: Vatican Observatory.

Ayala, F. J. (1998b). Human nature: One evolutionist's view. In W. S. Brown, N. Murphy, & H. N. Malony (Eds.), *Whatever happened to the soul? Scientific and theological portraits of human nature* (pp. 31–48). Minneapolis, MN: Fortress Press.

Ayer, A. J. (1952). *Language truth and logic.* New York: Dover.

Ayer, A. J. (1966). *Logical positivism.* Glencoe, IL: The Free Press.

Ayer, A. J., & Copleston, F. (1994). Logical positivism—a debate. In P. Moser, & D. Mulder (Eds.), *Contemporary approaches to philosophy* (pp. 141–170). New York: Macmillan. (Original work published 1965).

Aygun, Z. K., & Imamoglu, E. O. (2002). Value domains of Turkish adults and university students. *The Journal of Social Psychology, 142,* 333–351.

Azari, N. P., Nickel, J., Wunderlich, G., Niedeggen, M., Hefter, H., Tellman, L., et al. (2001). Short communication: Neural correlates of religious experience. *European Journal of Neuroscience, 13,* 1649–1652.

Azhar, M. Z., & Varma, S. L. (1995). Religious psychotherapy as management of bereavement. *Acta psychiatricia Scandinavica, 91,* 233–235.

Bach, P. A., Gaudiano, B., Pankey, J., Herbert, J. D., & Hayes, S. C. (2006). Acceptance, mindfulness, values, and psychosis: Applying acceptance and commitment therapy (ACT) to the chronically mentally ill. In R. A. Baer (Ed.), *Mindfulness-based treatment approaches: Clinician's guide to evidence base and applications* (pp. 93–116). Amsterdam: Elsevier, Academic Press.

Bachs, J. (1994). Belief, unbelief, and religious experience. In J. Corveleyn, & D. Hutsebaut (Eds.), *Belief and unbelief: Psychological perspectives* (pp. 185–199). Amsterdam: Rodopi.

Bacon, F. (2000). *The new organon* (L. Jardine, & M. Silverthorne, Eds.), Cambridge: Cambridge University Press. (Original work published 1620).

Bacon, F. (2001). *The advancement of learning.* New York: Random House. (Original work published 1605).

Badcock, C. R. (2000). *Evolutionary psychology: A critical introduction.* Cambridge: Polity Press.

Bader, C., Dougherty, K., Froese, P., Johnson, B., Mencken, F. C., Park, J., et al. (2006). *American piety in the 21st century: New insights to the depth and complexity of religion in the US: Selected findings form the Baylor Religion Survey.* Waco, TX: Baylor Institute for Studies of Religion. Retrieved August 17, 2007 from http://www.baylor.edu/content/services/document.php/33304.pdf.

Baer, R. A. (2003). Mindfulness training as a clinical intervention: A conceptual and empirical review. *Clinical Psychology: Science and Practice, 10,* 125–143.

Baer, R. A., & Krietemeyer, J. (2006). Overview of mindfulness- and acceptance-based treatment approaches. In R. A. Baer (Ed.), *Mindfulness-based treatment approaches: Clinician's guide to evidence base and applications* (pp. 1–27). San Diego, CA: Elsevier.

Baetz, M., Griffin, R., Bowen, R., Koenig, H., & Marcoux, E. (2004). The association between spiritual and religious involvement and depressive symptoms in a Canadian population. *Journal of Nervous and Mental Disease, 192,* 818–822.

Bagchi, B., & Wenger, M. (1957). Electrophysiological correlates of some yogic exercises. *Electroenephalography and Clinical Neurophysiology, 7,* 132–149.

Bagchi, B., & Wenger, M. (1958). Simultaneous EEG and other recordings during some yogic practices. *Electroencephalography and Clinical Neurophysiology, 10,* 193.

Bayer, C. J., & Wright, B. R. E. (2001). "If you love me, keep my commandments": A meta-analysis of the effect of religion on crime. *Journal of Research in Crime and Delinquency, 38,* 3–21.

Baker, M., & Wang, M. (2004). Examining connections between values and practice in religiously committed U.K. clinical psychologists. *Journal of Psychology and Theology, 32,* 126–136.

Bakhtin, M. (1981). *The dialogic imagination: Four essays* (M. Colquitt (Ed.), C. Emerson, & M. Colquitt, Trans.). Austin, TX: University of Texas Press.

Balboni, T., Vanderwerker, L., Block, S., Paulk, M, Lathan, C., Peteet, J., & Prigerson, H. (2007). Religiousness and spiritual support among advanced cancer patients and associations with end-of-life treatment preferences and quality of life. *Journal of Clinical Oncology, 25,* 555–560.

Balboni, J. (1902). *Social and ethical interpretations in mental development: A study in social psychology.* New York: Macmillan.

Baldwin, J. (1930). Autobiography of James Mark Baldwin. In C. Murchison (Ed.), *History of psychology in autobiography* (Vol. 1, pp. 1–30). Worcester, MA: Clark University.

Baldwin, J. (1975). *Thought and things: A study of the development and meaning of thought or genetic logic.* New York: Arno. (Original work published 1906–1915).

Balk, D. E. (1999). Bereavement and spiritual change. *Death Studies, 23,* 485–493.

Ball, J., Armistead, L., & Austin, B. (2003). The relationship between religiosity and adjustment among African American, female, urban adolescents. *Journal of Adolescence, 26,* 431–446.

Ball, R., & Goodyear, R. (1991). Self-reported professional practices of Christian psychotherapists. *Journal of Psychology and Christianity, 10,* 144–153.

Balswick, J., King, P., & Reimer, K. (2005). *The reciprocating self: Human development in theological perspective.* Downers Grove, IL: InterVarsity Press.

Baltes, P. B., & Staudinger, U. M. (2000). Wisdom: A metaheuristic (pragmatic) to orchestrate mind and virtue toward excellence. *American Psychologist, 55,* 122–136.

Bambrough, R. (1978). Intuition and the inexpressible. In S. T. Katz (Ed.), *Mysticism and philosophical analysis* (pp. 200–213). New York: Oxford University Press.

Bankart, C. (2003). Five manifestations of the Buddha in the west, a brief history. In K. Dockett, G. Dudley- Grant, & C. Bankart (Eds.), *Psychology and Buddhism from individual to global community* (pp. 45–69). New York: Kluwer Academic/Plenum.

Bankart, C. P., & Vincent, M. A. (2001). Beyond individualism and isolation: A study of communion in adolescent males. *The Journal of Social Psychology, 128,* 675–683.

Banschick, M. (1992). God-representations in adolescence. In M. Finn, & J. Gartner (Eds.), *Object relations theory and religion* (pp. 73–85). Westport, CT: Praeger.

Banziger, S., van Uden, M., & Janssen, J. (2008). Praying and coping: The relation between varieties of praying and religious coping styles. *Mental Health, Religion & Culture, 11,* 101–118.

Barbour, I. (1997). *Religion and science: Historical and contemporary issues.* San Francisco, CA: HarperSanFrancisco.

Barbour, I. (1998). Five models of God and evolution. In R. Russell, W. Stoeger, & F. Ayala (Eds.), *Evolutionary and molecular biology: Scientific perspectives on divine action* (pp. 419–442). Vatican City: Vatican Observatory.

Barbour, I. (2002). Neuroscience, artificial intelligence, and human nature: Theological and philosophical reflections. In R. Russell, N. Murphy, T. Meyering, & M. Arbib. (Eds.), *Neuroscience and the person* (pp. 249–280). Vatican City State: Vatican Observatory.

Barbre, C. (2004). The wages of dying: Catastrophe transformed. In F. Kelcourse (Ed.), *Human Development and Faith, life-cycle stages of body, mind and soul* (pp. 285–307). St. Louis, MO: Chalice Press.

Barnett, K. L., Duvall, N. S., Edwards, K. J., & Hall, M. E. L. (2005). Psychological and spiritual predictors of domains of functioning and effectiveness of short-term missionaries. *Journal of Psychology and Theology, 33,* 27–40.

Barnouw, J. (1981). The separation of reason and faith in Bacon and Hobbes, and Leibniz's theodicy. *Journal of the History of Ideas, 42,* 607–628.

Barrett, J. L. (1998). Cognitive constraints on Hindu concepts of the divine. *Journal for the Scientific Study of Religion, 37,* 608–619.

Barrett, J. L. (1999). Theological corrections: Cognitive constraint and the study of religion. *Method & Theory in the Study of Religion, 11,* 325–339.

Barrett, J. L., & Keil, F. C. (1996). Conceptualizing a nonnatural entity: Anthropomorphism in God concepts. *Cognitive Psychology, 31,* 219–247.

Barrett, J. L., & Richert, R. A. (2003). Anthropomorphism or preparedness? Exploring children's God concepts. *Review of Religious Research, 44,* 300–312.

Barrett, L., Dunbar, R., & Lycett, J. (2002). *Human evolutionary psychology.* Princeton, NJ: Princeton University Press.

Barrow, J., Tippler, F., & Wheeler, J. (1988). *The anthropic cosmological principle.* New York: Oxford University Press.

Barry, W. A. (2001). *Letting God come close: An approach to the Ignatian spiritual exercises.* Chicago: Jesuit Way.

Barth, K. (1932). *Church dogmatics, Volume 1, Part 1: The doctrine of the Word of God* (G. Thomson, Trans.). Edinburgh: T & T Clark.

Bartholomew, K., & Horowitz, L. (1991). Attachment styles among young adults: A test of a four-category model. *Journal of Personality and Social Psychology, 61,* 226–244.

Bartkowski, J. P. (2007). Connections and contradictions: Exploring the complex linkages between faith and family. In N. T. Ammerman (Ed.), *Everyday religion: Observing modern religious lives* (pp. 153–166). New York: Oxford University Press.

Bartocci, G. (2004). Transcendence techniques and psychobiological mechanisms underlying religious experience. *Mental Health, Religion & Culture, 7,* 171–181.

Bartoli, E. (2007). Religious and spiritual issues in psychotherapy practice: Training the trainer. *Psychotherapy: Theory, Research, Practice, Training, 44,* 54–65.

Bartos, E. (1999). *Deification in Eastern Orthodox theology: An evaluation and critique of the theology of Dumitru Staniloae.* Carlisle, UK: Paternoster.

Basil, St. (1999). *Ascetical works* (M. Wagner Trans.). Washington, DC: Catholic University of America.

Baskin, T. W., & Enright, R. D. (2004). Intervention studies on forgiveness: A meta-analysis. *Journal of Counseling and Development, 82,* 79–90.

Bass, D. (1994). Congregations and the bearing of traditions. In J. Wind, & J. Lewis (Eds.), *American congregations, Volume 2: New perspectives in the study of congregations* (pp. 169–191). Chicago: University of Chicago Press.

Bassett, R. L., Bassett, K. M., Lloyd, M. W., & Johnson, J. L. (2006). Seeking forgiveness: Considering the role of moral emotions. *Journal of Psychology and Theology, 34,* 111–124.

Bassett, R. L., Camplin, W., Humphrey, D., Dorr, C., Biggs, S., Distaffen, R., et al. (1991). Measuring Christian maturity: A Comparison of several scales. *Journal of Psychology and Theology, 19,* 84–93.

Batson, C. D. (1997). An agenda item for psychology of religion: Getting respect. In B. Spilka, & D. N. McIntosh (Eds.), *The psychology of religion: Theoretical approaches* (pp. 3–10). Boulder, CO: Westview Press.

Batson, C. D. (1998). Altruism and prosocial behavior. In D. T. Gilbert, S. T. Fiske, & G. Lindzey (Eds.), *The handbook of social psychology* (4th ed., Vol. 2, pp. 282–316). Boston, MA: McGraw-Hill.

Batson, C. D., Ahmad, N., Lishner, D. A., & Tsang, J.-A. (2002). Empathy and altruism. In C. R. Synder, & S. J. Lopez (Eds.), *Handbook of positive psychology* (pp. 485–498). Oxford: Oxford University Press.

Batson, C. D., & Schoenrade, P. A. (1991a). Measuring religion as quest: (1) Validity concerns. *Journal for the Scientific Study of Religion, 30,* 416–429.

Batson, C. D., & Schoenrade, P. A. (1991b). Measuring religion as quest: (2) Reliability concerns. *Journal for the Scientific Study of Religion, 30,* 430–447.

Batson, C. D., Schoenrade, P., & Pych, V. (1985). Brotherly love or self-concern? Behavioural consequences of religion. In L. Brown (Ed.), *Advances in the psychology of religion* (pp. 185–208). Elmsford, NY: Pergamon.

Batson, C. D., Schoenrade, P., & Ventis, W. L. (1993). *Religion and the individual: A social-psychological perspective.* New York: Oxford University Press.

Baumeister, R. F. (1991). *Meanings of life.* New York: Guilford Press.

Baumeister, R. F. (1998). The self. In D. T. Gilbert, S. T. Fiske, & G. Lindzey (Eds.), *The handbook of social psychology* (4th ed., Vol. 1, pp. 680–740). Boston, MA: McGraw-Hill.

Baumeister, R. F., & Exline, J. J. (1999). Virtue, personality and social relations: Self-control as the moral muscle. *Journal of Personality, 67,* 1165–1194.

Baumeister, R. F., & Exline, J. J. (2002). Mystical self-loss: A challenge for psychological theory. *The International Journal for the Psychology of Religion, 12,* 15–20.

Baumeister, R. F., & Leary, M. R. (1995). The need to belong: Desire for interpersonal attachments as a fundamental human motivation. *Psychological Bulletin, 117,* 497–529.

Beauchamp-Turner, D. L., & Levinson, D. M. (1992). Effects of meditation on stress, health, and affect. *Medical Psychotherapy, 5,* 123–132.

Bebis, G. (1989). Introduction. In Nicodemus, *Nicodemos of the Holy Mountain: A handbook of spiritual counsel* (pp. 5–65). New York: Paulist Press.

Beck, R. (2006). God as a secure base: Attachment to God and theological exploration. *Journal of Psychology and Theology, 34,* 125–132.

Beck, R., & Jessup, R. K. (2004). The multidimensional nature of quest motivation. *Journal of Psychology and Theology, 32,* 283–294.

Becker, K. (2001). *Unlikely companions: C.G. Jung on the Spiritual Exercises of Ignatius of Loyola: An exposition and critique based on Jung's lectures and writings.* Leominster, UK: Gracewing.

Becker, P. E., & Dhingra, P. H. (2001). Religious involvement and volunteering: Implications for civil society. *Sociology of Religion, 62,* 315–335.

Bedard, M., Felteau, M., Mazmanian, D., Fedyk, K., Klein, R., Richardson, J., et al. (2003). Pilot evaluation of a mindfulness-based intervention to improve quality of life among individuals who sustained traumatic brain injuries. *Disability and Rehabilitation, 25,* 722–731.

Begbie, J. (2001). Prayer and music. In F. Watts (Ed.), *Perspectives on prayer* (pp. 67–80). London: SPCK.

Beit-Hallahmi, B. (1985). Religiously based differences in approach to the psychology of religion: Freud, Fromm, Allport and Zilboorg. In L. B. Brown (Ed.), *Advances in the psychology of religion* (pp. 18–33). Oxford: Pergamon Press.

Beit-Hallahmi, B. (1995). Object relations theory and religious experience. In R. Hood, Jr. (Ed.), *Handbook of religious experience* (pp. 254–268). Birmingham, AL: Religious Education.

Beit-Hallahmi, B. (1996). Religion as psychopathology: Exploring a metaphor. In J. A. van Belzen, & J. M. van der Lans (Series Eds.) & H. Grzymala-Moszczynska, & B. Beit-Hallahmi (Vol. Eds.), *International series in the psychology of religion: Vol. 4. Religion, psychopathology, and coping* (pp. 71–85). Amsterdam: Rodopi.

Beit-Hallahmi, B., & Argyle, M. (1997). *The psychology of religious behaviour, belief, and experience.* London: Routledge.

Bell, C. (1992). *Ritual theory, ritual practice.* New York: Oxford University Press.

Bell, C. (1997). *Ritual: Perspectives and dimensions.* New York: Oxford University Press.

Belling, C. (2004). The death of the narrator. In B. Hurwitz, T. Greenhalgh, & V. Skultans (Eds.), *Narrative research in health and illness* (pp. 146–155). Malden, MA: Blackwell Publishing.

Bellinger, C. (2001). *The genealogy of violence: Reflections on creation, freedom and evil.* New York: Oxford University Press.

Bellous, J., de Roos, S., & Summey, W. (2004). A child's concept of God. In D. Ratcliff (Ed.), *Children's spirituality: Christian perspectives, research, and applications* (pp. 201–218). Eugene, OR: Cascade.

Beloff, J. (1993). *Parapsychology: a concise history.* New York: At Martin's Press.

Belzen, J. A. (1995). On religious experience: Role theory and contemporary narrative psychology. In N. G. Holm, & J. A. Belzen (Eds.), *Sunden's role theory: An impetus to contemporary psychology of religion.* Abo, Sweden: Abo Akademi.

Belzen, J. A. (1996). Methodological perspectives on psychopathology and religion: A historical review. In J. A. van Belzen, & J. M. van der Lans (Series Eds.) & H. Grzymala-Moszczynska, & B. Beit-Hallahmi (Vol. Eds.), *International series in the psychology of religion: Vol. 4. Religion, psychopathology, and coping* (pp. 23–33). Amsterdam: Rodopi.

Belzen, J. A. (Ed.). (1997). *Hermeneutical approaches in psychology of religion.* Amsterdam: Rodopi.

Belzen, J. A. (1999). The cultural psychological approach to religion: Contemporary debates on the object of the discipline. *Theory and Discipline, 9*(2), 229–255.

Belzen, J., & Hood. R. (2006). Methodological issues in the psychology of religion: Toward another paradigm? *Journal of Psychology, 140,* 5–28.

Benda, B., & Corwyn, R. (1997). Religion and delinquency: The relationship after considering family and peer influences. *Journal for the Scientific Study of Religion, 36,* 81–92.

Bender, C. J. (2007). Touching the transcendent: Rethinking religious experience in the sociological study of religion. In N. T. Ammerman (Ed.), *Everyday religion: Observing modern religious lives* (pp. 201–218). New York: Oxford University Press.

Benedict, St. (2001). *The rule of St. Benedict* (L. Doyle, Trans.). Collegeville, MN: Liturgical Press.

Benjamin, J. (1999). Recognition and destruction: An outline of intersubjectivity. In S. Mitchell,&L.Aron(Eds.),*Relationalpsychoanalysis:Theemergenceofatradition*(pp.181–210). Hillsdale, NJ: Analytic. (Original work published 1990).

Benjamins, M. R., Musick, M. A., Gold, D. T., & George, L. K. (2003). Age-related declines in activity level: The relationship between chronic illness and religious activities. *The Journals of Gerontology, 58B*(6), S377–S385.

Benner, D. G. (2005). Intensive soul care: Integrating psychotherapy and spiritual direction. In L. Sperry, & E. P. Shafranske (Eds.), *Spiritually oriented psychotherapy* (pp. 287–306). Washington, DC: American Psychological Association.

Bennett, M. R., & Hacker, P. M. S. (2003). *Philosophical foundations of neuroscience.* Malden, MA: Blackwell.

Benson, B., & Wirzba, N. (2005). Introduction. In B. Benson, & N. Wirzba (Eds.), *The phenomenology of prayer* (pp. 1–9). New York: Fordham University Press.

Benson, P. L., Donahue, M. J., & Erickson, J. A. (1989). Adolescence and religion: A review of the literature from 1970 to 1986. *Research in the Social Scientific Study of Religion, 1,* 153–181.

Benson, P. L., Leffert, N., Scales, P. C., & Blyth, D. A. (1998). Beyond the "Village" rhetoric: Creating healthy communities for children and adolescents. *Applied Developmental Science, 2,* 138–159.

Benson, P. L., Masters, K., & Larson, D. (1997). Religious influences on child and adolescent development. In N. Alessi (Ed.), *Handbook of child and adolescent psychiatry, Volume 4: Varieties of development* (pp. 206–219). New York: Wiley.

Benson, P. L., Roehlkepartain, E. C., & Rude, S. P. (2003). Spiritual development in childhood and adolescence: Toward a field of inquiry. *Applied Developmental Science, 7*, 204–212.

Benson, P. L., & Spilka, B. (1973). God image as a function of self-esteem and locus of control. *Journal for the Scientific Study of Religion, 12*, 297–310.

Berenbaum, H., Raghavan, C., Huynh-Nhu, L., Vernon, L., & Gomez, J. (1999). Disturbances in emotion. In D. Kahneman, E. Diener, & N. Schwarz (Eds.), *Well-being: The foundations of hedonic psychology* (pp. 267–287). New York: Russell Sage Foundation.

Berg, P. (2002). Luther and the our father. *Logia, 11*, 3–11.

Berger, B. G., & Owen, D. R. (1992). Mood alteration with yoga and swimming: Aerobic exercise may not be necessary. *Perceptual and Motor Skills, 75*, 1331–1343.

Berger, P. L. (1967). *The sacred canopy: Elements of a sociological theory of religion.* New York: Anchor.

Berger, P. L. (1974). Some second thoughts on substantive versus functional definitions of religion. *Journal for the Scientific Study of Religion, 13*, 125–133.

Berger, P. L. (1999). The desecularization of the world: A global overview. In P. L. Berger (Ed.), *The desecularization of the world: Resurgent religion and world politics* (pp. 1–18). Washington, DC and Grand Rapids, MI: Ethics and Public Policy Center and William B. Eerdmans.

Berger, P. L. (2007). Foreword. In N. T. Ammerman (Ed.), *Everyday religion: Observing modern religious lives* (pp. v–viii). New York: Oxford University Press.

Berger, P. L., & Luckmann, T. (1966). *The social construction of reality: A treatise in the sociology of knowledge.* New York: Anchor.

Bergin, A. (1983). Religiosity and mental health: A critical reevaluation and meta-analysis. *Professional Psychology: Research and Practice, 14*, 170–184.

Bergin, A., & Payne, I. R. (1997). Proposed agenda for a spiritual strategy in personality and psychotherapy. In B. Spilka, & D. N. McIntosh (Eds.), *The psychology of religion: Theoretical approaches* (pp. 54–66). Boulder, CO: Westview Press.

Bergman, S. (1996). Introduction: Twentieth-century martyrs: A meditation. In S. Bergman (Ed.), *Martyrs: Contemporary writers on modern lives of faith* (pp. 1–20). Maryknoll, NY: Orbis Books.

Bering, J. M. (2004). The evolutionary history of an illusion: Religious causal beliefs in children and adults. In B. J. Ellis, & D. F. Bjorklund (Eds.), *Origins of the social mind: Evolutionary psychology and child development* (pp. 411–437). New York: Guilford Press.

Bernard of Clairvaux, St. (1987). *Bernard of Clairvaux: Selected works* (G. Evans, Trans.). New York: Paulist. (Original work published c. 1150).

Bernard, H. R. (2002). *Research methods in anthropology: Qualitative and quantitative approaches* (3rd ed.). Walnut Creek, CA: AltaMira Press.

Bernhardt, S. (1990). Are pure consciousness events unmediated? In R. K. C. Forman (Ed.), *The problem of pure consciousness: Mysticism and philosophy* (pp. 220–236). New York: Oxford University Press.

Berry, J. W., Worthington, E. L., Jr., O'Connor, L. E., Parrott, L., III., & Wade, N. G. (2005). Forgivingness, vengeful rumination, and affective traits. *Journal of Personality 73*, 183–225.

Berthold, F., Jr. (1968). Theology and self-understanding: The Christian model of man as sinner. In P. Homans (Ed.), *The dialogue between theology and psychology* (pp. 11–32). Chicago: University of Chicago Press.

Bertman, S. (1999). A handful of quietness: Measuring the meaning of our years. In L. E. Thomas, & S. Eisenhandler (Eds.), *Religion, belief and spirituality in late life* (pp. 3–12). New York: Springer.

Besecke, K. (2007). Beyond literalism: Reflexive spirituality and religious meaning. In N. T. Ammerman (Ed.), *Everyday religion: Observing modern religious lives* (pp. 169–186). New York: Oxford University Press.

Beyer, P. (1997). Religious vitality in Canada: The complimentarity of religious market and secularization perspectives. *Journal for the Scientific Study of Religion, 36*, 272–288.

Bickel, C., Ciarrocchi, J., Sheers, N., & Estadt, B. (1998). Perceived stress, religious coping styles and depressive affect. *Journal of Psychology and Christianity, 17*, 33–42.

Bickle, J. (2006). Reducing mind to molecular pathways: Explicating the reductionism implicit in current cellular and molecular neuroscience. *Synthese, 151,* 411–434.

Bickhard, M. (2001). The tragedy of operationalism. *Theory and Psychology, 11,* 35–44.

Bidwell, D. R. (2000). Carl Jung's memories, dreams, reflections: A critique informed by postmodernism. *Pastoral Psychology, 49,* 13–22.

Bielefeldt, C. (1988). *Dogen's manuals of Zen meditation.* Berkeley, CA: University of California Press.

Bilu, Y. (1988). The inner limits of communitas: A covert dimension of pilgrimage experience. *Ethos, 16,* 302–325.

Birch, C. (1998). Neo-Darwinism, self-organization, and divine action in evolution. In R. Russell, W. Stoeger S. J., & F. Ayala (Eds.), *Evolutionary and molecular biology scientific perspectives on divine action* (pp. 225–250). Vatican City State: Vatican Observatory.

Bishop, J. (2007). How a modest fideism may constrain theistic commitments: Exploring an alternative to classical theism. *Philosophia, 35,* 387–402.

Bishop, J., Lacour, M. A., Nutt, N., Vivian, Y., & Lee, J. Y. (2004). Reviewing a decade of change in the student cultures. *Journal of College Students Psychotherapy, 18*(3), 3–30.

Bishop, P. (Ed.). (1999). *Jung in contexts: A reader.* New York: Routledge.

Bishop, S. R. (2002). What do we really know about mindfulness-based stress reduction? *Psychosomatic Medicine, 64,* 71–84.

Bishop, S. R., Lau, M., Shapiro, S., Carlson, L., Anderson, N. D., Carmody, J., et al. (2004). Mindfulness: A proposed operational definition. *Clinical Psychology, 11,* 230–241.

Bitner, R., Hillman, L., Victor, B., & Walsh, R. (2003). Subjective effects of antidepressants: A pilot study of the varieties of antidepressant-induced experiences in mediators. *The Journal of Nervous and Mental Disease, 191,* 660–667.

Bjorck, J. P. (2007). Faith, coping, and illusory control: Psychological constructs with theological ramifications. *Journal of Psychology and Christianity, 25,* 195–206.

Bjorck, J. P., & Cohen, L. (1993). Coping with threats, losses, and challenges. *Journal of Social and Clinical Psychology, 12,* 56–72.

Bjorck, J. P., Lee, Y. S., & Cohen, L. (1997). Control beliefs and faith as stress moderators for Korean American versus Caucasian American protestants. *American Journal of Community Psychology, 25,* 61–72.

Bjorck, J. P., & Thurman, J. W. (2007). Negative life events, patterns of positive and negative religious coping, and psychological functioning. *Journal for the Scientific Study of Religion, 46,* 159–167.

Black, H. K. (1995). "Wasted lives" and the hero grown old: Personal perspective of spirituality by aging men. *Journal of Religious Gerontology, 9*(3), 35–48.

Blanton, P. G. (2005). Narrative family therapy and spiritual direction: Do they fit? *Journal of Psychology and Christianity, 24,* 68–79.

Blasi, A. (1983). Moral cognition and moral action: A theoretical perspective. *Developmental Review, 3,* 178–210.

Blasi, A. (2002). Visitation to disaster sites. In W. H. Swatos, & L. Tomasi (Eds.), *From medieval pilgrimage to religious tourism: The social and cultural economics of piety* (pp. 159–180). Westport, CT: Praeger.

Blass, D. M. (2001). A conceptual framework for the interaction between psychiatry and religion. *International Review of Psychiatry, 13,* 79–85.

Blatt, S., & Blass, R. (1990). Attachment and separateness: A dialectical model of the products and processes of development throughout the life cycle. *The Psychoanalytic Study of the Child, 45,* 107–127.

Blieszner, R., & Ramsey, J. L. (2002). Uncovering spiritual resiliency through feminist qualitative methods. *Journal of Religious Gerontology, 14*(12), 31–49.

Bloch, M. (2004). Ritual and defense. In H. Whitehouse, & J. Laidlaw (Eds.), *Ritual and memory: Toward a comparative anthropology of religion* (pp. 65–78). Walnut Creek, CA: AltaMira.

Bloom, D. (2003). *The evolution of morality and religion.* Cambridge: Cambridge University Press.

Bloom, H. (1992). *The American religion: The emergence of the post-Christian nation.* New York: Simon & Schuster.

Bluck, S., & Habermas, T. (2001). Extending the study of autobiographical memory: Thinking back about life across the life span. *Review of General Psychology, 5*, 135–147.

Bockian, M. J., Glenwick, D. S., & Bernstein, D. P. (2005). The applicability of the stages of change model to Jewish conversion. *The International Journal for the Psychology of Religion, 15*, 35–50.

Bockus, F. M. (1968). The archetypal self: Theological values in Jung's psychology. In P. Homans (Ed.), *The dialogue between theology and psychology* (pp. 221–247). Chicago: The University of Chicago Press.

Bodhidharma. (1987). *The Zen teachings of Bodhidharma* (R. Pine, Trans.). New York: North Point Press.

Bogart, G. (1991). The use of meditation in psychotherapy: A review of the literature. *American Journal of Psychotherapy, XLV*, 383–412.

Bogart, G. (1997). *The nine stages of spiritual apprenticeship: Understanding the student-teacher relationship.* Richmond, CA: Dawn Mountain Press.

Bollas, C. (1978). The transformational object. *International Journal of Psycho-Analysis, 60*, 97–107.

Bolshakoff, S. (1976). *Russian mystics.* Kalamazoo, MI: Cistercian Press.

Bonnycastle, C. R. (2004). The role of religion in contemporary social service. *Canadian Review of Social Policy, 53*, 68–87.

Boorer, S. (1997). The dark side of God? A dialogue with Jung's interpretation of the book of job. *Pacifica, 10*, 277–297.

Booth, G. (1958). Science and spiritual healing. In S. Doniger (Ed.), *Religion and health: A symposium* (pp. 65–77). New York: Association.

Booth, H. (1981). *Edwin Diller Starbuck: Pioneer in the psychology of religion.* Washington, DC: University Press of America.

Booth, J., & Martin, J. (1998). Spiritual and religious factors in substance use, dependence, and recovery. In H. Koenig (Ed.), *Handbook of religion and mental health* (pp. 175–200). San Diego, CA: Academic Press.

Borg, J., Andree, B., Soderstrom, T., & Farde, L. (2003). The serotonin system and spiritual experiences. *The American Journal of Psychiatry, 160*, 1965–1969.

Boring, E. (1950). *A history of experimental psychology* (2nd ed.). New York: Appleton-Century-Crofts.

Bosma, H. A., & Kunner, E. S. (2001). Determinants and mechanisms in ego identity development: A review and synthesis. *Developmental Review, 21*, 39–66.

Bosworth, H. B., Park, K., McQuoid, D. R., Hays, J. C., & Steffens, D. C. (2003). The impact of religious practice and religious coping on geriatric depression. *International Journal of Geriatric Psychiatry, 18*, 905–914.

Boudewijnse, H. B. (1990). The ritual studies of Victor Turner: An anthropological approach and its psychological impact. In H.-G. Heimbrock, & H. Boudewijnse (Eds.), *Current studies on rituals: Perspectives for the psychology of religion* (pp. 1–18). Amsterdam: Rodopi.

Bourdieu, P. (1977). *Outline of a theory of practice* (R. Nice, Trans.). New York: Cambridge University Press.

Bourdieu, P. (1985). The forms of capital. In J. G. Richardson (Ed.), *Handbook of theory and research for the sociology of education* (pp. 241–258). New York: Greenwood Press.

Bourdieu, P. (1990). Critique of theoretical reason. In R. Nice (Trans.), *The logic of practice* (pp. 23–141). Stanford, CA: Stanford University Press. (Original work published 1980).

Bowen, M. (2005). Dimensions of the human person in relationship and the practice of supervision. In M. R. Bumpus, & R. B. Langer (Eds.), *Supervision of spiritual directors* (pp.65–81). Harrisburg, PA: Morehouse.

Bower, F. (1999). Metaphor, mysticism and madness. A response to the three papers on 'Is analytical psychology a religion?' by Storr, Shamdasani and Segal. *Journal of Analytical Psychology, 44*, 563–570.

Bowie, F. (2000). *The anthropology of religion: An introduction.* Oxford: Blackwell.

Bowlby, J. (1988). *A secure base: Parent-child attachment and health human development.* New York: Basic.

Boyatzis, C. (2003). Religious and spiritual development: An introduction. *Review of Religious Research, 44,* 213–219.

Boyatzis, C. (2004). Exploring scientific and theological perspectives on children's spirituality. In D. Ratcliff (Ed.), *Children's spirituality: Christian perspectives, research, and applications* (pp. 182–200). Eugene, OR: Cascade.

Boyatzis, C., Dollahite, D., & Marks, L. (2006). The family as a context for religious and spiritual development in children and youth. In E. Roehlkepartain, P. King, L. Wagener, & P. Benson (Eds.), *The handbook of spiritual development in childhood and adolescence* (pp. 297–309). Thousand Oaks, CA: Sage.

Boyatzis, C., & Janicki, D. L. (2003). Parent-child communication about religion: Survey and diary data on unilateral transmission and bi-directional reciprocity styles. *Review of Religious Research, 44,* 252–270.

Boyer, P. (1994). *The naturalness of religious ideas: A cognitive theory of religion.* Berkeley, CA: University of California Press.

Boyer, P. (2001). *Religion explained: The evolutionary origins of religious thought.* New York: Basic Books.

Boyer, P. (2005). A reductionistic model of distinct modes of religious transmission. In H. Whitehouse, & R. N. McCauley (Eds.), *Mind and religion: Psychological and cognitive foundations of religiosity* (pp. 3–29). Lanham, MD: AltaMira Press.

Boyer, P., & Ramble, C. (2001). Cognitive templates for religious concepts: Cross-cultural evidence for recall of counter-intuitive representations. *Cognitive Science, 25,* 535–564.

Braam, A. W., Beekman, A. T. F., van Tilburg, T. G., Deeg, D. J. H., & van Tilburg, W. (1997). Religious involvement in older Dutch citizens. *Social Psychiatry and Psychiatric Epidemiology, 32,* 284–291.

Braam, A. W., Hein, E., Deeg, D. J. H., Twisk, J. W. R., Beekman, A. T. F., & van Tilburg, W. (2004). Religious involvement and 6-year course of depressive symptoms in older Dutch citizens: Results from the longitudinal aging study Amsterdam. *Journal of Aging and Health, 16,* 467–489.

Braam, A. W., Sonnenberg, C. M., Beekman, A. T. F., Deeg, D. J. H., & van Tilburg, W. (2000). Religious denomination as a symptom-formation factor of depression in older Dutch citizens. *International Journal of Geriatric Psychiatry, 15,* 458–466.

Braam, A. W., van den Eeden, P., Prince, M. J., Beekman, A. T. F., Kivela, S.-L., Lawlor, B. A., et al. (2001). Religion as a cross-cultural determinant of depression in elderly Europeans: Results from the EURODEP collaboration. *Psychological Medicine, 31,* 803–814.

Braaten, C., & Jenson, R. (1995). Preface. In C. Braaten, & R. Jenson (Eds.), *Either/or: The gospel of neopaganism* (pp. 1–6). Grand Rapids, MI: Eerdmans.

Bradley, D. E. (1995). Religious involvement and social resources: Evidence from the data set "Americans' changing lives". *Journal for the Scientific Study of Religion, 34,* 259–267.

Bradley, N. (1978). *Communitas and transcendence: A critique of Victor Turner's conception of the function of ritual.* Rome: Pontificiae Universitatis Gregorianae.

Braud, W. G. (2002). Thoughts on the ineffability of the mystical experience. *The International Journal for the Psychology of Religion, 12,* 141–160.

Brawer, P., Handal, A., Fabricatore, R., & Wajda-Johnston, V. (2002). Training and education in religion/spirituality within APA-accredited clinical programs. *Professional Psychology: Research and Practice, 33,* 203–206.

Breakey, W. R. (2001). Psychiatry, spirituality and religion. *International Review of Psychiatry, 13,* 61–66.

Bréchon, P. (2003). Integration into Catholicism and Protestantism in Europe: The impact on moral and political values. In L. Halman, & O. Riis (Eds.), *Religion in secularizing society: The Europeans' religion at the end of the 20th century* (pp. 114–161). Leiden; Boston: Brill.

Brenneman, Jr., W. L. (1993). Pilgrimage and place: The reciprocal relationship of topographical context and religious image at Medjugorje. *Architecture & Behaviour Journal, 9,* 205–212.

Breslin, F. C., Zack, M., & McMain, S. (2002). An information-processing analysis of mindfulness: Implications for relapse prevention in the treatment of substance abuse. *Clinical Psychology: Science and Practice, 9*, 275–299.

Breslin, M., & Lewis, C. (2008). Theoretical models of the nature of prayer and health: A review. *Mental Health, Religion & Culture, 11*, 9–21.

Bretherton, R. (2006). Can existential psychotherapy be good news? Reflections on existential psychotherapy from a Christian perspective. *Mental Health, Religion & Culture, 9*, 265–275.

Brett, C. (2003). Psychotic and mystical states of being: Connections and distinctions. *Philosophy, Psychiatry & Psychology, 9*, 321–341.

Brewer, M. B., & Brown, R. J. (1998). Intergroup relations. In D. T. Gilbert, S. T. Fiske, & G. Lindzey (Eds.), *The handbook of social psychology* (4th ed., Vol. 2, pp. 554–594). Boston, MA: McGraw-Hill.

Brewi, J., & Brennan, A. (1988). *Celebrate mid-life: Jungian archetypes and mid-life spirituality.* New York: Crossroad.

Bridgman, P. (1950). *Reflections of a physicist.* New York: Philosophical Library.

Bridgman, P. (1959). *The way things are.* Cambridge, MA: Harvard University Press.

Bridgman, P. (1993). *The logic of modern physics* (Reprint ed.). Salem, NH: Ayer. (Original work published 1927).

Briggs, S. (1997). A history of our own: What would a feminist history of theology look like? In R. S. Chopp, & S. G. Davaney (Eds.), *Horizons in feminist theology: Identity, tradition, and norms* (pp. 165–178). Minneapolis, MN: Fortress Press.

Brock, S. (1999). The prayer of the heart in Syriac tradition. In E. Ferguson (Ed.), *Forms of devotion: Conversion, worship, spirituality, and asceticism* (pp. 133–144). New York: Garland.

Broderick, W. (1991). The dynamic of the second week. In P. Sheldrake (Ed.), *The way of Ignatius Loyola: Contemporary approaches to the spiritual exercises* (pp. 86–95). St. Louis, MO: The Institute of Jesuit Sources.

Brokaw, B., & Edwards, K. (1994). The relationship of God image to level of object relations development. *The Journal of Psychology and Theology, 22*, 352–371.

Bromiley, G. (1978). *Historical theology: An introduction.* Grand Rapids, MI: Eerdmans.

Bromley, D., & Melton, J. (2002). Violence and religion in perspective. In D. Bromley, & J. Melton (Eds.), *Cults, religion, and violence.* Cambridge: Cambridge University Press.

Bronfenbrenner, U. (1977). Toward an experimental ecology of human development. *American Psychologist, 32*, 513–531.

Bronfenbrenner, U. (1995). Developmental ecology through space and time: A future perspective. In P. Moen, G. Elder, & K. Luscher (Eds.), *Examining lives in context: Perspectives on the ecology of human development* (pp. 619–647). Washington, DC: American Psychological Association.

Bronfenbrenner, U., & Evans, G. W. (2000). Developmental science in the 21st century: Emerging questions, theoretical models, research designs and empirical findings. *Social Development, 9*, 115–125.

Brooke, J. H. (1991). *Science and religion: Some historical perspectives.* Cambridge: Cambridge University Press.

Broom, D. M. (2003). *The evolution of morality and religion.* Cambridge: Cambridge University Press.

Broughton, J. M. (1981a). Piaget's structural developmental psychology: I. Piaget and structuralism. *Human Development, 24*, 78–109.

Broughton, J. M. (1981b). Piaget's structural developmental psychology: II. Logic and psychology. *Human Development, 24*, 195–224.

Broughton, J. M. (1981c). Piaget's structural developmental psychology: III. Function and the problem of knowledge. *Human Development, 24*, 257–285.

Broughton, J. M. (1981d). Piaget's structural developmental psychology: IV. Knowledge without a self and without history. *Human Development, 24*, 320–346.

Broughton, J. M. (1981e). Piaget's structural developmental psychology: V. Ideology-critique and the possibility of a critical developmental theory. *Human Development, 24*, 382–411.

Brown, D. (1986). The stages of meditation in cross-cultural perspective. In K. Wilber, J. Engler, & D. Brown (Eds.), *Transformations of consciousness: Conventional and contemplative perspectives on development* (pp. 219–283). Boston, MA: New Science Library.

Brown, D., & Engler, J. (1986a). The stages of mindfulness meditation: A validation study. Part I: Study and results. In K. Wilber, J. Engler, & D. Brown (Eds.), *Transformations of consciousness: Conventional and contemplative perspectives on development* (pp. 161–191). Boston, MA: New Science Library.

Brown, D., & Engler, J. (1986b). The stages of mindfulness meditation: A validation study. Part II: Discussion. In K. Wilber, J. Engler, & D. Brown (Eds.), *Transformations of consciousness: Conventional and contemplative perspectives on development* (pp. 193–217). Boston, MA: New Science Library.

Brown, H. (2000). *William James on radical empiricism and religion.* Toronto: University of Toronto Press.

Brown, L. (1994). *The human side of prayer: The psychology of praying.* Birmingham, AL: Religious Education Press.

Brown, L., & Robinson, S. E. (1993). The relationship between meditation and/or exercise and three measures of self-actualization. *Journal of Mental Health Counseling, 15,* 85–93.

Brown, W. S. (1998a). Cognitive contributions to soul. In W. S. Brown, N. Murphy, & H. N. Malony (Eds.), *Whatever happened to the soul? Scientific and theological portraits of human nature* (pp. 99–125). Minneapolis, MN: Fortress Press.

Brown, W. S. (1998b). Conclusion: Reconciling scientific and biblical portraits of human nature. In W. S. Brown, N. Murphy, & H. N. Malony (Eds.), *Whatever happened to the soul? Scientific and theological portraits of human nature* (pp. 213–228). Minneapolis, MN: Fortress Press.

Browning, D. S. (1978). Erikson and the search for a normative image of man. In P. Homans (Ed.), *Childhood and selfhood: Essays on tradition, religion, and modernity in the psychology of Erik H. Erikson* (pp. 264–292). Cranbury, NJ: Associated University Presses.

Browning, D. S. (1980). *Pluralism and personality: William James and some contemporary cultures of psychology.* Lewisburg, PA: Bucknell University Press.

Browning, D. S. (1968). Faith and the dynamics of knowing. In P. Homans (Ed.), *The dialogue between theology and psychology* (pp. 111–134). Chicago: University of Chicago Press.

Browning, D. S. (1973). *Generative man: Psychoanalytic perspectives.* Philadelphia: Westminster John Knox Press.

Browning, D. S. (1991). *A fundamental practical theology: Descriptive and strategic proposals.* Minneapolis, MN: Fortress Press.

Browning, D. S. (1994). Congregational studies as practical theology. In J. Wind, & J. Lewis (Eds.), *American congregations, Volume 2: New perspectives in the study of congregations* (pp. 192–221). Chicago: University of Chicago Press.

Browning, D. S. (1999). Towards a fundamental and strategic practical theology. In F. Schweitzer, & J. van der Ven (Eds.), *Practical theology: International perspectives* (pp. 53–74). New York: Peter Lang.

Browning, D. S. (2002). Science and religion on the nature of love. In S. G. Post, L. G. Underwood, J. P. Schloss, & W. B. Hurlbut (Eds.), *Altruism & altruistic love: Science, philosophy, & religion in dialogue* (pp. 335–345). New York: Oxford University Press.

Browning, D. S., & Cooper, T. D. (2004). *Religious thought and the modern psychologies* (2nd ed.). Minneapolis, MN: Augsburg Fortress.

Bruce, M., & Cockreham, D. (2004). Enhancing the spiritual development of adolescent girls. *Professional School Counseling, 7,* 334–342.

Bruce, S. (1993). Religion and rational choice: A critique of economic explanations of religious behavior. *Sociology of Religion, 54,* 193–205.

Bruce, S. (2000). The supply-side model of religion: The Nordic and Baltic states. *Journal for the Scientific Study of Religion, 39,* 32–46.

Bruce, S. (2001). The social process of secularization. In R. K. Fenn (Ed.), *The Blackwell companion to sociology of religion* (pp. 249–263). Oxford, UK: Blackwell.

Bruce, S. (2002). *God is dead: Secularization in the west.* Malden, MA: Blackwell.

Bruner, J. (1986). *Actual minds, possible worlds.* Cambridge, MA: Harvard University Press.

Bruner, J. (1991). The narrative construction of reality. *Critical Inquiry, 18*, 1–21.

Buckley, M. J. (1991). The structure of the rules for discernment. In P. Sheldrake (Ed.), *The way of Ignatius Loyola: Contemporary approaches to the spiritual exercises* (pp. 219–237). St. Louis, MO: The Institute of Jesuit Sources.

Buckley, M. J. (1995). Ecclesial mysticism in the Spiritual exercises of Ignatius. *Theological Studies, 56*, 441–463.

Buddhaghosa, B. (1999). *The path of purification (Visuddhimagga).* (B. Nanamoli, Trans.). Seattle, WA: BPS Pariyatti.

Budziszewski, J. (1998). C.G. Jung's war on the Christian faith. *Christian Research Journal, 21*(3), 28–33.

Buffetrille, K. (1998). Reflections on pilgrimages to sacred mountains, lakes and caves. In A. C. McKay (Ed.), *Pilgrimage in Tibet* (pp. 18–34). Surrey, Richmond: Curzon, International Institute for Asian Studies.

Bufford, R., Paloutzian, R., & Ellison, C. (1991). Norms for the spiritual well-being scale. *Journal of Psychology and Theology, 19*, 56–70.

Buller, D. J. (1999). DeFreuding evolutionary psychology: Adaptation and human motivation. In V. G. Hardcastle (Ed.), *Where biology meets psychology: Philosophical essays* (pp. 99–114). Cambridge, MA: MIT Press.

Buller, D. (2005). *Adapting minds: Evolutionary psychology and the persistent quest for human nature.* Cambridge, MA: Bradford/MIT.

Bunge, M. (2001). Introduction. In M. Bunge (Ed.), *The child in Christian thought* (pp. 1–28). Grand Rapids, MI: Eerdmans.

Bunting, I. (2000). Pastoral care at the end of the twentieth century. In G. R. Evans (Ed.), *A history of pastoral care* (pp. 383–399). London: Cassell.

Burke, M., Hackney, H., Hudson, P., Miranti, J., Watts, G., & Epp, L. (1999). Spirituality, religion, and CACREP curriculum standards. *Journal of Counseling and Development, 77*, 251–257.

Burke, P. (1999). Spirituality: A continually evolving component in women's identity development. In L. E. Thomas, & S. Eisenhandler (Eds.), *Religion, belief and spirituality in late life* (pp. 113–136). New York: Springer.

Burman, E. (1994). *Deconstructing developmental psychology.* London: Routledge.

Burns, S. (2004). Forgiveness in challenging circumstances. In F. Watts, & L. Gulliford (Eds.), *Forgiveness in context: Theology and psychology in creative dialogue* (pp. 144–159). New York: T & T Clark.

Burns-Smith, C. (1999). Theology and Winnicott's object relations theory: A conversation. *Journal of Psychology and Theology, 27*, 3–19.

Burnstein, E. (2005). Altruism and genetic relatedness. In D. Buss (Eds.), *The handbook of evolutionary psychology* (pp. 528–551). New York: John Wiley & Sons.

Burris, C. T. (1994). Curvilinearity and religious types: A second look at intrinsic, extrinsic, and quest relations. *The International Journal for the Psychology of Religion, 4*, 245–260.

Burris, C. T., Batson, C. D., Altstaedten, M., & Stephens, K. (1994). "What a friend…": Loneliness as a motivator of intrinsic religion. *Journal for the Scientific Study of Religion, 33*, 326–334.

Burris, C. T., Jackson, L. M., Tarpley, W. R., & Smith, G. J. (1996). Religion as quest: The self-directed pursuit of meaning. *Personal and Social Psychology Bulletin, 22*, 1068–1076.

Burton, T. (1993). *Serpent-handling believers.* Knoxville, TN: University of Tennessee Press.

Bushell, W. (1995). Psychophysiological and comparative analysis of ascetico-meditational discipline: Toward a new theory of asceticism. In V. Wimbush, & R. Valantasis (Eds.), *Asceticism* (pp. 553–575). New York: Oxford University Press.

Bushman, B., Ridge, R., Das, E., Key, C., & Busath, G. (2007). When God sanctions killing: Effect of scriptural violence on aggression. *Psychological Science, 18*, 204–207.

Buss, D. M. (1995). Evolutionary psychology: A new paradigm for psychological science. *Psychological Inquiry, 6*, 1–30.

Buss, D. M. (2001). Human nature and culture: An evolutionary psychological perspective. *Journal of Personality, 69*, 955–978.

Buss, D. M. (2002). Sex, marriage, and religion: What adaptive problems do religious phenomena solve? *Psychological Inquiry, 13*, 201–238.

Buss, D. M., & Reeve, H. K. (2003). Evolutionary psychology and developmental dynamics: Comment on Lickliter and Honeycutt (2003). *Psychological Bulletin, 129*, 848–853.

Bussing, A., Ostermann, T., & Matthiessen, P. (2005). The role of religion and spirituality in medical patients in Germany. *Journal of Religion and Health, 44*, 321–340.

Butchvarov, P. (1999). Metaphysics. In R. Audi (ed.), *The Cambridge dictionary of philosophy* (2nd ed., pp. 563–566). Cambridge: Cambridge University Press.

Butler, D. C. (2003). *Western mysticism: Augustine, Gregory and Bernard on contemplation and the contemplative life*. Mineola, NY: Dover Publications.

Butter, E. M., & Pargament, K. I. (2003). Development of a model for clinical assessment of religious coping: Initial validation of the process evaluation model. *Mental Health, Religion and Culture, 6*, 175–194.

Byrd, K. R., Hageman, A., & Isle, D. B. (2007). Intrinsic motivation and subjective well-being: The unique contribution of intrinsic religious motivation. *International Journal for the Psychology of Religion, 17*, 141–156.

Byrd, K. R., Lear, D., & Schwenka, S. (2000). Mysticism as a predictor of subjective well-being. *The International Journal for the Psychology of Religion, 10*, 259–269.

Byrd, R. (2001). Positive therapeutic effects of intercessory prayer in a coronary care unit population. In L. Francis, & J. Astley (Eds.), *Psychological perspectives on prayer* (pp. 156–163). Leominster, UK: Gracewing.

Byrne, L. (Ed.). (1990). *Traditions of spiritual guidance*. Collegeville, MN: Liturgical.

Byrne, L. (1991). The spiritual exercises: A process and a text. In P. Sheldrake (Ed.), *The way of Ignatius Loyola: Contemporary approaches to the spiritual exercises* (pp. 17–27). St. Louis, MO: The Institute of Jesuit Sources.

Cacioppo, J. T. (2002). Social neuroscience: Understanding the pieces fosters understanding the whole and vice versa. *American Psychologist, 57*, 819–831.

Cady, L. E. (1997). Identity, feminist theory, and theology. In R. S. Chopp, & S. G. Davaney (Eds.), *Horizons in feminist theology: Identity, tradition, and norms* (pp. 17–32). Minneapolis, MN: Fortress Press.

Cahn, B. R., & Polich, J. (2006). Meditation states and traits: EEG, ERP, and neuroimaging studies. *Psychological Bulletin, 132*, 180–211.

Calvin, J. (1960). *Institutes of the Christian religion* (2 vols.) (J. McNeill, Ed., & F. Battles, Trans.). Philadelphia: Westminster.

Campbell, D. (1974). Downward causation in hierarchically organized systems. In F. J. Ayala, & T. Dobzhansky (Eds.), Studies in the philosophy of biology: Reduction and related problems (pp. 179–186). London: Macmillan.

Campbell, H. (2004). Challenges created by online religious networks. *Journal of Media and Religion, 3*, 81–99.

Canning, R. (Trans.). (1986). *The rule of St. Augustine*. Garden City, NY: Image.

Canter, P. H. (2003). The therapeutic effects of meditation. *British Medical Journal, 326*, 1049–1050.

Cantor, N., & Sanderson, C. A. (1999). Life task participation and well-being: The importance of taking part in daily life. In D. Kahneman, E. Diener, & N. Schwarz (Eds.), *Well-being: The foundations of hedonic psychology* (pp. 230–243). New York: Russell Sage Foundation.

Caporael, L. R., & Brewer, M. B. (2000). Metatheories, evolution and psychology: Once more with feeling. *Psychological Inquiry, 11*, 23–26.

Capper, D. (2002). Guru devotion and the American Buddhist experience. *Studies in Religion and Society, 57*, 1–237.

Capps, D. (1984). Erikson's life-cycle theory: Religious dimensions. *Religious Studies Review, 10*, 120–127.

Capps, D. (1996a). Do not despair of this world: A posthumous review of Erik H. Erikson's writings. *Religious Studies Review, 22*, 323–332.

Capps, D. (1996b). Erikson's "inner space": Where art and religion converge. *Journal of Religion and Health, 35*, 93–115.

Capps, D. (1997a). Childhood fears, adult anxieties, and the longing for inner peace: Eric Erikson's psychoanalytic psychology of religion. In J. Jacobs, & D. Capps (Eds.), *Religion, society, and psychoanalysis: Readings in contemporary theory* (pp. 127–164). Cumnor Hill, Oxford: WestviewPress.

Capps, D. (1997b). *Men, religion, and melancholia: James, Otto, Jung, and Erikson.* New Haven: Yale University Press.

Cardena, E., Lynn, S., & Krippner, S. (Eds.). (2000). *Varieties of anomalous experience: Examining the scientific evidence.* Washington, DC: American Psychological Association.

Carlson, C., Bacaseta, P., & Simanton, D. (1988). A controlled evaluation of devotional meditation and progressive relaxation. *Journal of Psychology and Theology, 16*, 362–368.

Carnap, R. (1949a). Logical foundations of the unity of science. In H. Feigl, & W. Sellars (Eds.), *Readings in philosophical analysis* (pp. 408–423). New York: Appleton-Century-Crofts. (Original work published 1938).

Carnap, R. (1949b). Truth and confirmation. In H. Feigl, & W. Sellars (Eds.), *Readings in philosophical analysis* (pp. 119–127). New York: Appleton-Century-Crofts.

Carnap, R. (1995). *An introduction to the philosophy of science* (M. Gardner, Ed.), New York: Dover.

Carney, C. E., & Segal, Z. V. (2005). Mindfulness-based cognitive therapy for depression. In L. VandeCreek (Ed.), *Innovations in clinical practice: Focus on adults* (pp. 5–17). Sarasota, FL: Professional Resource Press.

Carpendale, J. I. M. (2000). Kohlberg and Piaget on stages and moral reasoning. *Developmental Review, 20*, 181–205.

Carr, D. (2004). Time zones: Phenomenological reflections on cultural time. In D. Carr, & C. Chan-Fai (Eds.), *Space, time, and culture* (pp. 3–13). Dordrecht: Kluwer Academic.

Carrette, J. (2000). Post-structuralism and the psychology of religion: The challenge of critical psychology. In D. Jonte-Pace, & W. Parsons (Eds.), *Religion and psychology: Mapping the terrain* (pp. 110–126). London: Routledge.

Carroll, S. (1993). Spirituality and purpose in life in alcoholism recovery. *Journal of Studies on Alcohol, 54*, 297–301.

Carter, J., & Narramore, B. (1979). The integration of psychology and theology. Grand Rapids, MI: Zondervan.

Cartwright, K. B. (2001). Cognitive developmental theory and spiritual development. *Journal of Adult Development, 8*, 213–220.

Casey, M. (1995). Sacred reading: The ancient art of Lectio Divina. Liguori, MO: Liguori/ Triumph.

Casey, M. (1996). *Toward God: The ancient wisdom of Western prayer.* Liguori, MO: Liguori/ Triumph.

Caspi, O., & Burleson, K. O. (2005). Methodological challenges in meditation research. *ADVANCES, 21*, 4–11.

Cassian, J. (1999). *The monastic institutes* (J. Bertram, Trans.). London: Saint Austin.

Castillo, R. J. (1990). Depersonalization and meditation. *Psychiatry, 53*, 158–168.

Cauchi, M. (2005). The infinite supplicant: On a limit and a prayer. In B. Benson, & N. Wirzba (Eds.), *The phenomenology of prayer* (pp. 217–231). Bronx, NY: Fordham University Press.

Cauthen, N., & Prymak, C. (1977). Meditation versus relaxation: An examination of the physiological effects of relaxation training and of different levels of experience with transcendental meditation. *Journal of Consulting and Clinical Psychology, 45*, 496–497.

Cecero, J., Bedrosian, D., Fuentes, A., & Bornstein, R. (2006). Religiosity and health dependency as predictors of spiritual well-being. *International Journal for the Psychology of Religion, 16*, 225–238.

Cela-Conde, C. (1998). The hominid evolutionary journey: A summary. In R. Russell, W. Stoeger, & F. Ayala (Eds.), *Evolutionary and molecular biology: Scientific perspectives on Divine action* (pp. 59–78). Vatican City State: Vatican Observatory.

Cela-Conde, C., & Marty, G. (1998). Beyond biological evolution: Mind, morals, and culture. In R. Russell, W. Stoeger, & F. Ayala (Eds.), *Evolutionary and molecular biology: Scientific perspectives on Divine action* (pp. 445–462). Vatican City State: Vatican Observatory.

Chadwick, P. (2001). Sanity to supersanity to insanity: A personal journey. In I. Clark (Ed.), *Psychosis and spirituality: Exploring the new frontier* (pp. 75–89). London: Whurr.

Chae, M. H., Kelly, D. B., Brown, C. F., & Bolden, M. A. (2004). Relationship of ethnic identity and spiritual development: An exploratory study. *Counseling and Values, 49*, 15–26.

Chalfant, H. P., Heller, P. L., Roberts, A., Briones, D., Aguirre-Hochbaum, S., & Farr, W. (1990). The clergy as a resource for those encountering psychological distress. *Review of Religious Research, 31*, 305–313.

Chamberlain, T., & Hall, C. (2000). *Research on the relationship between religion and health: Realized religion.* Philadelphia: Templeton Foundation Press.

Chandy, J. M., Blum, R. W., & Resnick, M. D. (1996). History of sexual abuse and parental alcohol misuse: Risk, outcomes and protective factors in adolescents. *Child and Adolescent Social Work Journal, 13*, 411–432.

Chang, B., Skinner, K. M., Zhou, C., & Kazis, L. E. (2003). The relationship between sexual assault, religiosity, and mental health among male veterans. *International Journal of Psychiatry in Medicine, 33*, 223–239.

Chapman, G. C. (1997). Jung and Christology. *Journal of Psychology and Theology, 25*, 414–426.

Chapman, H. J. (1988). *Jung's three theories of religious experience.* Lewiston, NY: Edwin Mellen Press.

Chapple, C. (1990). The unseen seer and the field: Consciousness in Samkhya and Yoga. In R. K. C. Forman (Ed.), *The problem of pure consciousness: Mysticism and philosophy* (pp. 53–70). New York: Oxford University Press.

Charet, F. X. (2000). Understanding Jung: Recent biographies and scholarship. *Journal of Analytical Psychology, 45*, 195–216.

Charry, E. (2001). Theology after psychology. In M. McMinn, & T. Phillips (Eds.), *Care for the soul: Exploring the intersection of psychology and theology* (pp. 118–133). Downers Grove, IL: InterVarsity Press.

Chatters, L. M. (2000). Religion and health: Public health research and practices. *Annual Review of Public Health, 21*, 335–367.

Chaves, M. (1995). Symposium: On the rational choice approach to religion. *Journal for the Scientific Study of Religion, 34*, 98–104.

Chaves, M., & Stephens, L. (2003). Church attendance in the United States. In M. Dillon (Ed.), *Handbook of the sociology of religion* (pp. 85–95). Cambridge: Cambridge University Press.

Chela-Flores, J. (1998). The phenomenon of the eukaryotic cell. In R. Russell, W. Stoeger, & F. Ayala (Eds.), *Evolutionary and molecular biology: Scientific perspectives on divine action* (pp. 79–98). Vatican City State: Vatican Observatory.

Chen, C. P. (2005). Morita therapy: A philosophy of yin/yang coexistence. In R. Moodley, & W. West (Eds.), *Integrating traditional healing practices into counseling and psychotherapy* (pp. 221–232). Thousand Oaks, CA: Sage.

Chen, C., Dormitzer, C. M., Bejarano, J., & Anthony, J. C. (2004). Religiosity and the earliest stages of adolescent drug involvement in seven countries of Latin America. *American Journal of Epidemiology, 159*, 1180–1188.

Cheston, S. E., Piedmont, R. L., Eanes, B., & Lavin, L. P. (2003). Changes in clients' images of God over the course of outpatient therapy. *Counseling and Values, 47*, 96–108.

Chihara, T. (1989). Zen meditation and time-experience. *Psychologia, 32*, 211–220.

Chirban, J. (1986). Developmental stages in eastern orthodox Christianity. In K. Wilber, J. Engler, & D. Brown (Eds.), *Transformations of consciousness: Conventional and contemplative perspectives on development* (pp. 285–314). Boston, MA: New Science Library.

Chirban, J. (2001). Assessing religious and spiritual concerns in psychotherapy. In T. Plante, & A. Sherman (Eds.), *Faith and health: Psychological perspectives* (pp. 265–290). New York: Guilford Press.

Chittick, W. (1983). *The Sufi path of love: The spiritual teachings of Rumi.* Albany: State University of New York Press.

Chittick, W. (2005). Sufism: Name and reality. In R. Baker, & G. Henry (Eds.), *Merton & Sufism: The untold story* (pp. 15–31). Louisville, KY: Fons Vitae.

Chodorow, N. (1999). Toward a relational individualism: The mediation of self through psychoanalysis. In S. Mitchell, & L. Aron (Eds.), *Relational psychoanalysis: The emergence of a tradition* (pp. 109–130). Hillsdale, NJ: Analytic. (Original work published 1986).

Chopp, R. S. (1997). Theorizing feminist theology. In R. S. Chopp, & S. G. Davaney (Eds.), *Horizons in feminist theology: Identity, tradition, and norms* (pp. 215–231). Minneapolis, MN: Fortress Press.

Chrysostomos, A. (2007). *A guide to orthodox psychotherapy: The science, theology, and spiritual practice behind it and its clinical applications.* Lanham, MD: University Press of America.

Chrysostomos, B. (1988). Demonology in the Orthodox Church: A psychological perspective. *Greek Orthodox Theological Review, 33,* 45–61.

Chryssavgis, J. (2000). *Soul mending: The art of spiritual direction.* Brookline, MA: Holy Cross Orthodox.

Chryssavgis, J. (2002). Paths of continuity: Contemporary witnesses of the Hesychast experience. In J. Cutsinger (Ed.), *Paths to the heart: Sufism and the Christian East* (pp. 112–137). Bloomington, IN: World Wisdom.

Churchland, P. (1995). Eliminative materialism and the propositional attitudes. In P. Moser and J. Trout (Eds.), *Contemporary materialism: A reader* (pp. 150–179). London: Routledge.

Churchland, P. (1996). *The engine of reason, the seat of the soul: A philosophical journey into the brain.* Cambridge, MA: MIT Press.

Cicirelli, V. (2006). Can science and Christian religions coexist: Compatibility or conflict? In S. Ambrose (Ed.), *Religion and psychology: New research* (pp. 257–275). New York: Nova Science.

Claridge, G. (2001). Spiritual experience: Healthy psychoticism. In I. Clarke (Ed.), *Psychosis and spirituality* (pp. 90–107). Philadelphia, PA: Whurr.

Clark, M. S., Ouellette, R., Powell, M. C., & Millberg, S. (1987). Recipient's mood, relationship type, and helping. *Journal of Personality and Social Psychology, 53,* 94–103.

Clark, P. Y. (1995). The "cogwheeling" of Don Browning: Examining his Erikson perspective. *Pastoral Psychology, 43,* 141–161.

Clarke, C., Bannon, F. J., & Denihan, A. (2003). Suicide and religiosity: Masaryk's theory revisited. *Social Psychiatry and Psychiatric Epidemiology, 38,* 502–506.

Clarke, C. (2001a). Construction and reality: Reflections on philosophy and spiritual/psychotic experience. In I. Clarke (Ed.), *Psychosis and spirituality: Exploring the new frontier* (pp.143–162). Philadelphia, PA: Whurr.

Clarke, I. (2001b). Cognitive behaviour therapy for psychosis. In I. Clark (Ed.), *Psychosis and spirituality: Exploring the new frontier* (pp. 11–14). London: Whurr.

Clarke, I. (2001c). Psychosis and spirituality: The discontinuity model. In I. Clarke (Ed.), *Psychosis and spirituality: Exploring the new frontier* (pp.129–142). Philadelphia, PA: Whurr.

Clarke, S. (2005). Created in whose image? Religious characters on network television. *Journal of Media and Religion, 4,* 137–153.

Clayton, P. (2002). Neuroscience, the person and God: An emergentist account. In R. Russell, N. Murphy, T. Meyering, & M. Arbib (Eds.), *Neuroscience and the person* (pp. 181–214). Vatican City State: Vatican Observatory.

Cleary, T. (Trans.). (1993). *The flower ornament scripture: A translation of the Avatamsaka Sutra.* Boston: Shambhala.

Cleary, T. (Trans.). (1996). *Unlocking the Zen Koan: A new translation of the Zen classic Wumenguan.* Berkeley, CA: North Atlantic Books.

Cleary, T. (Trans.). (2005). *The blue cliff record.* Boston: Shambhala.

Clement, F. (2003). The pleasure of believing: Toward a naturalistic explanation of religious conversions. *Journal of Cognition and Culture, 3*, 69–89.

Clift, J., & Clift, W. (1996). *The archetype of pilgrimage.* New York: Paulist Press.

Clift, W. B. (1982). *Jung and Christianity: The challenge of reconciliation.* New York: Crossroad.

Clinebell, H. (1984). *Basic types of pastoral care and counseling: Resources for the ministry of healing and growth* (Rev. ed.). Nashville, TN: Abingdon Press.

Clinebell, H. (1990). The Emmanuel movement: Religion plus psychotherapy. In R. V. Kendall (Ed.), *Understanding and counseling the alcoholic through religion and psychology* (Rev. ed.) (pp. 175). Nashville, TN: Abingdon Press.

Clinebell, H. (1993). *Understanding and counseling the alcoholic* (Rev. ed.). Nashville, TN: Abingdon Press.

Cloutier, D. (2003). The pressures to die: Reconceiving the shape of Christian life in the face of physician-assisted suicide. In S. Hauerwas, C. Stoneking, K. Meador, & D. Cloutier (Eds.), *Growing old in Christ* (pp. 247–266). Grand Rapids: Eerdmans.

Coate, M. A. (2004). The capacity for forgiveness. In F. Watts, & L. Gulliford (Eds.), *Forgiveness in context: Theology and psychology in creative dialogue* (pp. 123–143). New York: T & T Clark.

Cochran, J. K., Beeghley, L., & Bock, E. W. (1992). The influence of religious stability and homogamy on the relationship between religiosity and alcohol use among protestants. *Journal for the Scientific Study of Religion, 31*, 441–456.

Cohen, A. B. (2002). The importance of spirituality in well-being for Jews and Christians. *Journal of Happiness Studies, 3*, 287–310.

Cohen, E. (1992). Pilgrimage and tourism: Convergence and divergence. In A. Morinis (Eds.), *Sacred journeys: The anthropology of pilgrimage* (pp. 47–61). Westport, CT: Greenwood Press.

Cohen, I. B. (Ed.). (1990). *Puritanism and the rise of modern science: The Merton thesis.* New Brunswick, NJ: Rutgers University Press.

Cohen, S. (2004). Social relationships and health. *American Psychologist, 59*, 676–684.

Cohen, S., & Lemay, E. (2007). Why would social networks be linked to affect and health practices? *Health Psychology, 26*, 410–417.

Cohen, S., & Pressman, S. (2006). Positive affect and health. *Current Directions in Psychological Science, 15*, 122–125.

Colby, A. (2002). Moral understanding, motivation, and identity. *Human Development, 45*, 130–135.

Cole, B. S. (2005). Spiritually-focused psychotherapy for people diagnosed with cancer: A pilot outcome study. *Mental Health, Religion & Culture, 8*, 217–226.

Cole, M., & Wertsch, J. V. (1996). Beyond the individual-social antinomy in discussions of Piaget and Vygotsky. *Human Development, 39*, 250–256.

Cole, V. L. (2003). Healing principles: A model for the use of ritual in psychotherapy. *Counseling and Values, 47*, 184–194.

Coleman, G. (2004). Clergy sexual abuse and homosexuality. In T. Plante (Ed.), *Sin against the innocents: Sexual abuse by priests and the role of the Catholic church* (pp. 73–84). Westport, CT: Praeger.

Coleman, P. G., Ivani-Chalian, C., & Robinson M. (2004). Religious attitudes among British older people: Stability and change in a 20-year longitudinal study. *Ageing & Society, 24*, 167–188.

Coles, R. (1990). *The spiritual life of children.* Boston: Houghton Mifflin.

Collcutt, M. (1988). Epilogue: Problems of authority in Western Zen. In K. Kraft (Ed.), *Zen: Tradition and transition* (pp. 199–207). New York: Grove Press.

Collings, G. H., Jr. (1989). Stress containment through meditation. *Prevention in Human Services, 6*, 141–150.

Collins, G. R. (1988). *Can you trust psychology?* Downers Grove, IL: InterVarsity Press.

Collins, R. (1997). Stark and Bainbridge, Durkheim and Weber: Theoretical comparisons. In L. A. Young (Ed.), *Rational choice theory and religion: Summary and assessment* (pp. 161–180). New York: Routledge.

Compton, W. C. (1991). Self-report of attainment in experienced Zen meditators: A cautionary note on objective measurement. *Psychologia, 34*, 15–17.

Compton, W. M., Conway, K. P., Stinson, F. S., & Grant, B. F. (2006). Changes in prevalence of major depression and comorbid substance use disorders in the United States between 1991–1992 and 2001–2002. *American Journal of Psychiatry, 163*, 2141–2147.

Comte, A. (1998a). Course on positive philosophy. In G. Lenzer (Ed.), *Auguste Comte and positivism: The essential writings* (pp. 71–306). New Brunswick, NJ: Transaction. (Original work published 1830–1842).

Comte, A. (1998b). System of positive polity. In G. Lenzer (Ed.), *Auguste Comte and positivism: The essential writings* (pp. 309–492). New Brunswick, NJ: Transaction. (Original work published 1851–1854).

Conrad, P. (2007). *The medicalization of society: On the transformation of human conditions into treatable disorders.* Baltimore, MD: Johns Hopkins University Press.

Contrada, R. J., Goyal, T. M., Cather, C., Rafalson, L., Idler, E. L., & Krause, T. J. (2004). Psychosocial factors in outcomes of heart surgery: The impact of religious involvement and depressive symptoms. *Health Psychology, 23*, 227–238.

Conze, E. (1956). *Buddhist meditation.* London: George Allen and Unwin.

Conze, E. (1975). *The large sutra on perfect wisdom.* Berkeley, CA: University of California Press.

Conze, E. (Trans.). (2001). *Buddhist wisdom: The Diamond Sutra and the Heart Sutra.* New York: Vintage.

Cook, C. (2004). Addiction and spirituality. *Addiction, 99*, 539–551.

Cook-Greuter, S. (2000). Mature ego development: A gateway to ego transcendence? *Journal of Adult Development, 7*, 227–240.

Cook-Greuter, S., & Soulen, J. (2007). The developmental perspective in integral counseling. *Counseling and Values, 51*, 180–192.

Coomaraswamy, A. (2007). Paths that lead to the same summit. In M. Lings, & C. Minnaar (Eds.), *The underlying religion: An introduction to the perennial philosophy* (pp. 217–229). Bloomington, IN: World Wisdom. (Original work published 1979).

Cooper, T. D. (2003). *The problem of identity in theology & psychology: Sin, pride & self-acceptance.* Downers Grove, IL: InterVarsity Press.

Cooper, T. D. (2006). *Paul Tillich and psychology: Historic and contemporary explorations in theology, psychotherapy, and ethics.* Macon, GA: Mercer University Press.

Cooper, T. D. (2007). *Dimensions of evil: Contemporary perspectives.* Minneapolis, MN: Fortress.

Corbett, L., & Stein, M. (2005). Contemporary Jungian approaches to spiritually oriented psychotherapy. In L. Sperry, & E. P. Shafranske (Eds.), *Spiritually oriented psychotherapy* (pp. 51–73). Washington, DC: American Psychological Association.

Corby, J. C., Roth, W. T., Zarcone, V. P., & Kopell, B. S. (1978). Psychophysiological correlates of the practice of Tantric Yoga meditation. *Archives of General Psychiatry, 35*, 571–577.

Corveleyn, J. (1996). The psychological explanation of religion as wish-fulfillment. A testcase: The belief in immortality. In J. A. van Belzen, & J. M. van der Lans (Series Eds.) & H. Grzymala-Moszczynska, & B. Beit-Hallahmi (Vol. Eds.), *International series in the psychology of religion: Vol. 4. Religion, psychopathology, and coping* (pp. 57–70). Amsterdam: Rodopi.

Corwyn, R. F., & Benda, B. B. (2000). Religiosity and church attendance: The effects on use of "hard drugs" controlling for sociodemographic and theoretical factors. *The International Journal for the Psychology of Religion, 10*, 241–258.

Cosmides, L., Tooby, J., & Barkow, J. H. (1992). Introduction: Evolutionary psychology and conceptual integration. In J. H. Barkow, L. Cosmides, & J. Tooby (Eds.), *The adapted mind: Evolutionary psychology and the generation of culture* (pp. 3–15). New York: Oxford University Press.

Coulson, C. A. (1955). *Science and Christian belief.* Chapel Hill, NC: University of North Carolina Press.

la Cour, P., Avlund, K., & Schultz-Larsen, K. (2006). Religion and survival in a secular region. A twenty year follow-up of 734 Danish adults born in 1914. *Social Science & Medicine, 62*, 157–164.

Court, J. (1997). Church-related counseling in Australia. *Journal of Psychology and Christianity, 16*, 142–147.

Cowan, D. E. (2005). Online u-topia: Cyberspace and the mythology of placelessness. *Journal for the Scientific Study of Religion, 44*, 257–263.

Coward, H. (1985). *Jung and eastern thought.* Albany, NY: State University of New York Press.

Coward, H. (1992). Jung's commentary on the *Amitayur Dhyana Sutra.* In D. Meckel, & R. Moore (Eds.), *Self and liberation: The Jung-Buddhism dialogue* (pp. 247–260). New York: Paulist Press.

Coward, H. (1995). Response to John Dourley's "The religious significance of Jung's psychology". *The International Journal for the Psychology of Religion, 5*, 95–100.

Coyle, C., & Enright, R. (1997). Forgiveness intervention with postabortion men. *Journal of Consulting and Clinical Psychology, 65*, 1042–1046.

Cranson, R. W., Orme-Johnson, D. W., Gackenbach, J., Dillbeck, C. D., Jones, C. H., & Alexander, C. N. (1991). Transcendental meditation and improved performance on intelligence-related measures: A longitudinal study. *Personality and Individual Differences, 12*, 1105–1116.

Craven, J. L. (1989). Meditation and psychotherapy. *Canadian Journal of Psychiatry, 34*, 348–353.

Crawford, M. E., Handal, P. J., & Wiener, R. L. (1989). The relationship between religion and mental health/distress, *Review of Religious Research, 31*, 16–22.

Criswell, E., & Patel, K. (2003).The yoga path: Awakening from the dream. In S. Mijares (Eds.), *Modern psychology and ancient wisdom: Psychological healing practices from the world's religious traditions* (pp. 201–226). New York: Haworth Integrative Healing Press.

Crossley, J. P, & Salter, D. P. (2005). A question of finding harmony: A grounded theory study of clinical psychologists' experience of addressing spiritual beliefs in therapy. *Psychology and Psychotherapy: Theory, Research and Practice, 78*, 295–313.

Crossley, M. (2000). *Introducing narrative psychology: Self, trauma and the construction of meaning.* Buckingham, UK: Open University Press.

Crosswell, A. G. (2000). Objects and idols: The significance of internal object relationships for the religious quest. *The Journal of Pastoral Care, 54*, 45–54.

Crowe, B. (2005). Heidegger and the prospect of a phenomenology of prayer. In B. Benson, & N. Wirzba (Eds.), *The phenomenology of prayer* (pp. 119–133). Bronx, NY: Fordham University Press.

Crowther, M., Parker, M., Achenbaum, W., Larimore, W., & Koenig, H. (2002). Rowe, & Kahn's model of successful aging revisited: Positive spirituality, the forgotten factor. *The Gerontologist, 42*, 613–620.

Crutchfield, J., Farmer, J., Packard, N., & Shaw, R. (1995). Chaos. In R. Russell, N. Murphy, & A. Peacocke (Eds.), *Chaos and complexity: Scientific perspectives on divine action* (pp.35–48). Vatican City State: Vatican Observatory.

Csanyi, D. A. (1982). Faith development and the age of readiness for the Bible. *Religious Education, 77*, 518–524.

Csikszentmihalyi, M. (1990). *Flow: The psychology of optimal experience.* New York: HarperPerennial.

Csikszentmihalyi, M. (1999). If we are so rich, why aren't we happy? *American Psychologist, 54*, 821–827.

Cummings, J. (1985). *Clinical neuropsychiatry.* Orlando, FL: Grune & Stratton.

Cummings, S. M., Neff, J. A., & Husaini, B. A. (2003). Functional impairment as a predictor of depressive symptomatology: The role of race, religiosity, and social support. *Health & Social Work, 28*, 23–32.

Curlin, F., Dugdale, L., Lantos, J., & Chin, M. (2007). Do religious physicians disproportionately care for the underserved? *Annals of Family Medicine, 5*, 353–360.

Curlin, F., Lawrence, R., Chin, M., & Lantos, J. (2007). Religion, conscience, and controversial clinical practices. *New England Journal of Medicine, 356*, 593–600.

Curlin, F., Lawrence, R., Odell, S., Chin, M., Lantos, J., Koenig, H., & Meador, K. (2007). Religion, spirituality, and medicine: Psychiatrists' and other physicians' differing observations, interpretations, and clinical approaches. *American Journal of Psychiatry, 164*, 1825–1831.

Cushman, P. (1995). *Constructing the self, constructing America: A cultural history of psychotherapy.* Cambridge, MA: Perseus.

Cutsinger, J. (2002). Hesychia: An Orthodox opening to esoteric ecumenism. In J. Cutsinger (Ed.), *Paths to the heart: Sufism and the Christian East* (pp. 225–260). Bloomington, IN: World Wisdom.

Cutsinger, J. (2003). The ladder of divine ascent: The yoga of hesychasm. In B. Dieker, & J. Montaldo (Eds.), *Merton & Hesychasm: The prayer of the heart: The Eastern Church* (pp. 75–89). Louisville, KY: Fons Vitae.

Daaleman, T. P., Perera, S., & Studenski, S. A. (2004). Religion, spirituality, and health status in geriatric outpatients. *Annals of Family Medicine, 2,* 49–53.

Dahlsgaard, K., Peterson, C., & Seligman, M. E. P. (2005). Shared virtue: The convergence of valued human strengths across culture and history. *Review of General Psychology, 9,* 203–213.

Damasio, A. (2002). A note on the neurobiology of emotions. In S. G. Post, L. G. Underwood, J. P. Schloss, & W. B. Hurlbut (Eds.), *Altruism & altruistic love: Science, philosophy, & religion in dialogue* (pp. 264–271). New York: Oxford University Press.

Damasio, A. (2003). *Looking for Spinoza: Joy, sorrow and the feeling brain.* Orlando, FL: Harcourt.

D'Andrade, R. (1995). *The development of cognitive anthropology.* Cambridge: Cambridge University Press.

Danner, D. D., Snowdon, D. A., & Friesen, W. V. (2001). Positive emotions in early life and longevity: Findings from the nun study. *Journal of Personality and Social Psychology, 80,* 804–813.

Dante Alighieri. (1995). *The divine comedy.* New York: Alfred A. Knopf. (Original work published 1314–1321).

D'Antonio, W. V. (1995). Small faith communities in the Roman Catholic church: New approaches to religion, work, and family. In N. T. Ammerman, & W. C. Roof (Eds.), *Work, family, and religion in contemporary society* (pp. 237–259). New York: Routledge.

d'Aquili, E., & Newberg, A. (1999). *The mystical mind: Probing the biology of religious experience.* Minneapolis: Fortress Press.

Darden, R. (2005). Spiritual assessment and treatment strategies. *The Christian Journal of Eating Disorders, 4,* 14–16.

Darwin, C. (1872). *The origin of species by means of natural selection, or the preservation of favoured races in the struggle for life* (6th ed.). London: John Murray.

Dasgupta, S. B. (1974*). An introduction to Tantric Buddhism.* London: Shambhala.

Davaney, S. G. (1997a). Continuing the story, but departing the text: A historicist interpretation of feminist norms. In R. S. Chopp, & S. G. Davaney (Eds.), *Horizons in feminist theology: Identity, tradition, and norms* (pp. 198–214). Minneapolis, MN: Fortress Press.

Davaney, S. G. (1997b). Introduction. In R. S. Chopp, & S. G. Davaney (Eds.), *Horizons in feminist theology: Identity, tradition, and norms* (pp. 1–16). Minneapolis, MN: Fortress Press.

Davidman, L. (2007). The new voluntarism and the case of unsynagogued Jews. In N. T. Ammerman (Ed.), *Everyday religion: Observing modern religious lives* (pp. 51–67). New York: Oxford University Press.

Davidson, A. (1990). Spiritual exercises and ancient philosophy: An introduction to Pierre Hadot. *Critical Inquiry, 16,* 475–482.

Davidson, R. J. (2003). Affective neuroscience and psychophysiology: Toward a synthesis. *Psychophysiology, 40,* 655–665.

Davidson, R. J. (2005). Well-being and affective style: Neural substrates and biobehavioural correlates. In F. Huppert, N. Baylis, & B. Keverne (Eds.), *The science of well-being* (pp. 107–139). Oxford: Oxford University Press.

Davidson, R. J., Goleman, D., & Schwartz, G. (1976). Attentional and affective concomitants of meditation: A cross-sectional study. *Journal of Abnormal Psychology, 85,* 235–238.

Davidson, R. J., Kabat-Zinn, J., Shumacher, J., Rosenkranz, M., Muller, D., Santorelli, S. F., et al. (2003). Alterations in brain and immune function produced by mindfulness meditation. *Psychosomatic Medicine, 65,* 564–570.

Davidson, R. J., Pizzagalli, D., Nitschke, J., & Putnam, K. (2002). Depression: Perspectives from affective neuroscience. *Annual Review of Psychology, 53*, 545–574.

Davie, G. (1999). Europe: The exception that proves the rule? In P. L. Berger (Ed.), *The desecularization of the world: Resurgent religion and world politics* (pp. 65–83). Washington, DC and Grand Rapids, MI: Ethics and Public Policy Center and William B. Eerdmans.

Davie, G. (2000). Religion in modern Britain: Changing sociological assumptions. *Sociology, 34,* 113–128.

Davie, G. (2001). Patterns of religion in western Europe: An exceptional case. In R. K. Fenn (Ed.), *The Blackwell companion to sociology of religion* (pp. 264–278). Oxford: Blackwell.

Davie, G. (2003). The evolution of the sociology of religion: Theme and variations. In M. Dillon (Ed.), *Handbook of the sociology of religion* (pp. 61–75). Cambridge: Cambridge University Press.

Davie, G. (2007). Vicarious religion: A methodological challenge. In N. T. Ammerman (Ed.), *Everyday religion: Observing modern religious lives* (pp. 21–35). Oxford: Oxford University Press.

Davies, M. F., Griffin, M., & Vice, S. (2001). Affective reactions to auditory hallucinations in psychotic, evangelical and control groups. *British Journal of Clinical Psychology, 40*, 361–370.

Davies, P. (1998). Teleology without: Purpose through. In R. Russell, W. Stoeger, & F. Ayala (Eds.), *Evolutionary and molecular biology: Scientific perspectives on divine action* (pp. 151–162). Vatican City State: Vatican Observatory.

Davies, P. (1993). *The mind of God: The scientific basis for a rational world*. New York: Simon & Schuster.

Davies, P. C. W. (1996). The intelligibility of nature. In R. Russell, N. Murphy, & C. J. Isham (Eds.), *Quantum cosmology and the laws of nature: Scientific perspectives on divine action* (2nd ed., pp. 149–164). Vatican City State: Vatican Observatory.

Davies, P. S. (1999). The conflict of evolutionary psychology. In V. G. Hardcastle (Ed.), *Where biology meets psychology: Philosophical essays* (pp. 67–81). Cambridge, MA: MIT Press.

Davis, C. F. (1989). *The evidential force of religious experience*. Oxford, NY: Claredon Press.

Davis III, C. (2004). The Qur'an, Muhammad, and Jihad in context. In J. Ellens (Ed.), *The destructive power of religion: Violence in Judaism, Christianity, and Islam, Volume 1: Sacred scriptures, ideology, and violence* (pp. 233–254). Westport, CT: Praeger.

Davis, P. G. (1996). The Swiss Maharishi: Discovering the real Carl Jung and his legacy today. *Touchstone, 9*, 10–14.

Davis, T. L., Kerr, B. A., & Kurpius, S. E. R. (2003). Meaning, purpose, and religiosity in at-risk youth: The relationship between anxiety and spirituality. *Journal of Psychology and Theology, 31*, 356–365.

Dawkins, R. (1987). *The blind watchmaker: Why the evidence of evolution reveals a universe without design*. New York: W.W. Norton.

Dawkins, R. (1989). *The selfish gene*. Oxford: Oxford University Press.

Dawkins, R. (1993). *Viruses of the mind*. London: British Humanists Association.

Dawkins, R. (1997). Human chauvinism. *Evolution, 51*, 1015–1020.

Dawson, L. (2004). Religion and the quest for virtual community. In L. Dawson, & D. Cowan (Eds.), *Religion online: Finding faith on the Internet* (pp. 75–89). New York: Routledge.

Dawson, L. (2006). *Comprehending cults: The sociology of new religious movements* (2nd ed.). Oxford: Oxford University Press.

Dawson, L., & Cowan, D. (2004). Introduction. In L. Dawson, & D. Cowan (Eds.), *Religion online: Finding faith on the Internet* (pp. 1–16). New York: Routledge.

Dawson, L., & Hennebry, J. (2004). New religions and the Internet: Recruiting in a new public space. In L. Dawson, & D. Cowan (Eds.), *Religion online: Finding faith on the Internet* (pp. 151–173). New York: Routledge.

Dawson, T. L. (2002). New tools, new insights: Kohlberg's moral judgment stages revisited. *International Journal of Behavioral Development, 26*, 154–166.

Day, J. M. (1993). Speaking of belief: Language, performance, and narrative in the psychology of religion. *The International Journal for the Psychology of Religion, 3*, 213–229.

Day, J. M. (1994). Moral development, belief, and unbelief: Young adult accounts of religion in the process of moral growth. In J. Corveleyn, & D. Hutsebaut (Eds.), *Belief and unbelief: Psychological perspectives* (pp. 155–173). Amsterdam: Rodopi.

Day, M. (2005). Rethinking naturalness: Modes of religiosity and religion in the round. In H. Whitehouse, & R. McCauley (Eds.), *Mind and religion: Psychological and cognitive foundations of religiosity* (pp. 85–106). Walnut Creek, CA: AltaMira.

Day, W. F. (1998). The historical antecedents of contemporary behaviorism. In R. W. Rieber & K. D. Salzinger (Eds.), *Psychology: Theoretical-historical perspectives* (pp. 301–352). Washington, DC: American Psychological Association.

Daya, R. (2005). Buddhist moments in psychotherapy. In R. Moodley, & W. West (Eds.), *Integrating traditional healing practices into counseling and psychotherapy* (pp. 182–193). Thousand Oaks, CA: Sage Publications.

Deatherage, G. (1975). The clinical use of "mindfulness" meditation techniques in short-term psychotherapy. *Journal of Transpersonal Psychology, 7,* 133–143.

DeBerry, S., David, S., & Reinhard, K. E. (1989). A comparison of meditation-relaxation and cognitive/behavioral techniques for reducing anxiety and depression in a geriatric population. *Journal of Geriatric Psychiatry, 22,* 231–247.

de Certeau, M. (1984). *The practice of everyday life.* Berkeley, CA: University of California Press.

de Certeau, M. (1992). *The mystic fable: Volume One: The sixteen and seventeenth centuries* (M. Smith, Trans.). Chicago: University of Chicago Press.

DeConick, A. D. (Ed.). (2001). "Early Jewish and Christian mysticism": A collage of working definitions. *Society of Biblical Literature Seminar Papers, 40,* 278–304.

de Fuentes, N. (2004). Clergy sexual misconduct oversight review boards. In T. Plante (Ed.), *Sin against the innocents: Sexual abuse by priests and the role of the Catholic church* (pp. 47–59). Westport, CT: Praeger.

Deikman, A. (1990). Deautomatization and the mystic experience. In C. Tart (Ed.), *Altered states of consciousness* (3rd ed., pp. 34–57). San Francisco: HarperSanFrancisco.

Deikman, A. (2000). A functional approach to mysticism. In J. Andresen, & R. K. C. Forman (Eds.), *Cognitive models and spiritual maps: Interdisciplinary explorations of religious experience* (pp. 75–91). Thorverton, UK: Imprint Academic.

Dein, S., & Stygall, J. (1997). Does being religious help or hinder coping with chronic illness? A critical literature review. *Palliative Medicine, 11,* 291–298.

de Kock, W. (2000). Fowler and faithful change. *Scriptura, 72,* 87–95.

Delaney, H., & DiClemente, C. (2004). Psychology's roots: A brief history of the influence of Judeo-Christian perspectives. In W. Miller, & H. Delaney (Eds.), *Judeo-Christian perspectives on psychology* (pp. 31–54). Washington, DC: American Psychological Association.

Delmonte, M. M. (1990). The relevance of meditation to clinical practice: An overview. *Applied Psychology, 39,* 331–354.

Demerath, N. J. (1995). Rational paradigms, a-rational religion, and the debate over secularization. *Journal for the Scientific Study of Religion, 34,* 105–112.

Demerath, N. J. (2000). The varieties of sacred experience: Finding the sacred in a secular grove. *Journal for the Scientific Study of Religion, 39,* 1–11.

Dennett, D. (2006). *Breaking the spell: Religion as a natural phenomenon.* New York: Viking Press.

Denton, M. L., & Smith, C. (2001). *Methodological issues and challenges in the study of American youth and religion.* Chapel Hill, NC: National Study of Youth and Religion.

de Paiva, G. J. (1994). Religious itineraries of academics: A psychological discussion. In J. Corveleyn, & D. Hutsebaut (Eds.), *Belief and unbelief: Psychological perspectives* (pp. 137–154). Amsterdam: Rodopi.

Dervic, K., Oquendo, M. A., Grunebaum, M. F., Ellis, S., Burke, A. K., & Mann, J. J. (2004). Religious affiliation and suicide attempt. *The American Journal of Psychiatry, 161*(12); 2303–2308.

de Silva, P. (2000). *An introduction to Buddhist psychology* (5th ed.). Lanham MD: Rowman & Littlefield.

Desjardins, L., & Tamayo, A. (1981). Parental and divine figures of Christians and Hindus according to belief system. In A. Vergote, & A. Tamayo (Eds.), *The parental figures and the representation of God* (pp. 116–125). The Hague: Mouton.

de St. Aubin, E. (1999). Personal ideology: The intersection of personality and religious beliefs. *Journal of Personality, 67*, 1105–1139.

Dewey, J., & Tufts, J. (1932). *Ethics*. New York: H. Holt.

Dickie, J. R., Eshleman, A. K., Merasco, D. M., Shepard, A., Vander Wilt, M., & Johnson, M. (1997). Parent-child relationships and children's images of God. *Journal for the Scientific Study of Religion, 36*, 25–43.

Diduca, D., & Joseph, S. (1997). Schizotypal traits and dimensions of religiosity. *British Journal of Clinical Psychology, 36*, 635–638.

Dieker, B. (2005). Merton's Sufi lectures to Cistercian novices, 1966–1968. In R. Baker, & G. Henry (Eds.), *Merton & Sufism: The untold story* (pp. 130–162). Louisville, KY: Fons Vitae.

Diener, E. (2000). Subjective well-being: The science of happiness and a proposal for a national index. *American Psychologist, 55*, 34–43.

Diener, E., & Clifton, D. (2002). Life satisfaction and religiosity in broad probability samples. *Psychological Inquiry, 13*, 206–209.

Diener, E., & Diener, C. (1996). Most people are happy. *Psychological Science, 7*, 181–185.

Diener, E., & Lucas, R. E. (1999). Personality and subjective well-being. In D. Kahneman, E. Diener, & N. Schwarz (Eds.), *Well-being: The foundations of hedonic psychology* (pp. 213–229). New York: Russell Sage Foundation.

Diener, E., Lucas, R. E., & Oishi, S. (2002). Subjective well-being: The science of happiness and life satisfaction. In C. R. Synder, & S. J. Lopez (Eds.), *Handbook of positive psychology* (pp. 63–73). Oxford: Oxford University Press.

Diener, E., Lucas, R. E., & Scollon, C. N. (2006). Beyond the hedonic treadmill: Revising the adaptation theory of well-being. *American Psychologist, 61*, 305–314.

Diener, E., & Oishi, S. (2000). Money and happiness: Income and subjective well-being across nations. In E. Diener, & E. M. Suh (Eds.), *Culture and subjective well-being* (pp. 185–218). Cambridge, MA: MIT Press.

Diener, E., & Suh, E. M. (1999). National differences in subjective well-being. In D. Kahneman, E. Diener, & N. Schwarz (Eds.), *Well-being: The foundations of hedonic psychology* (pp. 434–450). New York: Russell Sage Foundation.

Diener, E., Suh, E. M., Lucas, R. E., & Smith, H. L. (1999). Subjective well-being: Three decades of progress. *Psychological Bulletin, 125*, 276–302.

Dillbeck, M. C., & Alexander, C. N. (1989). Higher states of consciousness: Maharishi Mahesh Yogi's vedic psychology of human development. *The Journal of Mind and Behavior, 10*, 307–334.

Dillbeck, M. C., & Orme-Johnson, D. W. (1987). Physiological differences between transcendental meditation and rest. *American Psychologist, 42*, 879–881.

Dillon, M., & Wink, P. (2003). Religiousness and spirituality: Trajectories and vital involvement in late adulthood. In M. Dillon (Ed.), *Handbook of the sociology of religion* (pp. 179–189). Cambridge: Cambridge University Press.

Dillon, M., & Wink, P. (2007). *In the course of a lifetime: Tracing religious belief, practice, and change*. Berkeley, CA: University of California Press.

Dillon, M., Wink, P., & Fay, K. (2003). Is spirituality detrimental to generativity? *Journal for the Scientific Study of Religion, 42*, 427–442.

Doblin, R. (1991). Pahnke's "Good Friday experiment": A long-term follow-up and methodological critique. *The Journal of Transpersonal Psychology, 23*, 1–28.

Dockett, K., & North-Schulte, D. (2003). Transcending self and other Mahayana principles of integration. In K. Dockett, G. Dudley-Grant, & C. Bankart (Eds.), *Psychology and Buddhism: From individual to global community* (pp. 215–237). New York: Kluwer Academic/Plenum.

Dogen. (1985). *Moon in a dewdrop: Writings of Zen Master Dogen* (K. Tanahashi, Ed.), New York: North Point Press.

Dogen. (1996). *Dogen's pure standards for the Zen community: A translation of the* Eithei Shingi (T. Leighton, Ed. & S. Okumura, Trans.). Albany, NY: State University of New York Press.

Domenjo, B. (2000). Thoughts on the influences of Brentano and Comte on Freud's work. *Psychoanalysis and History, 2,* 110–118.

Don, N. S. (1977–78). The transformation of conscious experience and its EEG correlates. *Journal of Altered States of Consciousness, 3,* 147–167.

Donahue, M. J. (1985). Intrinsic and extrinsic religiousness: Review and meta-analysis. *Journal of Personality and Social Psychology, 48,* 400–419.

Donahue, M. J., & Benson, P. L. (1995). Religion and the well-being of adolescents. *Journal of Social Issues, 51*(2), 145–160.

Donden, Y. (1986). *Health through balance: An introduction to Tibetan medicine* (J. Hopkins, Trans.). Ithaca, NY: Snow Lion.

Donelson, E. (1999). Psychology of religion and adolescents in the United States: Past to present. *Journal of Adolescence, 22,* 187–204.

Doniger, W. (2000). Post-modern and –colonial –structural comparisons. In K. Patton, & B. Ray (Eds.), *A magic still dwells: Comparative religion in the postmodern age* (pp. 63–74). Berkeley, CA: University of California.

Donner, N. (1987). Sudden and graduate intimately conjoined: Chih-i's T'ien-t'ai view. In P. Gregory (Ed.), *Sudden and gradual: Approaches to enlightenment in Chinese thought* (pp. 201–226). Honolulu, HI: University of Hawaii Press.

D'Onofrio, B. M., Eaves, L. J., Murrelle, L., Maes, H. H., & Spilka, B. (1999). Understanding biological and social influences on religious affiliation, attitudes, and behaviors: A behavior genetic perspective. *Journal of Personality, 67,* 953–984.

Dorsett, L. (2004). *Seeking the secret place: The spiritual formation of C.S. Lewis.* Grand Rapids, MI: Brazos Press.

Dossey, L. (1997). *Healing words: The power of prayer and the practice of medicine.* New York: Harper.

Dougherty, K., Johnson, B., & Polson, E. (2007). Recovering the lost: Remeasuring U.S. religious affiliation. *Journal for the Scientific Study of Religion, 46,* 483–499.

Douglas, M. (1996). *Natural symbols: Explorations in cosmology.* London: Routledge.

Douglas-Klotz, N. (2001). Missing stories: Psychosis, spirituality, and the development of western religious hermeneutics. In I. Clarke (Ed.), *Psychosis and spirituality: Exploring the new frontier* (pp. 53–75). London: Whurr.

Douglas-Klotz, N. (2003).The key in the dark: Self and soul transformation in the Sufi tradition. In S. Mijares (Ed.), *Modern psychology and ancient Wisdom: Psychological Healing Practices from the world's religious traditions* (pp. 149–172). New York: Haworth Integrative Healing Press.

Dourley, J. P. (1995a). Jung and the religious alternative: The rerooting. *Psychology of Religion, 6,* 134–298.

Dourley, J. P. (1995b). The religious significance of Jung's psychology. *The International Journal for the Psychology of Religion, 5,* 73–89.

Dourley, J. P. (2001). Jung, mysticism and a myth in the making. *Studies in Religion, 30,* 65–78.

Dowling, E., Gestsdottir, S. Anderson, P., von Eye, A., Almerigi, J., & Lerner, R. (2004). Structural relations among spirituality, religiosity, and thriving in adolescence. *Applied Developmental Science, 8,* 7–16.

Downing, F. L. (1998). The dangerous journey home: Charting the religious pilgrimage in Fowler and Peck. *Perspectives in Religious Studies, 25,* 249–266.

Doyle, T. P. (2004). Canon law and the clergy sex abuse crisis: The failure from above. In T. Plante (Ed.), *Sin against the innocents: Sexual abuse by priests and the role of the Catholic church* (pp. 25–37). Westport, CT: Praeger.

Doyle, T. P. (2006). Clericalism: Enabler of clergy sexual abuse. *Pastoral Psychology, 54,* 189–213.

Drake, C. (1996). Jung and his critics. In R. Segal (Ed.), *Psychology and myth* (pp. 141–153). New York: Garland.

Drees, W. B. (1998). Evolutionary naturalism and religion. In R. J. Russell, W. R. Stoeger, & F. J. Ayala (Eds.), *Evolutionary and molecular biology: Scientific perspectives on divine action*. Vatican City: Vatican Observatory.

Drees, W. B. (1999). *Religion, science, and naturalism*. Cambridge: Cambridge University Press.

Driscoll, J. (2005). *Steps to spiritual perfection: Studies on spiritual progress in Evagrius Ponticus*. New York: Newman Press.

Driskill, J. D. (1989). Meditation as a therapeutic technique. *Pastoral Psychology, 38*, 83–103.

Driver, S. (2002). *John Cassian and the reading of Egyptian monastic culture*. New York: Routledge.

Druker, S. (1994). The ethics of enlightenment: An expanded perspective on the highest stage of moral development. In M. Miller, & S. Cook-Greuter (Eds.), *Transcendence and mature thought in adulthood: The further reaches of adult development* (pp. 207–236). Lanham, MD: Rowman & Littlefield.

Dubs, G. (1987). Psycho-spiritual development in Zen Buddhism: A study of resistance in meditation. *The Journal of Transpersonal Psychology, 19*, 19–86.

Dudley, C. S., & Roozen, D. A. (2001). Faith communities today: A report on religion in the United States today. Hartford Seminary: Hartford Institute for Religion Research. Retrieved August 22, 2007 from http://fact.hartsem.edu/Final%20FACTrpt.pdf.

Dudley, R. L., & Wisbey, R. L. (2000). The relationship of parenting styles to commitment to the church among young adults. *Religious Education, 95*, 1–9.

Dudley-Grant, G. (2003). Buddhism, psychology, and addiction theory in psychotherapy. In K. Dockett, G. Dudley-Grant, & C. Bankart (Eds.), *Psychology and Buddhism: From individual to global community* (pp. 105–124). New York: Kluwer Academic/Plenum.

Dueck, A., & Parsons, T. D. (2004). Integration discourse: Modern and postmodern. *Journal of Psychology and Theology, 32*, 232–247.

Dulles, A. (2002). *Models of the church* (Expanded ed.). New York: Doubleday.

Dumoulin, H. (1979). *Zen enlightenment: Origins and meaning*. New York: Weatherhill.

Dumoulin, H. (2005). *Zen Buddhism: A history. Volume 1: India and China* (J. Heisig, & P. Knitter, Trans.). Bloomington, IN: World Wisdom.

Dumoulin, H. (1990). *Zen Buddhism: A history. Volume 2: Japan* (J. Heisig, & P. Knitter,Trans.). New York: Macmillan.

Duncan, S. C., Duncan, T. E., Strycker, L. A., & Chaumeton, N. R. (2002). Relations between youth antisocial and prosocial activities. *Journal of Behavioral Medicine, 25*, 425–438.

Dutney, A. (2005). Hoping for the best: Christian theology of hope in the meaner Australia. In J. Eliott (Ed.), *Interdisciplinary perspectives on hope* (pp. 49–60). New York: Nova Science.

Dwairy, M. (2006). *Counseling and psychotherapy with Arabs and Muslims: A culturally sensitive approach*. New York: Teachers College Press.

Dykstra, C. (1986). Youth and the language of faith. *Religious Education, 81*, 163–184.

Dysinger, L. (2005). *Psalmody and prayer in the writings of Evagrius Ponticus*. Oxford: Oxford University Press.

Easwaran, E. (Trans.). (1996). *The Upanishads*. New Delhi: Penguin.

Eaves, L., Martin, N., & Heath, A. (1990). Religious affiliation in twins and their parents: Testing a model of cultural inheritance. *Behavior Genetics, 20*, 1–22.

Ebmeier, K. P., Donaghey, C., & Steele, J. D. (2006). Recent developments and current controversies in depression. *Lancet, 367*(9505), 153–167.

Eck, D. (2000). Dialogue and method: Reconstructing the study of religion. In K. Patton, & B. Ray (Eds.), *A magic still dwells: Comparative religion in the postmodern age* (pp. 131–149). Berkeley, CA: University of California.

Eckel, M. (2000). Contested identities: The study of Buddhism in the postmodern world. In K. Patton, & B. Ray (Eds.), *A magic still dwells: Comparative religion in the postmodern age* (pp. 55–62). Berkeley, CA: University of California.

Eckhart, M. (1981). *Meister Eckhart: The essential sermons, commentaries, treatises, and defense* (E. Colledge, & B. McGinn, Trans.). Malwah, NJ: Paulist Press.

Eckhart, M. (1986). *Meister Eckhart: Teacher and preacher* (B. McGinn, Ed.), Malwah, NJ: Paulist Press.

Eckstrom, K. (2004). Fine arts majors most religious, survey finds. *Christian Century, 121*(9), 18–19.

Edie, J. (1987). *William James and phenomenology.* Bloomington, IN: Indiana University Press.

Edinger, E. (1992). *Transformation of the God-image: An elucidation of Jung's answer to Job.* Toronto: Inner City Books.

Edwards, D., Ashmore, M., & Potter, J. (1995). Death and furniture: The rhetoric politics and theology of bottom line arguments against relativism. *History of the Human Sciences, 8,* 25–49.

Edwards, J. (2004). *The religious affections.* Carlisle, PA: Banner of Truth Trust.

Edwards, T. (1980). *Spiritual friend: Reclaiming the gift of spiritual direction.* Mahwah, NJ: Paulist Press.

Edwards, T. (2001). *Spiritual director, spiritual companion: Guide to tending the soul.* New York: Paulist Press.

Eggers, S. (2003). Older adult spirituality: What is it? A factor analysis of three related instruments. *Journal of Religious Gerontology, 14*(4), 3–33.

Eichelman, B. (2007). Religion, spirituality and medicine. *American Journal of Psychiatry, 164,* 1774–1775.

Eigen, M. (1999). The area of faith in Winnicott, Lacan and Bion. In S. Mitchell, & L. Aron (Eds.), *Relational psychoanalysis: The emergence of a tradition* (pp. 1–37). Hillsdale, NJ: Analytic. (Original work published 1981).

Eigen, M. (2001). Mysticism and psychoanalysis. *Psychoanalytic Review, 88,* 455–481.

Eisenberg-Berg, N., & Neal, C. (1979). Children's moral reasoning about their own spontaneous prosocial behavior. *Developmental Psychology, 15,* 228–229.

Eisinga, R., Billiet, J., & Felling, A. (1999). Christian religion and ethnic prejudice in cross-national perspective: A comparative analysis of the Netherlands and Flanders (Belgium). *International Journal of Comparative Sociology, 40,* 375–393.

Ekman, P., Davidson, R., Ricard, M., & Wallace, B. A. (2005). Buddhist and psychological perspectives on emotions and well-being. *Current Directions in Psychological Science, 14,* 59–63.

El Azayem, G. A., & Hedayat-Diba, Z. (1994). The psychological aspects of Islam: Basic principles of Islam and their psychological corollary. *International Journal for the Psychology of Religion, 4,* 41–50.

Elder, G., Jr. (1995). The life course paradigm: Social change and individual development. In P. Moen, G. Elder, Jr., & K. Luscher (Eds.), *Examining lives in context: Perspectives on the ecology of human development* (pp. 101–139). Washington, DC: American Psychological Association.

Elhard, L. (1968). Living faith: Some contributions of the concept of ego-identity to the understanding of faith. In P. Homans (Ed.), *The dialogue between theology and psychology* (pp. 135–161). Chicago: University of Chicago Press.

Eliade, M. (1963). *Myth and reality* (W. Trask, Trans.). New York: Harper & Row.

Eliassen, A. H., Taylor, J., & Lloyd, D. A. (2005). Subjective religiosity and depression in the transition to adulthood. *Journal for the Scientific Study of Religion, 44,* 187–199.

Elkind, D. (1962). The child's conception of his religious denomination II: The Catholic child. *Journal of Genetic Psychology, 101,* 185–193.

Elkind, D. (1964). Piaget's semi-clinical interview and the study of spontaneous religion. *Journal for the Scientific Study of Religion, 4,* 40–47.

Elkind, D. (1970). The origins of religion in the child. *Review of Religious Research, 12,* 35–42.

Elkins, D. (1995). Psychotherapy and spirituality: Toward a theory of the soul. *Journal of Humanistic Psychology, 35,* 78–98.

Elkind, D. (1996). Inhelder and Piaget on adolescence and adulthood: A postmodern appraisal. *Psychological Science, 7,* 216–220.

Elkind, D. (1999). Religious development in adolescence. *Journal of Adolescence, 22,* 291–295.

Elkind, D., & Elkind, S. F. (1962). Varieties of religious experiences in young adolescence. *Journal for the Scientific Study of Religion, 2,* 102–112.

Elkins, D. N. (1998). *Beyond religion: A personal program for building a spiritual life outside the walls of traditional religion.* Wheaton, IL: Theosophical.

Elkins, D. N. (2005). A humanistic approach to spiritually oriented psychotherapy. In L. Sperry, & E. P. Shafranske (Eds.), *Spiritually oriented psychotherapy* (pp. 131–151). Washington, DC: American Psychological Association.

Elkins, D. N., Lipari, J., & Kozora, C. J. (1999). Attitudes and values of humanistic psychologists: Division 32 survey results. *The Humanistic Psychologist, 27,* 329–342.

Ellens, J. (2004a). Fundamentalism, orthodoxy, and violence. In J. Ellens (Ed.), *The destructive power of religion: Violence in Judaism, Christianity and Islam, Volume 4: Contemporary views on spirituality and violence* (pp. 119–142). Westport, CT: Praeger.

Ellens, J. (2004b). Introduction: The interface of religion, psychology, and violence. In J. Ellens (Ed.), *The destructive power of religion: Violence in Judaism, Christianity and Islam, Volume 2: Religion, psychology, and violence* (pp. 1–10). Westport, CT: Praeger.

Ellens, J. (2004c). Introduction: Spirals of Violence. In J. Ellens (Ed.), *The destructive power of religion: Violence in Judaism, Christianity and Islam, Volume 4: Contemporary views on spirituality and violence* (pp. 1–18). Westport, CT: Praeger.

Ellens, J. (2004d). Introduction: Toxic texts. In J. Ellens (Ed.), *The destructive power of religion: Violence in Judaism, Christianity and Islam, Volume 3: Models and cases of violence in religion* (pp. 1–14). Westport, CT: Praeger.

Ellens, J. (2004e). Religious metaphors can kill. In J. Ellens (Ed.), *The destructive power of religion: Violence in Judaism, Christianity and Islam, Volume 1: Sacred scriptures, ideology, and violence* (pp. 255–272). Westport, CT: Praeger.

Eller, C. (1991). Relativizing the patriarchy: The sacred history of the feminist spirituality movement. In M. Eliade, J. Kitagawa, & C. Long, C. (Eds.), *History of religions* (pp. 279–295). Chicago, IL: University of Chicago Press.

Elliott, C. (2001). Prayer and society. In F. Watts (Ed.), *Perspectives on prayer* (pp. 15–26). London: SPCK.

Ellis, A. (1985). *The case against religion: A psychotherapist's view and the case against religiosity.* Austin, TX: American Atheist Press.

Ellis, B. J., & Ketelaar, T. (2000). On the natural selection of alternative models: Evolution of explanations in evolutionary psychology. *Psychological Inquiry, 11,* 56–68.

Ellis, B. J., & Ketelaar, T. (2002). Clarifying the foundations of evolutionary psychology: A reply to Lloyd and Feldman. *Psychological Inquiry, 13,* 157–164.

Ellis, G. (1998). The thinking underlying the new 'scientific' world-views. In R. Russell, W. Stoeger, S. J., & F. Ayala (Eds.), *Evolutionary and molecular biology scientific perspectives on divine action* (pp. 251–180). Vatican City State: Vatican Observatory.

Ellis, G. (2002). Intimations of transcendences: Relations in the mind and God. In R. Russell, N. Murphy, T. Meyering, & M. Arbib (Eds.), *Neuroscience and the person: Scientific perspectives on divine action* (pp. 449–474). Vatican City State: Vatican Observatory.

Ellis, G., & Stoeger, W. (1996). Introduction to general relativity and cosmology. In R. Russell, N. Murphy, & C. Isham (Eds.), *Quantum cosmology and the laws of nature* (2nd ed., pp. 35–50). Vatican City State: Vatican Observatory.

Ellison, C. G. (1991). Religious involvement and subjective well-being. *Journal of Health and Social Behavior, 32,* 80–99.

Ellison, C. G. (1995). Rational choice explanations of individual religious behavior: Notes on the problem of social embeddedness. *Journal for the Scientific Study of Religion, 34,* 89–97.

Ellison, C. G. (1998). Introduction to the symposium: Religion, health, and well-being. *Journal for the Scientific Study of Religion, 37,* 692–694.

Ellison, C. G., Boardman, J. D., Williams, D. R., & Jackson, J. S. (2001). Religious involvement, stress, and mental health: Findings from the 1995 Detroit area study. *Social Forces, 80*, 215–249.

Ellison, C. G., Gay, D. A., & Glass, T. A. (1989). Does religious commitment contribute to individual life satisfaction? *Social Forces, 68*, 100–123.

Ellison, C. G., & George, L. K. (1994). Religious involvement, social ties, and social support in a southeastern community. *Journal for the Scientific Study of Religion, 33*, 46–61.

Ellison, C. G., & Levin, J. S. (1998). The religion-health connection: Evidence, theory, and future directions. *Health Education and Behavior, 25*, 700–720.

Ellison, C. W. (1983). Spiritual well-being: Conceptualization and measurement. *Journal of Psychology and Theology, 11*, 330–340.

Ellison, C. W., & Smith, J. (1991). Toward an integrative measure of health and well-being. *Journal of Psychology and Theology, 19*, 35–48.

Elson, B. D., Hauri, P., & Cunis, D. (1977). Physiological changes in Yoga meditation. *Psychophysiology, 14*, 52–57.

Emavardhana, T., & Tori, C. D. (1997). Changes in self-concept, ego defense mechanisms, and religiosity following seven-day Vipassana meditation retreats. *Journal for the Scientific Study of Religion, 36*, 194–206.

Emde, R. N., Biringen, Z., Clyman, R. B., & Oppenheim, D. (1991). The moral self of infancy: Affective core and procedural knowledge. *Developmental Review, 11*, 251–270.

Emmons, R. A. (1999). *The psychology of ultimate concerns: Motivation and spirituality in personality.* New York: Guilford Press.

Emmons, R. A. (2004). The psychology of gratitude: An introduction. In R. Emmons, & M. McCullough (Eds.), *The psychology of gratitude* (pp. 3–16). Oxford: Oxford University Press.

Emmons, R. A. (2006). Spirituality. In M. Czikszentmihalyi, & I. Czikszentmihalyi (Eds.), *A life worth living: Contributions to positive psychology* (pp. 62–81). New York: Oxford University Press.

Emmons, R. A., & Crumpler, C. A. (1999). Religion and spirituality? The role of sanctification and the concept of God. *International Journal for the Psychology of Religion, 9*, 17–24.

Emmons, R. A., & Kneezel, T. T. (2005). Giving thanks: Spiritual and religious correlates of gratitude. *Journal of Psychology and Christianity, 24*, 140–148.

Emmons, R. A., & McCullough, M. E. (2003). Counting blessings versus burdens: An experimental investigation of gratitude and subjective well-being in daily life. *Journal of Personality and Social Psychology, 84*, 377–389.

Emmons, R. A., & Shelton, C. M. (2002). Gratitude and the science of positive psychology. In C. R. Synder, & S. J. Lopez (Eds.), *Handbook of positive psychology* (pp. 459–471). Oxford: Oxford University Press.

Engelhardt, H. T. (1986). *The foundations of bioethics.* New York: Oxford University Press.

Engler, J. (1984). Therapeutic aims in psychotherapy mediation: Developmental stages in the representation of self. *Journal of Transpersonal Psychology, 16*, 25–61.

Engler, J. (1986). Therapeutic aims in psychotherapy and meditation. In K. Wilber, J. Engler, & D. Brown (Eds.), *Transformations of consciousness: Conventional and contemplative perspectives on development* (pp. 17–51). Boston: New Science Library.

Engler, J. (2003). Being somebody and being nobody: A reexamination of the understanding of self in psychoanalysis and Buddhism. In J. Safran (Ed.), *Psychoanalysis and Buddhism: An unfolding dialogue* (pp. 35–80). Boston: Wisdom.

English, O. S. (1954). Understanding human nature. In S. Doniger (Ed.), *Religion and human behavior* (pp. 107–124). New York: Association Press.

Enright, R. (2001). *Forgiveness is a choice: A step-by-step process for resolving anger and restoring hope.* Washington, DC: American Psychological Association.

Enright, R., Eastin, D., Golden, S., Sarinopoulis, I., & Freedman, S. (1992). Interpersonal forgiveness within the helping professions: An attempt to resolve differences of opinion. *Counseling and Values, 36*, 84–103.

Enright, R., & Fitzgibbons, R. (2000). *Helping clients forgive: An empirical guide for resolving anger and restoring hope.* Washington, DC: American Psychological Association.

Eppley, K. R., Abrams, A. I., & Shear, J. (1989). Differential effects of relaxation techniques on trait anxiety: A meta-analysis. *Journal of Clinical Psychology, 45,* 957–974.

Epstein, M. (1995). *Thoughts without a thinker: Psychotherapy from a Buddhist perspective.* New York: Basic Books.

Epstein, M., & Lieff, J. (1986). Psychiatric complications of meditation practice. In K. Wilber, J. Engler, & D. Brown (Eds.), *Transformations of consciousness: Conventional and contemplative perspectives on development* (pp. 53–63). Boston: New Science Library.

Epstein, R. (1999). Mindful practice. *JAMA: Journal of the American Medical Association, 282,* 833–839.

Epstein, S. (1994). Integration of the cognitive and the psychodynamic unconscious. *American Psychologist, 49,* 709–724.

Eriksen, K., Marston, G., & Korte, T. (2002). Working with God: Managing conservative Christian beliefs that may interfere with counseling. *Counseling and Values, 47,* 48–68.

Erikson, E. (1950). *Childhood and society.* New York: Norton.

Erikson, E. (1958). *Young man Luther: A study in psychoanalysis and history.* New York: W. W. Norton.

Erikson, E. (1964). *Insight and responsibility lectures on the ethical implications of psychoanalytical insight.* New York: W.W. Norton.

Erikson, E. (1966). Ontogeny of ritualization. In R. Loewenstein, L. Newman, M. Schur, & A. Solnit (Eds.), *Psychoanalysis—A general psychology: Essays in honor of Heinz Hartmann* (pp. 601–621). New York: International Universities Press.

Erikson, E. (1968). *Identity: Youth and crisis.* New York: W.W. Norton.

Erikson, E. (1969). *Gandhi's truth: On the origins of militant nonviolence.* New York: W.W. Norton.

Erikson, E. (1977). *Toys and reasons: Stages in the ritualization of experience.* New York: W. W. Norton.

Erikson, E. (1982). *The life cycle completed.* New York: W. W. Norton.

Erikson, E. (1987). *A way of looking at things: Selected papers of Erik H. Erikson, 1930–1980* (S. P. Schlein, Ed.), New York: Norton.

Erikson, E. (1996). The Galilean sayings and the sense of "I." *Psychoanalysis and Contemporary Thought, 19,* 291–337. (Original work published 1981).

Erikson, E., Erikson, J., & Kivnick, H. (1986). *Vital involvement in old age.* New York: W. W. Norton.

Erndl, K. (2004). Afterward. In K. Pechilis (Ed.), *The graceful guru: Hindu female gurus in India and the United States* (pp. 245–251). New York: Oxford University Press.

Eshleman, A. K., Dickie, J. R., Merasco, D. M., Shepard, A., & Johnson, M. (1999). Mother God, father God: Children's perceptions of God's distance. *International Journal for the Psychology of Religion, 9,* 139–146.

Eugene, T. (1997). Late-life experiences: A cross-cultural comparison. *Journal of Aging Studies, 11,* 155–170.

Evagrius, P. (1972). *The Praktikos: Chapters on prayer.* Spencer, MA: Cistercian Press.

Evans, C. S. (2004). The relational self: Psychological and theological perspectives. In W. Miller, & H. Delaney (Eds.), *Judeo-Christian perspectives on psychology* (pp. 73–93). Washington, DC: American Psychological Association.

Exline, J. J. (2002a). The picture is getting clearer, but is the scope too limited? Three overlooked questions in the psychology of religion. *Psychology Inquiry, 13,* 245–247.

Exline, J. J. (2002b). Stumbling blocks on the religious road: Fractured relationships, nagging vices, and the inner struggle to believe. *Psychological Inquiry, 13,* 182–189.

Exline, J. J., Baumeister, R. F., Bushman, B. J., Campbell, W. K., & Finkel, E. J. (2004). Too proud to let go: Narcissistic entitlement as a barrier to forgiveness. *Journal of Personality and Social Psychology, 87,* 894–912.

Exline, J. J., Worthington, E. L., Jr., Hill, P., & McCullough, M. E. (2003). Forgiveness and justice: A research agenda for social and personality psychology. *Personality and Social Psychology Review, 7,* 337–348.

Exline, J. J., Yali, A. M., & Sanderson, W. C. (2000). Guilt, discord, and alienation: The role of religious strain in depression and suicidality. *Journal of Clinical Psychology, 56,* 1481–1496.

Faber, H. (1990). The meaning of ritual in the liturgy. In H.-G. Heimbrock, & H. Boudewijnse (Eds.), *Current studies on rituals: Perspectives for the psychology of religion* (pp. 43–57). Amsterdam: Rodopi.

Fabricatore, A. N., Handal, P. J., Rubio, D. M., & Gilner, F. H. (2004). Stress, religion, and mental health: Religious coping in mediating and moderating roles. *The International Journal for the Psychology of Religion, 14,* 91–108.

Fader, L. (1986). D. T. Suzuki's contribution to the West. In M. Abe (Ed.), *A Zen life: D.T. Suzuki remembered* (pp. 95–109). New York: Weatherhill Press.

Falkenstrom, F. (2003). A Buddhist contribution to the psychoanalytic psychology of self. *International Journal of Psychoanalysis, 84,* 1551–1568.

Fallot, R. D. (2001). Spirituality and religion in psychiatric rehabilitation and recovery from mental illness. *International Review of Psychiatry, 13,* 110–116.

Farah, M. (2008). Neuroethics and the problem of other minds: Implications of neuroscience for the moral status of brain-damaged patients and nonhuman animals. *Neuroethics, 1,* 9–18.

Farb, N., Segal, Z., Mayberg, H., Bean, J., McKeon, D., & Fatima, Z., et al. (2007). Attending to the present: Mindfulness meditation reveals distinct neural modes of self-reference. *Social Cognitive and Affective Neuroscience, 2,* 313–322.

Faucher, L. (2006). What's behind a smile? the return of mechanism: Reply to Schaffner. *Synthese, 151,* 403–409.

Feigl, H. (1949a). Operationism and scientific method. In H. Feigl, & W. Sellars (Eds.), *Readings in philosophical analysis* (pp. 498–509). New York: Appleton-Century-Crofts.

Feigl, H. (1949b). Some remarks on the meaning of scientific explanation. In H. Feigl, & W. Sellars (Eds.), *Readings in philosophical analysis* (pp. 510–514). New York: Appleton-Century-Crofts.

Feigl, H. (1956). Some major issues and developments in the philosophy of science of logical empiricism. In H. Feigl (Ed.), *Minnesota studies in the philosophy of science: The foundations of science and the concepts of psychology and psychoanalysis* (pp. 3–37). Minneapolis, MN: University of Minnesota Press.

Feigl, H. (1980). The scientific outlook: Naturalism and humanism. In E. D. Klemke, Robert Hollinger, & A. David Kline (Eds.), *Introductory readings in the philosophy of science* (pp. 427–437). Buffalo, NY: Prometheus Books.

Feldman, D. B., & Snyder, C. R. (2005). Hope and the meaningful life: Theoretical and empirical associations between goal-directed thinking and life meaning. *Journal of Social and Clinical Psychology, 24,* 401–421.

Ferraro, K. F., & Kelley-Moore, J. A. (2000). Religious consolation among men and women: Do health problems spur seeking? *Journal for the Scientific Study of Religion, 39,* 220–234.

Ferraro, K. F., & Kelley-Moore, J. A. (2001). Religious seeking among affiliates and non-affiliates: Do mental and physical health problems spur religious coping? *Review of Religious Research, 42,* 229–251.

Ferriss, A. L. (2002). Religion and the quality of life. *Journal of Happiness Studies, 3,* 199–215.

Fetz, R. L. (1988). On the formation of ontological concepts: The theories of Whitehead and Piaget. *Process Studies, 17,* 262–272.

Fetzer Institute/National Institute on Aging Working Group. (1999). *Multidimensional measurement of religiousness/spirituality for use in health research.* Kalamazoo, MI: John E. Fetzer Institute.

Feuerbach, L. (1957). *The essence of Christianity* (G. Elliot, Trans.). New York: Harper, & Brothers. (Original translation published 1854; original work published 1841).

Feuerstein, G. (1989). *The Yoga-sutra of Patanjali: A new translation and commentary.* Rochester, VT: Inner Traditions.

Feuerstein, G. (2001). *The yoga tradition: Its history, literature, philosophy and practice.* Prescott, AZ: Hohm Press.

Feyerabend, P. (1993). *Against method* (3rd ed.). London: Verso.

Fiala, W. E., Bjorck, J. P., & Gorsuch, R. (2002). The religious support scale: Construction, validation, and cross-validation. *American Journal of Community Psychology, 30,* 761–786.

Fiddes, P. (2002). The quest for a place which is 'not-a-place': The hiddenness of God and the presence of God. In O. Davies, & D. Turner (Eds.), *Silence and the Word: Negative theology and incarnation* (pp. 35–60). Cambridge: Cambridge University Press.

Fiese, B. H., & Tomcho, T. J. (2001). Finding meaning in religious practices: The relation between religious holiday rituals and marital satisfaction. *Journal of Family Psychology, 15,* 597–609.

Finke, R. (1997). Supply-side explanations for religious change. In L. A. Young (Ed.), *Rational choice theory and religion: Summary and assessment* (pp. 45–64). New York: Routledge.

Finlan, S., & Kharlamov, V. (2006). Introduction. In S. Finlan, & V. Kharlamov (Eds.), *Theosis: Deification in Christian theology* (pp. 1–15). Eugene, OR: Pickwick.

Finn, M. (1992). Transitional space and Tibetan Buddhism: The object relations of meditation. In M. Finn, & J. Gartner (Eds.), *Object relations theory and religion: Clinical applications* (pp. 109–118). Westport, CT: Praeger.

Finney, J., & Malony, H. N., Jr. (1985). Empirical studies of Christian prayer: A review of the literature. *Journal of Psychology and Theology, 13,* 104–115.

Finney, J., & Malony, H. (2001). An empirical study of contemplative prayer as an adjunct to psychotherapy. In L. Francis, & J. Astley (Eds.), *Psychological perspectives on prayer* (pp. 359–367). Leominster, UK: Gracewing.

Fiori, K., Brown, E., Cortina, K., & Antonucci, T. (2006). Locus of control as a mediator of the relationship between religiosity and life satisfaction: Age, race, and gender differences. *Mental Health, Religion, & Culture, 9,* 239–263.

Fiori, K. L., Hays, J. C., & Meador, K. G. (2004). Spiritual turning points and perceived control over the life course. *International Journal of Aging and Human Development, 59,* 391–420.

Firth, S. (1999). Spirituality and age in British Hindus, Sikhs, and Muslims. In A. Jewell (Ed.), *Spirituality and ageing* (pp. 158–173). London: Jessica Kingsley.

Fisher, K. (1988). *Women at the well: Feminist perspectives on spiritual direction.* New York: Paulist Press.

Fiske, A. P., Kitayama, S., Markus, H. R., & Nisbett, R. E. (1998). The cultural matrix of social psychology. In D. T. Gilbert, S. T. Fiske, & G. Lindzey (Eds.), *The handbook of social psychology* (4th ed., Vol. 2, pp. 915–981). Boston, MA: McGraw-Hill.

Fiske, S. T. (1998). Stereotyping, prejudice, and discrimination. In D. T. Gilbert, S. T. Fiske, & G. Lindzey (Eds.), *The handbook of social psychology* (4th ed., Vol. 2, pp. 357–411). Boston, MA: McGraw-Hill.

Fitchett, G. (1993). *Assessing spiritual needs: A guide for caretakers.* Minneapolis, MN: Augsburg Fortress.

Fitchett, G., Rybarczyk, B. D., DeMarco, G. A., & Nicholas, J. (1999). The role of religion in medical rehabilitation outcomes: A longitudinal study. *Rehabilitation Psychology, 44,* 333–353.

Flannelly, K. J., Koenig, H. G., Ellison, C. G., Galek, K., & Krause, N. (2006). Belief in life after death and mental health findings from a national survey. *The Journal of Nervous and Mental Disease, 194,* 524–529.

Flannelly, K. J., Weaver, A. J., Smith, W. J., & Handzo, G. F. (2003). Psychologists and health care chaplains doing research together. *Journal of Psychology ad Christianity, 22,* 327–332.

Fleischman, P. R. (2000). *Karma and chaos.* Seattle, WA: Vipassana Research.

Flood, G. (1996). *An introduction to Hinduism.* Cambridge: Cambridge University Press.

Flood, G. (2004). *The ascetic self: Subjectivity, memory and tradition.* Cambridge: Cambridge University Press.

Folkman, S., & Lazarus, R. S. (1985). If it changes it must be a process: Study of emotion and coping during three stages of a college examination. *Journal of Personality and Social Psychology, 48,* 150–170.

Foltz, F., & Foltz, F. (2003). Religion on the internet: Community and virtual existence. *Bulletin of Science, Technology & Society, 23*, 321–330.

Forest, J. (1997). *Praying with icons*. Maryknoll, NY: Orbis Books.

Forest, J. (2003). Thomas Merton and the silence of the icons. In B. Dieker, & J. Montaldo (Eds.), *Merton & Hesychasm: The prayer of the heart: The Eastern Church* (pp. 225–233). Louisville, KY: Fons Vitae.

Forman, R. K. C. (1990a). Eckhart, Gezucken, and the ground of the soul. In R. K. C. Forman (Ed.), *The problem of pure consciousness: Mysticism and philosophy* (pp. 98–120). New York: Oxford University Press.

Forman, R. K. C. (1990b). Introduction: Mysticism, constructivism, and forgetting. In R. K. C. Forman (Ed.), *The problem of pure consciousness: Mysticism and philosophy* (pp. 3–49). New York: Oxford University Press.

Forman, R. K. C. (Ed.). (1998a). *The innate capacity: Mysticism, psychology, and philosophy*. New York: Oxford University Press.

Forman, R. K. C. (1998b). What does mysticism have to teach us about consciousness? *Journal of Consciousness Studies, 5*, 185–201.

Forrester, B. (1999). Can theology be practical? In F. Schweitzer, & J. van der Ven (Eds.), *Practical theology: International perspectives* (pp. 15–28). Frankfurt am Main: Peter Lang.

Forthun, L. F., Bell, N. J., Peek, C. W., & Sun, S. (1999). Religiosity, sensation seeking, and alcohol/drug use in denominational and gender contexts. *Journal of Drug Issues, 29*, 75–90.

Foskett, J. (2001). Soul space: The pastoral care of people with major mental health problems. *International Review of Psychiatry, 13*, 101–109.

Foss, L., & Warnke, M. (2003). Fundamentalist protestant Christian women: Recognizing cultural and gender influences on domestic violence. *Counseling and Values, 48*, 14–23.

Foucault, M. (1965). *Madness and civilization: A history of insanity in the Age of Reason*. (R. Howard, Trans.). New York: Vintage.

Foucault, M. (1976). *Mental illness and psychology* (A. Sheridan, Trans.). Berkeley, CA: University of California Press.

Foulk, T. G. (1988). The Zen institution in modern Japan. In K. Kraft (Ed.), *Zen: Tradition and transition* (pp. 157–177). New York: Grove Press.

Fowler, J. W. (1981). *Stages of faith: The psychology of human development and the quest for meaning*. San Francisco: Harper & Row.

Fowler, J. W. (1987). *Faith development and pastoral care* (D. Browning, Ed.), Philadelphia: Fortress Press.

Fowler, J. W. (1989). Strength for the journey: Early childhood development in selfhood and faith. In D. Blazer (Ed.), *Faith development in early childhood* (pp. 1–36). Kansas City, MO: Sheed & Ward.

Fowler, J. W. (1991). Stages in faith consciousness. In F. Oser, & W. G. Scarlett (Eds.), *Religious development in childhood and adolescence* (pp. 27–45). San Francisco: Jossey-Bass.

Fowler, J. W. (1996). *Faithful change: The personal and public challenges of postmodern life*. Nashville, TN: Abingdon Press.

Fowler, J. W. (1999a). The emerging new shape of practical theology. In F. Schweitzer, & J. van der Ven (Eds.), *Practical theology: International perspectives* (pp. 75–92). Frankfurt am Main: Peter Lang.

Fowler, J. W. (1999b). Perspectives on adolescents: Personhood and faith. *Family Ministry, 13*, 22–32.

Fowler, J. W. (1999c). Practical theology and the social sciences. In F. Schweitzer, & J. van der Ven (Eds.), *Practical theology: International perspectives* (pp. 259–265). Frankfurt am Main: Peter Lang.

Fowler, J. W. (2001). Faith development theory and the postmodern challenges. *The International Journal for the Psychology of Religion, 11*, 159–172.

Fowler, J. W., & Dell, M. L. (2004). Stages of faith and identity: Birth to teens. *Child and Adolescent Psychiatric Clinics of North America, 13*(1), 17–33.

Fowler, J., & Dell, M. (2006). Stages of faith from infancy through adolescence: Reflections on three decades of faith development theory. In E. Roehlkepartain, P. King, L. Wagener, & P. Benson (Eds.), *The handbook of spiritual development in childhood and adolescence* (pp. 34–45). Thousand Oaks, CA: Sage.

Fox, J. W. (1992). The structure, stability, and social antecedents of reported paranormal experiences. *Sociological Analysis, 53*, 417–431.

Frager, R. (1989). Transpersonal psychology: Promise and prospects. In R. S. Valle, & S. Halling (Eds.), *Existential-phenomenological perspectives in psychology: Exploring the breadth of human experience* (pp. 289–309). New York: Plenum Press.

Frame, M. W. (2003). *Integrating religion and spirituality into counseling: A comprehensive approach*. Pacific Grove, CA: Brooks/Cole.

Francis, L., & Evans, T. (2001a). The psychology of Christian prayer: A review of empirical research. In L. Francis, & J. Astley (Eds.), *Psychological perspectives on prayer* (pp. 2–22). Leominster, UK: Gracewing.

Francis, L., & Evans, T. (2001b). The relationship between personal prayer and purpose in life among churchgoing and non-churchgoing twelve-to-fifteen-year-olds in the UK. In L. Francis, & J. Astley (Eds.), *Psychological perspectives on prayer* (pp. 271–282). Leominster, UK: Gracewing.

Francis, L., Fearn, M., & Lewis, C. A. (2005). The impact of personality and religion on attitudes toward alcohol among 16–18 year olds in northern Ireland. *Journal of Religion and Health, 44*, 267–289.

Francis, L., Lewis, J., Brown, L., Philipchalk, R., Lester, D. (1995). Personality and religion among undergraduate students in the United Kingdom, United States, Australia and Canada. *Journal of Psychology and Christianity, 14*, 250–262.

Francis, L., & Robbins, M. (2008). Psychological type and prayer preferences: A study among Anglican clergy in the United Kingdom. *Mental Health, Religion & Culture, 11*, 67–84.

Francis, L., Robbins, M., Lewis, C., & Barnes, L. P. (2008). Prayer and psychological health: A study among sixth-form pupils attending Catholic and Protestant schools in Northern Ireland. *Mental Health, Religion & Culture, 11*, 85–92.

Francis, L., & Wilcox, C. (1998). Religiosity and femininity: Do women really hold a more positive attitude toward Christianity? *Journal for the Scientific Study of Religion, 37*, 462–469.

Frank, A. W. (2004). Narratives of spirituality and religion in end-of-life care. In B. Hurwitz, T. Greenhalgh, & V. Skultans (Eds.), *Narrative research in health and illness* (pp. 132–145). Malden, MA: Blackwell.

Frank, P. (1977). Psychoanalysis and logical positivism. In M. Mujeeb-ur-Rahman (Ed.), *The Freudian paradigm: Psychoanalysis and scientific thought* (pp. 101–106). Chicago, IL: Nelson-Hall.

Franklin, R. L. (1990). Experience and interpretation in mysticism. In R. K. C. Forman (Ed.), *The problem of pure consciousness: Mysticism and philosophy* (pp. 288–301). New York: Oxford University Press.

Frantz, T. T., Trolley, B. C., & Johil, M. P. (1996). Religious aspects of bereavement. *Pastoral Psychology, 44*, 151–163.

Frawley, D. (1999). *Yoga and Ayurveda: Self-healing and self-realization*. Twin Lakes, WI: Lotus Press.

Frederick, S., & Loewenstein, G. (1999). Hedonic adaptation. In D. Kahneman, E. Diener, & N. Schwarz (Eds.), *Well-being: The foundations of hedonic psychology* (pp. 302–329). New York: Russell Sage.

Fredrickson, B. (2001). The role of positive emotions in positive psychology: The broaden-and-build theory of positive emotions. *American Psychologist, 56*, 218–226.

Fredrickson, B. (2005). The broaden-and-build theory of positive emotions. In F. Huppert, N. Baylis, & B. Keverne (Eds.), *The science of well-being* (pp. 217–238). Oxford: Oxford University Press.

Fredrickson, B. (2006). The broaden-and-build theory of positive emotions. In M. Czikszentmihalyi, & I. Czikszentmihalyi (Eds.), *A life worth living: Contributions to positive psychology* (pp. 85–103). Oxford: Oxford University Press.

Fredrickson, B., & Losada, M. (2005). Positive affect and the complex dynamics of human flourishing. *American Psychologist, 60,* 678–686.

Freedman, S., & Enright, R. (1996). Forgiveness as an intervention goal with incest survivors. *Journal of Consulting and Clinical Psychology, 64,* 983–992.

Freeman, D., Garety, P. A. A., Bebbington, P. E., Smith, B., Rollinson, R., Fowler, D., et al. (2005). Psychological investigation of the structure of paranoia in a non-clinical population. *British Journal of Psychiatry, 186,* 427–435.

Freeman, M. (1993). *Rewriting the self: History, memory, narrative.* London: Routledge.

Freeman, M. (2003). The priority of the other: Mysticism's challenge to the legacy of the self. In J. Belzen, & A. Geels (Eds.), *Mysticism: A variety of psychological perspectives* (pp. 213–224). Amsterdam: Rodopi.

French, S., & Joseph, S. (1999). Religiosity and its association with happiness, purpose in life, and self-actualisation. *Mental Health, Religion & Culture, 2,* 117–120.

Frenken, R. (2000). Childhood and fantasies of medieval mystics. *The Journal of Psychohistory, 28,* 150–172.

Freud, S. (1950). *Totem and taboo.* New York: W.W. Norton. (Original work published 1913).

Freud, S. (1953). Project for a scientific psychology. In J. Strachey (Ed. & Trans.), *The standard edition of the complete works of Sigmund Freud: Volume I (1886–1896)* (pp. 295–397). London: Hoargarth. (Original work published 1895).

Freud, S. (1961a). *Civilization and its discontent.* New York: W. W. Norton.

Freud, S. (1961b). *The future of an Illusion.* New York: W.W. Norton. (Original work published 1927).

Freyd, J., & Johnson, J. (1992). The evolutionary psychology of priesthood celibacy. *Behavioral and Brain Sciences, 15,* 385.

Friedland, R., & Hecht, R. (2006). The powers of place. In O. Stier, & J. Landres (Eds.), *Religion, violence, memory, and place* (pp. 17–36). Bloomington, IN: Indiana University Press.

Frijda, N. H. (1999). Emotions and hedonic experience. In D. Kahneman, E. Diener, & N. Schwarz (Eds.), *Well-being: The foundations of hedonic psychology* (pp. 190–210). New York: Russell Sage.

Frohlich, M. (1993). *The intersubjectivity of the mystic: A study of Teresa of Avila's Interior Castle.* Atlanta, GA: Scholars Press.

Fromm, E. (1950). *Psychoanalysis and religion.* New Haven: Yale University Press.

Fromm, E. (1963). *The dogma of Christ and other essays on religion, psychology and culture.* New York: Holt, Rinehart and Winston.

Fromm, E. (1986). Memories of D. T. Suzuki. In M. Abe (Eds.), *A Zen life: D.T. Suzuki remembered* (pp. 127–131). New York: Weatherhill Press.

Fromm, G. H. (1992). Neurophysiological speculations on Zen enlightenment. *The Journal of Mind and Behavior, 13,* 163–170.

Fry, P. S. (2000). Religious involvement, spirituality, and personal meaning for life: Existential predictors of psychological wellbeing in community-residing and institutional care elders. *Aging & Mental Health, 4,* 375–387.

Fuchs, A. H. (2002). Contributions of American mental philosophers to psychology in the United States. In W. E. Pickren, & D. A. Dewsbury (Eds.), *Evolving perspectives on the history of psychology* (pp. 79–99). Washington, DC: American Psychological Association.

Fulkerson, M. M. (1997). Contesting the gendered subject: A feminist account of the Imago Dei. In R. S. Chopp, & S. G. Davaney (Eds.), *Horizons in feminist theology: Identity, tradition, and norms* (pp. 99–115). Minneapolis, MN: Fortress Press.

Fuller, R. C. (1996). Erikson, psychology, and religion. *Pastoral Psychology, 44,* 371–383.

Fuller, R. C. (1988). *Religion and the life cycle.* Philadelphia: Fortress Press.

Fulton, A. S. (1997). Identity status, religious orientation, and prejudice. *Journal of Youth and Adolescence, 26,* 1–11.

Funk, J. (1994). Unanimity and disagreement among transpersonal psychologists. In M. Miller, & S. Cook-Greuter (Eds.), *Transcendence and mature thought in adulthood: The further reaches of adult development* (pp. 3–36). Lanham, MD: Rowman & Littlefield.

Funk, R. (2003). *Erich Fromm: His life and ideas* (I. Portman, & M. Kunkel, Trans.). New York: Continuum.

Furrow, J., King, P. E., & White, K. (2004). Religion and positive youth development: Identity, meaning and prosocial concerns. *Applied Developmental Science, 8,* 17–26.

Futterman, A., Dillon, J., Garand, F., & Haugh, J. (1999). Religion as a quest and the search for meaning in later life. In L. E. Thomas, & S. Eisenhandler (Eds.), *Religion, belief, and spirituality in late adult life* (pp. 153–177). New York: Springer.

Gabriel, Y. (2004). The voice of experience and the voice of the expert--can they speak to each other? In B. Hurwitz, T. Greenhalgh, & V. Skultans (Eds.), *Narrative research in health and illness* (pp. 168–185). Malden, MA: Blackwell.

Gadamer, H. G. (1981). *Reason in the age of science* (F. G. Lawrence, Trans.). Cambridge, MA: MIT Press.

Gadamer, H. G. (1989). *Truth and method* (2nd rev. ed.) (J. Weinsheimer, & D. Marshall, Trans.). New York: Continuum.

Gaines, A. (1998). Religion and culture in psychiatry: Christian and secular psychiatric theory and practice in the United States. In H. Koenig (Ed.), *Handbook of religion and mental health* (pp. 292–320). San Diego, CA: Academic.

Gale, R. (1999). *The divided self of William James.* Cambridge: Cambridge University Press.

Gall, T., Basque, V., Damasceno-Scott, M., & Vardy, G. (2007). Spirituality and the current adjustment of adult survivors of childhood sexual abuse. *Journal for the Scientific Study of Religion, 46,* 101–117.

Gallup International Association. (1999). *Gallup international millennium survey.* Retrieved May 24, 2005 from www.gallup-international.com.

Galton, F. (2001). Statistical inquiries into the efficacy of prayer. In L. Francis, & J. Astley (Eds.), *Psychological perspectives on prayer* (pp. 139–141). Leominster, UK: Gracewing.

Ganje-Fling, M., & McCarthy, P. (1991). A comparative analysis of spiritual direction and psychotherapy. *Journal of Psychology and Theology, 19,* 103–117.

Ganzevoort, R. R. (1994). Crisis experiences and the development of belief and unbelief. In J. Corveleyn, & D. Hutsebaut (Eds.), *Belief and unbelief: Psychological perspectives* (pp. 21–36). Amsterdam: Rodopi.

Gar, N., Hudson, J., & Rapee, R. (2005). Family factors and the development of anxiety disorders. In J. Hudson, & R. Rapee (Eds.), *Psychopathology and the family* (pp. 125–145). Amsterdam: Elsevier.

Gartner, J. (1992). The capacity to forgive: An object relations perspective. In M. Finn, & J. Gartner (Eds.), *Object relations theory and religion* (pp. 21–33). Westport, CT: Praeger.

Gartner, R. B. (2004). Predatory priests: Sexually abusing Fathers. *Studies in Gender and Sexuality, 5,* 31–56.

Garzon, F. L. (2005). Inner healing prayer in "spirit-filled" Christianity. In R. Moodley, & W. West (Eds.), *Integrating traditional healing practices into counseling and psychotherapy* (pp. 148–158). Thousand Oaks, CA: Sage.

Gay, P. (1998). *Freud: A life for our time.* New York: W. W. Norton.

Geary, D. C., & Bjorklund, D. F. (2000). Evolutionary developmental psychology. *Child Development, 71,* 57–65.

Geels, A. (1996). Religious visions in contemporary Sweden. In J. A. van Belzen, & J. M. van der Lans (Series Eds.) & H. Grzymala-Moszczynska, & B. Beit-Hallahmi (Vol. Eds.), *International series in the psychology of religion, Vol. 4: Religion, psychopathology, and coping* (pp. 193–206). Amsterdam: Rodopi.

Geels, A., & Belzen, J. (2003). A vast domain and numerous perspectives: Introduction to the volume. In J. Belzen, & A. Geels (Eds.), *Mysticism: A variety of psychological perspectives* (pp. 7–15). Amsterdam: Rodopi.

Geerts, H. (1990). An inquiry into the meanings of ritual symbolism: turner and Peirce. In H.-G. Heimbrock, & H. Boudewijnse (Eds.), *Current studies on rituals: Perspectives for the psychology of religion* (pp. 19–32). Amsterdam: Rodopi.

Geertz, C. (1973). *The interpretation of cultures.* New York: Basic Books.

Gelderloos, P., & Beto, Z. H. A. D. (1989). The transcendental meditation and TM-Sidhi program and reported experiences of transcendental consciousness. *Psychologia, 32*, 91–103.

Gelderloos, P., Hermans, H., Ahlscruom, H., & Jacoby, R. (2001). Transcendence and psychological health: Studies with long-term participants of the transcendental meditation and TM-Sidhi program. *The Journal of Psychology, 124*, 177–197.

Gellhorn, E., & Kiely, W. F. (1972). Mystical states of consciousness: Neuropsychological and clinical aspects. *Journal of Nervous and Mental Disease, 154*, 399–405.

George, L. K., Ellison, C. G., & Larson, D. B. (2002). Explaining the relationships between religious involvement and health. *Psychological Inquiry, 13*, 190–200.

Gergen, K. (1991). *The saturated self: Dilemmas of identity in contemporary life.* New York: Basic Books.

Gergen, K. (1994). *Realities and relationships: Soundings in social construction.* Cambridge MA: Harvard University Press.

Gergen, K. (1999). *An invitation to social construction.* London: Sage.

Germer, C. K. (2005a). Mindfulness: What is it? What does it matter? In C. K. Germer, R. D. Siegel, & P. R. Fulton (Eds.), *Mindfulness and psychotherapy* (pp. 3–27). New York: Guilford Press.

Germer, C. K. (2005b). Teaching mindfulness in therapy. In C. K. Germer, R. D. Siegel, & P. R. Fulton (Eds.), *Mindfulness and psychotherapy* (pp. 113–129). New York: Guilford Press.

al-Ghazali. (1980). *Deliverance from error: An annotated translation of al-Munqidh min al Dalal and other relevant works of al-Ghazali* (R. McCarthy, Trans.). Louisville, KY: Fons Vitae. (Original work published 1116).

Ghoncheh, S., & Smith, J. (2004). Progressive muscle relaxation, yoga stretching, and ABC relaxation theory. *Journal of Clinical Psychology, 60*, 131–136.

Gibson, T. S. (2004). Proposed levels of Christian spiritual maturity. *Journal of Psychology and Theology, 32*, 295–304.

Gilkey, L. (1994). The Christian congregation as a religious community. In J. Wind, & J. Lewis (Eds.), *American congregations, Volume 2: New perspectives in the study of congregations* (pp. 100–132). Chicago: University of Chicago Press.

Gill, R. (2001). The future of religious participation and belief in Britain and beyond. In R. K. Fenn (Ed.), *The Blackwell companion to sociology of religion* (pp. 279–291). Oxford,: Blackwell.

Gillath, O., Shaver, P. R., & Mikulincer, M. (2005). An attachment–theoretical approach to compassion and altruism. In P. Gilbert (Ed.), *Compassion: Conceptualisations, research and use in psychotherapy* (pp. 121–147). London: Routledge.

Gillespie, C. (2001). *Psychology and American Catholicism.* New York: Crossroad.

Gilligan, C. (1982). *In a different voice: Psychological theory and women's development.* Cambridge, MA: Harvard University Press.

Gilligan, C., Murphy, J. M., & Tappan, M. (1990). Moral development beyond adolescence. In C. Alexander, & E. Langer (Eds.), *Higher stages of human development* (pp. 208–225). New York: Oxford University Press.

Gilman, R., Dooley, J., & Florell, D. (2006). Relative levels of hope and their relationship with academic and psychological indicators among adolescents. *Journal of Social and Clinical Psychology, 25*, 166–178.

Gimello, R. M. (1978). Mysticism and meditation. In S. T. Katz (Ed.), *Mysticism and philosophical analysis* (pp. 170–199). New York: Oxford University Press.

Girard, R. (1977). *Violence and the sacred* (P. Gregory, Trans.). Baltimore: Johns Hopkins University Press.

Girard, R. (1986). *The scapegoat* (Y. Freccero, Trans.). Baltimore: Johns Hopkins University Press.

Girard, R. (1987). *Things hidden since the foundation of the world* (S. Bann. & M. Metteer, Trans.). Stanford, CA: Stanford University Press.

Glaser, J. L. (1994). Clinical applications of Maharishi Ayur-Veda in chemical dependency disorders. *Alcoholism Treatment Quarterly, 11*(3–4), 367–394.

Glock, C. Y., & Stark, R. (1965). *Religion and society in tension.* Chicago, IL: Rand McNally.

Godby, K. E. (2002). Mystical experience: Unveiling the veiled. *Pastoral Psychology, 50*, 231–242.

Godfrey, K. F. (2006). Postfoundationalist rationality and progress in the theology of religious conversion. *Asia Journal of Theology, 20,* 142–154.

Goehring, J. E. (1999). Withdrawing from the desert: Pachomius and the development of village monasticism in upper Egypt. In E. Ferguson (Ed.), *Forms of devotion: Conversion, worship, spirituality, and asceticism* (pp. 233–252). New York: Garland.

Gold, L., & Mansager, E. (2000). Spirituality: Life task or life process? *The Journal of Individual Psychology, 56,* 266–276.

Goldie, P. (2004). Narrative, emotion, and understanding. In B. Hurwitz, T. Greenhalgh, & V. Skultans (Eds.), *Narrative research in health and illness* (pp. 156–167). Malden, MA: Blackwell.

Goldman, R. (1968). *Readiness for religion: A basis for developmental religious education.* New York: Seabury.

Goldsmith, T. H. (1994). *The biological roots of human nature: Forging links between evolution and behavior.* New York: Oxford University Press.

Goldstein, J., & Kornfield, J. (2001). *Seeking the heart of wisdom: The path of insight meditation.* Boston, MA: Shambhala.

Gollnick, J. (2001). Development of the God-image in Carl Jung's psychology and spirituality. *Studies in Religion, 30,* 179–192.

Golsworthy, R., & Coyle, A. (1999). Spiritual beliefs and the search for meaning among older adults following partner loss. *Mortality, 4,* 21–40.

Gomez, L. (1987). Purifying gold: The metaphor of effort and intuition in Buddhist thought and practice. In P. Gregory (Ed.), *Sudden and gradual: Approaches to enlightenment in Chinese thought* (pp. 67–165). Honolulu, HI: University of Hawaii Press.

Gomez, L. (1995). Oriental wisdom and the cure of souls: Jung and the Indian East. In D. Lopez, Jr. (Ed.), *Curators of the Buddha: The study of Buddhism under colonialism* (pp. 197–250). Chicago: University of Chicago Press.

Gonsiorek, J. (2004). Barriers to responding to the clergy sexual abuse crisis within the Roman Catholic Church. In T. Plante (Ed.), *Sin against the innocents: Sexual abuse by priests and the role of the Catholic church* (pp. 139–153.). Westport, CT: Praeger.

Goodich, M. E. (1989). *From birth to old age: The human life cycle in medieval thought, 1250–1350.* Lanham: University Press of America.

Goodman, R. S., Walton, K. G., Orme-Johnson, D. W., & Boyer R. (2003). The transcendental meditation program: A consciousness-based developmental technology for rehabilitation and crime prevention. *Journal of Offender Rehabilitation, 36,* 1–33.

Goodwin, A. (1998). Freud and Erikson: Their contributions to the psychology of God-image formation. *Pastoral Psychology, 47,* 97–117.

Gooren, H. (2007). Reassessing conventional approaches to conversion: Toward a new synthesis. *Journal for the Scientific Study of Religion, 46,* 337–353.

Goosen, G., & Dunner, K. (2001). Secondary students and changing attitudes to prayer. In L. Francis. & J. Astley (Eds.), *Psychological perspectives on prayer* (pp. 92–97). Leominster, UK: Gracewing.

Gorski, P. S. (2003). Historicizing the secularization debate: An agenda for research. In M. Dillon (Ed.), *Handbook of the sociology of religion* (pp. 110–122). Cambridge: Cambridge University Press.

Gorsuch, R. L. (1968). The conceptualization of God as seen in adjective ratings. *Journal for the Scientific Study of Religion, 7,* 56–64.

Gorsuch, R. L. (1984). Measurement: The boon and bane of investigating religion. *American Psychologist, 39,* 228–236.

Gorsuch, R. L. (1988). Psychology of religion. *Annual Review of Psychology, 39,* 201–221.

Gorsuch, R. L. (1993). Religion and prejudice: Lessons not learned from the past. *The International Journal for the Psychology of Religion, 3,* 29–31.

Gorsuch, R. L. (1995). Religious aspects of substance abuse and recovery. *Journal of Social Issues, 51*(2), 65–83.

Gorsuch, R. L. (1997). Toward motivational theories of intrinsic religious commitment. In B. Spilka, & D. N. McIntosh (Eds.), *The psychology of religion: Theoretical approaches* (pp. 11–22). Boulder, CO: Westview Press.

Gorsuch, R. L. (2002a). *Integrating psychology and spirituality?* Westport, CT: Praeger.

Gorsuch, R. L. (2002b). The pyramid of sciences and of humanities. *American Behavioral Scientist, 45*, 1822–1838.

Gorsuch, R. L. (2003). James on the similarities and differences between religious and psychic phenomena. *Streams of William James, 5*, 26–29.

Gorsuch, R. L., & Barnes, M. L. (1973). Stages of ethical reasoning and moral norms of Carib youths. *Journal of Cross-Cultural Psychology, 4*, 283–301.

Gorsuch, R. L., & McPherson, S. E. (1989). Intrinsic/extrinsic measurement: I/E-revised and single-item scales. *Journal for the Scientific Study of Religion, 28*, 348–354.

Gorsuch, R. L. & Spilka, B. (1987). Retrospective review: The Varieties in historical and contemporary contexts. *Contemporary Psychology, 32*, 773–778.

Gorsuch, R. L., & Venable, G. D. (1983). Development of an "age universal" I-E scale. *Journal for the Scientific Study of Religion, 22*, 181–187.

Gould, G. (1993). *The desert fathers on monastic community.* Oxford: Oxford University Press.

Gould, S. J. (1988). Trends as changes in variance. *Journal of Paleontology, 62*, 319–329.

Gould, S. J. (1997). Darwinian fundamentalism. *New York Review of Books, 44*(10), 34–37. Retrieved August 10, 2006 from http://www.nybooks.com/articles/1151.

Gould, S. J. (1999). *Rocks of ages: Science and religion in the fullness of life.* New York: Ballantine.

Gould, S. J., & Lewontin, R. C. (1979). The spandrels of San Marco and the Panglossian paradigm: A critique of the adaptionist programme. *Proceedings of the Royal Society of London B, 205*, 581–598.

Gould, S. J., & Vrba, E. S. (1982). Exaptation: A missing term in the science of form. *Paleobiology, 8*, 4–15.

Grams, A. (2001). Learning, aging, and other predicaments. In S. McFadden, & R. Atchley (Eds.), *Aging and the meaning of time: A multidisciplinary exploration* (pp. 99–111). New York: Springer.

Goyeche, J. R. M., Chihara, T., & Shimizu, H. (1972). Two concentration methods: A preliminary comparison. *Psychologia, 15*, 110–111.

Granqvist, P. (2003). Attachment theory and religious conversions: A review and a resolution of the classic and contemporary paradigm chasm. *Review of Religious Research, 45*, 172–187.

Granqvist, P., & Dickie, J. (2006). Attachment and spiritual development in childhood and adolescence. In E. Roehlkepartain, P. King, L. Wagener, & P. Benson (Eds.), *The handbook of spiritual development in childhood and adolescence* (pp. 197–210). Thousand Oaks, CA: Sage.

Granqvist, P., & Hagekull, B. (2000). Religiosity, adult attachment, and why "singles" are more religious. *International Journal for the Psychology of Religion, 10*, 111–123.

Granqvist, P., & Kirkpatrick, L. A. (2004). Religious conversion and perceived childhood attachment: A meta-analysis. *The International Journal for the Psychology of Religion, 14*, 223–250.

Grant, E. (1986). Science and theology in the Middle Ages. In D. C. Lindberg, & R. L. Numbers (Eds.), *God and nature: Historical essays on the encounter between Christianity and science* (pp.49–71). Berkeley, CA: University of California Press.

Grantham, T., & Nichols, S. (1999). Evolutionary psychology: Ultimate explanations and Panglossian predictions. In V. G. Hardcastle (Ed.), *Where biology meets psychology: Philosophical essays* (pp. 47–66). Cambridge, MA: MIT Press.

Green, E., & Green, A. (1977). *Beyond biofeedback.* New York: Delta.

Greenway, A., Milne, L., & Clarke, V. (2003). Personality variables, self-esteem and depression and an individual's perception of God. *Mental Health, Religion & Culture, 6*, 45–.58.

Gregory the Great, St. (1978). *Pastoral care* (H. Davis, Trans.). New York: Newman.

Gregory, of Nazianzen, St. (1994). Select orations. In P. Schaff (Ed.), *The Nicene and Post-Nicene Fathers, Second Series, Volume 7: Cyril of Jerusalem, Gregory Nazianzen* (pp. 299–604). New York: Peabody, MA: Hendrickson. Original work written c. 380 A.D.

Greinacher, N. (1999). The importance of religion: The place of the organized churches in today's secular society. In F. Schweitzer, & J. van der Ven (Eds.), *Practical theology: International perspectives* (pp. 245–258). Frankfurt am Main: Peter Lang.

Grenz, S. J. (2001). *The social God and the relational self: A Trinitarian theology of the Imago Dei*. Louisville, Kentucky: Westminster John Knox Press.

Grib, A. A. (1996). Quantum cosmology, the role of the observer, quantum logic. In R. Russell, N. Murphy, & C. J. Isham (Eds.), *Quantum cosmology and the laws of nature: Scientific perspectives on divine action* (2nd ed., pp.165–184). Vatican City State: Vatican Observatory.

Griffin, D. R. (1997). *Parapsychology, philosophy, and spirituality: A postmodern exploration*. Albany, NY: State University of New York Press.

Griffin, D. R. (2000). *Religion and scientific naturalism: Overcoming the conflicts*. Albany, NY: State University of New York Press.

Griffin, G. A., Gorsuch, R. L., & Davis, A. (1987). A cross-cultural investigation of religious orientation, social norms, and prejudice. *Journal for the Scientific Study of Religion, 26*, 358–365.

Griffith, B. A., & Griggs, J. C. (2001). Religious identity status as a model to understand, assess, and interact with client spirituality. *Counseling and Values, 46*, 14–25.

Griffiths, P. (1990). Pure consciousness and Indian Buddhism. In R. K. C. Forman (Ed.), *The problem of pure consciousness: Mysticism and philosophy* (pp. 71–97). New York: Oxford University Press.

Groeschel, B. (1995). *Spiritual passages: The psychology of spiritual development*. New York: Crossroad.

Grof, S. (1985). *Beyond the brain: Birth, death, and transcendence in psychotherapy*. Albany, NY: State University of New York Press.

Grof, S. (2003). Implications of modern consciousness research for psychology: Holotropic Experiences and their healing and heuristic potential. *The Humanistic Psychologist, 31*(2/3), 50–83.

Grogan, B. (1991a). The one who gives the exercises. In P. Sheldrake (Ed.), *The way of Ignatius Loyola: Contemporary approaches to the spiritual exercises* (pp. 179–190). St. Louis, MO: The Institute of Jesuit Sources.

Grogan, B. (1991b). 'To make the exercises better': The additions. In P. Sheldrake (Ed.), *The way of Ignatius Loyola: Contemporary approaches to the spiritual exercises* (pp. 41–52). St. Louis, MO: The Institute of Jesuit Sources.

Grogan, B. (1991c). The two standards. In P. Sheldrake (Ed.), *The way of Ignatius Loyola: Contemporary approaches to the spiritual exercises* (pp. 96–102). St. Louis, MO: The Institute of Jesuit Sources.

Grossman, P., Niemann, L., Schmidt, S., & Walach, H. (2004). Mindfulness-based stress reduction and health benefits: A meta-analysis. *Journal of Psychosomatic Research, 57*, 35–43.

Grotstein, J. (1992). Reflections on a century of Freud: Some paths not chosen. *British Journal of Psychotherapy, 9*, 181–187.

Grover, S. (1980). An examination of Kohlberg's cognitive-developmental model of morality. *The Journal of Genetic Psychology, 136*, 137–143.

Grzymala-Moszczynska, H. (1996). Religion as transgression: Psychological mechanisms involved in religion and mental health. In H. Grzymala-Moszczynska, & B. Beit-Hallahmi (Eds.), *International series in the psychology of religion: Vol. 4. Religion, psychopathology, and coping* (pp. 87–93). Amsterdam: Rodopi.

Gschwandtner, C. (2005).Praise-pure and personal? Jean-Luc Marion's phenomenologies of prayer. In B. Benson, & N. Wirzba (Eds.), *The phenomenology of prayer* (pp. 168–184). Bronx, NY: Fordham University Press.

Gubi, P. M. (2001). An exploration of the use of Christian prayer in mainstream counselling. *British Journal of Guidance & Counselling, 29*, 425–434.

Guenther, M. (1992). *Holy listening: The art of spiritual direction*. Cambridge, MA: Cowley.

Guenther, M. (2000). Companions at the threshold: Spiritual direction with the dying. In N. Vest (Ed.), *Still listening: New horizons in spiritual direction* (pp. 105–118). Harrisburg, PA: Morehouse.

Gulliford, L. (2004a). The healing of relationships. In F. Watts, & L. Gulliford (Eds.), *Forgiveness in context: Theology and psychology in creative dialogue* (pp. 106–122). London: T & T Clark International.

Gulliford, L. (2004b). Intrapersonal forgiveness. In F. Watts, & L. Gulliford (Eds.), *Forgiveness in context: Theology and psychology in creative dialogue* (pp. 83–105). London: T & T Clark International.

Gunn, R. J. (2000). *Journeys into emptiness*. Mahwah, NJ: Paulist Press.

Gunnoe, M. L., Hetherington, E. M., & Reiss, D. (1999). Parental religiosity, parenting style, and adolescent social responsibility. *Journal of Early Adolescence, 19*, 199–225.

Gunnoe, M. L., & Moore, K. A. (2002). Predictors of religiosity among youth aged 17–22: A longitudinal study of the national survey of children. *Journal for the Scientific Study of Religion, 41*, 613–622.

Gunton, C. (1991). *The promise of Trinitarian theology*. Edinburgh: T & T Clark.

Gunton, C. (1993). *The one, the three and the many: God, creation and the culture of modernity*. Cambridge: Cambridge University Press.

Guntrip, H. (1949). *Psychology for ministers and social workers*. London: Independent.

Guntrip, H. (1957). *Psychotherapy and religion*. New York: Harper and Brothers.

Guntrip, H. (1969). Religion in relation to personal integration. *British Journal of Medical Psychology, 42*, 323–333.

Guntrip, H. (1973). *Psychoanalytic theory, therapy and the self*. New York: Basic.

Guntrip, H. (1996). My experience of analysis with Fairbairn and Winnicott: How complete a result does psychoanalytic therapy achieve? *International Journal of Psycho-Analysis, 77*, 739–754.

Gupta, B., & Lucas, C. (1995). Hindu mysticism. In D. Bishop (Ed.), *Mysticism and the mystical experience: East and West* (pp. 273–298). Cranbury, NJ: Associated University Press.

Gur, M., Miller, M., Warner, W., Wickramaratne, P., & Weissman, M. (2005). Maternal depression and the intergenerational transmission of religion. *The Journal of Nervous and Mental Disease, 193*, 338–345.

Gurdjieff, G. (1999). *Life is real only then, when 'I am'* (All and Everything, Third Series). London: Arkana.

Guthrie, S. (1993). *Faces in the clouds: A new theory of religion*. New York: Oxford University Press.

Guthrie, S. (2001). Why gods? A cognitive theory. In J. Andresen (Ed.), *Religion in mind: Cognitive perspectives on religious belief, ritual, and experience* (pp. 94–112). Cambridge: Cambridge University Press.

Habets, M. (2006). Reforming theosis. In S. Finlan, & V. Kharlamov (Eds.), *Theosis Deification in Christian theology* (pp. 146–167). Eugene, OR: Pickwick.

Hacker, F. (1974). Freud, Marx, and Kierkegaard. In B. Nelson (Ed.), *Freud and the 20th century* (pp. 125–142). Gloucester, MA: Peter Smith.

Hackney, C. H. (2007). Possibilities for a Christian positive psychology. *Journal of Psychology and Theology, 35*, 211–221.

Hackney, C. H., & Sanders, G. S. (2003). Religiosity and mental health: A meta-analysis of recent studies. *Journal for the Scientific Study of Religion, 42*, 43–55.

Haddad, S. (2003).Islam and attitudes toward U.S. policy in the Middle East: Evidence from survey research in Lebanon. *Studies in Conflict & Terrorism, 26*, 135–154.

Hadot, P. (1986a). Neoplatonist spirituality: I. Plotinus and Porphyry. In A. Armstrong (Ed.), *Classical Mediterranean spirituality: Egyptian, Greek, Roman* (pp. 230–249). New York: Crossroad.

Hadot, P. (1986b). The spiritual guide. In A. Armstrong (Ed.), *Classical Mediterranean spirituality: Egyptian, Greek, Roman* (pp. 436–459). New York: Crossroad.

Hadot, P. (1993). *Plotinus or the simplicity of vision* (M Chase, Trans.). Chicago, IL: The University of Chicago Press.

Hadot, P. (1995). *Philosophy as a way of life: Spiritual exercises from Socrates to Foucault* (A. Davidson, Ed., M. Chase, Tr.). Malden, MA: Blackwell.

Hadot, P., Davidson, A., & Wissing, P. (1990). Forms of life and forms of discourse in ancient philosophy. *Critical Inquiry, 16*, 483–505.

Hage, S. M. (2006). A closer look at the role of spirituality in psychology training programs. *Professional Psychology: Research and Practice, 37*, 303–310.

Hagedorn, W. B. (2005). Counselor self-awareness and self-exploration of religious and spiritual beliefs: Know thyself. In C. Cashwell, & J. S. Young (Eds.), *Integrating spirituality and religion into counseling: A guide to competent practice* (pp. 63–84). Alexandria, VA: American Counseling Association.

Hagen, E. (2005).Controversial issues in evolutionary psychology. In D. Buss (Ed.), *The handbook of evolutionary psychology* (pp. 145–176). New York: John Wiley & Sons.

Hagglund, T. (2001). Timelessness as a positive and negative experience. *The Scandinavian Psychoanalytic Review, 24*, 83–92.

Haig, B. D. (2002). Truth, method, and postmodern psychology. *American Psychologist, 57*(6–7), 457–458.

Halama, P. (2003). Meaning and hope: Two factors of positive psychological functioning in late adulthood. *Studia Psychologica, 45*, 103–110.

Hall, G. S. (1905). *Adolescence: Its psychology and its relations to physiology, anthropology, sociology, sex, crime, religion and education. Volume I.* New York: D. Appleton.

Hall, G. S. (1916). *Adolescence: Its psychology and its relations to physiology, anthropology, sociology, sex, crime, religion and education. Volume II.* New York: D. Appleton.

Hall, G. S. (1923). *Jesus the Christ in the light of psychology.* New York: D. Appleton. (Original work published 1917).

Hall, G. S. (1924). *Life and confessions of a psychologist.* New York: D. Appleton.

Hall, T. A. (1988). *Too deep for words: Rediscovering Lectio Divina.* New York: Paulist Press.

Hall, T. A. (1995). Spiritual effects of childhood sexual abuse in adult Christian women. *Journal of Psychology and Theology, 23*, 129–134.

Hall, T. W., & Brokaw, B. F. (1995). The relationship of spiritual maturity to level of object relations development and God image. *Pastoral Psychology, 43*, 373–391.

Hall, T. W., Brokaw, B. F., Edwards, K. J., & Pike, P. L. (1998). An empirical exploration of psychoanalysis and religion: Spiritual maturity and object relations development. *Journal for the Scientific Study of Religion, 37*, 303–313.

Hall, T. W., & Edwards, K. J. (1996). The initial development and factor analysis of the spiritual assessment inventory. *Journal of Psychology and Theology, 24*, 233–246.

Hall, T. W., & Edwards, K. J. (2002). The spiritual assessment inventory: A theistic model and measure for assessing spiritual development. *Journal for the Scientific Study of Religion, 41*, 341–357.

Halman, L., & Pettersson, T. (2003a). Differential patterns of secularization in Europe: Exploring the impact of religion on social values. In L. Halman, & O. Riis (Eds.), *Religion in secularizing society: The Europeans' religion at the end of the 20th century* (pp. 48–75). Leiden: Brill.

Halman, L., & Pettersson, T. (2003b). Religion and social capital revisited. In L. Halman, & O. Riis (Eds.), *Religion in secularizing society: The Europeans' religion at the end of the 20ᵗʰ century* (pp. 162–184). Leiden: Brill.

Halman, L., & Pettersson, T. (2003c). Globalization and patterns of religious belief systems. In L. Halman, & O. Riis (Eds.), *Religion in secularizing society: The Europeans' religion at the end of the 20th century* (pp. 185–204). Leiden: Brill.

Halman, L., & Riis, O. (2003). Contemporary European discourses on religion and morality. In L. Halman, & O. Riis (Eds.), *Religion in secularizing society: The Europeans' religion at the end of the 20ᵗʰ century* (pp. 1–21). Leiden: Brill.

Hamer, D. H. (1996). The heritability of happiness. *Nature Genetics, 14*, 125–126.

Hamilton, D. M., & Jackson, M. H. (1998). Spiritual development: Paths and processes. *Journal of Instructional Psychology, 25*, 262–270.

Hamilton, W. D. (1964). The genetical evolution of social behaviour: I. *Journal of Theoretical Biology, 7*, 1–16.

Hanh, T. (2002). *Friends on the path: Living spiritual communities* (J. Lawlor, Ed.), Berkeley, CA: Parallax Press.

Happel, S. (1995). Divine providence and instrumentality: Metaphors for time in self-organizing systems and divine action. In R. Russell, N. Murphy, & A. Peacocke (Eds.), *Chaos and complexity: Scientific perspectives on divine action* (pp. 177–203). Vatican City State: Vatican Observatory.

Happel, S. (1996). Metaphors and time asymmetry: Cosmologies in physics and Christian meanings. In R. Russell, N. Murphy, & C. J. Isham (Eds.), *Quantum cosmology and the laws of nature: Scientific perspectives on divine action* (2nd ed., pp. 105–138). Vatican City State: Vatican Observatory.

Happel, S. (2002). The soul and neuroscience: Possibilities for divine action. In R. Russell, N. Murphy, T. Meyering, & M. Arbib (Eds.), *Neuroscience and the person: Scientific perspectives on divine action* (pp. 281–304). Vatican City State: Vatican Observatory.

Haque, A., & Masuan, K. A. (2002). Religious psychology in Malaysia. *The International Journal for the Psychology of Religion, 12,* 277–289.

Hardy, A., Sir. (1983). *The spiritual nature of man: A study of contemporary religious experience.* Oxford: Oxford University Press.

Hardy, D. S. (2000). A Winnicottian redescription of Christian spiritual direction relationships: Illustrating the potential contribution of psychology of religion to Christian spiritual practice. *Journal of Psychology and Theology, 28,* 263–275.

Harker, K. (2001). Immigrant generation, assimilation, and adolescent psychological well-being. *Social Forces, 79,* 969–1004.

Harmless, W. (2004). *Desert Christians: An introduction to the literature of early monasticism.* Oxford: Oxford University Press.

Harms, E. (1944). The development of religious experience in children. *The American Journal of Sociology, 50,* 112–122.

Harper, M., & Gill, C. (2005). Assessing the client's spiritual domain. In C. Cashwell, & J. S. Young (Eds.), *Integrating spirituality and religion into counseling: A guide to competent practice* (pp. 31–62). Alexandria, VA: American Counseling Association.

Harris, J. I., Erbes, C. R., Engdahl, B. E., Olson, R. H. A., Winskowski, A., M., & McMahill, J. (2008). Christian religious functioning and trauma outcomes. *Journal of Clinical Psychology, 64,* 17–29.

Harris, S., Sheth, S., & Cohen, M. (2007). Functional neuroimaging of belief, disbelief, and uncertainty. *Annals of Neurology.* Retrieved from www3.interscience.wiley.com on February 12, 2008.

Harris, W., Gowda, M., Kolb, J., Strychacz, C., Vacek, J., et al. (2001). A randomized, controlled trail of the effects of remote, intercessory prayer on outcomes in patients admitted to the coronary care unit. In L. Francis, & J. Astley (Eds.), *Psychological perspectives on prayer* (pp. 164–176). Leominster, UK: Gracewing.

Harrison, L. J., Manocha, R., & Rubia, K. (2004). Sahaja yoga meditation as a family treatment programme for children with attention deficit-hyperactivity disorder. *Clinical Child Psychology and Psychiatry, 9,* 479–497.

Harrison, M. O., Koenig, H. G., Hays, J. C., Eme-Akwari, A. G., & Pargament, K. I. (2001). The epidemiology of religious coping: A review of recent literature. *International Review of Psychiatry, 13,* 86–93.

Hart, T. (2006). Spiritual experiences and capacities of children and youth. In E. Roehlkepartain, P. King, L. Wagener, & P. Benson (Eds.), *The handbook of spiritual development in childhood and adolescence* (pp. 163–177). Thousand Oaks, CA: Sage.

Harter, S. (2002). Authenticity. In C. R. Snyder, & S. J. Lopez (Eds.), *Handbook of positive psychology* (pp. 382–394). Oxford: Oxford University Press.

Hartford Institute for Religion Research (2003). *Meet your neighbors: Interfaith FACTs,* Hartford Seminary. Retrieved from http://fact.hartsem.edu/MeetNgbors1.pdf on March 8, 2005.

Hartsman, E. (2002). Jewish anthropology: The stuff between. In R. Olson (Ed.), *Religious theories of personality and psychotherapy: East meets West* (pp. 211–246). New York: Haworth Press.

Hartung, J. (1992). Getting real about rape. *Behavioral and Brain Sciences, 15,* 390–392.

Harvey, P. (1990). *An introduction to Buddhism.* Cambridge: Cambridge University Press.

Hatchett, B. F. (1999). Alcohol problems among older African American women. *Journal of Religion and Health, 38,* 149–154.

Hateley, B. (1984). Spiritual well-being through life histories. *Journal of Religion and Aging, 1,* 63–71.

Hathaway, W. L., & Pargament, K. I. (1990). Intrinsic religiousness, religious coping, and psychosocial competence: A covariance structure analysis. *Journal for the Scientific Study of Religion, 29,* 423–441.

Hauerwas, S., & Yordy, L. (2003). Captured in time: Friendship and aging. In S. Hauerwas, C. Stoneking, K. Meador, & D. Cloutier (Eds.), *Growing old in Christ* (pp. 169–184). Grand Rapids, MI: Eerdmans.

Haugt, J. (1998). Darwin's gift to theology. In R. Russell, W. Stoeger S. J., & F. Ayala (Eds.), *Evolutionary and molecular biology: Scientific perspectives on divine action* (pp. 393–418). Vatican City State: Vatican Observatory.

Hauke, C. (2000). *Jung and the postmodern: The interpretation of realities.* London: Routledge.

Haule, J. R. (2000). Jung's practice of analysis: A Euro-American parallel to Ch'an Buddhism. *The Journal of Individual Psychology, 56,* 353–365.

Hausherr, I. (1990). *Spiritual direction in the early Christian east* (A. P. Gythiel, Trans.). Kalamazoo, MI: Cistercian Press.

Hawkins, M. A. (2003). Effectiveness of the Transcendental Meditation program in criminal rehabilitation and substance abuse recovery: A review of the research. *Journal of Offender Rehabilitation, 36,* 47–65.

Hawley, K. (2006). Science as a guide to metaphysics? *Synthese, 149,* 451–470.

Hay, D. (1979). Religious experience amongst a group of post-graduate students: A qualitative study. *Journal for the Scientific Study of Religion, 18,* 164–182.

Hay, D. (1999). Psychologists interpreting conversion: Two American forerunners of the hermeneutics of suspicion. *History of the Human Sciences, 12,* 55–72.

Hay, D. (2001). The cultural context of stage models of religious experience. *International Journal for the Psychology of Religion, 11,* 241–246.

Hay, D., & Morisy, A. (1978). Reports of ecstatic, paranormal, or religious experience in Great Britain and the United States: A comparison of trends. *Journal for the Scientific Study of Religion, 17,* 255–268.

Hay, D., & Nye, R. (2006). *The spirit of the child* (rev. ed.). Philadelphia: Jessica Kingsley.

Hay, D., Reich, K. H., & Utsch, M. (2006). Spiritual development: Intersections and divergence with religious development. In E. Roehlkepartain, P. King, L. Wagener, & P. Benson (Eds.), *The handbook of spiritual development in childhood and adolescence* (pp. 46–59). Thousand Oaks, CA: Sage.

Hayes, L. J. (1997). Understanding mysticism. *Psychological Record, 47,* 573–597.

Hayes, R. (2003). Classical Buddhist model of a healthy mind. In K. Dockett, G. Dudley-Grant, & C. Bankart (Eds.), *Psychology and Buddhism: From individual to global community* (pp. 161–170). New York: Kluwer Academic/Plenum.

Hayes, S., Strosahl, K., & Wilson, K. (2003). *Acceptance and commitment therapy: An experiential approach to behavior change.* New York: Guilford.

Haynes, L. (1998). Responses to "restoring the substance to the soul of psychology": Clinical and spiritual development applications. *Journal of Psychology ad Theology, 26,* 44–54.

Hays, J. C., Meador, K. G., Branch, P. S., & George, L. K. (2001). The spiritual history scale in four dimensions (SHS-4): Validity and reliability. *The Gerontologist: Special Issue, 41,* 239–249.

Hays, R., & Hays, J. (2003). The Christian practice of growing old: The witness of Scripture. In S. Hauerwas, C. Stoneking, K. Meador, & D. Cloutier (Eds.), *Growing old in Christ* (pp. 3–18). Grand Rapids, MI: Eerdmans.

Hazra, K. L. (1988). *Constitution of the Buddhist Sangha.* Delhi: B.R. Publishing.

Heath, A. C., Madden, P. A. F., Grant, J. D., McLaughlin, T. L., Todorov, A. A., & Bucholz, K. K. (1999). Resiliency factors protecting against teenage alcohol use and smoking: Influences of religion, religious involvement and values, and ethnicity in the Missouri adolescent female twin study. *Twin Research, 2,* 145–155.

Hebert, R., & Tan, G. (2004). Quantitative EEG phase evaluation of transcendental meditation. *Journal of Neurotherapy, 8,* 120–121.

Hebl, J., & Enright, R. (1993). Forgiveness as a psychotherapeutic goal with elderly females. *Psychotherapy, 30,* 658–667.

Hechter, M. (1997). Religion and rational choice theory. In L. A. Young (Ed.), *Rational choice theory and religion: Summary and assessment* (pp. 147–159). New York: Routledge.

Heckhausen, J., Dixon, R. A, & Baltes, P. B. (1989). Gains and losses in development throughout adulthood as perceived by different adult age groups. *Developmental Psychology, 25,* 109–121.

Heelas, P. (1996). *The new age movement: The celebration of the self and the sacralization of modernity.* Oxford: Blackwell.

Hefner, P. (1998). Biocultural evolution: A clue to the meaning of nature. In R. Russell, W. Stoeger S. J., & F. Ayala (Eds.), *Evolutionary and molecular biology scientific perspectives on divine action* (pp. 329–356). Vatican City State: Vatican Observatory.

Heidegger, M. (1962). *Being and time* (J. Macquarrie, & E. Robinson, Trans.). San Francisco: HarperSanFrancisco.

Heiler, F. (1932). *Prayer: A study in the history and psychology of religion.* New York: Oneworld.

Heilman, S. C., & Witztum, E. (2000). All in faith: Religion as the idiom and means of coping with distress. *Mental Health, Religion & Culture, 3,* 115–124.

Heimbrock, H. (1990). Ritual and transformation: A psychoanalytic perspective. In H. Heimbrock, & H. B. Boudewijnse (Eds.), *Current studies on rituals: Perspectives for the psychology of religion* (pp. 33–42). Amsterdam: Rodopi.

Heisig, J. W. (1999). Jung, Christianity, and Buddhism. *Nazan Bulletin, 23,* 74–104.

Helal, G. (1999). The methodological and epistemological foundation of C.G. Jung's theory of religion and its relationship to ultimate reality and meaning. *Ultimate Reality and Meaning, 22,* 294–306.

Helland, C. (2004). Popular religion and the World Wide Web: A match made in (cyber) heaven. In L. Dawson, & D. Cowan (Eds.), *Religion online: Finding faith on the Internet* (pp. 23–35). New York: Routledge.

Heller, M. (1988). Adventures of the concept of mass and matter. *Philosophy in Science, 3,* 15–35.

Heller, M. (1995). Chaos, probability and the comprehensibility of the world. In R. Russell, N. Murphy, & A. Peacocke (Eds.), *Chaos and complexity: Scientific perspectives on divine action* (pp. 107–121). Vatican City State: Vatican Observatory.

Hellwig, M. (1991). 'The call of the king' and justice. In P. Sheldrake (Ed.), *The way of Ignatius Loyola: Contemporary approaches to the spiritual exercises* (pp. 77–85). St. Louis, MO: The Institute of Jesuit Sources.

Helminiak, D. A. (1981). Meditation-psychologically and theologically. *Pastoral Psychology, 30*(10), 6–20.

Helminiak, D. A. (1987). *Spiritual development: An interdisciplinary study.* Chicago: Loyola University Press.

Helminiak, D. A. (1996). A scientific spirituality: The interface of psychology and theology. *International Journal for the Psychology of Religion, 6,* 1–19.

Helminiak, D. A. (2001). Treating spiritual issues in secular psychotherapy. *Counseling and Values, 45,* 163–189.

Helve, H. (1994). The development of religious belief systems from childhood to adulthood: A longitudinal study of young Finns in the context of the Lutheran church. In J. Corveleyn, & D. Hutsebaut (Eds.), *Belief and unbelief: Psychological perspectives* (pp. 63–85). Amsterdam: Rodopi.

Hempel, C. (1949). The logical analysis of psychology. In H. Feigl, & W. Sellars (Eds.), *Readings in philosophical analysis* (pp. 373–384). New York: Appleton-Century-Crofts. (Original work published 1935).

Hempel, C. (2001a). Explanation and prediction by covering laws. In J. Fetzer (ed.), *The philosophy of Carl G. Hempel* (pp. 69–86). New York; Oxford University Press. Original work published 1963).

Hempel, C. (2001b). On the structure of scientific theories. In J. Fetzer (ed.), *The philosophy of Carl G. Hempel* (pp. 49–66). New York; Oxford University Press. (Original work published 1969).

Hendricks, W. L. (1986). *A theology for aging.* Nashville, TN: Broadman Press.

Hendrix, S. (1995). Beyond Erikson: The relational Luther. *Lutheran Theological Seminary Bulletin, 75,* 3–12.

Henking, S. (2000). Does (the history of) religion and psychological studies have a subject? In D. Jonte-Pace, & W. Parsons (Eds.), *Religion and psychology: Mapping the terrain* (pp. 59–74). London: Routledge.

Herbert, R., & Tan, G. (2004). Quantitative EEG Phase Evaluation of Transcendental Meditation. *Journal of Neurotherapy, 8,* 120–121.

Herman, J. (2000). The contextual illusion: Comparative mysticism and postmodernism. In K. Patton, & B. Ray (Eds.), *A magic still dwells: Comparative religion in the postmodern age* (pp. 92–100). Berkeley, CA: University of California Press.

Hermans, H. (1998). Meaning as an organized process of valuation: A self-confrontational approach. In P. Wong, & P. Fry (Eds.), *The human quest for meaning: A handbook of psychological research and clinical applications* (pp. 317–334). Mahwah, NJ: Lawrence Erlbaum.

Hermans, H. (2001). The dialogical self: Toward a theory of personal and cultural positioning. *Culture & Psychology, 7,* 243–281.

Hermans, H., & Josephs, I. (2003). The dialogical self: Between mechanism and innovation. In I. Josephs (Ed.), *Dialogicality in development* (pp. 111–126). Westport, CT: Praeger.

Hermans, H., Kempen, H., & van Loon, R. (1992). The dialogical self: Beyond individualism and rationalism. *American Psychologist, 47,* 23–33.

Herrera, L. P. (2000). The tradition of Ignatius of Loyola: A holistic spirituality. *Journal of Individual Psychology, 56,* 305–315.

Herrick, J. A. (2003). *The making of the new spirituality: The eclipse of the Western religious tradition.* Downers Grove, IL: InterVarsity Press.

Hertel, B. (1995). Work, family, and faith: Recent trends. In N. Ammerman, & W. Roof (Eds.), *Work, family, and religion in contemporary society* (pp. 81–121). New York: Routledge.

Herth, K. (1990). Relationship of hope, coping styles, concurrent losses, and setting to grief resolution in the elderly widow(er). *Research in Nursing & Health, 13,* 109–117.

Hervieu-Leger, D. (2000). *Religion as a chain of memory* (S. Lee, Trans.). New Brunswick, NJ: Rutgers University Press.

Hervieu-Leger, D. (2001). Individualism, the validation of faith, and the social nature of religion in modernity (M. Davis, Trans.). In R. K. Fenn (Ed.), *The Blackwell companion to sociology of religion* (pp. 161–175). Oxford: Blackwell.

Herzog, H., Lele, V. R., Kuwert, T., Langen, K., Kops, E. R., & Feinendegen, L. E. (1990). Changed pattern of regional glucose metabolism during yoga meditative relaxation. *Neuropsychobiology, 23,* 182–187.

Heynekamp, E. E. (2002). Coming home: The difference it makes. In P. Young-Eisendrath, & S. Muramoto (Eds.), *Awakening and insight: Zen Buddhism and psychotherapy* (pp. 252–262). New York: Taylor & Francis.

Higgins, E. T., Grant, H., & Shah, J. (1999). Self-regulation and quality of life: Emotional and non-emotional life experiences. In D. Kahneman, E. Diener, & N. Schwarz (Eds.), *Well-being: The foundations of hedonic psychology* (pp. 244–266). New York: Russell Sage Foundation.

Higgins-D'Alessandro, A., & Cecero, J. J. (2003). The social nature of saintliness and moral action: A view of William James's *Varieties* in relation to St Ignatius and Lawrence Kohlberg. *Journal of Moral Education, 32,* 357–371.

Hill, C. I. (1986). A developmental perspective on adolescent "rebellion" in the church. *Journal of Psychology and Theology, 14,* 306–318.

Hill, D. R., & Persinger, M. A. (2003). Application of transcerebral, weak (1 MICROT) complex magnetic fields and mystical experiences: Are they generated by field-induced dimethyltryptamine release from the pineal organ? *Perceptual and Motor Skills, 97,* 1049–1050.

Hill, P. C. (1997). Toward an attitude process model of religious experience. In B. Spilka, & D. N. McIntosh (Eds.), *The psychology of religion: Theoretical approaches* (pp. 184–193). Boulder, CO: Westview Press.

Hill, P. C., & Hall, T. W. (2002). Relational schemas in processing one's image of God and self. *Journal of Psychology and Christianity, 21*, 365–373.

Hill, P. C., & Hood, R. W., Jr. (1999). Affect, religion, and unconscious processes. *Journal of Personality, 67*, 1015–1046.

Hill, P. C., & Pargament, K. I. (2003). Advances in the conceptualization and measurement of religion and spirituality: Implications for physical and mental health research. *American Psychologist, 58*, 64–74.

Hill, P. C., Pargament, K. I., Hood, R. W., McCullough, M. E., Swyers, J. P., Larson, D. B., et al. (2000). Conceptualizing religion and spirituality: Points of commonality, points of departure. *Journal for the Theory of Social Behavior, 30*, 51–77.

Hill, T. D., Burdette, A. M., Angel, J. L., & Angel, R. J. (2006). Religious attendance and cognitive functioning among older Mexican Americans. *Journal of Gerontology: Psychological Sciences, 61B*(1), P3–P9.

Hillman, J. (1967). *Insearch: Psychology and religion.* New York: Charles Scriber's Sons.

Hills, P., Francis, L. J., Argyle, M., & Jackson, C. J. (2004). Primary personality trait correlates of religious practice and orientation. *Personality and Individual Differences, 36*, 61–73.

Hiltner, S. (1954a). Pastoral psychology and pastoral counseling. In S. Doniger (Eds.), *Religion and human behavior* (pp. 179–195). New York: Association Press.

Hiltner, S. (1954b). Pastoral psychology and constructive theology. In S. Doniger (Eds.), *Religion and human behavior* (pp. 196–216). New York: Association Press.

Hinde, R. A. (1991). When is an evolutionary approach useful? *Child Development, 62*, 671–675.

Hinde, R. A. (2002). The adaptionist approach has limits. *Psychological Inquiry, 6*, 50–53.

Hinde, R. A. (2005). Modes theory: Some theoretical considerations. In H. Whitehouse, & R. McCauley (Eds.), *Mind and religion: Psychological and cognitive foundations of religiosity* (pp. 31–55). Walnut Creek, CA: AltaMira.

Hinterkopf, E. (2005). The experiential focusing approach. In L. Sperry, & E. P. Shafranske (Eds.), *Spiritually oriented psychotherapy* (pp. 207–233). Washington, DC: American Psychological Association.

Hirai, T., Izawa, S., & Koga, E. (1959). EEG and Zen Buddhism. *Electroencephalography and Clinical Neurophysiology, 18*, 52.

Hoare, C. (2000). Morality, ethics, spirituality, and prejudice in the writings of Erik H. Erikson. In M. Miller, & A. West (Eds.), *Spirituality, ethics, and relationship in adulthood: Clinical and theoretical explorations* (pp. 31–56). Madison, CT: Psychosocial.

Hoare, C. H. (2002). *Erikson on development in adulthood: New insights from the unpublished papers.* NewYork: Oxford University Press.

Hobbes, T. (1962). *Leviathan* (J. Plamenatz, Ed.), Glasgow, UK: William Collins. (Original work published 1651).

Hodge, D. R. (2003). *Spiritual assessment: Handbook for helping professionals.* Botsford, CT: NACSW Press.

Hodges, S. (2002). Mental health, depression, and dimensions of spirituality and religion. *Journal of Adult Development, 9*, 109–115.

Hodgkinson, V., Weitzman, M., & Kirsch, A. (1990). From commitment to action: How religious involvement affects giving and volunteering. In R. Wuthnow, & V. Hodgkinson (Eds.), *Faith and philanthropy in America: Exploring the role of religion in America's voluntary sector* (pp. 93–114). San Francisco: Jossey-Bass.

Hoffman, M. (2004). From enemy combatant to strange bedfellow: The role of religious narratives in the work of W.R.D. Fairbairn and D.W. Winnicott. *Psychoanalytic Dialogues, 14*, 769–804.

Hofstede, G. (1980). *Culture's consequences: International differences in work-related values.* Beverly Hills, CA: Sage.

Hogan, P. (2004). Literature, God, & the unbearable solitude of consciousness. *Journal of Consciousness Studies, 11*(5/6), 116–142.

Hoge, D. R., & Petrillo, G. H. (1978). Development of religious thinking in adolescence: A test of Goldman's theories. *Journal for the Scientific Study of Religion, 17,* 139–154.

Holdrege, B. (2000). What's beyond the post? Comparative analysis as critical method. In K. Patton, & B. Ray (Eds.), *A magic still dwells: Comparative religion in the postmodern age* (pp. 77–91). Berkeley, CA: University of California.

Holifield, E. B. (1983). *A history of pastoral care in America: From salvation to self-realization.* Nashville, TX: Abingdon Press.

Hollenback, J. (1996). *Mysticism: Experience, response, and empowerment.* University Park, PA: Pennsylvania State University Press.

Hollinger, D. (1997). James, Clifford, and the scientific conscience. In R. Putnam (Ed.), *The Cambridge companion to William James* (pp. 69–83). Cambridge: Cambridge University Press.

Hollon, S. D., Thase, M. E., & Markowitz, J. C. (2002). Treatment and prevention of depression. *Psychological Science in the Public Interest, 3,* 39–77.

Holm, N. (1995). Role theory and religious experience. In R. Hood (Ed.), *Handbook of religious experience* (pp. 397–420). Birmingham, AL: Religious Education.

Holm, N. (1997). An integrated role theory for the psychology of religion: Concepts and perspectives. In B. Spilka, & D. N. McIntosh (Eds.), *The psychology of religion: Theoretical approaches* (pp. 73–85). Boulder, CO: Westview Press.

Holmes, A. (2000). *A life pleasing to God: The spirituality of the rules of St. Basil.* Kalamazoo, MI: Cistercian Press.

Homans, P. (1968a). Introduction. In P. Homans (Ed.), *The dialogue between theology and psychology* (pp. 1–10). Chicago: The University of Chicago Press.

Homans, P. (1968b). Toward a psychology of religion: By way of Freud and Tillich. In P. Homans (Ed.), *The dialogue between theology and psychology* (pp. 53–81). Chicago: The University of Chicago Press.

Homans, P. (1970). *Theology after Freud: An interpretive inquiry.* Indianapolis, IN: Bobbs-Merrill.

Homans, P. (1978a). Introduction. In P. Homans (Ed.), *Childhood and selfhood: Essays on tradition, religion, and modernity in the psychology of Erik H. Erikson* (pp. 13–56). Lewisburg, PA: Bucknell University Press.

Homans, P. (1978b). The significance of Erikson's psychology for modern understandings of religion. In P. Homans (Ed.), *Childhood and selfhood: Essays on tradition, religion, and modernity in the psychology of Erik H. Erikson* (pp. 231–263). Lewisburg, PA: Bucknell University Press.

Homans, P. (1995). *Jung in context: Modernity and the making of a psychology* (2nd ed.). Chicago: University of Chicago.

Honen. (1998). *Honen's Senchakushu: Passages on the selection of the Nembutsu in the original vow.* Honolulu: University of Hawaii Press.

Hood, R. W., Jr. (1973). Religious orientation and the experience of transcendence. *Journal for the Scientific Study of Religion, 12,* 441–448.

Hood, R. W., Jr. (1975). The construction and preliminary validation of a measure of reported mystical experience. *Journal for the Scientific Study of Religion, 14,* 29–41.

Hood, R. W., Jr. (1978). Anticipatory set and setting: Stress incongruities as elicitors of mystical experience in solitary nature situations. *Journal for the Scientific Study of Religion, 17,* 279–287.

Hood, R. W., Jr. (1994). Self and self-loss in mystical experience. In T. M. Brinthaupt, & R. P. Lipka (Eds.), *Changing the self: Philosophies, techniques, and experiences* (pp. 279–305). Albany, NY: State University of New York Press.

Hood, R. W., Jr. (1997). The empirical study of mysticism. In B. Spilka, & D. N. McIntosh (Eds.), *The psychology of religion: Theoretical approaches* (pp. 222–232). Boulder, CO: Westview Press.

Hood, R. W., Jr. (2001). *Dimensions of mystical experiences: Empirical studies and psychological links.* Amsterdam: Rodopi.

Hood, R. W., Jr. (2002). The mystical self: Lost and found. *International Journal for the Psychology of Religion, 12,* 1–14.

Hood, R. W., Jr. (2003). Conceptual and empirical consequences of the unity thesis. In J. Belzen, & A. Geels (Ed.), *Mysticism: A variety of psychological perspectives* (pp. 17–54). Amsterdam: Rodopi.

Hood, R. W., Jr., Ghorbani, N., Waston, P. J., Ghramaleki, A. F., Bing, M. N, Davison, H. K., et al. (2001). Dimensions of the mysticism scale: Confirming the three-factor structure in the United States and Iran. *Journal for the Scientific Study of Religion, 40*, 691–705.

Hood, R. W., Jr., Hill, P. C., & Williamson, W. P. (2005). *The psychology of religious fundamentalism.* New York: Guilford.

Hood, R. W., Jr., Morris, R. J., & Watson, P. J. (1989). Prayer experience and religious orientation. *Review of Religious Research, 31*, 39–45.

Hood, R. W., Jr., Spilka, B., Hunsberger, B., & Gorsuch, R. (1996). *The psychology of religion: An empirical approach* (2nd ed.). New York: Guilford.

Hood, R., Jr., & Williamson, W. P. (2000). An empirical test of the unity thesis: The structure of mystical descriptors in various faith samples. *Journal of Psychology and Christianity, 19*, 232–244.

Hoover, S. M., Clark, L. S., & Rainie, L. (2004). *Faith online: 64% of wired Americans have used the Internet for spiritual or religious purposes.* Retrieved online on August 22, 2007 at http://www.pewinternet.org/pdfs/PIP_Faith_Online_2004.pdf.

Hopewell, J. (1987). *Congregation: Stories and structures.* Philadelphia: Fortress Press.

Hortacsu, N., & Cem-ersoy, N. (2005). Values, identities and social constructions of the European Union among Turkish university youth. *European Journal of Social Psychology, 35*, 107–121.

Horwtiz, A. (2002). *Creating mental illness.* Chicago: University of Chicago.

Horwitz, A., & Wakefield, J. (2007). *The loss of sadness: How psychiatry transformed normal sorrow into depressive disorder.* Oxford: Oxford University Press.

Houdek, F. (1996). *Guided by the Spirit: A Jesuit perspective on spiritual direction.* Chicago: Jesuit Way.

House, R. (2001). Psychopathology, psychosis and the kundalini: Postmodern perspectives on unusual subjective experience. In I. Clarke (Ed.), *Psychosis and spirituality: Exploring the new frontier* (pp. 107–127). London: Whurr.

Houtman, D., & Aupers, S. (2007). The spiritual turn and the decline of tradition: The spread of post-Christian spirituality in 14 Western countries, 1981–2000. *Journal for the Scientific Study of Religion, 46*, 305–320.

Howard, G. S., Youngs, W. H., & Siatczynski, A. M. (1989). A research strategy for studying telic human behavior. *The Journal of Mind and Behavior, 10*, 393–411.

Howard, N. C., McMinn, M. R., Bissell, L. D., Faries, S. R., & VanMeter, J. B. (2000). Spiritual directors and clinical psychologists: A comparison of mental health and spiritual values. *Journal of Psychology and Theology, 28*, 308–320.

Hudson, W. (1996). Jung on myth and the mythic. In R. Segal (Ed.), *Psychology and myth* (pp. 197–213). New York: Garland.

Hughes, C., & Plomin, R. (2000). Individual differences in early understanding of mind: Genes, non-shared environment and modularity. In P. Carruthers, & A. Chamberlain (Eds.), *Evolution and the human mind: Modularity, language and meta-cognition* (pp. 47–61). Cambridge: Cambridge University Press.

Hughes, G. W. (1991). Forgotten truths. In P. Sheldrake (Ed.), *The way of Ignatius Loyola: Contemporary approaches to the spiritual exercises* (pp. 28–37). St. Louis, MO: The Institute of Jesuit Sources.

Hughes, G. W. (1999). Is there a spirituality for the elderly? An Ingatian approach. In A. Jewell (Ed.), *Spirituality and ageing* (pp. 14–20). London: Jessica Kingsley.

Hume, D. (2001). *A treatise of human nature.* New York: Oxford University Press (Original work published 1739–1740).

Hummel, C., Rey, J.-C., & d'Epinay, C. (1995). Children's drawing of grandparents: A quantitative analysis of images. In M. Featerhstone, & A. Wernick (Eds.), *Images of aging: Cultural representations of later life* (pp. 149–170). London: Routledge.

Hummer, R. A., Rogers, R. G., Nam, C. B., & Ellison, C. G. (1999). Religious involvement and U.S. adult mortality. *Demography, 36*, 273–285.

Hunsberger, B. (1996). Religious fundamentalism, right-wing authoritarianism, and hostility toward homosexuals in non-Christian religious groups. *International Journal for the Psychology of Religion, 6*, 39–49.

Hunsberger, B., & Altemeyer, B. (2006). *Atheists: A groundbreaking study of America's nonbelievers.* Amherst, NY: Prometheus.

Hunsberger, B., Pratt, M., & Pancer, S. M. (2001). Religious versus nonreligious socialization: Does religious background have implications for adjustment? *International Journal for the Psychology of Religion, 11*, 105–128.

Hunt, H. T. (1989). The relevance of ordinary and non-ordinary states of consciousness for the cognitive psychology of meaning. *The Journal of Mind and Behavior, 10*, 347–359.

Hunt, H. T. (2003). *Lives in spirit: Precursors and dilemmas of a secular Western mysticism.* Albany, NY: State University of New York Press.

Hunter, H. (1998). Adolescent attraction to cults. *Adolescence, 33*(131), 709–714.

Hurlbut, W. B. (2002). Empathy, evolution, and altruism. In S. G. Post, L. G. Underwood, J. P. Schloss, & W. B. Hurlbut (Eds.), *Altruism & altruistic love: Science, philosophy, & religion in dialogue* (pp. 309–327). New York: Oxford University Press.

Hurlbut, W. B., & Kalanithi, P. (2001). Evolutionary theory and the emergence of moral nature. *Journal of Psychology and Theology, 29*, 330–339.

Hurwitz, B. (2004). The temporal construction of medical narratives. In B. Hurwitz, T. Greenhalgh, & V. Skultans (Eds.), *Narrative research in health and illness* (pp. 414–427). Malden, MA: Blackwell.

Hussain, F. A., & Cochrane, R. (2003). Living with depression: Coping strategies used by South Asian women, living in the UK, suffering from depression. *Mental Health, Religion & Culture, 6*, 21–45.

Husserl, E. (1970). *The crisis of European sciences and transcendental phenomenology* (D. Carr, Trans.). Evanston, IL: Northwestern University Press. (Original work published 1954).

Hustwit, J. R. (2007). Can models of God compete? *Philosophia, 35*, 433–439.

Huxley, A. (2004). *The perennial philosophy: An interpretation of the great mystics, East and West.* New York: Perennial Classics. (Original work published 1945).

Hyde, K. (1990). *Religion in childhood and adolescence: A comprehensive review of the research.* Birmingham, AL: Religious Education.

Iannaccone, L. R. (1990). Religious practice: A human capital approach. *Journal for the Scientific Study of Religion, 29*, 297–314.

Iannaccone, L. R. (1994). Why strict churches are strong. *American Journal of Sociology, 99*, 1180–1211.

Iannaccone, L. R. (1995a). Second thoughts: A response to Chaves, Demerath, and Ellison. *Journal for the Scientific Study of Religion, 34*, 113–120.

Iannaccone, L. R. (1995b). Voodoo economics? Reviewing the rational choice approach to religion. *Journal for the Scientific Study of Religion, 34*, 76–89.

Iannaccone, L. R. (1996). Strictness and strength revisited: Reply to Marwell. *American Journal of Sociology, 101*, 1103–1108.

Iannaccone, L. R. (1997a). Framework for the scientific study of religion. In L. A. Young (Ed.), *Rational choice theory and religion: Summary and assessment* (pp. 25–44). New York: Routledge.

Iannaccone, L. R. (1997b). Skewness explained: A rational choice model of religious giving. *Journal for the Scientific Study of Religion, 36*, 141–157.

Iannaccone, L. R., & Everton, S. F. (2004). Never on sunny days: Lessons from weekly attendance counts. *Journal for the Scientific Study of Religion, 43*, 191–207.

Idler, E. L. (1995). Religion, health, and nonphysical senses of self. *Social Forces, 74*, 683–704.

Idler, E. L., & Kasl, S. V. (1997a). Religion among disabled and nondisabled persons I: Cross-sectional patterns in health practices, social activities, and well-being. *Journal of Gerontology: Social Sciences, 52B*(6), S294–S305.

Idler, E. L., & Kasl, S. V. (1997b). Religion among disabled and nondisabled persons II: Attendance at religious services as a predictor of the course of disability. *Journal of Gerontology: Social Sciences, 52B(6)*, S306–S316.

Idler, E., Kasl, S., & Hays, J. (2001). Patterns of religious practice and belief in the last year of life. *Journal of Gerontology: Social Sciences, 56B(6)*, S326–S334.

Idler, E. L., Musick, M. A., Ellison, C. G., George, L. K., Krause, N., Ory, M. G., et al. (2003). Measuring multiple dimensions of religion and spirituality for health research: Conceptual background and findings from the 1998 general social survey. *Research on Aging, 25*, 327–365.

Ignatius, of Loyola Saint. (1978). *The Spiritual Exercises of Saint Ignatius Loyola* (L. Delmage, Trans.). Boston: Daughters of St. Paul.

Inagaki, H. (1995). *The three pure land sutras: A study and translation from Chinese.* Kyoto: Nagata Bunshodo.

Inayat, Q. (2001). The relationship between integrative and Islamic counseling. *Counselling Psychology Quarterly, 14*, 381–386.

Inge, W. R. (1910). *Faith and its psychology.* New York: Charles Scribner's Sons.

Ingersoll, R. E. (1994). Spirituality, religion, and counseling: Dimensions and relationships. *Counseling & Values, 38*, 98–111.

Ingersoll-Dayton, B., Krause, N., & Morgan, D. (2002). Religious trajectories and transitions over the life course. *International Journal of Aging and Human Development, 55*, 51–70.

Inglehart, R., & Klingemann, H.-D. (2000). Genes, culture, democracy, and happiness. In E. Diener, & E. M. Suh (Eds.), *Culture and subjective well-being* (pp. 165–183). Cambridge, MA: MIT Press.

Inglehart, R., & Welzel, C. (2005). *Modernization, cultural change, and democracy: The human development sequence.* Cambridge: Cambridge University Press.

Inhelder, B., & Piaget, J. (1958). *The growth of logical thinking from childhood to adolescence: An essay on the construction of formal operational structures* (A. Parsons, & S. Milgram, Trans.). New York: Basic Books.

Institute of Medicine. (2001). *Crossing the quality chasm: A new health system for the 21st century.* Washington, DC: National Academy Press.

Irenaeus. (2001). Against heresies. In P. Schaff (Ed.), *The Ante-Nicene Fathers, Volume 1: The apostolic fathers with Justin Martyr and Irenaeus* (pp. 513–954). Grand Rapids, MI: Eerdmans. (Original work written c. 185).

Irving, L. M., Snyder, C. R., Cheavens, J., Gravel, L., Hanke, J., Hilberg, P., et al. (2004). The relationships between hope and outcomes at the pretreatment, beginning, and later phases of psychotherapy. *Journal of Psychotherapy Integration, 14*, 419–443.

Irwin, R. (2002). *Human development and the spiritual life: How consciousness grows towards transformation.* New York: Kluwer/Academic Plenum.

Israel, E., & Beiman, I. (1977). Live versus recorded relaxation training: A controlled investigation. *Behavior Therapy, 8*, 251–254.

Ivens, M. (1991). The eighteenth annotation and the early directories. In P. Sheldrake (Ed.), *The way of Ignatius Loyola: Contemporary approaches to the spiritual exercises* (pp. 238–247). St. Louis, MO: The Institute of Jesuit Sources.

Ivens, M. (1998). *Understanding the spiritual exercises.* Leominster, UK: Gracewing.

Jackson, D., Mueller, C., Dolski, I., Dalton, K., Nitschke, J., & Urry, H., et al. (2003). Now you feel it, now you don't: Frontal brain electrical asymmetry and individual differences in emotion regulation. *Psychological Science, 14*, 612–617.

Jackson, M. (2001). Psychotic and spiritual experience: A case study comparison. In I. Clarke (Ed.), *Psychosis and spirituality: Exploring the new frontier* (pp.165–191).London: Whurr.

Jackson, M., & Fulford, K. W. M. (1997). Spiritual experience and psychopathology. *Philosophy, psychiatry & psychology: PPP, 4*, 41–65.

Jacobs, A. (2003). Afterward. In K. R. Chase, & A. Jacobs (Eds.), *Must Christianity be violent? Reflections on history, practice and theology* (pp. 224–235). Grand Rapids, MI: Brazos Press.

James, B., & Samuels, C. (1999). High stress life events and spiritual development. *Journal of Psychology and Theology, 27*, 250–260.

James, W. (1890). *The principles of psychology, Volume 1.* New York: Dover.

James, W. (1897). *The will to believe and other essays in popular philosophy.* New York: Longmans Green.

James, W. (1961). *The varieties of religious experience.* New York: Collier. (Original work published 1902).

James, W. (1996a). *Essays in radical empiricism.* Lincoln, NE: University of Nebraska Press. (Original work published 1912).

James, W. (1996b). *A pluralistic universe.* Lincoln, NE: University of Nebraska Press. (Original work published 1909).

James, W. (2003). *Pragmatism.* New York: Barnes & Noble. (Original work published 1907).

Janssen, J., de Hart, J., & den Draak, C. (1990). Praying as an individualized ritual. In H.-G. Heimbrock, & H. Boudewijnse (Eds.), *Current studies on rituals: Perspectives for the psychology of religion* (pp. 71–85). Amsterdam: Rodopi.

Jaspers, K. (1963). *General psychopathology, Volume I* (J. Hoenig, & M. Hamilton, Trans.). Baltimore: Johns Hopkins.

Jaspers, K. (1969). *Philosophy, Volume 1* (E. Ashton, Trans.). Chicago, IL: The University of Chicago Press. (Original work published 1932).

Jeeves, M. (1997). *Human nature at the millennium: Reflections on the integration of psychology and Christianity.* Grand Rapids, MI: Baker Books.

Jeeves, M. (1998). Brain, mind, and behavior. In W. S. Brown, N. Murphy, & H. N. Malony (Eds.), *Whatever happened to the soul? Scientific and theological portraits of human nature* (pp. 73–98). Minneapolis, MN: Fortress Press.

Jenkins, P. (1996). *Pedophiles and priests: Anatomy of a contemporary crisis.* New York: Oxford University Press.

Jensen, J. (2002). The complex worlds of religion: Connecting cultural and cognitive analysis. In I. Pyysiainen, & V. Anttonen (Eds.), *Current approaches in the cognitive science of religion* (pp. 203–228). London: Continuum.

Jensen, L. A. (2003). Coming of age in a multicultural world: Globalization and adolescent cultural identity formation. *Applied Developmental Science, 7*, 189–196.

Jenson, R. W. (1995). God, space, and architecture. In R. W. Jenson (Ed.), *Essays in theology of culture* (pp. 9–15). Grand Rapids, MI: Eerdmans.

Jenson, R. W. (1997). *Systematic theology, Volume I.* New York: Oxford University Press.

Jernigan, H. L. (2001). Spirituality in older adults: A cross-cultural and interfaith perspective. *Pastoral Psychology, 49*, 413–437.

Jessor, R., Turbin, M., & Costa, F. (1998). Protective factors in adolescent health behavior. *Journal of Personality and Social Psychology, 75*, 788–800.

Jevning, R., Anand, R., Biedebach, M., & Fernando, G. (1996). Effects on regional cerebral blood flow of transcendental meditation. *Physiology & Behavior, 59*, 399–402.

Jevning, R., Wallace, R. K., & Bieidebach, M. (1992). The physiology of meditation: A review. A wakeful hypometabolic integrated response. *Neuroscience and Biobehavioral Reviews, 16*, 415–424.

Johansen, T. M. (2005). Applying individual psychology to work with clients of the Islamic faith. *The Journal of Individual Psychology, 61*, 174–184.

John, Climacus St. (1979). *The ladder of divine ascent* (Rev. ed.). Boston, MA: Holy Transfiguration Monastery.

John of the Cross, St. (1973). *The collected works of St. John of the Cross* (K. Kavanaugh, & O. Rodriguez, Trans.). Washington, DC: Institute of Carmelite Studies.

Johnson, B., Jang, S., Larson, D., & Li, S. (2001). Does adolescent religious commitment matter? A reexamination of the effects of religiosity on delinquency. *Journal of Research in Crime and Delinquency, 38*, 22–44.

Johnson, C., & Boyatzis, C. (2006). Cognitive-cultural foundations of spiritual development. In E. Roehlkepartain, P. King, L. Wagener, & P. Benson (Eds.), *The handbook of spiritual development in childhood and adolescence* (pp. 211–223). Thousand Oaks, CA: Sage.

Johnson, E. L. (1996a). The call of wisdom: adult development within Christian community, part I: The crisis of modern theories of post formal development. *Journal of Psychology and Theology, 24,* 84–102.

Johnson, E. L. (1996b). The call of wisdom: Adult development within Christian community, Part II: Towards a covenantal constructivist model of post-formal development. *Journal of Psychology and Theology, 24,* 93–103.

Johnson, E. L. (1997). Christ, the Lord of psychology. *Journal of Psychology and Theology, 25,* 11–27.

Johnson, R. (2004). Psychoreligious roots of violence: The search for the concrete in a world of abstractions. In J. Ellens (Ed.), *The destructive power of religion: Violence in Judaism, Christianity and Islam, Volume 4: Contemporary views on spirituality and violence* (pp. 195–210). Westport, CT: Praeger.

Johnston, W. (1995). *Mystical theology: The science of love.* New York: HarperCollins.

Johnston, W. (1997). *Christian Zen* (3rd ed.). New York: Fordham University Press.

Jones, J. (1997). Playing and believing: The use of D.W. Winnicott in the psychology of religion. In J. Jacobs, & D. Capps (Eds.), *Religion, society, and psychoanalysis: Readings in contemporary theory* (pp. 106–126). Boulder, CO: Westview Press.

Jones, L. G. (1995a). *Embodying forgiveness: A theological analysis.* Grand Rapids, MI: Eerdmans.

Jones, L. G. (1995b). The psychological captivity of the church in the United States. In C. Braaten, & R. Jenson (Eds.), *Either/or: The Gospel or Neopaganism* (pp. 97–113). Grand Rapids, MI: Eerdmans.

Jones, R. (1993). *Mysticism examined: Philosophical inquiries into mysticism.* Albany, NY: State University of New York Press.

Jones, S. (1994). A constructive relationship for religion with the science and profession of psychology: Perhaps the boldest model yet. *American Psychologist, 49,* 184–199.

Jones, S. (1996). A constructive relationship for religion with the science and profession of psychology: Perhaps the boldest model yet. In E. Shafranske (Ed.), *Religion and the clinical practice of psychology* (pp. 113–147). Washington, DC: American Psychological Association.

Jones, S. (1997). Women's experience between a rock and a hard place: Feminist, womanist and mujerista theologies in North America. In R. S. Chopp, & S. G. Davaney (Eds.), *Horizons in feminist theology: Identity, tradition, and norms* (pp. 33–53). Minneapolis, MN: Fortress Press.

Jones, S. (2006). Integration: Defending it, describing it, doing it. *Journal of Psychology and Theology, 34,* 252–259.

Jones, S., & Butman, R. (1991). *Modern psychotherapies: A comprehensive Christian appraisal.* Downers Grove, IL: InterVarsity Press.

Jones, S., & Jones, L. G. (2003). Worship, the Eucharist, baptism, and aging. In S. Hauerwas, C. Stoneking, K. Meador, & D. Cloutier (Eds.), *Growing old in Christ* (pp. 185–201). Grand Rapids: Eerdmans.

Jonte-Pace, D. (1997). Julia Kristeva and the psychoanalytic study of religion: Rethinking Freud's cultural texts. In J. Jacobs, & D. Capps (Eds.), *Religion, society, and psychoanalysis: Readings in contemporary theory* (pp. 240–267). Boulder, CO: Westview Press.

Jonte-Pace, D. (1999). In defense of an unfriendly Freud: Psychoanalysis, feminism, and theology. *Pastoral Psychology, 47,* 175–181.

Jonte-Pace, D. (2006). New directions in the feminist psychology of religion. *Journal of Feminist Studies in Religion, 13,* 63–74.

Joseph, S., & Diduca, D. (2001). Schizotypy and religiosity in 13–18 year old school pupils. *Mental Health, Religion & Culture, 4,* 63–69.

Joseph, S., Smith, D., & Diduca, D. (2002). Religious orientation and its association with personality, schizotypal traits and manic-depressive experiences. *Mental Health, Religion & Culture, 5*, 73–81.

Jourdan, J. (1994). Near-death and transcendental experiences: Neurophysiological correlates of mystical traditions. *Journal of Near-Death Studies, 12*, 177–200.

Judy, D. H. (1996). Transpersonal psychology: Roots in Christian mysticism. In B. W. Scotton, A. B. Chinen, & J. R. Battista (Eds.), *Textbook of transpersonal psychiatry and psychology* (pp. 134–144). New York: BasicBooks.

Juergensmeyer, M. (2003). *Terror in the mind of God: The global rise of religious violence* (3rd ed.). Berkeley, CA: University of California Press. (Original work published 2000).

Jung, C. G. (1953). *The symbolic life: Miscellaneous writings* (R. Hull, Trans.). (Collected works, Volume 18). Princeton, NJ: Princeton University Press.

Jung, C. G. (1963). *Mysterium coniunctionis: An inquiry into the separation and synthesis of psychic opposites in alchemy* (R. F. C. Hull, Trans.). (Collected works, Volume 14). New York: Pantheon Books. (Original work published 1955–1956).

Jung, C. G. (1964). The spiritual problem of modern man. In R. F. C. Hull (Trans.), *Civilization in transition* (2nd ed., pp. 74–94). Princeton, NJ: Princeton University Press. (Original work published 1928).

Jung, C. G. (1966). *The spirit in man, art, and literature* (R. Hull, Trans.). (Collected works, Volume 15). Princeton NJ: Princeton University Press.

Jung, C. G. (1967a). *Symbols of transformation* (2nd ed., R. Hull, Trans.). (Collected works, Volume 5). Princeton, NJ: Princeton University Press.

Jung, C. G. (1967b). *Alchemical studies* (R. Hull, Trans.). (Collected works, Volume 13). Princeton, NJ: Princeton University Press.

Jung, C. G. (1967c). *Two essays on analytical psychology* (G. Adler, & R. F. C. Hull, Ed. & Trans.). (Collected works, Volume 7). Princeton, NJ: Princeton University Press.

Jung, C. G. (1968). *Psychology and alchemy* (R. Hull, Trans.). (Collected works, Volume 12). Princeton, NJ: Princeton University Press.

Jung, C. G. (1969a). *Aion: Researches into the phenomenology of the self* (2nd ed., R. Hull, Trans.). (Collected works, Volume 9b). Princeton, NJ: Princeton University Press.

Jung, C. G. (1969b). *The archetypes and the collective unconscious* (2nd ed., R. Hull, Trans.). (Collected works, Volume 9a). Princeton, NJ: Princeton University Press.

Jung, C. G. (1969c). *Psychology and religion: West and east* (2nd ed., R. Hull, Trans.) (Collected works, Volume 11). Princeton, NJ: Princeton University Press.

Jung, C. G. (1969d). The stages of life. In R. F. C. Hull (Trans.), *The structure and dynamics of the psyche* (2nd ed., pp. 387–403) (Collected works, Volume 8). Princeton, NJ: Princeton University Press. (Original work published 1930).

Jung, C. G. (1970). *Civilization in transition.* R. Hull, Trans. (Collected works, Volume 10). Princeton, NJ: Princeton University Press.

Jung, C. G. (1973). *Synchronicity: An acausal connecting principle* (2nd ed.). Princeton, NJ: Princeton University Press. (Original work published 1952).

Jung, C. G. (1975). Psychological commentary on Kundalini yoga: Lectures one and two. In *Spring: An annual of Jungian psychology and archetypal thought* (pp. 1–32). New York: Spring.

Jung, C. G. (1976). Psychological commentary on Kundalini yoga: Lectures three and four. In *Spring: An annual of Jungian psychology and archetypal thought* (pp. 1–31). New York: Spring.

Jung, C. G. (1977). Exercitia spiritualia of St. Ignatius of Loyola: Notes on Lectures. *Spring, 1977*, 183–200. (Original work published 1939).

Jung, C. G. (1978). Exercitia spiritualia of St. Ignatius of Loyola: Notes on lectures. *Spring, 1978*, 28–36. (Original work published 1939).

Jung, C. G. (1989). *Memories, dreams, reflections* (A. Jaffe, Ed., C. Winston, & R. Winston, Trans.). New York: Vintage. (Original work published 1963).

Jung, C. (2001). *Modern man in search of a soul* (2nd ed.). W. Dell, & C. Baynes, Trans. London: Routledge. (Original work published 1933).

Juthani, N. V. (1998). Understanding and treating Hindu patients. In H. Koenig (Ed.), *Handbook of religion and mental health* (pp. 271–278). San Diego, CA: Academic.

Juthani, N. V. (2001). Psychiatric treatment of Hindus. *International Review of Psychiatry, 13,* 125–130.

Kabat-Zinn, J. (2003a). Mindfulness-based interventions in context: Past, present, and future. *Clinical Psychology: Science and Practice, 10,* 144–156.

Kabat-Zinn, J. (2003b). Mindfulness-based stress reduction (MBSR). *Constructivism in the Human Sciences, 8,* 73–107.

Kabat-Zinn, J. (2005a). *Coming to our senses: Healing ourselves and the world through mindfulness.* New York: Hyperion.

Kabat-Zinn, J. (2005b). *Wherever you go, there you are: Mindfulness meditation in everyday life.* New York: Hyperion. (Original work published 1994).

Kabat-Zinn, J., Lipworth, L., & Burney, R. (1985). The clinical use of mindfulness meditation for the self-regulation of chronic pain. *Journal of Behavioral Medicine, 8,* 163–190.

Kabat-Zinn, J., Massion, A., Kristeller, J., Peterson, L., Fletcher, K., & Pbert, L., et al. (1992). Effectiveness of a meditation-based stress reduction program in the treatment of anxiety disorders. *American Journal of Psychiatry, 149,* 936–943.

Kabbani, M. (2004). *The Naqshbandi Sufi tradition guidebook of daily practices and devotions.* Washington, DC: Islamic Supreme Council of America.

Kadloubovsky, E., & Palmer, G. E. H. (Trans.). (1992). *Writings from the 'Philokalia' on prayer of the heart.* London: Faber and Faber. (Original work published 1951).

Kadri, N., Manoudi, F., Berrada, S., & Moussaoui, D. (2004). Stigma impact on Moroccan families of patients with schizophrenia. *The Canadian Journal of Psychiatry, 49,* 625–629.

Kaelber, W. (1995). Understanding asceticism--Testing a typology: Response to the three preceding papers. In V. Wimbush, & R. Valantasis (Eds.), *Asceticism* (pp. 320–328). New York: Oxford University Press.

Kahn, P. J., & Greene, A. L. (2004). "Seeing conversion whole": Testing a model of religious conversion. *Pastoral Psychology, 52,* 233–258.

Kakigi, R., Nakata, H., Inui, K., Hiroe, N., Nagata, O., Honda, M., et al. (2005). Intracerebral pain processing in a yoga master who claims not to feel pain during meditation. *European Journal of Pain, 9,* 581–589.

Kalam, T. (1980). The role of spiritual guides from a psychologist's point of view. *Journal of Dharma, 5,* 262–269.

Kalam, T. (1990). Popular devotions: A psychological approach. *Journal of Dharma, 15,* 204–211.

Kaldestad, E. (1996). Religious orientation, religious activity and mental health. In J. A. van Belzen, & J. M. van der Lans (Series Eds.) & H. Grzymala-Moszczynska, & B. Beit-Hallahmi (Vol. Eds.), *International series in the psychology of religion: Vol. 4. Religion, psychopathology, and coping* (pp. 209–224). Amsterdam: Rodopi.

Kaldor, P., Francis, L. J., & Fisher, J. W. (2002). Personality and spirituality: Christian prayer and eastern meditation are not the same. *Pastoral Psychology, 50,* 165–172.

Kallstad, T. (1987). The application of the religio-psychological role theory. *Journal for the Scientific Study of Religion, 26,* 367–374.

Kamilar, S. (2002). A Buddhist psychology. In R. Olson (Ed.), *Religious theories of personality and psychotherapy: East meets west* (pp. 85–140). New York: Haworth Press.

Kane, D., Cheston, S. E., & Greer, J. (1993). Perceptions of God by survivors of childhood sexual abuse: An exploratory study in an underresearched area. *Journal of Psychology and Theology, 21,* 228–237.

Kanin, E. J. (1985). Date rapists: Differential sexual socialization and relative deprivation. *Archives of Sexual Behavior, 14,* 291–231.

Kant, I. (1960). *Religion within the limits of reason alone.* New York: Harper and Row. (Original work published 1794).

Kant, I. (1965). *Critique of pure reason* (N. Smith, Trans.). New York: St. Martin's. (Original work published 1787).

Kant, I. (1987). *Critique of judgment*. Indianapolis, IN: Hackett. (Original work published 1790).

Kant, I. (2002). *Critique of practical reason*. Indianapolis, IN: Hackett. (Original work published 1788).

Kapleau, P. (1988). The private encounter with the master. In K. Kraft (Ed.), *Zen: Tradition and transition* (pp. 44–69). New York: Grove Press.

Karcher, S. (1999). Jung, the Tao, and the classic of change. *Journal of Religion and Health, 38,* 287–304.

Kärkkäinen, V.-M. (2002). *An introduction to ecclesiology: Ecumenical, historical & global perspectives*. Downers Grove, IL: InterVarsity Press.

Kärkkäinen, V.-M. (2004). *One with God: Salvation as deification and justification*. Collegeville, MN: Liturgical Press.

Kasamatsu, A., & Hirai, T. (1969). An electroencephalographic study on the Zen meditation (Zazen). *Psychologia: An International Journal of Psychology in the Orient, 12,* 205–225.

Kaskutas, L. E., Turk, N., Bond, J., & Weisner, C. (2003). The role of religion, spirituality and Alcoholics Anonymous in sustained sobriety. *Alcoholism Treatment Quarterly, 21,* 1–16.

Kass, J., & Lennox., S. (2004). Emerging models of spiritual development: A foundation for mature, moral, and heath-promoting behavior. In W. Miller, & H. Delaney (Eds.), *Judeo-Christian perspectives on psychology: Human nature, motivation, and change* (pp. 185–204). Washington, DC: American Psychological Association.

Kasser, T. (2002). *The high price of materialism*. Cambridge, MA: MIT Press.

Kasser, T. (2006). Materialism and its alternatives. In M. Czikszentmihalyi, & I. Czikszentmihalyi (Eds.), *A life worth living: Contributions to positive psychology* (pp. 200–214). New York: Oxford University Press.

Kasulis, T. (1992). Zen Buddhism, Freud, and Jung. In D. Meckel, & R. Moore (Eds.), *Self and liberation: The Jung-Buddhism dialogue* (pp. 143–165). New York: Paulist Press.

Katz, S. T. (1978). Language, epistemology, and mysticism. In S. T. Katz (Ed.), *Mysticism and philosophical analysis* (pp. 22–74). New York: Oxford University Press.

Katz, S. T. (1995). Imagining the life-span: From premodern miracles to postmodern fantasies. In M. Featherstone, & A. Wernick (Eds.), *Images of aging: Cultural representations of later life* (pp. 61–78). London: Routledge.

Kaviratna, H. (Trans.). (1980). *Dhammapada: wisdom of the Buddha*. Pasadena, CA: Theosophical University Press.

Kawai, H. (2002). What is I?: Reflections from Buddhism and psychotherapy. In P. Young-Eisendrath, & S. Muramoto (Eds.), *Awakening and insight: Zen Buddhism and psychotherapy* (pp. 135–148). New York: Taylor & Francis.

Kawai, N., Honda, M., Nakamura, S., Samatra, P., Sukardika, K., Nakatani, Y., et al. (2001). Catecholamines and opioid peptides increase in plasma in humans during possession trances. *Neuroreport, 12,* 3419–3423.

Kawamura, L. (1995). Mysticism in a Buddhist context. In D. Bishop (Ed.), *Mysticism and the mystical experience: East and West* (pp. 260–272). Selinsgrove, PA: Susquehanna University Press.

Kay, W., & Francis, L. (1996). *Drift from the churches: Attitude toward Christianity during childhood and adolescence*. Cardiff, Wales: University of Wales Press.

Kazdin, A. (2008). Evidence-based treatment and practice: New opportunities to bridge clinical research and practice, enhance the knowledge base, and improve patient care. *American Psychologist, 63,* 146–159.

Kazemipur, A., & Rezaei, A. (2003). Religious life under theocracy: The case of Iran. *Journal for the Scientific Study of Religion, 42,* 347–361.

Kearney, M. (1984). *World view*. Novato, CA: Chandler & Sharp.

Kearns, C. (2005). Irigaray's between east and west: Breath, pranayama, and the phenomenology of prayer. In B. Benson, & N. Wirzba (Eds.), *The phenomenology of prayer* (pp. 103–118). Bronx, NY: Fordham University Press.

Keating, T. (1992). *Open mind, open heart: The contemplative dimension of the gospel*. New York: Continuum. Original work published 1986).

Keating, T. (1995). *Invitation to love: The way of Christian contemplation.* New York: Continuum. (Original work published 1992).

Keenan, J. (2007). The limits of Thomas Merton's understanding of Buddhism. In B. Thurston (Ed.), *Merton & Buddhism: Wisdom, emptiness, and everyday mind* (pp. 118–133). Louisville, KY: Fons Vitae.

Keizan. (2002). *Transmission of light: Denkoroku* (T. Cleary, Trans.). Boston: Shambhala.

Keks, N., & D'Souza, R. (2003). Spirituality and psychosis. *Australasian Psychiatry, 11,* 170–171.

Kelcourse, F. B. (Ed.). (2004). *Human development and faith: Life-cycle stages of body, mind and soul.* St. Louis, MO: Chalice Press.

Keller, C. A. (1978). Mystical literature. In S. T. Katz (Ed.), *Mysticism and philosophical analysis* (pp. 75–100). New York: Oxford University Press.

Keller, C. (1997). Seeking and sucking: On relation and essence in feminist theology. In R. S. Chopp, & S. G. Davaney (Eds.), *Horizons in feminist theology: Identity, tradition, and norms* (pp. 54–78). Minneapolis, MN: Fortress Press.

Kelly, J. (1978). *Early Christian doctrines.* Rev. Ed. New York: Harper & Row.

Keltner, D., Gruenfeld, D., & Anderson, C. (2003). Power, approach, and inhibition. *Psychological Review, 110,* 265–284.

Keltner, D., & Haidt, J. (2003). Approaching awe, a moral, spiritual, and aesthetic emotion. *Cognition and Emotion, 17,* 297–314.

Kemp, C. (1947). *Physicians of the soul: A history of pastoral counseling.* New York: Macmillan.

Kendler, K. S., Gardner, C. O., & Prescott, C. A. (1997). Religion, psychopathology, and substance use and abuse: A multimeasure, genetic-epidemiological study. *The American Journal of Psychiatry, 154,* 322–329.

Kendler, K. S., Liu, X., Gardner, C. O., McCullough, M. E., Larson, D., & Prescott, C. A. (2003). Dimensions of religiosity and their relationship to lifetime psychiatric and substance use disorder. *The American Journal of Psychiatry, 160,* 496–503.

Kennedy, G. (1998). Religion and depression. In H. Koenig (Ed.), *Handbook of religion and mental health* (pp. 129–145). San Diego, CA: Academic Press.

Kennedy, G. J., Kelman, H. R., Thomas, C., & Chen, J. (1996). The relation of religious preference and practice to depressive symptoms among 1,855 older adults. *Journal of Gerontology: Psychological Sciences, 51B*(6), P301–P308.

Kennedy, P., & Drebing, C. E. (2002). Abuse and religious experience: A study of religiously committed evangelical adults. *Mental Health, Religion & Culture, 5,* 225–237.

Kenney, D. (2000). Psychological foundations of stress and coping: A developmental perspective. In D. Kenney, J. Carlson, F. J. McGuigan, & J. Sheppard (Eds.), *Stress and health: Research and clinical applications* (pp. 73–104). Amsterdam: Harwood Academic.

Kerestes, M., Youniss, J., & Metz, E. (2004). Longitudinal patterns of religious perspective and civic integration. *Applied Developmental Science, 8,* 39–46.

Ketelaar, T., & Ellis, B. J. (2000). Are evolutionary explanations unfalsifiable? Evolutionary psychology and the Lakatosian philosophy of science. *Psychological Inquiry, 11,* 1–21.

Keyes, C. L. M. (2002). The mental health continuum: From languishing to flourishing in life. *Journal of Health and Social Behavior, 43,* 207–222.

Keyes, C. L. M., & Lopez, S. J. (2002). Toward a science of mental health: Positive directions in diagnosis and interventions. In C. R. Snyder, & S. J. Lopez (Eds.), *Handbook of positive psychology* (pp. 45–59). Oxford: Oxford University Press.

Keyes, C. L M., Shmotkin, D., & Ryff, C. (2002). Optimizing well-being: The empirical encounter of two traditions. *Journal of Personality and Social Psychology, 82,* 1007–1022.

Khalili, S., Murken, S., Reich, K. H., Shah, A. A., & Vahabzadeh, A. (2002). Religion and mental health in cultural perspective: Observations and reflections after the first international congress on religion and mental health, Tehran, 16–19 April 2001. *The International Journal for the Psychology of Religion, 12,* 217–237.

Khong, B. (2003).The Buddha teaches an attitude, not an affiliation. In S. Segall (Ed.), *Encountering Buddhism: Western psychology and Buddhist teachings* (pp. 61–74). Albany, NY: State University of New York Press.

Khouzam, H. R. (1996). Prayer and the treatment of depression in a case of prostate cancer. *Clinical Gerontologist, 17*, 69–73.

Kiecolt-Glaser, J. K., & Glaser, R. (1995). Psychoneuroimmunology and health consequences: Data and shared mechanisms. *Psychosomatic Medicine, 57*, 269–274.

Kier, F., & Davenport, D. (2004). Unaddressed problems in the study of spirituality and health. *American Psychologist, 59*, 53–54.

Kilcourse, G. (2004). Thomas Merton's inclusive and engaged spirituality. *Perspectives in Religious Studies, 31*, 21–35.

Kim, D., Moon, Y., Kim, H., Jung, J., Park, H., Suh, H., et al. (2005). Effect of Zen meditation on serum nitric oxide activity and lipid peroxidation. *Progress in Neuro-Psychopharmacology and Biological Psychiatry, 29*, 327–331.

Kim, J. (2006). Emergence: Core ideas and issues. *Synthese, 151*, 547–559.

Kim, J., Stewart, R., Glozier, N., Prince, M., Kim, S., Yang, S., et al. (2005). Physical health, depression and cognitive function as correlates of disability in an older Korean population. *International Journal of Geriatric Psychiatry, 20*, 160–167.

Kimball, C. (2002). *When religion becomes evil.* New York: Harper Collins.

King, C. (2002). Embracing diversity in the mindfulness, diversity, and social change Sangha. In T. Hanh, & J. Lawlor (Ed.), *Friends on the path: Living spiritual communities* (pp. 215–223). Berkeley, CA: Parallax Press.

King, D. E., & Bushwick, B. (1994). Beliefs and attitudes of hospital inpatients about faith healing and prayer. *Journal of Family Practice, 39*, 349–352.

King, D. E., Cummings, D., & Whetstone, L. (2005). Attendance at religious services and subsequent mental health in midlife women. *International Journal of Psychiatry in Medicine, 35*, 287–297.

King, P., & Boyatzis, C. (2004). Exploring adolescent spiritual and religious development: Current and future theoretical and empirical perspectives. *Applied Developmental Science, 8*, 2–6.

King, P., & Furrow, J. L. (2004). Religion as a resource for positive youth development: Religion, social capital, and moral outcomes. *Developmental Psychology, 40*, 703–713.

King, V., Elder, G. H., Jr., & Whitbeck, L. B. (1997). Religious involvement among rural youth: An ecological and life-course perspective. *Journal of Research on Adolescence, 7*, 431–456.

King, W. (1980). *Theravada meditation: The Buddhist transformation of yoga.* University Park: PA: Pennsylvania State University Press.

Kings, S. (1997). Jung's hermeneutics of scripture. *The Journal of Religion, 77*, 233–251.

Kinney, J. M., Ishler, K. J., Pargament, K. I., & Cavanaugh, J. C. (2003). Coping with the uncontrollable: The use of general and religious coping by caregivers to spouses with dementia. *Journal of Religious Gerontology, 14*(2/3), 171–188.

Kinsley, D. (1995). *Health, healing, and religion: A cross-cultural perspective.* Upper Saddle River, NJ: Prentice Hall.

Kirby, S. E., Coleman, P. G., & Daley, D. (2004). Spirituality and well-being in frail and nonfrail older adults. *Journal of Gerontology: Psychological Sciences, 59B*(3), P123–P129.

Kirkpatrick, L. A. (1989). A psychometric analysis of the Allport-Ross and Feagin measures of intrinsic-extrinsic religious orientation. In M. Lynn, & D. Moberg (Eds.), *Research in the social scientific study of religion* (Vol. 1, pp. 1–30). Greenwich, CT: JAI Press.

Kirkpatrick, L. A. (1992). An attachment-theory approach to the psychology of religion. *The International Journal for the Psychology of Religion, 2*, 3–28.

Kirkpatrick, L. A. (1997). A longitudinal study of changes in religious belief and behavior as a function of individual differences in adult attachment style. *Journal for the Scientific Study of Religion, 36*, 207–217.

Kirkpatrick, L. A. (1998). God as a substitute attachment figure: A longitudinal study of adult attachment style and religious change in college students. *Personality and Social Psychology Bulletin, 24*, 961–973.

Kirkpatrick, L. A. (1999). Toward an evolutionary psychology of religion and personality. *Journal of Personality, 67*, 921–952.

Kirkpatrick, L. A. (2005). *Attachment, evolution, and the psychology of religion.* New York: Guilford.

Kirkpatrick, L. A., & Hood, R. W., Jr. (1990). Intrinsic-extrinsic religious orientation: The "boon" or "bane" of contemporary psychology of religion? *Journal for the Scientific Study of Religion, 29*, 442–462.

Kirkpatrick, L. A., & Shaver, P. R. (1990). Attachment theory and religion: Childhood attachments, religious beliefs, and conversions. *Journal for the Scientific Study of Religion, 29*, 315–334.

Kirkpatrick, L. A., & Shaver, P. R. (1992). An attachment-theoretical approach to romantic love and religious belief. *Personality and Social Psychology Bulletin, 18*, 266–275.

Kirov, G., Kemp, R., Kirov, K., & David, A. S. (1998). Religious faith after psychotic illness. *Psychopathology, 31*, 234–245.

Kirsh, G. A., & Kuiper, N. A. (2002). Individualism and relatedness themes in the context of depression, gender, and a self-schema model of emotion. *Canadian Psychology, 43*, 76–90.

Kisala, R. (2003). Japanese religiosity and morals. In L. Halman, & O. Riis (Eds.), *Religion in secularizing society: The Europeans' religion at the end of the 20th century* (pp. 205–222). Leiden: Brill.

Kistler, M. (2006). New perspectives on reduction and emergence in physics, biology and psychology. *Synthese, 151*, 311–312.

Kjaer, T. W., Bertelsen, C., Piccini, P., Brooks, D., Alving, J., & Lou, H. C. (2002). Increased dopamine tone during meditation-induced change of consciousness. *Cognitive Brain Research, 13*, 255–259.

Klaassen, D. W., & McDonald, M. J. (2002). Quest and identity development: Re-examining pathways for existential search. *The International Journal for the Psychology of Religion, 12*, 189–200.

Kliger, R. (1994). Somatization: Social control and illness production in a religious cult. *Culture, Medicine and Psychiatry, 18*, 215–245.

Klinger, E. (1998). The search for meaning in evolutionary perspective and its clinical implications. In P. Wong, & P. Fry (Eds.), *The human quest for meaning: A handbook of psychological research and clinical applications* (pp. 27–50). Mahwah, NJ: Lawrence Erlbaum.

Kloos, B., Horneffer, K., & Moore, T. (1995). Before the beginning: Religious leaders' perceptions of the possibility for mutually beneficial collaboration with psychologists. *Journal of Community Psychology, 23*, 275–291.

Klostermaier, K. (2000a). *Hinduism: A short history.* Oxford: Oneworld.

Klostermaier, K. (2000b). *Hindu writings: A short introduction to the major sources.* Oxford: Oneworld.

Kneezel, T., & Emmons, R. (2006). The relation between spiritual development and identity processes. In E. Roehlkepartain, P. King, L. Wagener, & P. Benson (Eds.), *The handbook of spiritual development in childhood and adolescence* (pp. 266–278). Thousand Oaks, CA: Sage.

Knight, J., Sherritt, L., Harris, S. K., Holder, D., Kulig, J., & Shrier, L., et al. (2007). Alcohol use and religiousness/spirituality among adolescents. *Southern Medical Journal, 100*, 349–355.

Knox, S., Virginia, S. G., & Lombardo, J. P. (2002). Depression and anxiety in Roman Catholic secular clergy. *Pastoral Psychology, 50*, 345–359.

Koch, S. (1992). Foreword: Wundt's creature at age zero-and as centenarian: Some aspects of the institutionalization of the "new psychology." In S. Koch & D. E. Leary (Eds.), *A century of psychology as science* (pp. 7–35). Washington, DC: American Psychological Association. (Original work published 1985).

Kocher, P. H. (1953). *Science and religion in Elizabethan England.* San Marino, CA: The Huntington Library.

Koenig, H. G. (1994). *Aging and God: Spiritual pathways to mental health in midlife and later years.* New York: Hayworth.

Koenig, H. G. (1995). Religion as cognitive schema. *The International Journal for the Psychology of Religion, 5*, 31–37.

Koenig, H. G. (2000). Religion and medicine I: Historical background and reasons for separation. *International Journal of Psychiatry in Medicine, 30*, 385–398.

Koenig, H. G. (2001a). Religion and medicine II: Religion, mental health, and related behaviors. *International Journal of Psychiatry in Medicine, 31*, 97–109.

Koenig, H. G. (2001b). Religion and medicine IV: Religion, physical health, and clinical implications. *International Journal of Psychiatry in Medicine, 31*, 321–336.

Koenig, H. G. (2002). *Spirituality in patient care: Why, how, when, and what.* Philadelphia: Templeton Foundation.

Koenig, H. G. (2003). Health care and faith communities: How are they related? *Journal of General Internal Medicine, 18*, 962–963.

Koenig, H. G. (2006). Religion, spirituality and aging. *Aging & Mental Health, 10*, 1–3.

Koenig, H. G., Cohen, H. J., Blazer, D. G., Kudler, H. S., Krishnan, K. R., & Sibert, T. E. (1995). Religious coping and cognitive symptoms of depression in elderly medical patients. *Psychosomatics, 36*, 369–375.

Koenig, H. G., Cohen, H. J., Blazer, D. G., Pieper, C., Meador, K. G., Shelp, F., et al. (1992). Religious coping and depression among elderly, hospitalized medically ill men. The American Journal of Psychiatry, 149, 1693–1700.

Koenig, H. G., George, L. K., & Peterson, B. L. (1998). Religiosity and remission of depression in medically ill older patients. *The American Journal of Psychiatry, 155*, 536–542.

Koenig, H. G., George, L. K., & Titus, P. (2004). Religion, spirituality, and health in medically ill hospitalized older patients. *Journal of the American Geriatrics Society, 52*, 554–562.

Koenig, H. G., Hays, J. C., Larson, D. B., George, L. K., Cohen, H. J., McCullough, M. E., et al. (1999). Does religious attendance prolong survival? A six-year follow-up study of 3,968 older adults. *Journal of Gerontology: Medical Sciences, 54A*(7), M370–M376.

Koenig, H. G., Idler, E., Kasl, S., Hays, J. C., George, L. K., Musick, M., et al. (1999). Religion, spirituality and medicine: A rebuttal to skeptics. *International Journal of Psychiatry in Medicine, 29*, 123–131.

Koenig, H. G., & Larson, D. B. (2001). Religion and mental health: Evidence for an association. *International Review of Psychiatry, 13*, 67–78.

Koenig, H., Lawson, D., & McConnell, M. (2004). *Faith in the future: Healthcare, aging, and the role of religion.* Philadelphia: Templeton Foundation.

Koenig, H. G., McCullough, M. E., & Larson, D. B. (2001). *Handbook of religion and health.* Oxford: Oxford University Press.

Koerner, K., & Linehan, M. (2000). Research on dialectical behavior therapy for patients with borderline personality disorder. *Psychiatric Clinics of North America, 23*, 151–167.

Kohlberg, L. (1981). *The philosophy of moral development: Moral stages and the idea of justice. Essays on moral development, Volume I.* San Francisco: Harper & Row.

Kohlberg, L. (1982). Moral development. In J. Broughton, & D. Freeman-Moir (Eds.), *The cognitive-developmental theory of James Mark Baldwin: Current theory and research in genetic epistemology* (pp. 277–325). Norwood, NJ: Ablex.

Kohlberg, L. (1984). *The psychology of moral development: The nature and validity of moral stages. Essays on moral development, Volume II.* San Francisco: Harper & Row.

Kohlberg, L., & Ryncarz, R. (1990). Beyond justice reasoning: Moral development and consideration of a seventh stage. In C. Alexander, & E. Langer (Eds.), *Higher stages of human development: Perspectives on adult growth* (pp. 191–225). New York: Oxford University Press.

Kojetin, B. A., McIntosh, D. N., Bridges, R. A., & Spilka B. (1987). Quest: Constructive search or religious conflict? *Journal for the Scientific Study of Religion, 26*, 111–115.

Konstam, V., Holmes, W., & Levine, B. (2003). Empathy, selfism, and coping as elements of the psychology of forgiveness: A preliminary study. *Counseling and Values, 47*, 172–183.

Kopp, S. (1971). *Guru metaphors from a psychotherapist.* Palo Alto, CA: Science and Behavior Books.

Kornfield, J. (1979). Intensive insight meditation: A phenomenological study. *The Journal of Transpersonal Psychology, 11*, 41–58.

Korotkov, D. (1998). The sense of coherence: Making sense out of chaos. In P. Wong, & P. Fry (Eds.), *The human quest for meaning: A handbook of psychological research and clinical applications* (pp. 51–70). Mahwah, NJ: Lawrence Erlbaum.

Kose, A., & Loewenthal, K. M. (2000). Conversion motifs among British converts to Islam. *International Journal for the Psychology of Religion, 10*, 101–110.

Kosek, R. B. (1996). The contribution of object relations theory in pastoral counseling. *The Journal of Pastoral Care, 50*, 371–381.

Koss-Chioino, J. D. (2003). Jung, spirits and madness: Lessons for cultural psychiatry. *Transcultural Psychiatry, 40*, 164–180.

Koteskey, R. L., Little, M., & Matthews, M. (1991). Adolescent identity and depression. *Journal of Psychology and Christianity, 10*, 48–53.

Koteskey, R. L., Walker, J. S., & Johnson, A. W. (1990). Measurement of identity from adolescence to adulthood: Cultural, community, religious, and family factors. *Journal of Psychology and Theology, 18*, 54–64.

Kotre, J., & Kotre, K. (1998). Intergenerational buffers: "The damage stops here." In D. McAdams, & E. de St. Aubin (Eds.), *Generativity and adult development: How and why we care for the next generation* (pp. 367–390). Washington, DC: American Psychological Association.

Kotsch, W. E. (2000). Jung's mediatory science as a psychology beyond objectivism. *Journal of Analytical Psychology, 45*, 217–244.

Koyre, A. (1965). *Newtonian studies*. Cambridge, MA: Harvard University Press.

Kraft, K. (1988). Recent developments in North American Zen. In K. Kraft (Ed.), *Zen: Tradition and transition* (pp. 178–198). New York: Grove Press.

Kraus, D. (1999). Psychological studies of new religious movements: Findings from German-speaking countries. *International Journal for the Psychology of Religion, 9*, 263–281.

Krause, M., Chatters, L., Meltzer, T., & Morgan, D. (2000). Using focus groups to explore the nature of prayer in late life. *Journal of Aging Studies, 14*, 191–212.

Krause, N. (2002). Church-based social support and health in old age: Exploring variations by race. *Journal of Gerontology: Social Sciences, 57B*(6), S332–S347.

Krause, N. (2003). Religious meaning and subjective well-being in late life. *Journal of Gerontology: Social Sciences, 58B*(3), S160–S170.

Krause, N. (2006). Church-based social support and mortality. *Journal of Gerontology: Social Sciences, 61B*(3), S140–S146.

Krause, N. (2007). Social involvement in religious institutions and God-mediated control beliefs: A longitudinal investigation. *Journal for the Scientific Study of Religion, 46*, 519–537.

Krause, N., Ellison, C. G., & Wulff, K. M. (1998). Church-based emotional support, negative interaction, and psychological well-being: Findings from a national sample of Presbyterians. *Journal for the Scientific Study of Religion, 37*, 725–741.

Krause, N., Liang, J., Shaw, B. A., Sugisawa, H., Kim, H., & Sugihara, Y. (2002). Religion, death of a loved one, and hypertension among older adults in Japan. *Journal of Gerontology: Social Sciences, 57B*(2), S96–S107.

Krause, N., & Tran, T. V. (1989). Stress and religious involvement among older Blacks. *Journal of Gerontology: Social Sciences, 44*(1), S4–S13.

Krauss, S. W., & Flaherty, R. W. (2001). The effects of tragedies and contradictions on religion as a quest. *Journal for the Scientific Study of Religion, 40*, 113–122.

Krebs, D. (2005).The evolution of morality. In D. Buss (Ed.), *The handbook of evolutionary psychology* (pp. 747–775). Hoboken, NJ: John Wiley & Sons.

Kreidie, H. (2004). Religion and identity: Deciphering and construals of Islamic fundamentalism. In K. Hoover (Ed.), *The future of identity: Centennial reflections on the legacy of Erik Erikson* (pp. 137–165). Lanham, MD: Lexington Books.

Kreitler, S., & Kreitler, H. (1991). Cognitive orientation and physical disease or health. *European Journal of Personality, 5*, 109–129.

Kristensen, K. B., Pedersen, D. M., & Williams, R. N. (2001). Profiling religious maturity: The relationship of religious attitude components to religious orientations. *Journal for the Scientific Study of Religion, 40*, 75–86.

Kristeva, J. (1987). *In the beginning was love: Psychoanalysis and faith* (A. Goldhammer, Trans.). New York: Columbia University Press.

Kruger, D. J. (2002). The deconstruction of constructivism. *American Psychologist, 57*(6–7), 456–457.

Kuhn, T. (1996). *The structure of scientific revolutions* (3rd ed.). Chicago: University of Chicago Press. (Original work published 1962).

Kulik, A., & Szewczyk, L. (2002). Sense of meaning of life and the emotional reaction among young people pursuing different types of meditation. *Studia Psychologica, 44*, 155–166.

Kumar, K. G., & Ali, M. H. (2002). Mediation: A harbinger of subjective well-being. *Journal of Personality and Personal Studies, 19*, 93–102.

Kunkel, M. A., Cook, S., Meshel, D., Daughtry, D., & Hauenstein, A. (1999). God images: A concept map. *Journal for the Scientific Study of Religion, 38*, 193–202.

Kunnen, E. S., & Wassinck, M. E. K. (2003). An analysis of identity change in adulthood. *Identity: An International Journal of Theory and Research, 3*, 347–366.

Kurtz, E., & Ketcham, K. (1992). *The spirituality of imperfection: Storytelling and the search for meaning.* New York: Bantam Books.

Kurup, R. K., & Kurup, P. A. (2003). Hypothalamic digoxin, hemispheric chemical dominance, and spirituality. *International Journal of Neuroscience, 113*, 383–393.

Kutz, I., Borysenko, J. Z., & Benson, H. (1985). Meditation and psychotherapy: A rationale for the integration of dynamic psychotherapy, the relaxation response, and mindfulness meditation. *American Journal of Psychiatry, 142*, 1–8.

Labouvie-Vief, G. (1996). Emotion, thought, and gender. In C. Magai, & S. H. McFadden (Eds.), *Handbook of emotion, adult development, and aging* (pp. 101–117). San Diego, CA: Academic Press.

Lad, V. M. A. Sc. (2002). *Textbook of Ayurveda: fundamental principles.* Albuquerque, New Mexico: Ayurvedic Press.

Ladd, K. L., McIntosh, D., & Spilka, B. (1998). Children's God concepts: Influences of denomination, age, and gender. *The International Journal for the Psychology of Religion, 8*, 49–56.

Ladd, K. L., & Spilka, B. (2002). Inward, outward and upwards: Cognitive aspects of prayer. *Journal for the Scientific Study of Religion, 41*, 475–484.

Ladd, K. L., & McIntosh, D. (2008). Meaning, god, and prayer: Physical and metaphysical aspects of social support. *Mental Health, Religion & Culture, 11*, 23–38.

Laidlaw, J. (2004a). Introduction. In H. Whitehouse, & J. Laidlaw (Eds.), *Ritual and memory: Toward a comparative anthropology of religion* (p. 19). Walnut Creek, CA: AltaMira.

Laidlaw, J. (2004b). Embedded modes of religiosity in Indic renouncer religions. In H. Whitehouse, & J. Laidlaw (Eds.), *Ritual and memory: Toward a comparative anthropology of religion* (pp. 89–109). Walnut Creek, CA: AltaMira.

Laird, S. P., Snyder, C. R., Rapoff, M. A., & Green, S. (2004). Measuring private prayer: Development, validation, and clinical application of the multidimensional prayer inventory. *The International Journal for the Psychology of Religion, 14*, 251–272.

Lakatos, I. (1978). *The methodology of scientific research programmes: Philosophical papers, Volume 1* (J. Worrall, & G. Currie, Eds.), Cambridge: Cambridge University Press.

Lam, P.-Y. (2002). As the flocks gather: How religion affects voluntary association participation. *Journal for the Scientific Study of Religion, 41*, 405–422.

Lamb, S. (2005). Forgiveness therapy: The context and conflict. *Journal of Theoretical and Philosophical Psychology, 25*, 61–80.

Lambert, C., & Kurpius, S. (2004). Relationship of gender role identity and attitudes with images of God. In R. Dayringer, & D. Oler (Eds.), *The image of God and the psychology of religion* (pp. 55–75). New York: Haworth Pastoral.

LaMothe, R. (1999). Faith as a vital concern in human development: Structuring subjectivity and intersubjectivity. *Journal of Psychology and Theology, 27*, 230–240.

Lampton, C., Oliver, G. J., Worthington, E. L., Jr., & Berry, J. W. (2005). Helping Christian college students become more forgiving: An intervention study to promote forgiveness as part of a program to shape Christian character. *Journal of Psychology and Theology, 33,* 278–290.

Lane, R. (2001). *The loss of happiness in market democracies.* New Haven: Yale University Press.

Lange, R., & Thalbourne, M. (2007). The Rasch scaling of mystical experiences: Construct validity and correlates of the Mystical Experience Scale (MES). *International Journal for the Psychology of Religion, 17,* 121–140.

Langer, E., Chanowitz, B., Palmerino, M., Jacobs, S., Rhodes, M., & Thayer, P. (1990). Non-sequential development and aging. In C. Alexander, & E. Langer (Eds.), *Higher stages of human development* (pp. 3–32). New York: Oxford University Press.

Langer, E., & Moldoveanu, M. (2000a). The construct of mindfulness. *Journal of Social Issues, 56*(1), 1–9.

Langer, E., & Moldoveanu, M. (2000b). Mindfulness research and the future. *Journal of Social Issues, 56*(1), 129–139.

Langer, N. (2004). Resiliency and spirituality: Foundations of strengths perspective counseling with the elderly. *Educational Gerontology, 30,* 611–617.

Langer, R. (2005). Seeing with clarity: Defining the supervision task. In M. R. Bumpus, & R. B. Langer (Eds.), *Supervision of spiritual directors: Engaging in holy mystery* (pp. 33–46). Harrisburg, PA: Morehouse.

Larchet, J.-C. (2005). *Mental disorders and spiritual healing: Teachings from the early Christian East* (R. P. Coomaraswamy, & G. J. Champoux, Trans.). Hillsdale, NY: Sophia Perennis.

Larsen, E. (2000). *Wired churches, wired temples: Taking congregations and missions into cyberspace.* Washington, DC: Pew Internet & American Life Project. Retrieved August 22, 2006 from http://www.pewinternet.org/PPF/r/28/report_display.asp.

Larsen, E. (2004). Cyberfaith: How Americans pursue religion online. In L. Dawson, & D. Cowan (Eds.), *Religion online: Finding faith on the Internet* (pp. 17–20). New York: Routledge.

Larsen, E., & Rainie, L. (2001). *CyberFaith: How Americans pursue religion online.* Washington, DC: Pew Internet & American Life Project. Retrieved August 22, 2006 from www.pewinternet.org/pdfs/PIP_CyberFaith_Report.pdf.

Larson, C., Nitschke, J., & Davidson, R. (2007). Common and distinct patterns of affective response in dimensions of anxiety and depression. *Emotion, 7,* 182–191.

Larson, D. B., Hohmann, A. A., Kessler, L. G., Meador, K. G., Boyd, J. H., & McSherry, E. (1988). The couch and the cloth: The need for linkage. *Hospital and Community Psychiatry, 39,* 1064–1069.

Larson, D. B., & Larson, S. S. (2003). Spirituality's potential relevance to physical and emotional health: A brief review of quantitative research. *Journal of Psychology and Theology, 31,* 37–51.

Larson, D. B., Sherrill, K., Lyons, J., Craigie, F., Thielman, S. Greenwold, M., et al. (1992). Associations between dimensions of religious commitment and mental health reported in the *American Journal of Psychiatry* and *Archives of General Psychiatry:* 1978–1989. *American Journal of Psychiatry, 149,* 557–559.

Larson, E., & Witham, L. (1998). Leading scientists still reject God. *Nature, 394,* 313.

Larson, R. W., & Verma, S. (1999). How children and adolescents spend time across the world:

Lash, N. (1996). *The beginning and the end of 'religion'.* Cambridge: Cambridge University Press.

Laski, M. (1962). *Ecstasy: A study of some secular and religious experiences.* Bloomington, IN: Indiana University Press.

Latourette, K. (1975a). *A history of Christianity: Volume I: Beginnings to 1500* (Rev. ed.). New York: Harper & Row.

Latourette, K. (1975b). *A history of Christianity: Volume II: Reformation to the present* (Rev. ed.). New York: Harper & Row.

Lau, M. Y. (2002). Postmodernism and the values of science. *American Psychologist, 57,* 1126.

Laughlin, C. D., Jr., McManus, J., & d'Aquili, E. G. (1993). Mature contemplation. *Zygon, 28,* 133–176.

Laungani, P. (2005). Hindu spirituality and healing practices. In R. Moodley, & W. West (Eds.), *Integrating traditional healing practices into counseling and psychotherapy* (pp. 138–147). Thousand Oaks, CA: Sage.

Laurencelle, R. M., Abell, S. C., & Schwartz, D. J. (2002). The relation between intrinsic religious faith and psychological well-being. *The International Journal for the Psychology of Religion, 12*, 109–123.

Lawlor, J. (2002a). Introduction. In T. Hanh, & J. Lawlor (Ed.), *Friends on the path: Living spiritual communities* (pp. 1–6). Berkeley, CA: Parallax.

Lawlor, J. (2002b). Sharing the path: An overview of lay Sangha practice. In T. Hanh, & J. Lawlor (Ed.), *Friends on the path: Living spiritual communities* (pp. 51–86). Berkeley, CA: Parallax.

Lawlor, J. (2002c). Walking on ice. In T. Hanh, & J. Lawlor (Ed.), *Friends on the path: Living spiritual communities* (pp. 159–164). Berkeley, CA: Parallax.

Lawrence, P. (1965). Children's thinking about religion: A study of concrete operational thinking. *Religious Education, 60*, 111–116.

Lawson, R., Drebing, C., Berg, G., Vincellette, A., & Penk, W. (1998). The long term impact of child abuse on religious behavior and spirituality in men. *Child Abuse and Neglect, 22*, 369–380.

Lawton, M. P. (1996). Quality of life and affect in later life. In C. Magai, & S. H. McFadden (Eds.), *Handbook of emotion, adult development, and aging* (pp. 327–348). San Diego, CA: Academic Press.

Lax, W. (1996). Narrative, social contructionism, and Buddhism. In H. Rosen, & K. Kuehlwein (Eds.), *Constructing realities: Meaning-making perspectives for psychotherapists* (pp. 195–220). San Francisco, CA: Jossey-Bass.

Lazar, A. (2004). Cultural influences on religious experience and motivation. *Review of Religious Research, 46*, 64–71.

Lazar, A., & Kravetz, S. (2005a). A motivational systems theory approach to the relation between religious experiences and religious motives. *The International Journal for the Psychology of Religion, 15*, 63–72.

Lazar, A., & Kravetz, S. (2005b). Responses to the mystical scale by religious Jewish persons: A comparison of structural models of mystical experience. *The International Journal for the Psychology of Religion, 15*, 51–61.

Lazar, A., Kravetz, S., & Frederich-Kedem, P. (2002). The multidimensionality of motivation for Jewish religious behavior: Content, structure, and relationship to religious identity. *Journal for the Scientific Study of Religion, 41*, 500–519.

Lazar, S. W. (2005). Mindfulness research. In C. K. Germer, R. D. Siegel, & P. R. Fulton (Eds.), *Mindfulness and psychotherapy* (pp. 220–238). New York: Guilford Press.

Lazarus, R. S. (1993). Coping theory and research: Past, present, and future. *Psychosomatic Medicine, 55*, 234–247.

Leahey, T. (1987). *A history of psychology: Main currents in psychological thought*. Englewood Cliffs, NJ: Prentice-Hall. (Original work published 1980).

Leahey, T. (2002). History without the past. In W. E. Pickren, & D. A. Dewsbury (Eds.), *Evolving perspectives on the history of psychology* (pp. 15–20). Washington, DC: American Psychological Association. (Original work published 1986).

Leak, G. K., Gardner, L. E., & Parsons, C. J. (1998). Jealousy and romantic attachment: A replication and extension. *Representative Research in Social Psychology, 22*, 21–27.

Leary, D. (2003). A profound and radical change: How William James inspired the reshaping of American psychology. In R. J. Sternberg (Ed.), *The anatomy of impact: What makes the great works of psychology great* (pp. 19–42). Washington, DC: American Psychological Association.

Leas, R., & Thomas, J. (2005). *A brief history of the Association for Clinical Pastoral Education*. Retrieved May 30, 2006 from http://www.acpe.edu/cpehistory.htm#acpe.

Leavy, S. A. (1995). Roots of unitive experience. *The Psychoanalytical Review, 82*, 349–370.

Leder, D. (1996). Spiritual community in later life: A modest proposal. *Journal of Aging Studies, 10*, 103–116.

LeDoux, J. (2002). *Synaptic self: How our brains become who we are*. New York: Viking.

Lee, C. (2004). Agency and purpose in narrative therapy: Questioning the postmodern rejection of metanarrative. *Journal of Psychology and Theology, 32*, 221–231.

Lee, S. (2002). In a secular spirit: Strategies of clinical pastoral education. *Health Care Analysis, 10*, 339–356.

Leech, K. (2001). *Soul friend: Spiritual direction in the modern world.* Harrisburg, PA: Morehouse.

LeFevre, P. (1968). The snare of truth. In P. Homans (Ed.), *The dialogue between theology and psychology* (pp. 33–52). Chicago: University of Chicago Press.

Leffert, N., Benson, P. L., Scales, P. C., Sharma, A. R., Drake, D. R., & Blyth, D. A. (1998). Developmental assets: Measurement and prediction of risk behaviors among adolescents. *Applied Development Science, 2*, 209–230.

Leggett, T. (1981). *Sankara on the Yoga-sutra-a (Vol. I: Samadhi).* London: Routledge & Kegan Paul.

Lerner, R., & von Eye, A. (1992). Sociobiology and human development: Arguments and evidence. *Human Development, 35*, 12–33.

Leserman, J., Stuart, E. M., Mamish, M. E., & Benson, H. (1989). The efficacy of the relaxation response in preparing for cardiac surgery. *Behavioral Medicine, 15*, 111–117.

Leuba, J. H. (1912). *A psychological study of religion: Its origin, function and future.* New York: Macmillan.

Leuba, J. H. (1925). *The psychology of religious mysticism.* New York: Harcourt, Brace.

Levenson, M. R., & Crumpler, C. A. (1996). Three models of adult development. *Human Development, 39*, 135–149.

Levin, J. S. (1994). Religion and health: Is there an association, is it valid, and is it causal? *Social Science & Medicine, 38*, 1475–1482.

Levin, J. S. (1996). How religion influences morbidity and health: Reflections on natural history, salutogenesis, and host resistance. *Social Science & Medicine, 43*, 849–864.

Levin, J. S. (2001). *God, faith, and health: Exploring the spirituality-healing connection.* New York: John Wiley & Sons.

Levin, J. S. (2002). Is depressed affect a function of one's relationship with God? Findings from a study of primary care patients. *International Journal of Psychiatry in Medicine, 32*, 379–393.

Levin, J. S. (2003). Spiritual determinants of health and healing: An epidemiological perspective on salutogenic mechanisms. *Alternative Therapies, 9*, 48–57.

Levin, J. S., & Chatters, L. M. (1998). Religion, health, and psychological well-being in older adults: Findings from three national surveys. *Journal of Aging and Health, 10*, 504–531.

Levin, J. S., Chatters, L., & Taylor, R. (2005). Religion, health and medicine in African Americans: Implications for physicians. *Journal of the National Medical Association, 97*, 237–249.

Levin, J. S., & Markides, K. S. (1985). Religion and health in Mexican Americans. *Journal of Religion and Health, 24*, 60–69.

Levin, J. S., Markides, K. S., & Ray, L. A. (1996). Religious attendance and psychological well-being in Mexican Americans: A panel analysis of three-generations data. *The Gerontologist, 36*, 454–463.

Levin, J. S., & Taylor, R. J. (1998). Panel analyses of religious involvement and well-being in African Americans: Contemporaneous vs. longitudinal effects. *Journal for the Scientific Study of Religion, 37*, 695–709.

Levin, J. S., & Vanderpool, H. (1989). Is religion therapeutically significant for hypertension? *Social Science & Medicine, 29*, 69–78.

Levinas, E. (1969). *Totality and infinity: An essay on exteriority* (New ed., A. Lingis, Trans.). Pittsburgh, PA: Duquesne University Press.

Levinas, E. (1998). *Otherwise than being: Or beyond essence* (R. A. Cohen, Trans.). Pittsburgh, PA: Duquesne University Press.

Levinson, D. (1978). *The seasons of a man's life.* New York: Ballantine.

Levinson, D. (1996). *The seasons of a woman's life.* New York: Knopf.

Levi-Strauss, C. (1963). *Structural anthropology* (C. Jacobson, & B. Schoepf, Trans.). New York: Basic.

Levitt, P. (2007). Redefining the boundaries of belonging: The transnationalization of religious life. In N. T. Ammerman (Ed.), *Everyday religion: Observing modern religious lives* (pp. 103–120). Oxford: Oxford University Press.

Levy, L. H. (2000). Self-help groups. In J. Rappaport, & E. Seidman (Eds.), *Handbook of community psychology* (pp. 591–613). New York: Kluwer Academic/Plenum.

Levy, K. M., & Blatt, S. J. (1999). Attachment theory and psychoanalysis: Further differentiation within insecure attachment pattern. *Psychoanalytic Inquiry, 19*, 541–575.

Lewis, C. A. (2002). Church attendance and happiness among northern Irish undergraduate students: No association. *Pastoral Psychology, 50*, 191–195.

Lewis, C. A., & Cruise, S. M. (2006). Religion and happiness: Consensus, contradictions, comments and concerns. *Mental Health, Religion & Culture, 9*, 213–225.

Lewis, C. S. (1955). *Surprised by joy: The shape of my early life.* New York: Harcourt Brace Jovanovich.

Lewis, E. (2004). Posture as a metaphor for biblical spirituality. In J. Ellens (Ed.), *The destructive power of religion: Violence in Judaism, Christianity and Islam, Volume 4: Contemporary views on spirituality and violence* (pp. 143–174). Westport, CT: Praeger.

Lewis, M. M. (2001). Spirituality, counseling, and elderly: An introduction to the spiritual life review. *Journal of Adult Development, 8*, 231–240.

Lewis-Hall, M. E., Duvall, N. S., Edwards, K. J., & Pike, P. L. (1999). The relationship of object relations development to cultural adjustment in a missionary sample. *Journal of Psychology and Theology, 27*, 139–153.

Liebert, E. (2000). *Changing life patterns: Adult development in spiritual direction.* St. Louis, MO: Chalice.

Liebert, E. (2005). Supervision as widening the horizons. In M. R. Bumpus, & R. B. Langer (Eds.), *Supervision of spiritual directors: Engaging in holy mystery* (pp. 125–145). Harrisburg, PA: Morehouse.

Lietaer, H., & Corveleyn, J. (1995). Psychoanalytical interpretation of the demoniacal possession and the mystical development of Sister Jeanne des Anges from Loudun (1605–1665). *The International Journal for the Psychology of Religion, 5*, 259–276.

Lifton, R. (1999). *The Protean self: Human resilience in an age of fragmentation.* New York: BasicBooks. (Original work published 1993).

Lin, W.-F., Mack, D., Enright, R. D., Krahn, D., & Baskin, T. W. (2004). Effects of forgiveness therapy on anger, mood, and vulnerability to substance use among inpatient substance-dependent clients. *Journal of Consulting and Clinical Psychology, 72*, 1114–1121.

Lindbeck, G. A. (1984). *The nature of doctrine: Religion and theology in a postliberal age.* Louisville, KY: Westminster John Knox Press.

Lindberg, D. (1992). *The beginnings of Western science: The European scientific tradition in philosophical, religious, and institutional context, 600 B.C. to A.D. 1450.* Chicago: University of Chicago Press.

Linehan, M. M. (1993a). *Cognitive-behavioral treatment of borderline personality disorder.* New York: Guilford.

Linehan, M. M. (1993b). *Skills training manual for treating borderline personality disorder.* New York: Guilford Press.

Linehan, M. M., Armstrong, H. E., Suarez, A., Allmon, D., & Heard, H. L. (1991). Cognitive-behavioral treatment of chronically parasuicidal borderline patients. *Archives of General Psychiatry, 48*, 1060–1064.

Linehan, M. M., Comtois, K. A., Murray, A. M., Brown, M. Z., Gallop, R. J., Heard, H. L., et al. (2006). Two–year randomized controlled trail and follow-up of dialectical behavior therapy vs. therapy by experts for suicidal behaviors and borderline personality disorder. *Archives of General Psychiatry, 63*, 757–766.

Linehan, M. M., Tutek, D. A., Heard, H. L., & Armstrong, H. E. (1994). Interpersonal outcome of cognitive behavioral treatment for chronically suicidal borderline patients. *American Journal of Psychiatry, 151*, 1771–1776.

Linley, P. A., & Joseph, S. (2004). Positive change following trauma and adversity: A review. *Journal of Traumatic Stress, 17,* 11–21.

Lippman, L., & Keith, J. (2006). The demographics of spirituality among youth: International perspectives. In E. Roehlkepartain, P. King, L. Wagener, & P. Benson (Eds.), *The handbook of spiritual development in childhood and adolescence* (pp. 109–123). Thousand Oaks, CA: Sage.

Lisak, D., & Ivan, C. (1995). Deficits in intimacy and empathy in sexually aggressive men. *Journal of Interpersonal Violence, 10,* 296–308.

Litchfeild, A. W., Thomas, D. L., & Dao Li, B. (1997). Dimensions of religiosity as mediators of the relations between parenting and adolescence deviant behavior. *Journal of Adolescent Research, 12,* 199–226.

Lloyd, E., & Feldman, M. (2002). Evolutionary psychology: A view from evolutionary biology. *Psychological Inquiry, 13,* 150–156.

Locke, E. A. (2002). The dead end of postmodernism. *American Psychologist, 57*(6–7), 458.

Loder, J. (1999). Normativity and context in practical theology. In F. Schweitzer, & J. Van Der Ven (Eds.), *Practical theology: International perspectives* (pp. 359–382). New York: Peter Lang.

Loder, J. (1998). *The logic of the spirit: Human development in theological perspective.* San Francisco: Jossey-Bass.

Loewenstein, E. (1991). Psychoanalytic life history: Is coherence, continuity, and aesthetic appeal necessary? *Psychoanalysis and Contemporary Thought, 14,* 3–28.

Loewenthal, K. M., Cinnirella, M., Evdoka, G., & Murphy, P. (2001). Faith conquers all? Beliefs about the role of religious factors in coping among different cultural-religious groups in the UK. *British Journal of Medical Psychology, 74,* 293–303.

Lofland, J., & Skonovd, N. (1981). Conversion motifs. *Journal for the Scientific Study of Religion, 20,* 373–385.

Lohse, B. (1999). *Martin Luther's theology: Its historical and systematic development* (R. Harrisville, Trans. & Ed.), Minneapolis: Fortress Press.

Long, A. (1986). Epicureans and stoics. In A. H. Armstrong (Ed.), *Classical Mediterranean spirituality* (pp. 135–153). New York: Crossroad.

Long, D., Elkind, D., & Spilka, B. (1967). Child's conception of prayer. *Journal for the Scientific Study of Religion, 6,* 101–109.

Lonsdale, D. (1991). 'The Serpent's Tail': Rules for Discernment. In P. Sheldrake (Ed.), *The way of Ignatius Loyola: Contemporary approaches to the spiritual exercises* (pp. 165–175). St. Louis, MO: The Institute of Jesuit Sources.

Lonsdale, D. (2000). *Eyes to see, ears to hear: An introduction to Ignatian spirituality.* Maryknoll, NY: Orbis.

Loomba, R. M. (1942). The religious development of the child. *Indian Journal of Psychology, 17,* 161–172.

Loori, J. D. (1999). *Riding the ox home: Stages on the path of enlightenment.* Boston: Shambhala.

Lopez, S., Edwards, L., Teramoto-Pedrotti, J., Prosser, E., LaRue, S., Vehige-Spalitto, S., et al. (2006). Beyond the DSM-IV: Assumptions, alternatives, and alterations. *Journal of Counseling and Development, 84,* 259–267.

Loseries-Leick, A. (1998). On the sacredness of Mount Kailasa in the Indian and Tibetan sources. In A. McKay (Ed.), *Pilgrimage in Tibet* (pp. 143–164). Richmond, Surrey: Curzon.

Lossky, V. (1974). *In the image and likeness of God* (J. Erickson, & T. Bird, Eds.), Crestwood, NY: St. Vladimir's Seminary Press.

Lossky, V. (1998). *The mystical theology of the Eastern church.* Crestwood, NY: St. Vladimir's Seminary Press. (Original work published 1957).

Lotufo, Z., Jr., & Martins, J. C. (2004). Revenge and religion. In J. Ellens (Ed.), *The destructive power of religion: Violence in Judaism, Christianity and Islam, Volume 2: Religion, psychology, and violence* (pp. 131–153). Westport, CT: Praeger.

Lou, H. C., Kjaer, T. W., Friberg, L., Wildschiodtz, G., Holm, S., & Nowak, M. (1999). A ^{15}O-H$_2$O PET study of meditation and the resting state of normal consciousness. *Human Brain Mapping, 7*, 98–105.

Louchakova, O. (2007). Spiritual heart and direct knowing in the prayer of the heart. *Existential Analysis, 18*, 81–102.

Louchakova, O., & Warner, A. (2003). Via Kundalini: Psychosomatic excursions in transpersonal psychology. *The Humanistic Psychologist, 31*(2/3), 115–158.

Lourenco, O. (2003). Making sense of Turiel's dispute with Kohlberg: The case of the child's moral competence. *New Ideas in Psychology, 21*, 43–68.

Louth, A. (1996). *Maximus the Confessor.* London: Routledge.

Love, P. G. (2002). Comparing spiritual development and cognitive development. *Journal of College Student Development, 43*, 357–373.

Loveland, M. T. (2003). Religious switching: Preference development, maintenance, and change. *Journal for the Scientific Study of Religion, 42*, 147–157.

Lovheim, M. (2004). Young people, religious identity, and the internet. In L. Dawson, & D. Cowan (Eds.), *Religion online: Finding faith on the Internet* (pp. 59–73). New York: Routledge.

Lövheim, M. (2007). Virtually boundless? Youth negotiating tradition in cyberspace. In N. T. Ammerman (Ed.), *Everyday religion: Observing modern religious lives* (pp. 83–100). Oxford: Oxford University Press.

Lownsdale, S. (1997). Faith development across the life span: Fowler's integrative work. *Journal of Psychology and Theology, 25*, 49–63.

Luckmann, T. (1967). *The invisible religion: The problem of religion in modern society.* New York: Macmillan.

Ludwig, A. (1990). Altered states of consciousness. In C. Tart (Ed.), *Altered states of consciousness* (3rd ed., pp. 18–33). San Francisco: HarperSanFrancisco.

Ludwig, T. (2000). *The sacred paths: Understanding the religions of the world* (3rd ed.). New York: Prentice Hall.

Luibheid, C. (1982). *John Climacus: The ladder of divine ascent.* New York: Paulist Press.

Lukoff, D., & Lu, F. (1999). Cultural competence includes religious and spiritual issues in clinical practice. *Transpersonal Psychiatry, 29*, 469–472.

Lukoff, D., & Lu, F. (2005). A transpersonal-integrative approach to spiritually oriented psychotherapy. In L. Sperry, & E. P. Shafranske (Eds.), *Spiritually oriented psychotherapy* (pp. 177–205). Washington, DC: American Psychological Association.

Lukoff, D., Lu, F., & Turner, R. (1992). Toward a more culturally sensitive DSM-IV: Psychoreligious and psychospiritual problems. *Journal of Nervous and Mental Disease, 180*, 673–682.

Lukoff, D., Lu, F., & Turner, R. (1996). Diagnosis: A transpersonal clinical approach to religious and spiritual problems. In B. Scotton, A. Chinen, & J. Battista (Eds.), *Textbook of transpersonal psychiatry and psychology* (pp. 231–249). New York: Basic Books.

Lukoff, D., Lu, F., & Turner R. (1998). From spiritual emergency to spiritual problem: The transpersonal roots of the new DSM-IV category. *The Journal of Humanistic Psychology, 38*(2), 21–50.

Lumumba, H. (2003). The impact of Al-Islam on the African American population. *Counseling and Values, 47*, 210–219.

Luria, A. (1973). *The working brain: An introduction to neuropsychology* (B. Haigh, Trans.). New York: Basic.

Luther, M. (1968a). Personal prayer book, 1522. In G. K. Wiencke (Ed.), *Luther's works, Vol. 43: Devotional writings II* (M. Bertram, Trans.) (pp. 3–45). Philadelphia: Fortress Press.

Luther, M. (1968b). A simple way to pray, 1535. In G. K. Wiencke (Ed.), *Luther's works, Vol. 43: Devotional writings II* (M. Bertram, Trans.) (pp. 187–211). Philadelphia: Fortress Press.

Luther, M. (1969a). An exposition of the Lord's prayer for simple laymen, 1519. In M. O. Dietrich (Ed.), *Luther's works, Vol. 42: Devotional writings I* (M. Bertram, Trans.) (pp. 15–81). Philadelphia: Fortress Press.

Luther, M. (1969b). A meditation on Christ's passion, 1519 In M. O. Dietrich (Ed.), *Luther's works, Vol. 42: Devotional writings I* (M. Bertram, Trans.) (pp. 3–14). Philadelphia: Fortress Press.

Luther, M. (2002). *Luther's works on CD-ROM* (J. Pelikan, & H. Lehmann, Eds.), Philadelphia and St. Louis: Fortress and Concordia Press.

Lutz, A., & Borgman, D. (2002). Teenage spirituality and the internet. *Cultic Studies Review, 1,* 137–151.

Lutz, A., Brefczynski-Lewis, J., Johnstone, T., & Davidson, R. J. (2008). Regulation of the neural circuitry of emotion by compassion meditation: Effects of meditative expertise. *PLoS ONE, 3*(3), 1–10.

Lutz, A., Greischar, L. L., Rawlings, N. B., Ricard, M., & Davidson, R. J. (2004). Long-term meditators self-induce high-amplitude gamma synchrony during mental practice. *Proceedings of the National Academy of Sciences, 101,* 16369–16373.

Luyten, P., & Corveleyn, J. (2007). Attachment and religion: The need to leave our secure base: A comment on the discussion between Granqvist, Rizzuto, and Wulff. *International Journal for the Psychology of Religion, 17,* 81–97.

Lykken, D., & Tellegen, A. (1996). Happiness is a stochastic phenomenon. *Psychological Science, 7,* 186–189.

Lyon, K. B. (2004). Faith and development in late adulthood. In F. Kelcourse (Ed.), *Human Development and Faith, life-cycle stages of body, mind and soul* (pp. 269–284). St. Louis, MO: Chalice Press.

Lyotard, J.-F. (1984). *The postmodern condition: A report on knowledge* (G. Bennington, & B. Massumi, Trans.). Minneapolis: University of Minnesota Press.

Lysaught, M. T. (2003). The pressures to die: Reconceiving the shape of Christian life in the face of physician-assisted suicide. In S. Hauerwas, C. Stoneking, K. Meador, & D. Cloutier (Eds.), *Growing old in Christ* (pp. 267–301). Grand Rapids: Eerdmans.

Ma, S. H., & Teasdale, J. (2004). Mindfulness-based cognitive therapy for depression: Replication and exploration of differential relapse prevention effects. *Journal of Consulting and Clinical Psychology, 72,* 31–40.

Mabee, C. (2004). Reflections on monotheism and violence. In J. Ellens (Ed.), *The destructive power of religion: Violence in Judaism, Christianity and Islam, Volume 4: Contemporary views on spirituality and violence* (pp. 111–118). Westport, CT: Praeger.

MacDonald, D. A. (2000). Spirituality: Description, measurement, and relation to the five factor model of personality. *Journal of Personality, 68,* 153–197.

MacDonald, D. A., & Holland, D. (2002). Spirituality and complex partial epileptic-like signs. *Psychological Reports, 91,* 785–792.

MacInnes, E. (2003). *Zen contemplation for Christians.* Lanham, MD: Sheed & Ward.

MacIntyre, A. (1984). *After virtue: A study in moral theory* (2nd ed.). Notre Dame, IN: University of Notre Dame Press.

MacIntyre, A. (1988). *Whose justice? Which rationality?* Notre Dame, IN: University of Notre Dame Press.

MacIntyre, A. (1990). *Three rival versions of moral inquiry: Encyclopaedia, genealogy, and tradition.* Notre Dame, IN: University of Notre Dame Press.

MacIntyre, A. (1992). How psychology makes itself true- or false. In S. Koch, & D. E. Leary (Eds.), *A century of psychology as science* (pp. 897–920). Washington DC: American Psychological Association.

MacIntyre, A., & Ricoeur, P. (1969). *The religious significance of atheism.* New York: Columbia University Press.

Mackay, N. (1989). *Motivation and explanation: An essay on Freud's philosophy of science.* Madison, CT: International Universities.

Mackenzie, E. R., Rajagopal, D. E., Meilbohm, M., & Lavizzo-Mourey, R. (2000). Spiritual support and psychological well-being: Older adults' perceptions of the religion and health connection. *Alternative Therapies in Health and Medicine, 6*(6), 37–45.

MacKinlay, E. (2001). The spiritual dimension of caring: Applying a model for spiritual tasks of ageing. *Journal of Religious Gerontology, 12*(3/4), 151–166.

MacKinlay, E. (2002). Mental health and spirituality in later life: Pastoral approaches. *Journal of Religious Gerontology, 13*(3/4), 129–147.

Macmurray, J. (1957). *The self as agent.* Amherst, NY: Humanity Books.

MacNutt, F. (1999). *Healing* (Rev. ed.). Notre Dame, IN: Ave Maria.

Macquarrie, J. (1982). *In search of humanity: A theological and philosophical approach.* New York: Crossroad.

Maddi, S. (1998). Creating meaning through making decisions. In P. Wong, & P. Fry (Eds.), *The human quest for meaning: A handbook of psychological research and clinical applications* (pp. 3–26). Mahwah, NJ: Lawrence Erlbaum Associates.

Maddux, J. E. (2002). Stopping the "madness": Positive psychology and the deconstruction of the illness ideology and the *DSM.* In C. R. Snyder, & S. J. Lopez (Eds.), *Handbook of positive psychology* (pp. 13–25). Oxford: Oxford University Press.

Madell, G. (2003). Materialism and the first person. In M. O'Hear (Ed.), *Minds and persons* (pp. 123–140). Cambridge: Cambridge University Press.

Magaletta, P. (1996). An object relations paradigm for spiritual development with highlights from Merton's spiritual journey. *Pastoral Psychology, 45,* 21–28.

Magee, J. (2001). Mysticism and reframing memories in life review groups. *Journal of Religious Gerontology, 13*(1), 65–73.

Magid, B. (2003). Your ordinary mind. In J. Safran (Ed.), *Psychoanalysis and Buddhism: An unfolding dialogue* (pp. 251–286). Boston: Wisdom.

Mahalik, J. R., & Lagan, H. D. (2001). Examining masculine gender role conflict and stress in relation to religious orientation and spiritual well-being. *Psychology of Men and Masculinity, 2,* 24–33.

Mahoney, A., Pargament, K. I, Murray-Swank, A., & Murray-Swank, N. (2003). Religion and the sanctification of family relationships. *Review of Religious Research, 44,* 220–236.

Mahoney, A., & Tarakeshwar, N. (2005). Religion's role in marriage and parenting in daily life and during family crises. In R. F. Paloutzian, & C. L. Park (Eds.), *Handbook of the psychology of religion and spirituality* (pp. 177–192). New York: Guilford Press.

Mailey, B. (2004). The doctrinal mode and evangelical Christianity in the United States. In H. Whitehouse, & J. Laidlaw (Eds.), *Ritual and memory: Toward a comparative anthropology of religion* (pp. 79–87). Walnut Creek, CA: AltaMira.

Majercik, R. (1995). Plotinus and Greek mysticism. In D. Bishop (Ed.), *Mysticism and the mystical experience: East and West* (pp. 38–61). Selinsgrove, PA: Susquehanna University Press.

Makrakis, A. (1977). *The Logos and the Holy Spirit in the unity of Christian thought: According to the teachings of the Orthodox Church: Volume II Psychology: An Orthodox Christian perspective* (D. Cummings, Trans.). Chicago, IL: Orthodox Christian Educational Society.

Malamuth, N. M., & Brown, L. M. (1994). Sexually aggressive men's perceptions of women's communications: Testing three explanations. *Journal of Personality and Social Psychology, 67,* 699–712.

Maldonado, D. (1994). Religiosity and religious participation among Hispanic elderly. *Journal of Religious Gerontology, 9*(1), 41–61.

Malina, B. (1995). Pain, power, and personhood: Ascetic behavior in the ancient Mediterranean. In V. Wimbush, & R. Valantasis (Eds.), *Asceticism* (pp. 162–177). New York: Oxford University Press.

Mallery, P., Mallery, S., & Gorsuch, R. (2000). A preliminary taxonomy of attributions to God. *The International Journal for the Psychology of Religion, 10,* 135–156.

Malley, B. (2004). The doctrinal mode and evangelical Christianity in the United States. In H. Whitehouse, & J. Laidlaw (Eds.), *Ritual and memory: Toward a comparative anthropology of religion* (pp. 79–87). Walnut Creek, CA: AltaMira.

Maloney, G. (1992). *Pseudo-Macarius: The fifty spiritual homilies and the great letter.* New York: Paulist Press.

Malony, H. N. (2000). The psychological evaluation of religious professionals. *Professional Psychology: Research and Practice, 31,* 521–525.

Maltby, J. (1999). Personality dimensions of religious orientation. *The Journal of Psychology, 133,* 631–640.

Maltby, J. (2005). Protecting the sacred and expressions of rituality: Examining the relationship between extrinsic dimensions of religiosity and unhealthy guilt. *Psychology and Psychotherapy: Theory, Research and Practice, 78*, 77–93.

Maltby, J., & Day, L. (2000). Depressive symptoms and religious orientation: Examining the relationship between religiosity and depression within the context of other correlates of depression. *Personality and Individual Differences, 28*, 383–393.

Maltby, J., & Day, L. (2002). Religious experience, religious orientation and schizotypy. *Mental Health, Religion and Culture, 5*, 163–174.

Maltby, J., & Day, L. (2003). Religious orientation, religious coping and appraisals of stress: Assessing primary appraisal factors in the relationship between religiosity and psychological well-being. *Personality and Individual Differences, 34*, 1209–1224.

Maltby, J., Day, L., & Barber, L. (2005). Forgiveness and happiness: The differing contexts of forgiveness using the distinction between hedonic and eudaimonic happiness. *Journal of Happiness Studies, 6*, 1–13.

Maltby, J., Garner, I., Lewis, C. A., & Day, L. (2000). Religious orientation and schizotypal traits. *Personality and Individual Differences, 28*, 143–151.

Maltby, J., Lewis, C., & Day, L. (2008). Prayer and subjective well-being: The application of a cognitive-behavioural framework. *Mental Health, Religion & Culture, 11*, 119–129.

Mansager, E. (2000). Individual psychology and the study of spirituality. *The Journal of Individual Psychology, 56*, 371–388.

Mansager, E. (2002). Religious and spiritual problem v-code: An Adlerian assessment. *The Journal of Individual Psychology, 58*, 374–387.

Mansager, E., Gold, L., Griffith, B., Kal, E., Manaster, G., McArter, G., et al. (2002). Spirituality in the Adlerian forum. *The Journal of Individual Psychology, 58*, 177–196.

Mansfield, D. (1991a). The exercises and contemplative prayer. In P. Sheldrake (Ed.), *The way of Ignatius Loyola: Contemporary approaches to the spiritual exercises* (pp. 191–202). St. Louis, MO: The Institute of Jesuit Sources.

Mansfield, D. (1991b). Praying the passion. In P. Sheldrake (Ed.), *The way of Ignatius Loyola: Contemporary approaches to the spiritual exercises* (pp. 103–114). St. Louis, MO: The Institute of Jesuit Sources.

Marcia, J. (1966). Development and validation of ego-identity status. *Journal of Personality and Social Psychology, 3*, 551–558.

Marcia, J. (1980). Identity in adolescence. In J. Adelson (Ed.), *Handbook of adolescent psychology* (pp. 159–187). New York: Wiley.

Marechal, J. (2004). *The psychology of the mystics* (A. Thorold, Trans.). Mineola, NY: Dover. (Original work published 1927).

Marek, J. (1988). A Buddhist theory of human development. In R. Thomas (Ed.), *Oriental theories of human development: Scriptural and popular beliefs from Hinduism, Buddhism, Confucianism, Shinto, and Islam* (pp. 75–115). New York: Peter Lang.

Mariani, P. (2002). *Thirty days: On retreat with the exercises of St. Ignatius.* New York: Viking Compass.

Maritain, J. (1957). Freudianism and psychoanalysis: A Thomist view. In B. Nelson (Ed.), *Freud and the 20th Century* (pp. 230–258). Cleveland, OH: Meridian.

Markham, D., & Mikail, S. (2004). Perpetrators of clergy abuse of minors: Insights from attachment theory. In T. Plante (Ed.), *Sin against the innocents: Sexual abuse by priests and the role of the Catholic church* (pp. 101–114). Westport, CT: Praeger.

Markstrom, C. A.(1999). Religious involvement and adolescent psychosocial development. *Journal of Adolescence, 22*, 205–221.

Markstrom, C. A., & Kalmanir, H. M. (2001). Linkages between the psychosocial stages of identity and intimacy and the strengths of fidelity and love. *Identity: An International Journal of Theory and Research, 1*, 179–196.

Markstrom-Adams, C., Hofstra, G., & Dougher, K. (1994). The ego-virtue of fidelity: A case for the study of religion and identity formation in adolescence. *Journal of Youth and Adolescence, 23*, 453–469.

Markstrom-Adams, C., & Smith, M. (1996). Identity formation and religious orientation among high school students from the United States and Canada. *Journal of Adolescence, 19,* 247–261.

Markus, R. A. (1999). How on earth could places become holy? Origins of the Christian idea of holy places. In E. Ferguson (Ed.), *Forms of devotion: Conversion, worship, spirituality, and asceticism* (pp. 183–197). New York: Garland.

Marlatt, G. (2002). Buddhist philosophy and the treatment of addictive behavior. *Cognitive and Behavioral Practices, 9,* 44–50.

Marlatt, G., & Kristeller, J. (1999). Mindfulness and meditation. In W. Miller (Ed.), *Integrating spirituality into treatment: Resources for practitioners* (pp. 67–84). Washington, DC: American Psychological Association.

Marlatt, G., Witkiewitz, K., Dillworth, T., Bowen, S. Parks, G., Macpherson, L., et al. (2004). Vipassana meditation as a treatment for alcohol and drug use disorders. In S. Hayes, V. Follette, & M. Linehan (Eds.), *Mindfulness and acceptance: Expanding the cognitive-behavioral tradition* (pp. 261–287). New York: Guilford.

Marler, P. (1995). Lost in the fifties: The changing family and the nostalgic church. In N. Ammerman, & W. Roof (Eds.), *Work, family, and religion in contemporary society* (pp. 23–60). New York: Routledge.

Marler, P. L., & Hadaway, C. K. (2002). "Being religious" or "being spiritual" in America: A zero-sum proposition? *Journal for the Scientific Study of Religion, 41,* 289–300.

Marras, A. (2006). Emergence and reduction: Reply to Kim. *Synthese, 151,* 561–569.

Marsden, G., & Longfield, B. (Eds.). (1992). *The secularization of the academy.* Oxford: Oxford University Press.

Martin, D. (1978). *A general theory of secularization.* New York: Harper & Row.

Martin, D. (Trans.). (1997). *Carthusian spirituality: The writings of Hugh of Balma and Guigo de Ponte.* New York: Paulist Press.

Martin, L. (2002). *Sacred doorways: A beginner's guide to icons.* Brewster, MA: Paraclete Press.

Martin, T., Kirkcaldy, B., & Siefen, G. (2003). Antecedents of adult wellbeing: Adolescent religiosity and health. *Journal of Managerial Psychology, 18,* 453–470.

Martin, T., White, J. M., & Perlman, D. (2003). Religious socialization: The channeling hypothesis of parental influence on adolescent faith maturity. *Journal of Adolescent Research, 18,* 169–187.

Marty, M. (1994). Public and private: Congregation as meeting place. In J. Wind, & J. Lewis (Eds.), *American congregations, Volume 2: New perspectives in the study of congregations* (pp. 133–166). Chicago: University of Chicago Press.

Marty, M., & Appleby, R. S. (Eds.). (1991). *Fundamentalisms observed.* Chicago: University of Chicago Press.

Marty, M., & Appleby, R. S. (Eds.). (1993). *Fundamentalisms and society: Reclaiming the sciences, the family, and education.* Chicago: University of Chicago Press.

Marty, M., & Appleby, R. S. (Eds.). (1994). *Accounting for fundamentalisms: The dynamic character of movements.* Chicago: University of Chicago Press.

Marty, M., & Appleby, R. S. (Eds.). (1995). *Fundamentalisms comprehended.* Chicago: University of Chicago Press.

Martyn, D. (1992*). The man in the yellow hat: Theology and psychoanalysis in child therapy.* Atlanta, GA: Scholars Press.

Marwell, G. (1996). We still don't know if strict churches are strong, much less why: Comment on Iannaccone. *American Journal of Sociology, 101,* 1097–1108.

Marzanski, M., & Bratton, M. (2002a). Mystical states or mystical life? Buddhist, Christian and Hindu perspectives. *Philosophy, Psychiatry, & Psychology, 9,* 349–351.

Marzanski, M., & Bratton, M. (2002b). Psychopathological symptoms and religious experience: A critique of Jackson and Fulford. *Philosophy, Psychiatry, & Psychology, 9,* 359–371.

Maselko, J., & Buka, S. (2008). Religious activity and lifetime prevalence of psychiatric disorder. *Social Psychiatry & Psychiatric Epidemiology, 43,* 18–24.

Maselko, J., Kubzansky, L., Kawachi, I., Staudenmayer, J., & Berkman, L. (2006). Religious service attendance and decline in pulmonary function in a high-functioning elderly cohort. *Annals of Behavioral Medicine, 32*, 245–253.

Masis, K. V. (2002). American Zen and psychotherapy: An ongoing dialogue. In P. Young-Eisendrath, & S. Muramoto (Eds.), *Awakening and insight: Zen Buddhism and psychotherapy* (pp. 149–171). New York: Taylor & Francis.

Maslow, A. H. (1964). *Religions, values, and peak-experiences.* Columbus, OH: Ohio State University Press.

Maslow, A. H. (1969). The further reaches of human nature. *The Journal of Transpersonal Psychology, 1*, 1–9.

Maslow, A. H. (1970). *Motivation and personality* (2nd ed.). New York: Harper & Row.

Maslow, A. H. (1999). *Toward a psychology of being* (3rd ed.). New York: John Wiley & Sons.

Mason, J. (2002). *Qualitative researching* (2nd ed.). London: Sage.

Masten, A. S., & Reed, M.-G. J. (2002). Resilience in development. In C. R Snyder, & S. J. Lopez (Eds.), *Handbook of positive psychology* (pp. 74–88). Oxford: Oxford University Press.

Masters, K. S. (2005). Research on the healing power of distant intercessory prayer: Disconnect between science and faith. *Journal of Psychology and Theology, 33*, 268–277.

Masters, R., & Houston, J. (2000). *The varieties of psychedelic experiences: The classic guide to the effects of LSD on the human psyche.* Rochester, Vermont: Park Street Press.

Maton, K. I. (1989). The stress-buffering role of spiritual support: Cross-sectional and prospective investigations. *Journal for the Scientific Study of Religion, 28*, 310–323.

Maton, K. I., & Wells, E. A. (1995). Religion as a community resource for well-being: Prevention, healing, and empowerment pathways. *Journal of Social Issues, 51*(2), 177–193.

Matt, D. C. (1990). Ayin: The concept of nothingness in Jewish mysticism. In R. K. C. Forman (Ed.), *The problem of pure consciousness: Mysticism and philosophy* (pp. 121–159). New York: Oxford University Press.

Mattis, J., Ahluwalia, M., Cowie, S.-A., & Kirkland-Harris, A. (2006). Ethnicity, culture, and spiritual development. In E. Roehlkepartain, P. King, L. Wagener, & P. Benson (Eds.), *The handbook of spiritual development in childhood and adolescence* (pp. 283–296). Thousand Oaks, CA: Sage.

Mavrodes, G. (1978). Real v. deceptive mystical experiences. In S. T. Katz (Ed.), *Mysticism and philosophical analysis* (pp. 235–258). New York: Oxford University Press.

Maximus, C. St. (2003). *On the cosmic mystery of Jesus Christ: Selected writings from St. Maximus the Confessor* (P. M. Blowers, & R. L. Wilken, Trans.). Crestwood, NY: St Vladimir's Seminary Press.

May, G. (1982). *Will and spirit.* New York: Harper San Francisco.

May, G. (1988). *Addiction and grace.* San Francisco: Harper & Row.

May, G. (1992). *Care of mind, care of spirit.* San Francisco: HarperSanFrancisco.

May, G. (2004). *The dark night of the soul: A psychiatrist explores the connection between darkness and spiritual growth.* San Francisco: HarperSanFrancisco.

Maynard, E. A., Gorsuch, R. L., & Bjorck, J. P. (2001). Religious coping style, concept of God, and personal religious variables in threat, loss, and challenge situations. *Journal for the Scientific Study of Religion, 40*, 65–74.

McAdams, D. P. (1996). Personality, modernity, and the storied self: A contemporary framework for studying persons. *Psychological Inquiry, 7*, 295–321.

McAdams, D. P. (1997). *The stories we live by: Personal myths and the making of the self.* New York: Guilford.

McAdams, D. P. (2001). The psychology of life stories. *Review of General Psychology, 5*, 100–122.

McAdams, D. P. (2006). *The redemptive self: Stories Americans live by.* Oxford: Oxford University Press.

McAdams, D. P., & Bauer, J. (2004). Gratitude in modern life: Its manifestations and development. In R. Emmons, & M. McCullough (Eds.), *The psychology of gratitude* (pp. 81–99). Oxford: Oxford University Press.

McAdams, D. P., & de St. Aubin, E. (1998). Epilogue: Emerging themes and future directions. In D. P. McAdams, & E. de St. Aubin (Eds.), *Generativity and adult development: How and why we care for the next generation* (pp. 483–491). Washington, DC: American Psychological Association.

McAdams, D. P., Hart, H. M., & Maruna, S. (1998). The anatomy of generativity. In D. P. McAdams, & E. de St. Aubin (Eds.), *Generativity and adult development: How and why we care for the next generation* (pp. 7–43). Washington, DC: American Psychological Association.

McCauley, R., & Whitehouse, H. (2005). Introduction: New frontiers in the cognitive science of religion. *Journal of Cognition and Culture, 5*(1–2), 1–13.

McClenon, J. (1997). Shamanic healing, human evolution, and the origin of religion. *Journal for the Scientific Study of Religion, 36*, 345–354.

McCrae, R. R. (1999). Mainstream personality psychology and the study of religion. *Journal of Personality, 67*, 1209–1218.

McCullough, M. E. (1995). Prayer and health: Conceptual issues, research review, and research agenda. *Journal of Psychology and Theology, 23*, 15–29.

McCullough, M. E. (1999). Research on religion-accommodative counseling: Review and meta-analysis. *Journal of Counseling Psychology, 46*, 92–98.

McCullough, M. E. (2001a). Forgiving. In C. R. Snyder (Ed.), *Coping with stress: Effective people and processes* (pp. 93–113). Oxford: Oxford University Press.

McCullough, M. E. (2001b). Religious involvement and mortality: Answers and more questions. In T. Plante, & A. Sherman (Eds.), *Faith and health: Psychological perspectives* (pp. 53–74). New York: Guilford Press.

McCullough, M. E., Hoyt, W. T., Larson, D. B., Koenig, H. G., & Thoresen, C. (2000). Religious involvement and mortality: A meta-analytic review. *Health Psychology, 19*, 211–222.

McCullough, M. E., Kilpatrick, S. D., Emmons, R. A., & Larson, D. B. (2001). Is gratitude a moral affect? *Psychological Bulletin, 127*, 249–266.

McCullough, M. E., & Larson, D. B. (1999). Religion and depression: A review of the literature. *Twin Research, 2*, 126–136.

McCullough, M. E., Pargament, K., & Thoresen, C. (2000). The psychology of forgiveness: History, conceptual issues, and overview. In M. McCullough, K. Pargament, & C. Thoresen (Eds.), *Forgiveness: Theory, research and practice* (pp. 1–14). New York: Guilford Press.

McCullough, M. E., & Smith, T. (2003). Religion and health: Depressive symptoms and mortality as case studies. In M. Dillon (Ed.), *Handbook of the sociology of religion* (pp. 190–204). Cambridge: Cambridge University Press.

McCullough, M. E., & Tsang, J.-A. (2004). Parent of the virtues? The prosocial contours of gratitude. In R. Emmons, & M. McCullough (Eds.), *The psychology of gratitude* (pp. 123–141). Oxford: Oxford University Press.

McCullough, M. E., & Worthington, E. L., Jr. (1999). Religion and the forgiving personality. *Journal of Personality, 67*, 1141–1164.

McCullough, M. E., Worthington, E., Jr., & Rachal, K. (1997). Interpersonal forgiving in close relationships. *Journal of Personality and Social Psychology, 73*, 321–336.

McDargh, J. (1983). *Psychoanalytic object relations theory and the study of religion: On faith and the imaging of God.* Lanham, MD: University Press of America.

McDargh, J. (1986). God, mother and me: An object relational perspective on religious material. *Pastoral Psychology, 34*, 251–263.

McDargh, J. (1992). The deep structure of religious representations. In M. Finn, & J. Gartner (Eds.), *Object relations theory and religion* (pp. 1–19). Westport, CT: Praeger.

McDargh, J. (1993). Concluding clinical postscript: On developing a psychotheological perspective. In M. Randour (Ed.), *Exploring sacred landscapes: Religious and spiritual experiences in psychotherapy* (pp. 172–193). New York: Columbia University Press.

McDargh, R. (1997). Creating a new research paradigm for the psychoanalytic study of religion: The pioneering work of Ana-Maria Rizzuto. In J. Jacobs, & D. Capps (Eds.), *Religion, society, and psychoanalysis: Readings in contemporary theory* (pp. 181–199). Boulder, CO: Westview Press.

McDonald, A., Beck, R., Allison, S., & Norsworthy, L. (2005). Attachment to God and parents: Testing the correspondence vs. compensation hypotheses. *Journal of Psychology and Christianity, 24*, 21–28.

McFadden, S. H. (1999). Religion, personality, and aging: A life span perspective. *Journal of Personality, 67*, 1081–1104.

McFadden, S. H., & Levin, J. S. (1996). Religion, emotions, and health. In C. Magai, & S. H. McFadden (Eds.), *Handbook of emotion, adult development, and aging* (pp. 349–365). San Diego, CA: Academic Press.

McGinn, B. (1991). *The foundations of mysticism: Origins to the fifth century.* New York: Crossroad.

McGinn, B. (1996). *The growth of mysticism: Gregory the Great through the 12th century.* New York: Crossroad Herder.

McGinn, B. (1998). *The flowering of mysticism: Men and women in the new mysticism, 1200–1350.* New York: Crossroad Herder.

McGinn, B. (2001). *The mystical thought of Meister Eckhart: The man from whom God hid nothing.* New York: Crossroad.

McGinn, B. (2002). Vere tu es Deus absconditus: The hidden God in Luther and some mystics. In O. Davies, & D. Turner (Eds.), *Silence and the Word: Negative theology and incarnation* (pp. 94–114). Cambridge: Cambridge University Press.

McGinn, B. (2005). *The harvest of mysticism in medieval Germany (1300–1500).* New York: Herder & Herder.

McGrath, A. (2005). *Dawkins' God: Genes, memes, and the meaning of life.* Malden, MA: Blackwell.

McGrath, P. (2006). Defining spirituality: From meaning-making to connection. In S. Ambrose (Ed.), *Religion and psychology: New research* (pp. 223–239). New York: Nova Science.

McGuinness, D., Pribram, K., & Pirnazar, M. (1990). Upstaging the stage model. In C. Alexander, & E. Langer (Eds.), *Higher stages of human development* (pp. 97–113). New York: Oxford University Press.

McGuire, M. (2007). Embodied practices: Negotiation and resistance. In N. T. Ammerman (Ed.), *Everyday religion: Observing modern religious lives* (pp. 187–200). Oxford: Oxford University Press.

McGuire, W. (2003). Jung, Evan-Wentz and various other gurus. *Journal of Analytical Psychology, 48*, 433–445.

McIntosh, D. N. (1997). Religion-as-schema, with implications for the relation between religion and coping. In B. Spilka, & D. N. McIntosh (Eds.), *The psychology of religion: Theoretical approaches* (pp. 171–183). Boulder, CO: Westview Press.

McIntosh, D. N., Silver, R. C., & Wortman, C. B. (1993). Religion's role in adjustment to a negative life event: Coping with the loss of a child. *Journal of Personality and Social Psychology, 65*, 812–821.

McKay, A. (1998). Introduction. In A. McKay (Ed.), *Pilgrimage in Tibet* (pp. 1–17). Richmond, UK: Curzon.

McKay, B. E., & Persinger, M. A. (2006). Weak, physiologically patterned magnetic fields do not affect maze performance in normal rats, but disrupt seized rats normalized with ketamine: Possible support for a neuromatrix concept? *Epilepsy & Behavior, 8*, 137–144.

McKay, K., Hill, M., Freedman, S., & Enright, R. (2007). Toward a feminist empowerment model of forgiveness psychotherapy. *Psychotherapy: Theory, Research, Practice, Training, 44*, 14–29.

McKinney, J. P., & McKinney, K. G. (1999). Prayer in the lives of late adolescents. *Journal of Adolescence, 22*, 279–290.

McMahan, O. (2002). A living stream: Spiritual direction within the Pentecostal/charismatic tradition. *Journal of Psychology and Theology, 30*, 336–345.

McMinn, M. R. (1996). *Psychology, theology, and spirituality in Christian counseling.* Wheaton, IL: Tyndale House.

McMinn, M. R., Aikins, D. C., & Lish, R. A. (2003). Basic and advanced competence in collaborating with clergy. *Professional Psychology: Research and Practice, 34*, 197–202.

McMinn, M. R., Chaddock, T., Edwards, L., Lim, B., & Campbell, C. (1998). Psychologists collaborating with clergy. *Professional Psychology: Research and Practice, 29*, 564–570.

McMinn, M. R., Meek, K., Canning, S., & Pozzi, C. (2001). Training psychologists to work with religious organizations: The Center for Church-Psychology Collaboration. *Professional Psychology: Research and Practice, 32*, 324–328.

McMinn, M. R., Ruiz, J. N., Marx, D., Wright, J. B., & Gilbert, N. B. (2006). Professional psychology and the doctrines of sin and grace: Christian leaders' perspectives. *Professional Psychology: Research and Practice, 37*, 295–302.

McNamara, L. J. (2002). Theological perspectives on ageing and mental health. *Journal of Religious Gerontology, 13*(3/4), 1–16.

McNeill, J. T. (1951). *A history of the cure of souls*. New York: Harper & Row.

McPherson, M., Smith-Lovin, L., & Brashears, M. (2006). Social isolation in America: Changes in core discussion networks over two decades. *American Sociological Review, 71*, 353–375.

McRae, J. R. (1986). *The Northern School and the formation of early Ch'an Buddhism: Studies in East Asian Buddhism 3*. Honolulu: University of Hawaii Press.

McVerry, P. (1991). The first week and social sin. In P. Sheldrake (Ed.), *The way of Ignatius Loyola: Contemporary approaches to the spiritual exercises* (pp. 66–76). St. Louis, MO: The Institute of Jesuit Sources.

Mead, M. (1962). The immortality of man. In S. Doniger (Ed.), *The nature of man in theological and psychological perspective* (pp. 201–217). New York: Harper & Brothers.

Meador, K., & Henson, S. (2003). Growing old in a therapeutic culture. In S. Hauerwas, C. Stoneking, K. Meador, & D. Cloutier (Eds.), *Growing old in Christ* (pp. 90–111). Grand Rapids: Eerdmans.

Meador, K., Koenig, H., Hughes, D., & Blazer, D. (1992). Religious affiliation and major depression. *Hospital & Community Psychiatry, 43*, 1204–1208.

Mechthild, of Magdeburg. (1998). *Mechthild of Magdeburg: The flowing light of the Godhead*. New York: Paulist Press.

Meckel, D., & Moore, R. (Eds.). (1992). *Self and liberation the Jung-Buddhism dialogue*. New York: Paulist Press.

Mehrabian, A., Stefl, C. A., & Mullen, M. (1997). Emotional thinking in the adult: Individual differences in mysticism and globality-differentiation. *Imagination, Cognition and Personality, 16*, 325–355.

Mehta, K. K. (1997). The impact of religious beliefs and practices on aging: A cross-cultural comparison. *Journal of Aging Studies, 11*, 101–114.

Meier, A., & Meier, M. (2004). The formation of adolescents' image of God: Predictors and age and gender differences. In R. Dayringer, & D. Oler (Eds.), *The image of God and the psychology of religion* (pp. 91–111). New York: Haworth Pastoral.

Meilman, P. (1979). Cross-sectional age changes in ego identity status during adolescence. *Developmental Psychology, 15*, 230–231.

Meisenhelder, J. B., & Chandler, E. N. (2000). Prayer and health outcomes in church members. *Alternative Therapies in Health and Medicine, 6*, 56–60.

Meissner, W. W. (1984). *Psychoanalysis and religious experience*. New Haven, CT: Yale University Press.

Meissner, W. W. (1987). *Life and faith: Psychology perspectives on religious experiences*. Washington, DC: Georgetown University Press.

Meissner, W. W. (1992). *Ignatius of Loyola: The psychology of a saint*. New Haven, CT: Yale University Press.

Meissner, W. W. (2000). *The cultic origins of Christianity: The dynamics of religious development*. Collegeville, MN: Liturgical Press.

Meissner, W. W. (2001). So help me God! Do I help God or does God help me? In S. Akhtar, & H. Parens (Eds.), *Does God help? Developmental and clinical aspects of religious belief* (pp. 77–126). Northvale, NJ: Jason Aronson.

Meissner, W. W. (2003). Aspects of the mystical life of Ignatius of Loyola. In J. Belzen, & A. Geels (Eds.), *Mysticism: A variety of psychological perspectives* (pp. 293–327). Amsterdam: Rodopi.

Melbourne Academic Mindfulness Interest Group (2006). Mindfulness-based psychotherapies: A review of conceptual foundations, empirical evidence and practical considerations. *Australian and New Zealand Journal of Psychiatry, 40*, 285–294.

Menninger, K. (1954). Religio psychiatri. In S. Doniger (Ed.), *Religion and human behavior* (pp. 1–19). New York: Association Press.

Menninger, K. (1962). Hope. In S. Doniger (Ed.), *The nature of man in theological and psychological perspective* (pp. 183–200). New York: Harper, & Brothers.

Mensch, E. (2005). Prayer as Kenosis. In B. Benson, & N. Wirzba (Eds.), *The phenomenology of prayer* (pp. 63–74). Bronx, NY: Fordham University Press.

Mercer, C., & Durham, T. W. (1999). Religious mysticism and gender orientation. *Journal for the Scientific Study of Religion, 38*, 175–182.

Meredith, A. (1999). *Gregory of Nyssa*. London: Routledge.

Merrill, R. M., & Salazar, R. D. (2002). Relationship between church attendance and mental health among Mormons and non-Mormons in Utah. *Mental Health, Religion & Culture, 5*, 17–33.

Merton, T. (1960). *Spiritual direction and meditation*. Collegeville, MN: Liturgical Press.

Merton, T. (1961). *New seeds of contemplation*. New York: New Directions.

Merton, T. (1966). *Conjectures of a guilty bystander*. Garden City, NY: Doubleday.

Merton, T. (1971). *Contemplative prayer*. Garden City, NY: Image Books.

Merton, T. (1973). *The climate of monastic prayer*. Washington, DC: Consortium Press.

Merton, T. (1985). *Disputed questions*. San Diego, CA: Harcourt Brace Jovanovich.

Merton, T. (1991). The neurotic personality in the monastic life. *The Merton Annual, 4*, 5–19.

Merton, T. (2003a). *The inner experience: Notes on contemplation* (W. H. Shannon, Ed.), San Francisco: HarperSanFracisco.

Merton, T. (2003b). Love for God and mutual charity: Thomas Merton's lectures on hesychasm to the novices at the Abbey of Gethsemani. In B. Dieker, & J. Montaldo (Eds.), *Merton & Hesychasm: The prayer of the heart: The Eastern Church* (pp. 447–472). Louisville, KY: Fons Vitae.

Merton, T. (2003c). Orthodoxy and the world. In B. Dieker, & J. Montaldo (Eds.), *Merton & Hesychasm: The prayer of the heart: The Eastern Church* (pp. 473–484). Louisville, KY: Fons Vitae.

Merton, T. (2005a). Final integration: Toward a "monastic therapy." In R. Baker, & G. Henry (Eds.), *Merton & Sufism: The untold story* (pp. 266–277). Louisville, KY: Fons Vitae.

Merton, T. (2005b). *Cassian and the fathers: Initiation into the monastic tradition* (P. O'Connell, Ed.), Kalamazoo, MI: Cistercian Press.

Merton, T. (2006). *Pre-Benedictine monasticism: Initiation into the monastic tradition 2* (P. O'Connell, Ed.), Kalamazoo, MI: Cistercian Press.

Merton, T. (2008). *An introduction to Christian mysticism: Initiation into the monastic tradition 3* (P. O'Connell, Ed.), Kalamazoo, MI: Cistercian Press.

Metzner, R. (1989). States of consciousness and transpersonal psychology. In R. S. Valle, & S. Halling (Eds.), *Existential-phenomenological perspectives in psychology: Exploring the breadth of human experience* (pp. 329–338). New York: Plenum Press.

Meyendorff, J. (1998a). *St. Gregory Palamas and orthodox spirituality* (A. Fiske, Trans.). Crestwood, NY: St. Vladimir's Seminary Press.

Meyendorff, J. (1998b). *A study of Gregory Palamas* (G. Lawrence, Trans.). Crestwood, NY: St. Vladimir's Seminary Press. (Original work published 1959).

Michael, S. T., & Snyder, C. R. (2005). Getting unstuck: The roles of hope, finding meaning, and rumination in the adjustment to bereavement among college students. *Death Studies, 29*, 435–458.

Midgley, M. (2002). *Evolution as a religion*. London: Routledge. (Original work published 1985).

Milhailoff, V. (2005). *Breaking the chains of addiction*. Salisbury, MA: Regina Orthodox.

Millbank, J. (2003). Violence: Double passivity. In K. R. Chase, & A. Jacobs (Eds.), *Must Christianity be violent? Reflections on history, practice, and theology* (pp. 183–200). Grand Rapids, MI: Brazos Press.

Miller, A. S., & Hoffman, J. P. (1995). Risk and religion: An explanation of gender differences in religiosity. *Journal for the Scientific Study of Religion, 34*, 63–75.

Miller, A. S., & Stark, R. (2002). Gender and religiousness: Can socialization explanations be saved? *American Journal of Sociology, 107*, 1399–1423.

Miller, G. (1999). The development of the spiritual focus of counseling and counselor education. *Journal of Counseling & Development, 77*, 498–501.

Miller, G. A. (2003). The cognitive revolution: A historical perspective. *Trends in Cognitive Science, 7*, 141–144.

Miller, G. T. (2000). Baptists and neo-evangelical theology. *Baptist History and Heritage, 35*(1), 20–38.

Miller, L. (2005). Interpersonal psychotherapy from a spiritual perspective. In L. Sperry, & E. P. Shafranske (Eds.), *Spiritually oriented psychotherapy* (pp. 153–175). Washington, DC: American Psychological Association.

Miller, L., Warner, V., Wickramaratne, P., & Weissman, M. (1997). Religiosity and depression: Ten-year follow-up of depressed mothers and offspring. *Journal of the American Academy of Child & Adolescent Psychiatry, 36*, 1416–1425.

Miller, L., Warner, V., Wickramaratne, P., Weissman, M. (1999). Religiosity as a protective factor in depressive disorder. *The American Journal of Psychiatry, 156*, 808–809.

Miller, L., Weissman, M., Gur, M., & Greenwald, S. (2002). Adult religiousness and history of childhood depression: Eleven-year follow-up study. *The Journal of Nervous and Mental Disease, 190*, 86–93.

Miller, M. (2000). The interplay of object relations and cognitive development: Implications for spiritual growth and the transformation of images. In M. Miller, & A. West (Eds.), *Spirituality, ethics, and relationship in adulthood: Clinical and theoretical explanations* (pp. 307–335). Madison, CT: Psychosocial.

Miller, M. E. (2002). Zen and psychotherapy: From neutrality, through relationship, to the emptying place. In P. Young-Eisendrath, & S. Muramoto (Eds.), *Awakening and insight: Zen Buddhism and psychotherapy* (pp. 81–92). New York: Taylor & Francis.

Miller, R. (2001). The positive effect of prayer on plants. In L. Francis, & J. Astley (Eds.), *Psychological perspectives on prayer* (pp. 153–155). Leominster, UK: Gracewing.

Miller, W. R., & Thoresen, C. E. (2003). Spirituality, religion, and health: An emerging research field. *American Psychologist, 58*, 24–35.

Miner, M. (2007). Back to the basics in attachment to God: Revisiting theory in light of theology. *Journal of Psychology and Theology, 35*, 112–122.

Minnaar, C. (2007). Introduction. In M. Lings, & c. Minnaar (Eds.), *The underlying religion: An introduction to the perennial philosophy* (pp. xi–xxi). Bloomington, IN: World Wisdom.

Mischey, E. J. (1981). Faith, identity, and morality in late adolescence. *Character Potential, 9*, 175–185.

Mitchell, J., & Weatherly, D. (2000). Beyond church attendance: Religiosity and mental health among rural older adults. *Journal of Cross-Cultural Gerontology, 15*, 37–54.

Mitchell, L., & Romans, S. (2003). Spiritual beliefs in bipolar affective disorder. Their relevance for illness management. *Journal of Affective Disorders, 75*, 247–257.

Mithen, S. (2000). Mind, brain and material culture: An archaeological perspective. In P. Carruthers, & A. Chamberlain (Eds.), *Evolution and the human mind: Modularity, language and meta-cognition* (pp. 207–217). Cambridge: Cambridge University Press.

Moacanin, R. (1992). Tantric Buddhism and Jung: Connections, similarities, differences. In D. Meckel, & R. Moore (Eds.), *Self and liberation: The Jung-Buddhism dialogue* (pp. 275–301). New York: Paulist Press.

Moaddel, M. (2005). *Islamic modernism, nationalism, and fundamentalism: Episode and discourse.* Chicago, IL: The University of Chicago Press.

Moaddel, M., & Talattof, K. (Eds.). (2002). Modernist and fundamentalist debates in Islam. New York: Palgrave Macmillan.

Moberg, D. (2002a). Research on spirituality. In D. Moberg (Ed.), *Aging and spirituality: Spiritual dimensions of aging theory, research, practice, and policy* (pp. 55–69). New York: Haworth Pastoral.

Moberg, D. (2002b). The spiritual life review. In D. Moberg (Ed.), *Aging and spirituality: Spiritual dimensions of aging theory, research, practice, and policy* (pp. 159–176). New York: Haworth Pastoral.

Moghaddam, F. M. (2005). Psychological processes and "The staircase to terrorism". *American Psychologist, 60,* 1039–1041.

Mohamed, Y. (1995). Fitrah and its bearing on the principles of psychology. *The American Journal of Islamic Social Sciences, 12,* 1–18.

Mohan, Y., Mohan, K. K., Roy, G., Basu, S., & Viranjini, G. (2004). Spiritual well-being: An empirical study with yogic perspectives. *Journal of Indian Psychology, 22,* 41–57.

Mol, H. (1989). The secularization of Canada. In M. Lynn, & D. Moberg (Eds.), *Research in the social scientific study of religion, Volume 1* (pp. 197–215). Greenwich, CT: JAI Press.

Möller-Leimkühler, A. M. (2003). The gender gap in suicide and premature death or: Why are men so vulnerable? *European Archives of Psychiatry and Clinical Neuroscience, 253,* 1–8.

Moltmann, J. (1967). *Theology of hope: On the ground and the implications of a Christian eschatology.* New York: Harper & Row.

Moltmann, J. (1980). *Experiences of God.* Philadelphia: Fortress Press.

Montaldo, J. (2003). Contemplation and the cosmos: Chapter VIII of Thomas Merton's lecture notes on theology and mysticism. In B. Dieker, & J. Montaldo (Eds.), *Merton & Hesychasm: The prayer of the heart: The Eastern Church* (pp. 431–445). Louisville, KY: Fons Vitae.

Mookherjee, H. N. (1998). Perceptions of well-being among the older metropolitan and non metropolitan populations in the United States. *The Journal of Social Psychology, 138,* 72–82.

Moon, G. W. (2002a). Introduction to special issue on spiritual direction: Part one. *Journal on Psychology and Sociology, 30,* 261–263.

Moon, G. W. (2002b). Spiritual direction: Meaning, purpose, and implications for mental health professionals. *Journal of Psychology and Theology, 30,* 264–275.

Moore, G. E. (1903). *Principia ethica.* Cambridge: Cambridge University Press.

Moore, R. (2001). *The archetype of initiation: Sacred space, ritual process, and personal transformation* (M. Havlick, Jr., Ed.), Philadelphia: Xlibris

Moore, P. (1978). Mystical experience, mystical doctrine, mystical technique. In S. T. Katz (Ed.), *Mysticism and philosophical analysis* (pp. 101–131). New York: Oxford University Press.

Monk-Turner, E. (2003). The benefits of meditation: Experimental findings. *The Social Science Journal, 40,* 465–470.

Morey, J. R. (2005). Winnicott's splitting headache: Considering the gap between Jungian and object relations concepts. *Journal of Analytical Psychology, 50,* 333–350.

Morgan, D. (1998). *Visual piety: A history and theory of popular religious images.* Berkeley, CA: University of California Press.

Morinis, E. (1984). *Pilgrimage in the Hindu tradition: A case study of West Bengal.* Delhi: Oxford University Press.

Morinis, E. (1992). Introduction. In E. Morinis (Ed.), *Sacred journeys: The anthropology of pilgrimage* (pp. 1–28). Westport, CT: Greenwood Press.

Morris, P. A. (1982). The effect of pilgrimage on anxiety, depression and religious attitude. *Psychological Medicine, 12,* 291–294.

Moser, P., & Trout, J. (1995). *Contemporary materialism: A reader.* London: Routledge.

Mott, M. (1984). *The seven mountains of Thomas Merton.* Boston: Houghton Mifflin.

Mounce, H. (1997). *The two pragmatisms: From Peirce to Rorty.* London: Routledge.

Moustakas, C. (1994). *Phenomenological research methods.* Thousand Oaks, CA: Sage.

Mueller, P. S., Plevak, D. J., & Rummans, T. A. (2001). Religious involvement, spirituality, and medicine: Implications for clinical practice. *Mayo Clinic Proceedings, 76,* 1225–1235.

Mukherjee, A. (2002). Hindu psychology and the Bhagavad Gita. In R. Olson (Ed.), *Religious theories of personality and psychotherapy: East meets west* (pp. 19–84). New York: Haworth Press.

Muktananda, S. (1980). *The perfect relationship.* South Fallsburg, NY: SYDA Foundation.

Mulqueen, J., & Elias, J. L. (2000). Understanding spiritual development through cognitive development. *Journal of Pastoral Counseling, 35,* 99–112.

Muramoto, S. (2002a). Buddhism, religion and psychotherapy in the world today. In P. Young-Eisendrath, & S. Muramoto (Eds.), *Awakening and insight: Zen Buddhism and psychotherapy* (pp. 15–29). East Sussex, UK: Brunner-Routledge.

Muramoto, S. (2002b). Jung and Buddhism. In P. Young-Eisendrath, & S. Muramoto (Eds.), *Awakening and insight: Zen Buddhism and psychotherapy* (pp. 122–134). New York: Taylor & Francis.

Murata, T., Takahashi, T., Hamada, T., Omori, M., Kosaka, H., Yoshida, H., et al. (2004). Individual trait anxiety levels characterizing the properties of Zen meditation. *Neuropsychobiology, 50,* 189–194.

Murken, S., & Shah, A. A. (2002). Naturalistic and Islamic approaches to psychology, psychotherapy, and religion: Metaphysical assumptions and methodology – a discussion. *The International Journal for the Psychology of Religion, 12,* 239–254.

Murphy, D., & Stich, S. (2000). Darwin in the madhouse: Evolutionary psychology and the classification of mental disorders. In P. Carruthers, & A. Chamberlain (Eds.), *Evolution and the human mind: Modularity, language and meta-cognition* (pp. 62–92). Cambridge: Cambridge University Press.

Murphy, G. (1928). A note on method in the psychology of religion. *The Journal of Philosophy, 25,* 337–345.

Murphy, J. M., Horton, N. J., Laird, N. M., Monson, R. R., Sobol, A. M., & Leighton, A. H. (2004). Anxiety and depression: A 40-year perspective on relationships regarding prevalence, distribution, and comorbidity. *Acta Psychiatrica Scandinavica, 109,* 355–375.

Murphy, J. M., Laird, N. M., Monson, R. R., Sobol, A. M., & Leighton, A. H. (2000a). A 40-year perspective on the prevalence of depression: The Stirling County Study. *Archives of General Psychiatry, 57,* 209–215.

Murphy, J. M., Laird, N. M., Monson, R. R., Sobol, A. M., & Leighton, A. H. (2000b). Incidence of depression in the Stirling County Study: Historical and comparative perspectives. *Psychological Medicine, 30,* 505–514.

Murphy, J. M., Nierenberg, A. A., Laird, N. M., Monson, R. R., Sobol, A. M., & Leighton, A. H. (2002). Incidence of major depression: Prediction from subthreshold categories in the Stirling County Study. *Journal of Affective Disorders, 68,* 251–259.

Murphy, N. (1995). Divine action in the natural order: Buridan's ass and Schrodinger's cat. In R. Russell, N. Murphy, & A. Peacocke (Eds.), *Chaos and complexity: Scientific perspectives on divine action* (pp. 325–357). Vatican City State: Vatican Observatory.

Murphy, N. (1998a). Human nature: Historical, scientific, and religious issues. In W. S. Brown, N. Murphy, & H. N. Malony (Eds.), *Whatever happened to the soul? Scientific and theological portraits of human nature* (pp. 1–29). Minneapolis, MN: Fortress Press.

Murphy, N. (1998b). Nonreductive physicalism: Philosophical issues. In W. S. Brown, N. Murphy, & H. N. Malony (Eds.), *Whatever happened to the soul? Scientific and theological portraits of human nature* (pp. 127–148). Minneapolis, MN: Fortress Press.

Murphy, N. (1998c). Supervenience and nonreducibility of ethics to biology. In R. Russell, W. Stoeger, & F. Ayala (Eds.), *Evolutionary and molecular biology: Scientific perspectives on divine action* (pp. 463–490). Vatican City State: Vatican Observatory.

Murphy, N. (2002). Introduction. In R. Russell, N. Murphy, T. Meyering, & M. Arbib (Eds.), *Neuroscience and the person: Scientific perspective on Divine action* (pp. i–xxxv). Vatican City State: Vatican Observatory.

Murphy, N. (2005). Philosophical resources for integration. In A. Dueck, & C. Lee (Eds.), *Why psychology needs theology: A radical reformation perspective* (pp. 3–27). Grand Rapids, MI: Eerdmans.

Murphy, N., & Ellis, G. (1996). *On the moral nature of the universe: Theology, cosmology, and ethics.* Minneapolis, MN: Fortress Press.

Murphy, P. E., Ciarrocchi, J. W., Piedmont, R. L., Cheston, S., Peyrot, M, & Fitchett, G. (2000). The relation of religious belief and practices, depression, and hopelessness in persons with clinical depression. *Journal of Consulting and Clinical Psychology, 68*, 1102–1106.

Mursell, G. (2001a). *English spirituality: From earliest times to 1700*. London: Westminster John Knox.

Mursell, G. (2001b). *English spirituality: From 1700 to the present*. London: Westminster John Knox.

Musgrave, C. (1997). The near-death experience: A study of spiritual transformation. *Journal of Near-Death Studies, 15*, 187–201.

Musgrave, C., Allen, C. E., & Allen, G. J. (2002). Spirituality and health for women of color. *American Journal of Public Health, 92*, 557–560.

Musick, M. A. (2000). Theodicy and life satisfaction among Black and White Americans. *Sociology of Religion, 61*, 267–287.

Musick, M. A., Blazer, D. G., & Hays, J. C. (2000). Religious activity, alcohol use, and depression in a sample of elderly Baptists. *Research on Aging, 22*, 91–116.

Musick, M. A., Traphagan, J. W., Koenig, H. G., & Larson, D. B. (2000). Spirituality in physical health and aging. *Journal of Adult Development, 7*, 73–86.

Myers, D. G. (1996). On professing psychological science and Christian faith. *Journal of Psychology and Christianity, 15*, 143–149.

Myers, D. G. (1999). Close relationships and quality of life. In D. Kahneman, E. Diener, & N. Schwarz (Eds.), *Well-being: The foundations of hedonic psychology* (pp. 374–391). New York: Russell Sage Foundation.

Myers, D. G., & Diener, E. (1995). Who is happy? *Psychological Science, 6*, 10–19.

Nagarjuna. (1995). *The fundamental wisdom of the middle way: Nagarjuna's Mulamadhyamakakarika* (J. L. Garfield, Trans.). New York: Oxford University Press.

Nagel, T. (1970). Armstrong on the mind. *The Philosophical Review, 79*, 394–403.

Nagel, T. (1974). What is it like to be a bat? *The Philosophical Review, 83*, 435–450.

Nagel, T. (1986). *The view from nowhere*. New York: Oxford University Press.

Nagendra, H. R., & Nagarathna, R. (1986). An integrated approach of yoga therapy for bronchial asthma: A 3–54-month perspective study. *Journal of Asthma, 23*, 123–137.

Nanamoli, B., & Bodhi, B. (Trans.). (2001). *The middle length discourses of the Buddha: A translation of the Majjhima Nikaya* (2nd ed.). Boston: Wisdom.

Nasr, S. H. (2002). The heart of the faithful is the throne of the All-Merciful. In J. Cutsinger (Ed.), *Paths to the heart: Sufism and the Christian East* (pp. 32–45). Bloomington, IN: World Wisdom.

Nazar, F., & Kouzekanani, K. (2003). A cross-cultural study of children's perceptions of selected religious concepts. *Alberta Journal of Educational Research, 49*, 155–162.

Nealon-Woods, M. A., Ferrari, J. R., & Jason, L. A. (1995). Twelve-step program use among Oxford House residents: Spirituality or social support in sobriety? *Journal of Substance Abuse, 7*, 311–318.

Neimeyer, R., & Levitt, H. (2001). Coping and coherence: A narrative perspective on resilience. In C. R. Snyder (Ed.), *Coping with stress: Effective people and processes* (pp. 47–92). Oxford: Oxford University Press.

Neitz, M. J., & Mueser, P. R. (1997). Economic man and the sociology of religion: A critique of the rational choice approach. In L. A. Young (Ed.), *Rational choice theory and religion: Summary and assessment* (pp. 105–118). New York: Routledge.

Nelson, C. J., Rosenfeld, B., Breitbart, W., & Galietta, M. (2002). Spirituality, religion, and depression in the terminally ill. *Psychosomatics, 43*, 213–220.

Nelson, J. M. (2006). Missed opportunities in dialogue between psychology and religion. *Journal of Psychology and Theology, 34*, 205–216.

Nesse, R. M. (2005). Evolutionary psychology and mental health. In D. Buss (Ed.), *The handbook of evolutionary psychology* (pp. 903–930). Hoboken, NJ: John Wiley & Sons.

Nestingen, J. A. (2002). The Lord's prayer in Luther's catechism. *Word & World, 22*(1), 36–48.

Neufeld, K. (1979). Child-rearing, religion, and abusive parents. *Religious Education, 74*, 234–244.

Newberg, A., & d'Aquili, E. G. (2000). The neuropsychology of religious and spiritual experience. *Journal of Consciousness Studies, 7*, 251–266.

Newberg, A., & Iversen, J. (2003). The neural basis of the complex mental task of meditation: Neurotransmitter and neurochemical considerations. *Medical Hypotheses, 61*, 282–291.

Newberg, A., & Newberg, S. (2005). The neuropsychology of religious and spiritual experience. In R. F. Paloutzian, & C. L. Park (Eds.), *Handbook of the psychology of religion and spirituality* (pp. 199–216). New York: Guilford.

Newberg, A., Newberg, S., & d'Aquili, E. (1997). The philosophy and psychology of consciousness. *American Psychologist, 52*, 177–178.

Newberg, A., Wintering, N., Morgan, D., & Waldman, M. (2006). The measurement of regional cerebral blood flow during glossolalia: A preliminary SPECT study. *Psychiatry Research: Neuroimaging, 148*, 67–71.

Newman, J. W. (1996). *Disciplines of attention: Buddhist insight meditation, the Ignatian spiritual exercises, and classical psychoanalysis.* New York: Peter Lang.

Newman, P. R., & Newman, B. M. (1988). Differences between childhood and adulthood: The identity watershed. *Adolescence, 23*(91), 551–557.

Nicholson, I. A. M. (1998). Gordon Allport, character, and the "culture of personality," 1897–1937. *History of Psychology, 1*, 52–68.

Nicodemos. (1989). *Nicodemos of the holy mountain: A handbook of spiritual counsel* (P. A. Chamberas, Trans.). New York: Paulist Press.

Nidich, S. I., Nidich, R. J., & Alexander, C. N. (2000). Moral development and higher states of consciousness. *Journal of Adult Development, 7*, 217–225.

Niebuhr, R. (1955). *The self and the dramas of history.* New York: Charles Scribner's Sons.

Niebuhr, R. (1957). Human creativity and self-concern in Freud's thought. In B. Nelson (Ed.), *Freud and the 20th Century* (pp. 259–276). Cleveland, OH: Meridian.

Niebuhr, R. (1996a). *The nature and destiny of man: A Christian interpretation. Volume I: Human nature.* Louisville, KY: Westminster John Knox Press. (Original work published 1941).

Niebuhr, R. (1996b). *The nature and destiny of man: A Christian interpretation. Volume II: Human density.* Louisville, KY: Westminster John Knox Press. (Original work published 1943).

Nikodimos, St., & Makarios, St. (1979). *The Philokalia, Volume 1* (G. Palmer, P. Sherrard, & K. Ware, Eds. and Trans.). London: Faber & Faber. (Original work published 1782).

Nikodimos, St., & Makarios, St. (1981). *The Philokalia, Volume 2* (G. Palmer, P. Sherrard, & K. Ware, Eds. and Trans.). London: Faber & Faber. (Original work published 1782).

Nikodimos, St., & Makarios, St. (1984). *The Philokalia, Volume 3* (G. Palmer, P. Sherrard, & K. Ware, Eds. and Trans.). London: Faber & Faber. (Original work published 1782).

Nikodimos, St., & Makarios, St. (1995). *The Philokalia, Volume 4* (G. Palmer, P. Sherrard, & K. Ware, Eds. and Trans.). London: Faber & Faber. (Original work published 1782).

Nixon, L. (1996). Factors predispositional of creativity and mysticism: A comparative study of Charles Darwin and Therese of Lisieux. *Advanced Development, 7*, 81–100.

Noam, G., & Wolf, M. (1993). Psychology and spirituality: Forging a new relationship. In M. Randour (Ed.), *Exploring sacred landscapes: Religious and spiritual experiences in psychotherapy* (pp. 194–207). New York: Columbia University Press.

Noblitt, J., & Perskin, P. (2000). *Cult and ritual abuse: Its history, anthropology, and recent discovery in contemporary America.* Westport, CT: Praeger.

Noda, S. J. (2000). The concept of holism in individual psychology and Buddhism. *The Journal of Individual Psychology, 56*, 285–295.

Noffke, J. L., & McFadden, S. H. (2001). Denominational and age comparisons of God concepts. *Journal for the Scientific Study of Religion, 40*, 747–756.

Nolen-Hoeksema, S., & Rusting, C. L. (1999). Gender differences in well-being. In D. Kahneman, E. Diener, & N. Schwarz (Eds.), *Well-being: The foundations of hedonic psychology* (pp. 330–350). New York: Russell Sage Foundation.

Noll, M. A. (2003). Have Christians done more harm than good? In K. R. Chase, & A. Jacobs (Eds.), *Must Christianity be violent? Reflections on history, practice and theology* (pp. 79–93). Grand Rapids, MI: Brazos Press.

Noll, R. (1997). *The Aryan Christ: The secret life of Carl Jung.* New York: Random House.

Nooney, J., & Woodrum, E. (2002). Religious coping and church-based social support as predictors of mental health outcomes: Testing a conceptual model. *Journal for the Scientific Study of Religion, 41,* 359–368.

Nordin, K., Wasteson, E., Hoffman, K., Glimelius, B., & Sjoden, P. (2001). Discrepancies between attainment and importance of life values and anxiety and depression in gastrointestinal cancer patients and their spouses. *Psycho-Oncology, 10,* 479–489.

Norman, J. (2004). Gender bias in the diagnosis and treatment of depression. *International Journal of Mental Health, 33,* 32–43.

Norris, P., & Inglehart, R. (2004). *Sacred and secular: Religion and politics worldwide.* Cambridge: Cambridge University Press.

Nouwen, H. (1975). *Reaching out: The three movements of the spiritual life.* New York: Image.

Nucci, L., & Turiel, E. (1993). God's word, religious rules, and their relation to Christian and Jewish children's concepts of morality. *Child Development, 64,* 1475–1491.

Numbers, R. (2003). Science without God: Natural laws and Christian beliefs. In D. Lindberg, & R. Numbers (Eds.), *When science and Christianity meet* (pp. 265–285). Chicago: University of Chicago Press.

Nussbaum, M. (1990). *Love's knowledge.* New York: Oxford University Press.

Nye, R. (2004). Christian perspectives on children's spirituality: Social science contributions? In D. Ratcliff (Ed.), *Children's spirituality: Christian perspectives, research, and applications* (pp. 90–107). Eugene, OR: Cascade.

Oates, W. (1955). *Religious factors in mental illness.* New York: Association Press.

Oates, W. (1958). The pastor and faith healing. In S. Doniger (Ed.), *Religion and health, a symposium* (pp. 13–32). New York: Association Press.

O'Connor, K. V. (2001). What is our present? An Antipodean perspective on the relationship between "psychology" and "religion". In D. Jonte-Pace, & W. B. Parsons (Eds.), *Religion and psychology: Mapping the terrain: Contemporary dialogues, future prospects* (pp. 75–93). London: Routledge.

O'Connor, M. (2002). Spiritual *Dark Night* and psychological depression: Some comparisons and considerations. *Counseling and Values, 46,* 137–148.

O'Connor, R. (2005). *Undoing perpetual stress: The missing connection between depression, anxiety, and 21st century illness.* New York: Berkley Books.

O'Connor, S., & Vandenberg, B. (2005). Psychosis or faith? Clinicians' assessment of religious beliefs. *Journal of Consulting and Clinical Psychology, 73,* 610–616.

Oden, T. C. (1984). *Care of souls in the classic tradition.* Minneapolis, MN: Fortress Press.

Okagaki, L., & Bevis, C. (1999). Transmission of religious values: Relations between parents' and daughters' beliefs. *The Journal of Genetic Psychology, 160,* 303–318.

Okano, M. (2002). The consciousness-only school: An introduction and a brief comparison with Jung's psychology. In P. Young-Eisendrath, & S. Muramoto (Eds.), *Awakening and insight: Zen Buddhism and psychotherapy* (pp. 224–234). New York: Taylor & Francis.

Okasha, A. (1999). Mental health in the Middle East: An Egyptian perspective. *Clinical Psychology Review, 19,* 917–933.

Okholm, D. (2001). To vent or not to vent? What contemporary psychology can learn from ascetic theology about anger. In M. McMinn, & T. Phillips (Eds.), *Care for the soul: Exploring the intersection of psychology & theology* (pp. 164–186). Downers Grove, IL: InterVarsity Press.

Oksanen, A. (1994). *Religious conversion: A meta- analytical study.* Lund, Sweden: Lund University Press.

Olafson, F. (2001). *Naturalism and the human condition: Against scientism.* London: Routledge.

O'Leary, S. (2004). Cyberspace as sacred space: Communicating religion on computer networks. In L. Dawson, & D. Cowan (Eds.), *Religion online: Finding faith on the Internet* (pp. 37–58). New York: Routledge.

Oliner, S. P. (2002). Extraordinary acts of ordinary people: Faces of heroism and altruism. In S. G. Post, L. G. Underwood, J. P. Schloss, & W. B. Hurlbut (Eds.), *Altruism & altruistic love: Science, philosophy, & religion in dialogue* (pp. 123–139). New York: Oxford University Press.

Olivelle, P. (2004a). *The Asrama system: The history and hermeneutics of a religious institution.* New Delhi: Munshiram Manoharlal.

Olivelle, P. (Trans.). (2004b). The law code of Manu. New York: Oxford University Press.

Oliver, J. M., & Paull, J. C. (1995). Self-esteem and self-efficacy: Perceived parenting and family climate and depression in university students. *Journal of Clinical Psychology, 51,* 467–481.

Olson, D. V. A., & Perl, P. (2001). Variations in strictness and religious commitments within and among five denominations. *Journal for the Scientific Study of Religion, 40,* 757–764.

Olson, D. V. A., & Perl, P. (2005). Free and cheap riding in strict, conservative churches. *Journal for the Scientific Study of Religion, 44,* 123–142.

Olson, R., & McBeath, B. (2002). Convergence and divergence. In R. Olson (Ed.), *Religious theories of personality and psychotherapy: East meets west* (pp. 359–408). New York: Haworth Press.

Oman, D., & Thoresen, C. E. (2003). Spiritual modeling: A key to spiritual and religious growth? *The International Journal for the Psychology of Religion, 13,* 149–165.

Omori, S. (1996). *An introduction to Zen training: A translation of Sanzen Nyumon* (D. Hosokawa, & R. Yoshimoto, Trans.). London: Kegan Paul International.

O'Murchu, D. (1994). Spirituality, recovery, and transcendental meditation. In D. O'Connell, & C. Alexander (Eds.), *Self-recovery: Treating addictions using transcendental meditation and Maharishi Ayur-Veda* (pp. 169–184). Binghamptom, NY: Haworth Press.

Onda, A. (2002). The development of Buddhist psychology in modern Japan. In P. Young-Eisendrath, & S. Muramoto (Eds.), *Awakening and insight: Zen Buddhism and psychotherapy* (pp. 242–251). New York: Taylor & Francis.

Oppenheimer, J. E., Flannelly, K. J., & Weaver, A. J. (2004). A comparative analysis of the psychological literature on collaboration between clergy and mental-health professionals- perspectives from secular and religious journals: 1970–1999. *Pastoral Psychology, 53,* 153–162.

Origen. (1994). De principiis. In A. Roberts, & J. Donaldson (Eds.), *The Ante-Nicene Fathers, Volume 4: Fathers of the Third Century* (pp. 239–384). Peabody, MA: Hendrickson. (Original work written c. 185).

Orme-Johnson, D. (1988). The cosmic psyche: An introduction to Maharishi's Vedic psychology: The fulfillment of modern psychology. *Modern Science and Vedic Science, 2,* 113–163.

Orme-Johnson, D. (1994). Transcendental meditation as an epidemiological approach to drug and alcohol abuse: Theory, research, and financial impact evaluation. *Alcoholism Treatment Quarterly, 11*(1–2), 119–168.

Orme-Johnson, D., Zimmerman, E., & Hawkins, M. (1997). Maharishi's Vedic psychology: The science of the cosmic psyche. In H. Kao, & D. Sinha (Eds.), *Asian perspectives on psychology* (pp. 282–308). New Delhi: Sage.

Ornstein, R. (1991). *The evolution of consciousness: Of Darwin, Freud, and cranial fire: The origins of the way we think.* New York: Prentice Hall.

Orsillo, S., Roemer, L., Lerner, B., & Tull, M. (2004). Acceptance, mindfulness, and cognitive-behavioral therapy. In S. Hayes, V. Follette, & M. Linehan (Eds.), *Mindfulness and acceptance: Expanding the cognitive-behavioral tradition* (pp. 66–95). New York: Guilford.

Oser, F. (1991a). The development of religious judgment. In F. Oser, & W. G. Scarlett (Eds.), *Religious development in childhood and adolescence* (pp. 5–25). San Francisco: Jossey-Bass.

Oser, F. (1991b). Toward a logic of religious development: A reply to my critics. In J. Fowler, K. Nipkow, & F. Schweitzer (Eds.), *Stages of faith and religious development: Implications for church, education, and society* (pp. 37–64). New York: Crossroad.

Oser, F. (1997). Research on religious judgment, Part II: A conversation with Professor Fritz Oser University of Fribourg, Switzerland. *Journal of Research and Christian Education, 6,* 65–78.

Oser, F., & Gmunder, P. (1991). *Religious judgment: A developmental perspective.* Birmingham, AL: Religious Education.

Oser, F. K., Reich, K. H., & Bucher, A. A. (1994). Development of belief and unbelief in childhood and adolescence. In J. Corveleyn, & D. Hutsebaut (Eds.), *Belief and unbelief: Psychological perspectives* (pp. 39–62). Amsterdam: Rodopi.

Otto, R. (1932). *Mysticism east and west: A comparative analysis of the nature of mysticism.* New York: Macmillan.

Otto, R. (1950). *The idea of the holy* (2nd ed.) (J. Harvey, Trans.). London: Oxford University Press. (Original work published 1923).

Ouspensky, L., & Lossky, V. (1999). *The meaning of icons* (2nd ed.) (G. E. H. Palmer, & E. Kadloubovsky, Trans.). Crestwood, NY: St. Vladimir's Seminary Press. (Original work published 1952).

Outler, A. (1954). *Psychotherapy and the Christian message.* New York: Harper & Brothers.

Ouwehand, E. (1990). Women's rituals: Reflections on developmental theory. In H.-G. Heimbrock, & H. B. Boudewijnse (Eds.), *Current studies on rituals: Perspectives for the psychology of religion* (pp. 135–150). Amsterdam: Rodopi.

Overcash, W. S., Calhoun, L. G., Cann, A., & Tedeschi, R. G. (1996). Coping with crises: An examination of the impact of traumatic events on religious beliefs. *The Journal of Genetic Psychology, 157,* 455–464.

Overton, W. F. (1998). Developmental psychology: Philosophy, concepts, and methodology. In W. Damon, & R. M. Lerner (Eds.), *Handbook of child psychology: Theoretical models of development, Volume 1* (5th ed., pp. 107–188). New York: Wiley.

Oxman, T. E., Freeman, Jr., D. H., & Manheimer, E. D. (1995). Lack of social participation or religious strength and comfort as risk factors for death after cardiac surgery in the elderly. *Psychosomatic Medicine, 57,* 5–15.

Oxman, T. E., Rosenberg, S. D., Schnurr, P. P., Tucker, G. J., & Gala, G. (1988). The language of altered states. *Journal of Nervous and Mental Disease, 176,* 401–408.

Oyserman, D., Coon, H. M., & Kemmelmeier, M. (2002). Rethinking individualism and collectivism: Evaluation of theoretical assumptions and meta-analyses. *Psychological Bulletin, 128,* 3–72.

Ozorak, E. W. (1989). Social and cognitive influences on the development of religious beliefs and commitment in adolescence. *Journal for the Scientific Study of Religion, 28,* 448–463.

Ozorak, E. W. (1997). In the eye of the beholder: A social-cognitive model of religious belief. In B. Spilka, & D. N. McIntosh (Eds.), *The psychology of religion: Theoretical approaches* (pp. 194–203). Boulder, CO: Westview Press.

Pace, E. (2007). Religion as communication: The changing shape of Catholicism in Europe. In N. T. Ammerman (Ed.), *Everyday religion: Observing modern religious lives* (pp. 37–49). Oxford: Oxford University Press.

Packer, M. J. (1985). Hermeneutic inquiry in the study of human conduct. *American Psychologist, 40,* 1081–1093.

Packer, M. J. (1988). Hermeneutic inquiry: A response to criticisms. *American Psychologist, 43,* 133–136.

Packer, M. J., & Addison, R. B. (Eds.). (1989). *Entering the circle: Hermeneutic investigation in psychology.* Albany, NY: State University of New York Press.

Paden, W. (2000). Elements of a new comparativism. In K. Patton, & B. Ray (Eds.), *A magic still dwells: Comparative religion in the postmodern age* (pp. 182–192). Berkeley, CA: University of California Press.

Palmer, C. T. (1991). Human rape: Adaptation or by-product? *The Journal of Sex Research, 28,* 365–386.

Pahnke, W. (1966). Drugs and mysticism. *International Journal of Parapsychology, 8,* 295–314.

Pahnke, W., & Richards, W. A. (1966). Implications of LSD and experimental mysticism. *The Journal of Transpersonal Psychology, 1,* 69–102.

Palamas, G. (1983). *The triads* (J. Meyendorff, Ed., N. Gendle, Trans.). Mahwah, NJ: Paulist Press.

Paloutzian, R. (2005). Religious conversion and spiritual transformation: A meaning-system analysis. In R. Paloutzian, & C. Park (Eds.), *Handbook of the psychology of religion and spirituality* (pp. 331–347). New York: Guilford.

Paloutzian, R., & Ellison, C. (1982). Loneliness, spiritual well-being, and the quality of life. In L. Peplau, & D. Perlman (Eds.), *Loneliness: A sourcebook of current theory, research and therapy* (pp. 224–237). New York: Wiley.

Paloutzian, R., & Kirkpatrick, L. A. (1995). The scope of religious influences on personal and societal well-being. *Journal of Social Issues, 51*(2), 1–11.

Paloutzian, R., Richardson, J. T., & Rambo, L. R. (1999). Religious conversion and personality change. *Journal of Personality, 67*, 1047–1079.

Pankhania, J. (2005). Yoga and its practice in psychological healing. In R. Moodley, & W. West (Eds.), *Integrating traditional healing practices into counseling and psychotherapy* (pp. 246–256). Thousand Oaks, CA: Sage.

Pannenberg, W. (1983). *Christian spirituality*. Philadelphia, PA: Westminster.

Pannenberg, W. (1985). *Anthropology in theological perspective* (M. O'Connell, Trans.). Edinburgh: T & T Clark.

Pannenberg, W. (1988). *Systematic theology, Volume I.* (G. Bromiley, Trans.). Grand Rapids, MI: Eerdmans.

Pannenberg, W. (1996). How to think about secularism. *First Things: The Journal of Religion, Culture, and Public Life, 64*, 27–32.

Pardini, D. A., Plante, T. G., Sherman, A., & Stump, J. E. (2000). Religious faith and spirituality in substance abuse recovery: Determining the mental health benefits. *Journal of Substance Abuse Treatment, 19*, 347–354.

Pargament, K. I. (1990). God help me: Toward a theoretical framework of coping for the psychology of religion. *Research in the Social Scientific Study of Religion, 2*, 195–224.

Pargament, K. I. (1997). *The psychology of religion and coping: Theory, research and practice* (New ed.). New York: Guilford.

Pargament, K. I. (1999). The psychology of religion and spirituality: Yes and no. *The International Journal for the Psychology of Religion, 9*, 3–16.

Pargament, K. I. (2002a). The bitter and the sweet: An evaluation of the costs and benefits of religiousness. *Psychological Inquiry, 13*, 168–181.

Pargament, K. I. (2002b). Is religion nothing but…? Explaining religion versus explaining religion away. *Psychological Inquiry, 13*, 239–244.

Pargament, K. I., Cole, B., Vandecreek, L., Belavich, T., Brant, C., & Perez, L. (1999). The vigil: Religion and the search for control in the hospital waiting room. *Journal of Health Psychology, 4*, 327–341.

Pargament, K. I., Ensing, D. S., Falgout, K., Olsen, H., Reilly, B., Van Haitsma, K., et al. (1990). God help me: (I): Religious coping efforts as predictors of the outcomes to significant negative life events. *American Journal of Community Psychology, 18*, 793–824.

Pargament, K. I., Kennell, J., Hathaway, W., Grevengoed, N., Newman, J., & Jones, W. (1988). Religion and the problem-solving process: Three styles of coping. *Journal for the Scientific Study of Religion, 27*, 90–104.

Pargament, K. I., Koenig, H. G., & Perez, L. M. (2000). The many methods of religious coping: Development and initial validation of the RCOPE. *Journal of Clinical Psychology, 56*, 519–543.

Pargament, K. I., Koenig, H. G., Tarakeshwar, N., & Hahn, J. (2001). Religious struggle as a predictor of mortality among medically ill elderly patients: A 2-year longitudinal study. *Archives of International Medicine, 161*, 1881–1884.

Pargament, K. I., Magyar, G. M., Benore, E., & Mahoney, A. (2005). Sacrilege: A study of sacred loss and desecration and their implications for health and well-being in a community sample. *Journal for the Scientific Study of Religion, 44*, 59–78.

Pargament, K. I., & Mahoney, A. (2002). Spirituality: Discovering and conserving the sacred. In C. R. Synder, & S. J. Lopez (Eds.), *Handbook of positive psychology* (pp. 646–659). Oxford: Oxford University Press.

Pargament, K. I., & Mahoney, A. (2005). Sacred matters: Sanctification as a vital topic for the psychology of religion. *International Journal for the Psychology of Religion, 15*, 179–198.

Pargament, K. I., & Maton, K. I. (2000). Religion in American life: A community psychology perspective. In J. Rappaport, & E. Seidman (Eds.), *Handbook of community psychology* (pp. 495–522). New York: Kluwer Academic/Plenum.

Pargament, K. I., & Park, C. L. (1995). Merely a defense? The variety of religious means. *Journal of Social Issues, 51*(2), 13–32.

Pargament, K. I., & Park, C. L. (1997). In times of stress: The religion-coping connections. In B. Spilka, & D. N. McIntosh (Eds.), *The psychology of religion: Theoretical approaches* (pp. 43–53). Boulder, CO: Westview Press.

Pargament, K. I., Poloma, M., & Tarakeshwar, N. (2001). Methods of coping from the religions of the world: The Bar Mitzvah, karma, and spiritual healing. In C. R. Snyder (Ed.), *Coping with stress: Effective people and processes* (pp. 259–284). Oxford: Oxford University Press.

Pargament, K. I., Silverman, W., Johnson, S., Echemendia, R., & Snyder, S. (1983). The psychosocial climate of religious congregations. *American Journal of Community Psychology, 11*, 351–381.

Pargament, K. I., Smith, B. W., Koenig, H. G., & Perez, L. (1998). Patterns of positive and negative religious coping with major life stressors. *Journal for the Scientific Study of Religion, 37*, 710–724.

Parikh, B. (1980). Development of moral judgment and its relation to family environment factors in Indian and American families. *Child Development, 51*, 1030–1039.

Park, C. (2005). Religion and meaning. In R. F. Paloutzian, & C. L. Park (Eds.), *Handbook of the psychology of religion and spirituality* (pp. 295–314). New York: Guilford.

Park, J. H., Meyers, L. S., & Czar, G. C. (1998). Religiosity and spirituality: An exploratory analysis using the CPI 3-vector model. *Journal of Social Behavior & Personality, 13*, 541–552.

Park, J. Z., & Smith, C. (2000). "To whom much has been given…": Religious capital and community voluntarism among churchgoing protestants. *Journal for the Scientific Study of Religion, 39*, 272–286.

Parker, M. (1985). Identity and the development of religious thinking. In A. Waterman (Ed.), *Identity in adolescence: Processes and contents* (pp. 43–60). San Francisco: Jossey-Bass.

Parker, M., Roff, L. L., Klemmack, D. L., Koenig, H. G., Baker, P., & Allman, R. M. (2003). Religiosity and mental health in southern, community-dwelling older adults. *Aging & Mental Health, 7*, 390–397.

Parks, G. A. (2004). Transcendental meditation in criminal rehabilitation and crime prevention. The *Behavior Therapist, 27*, 179–182.

Parks, S. (1991). The North American critique of James Fowler's theory of faith development. In J. Fowler, K. Nipkow, & F. Schweitzer (Eds.), *Stages of faith and religious development: Implications for church, education, and society* (pp. 101–115). New York: Crossroad.

Parsons, W. (1999). *The enigma of the oceanic feeling: Revisioning the psychoanalytic theory of mysticism.* Oxford, NY: Oxford University Press.

Parsons, W. (2000). Themes and debates in the psychology-comparativist dialogue. In D. Jonte-Pace, & W. Parsons (Eds.), *Religion and psychology: Mapping the terrain* (pp. 229–253). London: Routledge.

Partridge, C. (2004). Alternative spiritualities, new religions, and the reenchantment of the West. In J. Lewis (Ed.), *The Oxford handbook of new religious movements* (pp. 39–67). Oxford: Oxford University Press.

Passmore, J. (1967). Logical positivism. In P. Edwards (Ed.), *The encyclopedia of philosophy* (Vol. 5). New York: Macmillan.

Patanjali (2003). *Yoga-Darshana: The Sutras of Patanjali with the Bhasya of Vyasa* (2nd ed., G. Jha, Trans.). Fremont, CA: Asian Humanities Press.

Paton, J. J., Belova, M. A., Morrison, S. E., & Salzman, C. D. (2006). The primate amygdala represents the positive and negative value of visual stimuli during learning. *Nature, 439*(7078), 865–870.

Patrick, J., & Kinney, J. (2003). Why believe? The effects of religious beliefs on emotional well being. In S. McFadden, M. Brennan, & J. Patrick (Eds.), *New directions in the study of late life religiousness and spirituality* (pp. 153–170). Binghampton, NY: Haworth Pastoral Press.

Patton, K. (2000). Juggling torches: Why we still need comparative religion. In K. Patton, & B. Ray (Eds.), *A magic still dwells: Comparative religion in the postmodern age* (pp. 153–171). Berkeley, CA: University of California Press.

Patton, K., & Ray, B. (2000). Introduction. In K. Patton, & B. Ray (Eds.), *A magic still dwells: Comparative religion in the postmodern age* (pp. 1–19). Berkeley, CA: University of California Press.

Paul, L. K. (1999). Jesus as object: Christian conversion as interpreted through the perspective of Fairborn's object relations theory. *Journal of Psychology and Theology, 27*, 300–308.

Payne, B. P. (1990). Research and theoretical approaches to spirituality and aging. *Generations, 14*(4), 11–14.

Payne, R. K. (2002). Locating Buddhism, locating psychology. In P. Young-Eisendrath, & S. Muramoto (Eds.), *Awakening and insight: Zen Buddhism and psychotherapy* (pp. 172–186). New York: Taylor & Francis.

Peace, R. (1998a). *Spiritual autobiography: Discovering and sharing your spiritual story.* Colorado Springs, CO: Navpress.

Peace, R. (1998b). *Spiritual journaling: Recording your journey toward God.* Colorado Springs, CO: Navpress.

Peacocke, A. (1993). *Theology for a scientific age: Being and becoming-natural, divine, and human.* Minneapolis, MN: Fortress Press.

Peacocke, A. (1995). God's interaction with the world: The implications of deterministic "Chaos" and of interconnected and interdependent complexity. In R. Russell, N. Murphy, & A. Peacocke (Eds.), *Chaos and complexity: Scientific perspectives on divine action* (pp. 263–287). Vatican City State: Vatican Observatory.

Peacocke, A. (1998). Biological evolution: A clue to the meaning of nature. In R. Russell, W. Stoeger, & F. Ayala (Eds.), *Evolutionary and molecular biology: Scientific perspectives on divine action* (pp. 357–376). Vatican City State: Vatican Observatory.

Peacocke, A. (2002). A sound of sheer silence: how does God communicate with humanity. In R. Russell, N. Murphy, T. Meyering, & M. Arbib (Eds.), *Neuroscience and the person: Scientific perspectives on divine action* (pp. 215–248).Vatican City State: Vatican Observatory.

Pearce, L. D., & Axinn, W. G. (1998). The impact of family religious life on the quality of mother-child relations. *American Sociological Review, 63*, 810–828.

Pearce, M. J., Chen, J., Silverman, G. K., Kasl, S. V., Rosenheck, R., & Prigerson, H. G. (2002). Religious coping, health, and health service use among bereaved adults. *International Journal of Psychiatry in Medicine, 32*, 179–199.

Pearlin, L. (2002). Some institutional and stress process perspectives on religion and health. *Psychological Inquiry, 13*, 217–220.

Pechilis, K. (2004). Introduction: Hindu female gurus in historical and philosophical context. In K. Pechilis (Ed.), *The graceful guru: Hindu female gurus in India and the United States* (pp. 3–49). Oxford: Oxford University Press.

Peele, S. (1997). Utilizing culture and behaviour in epidemiological models of alcohol consumption and consequences for western nations. *Alcohol & Alcoholism, 32*, 51–64.

Pekala, R., & Cardena, E. (2000). Methodological issues in the study of altered states of consciousness and anomalous experiences. In E. Cardena, S. Lynn, & S. Krippner (Eds.), *Varieties of anomalous experience: Examining the scientific evidence* (pp. 47–82). Washington, DC: American Psychological Association.

Peltzer, K. (2004). Preventive health behavior, personality and religiosity among Black and White South Africans. *Studia Psychologica, 46*, 37–48.

Pendleton, S., Benore, E., Jonas, K., Norwood, W., & Herrmann, C. (2004). Spiritual influences in helping children to cope with life stressors. In D. Ratcliff (Ed.), *Children's spirituality: Christian perspectives, research, and applications* (pp. 358–382). Eugene, OR: Cascade.

Pendleton, S., Cavalli, K., Pargament, K., & Nasr, S. (2002). Religious/spiritual coping in childhood cystic fibrosis: A qualitative study. *Pediatrics, 109*, 1–11.

Pennington, M. B. (1998). *Lectio Divina: Renewing ancient practice of praying the scriptures.* New York: Crossroad.

Pennington, M. B. (2001). *Centering prayer: Renewing an ancient Christian prayer form.* New York: Image Books.

Pennington, M. B. (2003). Thomas Merton and Byzantine spirituality. In B. Dieker, & J. Montaldo (Eds.), *Merton & Hesychasm: The prayer of the heart: The Eastern Church* (pp. 153–168). Louisville, KY: Fons Vitae.

Pennington, M. B. (2004). A spiritual master: Dom Thomas Keating. *Perspectives in Religious Studies, 31,* 47–54.

Perez-Ramos, A. (1988). *Francis Bacon's idea of science.* Oxford: Clarendon Press.

Perez-Ramos, A. (1997). Bacon's legacy. In M. Peltonen (Ed.), *The Cambridge companion to Bacon* (pp. 25–46). Cambridge: Cambridge University Press.

Perkins, H. W. (1985). Religious traditions, parents, and peers as determinants of alcohol and drug use among college students. *Review of Religious Research, 27,* 15–31.

Perl, P., & Olson, D. V. A. (2000). Religious market share and intensity of church involvement in five denominations. *Journal for the Scientific Study of Religion, 39,* 12–31.

Perovich, A. N., Jr. (1990). Does the philosophy of mysticism rest on a mistake? In R. K. C. Forman (Ed.), *The problem of pure consciousness: Mysticism and philosophy* (pp. 237–253). New York: Oxford University Press.

Persinger, M. A. (1987). *Neuropsychological bases of God beliefs.* New York: Praeger.

Persinger, M. A. (2001). The neuropsychiatry of paranormal experiences. *Journal of Neuropsychiatry and Clinical Neuroscience, 13,* 515–524.

Persinger, M. A., & Healey, F. (2002). Experimental facilitation of the sensed presence: Possible intercalation between the hemispheres induced by complex magnetic fields. *Journal of Nervous and Mental Disease, 190,* 533–541.

Persinger, M. A., & Makarec, K. (1987). Temporal lobe epileptic signs and correlative behaviors displayed by normal populations. *Journal of General Psychology, 114,* 179–195.

Peters, E. (2001). Are delusions on a continuum? The case of religious and delusional beliefs. In I. Clarke (Ed.), *Psychosis and spirituality* (pp.191–209). London: Whurr.

Peters, E., Day, S., McKenna, J., & Orbach, G. (1999). Delusional ideation in religious and psychotic populations. *British Journal of Clinical Psychology, 38,* 83–96.

Peters, E., Joseph, S. A., & Garety, P. A. (1999). Measurement of delusional ideation in the normal population: Introducing the PDI (Peters et al. Delusions Inventory). *Schizophrenia Bulletin, 25,* 553–576.

Peters, T. (1996). The Trinity in and beyond time. In R. J. Russell, N. Murphy, & C. J. Isham (Eds.), *Quantum cosmology and the laws of nature: Scientific perspectives on divine action* (2nd ed., pp. 263–289). Vatican City State: Vatican Observatory.

Peters, T. (2002). Resurrection of the very Embodied soul. In R. Russell, N. Murphy, T. Meyering, & M. Arbib (Eds.), *Neuroscience and the person: Scientific perspectives on divine action* (pp. 304–325). Vatican City State: Vatican Observatory.

Peters, T. (2007). Models of God. *Philosophia, 35,* 273–288.

Peters, T. C. (2000). *Cherish the Word: reflections on Luther's spirituality.* St. Louis, MO: Concordia Publishing House.

Petersen, L. R., & Roy, A. (1985). Religiosity, anxiety, and meaning and purpose: Religion's consequences for psychological well-being. *Review of Religious Research, 27,* 49–62.

Peterson, C. (1999). Personal control and well-being. In D. Kahneman, E. Diener, & N. Schwarz (Eds.), *Well-being: The foundations of hedonic psychology* (pp. 288–301). New York: Russell Sage Foundation.

Peterson, C. (2006). The Values in Action (VIA) classification of strengths. In M. Czikszentmihalyi, & I. Czikszentmihalyi (Eds.), *A life worth living: Contributions to positive psychology* (pp. 29–48). New York: Oxford University Press.

Peterson, C., & Seligman, M. (2004). *Character strengths and virtues: A handbook and classification.* Washington, DC: American Psychological Association.

Peterson, G. (2003). Demarcation and the scientistic fallacy. *Zygon, 38,* 751–761.

Petts, R., & Knoester, C. (2007). Parents' religious heterogamy and children's well-being. *Journal for the Scientific Study of Religion, 46,* 373–389.

The Pew Research Center & The Pew Forum on Religion and Public Life. (2002, March 20). *Americans struggle with religion's role at home and abroad.* Retrieved August 22, 2007 from http://pewforum.org/publications/surveys/religion.pdf.

Piaget, J. (1916). *La mission de l'idee.* Lausanne: Edition la concorde.

Piaget, J. (1954). *The construction of reality in the child* (M. Cook, Trans.). New York: Basic Books.

Piaget, J. (1968). *Six psychological studies* (A. Tenzer, & D. Elkind, Trans.). New York: Random House.

Piaget, J. (1971). *Psychology and epistemology* (A. Rosin, Trans.). New York: Orion.

Piaget, J. (1982). Reflections on Baldwin. In J. Broughton, & D. Freeman-Moir (Eds.), *The cognitive-developmental psychology of James Mark Baldwin: Current theory and research in genetic epistemology* (pp. 80–86). Norwood, NJ: Ablex.

Piaget, J. (1997). *The moral judgment of the child* (M. Gabain, Trans.). New York: Free Press. (Original work published 1932).

Piaget, J., & Inhelder, B. (1969). *The psychology of the child* (H. Weaver, Trans.). New York: Basic Books.

Pickering, J. (1997). Selfhood is a process. In J. Pickering (Ed.), *The authority of experience: Essays on Buddhism and psychology* (pp. 152–169). Richmond, UK: Curzon.

Pickering, M. (1993). *Auguste Comte: An intellectual biography, Volume 1.* Cambridge: Cambridge University Press.

Piedmont, R. L. (1999). Does spirituality represent the sixth factor of personality? Spiritual transcendence and the five-factor model. *Journal of Personality, 67,* 985–1013.

Piedmont, R. L. (2005). The role of personality in understanding religious and spiritual constructs. In R. F. Paloutzian, & C. L. Park (Eds.), *Handbook of the psychology of religion and spirituality* (pp. 253–273). New York: Guilford.

Pierre, J. M. (2001). Faith or delusion? At the crossroads of religion and psychosis. *Journal of Psychiatric Practice, 7,* 163–172.

Pilkington, K., Kirkwood, G., Rampes, H., & Richardson, J. (2005). Yoga for depression: The research evidence. *Journal of Affective Disorders, 89*(1–3), 13–24.

Pike, N. (1978). On mystic visions as sources of knowledge. In S. T. Katz (Ed.), *Mysticism and philosophical analysis* (pp. 214–234). New York: Oxford University Press.

Pillemer, D. B. (2001). Momentous events and the life story. *Review of General Psychology, 5,* 123–134.

Pingleton, J. (1997). Why don't we forgive: A Biblical and object relations theoretical model for understanding failures in the forgiveness process. *Journal of Psychology and Theology, 25,* 403–413.

Pine, R. (Trans.). (1987). *The Zen teachings of Bodhidharma.* New York: North Point.

Pingleton, J. (1997). Why we don't forgive: A biblical and object relations theoretical model for understanding failures in the forgiveness process. *Journal of Psychology and Theology, 25,* 403–413.

Plante, T. (2004). Introduction. In T. Plante (Ed.), *Sin against the innocents: Sexual abuse by priests and the role of the Catholic church* (pp. xvii–xxvii). Westport, CT: Praeger.

Plante, T., & Canchola, E. L. (2004). The association between strength of religious faith and coping with American terrorism regarding the events of September 11, 2001. *Pastoral Psychology, 52,* 269–278.

Plante, T., Saucedo, B., & Rice, C. (2001). The association between strength of religious faith and coping with daily stress. *Pastoral Psychology, 49,* 291–300.

Plante, T., & Sharma, N. (2001). Religious faith and mental health outcomes. In T. Plante, & A. Sherman (Eds.), *Faith and health: Psychological perspectives* (pp. 240–264). New York: Guilford.

Plato. (1997). *Complete works* (J. Cooper, Ed.), Indianapolis: Hackett.

Ple, B. (2000). Auguste Comte on positivism and happiness. *Journal of Happiness Studies, 1*(4), 423–445.

Pleasants, P. R. (2004). He was ancientfuture before ancientfuture was cool. *Perspectives in Religious Studies, 31*, 83–113.

Pleh, C. (2006). Positive psychology traditions in classical European psychology. In M. Czikszentmihalyi, & I. Czikszentmihalyi (Eds.), *A life worth living: Contributions to positive psychology* (pp. 19–28). New York: Oxford University Press.

Plotinus. (1991). *The Enneads* (S. MacKenna, Trans.). New York: Penguin Books.

Plotkin, H. (2004). *Evolutionary thought in psychology: A brief history.* Malden, MA: Blackwell.

Poirier, P. (2006). Finding a place for elimination in inter-level reductionist activities: Reply to Wimsatt. *Synthese, 151*, 477–483.

Poland, W. S. (1977). Pilgrimage: Action and tradition in self-analysis. *Journal of the American Psychoanalytic Association, 25*, 399–416.

Polanyi, M. (1962). *Personal knowledge: Towards a post-critical philosophy.* London: Routledge & Kegan Paul.

Polivy, J., & Herman, C. P. (2002). If at first you don't succeed: False hopes of self-change. *American Psychologist, 57*, 677–689.

Polkinghorne, D. E. (1988). *Narrative knowing and the human sciences.* Albany, NY: State University of New York Press.

Polkinghorne, D. E. (2004). *Practice and the human sciences: The case for a judgment-based practice of care.* Albany, NY: State University of New York Press.

Polkinghorne, J. (1995). The metaphysics of divine action. In R. Russell, N. Murphy, & A. Peacocke (Eds.), *Chaos and complexity: Scientific perspectives on divine action* (pp. 147–156). Vatican City State: Vatican Observatory.

Polkinghorne, J. (1999a). The laws of nature and the laws of physics. In R. Russell, N. Murphy, & C. J. Isham (Eds.), *Quantum cosmology and the laws of nature: Scientific perspectives on divine action* (2nd Ed., pp. 429–440). Vatican City State: Vatican Observatory.

Polkinghorne, J. (1999b). *Science & theology: An introduction.* Minneapolis, IN: Fortress Press.

Polkinghorne, J. (2001). Prayer and science. In F. Watts (Ed.), *Perspectives on prayer* (pp. 27–38). London: SPCK.

Poloma, M. M., & Pendelton, B. F. (1989). Exploring types of prayer and quality of life: A research note. *Review of Religious Research, 31*, 46–53.

Poloma, M. M., & Pendelton, B. F. (1990). Religious domains and general well-being. *Social Indicators Research, 22*, 255–276.

Poloma, M. M., & Pendelton, B. F. (1991). The effects of prayer and prayer experiences. *Journal of Psychology and Theology, 19*, 71–83.

Pontoriero, E. (2006). Remembering Auschwitz: Emmanuel Levinas on religion and violence. In C. Crockett (Ed.), *Religion and violence in a secular world: Toward a new political theology* (pp. 85–107). Charlottesville, VA: University of Virginia Press.

Pope, S. J. (2002). Relating self, others, and sacrifice in the ordering of love. In S. G. Post, L. G. Underwood, J. P. Schloss, & W. B. Hurlbut (Eds.), *Altruism & altruistic love: Science, philosophy, & religion in dialogue* (pp. 168–181). New York: Oxford University Press.

Popper, K. R., Sir. (2002). *The logic of scientific discovery.* London: Routledge. (Original work published 1935).

Post, S. G. (1993). Psychiatry and ethics: The problematics of respect for religious meanings. *Culture, Medicine and Psychiatry, 17*, 363–383.

Post, S. G., Puchalski, C. M., & Larson, D. B. (2000). Physicians and patient spirituality: Professional boundaries, competency, and ethics. *Annals of Internal Medicine, 132*, 578–583.

Potvin, R. (1977). Adolescent God images. *Review of Religious Research, 19*, 43–53.

Powell, L. H., Shahabi, L., & Thoresen, C. E. (2003). Religion and spirituality: Linkages to physical health. *American Psychologist, 58*, 36–52.

Power, F. C. (1991). Hard versus soft stages of faith and religious development: A Piagetian critique. In J. Fowler, K. Nipkow, & F. Schweitzer (Eds.), *Stages of faith and religious development: Implications for church, education, and society* (pp. 116–129). New York: Crossroad.

Powers, D., Cramer, R., & Grubka, J. (2007). Spirituality, life stress, and affective well-being. *Journal of Psychology and Theology, 35*, 235–243.

Powers, J. (1995). *Introduction to Tibetan Buddhism.* Ithaca, NY: Snow Lion.

Powlison, D. (2000). A Biblical counseling view. In E. Johnson, & S. Jones (Eds.), *Psychology and Christianity* (pp. 196–225). Downers Grove, IL: InterVarsity Press.

Powlison, D. (2001). Questions at the crossroads: The care of souls and modern psychotherapies. In M. McMinn, & T. Phillips (Eds.), *Care for the soul: Exploring the intersection of psychology and theology* (pp. 23–61). Downers Grove, IL: InterVarsity Press.

Powlison, D. (2003). *Seeing with new eyes: Counseling and the human condition through the lens of scripture.* Phillipsburg, NJ: P&R.

Pratt, J. B. (1971). *The religious consciousness: A psychological study.* New York: Hafner. (Original work published 1920).

Prebish, C. (2004). The Cybersangha: Buddhism on the internet. In L. Dawson, & D. Cowan (Eds.), *Religion online: Finding faith on the Internet* (pp. 135–147). New York: Routledge.

Presser, S., & Chaves, M. (2007). Is religious service attendance declining? *Journal for the Scientific Study of Religion, 46*, 417–423.

Presser, S., & Stinson, L. (1998). Data collection mode and social desirability bias in self-reported religious attendance: Church attendance in the United States. *American Sociological Review, 63*, 137–145.

Pressman, S., & Cohen, S. (2005). Does positive affect influence health? *Psychological Bulletin, 131*, 925–971.

Price, A. F., & Wong, M.-L. (Trans.) (1990). *The diamond Sutra and the Sutra of Hui-neng.* Boston: Shambhala.

Pridmore, S., & Pasha, M. I. (2004). Psychiatry and Islam. *Australasian Psychiatry, 12*, 380–385.

Prigge, N., & Kessler, G. E. (1990). Is mystical experience everywhere the same? In R. K. C. Forman (Ed.), *The problem of pure consciousness: Mysticism and philosophy* (pp. 269–287). New York: Oxford University Press.

Pritt, A. F. (1998). Spiritual correlates of reported sexual abuse among Mormon women. *Journal for the Scientific Study of Religion, 37*, 273–285.

Procter, M., & Hornsby-Smith, M. P. (2003). Individual religiosity, religious context and values in Europe and North America. In L. Halman, & O. Riis (Eds.), *Religion in secularizing society: The Europeans' religion at the end of the 20th century* (pp. 92–113). Leiden: Brill.

Progoff, I. (1980). *The practice of process meditation: The intensive journal way to spiritual experience.* New York: Dialogue House.

Progoff, I. (1992). *At a journal workshop.* Los Angeles, CA: Tarcher.

Propst, L. R. (1988). *Psychotherapy in a religious framework: Spirituality in the emotional healing process.* New York: Human Sciences Press.

Proudfoot, W. (1985). *Religious experience.* Berkeley, CA: University of California.

Proudfoot, W., & Shaver, P. R. (1997). Attribution theory and the psychology of religion. In B. Spilka, & D. N. McIntosh (Eds.), *The psychology of religion: Theoretical approaches* (pp. 139–152). Boulder, CO: Westview Press.

Pruyser, P. W. (1975). Aging: Downward, upward, or forward. *Pastoral Psychology, 24*, 102–118.

Pruyser, P. W. (1985). Forms and functions of the imagination in religion. *Bulletin of the Menninger Clinic, 49*, 353–370.

Pseudo-Dionysius, the Areopagite. (1987). *Pseudo-Dionysius: The complete works* (C. Luibheid, Trans.). New York: Paulist Press.

Psychodynamic Diagnostic Manual Task Force. (2006). *Psychodynamic diagnostic manual.* Silver Spring, MD: Alliance of Psychoanalytic Organizations.

Puchalski, C., Larson, D. B., & Lu, F. G. (2001). Spirituality in psychiatry residency training programs. *International Review of Psychiatry, 13*, 131–138.

Puchalski, C., & Romer, A. L. (2000). Taking a spiritual history allows clinicians to understand patients more fully. *Journal of Palliative Medicine, 3*, 129–137.

Puente, A., & Beiman, I. (1980). The effects of behavior therapy, self-relaxation, and Transcendental Meditation on cardiovascular stress response. *Journal of Clinical Psychology, 36,* 291–295.

Puffer, K. A., & Miller, K. J. (2001). The church as an agent of help in the battle against late life depression. *Pastoral Psychology, 50,* 125–136.

Puhakka, K. (2003). Awakening from the spell of reality: Lessons from Nagarjuna. In S. Segall (Ed.), *Encountering Buddhism: Western psychology and Buddhist teachings* (pp. 131–143). Albany, NY: State University of New York Press.

Putnam, H. (2002). *The collapse of the fact/value dichotomy and other essays.* Cambridge, MA: Harvard University Press.

Putnam, R. D. (2000). *Bowling alone: The collapse and revival of American community.* New York: Simon & Schuster.

Putnam, R. D. (2002). Conclusions. In R. Putnam (Ed.), *Democracies in flux: The evolution of social capital in contemporary society* (pp. 393–416). Oxford: Oxford University Press.

Putnam, R. D., & Goss, K. (2002). Introduction. In R. Putnam (Ed.), *Democracies in flux: The evolution of social capital in contemporary society* (pp. 3–19). Oxford: Oxford University Press.

Putt, B. K. (2005). "Too deep for words:" The conspiracy of divine "soliloquy." In B. Benson, & N. Wirzba (Eds.), *The phenomenology of prayer* (pp. 142–153). New York: Fordham University Press.

Putuwar, S., Rev. (1991). *The Buddhist Sangha: Paradigm of the ideal human society.* Lanham, MD: University Press of America.

Pyysiainen, I. (2001a). *How religion works: Towards a new cognitive science of religion.* Leiden: Brill.

Pyysiainen, I. (2001b). Cognition, emotion, and religious experience. In J. Andresen (Ed.), *Religion in mind* (pp. 70–94). Cambridge, UK: Cambridge University Press.

Pyysiainen, I. (2002). Introduction: Cognition and culture in the construction of religion. In I. Pyysiainen, & V. Anttonen (Eds.), *Current approaches in the cognitive science of religion* (pp. 1–13). London: Continuum.

Pyysiainen, I. (2005). Religious conversion and modes of religiosity. In H. Whitehouse, & R. McCauley (Eds.), *Mind and religion: Psychological and cognitive foundations of religiosity* (pp. 149–166). Walnut Creek, CA: AltaMira.

Quine, W. V. O., & Ullian, J. S. (1978). *The web of belief.* New York: McGraw-Hill.

Raab, K. A. (2003). Mysticism, creativity, and psychoanalysis: Learning from Marion Milner. *The International Journal for the Psychology of Religion, 13,* 79–96.

Rabinow, P. (1986). Representations are social facts: Modernity and post-modernity in anthropology. In J. Clifford, & G. Markus (Eds.), *Writing culture: The poetics and politics of ethnography* (pp. 234–261). Berkeley, CA: University of California.

Radin, D. (1997). *The conscious universe: The scientific truth of the psychic phenomena.* New York: HarperEdge.

Ragan, C., Malony, H. N., & Beit-Hallahmi, B. (1980). Psychologists and religion: Professional factors and personal belief. *Review of Religious Research, 21,* 208–217.

Rahner, K. (1963). *Theological investigations, Volume II: Man in the church* (K.-H. Kurger, Trans.). Baltimore, MD: Helicon Press.

Rahner, K. (1965). *Spiritual exercises* (K. Baker, Trans.). New York: Herder and Herder.

Rahner, K. (1974). *The Trinity* (J. Donceel, Trans.). New York: Seabury.

Rahner, K. (1975). *Theological investigation, Volume 13: Theology, anthropology, Christology.* London: Darton, Longman & Todd.

Rambo, L. (1995). *Understanding religious conversion.* New Haven: Yale University Press.

Ramel, W., Goldin, P. R., Carmona, P. E., & McQuaid, J. R. (2004). The effects of mindfulness meditation on cognitive processes and affect in patients with past depression. *Cognitive Therapy and Research, 28,* 433–455.

Ramsey, J., & Blieszner, R. (1999). *Spiritual resiliency in older women: Models of strength for challenges through the life span.* Thousand Oaks, CA: Sage.

Ramsey, J. L., & Blieszner, R. (2000). Community, affect, and family relations: A cross-cultural study of spiritual resiliency in eight old women. *Journal of Gerontology, 11,* 39–64.

Ramzy, I. (1977). From Aristotle to Freud: A few notes on the roots of psychoanalysis. In M. Mujeeb-ur-Rahman (Ed.), *The Freudian paradigm: Psychoanalysis and scientific thought* (pp. 21–34). Chicago, IL: Nelson-Hall.

Rand, M. L. (2004). Vicarious trauma and the Buddhist doctrine of suffering. *Annals of the American Psychotherapy Association, 7*(1), 40–41.

Randall, W. L. (1995). *The stories we are: An essay on self-creation.* Toronto: University of Toronto Press.

Rao, K. R. (1994). Anomalies of consciousness: Indian perspectives and research. *The Journal of Parapsychology, 58,* 149–187.

Rappaport, R. (1999). *Ritual and religion in the making of humanity.* Cambridge: Cambridge University Press.

Ratcliff, D., & May, S. (2004). Identifying children's spirituality. In D. Ratcliff (Ed.), *Children's spirituality: Christian perspectives, research, and applications* (pp. 7–21). Eugene, OR: Cascade.

Ratner, C. (1989). A sociohistorical critique of naturalistic theories of color perception. *The Journal of Mind and Behavior, 10,* 361–372.

Ray, B. (2000). Discourse about difference: Understanding African ritual language. In K. Patton, & B. Ray (Eds.), *A magic still dwells: Comparative religion in the postmodern age* (pp. 101–116). Berkeley, CA: University of California.

Ray, R. E., & McFadden, S. H. (2001). The web and the quilt: Alternatives to the heroic journey toward spiritual development. *Journal of Adult Development, 8,* 201–211.

Rayburn, C. A. (2004). Religion, spirituality, and health. *American Psychologist, 59,* 52–53.

Reed, G. L., & Enright, R. D. (2006). The effects of forgiveness therapy on depression, anxiety, and posttraumatic stress for women after spousal emotional abuse. *Journal of Consulting and Clinical Psychology, 74,* 920–929.

Reger, G. M., & Rogers, S. A. (2002). Diagnostic differences in religious coping among individuals with persistent mental illness. *Journal of Psychology and Christianity, 21,* 341–348.

Regnerus, M. D. (2000). Shaping schooling success: Religious socialization and educational outcomes in metropolitan public schools. *Journal for the Scientific Study of Religion, 39,* 363–370.

Regnerus, M. D. (2003). Linked lives, faith, and behavior: Intergenerational religious influence on adolescent delinquency. *Journal for the Scientific Study of Religion, 42,* 189–203.

Regnerus, M. D., Smith, C., & Fritsch, M. (2003). *Religion in the lives of American adolescents: A review of the literature.* Research report of the National Study of Youth and Religion, Number 3. Chapel Hill, NC: National Study of Youth and Religion.

Regnerus, M. D., Smith, C., & Sikkink, D. (1998). Giving and volunteering – Who gives to the poor? The influence of religious tradition and political location on the personal generosity of Americans toward the poor. *Journal for the Scientific Study of Religion, 37,* 481–493.

Regnerus, M. D., Smith, C., & Smith, B. (2004). Social context in the development of adolescent religiosity. *Applied Developmental Science, 8,* 27–38.

Reich, K. (1990). Rituals and social structure: The moral dimension. In H.-G. Heimbrock, & H. B. Boudewijnse (Eds.), *Current studies on rituals: Perspectives for the psychology of religion* (pp. 121–134). Amsterdam: Rodopi.

Reich, K. H. (1993). Cognitive-developmental approaches to religiousness: Which version for which purpose? *The International Journal for the Psychology of Religion, 3,* 145–171.

Reid, A. (2004). Gender and sources of subjective well-being. *Sex Roles, 51*(11/12), 617–629.

Reid, D. (1997). *Energies of the spirit: Trinitarian models in Eastern Orthodox and Western theology.* Atlanta, GA: Scholars.

Reiss, S. (2000). Why people turn to religion: A motivation analysis. *Journal for the Scientific Study of Religion, 39,* 47–52.

Reiss, S., & Havercamp, S. M. (1998). Toward a comprehensive assessment of fundamental motivation: Factor structure of the Reiss profiles. *Psychological Assessment, 10,* 97–106.

Rew, L., & Wong, Y. J. (2006). A systematic review of associations among religiosity/spirituality and adolescent health attitudes and behaviors. *Journal of Adolescent Health, 38,* 433–442.

Reynolds, B. (2004). *Embracing reality: The integral vision of Ken Wilber: A historical survey and chapter-by-chapter guide of Wilber's major works.* New York: Tarcher/Penguin.

Rice, H. (2000). Generations, our difference and similarities: How generational studies enlighten spiritual direction. In N. Vest (Ed.), *Still listening: New horizons in spiritual direction* (pp. 63–76). Harrisburg, PA: Morehouse.

Rich, J. M., & Devitis, J. L. (1985). *Theories of moral development.* Springfield, IL: Charles C. Thomas.

Richard, of St. Victor. (1979). *The twelve patriarchs; The mystical ark; Book three of the Trinity* (G. Zinn, Trans.). New York: Paulist Press. (Original work published c. 1160).

Richards, P. S. (2005). Theistic integrative psychotherapy. In L. Sperry, & E. P. Shafranske (Eds.), *Spiritually oriented psychotherapy* (pp. 259–285). Washington, DC: American Psychological Association.

Richards, P. S., & Bergin, A. (1997). *A spiritual strategy for counseling and psychotherapy.* Washington, DC: American Psychological Association.

Richards, P. S., & Bergin, A. E. (2004). A theistic spiritual strategy for psychotherapy. In P. S. Richards, & A. E. Bergin (Eds.), *Casebook for a spiritual strategy in counseling and psychotherapy* (pp. 1–32). Washington, DC: American Psychological Association.

Richardson, C. (1958). Spiritual healing in the light of history. In S. Doniger (Ed.), *Religion and health: A symposium* (pp. 53–64). New York: Association Press.

Richardson, F. C. (1996). Spirituality and human science: Helminiak's proposal. *The International Journal for the Psychology of Religion, 6,* 27–31.

Richardson, F. C. (2006). Psychology and religion: Hermeneutic reflections. *Journal of Psychology and Theology, 34,* 232–245.

Richardson, R. C. (2000). Epicycles and explanations in evolutionary psychology. *Psychological Inquiry, 11,* 46–49.

Richman, L. S., Kubzansky, L., Maselko, J., Kawachi, I., Choo, P., & Bauer, M. (2005). Positive emotion and health: Going beyond the negative. *Health Psychology, 24,* 422–429.

Richmond, L. J. (2004a). Religion, spirituality, and health: A topic not so new. *American Psychologist, 59,* 52.

Richmond, L. J. (2004b). When spirituality goes awry: Students in cults. *Professional School Counseling, 7,* 367–375.

Ricoeur, P. (1966). *Freedom and nature: The voluntary and the involuntary* (E. Kohak, Trans.). Evanston, IL: Northwestern University Press. (Original work published 1950).

Ricoeur, P. (1970). *Freud and philosophy: An essay on interpretation* (D. Savage, Trans.). New Haven, CT: Yale University Press.

Ricoeur, P. (1974). *The conflict of interpretations* (D. Ihde, Ed.), Evanston, IL: Northwestern University Press.

Ricoeur, P. (1976). *Interpretation theory: Discourse and the surplus of meaning.* Fort Worth, TX: Texas Christian University Press.

Ricoeur, P. (1981). *Hermeneutics and the human sciences: Essays on language, action, and interpretation* (J. Thompson, Ed. & Trans.). Cambridge: Cambridge University Press.

Ricoeur, P. (1984). *Time and narrative, Volume 1* (K. McLaughlin, & D. Pellauer, Eds.), Chicago: University of Chicago.

Ricoeur, P. (1992). *Oneself as another* (K. Blamey, Trans.). Chicago: University of Chicago Press.

Ricoeur, P. (1995). *Figuring the sacred: Religion, narrative, and imagination* (D. Pellauer, Trans.). Minneapolis: Fortress.

Ricoeur, P. (2007). *The course of recognition* (D. Pellauer, Tr.). Cambridge, MA: Harvard University.

Rieff, P. (1966). *The triumph of the therapeutic: Uses of faith after Freud.* New York: Harper & Row.

Riley, D. (2004). Hatha yoga and the treatment of illness. *Alternative Therapies in Health and Medicine, 10*(2), 20–21.

Rippentrop, A. E., Altmaier, E. M., Chen, J. J., Found, E. M., & Keffala, V. J. (2005). The relationship between religion/spirituality and physical health, mental health, and pain in a chronic pain population. *Pain, 116,* 311–321.

Riso, D. R., & Hudson, R. (2000). *Understanding the Enneagram: The practical guide to person-ality types.* Boston: Houghton Mifflin.

Ritskes, R., Ritskes-Hoitinga, M., Stodkilde-Jorgensen, H., Baerentsen, K., & Hartman, T. (2003). MRI scanning during Zen meditation: The picture of enlightenment. *Constructivism in the Human Sciences, 8,* 85–90.

Rizzuto, A.-M. (1974). Object relations and the formation of the image of God. *British Journal of Medical Psychology, 47,* 83–99.

Rizzuto, A.-M. (1976). Freud, God, the devil and the theory of object representation. *International Review of Psycho-analysis, 3,* 165–180.

Rizzuto, A.-M. (1979). *The birth of the living God: A psychoanalytic study.* Chicago: The Univer-sity of Chicago Press.

Rizzuto, A.-M. (1991). Religious development: A psychoanalytic point of view. In F. Oser, & W. G. Scarlett (Eds.), *Religious development in childhood and adolescence* (pp. 47–60). San Francisco: Jossey-Bass.

Rizzuto, A.-M. (1993). Exploring sacred landscapes. In M. L. Randour (Ed.), *Exploring sacred landscapes: Religious and spiritual experiences in psychotherapy* (pp. 16–33). New York: Columbia University Press.

Rizzuto, A.-M. (2001a). Does God help? What God? Helping whom? The convolutions of divine help. In S. Akhtar, & H. Parens (Eds.), *Does God help? Developmental and clinical aspects of religious belief* (pp. 21–51). Northvale, NJ: Jason Aronson.

Rizzuto, A.-M. (2001b). Religious development beyond the modern paradigm discussion: The psychoanalytic point of view. *The International Journal for the Psychology of Religion, 11,* 201–214.

Rizzuto, A.-M. (2004). Roman catholic background and psychoanalysis. *Psychoanalytic Psychol-ogy, 21,* 436–441.

Rizzuto, A.-M. (2005). Psychoanalytic considerations about spiritually oriented psychotherapy. In L. Sperry, & E. P. Shafranske (Eds.), *Spiritually oriented psychotherapy* (pp. 31–50). Washington, DC: American Psychological Association.

Roberts, C. W. (1989). Imaging God: Who is created in whose image? *Review of Religious Research, 30,* 375–386.

Roberts, R. C. (1997a). Introduction: Christian psychology? In R. C. Roberts, & M. R. Talbot (Eds.), *Limning the psyche: Explorations in Christian psychology* (pp. 1–19). Grand Rapids, MI: Eerdmans.

Roberts, R. C. (1997b). Parameters of a Christian psychology. In R. C. Roberts, & M. R. Talbot (Eds.), *Limning the psyche: Explorations in Christian psychology* (pp. 74–101). Grand Rap-ids, MI: Eerdmans.

Roberts, R. (2004). The blessings of gratitude: A conceptual analysis. In R. Emmons, & M. McCullough (Eds.), *The psychology of gratitude* (pp. 58–78). Oxford: Oxford University Press.

Robbins, J. (2005). Who prays? Levinas on irremissible responsibility. In B. Benson, & N. Wirzba (Eds.), *The phenomenology of prayer* (pp. 32–50). New York: Fordham University Press.

Robbins, M., & Francis, L. (1996). Are religious people happier? A study among undergraduates. In L. Francis, W. Kay, & W. Campbell (Eds.), *Research in religious education* (pp. 207–217). Leominster, UK: Gracewing.

Robbins, M., Francis, L., & Edwards, B. (2008). Prayer, personality and happiness: A study among undergraduate students in Wales. *Mental Health, Religion & Culture, 11,* 93–99.

Robins, C. J. (2002). Zen principles and mindfulness practice in dialectical behavior therapy. *Cog-nitive and Behavioral Practice, 9,* 50–57.

Robinson, E., Cranford, J., Webb, J., & Brower, K. (2007). Six-month changes in spirituality, reli-giousness, and heavy drinking in a treatment-seeking sample. *Journal of Studies on Alcohol and Drugs, 68,* 282–290.

Robinson, J., & Nussbaum, J. (2004). Grounding research and medical education about religion in actual physician-patient interaction: Church attendance, social support, and older adults. *Health Communication, 16,* 63–85.

Robinson, M., Thiel, M., Backus, M., & Meyer, E. (2006). Matters of spirituality at the end of life in the pediatric intensive care unit. *Pediatrics, 118*, e719–e729.

Robinson, P. W. (1999). Luther's explanation of *Daily Bread* in light of medieval preaching. *Lutheran Quarterly, 13*, 435–447.

Robinson, S. (1995). Christian asceticism and the emergence of the monastic tradition. In V. Wimbush, & R. Valantasis (Eds.), *Asceticism* (pp. 49–57). New York: Oxford University Press.

Rodriguez-Hanley, A., & Snyder, C. R. (2000). The demise of hope: On losing positive thinking. In C. R. Snyder (Ed.), *Handbook of hope: Theory, measures, & applications* (pp. 39–54). San Diego: Academic Press.

Roehlkepartain, E. (2004). The co-construction of spiritual meaning in parent-child communication. In D. Ratcliff (Ed.), *Children's spirituality: Christian perspectives, research, and applications* (pp. 182–200). Eugene, OR: Cascade.

Roehlkepartain, E., Benson, P., King, P., & Wagener, L. (2006). Spiritual development in childhood and adolescence: Moving to the scientific mainstream. In E. Roehlkepartain, P. King, L. Wagener, & P. Benson (Eds.), *The handbook of spiritual development in childhood and adolescence* (pp. 1–15). Thousand Oaks, CA: Sage.

Roehlkepartain, E., & Patel, E. (2006). Congregations: Unexamined crucibles for spiritual development. In E. Roehlkepartain, P. King, L. Wagener, & P. Benson (Eds.), *The handbook of spiritual development in childhood and adolescence* (pp. 324–336). Thousand Oaks, CA: Sage.

Roes, F. L., & Raymond, M. (2003). Belief in moralizing gods. *Evolution and Human Behavior, 24*, 126–135.

Roesch, S. C., & Vaughn, A. A. (2006). Evidence for the factorial validity of the dispositional hope scale: Cross-ethnic and cross-gender measurement equivalence. *European Journal of Psychological Assessment, 22*, 78–84.

Roff, W. (2001). Pilgrimage and the history of religions: Theoretical approaches to the Hajj. In R. C. Martin (Ed.), *Approaches to Islam in religious studies* (pp. 78–86). Oxford: Oneworld.

Rogers, C. (1957). A note on the "nature of man." *Journal of Counseling Psychology, 4*, 199–203.

Rogers, C. (1962). Niebuhr on the nature of man. In S. Doniger (Ed.), *The nature of man in theological and psychological perspective* (pp. 53–56). New York: Harper.

Rogers, F. G. (2002). Spiritual direction in the Orthodox Christian tradition. *Journal of Psychology and Theology, 30*, 276–289.

Rogers, S. A., Poey, E. L., Reger, G. M., Tepper, L., & Coleman, E. M. (2002). Religious coping among those with persistent mental illness. *The International Journal for the Psychology of Religion, 12*, 161–175.

Roof, W. C. (1989). Multiple religious switching: A research note. *Journal for the Scientific Study of Religion, 28*, 530–535.

Roof, W. C. (1993). *A generation of seekers: The spiritual journeys of the baby boom generation.* San Francisco: HaperSanFrancisco.

Roof, W. C. (1999). *Spiritual marketplace: Baby boomers and the remaking of American religion.* Princeton, NJ: Princeton University Press.

Roof, W. C. (2003). Religion and spirituality: Toward an integrated analysis. In M. Dillon (Ed.), *Handbook of the sociology of religion* (pp. 137–148). Cambridge: Cambridge University Press.

Roof, W. C., & Gesch, L. (1995). Boomers and the culture of choice: Changing patterns of work, family, and religion. In N. T. Ammerman, & W. C. Roof (Eds.), *Work, family, and religion in contemporary society: Remaking our lives* (pp. 61–79). New York: Routledge.

Rosenbaum, R. (2003). Reflections on mirroring. In S. Segall (Ed.), *Encountering Buddhism: Western psychology and Buddhist teachings* (pp. 143–164). Albany, NY: State University of New York Press.

Roskes, E. J., Dixon, L., & Lehman, A. (1998). A survey of the views of trainees in psychiatry regarding religious issues. *Mental Health, Religion & Culture, 1*, 45–55.

Roskies, A. (2008). Neuroimaging and inferential distance. *Neuroethics, 1*, 19–30.

Ross, M., & Konrath, S. (2002). Synergies. *Psychological Inquiry, 13*, 223–226.

Ross, C., Weiss, D., & Jackson, L. (1996). The relation of Jungian psychological type to religious attitudes and practices. *International Journal for the Psychology of Religion, 6*, 263–279.

Rossi, P. (1997). Bacon's idea of science. In M. Peltonen (Ed.), *The Cambridge companion to Bacon* (pp. 25–46). Cambridge: Cambridge University Press.

Rossi, V. (2002). Presence, participation, performance: The remembrance of God in the early Hesychast fathers. In J. Cutsinger (Ed.), *Paths to the heart: Sufism and the Christian East* (pp. 64–111). Bloomington, IN: World Wisdom.

Rossler, D. (1999). The unity of practical theology. In F. Schweitzer, & J. Van Der Ven (Eds.), *Practical theology: International perspectives* (pp. 29–38). New York: Peter Lang.

Rothberg, D. (1990). Contemporary epistemology and the study of mysticism. In R. K. C. Forman (Ed.), *The problem of pure consciousness: Mysticism and philosophy* (pp. 163–210). New York: Oxford University Press.

Rothberg, D. (1998). Ken Wilber and the future of transpersonal inquiry: An introduction to the conversation. In D. Rothberg, & S. Kelly (Eds.), *Ken Wilber in dialogue: Conversations with leading transpersonal thinkers* (pp. 1–27). Wheaton, IL: Quest Books.

Rowatt, W., & Kirkpatrick, L. A. (2002). Two dimensions of attachment to God and their relation to affect, religiosity, and personality constructs. *Journal for the Scientific Study of Religion, 41*, 637–651.

Rowatt, W., & Schmitt, D. (2003). Associations between orientations and varieties of sexual expression. *Journal for Scientific Study of Religion, 42*, 455–465.

Rowe, J. W., & Kahn, R. L. (1997). Successful aging. *The Gerontologist, 37*, 433–440.

Rubenson, S. (1995). Christian asceticism and the emergence of the monastic tradition. In V. Wimbush, & R. Valantasis (Eds.), *Asceticism* (pp. 49–57). New York: Oxford University Press.

Rubin, J. (1996). *Psychotherapy and Buddhism: Toward an integration.* New York: Plenum Press.

Rubin, J. (2003). Close encounters of a new kind: Toward an integration of psychoanalysis and Buddhism. In S. Segall (Ed.), *Encountering Buddhism: Western psychology and Buddhist teachings* (pp. 31–60). Albany, NY: State University of New York Press.

Rubinstein, G. (1997). Authoritarianism, political ideology, and religiosity among students of different faculties. *The Journal of Social Psychology, 137*, 559–567.

Rudinger, G., & Rietz, C. (2001). Structural equations modeling in longitudinal research on aging. In J. Birren, & K. W. Schaie (Eds.), *Handbook of the psychology of aging* (5th ed., pp. 29–52). San Diego, CA: Academic.

Ruffing, J. (2000). *Spiritual direction: Beyond the beginnings.* New York: Paulist Press.

Rumi, J. (2004). *The masnavi: Book one* (J. Mojaddedi, Trans.). Oxford: Oxford University Press.

Rumi, J. (2007). *The masnavi: Book two* (J. Mojaddedi, Trans.). Oxford: Oxford University Press.

Ruse, M. (2000). *The evolution wars: A guide to the debates.* Santa Barbara, CA: ABC-CLIO.

Ruse, M. (2001). *Can a Darwinian be a Christian? The relationship between science and religion.* New York: Cambridge University Press.

Ruse, M. (2002). A Darwinian naturalist's perspective on altruism. In S. G. Post, L. G. Underwood, J. P. Schloss, & W. B. Hurlbut (Eds.), *Altruism & altruistic love: Science, philosophy, & religion in dialogue* (pp. 151–167). New York, NY: Oxford University Press.

Russell, B. (1966). Logical atomism. In A. J. Ayer (Ed.), *Logical positivism* (pp. 31–50). Glencoe, IL: Free Press. (Original work published 1924).

Russell, B. (1997). *Religion and science.* New York: Oxford University Press. (Original work published 1935).

Russell, B. (2001). *The scientific outlook* (2nd ed.). London: Routledge. (Original work published 1949).

Russell, R. (1998). Special providence and genetic mutation: A new defense of theistic evolution. In R. Russell, W. Stoeger S. J., & F. Ayala (Eds.), *Evolutionary and molecular biology: Scientific perspectives on divine action* (pp. 191–224). Tucson, AZ: Vatican Observatory.

Russell, R., & Lucariello, J. (1992). Narrative, yes: Narrative ad infinitum, no! *American Psychologist, 47*, 671–672.

Russell, R., & Wandrei, M. (1996). Narrative and the process of psychotherapy: Theoretical foundations and empirical support. In H. Rosen, & K. Kuehlwein (Eds.), *Constructing reali-*

ties: Meaning-making perspectives for psychotherapists (pp. 307–335). San Francisco, CA: Jossey-Bass.

Russell, N. (2004). *The doctrine of deification in the Greek patristic tradition.* New York: Oxford University Press.

Russell, W. M. (2002). Luther, prayer, and the reformation. *Word & World, 22*(1), 49–54.

Ruth, J.-E., & Vilkko, A. (1996). Emotions in the construction of autobiography. In C. Magai, & S. H. McFadden (Eds.), *Handbook of emotion, adult development, and aging* (pp. 167–181). San Diego, CA: Academic Press.

Ryan, R., & Deci, E. (2001). On happiness and human potentials: A review of research on hedonic and eudaimonic well-being. *Annual Review of Psychology, 52,* 141–166.

Ryan, R., & Deci, E. (2006). Self-regulation and the problem of human autonomy: Does psychology need choice, self-determination, and will? *Journal of Personality, 74,* 1557–1585.

Ryan, R. B., & Kumar, V. K. (2005). Willingness to forgive: Relationships with mood, anxiety and severity of symptoms. *Mental Health, Religion & Culture, 8,* 13–16.

Ryff, C. (1989). Happiness is everything, or is it? Explorations on the meaning of psychological well-being. *Journal of Personality and Social Psychology, 57,* 1069–1081.

Ryff, C., & Keyes, C. (1995). The structure of psychological well-being revisited. *Journal of Personality and Social Psychology, 69,* 719–727.

Ryff, C., & Singer, B. (1998). The contours of positive human health. *Psychological Inquiry, 9,* 1–28.

Sabom. M. (1998). *Lights and death: One doctor's fascinating account of near-death experiences.* Grand Rapids, MI: Zondervan.

Sacks, H. L. (1979). The effect of spiritual exercises on the integration of self-system. *Journal for the Scientific Study of Religion, 18,* 46–50.

Sagan, C. (1997). *The demon-haunted world: Science as a candle in the dark.* New York: Random House Press.

Said, E. (1978). *Orientalism.* New York: Pantheon Books.

Saliba, J. (2004). Psychology and the new religious movements. In J. Lewis (Ed.), *The Oxford handbook of new religious movements* (pp. 317–332). Oxford: Oxford University Press.

Salmon, P., Sephton, S., Weissbecker, I., Hoover, K., Ulmer, C., & Studts, J. L. (2004). Mindfulness meditation in clinical practice. *Cognitive and Behavioral Practice, 11,* 434–446.

Samsel, P. (2002). A unity with distinctions: Parallels in the thought of St Gregory Palamas and Ibn Arabi. In J. Cutsinger (Ed.), *Paths to the heart: Sufism and the Christian East* (pp. 190–224). Bloomington, IN: World Wisdom.

Samuels, R. (2000). Massively modular minds: Evolutionary psychology and cognitive architecture. In P. Carruthers, & A. Chamberlain (Eds.), *Evolution and the human mind: Modularity, language and meta-cognition* (pp. 13–46). Cambridge: Cambridge University Press.

Sandage, S., & Shults, F. L. (2007). Relational spirituality and transformation: A relational integration model. *Journal of Psychology and Christianity, 26,* 261–269.

Sander, M. (1998). Cyprian's on the Lord's prayer: A patristic signpost in Luther's penitential theology. *Logia, 7,* 13–18.

Sands, D. (1994). Introducing Maharishi Ayur-Veda into clinical practice. In D. O'Connell, & C. Alexander (Eds.), *Self-recovery: Treating addictions using transcendental meditation and Maharishi Ayur-Veda* (pp. 335–366). Binghampton, NY: Haworth Press.

Sanford, A. (1966). *The healing gifts of the Spirit.* San Francisco: HarperSanFrancisco.

Sankaracarya. (1975). *Shankara's crest-jewel of discrimination: Timeless teachings on nonduality (Viveka-Chudamani)* (S. Prabhavananda, & C. Isherwood, Trans.). Hollywood, CA: Vedanta Press.

Saper, R. B., Eisenberg, D. M., David, R. B., Culpepper, L., & Phillips, R. (2004). Prevalence and patterns of adult yoga use in the United States: Results of a national survey. *Alternative Therapies in Health and Medicine, 10,* 44–49.

Sarbin, T. R. (1986). The narrative as a root metaphor for psychology. In T. R. Sarbin (Ed.), *Narrative psychology: The storied nature of human conduct* (pp. 3–21). New York: Praeger.

Saroglou, V. (2002). Beyond dogmatism: The need for closure as related to religion. *Mental Health, Religion & Culture, 5*, 183–194.

Sato, K., Kataoka, H., DeMartino, R., Abe, M., & Kawai, H. (1992). What is the true self? A discussion. In D. Meckel, & R. Moore (Eds.), *Self and liberation: The Jung-Buddhism dialogue* (pp. 119–127). New York: Paulist Press.

Savage, S. (2001). Prayer and the body. In F. Watts (Ed.), *Perspectives on prayer* (pp. 97–109). London: SPCK.

Saver, J., & Rabin, J. (1997). The neural substrates of religious experience. *The Journal of Neuropsychiatry and Clinical Neurosciences, 9*, 498–510.

Scaer, D. P. (1983). The concept of Anfechtung in Luther's thought. *Concordia Theological Quarterly, 47*, 15–30.

Scarlett, W. G. (2006). Toward a developmental analysis of religious and spiritual development. In E. Roehlkepartain, P. King, L. Wagener, & P. Benson (Eds.), *The handbook of spiritual development in childhood and adolescence* (pp. 21–33). Thousand Oaks, CA: Sage.

Scarlett, W. G., & Perriello, L. (1991). The development of prayer in adolescence. In F. Oser, & W. G. Scarlett (Eds.), *Religious development in childhood and adolescence* (pp. 63–76). San Francisco: Jossey-Bass.

Schaefer, C. A., & Gorsuch, R. L. (1991). Psychological adjustment and religiousness: The multivariate belief-motivation theory of religiousness. *Journal for the Scientific Study of Religion, 30*, 448–461.

Schaefer, C. A., & Gorsuch, R. L. (1992). Dimensionality of religion: Belief and motivation as predictors of behavior. *Journal of Psychology and Christianity, 11*, 244–254.

Schaefer, J. A., & Moos, R. H. (1992). Life crises and personal growth. In B. N. Carpenter (Ed.), *Personal coping: Theory, research, and application* (pp. 149–170). Westport, CT: Praeger.

Schaer, H. (1950). *Religion and the cure of souls in Jung's psychology* (R. F. C. Hull, Trans.). New York: Pantheon Books.

Schaffner, A. D., & Dixon, D. N. (2003). Religiosity, gender, and preferences for religious interventions in counseling: A preliminary study. *Counseling and Values, 48*, 24–33.

Schaffner, K. F. (2006). Reduction: The Cheshire cat problem and a return to roots. *Synthese, 151*, 377–402.

Schaie, K. W., & Hofer, S. (2001). Longitudinal studies in aging research. In J. Birren, & K. W. Schaie (Eds.), *Handbook of the psychology of aging* (5th ed., pp. 53–77). San Diego, CA: Academic.

Scharron-del-Rio, M., & Bernal, G. (2001). Are empirically supported treatments valid for ethnic minorities? Toward an alternative approach for treatment research. *Cultural Diversity and Ethnic Minority Psychology, 7*, 328–342.

Schechner, R. (1988). Preface. In V. Turner, *The anthropology of performance* (pp. 7–20). New York: PAJ.

Scheier, M., Wrosch, C., Baum, A., Cohen, S., Martire, L., Matthews, K., et al. (2006). The life engagement test: Assessing purpose in life. *Journal of Behavioral Medicine, 29*, 291–298.

Scherer-Dickson, N. (2004). Current developments of metacognitive concepts and their clinical implications: Mindfulness-based cognitive therapy for depression. *Counseling Psychology Quarterly, 17*, 223–234.

Schimmel, A. (1975). *Mystical dimensions of Islam.* Chapel Hill, NC: University of North Carolina Press.

Schimmel, A. (2000). Reason and mystical experience in Sufism. In F. Daftary (Ed.), *Intellectual traditions in Islam* (pp. 130–145). London: I. B. Tauris.

Schimmel, S. (1997). *The seven deadly sins: Jewish, Christian, and classical reflection on human psychology.* New York: Oxford University Press.

Schleiermacher, F. (1999). *The Christian faith* (New ed.). London: T. & T. Clark. (Original work published 1830).

Schlick, M. (1949a). Is there a factual *a priori*? In H. Feigl, & W. Sellars (Eds.), *Readings in philosophical analysis* (pp. 277–285). New York: Appleton-Century-Crofts. (Original work published 1930).

Schlick, M. (1949b). Meaning and verification. In H. Feigl, & W. Sellars (Eds.), *Readings in philosophical analysis* (pp. 146–170). New York: Appleton-Century-Crofts. (Original work published 1936).

Schlick, M. (1949c). On the relation between psychological and physical concepts. In H. Feigl, & W. Sellars (Eds.), *Readings in philosophical analysis* (pp. 393–407). New York: Appleton-Century-Crofts. (Original work published 1935).

Schloss, J. P. (2002a). Conclusion to part III. In S. G. Post, L. G. Underwood, J. P. Schloss, & W. B. Hurlbut (Eds.), *Altruism & altruistic love: Science, philosophy, & religion in dialogue* (pp. 243–245). New York: Oxford University Press.

Schloss, J. P. (2002b). Emerging accounts of altruism: "Love creation's final law"? In S. G. Post, L. G. Underwood, J. P. Schloss, & W. B. Hurlbut (Eds.), *Altruism & altruistic love: Science, philosophy, & religion in dialogue* (pp. 212–242). New York: Oxford University Press.

Schmidt, W. S. (1999). Valuing the intersubjective: Reflections on object relations in psychoanalytic theory. *American Journal of Pastoral Counseling, 2,* 75–80.

Schmied, K. (2002). On the path to liberation: Insights and experiences with communities. In T. Hanh, & J. Lawlor (Ed.), *Friends on the path: Living spiritual communities* (pp. 159–164). Berkeley, CA: Parallax.

Schneider, R. H., Alexander, C. N., Salerno, J. W., Robinson, D. K., Fields, J. Z., & Nidich, S. I. (2002). Disease prevention and health promotion in the aging with a traditional system of natural medicine: Maharishi Vedic medicine. *Journal of Aging and Health, 14,* 57–78.

Schneiders, S. M. (1994). A Hermeneutical approach to the study of Christian spirituality. *Christian Spirituality Bulletin, 2,* 9–14.

Schneiders, S. M. (1998). The study of Christian spirituality: Contours and dynamics of a discipline. *Christian Spirituality Bulletin, 6*(1), 3–12.

Schnittker, J. (2001). When is faith enough? The effects of religious involvement on depression. *Journal for the Scientific Study of Religion, 40,* 393–411.

Schreiter, R. J. (1998). *The ministry of reconciliation: Spirituality and strategies.* Maryknoll, NY: Orbis Books.

Schottenbauer, M., Fallot, R., Azrin, S., & Coursey, R. (2004). Concepts of God and therapeutic alliance among people with severe mental disorders. In R. Dayringer, & D. Oler (Eds.), *The image of God and the psychology of religion* (pp. 27–39). New York: Haworth Pastoral.

Schottenbauer, M., Fallot, R., & Tyrrell, C. (2004). Attachment, well-being, and religious participation among people with severe mental disorders. In R. Dayringer, & D. Oler (Eds.), *The image of God and the psychology of religion* (pp. 13–25). New York: Haworth Pastoral.

Schulman, M. (2002). How we become moral: The sources of moral motivation. In C. R. Synder, & S. J. Lopez (Eds.), *Handbook of positive psychology* (pp. 499–512). London; New York: Oxford University Press.

Schuon, F. (1984). *The transcendent unity of religions.* Wheaton, IL: Theosophical Publishing House.

Schuon, F. (2007). The perennial philosophy. In M. Lings, & C. Minnaar (Eds.), *The underlying religion: An introduction to the perennial philosophy* (pp. 243–248). Bloomington, IN: World Wisdom. (Original work published 1991).

Schwab, R., & Petersen, K. U. (1990). Religiousness: Its relation to loneliness, neuroticism and subjective well-being. *Journal for the Scientific Study of Religion, 29,* 335–345.

Schwadel, P., & Smith, C. (2005). *Portraits of Protestant teens: A report on teenagers in major U.S. denominations.* Chapel Hill, NC: National Study of Youth and Religion.

Schwartz, K., Bukowski, W., & Aoki, W. (2006). Mentors, friends, and gurus: Peer and nonparent influences on spiritual development. In E. Roehlkepartain, P. King, L. Wagener, & P. Benson (Eds.), *The handbook of spiritual development in childhood and adolescence* (pp. 310–323). Thousand Oaks, CA: Sage.

Schwartz, S. H., & Melech, G. (2000). National differences in micro and macro worry: Social, economic, and cultural explanations. In E. Diener, & E. M. Suh (Eds.), *Culture and subjective well-being* (pp. 219–256). Cambridge, MA: MIT Press.

Schweitzer, F. (1991). Developmental views of the religion of the child: Historical antecedents. In J. Fowler, K. Nipkow, & F. Schweitzer (Eds.), *Stages of faith and religious development: Implications for church, education, and society* (pp. 67–81). New York: Crossroad.

Schweitzer, F., & Mette, N. (1999). The cultural context of practical theology: A German perspective. In F. Schweitzer, & J. Van Der Ven (Eds.), *Practical theology: International perspectives* (pp. 447–454). New York: Peter Lang.

Scott, D. G. (2003). Spirituality in child and youth care: Considering spiritual development and "relational consciousness." *Child & Youth Care Forum, 32*, 117–131.

Scott, G., Ciarrochi, J., & Deane, F. P. (2004). Disadvantages of being an individualist in an individualistic culture: Idiocentrism, emotional competence, stress, and mental health. *Australian Psychologist, 39*, 143–153.

Scotton, B. (1996). Introduction and definition of transpersonal psychiatry. In B. Scotton, A. Chinen, & J. Battista (Eds.), *Textbook of transpersonal psychiatry and psychology* (pp. 3–8). New York: Basic Books.

Scotton, B. (1998). Treating Buddhist patients. In H. Koenig (Ed.), *Handbook of religion and mental health* (pp. 263–271). San Diego, CA: Academic.

Searle, J. (1993). The Critique of cognitive reason. In A. Goldman (Ed.), *Readings in philosophy and cognitive science* (pp. 833–847). Cambridge, MA: MIT Press.

Seeman, T., Dubin, L. F., & Seeman, M. (2003). Religiosity/spirituality and health: A critical review of the evidence for biological pathways. *American Psychologist, 58*, 53–63.

Segal, R. A. (1999). Is analytical psychology a religion? Rationalist and romantic approaches to religion and modernity. *Journal of Analytical Psychology, 44*, 547–560.

Segal, Z., Teasdale, J., & Williams, J. (2004). Mindfulness-based cognitive therapy: Theoretical rationale and empirical status. In S. Hayes, V. Follette, & M. Linehan (Eds.), *Mindfulness and acceptance: Expanding the cognitive-behavioral tradition* (pp. 45–65). New York: Guilford Press.

Segal, Z., Williams, J. M. G., & Teasdale, J. D. (2001). *Mindfulness-based cognitive therapy for depression.* New York: Guilford Press.

Segall, S. (2003). Psychotherapy practice as Buddhist practice. In S. Segall (Eds.), *Encountering Buddhism: Western psychology and Buddhist teachings* (pp. 165–178). Albany, NY: State University of New York Press.

Segalla, R. A. (2003). Meditation and group psychotherapy. *Psychoanalytic Inquiry, 23*, 784–799.

Seifert, L. S. (2002). Toward a psychology of religion, spirituality, meaning-search, and aging: Past research and a practical application. *Journal of Adult Development, 9*, 61–70.

Seigfried, C. H. (1990). *William James's radical reconstruction of philosophy.* Albany, NY: State University of New York Press.

Sekida, K. (1975). *Zen training: Methods and philosophy* (A. Grimstone, Ed.), New York: Weatherhill.

Selengut, C. (2003). *Sacred fury: Understanding religious violence.* Walnut Creek, CA: AltaMira.

Seligman, M. E. (1990).Why is there so much depression today? The waxing of the individual and the waning of the commons. In R. Ingram (Ed.), *Contemporary psychological approaches to depression: Theory, research and treatment* (pp. 1–9). New York: Plenum.

Seligman, M. E. (2002). Positive psychology, positive prevention, and positive therapy. In C. R. Snyder, & S. J. Lopez (Eds.), *Handbook of positive psychology* (pp. 3–9). New York: Oxford University Press.

Seligman, M. E., & Csikszentmihalyi, M. (2000). Positive psychology: An introduction. *American Psychologist, 55*, 5–14.

Seligman, M., Steen, T. A., Park, N., & Peterson, C. (2005). Positive psychology progress: Empirical validation of interventions. *American Psychologist, 60*, 410–421.

Seltzer, E. (1977). A comparison between John Dewey's theory of inquiry and Jean Piaget's genetic analysis of intelligence. *The Journal of Genetic Psychology, 130*, 323–335.

Senn, F. C. (1986). Lutheran spirituality. In F. C. Senn (Ed.), *Protestant spiritual traditions* (pp. 9–54). New York: Paulist Press.

Senne, E. (2002). Spiritual care in the new pluralistic context. In R. Gilbert (Ed.), *Health care & spirituality: Listening, assessing, caring* (pp. 65–74). Amityville, NY: Baywood.

Sensky, T. (1983). Religiosity, mystical experience and epilepsy. In F. C. Rose (Ed.), *Research progress in epilepsy* (pp. 214–220). London: Pitman.

Serrano, M. 1966. *C. G. Jung and Hermann Hesse: A record of two friendships* (F. MacShane, Trans.). New York: Schocken.

Sethi, S., & Bhargava, S. C. (2003). Relationship of meditation and psychosis: Case studies. *Australian and New Zealand Journal of Psychiatry, 37*, 382.

Seybold, K. S., & Hill, P. C. (2001). The role of religion and spirituality in mental and physical health. *Current Directions in Psychological Science, 10*, 21–24.

Shafranske, E. P. (1992). God-representation as the transformational object. In M. Finn, & J. Gartner (Eds.), *Object relations theory and religion* (pp. 57–72). Westport, CT: Praeger.

Shafranske, E. P. (2001). The religious dimension of patient care within rehabilitation medicine: The role of religious attitudes, beliefs, and professional practices. In T. Plante, & A. Sherman (Eds.), *Faith and health: Psychological perspectives* (pp. 311–338*)*. New York: Guilford.

Shafranske, E., & Gorsuch, R. (1984). Factors associated with the perception of spirituality in psychotherapy. *Journal of Transpersonal Psychology, 16*, 231–241.

Shafranske, E. P, & Malony, H. N. (1990). Clinical psychologists' religious and spiritual orientations and their practice of psychotherapy. *Psychotherapy, 27*, 72–78.

Shafranske, E. P., & Sperry, L. (2005). Addressing the spiritual dimension in psychotherapy: Introduction and overview. In L. Sperry, & E. P. Shafranske (Eds.), *Spiritually oriented psychotherapy* (pp. 11–29). Washington, DC: American Psychological Association.

Shah-Kazemi, R. (2002). The metaphysics of interfaith dialogue: Sufi perspectives on the universality of the Quranic message. In J. Cutsinger (Ed.), *Paths to the heart: Sufism and the Christian East* (pp. 140–189). Bloomington, IN: World Wisdom.

Shah-Kazemi, R. (2006). *Paths to transcendence: According to Shankara, Ibn Arabi, and Meister Eckhart.* Bloomington, IN: World Wisdom.

Shahabi, L., Powell, L. H., Musick, M. A., Pargament, K. I., Thoresen, C. E., Williams, D., et al. (2002). Correlates of self-perceptions of spirituality in American adults. *Annals of Behavioral Medicine, 24*, 59–68.

Shamdasani, S. (1999). Is analytical psychology a religion? In statu nascendi. *Journal of Analytical Psychology, 44*, 539–545.

Shamdasani, S. (2000). Misunderstanding Jung: The afterlife of legends. *Journal of Analytical Psychology, 45*, 459–472.

Shanahan, T. (2004). *The evolution of Darwinism: Selection, adaptation, and progress in evolutionary biology.* Cambridge: Cambridge University Press.

Shannahoff-Khalsa, D. S. (2003). Kundalini yoga meditation techniques for the treatment of obsessive-compulsive and OC spectrum disorders. *Brief Treatment and Crisis Intervention, 3*, 369–382.

Shannon, W. (2000). *Thomas Merton's paradise journey: Writings on contemplation.* Wellwood, UK: Burns & Oates.

Shapiro, D. H., Jr. (1982). Overview: Clinical and physiological comparison of meditation with other self-control strategies. *American Journal of Psychiatry, 139*, 267–274.

Shapiro, D. H., Jr. (1992a). Adverse effects of meditation: A preliminary investigation of long-term mediators. *International Journal of Psychosomatics, 39*, 62–67.

Shapiro, D. H., Jr. (1992b). A preliminary study of long-term meditators: Goals, effects, religious orientation, cognitions. *The Journal of Transpersonal Psychology, 24*, 23–39.

Shapiro, D. H., Jr., & Walsh, R. N. (Eds.). (1984). *Meditation: Classic and contemporary perspectives.* New York: Aldine.

Shapiro, L. A. (1999). Presence of mind. In V. G. Hardcastle (Ed.), *Where biology meets psychology: Philosophical essays* (pp. 83–98). Cambridge, MA: MIT Press.

Shapiro, S. L., & Walsh, R. (2003). An analysis of recent meditation research and suggestions for future directions. *The Humanistic Psychologist, 31*, 86–114.

Sharma, H., & Clark, C. (1998). *Contemporary Ayurveda: Medicine and research in Maharishi Ayur-Veda*. New York: Churchhill Livingstone.

Shea, E. (1991). Spiritual direction and social consciousness. In P. Sheldrake (Ed.), *The way of Ignatius Loyola: Contemporary approaches to the spiritual exercises* (pp. 203–215). St. Louis, MO: The Institute of Jesuit Sources.

Sheldrake, P. (1991). Introduction. In P. Sheldrake (Ed.), *The way of Ignatius Loyola: Contemporary approaches to the spiritual exercises* (pp. 1–13). St. Louis, MO: The Institute of Jesuit Sources.

Sheldrake, P. (1995). *Spirituality and history: Questions of interpretation and method* (Rev. ed.). London: SPCK.

Sheldrake, P. (1998). *Spirituality and theology: Christian living and the doctrine of God*. Maryknoll, NY: Orbis Books.

Sheldon, K. M., & Kasser, T. (1995). Coherence and congruence: Two aspects of personality integration. *Journal of Personality and Social Psychology, 68*, 531–543.

Shelton, S. F., & Mabe, P. A. (2006). Spiritual coping among chronically ill children. In S. Ambrose (Ed.), *Religion and psychology: New research* (pp. 53–71). New York: Nova Science.

Sheng-Yen. (1988). Zen meditation. In K. Kraft (Ed.), *Zen: Tradition and transition* (pp. 30–43). New York: Grove Press.

Sheridan, L. P., & North, A. C. (2004). Representations of Islam and Muslims in psychological publications. *The International Journal for the Psychology of Religion, 14*, 149–159.

Sherkat, D. E. (1997). Preferences and social constraints into rational choice theories of religious behavior. In L. A. Young (Ed.), *Rational choice theory and religion: Summary and assessment* (pp. 65–85). New York: Routledge.

Sherkat, D. E. (1998). Counterculture or continuity? Competing influences on baby boomers' religious orientations and participation. *Social Forces, 76*, 1087–1115.

Sherkat, D. (2001). Tracking the restructuring of American religion: Religious affiliation and patterns of religious mobility, 1973–1998. *Social Forces, 79*, 1459–1493.

Sherkat, D. E. (2002). Sexuality and religious commitment in the United States: An empirical examination. *Journal for the Scientific Study of Religion, 41*, 313–323.

Sherkat, D. E., & Darnell, A. (1999). The effect of parents' fundamentalism on children's educational attainment: Examining differences by gender and children's fundamentalism. *Journal for the Scientific Study of Religion, 38*, 23–35.

Sherkat, D. E., & Ellison, C. G. (1997). The cognitive structure of a moral crusade: Conservative Protestantism and opposition to pornography. *Social Forces, 75*, 957–982.

Sherkat, D. E., & Ellison, C. G. (1999). Recent developments and current controversies in the sociology of religion. *Annual Review of Sociology, 25*, 363–394.

Sherkat, D. E., & Wilson, J. (1995). Preferences, constraints, and choices in religious markets: An examination of religious switching and apostasy. *Social Forces, 73*, 993–1026.

Sherr, M. E., & Straughan, H. H. (2005). Volunteerism, social work, and the church: A historic overview and look into the future. *Social Work & Christianity, 32*, 97–115.

Sherwood, P. (Trans.) (1955). *St. Maximus the Confessor: The ascetic life, the four centuries on charity*. New York: Newman.

Shields, J., Broome, K., Delany, P., Fletcher, B., & Flynn, P. (2007). Religion and substance abuse treatment: Individual and program effects. *Journal for the Scientific Study of Religion, 46*, 355–371.

Shimano, E. (1988). Zen koans. In K. Kraft (Ed.), *Zen: Tradition and transition* (pp. 70–87). New York: Grove Press.

Shirley, J. (2004). *Gurdjieff: An introduction to his life and ideas*. New York: Penguin.

Shoemaker, S. (1999). Physicalism. In R. Audi (ed.), *The Cambridge dictionary of philosophy* (2nd ed., pp. 706–707). Cambridge: Cambridge University Press.

Shore, J. (2002). A Buddhist model of the human self: Working through the Jung-Hisamatsu discussion. In P. Young-Eisendrath, & S. Muramoto (Eds.), *Awakening and insight: Zen Buddhism and psychotherapy* (pp. 30–44). New York: Taylor & Francis.

Shorey, H. S., Snyder, C. R., Rand, K. L., Hockemeyer, J. R., & Feldman, D. B. (2002). Authors' response: Somewhere over the rainbow: Hope theory weathers its first decade. *Psychological Inquiry, 13*, 322–331.

Shorey, H. S., Snyder, C. R., Yang, X., & Lewin, M. R. (2003). The role of hope as a mediator in recollected parenting, adult attachment, and mental health. *Journal of Social and Clinical Psychology, 22*, 685–713.

Shults, F. L. (2003). *Reforming theological anthropology: After the philosophical turn to relationality.* Grand Rapids, MI: Eerdmans.

Shults, F. L., & Sandage, S. (2006). *Transforming spirituality: Integrating theology and psychology.* Grand Rapids, MI: Baker Academic.

Shuman, J. (2003). The last gift: The elderly, the Church, and the gift of a good death. In S. Hauerwas, C. Stoneking, K. Meador, & D. Cloutier (Eds.), *Growing old in Christ* (pp. 151–168). Grand Rapids: Eerdmans.

Shuman, J., & Meador, K. (2003). *Heal thyself: Spirituality, medicine, and the distortion of Christianity.* Oxford: Oxford University Press.

Siddle, R., Haddock, G., Tarrier, N., & Faragher, E. B. (2002). Religious delusions in patients admitted to hospital with schizophrenia. *Social Psychiatry and Psychiatric Epidemiology, 37*, 130–138.

Siddle, R., Haddock, G., Tarrier, N., & Faragher, E. B. (2004). Religious beliefs and religious delusions: Response to treatment in schizophrenia. *Mental Health, Religion & Culture, 7*, 211–223.

Simon, W. M. (1963). *European Positivism in the nineteenth century: An essay in intellectual history.* Ithaca, NY: Cornell University Press.

Simpson, D., Newman, J., & Fuqua, D. (2005). *Further evidence regarding the validity of the quest orientation.* Paper presented at the annual meeting of the American Psychological Association, Washington, DC.

Simpson, J. A., & Campbell, L. (2005). Methods of evolutionary sciences. In D. M. Buss (Ed.), *The handbook of evolutionary psychology* (pp. 119–144). Hoboken, NJ: John Wiley & Sons.

Singer, J. A. (1996). The story of your life: A process perspective on narrative and emotion in adult development. In C. Magai, & S. H. McFadden (Eds.), *Handbook of emotion, adult development, and aging* (pp. 443–463). San Diego, CA: Academic Press.

Singer, J. A., & Bluck, S. (2001). New perspectives on autobiographical memory: The integration of narrative processing and autobiographical reasoning. *Review of General Psychology, 5*, 91–99.

Singer, M., & Lalich, J. (1995). *Cults in our midst.* San Francisco: Jossey-Bass.

Sinkewicz, R. (Trans.). (2003). *Evagrius of Pontus: The Greek ascetic corpus.* Oxford: Oxford University Press.

Sinnott, J. D. (1994). Development and yearning: Cognitive aspects of spiritual development. *Journal of Adult Development, 1*, 91–99.

Sinnott, J. D. (1998). *The development of logic in adulthood: Postformal thought and its applications.* New York: Plenum.

Sinnott, J. D. (2000). Cognitive aspects of unitative states: Spiritual self-realization, intimacy, and knowing the unknowable. In M. Miller, & A. West (Eds.), *Spirituality, ethics, and relationship in adulthood: Clinical and theoretical explorations* (pp. 177–198). Madison, CT: Psychosocial.

Sinnott, J. D. (2001). Introduction: Special issue on spirituality and adult development, Part I. *Journal of Adult Development, 8*, 199–200.

Sinnott, J. D. (2002a). Introduction: Special issue on spirituality and adult development, Part II. *Journal of Adult Development, 9*, 1–2.

Sinnott, J. D. (2002b). Introduction: Special issue on spirituality and adult development, Part III. *Journal of Adult Development, 9*, 95–96.

Sjoerup, L. (1997). Mysticism and gender. *Journal of Feminist Studies in Religion, 13*(2), 45–68.

Skinnider, M. (1991). The exercises in daily life. In P. Sheldrake (Ed.), *The way of Ignatius Loyola: Contemporary approaches to the spiritual exercises* (pp. 131–141). St. Louis, MO: The Institute of Jesuit Sources.

Slee, N. (1990). Getting Away from Goldman: Changing Perspectives on the Development of Religious Thinking. *The Modern Churchman, 32,* 1–9.

Slife, B. D. (1993). *Time and psychological explanation.* Albany, NY: State University of New York Press.

Slife, B. D. (1995). Information and time. *Theory & Psychology, 5,* 533–550.

Slife, B. D. (2000). Are discourse communities incommensurable in a fragmented psychology? The possibility of disciplinary coherence. *Journal of Mind and Behavior, 21,* 261–271.

Slife, B. D. (2005). Are the natural science methods of psychology comparable with theism? In A. Dueck, & C. Lee (Eds.), *Why psychology needs theology: A Radical Reformation perspective* (pp. 163–184). Grand Rapids, MI: Eerdmans.

Slife, B. D., Hope, C., & Nebeker, R. S. (1999). Examining the relationships between religious spirituality and psychological science. *Journal of Humanistic Psychology, 39*(2), 51–85.

Slife, B. D., & Hopkins, R. O. (2005). Alternative assumptions for neuroscience: Formulating a true monism. In B. D. Slife, J. S. Reber, F. C. Richardson (Eds.), *Critical thinking about psychology: Hidden assumptions and plausible alternatives* (pp. 121–147). Washington, DC: American Psychological Association.

Slife, B. D., Mitchell, L. J., & Whoolery, M. (2004). A theistic approach to therapeutic community: Non-naturalism and the Alldredge Academy. In P. S. Richards, & A. Bergin (Eds.), *Casebook for a spiritual strategy in counseling and psychotherapy* (pp. 35–54). Washington, DC: American Psychological Association.

Slife, B. D., & Richards, P. S. (2001). How separable are spirituality and theology in psychotherapy? *Counseling and Values, 45,* 190–206.

Slife, B. D., & Whoolery, M. (2006). Are psychology's main methods biased against the worldview of many religious people? *Journal of Psychology and Theology, 34,* 217–231.

Sloan, R. P., & Bagiella, E. (2002). Claims about religious involvement and health outcomes. *Annals of Behavioral Medicine, 24,* 14–21.

Sloan, R. P., Bagiella, E., & Powell, T. (2001). Without a prayer: Methodological problems, ethical challenges, and misinterpretations in the study of religion, spirituality, and medicine. In T. G. Plante, & A. C. Sherman (Eds.), *Faith and health: Psychological perspectives* (pp. 339–354). New York: Guilford.

Sloat, D. (2004a). Imposed shame: The origin of violence and worthlessness. In J. H. Ellens (Ed.), *The destructive power of religion: Violence in Judaism, Christianity, and Islam: Volume 3 Models and cases of violence in religion* (pp. 175–192). Westport, CT: Praeger.

Sloat, D. (2004b). Terrorizing the self to save the soul: The destructive power of legalistic Christianity. In J. H. Ellens (Ed.), *The destructive power of religion: Violence in Judaism, Christianity, and Islam: Volume 3 Models and cases of violence in religion* (pp. 151–174). Westport, CT: Praeger.

Smart, N. (1978). Understanding religious experience. In S. T. Katz (Ed.), *Mysticism and philosophical analysis* (pp. 10–21). New York: Oxford University Press.

Smart, N. (1993). *Buddhism and Christianity: Rivals and allies.* Honolulu, HI: University of Hawaii Press.

Smart, N. (1996). *Dimensions of the sacred: An anatomy of the world's beliefs.* Berkeley, CA: University of California.

Smart, N. (1998). *The world's religions* (2nd ed.). Cambridge: Cambridge University Press.

Smart, N. (1999a). *Worldviews: Crosscultural explorations of human beliefs* (3rd ed.). Upper Saddle River, NJ: Prentice Hall.

Smart, N. (1999b). *Dimensions of the sacred: An anatomy of the world's beliefs.* University of California Press.

Smith, B. W., Pargament, K. I., Brant, C., & Oliver, J. M. (2000). Noah revisited: Religious coping by church members and the impact of the 1993 Midwest flood. *Journal of Community Psychology, 28,* 169–186.

Smith, C. (2003a). Religious participation and network closure among American adolescents. *Journal for the Scientific Study of Religion, 42,* 259–267.

Smith, C. (2003b). Theorizing religious effects among American adolescents. *Journal for the Scientific Study of Religion, 42*, 17–30.

Smith, C. (2005). *Soul searching: The religious and spiritual lives of American teenagers.* New York: Oxford University Press.

Smith, C., & Denton, M. L. (2003). *Methodological design and procedures for the National Study of Youth and Religion (NSYR): Longitudinal telephone survey (Waves 1 & 2).* Chapel Hill, NC: The National Study of Youth and Religion. Retrieved June 27, 2007, from http://www.youthandreligion.org/research/docs/methods_report_only_08.2006.pdf.

Smith, C., Denton, M. L., Faris, R., & Regnerus, M. (2002). Mapping American adolescent religious participation. *Journal for the Scientific Study of Religion, 41*, 597–612.

Smith, C., & Faris, R. (2002a). *Religion and American adolescent delinquency, risk behaviors and constructive social activities.* Chapel Hill, NC: The National Study of Youth and Religion.

Smith, C., & Faris, R. (2002b). *Religion and the life attitudes and self-images of American adolescents.* Chapel Hill, NC: The National Study of Youth and Religion.

Smith, C., Faris, R., & Denton, M. L. (2004). *Are American youth alienated from organized religion?* Chapel Hill, NC: The National Study of Youth and Religion.

Smith, C., & Kim, P. (2003). *Family religious involvement and the quality of parental relationships for families with early adolescents.* Chapel Hill, NC: The National Study of Youth and Religion.

Smith, C., & Sikkink, D. (2003). Social predictors of retention in and switching from the religious faith of family of origin: Another look using religious tradition self-identification. *Review of Religious Research, 45*, 188–206.

Smith, D. (2007). A phenomenological reflection on the experience of hope. *The Humanistic Psychologist, 35*, 81–104.

Smith, H. (2000). Methodology, comparisons, and truth. In K. Patton, & B. Ray (Eds.), *A magic still dwells: Comparative religion in the postmodern age* (pp. 172–181). Berkeley, CA: University of California.

Smith, J. C. (2004a). Alterations in brain and immune function produced by mindfulness meditation: Three caveats. *Psychosomatic Medicine, 66*, 148–152.

Smith, J. C., Amutio, A., Anderson, J. P., & Aria, L. A. (1996). Relaxation: Mapping an uncharted world. *Biofeedback and Self-Regulation, 21*, 63–90.

Smith, J. Z. (1982). *Imaging religion: From Babylon to Jerusalem.* Chicago: University of Chicago.

Smith, P. K. (2004b). Play: Types and functions in human development. In B. J. Ellis, & D. F. Bjorklund (Eds.), *Origins of the social mind: Evolutionary psychology and child development* (pp. 271–291). New York: The Guilford Press.

Smith, R. J. (2001). The place of facts in a world of values: Subject and object in a postmodern world. *Journal of Theoretical and Philosophical Psychology, 21*, 153–172.

Smith, T. B. (2000). Cultural values and happiness. *American Psychologist, 55*, 1162a.

Smith, T. B., McCullough, M. E., & Poll, J. (2003). Religiousness and depression: Evidence for a main effect and the moderating influence of stressful life events. *Psychological Bulletin, 129*, 614–636.

Snell, R. S. (2000). Studying moral ethos using an updated Kohlbergian model. *Organization Studies, 21*, 267–295.

Snibbe, A., & Markus, H. (2002). The psychology of religion and the religion of psychology. *Psychological Inquiry, 13*, 229–234.

Snyder, C. R. (1995). Conceptualizing, measuring, and nurturing hope. *Journal of Counseling & Development, 73*, 355–360.

Snyder, C. R. (2000a). Genesis: The birth and growth of hope. In C. R. Snyder (Ed.), *Handbook of hope: Theory, measures, & applications* (pp. 25–38). San Diego: Academic Press.

Snyder, C. R. (2000b). The past and possible future of hopes. *Journal of Social and Clinical Psychology, 19*, 11–28.

Snyder, C. R. (2002). Hope theory: Rainbows in the mind. *Psychological Inquiry, 13*, 249–275.

Snyder, C. R., Harris, C., Anderson, J. R., Holleran, S. A., Irving, L. M., Sigmon, S. T., et al. (1991). The will and the ways: Development and validation of an individual-differences measure of hope. *Journal of Personality and Social Psychology, 60*, 570–585.

Snyder, C. R., Ilardi, S. S., Cheavens, J., Michael, S. T., Yamhure, L., & Sympson, S. (2000). The role of hope in cognitive-behavior therapies. *Cognitive Therapy and Research, 24*, 747–762.

Snyder, C. R., Lehman, K. A., Kluck, B., & Monsson, Y. (2006). Hope for rehabilitation and vice versa. *Rehabilitation Psychology, 51*, 89–112.

Snyder, C. R., & Lopez, S. J. (2002). The future of positive psychology: A declaration of independence. In C. R Snyder, & S. J. Lopez (Eds.), *Handbook of positive psychology* (pp. 751–767). New York: Oxford University Press.

Snyder, C. R., & McCullough, M. E. (2000). A positive psychology field of dreams: "If you build it, they will come…". *Journal of Social and Clinical Psychology, 19*, 151–160.

Snyder, C. R., & Rand, K. L. (2003). The case against false hope. *American Psychologist, 58*, 820–822.

Snyder, C. R., Rand, K. L., King, E. A., Feldman, D. B., & Woodward, J. T. (2002). False hope. *Journal of Clinical Psychology, 58*, 1003–1022.

Snyder, C. R., Rand, K. L., & Sigmon, D. R. (2002). Hope theory: A member of the positive psychology family. In C. R Snyder, & S. J. Lopez (Eds.), *Handbook of positive psychology* (pp. 257–276). New York: Oxford University Press.

Snyder, C. R., Sigmon, D., & Feldman, D. (2002). Hope for the sacred and vice versa: Positive goal-directed thinking and religion. *Psychological Inquiry, 13*, 234–238.

Snyder, C. R., Sympson, S. C., Ybasco, F. C., Borders, T. F., Babyak, M. A., & Higgins, R. L. (1996). Development and validation of the State Hope Scale. *Journal of Personality and Social Psychology, 70*, 321–335.

Snyder, C. R., & Taylor, J. D. (2000). Hope as a common factor across psychotherapy approaches: A lesson from the Dodo's verdict. In C. R. Snyder (Ed.), *Handbook of hope: Theory, measures, & applications* (pp. 89–108). San Diego: Academic Press.

Sober, E. (2002). The ABCs of altruism. In S. G. Post, L. G. Underwood, J. P. Schloss, & W. B. Hurlbut (Eds.), *Altruism & altruistic love: Science, philosophy, & religion in dialogue* (pp. 17–28). New York: Oxford University Press.

Sobom, M. (1998). *Light and death: One doctor's fascinating account of near-death experiences.* Grand Rapids, MI: Zondervan.

Socha, P. (1996). A model of sequential development of religious orientation as a criterion of mental health. In H. Grzymala-Moszczynska, & B. Beit-Hallahmi (Eds.), *International series in the psychology of religion: Vol. 4. Religion, psychopathology, and coping* (pp. 139–157). Amsterdam: Rodopi.

Soko, M. (1988). My struggle to become a Zen monk. In K. Kraft (Ed.), *Zen: Tradition and transition* (pp. 13–29). New York: Grove Press.

Sommer, K., & Baumeister, R. (1998). The construction of meaning from life events: Empirical studies of personal narratives. In P. Wong, & P. Fry (Eds.), *The human quest for meaning: A handbook of psychological research and clinical applications* (pp. 143–162). Mahwah, NJ: Erlbaum.

Sommer, S. M. (1997). The experience of long-term recovering alcoholics in alcoholics anonymous: Perspectives on therapy. *Alcoholism Treatment Quarterly, 15*, 75–80.

Sommers, S., & Kosmitzki, C. (1988). Emotion and social context: An American-German comparison. *British Journal of Social Psychology, 27*, 35–49.

Sorajjakool, S. (1998). Gerontology, spirituality, and religion. *The Journal of Pastoral Care, 52*, 147–156.

Sorotzkin, B. (1998). Understanding and treating perfectionism in religious adolescents. *Psychotherapy, 35*, 87–95.

Soto, A. M., & Sonnenschein, C. (2006). Emergentism by default: A view from the bench. *Synthese, 151*, 361–376.

Spanos, N. P., & Moretti, P. (1988). Correlates of mystical and diabolical experiences in a sample of female university students. *Journal for the Scientific Study of Religion, 27*, 105–116.

Sparkman, G. T. (1986). Proposals on religious development: A brief review. *Review and Expositor, 83*(1), 93–109.

Speeth, K. (1989). *The Gurdjieff work.* New York: Tarcher.

Sperry, L. (2001). *Spirituality in clinical practice: Incorporating the spiritual dimension in psychotherapy and counseling.* Philadelphia: Brunner-Routledge.

Sperry, L. (2005). Integrative spiritually oriented psychotherapy. In L. Sperry, & E. P. Shafranske (Eds.), *Spiritually oriented psychotherapy* (pp. 307–329). Washington, DC: American Psychological Association.

Sperry, L., & Mansager, E. (2004). Holism in psychotherapy and spiritual direction: A course correction. *Counseling and Values, 48*, 149–160.

Sperry, L., & Mansager, E. (2007). The relationship between psychology and spirituality: An initial taxonomy for spiritually oriented counseling and psychotherapy. *Journal of Individual Psychology, 63*, 359–370.

Sperry, L., & Shafranske, E. P. (2005a). Approaches to spiritually oriented psychotherapy: A comparative analysis. In L. Sperry, & E. P. Shafranske (Eds.), *Spiritually oriented psychotherapy* (pp. 333–350). Washington, DC: American Psychological Association.

Sperry, L., & Shafranske, E. P. (2005b). Introduction. In L. Sperry, & E. P. Shafranske (Eds.), *Spiritually oriented psychotherapy* (pp. 3–7). Washington, DC: American Psychological Association.

Spidlik, T. (1986). *The spirituality of the Christian East: A systematic handbook* (A. Gythiel, Trans.). Kalamazoo, MI: Cistercian Press.

Spidlik, T. (2005). *Prayer: The spirituality of the Christian East* (Vol.2) (A. Gythiel, Trans.). Kalamazoo, MI: Cistercian Press. (Original work published 1986).

Spilka, B. (1986). Spiritual issues: Do they belong in psychological practice? Yes-But! *Psychotherapy In Private Practice, 4*(4), 93–100.

Spilka, B. (1987). Religion and science in early American psychology. *Journal of Psychology and Theology, 15*, 3–9.

Spilka, B., Armatas, P., & Nussbaum, J. (1964). The concepts of God: A factor-analytic approach. *Review of Religious Research, 6*, 28–36.

Spilka, B., & Bridges, R. (1989). Theology and psychological theory: Psychological implications of some modern theologies. *Journal of Psychology and Theology, 17*, 343–351.

Spilka, B., Hood, R. W., Jr., Hunsberger, B., & Gorsuch, R. (2003). *The psychology of religion: An empirical approach* (3rd ed.). New York: Guilford.

Spilka, B., Ladd, K. L., McIntosh, D. N., Milmoe, S., & Bickel, C. (1996). The content of religious experience: The roles of expectancy and desirability. *The International Journal for the Psychology of Religion, 6*, 95–105.

Spilka, B., Shaver, P. R., & Kirkpatrick, L. A. (1997). A general attribution theory for the psychology of religion. In B. Spilka, & D. N. McIntosh (Eds.), *The psychology of religion: Theoretical approaches* (pp. 153–170). Boulder, CO: Westview Press.

Spohn, W. (2004). Episcopal responsibility for the sexual abuse crisis. In T. Plante (Ed.), *Sin against the innocents: Sexual abuse by priests and the role of the Catholic church* (pp. 155–167). Westport, CT: Praeger.

Springer, S., & Deutsch, G. (1998). *Left brain, right brain: Perspectives from cognitive neuroscience* (5th ed.). New York: W. H. Freeman.

Stace, W. T. (1960a). *Mysticism and philosophy.* New York: J. B. Lippincott.

Stace, W. T. (1960b). *The teachings of the mystics: Being selections from the great mystics and mystical writings of the world.* New York: New American Library.

Stack, S. (1991). The effect of religiosity on suicide in Sweden: A time series analysis. *Journal for the Scientific Study of Religion, 30*, 462–468.

Stack, S., Wasserman, I., & Kern, R. (2004). Adult social bonds and use of Internet pornography. *Social Science Quarterly, 85*, 75–88.

Stam, H. J. (1992). The demise of logical positivism: Implications of the Duhem-Quine thesis for psychology. In C. Tolman (Ed.), *Positivism in psychology: Historical and contemporary problems* (pp. 17–24). New York: Springer-Verlag.

Starbuck, E. D. (1915). *The psychology of religion: An empirical study of the growth of religious consciousness.* New ed. London: Walter Scott. (Original work published 1899).

Stark, R. (1997a). Bringing theory back in. In L. A. Young (Ed.), *Rational choice theory and religion: Summary and assessment* (pp. 3–23). New York: Routledge.

Stark, R. (1997b). A taxonomy of religious experience. In B. Spilka, & D. N. McIntosh (Eds.), *The psychology of religion: Theoretical approaches* (pp. 209–221). Boulder, CO: Westview Press.

Stark, R., & Bainbridge, W. S. (1997). Toward a theory of religion: Religious commitment. In B. Spilka, & D. N. McIntosh (Eds.), *The psychology of religion: Theoretical approaches* (pp. 27–42). Boulder, CO: Westview Press.

Stark, R., & Glock, C. (1968). *American piety: The nature of religious commitment.* Berkeley, CA: University of California Press.

Staudinger, U. M. (2001). Life reflection: A social-cognitive analysis of life review. *Review of General Psychology, 5,* 148–160.

St. Clair, M. (1994). *Human relationships and the experience of God: Object relations and religion.* New York: Paulist Press.

St. Clair, M. (2000). *Object relations and self psychology: An introduction* (3rd ed.). Belmont, CA: Brooks/Cole.

Steffen, P. R., Hinderliter, A. L., Blumenthal, J. A., & Sherwood, A. (2001). Religious coping, ethnicity, and ambulatory blood pressure. *Psychosomatic Medicine, 63,* 523–530.

Steinbock, A. (2004). Personal givenness and cultural *a prioris*. In D. Carr & C. Chan-Fai (Eds.), *Space, time, and culture* (pp. 159–176). Dordrecht: Kluwer Academic.

Stenmark, M. (2001). *Scientism: Science, ethics and religion.* Aldershot, UK: Ashgate.

Stenmark, M. (2004). *How to relate science and religion: A multidimensional model.* Grand Rapids, MI: Eerdmans.

Stern, D. (2000). *The interpersonal world of the infant: A view from psychoanalysis and developmental psychology.* New York: Basic.

Sternberg, R. J. (2000). Images of mindfulness. *Journal of Social Issues, 56*(1), 11–26.

Stewart, C. (1999). Monastic journey according to John Cassian. In E. Ferguson (Ed.), *Forms of devotion: Conversion, worship, spirituality, and asceticism* (pp. 311–322). New York: Garland.

Stifoss-Hanssen, H. (1995). Roles constitute religious experience: Fiction and fact in Hjalmar Sunden's role theory, attribution theory and psychodynamic theory. In N. Holm, & J. Belzen (Eds.), *Sunden's role theory: An impetus to contemporary psychology of religion* (pp. 105–127). Abo: Abo Akademi.

Stifoss-Hanssen, H. (1999). Religion and spirituality: What a European ear hears. *The International Journal for the Psychology of Religion, 9,* 25–33.

Stigler, J. W., Shweder, R. A., & Herdt, G. H. (Eds.). (1990). *Cultural psychology: Essays on comparative human development.* New York: Cambridge University Press.

Stinnette, C. R., Jr. (1968). Reflection and transformation: Knowing and change in psychotherapy and in religious faith. In P. Homans (Ed.), *The dialogue between theology and psychology* (pp. 83–110). Chicago: University of Chicago Press.

Stirling, M. C. (2004). Violent religion: Rene Girard's theory of culture. In J. Ellens (Ed.), *The destructive power of religion: Violence in Judaism, Christianity and Islam* (pp. 11–50). Westport, CT: Praeger.

St Louis, D. (1991). The Ignatian examen. In P. Sheldrake (Ed.), *The way of Ignatius Loyola: Contemporary approaches to the spiritual exercises* (pp. 154–164). St. Louis, MO: The Institute of Jesuit Sources.

Stoddart, W. (2007). Mysticism. In M. Lings, & c. Minnaar (Eds.), *The underlying religion: An introduction to the perennial philosophy* (pp. 230–242). Bloomington, IN: World Wisdom. (Original work published 1998).

Stoeber, M. (1994). *Theo-monistic mysticism: A Hindu-Christian comparison.* New York: St. Martin's Press.

Stoeber, M. (2001). Mysticism and the spiritual life: Reflections on Karl Rahner's view of mysticism. *Toronto Journal of Theology, 17*, 263–275.

Stoeger, W. R. (1995). Describing God's action in the world in light of scientific knowledge of reality. In R. Russell, N. Murphy, & A. Peacocke (Eds.), *Chaos and complexity: Scientific perspectives on Divine action* (pp. 239–261). Vatican City State: Vatican Observatory.

Stoeger, W. R. (1996). Contemporary physics and the ontological status of the laws of nature. In R. J. Russell, N. Murphy, & C. J. Isham (Eds.), *Quantum cosmology and the laws of nature: Scientific perspectives on Divine action* (2nd ed., pp. 207–231). Vatican City State: Vatican Observatory.

Stoeger, W. R. (1998). The immanent directionality of the evolutionary process, and its relationship to teleology. In R. Russell, W. Stoeger, & F. Ayala (Eds.), *Evolutionary and molecular biology: Scientific perspectives on Divine action* (pp. 163–190). Vatican City State: Vatican Observatory.

Stoeger, W. R. (2002). The mind-brain problem, the laws of nature, and constitutive relationships. In R. Russell, N. Murphy, T. Meyering, & M. Arbib (Eds.), *Neuroscience and the person: Scientific perspectives on Divine action* (pp. 129–146). Vatican City State: Vatican Observatory.

Stone, C. (2004). Liberating images of God. In R. Dayringer, & D. Oler (Eds.), *The image of God and the psychology of religion* (pp. 1–11). New York: Haworth Pastoral.

Stone, H. W. (1998). Summoning hope in those who are depressed. *Pastoral Psychology, 46*, 431–445.

Stoneking, C. (2003). Modernity: The social construction of aging. In S. Hauerwas, C. Stoneking, K. Meador, & D. Cloutier (Eds.), *Growing old in Christ* (pp. 63–89). Grand Rapids, MI: Eerdmans.

Storr, A. (1999). Is analytical psychology a religion? Jung's search for a substitute for lost faith. *Journal of Analytical Psychology, 44*, 531–537.

Strauss, A. L., & Corbin, J. M. (1998). *Basics of qualitative research: Techniques and procedures for developing grounded theory* (2nd ed.). Thousand Oaks, CA: Sage.

Strawbridge, W. J., Cohen, R. D., Shema, S. J., & Kaplan, G. A. (1997). Frequent attendance at religious services and mortality over 28 years. *American Journal of Public Health, 87*, 957–961.

Strawbridge, W. J., Shema, S. J., Cohen, R. D., & Kaplan, G. A. (2001). Religious attendance increases survival by improving and maintaining good health behaviours, mental health, and social relationships. *Annals of Behavioral Medicine, 23*, 68–74.

Strawbridge, W. J., Shema, S. J., Cohen, R. D., Roberts, R. E., & Kaplan, G. A. (1998). Religiosity buffers effects of some stressors on depression but exacerbates others. *The Journals of Gerontology. Series B, Psychological Sciences and Social Sciences, 53*(3), S118–S126.

Strawn, B. D., & Leffel, G. M. (2001). John Wesley's orthokardia and Harry Guntrip's "Heart of the Personal": Convergent aims and complementary practices in psychotherapy and spiritual formation. *Journal of Psychology and Christianity, 20*, 351–359.

Strawser, M. S., Storch, E. A., Geffken, G. R., Killiany, E. M., & Baumeister, A. L. (2004). Religious faith and substance problems in undergraduate college students: A replication. *Pastoral Psychology, 53*, 183–188.

Strawson, P. F. (1985). *Skepticism and naturalism: Some varieties: The Woodbridge lectures, 1983*. London: Methuen.

Streib, H. (2001a). Faith development theory revisited: The religious styles perspective. *The International Journal for the Psychology of Religion, 11*, 143–158.

Streib, H. (2001b). The symposium on faith development theory and the modern paradigm. *The International Journal for the Psychology of Religion, 11*, 141–142.

Streng, F. J. (1978). Language and mystical awareness. In S. T. Katz (Ed.), *Mysticism and philosophical analysis* (pp. 141–169). New York: Oxford University Press.

Stroup, G. (1981). *The promise of narrative theology*. Atlanta, GA: John Knox.

Struch, N., & Schwartz, S. (1989). Intergroup aggression: Its predictors and distinctness from ingroup bias. *Journal of Personality and Social Psychology, 56*, 364–373.

Stuckey, J. C. (2001). Blessed assurance: The role of religion and spirituality in Alzheimer's disease caregiving and other significant life events. *Journal of Aging Studies, 15*, 69–84.

Stuckey, J. C. (2003). Faith, aging, and dementia: Experiences of Christian, Jewish, and non-religious spousal caregivers and older adults. *Dementia, 2*, 337–352.

Studzinski, R. (1985). *Spiritual direction and midlife development.* Chicago: Loyola University Press.

Sturgill, A. (2004). Scope and purposes of church websites. *Journal of Media and Religion, 3*, 165–176.

Suh, E., Diener, E., & Fujita, F. (1996). Events and subjective well-being: Only recent events matter. *Journal of Personality and Social Psychology, 70*, 1091–1102.

Sutich, A. J. (1969). Some considerations regarding transpersonal psychology. *The Journal of Transpersonal Psychology, 1*, 11–20.

Suzuki, D. T. (1949). *Essays in Zen Buddhism.* New York: Grove Press.

Suzuki, D. T. (1955). *Studies in Zen.* London: Rider.

Suzuki, D. T. (1986a). An autobiographical account. In F. Haar, & M. Abe, *A Zen life: D. T. Suzuki remembered* (pp. 13–26). New York: Weatherhill.

Suzuki, D. T. (1986b). Early memories. In F. Haar, & M. Abe, *A Zen life: D. T. Suzuki remembered* (pp. 3–12). New York: Weatherhill.

Suzuki, D. T. (1996). *Zen Buddhist: Selected writings of D. T. Suzuki* (W. Barrett, Ed.), New York: Doubleday.

Suzuki, D. T. (1999). *Studies in the Lankavatara Sutra.* London: Routledge.

Suzuki, D. T. (2002). *Mysticism: Christian and Buddhism.* New York: Routledge. (Original work published 1957).

Suzuki, D. T., Fromm, E., & De Martino, R. (1960). *Zen Buddhism and psychoanalysis.* New York: Grove Press.

Suzuki, S. (1970). *Zen mind, beginner's mind* (T. Dixon, Ed.), New York: Weatherhill.

Symons, D. (1995). On the use and misuse of Darwinism in the study of human behavior. In J. H. Barkow, L. Cosmides, & J. Tooby (Eds.), *The adapted mind: Evolutionary psychology and the generation of culture* (pp. 137–162). New York: Oxford University Press.

Tacey, D. J. (2001). *Jung and the New Age.* Philadelphia, PA: Brunner-Routledge.

Tacon, A. M., McComb, J., Caldera, Y., & Randolph, P. (2003). Mindfulness meditation, anxiety reduction, and heart disease: A pilot study. *Family & Community Health, 26*, 25–33.

Takahashi, M., & Ide, S. (2003). Implicit theories of spirituality across three generations: A cross-cultural comparison in the U.S. and Japan. *Journal of Religious Gerontology, 15*(4), 15–38.

Takahashi, T., Murata, T., Hamada, T., Omori, M., Kosaka, H., Kikuchi, M., et al. (2005). Changes in EEG and autonomic nervous activity during meditation and their association with personality traits. *International Journal of Psychophysiology, 55*, 199–207.

Talbot, M. R. (1997). Starting from scripture. In R. C. Roberts, & M. R. Talbot (Eds.), *Limning the psyche: Explorations in Christian psychology* (pp. 102–122). Grand Rapids, MI: Eerdmans.

Tamayo, A. (1981). Cultural differences in the structure and significance of the parental figures. In A. Vergote, & A. Tamayo (Eds.), *The parental figures and the representation of God: A psychological and cross-cultural study* (pp. 73–95). New York: Mouton.

Tamminen, K. (1991). *Religious development in childhood and youth: An empirical study.* Helsinki: Suomalainen Tiedeakatemia.

Tamminen, K. (1994a). Comparing Oser's and Fowler's developmental stage. *Journal of Empirical Theology, 7*, 52–74.

Tamminen, K. (1994b). Religious experiences in childhood and adolescence: A viewpoint of religious development between the ages of 7 and 20. *The International Journal for the Psychology of Religion, 4*, 61–85.

Tan, S.-Y. (1991). *Lay counseling: Equipping Christians for a helping ministry.* Grand Rapids, MI: Zondervan.

Tan, S.-Y. (1996). Religion in clinical practice: Implicit and explicit integration. In E. P. Shafranske (Ed.), *Religion and the clinical practice of psychology* (pp. 365–387). Washington, DC: American Psychological Association.

Tan, S.-Y. (2001a). Empirically supported treatments. *Journal of Psychology and Christianity, 20*, 282–286.

Tan, S.-Y. (2001b). Integration and beyond: Principled, professional, and personal. *Journal of Psychology and Christianity, 20*, 18–28.

Tan, S.-Y. (2002). Empirically informed principles of treatment selection: Going beyond empirically supported treatments. *Journal of Psychology and Christianity, 21*, 54–56.

Tan, S.-Y. (2003a). Empirically supported therapy relationships: Psychotherapy relations that work. *Journal of Psychology and Christianity, 22*, 64–47.

Tan, S.-Y. (2003b). Integrating spiritual direction into psychotherapy: Ethical issues and guidelines. *Journal of Psychology and Theology, 31*, 14–23.

Tan, S.-Y. (2007). Use of prayer and scripture in cognitive-behavioral therapy. *Journal of Psychology and Christianity, 26*, 101–111.

Tan, S.-Y., & Dong, N. J. (2001). Spiritual interventions in healing and wholeness. In T. G. Plante, & A. C. Sherman (Eds.), *Faith and health: Psychological perspectives* (pp. 291–310). New York: Guildford.

Tan, S.-Y., & Johnson, W. B. (2005). Spiritually oriented cognitive-behavioral therapy. In L. Sperry, & E. P. Shafranske (Eds.), *Spiritually oriented psychotherapy* (pp. 77–103). Washington, DC: American Psychological Association.

Tanahashi, K. (1985). *Moon in a dewdrop: Writings of Zen master Dogen.* San Francisco: North Point Press.

Tangney, J. P. (2002). Humility. In C. R. Snyder, & S. J. Lopez (Eds.), *Handbook of positive psychology* (pp. 411–419). New York: Oxford University Press.

Tanuwidjaja, F. H. (1974). Religious thinking of Indonesian children from childhood to adolescence. *The South East Asia Journal of Theology, 15*, 117–118.

Tart, C. (1975). *States of consciousness.* New York: E. P. Dutton.

Tart, C. (Ed.). (1992). *Transpersonal psychologies: Perspectives on the mind from seven great spiritual traditions.* New York: Harper San Francisco.

Tate, Y., & Parker, S. (2007). Using Erikson's developmental theory to understand and nurture spiritual development in Christians. *Journal of Psychology and Christianity, 26*, 216–226.

Tateyama, M., Asai, M., Hashimoto, M., Bartels, M., & Kasper, S. (1998). Transcultural study of schizophrenic delusions. Tokyo versus Vienna and Tubingen (Germany). *Psychopathology. 31*, 59–68.

Tateyama M, Asai M, Kamisada M, Hashimoto M, Bartels M, & Heimann, H. (1993). Comparison of schizophrenic delusions between Japan and Germany. *Psychopathology, 26*(3–4), 151–158.

Tatsuo, H. (2002). The problematic of mind in Gotama Buddha. In P. Young-Eisendrath, & S. Muramoto (Eds.), *Awakening and insight: Zen Buddhism and psychotherapy* (pp. 235–241). New York: Taylor & Francis Group.

Taves, A. (1999). *Fits, trances, & visions: Experiencing religion and explaining experiences from Wesley to James.* Princeton, NJ: Princeton University Press.

Taylor, C. (1989). *Sources of the self: The making of the modern identity.* Cambridge, MA: Harvard University Press.

Taylor, C. (2002). *Varieties of religion today: William James revisited.* Cambridge, MA: Harvard University Press.

Taylor, C. (2007). *A secular age.* Cambridge, MA: Belknap.

Taylor, E (1984). *William James on exceptional mental states: The 1896 Lowell lectures.* Amherst: University of Massachusetts Press.

Taylor, E. (1998). William James on the demise of positivism in American psychology. In R. W. Rieber & K. D. Salzinger (Eds.), *Psychology: Theoretical-historical perspectives* (pp. 101–132). Washington, DC: American Psychological Association.

Taylor, E. (1999). *Shadow culture: Psychology and spirituality in America.* Washington, DC: Counterpoint.

Taylor, E. (2003). Some vicissitudes of constructing a cross-cultural comparative psychology of mystical states. In J. Belzen, & A. Geels (Eds.), *Mysticism: A variety of psychological perspectives* (pp. 179–212). Amsterdam: Rodopi.

Taylor, R. J., Ellison, C. G., Chatters, L. M., Levin, J. S., & Lincoln, K. D. (2000). Mental health services in faith communities: The role of clergy in Black churches. *Social Work, 45*, 73–87.

Teasdale, J., Moore, R., Hayhurst, H., Pope, M., Williams, S., & Segal, Z. (2002). Metacognitive awareness and prevention of relapse in depression: Empirical evidence. *Journal of Consulting and Clinical Psychology, 70,* 275–287.

Teasdale, J., Segal, Z. V., Williams, J. M., Ridgeway, V. A., Soulsby, J. M., & Lau, M. A. (2000). Prevention of relapse/recurrence in major depression by mindfulness-based cognitive therapy. *Journal of Consulting and Clinical Psychology, 68,* 615–623.

Tedeschi, R., & Calhoun, L. (1995). *Trauma and transformation: Growing in the aftermath of suffering.* Thousand Oaks, CA: Sage.

Templeton, J., & Eccles, J. (2006). The relation between spiritual development and identity processes. In E. Roehlkepartain, P. King, L. Wagener, & P. Benson (Eds.), *The handbook of spiritual development in childhood and adolescence* (pp. 252–265). Thousand Oaks, CA: Sage.

Teo, A. (2002). Human altruism in evolutionary psychological perspective: A critique. *Journal of Psychology and Christianity, 21,* 169–180.

Teo, T., & Febbraro, A. R. (2002). Attribution errors in the postmodern landscape. *American Psychologist, 57,* 458–460.

Teresa of Avila, St. (1979). *The interior castle* (K. Kavanaugh, & O. Rodriguez, Trans.). Malwah NJ: Paulist.

Teresa of Avila, St. (1991). *The way of perfection* (E. Peers, Trans. & Ed.), New York: Image (Original work published 1583).

Thalbourne, M. A. (1995). Psychological characteristics of believers in the paranormal: A replicative study. *Journal of the American Society for Psychical Research, 89,* 154–163.

Thalbourne, M. A. (2004). A note on the Greely measure of mystical experience. *The International Journal for the Psychology of Religion, 14,* 215–222.

Thalbourne, M. A., Crawley, S. E., & Houran, J. (2003). Temporal lobe lability in the highly transliminal mind. *Personality and Individual Differences, 35,* 1965–1974.

Thalbourne, M. A., & Delin, P. S. (1999). Transliminality: Its relation to dream life, religiosity, and mystical experience. *The International Journal for the Psychology of Religion, 9,* 45–61.

Thalbourne, M. A., & French, C. (1995). Paranormal belief, manic-depressiveness, and magical ideation: A replication. *Personality and Individual Differences, 18,* 291–292.

Thalbourne, M. A., & Hensley, J. (2001). Religiosity and belief in the paranormal. *Journal of the Society for Psychical Research, 65,* 47.

Thandeka. (1997). The self between feminist theory and theology. In R. S. Chopp, & S. G. Davaney (Eds.), *Horizons in feminist theology: Identity, tradition, and norms* (pp. 79–98). Minneapolis, MN: Fortress Press.

Theophan, St. (1995). *The spiritual life and how to be attuned to it* (A. Dockham, Trans.). Platina, CA: St. Herman of Alaska Brotherhood.

Thiel, M. M., & Robinson, M. R. (1997). Physicians' collaboration with chaplains: Difficulties and benefits. *The Journal of Clinical Ethics, 8,* 94–103.

Thomas, A., St. (1998). *St. Thomas Aquinas and the Summa Theologica.* Gervais, OR: Harmony Media. CD-ROM.

Thomas, L. E. (1991). Dialogues with three religious renunciates and reflections on wisdom and maturity. *International Journal of Aging and Human Development, 32,* 211–227.

Thomas, L. E. (1994). Reflections on death and dying by spiritually mature elders. *OMEGA: Journal of Death and Dying, 29,* 177–185.

Thomas, L. E. (1997). Late-life effect of early mystical experiences: A cross-cultural comparison. *Journal of Aging Studies, 11,* 155–169.

Thomas, L. E., & Cooper, P. E. (1978). Measurement and incidents of mystical experiences: An exploratory study. *Journal for the Scientific Study of Religion, 17,* 433–437.

Thompson, E. H., Jr. (1991). Beneath the status characteristic: Gender variations in religiousness. *Journal for the Scientific Study of Religion, 30,* 381–394.

Thompson, E. H., Jr., & Remmes, K. R. (2002). Does masculinity thwart being religious? An examination of older men's religiousness. *Journal for the Scientific Study of Religion, 41,* 521–532.

Thoresen, C. E. (1999). Spirituality and health: Is there a relationship? *Journal of Health Psychology, 4*, 291–300.

Thoresen, C. E., Harris, A. H. S., & Oman, D. (2001). Spirituality, religion, and health: Evidence, issues, and concerns. In T. Plante, & A. Sherman (Eds.), *Faith and health: Psychological perspectives* (pp. 15–52). New York: Guilford.

Thornhill, R., & Thornhill, N. W. (1992). The evolutionary psychology of men's coercive sexuality. *Behavioral and Brain Sciences, 15*, 363–421.

Thorson, J. A., & Powell, F. C. (2000). Developmental aspects of death anxiety and religion. In J. A. Thorson (Ed.), *Perspectives on spiritual well-being and aging* (pp. 142–158). Springfield, IL: Charles C. Thomas.

Thrangu, R. (2004). *Medicine Buddha teachings* (Y. Gyamtso, Trans. & T. Namgyal, Ed.), Ithaca, NY: Snow Lion.

Thunberg, L. (1995). *Microcosm and mediator: The theological anthropology of Maximus the Confessor* (2nd ed.). Chicago: Open Court.

Thurston, B. (2005). Thomas Merton's interest in Islam: The example of *dhikr*. In R. Baker, & G. Henry (Eds.), *Merton & Sufism: The untold story* (pp. 40–50). Louisville, KY: Fons Vitae.

Tilak, S. (1989). *Religion and aging in the Indian tradition*. Albany, NY: State University of New York Press.

Tillich, P. (1951). *Systematic theology, Volume I: Reason and revelation; Being and God*. Chicago: The University of Chicago Press.

Tillich, P. (1957). *Systematic theology, Volume II: Existence and the Christ*. Chicago: The University of Chicago Press.

Tillich, P. (1958). The relation of religion and health. In S. Doniger (Eds.), *Religion and health, a symposium* (pp. 13–32). New York: Association Press.

Tillich, P. (1962). Existentialism, psychotherapy, and the nature of man. In S. Doniger (Ed.), *The nature of man in theological and psychological perspective* (pp. 42–52). New York: Harper & Brothers.

Tillich, P. (1963a). *Christianity and the encounter of the world religions*. New York: Columbia University Press.

Tillich, P. (1963b). *Systematic theology, Volume III: Life and the Spirit; History and the kingdom of God*. Chicago: The University of Chicago Press.

Tillich, P. (2000). *The courage to be* (2nd ed.). New Haven: Yale University Press. (Original work published 1952).

Ting, R., & Watson, T. (2007). Is suffering good? An explorative study on the religious persecution among Chinese pastors. *Journal of Psychology and Theology, 35*, 202–210.

Tisdale, T. C., Key, T. L., Edwards, K. J., Brokaw, B. F., Kemperman, S. R., Cloud, H., et al. (1997). Impact of treatment on God image and personal adjustment, and correlations of God image to personal adjustment and object relations development. *Journal of Psychology and Theology, 25*, 227–239.

Tisdale, T. (2003). Listening and responding to spiritual issues in psychotherapy: An interdisciplinary perspective. *Journal of Psychology and Christianity, 22*, 262–272.

Tjeltveit, A. (1999). *Ethics and values in psychotherapy*. London: Routledge.

Tomkins, S., & Demos, E. V. (1995). *Exploring affect: The selected writings of Silvan S. Tomkins*. Cambridge: Cambridge University Press.

Tong, B. R. (2003). Taoist mind-body resources for psychological health and healing. In S. Mijares (Ed.), *Modern psychology and ancient wisdom: Psychological healing practices from the world's religious traditions* (pp. 175–198). New York: Haworth Integrative Healing Press.

Tooby, J., & Cosmides, L. (1992). The psychological foundations of culture. In J. H. Barkow, L. Cosmides, & J. Tooby (Eds.), *The adapted mind: Evolutionary psychology and the generation of culture* (pp. 19–136). New York: Oxford University Press.

Tooby, J., & Cosmides, L. (2005). Conceptual foundations of evolutionary psychology. In D. Buss (Ed.), *Handbook of evolutionary psychology* (pp. 5–67). New York: John Wiley.

Toomela, A. (2003). Culture as a semiosphere: On the role of culture in the culture-individual relationship. In I. Josephs (Ed.), *Dialogicality in development* (pp. 129–163). Westport, CT: Praeger.

Tornstam, L. (1997). Gerotranscendence: The contemplative dimension of aging. *Journal of Aging Studies, 11*, 143–154.

Tornstam, L. (1999). Late-life transcendence: A new developmental perspective on aging. In L. E. Thomas, & S. Eisenhandler (Eds.), *Religion, belief, and spirituality in late life* (pp. 178–202). New York: Springer.

Torrance, T. (1994). *Trinitarian perspectives: Toward doctrinal agreement.* Edinburgh: T & T Clark.

Tracy, D. (1975). *Blessed rage for order: The new pluralism in theology.* New York: Seabury Press.

Tracy, D. (1983). Foundations of practical theology. In D. Browning (Ed.), *Practical theology* (pp. 61–82). San Francisco: Harper & Row.

Tracy, T. (1995). Particular providence and the God of the gaps. In R. Russell, N. Murphy, & A. Peacocke (Eds.), *Chaos and complexity: Scientific perspectives on divine action* (pp. 289–324). Vatican City State: Vatican Observatory.

Travis, F., & Arenander, A. (2004). EEG asymmetry and mindfulness meditation. *Psychosomatic Medicine, 66*, 147–148.

Travis, F., Arenander, A., & DuBois, D. (2004). Psychological and physiological characteristics of a proposed object-referral/self-referral continuum of self-awareness. *Consciousness and Cognition, 13*, 401–420.

Travis, F., Olson, T., Egenes, T., & Gupta, H. K. (2001). Physiological patterns during practice of transcendental meditation technique compared with patterns while reading Sanskrit and a modern language. *International Journal of Neuroscience, 109*, 71–80.

Travis, F., & Pearson, C. (2000). Pure consciousness: Distinct phenomenological and physiological correlates of "consciousness itself". *International Journal of Neuroscience, 100*, 77–89.

Travis, F., Tecce, J., Arenander, A., & Wallace, R. K. (2002). Patterns of EEG coherence, power, and contingent negative variation characterize the integration of transcendental and waking states. *Biological Psychology, 61*, 293–319.

Travis, F., & Wallace, R. K. (1999). Autonomic and EEG patterns during eyes-closed rest and transcendental meditation (TM) practice: The basis for a neural model of TM practice. *Consciousness and Cognition, 8*, 302–318.

Travis, T., Kondo, C., & Knott, J. (1976). Heart rate, muscle tension, and alpha production of transcendental meditation and relaxation controls. *Biofeedback and Self-Regulation, 1*, 387–394.

Treanor, B. (2005). Plus de secret: The paradox of prayer. In B. Benson, & N. Wirzba (Eds.), *The phenomenology of prayer* (pp. 154–167). Bronx, NY: Fordham University Press.

Tremlin, T. (2005). Divergent religion: A dual-process model of religious thought, behavior, and morphology. In H. Whitehouse, & R. McCauley (Eds.), *Mind and religion: Psychological and cognitive foundations of religiosity* (pp. 69–83). Walnut Creek, CA: AltaMira.

Triandis, H. (1995). *Individualism and collectivism.* Boulder, CO: Westview.

Trice, P. D., & Bjorck, J. P. (2006). Pentecostal perspectives on causes and cures of depression. *Professional Psychology: Research and Practice, 37*, 283–294.

Trier, K., & Shupe, A. (1991). Prayer, religiosity, and healing in the heartland, USA: A research note. *Review of Religious Research, 32*, 351–358.

Trivers, R. (1972). Parental investment and sexual selection. In B. Campbell (Ed.), *Sexual selection and the descent of man* (pp. 136–179). Chicago, IL: Aldine.

Trzebinski, J., & Zieba, M. (2004). Basic hope as a world-view: An outline of concept. *Polish Psychological Bulletin, 35*, 173–182.

Tsang, J.-A., & Rowatt, W. (2007). The relationship between religious orientation, right-wing authoritarianism, and implicit sexual prejudice. *International Journal for the Psychology of Religion, 17*, 99–120.

Tschannen, O. (1991). The secularization paradigm: A systematization. *Journal for the Scientific Study of Religion, 30*, 395–415.

Tsongkhapa. (1999).*The fulfillment of all hopes: Guru devotion in Tibetan Buddhism* (G. Sparham, Trans.). Boston: Wisdom.

Tu, W. (1999). The quest for meaning: Religion in the People's Republic of China. In P. L. Berger (Ed.), *The desecularization of the world: Resurgent religion and world politics* (pp. 85–101). Washington, DC and Grand Rapids, MI: Ethics and Public Policy Center and William B. Eerdmans.

Tupper, E. F. (1973). *The theology of Wolfhart Pannenberg.* Philadelphia: Westminster Press.

Turner, D. (1995). *The darkness of God: Negativity in Christian mysticism.* New York: Cambridge University Press.

Turner, D. (2002). Apophaticism, idolatry and the claims of reason. In O. Davies, & D. Turner (Eds.), *Silence and the Word: Negative theology and incarnation* (pp. 11–34). Cambridge: Cambridge University Press.

Turner, R. P., Lukoff, D., Barnhouse, R. T., & Lu, F. G. (1995). Religious or spiritual problem: A culturally sensitive diagnostic category in the DSM-IV. *The Journal of Nervous and Mental Disease, 183,* 435–444.

Turner, V. W.(1969). *The ritual process: Structure and anti-structure.* Hawthorne, NY: Aldine De Gruyter.

Turner, V. W. (1988). *The anthropology of performance.* New York: PAJ.

Turner, V. W., & Turner, E. L. B. (1978). *Image and pilgrimage in Christian culture: Anthropological perspectives.* New York: Columbia University Press.

Tyler, S. (1986). Post-modern ethnography: From document of the occult to occult document. In J. Clifford, & G. Markus (Eds.), *Writing culture: The poetics and politics of ethnography* (pp. 122–140). Berkeley, CA: University of California Press.

Tylor, E. B. (1871). *Primitive culture: Researches into the development of mythology, philosophy, religion, art, and custom.* London: J. Murray.

Ulanov, A. B. (1997). Jung and religion: The opposing self. In P. Young-Eisendrath, & T. Dawson (Eds.), *The Cambridge companion to Jung* (pp. 296–313). Cambridge: Cambridge University Press.

Ulanov, A. B. (1999). *Religion and the spiritual in Carl Jung.* New York: Paulist Press.

Ulanov, A. B. (2001). *Finding space: Winnicott, God, and psychic reality.* Louisville, KY: Westminster John Knox.

Ulanov, A. B., & Ulanov, B. (1982). *Primary speech: A psychology of prayer.* Atlanta, GA: J. Knox.

Ullman, C. (1989). *The transformed self: The psychology of religious conversion.* New York: Plenum Press.

Underhill, E. (1990). *Mysticism.* New York: Image. (Original work published 1911).

Underwood, R. L. (1997). Primordial texts: An object relations approach to Biblical hermeneutics. *Pastoral Psychology, 45,* 181–192.

Unno, T. (2002). *Shin Buddhism: Bits of rubble turn into gold.* New York: Doubleday.

Urry, H., Nitschke, J., Dolski, I., Jackson, D., Dalton, K., Mueller, C., et al. (2004). Making a life worth living: Neural correlates of well-being. *Psychological Science, 15,* 367–372.

Utts, J. M. (1996). An assessment of the evidence for psychic functioning. *Journal of Scientific Exploration, 10*(1), 3–30.

Valle, R. S. (1989). The emergence of transpersonal psychology. In R. S. Valle, & S. Halling (Eds.), *Existential-phenomenological perspectives in psychology: Exploring the breadth of human experience* (pp. 257–268). New York: Plenum Press.

Valle, R. S., King, M., & Halling, S. (1989). An introduction to existential-phenomenological thought in psychology. In R. S. Valle, & S. Halling (Eds.), *Existential-phenomenological perspectives in psychology: Exploring the breadth of human experience* (pp. 3–16). New York: Plenum Press.

Vallerand, R. (2008). On the psychology of passion: In search of what makes people's lives most worth living. *Canadian Psychology, 49(1),* 1–13.

Valsiner, J. (2000). *Culture and human development.* London: Sage.

Vande Kemp, H. (1985). Psychotherapy as a religious process: A historical heritage. *The Psychotherapy Patient, 1,* 135–146.

Vande Kemp, H. (1992). G. Stanley Hall and the Clark school of religious psychology. *American Psychologist, 47,* 290–298.

Vande Kemp, H. (1996). Historical perspective: Religion and clinical psychology in America. In
    E. Shafranske (Ed.), *Religion and the clinical practice of psychology* (pp. 71–112). Washington,
    DC: American Psychological Association.
Vande Kemp, H. (1998). Christian psychologies for the twenty-first century: Lessons from history.
    Journal for Psychology and Christianity, 17, 197–209.
Vande Kemp, H. (1999). Commentary on the special issue: Religion in the psychology of personal-
    ity. *Journal of Personality, 67*, 1195–1207.
Vande Kemp, H. (2000). Gordon Allport's pre-1950 writings on religion: The archival record.
    In J. A. Belzen (Ed.), *Aspects in contexts: Studies in the history of psychology of religion*
    (pp. 129–172). Amsterdam: Rodopi.
Vandenberg, B., & O'Connor, S. (2005). Psychosis or faith? Clinicians' assessment of religious
    beliefs. *Journal of Consulting and Clinical Psychology, 73*, 610–616.
van der Lans, J. (1987). The value of Sunden's role-theory demonstrated and tested with respect
    to religious experiences in meditation. *Journal for the Scientific Study of Religion, 26*,
    401–412.
van der Lans, J. (1996). Religion as a meaning system: A conceptual model for research and coun-
    seling. In J. A. van Belzen, & J. van der Lans (Series Eds.) & H. Grzymala-Moszczynska, &
    B. Beit-Hallahmi (Vol. Eds.), *International series in the psychology of religion: Vol. 4. Reli-
    gion, psychopathology, and coping* (pp. 95–105). Amsterdam: Rodopi.
van der Lans, J., & Geerts, H. (1990). The impact of the liturgical setting. An empirical study
    from the perspective of environmental psychology. In H.-G. Heimbrock, & H. Boudewijnse
    (Eds.), *Current studies on rituals: Perspectives for the psychology of religion* (pp. 87–102).
    Amsterdam: Rodopi.
Vandermeersch, P. (1990). Psychotherapeutic and religious rituals: The issue of secularization. In
    H.-G. Heimbrock, & H. B. Boudewijnse (Eds.), *Current studies on rituals: Perspectives for
    the psychology of religion* (pp. 151–164). Amsterdam: Rodopi.
Vandermeersch, P. (2000). The failure of second naivete: Some landmarks in the French psychol-
    ogy of religion. In J. A. Belzen (Ed.), *Aspects in contexts: Studies in the history of psychology
    of religion* (pp. 235–279). Amsterdam: Rodopi.
Van Dierendonck, D., & Mohan, K. (2006). Some thoughts on spirituality and eudaimonic well-
    being. *Mental Health, Religion & Culture, 9*, 227–238.
van Gennep, A. (1960). *The rites of passage* (M. Vizedom, & G. Caffee, Trans.). Chicago:
    University of Chicago Press.
van IJzendoorn, M. H. (1995). Adult attachment representations, parental responsiveness, and
    infant attachment: A meta-analysis on the predictive validity of the adult attachment inter-
    view. *Psychological Bulletin, 117*, 387–403.
Van Ness, P. H., & Kasl, S. V. (2003). Religion and cognitive dysfunction in an elderly cohort.
    The Journals of Gerontology. Series B, Psychological Sciences and Social Sciences, 58(1),
    S21–S29.
van Spengen, W. (1998). On the geographical and material contextuality of Tibetan pilgrimage. In
    A. C. McKay (Eds.), *Pilgrimage in Tibet* (pp. 35–51). Surrey: Curzon.
van Uden, M., & Pieper, J. (1990).Christian pilgrimage: Motivational structures and ritual func-
    tions. In H.-G. Heimbrock, & H. B. Boudewijnse (Eds.), *Current studies on rituals: Perspec-
    tives for the psychology of religion* (pp. 165–176). Amsterdam: Rodopi.
Van Uden, M. H., & Pieper, J. Z. (1996). Mental health and religion: A theoretical survey. In
    J. A. van Belzen, & J. M. van der Lans (Series Eds.) & H. Grzymala-Moszczynska, &
    B. Beit-Hallahmi (Vol. Eds.), *International series in the psychology of religion: Vol. 4. Reli-
    gion, psychopathology, and coping* (pp. 35–55). Amsterdam: Rodopi.
Van Waning, A. (2002). A mindful self and beyond: Sharing in the ongoing dialogue of Buddhism
    and psychoanalysis. In P. Young-Eisendrath, & S. Muramoto (Eds.), *Awakening and insight:
    Zen Buddhism and psychotherapy* (pp. 93–105). New York: Taylor & Francis Group.
Varela, F. (2001). Why a proper science of mind implies the transcendence of nature. In J. Andresen
    (Ed.), *Religions in mind: Cognitive perspectives of religious belief, ritual, and experience*
    (pp. 207–236). Cambridge: Cambridge University Press.

Varela, F., & Thompson, E., & Rosch, E. (1991). *The embodied mind: Cognitive science and human experiences.* London, England: MIT Press.

Vash, C. L. (1994). *Personality and adversity: Psychospiritual aspects of rehabilitation.* New York: Springer.

Vasudev, J., & Hummel, R. C. (1987). Moral stage sequence and principled reasoning in an Indian sample. *Human Development, 30,* 105–118.

Veale, J. (1991a). The first week: Practical questions. In P. Sheldrake (Ed.), *The way of Ignatius Loyola: Contemporary approaches to the spiritual exercises* (pp. 53–65). St. Louis, MO: The Institute of Jesuit Sources.

Veale, J. (1991b). Ignatian prayer or Jesuit spirituality. In P. Sheldrake (Ed.), *The way of Ignatius Loyola: Contemporary approaches to the spiritual exercises* (pp. 248–260). St. Louis, MO: The Institute of Jesuit Sources.

Veenhoven, R. (1999). Quality-of-life in individualistic society. *Social Indicators Research, 48,* 159–186.

Veenhoven, R. (2000). Freedom and happiness: A comparative study in forty-four nations in the early 1990s. In E. Diener, & E. M. Suh (Eds.), *Culture and subjective well-being* (pp. 257–288). Cambridge, MA: MIT Press.

Veilleux, A. (Trans.). (1980). *Pachomian koinonia, Volume 1: The life of Saint Pachomius and his disciples.* Kalamazoo, MI: Cistercian Press.

Veilleux, A. (Trans.). (1981). *Pachomian koinonia, Volume 2: Pachomian chronicles and rules.* Kalamazoo, MI: Cistercian Press.

Velmans, M. (2000). *Understanding Consciousness.* Philadelphia, PA: Routledge.

Ventis, W. L. (1995). The relationships between religion and mental health. *Journal of Social Issues, 51*(2), 33–47.

Vercruysse, G., & de Neuter, P. (1981). Maternal and paternal dimensions in the parental and divine figures. In A. Vergote, & A. Tamayo (Eds.), *The parental figures and the representation of God* (pp. 43–71). The Hague: Mouton.

Vergote, A. (1969). *The religious man: A psychological study of religious attitudes* (M.-B. Said, Trans.). Dayton, OH: Pfalaum.

Vergote, A. (1981a). Overview and theoretical prospects. In A. Vergote, & A. Tamayo (Eds.), *The parental figures and the representation of God* (pp. 185–225). The Hague: Mouton.

Vergote, A. (1981b). The parental figures: Symbolic functions and medium for the representation of God. In A. Vergote, & A. Tamayo (Eds.), *The parental figures and representation of God: A psychological and cross-cultural study* (pp. 1–23). The Hague: Mouton.

Vergote, A. (1988). *Guilt and desire: Religious attitudes and their pathological derivatives* (M. H. Wood, Trans.). New Haven, CT: Yale University Press.

Vergote, A. (1994). Epilogue. In J. Conveleyn, & D. Hutsebaut (Eds.), *Belief and unbelief: Psychological perspectives* (pp. 233–243). Amsterdam: Rodopi.

Vergote, A. (1997). *Religion, belief and unbelief: A psychological study.* Amsterdam/Atlanta, GA: Leuven University Press.

Vergote, A. (1998). *Psychoanalysis, phenomenological anthropology and religion* (J. Corveleyn, & D. Hutsebaut, Eds.), Leuven: Leuven University Press.

Vergote, A. (2003). Plying between psychology and mysticism. In J. Belzen, & A. Geels (Eds.), *Mysticism: A variety of psychological perspectives* (pp. 81–107). Amsterdam: Rodopi.

Verma, S., & Maria, M. (2006). The changing global context of adolescent spirituality. In E. Roehlkepartain, P. King, L. Wagener, & P. Benson (Eds.), *The handbook of spiritual development in childhood and adolescence* (pp. 124–136). Thousand Oaks, CA: Sage.

Vianello, R. (1991). Religious beliefs and personality traits in early adolescence. *International Journal of Adolescence and Youth, 2,* 287–296.

Vianello, R., & Marin, M. L. (1989). Belief in a kind of justice immanent in things: A revision of the Piagetian hypothesis. *Early Child Development and Care, 46,* 57–61.

Viau, M. (1999). Practical theology: Instigator of a new apologetic. In F. Schweitzer, & J. van der Ven (Eds.), *Practical Theology-International Perspectives* (pp. 39–51). New York: Peter Lang.

Vick, R. D., Sr., Smith, L. M., & Herrera, C. I. R. (1998). The healing circle: An alternative path to alcoholism recovery. *Counseling and Values, 42,* 133–141.

Vidal, F. (1987). Jean Piaget and the liberal Protestant tradition. In M. Ash, & W. Woodward (Eds.), *Psychology in twentieth-century thought and society* (pp. 271–294). New York: Cambridge University Press.

Viney, W., & King, D. B. (1998). *A history of psychology: Ideas and context* (2nd ed.). Boston: Allyn & Bacon.

Vishnevskaya, E. (2006). Divination and spiritual progress in Maximus the Confessor. In S. Finlan, & V. Kharlamov (Eds.), *Theosis: Deification in Christian theology* (pp. 134–145). Eugene, OR: Pickwick.

Visscher, A., & Stern, M. (1990). Family rituals as medium in Christian faith transmission. In H. B. Heimbrock, & H-G Boudewijnse (Eds.), *Current studies on rituals: Perspectives for the psychology of religion* (pp. 103–118). Atlanta, GA: Rodopi.

Vitz, P. C. (1977). *Psychology as religion: The cult of self-worship*. Grand Rapids, MI: Eerdmans.

Vitz, P. C. (1990). The use of stories in moral development: new psychological reasons for an old education method. *American Psychologist, 45*, 709–720.

von Balthasar, H. (1967). *A theological anthropology*. New York: Sheed and Ward.

von Balthasar, H. (1986). *Prayer* (G. Harrison, Trans.). San Francisco: Ignatius Press.

von Balthasar, H. (1995). *Presence and thought: An essay on the religious philosophy of Gregory of Nyssa* (M. Sebanc, Trans.). San Francisco: Ignatius Press.

von Balthasar, H. (2000). *The Christian and anxiety* (D. Martin, & M. Miller, Trans.). San Francisco: Ignatius Press.

von Hugel, F. (1999). *The mystical element of religion: As studied in Saint Catherine of Genoa and her friends*. New York: Crossroad. (Original work published 1908).

Voss, S. L. (1996). The church as an agent in rural mental health. *Journal of Psychology and Theology, 24*, 114–123.

Voyé, L. (2002). Popular religion and pilgrimages in Western Europe. In W. H. Swatos, & L. Tomasi (Eds.), *From medieval pilgrimage to religious tourism: The social and cultural economics of piety* (pp. 115–135). Westport, CT: Praeger.

Vygotsky, L. S. (1986). *Thought and language* (Rev. ed.). Cambridge, Massachusetts: The Massachusetts Institute of Technology. Original work published 1934.

Wade, N. G., Bailey, D. C., & Shaffer, P. (2005). Helping clients heal: Does forgiveness make a difference? *Professional Psychology: Research and Practice, 36*, 634–641.

Wade, N. G., & Worthington, E. L., Jr. (2003). Overcoming interpersonal offenses: Is forgiveness the only way to deal with unforgiveness? *Journal of Counseling and Development, 81*, 343–353.

Wade, N. G., & Worthington, E. L., Jr. (2005). In search of a common core: A content analysis of interventions to promote forgiveness. *Psychotherapy: Theory, Research, Practice, Training, 42*, 160–177.

Waelde, L. C. (2003). Dissociation and meditation. *Journal of Trauma & Dissociation, 5*, 147–162.

Waelde, L. C., Thompson, L., & Gallagher-Thompson, D. (2004). A pilot study of a yoga and meditation intervention for dementia caregiver stress. *Journal of Clinical Psychology, 60*, 677–687.

Wagener, L., Furrow, J. L., King, P. E., Leffert, N., & Benson, P. (2003). Religious involvement and developmental resources in youth. *Review of Religious Research, 44*, 271–284.

Wagener, L, & Malony, H. N. (2006). Spiritual and religious pathology in childhood and adolescence. In E. Roehlkepartain, P. King, L. Wagener, & P. Benson (Eds.), *The handbook of spiritual development in childhood and adolescence* (pp. 137–149). Thousand Oaks, CA: Sage.

Wagnild, G., & Young, H. (1990). Resilience among older women. *IMAGE: Journal of Nursing Scholarship, 22*, 252–255.

Wahass, S., & Kent, G. (1997). The modification of psychological interventions for persistent auditory hallucinations to an Islamic culture. *Behavioural and Cognitive Psychotherapy, 25*, 351–364.

Walker, D. F., & Gorsuch, R. L. (2002). Forgiveness within the Big Five personality model. *Personality and Individual Differences, 32*, 1127–1137.

Walker, D. F., & Gorsuch, R. L. (2004). Dimensions underlying sixteen models of forgiveness and reconciliation. *Journal of Psychology and Theology, 32*, 12–25.

Walker, D. F., Gorsuch, R. L., & Tan, S.-Y. (2004). Therapists' integration of religion and spirituality in counseling: A meta-analysis. *Counseling and Values, 49*, 69–80.

Walker, L. J., & Pitts, R. C. (1998a). Data can inform the theoretical skew in moral psychology: A rejoinder to Hart. *Developmental Psychology, 34*, 424–425.

Walker, L. J., & Pitts, R. C. (1998b). Naturalistic conceptions of moral maturity. *Developmental Psychology, 34*, 403–419.

Walker, L., & Reimer, K. (2006). The relationship between moral and spiritual development. In E. Roehlkepartain, P. King, L. Wagener, & P. Benson (Eds.), *The handbook of spiritual development in childhood and adolescence* (pp. 224–238). Thousand Oaks, CA: Sage.

Wallace, B., & Shapiro, S. (2006). Mental balance and well-being: Building bridges between Buddhism and Western psychology. *American Psychologist, 61*, 690–701.

Wallace, Jr., J. M., & Forman, T. A. (1998). Religion's role in promoting health and reducing risk among American youth. *Health Education and Behavior, 25*, 721–741.

Wallace, M. I. (2000). From phenomenology to scripture? Paul Ricoeur's hermeneutical philosophy of religion. *Modern Theology, 16*, 301–313.

Wallace, R., & Benson, H. (1972). The physiology of meditation. *Scientific American, 226*, 84–90.

Waller, N. G., Kojetin, B. A., Bouchard, Jr., T. J., Lykken, D. T., & Tellegen, A. (1990). Genetic and environmental influences on religious interests, attitudes, and values: A study of twins reared apart and together. *Psychological Science, 1*, 138–142.

Wallwork, E. (1982). Religious development. In J. Broughton, & D. Freeman-Moir (Eds.), *The cognitive-developmental psychology of James Mark Baldwin: Current theory and research in genetic epistemology* (pp. 335–388). Norwood, NJ: Ablex.

Walsh, R. (1977). Initial meditative experiences: Part I. *The Journal of Transpersonal Psychology, 9*, 151–192.

Walsh, R. (1978). Initial meditative experiences: Part II. *The Journal of Transpersonal Psychology, 10*, 1–28.

Walsh, R. (1980). The consciousness disciplines and the behavioral sciences: Questions of comparison and assessment. *American Journal of Psychiatry, 137*, 663–673.

Walsh, R. (1998). Developmental and evolutionary synthesis in the recent writings of Ken Wilber. In D. Rothberg, & S. Kelly (Eds.), *Ken Wilber in dialogue: Conversations with leading transpersonal thinkers* (pp. 30–52). Wheaton, IL: Quest Books.

Walsh, R., Goleman, D., Kornfield, J., Pensa, C., & Shapiro, D. (1978). Meditation: Aspects of research and practice. *Journal of Transpersonal Psychology, 10*, 113–133.

Walsh, R., King, M., Jones, L., Tookman, A., & Blizard, R. (2002). Spiritual beliefs may affect outcome of bereavement: prospective study. *Behavioural Medicine Journal, 325*, 1551–1555.

Walsh, R., & Shapiro, S. L. (2006). The meeting of meditative disciplines and Western psychology: A mutually enriching dialogue. *American Psychologist, 61*, 227–239.

Walshe, M. (Trans.). (1995). *The long discourses of the Buddha: A translation of the Digha Nikaya.* Boston: Wisdom.

Walton, K., & Levitsky, D. (1994).A neuroendocrine mechanism for the reduction of drug use and addictions by transcendental meditation. In, D. O'Connell, & C. Alexander (Eds.), *Self-recovery: Treating addictions using transcendental meditation and Maharishi Ayur-Veda* (pp. 89–105). Binghampton, NY: The Haworth Press.

Walton, K., Schneider, R. H., Nidich, S. I., Salerno, J. W., Nordstrom, C. K., & Bairey Merz, C. N. (2002). Psychosocial stress and cardiovascular disease part 2: Effectiveness of the transcendental meditation program in treatment and prevention. *Behavioral Medicine, 28*, 106–123.

Walzer, M. (1994). *Thick and thin: Moral argument at home and abroad.* Notre Dame, IN: University of Notre Dame Press.

Ward, B. (Trans.). (1975). *The sayings of the desert fathers: The alphabetical collection..* Kalamazoo, MI: Cistercian Press.

Ward, K. (1996). God as a principle of cosmological explanation. In R. Russell, N. Murphy, & C. J. Isham (Eds.), *Quantum Cosmology and the laws of nature: Scientific perspectives on divine action* (2nd ed., pp. 247–262). Vatican City State: Vatican Observatory.

Ware, K. (1986a). The human person as an icon of the Trinity. *Sobornost, 8*, 6–23.

Ware, K. (1986b). *The power of the name: The Jesus prayer in Orthodox spirituality* (New ed.). Oxford, UK: SLG Press.

Ware, K. (1990). Foreword. In I. Hausherr, *Spiritual direction in the early Christian East* (A. Gythiel, Trans.) (pp. vii–xxxiii). Kalamazoo, MI: Cistercian Press.

Ware, K. (1995). The way of the ascetics: Negative or affirmative? In V. L. Wimbush, & R. Valantasis (Eds.), *Asceticism* (pp. 3–15). New York: Oxford University Press.

Ware, K. (2002). How do we enter the heart? In J. Cutsinger (Ed.), *Paths to the heart: Sufism and the Christian East* (pp. 2–23). Bloomington, IN: World Wisdom.

Ware, K. (2003a). How do we enter the heart, and what do we find when we enter? In B. Dieker, & J. Montaldo (Eds.), *Merton & Hesychasm: The prayer of the heart: The Eastern Church* (pp. 3–16). Louisville, KY: Fons Vitae.

Ware, K. (2003b). The power of the name: The Jesus prayer in Orthodox spirituality. In B. Dieker, & J. Montaldo (Eds.), *Merton & Hesychasm: The prayer of the heart: The Eastern Church* (pp. 41–74). Louisville, KY: Fons Vitae.

Ware, K. (2003c). Silence in prayer: The meaning of hesychia. In B. Dieker, & J. Montaldo (Eds.), *Merton & Hesychasm: The prayer of the heart:The Eastern Church* (pp. 17–40). Louisville, KY: Fons Vitae.

Warner, R. S. (1994). The place of the congregation in the contemporary American religious configuration. In J. Wind, & J. Lewis (Eds.), *American congregations, Volume 2: New perspectives in the study of congregations* (pp. 54–99). Chicago: University of Chicago Press.

Washburn, M. (1998). The pre-trans fallacy reconsidered. In D. Rothberg, & S. Kelly (Eds.), *Ken Wilber in dialogue: Conversations with leading transpersonal thinkers* (pp. 62–84). Wheaton, IL: Quest Books.

Watanabe, T., Shapiro, D., & Schwartz, G. E. (1972). Meditation as an anoxic state: A critical review and theory. *Psychophysiology, 9*, 279.

Watlington, C. G., & Murphy, C. M. (2006). The roles of religion and spirituality among African American survivors of domestic violence. *Journal of Clinical Psychology, 62*, 837–857.

Watson, B. (Trans.). (1993). *The lotus sutra.* New York: Columbia University Press.

Watson, C. G., Tuorila, J., Detra, E., Gearhart, L. P., & Wielkiewicz, R. M. (1995). Effects of a Vietnam war memorial pilgrimage on veterans with posttraumatic stress disorder. *The Journal of Nervous and Mental Disease, 183*, 315–319.

Watson, D. (1986). Methodist spirituality. In F. C. Senn (Ed.), *Protestant spiritual traditions* (pp. 217–273). New York: Paulist Press.

Watson, P. J. (1993). Apologetics and ethnocentrism: Psychology and religion within an ideological surround. *The International Journal for the Psychology of Religion, 3*, 1–20.

Watson, P. J. (1994). Changing the religious self and the problem of rationality. In T. M. Brinthaupt, & R. P. Lipka (Eds.), *Changing the self: Philosophies, techniques, and experiences* (pp. 109–139). Albany, NY: State University of New York Press.

Watson, P. J., Ghorbani, N., Davison, H. K., Bing, M. N., Hood, R. W. Jr., & Ghramaleki, A. F. (2002). Negatively reinforcing personal extrinsic motivations: Religious orientation, inner awareness, and mental health in Iran and the United States. *The International Journal for the Psychology of Religion, 12*, 255–276.

Watson, P. J., Howard, R., Hood, R., Jr., & Morris, R. (1988). Age and religious orientation. *Review of Religious Research, 29*, 271–280.

Watson, P. J., Sawyers, P., Morris, R. J., Carpenter, M. L., Jimenez, R. S., Jonas, K. A., et al. (2003). Reanalysis within a Christian ideological surround: Relationships of intrinsic religious orientation with fundamentalism and right-wing authoritarianism. *Journal of Psychology and Theology, 31*, 315–328.

Watts, F. (2000). Psychological research questions about yoga. *Mental Health, Religion & Culture, 3*, 71–83.

Watts, F. (2001). Prayer and psychology. In F. Watts (Ed.), *Perspectives on prayer* (pp. 39–52). London: SPCK.

Watts, F. (2002a). Cognitive neuroscience and religious consciousness. In R. Russell, N. Murphy, T. Meyering, & M. Arbib (Eds.), *Neuroscience and the person* (pp. 327–346). Vatican City State: Vatican Observatory.

Watts, F. (2002b). Evolution, human nature and Christianity. *Epworth Review, 29*(1), 24–31.

Watts, F. (2002c). *Theology and psychology*. Aldershot, UK: Ashgate.

Watts, F. (2003). [Review of the book *Religion in mind: Cognitive perspectives on religious belief, ritual, and experience*]. *Zygon, 38*, 981–984.

Watts, F. (2004). Relating the psychology and theology of forgiveness. In F. Watts, & L. Gulliford (Eds.), *Forgiveness in context: Theology and psychology in creative dialogue* (pp. 1–10). London: T & T Clark International.

Watts, F. (2007). Emotion regulation and religion. In J. Gross (Ed.), *Handbook of emotion regulation* (pp. 504–520). New York: Guilford Press.

Watts, F., Dutton, K., & Gulliford, L. (2006). Human spiritual qualities: Integrating psychology and religion. *Mental Health, Religion & Culture, 9*, 277–289.

Watts, F., & Williams, M. (1988). *The psychology of religious knowing*. Cambridge: Cambridge University Press.

Weaver, A. J. (1995). Has there been a failure to prepare and support parish-based clergy in their role as frontline community mental health workers: A review. *Journal of Pastoral Care, 49*, 129–147.

Weaver, A. J., Flannelly, K., Flannelly, L., & Oppenheimer, J. (2003). Collaboration between clergy and mental health professionals: A review of professional health care journals from 1980 through 1999. *Counseling and Values, 47*, 162–171.

Weaver, A. J., Kline, A. E., Samford, J. A., Lucus, L. A., Larson, D., & Gorsuch, R. (1998). Is religion taboo in psychology? A systematic analysis of research on religion in seven major American Psychological Association journals: 1991–1994. *Journal of Psychology and Christianity, 17*, 220–233.

Weaver, A. J., Samford, J., Kline, A., Lucas, L., Larson, B., & Koenig, H. (1997). What do psychologists know about working with the clergy? An analysis of eight APA journals: 1991–1994. *Professional Psychology: Research and Practice, 5*, 471–474.

Weaver, A. J., Samford, J. A., Morgan, V. J., Lichton, A. I., Larson, D. B., & Garbarino, J. (2000). Research on religious variables in five major adolescent research journals: 1992 to 1996. *The Journal of Nervous and Mental Disease, 188*, 36–44.

Weaver, C. D. (2004). The spirituality of Martin Luther King Jr. *Perspectives in Religious Studies, 31*, 55–70.

Webb-Mitchell, B. (2001). Leaving development behind and beginning our pilgrimage. In M. McMinn, & T. Phillips (Eds.), *Care for the soul: Exploring the intersection of psychology and theology* (pp. 78–101). Downers Grove, IL: InterVarsity Press.

Wegela, K. K. (2003). Nurturing the seeds of sanity: A Buddhist approach to psychotherapy. In S. Mijares (Ed.), *Modern psychology and ancient wisdom: Psychological healing practices from the world's religious traditions* (pp. 17–42). New York: The Haworth Integrative Healing Press.

Wehr, D. (2000). Spiritual abuse: when good people do bad things. In P. Young-Eisendrath, & M. Miller (Eds.), *The psychology of mature spirituality: Integrity, wisdom, and transcendence* (pp. 47–61). London: Routledge.

Weigert, E. (1962). The psychoanalytic view of human personality. In S. Doniger (Ed.), *The nature of man in theological and psychological perspective* (pp. 3–21). New York: Harper & Brothers.

Weinberger, J. (1985). *Science, faith, and politics: Francis Bacon and the Utopian roots of the modern age: A commentary on Bacon's advancement of learning*. Ithaca, NY: Cornell University Press.

Weintraub, A. (2004). *Yoga for depression: A compassionate guide to relieve suffering through yoga*. New York: Broadway.

Weisberg, D., Keil, F., Goodstein, J., Rawson, E., & Gray, J. (2008). The seductive allure of neuroscience explanations. *Journal of Cognitive Neuroscience, 20*, 470–477.

Weiss, A., Bates, T., & Luciano, M. (2008). Happiness is a personal(ity) thing: The genetics of personality and well-being in a representative sample. *Psychological Science, 19*, 205–210.

Weissman, M., & Markowitz, J. (2000). *Comprehensive guide to interpersonal psychotherapy.* New York: Basic Books.

Welch, J. (1982). *Spiritual pilgrims: Carl Jung and Teresa of Avila.* New York: Paulist.

Welch, J. (1996). *The Carmelite way: An ancient path for today's pilgrim.* New York: Paulist Press.

Wells, R. W. (1918). The theory of recapitulation and the religious and moral discipline of children. *The American Journal of Psychology, 29*, 371–382.

Welton, G. L., Adkins, A. G., Ingle, S. L., & Dixon, W. A. (1996). God control: The fourth dimension. *Journal of Psychology and Theology, 24*, 13–25.

Wengert, T. (2004). Luther on prayer in the Large Catechism. *Lutheran Quarterly, 18*, 249–274.

West, M. (1979). Meditation. *British Journal of Psychiatry, 135*, 457–467.

Westen, D., & Bradley, R. (2005). Empirically supported complexity: Rethinking evidence–based practice in psychotherapy. *Current Directions in Psychological Science, 14*, 266–271.

Westen, D., Novotny, C. M., & Thompson-Brenner, H. (2004). The empirical status of empirically supported psychotherapies: Assumptions, findings, and reporting in controlled clinical trials. *Psychological Bulletin, 130*, 631–663.

Westgate, C. E. (1996). Spiritual wellness and depression. *Journal of Counseling and Development, 75*, 26–35.

Westphal, M. (2005). Prayer as the posture of the decentered self. In B. Benson, & N. Wirzba (Eds.), *The Phenomenology of Prayer* (pp. 13–31). Bronx, NY: Fordham University Press.

Wethington, E., Cooper, H., & Holmes, C. (1997). Turning points in midlife. In I. H. Gotlib, & B. Wheaton (Eds.), *Stress and adversity over the life course: Trajectories and turning points* (pp. 215–231). Cambridge: Cambridge University Press.

Wheaton, B., & Gotlib, I. (1997). Trajectories and turning points over the life course: Concepts and themes. In I. Gotlib, & B. Wheaton (Eds.), *Stress and adversity over the life course: Trajectories and turning points* (pp. 1–25). Cambridge: Cambridge University Press.

White, A. D. (1901). *A History of the warfare of science with theology.* New York: D. Appleton and Company.

White, D. (2000). The scholar as mythographer: Comparative Indo-European myth and postmodern concern. In K. Patton, & B. Ray (Eds.), *A magic still dwells: Comparative religion in the postmodern age* (pp. 47–54). Berkeley, CA: University of California.

White, J., Joseph, S., & Neil, A. (1995). Religiosity, psychoticism, and schizotypal traits. *Personality and Individual Differences, 19*, 847–851.

Whitehead, E. E., & Whitehead, J. D. (1979). *Christian life patterns: The psychological challenges and religious invitations of adult life.* Garden City, NY: Doubleday.

Whitehouse, G. (2000). Ricoeur on religious selfhood: A response to Mark Wallace. *Modern Theology, 16*, 315–323.

Whitehouse, H. (2004a). *Modes of religiosity: A cognitive theory of religious transmission.* Walnut Creek, CA: AltaMira Press.

Whitehouse, H. (2004b). Toward a comparative anthropology of religion. In H. Whitehouse, & J. Laidlaw (Eds.), *Ritual and memory: Toward a comparative anthropology of religion* (pp. 187–205). Walnut Creek, CA: AltaMira.

Whitehouse, H. (2005). The cognitive foundations of religiosity. In H. Whitehouse, & R. McCauley (Eds.), *Mind and religion: Psychological and cognitive foundations of religiosity* (pp. 207–232). Walnut Creek, CA: AltaMira.

Whittaker, M. L. (1932). Adolescent religion in relation to mental hygiene. *Religious Education, 27*, 811–817.

Wickham, J. F. (1991). Ignatian contemplation today. In P. Sheldrake (Ed.), *The way of Ignatius Loyola: Contemporary approaches to the spiritual exercises* (pp. 145–153). St. Louis: The Institute of Jesuit Sources.

Wikstrom, O. (1987). Attribution, roles and religion: A theoretical analysis of Sunden's role theory of religion and the attributional approach to religious experience. *Journal for the Scientific Study of Religion, 26*, 390–400.

Wikstrom, O. (1990). Ritual studies in the history of religions: A challenge for the psychology of religion. In H.-G. Heimbrock, & H. Boudewijnse (Eds.), *Current studies on rituals: Perspectives for the psychology of religion* (pp. 57–67). Amsterdam: Rodopi.

Wilber, K. (1986a). The spectrum of development. In K. Wilber, J. Engler, & D. Brown (Eds.), *Transformations of consciousness: Conventional and contemplative perspectives on development* (pp. 65–105). Boston: New Science Library.

Wilber, K. (1986b). The spectrum of psychopathology. In K. Wilber, J. Engler, & D. Brown (Eds.), *Transformations of consciousness: Conventional and contemplative perspectives on development* (pp. 107–126). Boston: New Science Library.

Wilber, K. (1986c). Treatment modalities. In K. Wilber, J. Engler, & D. Brown (Eds.), *Transformations of consciousness: Conventional and contemplative perspectives on development* (pp. 127–159). Boston: New Science Library.

Wilber, K. (1996). *The Atman project: A transpersonal view of human development* (2nd ed.). Wheaton, IL: Quest Books.

Wilber, K. (2000a). *Integral psychology: Consciousness, spirit, psychology, therapy.* Boston: Shambhala.

Wilber, K. (2000b). *Sex, ecology, spirituality: The spirit of evolution: The collected works of Ken Wilber* (Vol. 6). Boston: Shambhala.

Wilber, K., Engler, J., & Brown, D. P.(1986). *Transformations of consciousness: Conventional and contemplative perspectives on development.* Boston: New Science Library.

Wilcox, W. B. (1998). Conservative Protestant child-rearing: Authoritarian or Authoritative? *American Sociological Review, 63,* 796–809.

Wildman, W. J. (1998). Evaluating the teleological argument for divine action. In R. Russell, W. Stoeger, & F. Ayala (Eds.), *Evolutionary and molecular biology: Scientific perspectives on divine action* (pp. 117–150). Vatican City State: Vatican Observatory.

Wildman, W. J., & Brothers, L. (2002). A neuropsychological-semiotic model of religious experiences. In R. Russell, N. Murphy, T. Meyering, & M. Arbib (Eds.), *Neuroscience and the person* (pp. 347–416). Vatican City State: Vatican Observatory.

Wildman, W. J., & Russell, R. J. (1995). Chaos: A mathematical introduction with philosophical reflections. In R. Russell, N. Murphy, & A. Peacocke (Eds.), *Chaos and complexity: Scientific perspectives on divine action* (pp. 49–90). Vatican City State: Vatican Observatory.

Wilken, R. (1995). Maximus the Confessor on the affections in historical perspective. In V. L. Wimbush, & R. Valantasis (Eds.), *Asceticism* (pp. 412–423). New York: Oxford University Press.

Willard, D. (1998). Spiritual disciplines, spiritual formation, and the restoration of the soul. *Journal of Psychology and Theology, 26,* 101–109.

William, of Saint-Thierry. (1971). *The golden epistle: A letter to the brethren at Mont Dieu.* Kalamazoo, MI: Cistercian Press.

Williams, B. (2003). The worldview dimensions of individualism and collectivism: Implications for counseling. *Journal of Counseling and Development, 81,* 370–374.

Williams, D. R., Larson, D. B., Buckler, R. E., Heckmann, R. C., & Pyle, C. M. (1991). Religion and psychological distress in a community sample. *Social Science & Medicine, 32,* 1257–1262.

Williams, J. M. G., & Swales, M. (2004). The use of mindfulness-based approaches for suicidal patients. *Archives of Suicide Research, 8,* 315–329.

Williams, J. M. G., Teasdale, J. D., Segal, Z. V., & Soulsby, J. (2000). Mindfulness-based cognitive therapy reduces overgeneral autobiographical memory in formerly depressed patients. *Journal of Abnormal Psychology, 109,* 150–155.

Williams, R. (2002). The deflections of desire: negative theology in Trinitarian disclosure. In O. Davies, & D. Turner (Eds.), *Silence and the Word: Negative theology and incarnation* (pp. 115–135). Cambridge: Cambridge University Press.

Williams, R. (2003). Bread in the wilderness: The monastic ideal in Thomas Merton and Paul Evdokimov. In B. Dieker, & J. Montaldo (Eds.), *Merton & Hesychasm: The prayer of the heart: The Eastern Church* (pp. 175–196). Louisville, KY: Fons Vitae.

Williams, R. (2004). *The dwelling of the light: Praying with icons of Christ.* Grand Rapids, MI: Eerdmans.

Williamson, G. M., & Clark, M. S. (1989). Providing help and desired relationship type as determinants of changes in moods and self-evaluations. *Journal of Personality and Social Psychology, 56,* 722–734.

Wills, T. A., Gibbons, F. X., Gerrard, M., Murry, V. M., & Brody, G. H. (2003). Family communication and religiosity related to substance use and sexual behavior in early adolescence: A test for pathways through self-control and prototype perceptions. *Psychology of Addictive Behaviors, 17,* 312–323.

Wilson, B. (2001). Salvation, secularization, and de-moralization. In R. K. Fenn (Ed.), *The Blackwell companion to sociology of religion* (pp. 39–51). Oxford, UK: Blackwell.

Wilson, E. O. (1975). *Sociobiology: The new synthesis.* Cambridge, MA: Belknap Press of Harvard University Press.

Wilson, E. O. (1978). *On human nature.* Cambridge, MA: Harvard University Press.

Wilson, K. G., & Murrell, A. R. (2004). Values work in acceptance and commitment therapy: Setting a course for behavioral treatment. In S. C. Hayes, V. M. Follette, & M. M. Linehan (Eds.), *Mindfulness and acceptance: Expanding the cognitive-behavioral tradition* (pp. 120–151). New York: Guilford.

Wilson, W. (1998). Religion and psychoses. In H. Koenig (Ed.), *Handbook of religion and mental health* (pp. 161–173). San Diego, CA: Academic Press.

Wilson, W., Larson, D. B., & Meier, P. D. (1983). Religious life of schizophrenics. *Southern Medical Journal, 76,* 1096–1100.

Wilson, J., & Musick, M. (1997). Who cares? Toward an integrated theory of volunteer work. *American Sociological Review, 62,* 694–713.

Wilson, J., & Sherkat, D. E. (1994). Returning to the fold. *Journal for the Scientific Study of Religion, 33,* 148–161.

Wimsatt, W. C. (2006). Reductionism and its heuristics: Making methodological reductionism honest. *Synthese, 151,* 445–475.

Wind, J., & Lewis, J. (1994). Introduction. In J. Wind, & J. Lewis (Eds.), *American congregations, Volume 2: New perspectives in the study of congregations* (pp. 1–20). Chicago: University of Chicago Press.

Wink, P. (2003). Dwelling and seeking in late adulthood: The psychosocial implications of two types of religious orientations. *Journal of Religious Gerontology, 14*(2/3), 101–117.

Wink, P., & Dillon, M. (2002). Spiritual development across the adult life course: Findings from a longitudinal study. *Journal of Adult Development, 9,* 79–94.

Wink, P., & Dillon, M. (2003). Religiousness, spirituality and psychosocial functioning in late adulthood: Findings from a longitudinal study. *Psychology and Aging, 18,* 916–924.

Wink, P., Dillon, M., & Larsen, B. (2005). Religion as moderator of the depression-health connection: Findings from a longitudinal study. *Research on Aging, 27,* 197–220.

Wink, P., Dillon, M., & Prettyman, A. (2007). Religiousness, spiritual seeking, and authoritarianism: Findings from a longitudinal study. *Journal for the Scientific Study of Religion, 46,* 321–335.

Wink, W. (2004). The myth of redemptive violence. In J. H. Ellens (Ed.), *The destructive power of religion: Violence in Judaism, Christianity, and Islam Volume 3: Models and cases of violence in religion* (pp. 265–286). Westport, CT: Praeger.

Winnicott, D. W. (1953). Transitional objects and transitional phenomena: A study of the first not-me possession. *The International Journal of Psycho-Analysis, 34,* 89–97.

Winnicott, D. W. (1975). *Through paediatrics to psycho-analysis.* New York: Basic Books.

Winnicott, D. W. (1990). *The maturational processes and the facilitating environment.* London: Karnac Books.

Wirzba, N. (2005). Attention and responsibility: The work of prayer. In B. Benson, & N. Wirzba (Eds.), *The Phenomenology of Prayer* (pp. 88–102). Bronx, NY: Fordham University Press.

Wiseman, J. (2007). Thomas Merton and Theravada Buddhism. In B. Thurston (Ed.), *Merton & Buddhism: Wisdom, emptiness, and everyday mind* (pp. 31–50). Louisville, KY: Fons Vitae.

Wittgenstein, L. (1958). *Philosophical investigations* (3rd ed.) (G. Anscombe, Trans.). Upper Saddle River, NJ: Prentice Hall.

Wittgenstein, L. (1975). *Tractatus logico-philosophicus* (C. K. Ogden, Trans.). London: Routledge. (Original work published 1922).

Wittine, B. (1989). Basic postulates for a transpersonal psychotherapy. In R. S. Valle, & S. Halling (Eds.), *Existential-phenomenological perspectives in psychology: Exploring the breadth of human experience* (pp. 269–287). New York: Plenum Press.

Witvliet, C. V. (2001). Forgiveness and health: Review and reflections on a matter of faith, feelings, and physiology. *Journal of Psychology and Theology, 29,* 212–224.

Wong, P. T. P. (1998a). Meaning-centered counseling. In P. T. P. Wong, & P. S. Fry (Eds.), *The human quest for meaning: A handbook of psychological research and clinical applications* (pp. 395–436). Mahwah, NJ: Lawrence Erlbaum.

Wong, P. T. P. (1998b). Spirituality, meaning, and successful aging. In P. T. P. Wong, & P. S. Fry (Eds.), *The human quest for meaning: A handbook of psychological research and clinical applications* (pp. 359–394). Mahwah, NJ: Lawrence Erlbaum.

Wong, P. T. P., & Fry, P. (1998). Introduction. In P. Wong, & P. Fry (Eds.), *The human quest for meaning: A handbook of psychological research and clinical applications* (pp. xvii–xxvi). Mahwah, NJ: Lawrence Erlbaum.

Wong-McDonald, A., & Gorsuch, R. L. (2000). Surrender to God: An additional coping style? *Journal of Psychology and Theology, 28,* 149–161.

Wong-McDonald, A., & Gorsuch, R. L. (2004). A multivariate theory of God concept, religious motivation, locus of control, coping, and spiritual well-being. *Journal of Psychology and Theology, 32,* 318–334.

Woodberry, R. D., & Smith, C. S. (1998). Fundamentalism et al.: Conservative Protestants in America. *Annual Review of Sociology, 24,* 25–56.

Woodhead, L. (2001). Feminism and the sociology of religion: From gender-blindness to gendered difference. In R. K. Fenn (Ed.), *The Blackwell companion to sociology of religion* (pp. 67–84). Oxford, UK: Blackwell.

Woodhouse, M. B. (1990). On the possibility of pure consciousness. In R. K. C. Forman (Ed.), *The problem of pure consciousness: Mysticism and philosophy* (pp. 254–268). New York: Oxford University Press.

Woody, W. D. (2003). Varieties of religious conversion: William James in historical and contemporary contexts. *Streams of William James, 5*(1), 7–11.

Woolery, A., Myers, H., Sternlieb, B., & Zeltner, L. (2004). A yoga intervention for young adults with elevated symptoms of depression. *Alternative Therapies in Health and Medicine, 10,* 60–63.

Woolever, C., & Bruce, D. (2002). *A field guide to U.S. congregations.* Louisville, KY: Westminster John Knox.

Woolfolk, R. L. (1975). Psychophysiological correlates of meditation. *Archives of General Psychiatry, 32,* 1326–1333.

Woolfolk, R. (1998). *The cure of souls: Science, values and psychotherapy.* San Francisco: Jossey-Bass.

Worthington, E. L., Jr. (1988). Understanding the values of religious clients: A model and its application to counseling. *Journal of Counseling Psychology, 35,* 166–174.

Worthington, E. L., Jr. (1989). Religious faith across the life span: Implications for counseling and research. *The Counseling Psychologist, 17,* 555–612.

Worthington, E. L., Jr., Kurusu, T. A., Collins, W., Berry, J. W., Ripley, J. S., & Baier, S. N. (2000). Forgiving usually takes time: A lesson learned by studying interventions to promote forgiveness. *Journal of Psychology and Theology, 28,* 3–20.

Worthington, E. L., Jr., Kurusu, T. A., McCullough, M. E., & Sandage, S. J. (1996). Empirical research on religion and psychotherapeutic processes and outcomes: A 10-year review and research prospectus. *Psychological Bulletin, 119,* 448–487.

Worthington, E. L., Jr., Mazzeo, S. E., & Canter, D. E. (2005). Forgiveness-promoting approach: Helping clients REACH forgiveness through using a longer model that teaches reconciliation.

In L. Sperry, & E. P. Shafranske (Eds.), *Spiritually oriented psychotherapy* (pp. 235–257). Washington, DC: American Psychological Association.

Worthington, E. L., Jr., O'Connor, L. E., Berry, J. W., Sharp, C., Murray, R., & Yi, E. (2005). Compassion and forgiveness: Implications for psychotherapy. In P. Gilbert (Ed.), *Compassion: Conceptualisations, research and use in psychotherapy* (pp. 168–192). New York: Routledge.

Worthington, E. L., Jr., & Sandage, S. J. (2001). Religion and spirituality. *Psychotherapy, 38*, 473–478.

Worthington, E. L., Jr., & Scherer, M. (2004). Forgiveness is an emotion-focused coping strategy that can reduce health risks and promote health resilience: Theory, review, and hypotheses. *Psychology and Health, 19*, 385–405.

Worthington, E. L., Jr., Sharp, C. B., Lerner, A. J., & Sharp, J. R. (2006). Interpersonal forgiveness as an example of loving one's enemies. *Journal of Psychology and Theology, 34*, 32–42.

Worthington, E. L. Jr., & Wade, N. G. (1999). The psychology of unforgiveness and forgiveness and implications for clinical practice. *Journal of Social and Clinical Psychology, 18*, 385–418.

Worthington, E. L., Jr., Wade, N. G., Hight, T. L., Ripley, J. S., McCullough, M. E., Berry, J. T., et al. (2003). The religious commitment inventory-10: Development, refinement, and validation of a brief scale for research and counseling. *Journal of Counseling Psychology, 50*, 84–96.

Wozniak, R. H. (2001). Development and synthesis: An introduction to the life and work of James Mark Baldwin. In J. M. Baldwin (Ed.), *Mental development in the child and the race* (pp. v–xxxi). Bristol, UK: Thoemmes.

Wright, L., Frost, C., & Wisecarver, S. (1993). Church attendance, meaningfulness of religion, and depressive symptomatology among adolescents. *Journal of Youth and Adolescence, 22*, 559–568.

Wright, N. T. (1992). *The New Testament and the people of God*. Minneapolis, MN: Fortress.

Wright, S. A. (1995). Religious innovation in the mainline church: House churches, home cells, and small groups. In N. T. Ammerman, & W. C. Roof (Eds.), *Work, family, and religion in contemporary society* (pp. 261–282). New York: Routledge.

Wright, T. C. (2005). Edith Stein: Prayer and interiority. In B. E. Benson, & N. Wirzba (Eds.), *The phenomenology of prayer* (pp. 134–141). Bronx, NY: Fordham University Press.

Wrobleski, K. K., & Snyder, C. R. (2005). Hopeful thinking in older adults: Back to the future. *Experimental Aging Research, 31*, 217–233.

Wujastyk, D. (Ed. and Trans.). (2003). *The roots of Ayurveda*. New York: Penguin.

Wulff, D. (1997). *Psychology of religion: Classic & contemporary* (2nd ed.). New York: John Wiley & Sons.

Wulff, D. (2000). James Henry Leuba: A reassessment of a Swiss-American pioneer. In J. A. Belzen (Ed.), *Aspects in contexts: Studies in the history of psychology of religion* (pp. 25–44). Amsterdam: Rodopi.

Wulff, D. (2003). A field in crisis: Is it time for psychology of religion to start over? In P. Roelofsma, J. Corveleyn, & J. Van Saane (Eds.), *A hundred years of psychology of religion: Issues and trends in a century long quest* (pp. 1–17). Amsterdam: VU University Press.

Wuthnow, R. (1998). *After heaven: Spirituality in America since the 1950s*. Berkeley, CA: University of California Press.

Wuthnow, R. (1999). *Growing up religious: Christians and Jews and their journeys of faith*. Boston: Beacon Press.

Wuthnow, R. (2000). How religious groups promote forgiving: A national study. *Journal for the Scientific Study of Religion, 39*, 125–139.

Wuthnow, R. (2001). Spirituality and spiritual practice. In R. K. Fenn (Ed.), *The Blackwell companion to sociology of religion* (pp. 306–320). Oxford: Blackwell.

Wuthnow, R. (2002). Religious involvement and status-bridging social capital. *Journal for the Scientific Study of Religion, 41*, 669–684.

Wuthnow, R. (2004). *Saving America? Faith-based services and the future of civil society*. Princeton: Princeton University Press.

Wuthnow, R., Christiano, K., & Kuzlowski, J. (1980). Religion and bereavement: A conceptual framework. *Journal for the Scientific Study of Religion, 19*, 408–422.

Wuthnow, R., Hackett, C., & Hsu, B. Y. (2004). The effectiveness and trustworthiness of faith-based and other service organizations: A study of recipients' perceptions. *Journal for the Scientific Study of Religion, 43*, 1–17.

Wynn, T. (2000). Symmetry and the evolution of the modular linguistic mind. In P. Carruthers, & A. Chamberlain (Eds.), *Evolution and the human mind: Modularity, language and meta-cognition* (pp. 113–139). Cambridge: Cambridge University Press.

Wynot, J. J. (2004). *Keeping the faith: Russian Orthodox Monasticism in the Soviet Union, 1917–1939*. College Station, TX: Texas A&M University Press.

Yanchar, S. C., & Hill, J. R. (2003). What is psychology about? Toward an explicit ontology. *The Journal of Humanistic Psychology, 43*, 11–32.

Yangarber-Hicks, N. (2004). Religious coping styles and recovery from serious mental illnesses. *Journal of Psychology and Theology, 32*, 305–317.

Yarhouse, M., Butman, R., & McRay, B. (2005). *The modern psychopathologies: A comprehensive Christian appraisal*. Downers Grove, IL: InterVarsity Press.

Yarhouse, M. A., & Turcic, E. K. (2003). Depression, creativity, and religion: A pilot study of Christians in the visual arts. *Journal of Psychology and Theology, 31*, 348–355.

Yorston, G. A. (2001). Mania precipitated by meditation: A case report and literature review. *Mental Health, Religion & Culture, 4*, 209–213.

Young, A. (2004a). How narratives work in psychiatric science: An example from the biological psychiatry of PTSD. In B. Hurwitz, T. Greenhalgh, & V. Skultans (Eds.), *Narrative research in health and illness* (pp. 382–396). Malden, MA: Blackwell.

Young, G. (2004b). Reading and praying online: The continuity of religion online and online religion in internet Christianity. In L. Dawson, & D. Cowan (Eds.), *Religion online: Finding faith on the Internet* (pp. 93–105). New York: Routledge.

Young, L. A. (1997). Phenomenological images of religion and rational choice theory. In L. A. Young (Ed.), *Rational choice theory and religion: Summary and assessment* (pp. 133–145). New York: Routledge.

Young-Eisendrath, P. (2002). The transformation of human suffering: A perspective from psychotherapy and Buddhism. In P. Young-Eisendrath, & S. Muramoto (Eds.), *Awakening and insight: Zen Buddhism and psychotherapy* (pp. 67–80). New York: Taylor & Francis.

Young-Eisendrath, P., & Miller, M. E. (2000). Beyond enlightened self-interest: The psychology of mature spirituality in the twenty-first century. In P. Young-Eisendrath, & M. E. Miller (Eds.), *The psychology of mature spirituality: Integrity, wisdom, transcendence* (pp. 1–7). London: Routledge.

Young-Eisendrath, P., & Muramoto, S. (2002). Continuing a conversation from East to West: Buddhism and psychotherapy. In P. Young-Eisendrath, & S. Muramoto (Eds.), *Awakening and insight: Zen Buddhism and psychotherapy* (pp. 1–29). New York: Taylor & Francis.

Youniss, J., McLellan, J. A., & Yates, M. (1999). Religion, community service, and identity in American youth. *Journal of Adolescence, 22*, 243–253.

Yun, H. (2005). *Sutra of the medicine Buddha: With an introduction, comments, and prayers* (Rev. ed.). Hacienda Heights, CA: Buddha's Light.

Zaehner, R. C. (1961). *Mysticism: Sacred and profane*. New York: Oxford University Press.

Zagorin, P. (1998). *Francis Bacon*. Princeton, NJ: Princeton University Press.

Zahavi, D. (2004). Natural realism, anti-reductionism, and intentionality. The "Phenomenology" of Hilary Putnam. In D. Carr, & C. Chan-Fai (Eds.), *Space, time, and culture* (pp. 235–251). Dordrecht: Kluwer Academic.

Zautra, A. J., & Bachrach, K. M. (2000). Psychological dysfunction and well-being: Public health and social indicator approaches. In J. Rappaport, & E. Seidman (Eds.), *Handbook of community psychology* (pp. 165–185). New York: Kluwer Academic/Plenum.

Zhang, J., & Jin, S. (1996). Determinants of suicide ideation: A comparison of Chinese and American college students. *Adolescence, 31*(122), 451–467.

Zhuangzi. (1996). *The book of Chuang Tzu* (M. Palmer, Trans.). London: Penguin.

Zimbardo, P. (2007). *The Lucifer effect: Understanding how good people turn evil.* New York: Random House.

Zinnbauer, B. J., & Pargament, K. I. (1998). Spiritual conversion: A study of religious change among college students. *Journal for the Scientific Study of Religion, 37,* 161–180.

Zinnbauer, B. J., Pargament, K. I., Cole, B., Rye, M. S., Butter, E. M., Belavich, T. G., et al. (1997). Religion and spirituality: Unfuzzing the fuzzy. *Journal for the Scientific Study of Religion, 36,* 549–564.

Zinnbauer, B. J., Pargament, K. I., & Scott, A. B. (1999). The emerging meanings of religiousness and spirituality: Problems and prospects. *Journal of Personality, 67,* 889–919.

Zizioulas, J. (1985). *Being as communion.* Crestwood, NY: St. Vladimir's Seminary Press.

Zizioulas, J. (2006). *Communion and otherness: Further studies in personhood and the church* (P. McPartlan, Ed.), London: T & T Clark.

Zock, H. (1990). *A psychology of ultimate concern: Erik H. Erikson's contribution to the psychology of religion.* Amsterdam: Rodopi.

Zock, H. (1997). The predominance of the feminine sexual mode in religion: Erikson's contribution to the sex and gender debate in the psychology of religion. *International Journal for the Psychology of Religion, 7,* 187–198.

Zondag, H. J. (2004). Knowing you make a difference: Result awareness and satisfaction in the pastoral profession. *Review of Religious Research, 45,* 254–269.

Zuroff, D. C., & Schwarz, J. C. (1980). Transcendental meditation versus muscle relaxation: A two year follow up of a controlled experiment. *American Journal of Psychiatry, 137,* 1229–1231.

Author Index

Subject Index

Note: Boldface page numbers indicate the location where a term is defined.